The Development of Neolithic House Societies in Orkney

Investigations in the Bay of Firth, Mainland, Orkney (1994–2014)

Edited by

Colin Richards and Richard Jones

WIND*gather*
PRESS

View of the Bay of Firth study area from the east with the southern slopes of Wideford Hill in the foreground. To the west the Hills of Heddle and Cuween create a boundary with western Mainland and the Stenness–Brodgar monument complex. The Brodgar isthmus can be seen top left (Craig Taylor).

This book is dedicated to
Alasdair Whittle

And the memory of
Judith Robertson

Windgather Press is an imprint of Oxbow Books

Published in the United Kingdom in 2016 by
OXBOW BOOKS
10 Hythe Bridge Street, Oxford OX1 2EW

and in the United States by
OXBOW BOOKS
1950 Lawrence Road, Havertown, PA 19083

Hardback Edition: ISBN 978-1-90968-689-2
Digital Edition: ISBN 978-1-90968-690-8

A CIP record for this book is available from the British Library

Printed in the United Kingdom by Short Run Press, Exeter

For a complete list of Windgather titles, please contact:

United Kingdom	United States of America
Oxbow Books	Oxbow Books
Telephone (01865) 241249	Telephone (800) 791-9354
Fax (01865) 794449	Fax (610) 853-9146
Email: oxbow@oxbowbooks.com	Email: queries@casemateacademic.com
www.oxbowbooks.com	www.casemateacademic.com/oxbow

Oxbow Books is part of the Casemate group

Front cover: *Knap of Howar, Papa Westray (Colin Richards)*
Back cover: *The hills of northern Hoy dominate Mainland, Orkney (Colin Richards)*

Contents

Acknowledgements vii

List of Figures xi

List of Tables xix

1. Images of Neolithic Orkney 1
   Colin Richards and Richard Jones

2. Houses of the Dead: the transition from wood to stone architecture at Wideford Hill 16
   Colin Richards and Andrew Meirion Jones

3. Place in the Past: an early Neolithic house at the Knowes of Trotty barrow cemetery,
   Harray, Mainland, Orkney 41
   *Jane Downes, Paul Sharman, Adrian Challands, Erika Guttmann-Bond,
   Jo McKenzie, Roy Towers and Patricia D. Voke*

4. Local Histories of Passage Grave Building Communities: Brae of Smerquoy 64
   Christopher Gee, Colin Richards and Mairi Robertson

5. Good Neighbours: Stonehall Knoll, Stonehall Meadow and Stonehall Farm 91
   *Colin Richards, Kenny Brophy, Martin Carruthers, Andrew Meirion Jones,
   Richard Jones and Siân Jones*

6. At Stonehall Farm, Late Neolithic Life is Rubbish 128
   *Colin Richards, Richard Jones, Adrian Challands, Stuart Jeffrey, Andrew Meirion Jones,
   Siân Jones and Tom Muir*

7. The Settlement of Crossiecrown: the Grey and Red Houses 160
   *Nick Card, Jane Downes, Colin Richards, Richard Jones, Adrian Challands,
   Charles A. I. French and Antonia Thomas*

8. Reorientating the Dead of Crossiecrown: Quanterness and Ramberry Head 196
   Rebecca Crozier, Colin Richards, Judith Robertson and Adrian Challands

9. Materializing Neolithic House Societies in Orkney, introducing Varme Dale
   and Muckquoy 224
   Colin Richards, Jane Downes, Christopher Gee and Stephen Carter

10. Beside the Ocean of Time: a chronology of early Neolithic burial monuments
    and houses in Orkney 254
    Seren Griffiths

11.   Prehistoric Pottery from Sites within the Bay of Firth: Stonehall, Crossiecrown,
       Wideford Hill, Brae of Smerquoy, Muckquoy, Ramberry and Knowes of Trotty 303
       Andrew Meirion Jones, Richard Jones, Gemma Tully, Lara Maritan, Anna Mukherjee,
       Richard Evershed, Ann MacSween, Colin Richards and Roy Towers

12.   Flaked Lithic Artefacts from Neolithic Sites around the Bay of Firth: Wideford Hill,
       Knowes of Trotty, Brae of Smerquoy, Stonehall, Crossiecrown and Ramberry 413
       Hugo Anderson-Whymark, Richard Chatterton, Mark Edmonds and Caroline Wickham-Jones

13.   The Coarse Stone from Neolithic Sites around the Bay of Firth: Stonehall, Wideford Hill,
       Crossiecrown, Knowes of Trotty and Brae of Smerquoy 445
       Ann Clarke

             Appendix 1.   The Pumice from Crossiecrown and Stonehall 473
                           Ann Clarke
             Appendix 2.   The Black Stone Bead from Structure 1, Stonehall Farm 474
                           Alison Sheridan
             Appendix 3.   The Haematite and Related Iron-rich Materials 475
                           Effie Photos-Jones, Arlene Isbister and Richard Jones

14.   The Animal Remains from Stonehall and Crossiecrown 485
       Catherine Smith and Julie A. Roberts

             Appendix 1.   The Human Remains from Ramberry Head 488
                           David Lawrence

15.   Bay of Firth Environments from the 2nd to 4th Millennium BC: the evidence from Stonehall,
       Wideford Hill, Crossiecrown, Knowes of Trotty, Varme Dale and Brae of Smerquoy 495
       Jennifer Miller, Susan Ramsay, Diane Alldritt and Joanna Bending

             Appendix 1.   Palaeoenvironmental Investigation of a Peat Core from Stonehall 520
                           Susan Ramsay, Stephanie Leigh-Johnson and Rupert Housley

16.   The Micromorphological Analysis of Soils and Site Contexts at Stonehall and Crossiecrown 527
       Charles French

Bibliography 543
Index 561

Acknowledgements

This monograph charts the second phase of fieldwork undertaken to investigate the Neolithic of Mainland, Orkney, the first having been described in *Dwelling Among the Monuments* (Richards 2005) and the third in *Building the Great Stone Circles of the North* (Richards 2013). Initially, the project was funded by the University of Glasgow (New Initiatives Fund), and later by the British Academy, the Society of Antiquaries of Scotland, Orkney Islands Council, The Russell Trust, the University of Manchester and the Glasgow Archaeological Society. The project was also sponsored by Orcargo (and we thank David Laidlow for his enthusiasm and generosity) for several years. However, it was only with funding from Historic Scotland that the research reached a level that enabled a transformation of the project into the substantial form as reported in this volume. For this support we are indebted to Patrick Ashmore for initiating funding and subsequently Rod McCullagh who not only managed this project over many years but showed both great enthusiasm and patience for which we are most grateful. We are also very grateful to Lisa Brown at Historic Scotland for her help and guidance at the publication stage of this volume.

During the entire project we have worked in conjunction with the local community in a variety of ways and a number of people have been pivotal in this capacity. Bryce Wilson, former director of Tankerness House Museum, Kirkwall, Mainland, Orkney, always considered a formal relationship between our project and Orkney Museums to be essential. Consequently, Tom Muir participated in all our excavations and provided expert advice and great friendship and we cannot thank him enough. The late Anne Brundle always took great interest in our work and her enthusiasm was contagious. Even as a reporter Sigurd Towrie consistently visited the excavations and communicated our results to the island community through the *Orcadian* newspaper, and now as editor, he continues to report and promote island archaeology in a highly knowledgeable and exciting manner. He too has become a valued friend and we thank him for his long-term interest and commitment to disseminate our results. Throughout the duration of the project we have been fortunate enough to have the friendship, knowledge and support of the Regional Archaeologist Julie Gibson. During her tenure, and under her guidance, Orcadian archaeology has gone from strength to strength and is now a model for the entirety of Scotland. We cannot thank her enough for her continual enthusiasm and kindness. Andrew Appleby has always been an enthusiastic supporter of both our project and Orcadian archaeology in general and we thank him for his support. Caroline Wickham-Jones always provided valuable advice (especially when a hint of Mesolithic archaeology appeared) which is much appreciated. Virtually all the excavations comprising this project have required top-soil removal by expert machining, which for over twenty years has been provided by the finest JCB operators in Orkney, Ally Miller, and more recently Terry Todd and we thank them for their generosity and professionalism. Finally, a particular debt is owed to Donald Kirkpatrick for his consistent patience, support and friendship.

The theme of this volume revolves around a modification of Claude Lévi-Strauss' concept of *sociétés à maisons* and since the start of the project its theoretical orientation has been a major topic of discussion. Consequently, the following people are thanked for valuable discussions: Richard Bradley, Kenny Brophy, Giles Carey, Gabriel Cooney, Vicki Cummings, Jane Downes, Mark Edmonds, Seren Griffiths, Andy M. Jones, Siân Jones, Duncan Garrow, Dan Lee, Lesley McFadyen, Tom Muir, Mike Parker Pearson, Josh Pollard, John Raven, Niall Sharples, Antonia Thomas, Julian Thomas and Alasdair Whittle.

A number of people also gave complete access to their unpublished excavations and for this generosity we would like to thank Dan Lee and Antonia Thomas (Ha'Breck, Wyre), Mick Miles and Diana Coles (Green, Eday) and Nick Card (Ness of Brodgar, Mainland). Colin Renfrew kindly allowed access to his Quanterness archive at the University of Kent, and permitted the reproduction of photographs of his excavation in 1973.

Hugo Anderson-Whymark, Adam Stanford and Craig Taylor kindly provided a range of excellent photographs and they are warmly thanked.

Although of long duration, this project was constantly producing unexpected results right up to its conclusion in 2014. Consequently, it was exciting and fun to direct. It began in March 1994 when Adrian Challands and the two authors went to Orkney to undertake a gradiometer survey at Deepdale, Stromness. As the results of this survey were inconclusive, it was decided to shift the focus to a new study area taking in the coastal zone of the Bay of Firth. A year or so earlier, at an open evening arranged by the late Anne Brundle at Tankerness House Museum in Kirkwall, Mr Ronnie Flett had brought in a number of objects to be identified which included a broken macehead and several worked flints. When asked where this material came from, he explained that it had been collected from a corner of a field which lay directly below Cuween Hill chambered cairn. The name of this farm was Stonehall where we went on to work from 1994 to 2000. Our fieldwork at Stonehall was highly enjoyable, not least because of the interest, enthusiasm and kindness of Ronnie Flett and his wife Mabel. We cannot thank them enough.

Overall, the new study area seemed to fulfil the necessary requirements of possessing a good range of Neolithic settlement, with the additional bonus of associated chambered cairns. The following account is based upon the results of a prolonged period of fieldwork where seven Neolithic settlements were examined which spanned the entirety of the Neolithic period (*c*.3600–2000 cal BC). It is fair to say that the results of this research have substantially altered our understanding of the nature of habitation during the Orcadian Neolithic.

The Bay of Firth area in central Mainland, Orkney, is very fertile and the pasture tends to be ploughed and reseeded on a 5–8 year cycle. This allowed fieldwalking to be undertaken and we would like to thank both Scott Harcus and Ken Watson for allowing us to wander across the lands of Quanterness and Rennibister respectively. As good fortune would have it, the settlements at Crossiecrown and Wideford were located on the land of both farms and again we are indebted to both Scott and Ken, and their respective sons, William and Alastair for their permission and great interest in our work.

As the project progressed, a degree of reflexivity was required to accommodate the unexpected material being discovered. For example, our early aim of examining forms of settlement contemporary with Barnhouse had to accommodate a much wider chronological spread with a substantial component of habitation being of mid–late 4th millennium cal BC date. Between 1998 and 2006 Jane Downes undertook several projects examining early Bronze Age barrows and burial practices including Varme Dale, Rendall, which produced mid-4th millennium cal BC settlement evidence which is incorporated into this volume. Jane wishes to thank the landowner at Varme Dale (the late) Mr Fraser.

In 2013–14, in conjunction with Christopher Gee, a new site at Brae of Smerquoy was investigated on the lands of Billy Sinclair who we cannot thank enough for his enthusiasm, warmth and permission to work on his land. We would also like to extend this gratitude to Billy's neighbour, Mr John Brody for his interest, help and kindness during the fieldwork and excavation. Our particular thanks also go to the late Eoin Scott, who was extremely interested in the Redland sites and a good friend to Orkney archaeology. His interest extends in the current landowner Mr Robbie Tulloch and we thank him for enthusiastic support (and patience) of the investigation of the Muckquoy site and field survey in the surrounding area.

The important role of Jane Downes, Siân Jones and more recently, Christopher Gee in the project cannot be overstated, nor can the help of many students from the Universities of Glasgow, Manchester and University College Dublin who took part in the large excavations at Stonehall (co-directed by Colin Richards, Richard Jones and Siân Jones) and Crossiecrown (co-directed by Nick Card and Jane Downes) and the subsequent post-excavation work. Equally, the great help of University of the Highlands and Islands students and support of numerous local volunteers and others who came from further afield, especially in regard to Smerquoy (co-directed by Christopher Gee, Colin Richards and Mairi Robertson) is kindly acknowledged.

The contributions of supervisors Kenny Brophy, Martin Carruthers, Adrian Challands, Norma Challands, Stuart Jeffrey, Andrew M. Jones, Angus Mackintosh Judith Robertson, Mary Harris and Lesley McFadyen at Crossiecrown and Stonehall are gratefully acknowledged. Richard Jones is grateful to Lorna Campbell, Lorna Sharpe, Lesley Farrell, Chris Connor and Gert Petersen for their assistance in many different ways throughout the project. At the project's archiving stage in Glasgow, (the late) Anne Brundle gave much helpful advice, and several students were involved, especially Kristjana Eyjclfsson and Elizabeth Pierce, in that process.

The Wideford Hill excavations received funding from Historic Scotland and Orkney Island Council. The initial persistence of Richard Chatterton undoubtedly led to the discovery of the unknown area of the Wideford settlement and we are very grateful for his tenacity. The two periods of excavation were undertaken in variable conditions by a highly enthusiastic team for no huge reward (apart from the amazing archaeology) and we really appreciate the help of Nick Card, Martin Carruthers, Adrian Challands, Richard Chatterton, Stuart Jeffrey and Angus Mackintosh. Jane Downes and her students also joined in the excavations along with Tom Muir of Orkney Museums.

For Knowes of Trotty Jane Downes thanks the excavation co-director, Nick Card, and fieldworkers Paul Sharman, Adrian and Norma Challands, Alastair Wilson, Jakob Kainz, Roy Towers, Marion Chesters, John Chesters, Kathleen Ireland, Katy Chalmers, Mary Harris, (the late) Judith Robertson, Alastair Wright, Naomi Woodward, Matt Jones, Ann Johnston, Sean Mullan and Tom Whalley for their hard work and enthusiasm in the survey and excavation. The late David Coombs, and Keith Maud, of the University of Manchester collaborated in the first year of survey at the site and it was a pleasure to work with them. Many thanks also go to Alison Sheridan and the National Museums of Scotland for their very generous support; Regional Archaeologist Julie Gibson, and Rod McCullagh of Historic Scotland for their advice and help. As always, Frank Bradford took some wonderful photographs which are much appreciated.

Varme Dale was excavated as part of the Orkney Barrows Project, generously funded by Historic Scotland. Site director Jane Downes acknowledges the support of Julie Gibson, Orkney Archaeological Trust, and (the late) Anne Brundle and Tom Muir of Orkney Museums. Thanks go to the fieldwork team: Biddy Simpson, Tom Ullathorne, Danny Hind, Sue McCabe, Cathy Pink, Adrian Challands, Julie Roberts, Camilla Priede, Norma Challands, Leslie Macfadyen and Matilda Webb. Pat Wagner co-ordinated the environmental analysis at Sheffield University.

The Ramberry Head sites were reported by the landowner, Mr Scott Harcus who subsequently gave permission for excavation. These sites would have remained undetected without his keen eye and great interest and we thank him for his support. Excavations occurred in the spring of 2005 and were conducted by Colin Richards, Adrian Challands and the late Judith Robertson.

More recently, the Brae of Smerquoy was investigated on the lands of Billy Sinclair. Smerquoy was funded by grants from the Orkney Island Council and University of Manchester, and ORCA kindly supplied equipment. Billy Sinclair, Peter Brigham and the University of Manchester generously provided support with radiocarbon dating, as did the Orkney Archaeology Society, and we very much appreciate the support of Andrew Appleby. Of the many people who either volunteered or helped at Smerquoy, we would like to thank Hugo Anderson-Whymark, Andy Boyer, Peter Brigham, Mary-Anne and Andy Buntin, Robbie Cant, Giles Carey, Norma and Adrian Challands, Mr and Mrs Cullen, Vicki Cummings, Mr and Mrs Davis, Michael Ferguson, Alistair Foden, Kim Foden, Martin and Mansie Gee, Joyce Gray, George Gray, Seren Griffiths, Anne Johnston, Catherine Kriisa, Christopher Leask, Neil Leask, John Leith, Mark Littlewood, Ragnhild Ljosland, Dani Lord, Danny Muir, Tom Muir, Mick Page, Alan Price, Georgie Ritchie, Jeanne Rose, Mary Saunders, Lorraine Sharpe, Michael Sharpe, Kenneth Stander, Roy Towers, Joanna Wright and Peter Woodward. Seren Griffiths and Ben Geary are particularly thanked for their environmental and botanical advice and work at Smerquoy.

Muckquoy, Redland, was fieldwalked in the spring of 2013 by Colin Richards, Mairi Robertson and members of the Orkney Archaeological Society. Concurrent geophysical survey was undertaken by Christopher Gee and James Moore, and topographic survey by Mark Littlewood. Further geophysical survey and excavation occurred in the summer of 2013 and the team consisted of Christopher Gee, Alan Price, Dave Rae, Colin Richards, George Richie, Mairi Robertson and Roy Towers.

As can be imagined, the post-excavation component of this project was considerable involving a large number of specialists in different location and we thank all of them for their help in bringing this research to a satisfactory conclusion. In this vein Richard Jones thanks David Sneddon for the initial recording of much of the pottery at Stonehall, Jane Sievewright for the pottery drawings, Shane Donatello who carried out the phosphate determinations at Stonehall, and Lorna Campbell for preparation of many of the ceramic thin sections. For the experimental work he is primarily indebted to Bill Brown, Ken Ryan, Stephanie Durning, Fiona Stephens and John Irwin. In Orkney he is grateful to Andrew Appleby and Tom Muir for their assistance and advice. Finally, he is grateful to Ann MacSween and Alison Sheridan for advice and encouragement.

Andrew Meirion Jones would like to thank (the late) David Peacock, David Williams, Gemma Tully and Sandy Budden for help or assistance over the course of the project. Lara Maritan extends thanks to Emrys Phillips and the

British Geological Survey at Edinburgh for access to its collection of rock thin sections, Allan Hall for advice and assistance with the photomicroscopy and Lesley Farrell and Leonardo Tauro for kindly preparing thin sections. Anna Staples (née Mukherjee) and Richard Evershed are grateful to Jim Carter, Ian D. Bull and Rob Berstan for their technical assistance and the NERC for funding the Bristol node of the Life Sciences Mass Spectrometry Facility. The Wellcome Trust is thanked for providing a Bioarchaeology PhD studentship for Anna Mukherjee (061666/Z/00/Z). David Lawrence thanks Nick Card for providing background information on the Ramberry project and for the skeletal reports on the Knowes of Trotty and Loth Road, and Alison Sheridan for discussing the technique of carbonate dating as applied to cremated bone.

Alison Sheridan thanks Dr Kathy Eremin (formerly of NMS) for undertaking analysis of the Stonehall bead. Effie Photos-Jones is grateful to Allan Hall for commenting on an earlier draft of the section on haematite, and John Brown is gratefully acknowledged for the information on the recent hematite finds on Mainland. In relation to Chapter 16 Charles French thanks Julie Miller and Brian Pittman of the McBurney Geoarchaeology Laboratory, Department of Archaeology, University of Cambridge, for the manufacture of the thin sections, and Karen Hartshorn (then of the same Department) who carried out the basic descriptions and analyses of three thin section profiles (1–3) as part of her M. Phil dissertation in 1999.

The major task of illustration and artefact photography for this project was undertaken by a range of people including Hugo Anderson-Whymark, Anne Bankier, Steve Bellshaw, Adrian Challands, Ann Clarke, Crane Begg, Amanda Brend, Thomas Desalle, Christopher Gee, Patricia Voke, Lorraine McEwan, Michael Sharpe, Jill Sievewright, Antonia Thomas and Joanna Wright. Archiving this project was a major task that was effectively undertaken by Irene Garcia Rovira, and she has our warmest thanks. Alasdair Whittle and Vicki Cummings kindly read and commented on various elements of this text.

There have been so many people involved in this project some will have slipped through our net, however, we thank all those who have generously given their time and worked on what has been a highly enjoyable and exciting project in so many ways since its inception in 1994. Unfortunately, one of the people we worked with at Ramberry Head (Chapter 8), Judith Robertson died unexpectedly in 2007. Judith was a lovely person and great archaeologist, and it is fitting that this book is dedicated to her memory.

Finally, we thank Tara Evans, Julie Gardiner and Clare Litt at Oxbow for their considerable assistance and patience in bringing this volume to fruition.

Since before going to study archaeology at university, one of the authors (CR) became obsessed with the Neolithic period and was especially inspired by the writings of Alasdair Whittle. Significantly, some of Alasdair's early research was based in the Northern Isles (although it was Shetland!). Since that time he has become a good friend and continued to provide a range of stimulating books and papers on the British and European Neolithic. Consequently, we would like to also dedicate this volume to you too Alasdair.

Colin Richards, Manchester
Richard Jones, Glasgow

List of Figures

1.1 Location map of Orkney

1.2 View of Orkney from Caithness

1.3 The hills of northern Hoy dominate Mainland, Orkney

1.4 The stepped character of Orcadian sandstone cliffs

1.5 Map of Orkney identifying the main islands

1.6 Knap of Howar, Papa Westray

1.7 Plan of (a) Knap of Howar, House 2 and (b) Holm of Papa Westray North

1.8 View of the Bay of Firth from the east

1.9 The early prehistoric sites and topography of the Bay of Firth area of Mainland, Orkney

1.10 Bathymetry based reconstruction model for the Bay of Firth of the rise in sea level during the period *c.*5000–3500 BC

1.11 View over Finstown looking up the west coast of the Bay of Firth

1.12 The three Dr Jones' directing Trench E at Stonehall Farm, left to right, Andrew, Richard and Siân

1.13 Excavations at the Knowes of Trotty with the central cist of the main mound uncovered, the excavation of the early Neolithic house can be seen in the background

1.14 The discovery of the horned spiral in the Smurquoy Hoose occurred when the sun shone from the southeast

2.1 Robert Rendall's published plan of the 'flint field' at Wideford Hill

2.2 Location of excavated trench at Wideford Hill

2.3 Results of survey at Wideford Hill using a Geoscan FM36 fluxgate gradiometer

2.4 Topographic survey of the Wideford Hill settlement

2.5 Robert Rendall's unpublished distribution plan of the Wideford Hill 'flint-field'

2.6 Plan of the wooden buildings discovered in the excavated area

2.7 Detailed plan of Timber structure 1

2.8 Sectioned central scoop hearth [068] in Timber structure 1

2.9 Unstan ware sherd SF 958 recovered from the central hearth in Structure 1

2.10 Sections of postholes comprising Timber structure 1

2.11 Posthole [039], showing the outer packing *in situ* and inner post-pipe removed

2.12 View of Timber structure 1 under excavation from the south-east

2.13 Plan of Timber structure 2

2.14 Sections of postholes constituting Timber structure 2

2.15 Posthole [121] as initially revealed as a substantial void beneath the primary clay floor of Stonehouse 1

2.16 Scoop hearth [155] in Timber structure 2

2.17 Plan of 'Timber structure 3'

2.18 Sections of postholes and features constituting 'Timber structure 3'

2.19 Western view of the postholes comprising 'Timber structure 3'

2.20 The scoop hearth [036] in 'Timber structure 3'

2.21 Stone-packing surrounds excavated posthole [041]

2.22 Posthole [053]

2.23 Plan of Stonehouse 1 and associated work area [002] at Wideford Hill

2.24 View of Stonehouse 1 from the south

2.25 Plan of primary features within Stonehouse 1

2.26 East-facing section through scoop hearths within Stonehouse 1 showing stratigraphic relationships of the internal occupation ash deposits

2.27 Excavating the internal ash deposits spreading from the second scoop hearth [152]

2.28 The stone box arrangement in Stonehouse 1

2.29 The clay 'bowl' [146] in Stonehouse 1; the excavated earlier drain [140] can be seen stratified beneath the box-like structure [110]

2.30 Plan of secondary drains and internal features inside Stonehouse 1

2.31 The interior of Stonehouse 1 under excavation

2.32 West view of the rammed stone surface [002] under excavation

2.33 Plan of Stonehouse 1 and foundation slabs of Stone structure 2

2.34 The distribution of stone artefacts (a), ceramics (b) and worked flint (c) across the rammed stone deposit [002]

2.35   As Adrian Challands and Andrew M. Jones remove the rammed stone deposit [002], the underlying line of foundation stones [007] for Stone structure 2 becomes visible

3.1   Location of Knowes of Trotty, showing barrows and trench positions

3.2   Gradiometer survey of Knowes of Trotty

3.3   The Neolithic house under excavation with Mound 1 in background

3.4   First phases of the Knowes of Trotty house

3.5   Detail of wall [203], with Phase 2 walls [024] and [101] in front

3.6   East–west section through the Knowes of Trotty house

3.7   Unstan ware rim sherd (SF 6) from the wall core of the first Knowes of Trotty house

3.8   View from north to south of the Knowes of Trotty house

3.9   Primary hearth [302], feature [294] is under excavation in foreground

3.10   Pit [286] in northern end of building

3.11   Plan of Knowes of Trotty house: phase 2

3.12   View of house from south showing entrance to the rear chamber, and chamber partially excavated

3.13   Detail of recess in rear of house showing rubble tipping inward from collapsed wall

3.14   View of the phase 2/3 Knowes of Trotty house and hearth from the north, central hearth unexcavated

3.15   Hearth [215] sectioned

3.16   Detail of the porch looking west to house interior

3.17   External work areas under excavation, to left of picture

3.18   View of 'kiln' looking southwards

3.19   Axe fragment SF 280 from the 'kiln' debris

3.20   'Kiln' debris [263] sectioned in the trench edge

3.21   Knap of Howar grinders SF 135 and SF 299

3.22   Knowes of Trotty House: Phase 3

3.23   View of the barrow cemetery from the south with Mound 1 centre, berm clearly visible

3.24   The cist and orthostats present within Mound 1, Knowes of Trotty

3.25   View to the southwest with Neolithic house and Mound 1 under excavation, and the hills of Hoy visible on the horizon

4.1   Topographic situation of Brae of Smerquoy

4.2   Distribution of surface material at Brae of Smerquoy

4.3   Results of the geophysical survey at Brae of Smerquoy

4.4   Location of excavation trenches at Brae of Smerquoy

4.5   View of Trench 1 showing the differential preservation of the Smerquoy Hoose

4.6   Plan of the primary features in the Smerquoy Hoose

4.7   Drain [030] running through the outer wall

4.8   North-facing section across the Smerquoy Hoose

4.9   The front entrance into the Smerquoy Hoose

4.10   Horizontal pecked line running along the single stone forming the lowest course of the eastern wall of the front entrance

4.11   Decorated stone (SF 172) formed part of the lowest course of masonry in the inner wall-face of the house

4.12   Cuts for the facing and door jamb uprights of the side (west) entrance of the Smerquoy Hoose

4.13   Excavating the flagstones paving the side (west) entrance into the house

4.14   View of the orthostats [019] and [060] in the north-east corner of the house

4.15   Christopher Gee excavating the circular scoop hearth [145]

4.16   Plan of secondary features in the Smerquoy Hoose

4.17   View of the secondary features in the Smerquoy Hoose

4.18   The rectangular stone hearth

4.19   Section drawings of the pits in the southern area of Smerquoy Hoose

4.20   Graph showing dimensions of stakeholes (S-H), post-holes (P-H) and pits within the rear area of the house

4.21   The two ground end 'finger' stones SF 303 and SF 304

4.22   View of pit [091] behind the hearth showing the pick-dressed stone (SF 160)

4.23   In the foreground the pits at the rear of the Smerquoy are under excavation

4.24   Drawing showing phases (A–C) of the drains operating within the Smerquoy Hoose

4.25   Vertical view of external drain [052] showing white clay lining

4.26   Plans of central hearth showing (a) original hearth represented by cuts [184 and 192], (b) construction detail of reconstruction and (c) the realigned hearth

4.27   South-facing section through the stone hearth

4.28   Plan of Smerquoy Hoose showing later features

4.29   View of the Smerquoy Hoose porch-like structure from the southeast

4.30   The porch-like structure added to House 5 at Ha'Breck

4.31   Broken quern (SF 101) adjacent to ruined wall [062] in the house extension

4.32   The collapsed western outer casing wall [016] can be seen to the upper right beyond the drain running through the thickness of the outer wall

4.33   View of the Smerquoy Hoose showing rubble infill [005] spread across its interior

4.34 Broken gneiss macehead (SF 29) from the clay make-up [017] covering the house entrance

4.35 Plan of Trench 1 showing the clay surface covering exterior areas north of the Smerquoy Hoose

4.36 The sub-soil in Trench 2 was severely eroded and the deposits truncated

4.37 Plan of Trench 2 in 2013

4.38 Expanded Trench 2 in 2014 showing cuts into the glacial clay to form level platforms for work areas and sub-rectangular timber buildings

4.39 Detail showing the pick-dressed 'horned spiral' decoration on the stone (SF 172) adjacent to the front entrance passage

4.40 Pick dressed designs, including 'horned spirals' on the redeposited slab from Green, Eday

4.41 Pick dressed 'horned spirals' from Pierowall Quarry passage grave

4.42 The decorated stone *in situ* in Structure 12 at the Ness of Brodgar

4.43 Saddle quern lying at the field edge of the upper field

4.44 North-west view across the Bay of Firth from Trench 2

5.1 View of the Bay of Firth from Cuween passage grave with Wideford Hill in the distance

5.2 View of Cuween Hill passage grave from Stonehall

5.3 Situation (left) and trench locations (right) of the Stonehall sites

5.4 Looking towards Stonehall Knoll (Trench C) from Stonehall Farm (Trench B)

5.5 Plan of Trench C showing two stone house structures (Houses 4 and 5) representing early historic occupation of the knoll

5.6 The two early historic house structures (Houses 4 and 5) overlying Neolithic deposits

5.7 Section drawings of postholes [4057] and [4059]

5.8 View of the rear walling [1068] of Structure 1 showing position of postholes [4057 and 4059]

5.9 Tom Muir excavating the ash and midden deposits covering and slumping down from the eastern wall of Structure 1

5.10 East–west section across paved area [472] and elements of House 2 and Structure 1

5.11 Plan of Stonehall Knoll showing position of Structure 1 walling [1068]

5.12 Rear walling [1068] of Structure 1 from the east

5.13 Plan of Calf of Eday Long stalled cairn showing the small rear chamber encased within the cairn

5.14 Vertical view showing the uncovering of the flagstone paving [472] capping the summit of the knoll

5.15 Plan of House 2, showing surrounding paving and associated midden deposits

5.16 View looking at the main paved area [472] running up to the robbed wall of House 2

5.17 The stone hearth and related divisional uprights in House 2

5.18 North-facing section of midden deposits on eastern slope of the knoll beyond the entrance into House 2

5.19 Plan of House 3, Stonehall Knoll, showing the primary occupation deposits, ash spread [4042] (a), phosphate (b) and magnetic susceptibility values (c)

5.20 East–west section through House 3, Stonehall Knoll

5.21 Primary architecture of House 3, Stonehall Knoll

5.22 Plan of primary architecture of House 3, Stonehall Knoll

5.23 Stone hearth [4023] revealed beneath collapsed stone in House 3

5.24 Entrance passage into House 3

5.25 Stone boxes ran along the eastern side of the central area of House 3

5.26 Plan showing collapsed stone partitioning within House 3

5.27 Collapsed stone 'furniture' within House 3

5.28 Plan showing secondary attempts to shore the western wall of House 3

5.29 Secondary wall [1047] built inside the western wall of House 3

5.30 The outer buttress [1026] with upright wedge stones was built against the rear of House 3 to support the leaning outer wall

5.31 Western wall of House 3 from the north with upright wedge stones in the foreground

5.32 Distribution of flint (a), pottery (b) and stone (c) on Stonehall Knoll

5.33 Excavating the front compartment of House 3, Stonehall Meadow

5.34 Plan of upper deposits and paving in Stonehall Meadow House 3

5.35 Plan of Stonehall Meadow Houses 2 and 3 showing the features within the inner and paving within the outer compartments of the latter

5.36 View of the faced outer wall of Stonehall Meadow House 2 and faced inner wall of House 3

5.37 View of excavated Stonehall Meadow House 3 from the west. The curving walling at the rear gives the house a boat-shape

5.38 View of front area of Stonehall Meadow House 3, showing divisional slots, and flagstone paving [3026] and [3036]

5.39 Detail of pit [3074] covered by flagstone (a), uncovered showing barley-rich basal fill [3075] (b)

5.40 Pre-excavation view of the red ash [3068] spreading from the top of the scoop hearth [3070]

5.41   East-facing section of scoop hearth [3070] in Stonehall Meadow House 3

5.42   The linear slot [3079] and lateral slot [3077] projecting from the left-hand inner wall-face probably held stone or timber uprights forming 'bed-like' furniture within the inner compartment

5.43   North-facing section through Stonehall Meadow House 3

5.44   View of Stonehall Meadow House 3 showing the line of secondary paving and lateral wall [3046]

5.45   Phosphate values for primary floor [3047], House 3, Stonehall Meadow

5.46   The enlarged House 5 at Ha'Breck, Wyre, where masonry piers serve to subdivide internal space

5.47   Plan of occupation deposits in Trench A of Stonehall Meadow

5.48   View of occupation deposits in Trench A from the east

5.49   Distribution of worked flint (a), stone (b) and pottery (c) within Trench Z, Stonehall Meadow

5.50   Distribution of worked flint (a), stone (b) and pottery (c) within Trench A

5.51   Excavated remains of stratigraphically early House 2 beneath Structure 1 at Stonehall Farm

6.1   Map of Orkney showing known 'villages' of the 3rd millennium cal BC

6.2   Aerial view of the Stonehall Farm mound

6.3   The geophysical and geochemical surveys of the Stonehall sites

6.4   Plan of Trench B at Stonehall Farm

6.5   View of covered drain [514] running east–west across Trench B

6.6   The drain [514] had collapsed where it ran through the soft and unstable midden

6.7   Portion of Structure 1 uncovered in 1995

6.8   Plan of upper deposits within Structure 1

6.9   Structure 1 showing upper deposits

6.10   Northeast facing section showing midden formation and construction cut for Structure 1

6.11   Southeast facing section through Structure 1

6.12   Broken orthostats facing the inner wall of Structure 1

6.13   Excavating the cell in the right-hand corner of Structure 1

6.14   Basal slab [645] of the shallow stone box or cist set in the floor of Structure 1, two hammerstones can be seen *in situ*

6.15   Stone slab [642] in the floor of Structure 1 (lower) and after removal (upper)

6.16   Tom Muir excavated the cavity beneath capstone [642] on the last day of excavation in 1997

6.17   Flint (a) and stone tools (b) from beneath flagstone [642]

6.18   Highly decorated Grooved ware rim sherd SF 2684 from soil [641] among stonework [635 and 863]

6.19   Excavated stone-lined pit [640]

6.20   Plan of Structure 1 showing charcoal bands encircling central cist

6.21   Magnetic susceptibility readings taken across the lower floor surface [880] by Adrian Challands

6.22   Plan of Structure 1 showing the position of the clay bowl [815]

6.23   Yellow clay bowl [815] in floor of Structure 1

6.24   Upper deposits [542] exposed in central cist on removal of the capstone

6.25   Detail of central cist

6.26   Distribution of material culture within the interior of Structure 1

6.27   The exposed early Bronze Age cairn at Mousland

6.28   Black stone bead (SF 2520) from occupation layer [519]

6.29   Plan of Stonehall Farm Trenches B and E

6.30   View of House 1 at Stonehall Farm

6.31   Detail of the hearth and surrounding yellow clay floor within House 1

6.32   Excavating the main doorway into House 1

6.33   Plan of House 1

6.34   Excavating the central hearth in House 1

6.35   Section (west-facing) through House 1

6.36   The snapped stone uprights forming the rectangular box to the left of the entrance into House 1

6.37   Successive layers of yellow clay flooring surrounded the central hearth

6.38   Distribution of worked stone and flint at Stonehall Farm

6.39   Cleaning a colourful section of midden (section D–B) east of Structure 1 in Trench B at Stonehall Farm

6.40   Sections through the Stonehall Farm midden east of Structure 1

6.41   The conical profile of the midden heap can be clearly seen in the stratigraphy of the upper eastern section east of Structure 1

6.42   East-west section (north-facing) through the eastern midden running up to Structure 1

7.1   Situation of the Crossiecrown and Ramberry sites

7.2   Plot of the gradiometer survey of Crossiecrown, using a Philpot Electronics Gradiometer AM01

7.3   Trench location at Crossiecrown.

7.4   View of the curving early gulley or drain [526] cut into the glacial clay in the southern area of Trench 2

7.5   View of Trenches 1 and 2 looking to the north

7.6   Plan of Trench 1 (spit 3)

7.7   Distribution of worked stone, flint, and pottery in Trench 1

7.8   View of the southern midden forming the settlement mound (Trench 1) from the south

7.9   Section across interior of Structure 1; note the red midden [057] within the building

7.10   Trench 3 from the west

7.11   Plan of Trench 3

7.12   North-facing section through midden deposits in Trench 3

7.13   Andrew M. Jones and Richard Jones excavating sherds of Grooved ware vessel (SFs 316, 343 and 380) in north-eastern midden deposit [210]

7.14   Plan of Trench 2

7.15   Distribution of Pottery in Trench 2 at Crossiecrown

7.16   Structure 1 at the Ness of Brodgar

7.17   View of the Red House showing the well-preserved wall in the northeast recess and thickened rear wall in the foreground

7.18   Plan of modified Red House

7.19   The original casing wall [154] running around the west side of the Red House

7.20   Southwest facing (a) and southeast facing (b) sections through the Red House

7.21   Plan of the final Red House

7.22   View of the shelf-like recess from the south when the Red House was first uncovered

7.23   Drain running out of cell in the Red House

7.24   Stone mortar (SF 85) *in situ* at rear of the Red House cell

7.25   Small stone box [015] after the removal of its four uprights, boxes [013] and [136] can be seen in the background

7.26   Sections through the three stone boxes [013], [015] and [136] in the Red House

7.27   Lesley McFadyen supervises rear area of the remodelled Red House; note the thickened outer wall with midden core

7.28   The floor of the Red House with the sample square subdivision

7.29   Plan showing the grid over the Red House

7.30   The distribution of flint, stone, Grooved ware and pumice across the Red House floor

7.31   The polished stone axe (SF 63) from the right recess

7.32   Magnetic susceptibility distribution (a) across the Red House, and phosphate distribution (b) across the Red House

7.33   Distribution of (a) phosphorus, (b) calcium, (c) copper, (d) iron, (e) rubidium, (f) strontium, (g) zirconium and (h) lead across the interior of the Red House

7.34   Excavating ash layers within the large Red House hearth

7.35   Plan of the Grey House and the northern area of Trench 2

7.36   The Grey House under excavation as viewed from the northeast

7.37   View of the Grey House from the west

7.38   Paved area [193] south of the Grey House; note the extant earlier wall [566] redeployed as an outer casement wall

7.39   View of sectioned central hearth in the Grey House

7.40   Nick Card uncovers the polished gneiss tool (SF 654) deposited in the northeast recess of the Grey House

7.41   View of cell in northern area of the Grey House

7.42   Sections of small stone boxes [419] and [492] in the Grey House

7.43   South-facing section through the eastern side of the Grey House

7.44   Plan of the primary Red and Grey Houses

7.45   Hollow [213] under excavation, hearth [491] can be seen to the right

7.46   Plan of the northeast area of Trench 2, showing the extent and shape of the proposed timber and turf structure represented by hollow [213]

7.47   Detail of hearth [491] in the eastern area of Trench 2

8.1   View of Quanterness passage grave from Crossiecrown

8.2   The typology of chambered cairns as constructed by Stuart Piggott

8.3   The 1973 excavation trench running up the western side of Quanterness exposed the cairn material

8.4   The upper bone spread running up to the entrance to the northern cell

8.5   The bone spread in the central chamber at Quanterness

8.6   Aerial view of Cuween Hill passage grave

8.7   The orientation of the passage at Wideford Hill is roughly aligned on Cuween Hill passage grave to the west

8.8   SER values observed for the whole sample (subadult and adult)

8.9   Skeletal element representation at Quanterness

8.10   In the floor of the main chamber at Quanterness, below the main bone-spread, was a primary crouched inhumation in Pit A

8.11   Unlike Pit A, Pit B at Quanterness was a nicely constructed stone cist with a well-fitting capstone

8.12   After the capstone was removed from Pit B, the cist was seen to be built with sidestones but only decayed cranial fragments were present

8.13 The legs of the extended inhumation in Pit C cut into the upper bone spread layer within the central chamber of Quanterness

8.14 Ramberry Head from the southeast

8.15 At Ramberry Head, Site 1, deposits of cremated bone, pottery and stone artefacts were brought to the surface during ploughing in April, 2005

8.16 Gradiometer plot of survey undertaken over Sites 1 and 3 at Ramberry Head

8.17 Plan of Ramberry Head Site 1

8.18 View of the Ring Cairn from the west

8.19 Section view of the white clay foundation spread for the water-worn basal slab

8.20 Project geophysicist Adrian Challands excavates pottery (SF 12) from the central setting

8.21 Distribution plan of pottery recovered from Site 1

8.22 Magnetic susceptibility plot of Site 1

8.23 View of the encircling stone bank where it was preserved in a hollow to the east, running concentric to the central setting

8.24 Ard point (SF 17) incorporated in the encircling bank

8.25 Adrian Challands stands centrally within the spread of stone (Site 2) brought to the surface by ploughing

8.26 Beneath the ploughsoil at Site 2 a mass of collapsed stonework was exposed in the original trench

8.27 Plan of the Ramberry Head passage structure fully excavated

8.28 View from the southeast of the passage after it was first uncovered

8.29 View of excavated passage structure from the southwest

8.30 Plan of passage structure showing infill rubble and line of stones [043]

8.31 View of the passage structure (Site 2) under excavation

8.32 Plan showing the material complexity of the burial context at Ramberry Head Site 1

9.1 View of the Cuween-Wideford coastal zone from the north, the Holm of Grimbister occupies the foreground

9.2 Traditionally animals were transported by boat in Orkney

9.3 View of timber House 4, Trench A at Braes of Ha'Breck, Wyre

9.4 View of timber House 1, Trench C at Braes of Ha'Breck, Wyrek

9.5 Distribution of stalled chambered cairns in Rousay, Orkney

9.6 Knap of Howar from the air, the primary House 1 is seen as a substantially larger dwelling

9.7 Varme Dale barrow excavations from the northwest, the burnt layers can be seen to the right running around the outside of the mound

9.8 Plan of Varme Dale showing the excavation Trenches 2a and 2b

9.9 Section through Mound 2 at Varme Dale

9.10 The burnt deposits containing charred grain ran beneath the barrow

9.11 House 3 at Braes of Ha'Breck, Wyre showing the large spread of burnt barley grains at the rear of the house

9.12 House 3 at Braes of Ha'Breck was elongated and doubled in size by the addition of House 5

9.13 Planning in House 3 at Stonehall Meadow, Cuween Hill Passage grave is visible high up on the hillside

9.14 Northern view of the late 4th millennium cal BC house structure at Green, Eday

9.15 Barnhouse from the air

9.16 Grooved ware from the Stones of Stenness and Barnhouse displays identical decoration

9.17 House 2 at Barnhouse from the southwest

9.18 An unusual ground and polished camptonite object with knobs collected by Christopher Gee

9.19 Kerb running around Cairn S, Loughcrew, Ireland

9.20 Peristalith at Reineval, Sout Uist

9.21 Distribution of passage graves in Mainland, Orkney

9.22 The Stones of Stenness

9.23 The Ring of Brodgar

9.24 Macehead fragment (Orkney pestle)

9.25 The gathering of 'big houses' at the Ness of Brodgar

9.26 Aerial view of Skara Brae

9.27 Looking into Hut 1 at Skara Brae

9.28 Structure 8 at Barnhouse overlies part of the earlier village

9.29 Plan of the later configuration of houses at Skara Brae

9.30 Orcadian double houses span the 3rd and 2nd millennium cal BC: (a) Links of Noltland; (b) Skara Brae; (c) Wasbister; (d) Holm of Farray; (e) Auskerry; (f) Skaill, Deerness

9.31 'Double' houses 1 and 6 at Barnhouse

9.32 Location of Muckquoy, Redland, Mainland, Orkney

9.33 Immediate topography of Muckquoy, Redland

9.34 View of Muckquoy from the east during geophysical survey

9.35 Fragment of a gneiss pestle macehead recovered from fieldwalking at Muckquoy, Redland

9.36 Polished haematite recovered from fieldwalking

9.37 Gradiometer survey of Muckquoy, Redland

9.38 The south-eastern stone wall bounding the Ness of Brodgar

9.39 South-facing section through the peripheral midden at Muckquoy, Redland

9.40 Plan of 'ditch' [003] and slots [005], [008], [013], [040] and [042] at Muckquoy, Redland

9.41 Boundary slot [005] cutting upper midden deposits [002]

9.42 The base of posthole [037] showing in the base of slot [005]

9.43 Gradiometer survey of area around Muckquoy, Redland, undertaken by Christopher Gee

10.1 Map of Neolithic sites in Orkney with radiocarbon dates mentioned in the text, or shown in the model in Fig. 10.2

10.2 The model structure for the analysis of radiocarbon dates

10.3 The first part of the Bay of Firth component of the model

10.4 The second part of the Bay of Firth component of the model

10.5 The first part of the early Neolithic Orkney house component of the model

10.6 The second part of the early Neolithic house component of the model

10.7 The first part of the Orkney-Cromarty cairn component of the model

10.8 The second part of the Orkney-Cromarty cairn component of the model

10.9 The third part of the Orkney-Cromarty cairn component of the model

10.10 The first part of the passage grave (Maes Howe-type) component of the model

10.11 The second part of the passage grave (Maes Howe-type) component of the model

10.12 A model for radiocarbon result from the ditches sampled by Renfrew

10.13 Posterior density estimates associated with early Neolithic timber structures and stone-built stalled houses

10.14 Posterior density estimates associated with start of activity from early Neolithic Orkney-Cromarty cairns

10.15 Posterior density estimates associated with Maes Howe-type cairns from Quanterness, Maes Howe, Pierowall and Quoyness

10.16 A comparison of posterior density estimates from the model shown in Fig. 10.2

10.17 A comparison of posterior density estimates calculated in the model shown in Fig. 10.2

11.2.1 Wall thickness (cm) in all sherds from Stonehall Knoll, Meadow and Farm

11.2.2 Longest axis (cm) in all sherds from Stonehall Knoll, Meadow and Farm

11.2.3 Rim diameter (cm) in all sherds from Stonehall Knoll and Meadow

11.2.4 Plot of rim diameter against wall thickness for rims at Stonehall Knoll (K) and Stonehall Meadow (M)

11.2.5 Sherds from Stonehall Knoll

11.2.6 Percentage of the fabric made up by inclusions in all sherds from Stonehall Knoll, Meadow and Farm

11.2.7 Illustrated sherds from (a) Stonehall Meadow (Trench A), (b) Stonehall Meadow (Trench Z)

11.2.8 The distribution of pottery from Stonehall Farm (Trenches B and E)

11.2.9 Clay balls and architectural fragment SF 2139

11.2.10 Wall thickness (cm) of sherds at Stonehall Farm (Trenches B, E and F)

11.2.11 Rim and base diameters (cm) at Stonehall Farm (Trenches B, E and F)

11.2.12 Decorated and other pottery from Stonehall Farm (Trench B)

11.2.13 Pottery bases from Stonehall Farm (Trench B)

11.2.14 Distribution of decoration types at Stonehall Farm (Trenches B, E and F)

11.2.15 Distribution of the Sedimentary and Igneous +Sedimentary fabric groups identified at Stonehall Knoll, Meadow and Farm

11.2.16 Distribution of sizes of the maximum dimension of the largest inclusion observed in the thin sections of clays

11.3.1 Unstan ware sherd SF 774 from context [445], Trench 2 at Crossiecrown

11.3.2 Grooved ware rim sizes

11.3.3 Grooved ware from Crossiecrown

11.3.4 Decoration types for Grooved ware at Crossiecrown

11.3.5 Grooved ware SFs 150, 152 and 154 at Crossiecrown

11.3.6 Grooved ware fabrics in large, medium and small size vessels

11.3.7 Grooved ware use wear and vessel size at Crossiecrown

11.3.8 Beaker rims SF 467 and SF 1399 from Crossiecrown

11.3.9 The pot spread (SF 316, 380 and 343) in the northern midden at Crossiecrown

11.3.10 The Grooved ware vessel (SF 316, 380 and 343), from the midden in Trench 3, Crossiecrown

11.4.1 Pottery from Wideford Hill

11.4.2 Rim diameter ranges in Wideford Hill pottery

11.4.3 Wideford pottery fabrics and vessel size

11.5.1 Location of clays and igneous rock in the Stonehall-Grimbister area

11.5.2 Reconstruction of a round-based vessel, using a hollow scooped in the ground

11.5.3 Constructing a flat-based vessel using ribbon-shaped coils

11.5.4   Preheating a Grooved ware-type vessel at Stonehall (a), prepared firing area with Central 'grate' and Buller's bar (b)

11.5.5   (top) Stonehall firing 4 (see Table 11.5.4); (middle) raking out the ash after the firing; (bottom) close-up of pots (and Bullers bar) after firing

11.5.6   Characteristics of firings 2, 3 and 4 at Stonehall using two thermocouples

11.5.7   Magnetic and magnetic susceptibility plots at the experimental firing area at Stonehall (a), Magnetic and magnetic susceptibility plots at Trench D at Stonehall (b)

11.6.1   Photomicrographs of (a) Stonehall group α; (b) Stonehall group α; (c) grog fragment; (d) camptonite inclusion; (e) dolerite inclusion ; (f) Stonehall group β; (g) Stonehall group β

11.6.2   Photomicrographs of (a) Crossiecrown group A; (b) camptonite inclusion; (c) dolerite inclusion ; (d) monchiquite inclusion; (e) basalt inclusion; (f) Crossiecrown group G; (g) Quanterness 187

11.6.3   Location of dykes in the Bay of Firth area

11.7.1   Plot of $\Delta^{13}C$ against $\delta^{13}C_{16:0}$ values for (a) Grooved Ware and Early Neolithic sherds and surface residues from Stonehall, (b) the Grooved Ware and Beaker Ware sherds from Crossiecrown, and (c) Unstan Ware absorbed and surface residues from sherds from Wideford Hill

11.8.1   Illustrated sherds from Ramberry Head

11.9.1   Illustrated sherds from Brae of Smerquoy

11.9.2   The distribution of sherd thickness (cm) at Brae of Smerquoy

11.9.3   Illustrated sherds and clay ball from Muckquoy, Redland

11.9.4   The distribution of sherd thickness (cm) at Muckquoy, Redland

11.10.1   Rim sherds from the Knowes of Trotty

12.1   Flaked lithic artefacts from Wideford Hill. Illustrations 1–12

12.2   Flaked lithic artefacts from the Brae of Smerquoy. Illustrations 13–17

12.3   Flaked lithic artefacts from Stonehall Knoll. Illustrations 18–28

12.4   Flaked lithic artefacts from Stonehall Meadow. Illustrations 29–32

12.5   Flaked lithic artefacts from Stonehall Farm. Illustrations 33–62

12.6   Chisel arrowheads from Stonehall Farm. Illustrations 63–65

12.7   Flaked lithic artefacts from Crossiecrown. Illustrations 66–77

12.8   Arrowheads from Crossiecrown. Illustrations 75–79

12.9   The 'Stonehall Farm-type' scrapers from Crossiecrown. Illustrations 80–86

13.1   Worked stone from Stonehall

13.2   Worked stone from Wideford Hill

13.3   Worked stone from Crossiecrown

13.4   The sculpted stone (SF 184) from the floor of the Red House

13.5   Worked stone from Knowes of Trotty

13.6   Unstratified ground end 'finger' stone tool from Trench 1, Smerquoy

13.7   Unstratified 'Knap of Howar' grinder from Trench 1, Smerquoy

13.8   Broken sandstone axe recovered from fieldwalking in 2010

13.9   Worked stone from Ramberry Head

13.10   Cobble tool from 2013 fieldwalking at Muckquoy, Redland

13.1.1   Pumice SF 2088 from Stonehall

13.2.1   The black stone bead from Structure 1, Stonehall Farm

13.3.1   The *wet abrasion method* demonstrated on a white quartzite stone showing micronised pigment production

13.3.2   Streak test on ceramic plate of samples

13.3.3a   Crossiecrown haematite IP3 and IP2

13.3.3b   Crossiecrown haematite: top row IP1, 5, 9; lower row IP 11, 18

13.3.3c   Crossiecrown haematite IP1, 5 and 11 showing very finely striated and polished faceted surfaces

13.3.3d   Crossiecrown haematite: top IP8, 10; bottom IP4bis, IP14

13.3.4   (Modern) pot made of Orcadian clay showing painted decoration using haematite and iron-rich sandstone

13.3.5   Palm-sized specimen of shiny, black, botryoidal haematite found *in situ* between the sandstone boulders at Bay of Creekland, on Hoy

14.1.1   1mm^2 thin section through cremated bone

15.1   Comparison of cereals present in different phases at Knowes of Trotty

15.2   Comparison of fuel types present in different phases at Knowes of Trotty

15.3   Comparison of charcoal present in different phases at Knowes of Trotty

15.1.1   Stonehall peat profile

15.1.2   Time-depth plot

15.1.3   Stonehall pollen diagram

15.1.4   Stonehall macrofossil diagram

16.1   Location of profiles in respect to Structure 1, Stonehall Farm

16.2   Stonehall photomicrographs

16.3   Crossiecrown photomicrographs

List of Tables

2.1 Details of postholes comprising Timber structure 1

2.2 Radiocarbon sequence through scoop hearth [067]

2.3 Details of postholes comprising Timber structure 2

2.4 Details of postholes comprising Timber structure 3

4.1 Sizes of the pits within the innermost (southern) compartment

7.1 Radiocarbon dates through midden [204] in Trench 3

7.2 Summary of the soil micromorphology of the Red House floor

7.3 Summary statistics for 13 selected elements and ranges in the reference material

8.1 Radiocarbon dates for Cuween Hill passage grave

8.2 Minimum number of elements and number of identified specimens for Quanterness

10.1 Results from sites from the Bay of Firth landscape study area

10.2 Key posterior density estimates from the model shown in Fig. 10.2, the model shown in Fig. 10.12, and the calculations shown in Fig. 10.13

11.2.1 Associations of sherds on Stonehall Knoll

11.2.2 Rims from Stonehall Knoll, those in italics are illustrated in Fig. 11.2.5

11.2.3 Petrographic groups in pottery from Stonehall Knoll.

11.2.4 Associations of individual sherds from Stonehall Meadow (Trench A)

11.2.5 Associations of individual sherds from Stonehall Meadow (Trench Z)

11.2.6 Pottery from Stonehall Meadow (Trenches A and Z)

11.2.7 Sherds with carbonised residue and/or sooting from Stonehall Meadow

11.2.8 Petrographic groups in pottery from Stonehall Meadow (Trenches A and Z)

11.2.9 Clay balls from Stonehall Farm (Trench B)

11.2.10 Decorated and other pottery from Stonehall Farm (Trench B)

11.2.11 Bases from Stonehall Farm (Trench B bases)

11.2.12 Decorative types in Grooved ware from Stonehall Farm (Trenches B, E and F)

11.2.13 Incised decoration on Grooved ware from Stonehall Farm

11.2.14 Petrographic data for pottery from Stonehall Farm (Trenches B, E and F)

11.3.1 Early Neolithic rim forms

11.3.2 Characteristics of round-based vessels

11.3.3 Round-based vessel sherds showing sooting

11.3.4 Bevelled rims

11.3.5 Pointed rims

11.3.6 Rounded rims

11.3.7 Scalloped rims

11.3.8 Flat rims

11.3.9 Flat bases

11.3.10 Footed bases

11.3.11 Bases with rounded interiors and/or square exteriors

11.3.12 Bases with angled walls at 45 degree angle to base

11.3.13 Bases with angled walls at 90 degree angle to base

11.3.14 List of Beaker rim forms

11.3.15 Beaker sherds with evidence of twisted cord impressions

11.3.16 Beaker sherds with comb impression, incision and other impressed decoration

11.3.17 Sooting and residue on Beaker sherds

11.3.18 Unstan ware petrology

11.3.19 Grooved ware petrology

13.3.20 Beaker petrology

11.4.1 Bevelled rims

11.4.2 Club-shaped and flat, flat everted and inverted rims

11.4.3 Flat, lipped rims

11.4.4 Rounded rims

11.4.5 Vessels with finger or thumbnail impressions

11.4.6 Vessels with incised or stab-and-drag motifs

11.4.7 Other decorated vessels

11.4.8 Decoration on the upper rim

11.4.9 Undecorated Unstan vessels

11.4.10 Firing profile of Wideford Hill pottery assemblage

11.4.11 Evidence for repair or suspension holes

11.4.12 Catalogue of petrological samples

11.5.1 Characteristics of clays from Stonehall and environs

11.5.2 Comparison of the compositions of the clays and Neolithic pottery

11.5.3 Firings at Stonehall 1997

11.6.1 The main inclusions of the samples of Group α at Stonehall

11.6.2 The main inclusions of the samples of Group β at Stonehall

11.6.3 The main inclusions in the pottery at Crossiecrown

11.6.4 BGS thin-sections of the pottery at Stonehall and Crossiecrown and their locations on Orkney

11.7.1 Early Neolithic and Grooved ware sherds and surface (S) residues from Stonehall, Crossiecrown and Wideford Hill

11.7.2 Lipid assignments for Early Neolithic and Grooved Ware from Stonehall, Crossiecrown and Wideford Hill based on TLEs, TAGs, $\delta^{13}C$ and $\Delta^{13}C$ values

11.9.1 Sherds from Brae of Smerquoy

11.9.2 Sherds from Muckquoy

12.1 Summary struck lithic assemblage quantified by number and weight

12.2 Summary lithic assemblages shown as percentages of site total

12.3 Raw materials by site, excluding chips and unworked pebbles

12.4 The colour of struck flints from selected sites

12.5 Colour by key artefact type

12.6 Classification of reworked artefacts

12.7 The struck lithic assemblage from Wideford Hill by artefact type and raw material

12.8 The struck lithic assemblage from Knowes of Trotty by artefact type and raw material

12.9 The flint assemblage from the Knowes of Trotty by trench, context and artefact type

12.10 The struck lithic assemblage from the Brae of Smerquoy by artefact type and raw material

12.11 The struck lithic assemblage from Stonehall Knoll by artefact type and raw material

12.12 The struck lithic assemblage from Stonehall Meadow by artefact type and raw material

12.13 The struck lithic assemblage from Stonehall Farm by artefact type and raw material

12.14 The lithic assemblage from Stonehall Farm by Trench

12.15 Flints with facetted butts from Stonehall Knoll and Stonehall Farm

12.16 The struck lithic assemblage from Crossiecrown by artefact type and raw material

12.17 The struck lithic assemblage from Crossiecrown Trench 1 by phase

12.18 The struck lithic assemblage from Crossiecrown Trenches 2 and 3 by phase

12.19 The struck lithic assemblage from Ramberry by artefact type and raw material

13.1 Artefact types from the excavated trenches at Stonehall

13.2 Wideford Hill: course artefacts and context type

13.3 Cobble tool types from Wideford Hill

13.4 Stone assemblages from Orcadian fourth millennium cal BC sites

13.5 Distribution of stone artefacts in the Red House at Crossiecrown

13.6 Distribution of stone artefacts in the post-Red House occupation of Crossiecrown

13.7 Distribution of stone artefacts in the later occupation of Crossiecrown

13.8 Knowes of Trotty stone artefacts by trench

13.9 Stone tools from Smerquoy excavation 2013

13.10 Ramberry head: stone artefacts by site

13.1.1 Crossiecrown pumice by context

13.1.2 Stonehall pumice by context

13.3.1 Material from Crossiecrown

13.3.2 Material from Stonehall

14.1 Bone and teeth identification from Stonehall

14.2 Bone and teeth identification from Crossiecrown

14.1.1 Contexts that produced burnt bone or that were bulk sampled for flotation

14.1.2 Samples processed as part of this study

14.1.3 Finds recovered during processing

14.1.4 Overall identification of skeletal areas

14.1.5 Age range equivalents for descriptive terms used

15.1 The botanical evidence from Stonehall Meadow (Trench A)

15.2 The botanical evidence from Stonehall Meadow (Trench Z)

15.3 The botanical evidence from Stonehall Farm (Trench B)

15.4 The botanical evidence from Stonehall Farm (Trenches D and E)

15.5 Botanical evidence from Stonehall Knoll

15.6 Botanical evidence from Crossiecrown

15.7 Botanical evidence from Wideford Hill

15.8 Botanical evidence for Knowes of Trotty (a–f phased)

15.9 Botanical evidence from Varme Dale

15.1.1 Radiocarbon dates

15.1.2 Summary of vegetation zones

16.1 Profile descriptions at Stonehall

16.2 Summary of the main micromorphological features of profiles 1–6

16.3 Summary of the main features of the Stonehall hearth sequences

16.4 Summary of the micromorphological descriptions and interpretations for samples 15–17, Crossiecrown Trench 1, 1998

16.5 Summary of the micromorphological descriptions and interpretations for Crossiecrown Trench 2, 1999

16.6 Summary of the micromorphological descriptions and interpretations for Crossiecrown Trench 3, 1999

CHAPTER ONE

Images of Neolithic Orkney

Colin Richards and Richard Jones

1.1 Images of Neolithic Orkney

Orkney is an archipelago that lies off the rugged northeastern coast of Caithness in northern Scotland (Fig. 1.1). It is separated from the Scottish mainland by the volatile Pentland Firth, one of the roughest and unpredictable stretches of water in the world. On calm summer days the southern isles of Orkney appear colourful, tranquil and easily accessible across glassy waters when viewed from Caithness. However, even in these conditions this imagery is deceptive as treacherous currents are always present in the Pentland Firth. On stormy days Orkney becomes obscured and the Firth becomes a maelstrom of enormous seas. Deceptively reachable, and yet clearly defined as another world, this is the view of Orkney today, and as it would have appeared over five thousand years ago when viewed from the steep cliffs of the Scottish mainland (Fig. 1.2).

Although of similar geology, the topography of Orkney appears very different from that of Caithness. From the dominant hills of northern Hoy (Fig. 1.3), to the stepped terraces of Rousay, to the rolling hill-slopes of western Mainland, the Old Red Sandstone flagstone series creates a varied but 'subdued topography' (Mykura 1976, 1). Unlike Shetland or the Outer Hebrides, stone does not obviously appear to be a dominant component of the Orcadian terrain. Yet, before the 2nd millennium cal BC formation of peat (Davidson and R. L. Jones 1985, 28), dramatic cliff sections, projecting flagstone beds along the shore, and outcropping rock on the upper hill terraces would have together constituted highly visible constituents of landscape. The browns, yellows and reds of the different strata give the rock a warm and rich colouring, but on closer inspection it is the unusual laminate character of the flagstone that makes it so distinctive. At different scales it is this quality that gives rise to the stepped appearance of the towering cliffs

of Orkney (Fig. 1.4) and provides all the features of an excellent building material with variable strata thickness and geometric secondary jointing. Of course, it is these qualities that were exploited in Orcadian prehistory to create architecture that in many cases has endured.

Today, the archipelago (Fig. 1.5) can be described as a place of sea and sky, where open vistas are produced by expansive treeless landscapes, weakly punctuated by ridges, hills and lochs. The 'smooth contours clothed by green pasture or peat' (Ritchie 1995, 14) could easily describe the open landscapes of the majority of islands, and it is this picture of Orkney that colours the popular imagination. Because of the seemingly timeless qualities of the islands it is easy to project this image back into the past, for instance, it had been assumed that from the early Neolithic the vegetation had been reduced to 'scrub woodland cover' (Sharples 1992, 325), which in turn 'began to be replaced by more open vegetation about 3500 BC' (Davidson and R. L. Jones 1985, 25). This situation was lamented by R. L. Jones because 'if early man [*sic*] in Orkney adapted to a shrubland environment, as seems almost certainly to be the case on the basis of available palynological evidence, clearance phases...characteristic of neolithic peoples operating in forested conditions will not be found in the pollen spectra' (1979, 21). Indeed, it is this narrative of scant woodland cover being removed by early agricultural clearance in the middle of the 4th millennium cal BC that has been identified by Farrell *et al.* (2014) as the dominant discursive framework for interpreting vegetation cover at the beginning of the Neolithic.

This discourse now appears flawed, as recent pollen evidence demonstrates the continuation of woodland conditions beyond the mid-4th millennium cal BC on Mainland, Orkney (Farrell *et al.* 2014). The maintenance

Figure 1.1 Location map of Orkney.

Figure 1.2 View of Orkney from Caithness (Colin Richards).

Figure 1.3 The hills of northern Hoy dominate Mainland, Orkney (Colin Richards).

Figure 1.4 The stepped character of Orcadian sandstone cliffs (Colin Richards).

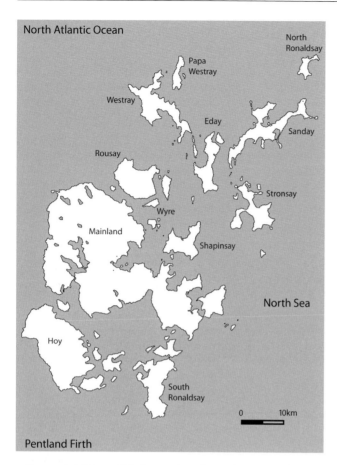

North Atlantic Ocean

Papa
Westray

North
Ronaldsay

Westray

Eday

Sanday

Rousay

Stronsay

Wyre

Mainland

Shapinsay

North Sea

Hoy

South
Ronaldsay

0   10km

Pentland Firth

Figure 1.5 Map of Orkney identifying the main islands.

of such areas of woodland provides an explanation for the presence of molluscs considered to indicate 'a former woodland environment' in a buried soil at Knap of Howar, Papa Westray (Evans and Vaughan 1983, 110). It may also account for the large quantity of birch, hazel and willow visible in the Orkney peats (Davidson and Jones 1985, 23). Perhaps, more importantly, the continuation of tracts of woodland makes the claim for timber houses being raised in the early Bronze Age more comprehensible (*e.g.* Buteux 1997; Downes and Thomas 2014, 82). Hence, rather than presenting open landscapes of sparse birch and hazel scrub, the archipelago may now be seen as possessing a highly attractive range of resources (Edwards 1996, 28). As Saville notes, 'apart from the uses which Mesolithic people would have had for timber (shelter, firewood, tools, *etc.*) and timber products (birch bark, resin, *etc.*), the hazel would provide nuts to eat, while understorey and open-ground bushes and plants would have produced numerous edible fruits, berries, leaves, shoots and roots' (2000, 97). Of course, exactly the same holds true for people tending domesticated

animals and cultivating cereals during the early to middle 4th millennium cal BC.

The form and chronology of the early Neolithic period in Orkney seemed relatively clear-cut when Anna Ritchie first published *Prehistoric Orkney* in 1995. Several years earlier she had directed two seasons of excavation at Knap of Howar on the small island of Papa Westray. The site comprised two juxtaposed buildings which had been previously excavated by Traill and Kirkness (1937, 314), who suggested an Iron Age date. Re-excavation by Ritchie soon revealed Knap of Howar to be Neolithic and the discovery of round-based pottery, including Unstan ware, was indicative of a date in the middle 4th millennium cal BC (Sheridan and Higham 2006, 202–203). The presence of Unstan ware was considered particularly significant as this represented the first instance of the ceramic being found in a context beyond the Orcadian chambered cairns (A. Ritchie 1983, 54, but see Davidson and Henshall 1989, 77).

Indeed, the preservation of the buildings at Knap of Howar is remarkable with walls standing over a metre and a half in height, and internal stone furniture remaining *in situ* (Fig. 1.6). In this respect Knap of Howar is comparable with Skara Brae or the Ness of Brodgar. Just as Skara Brae came to be seen as being typical of late Neolithic domestic architecture, so Knap of Howar assumed a similar status in regard to the earlier Neolithic period (Downes and Richards 2000, 167). Within the interior of Knap of Howar, internal space is demarcated by opposed orthostats projecting from the side walls creating a spatial structure based on linear sub-division (Fig. 1.7a). This architecture clearly resonates with the orthostatic 'stalling' within the 'Orkney-Cromarty' chambered cairns (Davidson and Henshall 1989, 19–36). Consequently, a comparison between chambered cairn and Knap of Howar architecture was inevitable and subsequently has been consistently made (*e.g.* Ritchie 1983, 58; Hodder 1984; Richards 1992, 66; 1995, Fig. 29), resulting in the former being conceived as 'houses of the dead' (Ritchie 1995, 44). Of course, such recognition is contingent on the chambered cairns replicating the architectural vocabulary of the house.

Although clearly identified (Ritchie 1983, 44–46), the evidence derived from Knap of Howar for an early period of habitation exhibiting no extant structural remains is often neglected in narratives of the Orcadian Neolithic. 'The basic stratigraphy of the site is simple' declares Anna Ritchie and indicates 'two main periods of activity. A layer of midden some 0.4m thick represents the primary phase but, apart from the remains of stone paving to the

Figure 1.6 (above) Knap of Howar, Papa Westray (Colin Richards).

Figure 1.7 (right) Plan of (A) Knap of Howar and (B) Knowe of Yarso (after Ritchie 1983; 1995).

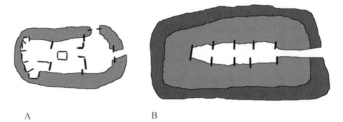

A   B

S of house 1, there was no trace in the excavated area of any contemporary structure' (1983, 44). It was upon this early midden that the Knap of Howar stone Houses 1 and 2 were erected. Of course, the masonry comprising these buildings could have been robbed from unidentified structures but this seems unlikely. Instead, the lack of structural evidence from this earlier period may suggest something entirely different, for example a primary phase of occupation constituted by less durable architecture. Given the spread and context of radiocarbon dates at Knap of Howar in conjunction with the site phasing, the primary (timber house?) occupation continues until *c.*3300 cal BC. If this is the case, rather than initially accompanying stone-built houses, the Orcadian stalled chambered cairns were actually built by people dwelling in timber houses, an occurrence which will be explored in the following chapters. The main point to be made here is that our images of a neatly ordered early Neolithic world are blurring and a new canvas is required.

1.2 Constructing Neolithic worlds

In *The prehistory of Orkney* Anna Ritchie lamented that 'since we cannot yet identify the very earliest colonists, it is impossible to trace the route by which they arrived on the southern shores of the Pentland Firth, whether by way of the east or west coasts of mainland Scotland' (1990a, 39). This line of enquiry has tended to be a problematic interpretative area because of a culture-history legacy. Without doubt the first agriculturists had to arrive by boat at islands forming the Orkney archipelago. However, was the 'Neolithic' really brought to Orkney by 'colonists'? The danger here is that such a question simply perpetuates an interpretative framework that attempts to identify Neolithic colonization incrementally spreading from the south of Britain (cf. Whittle *et al.* 2011, 866–71; Thomas 2013, 135–41) or even further south (Sheridan 2000; 2003). Such a discourse regarding the direction of colonization was initially proposed by Childe on the basis of the distribution of pottery styles and chambered cairns:

Similarly in the north of Scotland we can, on the ceramic evidence, no longer speak of a Windmill Hill culture, but an Unstan or Pentland culture infected with the ceramic and funerary traditions associated with megalithic passage graves. So the mariners who, whether as missionaries or chiefs, spread the megalithic religion had a share in instigating or leading the expansion of Windmill Hill culture over Scotland and Ireland.

(Childe 1940, 45).

In turn, this perspective was reiterated by Piggott who commented on the geographical spread of chambered cairns in a more detailed manner:

This distribution could be the result of the use of two routes, either exclusively one or the other, or a combination of both. The first would continue the Western Approaches up the Atlantic coasts beyond the Hebridean area of colonization… to make landfalls along the north coast of the mainland and in the Orkneys, and thence down the east coast to the Moray Firth. The second would utilize the natural highway of the Great Glen, stretching for some 80 miles north-east from the Firth of Lorne on the west coast to the Moray Firth on the east and affording a series of lochs for water transport. From the head of the Great Glen in the neighbourhood of Inverness, colonization could spread northwards by coasting voyages to Sutherland and Caithness, and ultimately to the Orkneys: as we shall see, typology makes it clear that a large number of Orcadian tombs must be derivatives from Caithness forms, so that a proportion of its colonists must have come from the Scottish mainland whichever route was used.

(Piggott 1954, 233–34).

Audrey Henshall, a student of Stuart Piggott, re-classified the chambered cairns of Scotland according to criteria of architectural similarity and variation (1963; 1972). Each type of chambered cairn was named on the basis of its geographic spread, for example, the Orkney-Cromarty group. Incorporated within this schema was the geographic spread or diffusion of chambered tombs across Scotland, thereby charting the extension of 'cultures'.

If we reject this particular culture history line of reasoning concerning the forces behind such distributions (*e.g.* S. Jones 1997) alternative interpretations are required. One narrative that will be pursued within this volume is that building is a social process and consequently the erection of, for instance, a chambered cairn represents a form of strategic practice (see also Richards 2013a). Motivation for such actions is multifaceted, encompassing a range of desires and intentions, however, the main point to make here is that building monuments can be seen as a social strategy as opposed to a 'cultural necessity'.

Hence, monument construction can be undertaken at different times and for a range of reasons, a divergence in practice that will be later identified as occurring in Neolithic Orkney (Chapter 9).

When Colin Renfrew first edited the *Prehistory of Orkney* in 1985, there appeared a degree of chronological and material order to the Orcadian Neolithic. Represented by the two pottery types, Unstan ware and Grooved wares, and associated styles of house and chambered cairn, the Neolithic could be pleasingly sub-divided into two discrete elements. Although unstated, such criteria and ordering of material culture bore great similarity to the methodology of cultural recognition employed by previous generations of prehistorians (*e.g.* Childe 1940; 1946; Piggott 1954, 232–56). However, such designations within culture-history discourse were avoided within Renfrew's scheme by providing chronological and social, as opposed to spatial definition. For instance, Unstan ware was positioned in the early Neolithic and Grooved ware in the late Neolithic periods respectively. A social evolutionary scheme was introduced which claimed to establish a sequential relationship of changing pottery styles and increasing monumentality coinciding nicely with the 4th and 3rd millennia cal BC (Renfrew 1979, Fig. 54). The same was suggested for the typological development of chambered cairns (*ibid.*, Fig. 55). Although chronologically divided, the early and late periods of the Orcadian Neolithic were in retrospect merely thinly veiled 'cultures', constituted on the basis of culture-history principles of the relatedness of different types of material culture.

Unfortunately, because they appeared as relatively discrete entities, it was extremely difficult to understand how an early Neolithic period composed of stalled cairns, single 'Knap of Howar type' farmsteads, Unstan ware, and so forth, could transform into a later Neolithic period composed of passage graves, villages and Grooved ware. Despite the attempt by Colin Renfrew to explain this transformation as a social phenomenon by charting the evolution from Unstan ware-using, early Neolithic segmentary societies into a Grooved ware-using, late Neolithic chiefdom (1979, 214–18; 2000), an Orcadian Neolithic composed of two entities remained (see for instance, MacSween 2007, 281).

In light of more sophisticated chronologies (*e.g.* Ashmore 2000a; 2005; Chapter 10), and an increase in available evidence, a more 'messy' picture of Neolithic habitation emerges and these basically 'cultural' entities become more frayed and ragged and their integrity further compromised. Equally, the coherence of the different constituents such as pottery style, house and tomb architecture begin to unravel, just as they had for Childe some 60 years ago (Richards 1995). Clearly, a different interpretative framework becomes necessary to accommodate new evidence and more sophisticated chronologies (see also Cooney 2003, 51–52; Richards 2013b, 81–83; Thomas 2013, 290–94).

1.3 Neolithic house societies

When Claude Lévi-Strauss conceived of a form of social organization based upon the 'house' – *sociétés à maisons* – it was essentially to provide a classification for social groups that appeared not to conform to established anthropological kinship structures. Hence, the *société à maisons* was principally identified as an institution, 'a corporate body holding an estate made up of material and immaterial wealth, which perpetuates itself through the transmission of its name, its goods, and its titles down a real or imaginary line, considered legitimate as long as this continuity can express itself in the language of kinship or affinity and, most often, of both' (Lévi-Strauss 1982, 174).

It should be remembered that when Lévi-Strauss gave the series of lectures in 1976–77 at the Collège de France where the *sociétés à maisons* idea was first outlined, the analytical integrity of kinship structures as a fundamental component of ethnographic research was already beginning to fracture (*e.g.* Schneider 1965; 1984). Obviously, social relations remained at the core of the discipline but the identification of idealized kinship structures had always been problematic as in reality relationships between people were far more variable and contingent. The notion of a house society was clearly situated in this debate as the anthropological examples used by Lévi-Strauss were those where kinship structures appeared either confused or unidentifiable (see Gillespie 2000b, 23). Specifically, *sociétés à maisons* provided an account of social organization that acknowledges the tension between relations based on what has been described as 'blood and soil' (*e.g.* Kuper 1982, 72; Gillespie 2000a, 1–3). The former (blood) relates to kinship, while the latter (soil) highlights the role of proximity or locality in the construction of social identities. Today, such a dichotomy has to some extent dissolved with any primacy or privileging of blood or kin relations being relegated in the face of the potency of practice-based, face-to-face social relationships (Carsten 2000). Interestingly, in archaeology a similar turn is noticeable in the increasing attention drawn to daily subsistence-

based practices characterizing social relationships during the earliest Neolithic in Britain (*e.g.* Schulting 2004; 2008; Cochrane and Jones 2012, 10–11; Thomas 2013). In short, the idea of house societies as formulated by Lévi-Strauss was to address a problem caused by anthropological discourses elevating 'elementary' kinship models, a problem which is of far less consequence to contemporary anthropology. Nor should it be forgotten that *sociétés à maisons* were conceived as a social 'type' within an evolutionary trajectory as opposed to a *social process*. Finally, criticism of the *sociétés à maisons* concept in terms of definitional clarity – or lack of it (see papers in Carsten and Hugh-Jones 1995) – has rendered a degree of uncertainty regarding the analytical potency of an idea described as being of 'startling scope' (Waterson 1995, 47).

Does this mean that *sociétés à maisons* is a redundant concept for any analysis of social process? Again, Waterson ponders the dual trajectories that the idea of *sociétés à maisons* initiates:

> Should we be using this simply as a jumping-off point from which to examine indigenous concepts? Or is what is needed a rigorous refinement of Lévi-Strauss 's definition, in order to decide exactly which societies may qualify as 'true' house societies and which may be excluded?
>
> (1995, 48).

This uncertainty encapsulates the ways in which *sociétés à maisons* has been deployed in different anthropological studies (Macdonald 1987; Carsten and Hugh-Jones 1995; Joyce and Gillespie 2000). Another potentially problematic aspect of the concept as originally formulated by Lévi-Strauss is that in being a social 'type', house societies assumed social evolutionary status (Lévi-Strauss 1987, 151; Carsten and Hugh-Jones 1995, 9–10). This feature of *sociétés à maisons* can be reformulated to suggest that the transformatory qualities of societies appearing to lack strong kin-based organization actually represent a *process articulated through social choices, strategies and practices deployed by competing groups under very particular historical conditions* (cf. Carsten and Hugh-Jones 1995, 36–42; Sissons 2010). Under such circumstances it should come as no surprise that the anchor point is the 'house', understood as a conceptual resource within extremely fluid social conditions. It is not so much that a 'house' provides a mechanism of creating stabilized social units, but that it is a consequence of a strategy of constructing and legitimizing identities under ever-shifting social conditions. It is this aspect of the idea of *sociétés à maisons* that has seen the concept deployed as an interpretative aid at its most effective (*e.g.* Marshall 2000), and is advocated here as a good way of thinking about the Orcadian Neolithic.

Before proceeding, it is important to address a particular area of obscurity and deficiency in Lévi-Strauss's original formulation of *sociétés à maisons*. If the 'house' is conceived as essentially an institution or abstract structuring principle, what is the status of the built house as a material and architectural construct? Equally, if the language of social reality is that of kinship and the house, does that extend to a physical manifestation or entity? Surely, if the house effectively materializes the social group (cf. Gillespie 2000a, 2) and is an instrument for the maintenance and continuity of a corporate group, should not the physical house be understood as both a social project and highly visible fetish of those qualities? Of course, the symbolic status of the materiality and architecture of the house as being redolent in layered and complex meanings is well attested (*e.g.* Waterson 1990; Fox 1993; Parker Pearson and Richards 1994). Here we recognise a duality of the house: as a fetish it is by default representational, and as a material entity it should be regarded as part of a process, a practical strategy which can be manipulated at different levels to serve particular social interests.

Let us begin with a central tenet of Lévi-Strauss, that of accounting for the apparent lack of strong kinship structures by virtue of residence and/or everyday practice constituting the main principle of social organization. This creates a corporate group (*personnes morales*) materialized by affiliation to a house and articulated through a language of the house (Gillespie 2000b, 46–47). Such language is not merely about kinship, economy and so forth, but crucially is also 'about common spaces and about buildings' (Carsten and Hugh-Jones 1995, 19). However, returning to the Orcadian Neolithic, just because houses appear to be such a strong and visible archaeological component, their presence does not necessarily translate, even in the modified form advocated here, into the existence of *sociétés à maisons* as defined by Lévi-Strauss. Howell phrases the applicability of the concept of house societies as an aid to interpretation in a slightly different manner:

> There would appear to be two possibilities: there are non-differentiated societies in which social and moral unity is found through the House; and there are differentiated societies where such a unity is found primarily in fixed kin and alliance categories and in the relation between these. If the latter societies can also be found to have 'Houses' then their meaning must be explained in different terms…
>
> (1995, 151).

We will heed both Howell (1995) and Waterson (1995: 2000) to some degree and attempt to unravel the role and manipulation of the material house as a component of both non-differentiated and differentiated social relationships. Within this volume it will be argued that in Orkney during the second half of the 4th millennium cal BC strong kin-based differentiation gives way to a particular form of *sociétés à maisons* precisely because once relatively stable identities become more volatile and unstable due to an expansion in external relationships induced by changing modes of practice within a developing 'Neolithic' (cf. Whittle 2000; Schulting 2008; Thomas 2013, 293). In short, we argue that 'subsistence matters' (Schulting 2004, 22), and nowhere does it matter more than in the changing social practices constituting the earliest Neolithic in Orkney.

Within the Orcadian Neolithic, the materiality and inhabitation of the physical house is strongly argued to not be independent of the *sociétés à maisons* concept (see Marshall 2000 for a diachronic view of physical houses and *sociétés à maisons*). Drawing on the fieldwork reported in this volume, we wish to explore the idea that the physical appearance of the house is a potent resource for materializing the apparent dichotomous alliance and descent principles. Consequently, we argue that some of the insights made by Lévi-Strauss (1982; 1987) in his basic formulation of *sociétés à maisons* are extremely relevant to interpreting the archaeological evidence and providing the parameters for a 'social' narrative of the material changes occurring in Orkney between the 4th and 2nd millennia cal BC.

1.4 Identifying Neolithic inhabitation of the Bay of Firth area of Mainland, Orkney

Considering that Orkney is a group of relatively small islands lying off the northeast coast of the Scottish mainland, its wealth of Neolithic archaeology is truly extraordinary. An assortment of houses, chambered cairns, stone circles, standing stones and passage graves provides an unusually comprehensive range of archaeological and architectural contexts. Yet, in the early 1990s there was a noticeable imbalance between 4th and 3rd millennium cal BC evidence, with house structures, and 'villages' being well represented in the latter but minimally in the former. As elsewhere in the British Isles, the archaeological visibility of the 4th millennium cal BC in Orkney tends to be dominated by the monumental presence of chambered cairns or tombs.

Figure 1.8 View of the Bay of Firth from the east (Colin Richards).

In order to address this discrepancy, and to break down the image of 'two Neolithics' identified earlier, a project of fieldwork and excavation was initiated in 1994 in the Cuween-Wideford area of central Mainland, Orkney (Fig. 1.8). This area was subsequently expanded to include the entirety of the Bay of Firth and the hills that provide a natural definition, a north–south spine running up the east side of west-central Mainland, Orkney (Figs 1.9 and 1.11).

The Bay of Firth coastal strip is essentially an area of fertile land enclosed to the east, south and west by a semicircle of hills which stretch north towards the parish of Evie. Although of similar topography as seen today (Fig. 1.9), by the middle centuries of the 4th millennium cal BC, tree cover was thinning and the land becoming more open (Bunting 1994; 1996). However, it seems likely that clumps of forest remained in sheltered areas (Farrell *et al.* 2014). One major difference, however, would be that the sea level within the bay was substantially lower at this time, possibly up to as much as a 2m difference (Bates *et al.* 2013). Such divergence gives considerable variation to the position of the coastline and significantly attaches the islands of the Holm of Grimbister and Damsay to the mainland, (Fig. 1.10).

Overall, the Bay of Firth constitutes an interesting study area for a number of reasons. First, although it is situated only *c.*7km east of the Stenness-Brodgar monumental complex of central western Mainland, the Bay of Firth is entirely separated by the Hill of Heddle and a spine of hills running north–south (Fig. 1.9). Second, such demarcation gives the Bay of Firth an enclosed, slightly isolated, character where vistas are open to the north (towards the Northern Isles), but restricted to the east, south and west. In many ways, this area of fertile ground is inward looking with a focus on the northern shoreline. Third, the enclosed character of the Bay of Firth is emphasized through the position of the passage graves on Cuween Hill and Wideford Hill which in facing outwards over the fertile coastal zone provide 'cultural' definition to the west and east respectively. As both passage grave entrances are orientated on one another across the coastal zone a front–back distinction is achieved which further enhances the enclosed feel of this area. Thus, in many ways, such a contained quality of landscape as is produced by the encircling hills serves to create an 'island' within an island. Consequently, Daniel and Powell's statement that 'the Maes Howe-Wideford Hill-Cuween group on the mainland of Orkney might perhaps be classified as a cemetery of Passage-Graves' (1949, 178) is unjustifiable on the ground. Finally, the fertile, gently

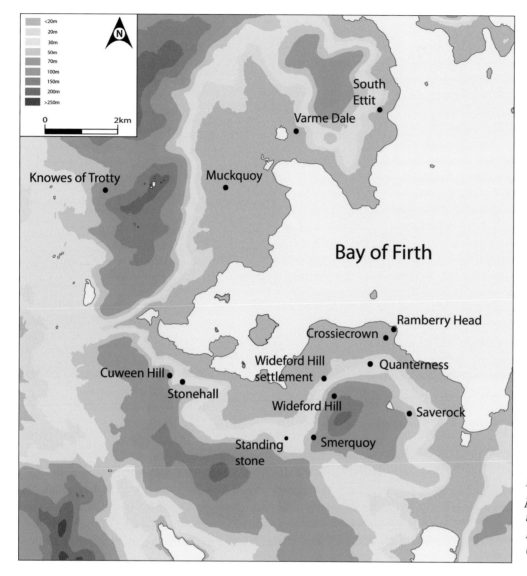

Figure 1.9 The early prehistoric sites and topography of the Bay of Firth area of Mainland, Orkney.

sloping terrain running from the lower reaches of the hills though cultivated land down to the shoreline presents an ideal arena for an examination of the nature of early prehistoric settlement patterns across a variety of landscape conditions. Interestingly, it was also one of Colin Renfrew's selected research transects in the fieldwork leading to the 1979 study *Investigations in Orkney*.

The *Cuween-Wideford Landscape Project* began in a modest manner being funded solely by a grant from the University of Glasgow. In many ways, this field-based research was considered an adjunct to the *Barnhouse-Maeshowe Project* (Richards 2005), in that there was a wish to examine the nature of 3rd millennium cal BC settlement beyond the great monuments and settlements of Barnhouse and the Ness of Brodgar (which was discovered in 2003 while excavations at Wideford Hill were in progress).

Of course, the best-laid plans and research strategies often require a degree of reflexivity and rethinking in light of unexpected results and eventualities. This research project was no exception. Fieldwork was initiated in 1994 by undertaking survey and excavation at Stonehall Farm, Firth (Chapters 5 and 6). This was accompanied by a programme of clay prospection, geophysical survey and fieldwalking across the differing terrain of the Bay of Firth coastal area. The location of Stonehall was not actually discovered by fieldwork but through the collecting activities of the farmer Mr Ronnie Flett who, together with his father, had picked up a number of flint artefacts and a macehead from a cultivated field situated to the west of Stonehall Farm. These finds were brought into Tankerness House Museum during an 'open evening' organized by Anne Brundle and Tom Muir. As can be imagined, great excitement ensued when

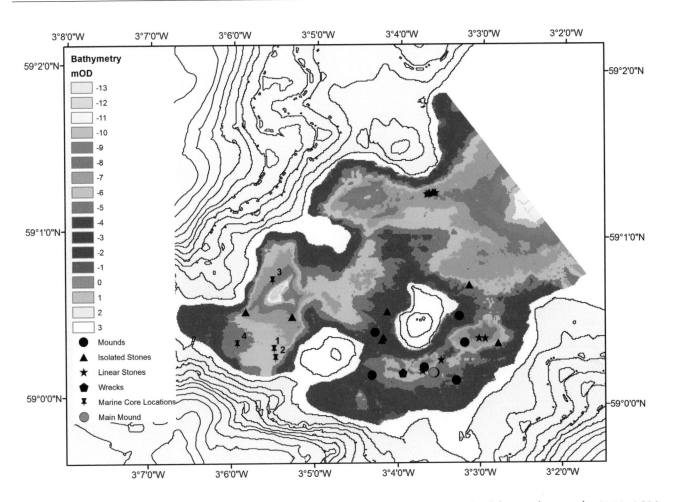

Figure 1.10 Bathymetry based reconstruction model for the Bay of Firth of the rise in sea level during the period c. 5000–3500 bc where there is a change from -6mOD to -4mOD. The edge of the dark brown area provides an approximate map of sea level at the onset of the Neolithic (by kind permission of C. R. Bates and the Rising Tide Project, University of St Andrews).

Ronnie disclosed the location of Stonehall Farm to be directly below Cuween Hill passage grave. Subsequent geophysical survey over the area identified as the source of the objects revealed discrete areas of magnetic enhancement coinciding with a number of low mounds (Fig. 6.3). From these results and observations it was decided to begin excavations at Stonehall, and in many ways this site became the centrepiece of the project.

Excavations at Stonehall ran over a six year period from 1994 to 2000 (Fig. 1.12). From the commencement of exploratory excavations it soon became apparent that well-preserved archaeological structural remains and deposits were present, representing spatially separated areas of settlement (Fig. 5.3). It also became clear that occupation ran over a considerable period beginning in the middle of the 4th millennium cal BC. Moreover, the nature of habitation varied quite dramatically. The

smaller discrete areas of enhancement were found to represent structural remains and midden deposits of early Neolithic date and the larger area (which could be seen as a broad low mound in the field) was found to be a late 4th millennium cal BC settlement that graduates into a late Neolithic 'village' or hamlet.

In conjunction with the Stonehall excavations, a number of fields were surveyed and walked in the study area – initially – with little success. Later, whilst walking fields to the east of the Bay of Firth we talked with Scott Harcus, the owner of Quanterness Farm, and he happened to mention that a number of years ago his father had cleared some 'building stone' from a discrete area of a field, which, rather fortuitously, was in the process of being ploughed. Sure enough at the place described, a low mound was present and the surface was covered with worked flints and stone tools;

Figure 1.11 View over Finstown looking up the west coast of the Bay of Firth (Colin Richards).

the large Neolithic settlement of Crossiecrown had been 'discovered' which Nick Card and Jane Downes excavated as part of the project between 1998 and 2000.

Crossiecrown lies on the coastal plain between the northern slopes of Wideford Hill and Ramberry Head (Chapters 7 and 8). The well-known passage grave of Quanterness, excavated by Colin Renfrew in the early 1970s, is clearly visible *c.*1km southwest of the site in an elevated position (Fig. 8.1). The finds from fieldwalking included a barbed and tanged arrowhead and a variety of stone tools assignable to the late 3rd and early 2nd millennia cal BC. This discovery initiated a detailed geophysical survey of the area (Fig. 7.2). Due to the scarcity of late 3rd millennium cal BC (early Bronze Age) settlement and the risk of further damage by ploughing, preliminary excavations were undertaken in 1998.

As a consequence of the discovery of Crossiecrown, our research aims expanded and we were extremely fortunate that, through the timely intervention of Patrick Ashmore, Historic Scotland became a significant

funder under the criteria of evaluating and investigating plough-damaged sites. The excavation of Crossiecrown was particularly informative regarding the continuity of occupation and recycling of stone in a constant process of demolition and rebuilding. One of the most exciting discoveries, although the significance of which was not fully appreciated at the time (as it should have been), was the use of red clay to both render and colour the internal wall of the 'Red House'. Now that additional evidence for the use of clay and pigments to colour internal features has been obtained from within buildings at the Ness of Brodgar settlement (Card and Thomas 2012; Antonia Thomas pers. comm.), the full significance of the Crossiecrown discovery comes sharply into focus.

Despite walking fields as they became available through pasture renewal from the late 1980s, the location of a flint scatter at the northern base of Wideford Hill, first discovered in 1929 by Robert Rendall when the land was being 'improved', remained elusive (Chapter 2). Indeed, knowledge of its existence had been influential in the selection of the Cuween-Wideford study area as ceramics from the surface collection had been identified as Unstan ware by Audrey Henshall (Davidson and Henshall 1989, 77). This suggested a 4th millennium cal BC date for the site. The 'flint field' was rediscovered in 1994, and a geophysical survey was undertaken, although the results were poor (see Fig. 2.3). Unfortunately, definition of the spread of surface material was restricted by partial ploughing of the entire field. Because of the disappointing geophysical results, this site was abandoned as viable for any further investigations.

However, just as the project was concluding in 2002, on the final day of fieldwork Richard Chatterton discovered an unpublished plot of surface finds at Wideford Hill in Tankerness House Museum, Kirkwall. This clearly revealed a concentration of surface material to lie much further west than was previously realized. Late in the afternoon, after a quick scan with the gradiometer and the excavation of a 1m² test-pit, it was clear that substantial occupation deposits existed below the ploughsoil in a discrete area (Fig. 2.5). Subsequent trial excavation and a longer season at Easter 2003 revealed the totally unexpected presence of circular timber buildings superseded by stone architecture. Both house forms were associated with round-based vessels including Unstan ware pottery.

At the same time, during an examination of the famous early Bronze Age barrow cemetery at Knowes of Trotty, Harray, Mainland, Orkney, geophysical survey undertaken by Adrian Challands located a magnetic anomaly to the north of the barrows. Excavations undertaken in 2002–2006 by Jane Downes and Paul Sharman unexpectedly uncovered a 4th millennium cal BC house structure nestling into the end of a low spur (Chapter 3). Geographically, the Knowes of Trotty house was not strictly within the study area as it was situated on the western side of the spine of hills separating west Mainland from the Bay of Firth (Figs 1.9 and 1.11). However, spatially it is in close vicinity to the Bay of Firth settlements being little more than 3km due west of the large Muckquoy settlement at Redland (Chapter 9). Consequently, it is included in this volume as an additional and important 4th millennium cal BC settlement which demonstrates consistent structural change. Moreover, its topographic location was of particular interest as contrary to expectation, like Stonehall, it was situated in an inland position, as opposed to being coastal or lochside. Occupation at Knowes of Trotty in the mid-late 4th millennium cal BC also introduces the status of a settlement site as a future social resource, as a place of

Figure 1.12 The three Dr Jones' directing Trench E at Stonehall Farm, left to right, Andrew, Richard and Siân.

'ancestral' significance. Here, early Neolithic habitation is a precursor to the amazing early Bronze Age linear barrow cemetery famed for its rich grave goods including gold and jet objects (Fig. 1.13).

While the original aim of the research was to discover and investigate other late Neolithic settlements in order to provide a contrast with Barnhouse, this aim was slowly being subverted by the actual results of fieldwork and through the extensive 4th millennium cal BC settlement component being discovered. Although unexpected, this evidence did in fact force a reappraisal of the nature of early Neolithic inhabitation of Mainland, Orkney. Given that sites such as Stonehall and Crossiecrown had a degree of longevity from the early to late Neolithic (and early Bronze Age in the case of Crossiecrown), an altered and broader interpretative perspective was clearly required.

Consequently, the research framework of the project was rethought with the focus being placed on the social processes and strategies that lay behind the extensive changes seen in the materiality and architecture of

Figure 1.13 Excavations at the Knowes of Trotty with the central cist of the main mound uncovered, the excavation of the early Neolithic house can be seen in the background. The stonework in the cairn is clearly visible and probably derives from the ruined house. From left to right: John Chesters, Judith Robertson, Nick Card, Jane Downes and Alison Sheridan (Frank Bradford).

houses, settlements and monuments over a 1500-year period of time. This allowed a degree of freedom to expand the studies of the broader changes in materials, especially ceramics (see Chapter 11). As discussed earlier, it also permitted a new interpretative framework to be employed drawing on a modified form of Claude Lévi-Strauss's concept of house societies (*sociétés à maisons*).

Finally, in 2010 during the writing-up stage of the project, Christopher Gee learned from Mr Billy Sinclair, who farms Smerquoy, St Ola, of an area in one of his fields where red ash and stone regularly comes to the surface during ploughing. Actually, it was Billy's father who had first encountered the red ashy soil and cleared 'building' stone off the field surface during and after ploughing

many years ago. The field was to be ploughed once again and Christopher seized the initiative and undertook fieldwalking and geophysical survey. Many Neolithic flint and stone tools, and pottery, were collected from the field surface and the subsequent gradiometer survey revealed extensive magnetically enhanced deposits (Fig. 4.3). This site lay at the southwest base of Wideford Hill assuming yet another inland location overlooking the Bay of Firth study area (Chapter 4). It simply could not be ignored and was partially investigated in the early summer of 2013. The results of the excavation were extraordinary in uncovering yet another late 4th millennium cal BC stone-built house, in this case with pecked decoration present on the internal wall-face (Fig. 1.14). This is the first known example of 'megalithic' art occurring within this form of architecture. Although not fully explored (and part of a new project looking at the origins of agriculture in the Northern Isles), Smerquoy would appear to follow a similar trajectory to Wideford Hill in charting the progression from timber to stone house construction (see Fig. 4.38).

In the spring of 2013, a substantial mounded site at Muckquoy on the lands of Redland Farm was ploughed allowing a programme of surface collection and geophysical survey to commence (Chapter 9). Actually, this site had been reported to the Orkney Archaeological Society in 2006 by the landowner, the late Eoin Scott and two previous seasons of fieldwalking in 2006 and 2011 had collected a range of material from the surface, including a rim sherd of Unstan ware and an unfinished polished stone macehead. The 2013 fieldwalking produced lithics, stone tools, a number of Grooved ware sherds, together with red-coloured pottery of likely early Bronze Age date. Fragments of polished stone axes, maceheads (Fig. 9.35) polished haematite (Fig. 9.36), and a bronze 'bangle' of late Bronze Age or Iron Age date (F. Hunter pers. comm.) were also recovered.

The accompanying gradiometer survey by Christopher Gee and James Moore produced stunning results in revealing the settlement to be enclosed. However, questions remained concerning the nature and date of the enclosure, as substantial walling defining occupation is only known at the Ness of Brodgar (Card 2010). In order to address these questions a small trench was opened in May 2013 and the 'enclosure' was identified as concentric lines of steep-sided, shallow slots and a truncated ditch. These are interpreted as the cuts of palisades or fences. The 'fence' trenches post-dated thick late Neolithic midden deposits containing Grooved ware. Although limited investigations

Figure 1.14 The discovery of the horned spiral in the Smurquoy Hoose occurred when the sun shone from the southeast (left to right: Billy Sinclair, Alan Price and Colin Richards).

were undertaken at Muckquoy, undoubtedly it is a well-preserved multi-period settlement dating back to the 4th millennium cal BC.

More recently, in March 2014, Christopher Gee and students from Orkney College fieldwalked a slight mound in a newly ploughed field at Saverock, St Ola. This exercise produced worked flint and stone, together with early Neolithic round-based pottery. Undoubtedly, the mound at Saverock represents yet another 4th millennium cal BC settlement, in this instance on the eastern lower slopes of Wideford Hill (Fig 1.9).

Overall, this field-based research project has been extremely successful in identifying Neolithic settlement in the Bay of Firth study area. Of the many discoveries, perhaps the most exciting and unexpected was the detection of timber structures at Wideford Hill representing the earliest Neolithic occupation. This volume contains reports on the excavation of a range of timber house structures and stone-built houses from the mid-late 4th millennium cal BC. Equally, four sites, Stonehall, Crossiecrown, Smerquoy and Muckquoy,

straddle the 4th and 3rd millennia cal BC. While research priorities have undoubtedly shifted over the duration of the *Cuween-Wideford Landscape Project*, the 3rd millennium cal BC Neolithic settlement of the Bay of Firth does make an interesting adjunct to the Stenness-Brodgar area of west Mainland, Orkney. However, it is the extensive early Neolithic component of the field project, in combination with two newly discovered and excavated mid-late 4th millennium cal BC settlements at Ha'Breck, Wyre (Thomas and Lee 2012) and Green, Eday (Miles 2010), that allows a more nuanced interpretation of an increasingly fascinating 500-year period of Orcadian prehistory. Previous to the project no definite early Neolithic settlements had been investigated on Mainland, Orkney. Now we arrive at the enviable position of being able to rethink the entirety of one of the richest areas, in terms of the range of material evidence for the Neolithic period in northwest Europe, and trace the development and fragmentation of *sociétés à maisons* over a 1500-year period of Northern Isles prehistory.

CHAPTER TWO

Houses of the Dead: the transition from wood to stone architecture at Wideford Hill

Colin Richards and Andrew Meirion Jones

2.1 The earliest Neolithic

The use of stone in the construction of houses has been a defining feature of the Orcadian Neolithic since Stuart Piggott (Warren *et al.* 1936; Piggott 1954, 32–32), revised Childe's (1931a) dating of Skara Brae. Of course, the presence of stone houses is not restricted solely to late Neolithic settlements such as Rinyo, Pool, Barnhouse, Links of Noltland, Ness of Brodgar and Skara Brae. The well-preserved structures at Knap of Howar, Papa Westray, also demonstrate sophistication in stone masonry (Fig. 1.6), and as noted in the previous chapter, the site has heavily influenced views of early Neolithic habitation in the Northern Isles.

There is, however, a problem concerning the status and chronology of stone architecture at Knap of Howar because the pair of houses do not actually form part of the primary occupation deposits. Representing an undetected structural phase of occupation, a 'primary' layer of midden was recorded as spreading across a substantial area. Through a series of test pits the midden was identified to be leveled at *c.*0.4m thickness, only tapering off at the periphery (Ritchie 1983, 45). The leveling was related to the construction of the two houses and the midden also provided material for the wall core of House 1. Apart from a discrete area of 'fragmentary paving, upright stone and grooves left by the removal of two upright stones' (*ibid.*, 46), no structural features of stone were discovered relating to this earlier period of habitation.

A rather similar situation was encountered when the early Neolithic deposits were excavated at Pool, Sanday. John Hunter observes that 'ironically, the earliest occupation

identified at Pool belonged not to the reddish-brown layers at the centre of the mound, but to an underlying series of darker deposits located at the NE of the site' (2007, 28). These deposits were grouped together but 'two phases were interpreted, an earlier tip-like sequence of deposits (Phase 1.1) and a subsequent phase which contained obvious evidence of structural remains (Phase 1.2)' (Hunter *et al.* 2007, 28). Accepting the restricted nature of excavation within this area of the extensive Pool settlement (*ibid.*, 28–31), there does appear to be a period of occupation associated with stone architecture overlying a preceding period of occupation with no stone structures. As with Knap of Howar, Unstan bowls formed part of the ceramic assemble of this early habitation (*ibid.*, 28).

From these two examples it can be seen that by the early 1990s there existed some indications that a less archaeologically visible period of settlement, with no stone houses, was present in Orkney during the middle centuries of the 4th millennium cal BC. A further factor was that the parallel stone architecture of stalled cairns and houses appeared as a mutually cohesive early Neolithic Orcadian 'package' (see Richards 1992, 66–67; Ritchie 1995, Fig. 29), though when we consider the Orcadian evidence against the broader picture of Neolithic settlement in Britain and Ireland it is now evident that timber settlement architecture co-existed alongside stone built mortuary architecture as in the specific example at Yarnton, Thames Valley and throughout the Irish Neolithic (*e.g.* Smyth 2014; Hey and Robinson 2011, 248–58).

In a chapter entitled 'Colonization of the Highlands and Islands' in *Neolithic Cultures of the British Isles*, Stuart

Piggott identified two routes of colonization, 'the first would continue the Western Approaches up the Atlantic coasts beyond the Hebrides area of colonization… to make landfalls along the north coast of mainland and in the Orkneys… the second would utilize the natural highway of the Great Glen… from the head of the Great Glen in the neighbourhood of Inverness, colonization could spread northwards by coasting voyages to Sutherland and Caithness, and ultimately to the Orkneys' (1954, 233–334). Although considered by Piggott (*ibid.*, 123) to hold far less cultural implication, it was the distribution of chambered cairns that marked the routes and landfalls of the Neolithic colonists as they spread north.

A legacy of this discourse is the acceptance of the primacy of chambered cairns in the establishment of Neolithic lifeways. However, the assumed architectural association of stone-built 'Knap of Howar' houses with tripartite and stalled chambered cairns, by default caused both buildings being employed to define the early Neolithic in Orkney. Consequently, stone houses would also appear to constitute a primary form in the colonization process of the Northern Isles.

This view of the initiation of the Orcadian Neolithic, and the primary status of the stone-constructed houses, had actually been questioned in the 1980s. For example, Anna Ritchie states that 'it is inherently unlikely that developed settlements such as Knap of Howar… should represent the homes of the first pioneering colonists' (1983, 39). Continuing, she muses that 'the earliest settlers need not have been tomb-builders, and there may have been a primary phase, as yet undetected in the archaeological record, during which a very limited range of Neolithic activities was practiced' (*ibid.*, 39). Side stepping the question of tomb-building for a moment, ironically, it is highly probable that the 'undetected primary phase' of settlement is actually present at Knap of Howar taking the form of the broad spread of midden constituting period 1 (*ibid.*, 44–46). At the same time that Anna Ritchie published Knap of Howar, fieldwalking across Mainland, Orkney, began to locate early Neolithic occupation sites employing blade lithic technology, such as Deepdale Bay, Stromness (Richards 2005a, 14–16). Yet, when geophysical survey was implemented no signs of stone buildings or extensive midden deposits emerged (see also Carey 2012, 56–66). Here an obvious question presented itself: what was the nature of the 'undetected primary phase' of Orcadian Neolithic settlement? In this chapter, through the investigation of the Wideford Hill settlement, this question will be addressed.

2.2 Rediscovering an early 'flint-field' at Wideford Hill, Mainland, Orkney

The naturalist, painter and poet, Robert Rendall, was a self-taught Orcadian who was fascinated by a wide range of subjects, including archaeology (Dickson 1990). In early September of 1929 he decided to examine a newly ploughed piece of hill ground at the base of the northern slopes of Wideford Hill. The marshy field had never been ploughed before, explained Rendall to an audience of the Orkney Antiquarian Society on the 11 December 1930, and 'scarcely had I walked up over the field before I found my first arrow-head' (1931, 21). He went on to describe how the 'decidedly peaty' soil was 'interspersed with considerable patches of yellow clay … and it is from these clayey patches that most of the flints were recovered' (*ibid.*). Unlike many of his contemporaries, Rendall meticulously recorded the surface material in the form of a drawn plan detailing the location of the clayey patches and artefacts from the 'flint-field' which was subsequently published in the *Proceedings of the Orkney Antiquarian Society* for 1931 (Fig. 2.1).

Additional areas of the 'flint-field' were ploughed between 1930–33 and Rendall assisted by Dr Ronald Mooney extended the collection. In a second paper read before the Orkney Antiquarian Society, Rendall discusses the flint and stone discoveries and focuses attention on the range of pottery recovered. Aided by Graham Callander, Director of the National Museum of Antiquities, Rendall recognized the Neolithic date of the ceramics and compared the decoration of several sherds to that present on pottery from Unstan and Taversoe Tuick (Rendall 1934, 22). 'Those, however, are chambered cairns, this an open station', reflected Rendall and then noted that 'the real importance, therefore, of the Wideford Hill site is that it is, as far as we know, the first open Neolithic "floor" to be discovered in our islands' (*ibid.*). Unfortunately, whilst accurately detailing the distribution of both flints and pottery within the field, Rendall (*e.g.* 1931, 20) neglected to provide the actual location of the flint-field. The only clue to its whereabouts was the name 'Wideford Hill' and the inclusion of the adjacent road between Stromness and Kirkwall on his ink drawing of the flint-field (Fig. 2.1).

Examination of the ceramics from Wideford Hill, held in Tankerness House Museum, Kirkwall, by Audrey Henshall confirmed that several Unstan bowls formed part of the surface assemblage (Davidson and Henshall 1989, 77). Hence, there was a definite 4th millennium cal BC component to the occupation of

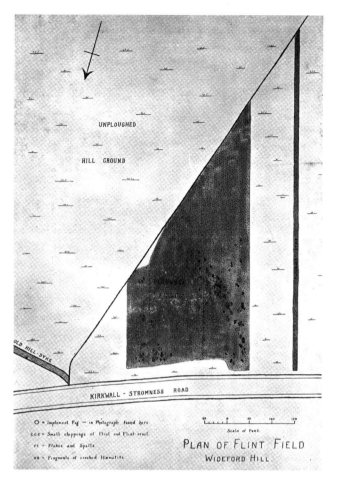

UNPLOUGHED

HILL GROUND

OLD HILL DYKE

KIRKWALL - STROMNESS ROAD

O = Implement Fig — in Photograph found here

CCC = Small chippings of Flint and Flint crust

FF = Flakes and Spalls

HH = Fragments of crushed Hæmatite

Scale of Feet.

PLAN OF FLINT FIELD
WIDEFORD HILL.

Figure 2.1 Robert Rendall's published plan of the 'flint field' at Wideford Hill (after Rendall 1931).

Wideford Hill. More interestingly, although Rendall noted the presence of 'numerous small flints' among the assemblage, he was equivocal over their belonging to 'epi-palaeolithic cultures' (Rendall 1934, 20). More recently Caroline Wickham-Jones (pers. comm.) and Alan Saville (2000, 95) have confirmed the inclusion of a Mesolithic component, taking the form of microliths, in the Wideford Hill assemblage (see Chapter 12).

Apart from the obvious importance of investigating an early Neolithic settlement on Mainland, Orkney, the inclusion of a Mesolithic component in the flint assemblage suggested that occupation at Wideford Hill may have extended back to the early 4th millennium cal BC. Several fields alongside the Finstown to Kirkwall Road were examined in an attempt to locate this scatter. In 1994 a good candidate for the 'flint field' was partially ploughed and fieldwalking revealed the presence of flint and stone artefacts on the surface. Because the field

was only partially cultivated the extent of the surface scatter was never adequately defined. Hence, while the actual location of the 'Wideford Hill flint field' was rediscovered (Fig. 2.2), its true extent remained unknown.

As Wideford Hill lay within the project study area, further work at the site was deemed essential. Another attempt to define the area of occupation through gradiometer survey over the area of surface scatter was conducted by Richard Jones and Lorna Sharpe in 1998. Unfortunately, the results were disappointing with no substantial magnetic anomalies representing occupation deposits being detected (Fig. 2.3). Further to this survey a series of test pits were dug across the area of the scatter in 1999, but again no trace of *in situ* archaeological deposits was discovered below the ploughsoil. To all intents and purposes this concluded the investigation into the Wideford Hill flint field and it was assumed that any stratified archaeological deposits had been truncated and destroyed due by a long history of cultivation extending back over 80 years.

In late September 2002, on what was intended to be the last day of the final week of fieldwork, during a re-examination of the lithic material from Wideford Hill in Tankerness House Museum, a second plan by Rendall of the 'flint field' was discovered by Richard Chatterton. The significance of this plan was that it included an additional area of high artefact density situated over a hundred metres west of the flint scatter detailed in the original published plan (Fig. 2.5). Realizing that we may have been searching in the wrong place all along, it was quickly decided to scan the new location with the gradiometer. This immediately revealed a substantial magnetic anomaly coinciding with a slightly raised area at the edge of the field (Fig. 2.4). Amid great excitement, as dusk approached, a 1×1m test pit was quickly excavated and directly below the ploughsoil there appeared the characteristic compact, charcoal-mottled deposits characteristic of Neolithic occupation.

Part of this mound was superficially examined over the next two days by opening a trial trench measuring 8m × 4m. The trench partially exposed the Neolithic rammed stone surface [002] upon which lay a range of stone tools, including polished stone axes, flint tools and decorated Unstan ware. Moreover, on the last day a deep void was discovered beneath the rammed stone surface, which was actually a sealed posthole [049] belonging to what was later identified as 'Timber structure 3'. However, this was not realized at the time as postholes of this size had never before been encountered in an Orcadian Neolithic context. Given the richness of the archaeological deposits it was decided to adjourn excavation until the following Easter.

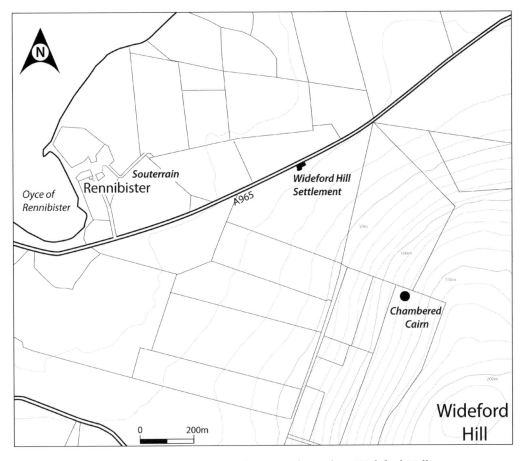

Figure 2.2 Location of excavated trench at Wideford Hill.

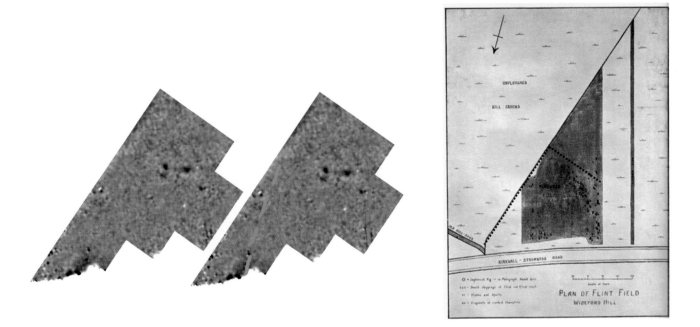

Figure 2.3 Results of survey at Wideford Hill using a Geoscan FM36 fluxgate gradiometer (sample and traverse interval 1m).

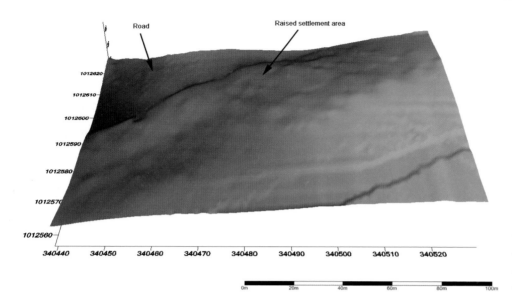

Figure 2.4 Topographic survey of the Wideford Hill settlement (Mark Littlewood).

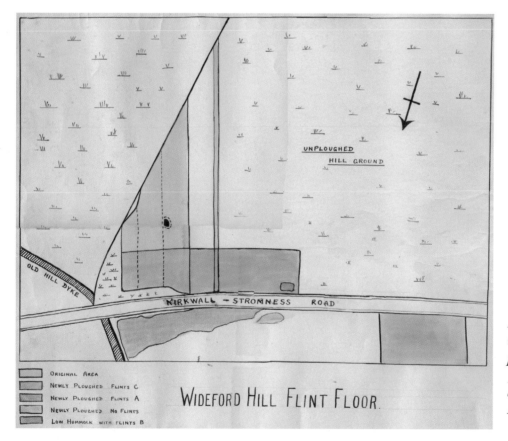

Figure 2.5 Robert Rendall's unpublished distribution plan of the Wideford Hill 'flint-field' (reproduced courtesy of Tankerness House Museum).

2.3 Excavating the timber house structures at Wideford Hill

During fine sunny weather in late March 2003, a trench measuring *c.*20m × 9m was opened to extend the area examined the previous year (Fig. 2.2). Overall, the area of habitation appeared to be positioned on the slight natural rise which was clearly visible from the south

but much less pronounced when viewed from the north (from the main road). On removing the ploughsoil it was immediately clear that the site had sustained severe damage from a variety of sources. To the north, adjacent to the A965 Kirkwall–Finstown road, part of the site had been removed by the cutting of a water pipeline and, of course, the main road itself. The area of occupation

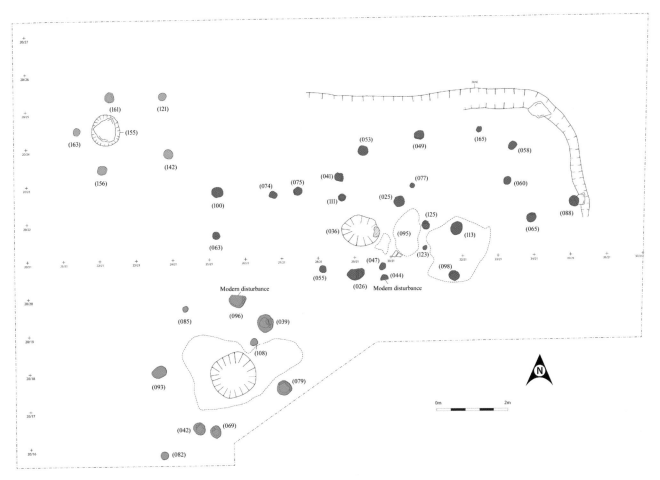

Figure 2.6 Plan of the wooden buildings discovered in the excavated area. Timber structure 1 (red), Timber structure 2 (green) and 'Timber structure 3' (blue).

sloped up from the roadside to a slight summit within the field, where unfortunately the deposits were completely truncated by the plough. Consequently, the preserved archaeological remains constituted a narrow strip, *c.*10m in width, running roughly parallel with the fence-line.

To everyone's surprise, the primary occupation of Wideford Hill was found to be represented by a series of structures or houses of timber construction. At least two sub-circular structures (Timber structures 1 and 2) were identified, whilst a likely third ('Timber structure 3') was situated further to the east. The level of uncertainty with regard to 'Timber structure 3' is due to the extensive distribution and pattern of postholes, some of which may represent additions to an original sub-circular building creating a more linear architectural arrangement (see Figs 2.6 and 2.17). The discovery of the substantial postholes of so many house-structures was truly remarkable

because, despite Anna Ritchie's suggested undetected primary phase of early Neolithic settlement (1983, 39), timber-constructed buildings were not assumed to be a likely component of the Orcadian Neolithic.

Importantly, it is worth noting that further timber structures almost certainly exist beyond the excavated area. After the second Rendall map of the 'flint-field' was identified the true extent of the flint scatter became clear (Fig. 2.5). In comparison to known Orcadian surface flint scatters (see sites in Richards 2005a), Wideford Hill scatter was more dispersed in extending nearly 300m from the northeastern corner of the field. Moreover, the surface material seemed to appear in small clusters (Rendall 1931; 1934) which suggests discrete residential units within a more dispersed or shifting pattern of occupation.

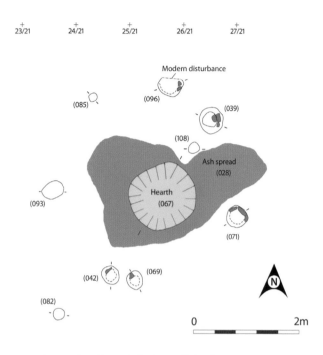

Figure 2.7 Detailed plan of Timber structure 1.

2.3.1 Timber structure 1

Situated in the southeast corner of the trench, Timber structure 1 was only uncovered after the trench was extended to explore an arrangement of postholes that was clearly running beyond the area of excavation. After the extension, the remains of a circular timber building, possibly incorporating a 'porch' arrangement, comprising nine postholes was exposed (Figs 2.7 and 2.13; Table 2.1). Centrally positioned within the ring of postholes was a scoop hearth [067] which contained three discrete ashy layers. The lower two, a primary layer of burnt orange ashy soil covered by a black layer of charcoal-rich soil incorporating burnt stones, related to consecutive episodes of burning (Fig. 2.8). Initially, the structure was thought to be a 'Mesolithic' house, but the presence of a sherd of Unstan ware (SF 958) in the lower ash fill of the hearth confirmed a date in the later 4th millennium cal BC (Fig. 2.9). The upper fill of the hearth was a dark brown silty-loam which merged with a thin and discontinuous layer of occupation material [028] which covered the eastern area of the timber building. The group of three radiocarbon dates obtained from ash from the scoop hearth (Table 2.2) are very consistent

Figure 2.8 Sectioned central scoop hearth [068] in Timber structure 1 (Richard Chatterton).

and in giving a range between 3360 and 2920 cal BC are indistinguishable from those derived from Stonehouse 1 and the associated rammed-stone work area [002] (see Chapter 10).

In some cases, the clay and stone packing material of the postholes remained *in situ* (Figs 2.10 and 2.11), thereby allowing the diameter of the posts to be calculated (Table 2.1). This effectively demonstrates that the timbers were left in place to decay and not removed on abandonment. Overall, the timbers utilized in Timber structure 1 were fairly substantial (Table 2.1), with the largest posthole [042], holding an upright of *c*.0.36m diameter set *c*.0.37m into the ground. The preponderance of birch charcoal within the postholes (see Table 15.7) provides some evidence of the timber species selected for the structural uprights. The presence of hazel and willow charcoal may well indicate the charred remains of woven panels fabricated for side-walling. A few residual charred cereal grains of six-row barley were recovered from posthole [034]. Carbonized cereal grains, birch and hazel charcoal, and unidentifiable burnt bone were generally represented throughout the hearth ash. In the intermediate ash fill [089], charred heather was also present which also may have been employed as roofing material.

Regarding the living space within the house structure, the circuit of timber posts had a diameter of *c*.3.5m,

and if it assumed that the roof projected beyond these uprights we can suggest an internal floor area of at least *c*.13m². This area compares with the internal area present within a circular late Neolithic house such as House 3 at Barnhouse (Downes and Richards 2005, 61–66).

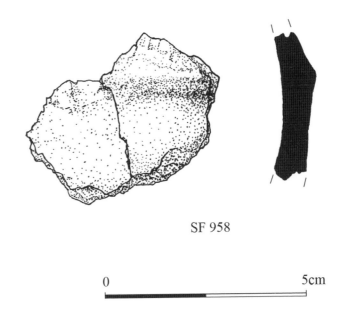

SF 958

0   5cm

Figure 2.9 Unstan ware sherd SF 958 recovered from the central hearth in Timber structure 1.

Table 2.1 Details of postholes comprising Timber structure 1.

Posthole	Fill	Fill description	Posthole diameter	Post diameter	Depth	Packing present
39	46	Light-brown silty loam with charcoal flecks	44cm	30cm	36cm	Yes
42	43	Dark-brown silty loam with charcoal flecks	36cm	32cm	37cm	Yes
69	70	Dark-brown silty loam	25cm	15 cm	24cm	Yes
71	72	Dark-brown silty loam with charcoal flecks	25cm	20cm	23cm	Yes
82	83	Dark-brown silty loam	22cm		23cm	No
85	84	Dark-brown silty loam with much charcoal	12cm		11cm	No
93	94	Dark-brown silty loam	40cm		28cm	No
96	97	Dark-brown silty loam	50cm*		24cm	Yes
108	109	Dark-brown silty loam	22cm		26cm	No

Table 2.2 Radiocarbon sequence through scoop hearth [067].

Location	Context No.	Date	Lab No.
Upper hearth fill	[068]	3360–3090 cal BC	GU-12492
Middle hearth fill	[115]	3350–3030 cal BC	GU-12495
Lower hearth fill	[089]	3340–2920 cal BC	GU-12493

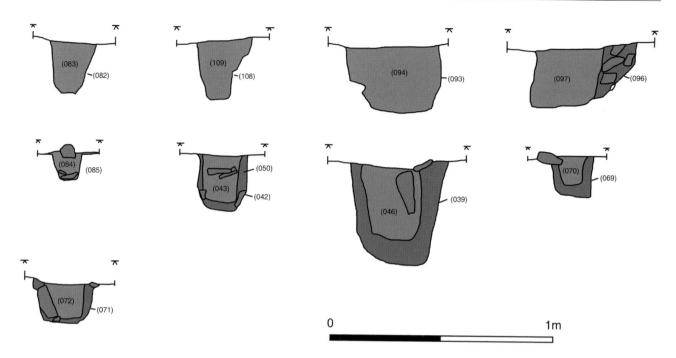

Figure 2.10 Sections of postholes comprising Timber structure 1.

Figure 2.11 Posthole [039], showing the outer packing in situ *and inner post-pipe removed (Colin Richards).*

Figure 2.12 View of Timber structure 1 under excavation from the south-east (Colin Richards).

2.3.2 Timber structure 2

Timber structure 2 only became apparent during the excavation of the floor deposits in Stonehouse 1 (Fig. 2.15). It comprised five postholes arranged in a sub-circular arrangement around a scoop hearth [155]. Overall, the diameters and depths of the postholes were smaller than those forming Timber structure 1, indicating this to have been of slighter construction (Fig. 2.14;

Table 2.3). The actual floor surface area of Structure 2 was relatively small with the timber posts having a diameter of just over two metres. Even with extended roof projection this gives a possible floor area of *c*.8m² around the scoop hearth.

A stratigraphic relationship between Timber structure 2 and Stonehouse 1 was provided by two postholes [121] and [142]. Posthole [121] was located adjacent to the

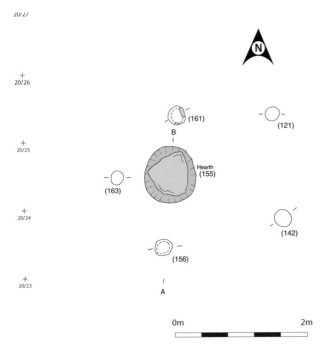

Figure 2.13 Plan of Timber structure 2 (see Fig. 2.23 for section A–B).

eastern wall [102] and had clearly contained a timber when the floor [104] of Stonehouse 1 had been laid because, on excavating the clay surface, the posthole opened up as a void (Fig. 2.15). A second posthole [142] was present further south and partially underlay the wall core material. Taken together, both postholes reveal the stone house to have been superimposed upon the timber structure but significantly this occurred before the below-ground timbers had completely decayed.

Although not centrally positioned, as seen within Timber structures 1 and 3, the off-centre scoop hearth [155] appeared to be associated with Timber structure 2. However, there is no stratigraphic evidence to link the postholes and the scoop hearth. Since Timber structures 1 and 3 incorporated a scoop hearth, there seem reasonable grounds to consider this to be a consistent architectural configuration. The scoop hearth [155] employed a horizontal stone as a base, and the remains of a loose black ash [154] lay sealed in the hollow (Fig. 2.16). A trampled primary occupation surface [127] ran across the central area of the superimposed Stonehouse

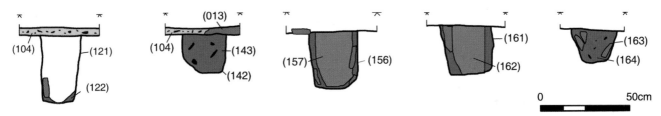

Figure 2.14 Sections of postholes constituting Timber structure 2.

Figure 2.15 Posthole [121] as initially revealed as a substantial void beneath the clay floor of Stonehouse 1 (Colin Richards).

Figure 2.16 Scoop hearth [155] in Timber structure 2 (Angus Mackintosh).

Table 2.3 Details of postholes comprising Timber structure 2.

Posthole	Fill No.	Fill description	Void	Posthole diameter	Post diameter	Depth	Packing present
121	122	Dark-brown silty loam	Yes	22cm	18–20cm	34cm	Yes
142	143	Dark-brown silty loam	No	23cm		13cm	No
156	157	Dark-brown silty loam	No	27cm	20cm	25cm	Yes
161	162	Black silty loam	No	28cm	17cm	20cm	Yes
163	164	Dark-brown silty loam	No	22cm	18cm	14cm	Yes

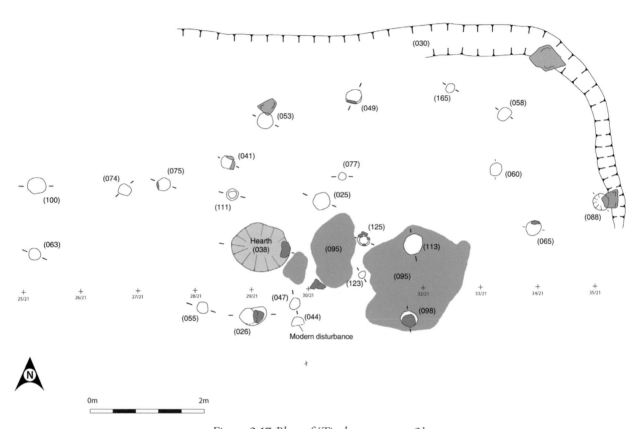

Figure 2.17 Plan of 'Timber structure 3'.

1 and there must be a strong possibility that this relates to both the inhabitation of Timber structure 2 and primary occupation of Stonehouse 1. The importance of this timber structure is that in being superimposed by a stone house, the rapid transformation from timber to stone architecture can be stratigraphically demonstrated.

The scoop hearth [155] of Timber structure 2 appears to perform a crucial role in this transformation process as it is maintained during the primary occupation of Stonehouse 1. In its continued use, the scoop hearth provides a dominant symbol of continuity in a drastic architectural and material change in residency. Unfortunately, due to the superimposition of Stonehouse 1 over Timber structure

2, there can be no definite attribution of any occupation deposits to the earlier timber house structure.

2.3.3 Timber structure 3

It is possible to recognize a third circular structure, akin to Structure 1, centered on the scoop hearth [036] (Figs 2.17 and 2.19). This building may have been rebuilt and even modified into a more rectangular form perhaps including the two westerly postholes [063 and 100]. Such sub-rectangular timber structures have been recognized at Ha'Breck, Wyre (Thomas and Lee 2012; Carey 2012, 29–31). Details of the postholes comprising this building

Table 2.4 Details of postholes comprising 'Timber structure 3'.

Posthole	Fill No.	Fill description	Void	Posthole diameter	Post diameter	Depth	Packing present
10/49	50	Compact clay	Yes	33 × 26cm	26cm	42cm	Yes
25	24	Dk brown silt	Yes	27 × 22cm	22cm	46cm	Yes
26*	27	Mid-brown silt with charcoal flecks	No	24/12cm*		24/18cm	Yes
41	33	Grey-brown silt	No	25cm	20cm	35cm	Yes
44**	45	Dk brown charcoal rich silt	No	24cm		32cm	No
47	48	Grey-brown silt	No	19cm		32cm	No
53	54	Mid-brown silt	No	22 × 17cm		33cm	No
55	56	Mid-brown silt	No	21cm		35cm	No
58	59	Yellow-brown silt	No	23 × 14cm		22cm	No
60	61	Dk brown silt	No	15cm		28cm	No
63	64	Dk red-brown silt	No	22cm	17cm	27cm	Yes
65	66	Dk brown silt	No	28cm	23cm	46cm	Yes
73	74	Dk brown silt	Yes	21cm		24cm	No
75	76	Dk brown silt	No	25cm	20cm	29cm	Yes
77	78	Dk brown silt	No	12cm		23cm	No
98	99	Dk brown silt with ash, charcoal, and burnt stone	No	20cm		22cm	No
100	101	Dk brown silt with charcoal flecks	No	31cm		24cm	No
111	112	Mid-brown silt	Yes	12cm		24cm	No
113	114	Lenses of silt, ash and burnt stones	No	31cm		37cm	No
123	124	Mid-brown silt	No	13cm		14cm	No
125	126	Lenses of silt and ash	No	13cm		28cm	No
165	166	Dk brown silt	No	12cm		20cm	No

*double or re-cut posthole
**damaged by drainage cut

or buildings are provided in Table 2.4. Accepting the difficulties of identifying phases of construction or clear structural forms within the 'Timber structure 3' posthole group, an early radiocarbon date of *3620–3350 cal BC (GU-12491)* from charred grain at the base of the void in the large sealed posthole [053] directly north of the scoop hearth [036] suggests a mid-4th millennium cal BC date for at least one of the timber buildings at Wideford Hill (see Chapter 10).

The scoop hearth [036] is the only fireplace related to the 'Timber structure 3' postholes. It is of typical oval shape and measures 0.8m × 0.6m. Filling the scoop hearth was burnt orange-brown ash overlying a darker ash layer (Fig. 2.20). Although the deposits within 'Timber structure 3' had suffered severe erosion from ploughing, particularly in the eastern area, a thin clay layer [095] occurred in places overlying the natural till. This layer was compact and charcoal flecked and almost certainly represents remnants of an occupation surface or floor. Two circular features, [098] and [113], that appeared similar to postholes, but could equally be interpreted as steep-sided pits, were positioned within the area covered by the clay

surface. Both contained a banded ash fill incorporating burnt stones [099 and 114].

Of all the groups of postholes, those surrounding the scoop hearth [036] are the most confusing and difficult to ascribe structural units (Figs 2.6 and 2.17). With no stratigraphic relationship to aid interpretation individual buildings are difficult to discern. The 'messy' picture is possibly compounded by the addition of partial components of separate structures. For instance, the easterly group of postholes [165], [058], [060] and [065] could relate to a different building. If this is the case then the shallow pit [088], *c.*0.33m in diameter and 0.2m deep, is possibly associated with that structure. A large slab angled down into the fill of the pit may well represent a slumped covering stone.

Further evidence of a sequence of construction and reconstruction to the buildings incorporated in the umbrella term 'Timber structure 3' is demonstrated by one posthole [165] being sealed beneath a large flagstone which formed part of the short line of foundation slabs [007] of Stone structure 2. These flagstones were in turn sealed by the later rammed-stone surface [002] which

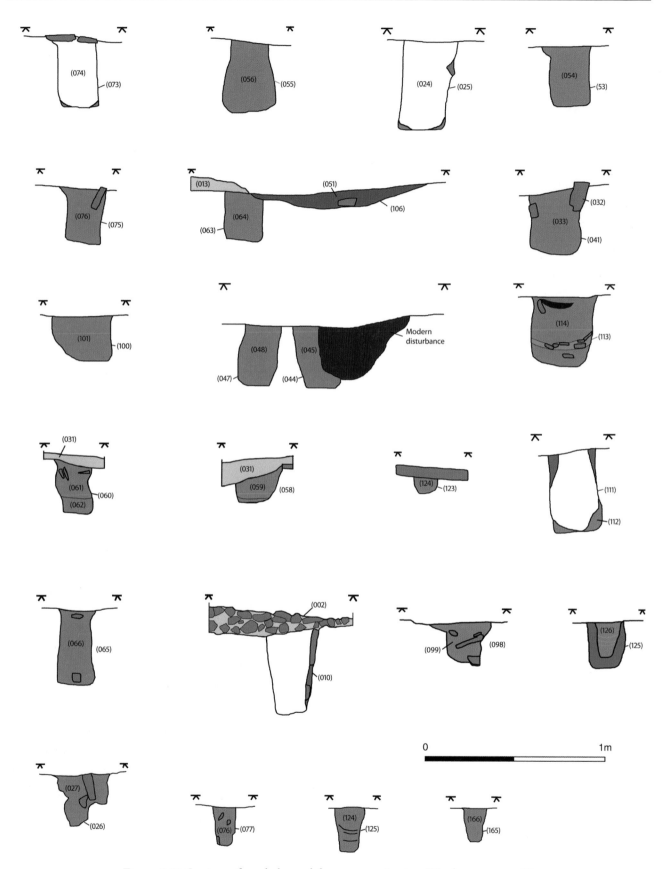

Figure 2.18 Sections of postholes and features constituting 'Timber structure 3'.

Figure 2.20 The scoop hearth [036] in 'Timber structure 3' (Colin Richards).

Figure 2.19 Western view of the postholes comprising 'Timber structure 3' (Colin Richards).

Figure 2.21 Stone-packing surrounds excavated posthole [041] (Colin Richards).

is an outside working area associated with the later Stonehouse 1. The remaining short stretch of flagstones seemed to form the southern side of a shallow gully [030] which also maintained an east–west direction. At its eastern end the gully curved around to the south where it disappeared through plough erosion. Another, later, gully [020] also followed a similar line but in this case continued on an east–west alignment cutting through gully [030]. These features are difficult to interpret (a short stretch of a possible third gully was present between the two) in relation to the postholes. Clearly they post-date some of the postholes, but the curving route of gully [030] is highly suggestive of it respecting a linear structure of some form. This may provide further tentative evidence for the presence of a sub-rectangular wooden structure. Postholes tended to have contained single timbers which were well packed with stone (Fig. 2.21), and rotted *in situ*; in the majority of cases there was no evidence for replacement.

A relative date for at least one element of the 'Timber structure 3' postholes, in the sequence of

Figure 2.22 Posthole [053] suddenly appearing as a void after the partial removal of the line of flagstones [007] representing the foundation of Stone structure 2. Excavated posthole [041] is visible in the bottom right corner (Colin Richards).

timber house construction at Wideford Hill, can be demonstrated stratigraphically. Several of the postholes were clearly sealed by the rammed-stone surface and ash lenses comprising the later work area [002] associated with Stonehouse 1. They were sealed when the below-ground posts remained as solid wood, consequently, they rotted *in situ* and as occurred with posthole [053] remained as voids (Figs 2.18 and 2.22). Hence, the construction of Stonehouse 1, Stone structure 2 and the associated work area [002] occurred relatively shortly after Timber structures 2 and 3 were either abandoned or dismantled.

Because of the difficulty of unraveling the building sequence constituting 'Timber structure 3' it is difficult to discuss floor areas, although the posts surrounding hearth scoop [036] enclose an area of similar dimensions to Timber structure 1. Of interest in this early Neolithic context is that posthole [041] contained substantial amounts of charred grain within its fill [033], while a second pit/posthole [044], which was disturbed by a modern field drain, contained an ashy fill [045] incorporating nearly 6000 charred cereal grains (see Chapter 15). Apart from Braes of Ha'Breck, Wyre (Thomas and Lee 2012), and probably Varme Dale, Evie (Chapters 9 and 15) this is the largest amount of carbonized cereal, mainly naked barley, recovered from an early Neolithic context in Orkney. Judging from the associated radiocarbon date (Chapter 10), this indicates that extensive cereal cultivation was occurring at Wideford Hill during the occupation of timber houses from the mid-4th millennium cal BC. Clearly, at this time cereals not only 'matter', but constitute a major component of subsistence in early Neolithic Orkney (cf. Schulting 2004, 2008; Stevens and Fuller 2012, 715).

2.4 Stone architecture at Wideford Hill: Stonehouse 1

Before the below-ground posts of two of the timber buildings had completely decayed, Stonehouse 1 was erected directly over Timber Structure 2. Unfortunately, on excavation the condition and survival of Stonehouse 1 was found to be very poor as it had been severely damaged through a combination of recent activities. Ploughing had effectively removed its rear area (south), and two water pipe trenches, running parallel to the road, had cut away the front (north), including the house entrance. Indeed, only a short section of the outer wall remained on the eastern side of the house. However, portions of the interior floor surfaces remained intact and from the route of an encircling outer drain [106] the overall shape of the

rear of the house could be approximated (Fig. 2.23). It is unlikely that this was a single building. Beyond the trench, directly west of Stonehouse 1, is an elevated area of ground (Fig. 2.4), and it is extremely likely that this is the site of a second stone structure creating a 'double house' arrangement.

Obviously, the positioning of Stonehouse 1 was influenced by Timber structure 2. Indeed, this house appears to have been directly centered on the hearth of the earlier timber building. As mentioned above, several postholes of a small circular structure were revealed on the removal of the house floor deposits [104]. One posthole [121] was actually present as a void, thereby demonstrating that it still contained an *in situ* timber when covered by the clay of the primary floor of Stonehouse 1 (Fig. 2.15). This reveals the construction of Stonehouse 1 occurred relatively shortly after the timber structure either fell out of use or was purposely felled. A substantial lump of birch charcoal (SF 948), presumably derived from a structural timber, was recovered from the base of the house floor which may relate to the destruction of the earlier wooden building.

Despite its poor survival, enough remained of Stonehouse 1 to determine its overall form. The house wall had an outer and inner masonry skin facing a clay core, giving a thickness of *c*.1.65m. No outer casing wall was detected. The remaining section of the outer wall, together with the route of a large drain [106] running around the outer perimeter of the eastern side of the house, revealed a typical sub-rectangular building orientated roughly north–south. The surviving section of walling incorporated a slight 'pinch' in the inner wall skin (Figs 2.23 and 2.24). Generally such a pinch in the wall coincides with an internally projecting orthostat, for example as seen at Smerquoy or Knap of Howar (Figs 1.6 and 4.5). However, in the case of Stonehouse 1 no such divisional orthostats or necessary cuts were detected. The absence of large divisional orthostats providing partitioning to the house interior is surprising, given that Stonehouse 1 is the primary form of stone architecture at Wideford Hill.

The earliest deposit attributable to the inhabitation of Stonehouse 1 is the ash-trampled clay layer [127], which in places had a black sheen reminiscent of house floor surfaces seen within houses at Smerquoy, Stonehall and Barnhouse. Unsurprisingly, this layer included a much more ashy component around the primary scoop hearth [155], which had also acted as a fireplace in the earlier Timber structure 2 (Fig. 2.16). Consequently, a strong possibility exists that the hearth continued to be used

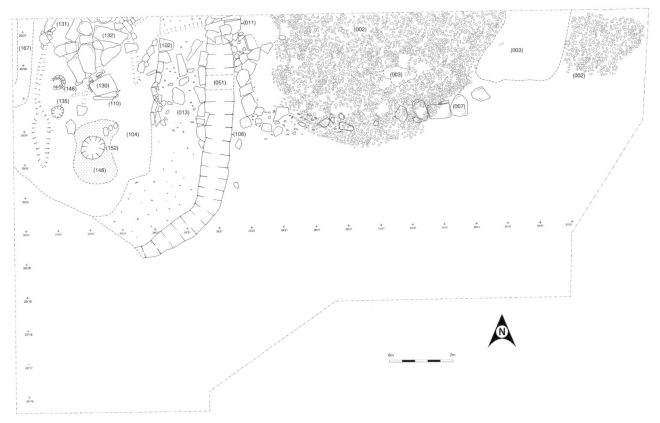

Figure 2.23 Plan of Stonehouse 1 and associated work area [002] at Wideford Hill.

and remained the focal point of the newly constructed stone house. This scoop hearth is also associated with the adjacent primary drain [140] which runs northwards through the house from a position to the west of the fire to drain in the large pit or sump [138] (Fig. 2.25).

Over the primary clay floor, a more general occupation layer [104] spread across the entire internal area of the house and again varied considerably in colour (red-orange around the hearth and black–dark-brown elsewhere). Associated with this occupation layer was a new scoop hearth [152] which is situated slightly south of the primary hearth [155] (Fig. 2.26). The new hearth was filled with a lower black ash [149] with an upper red ashy fill [148] which had spilled out across the adjacent floor surface (Fig. 2.27). This ash [148] had covered an orange-brown ashy layer [153] which must relate to primary use of hearth [152]. A radiocarbon date of *3340–2920 cal BC (GU-12497)* was obtained from a naked barley grain from upper ash spread [148].

The seemingly minor act of cutting a new hearth is argued here to be of considerable significance in relation to the embryonic *société à maisons*. Principally, it would appear to mark a partial disjuncture with the previous

timber house, a situation where, although maintaining a degree of importance, continuity (descent) is slowly becoming subordinate to the social and material potency of developing networks of 'horizontal' social relations. The abandoning of the original hearth and construction of a new scoop hearth is suggested here to illustrate the 'central feature of the house' (Hugh-Jones 1995, 7), and as a material metaphor of the 'household' (those who sit around it), serves to both balance and negotiate the antagonistic principles' of alliance and descent (cf. Lévi-Strauss 1982, 174–76). The new hearth arguably represents a desire on the part of those who now share it to physically acknowledge changing social circumstances, but within the security of continuity as materialized in the stone-built durable house. It is suggested that this balance between relatedness constituted through shared practices surrounding Neolithic lifeways (*e.g.* agriculture and exchange strategies), and claimed lines of descent and social continuity, provides a dynamic tension which structures the development of *sociétés à maisons* throughout the Orcadian Neolithic.

Slightly nearer the front area of the house was a shallow 'box-like' feature occupying a central position which was

Figure 2.24 View of Stonehouse 1 from the south; note the internal ash deposits spreading from the second scoop hearth [152] (Colin Richards).

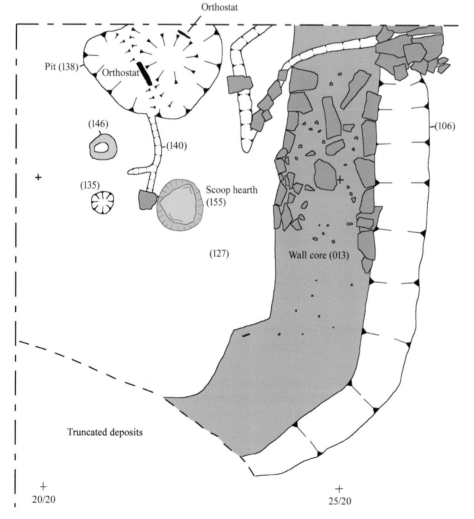

Figure 2.25 Plan of primary features within Stonehouse 1.

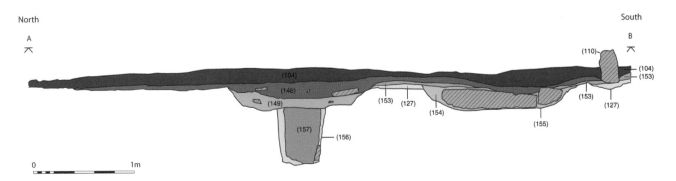

North | South

Figure 2.26 *East-facing section through scoop hearths [152] and [155] within Stonehouse 1 showing stratigraphic relationships of the internal occupation ash deposits.*

Figure 2.27 *Excavating the internal ash deposits spreading from the second scoop hearth [152] (Colin Richards).*

Figure 2.28 *The stone box arrangement in Stonehouse 1 (Colin Richards).*

initially interpreted as a hearth. This was because the covering slab had cracked and sunk in the centre giving the impression of surrounding stone uprights defining what appeared as ashy material [129] in the centre (see Fig. 2.28). The box was actually formed from two small uprights [110] with a large overlying slab [130]. This slab covered a shallow cavity in which black 'sticky' silt had collected. The function of the shallow stone box is difficult to interpret but a similar arrangement was present in the later occupation of the Smerquoy Hoose (Chapter 4). To the west of the stone box, what only can be described as a raised circle of yellow glacial clay had been hollowed out to create a clay 'bowl' [146]. This was filled with brown silt with charcoal flecks (Fig. 2.29). A small shallow pit [133], filled with loose black silty loam [134] was located c.0.6m south of the clay 'bowl'. A further elongated shallow pit running into a drain [158], orientated north-south, was positioned adjacent

Figure 2.29 *The clay 'bowl' [146] in Stonehouse 1 is visible towards the bottom of the picture. Above, the excavated earlier drain [140] can be seen stratified beneath the box-like structure [110] (Colin Richards).*

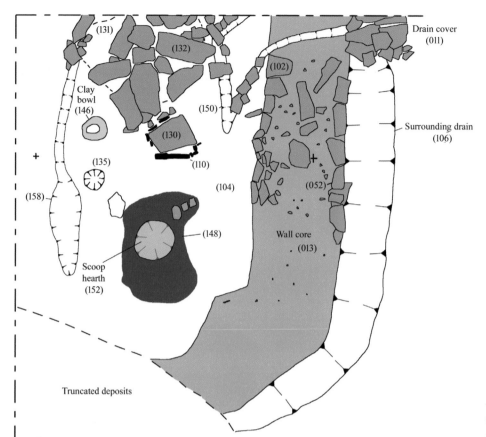

Figure 2.30 Plan of secondary drains and internal features inside Stonehouse 1.

to the assumed position of the truncated eastern outer wall and relates to secondary occupation of Stonehouse 1 (Fig. 2.30).

2.4.1 Hydrology

A fairly complicated drainage system was present within the northern area (front) of Stonehouse 1 which clearly relates to different periods of occupation (see also Chapter 4). Initially, a drain [140] ran in a northerly direction from a position adjacent to the primary scoop hearth [155], and flowed into a large amorphous pit [138] dug in the frontal area of the house, which is best interpreted as a sump or cistern (Fig. 2.25). At this time the large pit appears to have been covered by flagstones supported by diminutive stone uprights. A short length of drain, running in from the west, conjoins drain [140], and it is difficult to know if this additional stretch represents a chronological shift or activities occurring at different locations within the house.

A second drain [150] running north from the east side of the stone box is more complicated in that it splits shortly beyond its origin point. One channel, still slab covered in places, flowed out beneath the house wall into the large ditch or drain [106] running around the east perimeter of the house. This indicates that it is a primary element of construction. However, the second channel ran northwards and on excavation clearly exited beneath the house wall further to the north-east. The drain skirted the eastern edge of the cistern or large pit [138] which by this time had filled with black loose silt [139] and been re-surfaced with a spread of flagstones [132]. The flagstones were uneven due to subsidence into the relatively soft fill of the pit (Fig. 2.31). The presence of such a large covered pit within the confines of the frontal compartment of the house is unusual. Originally, it would have been covered by large flagstones supported by stone uprights. Indeed, two such small orthostats were discovered *in situ* set into the base of the pit. Childe seems to have encountered a similar pit or cistern beneath the floor of Hut 5 at Skara Brae: 'the impression produced by the ruin is that there had been a sort of covered cistern here that must have been broken down and filled in before the erection of hut 5' (1931a, 81–82). Because of the slope at Skara Brae, Childe posited the possibility of drains carrying fresh water into the cistern (*ibid.*, 82).

Figure 2.32 West view of the rammed-stone surface [002] under excavation. In the left foreground the large drain, with stone covering, runs around the outer wall of Stonehouse 1. Beyond this the remains of the curving wall [012] of Stone structure 2, and its partially removed E–W extension [007], can be clearly seen (Colin Richards).

Figure 2.31 The interior of Stonehouse 1 under excavation; to the left is the upper surface of the large pit or sump, note the flagstones sinking down into the fill. To the right the stone 'box' is visible. The yellow clay remnant of the west wall core is visible in the foreground (Colin Richards).

As demonstrated by the sophisticated drainage network in the Smerquoy Hoose (see Chapter 4), the hydrological processes in early Neolithic houses are relatively complex, a situation not present in the timber structures. The purpose of the large pit [138] in Stonehouse 1 is nonetheless difficult to determine. Whilst having a possible overflow which suggests the immersion of materials, certainly at one time waste liquid appears to flow directly into it via the drain [140]. There seems to be no resolution to the status of the pit or cistern in Stonehouse 1 though it appears to have been a functioning component of the dwelling during its earliest period of occupation. Clearly, there is a complex history of drainage represented by the sequence of channels which to some degree concur with the redundancy of the primary scoop hearth [155] and its replacement by a second fireplace [152].

2.5 Sedimenting practice in place: Stone structure 2 and the overlying rammed-stone working area

As noted above, around the eastern side of the outer wall of Stonehouse 1 ran a shallow ditch or drain. A semi-circle of medium flagstones [012] partially formed the east side of the drain and also defined the western edge of the rammed-stone surface [002]. Adjacent to the northern baulk of the trench a series of large flagstones [011] were present showing that the drain had originally been covered along its circuit (Fig. 2.32). As with the other deposits relating to Stonehouse 1, the drain was traced southwards until it began to curve around the rear of the house where it had been truncated and destroyed by ploughing.

The semi-circle of walling [012] in conjunction with the line of slabs [007] running east-west appear to be the remains of a ruined building known as Stone structure 2 (Figs 2.33 and 2.35). Initially, Stonehouse 1 and Stone structure 2 were contemporary units separated by the covered drain. Any trace of any internal architectural features within Stone structure 2 was entirely absent, although not all of the covering rammed-stone surface was removed by excavation. However, to the north of gully [030] and 'Timber structure 3', a layer of orange-brown ashy soil mixed with burnt stone [128] was sealed beneath the rammed-stone surface [002] and

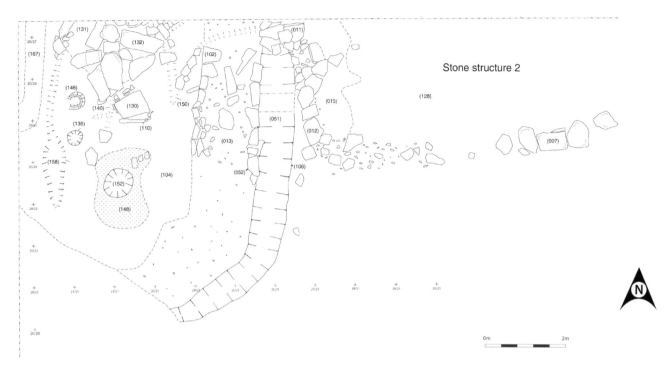

Figure 2.33 Plan of Stonehouse 1 and foundation slabs of Stone structure 2.

incorporated dumps of ash [003]. Radiocarbon dates of *3360–3090* and *3370–3090 cal BC (GU-12487* and *GU-12496)* were obtained from the lower layer [128], while ash dump [003] was dated to *3510–3100 cal BC (GU-12486)*. Given the stratigraphy, it seems possible these deposits could have been associated with earlier occupation and Stone structure 2.

Apart from its curved form, little more can be said of the architecture and role of Stone structure 2, besides the observation that at some time during the life of Stonehouse 1, it was demolished and the rammed-stone surface [002] laid down. This deposit entirely covered the area previously taken by Stone structure 2, and was composed of an extensive spread of compacted, variable sized, sandstone blocks and fragments, many of which were fire reddened. In function, it represented an open area where a number of tasks were undertaken, while in composition this deposit was in some ways similar to the spread of burnt stones uncovered adjacent to Houses 2 and 3 at Stonehall Meadow (see Chapter 5).

That the rammed stone surface had been consistently built-up during its life is clear from the thin bands of ash and soil that effectively interlaced the stones. A radiocarbon date of *3490–3090 cal BC (GU-12488)* was obtained from naked barley within an upper ash lense. Despite this interleaving, the stones were extremely

compact (the description 'rammed stone surface' being very apt) which made trowelling extremely difficult. This compaction was clearly due to continuous trampling as various tasks were taking place in this area. In particular areas the rammed stone surface incorporated spreads of red ash. A further feature was the inclusion of large amounts of pottery and broken stone and flint artefacts with the burnt stones (Fig. 2.34). The broken nature of so many stone tools causes Ann Clarke (see Chapter 13) to suggest that they may have been deliberately broken up to be incorporated within the surface (Fig. 2.34a). This interesting observation can be modified to include the possibility that periods of intensive work led to extensive tool breakage after prolonged use-life. Here specific tasks would be literally sedimented in place, not only by practice, but by practices of deposition. In many ways this specialized work area presages the specialized late Neolithic craft production areas at Barnhouse (the central area), suggesting that the regionalization of craft activities has some antiquity in Orcadian prehistory.

In such practices we see a marked departure from more ephemeral activities associated with the earlier timber houses. Marking particular places, time and time again, through sequential deposition hints at new material discourses coming into existence emphasizing place and continuity. In short, materials were literally

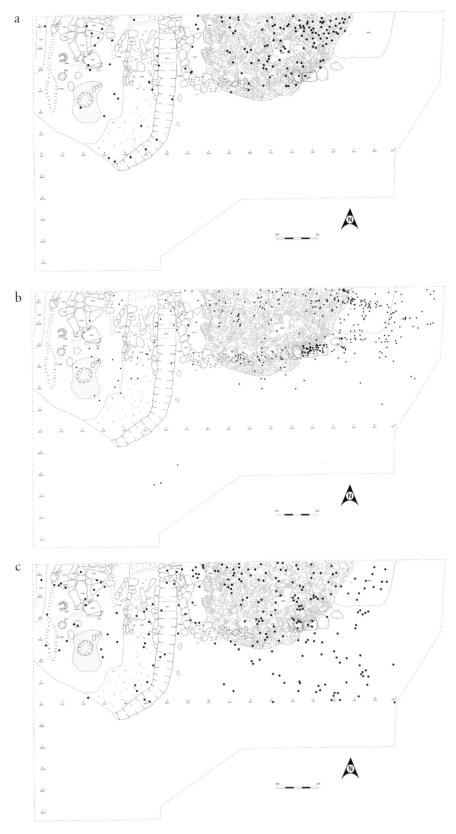

Figure 2.34 The distribution of stone artefacts (a), ceramics (b) and worked flint (c) across the rammed stone deposit [002].

thrown down after use to be absorbed and incorporated as part of an assemblage incorporating people things and memories. Because of the episodic re-surfacing, the various artefacts fused within the rammed-stone deposit become 'fossilized' and spatially representative of sequential activities occurring in the work area (Fig. 2.34).

Further to the south, the fire-reddened blocks and fragments of stone constituting the rammed-stone surface [002] began to thin out becoming mixed with a dark brown charcoal flecked silty soil [005]. Unfortunately, to the east, the compact stone surface [002] was truncated and gave way to a discrete orange-brown ashy old land surface [003] which lapped over the yellow glacial clay. All deposits further south or east had been completely removed by the plough.

2.6 Houses of the dead: the transformation from wood to stone architecture at Wideford Hill

Since the initial surface collection by Rendall, it has been recognized that the Wideford Hill flint assemblage includes microliths. Apart from the example recovered from the rammed-stone area [002], the other microliths have all come from the ploughsoil and are distributed across the field towards its northeast corner (Fig. 2.1). Given the ephemeral remains associated with the timber structures, it is unsurprising that a series of small test pits dug in 1999–2000 failed to locate subsurface deposits as in all probability only the postholes remain. Rendall (1931; 1934, 19–20) does mention that the flint-rich areas coincided with discrete spreads of clay which he describes as 'flint-floors'. These clay 'flint-floors' can be contrasted with the hummock, which represents the beginning of stone architecture at Wideford Hill. If the flint scatter is an index of habitation, the timber house structures encountered within the excavated trench are merely a component of a larger number spreading across the eastern extent of the Wideford 'flint field' corresponding to Robert Rendall's 'flint-floors' (Figs 2.1 and 2.5). Under these circumstances the stone-constructed Stonehouse 1 would lie at the northwest edge of an area of shifting settlement comprising timber-built round houses which may, in all probability, date back to the early–mid 4th millennium cal BC.

A number of voids and cavities caused by the decay of *in situ* timbers within the postholes of both Timber structures 2 and 3 were sealed beneath clay surfaces associated with the two stone buildings. Consequently, there was clearly a fairly rapid succession of occupation from timber to stone buildings. A similar rapid sequence

has been suggested for Knap of Howar where the stone constructed houses were built on a pre-existing midden (Ashmore 1996, 45). The single radiocarbon date from a sealed posthole [053] provided a mid-4th millennium cal BC context for one of the later timber roundhouses at Wideford Hill (see Chapter 10). Again this is consistent with radiocarbon dates obtained from the lowest midden at Knap of Howar, Papa Westray (Sheridan and Higham 2006, 202–203; 2007, 225).

Analysis of the charcoal from Wideford Hill shows the presence of willow, birch and hazel, and absence of pine (see Chapter 15). This effectively confirms the presence of woodland cover up to at least the mid-4th millennium cal BC as documented by Davidson and Jones (1990, 25) and Farrell *et al.* (2014). It also demonstrates that driftwood was not the essential building material previously assumed, and that indigenous woodland was far more prolific and quite capable of providing timbers of necessary size and strength for structural purposes.

How then is the shift in the materiality and architecture of the early Neolithic house best understood? As intimated above, the extensive nature of the Wideford Hill surface scatter may relate to a more transient mode of habitation. This phenomenon is certainly evident in the timber structures encountered within the excavated area. Where such a periodic shift in location occurs it hints at a perspective on dwelling that does not necessarily emphasize social continuity through maintenance of a particular place. Here, social relations and lines of descent, as manifest materially in the continuity of a house and social group, are not being articulated solely through continued residence as defined by a specific location. While at one level it is clear that a degree of maintenance of 'place' is present at Wideford Hill as revealed through the broad extent of the surface scatter, at another the degree of displacement expressed through shifting house location militates against social identity being entirely expressed materially and spatially through residence superimposition.

Within such a scheme there is also a problem in estimating the number of timber structures being occupied at any given time. It is possible, given their spatial proximity, that only one or two timber structures could have been occupied concurrently, or that multiple structures were occupied simultaneously for different uses or purposes. The internal space within Timber structure 1 is relatively small and it is unlikely to have contained a large domestic unit. This exposes yet another facet of the Wideford Hill timber buildings, that they may reflect social practices involving kin fragmentation, a characteristic which would

Figure 2.35 As Adrian Challands and Andrew M. Jones remove the rammed-stone deposit [002], the underlying line of foundation stones [007] for Stone structure 2 becomes visible (Colin Richards).

inevitably be manifest in changing residence rules and the spatial patterns of house size and location. Whilst timber architecture is present at Smerquoy (Chapter 4), little is currently known of the density or chronology of settlement. The timber buildings at Wideford Hill, because of their spatial definition and lack of stratigraphic relationships, provide little assistance in this area.

The significance of building habitations out of wood, a growing and seasonally changing material, should not be underestimated (Noble 2006a, 96–99; 2006b, 58–62). Building in wood undoubtedly introduces a finite 'life span' to any structure which will ultimately succumb to the ravages of time and decay. Here, analogies between the life cycle of timber houses, fertility and human household are entirely possible (cf. Noble 2006a, 99–99). But decay does not necessarily lead to abandonment and displacement as rebuilding can easily occur *in situ* with new timbers, as we see for example with the continuous maintenance and rebuilding of timber houses in house societies of the northwest coast of America (Marshall 2000). Yet, the lack of post replacement appears to be a feature of the timber structures revealed by excavation. Even if a decline in available timber in Orkney was a factor in this process (and judging from recent research, *e.g.* Farrell *et al.* 2014, it is not) this does not account for

the complete change in architecture between the timber and stone houses as witnessed at Wideford Hill.

Indeed, the change from timber to stone house construction is a fascinating transformation in terms of both the materiality and architecture of dwelling. As mentioned in the introduction to this chapter, the typological classification of chambered cairns was still a prevalent archaeological endeavour of Neolithic archaeology in the mid-twentieth century (*e.g.* Daniel 1950; Henshall 1963). Once types had been established their spatial or geographic distribution could be charted to discern archaeological cultures and their spread. In the case of the Orkney-Cromarty group of chambered cairns, originally identified by Piggott (1954, 232–56), they were considered to chart the northerly movement of Neolithic 'colonists' in the north of Scotland. Although outdated, this schema has substantial implications for understanding the change from timber to stone house architecture that we can now identify occurring at Wideford Hill, Smerquoy and Ha'Breck, Wyre (Thomas and Lee 2012). For example, regardless of the culture-history resonance of chambered cairn types, there is ample evidence that chambered cairns of stalled architecture were being built fairly early in the Orcadian sequence, certainly by *c.*3600–3500 cal BC (Barber 1997,

58–60; Schulting and Richards 2009, 66–74). They are, therefore, associated with early agriculturists regardless of the social mechanisms instigating their presence and construction.

Significantly, on the basis of radiocarbon dates obtained from Wideford Hill, Ha'Breck and Knap of Howar, the initial contemporaneity of stalled cairns and stone-built houses of similar 'stalled' architecture is unlikely. Instead, it appears that timber houses were being constructed well into the latter half of the 4th millennium cal BC (see Chapter 10). We suggest that stone houses were not being erected in Orkney until as late as *c*.3300 cal BC, which would seem to confirm Anna Ritchie's statement that 'it is inherently unlikely that developed settlements such as Knap of Howar… should represent the homes of the first pioneering colonists' (1983, 39). This observation has profound implications for the idea that the stalled chambered tombs should be conceived as 'houses of the dead' (Ritchie 1995, 44–45). The basis of this identification derives from the similarity in architecture between houses and stalled cairns (Hodder 1984; Richards 1992, 66–67), and the implication is that the latter were modeled on house architecture (Fig. 1.5). Such an assumption conforms to broader debates concerning the origins of monumentality (see Deboer 1997; Kirch 2000). However, the discovery of early Neolithic circular and sub-rectangular timber house architecture at Wideford Hill, Ha'Breck, Green and Smerquoy subverts this scheme. Instead of stalled cairn architecture being derived from the house, the opposite appears to be the case in that the materiality and architecture of the house is a replication of the stalled chambered cairn. Clearly, the question of why people should begin to build and dwell within houses resembling and referencing chambered cairns takes centre stage.

Given the distribution of Piggott's Orkney-Cromarty type of chambered cairn from just north of Inverness to Caithness and Orkney, it is clear that whilst not invoking archaeological cultures or movement of peoples, there exist contacts and social relationships extending well beyond the Northern Isles. Equally, the chambered cairns, as places of the dead in one form or another, are of ancestral consequence. To build a house referencing the materiality and architecture of the chambered cairn is to dwell within the 'tomb', and within the past. Under such circumstances a reversal occurs and the dwelling becomes the 'house of the dead', a place where past and present generations fuse. In short, the transformation in the house that occurs at Wideford Hill (and Ha'Breck, Green and Smerquoy) goes beyond material metaphor, because building and living in a 'house of the dead' powerfully articulates a merging of ancestry with origins. This is precisely the discursive

framework that mediates social relations within the context of developing Neolithic *sociétés à maisons* in Orkney.

At another level, the transformation from timber to stone houses could be said to balance two conflicting principles: continuity and dislocation. Dislocation is clearly manifest in the changing materiality and architecture of the dwelling, despite its clear relationship with the stalled architecture of the chambered cairn. Yet, this dislocation is mediated, to some degree, through a strategy of continuity, interestingly articulated through rapid succession and the continuity of the hearth. A close sequence of construction is clearly demonstrated by the occurrence of sealed voids of postholes beneath the clay floor of Stonehouse 1. This indicates that timber survived within the postholes in one form or another, only rotting subsequent to the laying of the clay floor. The continued use of the scoop hearth [155] of Timber structure 2 in the newly built Stonehouse 1 is remarkable. In this occurrence, perhaps for the first time, we witness the hearth transcending other elements of the house and relating directly to the continuity of occupation, and more importantly the people who share a hearth.

The stone-constructed houses are substantially larger buildings than their timber predecessors, and could potentially accommodate a greater number of people. This material enveloping of a larger social group is clearly a substantial shift from the smaller, possibly kin-based, timber dwellings. The advent of open communal working areas, as represented by the rammed-stone surface [002], also marks a point of departure. Here tasks are undertaken in specific places, time after time, and the materiality of these encounters is incorporated in the substance of the ground (or platform) upon which they occur. Clearly, not only are themes of communality, place and continuity being expressed through social practices, but the agency of deposition anticipates the creation of the great midden-constituted settlement mounds of the 3rd millennium cal BC.

Manifest in the architecture and materiality of the new stone house-form are horizontal relationships based on a shared hearth and wider social practices (as seen in the tasks occurring on the adjacent rammed-stone surface). Yet, this occurs within the architecture of a 'house of the dead' which materializes discourses of vertical relations emphasizing descent and ancestry. But, of course, this is exactly the language of the 'house' expected within a *société à maisons* as outlined by Lévi-Strauss (1982, 174–75). This distinction and a general trend towards broader social units and the importance attached to their continuity through the changing social practices of agricultural production will be explored further in Chapter 9.

CHAPTER THREE

Place in the Past: an early Neolithic house at the Knowes of Trotty barrow cemetery, Harray, Mainland, Orkney

Jane Downes, Paul Sharman, Adrian Challands,
Erika Guttmann-Bond, Jo McKenzie, Roy Towers and Patricia D. Voke

3.1 An unexpected discovery

The Knowes of Trotty in the parish of Harray is one of the finest examples of a linear Bronze Age barrow cemetery in the north of Britain. The site is most famously known for the spectacular 'Wessex' gold discs and amber beads discovered in 1858 (Petrie 1860), accompanying a cremation in the largest of the barrows, Mound 1 (Figs 3.1, 3.2 and 3.3). This barrow cemetery is aligned north-northeast–south-southwest and extends over *c.*350m, being the largest in Orkney. In 2001, a geophysical survey of the barrow cemetery by Adrian Challands was undertaken with the aim of locating features associated with Bronze Age burial rites. Among many features, a discrete sub-circular area of high magnetic response was identified in the northeast part of the cemetery (Anomaly 6, Fig. 3.2). The feature lay *c.*38 metres to the north of the small barrows 4 and 5 (Fig. 3.1), which lie at the north end of the longer line of the barrow cemetery. Excavation of this area of high magnetic response was undertaken as part of a programme of investigation in 2002 to examine a selection of the geophysical anomalies in the anticipation of finding pyre sites, flat cemeteries, mortuary structures and other features associated with the stages of mortuary rites (Downes forthcoming). To everyone's surprise a ruined house structure was revealed on removal of the turf and topsoil, the architecture of which was obviously 4th millennium cal BC in date (Fig. 3.3).

As can be imagined, the finding of an early Neolithic house was totally unexpected as the structural remains were not visible on the ground apart from a slight hollow which transpired to be the south end of the house. The house was first identified by the excavation of a small trench in 2002 (Trench B, Fig. 3.1) which was expanded in 2005, incorporating the earlier trench and located on a slight elongated hollow that was visible on the ground surface. This hollow represented the interior of a building with more than one phase of use and alteration, a stone-built hearth, and entrances probably to the north, and to the east. In 2006, the trench was extended 2 metres to the north, to examine the end wall and entranceways, and 4 metres to the east, to determine whether the area accessed through the eastern doorway was a conjoining building. The excavation was also extended in the southwest corner of the house to examine the wall phasing.

It was not possible to excavate all of the occupation deposits within the building due to time and financial constraints. Neither was it possible to excavate fully the building walls or the yard to the east of the house. These limitations to the excavation, coupled with the ruinous and truncated condition of parts of the building, have meant that several presumptions have been made, especially about the form of the earliest phases of the building and its entrances. The northern end of the housse was particularly truncated, as opposed to the southern end, which was better protected due to it being cut into the natural subsoil

It is most probable (68%) that the occupation of

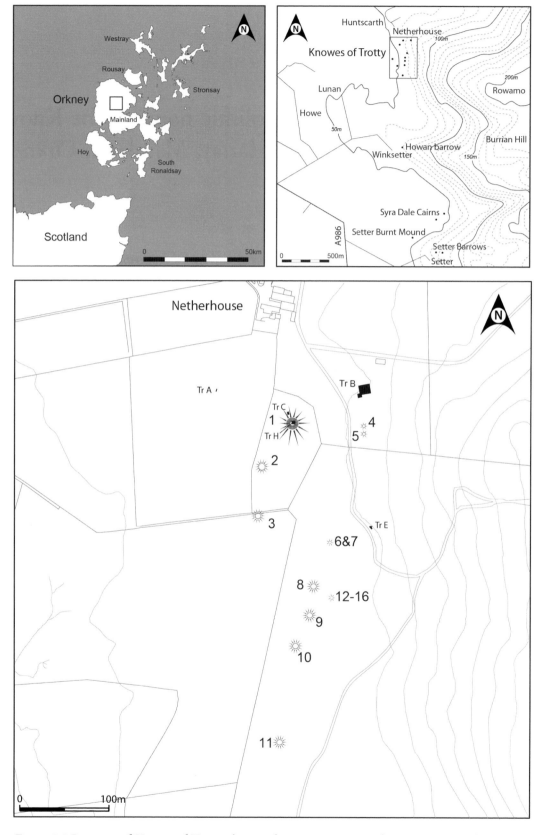

Figure 3.1 Location of Knowes of Trotty, showing barrow cemetery and excavation trench positions.

Figure 3.2 Gradiometer survey of Knowes of Trotty. Anomalies 1 and 2 represent Mound 1, the largest of the barrows, and anomaly 6 the early Neolithic house.

the building spanned less than 200 years, beginning sometime in the 34th to 32nd centuries cal BC (see Chapter 10). Three broad phases of reconstruction occurred during the occupation of the Knowes of Trotty house, a feature which is consistent with other stone houses of the second half of the 4th millennium cal BC, such as Stonehall Meadow House 3 (Chapter 5) and the Smerquoy Hoose (Chapter 4).

3.2 Phase 1: A new house

The site chosen to construct the house was on the edge of a low ridge with a slope down to the north and west, so in order to achieve a level foundation, the glacial till was cut back into the slope to accommodate the southern part of the house (Fig. 3.3). Along with a small area of level ground in front of the cut, a platform was created that measured some 14.5m × 7.5m. A sub-rectangular house was built on this, with its long axis

Figure 3.3 The Neolithic house under excavation with Mound 1 in background (Jane Downes).

oriented north-northeast–south-southwest (Fig. 3.4). The walling of the earliest phase could only be traced in places, mostly on the west side of the building where the wall was standing on the ground surface as opposed to the south and east sides where walling placed within the cut into the subsoil was buried under subsequent construction phases and remained unexcavated. On the west side, the house extended outside the excavated area and, due to the limited nature of the excavation, no parts of walling or internal features of the earliest building were fully exposed. In addition, the subsequent activities of rebuilding and modification obscured or removed parts of the initial house; all these factors combine to make a plan of the original building conjectural in places. It is possible to approximate the internal space as measuring 4.5m east–west by 9.0m north–south, which makes the Knowes of Trotty a little smaller than Knap of Howar House 1 which was *c*.10.0m long and 5.0m wide, and very similar dimensions (and orientation) to the Smerquoy Hoose *c*.4.00m east–west and *c*.9.50m north–south (Chapter 4).

Although conditions of preservation allowed the whole wall structure to be seen in only a few places, the masonry of the northern half of the house was constituted in typical Orcadian Neolithic construction style, with an inner and outer face and a clay or rubble core. The earliest stretch of walling [203], found on the site on the west side of the building, was revealed within an exploratory cutting through the walls within the inner part of the building, south of the orthostat partition (Fig. 3.4). This section of walling was completely overlain and replaced by the phase 2 walling. Wall [203] was built of substantial, well-finished, blocks of quarried stone (Fig. 3.5), and was of a better quality and of more substantial block masonry than walling elsewhere in the building. The stonework revealed was the inner wall face of the building, set against a cut into the glacial till which would have formed the wall core. In contrast, the outer wall face was set in an elevated position on the glacial till (Figs 3.4 and 3.6), a constructional feature also seen in the south west corner of the building. A sherd of Unstan ware pottery rim was recovered from the wall core backing these wall sections (SF 6, Fig. 3.7).

The earliest phase of building is represented on the west side by a 1.40m–1.80m wide wall, whose external faces were built mostly of coursed thin flags. Although there is a start of a gentle curve round, the southern end of the wall and the manner in which it turned to the east was not revealed, because again it lay below material deposited as part of the phase 2 building. It is not clear how much of internal wall face [144] was part of the first phase of construction; although it does key into the dividing orthostat [209] there is a cut behind it, which may have had the original walling set against it. This would have replaced by walling at a slightly different angle when the building was narrowed and shortened in phase 2.

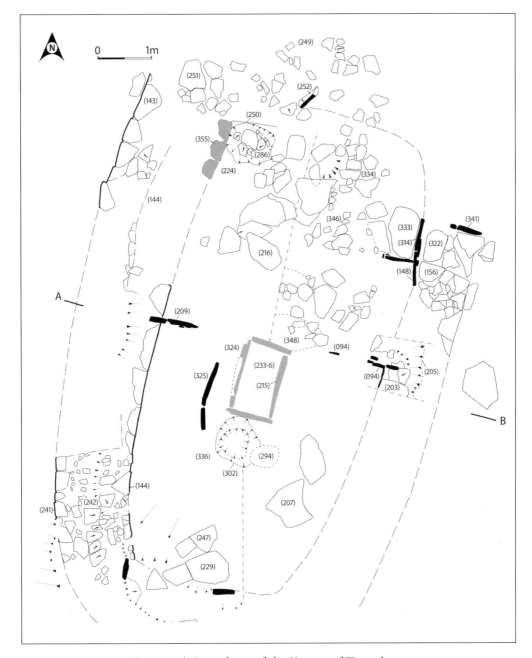

Figure 3.4 First phases of the Knowes of Trotty house.

The part of the internal face at the southwest end survived to eleven courses, attaining a height of at least 0.50m, set in a cut against the glacial till. The outer wall face, set up above the inner face on the natural surface, survived to only a single course. The wall core here simply comprised a mixture of flagstone and gritty silt, which interlocked with the rear of the wall faces. The large blocky stones at the south end of the building were angled inwards from the original wall line (Fig. 3.8), being remnants of the original wall which became

displaced to sit within the later rear chamber created in phase 2.

Thus, in the south and southeast parts of the house, the cut into the glacial till forming the lower part of the building was faced with stonework, with outer stone walling resting on the natural till ledge and forming the upper parts of the sides of the house, with a height difference of 0.50m (Fig. 3.8). This 'stepped' technique of outer wall construction is replicated in a number of 4th millennium cal BC houses, for example, Stonehall

Knoll House 3 and the Smerquoy Hoose. Similarly at Knap of Howar, Papa Westray an area of midden (Period I) was removed to create a level platform for house 1 and 2 (Period II) (Ritchie 1983, 44–46), and the inner wall-face was laid directly on boulder clay with the outer face laid on top of the lower midden, at a difference of some 0.35m between the inner and outer basal courses (*op. cit.*,

48). This building technique may well have originated earlier in the 4th millennium cal BC, as within Brae of Smerquoy Trench 2, a timber and turf-constructed building appears to utilize cuts into the glacial clay to provide a stepped outer wall (see Fig. 4.38). At the Knowes of Trotty the width of the original wall at the southwest end was 1.40m, comparable with the slightly larger Smerquoy Hoose whose wall averaged *c.*1.80m in thickness (Chapter 4).

The fragment of external wall face on the northwest side of the house (Fig. 3.4) is also presumed part of the original house wall. There were some level flagstones at what would have been the northwest corner, which could represent the remains of probable foundation stones below the wall core. It is assumed that there was originally an entranceway central to the northern end of the house, as at Knap of Howar and other examples of early Neolithic houses within this volume. The cracked and jagged upright stone [252] which protruded up through the disturbed wall material is interpreted as a displaced threshold stone or entranceway orthostat, the only evidence for the original northern entrance (Figs 3.4 and 3.8, foreground). The walls forming the northeast corner of the building were missing from phases 1 and 2, in part truncated because the archaeology is so close to the surface here and had modern disturbance evidenced by a pit, and in part due to phase 3 rebuilding. With evidence from comparable structures, the likely layout of this corner of the building can be postulated as sweeping in a gentle curve with its outer face just within the limits of the excavation trench.

Few primary occupation deposits, fixtures and fittings were completely exposed in the building. However, the division of space through the use of paired orthostats, as indicated by [209] to the west and [094] to the east, created a clear demarcation between the inner, lower compartment to the south and an elevated

Figure 3.5 Detail of wall [203], with Phase 2 walls [024] and [101] in front (ORCA).

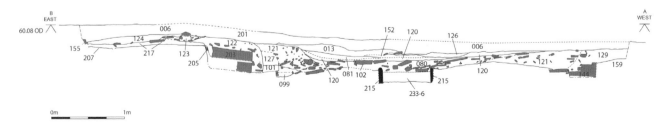

Figure 3.6 East–west section through the Knowes of Trotty house.

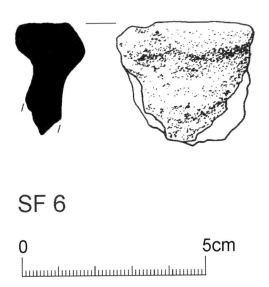

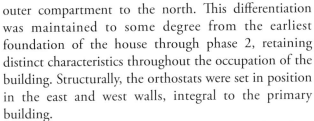

SF 6

0   5cm

Figure 3.7 Unstan ware rim sherd (SF 6) from the wall core of the first Knowes of Trotty house.

Figure 3.8 View from north to south of the Knowes of Trotty house (ORCA).

Figure 3.9 Primary hearth [302]. Feature [294] is under excavation in foreground (ORCA).

outer compartment to the north. This differentiation was maintained to some degree from the earliest foundation of the house through phase 2, retaining distinct characteristics throughout the occupation of the building. Structurally, the orthostats were set in position in the east and west walls, integral to the primary building.

In the southern half of the interior a clay floor belonging to the primary occupation was partially revealed. The floor was laid on a surface of rammed subsoil, so treated to form a durable level surface across the southern part of the house. Similar hard-packed material was set around two substantial and firmly bedded north-northeast–south-southwest oriented upright stones [325] positioned in line parallel to and 1.10m in from the west wall. These upright stones are most likely the remains of a 'bed' set along the west side of the house; a parallel to this feature was found at Stonehall Meadow House 3 (Fig. 5.42), represented by a cut 3.6m long which, like the orthostat setting at Knowes of Trotty, had a curved slot running inwards as it approached the divisional orthostat. However, the whole arrangement was reversed since the slot was on the right-hand side of the Knowes of Trotty house and the left within Stonehall Meadow House 3.

The rectangular stone-built hearth [215] was not dismantled during excavation and as a consequence any earlier features could not be examined. However, it is not the primary hearth of the house; the hearth stones

are later than the orthostats [325] and the hearth cuts through primary floor surfaces, including a spread of ashy material associated with an earlier hearth. The original hearth [302] instead was a wide shallow scoop 0.12 m deep (Figs 3.4 and 3.9). This hearth was filled with charcoal-rich bright red ashy silt remains and capped by a flagstone. The material in the scoop was very well preserved so it may have been capped by the flagstone immediately after the final deposition. Birch charcoal within this context [301] produced a radiocarbon date of *3350–3080 cal BC (SUERC 18239)*. This scoop hearth

Figure 3.10 Pit [286] in northern end of building (ORCA).

is similar to the primary hearth identified within the Smerquoy Hoose, Stonehall Meadow House 3 and Stonehouse 1 at Wideford Hill.

Within the inner, southern part of the building the flooring comprised layers of compact clay and silt, whereas in the outer, northern part the floor surfaces were flagged, and patched with smaller areas of paving interspersed with compact clayey flooring material. Large slabs and floor surfaces in the northern part of the house may originate in primary phases, and continue in use into subsequent phases.

In the northern part of the house, pit [286] represents the probable earliest feature on site, overlain by phase 2 walling. The pit, which was sub-oval and unevenly cut, was fairly shallow measuring 0.33m in depth (Fig. 3.10), and was lined roughly with flags [284] at the sides and bottom. Within one of the layers of fill in the pit [282] fragments of birch charcoal provided a date of *3500–3460 cal BC (SUERC 18239)*. Seven sherds of undecorated pottery from seven different vessels, and small fragments of burnt bone were recovered from the pit fill indicating it to have been filled with midden. The pit was sealed by paving (Fig. 3.10), probably in an effort to level the floor for continuing use, which was unsuccessful as it eventually sank into the soft fill of the pit. A similar amorphous pit was present in the floor of Stonehouse 1 at Wideford Hill, and it too had been covered by flagstones which promptly sank into its soft fill (see Fig. 2.31). The function of the Knowes of Trotty pit is equally unclear; it is too wide and shallow to have been a posthole, and there is no burning of the surfaces to indicate a fire-pit or oven. The pit could possibly have been associated with water coursing, relating to features similar to those encountered within the Smerquoy Hoose (Figs 4.6 and 4.24).

The entrance in the east side of the building was much better preserved than that to the north. The west side of the east entrance butted a north-northeast–south-southwest oriented orthostat [148] which would have formed the lower part of the interior house wall facing, and aligned with the primary walling. The line of the orthostat was continued by another orthostat with a worn top set into the entrance passage acting as the threshold (Fig. 3.4). The small amount of primary walling [203] visible with the threshold orthostat provided evidence for a wall of 1.40m thickness, comparable with walling in the southwest corner. The top of threshold orthostat [314] stood *c.*150mm proud of the stone flags in the house interior, indicating a step down into the house when entering from the east. The south side of the east entrance was formed by the wall facing at the end of the north-northeast–south-southwest oriented wall, [156], which was also faced on the external (east) side.

This entrance possibly led originally into an adjoining house to the east which subsequently was demolished. Based on comparisons between the Knowes of Trotty house and both Knap of Howar and Stonehall Meadow: the short passage way joining two houses is in the same position at each site. The adjoining house would have occupied a levelled platform at a higher level than the surviving house. At the Knowes of Trotty, wall [156] would thereby have been the inner wall face of both conjoined houses; although it could arguably be the partial original outer wall of the house it comprises blockier stones and is well finished, bearing more similarities in these respects to the inner-facing wall [203] than to the outer-wall faces seen elsewhere. The large flat slabs may be similar vestiges of paving within a building. The area to the east of the house became an external yard and work area in subsequent phases and this activity removed traces of phase 1 activity, in addition to which the higher level of this area has been more vulnerable to truncation.

3.3 Phase 2: making alterations

At a later time, the Knowes of Trotty house was rebuilt and it is this period of occupation which is archaeologically best preserved. However, it is difficult to allocate elements to discrete episodes because there seems to have been a continuous process of patching and rebuilding. Within the house, the secondary phase falls into two parts with the initial rebuilding and realigning of walls. This is probably coupled with the instatement of the stone-built central hearth and an associated build-up of floors and occupation layers. Further inhabitation results in

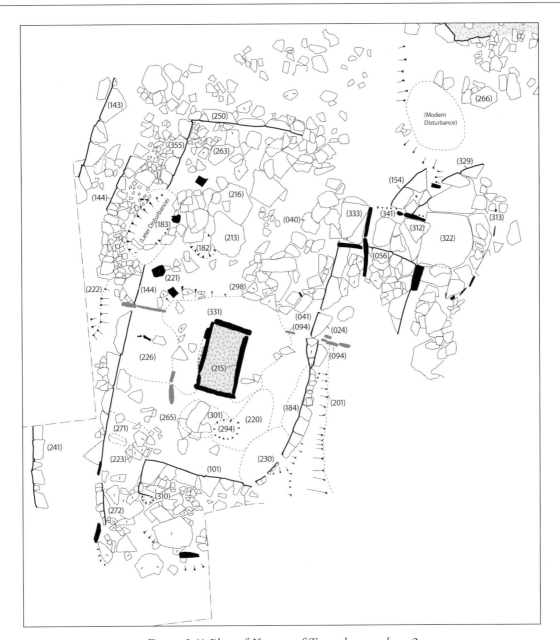

Figure 3.11 Plan of Knowes of Trotty house: phase 2.

laying new floors and accumulation of occupation layers coupled with structural alterations to the walling. Except for a pottery firing structure, activities in the external area associated with the building are difficult to define, and even more difficult to phase. This includes a sequence of messy surfaces, sporadic flags and the occasional deposition of rubble debris, disturbed both by humans and by soil processes such as gleying and solifluction.

The secondary rebuilding of the house, within the original structure, shortened and narrowed the house floor to 3.6m east–west by 6.8m north–south (Fig. 3.11). To the north of the building, new walling closed off entry

from this direction. The west wall remained virtually the same, except in its northern part where a couple of minor alterations occurred, comprising rebuilding a narrower northern half of the west wall with slightly smaller stone than the original. This part of walling post-dates the main northern wall rebuild, demonstrating a building that is constantly altered and structurally modified.

The most substantial alterations to the structure of the building comprised the burial of the original southern and eastern walls under a bank of rubble and re-deposited glacial till [122] (Fig. 3.6), followed by the construction of new internal wall faces against this bank. In effect this

Figure 3.12 View of house from south showing entrance to the rear chamber, and chamber partially excavated (ORCA).

Figure 3.13 Detail of recess in rear of house showing rubble tipping inward from collapsed wall (ORCA).

continued the idea of building an inner wall face at a lower level than the external wall face to the east. The southern (rear compartment) end of the house became markedly lower than the northern (front compartment) through processes of cleaning out and re-flooring with thin clay layers, whereas the north part became further elevated through accretion of re-paving and flooring with clay on existing flagged floor surfaces.

The new southern end of the wall was built as part of the same wall face as the south half of the east wall, with a sharp almost faceted curve forming the return. A new wall built within the south end of the building shortened the house and created a rear chamber (Figs 3.11, 3.12 and 3.13).

In the southwest corner of the building, the west end of the southern wall did not join with the west wall, but was faced off to create an entranceway permitting access into the rear chamber. The face of this entrance was formed quite crudely, with large voids in the masonry. There was a 0.18m-deep sub-circular posthole [310] (Fig. 3.11) at the rear face of wall immediately beside the entranceway, suggesting that the space could be shut off by a door or hanging. However, the area soon became unusable and was filled with more than one episode of collapsing masonry (probably from the original southern wall). This collapse was held back by the new wall, except where the tipping rubble sloped down through the chamber entranceway into the house (Fig. 3.13), where it interleaved with the phase 2 floor deposits. Although not so well-structured, this chamber echoes the series of compartments within a recess in the rear wall of House 2 at the Knap of Howar. This innermost part of the early Neolithic house was perhaps the most sacred area,

a feature which endured, developing into the 'dressers' or house altars of the later Neolithic houses.

The north end of the wall [024] formed the south side of the eastern entrance passage, thus lengthening the passage by 0.6m and creating a short length of passage on the internal side of the original threshold and the orthostat faced original wall (Fig. 3.11). At least the south side of this new part of the passage was lined with thin orthostats, facing off the northern end of the east wall. The creation of an internal section of the entrance passage by having a threshold orthostat, and/or orthostats set into the sides of the passage close to the internal end, seems to be a standard feature of later 4th millennium cal BC architecture, for example, the Smerquoy Hoose and Knap of Howar (Ritchie 1983, 42–47). The evidence for walling on the north side of the flagged entrance passage and the north east corner of the building is absent due to truncation.

The northern part of the new eastern wall [024] was built as a separate entity and in a different style from the southern section [101], with the orthostat from the earlier phase of the building acting as the division between the two. The northern section of inner wall face was built of larger stones than the southern part and set out slightly from the line of the southern wall face, which probably predates the northern section (Figs 3.5 and 3.11). In order to join these two disparate sections, wall [101] was brought inwards to the interior of the house a little; this modification replaced and marked the earlier orthostatic division with the characteristic 'pinch in' of the walling: a feature seen at Knap of Howar, Stonehall Knoll and Meadow and Wideford Hill. The orthostat divider on the east side probably retained its divisional function through phase 2.

Figure 3.14 View of the phase 2/3 Knowes of Trotty house and hearth from the north, central hearth unexcavated (ORCA).

The revised interior was of similar shape but smaller than the original house. It remained subdivided by the orthostats and dominated by a newly instated stone-built hearth. The north end of the hearth was aligned precisely with the central dividing line of the house formed by the orthostats and the pinch in the wall, confirming the continuing significance of this spatial division of the building. But at the same time the rake out/spreads of ash encircle the hearth which becomes more central to the interior in the new house (Figs 3.11 and 3.14). However, it should be noted that the inner or rear compartment (south) of the building is some 0.40m lower than the front compartment (north) which is level with the ground surface, so the rear of the house is physically lower than the front. It is almost certain that this disparity in height was present from the beginning and is not the result of a particularly uneven build-up of occupation deposits within the building. This demonstrates that the building must have been watertight, otherwise the southern end of the building would have been extremely damp making it difficult to keep a fire lit in a sunken hearth. This internal slope would also have created a subliminal psychological effect by requiring a person to walk 'down' to the hearth and the semi-subterranean rear of the house and up towards the exits to the outside world.

3.3.1 The hearth and associated floor deposits

The rectangular stone-built hearth was set into the floor of the building, cutting through the earlier occupation deposits and perhaps replacing an original scoop hearth. The long axis of the hearth was central to the width of the interior and maintained the same orientation as that of the building (Figs 3.11 and 3.14). The hearthstones were set in narrow sockets, with smaller stone packing supporting them within these cuts. The tops of the hearthstones stood 0.15m higher than the associated floor (Figs 3.6 and 3.15), and over time, they were scorched by the heat of the fire, which caused them to start laminating. The heat also resulted in the reddening of the firmly packed stony yellow clay at the base of, and in the layers surrounding, the hearth.

The fill of the hearth was excavated in four *c.*30 mm layers (Fig. 3.15), numbered [233], [234], [235] and [236] from top to bottom. In thin section, each of the layers showed clear individual characteristics which may inform upon the use-history and post-depositional processes within the hearth structure. The basal deposit [236] consists mainly of dark reddish-brown organic-rich material intermingled with lighter, mineral-dominated areas, but within the layer two distinct deposits were identified by a clear, undulating boundary separating, the thinner lowest lens [236a] from the deposit above [236b]. The lowest layer [236a] comprises a fine sand-sized quartz making up the majority of the deposit, with larger fragments of sandstone and siltstone providing the only variation from this. This can be interpreted as re-deposited subsoil forming a base to the hearth, with a high concentration of fuel residue material admixed, consisting almost entirely of burnt peat, which may

Figure 3.15 Hearth [215] sectioned (ORCA).

explain the presence of not only phytoliths but diatoms. Layer [236b] has a coarse mineral fraction of almost entirely a fine coarse sand similar to [236a], but larger sandstone and siltstone rock fragments are far rarer, likely to have become degraded. When this layer is viewed in oblique incident light the entire soil matrix appears a bright, strong red, a colour change which in fact largely defines the boundary between the two lenses of [236] – although clearly heated, lower lens [236a] is nothing like as fiercely red. This indicates strong domestic heating at temperatures of *c*.400°C (Simpson *et al.* 2003) concentrated within the upper part of this hearth deposit.

Hearth layers [234] and [235] probably represent the *in situ* final use of the hearth before it was decommissioned. These layers contain a mix of small charcoals, burnt peat fragments and aggregates of what appears to be burned soil material throughout, suggesting a mix of a small amount of wood, peat and turfs used as fuel.

The organic component of upper layer [234] appeared to be quite different to other layers in the hearth: lighter in colour and less dense, and a most significant feature of this layer was the number of large, whole diatoms seen in thin section. With peat identified as the key fuel source within the hearth deposits, this is not surprising; however, the presence of so many large diatoms showing no sign of heating or vitrification may indicate that a large amount of unburned peat material may have found its way into these contexts. One suggestion is that this layer may represent a dump of deliberately organic-rich, perhaps wet material added to damp or compress lower hearth layers. Another is that post-depositional processes may have included peat development in this part of the site as it became increasingly wet. In this uppermost layer of the hearth fill [234] the consequences

of iron movement such as iron-rich nodules and iron impregnation or depletion of larger rock fragments noted in thin section were more frequent, suggesting a degree of illuviation not indicated elsewhere. This is likely to have affected the entire sediment sequence in the hearth to some degree.

Both sub-layers [236-a] and [236-b] are mixed and disturbed. The presence of a series of small fragments of bone in deposit [236-b] is notable as these should be completely combusted at the temperatures indicated for this layer and these, along with the presence of several very clear, un-vitrified diatoms suggest a degree of mixing and introduction of extraneous materials for this layer which likely relates in part to the process of scraping the bottom of the hearth when cleaning it of fuel residues. The upper deposits in the hearth profile strongly suggest movement of materials downwards through water action, probably relating to phase 3 when this area of the site formed a sump for drainage – in particular, the lighter groundmass of deposit [234] displays particularly well the frequent incidence of iron-rich nodules and presence of fine clay and organic 'coatings', indicative of illuvial processes. The analysis of [235] further confirms this proposition, as large, wide cracks making a sub-angular blocky microstructure, accompanied by further frequent iron-rich nodules, suggest that this deposit saw repeated wetting-and-drying episodes.

The hearth is surrounded by a series of layers of burnt debris or rake-out from the hearth (Figs 3.11 and 3.14) punctuated with layers of more clayey material that appear to be deliberately laid floor surfaces. These form a halo effect around the central point of the hearth, especially to the north where they rise so that the edges of the layers are exposed upslope, like an onion cut across horizontally. A very similar effect was present in Structure 1, Stonehall Farm (Chapter 6). These rake-out layers indicate that there were many fires in the hearth, the remains of which must have been regularly cleaned out to prevent it from filling up. Charred birch from within rake out layer [340], a thin brown ashy spread to the northeast of the hearth, produced a radiocarbon date of *3360–3260 cal BC (SUERC 18244)*. The radiocarbon date obtained from charcoal within the rake out layer [331], immediately above [340], is *3350–3080 cal BC (SUERC 18243)*.

The sequence of 20–30mm thick flooring layers that were laid around the hearth comprised compacted sandy clay, with a silty peat ash content indicative of mixed derivation combining the clay subsoil with fire debris (peat ash and charcoal). These surfaces varied from extensive, often across the full length and width of the south half of the building, to more localised, tightly focussed around the hearth. They represent episodes of patching and re-levelling rather than floors that completely supersede the one below, in effect providing new, clean surface areas. Artefacts were rare within these layers indicating the house interior was kept clean, although one of the earliest floor deposits [323] of this phase, an extensive spread of mixed clay and subsoil derived material and ash covering almost the entirety of the southern half of the building, contained sherds of pottery from three different vessels (SFs 302 and 303) and a hammerstone (SF 304). In the southwest corner, the floor surface sloped up from the building interior through the entranceway into the rear chamber, interleaving with the collapsed masonry (Fig. 3.13), showing how the habitation of the building was a process that encompassed both activity and neglect, both building and collapse, all at the same time.

This sequence of five patchy floor levels and occupation deposits was sealed by an extensive 0.03m thick floor surface that also spread around the west central dividing orthostat into the north half of the building. This floor comprised introduced clay, probably tamped down to provide a hard surface, which became darker, greasy and mottled through trampling, littering and general occupation activities.

The deposits that built up on the floors around the hearth comprised a mixture of silts tinged with the reddish, pink and grey hues of peat ash, containing flecks and larger pieces of charcoal, indicating that much of the material was derived from raking out ashes from the hearth (Fig. 3.14). The layers tended to be 20–40mm thick and at least 2m × 2m in extent. Some were still soft whilst others were moderately firm, perhaps compacted by use of the area and heat from the hearth. Occasionally there were more discrete patches of material dumped around the edges of the building: for example, a distinct purplish-black sticky silty clay [297] spread extending from the south west corner against and around the end of the south wall and into the rear chamber (Fig. 3.13).

Almost all of the floors and occupation layers around the hearth spread to its northern side, thus extending into the north compartment of the building beyond the dividing line created by the original opposed central orthostats (Fig. 3.11). They blended the two areas, indicating that activities also spanned the divide to a certain extent, despite there being a clear difference in general traits such as the presence of flagstone surfaces and entrances in the north part and none in the south, as well as the fact that the levels in the north part were

at a higher level than those in the south. These deposits were sealed by another clay surface that overlapped the earliest, phase 1, primary clay surface in the north part and in turn had a flagstone floor laid over it. As in the south area, there was a sequence of surfaces (both clay and flagstone) and occupation layers, some of which sloped down towards the hearth interleaving with spreads of silt and burnt material (such as peat ash and charcoal) sloping up from the hearth.

3.3.2 Further phase 2 alterations to the house

The eastern entrance passage was lengthened to the interior of the building, a product of the house wall being rebuilt within the original. If there had been a conjoined building, it was razed to the ground before or during phase 2. Adaptations were made to the linking passage to create a porch and a new south-facing entrance, parallel to the house wall (Fig. 3.11).

The outer section of the entrance passage, east of the orthostat threshold, was a neatly paved surface [322] that also formed the floor of the porch (Fig. 3.16). A thin layer of silt lay on the flags and it was on this trample and flag surface that a double-skinned wall was built to create the small enclosed space of the porch, some 2.0m × 1.4m in size, with a doorway leading out to the south. The 0.6m wide wall forming the east side of the porch was not as solidly built as the walls of the main building. The arc of the inner face was constructed of a combination of flanked orthostats and stone blocks, whilst the outer face, where it survived, was built solely of stone blocks. One side of the entrance passage to the south utilised the external wall face of the main building, whilst the opposing side was

Figure 3.16 Detail of the porch looking west to house interior (ORCA).

formed by a stone block set against upright stones at the end of the inner wall face of the porch.

The floor of the porch was built up in a sequence of thin soil-based spreads and flags. The spreads comprised mixed silts and clays mottled with various colours of peat ash, all containing charcoal, indicating that waste, presumably from within the building, was either placed here, or perhaps dropped as ashes and domestic debris were removed from the house. The earliest of these layers [311], which lay directly on the flagstones, had been placed against the north and east sides of the space, with the main thoroughfare kept clear. This context contained a pottery rim with a flat interior lip (SF 309; Fig. 11.10.1) and a fragment of a thin pebble which appeared to have been ground unifacially to create a sharp edge stone tool (SF 284). Birch charcoal found in this context produced a radiocarbon date of *3350–3080 cal BC (SUERC 18242).*

The ensuing deposit was the culmination of material spread across the whole of the porch and the external section of the entrance passage. Interspersed with level flagstones, this provided a new floor surface. At this point there was some revision of the area which appears to link with the later episodes of the phase 2 occupation within the main building.

During phase 2, some further structural changes were made to the main building and the porch, and there was evidence of some cleared collapse while the building was in use as demonstrated by the interleaving of interior surface spreads and patches of wall collapse. The structural revisions and repairs of phase 2 activity do not indicate a significant change in the way the building was inhabited. For example, another fire-pit was dug on the south side of the hearth (Figs 3.9 and 3.11), maintaining the tradition of keeping fireplaces in the south half of the building. This fire-pit was a small scoop cut into the east edge of the original hearth pit. *Calluna* charcoal from within deposit [220] was dated to *3320–3230 cal BC (SUERC 18240).* The burnt fill of the fire pit extended beyond its edges to form a sub-circular spread 1.50m diameter to the south and southeast of the hearth [215]. This material seemed contemporary with a discrete patch of loose charcoal and burnt red clay [271] sloping up over the rubble collapse in the rear chamber in the south-west corner of the house. A radiocarbon date of *3320–3230 cal BC (SUERC 18240)* was obtained from birch charcoal from this spread [271].

Bulk samples from this context produced a highly abundant quantity of heather stems, rhizomes, and weed macrofossils from grassy and damp heathland environments. No charcoal was found in this deposit suggesting turf was the main source of fuel. The employment of turf as fuel is ideal for processes such as cereal grain drying which require long smouldering heat, rather than high temperatures. Two *Hordeum vulgare* sl. (barley) grains were also found in [220], indicating possible cereal drying, or cooking waste (see Chapter 15). The material from this context skews the weight for weight comparison data in favour of turf fuel, but it must be remembered that wood charcoal was found in varied amounts in nearly every sample from Phase 2, and largely spread by trampling and sweeping, so its importance as the probable main fuel source for the hearth should not be eclipsed by a single *in situ* deposit.

In the north part of the building, patching of old surfaces with more clay and flags continued; one of the clay spreads extended from the north into the south part of the house, indicating again the increasing centrality of the stone-built hearth in the house layout. A 2.90m broad arc of stone blocks [221], notable when compared to the usual thin flagstones, was instated in the northwest quadrant of house (Fig. 3.11). The blocks were unevenly spaced, with gaps of 0.27m to 0.60m between them. It is possible that these indicate the presence of a curved screen, or alternatively they indicate internal radial divisions, perhaps something like the 'cupboard' cells created with orthostats in the southeast end of House 2 at Knap of Howar (Ritchie 1983, 43–47).

New clean floors of compact clay were laid across much of the area to the south and west of the central hearth over the burnt spread from the fire-pit. In both the southern and northern parts of the house these surfaces were kept clean and, as with phase 1, there was remarkably little occupation debris (apart from hearth ash) recovered from the house interior throughout phase 2.

Revision of the porch appears to link with the second part of the phase 2 occupation within the main building, described above. Set on the north edge of a renewed floor surface which spread across the whole area of the porch was an arc of blocks [154], with a curved facing to the north, which can be seen to have been partially dislodged by the modern disturbance in this part of the site (Figs 3.11 and 3.16). These blocks formed the north wall of the porch.

The original flagged surface of the porch continued through to the outside, using flags of mixed sizes with larger gaps between them. The external flags at the southern doorway of the porch were replaced at least once. Much of the external area to the east and north east of the house comprised patches of flagstones, rubble and clay, and discrete small spreads of smaller stones in compacted clay, indicative of use as a yard where

Figure 3.17 External work areas under excavation, to left of picture (ORCA).

artefact manufacture was observable (Fig. 3.17). Of the 35 pieces of worked flint that were retrieved through the excavation (Chapter 12) seven pieces came from within a compacted layer along the east side of the house exterior, suggesting perhaps that this is a meaningful concentration indicating a work area.

3.4 The pottery 'kiln'

The most distinct feature in the external yard or work area was a pottery firing structure, or perhaps a kiln, located in the northeast corner of the excavation trench (Figs 3.11 and 3.18). This feature was distinguished by a vivid red fine silty spread [263] which extended to the north outwith the limits of the excavation. The firing structure was contained within a straight-edged arrangement of low stone walling two courses high on the west side, and possibly continuing in a curve towards the east side; thus the firing area appears to have been enclosed by a low wall. On the west outer side this

walling was only partially revealed and was overlain by a compacted metalled surface, representing heavy trampling and possibly related to the pottery firing area or other work activities. The pottery firing area was less well defined on the south east side because of truncation.

The firing structure base comprised brittle but compact bright red gritty silt and lumps of burnt clay [307], in a slight mound 0.06m thick, which lapped over onto burnt flag stones. The base, its contents and associated burnt material, were sealed by what is likely to be the remains of the demolition of its superstructure. A single pottery sherd was recovered from [307], but from the other kiln debris were 27 sherds, plus smaller fragments, of pottery representing 14 vessels, of which 13 sherds were from the same vessel. The majority of this pottery comprised undiagnostic body sherds, but included four rim fragments with internal bevels (SFs 230, 263, 285 and 295). An axe fragment (SF 280, Fig. 3.19) and one of the two 'Knap of Howar' grinders (SF 299, Fig. 3.21) also derived from this kiln debris.

Figure 3.18 View of 'kiln' looking southwards (Jane Downes).

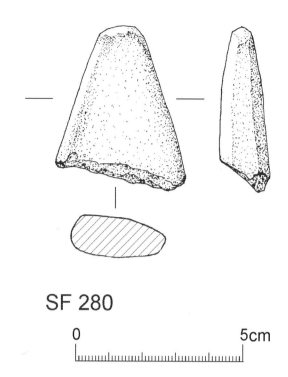

SF 280

0   5cm

Figure 3.19 Axe fragment SF 280 from the 'kiln' debris.

A micromorphological sample was taken through context [263] (Fig. 3.20) in which high levels of organic material were also seen throughout the silty dump of intensely heated material, with some of it burnt or partially-burned. Although no internal boundaries are visible within the thin section, there was more than one material type present. The more prevalent of these was a badly sorted medium to coarse silt, almost entirely made up of quartz, introduced through the use of peat and turfs as fuel. Within this matrix, however, are frequent, large (1–2 cm maximum diameter) amorphous patches of material which appear to be almost entirely organic, with only occasional mineral inclusions. While anthropogenic inclusions are present throughout the sample, the vast majority of these are concentrated within the darker, denser, organic-dominated patches. Carbonised fuel residue materials are present throughout the sample, and both some charcoal and more burnt peat can be identified. The feature which dominates all others is, as noted during excavation, evidence for intense heating: in oblique incident light, the entire sample is a bright red, indicating heating in the same temperature range (at least 400°C) as indicated for the lower lens of fill within in the stone-built hearth in the house (Simpson *et al.* 2003).

The majority of carbonised material within [236] is however unidentifiable to type, appearing as black, generally rounded, amorphous lumps of material. These, along with similarly shaped but non-carbonised lumps of brown amorphous organic material make up the majority of the dark, organic patches seen throughout the deposit. The overall impression is of a very coarse, granular soil structure, with these large, generally rounded aggregates of darker material held within the lighter, looser general

soil matrix with its frequent voids. There is considerable biological activity, and large areas of excremental soil fabric within the silt-dominated areas make the darker organic patches appear even denser. A distinctive feature of the deposit is the accumulation of amorphous red to yellow iron-rich material within the void space which is most likely organic in origin: it would appear that the high concentration of organic material in this deposit was originally higher still, and that much of it has degraded to a fine amorphous material permeating the entire deposit. Not all of the extant organic matter appears burned, suggesting that this deposit is not likely to have originated within the firing structure. However, the discrete, generally rounded, 'rolled' nature of the organic-dominated patches suggests that they may represent some deliberate construction process. It is therefore tentatively suggested that there could be some role for grassy materials, represented by these unburned organics, in the manufacturing process, perhaps by integration with burnt material as packing or fuel material. It is also possible that the unburnt organic material comprised part of the make-up of a superstructure.

The pottery firing structure was not overlain by subsequent archaeological layers, and the 'loose structure' observed in thin section indicated a dump of material which had certainly not seen compaction or trampling. It would appear that this area of the site, and perhaps the working area or yard as whole, was not used after the structure became redundant.

The identification of this feature as a pottery kiln is not a straightforward matter (hence why it has been referred to as a 'kiln' or pottery firing structure) as there is a dearth of evidence that structures such as 'kilns' were used in the firing of pottery during the Neolithic. Instead, Neolithic and Bronze Age pottery is thought to have been open fired in bonfire or pits with little control over the firing environment (Gibson 2002). There are essentially two methods for firing pottery: with and without a kiln (Rice 2005, 153). In a kiln the burning fuel is separated from the vessels to be fired, unlike non-kiln methods where the fuel surrounds and interleaves the vessels. Higher temperatures are usually reached through firings within kilns of this sort which are also normally of longer duration than a non-kiln method (Gibson and Woods 1997, 196). Although at Knowes of Trotty the pottery to be fired could have been separated from the fuel by a raft of logs resting on the stone or turf surrounding wall, this is not certain and so technically the Knowes of Trotty feature is not a true kiln but instead is a firing structure. It would appear that the pottery was fired enclosed by organic materials such as turfs, peat and grasses, forming a clamp.

Many of the sherds from the pottery firing area of the Knowes of Trotty excavation can be considered to be low-fired, and this view may be enhanced by the soil micromorphology which notes that analysis of context [263] within the 'kiln' area indicates heating in the temperature range of around 400°C. This is a very low

temperature for the firing of clay vessels, even by bonfire methods (cf. Table 11.5.3). Research by Gosselain (1992) and by Livingstone Smith (2001) has questioned the assumptions made by archaeologists about the nature of the firing process which produces the pottery sherds they examine. Gosselain (1992) argued that maximum firing temperatures were meaningless in differentiating the various firing procedures and the various physical structures which produced them. Instead, duration of both types of procedures is extremely variable and that average maximum temperatures for open firings fall between 550°C and 950°C, while those for kilns range between 650°C and 900°C (Livingstone Smith 2001). This suggests that, while open firings may produce lower maximum temperatures than kiln firings, this is not necessarily so. It should also lead to a questioning of the simple correlation which says that soft-fired sherds come from open firings while hard-fired sherds must come from kilns. Data from 80 firing sessions in various African states revealed that diversity and complexity in firing technologies observed has been significantly underestimated, suggesting a simple opposition of 'open' and 'kiln' firing simply does not hold, as the Knowes of Trotty example demonstrates.

There is an example from Scotland with which to compare the Knowes of Trotty example with, at Allt Chrysal, Barra, Outer Hebrides. At this site an area was discovered with *in situ* burning and pottery fragments found at the base of the deposit (Branigan and Foster 1995, 85). Examination of the feature identified baked blocks of turf which were very friable without any recognisable structural form. Although wasters were not evident (a prerequisite for the identification of a kiln)

Figure 3.20 'Kiln' debris [263] sectioned in the trench edge (Jane Downes).

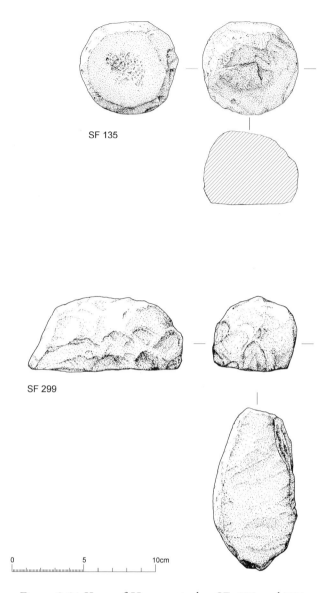

SF 135

SF 299

0   5   10cm

Figure 3.21 Knap of Howar grinders SFs 135 and 299.

it is obvious that there were activities involving the use of fire and several large fragments of different pottery vessels. The Knowes of Trotty kiln is comparable with this example, being erected on the ground surface rather than having a pit underneath. Although there was a relatively substantial quantity of pottery from the kiln-related contexts at the Knowes of Trotty, with 30% of the assemblage from the site deriving from here, as at Allt Chrysal there were no 'wasters', despite three amorphous 'lumps' of pottery from the vessel (SF 41) in [263].

An experimental pottery kiln which was built by Stephen Harrison (2008) and Andrew Appleby (2011) based on the findings at the Knowes of Trotty helps

shed light on the nature of this form of Neolithic kiln. A circular turf superstructure with an internal diameter of 1.0m was constructed on ground stripped of topsoil, within which a wood fire was set and left to die down after thirty minutes. The glowing embers were covered in peat, and then three tiers of vessels were interspersed with layers of peat mixed with animal dung. Peat blocks were used to close the kiln over, and the whole was covered in damp seaweed. The twenty vessels were successfully fired and then the superstructure dismantled to retrieve the pots. The experimental kiln demonstrated an effective kiln structure set on the ground surface, the basal remains of which were very similar to the deposits found at Knowes of Trotty, particularly the characteristic vibrant red colour of the burnt peat. The use of a mix of materials for fuel, and turfs for the superstructure may partially explain the soil micromorphology findings of burnt and unburnt organic material. If Neolithic pottery kilns were commonly constructed on the ground surface rather than with a pit as a base it is perhaps unsurprising that so little evidence for kiln firing has been recovered for in the majority of locations such ephemeral above-ground surface remains would have been removed through ploughing or other forms of truncation.

3.5 Starting again: refurbishing the Knowes of Trotty house

An episode of the spreading of collapsed walling and midden is evidenced by an extensive concave layer of rubble (Fig. 3.6, layers [121] and [080]) that spread across much of the hollow in the interior of the structure, in the southern part of the building where the surface was lower and more hollowed, obscuring walling to the south and east, and a little of the wall to the west. Layer [121] was confined to the southern half of the structure and its associated contexts contained a high proportion of the artefacts recovered during the excavation. Pottery finds comprised eight groups of pottery from six vessels; instances of sherds from the same vessels also deriving from wall core behind wall [024] affirms some of this material derived from collapsed walling. The second of the two Knap of Howar grinders (SF 135, Fig. 3.21), a sharpening stone (SF 53 see Chapter 13), and two stone disc fragments (SFs 57 and 131) derived from [121], and the clay bank that it sealed (Fig. 3.10).

The stone-built hearth was decommissioned during this episode, with a carefully placed layer of stones (Figs 3.14 and 3.22) sealing the deposits within. At the same level, and merging into layer [121], was a spread of flat

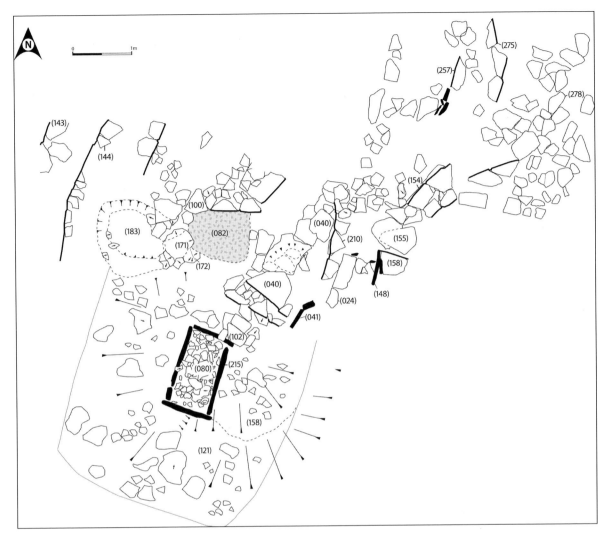

Figure 3.22 Knowes of Trotty House: Phase 3.

slabs and angular blocky stones unevenly spread across the interior of the house, dipping down into the hollow of the south end of the structure. A substantial paved drain was created (Fig. 3.22), flowing from a presumed building to the northeast. The paving over the drain was part of the levelling layer, and together represented attempts to make this wet part of the occupation area serviceable, or indeed to direct water into what was in effect a sump. The water flow from upslope, which this drain sought to direct, must have been controlled effectively by a drainage system throughout phases 1 and 2 as the lower end of the house remained dry throughout its occupation.

The levelling layers across the southern part of the building were elements of a re-orientation of the use of space which saw occupation focus more to the front

part of the house and out to the north east (Fig 3.22). Represented only by fragments of walling, it is hard to discern how many different buildings were present and what form they took.

A stretch of walling, that can be seen to seal off the east entranceway to the original house, probably formed one side of an entrance at the northeast of the original building, with the other side formed by walling [100] running east-westwards (Fig 3.22). The west end of the wall was truncated by a cut which represents an area of disturbance through stone robbing. This wall had a hearth [082] placed against it, set upon the surface of previous paving remains. Whilst the hearth was sub-rectangular it had no stone surround and it is tempting to think that originally stones had surrounded and contained the hearth, only to be removed as a final act as occurs in later Neolithic houses at Barnhouse (Richards 2005) and Structure 1, Stonehall Farm (Chapter 6). Radiocarbon dates from birch charcoal within the hearth material indicate that the final phase of occupation was dated to *3360–3080 cal bc (SUERC 18233)*. The last Neolithic activity identified in the house is a small stone box [171] (Fig. 3.22), which was cut into the hearth material on its northeast part and into hearth-related red ash spreads on its southwest. The box was filled with clay and stones. The function of this stone box is unknown, although its location directly cutting into hearth is probably significant; in this it echoes the box or cist replacing the hearth in Structure 1 at Stonehall Farm. For the latter, this is suggested to transform the entire nature of the building turning it into an 'ancestral' or 'big house', an emblem or microcosm of the *société à maisons* (see Chapters 7 and 9).

The method of construction of the phase 3 walling differs as there is hardly any external wall facing apparent, as the walling was perhaps set into a turf, soil or midden backing, and generally appears to have been narrower. What may have been located on the site in Phase 3 was either more transient occupation, or smaller buildings or shelters around work areas. The fragmentary walling surviving to the north east of the site could be the partial remains of a larger porch addition, similar to those at the Smerquoy Hoose (Chapter 4) and House 5, Braes of Ha'Breck (A. Thomas pers. comm.).

3.6 Making places

The landscape of this part of Mainland, Orkney, is characteristic glacial moraine, with hummocks and drumlins a distinguishing feature of glacial retreat. Such areas of 'hummocky moraine' appear to have been of particular interest to communities in Orkney throughout prehistory, being the site of early Neolithic settlement such as Knowes of Trotty and Stonehall, and the great passage grave of Maes Howe. In later prehistory, natural glacial hummocks appear to have been 'mistaken' for earlier, Neolithic, monuments as types of activity such as the insertion of Bronze Age burials occurs at both chambered cairns and glacial mounds.

Thus far the early Neolithic house has been described as though it was isolated in the landscape. The possibility of a dispersed group of houses similar to the residence pattern at Stonehall and Smerquoy is retained (the topography of these sites being quite similar), as the results of survey and excavation provided partial evidence for the presence of other Neolithic houses.

The arc of a circular anomaly measuring *c*.30m diameter on the gradiometer survey, located 170m to the east of the Neolithic house (Fig. 3.2, anomaly 39), was investigated by a small excavation trench (Trench A, Fig. 3.1) as it was thought to possibly represent the remains of midden surrounding a house or group of houses. However resistivity survey did not detect the presence of any obvious walling or other stone features within the confines of this anomaly. Thin section analysis of a sample taken through soils identified charred peat fragments, charcoal fragments and heat-reddened soil contained within the layer [018] between topsoil and natural till. The magnetic enhancement of the soil is due to this burnt component, although the soil is perhaps not burnt *in situ*, but derived from elsewhere. The layer also includes charred peat fragments and diatoms, which are commonly found in peat. As such the components within the soil are similar to the fuel residues within the hearth [215], and the material could be redeposited domestic debris relating to Neolithic settlement. This evidence could also be interpreted as burnt materials relating to Bronze Age cremation, redeposited in a manner similar to the burnt soil on the berm surrounding Mound 1 (Fig. 3.2, anomaly 1). However, a factor weighing in favour of domestic debris, as opposed to cremation-related deposits, is the lack of any fragments of burnt bone found in the soil thin section analysis.

Another probable non-funerary-related feature was identified through the gradiometer survey (Fig. 3.2, anomaly 13); located 150m to the south of the excavated Neolithic house and on the same contour line at the foot of the hill, this sub-circular anomaly of diameter c. 14 m was investigated through a small excavation, Trench E (Fig. 3.1). The excavation trench cut obliquely through the feature, and revealed the extremely truncated remains of a wall. The reason the site is so truncated is because it is located within the path of an un-metalled road, which is still used for driving cattle. Only the outer face survived and remnants of the wall core showing the wall to have been *c*.1.50m wide; in the technique of construction and its diameter this wall could very well be of Neolithic date.

Tantalising glimpses are therefore given of possible further Neolithic settlement to the west and south of the excavated Knowes of Trotty house. But what of the prominent sculpted drumlin upon which Mound 1 barrow is situated? Was this originally the site of another Neolithic house? It is apparent that the knoll or drumlin at Stonehall, upon which the early Neolithic Structure 1 and subsequent sequence of two houses were built, was a favoured situation (Fig. 5.4). This is revealed in the efforts

Figure 3.23 View of the barrow cemetery from the south with Mound 1 centre, berm clearly visible. The pasture field to the right of Mounds 1, 2 and 3 is the location of Trench A, anomaly 39 (Frank Bradford).

made to consolidate and maintain House 3, Stonehall Knoll despite pronounced subsidence problems (Chapter 5). At Knowes of Trotty, the drumlin surmounted by Mound 1 barrow has clearly been flattened, and this modification of the natural mound creates a berm around the barrow (Fig. 3.23). Excavation undertaken on the berm (Trench C, Fig. 3.1) revealed a stone kerb encircling the very outermost perimeter of the berm. The kerb acted as revetting to re-deposited natural boulder clay mixed with large flat slabs; further rubble and anthropogenic soils were encountered underneath and to the outside of the kerb. The re-excavation of the original excavation trench downwards through the centre of Mound 1 (Trench H, Figs 3.1 and 3.24) re-exposed the central cist, but as this cist was left *in situ* there was opportunity only to examine a very small area beneath the cist where loose subsoil, which did not appear to be *in situ*, was encountered. This deposit could have been a clay surface laid prior to erecting the cist. The evidence suggests a possibility that earlier buildings were razed and levelled at a point in the early Bronze Age when the platform was sealed with redeposited subsoil for the erection of the barrow, which was surrounded by a stone kerb.

The method of constructing the Mound 1 burial was very interesting with respect to the recreation, in a Bronze Age funerary context, of key aspects of early Neolithic house architecture. The burial cist within Mound 1 was unusually large – 1.45m long by 0.64m wide – and rectangular shaped, and as such was very similar in

length and shape to the hearth encountered in the early Neolithic house (1.38m long by 0.78m wide). This cist uniquely had the addition of two substantial orthostats placed at right angles to, and at the mid-point of, the long sides of the cist (Fig. 3.24). It is suggested that those creating this early Bronze Age funerary architecture were deliberately drawing upon the dominant features of the hearth and the orthostat dividers within the early Neolithic house. Here an analogy may be being expressed architecturally between the hearth and cist, an analogue played out in the reconstruction of Structure 1, Stonehall Farm, where a cist actually replaces a hearth in the centre of the building (see Chapter 6).

Another unusual feature of the Mound 1 burial was the incorporation of large amounts of flat slabs (Fig 3.24), and midden material, within the body of the burial mound. This material almost certainly comprises rubble and debris from the Neolithic house, either from a house upon this glacial mound, or from the one that was excavated (and note (above) the stone robbing trench encountered), or both. It should be noted, however, that there are other Orcadian examples of Bronze Age barrows being placed on early Neolithic house remains, for example at Varme Dale (Chapter 9). This trait is almost certainly a desire by these communities to draw power and authority to themselves and their emergent ancestors by emphasising origins, situating their burial monuments upon the remains of their 'founding-fathers' (cf. Bradley 2002).

Figure 3.24 The cist and orthostats present within Mound 1, Knowes of Trotty (Frank Bradford).

The significance of the appropriation of place as well as ancestry to Bronze Age people is explored more fully elsewhere (Downes in prep.). In terms of the landscape situation of the early Neolithic settlements and the spatial structring of emerging *sociétés à maisons* that are the subject of this volume, there appears to be an interesting consistency in topographic position. The dominance of the Knap of Howar as the only excavated early Neolithic settlement until recent years (added to the popular imagery of Skara Brae) has created an impression that 4th millennium cal BC settlement was predominantly coastal (see Chapter 1). However, the Knowes of Trotty is distinctly inland (being within the only land-locked parish in Orkney), and when the locations of the other settlements within the Bay of Firth area are considered, with the exception of Crossiecrown (Chapter 7), they are not close to the sea. Indeed, if contemporary sea levels were *c*.2 m lower than today (see Chapter 1), then the positions of habitation would have been even further inland. The Knowes of Trotty Neolithic settlement is several kilometres from the sea, which due to the topography is not actually visible from the site. Instead, views from the house covered gently undulating ground running down towards the Loch of Harray, 4.5km distance, across the Brodgar isthmus (which is not visible from the site), to the dramatic hills of Hoy in the distance (Fig. 3.25).

Instead of selecting coastal locations for settlement, what is notable is that the location selected for the majority of 4th millennium cal BC settlements detailed within this volume is at the foot of a hill, overlooking an area of cultivable land. Essentially these early Neolithic settlements hug the foot and lower slopes of the range

of hills that runs from Burgar Hill in Evie at the north of Mainland, to Wideford Hill in St Ola (Fig. 1.9). The excavated house at Knowes of Trotty is tucked in at the foot of Rowamo Hill, while Muckquoy lies 3 km to the east, on the opposite side of the same hill. The Wideford Hill settlement and Brae of Smerquoy are situated on the lower slopes of Wideford Hill. Stonehall occupies an equivalent position on the western side of the Cuween-Wideford landscape. Across the Bay of Firth from Wideford Hill, at the Bay of Isbister, the settlement of Varme Dale is situated on a terrace in the slope of a small hill at Gorseness (see Chapter 9).

In considering the landscape situation of the earlier Neolithic Orcadian settlements on the northern isles, it is interesting to note that where topography permits, the same phenomena can be observed. For instance, Rinyo, which is founded in the 4th millennium cal BC judging from the round-based pottery recovered (see Childe and Grant 1947), lies within the Sourin valley on the island of Rousay. In assuming this position it is situated about as far from the sea as is possible while still remaining within an area of cultivable land. Paralleling some of the Bay of Firth settlements, the steep hill of Faraclett, with the chambered cairns of Bigland Round and Faraclett on its upper terraces, towers above the Rinyo settlement.

On the smaller outer isles where the opportunities to select this apparently favoured situation are more limited due to terrain, cosmological ideals are adapted to the physical geography (cf. Downes and Thomas 2013); the settlements at Knap of Howar on Papa Westray, Pool on Sanday, and Green on Eday are at the foot of gently sloping ground, in all cases on low cliffs immediately at or close to the present-day shoreline. The Braes of Ha'Breck, Wyre, is situated away from the coast and on the hillslopes that the name suggests.

A corollary of settlements being founded at the foot of hills is the requirement to deal with water ingress as water runs off the hill slopes. Although at the Knowes of Trotty excavations did not proceed far enough in the stratigraphy to reveal the drainage system within the house, there would have undoubtedly been a complex similar to those revealed in the other houses such as the Brae of Smerquoy and Stonehall. The house at the Knowes of Trotty was located in a position where a large volume of water was being channelled naturally from the hill – and in more recent times the close proximity of the water mill and associated directing of the stream emphasises this feature of the location. Sufficient was flowing through the house to result in it collecting water in significant quantities during later phases as described

Figure 3.25 View to the southwest with Neolithic house and Mound 1 under excavation, and the hills of Hoy visible on the horizon (left) (Jane Downes).

above when the drainage system ceased to function effectively. At Rinyo, the drainage issue was particularly acute, as described in detail by the excavators (Childe and Grant 1939).

Thus, there was a deliberate intention to draw water through the house, and the example of the Smerquoy Hoose (Chapter 4) illustrates clearly the ingenious and sophisticated technology of the hydrology (Fig. 4.24). The house, therefore, acted as a conduit for a flow of substances which would, we can propose, have been regarded as more pure at the point of entry into the house than when exiting with the contamination of various types of waste. The flow then continued downhill, to lower houses and fields lying downslope. Consequently, the house may well have been perceived as participating within a series of homologies, and we could postulate metaphoric links between body and house wherein the 'generative substances of the land and body are tied together in a continuous cycle' (Fowler 2004, 109). In the embryonic *société à maisons* of 4th millennium cal BC Orkney, the role of the drainage system in conduit and confluence of the 'life blood' of households and group could have provided the material metaphors of unity through alliance and descent. Equally, through the process of becoming 'dirty' the hydrology of settlements

reinforced vertical (social and topographic) residence patterns and accordingly the disparities of relatedness (see Chapter 5).

What is clearly at play within this situation is an emphasis on vertical ranking in generative cosmologies wherein the occupation of a knoll or elevated place puts a 'house group' in the ascendant (socially, physically and metaphysically) as the houses below would be in receipt of more contaminated flows of substances. The positioning of passage graves in an upslope position in the Cuween-Wideford landscape, and the discovery of drains in chambered cairns where excavations were thorough enough to reveal them (*e.g.* Maes Howe and Taversoe Tuick), emphasise the role of ancestry and descent in such schema. The selection of hill slopes was about manipulation and control of the substances that flowed through the community, and about the creation of differences between house-groups relating to where they were situated within the 'flow'. If ancestors occupy an upper realm, a pattern of residence associating those house groups closest to chambered cairns by elevated dwelling on the tops of knolls, provides a social strategy by which house-groups through 'association with cosmological origins' asserted their primacy and imbuing themselves with 'ancestral qualities' (Helms 1998, 6).

CHAPTER FOUR

Local Histories of Passage Grave Building Communities: Brae of Smerquoy

Christopher Gee, Colin Richards and Mairi Robertson

4.1 Introduction

As introduced in Chapter 2, an important eventuality that has substantial bearing on the genesis of *sociétés à maisons* in Orkney during the 4th millennium cal BC concerns the nature and significance of the transition from timber to stone architecture. It will be recalled that this change was considered to be more than a mere substitution of building materials, for example as a response to dwindling forest cover, but represented a shift or disjunction in 'dwelling' involving a clear strategic intention to replicate the architecture and materiality of stalled cairns. Here an obvious question arises: under what social conditions would people elect to build and inhabit what were effectively houses of the dead? A related question also presents itself: if dwellings assume the form and materiality of the chambered cairn, should we consider the construction of a stone house as the creation of a form of monumentality? If answered in the affirmative, the 'monumental' house clearly relates to the ontological requirements of its inhabitants and in this form, a quest for 'authenticity' in regard to claimed ancestral connections. Equally, the building of the house in stone speaks of durability and permanence, while the internal architecture replicates a spatial configuration that has been argued to be concerned with changing states and connections or passage to another world – a world of 'others' in the form of deities and ancestors (see Section 2.6; Richards 1992). To build and inhabit the monumental house was undoubtedly a very different prospect from living within the timber house, an observation that highlights the possibility that the two buildings were anything but materially variant equivalent entities.

Certainly, over the last few years an argument has emerged concerning the origins of certain 'ceremonial' monuments being situated in the domestic house (*e.g.* Deboer 1997; Kirch 2000). This line of reasoning has also been extended to late Neolithic monumentality (*e.g.* Bradley 2005, 74; Thomas 2010; Pollard 2010, 100–103). However, in the construction of the earliest Orcadian stone houses this argument is clearly reversed in that the domestic house replicates a monument, the stalled cairn. In so doing, the house, as opposed to the tomb, effectively becomes a 'house of the dead' or rather a 'house of the ancestors' (*contra* Richards 1992; Ritchie 1995, 44–48). To dwell within such a construct can be construed as not only a process of entering another domain, but as a transcendent act which provides ontological legitimacy to social relationships emanating from the 'house'. It almost goes without saying that this can be recognized as a critical scheme for constructing social identity, and a sense of belonging, within embryonic *sociétés à maisons*.

It is difficult for us to estimate the extent of such 'houses' in Orkney during the latter part of the 4th millennium cal BC. Indeed, one of the aims of this research project was to determine the density of early prehistoric habitation within the Bay of Firth area, in central Mainland. Although several new sites were discovered, it is has only been towards the end of the project, with the recent discovery of Brae of Smerquoy, Muckquoy (Chapter 9) and Saverock (Fig. 1.9) that the potentially high density of early Neolithic settlement has been realized. It is to the Brae of Smerquoy that we now turn.

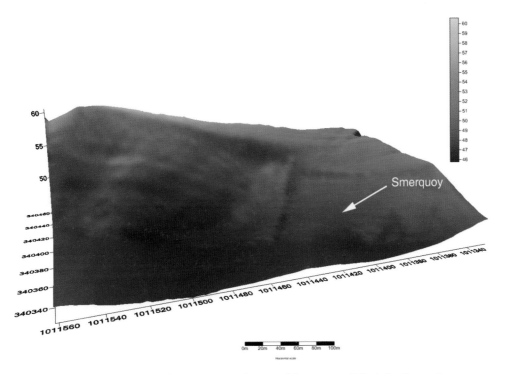

Figure 4.1 Topographic situation of Brae of Smerquoy (Mark Littlewood).

4.2 Discovery

Running along the base of Wideford Hill, on its southwest side is a group of small fields that were taken into cultivation in the mid-twentieth century by the father of the current landowner, Mr Billy Sinclair. In the northeast corner of one field is a slight and unprepossessing mound (Fig. 4.1) over which large stones and ashy deposits had always come to the surface after ploughing. This knowledge stayed within the family until Christopher Gee was informed in 2010. The field was due to be ploughed that year and a subsequent fieldwalking exercise located a range of flints, pottery and stone tools including the blade of a polished sandstone axe (Figs 4.2 and 13.8). This material appeared to be Neolithic, but there was nothing sufficiently diagnostic among the collection to establish a broad date within the 4th or 3rd millennium cal BC. Subsequent, geophysical survey identified several areas of high magnetic enhancement in the lower area of the field, the main anomaly coinciding with the slight raised mound, but interestingly a more dispersed spread of higher magnetic enhancement was present across areas upslope of the settlement mound (Fig. 4.3). Taken together, the results of the fieldwalking and geophysical surveys appear to show the presence of dispersed Neolithic occupation around a core settlement mound. The obvious questions arising from the surface

investigations concerned the extent and character of the settlement. Of particular interest was that the overall situation and widespread nature of Neolithic activity at Brae of Smerquoy seemed to bear a degree of similarity to that present at Stonehall (see Chapters 5 and 6). This included it being overshadowed by a passage grave.

Given the location of the Brae of Smerquoy within the Bay of Firth study area (Fig. 1.9), together with the 'Neolithic' character of the surface collection, a programme of fieldwork was undertaken in May–June 2013. The goals of this investigation were to establish a date of occupation (see Fig. 10.4), record any surviving structural remains and recover a material assemblage to compare with the other Neolithic sites examined within the Bay of Firth area.

4.3 Investigations at the Brae of Smerquoy

Within the parameters of the current project, excavations at the Brae of Smerquoy were confined to two areas, Trenches 1 and 2 (Fig. 4.4). After the topsoil was removed within the two trenches it was decided to concentrate on a stone-built house structure in Trench 1, known as the Smerquoy Hoose. In fact, Trench 1 was actually positioned to examine the raised mound and a smaller trench (Trench 2) was placed further upslope to assess

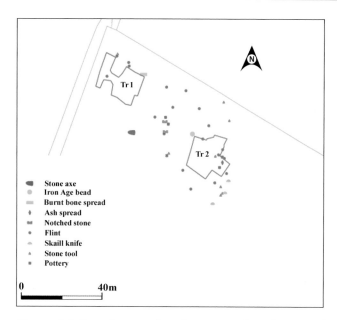

Figure 4.2 Distribution of surface material at the Brae of Smerquoy.

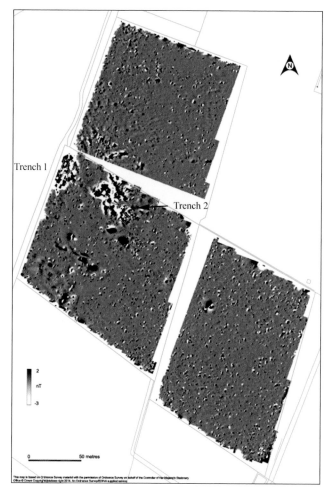

Figure 4.3 Results of the geophysical survey at the Brae of Smerquoy (Christopher Gee).

the broader spread of surface material and the more amorphous gradiometer results (Figs 4.2 and 4.3). The ploughsoil removed in both trenches by machine, was remarkably shallow, *c*.0.20m in depth. In Trench 1, directly below the topsoil, areas of midden, re-deposited yellow clay and spreads of stone rubble were encountered. Given the shallow topsoil it was unsurprising that ash deposits and stone had been brought to the surface by previous episodes of ploughing.

In cleaning the northern strip of Trench 1, spreads of midden material, isolated flagstones and large areas of re-deposited clay were revealed. A number of flint and stone artefacts were recovered from these deposits which may be assumed to represent the truncated remains of outside work areas. Due to time constraints no further excavation continued within this part of the trench. Further south, the upper course of a stone wall was soon revealed. The walling defined a sub-rectangular structure filled with stone rubble [005]. Overall, the structure seemed to be relatively well preserved, however in the very south of the trench the majority of archaeological deposits had been removed by ploughing, including the rear wall of the structure (Fig. 4.5). In this area, running east–west, a later linear drain with cover-stones was clearly visible cutting the yellow glacial clay.

As the excavation progressed, it soon became clear that the sub-rectangular structure was a house that due to its architectural similarity to Knap of Howar (Ritchie 1983), Stonehall Meadow and Knowes of Trotty, should

date to the mid-late 4th millennium cal BC (Chapter 10, Fig. 10.4). It was this structure, known as the Smerquoy Hoose, which initially provided the main focus of excavation and produced the first example of *in situ* pick-dressed decoration from an early Neolithic house.

4.4 Constructing the Smerquoy Hoose

The importance of considering the construction sequence of the Smerquoy Hoose is that it exposes the extent to which the internal spatial organization of 4th millennium cal BC buildings was pre-planned. In particular, the spatial configuration of specific practices within the house was architecturally demarcated. This is because it was necessary to organize and construct the drainage systems, and erect the divisional orthostats before the outer walls were built. During excavation it soon became

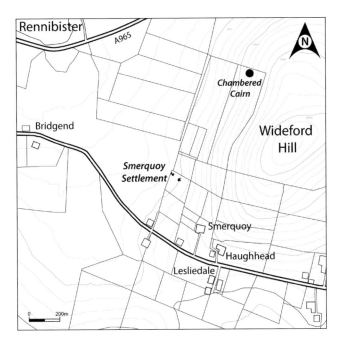

Figure 4.4 (above) Location of excavation trenches at Brae of Smerquoy.

Figure 4.5 (right) View of Trench 1 showing the differential preservation of the Smerquoy Hoose. The rear wall of the building had been removed by ploughing and cut by a more recent drain (Colin Richards).

clear that like the Knowes of Trotty house, the Smerquoy Hoose had a lengthy biography involving substantial modification and reconstruction.

Initially, the area to be occupied by the house was stripped of turf and topsoil down to the glacial till. Next, the slots for the western and eastern divisional orthostats were dug and the orthostats wedged in position with packing stones. Accompanying the erection of the divisional orthostats, the threshold upright of the side passageway was set in its cut, as were the associated door jambs, and facing uprights. The passage was then floored with flagstone paving set on a slightly elevated clay bed.

After these elements were positioned, a thick layer of yellow clay, *c.*0.06–0.16m, was laid across the entire area to be occupied by the house. This spread of clay acted as both a firm foundation for the outer walls and primary floor surface. An oval scoop hearth was dug just south of the lateral orthostats in slots [328], [312], [343] and [345]. At this time the primary channels of the drainage network were cut which necessarily reflected the precise positioning of specific tasks and activities to be undertaken within different parts of the house. First,

a large channel [132] ran east–west across the front (north) area of the house. This channel entered the house beneath the eastern wall, widening and deepening as it traversed the interior before exiting through a conduit [089] constructed in the west wall. A second drain [cuts 190 and 186] ran downslope from the eastern side of the scoop hearth, between the lateral orthostats, and conjoined with the channel [030] that appears to have also functioned as an overflow drain for pit [115]. This channel flowed out of the house through a conduit formed by a series of paired stone uprights beneath the west wall, just south of the side entrance (Fig. 4.7). At the rear (southwest) corner of the house, yet another drain [089] flowed out beneath the house wall (Fig. 4.6). Beyond the western outer wall, both drain channels emptied into a larger external drain [052] which was carefully lined at its base by a deposit of fine grey clay. This drain ran parallel to the western wall of the house, running away downslope in a northern direction.

After the preliminary elements of the Smerquoy Hoose were laid out, the outer walls were built. In construction the walls employed a technique first recognized at Knap

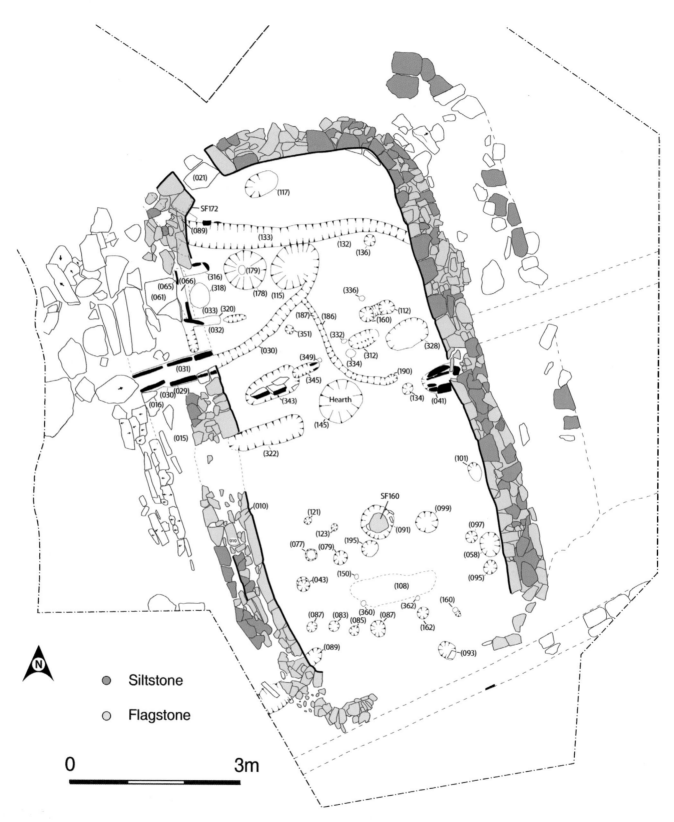

Figure 4.6 Plan of the primary features in the Smerquoy Hoose. Note the different stone types employed in the construction of the outer wall.

of Howar, Papa Westray (Ritchie 1983, 48). This involved a 'step-like' sequence of wall faces; first, the inner wall-face was built directly on the floor/foundation platform of yellow clay. Directly behind this wall-face, another spread of clay was butted up against the outer face of the inner wall skin to form a slightly elevated foundation upon which the outer face of the inner wall was built (Fig. 4.8). The thickness of this wall varied from 0.6m–0.8m which was structurally insufficient for either support or insulation. To remedy this, the foundation of clay (in the western area clay and midden), was extended *c*.1m beyond the outer face of the wall. Upon this foundation an outer casing wall was erected to create an overall wall thickness of nearly two metres. A clear indicator that the external walls were raised around the standing divisional orthostats is illustrated by the misalignment of the two sections of the western wall either side of the central 'pinch' and divisional orthostat (Fig. 4.6).

The construction of the house wall is also interesting in terms of the distribution of different stone types. During the excavation, as the masonry was being

Figure 4.7 Drain [030] running through the outer wall; the slumped lower courses of the collapsed outer casing wall can be seen in the background, and the paving slabs of the side entrance to the right (Colin Richards).

uncovered, the stone employed in the eastern wall was found to be extremely soft and in some cases was actually mistaken for mud. It was in fact a form of siltstone which displayed a very distinctive yellow-brown colour and eroded rounded appearance (Fig. 4.6). This stone was not only restricted to the inner wall, but also occurred in the remnants of outer casing wall. However, far less siltstone was present within the western wall, instead a harder grey-white flagstone, clearly derived from a different stratum and possibly location, formed identifiable sections of walling. The fracturing planes of the flagstone stratum allowed longer blocks to be extracted which led to a very different form of masonry.

The interior architecture of the Smerquoy Hoose is extremely similar to that seen in the nearby 4th millennium cal BC houses at Knowes of Trotty, House 2 at Stonehall Knoll and House 3 at Stonehall Meadow, and further afield houses at Ha'Breck, Wyre (Thomas and Lee 2012), Green, Eday (Coles and Miles 2013) and Knap of Howar, Papa Westray (Ritchie 1983). Unfortunately, the rear wall of the Smerquoy Hoose was destroyed through ploughing and the insertion of a later stone-lined drain, however, in its primary form the Smerquoy Hoose measured internally *c*.9.50m long and 4.00m wide.

There were two points of access into the house. A front entrance, measuring *c*.0.65m in width was positioned in an off-centred position adjacent to the northwest corner (Fig. 4.9). This entrance, although being paved by a single flagstone, did not have either projecting door jambs or a threshold stone form. A large stone formed the lowest course of the eastern side of the entrance passage. Along the length of this stone a horizontal groove was pick-dressed in an irregular manner, which could represent a method of marking stone for splitting at the quarry (Figs 4.9 and 4.10). During excavation, to everyone's astonishment, in the lowest course of masonry, adjacent to the doorway a stone block (SF 172) was found to display pick-dressed decoration on its outer surface. The pick-dressed design was of 'eyebrows' which continued down and joined to create a 'horned spiral' motif (Fig. 4.11). Significantly, excavation revealed that internal occupation deposits

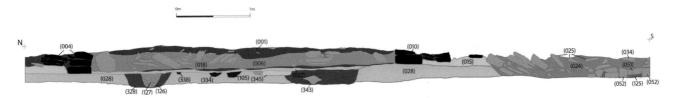

Figure 4.8 North-facing section across the Smerquoy Hoose.

Figure 4.9 The front entrance into the Smerquoy Hoose. Pick-dressed decoration can be just seen on the lower stone to left of the entrance (see also Fig. 4.11) (Colin Richards).

Figure 4.10 Horizontal pick-dressed line running along the single stone forming the lowest course of the eastern wall of the front entrance (Michael Sharpe).

Figure 4.11 Decorated stone (SF 172) formed part of the lowest course of masonry in the inner wall-face of the house (Colin Richards).

Figure 4.12 Cuts for the facing and door jamb uprights of the side (west) entrance of the Smerquoy Hoose (Colin Richards).

[022] had built up and partially covered the decoration demonstrating it to have been in place from an early stage in the occupation of the Smerquoy Hoose.

The second point of access into the house was a doorway through the western side wall. This was of a more typical construction in being extensively paved by a series of wide flagstones with an internal threshold stone which defined the point of entry into the house interior. At the threshold two orthostats had originally faced the passage, the northern of which remained *in situ*, but broken and slumped inwards, while the southern orthostat was absent and represented by a linear slot which extended into the interior of the house for a distance of *c*.1m (Fig. 4.12). When erect, an orthostat in this position would

have shielded the inner (southern) area of the house from anyone entering through the side doorway. Externally, the flagstones paving the doorway continued and curved around to the southwest (Fig. 4.13).

Also in the front compartment, an arrangement of orthostats [019 and 060] butting up against the inner-face of the eastern wall projected 0.85m into the interior. Together, the orthostats divided off a small section of the front corner of the house (Fig. 4.14).

4.5 Inside the Smerquoy Hoose

Internally, the Smerquoy Hoose was subdivided into a front and back area by a slight 'pinch' in the inner wall

Figure 4.13 *Excavating the flagstones paving the side (west) entrance into the house (Colin Richards).*

Figure 4.14 *View of the orthostats [019] and [060] in the north-east corner of the house (Colin Richards).*

face and opposed lateral divisional orthostats. Judging from the length of its slot [041], the eastern divisional orthostat was relatively short in projecting 0.60m from the side wall, while the western orthostat was much longer in being set in a cut [322] that extended 1.35m into the interior (Fig. 4.6). Further lateral orthostats set in slots [328], [312], [343] and [345] would have emphasized the interior sub-division and served to restrict access into the back area of the house. At this time a central scoop hearth [145] (Fig. 4.15) was positioned just inside, or rather behind, the divisional orthostats. A drain flowed from the left (east) side of the scoop hearth, through a gap between the orthostats and ran downslope (north) into drain [030] (Fig 4.6). The drain [089] running out beneath the rear corner of the house also functioned at this time.

4.5.1 Reconstruction

Through time substantial alterations occur within the Smerquoy Hoose. The scoop hearth appears to become redundant and was filled with clay and levelled off at floor level. As part of this alteration, the interior was 'opened-out' and a number of divisional orthostats were removed and their slots ([328], [312], [343] and [345]) filled with clay. A degree of balance is brought to the interior by placing a smaller divisional orthostat in slot [039] in the right-hand (west) side of the house (Fig. 4.16). Four hearth stones, measuring *c.*0.80m (E–W) × 1.20m (N–S), were set in slots to form a substantial rectangular fireplace (Fig. 4.18). Interestingly, the primary hearth appears to have been aligned on the front entrance passage making

Figure 4.15 *Christopher Gee excavating the circular scoop hearth [145] (Colin Richards).*

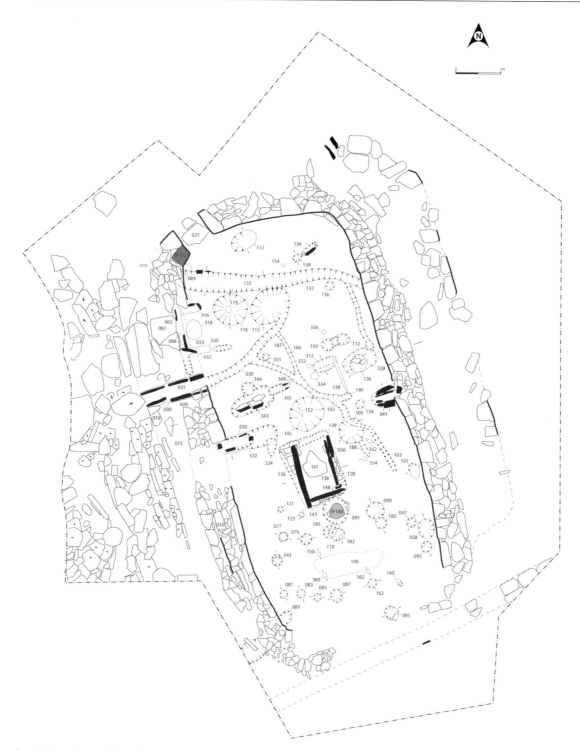

Figure 4.16 Plan of secondary features in the Smerquoy Hoose, the majority of the rear features are shown although their exact place in the interior sequence is unknown. The decorated 'horned spiral' stone is marked in brown.

it slightly askew in relation to the overall orientation of the house. Two stakeholes [152 and 182] of identical dimensions, c.0.07m in diameter and 0.17m deep, were positioned to the front and rear of the hearth, and almost

certainly pertain to some form of spit arrangement over the fire. Such support would have been ideal for cooking or smoking cuts of meat, fish or animal skins.

Figure 4.17 View of the secondary features in the Smerquoy Hoose (Colin Richards).

Figure 4.18 The rectangular stone hearth; the position of the original hearth stones can be seen by the off-set cuts (Colin Richards).

4.5.2 Pits

During the early life of the house a large number of different sized pits were dug throughout the interior of the house, but the majority were positioned directly behind the stone hearth at the rear of the house (Fig. 4.19). Of these, only two convincing postholes [195] and [077] were identified south and southwest of the hearth. Although extending across the rear of the house, the main concentration of the pits were dug in the inner right-hand (south-west) area of the house. While the sizes of the pits vary (Table 4.1), they do fall into relatively discrete groups (Fig. 4.20), and it is suggested that these groupings relate to quite different purposes. Some of the larger pits with their carefully rounded profiles, for example, pits [091], [058], [105] and [099], may well have been dug to contain and support medium – large round-based pots and relate to food preparation activities occurring adjacent to the hearth (see Fig. 4.19). In contrast, the smaller pits may have been dug to bury and conceal small objects. Despite the lack of such objects remaining in the pits situated to the rear of the hearth, part of a polished stone axe (SF 164) was discovered within pit [164] northwest of the hearth, and two shaped and polished 'finger' stones (SFs 303 and 304) deposited in a small cut at the base of slot [312] (Fig. 4.21).

A substantial pit [091], situated directly behind the hearth, did contain a large, heavily pick-dressed stone (SF 160) (Fig. 4.22). This stone appears to have been carefully placed in the pit overlying a broken hammerstone (SF 161). A similar sized pit [105], suggested to have acted as a container for a round-based ceramic vessel, was located adjacent to the hearth on its eastern side. The group of pits at the rear of the house tend to respect a broad area of burning [108] situated *c.*1.20m behind the hearth. Not only was there a spread of burnt material, but the clay floor [028] was actually scorched to such a degree that it displayed a mottled red colour (Fig. 4.23). The edges of the area of burning were relatively well defined and associated with several stakeholes (Fig. 4.16).

Although not clustered in the same manner as those at the rear of the house, a smaller number of pits were present scattered across the front area of the house (see Fig. 4.16). Inside the front entrance, to the east, was a shallow oval pit or scoop [117], measuring 0.60m × 0.38m which contained a cobble tool (SF 89) in its upper fill [118]. Directly in front of the side entrance another pit [318] was present which would almost certainly have been concealed beneath an entrance flagstone (Fig. 4.12). Although nothing was present or preserved within this pit, it may have contained a deposit of organic matter given its location at the threshold to the house.

A small pit [158] and stakehole [154] were positioned in the northeast area, north of drain [132]. Beyond the

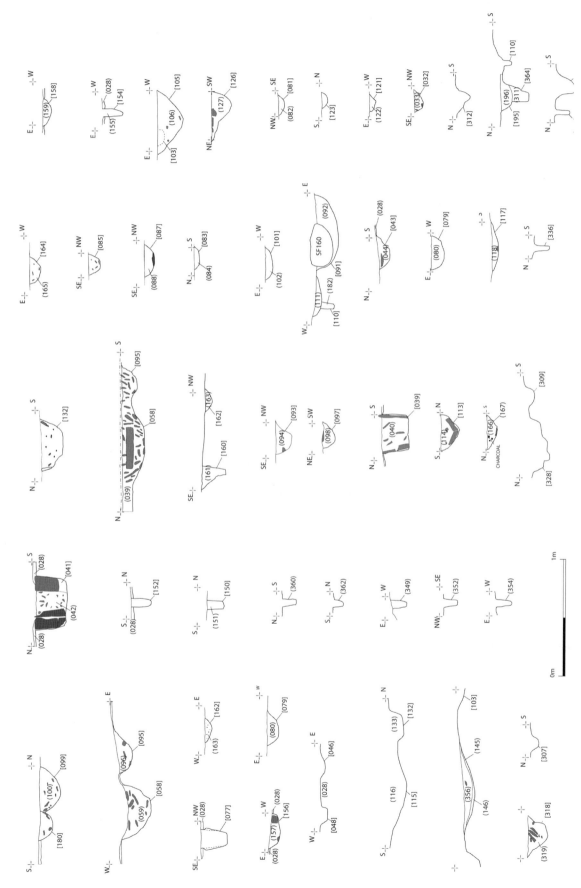

Figure 4.19 Section drawings of the pits in the southern area of Smerquoy Hoose.

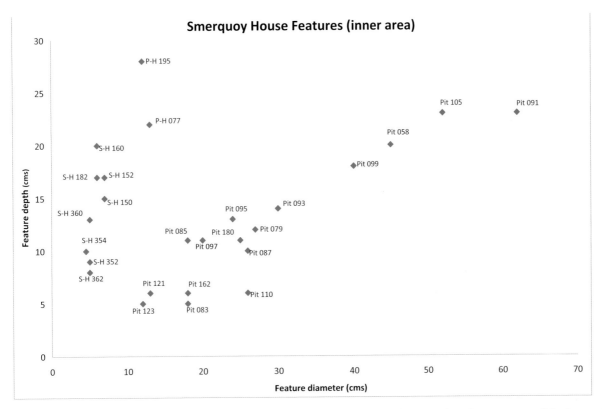

Smerquoy House Features (inner area)

Figure 4.20 Graph showing dimensions of stakeholes (S-H), postholes (P-H) and pits within the rear area of the house. Note the grouping of small and medium–large pits.

Figure 4.21 The two ground-end 'finger' stones SF 303 and SF 304 (a) had been placed in the basal cut of slot [312] (b) (Christopher Gee).

Pit	Fill	Diameter	Depth
095	096	24	13
058	059	45	20
099	100	40	18
093	094	30	14
160	161	6	20
162	163	18	6
087	088	26	10
085	086	18	11
083	084	18	5
081	082	18	6
180	181	25	11
097	098	20	11
110	111	26	6
091	092	62	23
150	151	7	15
079	080	27	12
123	124	12	5
077	078	17	14
121	122	13	6
043	044	26	10
182	183	6	17
152	153	7	17

Table 4.1 Sizes (in cm) of the pits within the innermost (southern) compartment.

drain, on the east side of the house, a series of pits ([136], [112], [166], [126] and [134]) had been dug running up through the interior. Only a single pit [164], containing a broken fragment of a polished stone axe (SF. 164), was positioned between drain [030] and divisional orthostat cut [039] in the western side of the house. A number of other pits, scoops and stakeholes had also been dug into the floor in the front area of the house. Of particular interest are the two large, centrally-placed, pits [115] and [176] which will be discussed below in relation to the complicated hydrology of the house. Given the extensive drainage system flowing through this part of the house, it is worth remembering that most of this area would in all probability have been covered by paving-stones as found, for instance, in the similar buildings at Stonehall Meadow (see Chapter 5) or Knap of Howar, Structure 1 (Ritchie 1983).

Figure 4.22 (left) View of pit [091] behind the hearth showing the pick-dressed stone (SF 160) (Colin Richards).

Figure 4.23 (below) In the foreground the pits at the rear of the Smerquoy are under excavation; the reddened scorched clay floor can be clearly seen between the excavators and the stone hearth (Colin Richards).

4.5.3 Hydrology

As seen in Stonehouse 1 at Wideford Hill (Chapter 2), hydrology appears to have played a major role in both the spatial organization of activities within the house and its overall architecture. Obviously, fresh water was an essential ingredient of life within the settlement in being not only required for drinking and cooking but also necessary for a range of other activities such as washing, dyeing fabrics, potting and so forth. As discussed in the previous chapter, concepts of pollution and purity would also have played a key role in the organization of drains, drainage and households (see also A. M. Jones and Richards 2005, 51–52). Given the location of the Smerquoy Hoose at the western base of Wideford Hill, drainage was also important in order to channel run-off water away from the house. As we have seen, the structure of the outer wall was designed to inhibit the penetration of water and dampness into the house; however, without further drainage sustained rainfall would in all probability have caused substantial problems for the inhabitants.

Conversely, as noted above, access to fresh water was a crucial aspect of daily life. The topographic position of the settlement could be seen as being partly selected with this in mind. Water running off Wideford Hill would have flowed close to Brae of Smerquoy. As discussed in Chapter 3, such an occurrence may partially account for inland habitations in the 4th millennium cal BC being frequently located at the foot of hillsides (*e.g.* Stonehall and Knowes of Trotty).

Three drainage networks served the Smerquoy Hoose. The first was within the innermost area of the house and channelled liquid out of its extreme right-hand corner. This drained liquid from specific activities occurring at the very back of the living area. The second drain ran from the eastern side of the hearth, down through the interior and out beneath the western wall (Fig. 4.7). This drain was clearly of continued importance to the inhabitants since it was altered up to three times (Fig. 4.24). First, a narrow drain ([190] and [186]) ran directly from the left (east) side of the scoop hearth [145] downslope into the large channel [030] (Fig. 4.24a). After the scoop hearth was decommissioned and a stone hearth constructed, the original drain [190] was extended and replaced by a secondary drain [188] which essentially followed the same route into drain [030]. This drain appears to have fallen out of use and is cut by the large pit [105]. Finally, yet another drain [103] was dug, cutting the in-filled pit [105] in the process, and once

again flowing downslope to run into channel [030] at a more westerly point. It seems entirely likely that each redirection of the drain concurred with a remodelling of the hearth (see section 4.4.4).

Apart from acting as a drain for waste liquids produced by activities occurring adjacent to the different hearths, drain [030] performed the dual role of channelling overflow liquid away from the large pit [115] situated in the front area of the house (Fig. 4.7). The need to provide an overflow for this pit clearly relates to practices involving some form of immersion. A further strand of evidence indicates that the liquid within the pit was heated as several pieces of burnt, fire-damaged igneous rock (*e.g.* SF 175) were present within its silty fill. This is exactly the type of stone that could be safely heated within the fire and subsequently employed to raise the temperature of liquid.

A more substantial channel [132] entered the house beneath the eastern wall and ran diagonally across the floor exiting through a conduit [089] in the northwest wall (see Fig. 4.12). This channel would have contained water derived from an un-located source upslope to the east of the house. Internally, it ran across the floor alongside the large pit [115], and is suggested to be the supplier of cold water that could be fed into this pit when required. There was some form of division between pit and channel (elevated clay formed a shallow lip between the two features) allowing control of the flow. Hence, at times unnecessary water was allowed to flow unimpeded through the house, and after exiting the western wall, to run into the large external drain. A shallower pit [178] of similar diameter was cut a few centimetres west of pit [115] and it too had pieces of burnt igneous rock (SF 176) present in its fill [189]. Together, these different features would appear to combine in practices involving the supply and heating of water in which objects and substances were immersed.

Curiously, the precautionary over-flow drain [030] channelled liquid away from the large pit and exited the house through a separate conduit (Fig. 4.24). This was unnecessary because any overflow could have been channelled back into the major drain [132] further to the west. Here then, we appear to be confronted with a clear example of avoidance between the contents of two channels and some form of purity – pollution distinction must have underlain this decision. But this strategy of avoidance is apparently only necessary or active within the confines of the house, because after draining beneath the house wall in the respective conduits, both empty, and effectively combine, in the large external drain.

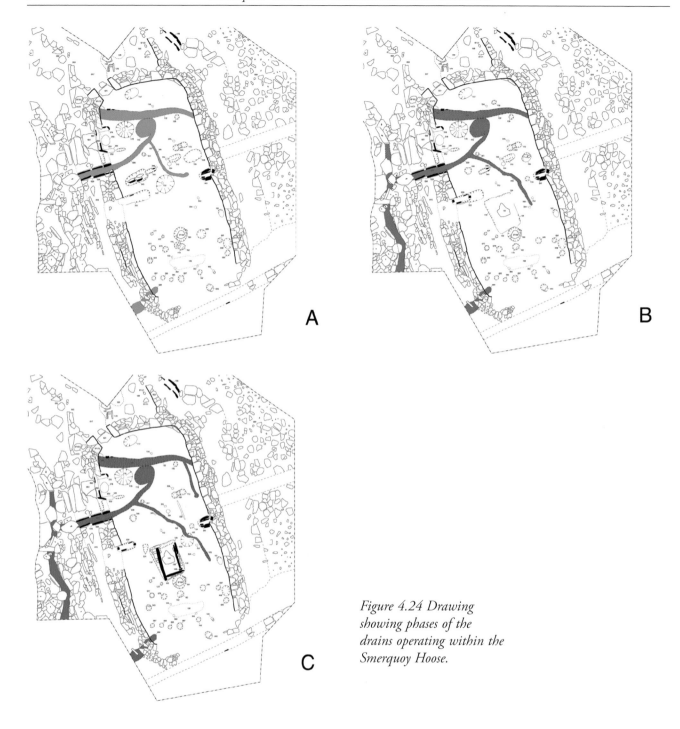

Figure 4.24 Drawing
showing phases of the
drains operating within the
Smerquoy Hoose.

Given this hydrological segregation the presence of a small channel [307] running downslope, roughly parallel with the eastern wall-face is very curious. This is because it drains into channel [132] before it reaches the two pits. Some resolution to this conundrum may be that channel [307] was a secondary feature as it cut the in-filled slot [328]. Importantly it appears to reveal a change in function of the larger channel [132] from supplier of water to that exclusively concerned with drainage (Fig. 4.24).

The subdivision of the drains in the Smerquoy Hoose into a tripartite structure could be attributed to functional differences beginning in the earliest period of occupation. The segregation also appears to be predicated on sources of waste liquids, for instance, from the inner (back) and outer (front) compartments of the house. Equally, it is worth reinforcing the observation that this system of drainage forms part of the 'fabric' of the house, being present from its initial construction. That all drainage systems ultimately serve to remove liquid waste from within the house reveals a requirement to employ a technology of separation that clearly transcends function. It is also worth noting that each of the channels exiting beneath the western wall appears to have fed liquid into the same external drain. This drain was built in a relatively poor manner in comparison with the carefully constructed drainage network within the house, however, it was carefully clay lined (Fig. 4.25). Indeed, it was probably subsidence occurring in this external area that caused the instability and eventual collapse of the western outer casement wall of the Smerquoy Hoose.

4.5.4 The fireplaces

The primary oval scoop hearth [145] within the Smerquoy Hoose, measuring *c*.0.6m (north–south) × 0.68m (east–west), is typical of fireplaces occurring within the earliest Orcadian houses of the 4th millennium cal BC. As discussed in Chapter 2, the scoop hearth was a central feature within the circular timber structures at the Wideford Hill settlement. Indeed, it was argued that the same scoop hearth remained in operation through the transition from Timber structure 2 to Stonehouse 1. In this maintenance of the fireplace we see the beginnings of a potent material metaphor of continuity being deployed in the face of a massive architectural and material shift in dwelling. Interestingly, there is divergence in the biography of hearths. For example, in some early Neolithic stone-built houses, such as Stonehall Meadow House 3 and Knap of Howar House 1, the scoop hearth is maintained, whilst at others it is superseded by a square or rectangular stone defined fireplace. One of the consequences of replacing a circular or oval scoop hearth by a stone-constructed hearth is that it provides orientation to both the fireplace and, in combination with the entrance, the house itself.

The oval scoop hearth within the Smerquoy Hoose was eventually filled with clay (Fig. 4.15) and replaced by a rectangular stone-built hearth (Fig. 4.18). However, excavation revealed that the stone hearth had subsequently been reconstructed which entailed reorientation (Fig. 4.26). Assuming the original hearthstones to be *c*.0.10m thick, the cuts [184 and 192] indicate a primary hearth with an internal area measuring 0.90m × 0.60m (Fig. 4.26a). This fireplace was orientated NNE–SSW, and it appears to have been aligned directly on the front entrance of the house (Fig. 4.17).

At a later date the hearth was remodelled (Fig. 4.26b). This was achieved by removing the original hearthstones

Figure 4.25 Vertical view of external drain [052] showing white clay lining (Colin Richards).

and inserting new stones, on excavation three of which remained *in situ*, in the changed position. The long axis of the rectangular hearth was now realigned into an almost N–S position. Each hearthstone was carefully supported, levelled and wedged into position by placing packing stones within the old cuts. Significantly, the old broken hearth stones were reused as packing and supports for the new stones. A single, small, upright stone [148] was set as an extension of the eastern hearthstone, its surface gently pick-dressed as if it had been used as a small anvil. Once wedged into place, the hearthstones were set in position by depositing yellow clay into the slots. A single flagstone was laid down to provide a base for the fireplace. On excavation, a primary ash fill [072] of bright red-orange colour was covered by a compact yellow-clay deposit [071] which may be interpreted as a final sealing of the hearth. Above this, however, a dark ashy deposit [070] merged with the overlying soil matrix [006] of the rubble house infill [005]. This deposit indicates a later use of the hearth (Fig. 4.27).

4.6 Continued occupation of the Smerquoy Hoose

Differences between activities occurring in the front and rear compartments resulted in divergent architecture and flooring. For instance, apart from its employment to fill redundant cuts and slots, no clay re-flooring was detected in the rear area although a substantial build-up of compact ashy occupation deposits had accumulated around and behind the hearth. These were subdivided into an upper [027] and lower [022] strata overlying the yellow clay floor [028]. Unsurprisingly, magnetic

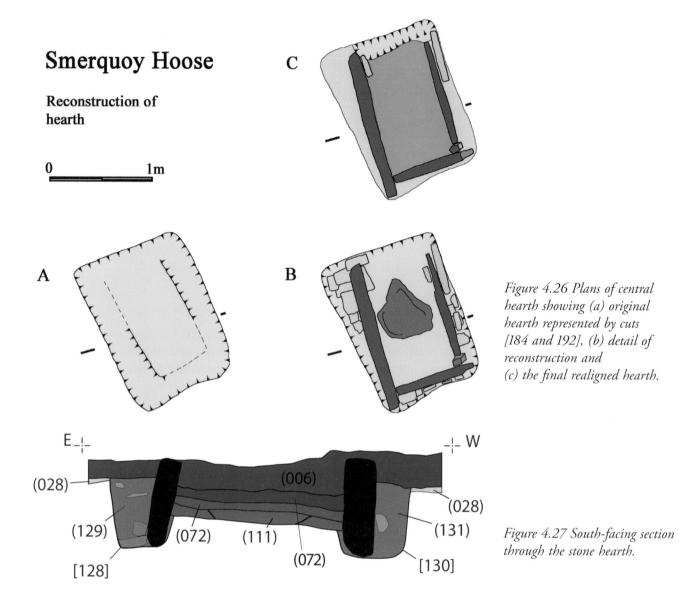

Smerquoy Hoose

Reconstruction of hearth

0 _____ 1m

Figure 4.26 Plans of central hearth showing (a) original hearth represented by cuts [184 and 192], (b) detail of reconstruction and (c) the final realigned hearth.

Figure 4.27 South-facing section through the stone hearth.

susceptibility readings simply confirmed the discrepancy between front and rear compartments with the latter displaying consistently higher readings during the period of occupation. Overall, the accumulation of occupation deposits in the rear area reached a depth of *c.*0.20m directly behind the hearth, as opposed to the front area of the house which displayed on average a depth of between 0.06 to 0.04m. However, it should not be forgotten that the front area of the house was almost certainly paved with flagstones.

Pit-digging activities appear to have reduced considerably through time as only two small pits [046 and 048], with charcoal-rich fills, and a single stone-lined pit [058] were cut through the upper occupation surface [027] at the rear of the Hoose (Fig. 4.28). This later evidence actually testifies to practices occurring nearly

a thousand years later than the initial occupation of the Smerquoy Hoose (see Chapter 10).

Associated with this later activity was an unusual arrangement of a flagstone flanked by two upright stones [056 and 057], positioned to the east of the hearth. In some ways this structure is reminiscent of Stonehouse 1 at Wideford Hill (Chapter 2), where its purpose appears equally nebulous. At this time the rectangular hearth appears to have fallen out of use and a scoop with ash [038] may represent a final temporary hearth.

As mentioned above, in contrast to a number of other early Neolithic Orcadian houses (*e.g.* Knowes of Trotty, Stonehall Meadow House 3, Knap of Howar), on excavation no paving was discovered in the front area of the Smerquoy Hoose. This absence is almost certainly deceptive. At a purely practical level, the extensive drainage

Figure 4.28 Plan of Smerquoy Hoose showing later features.

network within the front area of the house must have been at least partially covered by flagstones. These could easily have been removed at a later time when the practices surrounding the extensive pit and drainage network had ceased and the channels themselves became silted.

Regardless of the status of potentially robbed flagstones, at a later date a secondary grey clay floor [018] was laid down across the entire outer compartment of the house. Into this floor a small orthostat [064], measuring 0.42m long × 0.08m thick, was set up south of the eastern divisional

Figure 4.29 View of the Smerquoy Hoose porch-like structure from the southeast (Colin Richards).

Figure 4.30 The porch-like structure added to House 5 at Ha'Breck (Antonia Thomas).

Figure 4.31 Broken quern (SF 101) adjacent to ruined wall [062] in the house extension (Colin Richards).

upright (represented by cut [041]). On excavation the broken base of this orthostat remained *in situ*.

Accepting the limited size of the excavation trench, the Smerquoy Hoose appears to have stood in a relatively open area. Certainly to the east a partially paved area

[009], extended from the outer casing wall [119]. Overall, relatively few finds of flint or stone were recovered from this context, which suggests that this was not a working area involving deposition, as was present adjacent to Stonehouse 1 at Wideford Hill.

Quite late in the life of the Smerquoy Hoose, beyond the front entrance, a porch-like extension was added. The exact length of the extension is unknown as its walls ran beneath the adjacent baulk and were unexcavated (Figs 4.29). A similar extension to the front of the house was identified at Ha'Breck, Wyre (Fig. 4.30). Judging from the remaining masonry, the Smerquoy extension was not well built and consisted of a western outer wall [063] and double-faced eastern outer wall [062] abutting the outer wall of the original house.

The two outer walls of the extension defined an internal earthen occupation surface [168], which incorporated substantial spreads of ash and charcoal. A sub-circular spread of bright red ash [199] was present in the centre of the floor area and was surrounded by several horizontal flagstones. The red ash may either represent a shallow scoop hearth, or an area of ash spreading from a hearth outwith the area of excavation. A stone box [169], lined with small stone uprights, was set into the occupation surface. The stone box contained a dark-brown, silty loam fill but no artefacts were recovered. On the occupation surface [168], adjacent to the ruinous western outer wall was a broken pick-dressed quern (SF 101) (Fig. 4.31). On the opposite side of the extension a broken polissoir (SF 171) and a shaped 'macehead-like' igneous stone artefact (SF 151) were present in the occupation material [168].

Subsequently, the entire house appears to have been levelled (Fig. 4.33). The interior of the house was in-filled with rubble and soil, and the area around and within the entrance passage was covered with rubble and yellow clay [017]. This would appear to have occurred later in the Neolithic period as a broken gneiss macehead (SF 29) was deposited in the clay infill (Fig. 4.34).

The shape of the excavated trench prohibited extensive investigations directly at the front (north) of the Smerquoy Hoose (Fig. 4.35). Further north, a longer strip was uncovered and cleaned which exposed extensive areas of midden deposits covered by a yellow-brown, silty clay surface [002]. This material seems to have been laid to create an open working area and a number of flint and stone small finds were recovered from this surface. This clay also seemed to be associated with the spread of clay [017] that partially covered the Smerquoy Hoose entrance and porch-like extension. Interestingly, the silty clay [002] clearly overlay sections of buried masonry which appeared as areas of dry grey soil after the trench had been open for several days. A spread of ashy midden [007] was present in the centre of the northern part of the trench. In other places, orthostats projected through this surface demonstrating the presence of ruined earlier structural remains. In the northwest area of the trench a series of small uprights almost certainly charted the route of yet another drain.

Finally, structural failure overtook the Smerquoy Hoose. Initially, the stability of the outer casing wall of the house in its western circuit became compromised due to subsidence along the line of the external drain. Eventually, the casing wall collapsed and its lower courses slipped outwards to become trapped in the hollow resulting from the subsiding drain (Fig. 4.32). It is difficult to know whether the wall fell after abandonment or whether the collapse precipitated abandonment. Whichever is correct, the collapse of the casement wall would seem to mark the end of dwelling within the Smerquoy Hoose.

Figure 4.32 (top) The collapsed western outer casing wall [016] can be seen to the upper right beyond the drain running through the thickness of the outer wall (Colin Richards).

Figure 4.33 (centre) View of the Smerquoy Hoose showing rubble infill [005] spread across its interior (Colin Richards).

Figure 4.34 (bottom) Broken gneiss macehead (SF 29) from the clay make-up [017] covering the house entrance (Christopher Gee).

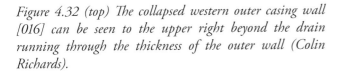

Figure 4.35 Plan of Trench 1 showing the clay surface covering exterior areas north of the Smerquoy Hoose.

4.7. The timber structures: Trench 2

In 2013, a second trench (Trench 2) measuring *c.*11m (N–S) × 7.5m (E–W) was opened further south of Trench 1 to investigate a series of amorphous magnetic anomalies running upslope that coincided with surface flint and stone artefacts. Due to this trench being positioned on previously cultivated sloping section of ground, it was of little surprise that the ploughsoil was very shallow and the sub-surface deposits were severely eroded (Fig. 4.36). Nevertheless, discrete spreads of burnt material survived *in situ* in hollows and scoops across the trench (Fig. 4.37). Although spreads of burnt stone were also present, particularly running out of the trench on the western side, it was impossible to determine their function.

Three main spreads of red-brown ashy occupation material were clearly defined. First, a large sub-oval spread of burnt stone mixed with ashy material [205] was present in the southern area of the trench. Excavation of this layer revealed that it was the remnants of an occupation deposit filling a broad shallow irregular hollow. Underlying this occupation material an *in situ* fireplace, represented by a spread of charcoal [206] had been laid directly on the glacial clay. The second major feature first appeared as a smaller, but clearer, sub-oval shaped shallow pit or scoop [203] filled with red-brown burnt material [202], including burnt stone, charcoal and notable amounts of degraded red clay. Excavation of the northwest quadrant of this feature revealed a smaller oval pit [214] filled with the same burnt material [202]. In the southeast quadrant another small cut [215] contained a flagstone supported by small stones (Fig. 4.37).

The third feature was a roughly linear spread of occupation material, again containing burnt stone and pottery, which ran east – west across the northern area of the trench (Fig. 4.36). Partial excavation of this material revealed it to cover a curving cut into the glacial clay. Ongoing excavations in 2014 revealed the cut to be a drain or gulley channelling water around an area strewn with burnt stone, below which was a deep cut into the glacial clay to collect water.

Adjacent to this area, two large sub-rectangular cuts had been dug into the glacial clay. These were to create level platforms for timber house structures (Fig. 4.38). Both structures had thin spreads of clay running around their outer circuits which would appear to provide a foundation for a thick turf wall. Overall, the sloping ground has allowed a covering of soil or colluvium to build up over the occupation material within the depressions, hence protecting the floor surfaces of the timber and turf buildings. The investigation of this earlier component of the Brae of Smerquoy settlement is on-going as part of a new project examining the beginning of agriculture and middens in the Northern Isles.

4.8 The Smerquoy Hoose decorated stone

The discovery of the pick-dressed 'horned spiral' decorated stone within the inner wall face of the Smerquoy Hoose

Figure 4.36 The sub-soil in Trench 2 was severely eroded and the deposits truncated. Note the linear band of burnt material [201] running across the northern (bottom) end of the trench (Colin Richards).

was a great surprise (Figs 4.11 and 4.39). Up until now, decorated stones have been uncovered in passage graves (Davidson and Henshall 1989, 82–84; Bradley *et al.* 2001) and settlements of the 3rd millennium cal BC, for example, Barnhouse, Ness of Brodgar, Pool, Skara Brae and Links of Noltland. A stone with similar pick-dressed designs was found redeposited in a later Neolithic context at Green, Eday (Fig. 4.40). In contrast, the majority of the decoration within the late Neolithic villages is grooved or incised. Another point of interest is that the 'horned spiral' motif tends to be restricted to the British Isles, and does not occur with any frequency as a component of Irish passage grave art (Bradley 1997, 110).

The Smerquoy Hoose stone is the earliest contextualized example of pick-dressed decoration yet discovered in

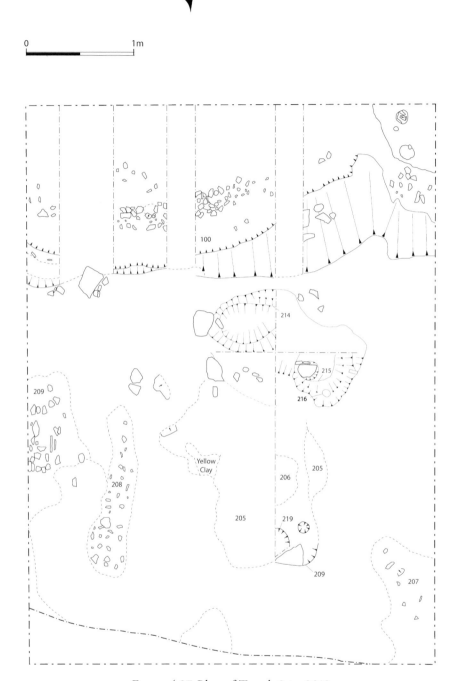

Figure 4.37 Plan of Trench 2 in 2013.

Orkney. Interestingly, pick-dressed decoration is not only present on the face of the stone, but a smaller example of the same motif was present on its side. In assuming this position, the smaller design was not only sealed from view by the adjacent masonry, but demonstrates it was executed before the stone was set in the wall. Overall, visibility appears to have been of minimal concern

since the stone was part of the basal course and soon became partially covered by primary occupation deposits building up in the front area of the house. Curiously, during excavation despite the execution by deep pick-dressing the decorated surface was only recognized when the sun was at an oblique angle. In fact, over the previous two weeks numerous people had worked next to the

Figure 4.38 Expanded Trench 2 in 2014 showing cuts into the glacial clay to form level platforms for work areas and sub-rectangular timber building (Colin Richards).

stone and failed to identify the decoration. This simply serves to demonstrate the inconspicuous nature of the design and position of the stone. Unlike the surrounding masonry, the decorated stone is fine-grained sandstone of a dark-brown matt appearance. How then are we to interpret the inclusion of this disparate stone in an innocuous position within the fabric of the Smerquoy Hoose?

The Smerquoy decorated stone appears anomalous within the house construction and in all probability is a re-used stone. The design of the Smerquoy pick-dressed stone strongly resembles the 'horned spirals' present on a slab recovered from the settlement of Green, Eday (Coles *et al.* 2010, 14) and the passage grave of Pierowall Quarry, Westray (Figs 4.40 and 4.41). There are also clear similarities between the Smerquoy design and the 'eyebrow' motifs present in the Holm of Papa Westray South passage grave (see Davidson and Henshall 1989, Plate 24), but there are also differences.

Figure 4.39 Detail showing the pick-dressed 'horned spiral' decoration on the stone (SF 172) adjacent to the front entrance passage (Michael Sharpe).

Figure 4.40 Pick dressed designs, including 'horned spirals' on the redeposited slab from Green, Eday (Antonia Thomas, courtesy of BEVARS).

Figure 4.41 Pick dressed 'horned spirals' from Pierowall Quarry passage grave (Sheila Garson: Orkney Islands Council).

Figure 4.42 The decorated stone in situ in Structure 12 at the Ness of Brodgar (Hugo Anderson-Whymark).

A similar stone, in terms of size and lithology, and to some extent design, was discovered in Structure 12 at the Ness of Brodgar in 2013 (Fig. 4.42). This too assumed a basal position in the inner wall face of the building and, although this may not be a primary element of construction (A. Thomas pers. comm.), whilst not exactly replicating the design of the Smerquoy stone, it is close enough for comparisons to be made. As at Smerquoy, the lithology of the Ness of Brodgar pick-dressed decorated stone in Structure 12 is inconsistent with the surrounding masonry and stands out as anomalous. Yet its basal situation and matt surface appearance makes the decorated stone equally inconspicuous. This situation is actually paralleled in another structure at the Ness of Brodgar, where yet another pick-dressed stone, displaying different size and lithology is built into the wall of

Structure 1 (N. Card pers. comm.). If the presence of the pick-dressed decorated stones at the Ness of Brodgar parallels the Smerquoy pick-dressed stone, then we may be witnessing an interesting practice of re-incorporating stones from earlier structures into new buildings. This is not a unique practice in the Orcadian Neolithic but replicates an occurrence recognized in hearth construction where older hearthstones are redeployed within new houses (see Downes and Richards 2005, 125–26).

Pick-dressed decoration is relatively rare in Orkney, for example, the majority of the massive amount of decoration adorning structures at the Ness of Brodgar and Skara Brae is incised. Pick-dressed decoration is not that common within chambered cairns either, and is unknown in stalled cairns. Examples of curvilinear pick-dressed decoration are known from the passage graves, Eday Manse, Holm of Papa Westray South and Pierowall Quarry (Sharples 1984; Davidson and Henshall 1989, 82–83). One possibility concerning the Smerquoy decorated stone is that it was derived from a demolished passage grave, but there is absolutely no evidence to support this idea. Nor is it chronologically consistent. On the contrary, pick-dressed decorated stones may have originally been an essential component of the fabric of early Neolithic stone houses in Orkney. Subsequently, stones could have been removed from ruined buildings and re-incorporated in later dwellings, and passage graves. Such material re-use is clearly a potent expression of continuity, establishing physical and metaphoric relationships between different times and places. In the context of *sociétés à maisons*, the maintenance of the 'house' through the generations is a defining characteristic. Claims to continuity may well be expressed through descent lines of real or fictive kin, but such claims could be potently materialized through the re-use of special or powerful stones embodying the 'fabric' of an origin house (in all respects).

4.9 Neolithic life at Smerquoy

Although the investigation of Trench 2 represents ongoing fieldwork, the results from this small area are extraordinary. It will be recalled that the timber structures at Wideford Hill were the first early Neolithic timber-constructed houses recorded in Orkney. Unfortunately, although the postholes and central scoop hearths were preserved, any floor surfaces had been truncated and lost through years of cultivation. Sub-rectangular timber houses have been subsequently identified at Ha'Breck, Wyre (Thomas and Lee 2012). Here too, ploughing had completely removed floor deposits from House 1, and a stone house (House 2) appears to have been built over the preceding timber structure (A. Thomas and D. Lee pers. comm.). The presence of sub-rectangular timber architecture in Trench 2 at Smerquoy, with well-preserved floor deposits, is clearly of great importance and further investigation is planned for future years. Within the remit of this monograph, the importance of a timber building positioned upslope from the Smerquoy Hoose lies in the similarity with the sequence of occupation identified at Wideford Hill (Chapter 2), Ha'Breck, Wyre and Green, Eday.

The geophysical survey and field collection at the Brae of Smerquoy revealed a broad spread of surface material and magnetic anomalies running diagonally across the field, including upslope areas to the south (Figs 4.2 and 4.3). The presence of at least two timber buildings in this location suggests a substantial occupation history to the site, in all probability running from the early-mid 4th millennium cal BC. This history appears to embrace clear spatial definition, in terms of a shifting settlement pattern as was suggested to be present at Wideford Hill. Indeed, the presence of spatially differentiated mid-4th millennium cal BC timber and turf buildings followed by stone architecture would parallel the sequence observed at Wideford Hill. Moreover, the presence of a large saddle quern (Fig. 4.43) at the edge of the field directly above the Smerquoy field is also suggestive of a far greater dispersal of habitation, as was suggested to be present at Wideford Hill.

Whether the Smerquoy Hoose represents the primary stone architecture erected at Brae of Smerquoy remains

Figure 4.43 Saddle quern lying at the field edge of the upper field (Christopher Gee).

to be seen, however the presence of a primary scoop oval hearth is highly suggestive. The secondary central stone hearth of the Smerquoy Hoose displayed an unusual history of modification and reorientation. The obvious question here is why at a later time the hearth was reorientated. Even if the original hearth stones had been damaged through continual exposure to heat, the hearth was not merely reconstituted; it was very carefully and purposefully realigned.

Evidence is slight regarding the specific activities occurring within the Smerquoy Hoose. The presence of a broken quern (SF 101) in the later porch-like structure together with a complete saddle quern being incorporated in field clearance of the upper field at Smerquoy (Fig. 4.43) is consistent with the on-site processing of cereals. Indeed, charred barley grains were present in numerous contexts within the Smerquoy Hoose. The burnt floor surface behind the hearth in the inner compartment of the house is difficult to interpret (Fig. 4.23), but to a lesser degree replicates the amazing burnt deposits at the rear of House 3 at Ha'Breck, Wyre (Fig. 9.10). Here, large amounts of burnt grain were recovered from a burnt floor surface which may indicate a form of cereal treatment through fire or roasting, as opposed to a disaster involving the burning down of the house. Overall, cereals feature strongly in 4th millennium cal BC habitation contexts, as opposed to later settlements, for example, Barnhouse where there is negligible evidence for cereal exploitation.

In conclusion, habitation of the Brea of Smerquoy is spatially extensive (Fig. 4.3) and would appear to span

Figure 4.44 North-west view across the Bay of Firth from Trench 2; Trench 1 is in the foreground and the broad settlement mound is just visible (Colin Richards).

a considerable time running from the mid-4th to early 2nd millennia cal BC. Occupation covers a substantial shift in the materiality of house construction and the nature of dwelling. As will be seen at Stonehall (Chapters 5 and 6), out of dispersed settlement a process of house conglomeration occurs resulting in the accumulation of midden and the emergence of a noticeable settlement mound (Fig. 4.44). It was not just the late dates for final activities within the Smerquoy Hoose that were surprising (see Chapter 10). The construction date of the Smerquoy Hoose was notably late in the 4th millennium cal BC. Whilst this serves to provide additional evidence for the late appearance of stone houses as discussed in Chapter 2, it also indicates a compression in styles of house architecture in the final two centuries of the 4th millennium cal BC.

Undoubtedly, the replacement of timber house construction by stone as seen at Smerquoy, Wideford Hill, Ha'Breck and Green will be discovered to be a feature of 4th millennium cal BC settlement replicated throughout Orkney. The argument forwarded in Chapter 2 (see also Chapter 9) that this transition represents the results of strategic practice as opposed to a response to the degradation of woodland is becoming indicated in the environmental record (Farrell *et al.* 2014). The landscape location of Smerquoy also reinforces the trend

commented on in the previous chapter of initial Neolithic settlement being essentially inland, and not adjacent to the seashore. This non-coastal settlement pattern emphasises fresh water sources and their management, and more importantly terrestrial resources as opposed to marine (see Richards and Schulting 2006; Thomas 2013, 414–17). Clearly, the sea was an important element in people's lives at this time; however, it was not the dominant subsidence and transport base that was originally indicated by the location of, and evidence from, Knap of Howar, Papa Westray (see A. Ritchie 1983; 1990).

Investigations at Smerquoy are ongoing and form part of a new project into the initiation of agriculture and middens in the Northern Isles. However, the partial elements of inhabitation discussed in this chapter are of significance to an overall picture of the development of *sociétés à maisons* in the Bay of Firth area during the early Neolithic period. It is tempting to draw out the degree of continuity and maintenance as expressed by the Smerquoy Hoose as an indicator of the changing trajectory and character of inhabitation that emerges with stone architecture. In the following chapters this pattern will be seen to be replicated at other sites investigated within the study area.

CHAPTER FIVE

Good Neighbours: Stonehall Knoll, Stonehall Meadow and Stonehall Farm

*Colin Richards, Kenny Brophy, Martin Caruthers, Andrew Meirion Jones,
Richard Jones and Siân Jones*

5.1 Introduction

High on the eastern slopes of Cuween Hill a small passage grave overlooks the coastal zone of the Bay of Firth, Mainland, Orkney (Fig. 5.1). Although elevated, the passage grave does not seem to be positioned for maximum visibility and is only silhouetted when viewed from low ground to the south (Figs 5.2 and 9.14). At that very spot, nestling in the lea of the hill, is the Neolithic settlement complex of Stonehall comprising three elements: Stonehall Knoll, Stonehall Meadow, and Stonehall Farm (Fig. 5.3). But just as is paralleled at Crossiecrown, Brae of Smerquoy and Wideford Hill, when settlement was founded at Stonehall the passage grave had yet to be constructed.

In this chapter we will describe and chart the organization of the Stonehall settlement complex as it developed through the 4th millennium cal BC. Part of this process of dwelling entailed the building of the passage grave on Cuween Hill, which although undated probably occurred towards the end of the 4th millennium cal BC. Here we may ponder on the social conditions that led to this construction and why a passage grave was built as opposed to a stalled cairn. These are interesting questions and in order to address them it is necessary to explore the nature of settlement at Stonehall in detail and draw out the subtleties that may lead to such social strategies being implemented. At the onset it is suggested that to build such a monument emphasises a contingent requirement to provide material expression and visible verification of claims to specific lines of descent within a particular *locale*.

Figure 5.1 View of the Bay of Firth area from Heddle Hill in the east (Colin Richards).

Figure 5.2 View of Cuween Hill passage grave from Stonehall (Colin Richards).

Lying in the lea of Cuween Hill, the Stonehall sites assume a very comfortable and secure location. To the rear, Cuween and Heddle Hills would have shielded the dwellings from the persistence of the westerly winds and gales. In this position it conforms to the general situation of inland early Neolithic habitation (see Chapter 3); Stonehall is ideally situated for protection and shelter. Yet, in possessing wide views to the northeast and out across the sea towards the Northern Isles, the settlement maintains a clear front–back spatial structure. The hills not only provide a natural barrier but also a conceptual partition between the semi-enclosed world of the Bay of Firth landscape and the open bowl of western Mainland; these are totally different domains, and the latter within a few centuries became transformed through massive displays of monumentality. This disjunction is a feature of all the settlements in the Cuween-Wideford

landscape; however, when these sites were founded, like the passage graves, the great stone circles had yet to be built (Richards 2013).

5.2 Stonehall Knoll

During the first season of fieldwork at Stonehall Farm the land owner, Mr Ronnie Flett, continually drew our attention to a prominent mound at the base of Cuween Hill (Fig. 5.4). He had always wondered whether this might be a chambered cairn set in a similar position to the mound of Quanterness which lies at the base of Wideford Hill (Fig. 8.1). The knoll at Stonehall lies in a rising area of rough grazing which after having been cleared and 'improved' at the beginning of the 20th century received little further cultivation. After this seed of curiosity had been planted it was only a matter of time before a limited exploratory excavation was undertaken. During a quiet period towards the end of the first season of excavation a trial trench was opened on the eastern upper slope of the knoll. Much to everyone's surprise, rather than the collapsed masonry of a passage grave or the sterile natural till of a glacial mound, ashy midden deposits, including flint flakes and sherds of round-based bowl were discovered directly below the topsoil. Clearly, a further area of early Neolithic habitation had been discovered little more than 100m away from Stonehall Meadow and Stonehall Farm (Fig. 5.3).

5.2.1 A Pictish House

As two other trenches (Trenches A and B) were being excavated that year a decision was made to leave the newly discovered site until the following fieldwork season. Subsequently, a larger trench (Trench C) was opened on the summit of the knoll. Excavation of Stonehall Knoll continued over two subsequent seasons in 1997 and 2000. Immediately below the turf, substantial quantities of rubble were encountered which on removal of the upper level resolved into the remains of two sub-circular structures with a third appearing in section on the northern down-slope (Fig. 5.5). The knoll was found to be of glacial origin upon which a series of stone structures were built over a four thousand year period. The latest building event was the construction of a Pictish 'figure-of-eight' house, which was actually the amalgam of two sequential sub-circular structures (Houses 4 and 5) dating to *c*.380–550 cal AD (Chapter 10). Overall, the buildings were found to be very clean and no associated artefacts discovered although certain

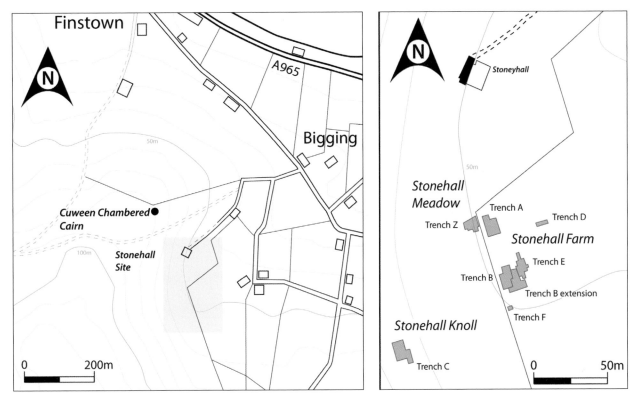

Figure 5.3 Situation (left) and trench locations (right) of the Stonehall sites.

Figure 5.4 Looking towards Stonehall Knoll (Trench C) from Stonehall Farm (Trench B). Stonehall Knoll settlement was founded on a natural moraine at the base of the hill, the adjacent mire can be seen as rough ground to the left (Siân Jones).

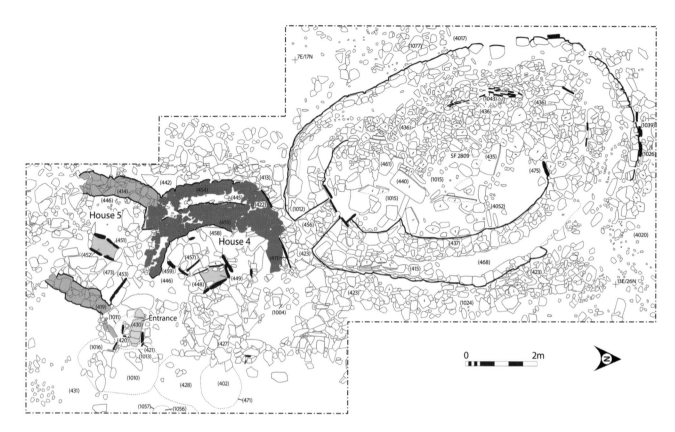

Figure 5.5 Plan of Trench C showing stone house structures (Houses 4 and 5) representing early historic occupation of the knoll.

upper ash deposits were associated with this early historic period of habitation.

The figure-of-eight design is a fairly typical form of architecture for the Pictish period (*e.g.* Ritchie 1990b, 197), but on Stonehall Knoll a sequence of addition was noticed in that House 5 was built onto pre-existing House 4 to form two compartments. Curiously, a disparity in construction existed between the two houses confirming sequential development. The eastern (lower) wall of House 4 had collapsed and remnants of the masonry ran downslope. In contrast, its western circuit remained extant and took the form of a double-faced inner wall [455] and outer faced external wall [454]. To the north, the passage of earlier Neolithic House 3 was carefully filled with rubble [456] which acted as a thick support for the lower portion of the outer wall.

In contrast, House 5 was constituted by a single, double-faced outer wall [414 and 419]. The interior of House 4 was partially paved with large flagstones [458], as was the eastern side of House 5, and a thin layer of yellow clay [446] acted as a floor surface for both compartments of the overall figure-of-eight house (Houses 4 and 5). A rectangular hearth was present in

each sub-circular compartment, both of which contained a similar mixed red-brown ashy deposit [449 and 452].

Entry into the figure-of-eight house was from the east in a fairly central location, and because of the sloping ground it involved a step up into the interior (Figs 5.5 and 5.6). Two uprights remained of packing for passage-facing orthostats and the passage was paved with a line of flagstones [430]. A low orthostat [453] provided a threshold stone dividing the two compartments of the house.

Apart from residual flints, no material culture was recovered from the figure-of-eight structure. The Pictish house had a number of associated ash deposits [428], [431], [1008], [1010] to the east, clearly a result of ash from the hearths being tipped downslope. A large pit [471] with a diameter of *c.*1m had been cut into the Neolithic deposits (see Fig. 5.13). It contained a charcoal-rich fill [402] composed mainly of willow round-wood which may indicate a wicker inner skin (see Chapter 15). Charcoal associated with pit [471] produced a radiocarbon date of *340–550 cal AD (GU-10331).* Beneath the early historic buildings, three main constructional events were uncovered representing prolonged Neolithic

Figure 5.6 The two early historic house structures (Houses 4 and 5) overlying Neolithic deposits (Colin Richards).

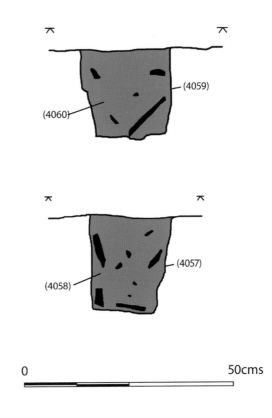

Figure 5.7 Section drawings of postholes [4057] and [4059].

Figure 5.8 View of the rear walling [1068] of Structure 1 showing position of postholes [4057 and 4059] (Colin Richards).

Figure 5.9 Tom Muir excavating the ash and midden deposits covering and slumping down from the eastern wall of Structure 1 (Colin Richards).

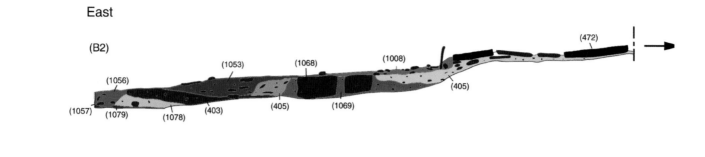

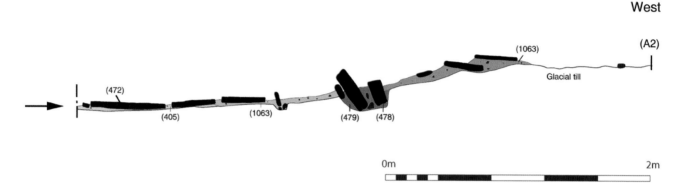

Figure 5.10 East–west section across paved area [472] and elements of House 2 and Structure 1.

occupation during the late 4th and early 3rd millennium cal BC.

5.2.2 Stonehall Knoll: Structure 1

The earliest Neolithic activity on Stonehall Knoll is represented by two postholes and a section of stone walling and series of structural features and associated deposits sealed beneath the paved area [472] on the summit of the glacial mound (Figs 5.7, 5.10 and 5.11). These remains were identified only after the removal of the upper deposits, and the survival of the walling is due to its employment as a foundation for the eastern edge of the flagstone paving. When excavations were undertaken at Stonehall Knoll (Trench C), the timber buildings at Wideford Hill, Ha'Breck, Green and Smerquoy had yet to be discovered. Consequently, it is fair to say that inadequate attention was given to the presence of the two postholes discovered adjacent to Structure 1. Posthole [4057] was *c.*0.2m in diameter and 0.22m deep, while posthole [4059] was 0.23m in diameter and 0.19m deep (Fig. 5.7). Both postholes contained a similar loose dark-brown loamy fill [4058 and 4060]. Clearly in retrospect, together these could easily form part of a small timber building much of which would lie beyond the limits of

excavation. Equally, that the line of the two postholes traverses the wall of Structure 1 provides additional evidence that these relate to an early timber structure preceding the stone building (Fig. 5.8).

The structural evidence of a stone building consists of the remains of a curving double-skinned wall [1068] representing the rear of a small structure (Fig. 5.11). Standing up to two courses in places, the walling was partly covered and sealed by the clay [405] laid as a foundation for the flagstones; beneath this the walling was engulfed by a thick grey-brown silt deposit [1069] (Figs 5.9 and 5.10).

Structure 1 was clearly quite small in size and orientated southwest–northeast (Fig. 5.12). Although most of the building had been demolished, broken fragments of two small opposed orthostats [4012 and 4016] remained. These internal features accorded with typical orthostatic 'stalling' present within 4th millennium cal BC stone architecture. The position of the cuts into the glacial till revealed the alignment of the building and indicated it to have been of an elongated shape (Fig. 5.11). Consequently, the entrance would have faced toward the southwest. Despite a careful examination, no further associated remains were discovered, particularly any evidence for a fireplace either in the form of a scoop or a series of cuts

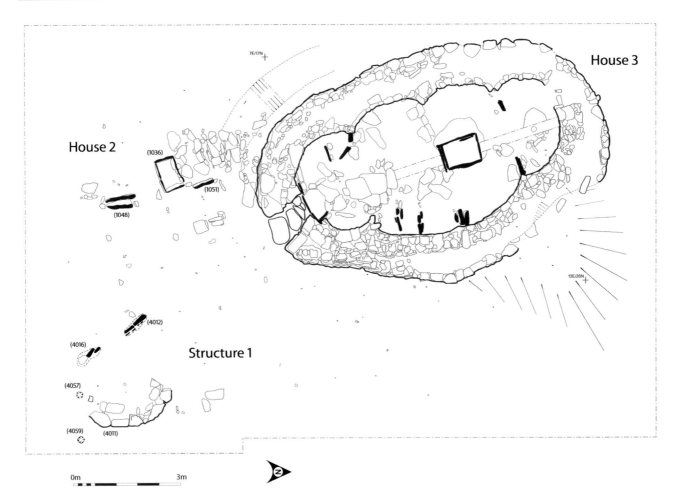

House 3

House 2

Structure 1

0m   3m

Figure 5.11 (above) Plan of Stonehall Knoll showing position of Structure 1.

Figure 5.12 (right) Rear walling [1068] of Structure 1 from the east (Colin Richards).

for the stones forming a square or rectangular-shaped hearth. The absence of a hearth throws serious doubt on an interpretation of this building having been a dwelling. A *caveat* should be inserted here that no evidence for fireplaces was discovered in the earliest structures encountered at Pool, Sanday (Hunter *et al.* 2007, 28–31). However, 'small patches of ash and burning' were present within Pool Structure 1, and the internal features were probably destroyed by later activity (*ibid.*, 31).However, a second building (Structure 2) overlay Structure 1 and this too contained no formal hearth (*ibid*).

Situated centrally on the summit of the knoll, Structure 1 at Stonehall assumed a prime position that was curiously avoided by each of the subsequent Neolithic buildings.

In terms of topographic location, the knoll overlooks the other areas of identified early Neolithic settlement at Stonehall (see Fig. 5.4). Such an elevated position is more consistent with the location of a chambered cairn rather than a dwelling. However, such close proximity to the areas of habitation and lack of a cairn militates against this being a place of burial. Instead, the lack of 'cairn' material and the curvature and thickness of the wall skin [1068] suggests a small structure resembling the building incorporated within the outer cairn of Calf of Eday Long (Fig 5.13). The Calf of Eday Long building is difficult to interpret given the situation at Pool where some early 'dwellings' possess no formal fireplaces. Noting its structural relationship with the stalled cairn, the encased building is clearly of early

construction (Davidson and Henshall 1989, 107; *contra* Calder 1937), and has a relatively thin outer wall with no indication of a cairn. Overall, it is difficult to interpret Structure 1 on Stonehall Knoll since it is just as likely to be a primary dwelling as a mortuary building, but either way it represents the founding of stone construction activities on the knoll.

5.2.3 Stonehall Knoll: House 2

At a later date, Structure 1 was demolished and the majority of masonry and internal stone furniture removed leaving just the lowest course of the rear wall. Once the building was removed the area was levelled by spreading a thin layer of yellow clay [405] across the top of the knoll. This layer, together with odd slabs of thin sandstone, formed the foundation of an extensive paved area of large flagstones [472]. The flagstones both capped and flattened the summit (Fig. 5.14), and were associated with the construction of a second stone building (House 2) on Stonehall knoll (Fig. 5.15).

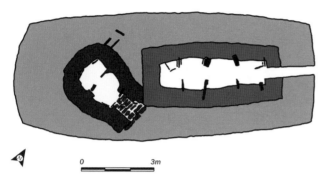

Figure 5.13 Plan of Calf of Eday Long stalled cairn showing the small rear chamber encased within the cairn (after Calder 1937).

Figure 5.14 Vertical view showing the uncovering of the flagstone paving [472] capping the summit of the knoll. Excavators include Tom Muir, Colin Richards, with Siân Jones (left) and Stephanie Durning (right) looking on (Kenny Brophy).

The same spread of clay that formed a foundation for the paved area provided the same role for the new house. Despite an absence of the outer walling of House 2, remnants of internal architecture were represented by a series of broken divisional orthostats or slots. Interestingly, of all the broken and removed internal stone furniture only the hearth stones remained relatively intact. The paving appeared to follow the outline of the missing house wall (Fig. 5.15) and it must be concluded that some of the flagstones acted as a secure footing for a slightly elevated outer wall skin. Typically, the internal spatial organization of House 2 was predetermined by the position of a series of orthostats and the hearth, which were positioned before the yellow clay floor was laid (Figs 5.16 and 5.17). As this

clay layer seemed to be a continuation of the yellow clay forming the foundation of the paved area, it seems as if the entire re-modelling of the knoll summit was undertaken as a unitary constructional event.

The house was clearly organized according to a linear spatial structure with its entrance facing east-northeast. The size of the orthostats indicates relatively subtle internal divisions within the house. Here we can contrast House 2 with houses elsewhere, for example, House 3 at Stonehall Meadow and the later phase of the Smerquoy Hoose, which posses more substantial divisional orthostats.

Because of the steep drop in slope beyond the entrance to House 2, a pile of stone slabs [1030] had been heaped

Figure 5.15 Plan of House 2, surrounding paving and associated midden deposits.

Figure 5.16 View looking at the main paved area [472] running up to the robbed wall of House 2. A line of flagstones [1071] (running beneath the top ranging rod) marks the path into the house. The well-preserved later House 3 can be seen in the background showing the relationship between the two houses. To the right of the trench the Pictish pit [471] can be seen fully excavated (Colin Richards).

Figure 5.17 The stone hearth and related divisional uprights in House 2 (Colin Richards).

up to wedge the orthostat [1029] in place. Even with this stone make-up in place, entry into House 2 would have involved walking up a steep slope or more likely approaching the entrance passage from the side (Figs 5.15 and 5.16). Militating against the awkwardness of such a sideways approach was the dramatic and dominating visual effect of this location. The frontage of House 2 would have assumed an imposing countenance in overlooking the houses and their inhabitants at both Stonehall Meadow and Stonehall Farm.

The entrance passage into House 2 was paved with flagstones set into the same spread of clay [405] that acted as the house floor. These flagstones continued up the central aisle between the remains of two opposed orthostats represented by an *in situ* broken upright [1048] to the right (north) of the paving, and a slot [1060] with packing stones to the left (south). Together the divisional orthostats would have defined an outer compartment within the house. At this point a stone-constructed drain was detected running beneath the line or pathway of flagstones [1071] and flowing downhill to the east where it ran out beneath the paved entrance passage. Stone rubble [1030] forming a stable surface beyond the house doorway would have been an effective soak-away and this may explain the cut [409] containing a fine brown silt [408] that ran directly downslope from the house entrance.

Continuing through the house, another pair of opposed orthostats combine to define a second compartment. A small upright [1074] set at right angles to the divisional orthostats probably faced the inner wall, giving an estimated width of 3–3.5m to the house at this point. The square hearth was positioned centrally just inside this division being composed of several upright slabs (Fig. 5.17). Below an upper rubble fill, which included a large flagstone measuring 0.9 × 0.4m, which completely sealed the hearth, a thin and partial layer of red ash remained *in situ*. The area around the hearth had several interesting components; what is interpreted as a low bench or shelf formed by 2–3 courses of masonry lay to its right (north). Alternatively, it is possible that this masonry represents the position of the inner wall face. The floor between the shelf or wall and the central hearth was paved by medium-sized flagstones [1080]. A broad area of the clay floor radiating from the hearth between the divisional orthostats [1049 and 1072] was heavily mottled due to ash being trampled into its surface, while a dense spread of black ash [1064] surrounded the hearth on its left-hand side (south).

Behind the hearth towards the rear of the house a further snapped small orthostat [1073] was set in a position that suggested that it was the northern one of a pair creating the final partitioning within the house interior. No corresponding slot was discovered to the south. Unfortunately, the entire rear area of the house had been demolished and removed.

5.2.3.1 Midden associated with the occupation of House 2
As mentioned above, directly in front of the House 2 entrance the eastern side of the knoll drops away sharply.

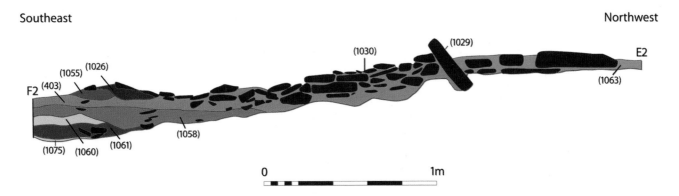

Figure 5.18 North-facing section of midden deposits on eastern slope of the knoll beyond the entrance into House 2.

An orthostat [1029] that defined and bounded the edge of the relatively level paved summit of the knoll was held in position by a series of stone slabs. These slabs seem to have been carefully laid on the glacial till, or more likely a thin old land surface that covered the eastern slope of the knoll. Equally, where the clay platform that provided the foundation for both the paving [472] and House 2 had slumped downslope it was directly overlain by a thick deposit of red ash [403]. This ash partially overlay and blended into a further dump of ash [1058], but there was no sharp division between the two deposits. Indeed, whilst these spreads of ash are distinctively different in places, there were also areas where they were intermixed with little definition. This blurring is because each deposit comprises numerous small episodes of ash dumping and refuse disposal occurring throughout the occupation of House 2. In short, the occupants consistently dumped ash downslope at the front of the house, which would have also had the additional effect of building up a surface at the house frontage.

Establishing a clear relationship between the depositional events outlined above and the occupation of House 2 is difficult. However, given the stratigraphic distinctions noted above is seems likely that in general terms the lower midden deposits [1058, 1060, 1061, 407 and 410] accumulated during this period of occupation (Fig. 5.18).

5.2.4 Stonehall Knoll: House 3

In the latter centuries of the 4th millennium cal BC, House 2 was completely demolished and a new dwelling was erected (House 3). The orientation of the new building was quite different to its predecessor in taking a south-southeast–north-northwest alignment with the entrance to the southeast. When appraising the sequence of construction on Stonehall Knoll it is evident that an unusual strategy of avoidance was being implemented. In avoiding the site of the demolished House 2, House 3 was positioned further to the north and consequently was precariously positioned across two slopes. Erecting the house on sloping ground made it inherently unstable and a consistent feature of its structural and occupational history is the constant requirement, on the part of its inhabitants, to rebuild and consolidate the house against subsidence and to prevent collapse.

Despite these structural problems, this was the best preserved Neolithic house that we encountered on Stonehall Knoll. Overall, the new house measured *c*.9.9m long by 6.2m at its widest point. In plan, the house assumed an elongated shape and as with the other earlier Neolithic buildings the internal spatial organization was achieved by lateral sub-divisions along the long axis. These divisions were created by orthostats projecting in from the inner wall-face, but in contrast to its predecessor House 2, and House 3 at Stonehall Meadow, the inner face of the outer wall of House 3 substantially 'pinched in' at the point of the internal divisions (Fig. 5.19a). Consequently, rather than simply sub-dividing a rectangular internal space, this had the effect of creating recesses within the fabric of the house. In other words, the interior architecture of the house changed and became virtually molded to the practices that were now occurring within its confines. It is also worth mentioning that whilst this house avoided the site of House 2, it was almost certainly built out of robbed stone derived from the former house.

Judging from the general clay floor layers, as opposed to discrete episodes, this house had two main periods of occupation, each of which appears to have run over a considerable time. Radiocarbon determinations suggest

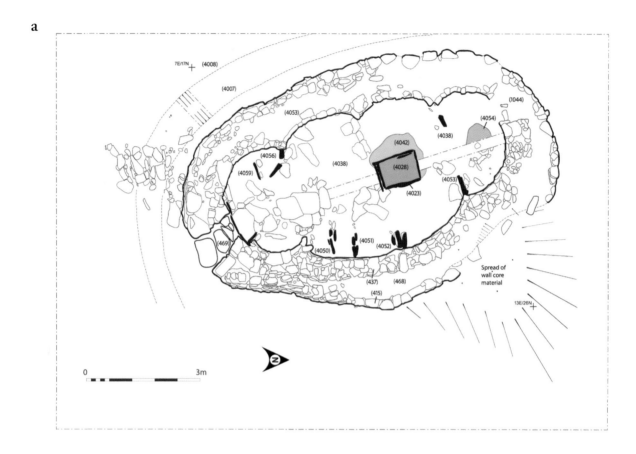

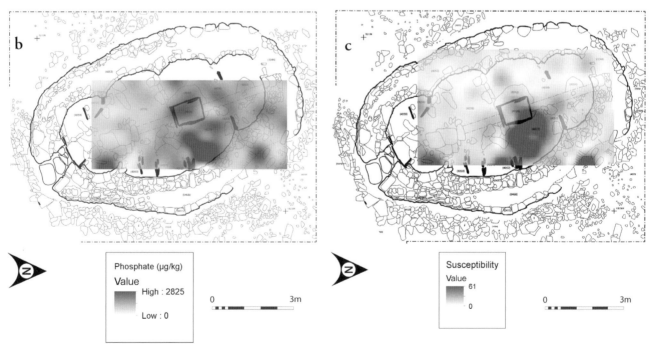

Figure 5.19 Plan of House 3, Stonehall Knoll, showing the primary occupation deposits, ash spread [4042] (a), phosphate (b) and magnetic susceptibility values (c). Note the way the 'pinches' of the inner face of the outer wall effectively mold the internal architecture to create internal recesses.

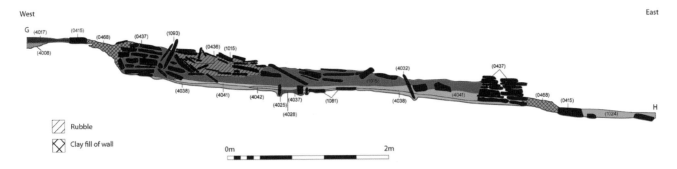

West   East

Figure 5.20 East–west section through House 3, Stonehall Knoll.

the overall duration of occupation to span c. 5-600 years beginning *c.*3300 cal BC (Chapter 10), but of course this need not be continuous. The later stages of occupation are marked by a constant battle to keep the house standing as its position on the hillslope results in subsiding walls and a damp west wall caused by water run-off from the higher slopes of Cuween Hill. Clearly, the resourcefulness that went into maintaining this house reveals its continued significance for its inhabitants.

Such a prolonged occupation of House 3 resulted in accumulative midden deposits building up on the eastern slope of the knoll. Also, the demolition of House 2 effectively cleared the summit of the knoll which still remained partially paved by flagstones [472]. Given the interesting and contrasting distribution of different materials (Fig. 5.32), which we argue is indicative of use and *in situ* discard, it is this area that provided an external working area directly associated with the occupation of House 3.

5.2.4.1 Construction, and occupation of House 3

As noted above, the selected site for House 3 ran across two slopes which inevitably caused structural problems and, consequently, a continual programme of maintenance and repair of the building. Clearly, a more central location on the summit of the knoll or even a position closer to the fairly level site of the demolished House 2 would have presented the better practical option, nonetheless what appears to be a strategy of avoidance was played out. In order to compensate for the slopes and to help create a degree of stability for House 3, a horizontal platform was achieved by cutting back into the glacial till of the hillside (Fig 5.20). A similar technique of excavating a level platform into the sloping glacial till occurred at the Knowes of Trotty house (Fig. 3.4) and is also employed for the timber structure at Brae of Smerquoy (Fig. 4.37) and higher upslope at Cuween

Figure 5.21 Primary architecture of House 3, Stonehall Knoll (Colin Richards).

Hill to provide a level platform for the construction of the passage grave.

Once the platform had been cut into the knoll, a relatively flat surface was available to lay the house floor and erect the outer wall (Figs 5.21 and 5.22). Initially, four slots were dug for the hearth stones [4023] which were subsequently wedged in place (Fig. 5.23). Similarly, the threshold upright [467] was inserted into its slot and together these elements effectively determined the orientation of the house. Next, a skim of grey–yellow clay [4038], *c.*0.02–0.05m thick, which acted as the house floor, was laid across the platform sealing the hearth and threshold slabs into place. An outer wall of double-skinned masonry encasing a lower clay core was then erected. Because of the pronounced west–east slope of the lower hillside, the outer masonry face [415] of the western wall was built on the elevated glacial till above the cut platform while the inner wall face [437] was grounded on the lower rear surface of the platform (Fig. 5.20). This high outer–low inner wall facing appears to be a consistent early Neolithic building technique. Within the project study area it is also employed in house wall construction at Knowes of Trotty and Brae

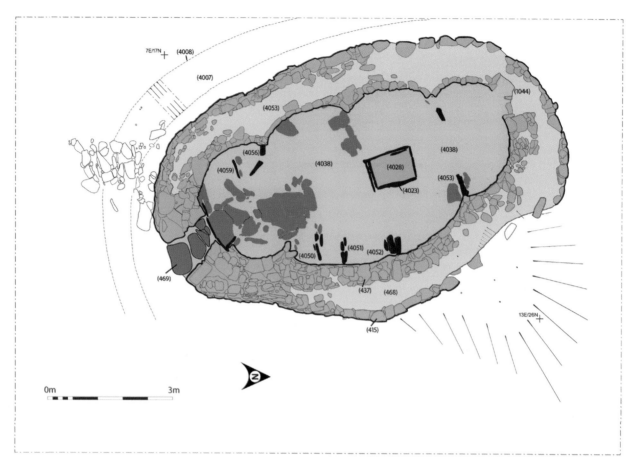

Figure 5.22 Plan of primary architecture of House 3, Stonehall Knoll.

of Smerquoy, and is a well documented characteristic of House 1 at Knap of Howar (Ritchie 1990a, 43).

The entrance passage into the house had a length of *c*.1.2m, and flared towards the outside from c. 0.6m at the inner door jambs increasing to 0.9m at the outer entrance. The length of the passage was floored with large flagstones [469] that did not run beneath the outer wall (Fig. 5.24). Externally, the paved entrance linked with a series of flagstones directly in front of the house. Internally, the paving ran up to the threshold slab which was positioned in line with the inner wall face, and two opposed orthostats projected from either side of the threshold upright to provide door jambs.

While the outer and inner wall faces of House 3 were being erected, a clay core [468] was introduced in order to both bind the walls and provide a waterproof seal. The cut platform and staggered wall foundation compensated to some degree for the lateral slope of the house but the longitudinal (south–north) slope off the knoll was clearly more problematic. Here a series of small orthostats [1039] were wedged against the lowest course

of masonry of the outer wall to prevent slippage at the rear of the house (Fig. 5.28). At a later time, presumably due to slippage, a buttress was built up against this wall (see Fig. 5.30).

The architecture and spatial organization of House 3 was unusual in comparison to late 4th millennium cal BC houses. Although the interior can be described as being constituted of segments or compartments organized in a linear manner, the method of sub-division deviated strongly from the more typical 'stalled' arrangement of large orthostats encountered at Knap of Howar, Smerquoy Hoose and Stonehall Meadow (see below). Instead, notches at the end point of each 'pinch' in the inner wall face allowed small stone uprights to be inserted so that the internal area of the house was divided into four compartments (Figs 5.21 and 5.22). Significantly, the slightly outward-bowed walling of compartments, as seen in the Smerquoy Hoose or Knap of Howar House 2, is exaggerated in Stonehall Knoll House 3, and for the first time the term 'recess' can be appropriately employed to describe the internal architecture.

Figure 5.23 Stone hearth [4023] revealed beneath collapsed stone in House 3 (Martin Carruthers).

Figure 5.24 Entrance passage into House 3 (Colin Richards).

Because of its position, House 3 was also continually prone to problems caused by water running off the upper hillside. Indeed, this situation caused us problems during excavation when the trench would fill with water for lengthy periods after rainfall. In order to provide some protection against water run-off, a shallow ditch [4008] had been dug around the western side of the house (Fig. 5.22). This seems to have been originally stone-lined and over a period of time filled with silt [4007].

Overall, the interior of House 3 seems to be quite fluid and open with no major architectural divisions. The central area contained the stone-built hearth composed of a nearly square setting of four upright stones measuring 1.1 × 0.8m (Fig. 5.23). Around this central area the inner wall-face arcs and 'pinches' were employed as much to define internal furniture as to sub-divide the central area into two units. There was, however, a stronger use of orthostats to separate the central area from the inner and outer compartments, but in the frontal region of the house, from the doorway to the hearth, this division is diluted by the presence of a line or pathway of flagstones [1081] (Fig. 5.22).

In the recessed architecture of the central area, the broken remains of stone uprights projecting from the inner wall face together with the slumped long divisional slabs revealed that stone boxes originally ran along the right-hand (east) side of the hearth (Fig. 5.25). A similar arrangement probably existed on the western side, as indicated by an orthostat [4056] projecting from the first 'pinch', however later rebuilding effectively removed traces of the primary furniture in this part of the house. Given the evidence of stone boxes on the left-hand side (west) during the secondary period of occupation it may be assumed that a similar degree of left–right symmetry existed in the primary occupation of House 3. In the architecture of the recesses and stone 'boxes' we may be

Figure 5.25 Stone boxes ran along the eastern side of the central area of House 3 (Colin Richards).

witnessing the stone 'box-beds' of later Neolithic houses in embryonic form.

Not all of the original furniture was maintained during the life of the house. For instance, the snapped partition upright [4049], projecting from the left-hand side of the outer compartment, which together with upright [4056] probably formed part of a stone box arrangement, had been clayed over by the secondary floor [4041]. A series of radiocarbon dates were obtained from occupation trampled into the secondary floor:

3360–3040 cal BC (GU-10316)
2930–2680 cal BC (GU-10326)
2630–2450 cal BC (GU-10325)

The divergence in the radiocarbon dates clearly relates to a degree of mixing of the upper layers within the central area of House 3. Such disturbance could easily

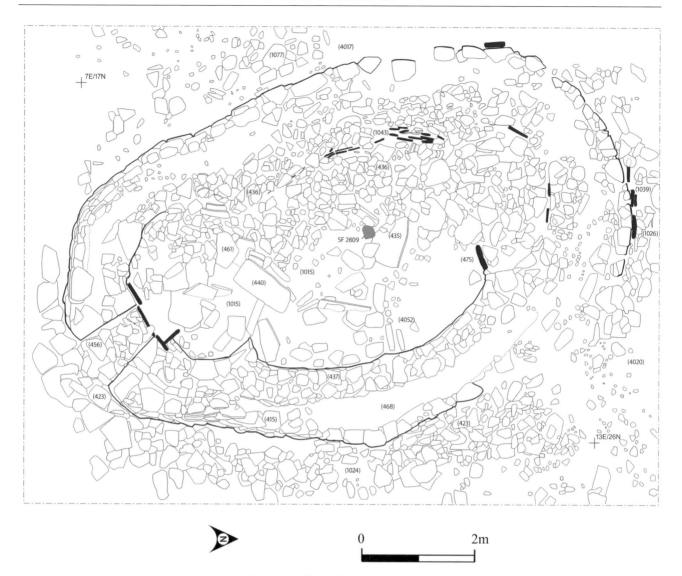

Figure 5.26 Plan showing collapsed stone partitioning within House 3.

Figure 5.27 Collapsed stone 'furniture' within House 3 (Colin Richards).

have occurred with the toppling of the stone furniture which damaged the clay floors. Given House 3 is the third building erected upon the knoll, and the dates derive from a secondary floor level, it would seem the knoll has a deep time depth running back into the 4th millennium cal BC.

Many of the activities within the house would have centred on the fireplace and as a result a deposit of red ash [4042] accrued to the left (west) and rear (north) of the hearth stones (Fig. 5.19a). Apart from the ash spread, a high and discrete phosphate anomaly was apparent on the other side (east) of the hearth which did however spread with decreasing value to the west (Fig. 5.19b). As may be expected, high magnetic susceptibility readings coincided with the ash spread [4042] but interestingly

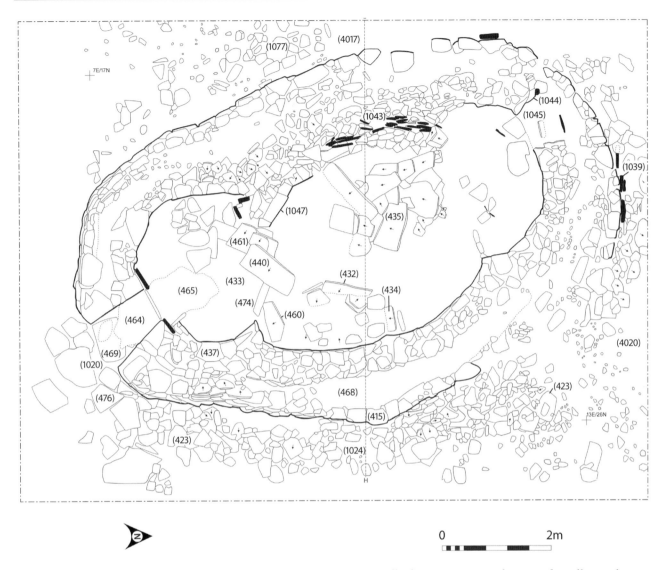

Figure 5.28 Plan showing secondary attempts to shore the western wall of House 3. Note the row of small upright stones [1039] securing the rear wall.

included high values that coincide with the phosphate values on the other side of the hearth (Fig. 5.19c). Together this evidence shows a concentration of activities was centred on the hearth and not in the recessed area. However, a further coincidence of high magnetic susceptibility and phosphate values occurred in the first chamber, on the right-hand side.

There was no general occupation layer present within the house, just a degree of discolouration to the upper surface of the clay floor [4038] and in places a dark sheen and mottled appearance. This was the result of substantial use and trampling of ash and organic material into the floor surface. Only in the rear compartment was a discrete spread of 'occupation' material [4054] encountered in the centre of the floor. Overall, the inside

of the house had clearly been kept meticulously clean during its occupation.

Much of the remodelling and alterations occurring within House 3 were a direct consequence of its being built in a poor location straddling two slopes. Giving the greatest trouble was the stability of the western wall which in all probability began to sag and slip inwards not long after the house was constructed. This was also a damp wall and even with the provision of the encircling ditch on its upward side must have been cold and moist to the touch. Unsurprisingly, these structural problems seem to have been a constant cause for concern and gave rise to the rebuilding and inner shoring, of the house wall along the western side (Figs 5.28 and 5.29). Again caused by building on a cross-slope, the problem of the

Figure 5.29 Secondary wall [1047] built inside the western wall of House 3 (Martin Carruthers).

Figure 5.30 The outer buttress [1026] with upright wedge stones was built against the rear of House 3 to support the leaning outer wall (Martin Carruthers).

Figure 5.31 Western wall of House 3 from the north with upright wedge stones in the foreground; the lower course of secondary inner-facing wall [1047] can be seen to the rear (Martin Carruthers).

western wall slumping inwards was exaggerated by the outward movement of the rear wall. In an attempt to prohibit structural movement a masonry outer buttress [1026] was erected against the outer wall-face of the rear wall (Fig. 5.30). A positive feature of drystone masonry is its flexibility in respect to slippage and movement; however, due to the structural forces at work on House 3, living in this dwelling would have involved constant maintenance and the ever-present possibility of collapse.

Over time the number of stone uprights wedged against the inner face of the western wall increased and were supplemented by a revetment-like new internal wall [1047], and the enlarged cavity was filled by rubble and clay and further stone wedges (Figs 5.28, 5.29 and 5.31). Although far from satisfactory this episode of refurbishment appears to have been successful as it increased the stability of the house for a substantial period of time.

Accompanying this structural modification was the laying of a new clay floor. On the grey-yellow clay surface of the front area [433] was a large irregular slab (SF 2807) that appears to have been employed as a polissoir. Radiocarbon determinations from ash (charcoal) trodden into the floor surface give a duration of occupation ranging from *c.*3300–2700 cal BC (see Chapter 10). Although the laying of the secondary floor (generic context [4041]) seems to represent a unitary event; *e.g.* as a single layer across the entire house, when uncovered during excavation the floor surface was of variable colouring in different areas of the interior. At the front of the house the clay floor was grey-yellow in colour, while around the hearth and to the rear it appeared as a slightly scorched mottled red-brown. Undoubtedly this distinction is partially due to the trampling of ash into the surface, however different household activities must have led to spillage and waste resulting in staining and discolouration. To the right of the hearth, a spread of red-black ashy material [4043], ran across the floor surface. The hearth itself remained in position without further embellishment, and its excavation revealed the presence of two distinct ash layers: an upper bright red ash [4028] and a lower dark red ash [4037].

Accepting the changes noted above, the internal layout of stone furniture seems to have been maintained during this period of reconstruction. For example, a pile of displaced collapsed orthostats from stone 'boxes' running along the left (west) side of the central area was discovered beneath general rubble collapse (Fig. 5.25). The re-flooring tended to respect and lap around similar structures in the right (east) hand area. The only notable difference between the primary and secondary periods of occupation is that the entrance between the first pair of opposed divisional orthostats seems to be enhanced by longitudinal uprights creating extended and more formal entry into the central area.

Despite a long history of remedial work, eventually the structure became more unstable. Finally, House 3 was abandoned in the early centuries of the 3rd millennium cal BC. Whether this was due to a dramatic collapse of the western wall or for another reason entirely is impossible to know, nonetheless, sealing the final deposits within House 3 are the collapsed remains of the western wall. Similarly, the eastern and gable walls collapsed downslope as represented by the spread of rubble to the east of the house.

5.2.4.2 Working inside and outside House 3: addressing questions of social and material differentiation

The presence of a range of stone tools (Fig. 5.32c), for instance, three smoothers, a grinding stone and a banded grinding slab within House 3, reveal that processing and manufacturing was in all probability occurring within the building (see Chapter 13). Equally, their presence inside the house could be a consequence of storage. Cooking aside, obviously some tasks may have required a degree of seclusion and sanction, such as those surrounding the human body, or creating certain objects of ritual significance. Interestingly, Miller *et al.* (Chapter 15) point to a discrepancy between House 3 on Stonehall Knoll and the other Stonehall sites in terms of the fuel burnt within the hearth (see also Chapter 16). Unusually, turf

was not employed, instead heather, birch, willow and rowan, and seaweed was present in the hearth ash. This variation in fuel will lead to fires of different temperature (higher) and apart from additional warmth, the fire may be employed for different tasks, including cooking meat on a spit arrangement.

For other activities a more social arena may have been preferred. In this context, it is quite easy to conjure up images of a range of tasks being undertaken outside the confines of the house. Indeed, given the elevated situation of House 3 (and its occupants), any physical movement, including daily practices, occurring on the knoll would have been an ever present and highly visible reminder of the social order of things and people. Such differentiation may take many guises. For example, the range of stone tools present on the knoll is different from Stonehall Meadow and Farm in emphasizing activities involving grinding in the manufacture of tools for specific purposes (see Chapter 13).

Further differentiation between Stonehall Knoll and the adjacent Stonehall sites may involve food processing and consumption. Miller *et al.* (Chapter 15) remark on the absence of grain from Stonehall Knoll, which is in marked contrast to Stonehall Meadow. Such discrepancy may well translate into variation in access to food and consumption. Although negligible, more flakes and a flaked cobble, all possibly employed for butchery, were present on Stonehall Knoll. Evidence may be slight, but is consistent with more meat being consumed by the inhabitants of Houses 2 and 3 on Stonehall Knoll.

In front of House 3, the demolition of House 2 had opened up the summit of the knoll for general outdoor tasks and activities. In particular, the large paved area [472] that had been originally laid in conjunction with House 2, became re-employed as a place for a range of tasks, some of which involved the use of worked flint. In terms of disposal we see an interesting pattern of discard where the main flagstone surface was kept relatively clean. The discarded lithics appear to encircle the paved area with unwanted material being simply thrown beyond the place of working to create a halo-effect (Fig. 5.32a). This distribution contrasts to some degree with the distribution of pottery that seems to be deposited mainly in the downslope midden (Fig. 5.32b).

Presumably as a consequence of continuous work activities, a thin ashy occupation deposit [1008] gradually covered the flagstones and spilt a short distance down the eastern slope of the knoll. Interestingly, this material contains quantities of charred seaweed which must relate to very specific activities (see Chapter 15). As may be

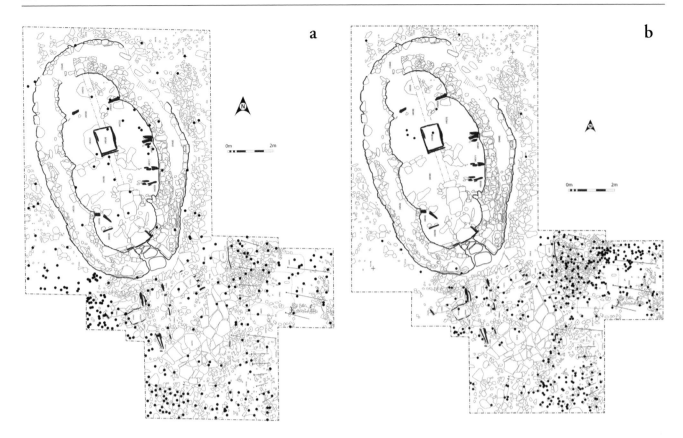

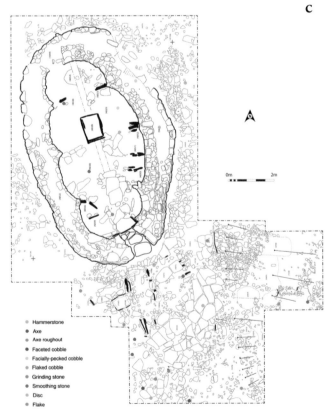

Figure 5.32 Distribution of flint (a), pottery (b) and stone (c) on Stonehall Knoll.

expected during the lengthy occupation of House 3, substantial amounts of ash and midden material [403] were continually dumped down the eastern slope of the knoll. As noted earlier, the fact that this red-orange-black ash spread incorporates numerous episodes of deposition undertaken over decades meant that layer definition was quite blurred in places. Hence, what was identified as the upper midden material [403], produced by ash disposal from House 3, displays localized diversity in colour and consistency. Equally, the division between the generic upper [403] and lower [1058] middens was clearly defined in some areas but unclear in others, much the same effect as was noted in the middens at Knap of Howar (Ritchie 1983).

Overall, occupation on the knoll spanned several hundred years and appears to incorporate practices of a distinctive character. Certainly, a different assemblage of stone tools in conjunction with a lack of cereal processing suggests possible dietary differences between those living on the knoll and those occupying lower habitations. There are also distinctive practices occurring on the knoll which involved the burning of seaweed. In terms of a history of inhabitation on the knoll, accepting a degree of uncertainty regarding the status of the postholes and Structure 1, two different houses were built and occupied. Living in an elevated position had its consequences, as the difficult structural history of House 3 aptly testifies. Nevertheless, the knoll was clearly a desirable place to live and it is difficult not to translate physical elevation into enhanced social position. The final house (House 3) displayed a distinctive internal architecture with much 'softer' internal divisions, which in many ways anticipate the changes manifest in later Neolithic houses where recesses are incorporated into the actual fabric of the structure (*e.g.* Downes and Richards 2005, Fig. 4.3).

If an elevated physical position equates to a similar social position then the situation of the Stonehall sites provides a form of social geography. This grouping also constituted a neighbourhood with all its implications concerning accruing social capital by living adjacent to those of higher social order. Such conglomeration could also be related to changing social practices of production and consumption (see Schulting 2004; 2008). This aggregation is also suggested to be a manifestation of discrete households conjoining to form a *société à maisons* where status competition is not only inter-group but also an intra-group social condition. Consequently, it is to the other households comprising the Stonehall *société à maisons* that we will now turn.

5.3 Stonehall Meadow

During our initial reconnaissance of Stonehall in 1994, the farmer, Mr Ronnie Flett, pointed out several areas within his field that had produced ash and building stone whenever it was cultivated. As we looked over the field, the places that he identified were clearly visible as different sized mounds (Fig. 5.4). A slighter mound in the northwest corner of the field was noted as a place where 'red ash' was brought to the surface during ploughing. The results of a subsequent gradiometer survey confirmed this mound to be an area of considerable magnetic enhancement (see Fig. 6.3).

This area (Trench A) was investigated in 1994, but as the complexity and duration of occupation at Stonehall became apparent it was decided to examine this mound further before the project ended. The initial excavations showed the deposits within the field to be severely truncated through ploughing and although vague traces of structural remains were present they were too badly

preserved to be confident of any particular architectural form. Trench A was actually positioned adjacent to a deep drainage ditch which bounded the western edge of the field. Examination of the exposed stratigraphy on either face of the ditch cutting showed the deposits to extend beyond the field boundary and continue uphill to the west into an area of rough pasture. As this field had experienced reduced cultivation it was decided to open another trench (Trench Z) on the opposite side of the ditch to Trench A. Consequently, the site now known as Stonehall Meadow comprises the structural remains and deposits as revealed in both trenches (see Fig. 5.3).

As suspected, in Trench Z thick deposits of colluvium covered the archaeological remains which unfortunately were not as well preserved as was hoped. Nonetheless, from the structural components a sequence comprising three different houses was discernible. House 1 was the earliest structure encountered being represented by a short stretch of walling that had been incorporated in the later House 3 (Figs 5.33 and 5.34). This section of walling included a blocked entrance to the north. Given the curvature of the wall, House 1 was probably of sub-rectangular shape and oriented on a rough north–south axis. Intriguingly, the nature of construction and the architecture of this short length of walling were reminiscent of the style of masonry present at Stonehall Knoll House 3 and Stonehouse 1 at Wideford Hill (see Chapter 2). However, Stonehall Meadow House 1 had clearly been demolished to allow the construction of the juxtaposed Houses 2 and 3.

Chronologically, House 2 was the next structure to be erected, being partially uncovered in extensions to Trench Z to the south. Although House 2 appears to be paired with House 3, as for instance is seen at Knap of Howar, it is clear that it was the primary construction of the two.

The partial remains of House 1 and almost the full extent of House 3 (with the exception of the northwest corner which was cut by a modern field ditch) were fully excavated. Unfortunately, the remains of House 2 were not located until very late in the excavation season due to being obscured by a thick layer of colluvium, and consequently were only partially investigated.

5.3.1. Initial occupation of Stonehall Meadow: House 1

The short section of walling, and blocked entrance, forming part of the front of House 3 represented the earliest identifiable structural phase of building (see Figs 5.33 and 5.34). This stretch of masonry clearly belonged to an earlier building which was identified as House 1.

Figure 5.33 Excavating the front compartment of House 3, Stonehall Meadow. Project illustrator and supervisor, Joanna Wright and Stuart Jeffrey (top right) examine the differently built section of masonry that was a remnant of the earlier House 1 (Colin Richards).

The line of the wall suggests that it formed part of an earlier house that originally extended to the south with its primary (blocked) entrance lying at its northern end. The surviving wall of House 1 was *c*.1.10m thick and was constructed in typical manner with inner and outer skins of masonry, surviving up to 5–7 courses in height, facing a core comprising a mixture of clay, midden and small stone chips. The drystone masonry comprised thin, well-fitting slabs. This wall was actually associated with two entrances: one on the northern side of the building, and another in the eastern section of the wall. The northern entrance was almost certainly the primary entrance into House 1, being neatly faced with interleaved stonework which was integral to the inner and outer wall faces. A large flagstone paved the entrance, but rather unusually there were no upright threshold stones, passage-facing slabs or door jambs. This entrance had been blocked

with large stones, probably when the wall was re-used as a component of the later House 3.

The inner skin of walling was also characterised by a small pinch in the wall as it curved round in the northeast corner, and a small orthostat projecting inwards from the pinch. Both the pinching and the character of the stonework very closely resembled the walling of House 3 on Stonehall Knoll. This structural sequence is surprising in that the primary house has a curving inner wall face with internal 'pinches' and no substantial orthostatic divisions. Admittedly little remained of the building; nonetheless, it appears to resemble the primary stone house at Wideford Hill (Chapter 2) as opposed to possessing large divisional orthostats reminiscent of 'Knap of Howar' architecture. However, it is the later house (House 3) at Stonehall Meadow that has strong inner–outer spatial demarcation created by orthostatic partitioning.

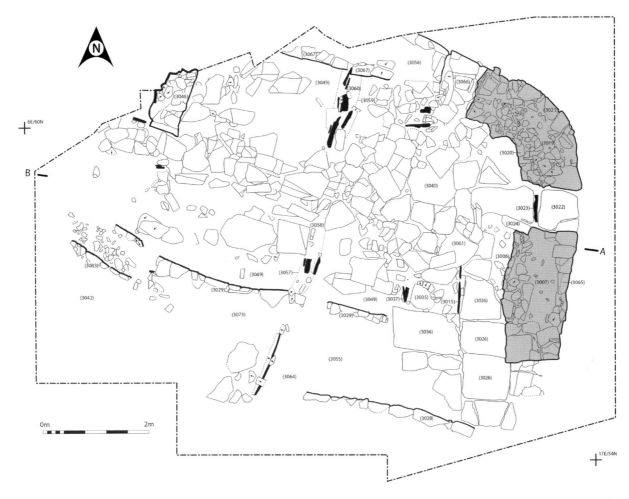

Figure 5.34 Plan of upper deposits and paving in Stonehall Meadow House 3, the shaded section of masonry is derived from the earlier House 1.

The wall attributed to the earlier House 1 was truncated in the south where it came to an abrupt and irregular end, and in the west where it was replaced by the later masonry of House 3 outer wall. This masonry was of a completely different style formed by a narrower inner skin, with longer slabs creating a neat inner wall-face extending in an almost straight line west–northwest. A number of internal features surviving within House 3 were clearly original components of House 1, either having a direct relationship with the walling or respecting associated elements.

In summary, these components consist of five large flagstones [3026 and 3036], two of which extended beneath the inner wall skin and, therefore, formed part of the primary House 1 foundation (Fig. 5.34). There were also a series of orthostats [3025] and [3037], and horizontal stones [3034] and [3035], that formed a box feature which respected the five flagstones, and an

orthostat [3091] projecting from the pinch in the inner skin of the wall. These internal features were associated with a grey clay foundation deposit [3039], [3041] and [3048] between and around the flagstones. On the basis of association with this deposit, most of the flagstones [3040] in the north-eastern part of the trench in the vicinity of the wall could also be associated with the primary House 1. The grey foundation deposit is clearly differentiated from the yellow clay foundation laid as part of the construction of the later western extensions that comprised House 3.

5.3.2 Structural reorientation – House 2

As mentioned above, House 2 was only identified late in the 2000 season of fieldwork after excavation of a single lateral trench extending south from the southern wall

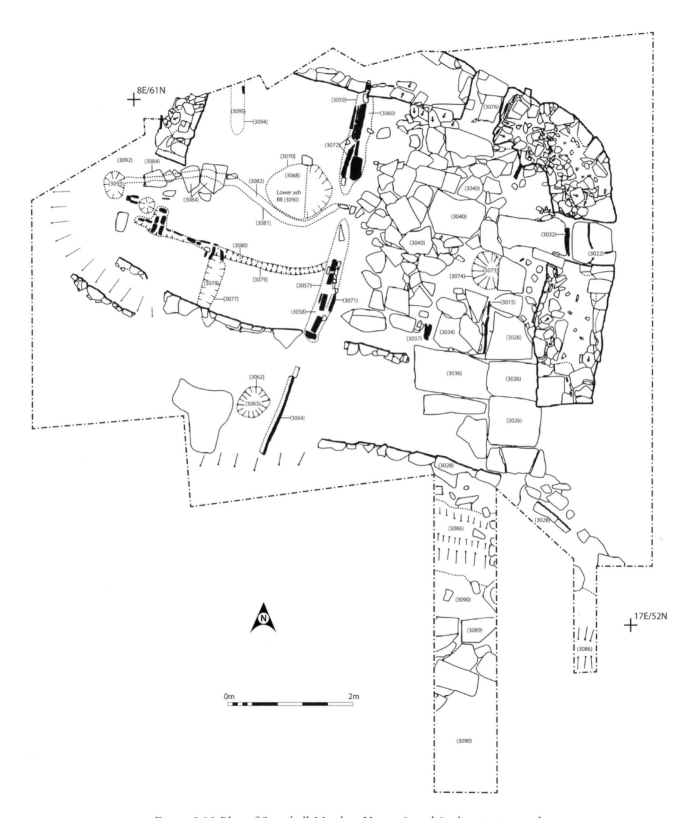

Figure 5.35 Plan of Stonehall Meadow Houses 2 and 3, showing internal.

Figure 5.36 View of the faced outer wall of Stonehall Meadow House 2 and faced inner wall of House 3 (Siân Jones).

Figure 5.37 View of excavated Stonehall Meadow House 3 from the west. The curving walling at the rear gives the house a boat-shape (Colin Richards).

of House 3 (Fig. 5.35). This revealed an outer wall skin [3028] and central wall core [3086] c.1m thick, overlying a grey clay foundation deposit [3090]. The narrow outer wall skin [3028] only survived 1–2 courses high, but was of a similar style to House 3 in displaying neatly faced masonry. A substantial number of cereal grains were recovered from the wall core of House 2 confirming that at least some of this material was derived from pre-existing midden deposits. The trench extension did not run far enough to locate the southern wall of House 2, but did reveal a series of flagstones [3089] running inside the inner wall face of the building.

House 2 is clearly later than House 1 as it cuts across the likely north–south axis of the latter. As seen at Knap of Howar, Stonehall Meadow House 2 was conjoined to House 3, which was built against its northern wall. House 2 was undoubtedly the primary structure as it possessed an externally faced outer wall [3028], indicating that it was free-standing at some point in its life. In contrast, the southern wall of House 3 adjoining House 2 possessed just an inner skin [3029] and the thick wall core [3055] was banked up directly up against the outer wall-face of House 2 (Fig. 5.36).

5.3.3 House 3

Of all the structures at Stonehall Meadow, House 3 was the best preserved and measured c.8m wide and at least 11m long (probably 12–13m) but the western end had been partially truncated by a modern field ditch. Although of sub-rectangular shape, the building had

rounded corners and the entire western gable end was rounded from the outside giving the building a 'boat-shaped' plan (Fig. 5.37). The interior of the house was characterised by much straighter walls and a more rectangular plan measuring 4.2m wide and 6.7m long. Two centrally positioned opposed orthostats provided sharp definition to the interior of the house, and partitioned the internal area into two roughly equal compartments.

5.3.3.1 The construction of House 3

As House 3 was relatively well preserved, it is possible to detail its sequence of construction. Initially, House 2 stood as a single building and at some later date a second house structure was erected against its northern wall. Not only did this extension negate the requirement of a southern outer facing wall for House 3, but the later house was also positioned in such a way as to utilize part of the basal courses of the ruined House 1 as a component of its frontage. This concurrence seems remarkably fortuitous until it is recalled that the consistent feature of Neolithic house construction, apart from on Stonehall Knoll, is that dwellings are built and rebuilt in the same location, but often in a slightly offset position and different entrance orientation (Downes and Richards 2005). Here we have clear evidence that this practice was also occurring in the early Neolithic period. Surely this practice relates to an altered sense of 'place', whilst maintaining relationships to previous generations as manifest in the change to stone architecture discussed in Chapters 2 and 9. In this context it is worth remembering that when House 3 was

Figure 5.38 View of front area of Stonehall Meadow House 3, showing divisional slots, and flagstone paving [3026] and [3036] (Colin Richards).

erected, the ruinous remains of House 1 must have been partly extant and visible.

To build House 3, an area was cleared to the north of House 2 presumably including some of the collapsed masonry of the ruined House 1. This enabled a section of its outer wall to be incorporated as part of the new building. The linear slots for the left [3057] and right [3059] stone orthostats that operated as divisional uprights within the interior were dug and the large orthostats wedged in position with packing stones. Charcoal recovered from the fill of the southern slot was solely composed of lumps of birch (see Chapter 15).

The threshold slab [3032] was also inserted into its cut and packed in position and together with the paired orthostats [3071 and 3072] effectively determined the internal architecture of the complete house. The next step was the laying of a spread of yellow clay [3047] that acted as both a floor for the interior and a level foundation surface for the outer wall, with the exception of the house frontage. The outer wall was then built and the masonry merged with the remaining section of House 1 walling. At the same time the old entranceway to House 1 was blocked and sealed by irregular masonry [3066]. Overall, the new walling was composed of slightly larger sandstone blocks. However, like the earlier walling it followed a typical method of construction that continued throughout the Neolithic with an inner [3067 and 3029] and outer [3096] masonry skin sandwiching a thick clay and midden core [3056]. Generally, the outer wall was substantial, particularly in the southern area where the core alone measured 1.4m in thickness and directly abutted the northern wall of House 2. The

inner skin of the western wall [3046] was much thicker, but it is difficult to estimate the overall thickness of this or the northern wall as they were both truncated on the outside by a modern field ditch which cut across the northwestern edge of the house.

Orientated east-southeast, the front entrance to House 3 was paved by three flagstones and had an inner threshold stone. Because the adjacent walling was re-used it is difficult to know whether this entrance had originally been part of House 1, but overall it is most likely to be a secondary feature associated with House 3. A variety of evidence leans towards this interpretation. For example, in contrast to the blocked entrance in the northern wall the sides were not faced by a neat course of stonework linked to the inner and out skins of the wall. Instead they were composed of a rough arrangement of stonework and, where they were most irregular, faced with a large orthostat [3024], which projected into the building. Overall, the evidence points towards a later breaching and modification of the wall to create this entrance.

5.3.3.2 Interior of House 3

The interior of House 3 was typically partitioned (see, for instance, House 1, Knap of Howar) into two roughly equal compartments by opposed orthostats, below ground some of the broken pieces remained *in situ*. The front (eastern) compartment, measuring *c*.4m wide by 3.6m long, was almost entirely paved with large flagstones [3026 and 3036] (Fig. 5.38). These were contiguous with the entrance and extended into the side inter-linking passage conjoining Houses 2 and 3. Smaller, more irregular areas of flagstones, paved the interior. On the left of the house when entering, just inside the flagstones leading into the inter-linking passage, a box-like structure, consisting of a series of orthostats [3015 and 3037] and a flagstone base and lid, was set into the clay floor. Located beneath a large flagstone [3061], adjacent to this box-like structure, was a pit [3074]. The pit was empty save for a loose silt [3075] filling its base (Fig. 5.39b), which produced the largest quantity of (naked) barley, from any of the samples taken at Stonehall. Given the presence of charcoal this is suggested to be a mainly empty grain storage pit, the contents of which had been accidentally or intentionally burned (see Chapter 15). A radiocarbon date from naked barley of *3360–3010 cal* BC *(GU-10332)* was obtained from the fill [3075].

Some of the flagstones paving the outer chamber of House 3 extended under the section of walling attributed to House 1 and, therefore, were originally part

Figure 5.39 Detail of pit [3074] covered by flagstone (a), uncovered showing barley-rich basal fill [3075] (b), (Siân Jones).

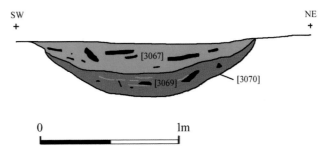

Figure 5.41 East-facing section of scoop hearth [3070] in Stonehall Meadow House 3.

Figure 5.40 Pre-excavation view of the red ash [3068] spreading from the top of the scoop hearth [3070] (Siân Jones).

of the foundation of the earlier building. Furthermore, most of the flagstones in this part of the house were associated with two sequential grey-brown clay layers [3039], [3041] and [3048], the former of which appears to have been a levelling deposit for the flagstones. This foundation deposit differs significantly from that present beneath the other walls of the house.

The rear compartment measured c.4.4m in width, and 3m in length. However, the width measurement belies a substantial curvature to the rear walls of the house (Fig. 5.37). Typically, the inner compartment was dominated by an oval-shaped scoop hearth [3070], measuring 0.8m × 1.1m (Fig. 5.40). Two distinct layers of ash, an upper red ash [3068], which also spread across the floor surface and a lower black ash [3069], filled the hearth scoop (Fig. 5.41), radiocarbon dates of *3340–2920 cal BC (GU-*

10329) and *3340–2920 cal BC (GU-10321)* were obtained from the respective hearth fills. On the left hand side of the room a long cut [3079], 0.1m wide, 3.6m long, and 0.15m deep, ran parallel to the wall and another much shorter and wider cut [3077], 0.25m wide × 1.1m long × 0.15m deep, ran laterally from the wall. These slots probably provided the foundation for orthostats, or, in the case of the longer cut which curves slightly, perhaps a wooden partition (Fig. 5.42). These interior features created a 'box-bed' type structure, which could just as easily been employed for storage as sleeping (*contra* Childe 1931a, 14–16). Interestingly, a similar arrangement on the other side of the house was present within the Knowes of Trotty house (Chapter 3). On the right-hand side, one short cut [3094], 0.2m wide, 0.8m long and c.0.15m deep, projected out from the wall towards the rear of the house and likely contained a stone orthostat screening off the back right hand corner of the room.

In contrast to the front, the rear compartment was unpaved, instead the floor was formed by a layer of the yellow clay [3047] with occupation material [3050] trampled into its surface. This compaction produced a black sheen to the floor surface which is seen in many Neolithic houses. Phosphate values on this surface reveal three broad areas of high values; one of these is associated directly with the hearth [3068], with two more on either side (Fig. 5.45). This is a very similar distribution to that seen within House 3 on the knoll and indicates a concentration of activities centred on the hearth. Some of the large flagstones recognized as part of the secondary

alterations (see below) may represent collapsed internal partitions and 'furniture', but their original location could not be ascertained with any certainty. A line of smaller stones were found to be the cover stones for a drain [3081], which was filled with a dark brown greasy silt [3082]. The drain ran from a pit [3092], through the middle of the inner chamber. The pit was situated at the rear of the house and contained a bright orange silt fill [3093].

The entire floor of the house (inner and outer compartments) was covered by thick spreads of red ash [3003 and 3025]. This is an unusual occurrence in a Neolithic house, where floors tend to be kept clean and ash is usually deposited outside the house with other midden material. Indeed, some mixed midden and ash deposits (upper layer [3018] and lower layer [3045]) had accumulated outside of the eastern and north-eastern walls [3017]; a polished stone axe (SF 7035) was recovered from the upper midden [3018]. The ash spreads within the building suggest that either the building was destroyed by fire or that once it had fallen out of use, the area was used for dumping ash from other houses.

There was also a secondary phase to the life of House 3. A lateral wall [3046] projected into the rear compartment (Fig. 5.44). Also, a line of paving stones extended through the gap between the opposed divisional orthostat slots, through the centre of the 'inner' chamber, and continued into what appears as an extended rear section of House 3. Unfortunately, the angled modern field drain cut through the rear of the house and had destroyed the modified rear section. More recent excavations of 4th millennium cal BC house structures at Ha'Breck, Wyre, have uncovered projecting walling, creating masonry 'piers' (Fig. 5.46). Again, a similar rear chamber was present within the later phases of the Knowes of Trotty house.

Figure 5.42 The linear slot [3079] and lateral slot [3077] projecting from the left-hand inner wall-face probably held stone or timber uprights forming 'bed-like' furniture within the inner compartment (Colin Richards).

5.3.4 Inhabiting Stonehall Meadow

Extensive spreads of red ash and burnt stone were characteristic of the midden deposits lying to the front

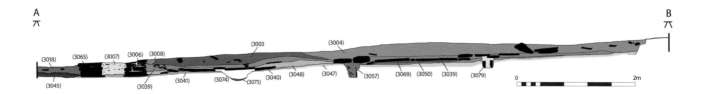

Figure 5.43 North-facing section through Stonehall Meadow House 3.

Figure 5.44 View of Stonehall Meadow House 3 showing the line of secondary paving and lateral wall [3046]. The curving rear wall, resembling a boat-shape is visible on the southern side (Colin Richards).

(east) of Stonehall Meadow House 3. It will be recalled that a correspondence of ashy deposits brought to the surface after ploughing, together with the results of the gradiometer survey (Fig. 6.3), led to the investigation of Trench A which was situated in the northwest corner of the Stonehall Farm field. When this was first examined we had no idea that substantial house structures survived on the other side of the large field ditch to the west. The subsequent excavation of house structures during the 2000 season confirmed that the deposits in Trench A were merely an extension of the settlement encountered in Trench Z (Fig. 5.3).

After the removal of ploughsoil in Trench A extensive deposits of red ash, burnt stone and midden, together with spreads of yellow clay and rubble were revealed (Figs 5.47 and 5.48). Unfortunately, it was also clear that these deposits had been very badly truncated by cultivation and cut by a series of modern field drains. Despite the eroded nature of the deposits traces of some structural remains were present. The most convincing elements were a line of flagstones leading to a stone upright [005]. This upright was set in a stone packed cut [032] and was almost certainly a threshold slab. Hence, another structure,

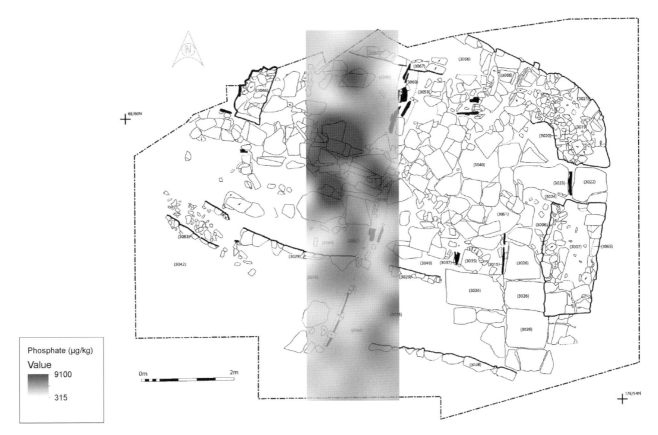

Figure 5.45 Phosphate values for primary floor [3047].

Figure 5.46 The enlarged House 5 at Ha'Breck, Wyre, where masonry piers serve to subdivide internal space (Antonia Thomas).

tentatively described as House 4, appeared to be present on the eastern side of the ditch which given the alignment of the threshold shared a similar north – south axis with the earliest building (House 1) in Trench Z. The threshold slab was flanked to the east and west by amorphous spreads of pale grey clay [035] which may represent part of the initial clay foundation spread for the walls of the building. Beyond the threshold slab, within the supposed interior of the building, a line of flagstones created internal paving that ran between two opposed broken orthostats. These were both set in stone-packed slots and a spread of rubble was present between them. To the north, two further broken orthostats seemed to respect the assumed alignment of the building as indicated by the threshold slab. Directly behind the north-eastern orthostat and enclosed by stone upright [009], was a hollow filled with numerous fire-reddened stones [018] and red ash [019], a

radiocarbon date of *3490–3090 cal BC (GU-10320)* from charred barley was obtained from the ash [019]. Further red ash [029] surrounded the hollow, and another radiocarbon date of *3360–3030 cal BC (GU-10330)* was obtained from charred barley from this deposit.

The central area of the trench was dominated by a large spread of re-deposited yellow clay [004]. Undoubtedly this constitutes a laid clay surface akin to a house floor. But if it was a floor surface its position seemed to bear no relationship to the linear projection of the supposed building, indeed it spread downslope to the east away from the paving and stone uprights. The clay surface did run laterally across what was thought to be the internal area of the building and lapped around the southern set of paired orthostats. Furthermore, the clay observed the circular hollow containing burnt stones and ash considered to be the remains of a hearth.

A similar coloured clay surface [028] was present in the northwest area of the trench which should correspond to the rear of the structure. However, apart from a semi-circular band running into the western baulk this surface appeared equally nebulous in relation to any supposed floor area. Encircling the clay surface was a homogeneous red-brown, charcoal-rich deposit [002] that contained large amounts of ash and burnt stone fragments. As this probable midden material ran downslope to the east it became more of a russet colour with discrete concentrations of burnt bone and charcoal [017].

Because of the truncated nature of these deposits it is difficult to provide an authoritative interpretation. Nonetheless, it is clear that a ruinous building, probably a house structure, was present on the summit of the low mound. It is equally clear that this is later than the deposition of ash and burnt material. This deposit probably built up during the early occupation of the dwellings within Trench Z. Indeed, the mound itself is little more than a large midden heap composed of burnt stones and ash.

At the time of excavation there was no suspicion that circular and rectangular timber structures were a pre-stone component of the earlier Neolithic in Orkney, consequently they were not looked for. Certainly, in Trench A the nature of investigation involved characterizing the deposits, as opposed to their complete excavation and removal. Therefore, it is not beyond the realms of possibility that an undetected, pre-stone, timber phase exists in this area.

That cereal cultivation was widely practiced during the occupation of Stonehall Meadow is demonstrated by the significant amount of barley incorporated in the midden

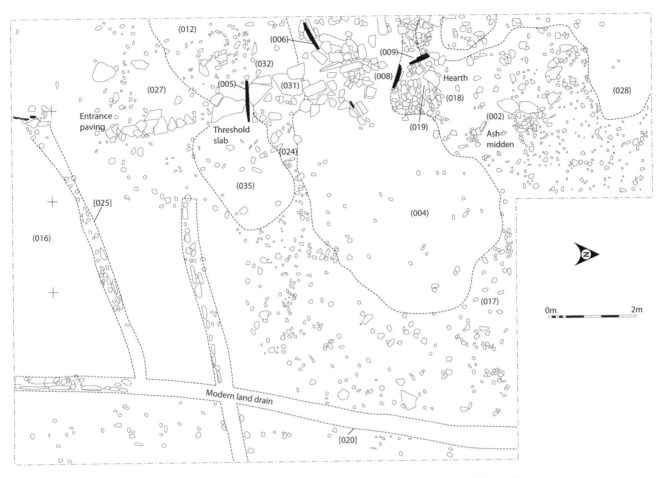

Figure 5.47 Plan of occupation deposits in Trench A of Stonehall Meadow.

core of House 2 and fill of pit [3074] in House 3 (Chapter 15). No querns, however, were present within House 3, or in the associated midden. The broad spread of rubble, incorporating burnt stone, ash and clay surfaces revealed in Trench A, almost certainly acted as a working area in front of the Trench Z Houses 2 and 3. In this area deposits of charred barley grains were associated with turf and heather stems, a combination indicative of cereal processing (see Chapter 15). This evidence contrasts strongly with that from Stonehall Knoll where no charred cereal grains were present, nor querns or rubbers.

A substantial proportion of the worked flint was recovered from the paved front compartment of House 3 (Fig. 5.49a), reinforcing the interpretation of this part of the house being more concerned with craft activities. As may be expected flints were also present in the area (Trench A) beyond the front of House 3 (Fig. 5.50a).

Figure 5.48 View of occupation deposits in Trench A from the east (Colin Richards).

a

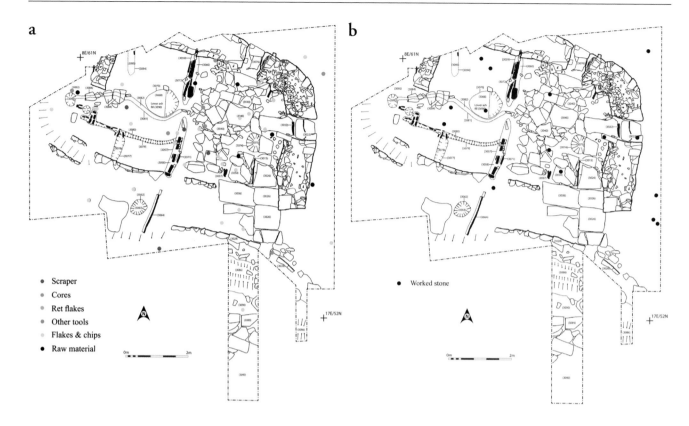

b

- Scraper
- Cores
- Ret flakes
- Other tools
- Flakes & chips
- Raw material

Worked stone

c

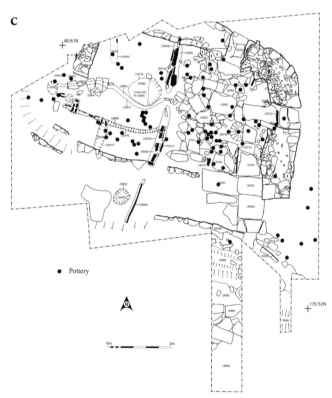

- Pottery

Figure 5.49 Distribution of worked flint (a), stone (b) and pottery (c) within Trench Z.

5.4 4th millennium cal BC settlement at Stonehall Farm

The third, and what becomes the most substantial, area of settlement, Stonehall Farm (see Chapter 6), was identified by Ronnie Flett as a part of the field where both ash and 'building' stone came to the surface when ploughed. It was also visible as a broad low mound which appeared to traverse the boundary fence and drainage ditch (as was the case with Stonehall Meadow). Gradiometer survey undertaken in 1994 substantiated the mound as the largest area of occupation (Fig. 6.3), which was consistently examined over the next five years (Trenches B, E and F).

Initially, we assumed this site to be a small late Neolithic 'village' or 'hamlet' which was confirmed through excavation (see Chapter 6). However, in 1999, at the base of the deepest midden, underlying the structures and deposits described in the following chapter, the remains of a probable house structure (House 2), was revealed. This was represented by a badly damaged wall and spread of collapsed masonry [875] adjacent to a flagstone (which may have been a collapsed orthostat). The remnant wall survived as three thin courses of masonry, reaching a height of 0.19m in a single section but elsewhere was completely ruinous. Wall collapse ran to the northeast into the main east–west section.

Figure 5.50 Distribution of worked flint (a), stone (b) and pottery (c) within Trench A.

Figure 5.51 Excavated remains of stratigraphically early House 2, beneath Structure 1 at Stonehall Farm, looking southwest (Colin Richards).

An associated upright [874] was set adjacent to the outer wall of later Structure 1 (Chapter 6). A pile of stone slabs lay around the orthostat and these seemed to join with a stone spread [812] at a higher level which had been formed into a stone surface by laying clay, directly outside the cell of overlying Structure 1. From this evidence it seems likely that the ruined remains of a primary stone building (House 2), beneath Structure 1, had been spread and compacted to form a stable surface for the erection of the later structure (Fig. 5.51).

Although tentative, from the linear nature of the spread of collapsed walling it is suggested that the earlier structure was rectangular-shaped building, typical of 4th millennium cal BC houses. The orientation of the orthostat and collapsed walling indicates the building to be aligned on a southeast–northwest axis. No convincing floor surface was discovered within the interior of the

building, nor was a hearth found, but these absences are probably due to the limited extent of excavation.

The presence of at least one deeply stratified house structure (House 2) at Stonehall Farm, together with the early radiocarbon dates (see Chapter 10), indicates this to be another location of mid–late 4th millennium cal BC occupation. Indeed, the radiocarbon dates obtained for the occupation of houses at Stonehall Knoll (Trench C), Stonehall Meadow (Trenches A and Z) and Stonehall Farm (Trenches B, E, and F), are indistinguishable (Chapter 10). Hence, there is a clear overlap in the occupation of each of the three sites. The earliest radiocarbon dates for Stonehall Farm not only come from the lower midden [809]: *3310–2900 cal BC (GU-10322)*, but from within Structure 1 *(3360–3030 cal BC (GU-10317)* and *3360–2930 cal BC (GU-10333))*. Although these dates are consistent, the radiocarbon sample *(GU-10333)* obtained from the fill of the central cist may well relate to the lower midden deposits upon which Structure 1 was built. It is these very deposits that are suggested to concur with the occupation of Stonehall Farm House 2.

In the far western area of the trench, adjacent to (and in some instances overlying) House 2, the lower midden was composed of a deep, rich, fairly homogeneous dark-brown soil [873] which actually contained numerous thin ashy lenses of variable thickness *c*.0.2–0.6cm (Figs 6.42 and 6.43). The overall midden layer [873] represents material accumulating on the natural till over a substantial period of time, reaching a height of up to 1.20m in places. It seems likely, therefore, that midden material began to accumulate around House 2 from its first occupation in the 4th millennium cal BC. Although noted to be stratigraphically ambiguous, early and late Neolithic flintwork was present at Stonehall Farm (Chapter 12.12), and a similar presence was considered to be present in the ceramics (Chapter 11.2.3.3). Overall, the evidence supports Stonehall Farm as a third location of early Neolithic settlement running parallel with the occupation of Stonehall Knoll and Meadow.

5.5 Living together at Stonehall in the 4th millennium cal BC: proximity, reproduction and social capital

One of the defining characteristics of *sociétés à maisons* is the identification of the 'house' as a relational category. Here, proximity, shared practices, division of labour and interaction, not just blood ties, are the principal fields for the establishment of close social relationships and corporate group affiliation. In this respect, the spatial organization of 4th millennium cal BC settlement at Stonehall is pivotal in charting the early development of Neolithic *sociétés à maisons* in Mainland, Orkney. Before the discovery of the breadth of habitation, as is observable at Stonehall, early Neolithic settlement was considered to comprise small-scale, isolated social units. As discussed in earlier chapters, this characterization of the nature and location of settlement was based solely on the evidence form Knap of Howar, Papa Westray (Ritchie 1983; 1990a). Following the evidence obtained of grouped early structures at Pool, Sanday (Hunter *et al.* 2007, 63–64), the investigation of different elements of Stonehall provides clear evidence that far from being composed of small isolated social units (farmsteads), in the second half of the 4th millennium cal BC settlement shows a degree of aggregation.

At least three different areas of co-existent settlement were discovered at Stonehall; Stonehall Knoll, Stonehall Meadow and Stonehall Farm, and it is not beyond the realms of possibility that further occupation is present beyond the area investigated. Yet, each site at Stonehall is distinctive and the selection of the summit of the knoll for habitation introduced an interesting 'vertical' dynamic to the organization of settlement. Here, elevation appears to be enjoyed as an important social structuring principle between those occupying different topographic positions (see also discussion concerning water flow and metaphor in Chapter 3). To live on the knoll was to overlook other households whilst assuming an ascendant position.

We have argued that the Stonehall Meadow houses were not alone in occupying the lower ground. Several radiocarbon dates obtained from Structure 1 and the primary midden at Stonehall Farm (Chapter 10), together with the likely building (House 2) beneath the midden, indicates another centre of concurrent habitation (see Chapter 6). This ocurrence begins to provide us with a picture of several houses, loosely grouped within 60–100m of one another. Both Stonehall Knoll and Stonehall Meadow reveal lengthy periods of occupation punctuated by demolition and construction.

Before examining the architectural differences between houses at each site, it is worth considering the social mechanisms articulating the residence pattern occurring at Stonehall during the latter half of the 4th millennium cal BC. This is especially important given our claims for evolving *sociétés à maisons* in early Neolithic Orkney. Naked barley was found in substantial amounts from the sample taken from pit [3074] in House 3 at Stonehall

Meadow, and deposits were also present within the wall core and working area beyond the front of Houses 2 and 3 (see Chapter 15). A surprisingly large deposit of charred grain has been recently discovered within the inner compartment of House 3 at Ha'Breck (Thomas and Lee 2012), while substantial amounts of barley were present within posthole [044] of Timber structure 3 at Wideford Hill (Chapters 2 and 15) and other early Orcadian sites (Chapters 9 and 10).

Large querns are also present at other 4th millennium cal BC settlements such as Knap of Howar, Papa Westray (Ritchie 1983) and Brae of Smerquoy (Fig. 4.43). Indeed, the large quern discovered as part of a drain lining in phase 1.2 at Pool, Sanday (Clarke 2007a, illus: 8.2.13), demonstrates a role in cereal processing during the earliest period of occupation (*ibid.*, 377). This range of evidence confirms that extensive cereal cultivation and processing was being practiced in Orkney from the first half of the 4th millennium cal BC. The initiation of mixed agriculture and changes in subsistence necessarily embody changes in social practices (*e.g.* Whittle 2000; Schulting 2008; Cummings and Harris 20011, 368; Thomas 2013, 404-8), specifically labour requirements would certainly rise at particular times of the year (for Orkney, see Sharples 1992, 324–26; Parker Pearson 2004, 138). Consequently, new or altered relations of co-operation and reciprocity would necessarily emerge. Alternative relational networks would therefore come into being which in turn would create new arenas for the negotiation of social position.

It is in this context that we can begin to see how residence and the creation of 'neighbourhoods' may become a crucial social strategy and resource. For instance, where you live, who your neighbours are, and what you do together, are not neutral situations, but potentially create groups and networks that translate into sources of social capital (*e.g.* Bourdieu 1984; Lin 1999, 30–31). The important point here is that a shifting economic or subsistence base may provide social conditions that are counter to established kinship relations and under which residence, locality and group membership may become alternative social strategies (see Chapter 9 for a more detailed discussion).

If living in close proximity, and the creation of neighbourhoods, becomes a salient feature in the development of Neolithic *sociétés à maisons* in Orkney, then the nature and organization of settlements, in terms of the similarities and differences of houses, households, and location should be particularly illuminating. This includes social practices, particularly differential access to, and control over, a range of resources. At Stonehall, each of the different house sites investigated appeared to be spatially discrete. Equally, a structural history of each Stonehall site charts the re-use or re-cycling of materials and the reproduction of houses and 'place' (a theme that will be extended in the following chapter). Despite the houses at Stonehall Knoll, Stonehall Meadow and Stonehall Farm forming a neighbourhood, each element comprises recognizably different architecture.

The occupation of Stonehall Knoll begins with Structure 1. This building is problematic to assign a function as it does not appear to have had a hearth. Hearths are essential to the maintenance of life in the Northern Isles, and even under the different climatic conditions of the 4th millennium cal BC would still be absolutely necessary. Consequently, Structure 1 does not appear as a dwelling as such. At a later time this nebulous structure was demolished and its stone employed in the building of House 2. Although virtually no walling remained of this building, the large area of paving capping the summit of the knoll was laid down to act as a formalized surrounding area and partial foundation. The architecture of House 2 is difficult to reconstruct, suffice is to note that it had a stone-constructed rectangular hearth, and was sub-divided into compartments by orthostats. However, these were not the substantial orthostats that demarcate linear space in such an emphatic manner as present at Stonehall Meadow, Brae of Smerquoy, Knowes of Trotty or Knap of Howar.

Finally, House 2 was totally demolished and a new reorientated house (House 3) built in an offset position. This situation causes considerable problems to the inhabitants as subsidence and structural instability become part of dwelling on the knoll. It could be argued that the architecture of House 3 anticipates the layout of the circular late Neolithic houses as are present within the 3rd millennium cal BC Orcadian villages. The main similarities lie in the more centrally placed hearth and the way the design of the outer wall combines with the inner stone uprights to create stone furniture and less intrusive internal divisions. In this way, the stone furniture and layout of the interior space is recessed and embedded in the actual fabric of the house.

Apart from the ascendant topographic position, there are a number of other forms of evidence that serve to identify a distinction in practices occurring between the occupants of Stonehall Knoll and those living at Stonehall Meadow and Farm. The absence of any evidence for the presence of cereals or their processing on the knoll is striking when contrasted with the range of

evidence from Stonehall Meadow. At the latter, charred cereal grains were present in a range of contexts and in considerable quantities, which together with other plant remains allows Miller *et al.* (Chapter 15) to identify cereal processing. Such an emphasis on cereal processing may even extend to differences in the selection of hearth fuel. Turf was employed as a fuel at Stonehall Meadow, which is suggested in Chapter 3 to provide a low and level heat necessary to facilitate cereal drying. It also demonstrates access to large areas of higher ground for its procurement.

In direct contrast, on the knoll, a combination of woods was used for fuel. Accepting that in Neolithic Orkney, as elsewhere, food and its preparation is an index of identity and social status (*e.g.* A. M. Jones 1999a; A. M. Jones and Richards 2003), different diets are an important indicator of social position. The presence of stone flakes and flaked stone may be indicative of butchery practices, but unfortunately the lack of bone survival restricts further comment. Certainly, more large vessels (Fig. 11.2.2) were present on the knoll, a further shred of evidence pointing towards a variation in food, cooking and practices of consumption.

At the general level of differential practices between the inhabitants of Stonehall Knoll and those occupying the Meadow and Farm sites, it is interesting that there is evidence for the exclusive exploitation of clay sources. Analysis of fabric differences in ceramics between the three Stonehall sites (Chapter 11), reveals a dominance of sedimentary fabric on the knoll, as opposed to sedimentary+igneous fabrics at Stonehall Meadow and Farm (Fig. 11.2.21). This distinction can be taken to represent the exclusive exploitation of different clay sources with included rock being incorporated in the source clay. The presence of a concentration of grinding stones on the Knoll, is suggested by Ann Clarke (Chapter 13) to represent a 'manufacturing base'. Although smaller numbers were present below at Stonehall Meadow, this discrepancy does suggest divergence in the scale of practices between the two sites. Indeed, we may wonder if axes were being roughly shaped at the Knoll.

As with Stonehall Knoll, there appears to be a long sequence of occupation at Stonehall Meadow, involving at least two episodes of house construction. Curiously, the initial House 1 seems to resemble the architecture of the later Stonehall Knoll House 3. However, House 1 is also similar to the primary Stonehouse at Wideford Hill. Perhaps of greater importance is that the deployment of substantial orthostats to demarcate compartments within the house does not constitute primary architecture at either Stonehall or Wideford Hill. This observation is very significant in that it demonstrates that 'stalled' cairn architecture is only drawn on in the domestic sphere at some time *after* stone is utilized as a house building material. At Stonehall, such pronounced 'stalled' architecture is only present at Stonehall Meadow.

Overall, the aggregation of settlement at Stonehall in the latter half of the 4th millennium cal BC is argued to be a product of changing social practices leading to a reconfiguring of social relations. The presence of at least three different, spatially discrete, house sites in close vicinity charts these changes in residence patterns. Unified, yet distinct, each house and its occupants emphasise continuity and descent through maintenance of place and lengthy sequences of rebuilding. The process of construction may bring new houses into existence; however, the re-use of materials from the preceding structure provides a form of material permanence. What is so noticeable about the Stonehall sites, particularly regarding the Knoll and Meadow, is the architectural diversity of the houses. Not only is their internal layout different, but externally they would have assumed very different appearances. Again, we may be seeing a degree of internal group differentiation, signalled visually through architecture.

This theme is also manifest in portable materials, particularly pottery. Although Unstan bowls are a strong component of the ceramic assemblage from the Wideford Hill settlement, they do not occur at Stonehall. Instead, exclusive local sources of clay are exploited at the household level to produce round-based forms which feature little or no decoration (see Chapter 11). Here,

through the medium of ceramic form and decoration, a unitary identity is being constructed in relation to 'other' social groupings. In this case the 'other' is represented by the inhabitants of nearby settlements. Alternatively, inter-household 'otherness' is also being expressed by exclusive access to clay sources and the practices surrounding pottery production. As an expression of material and practical differentiation, divergence in the manufacture of ceramics will continue through to the 3rd millennium cal BC (see A. M. Jones 2002; 2005).

At Stonehall, in these social strategies we see inevitable internal fracture lines appearing within emergent corporate groups, bound together through proximity and shared practices giving rise to forms of relatedness that extend beyond blood ties. Although group identity is constructed in relation to 'other' social groups, internally these *sociétés à maisons* may be riddled with household rivalry and competition. Accepting at Stonehall the presence of family groups relating to smaller 'houses' constituting the broader *société à maisons*, a perpetuation of names, material houses and household identity is an essential ingredient. That there is structural tension within this form of social organization is unsurprising as in the Orcadian context it is suggested to be based heavily on intra and inter-group rivalry and competition. As we will see in the following chapter, the social forces which produce the conglomeration of houses at Stonehall appear to gain momentum resulting in the move towards nucleation and the establishment of 'villages' which will come to define patterns of residence in 3rd millennium cal BC Orkney.

CHAPTER SIX

At Stonehall Farm, Late Neolithic Life is Rubbish

Colin Richards, Richard Jones, Adrian Challands, Stuart Jeffrey,
Andrew Meirion Jones, Siân Jones and Tom Muir

6.1 Introduction: living with neighbours and middens

If we were able to visit Stonehall at the beginning of the 3rd millennium cal BC, the settlement would take the appearance of a collection of spatially discrete houses in various states of repair. For instance, the structural instability and antiquity of the building on Stonehall Knoll (House 3) would be clearly visible in the contorted and bowed walls supported by external stone buttressing. Downslope from the Knoll, the pair of houses at Stonehall Meadow would initially appear to be in good repair, but closer inspection reveals a degree of subsidence and cracking where different sections of masonry conjoin. Further scrutiny reveals the ruined remains of earlier buildings, represented by sections of low masonry and upright stones covered in vegetation. Middens would be creeping downslope to the east of both the Stonehall Knoll and Meadow sites. In the case of the latter, midden spread created a substantial platform composed of red ash and burnt stones directly in front of Houses 2 and 3. However, one area of habitation, Stonehall Farm, would be noticeably different in that a number of smaller dwellings are set in close proximity with large amounts of ashy midden accumulating around their periphery. The nature and organization of settlement at Stonehall is in flux.

Interestingly, at this very time numerous settlements across Orkney were replicating this trajectory of change (Fig. 6.1). For example, at Crossiecrown (Chapter 7), and Muckquoy (Chapter 9), dwellings slowly aggregate among expanding mounds of midden. Perhaps the most famous settlement where this occurrence is well documented is Skara Brae on the west coast of Mainland, Orkney (Childe 1931a). As a phenomenon, expanding middens and conglomerating dwellings extends beyond Mainland, Orkney to the outer isles. Settlements at Pool and Bay of Stove, Sanday (Hunter *et al.* 2007; Bond *et al.* 1995), Rinyo, Rousay (Childe and Grant 1939; 1947), and Links of Noltland, Westray (Clarke and Sharples 1990; Moore and Wilson 2011) are all nucleated settlements associated with extensive midden deposits.

Although the process of increasing nucleation is a consistent feature of late Neolithic Orcadian settlements, their individual histories are mixed. Neither Barnhouse nor Skara Brae appears to posses any form of continuity or development from earlier occupation, for example, before *c.*3200 cal BC. This stands in direct contrast to Pool, Sanday (Hunter 2000), Rinyo, Rousay (Childe and Grant 1939; 1947), Crossiecrown (see Chapter 7), Muckquoy, Redland (see Chapter 9) and Ness of Brodgar (N. Card pers. comm.), where late Neolithic 'villages' or 'hamlets' appear to continue a sequence of occupation running back into the 4th millennium cal BC. Of course, a degree of settlement dislocation may have taken place, as occurs at the Bay of Stove, Sanday (Bond *et al.* 1995). This would give sites such as Barnhouse and Skara Brae the appearance of new developments. Taken together, there seems to have been a relatively fluid and mixed tradition of house architecture and settlement organization in operation running up to the end of the 4th millennium cal. BC. Yet, from the turn of the 3rd millennium cal BC we see a convergence in the trajectories of virtually all Orcadian settlements.

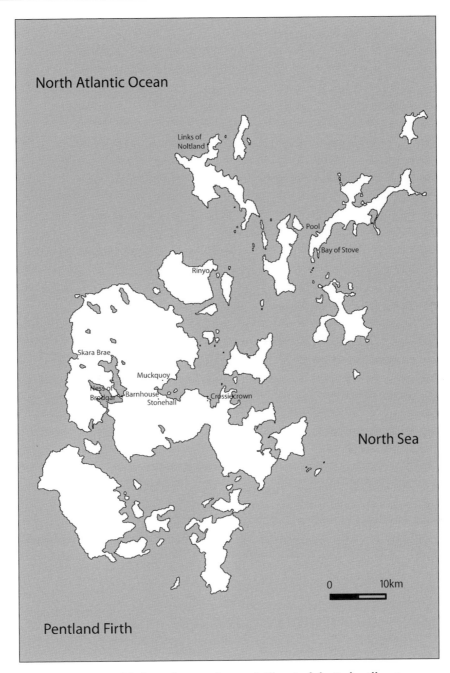

Figure 6.1 Map of Orkney showing known 'villages' of the 3rd millennium BC.

As outlined in the previous chapter, the occupation of Stonehall Knoll, Stonehall Meadow and Stonehall Farm clearly ran through the latter part of the 4th millennium cal. BC. Admittedly, detailed knowledge of the spatial organization of the buildings at Stonehall Farm during this early period is more limited than the other two sites. Significantly, this absence of knowledge is principally due to buildings being superimposed and subsumed within an ever-expanding midden heap which prohibited large-

scale excavation within the time available. Evaluating the significance of nucleation and the accumulation of extensive middens is, however, one of the dominant themes of this chapter.

During our first visit, the Stonehall Farm site was the most visible being represented by a broad low mound (Fig, 6.2). It was also the source of the majority of Ronnie Flett's collection of Neolithic flint and stone tools. Indeed, this was the area of the field at Stonehall

Figure 6.2 Aerial view of the Stonehall Farm mound (Angus Mackintosh).

that initially raised Ronnie's curiosity, not least because it was the only place where recognizable 'building' stone came to the surface when ploughed. For this reason the Stonehall Farm mound was the main target of excavation and its investigation was envisaged to fulfil the initial research objectives of the project (see Chapter 1). Our first task was to undertake a systematic surface geophysical and geochemical survey.

The gradiometer survey undertaken by Richard Jones and Adrian Challands (Fig. 6.3a), confirmed its large extent and revealed the Stonehall Farm site to traverse the drainage ditch bounding the western side of the field (as did the Stonehall Meadow site). More specifically and notwithstanding the gap in the magnetic survey to the southwest of the drainage ditch owing to the presence of an area of mire, there was a large central anomaly entirely consistent with extensive midden deposits. Its shape seemed to be roughly lobate with a hint of a 'stalk' at the northern end represented by the midden associated with the Meadow site (Trenches A and Z). As such, it contrasted somewhat with the 'cloverleaf' shape, with dimensions *c.*40 × 45m, observed in the corresponding magnetic survey at Crossiecrown (Fig. 7.2). Lying outside this core were the

houses on the Knoll, and most interestingly, apparent extensions marked **1** and **2** on Fig. 6.3a. A further anomaly was present to the east and in this instance was examined by a 2m × 8m trench (Trench D). Disappointingly, any midden deposits had been removed by the plough and all that remained was a spread of material over the glacial till (Jones and Brown 2000, 171). However, high magnetic susceptibility readings were obtained over the burnt area confirming that it had apparently been subjected to high temperature (20–660 m.s. units). The possibility that this deposit represented a pottery firing area cannot be ruled out (see Chapter 11.5).

Before considering anomalies **1** and **2**, it is worth remarking that the chief outcome of the magnetic survey has been to define the limits of the midden spread of the settlement, giving dimensions *c.*50 m wide (E–W) and 160m long (N–S); within those limits the magnetic signature of that midden appears quite uniform; for example on the east side of the drainage ditch there is continuous midden or occupation deposits extending from the south of the Farm site (Trenches B, E and F) right through to the Meadow site. Since the magnetic signature of midden is much stronger than that of flagstone, little or no detail of the individual houses was identified. Thus the anomaly at the Knoll corresponds not with the house but with the midden material running downslope.

To the southwest of Trench B lies an arced extension at anomaly **1**. There seems to be up to 10m of magnetically quiet ground separating anomaly **1** from the main settlement, giving it the appearance of creating an enclosure. Anomaly **1** has the character of midden but is less intense than in the main settlement; its width of roughly 5m is too large for it to be regarded an enclosure 'wall'. No *comparanda* are apparent either at Muckuoy (Fig. 9.37) or for example among the several locations surveyed at Tofts Ness and Pool on Sanday.

Anomaly **2** seems to differ from anomaly **1** but it is very difficult to suggest either what it represents or what it may be part of. Lying in the field towards the present Stonehall Farm, anomaly **3** is likely to be modern iron rubbish. Extension of the survey to the south of anomaly **1** along both sides of the drainage ditch for 200m revealed no evidence of either continuation of the settlement or other features. The same remarks apply to the north of the Meadow site towards and including the immediate environs of Stoneyhall Cottage.

Drawing in the phosphate distribution (Fig. 6.3c), greater enhancement occurs in the area between Stonehall Meadow (Trench A) and Stonehall Farm (Trenches B, E and F). There are further high phosphate concentrations first to the south of Trench B at the southerly extremity of the magnetically-defined settlement, and second close to anomaly **1**. Given this correspondence, and the similarity in readings with those at the Knoll and Meadow, it is likely to represent yet another area of occupation.

The corresponding magnetic susceptibility distribution (Fig. 6.3d) is interesting in the way it records significant enhancement between Stonehall Knoll and Meadow. This is important as it drives home the point that while different houses were separated, Stonehall was a fully integrated settlement unit, creating a form of 'neighbourhood'. Consequently, some communal activities would have occurred between houses. Of course, methodologically, the higher magnetic susceptibility readings could be a result of more recent burning activities.

Systematic magnetic survey to the north of Stonehall Meadow towards and including the immediate environs of Stoneyhall Cottage revealed no anomalies that would be consistent with a northerly extension of the settlement. Similar negative results were obtained in an area *c*.100 × 200m on either side of the drainage ditch to the south.

Although the gradiometer survey had been very successful in defining the different Stonehall sites (Fig. 6.3a), it was of little use in providing detailed information of the internal organization of the large Stonehall Farm mound. In an attempt to characterise the site, it was decided to run a trench (Trench B) from the summit of the mound in a northerly direction towards Stonehall Meadow. A second small trench (Trench F) was later opened *c*.12m south of Trench B (see Fig. 5.3). Excavation of Trench F revealed a similar sequence of midden deposits to those encountered in Trench B, and apart from an area of paving no structural evidence was present.

After removing the top soil, *in situ* stratified Neolithic deposits were immediately encountered. Within the southern area of the trench, on the summit of the mound, a mass of collapsed stonework and flagstones was revealed. Distinctive and colourful ashy midden deposits ran downslope to the north. Here several spreads or compacted mounds of burnt stone [509], [523], [524] and [525] were also visible, a feature that was to reoccur in the extension trench (Trench E) opened to the east. Two stone structures were revealed at a relatively high stratigraphic level over the next four years of excavation. In Trench E the truncated remains of a house structure (House 1) were immediately obvious, while in the southern area of Trench B, an unusual building (Structure 1), exhibiting curious architectural features was investigated over the next three seasons.

As far as can be determined by the limited trenches opened at Stonehall Farm, the mound consists of a core of superimposed house structures within a mound of midden that began to form during the latter part of the 4th millennium cal BC. The houses appear to be free-standing but concentrated towards the centre of the settlement mound. The periphery of the mound is composed solely of midden deposits spreading away from the dwellings. The process of building and rebuilding necessarily involved a degree of stabilization of the midden as demonstrated by the flagstone paving [302 and 604] encountered in the southern area of Trench B north of Structure 1. Here, several layers of flagstones served to stabilise and cover the surface of the midden (Fig. 6.7). The underlying deposits in this area were left unexcavated but it was visibly patchy with discrete dumps of red and black ash being intermingled with grey-brown clay containing substantial amounts of highly decayed animal bone. Because of the instability of the midden, the paving had sunk and individual flagstones were tipping in different directions. However, concealed beneath the paving was a major drain [514] running

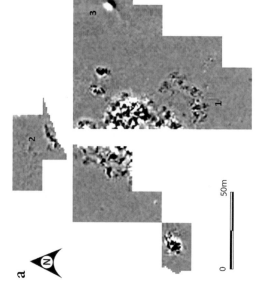

Figure 6.3 The geophysical and geochemical surveys of the Stoneball sites: (a) Gradiometer survey using a Geoscan FM36 fluxgate gradiometer (sample and traverse intervals 1m); black–white shades correspond to ± 10nT respectively; (b) Gradiometer graphic placed over the site plan; black–white shades correspond to ± 10nT respectively; (c) total phosphate survey of the Stoneball Meadow and Farm sites and environs (sample and traverse intervals 5m and 10m respectively). White to black corresponds to 0–5960 µgkg⁻¹ phosphate (data from Shane Donatello); (d) magnetic susceptibility measurements obtained from test pits at 5 metre intervals at Stoneball. White to black 0 to 44 m.s. units (data from Adrian Challands).

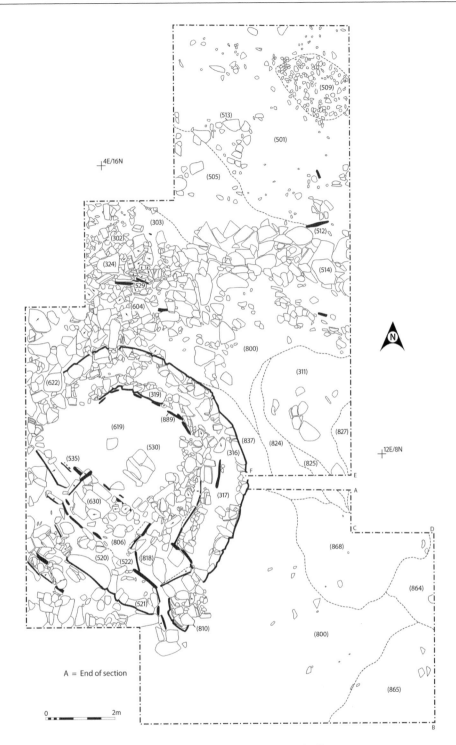

Figure 6.4 Plan of Trench B at Stonehall Farm.

west–east, that had been cut into the lower midden. To the east it was covered by a line of well-fitting flagstones [324] which also acted as a pathway to House 1 in Trench E (Figs 6.5 and 6.33). The drain typically ran beneath the entrance passage into this house where it was unexcavated. Again, most of the covering flagstones had

broken and slipped into the drain cavity, the structure of which was extremely unstable due to the softness and slippage of the underlying midden (Fig. 6.6). It was not established whether the small drain running out beneath the doorway of Structure 1 actually joined with the main drain, however given the level and direction of flow it

Figure 6.5 View of covered drain [514] running east–west across Trench B (Colin Richards).

Figure 6.6 The drain [514] had collapsed where it ran through the soft and unstable midden (Colin Richards).

Figure 6.7 Portion of Structure 1 uncovered in 1995 (note the stone cist capstone in the centre of the building) (Colin Richards).

would seem highly likely that they merged somewhere to the north of the building.

Without doubt, there remain further house structures west of Structure 1 from whence the main drain flowed. If it is assumed that this drain served Structure 1 and other buildings to the west and then formed part of the construction of House 1, a relationship is established between the different components of the site. In linking several buildings, this main drainage system provides an artery and index for the later structural history of Stonehall Farm. In the following sections the various components of this history will be unravelled beginning with the extraordinary alterations that occur throughout the life of a building named unimaginatively Structure 1.

6.2 Structure 1

The outer wall of a stone-built structure in Trench B was discovered during the first season of excavation at Stonehall Farm (Fig. 6.7). The majority of the interior was uncovered and excavated during the 1997 and 1999 seasons. When the outer walling was initially encountered it was assumed to be a typical late Neolithic house structure. However, the combination of an internal circuit of upright slabs facing the inner wall and the presence of a central stone covered 'cist' occupying the position normally reserved for the hearth made it clear that this structure represented something quite unusual. Further excavation in 1999 exposed the entirety of the building except the extreme west sector which had been destroyed by the adjacent field ditch (Fig. 6.8). Structure 1 had been built directly on earlier midden material which gave rise to an instability resulting in the shifting and subsidence of the outer wall. Nor was this a well-constructed building. Apart from a partial layer of clay and slabs [812], there was no trace of the expected clay platform acting as a foundation and floor; instead the outer wall was simply sitting on leveled midden deposits.

The overall interpretation of this building was quite challenging because during excavation it continually produced surprises in the form of concealed deposits, a complex internal structural sequence and lack of conformity with previously excavated 3rd millennium cal BC houses. Particular evidence, such as that demonstrating the presence of a primary central hearth is very secure. In contrast, other evidence, for instance the status of the original entrance is more ambiguous.

Almost certainly the initial structure was built as some

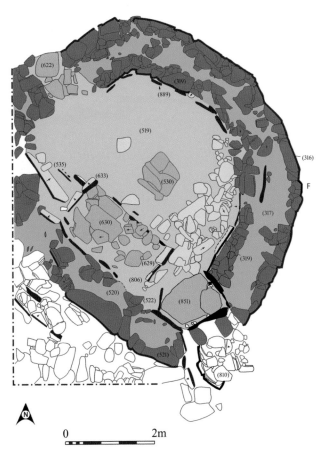

Figure 6.8 Plan of upper deposits within Structure 1.

Figure 6.9 Structure 1 showing upper deposits, the central capstone has been removed from the cist and the shallow stone box, containing the hoard of objects (see Fig. 6.16) is visible bottom right (Colin Richards).

form of dwelling with a typically situated central hearth. In plan it followed a circular form with the exception of the southwest sector where the wall was virtually straight so lending the structure a slightly D-shaped appearance (Figs 6.8 and 6.9). This plan is intriguing, especially the virtually straight southern wall. It is not beyond the realms of possibility that this wall could be a component of the remodeling incurred by this building, and that originally it did assume a more rounded shape.

6.2.1 Biography of Structure 1: the early house

To obtain a level surface to build Structure 1 a pre-existing midden heap was sculpted and partially leveled in its eastern area (see Fig. 6.10). Much of the upper deposits seem to have been dug through until the more compacted surface of the lower midden was exposed. Also, beneath the southeast of the building a surface composed of stone slabs in a clay matrix [812] may have been either laid down at this time or a pre-existing pile of stone slabs was consolidated and stabilised by laying clay.

Once a relatively firm and level surface of midden, clay and stone slabs had been formed, a number of uprights or orthostats for the internal furniture were positioned and held in place by packing stones wedged into cuts in the midden. This included the unusual ring of orthostats [889] facing the entire circumference of the inner wall (Figs 6.10, 6.11 and 6.12). As the ring of orthostats ran around the inner wall-face they connected with the facing slabs of the right-hand rear (southeast) cell.

The cell was composed of a series of orthostats facing a gap in the outer wall. The rear of the cell was simply formed by another large orthostat wedged in position by two large blocks (Fig. 6.13). It employed several layers of 'paving' to create the floor and a drain ran out to the southeast. The architecture of this cell requires further comment because of its unusual construction. As mentioned above, the rear orthostat was held in position by the two stone blocks, which is a very unusual construction and in all other examples of such cells (*e.g.* in the Red and Grey Houses at Crossiecrown) there is always an outer casing wall running behind the cell to provide both insulation and structural support. In Structure 1, this ephemeral form of brace would have provided no obstacle to wind and rain nor constituted structural integrity. Indeed, this arrangement was so flimsy that it appeared to be little more than temporary support wedged in place, allowing the cell to be accessed from the outside. However, if the entire building was partially cut into the lower midden, as was suspected, then further encasement would be unnecessary.

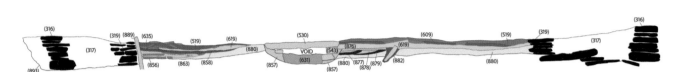

Figure 6.10 *Northeast facing section showing midden formation and construction cut for Structure 1.*

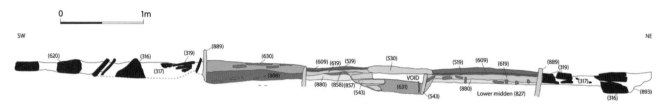

Figure 6.11 *Southeast facing section through Structure 1.*

In comparison with other examples of Neolithic architecture the entire construction of Structure 1 is of poor quality. Nowhere was this more clearly seen than in the structural arrangement of the northwest entrance which appeared to be little more than a breach through the wall. Although this area of the building was quite ruinous there were no passage facing orthostats or door 'jambs' which are a widespread feature of house architecture (see Childe 1931a, 12–14).

The construction of the outer wall, however, was more consistent with other late Neolithic buildings in having an outer and inner skin of masonry which faced a midden core. Despite the leveling of the midden, the underlying surface remained fairly uneven, and consequently in some places the outer and inner wall faces were built up from the same level (*e.g.* in the eastern area), while in others the basal course of the inner wall-face was slightly elevated.

As noted earlier, the layout of the building was asymmetrical with the northern wall curving around in a pronounced arc and the southern wall being virtually straight. There are also notable differences in construction between the two walls with the northern section being built with small stone slabs of which up to six courses survived. In contrast, the southern section was more coarsely built including, for instance, a large amorphous block of sandstone to form part of the outer wall-face. Equally, the construction of the inner wall-face was very haphazard and in many places it was nonexistent with the small orthostats being the only facing for the clay

and midden core. During the final season of excavation in 1999, when the trench was extended to the south, further stonework was discovered beyond the structure seemingly following its circumference. This consisted of a large block of stone associated with a broad arc of slumped masonry. Further west, a series of uprights and associated walling [620], situated outside the outer wall also seemed to follow a more curved course. Taken together this evidence suggests the existence of an early southern wall running on an arc from the southeast cell, which would have provided a more typical circular form to the earlier building.

Once the walls and uprights were positioned the primary grey clay floor [880] was laid down. Integral to the laying of the floor was the inclusion of a shallow stone box positioned adjacent to the left-hand (north) wall. It consisted of a large horizontal basal flagstone [645] supporting two short uprights which in turn supported an upper rectangular flagstone [642] (Figs 6.14 and 6.15). Together the flagstones sandwiched a small cavity, originally *c.*0.15m in depth, but on excavation one side was found to have collapsed.

The discovery and excavation of the stone box or cist was one of the most memorable events at Stonehall. It occurred in the early afternoon of the final day of the 1997 season which was intended to be the last examination of Structure 1. The large size of the flagstone [642] forming part of the floor had not been fully appreciated as it was virtually covered by the later clay floor [619]. Once the flagstone had been uncovered and recorded it was lifted

Figure 6.12 Broken orthostats facing the inner wall of Structure 1 (Adrian Challands).

Figure 6.13 Excavating the cell in the right-hand corner of Structure 1 (Richard Jones).

Figure 6.14 Basal slab [645] of the shallow stone box or cist set in the floor of Structure 1, two hammerstones can be seen in situ (Adrian Challands).

by Tom Muir (Fig. 6.16). After removal (and a thorough check for decoration), a glistening array of fine stone and flint objects were immediately visible lying within a fine silt [643] that had accumulated in the base of the cavity. These included a large polished quartz axe (SF 2658), a Knap of Howar grinder (SF 2657), and four fine knapping hammers (SFs 2656, 6349, 6350 and 6473) (Fig. 6.17a), together with flint knapping debris (Fig 6.17b).

Ann Clarke (see Chapter 13) comments that this group constitutes the most well-formed examples of all the cobble tools on site. She suggests that in comparison to other equivalent tools at Stonehall they had seen extensive use as hammerstones in flint knapping particularly using the bipolar technique. Once these objects had been inserted in the cavity they were sealed by the upper flagstone [642]. As no cut for the stone box was visible, it seems that it was positioned before the upper clay floors were laid down during the reconstruction of the house. On completion only a corner of the flagstone was visible as part of the upper floor surface [619]. While this undoubtedly constitutes a secondary 'foundation' deposit, it is difficult to know whether it was associated with human skeletal remains or any other organic material. Certainly no traces of

decayed bone were encountered in the small cavity but given the presence of such a gap and the fact that there was extremely poor bone survival at Stonehall this must remain a possibility.

It is also worth noting that many early Bronze Age burial cists seem to have grave goods placed either on top of the capstone or sandwiched between two capstones, as opposed to being directly associated with the burial deposits (J. Downes pers. comm.). Interestingly, in a number of cases the grave goods are coarse stone tools, particularly hammerstones and occasionally axes. Apart from the revealed flagstone covering this deposit, no stone furniture appears to have occupied this side of the building.

Figure 6.16 Tom Muir excavated the cavity beneath capstone [642] on the last day of excavation in 1997 (Colin Richards).

Figure 6.15 Stone slab [642] set in the floor of Structure 1 (lower) and after removal (upper) (Colin Richards).

When Structure 1 was uncovered there was a substantial spread of stones adjacent to the inner face of the rear (eastern) wall. Some of the stonework was clearly the collapse of the inner wall [319] and facing uprights [889]. Also, between the wall collapse and the cell were layers of flagstones and clay that probably represent a sequence of re-flooring over the primary layer of paving [856]. The area of wall collapse aroused curiosity because directly behind it was an anomalous upright apparently set within the wall core itself. Further investigation in 1997 was inconclusive; when the haphazard stonework was removed it was initially thought that a small stone-lined pit [640] was present adjacent to the orthostatic wall-facing (Fig. 6.19). Stonework appeared to have slumped into the upper fill [641] of the pit which contained a semi-decayed sheep's scapular associated with a highly decorated sherd of Grooved ware (SF 2684; Fig. 6.18). Later, however, this interpretation became less certain as the entire rear area of Structure 1 was found to be composed of a spread of closely set stonework and clay [635 and 863] overlaying

what is assumed to be the primary 'paving' [856]. While the changes occurring within Structure 1 did involve raising the floor (*e.g.* successive clay floors [880], [619] and [519], a more complex sequence is apparent in the rear area (Fig. 6.10). Here a basal spread of stonework [856] seems contemporary with the primary clay floor [880]. Over this is a succession of clay floors [863, 619 and 639], occupation [858] and flagstones [635]. Why the floor in the rear area should be made-up by stone slabs, as opposed to the clay that covers the main floor area of the structure, is difficult to explain. However, if a rear 'dresser' arrangement had once formed part of the original house architecture then stone packing necessary to support the uprights may have, after its demolition, become displaced and leveled to create a new surface.

As mentioned earlier there is ample evidence that Structure 1 was initially built with a central hearth. However, on excavation a cist with capstone was located within the centre of this building (Fig. 6.8). The stonework [543] forming the cist was set in a roughly square-shaped cut and was held in place by a deposit of yellow clay [857] (Figs 6.10, 6.11 and 6.25). If the cist stonework had been a primary element of construction, the clay floor [880] would have lapped up against it in a typical manner as seen with other primary constructional features. Instead, the primary clay floor had clearly been cut through in the construction of the cist. Once set in position, the lining stonework was held in place by a clay skin and covered by the upper clay floor [619]. The capstone of the cist had then been lowered into position and rested upon the upper clay floor. Having established the cist to be part of later

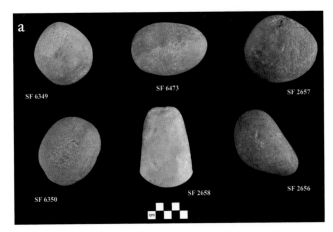

Figure 6.17 Stone tools (a) and flints (b) from beneath flagstone [642] (Michael Sharpe and Colin Richards).

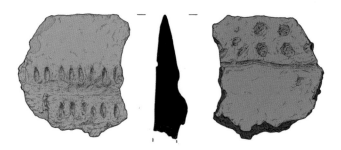

Figure 6.18 Highly decorated Grooved ware rim sherd SF 2684 from soil [641] among stonework [635 and 863].

Figure 6.19 Excavated stone-lined pit [640] (Colin Richards).

remodeling, a question arises concerning the nature of the original internal architecture of Structure 1.

It was only during the final examination of the structure in 1999, that the removal of what had previously been assumed to be a primary floor surface [619] exposed a lower clay floor [880]. This primary clay floor contained numerous fragments of charcoal trampled into its upper surface beyond the cut for the cist. Furthermore, concentric bands of ashy material [877 and 879] were clearly observable partly encircling the cist cut (Fig. 6.20). A series of magnetic susceptibility reading was taken across the lower floor surface which confirmed that burnt material was present (Fig. 6.21), and the phosphate distribution across the floor showed three anomalies close to the walls and one roughly above the cist. Significantly, the magnetic susceptibility readings showed that the burned material ran up to the central cist but was not included in its clay lining [857]. Moreover, the central cist showed no signs of having been subjected to heat. Further investigation showed that the concentric bands of ash visible in the floor surface were actually the upper

projection of two ashy occupation layers [877 and 879] sandwiched between spreads of clay flooring [876 and 878] partially encircling the central area (Figs 6.10 and 6.20). This stratigraphy represents two episodes of re-flooring, presumably around an original hearth (see Figs 6.10 and 6.11). Similar episodes of re-flooring are common around hearths, for instance, as seen at Knowes of Trotty and House 1 at Stonehall Farm and the eastern hearth in House 2 at Barnhouse (Richards 2005b, 135). From these various strands of evidence we can with some confidence assert that the ash was derived from a frequently used central hearth, measuring up to c.0.95 × 0.90m, which was subsequently dismantled and removed.

In the western area of the building a low stone upright [881] lay parallel to the original position of the removed northwest hearth stone at a distance of approx 0.80m, and bounded a thin ashy occupation deposit [858] overlying

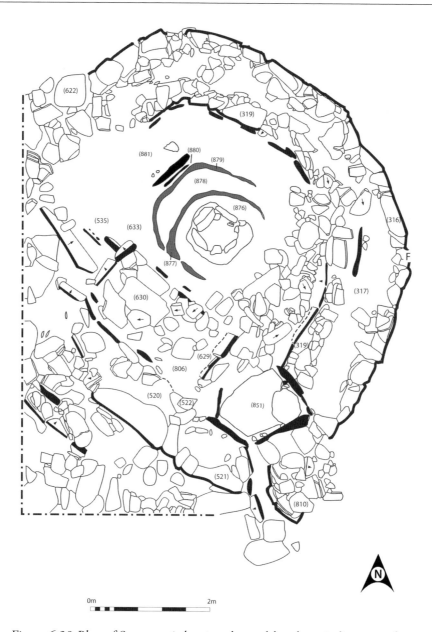

Figure 6.20 Plan of Structure 1 showing charcoal bands encircling central cist.

the final phase of re-flooring around the earlier hearth. At sometime after the build-up of occupation a 'bowl' formed by unbaked yellow clay [891] was created on the floor surface adjacent to the hearth (Figs 6.22 and 6.23). Initially, on discovering the upper circle of clay it was supposed that a clay 'oven' had been discovered of the type encountered by Childe and Grant (1939, 14–15), within House C at Rinyo, Rousay. However, the Rinyo example was composed of baked clay sitting on a flat stone slab and was of a more 'squared' shape with a small opening in one side (*ibid*, 14). On excavation, the upper clay floor [619] appeared to flow over the bowl which was sealed by

a small flagstone. Below the covering stone its contents [816] comprised large pieces of charred birch (see Chapter 15). The charcoal produced a late 4th millennium cal BC date range of *3360–3030 cal BC (GU-10317)*. Beyond the clay bowl a spread of similar clay [855] lay over the earlier floor deposits [862]. Due to inconclusive stratigraphy it is difficult to be totally certain whether the clay bowl relates to Structure 1 before or after the fireplace was replaced by a cist; on balance we would suggest the latter.

6.2.2 The later reconstruction

The substitution of the central hearth with a cist structure

Figure 6.21 Magnetic susceptibility readings taken across the lower floor surface [880] by Adrian Challands showed ash and burnt material ran up to the cut for the central cist. Readings were low (14–18 units) over the cist contents demonstrating they were not part of a hearth. In contrast, the surrounding floor area readings were moderately high (>56 units).

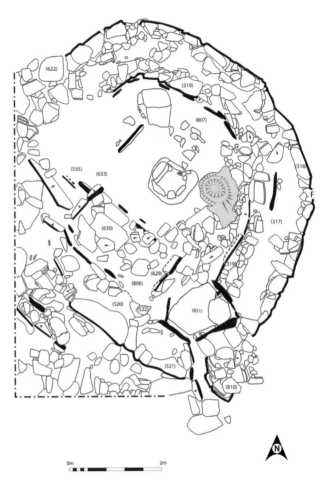

Figure 6.22 Plan of Structure 1 showing the position of the clay bowl [815].

Figure 6.23 Yellow clay bowl [815] in floor of Structure 1 (Adrian Challands).

drastically altered the character of Structure 1. Clearly this modification would have effectively ended any role as a permanent dwelling, but if the southern wall was rebuilt at this time it may suggest that the earlier 'house' was already in a ruinous condition. The reconstruction represented not merely an extraction of the fireplace but indicates that a degree of interchangeability and metaphorical linkage existed between hearth and burial cist.

The probable reconstruction of the southern wall substantially altered the right-hand side of the building and in plan it now assumed a 'D' shape. The new outer wall was poorly built as it ran inside the earlier one, cutting back from the southeast cell at a sharp angle in an almost straight line (Fig. 6.8). The wall was also thinner and the outer face [521] appeared more roughly constructed with large irregular blocks incorporated to form its

Figure 6.24 Upper deposits [542] exposed in central cist on removal of the capstone (Colin Richards).

Figure 6.25 Detail of central cist (Colin Richards).

base. Internally, an elongated 'platform' arrangement in conjunction with a large stone box was built along the straightened southwest wall. The platform was elevated and floored with flagstones [630] sitting on a thick deposit of clay and stone slabs. Its front was defined and faced by a combination of coursed masonry and small stone uprights. It was delineated at either end by orthostats projecting from the inner wall. The rearmost (west) orthostat also served as a divisional slab between the shelving and stone box arrangement. Unfortunately, this area of the structure was badly damaged but enough survived to recognise part of the box arrangement (Fig. 6.20). Both shelving and box were faced at the rear by a line of orthostats.

The most significant alteration to Structure 1 was the removal of the hearth and its replacement with a stone-covered cist. The contents of the central cist would also have been inserted at this time, and then sealed by the large capstone [530] (Fig. 6.8). The stratigraphic position of the cist and covering slab is well attested as the entire floor was resurfaced with a grey-brown silty clay [619] which ran up to the cap-stone of the central cist and effectively sealed it in position as part of the floor surface. On the removal of the capstone (Fig. 6.24), traces of highly decayed bone were found in the upper fill [542] of the small cist (more substantial amounts were recovered from the soil samples – see Chapter 15); nothing else was recovered from the silty fill. Any identification of the highly decayed bone was impossible; suffice to note its presence with the strong possibility that human skeletal material was originally present within the cist.

As mentioned above, the cist and its cover were sealed as part of the re-flooring by grey-brown clay [619] which ran across the interior of the structure. The only area apparently omitted from this flooring was adjacent to the cell in the southeast where further paving [638] was laid down. A threshold slab for the southeast cell was set in this material. The cell was subsequently re-floored by a further large flagstone [844] which effectively elevated the floor to match the level of the secondary flooring [619]. Running from the cell threshold slab, across the rear area of the structure, was a further spread of rough paving [635 and 638] laid down on a clay bedding [639].

During the later use of Structure 1, a thin layer of mottled orange-grey clay [609] was deposited as partial re-flooring over the secondary floor [619]. Above the upper clay floor, occupation material [519] accumulated unevenly across the interior. Buried within this occupation were two flint knives made of distinctive grey flint (SFs 2090–2091) deposited adjacent to a facing orthostat by the northeast wall (see Fig. 12.5). Given the close proximity of these flints it seems extremely likely that they were buried within a small bag. A large black bead (SF 2520; see Chapter 13.1), was also deposited within this layer adjacent to the southern platform which appeared to remain operational throughout the history of the structure (Fig. 6.28). As the internal floor layers of the structure accumulated, so both the paving [622] flooring the passageway into Structure 1 and the flagstones [818] flooring the southeast cell were built up to a similar level.

6.3 Structure 1 is a 'big house': a place with the living for the dead

On Mainland, Orkney, within both the late Neolithic villages of Skara Brae and Barnhouse, single structures, or big houses have been discovered which seem qualitatively different from the 'normal' dwellings. At Skara Brae, despite arguments to the contrary (Clarke 2004), Hut 7 is recognizably different for a number of reasons (see Richards 1991). The presence of a burial cist with capstone positioned beneath the right-hand 'box-bed' and wall also helps distinguish it as being qualitatively different from the other houses. The cist, measuring 1.07m long × 0.81m wide and 0.35m deep, held two contracted female skeletons (Bryce 1931, 185–86). On excavation it was found to be 'almost entirely filled with slimy midden material including innumerable limpet shells' (Childe 1931a, 141) which were assumed to have 'trickled in through the cracks in the cover-stone' (*ibid.*). This eventuality is very improbable and it seems more likely that the burials were covered in midden.

That Hut 7 was the only structure among the later houses at Skara Brae to contain a burial beneath the floor is incorrect. There is a report by Laing (1873, 76; Childe 1931a, 140) that human remains, including a lower jaw bone, were found beneath a stone 'pavement' in one of the houses (either Hut 1, 2 or 3). This is of interest for two reasons; first, it could easily have been a shallow stone-covered cist within the house floor. Second, the indication is that an entire skeleton was not present, only particular skeletal parts. This occurrence was probably mirrored in House 2 at Barnhouse (Richards 2005b, 137), where a cavity, measuring 0.86m long × 0.78m wide × 0.60m deep and covered by a shaped flagstone, was positioned adjacent to the eastern hearth. On excavation of the silt at its base, tiny fragments of disintegrating bone were present.

In this respect the central cist within Structure 1 at Stonehall Farm falls into a growing pattern of the burial of human skeletal remains within stone-covered cists inserted into floors of 'big houses' within settlements during the early 3rd millennium cal BC. In a little known paper, Marwick (1929, 20) states that at Skara Brae, after sand was washed off the masonry by rain, he clearly observed that the outer wall directly above the Hut 7 cist showed definite signs of having been rebuilt (and note Childe's (1931a, 140–41) description of the right-hand wall being of different construction). This demonstrates the Hut 7 cist to have been a later addition. While the Stonehall Farm, Structure 1 cist is also secondary, what makes it so unusual is that it replaced a hearth. To understand the significance of this occurrence it is necessary to trace the history of this building.

Because Structure 1 seemingly begins with the provision of a hearth it is tempting to assume that originally it was a normal dwelling. Although this may be the case there are several points to consider. The first concerns the quality of construction. Structure 1 was very badly built; not only was it unstable due to being erected on midden, but the masonry of the outer wall was also of poor quality. The northwest entrance was unusual in that there were no side-facing slabs. Overall, the impression is of a badly constructed building, which was destined to be structurally unsound, but of course, quality of construction does not necessarily provide an index of importance.

Judging from a recognizable cut lying beyond the east to northeast circuit of the outer wall face [521] (visible in section Fig 6.10), there seems good evidence that the upper part of the midden was partially excavated to provide a foundation hollow for Structure 1. The creation of a depression in the midden for house construction is also a feature of the later houses at Skara Brae (Childe 1931a, 10–11). However, Childe (*ibid.*), argued that the Skara Brae houses were not truly subterranean and, as at Barnhouse (Richards 2005c), the enveloping midden material built up around them during their occupation. Cutting down into the pre-existing midden may help to explain why the right-hand rear cell and lower masonry courses of Structure 1 were of such poor construction. A similar situation may have existed at Skara Brae, as Childe mentions the lower masonry to display primitive traits of 'merely piling slabs one on top of the other without breaking band for four or even five courses' (1931a, 10).

The internal stone furniture within Structure 1 at Stonehall Farm is atypical of Orcadian late Neolithic houses. Whilst a central hearth is argued to have been present during its early phase, there was no left-hand 'box-bed' or rear 'dresser' (but see above). Although, the absence of a 'dresser' is apparent in some later Neolithic house structures, for instance, House 7 at Barnhouse

Figure 6.26 Distribution of material culture within the interior of Structure 1.

Figure 6.27 The exposed early Bronze Age cairn at Mousland (Jane Downes).

BC *(GU-10317)* obtained from birch charcoal in the yellow clay bowl [815] is supported by a second date of *3360–2930 cal BC (GU-10333)* derived from birch charcoal in midden material [631] within the central cist. This context should relate to the remodelled hearth/cist, although the possibility exists that the midden material could easily derive from earlier deposits into which the cist had been cut. Overall, the construction and initial use of Structure 1 would seem to fall between 3300 and 3000 cal BC, and it is immediately obvious that this date range overlaps with the later occupation of both Stonehall Knoll and Stonehall Meadow.

The status of Structure 1 during its initial period of use is difficult to interpret. The presence of the central hearth together with the episodes of reflooring covering ash deposits is suggestive of a regime of extensive use. However, the interior architecture is atypical but that does not preclude occupation by a household. Regardless of whether Structure 1 was actually inhabited by a domestic unit during its earliest period of use, from a range of evidence we can be certain that other dwellings were occupied at this time within the settlement. This is based on the presence of the major drain [514] running from unexcavated structures to the west, which eventually links with House 1 (Trench E) and appears to also interconnect with a drain running out beneath the entrance to Structure 1. Moreover, the accumulation of surrounding midden continues throughout the life of Structure 1.

6.3.1 The fire is extinguished: the presence of the dead and the altered role of Structure 1

In contrast to the uncertainty regarding the nature of the initial occupation of Structure 1, we can have greater

(Downes and Richards 2005, 88–91), the open left-hand area is more unusual. The right-hand area comprised an elevated shelf-like arrangement with at least one stone box. Such an elevated shelf arrangement is present within the Red House at Crossiecrown (Chapter 7). Beyond the right-hand shelf and box was positioned a cell with a drain running out to the south. The position of the cell conforms to other late Neolithic house structures, for instance, the Grey and Red Houses at Crossiecrown (Chapter 7), House 3 at Barnhouse (Downes and Richards 2005) and House 9 at Skara Brae (Childe 1931a).

The material culture which can be confidently assigned to the earliest period of occupation is negligible which suggests that if Structure 1 was ever a 'normal' house then it was kept relatively clean. A highly decorated sherd of Grooved ware (SF 2684) from within stone slabs constituting the floor at the rear of the building may relate to the earliest use (Fig. 6.18). The late 4th millennium cal BC radiocarbon date of *3360–3030 cal* confidence that the removal of the central hearth and its replacement by a stone cist effectively ceases human occupation. As mentioned above, the secondary insertion of cists with capstones in particular later Neolithic buildings is part of a wider phenomenon in the creation of 'big houses'. However, the actual substitution of a hearth with a cist within a building is currently unique to Stonehall Farm. This act is very illuminating in terms of understanding the conceptual and physical significance of the hearth or fireplace at the centre of the house, and people's lives and their identity.

The inter-relationship between the architecture of the house and round burial cairns of the late 3rd and early 2nd millennium cal BC has been noted elsewhere (*e.g.* Downes 1994). Essentially, the square stone construction of the cist replicates that of a hearth in occupying a central position within a clayed surface which is bounded by a circular outer wall (see also discussion in Chapter 3). The imagery of the round burial cairn is strikingly similar to the house and the square cist unmistakably references the hearth (Fig. 6.27). While cists as cremation containers draw on similar principles of spatial order and transformation by fire, the apparent interchangeability of hearth and cist in Structure 1 introduces a further dimension of homology which places the dead at the 'centre' or heart of the house.

The primary significance of the hearth in Orcadian Neolithic dwellings has been stated many times (*e.g.* Clarke and Sharples 1990, 70; Richards 1990; Parker Pearson and Richards 1994). In being a primary element of house construction (Downes and Richards 2005, 60), the hearth was a dominant feature with enormous metaphorical potential. Its centrality within the house and to the maintenance of life easily translates into a mnemonic index of the house occupants. That fireplaces became synonymous with continuity, descent and especially the founders of the house is clearly witnessed at Barnhouse. Here, certain hearth stones were actually excavated, removed, and re-used in later dwellings within an active strategy involving claimed continuity and reconstitution of social identities (*ibid.*, 125–26; S. Jones and Richards 2005; Hill and Richards 2005, 162–64). The absence of hearths within chambered cairns also confirms a relationship between fire, hearths, warmth, sustenance and life. How then may we best understand the substitution seen within Structure 1?

The circular form of the late Neolithic house emphasises its centre, just as its spatial order embodies principles of concentricity and centrality that provided cosmological referents for understanding the late Neolithic Orcadian world (Richards 1996b; Bradley 1998, 116–24; Garrow *et*

al. 2005). In this scheme the hearth is central and can be seen as a form of *axis mundi* where different realms conjoin (Richards 1990; 1996b). For instance, Garnham (2004, 158–59) follows Eliade's (1959) tripartite scheme of an *axis mundi* being a point of conjunction linking different cosmological realms. Hence, the fireplace in its central position may have been understood as a form of conduit linking past, present and future generations.

The rebuilding of houses upon the site of previous houses is a feature of many late Neolithic settlements. As opposed to natural decay, this structural cycle of construction, demolition and reconstruction has been suggested to relate to rules surrounding social and physical position within the village, and perhaps being instigated by the death of one of the inhabitants (Richards 1991; Downes and Richards 2005, 126). Other circumstances involving an inauspicious event could invoke the abandonment or even demolition of a standing building and the burial of a deceased inhabitant. The central cist within Structure 1 was relatively small in measuring 0.58m long, 0.56m wide and 0.20m deep. Although the silt-filled cavity [542] between capstone and basal 'midden' infill [631] contained decayed bone, it was also very shallow in attaining a depth of only *c.*0.08m deep (see Fig. 6.25). Obviously, these proportions prohibit the burial of an entire corpse; instead, we may envisage the deposition of specific body parts or even a material representation of the deceased.

An alternative view of the conditions under which Structure 1 is transformed is not one of abandonment, possibly under inauspicious circumstances. On the contrary, the positioning of a receptacle for human remains centrally within a pre-existing building may constitute the 'safe' presencing of the dead within the domain of the living. In assuming this position the dead are both present and accessible to the inhabitants of Stonehall Farm, yet safely controlled and contained within a re-modeled building and beneath a substantial capstone. The unusual employment of small stone uprights facing the inner wall-face may also be another mechanism of containing or wrapping the dead. In housing ancestral remains at its centre it should also be remembered that Structure 1 also assumes a central 'ancestral' position within the small village, being a 'big house' it is both emblematic and a materialization of a *société à maisons*. This is a crucial identification which will be returned to below.

Apart from the insertion of the central cist another feature of Structure 1 is the presence of fine artefacts deposited within its confines (*e.g.* Fig. 6.28). From its

0   5cm

Figure 6.28 Black stone bead (SF 2520) from occupation layer [519] (Hugo Anderson-Whymark).

reconstruction a series of 'special' deposits had been buried within the floor of Structure 1. For example, the flagstone-covered stone box containing stone artefacts, including a beautiful quartz axe SF 2658 (Fig. 6.17b), two 'Stonehall Farm type' scrapers, a cortex-backed knife and 14 flakes and chips, seems to be part of the reconstruction of Structure 1 (see Chapter 12). Two fine flint knives (SFs 2090 and 2091) flaked from grey-coloured raw material were buried together (Fig. 12.5, Illus. 54 and 58), probably in a small pouch or bag, at a time after the cist replaced the central hearth, as was the large black stone bead SF 2520 (Figs 6.28 and 13.10). Taken together this collection is the finest array of artefacts recovered from Stonehall. Interestingly, similar deposits, including a fine polished stone chisel, were buried in the floor of House 2 at Barnhouse which also contained a burial cist (Richards 2005b, 140). More recently, a number of fine objects have been recovered from floor layers within the structures at the Ness of Brodgar (Card 2010). Further discussion of heirlooms (see Joyce 2000) and the role of 'big houses' (cf. Bradley 2005, 74–75) in the context of developing *sociétés à maisons* will be undertaken in Chapter 9.

6.4 The surrounding dwellings: House 1 at Stonehall Farm

There were several contemporary dwellings surrounding Structure 1 at Stonehall Farm, but only one (House 1) was investigated by excavation. The damaged and displaced walling of another structure situated to the west of Structure 1 was visible in the far side of the adjacent field drain. House 1 was uncovered in an extension trench (Trench E) positioned to the east of

Trench B (Fig 6.33). The extension was opened to further explore the settlement mound and attempt to trace the extent of the midden deposits over a wider distance. In particular, Trench E was also positioned to trace the main drain [514] as it ran to the east (Figs 6.5 and 6.29). Moreover, we considered it vital to identify further structural evidence, both to provide a comparison for Structure 1 and to gain a broader picture of house architecture at Stonehall Farm during the later period of its occupation. Initially an exploratory trench *c.*2 × 12m was excavated directly east of Trench B, which was subsequently extended several times after stonework and areas of yellow clay flooring were discovered. The majority of structural remains clearly belonged to a single building (House 1), but in the northern area of the extended trench, a curving spread of distinctive red midden [2020] and associated stretch of walling [2061] provided indication that a second dwelling lay in close proximity to the north.

House 1 was built on midden material [2015], which was mainly unexcavated, and consequently constructed late in the occupational sequence of Stonehall (Fig. 6.30). A radiocarbon date of *3090–2880 cal BC (GU-12878)* was obtained from a grain of naked barley from the upper midden [2015] in the northeast corner of Trench E.

House 1 was uncovered directly below a spread of burnt deposits [2002]. A fairly discrete area of the northern interior of the house, including the hearth, was covered by a spread of rubble embedded in a mixed matrix of grey clay and dark-brown loamy soil [2021 and 2029]. While relating to a make-up layer associated with the later burning activities, this rubble and clay effectively capped the hearth in a very discrete and particular manner and would appear to relate to a formal sealing of the hearth as part of the house closure.

Although severely truncated, the form of the internal features partially resembled other houses of the mid-3rd millennium cal BC, particularly those present in the final phases of occupation at Skara Brae (Childe 1931a). Where visible, the denuded remains of the wall of House 1, in conjunction with the shape of the clay floor and the internal architecture, demonstrate a sub-circular house with a roughly central hearth (Fig. 6.33). However, the most unusual characteristic of this house was the presence of two doorways through the outer wall. The main doorway leads into the western area of the house while a secondary doorway penetrates the northeast section of the outer wall. Due to the truncated condition of this building the exact status of the secondary doorway is difficult to establish. Initially, it was considered to be a possible entrance to a

6.29 Plan of Stonehall Farm Trenches B and E.

Figure 6.31 Detail of the hearth and surrounding yellow clay floor within House 1 (Siân Jones).

Figure 6.30 View of House 1 at Stonehall Farm (Colin Richards).

Figure 6.32 Excavating the main doorway into House 1 (Siân Jones).

cell (very similar to that present in Hut 1 at Skara Brae). However, an uneven line of paving [2018] runs out from the threshold upright appearing to follow a route beyond the considered circuit of the outer wall.

The main doorway in the western wall of House 1 was approached by an external pathway of slabs [2055] that ran up to the threshold stone, which was aligned with the outer wall face. The flagstones forming the path also served to cover the main drain [514] encountered running across Trench B (see Figs 6.5 and 6. 29). The entrance passage ran through the thickness of the wall and was paved with flagstones [2043] (Fig. 6.32). The second doorway leading out to the north was also defined by a threshold stone [2044], and as noted above, if the interpretation of the position of the circuit of the outer wall face is correct, then the line of external paving [2018] would run around its outer perimeter as opposed to being a cell encased in that wall. However, in contrast to the western entrance, the position of the threshold upright of the northern door does appear to have been set in line with the inner wall face.

Unfortunately, the walls of the house were mainly absent but short sections around the circuit, in the west and northeast, had survived to provide some guide to their original route and construction technique. As frequently seems to be the case with late Neolithic buildings, the structural elements of the house that are hidden tend to be poorly and inconsistently constructed. This is certainly the case with wall cores where a single dwelling may have a range of different materials used to fill the gap between the inner and outer wall faces, such as clay, different midden, soils, *etc.* This diversity is present within the outer wall of House 1. For instance, the best areas of preservation were either side of the western doorway and here the wall was *c.*1.10m thick and typically constructed with a yellow-grey clay and midden core [2035] bonding the inner and outer stone wall faces. Although less clear, a similar layout seems to have existed in the northeast of the house where

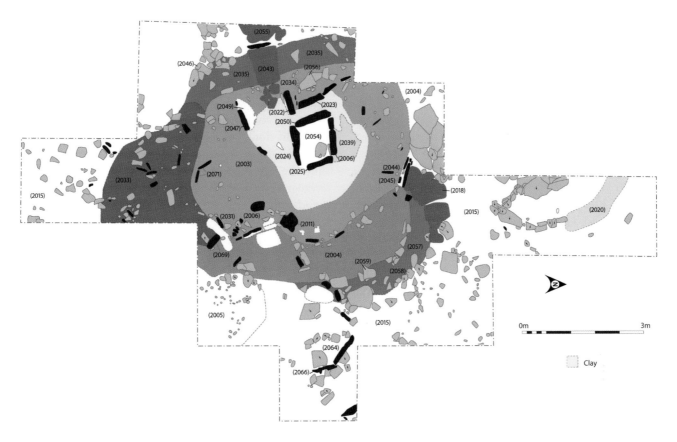

Figure 6.33 Plan of House 1.

a semi-circle of masonry was present. Here, the wall core was composed of grey clay mixed with brown loam. Two lines of collapsed stones seemed to represent the inner and outer masonry skins. The southern and eastern walls were far more problematic in terms of interpretation. A wide, linear whitish-grey clay and rubble spread [2033] was identified on the southern side of the house. Whilst this clay-rubble feature did appear to join up with the clay wall core on the southwest of the house, further examination did not reveal masonry faces. The white-grey clay and rubble [2033] can be interpreted either as spread of wall core material resulting from the collapse and robbing of the house wall or the remains of a foundation platform originally laid to support the outer wall.

At the rear of the house a series of orthostats present in the southeast appear to have been directly associated with the architecture of House 1 rather than another structure. However, one of these orthostats [2062] laterally cuts the remains of the northeast section of the house wall. The presence of a patch of clay [2067] of a similar colour and consistency to the house floor adjacent to orthostat [2062] also suggests that the area to the east, enclosed

by orthostats [2064] and [2066], was contiguous with the house. Comparison with the Skara Brae houses (especially Hut 1) indicates that these orthostats may be the severely disturbed facing uprights lining a cell in the eastern wall at the back of the house. If this is the case, the clay-rubble matrix [2033] is the damaged remains, or foundation layer, of the southern wall which thickened rapidly towards the east in order to accommodate the possible cell in the eastern wall (*i.e.* the rear) of the house.

6.4.1 House 1 Interior

As seen in the construction of houses at Barnhouse and elsewhere, the clay floor of House 1 was also laid after the internal stone furniture had been positioned. Here, however, the clay floor was restricted to the central area around the hearth (Fig. 6.31). The primary floor surface was formed of a spread of bright yellow clay, but to the north (left-hand side) and east (rear of the house), the clay became quite patchy being inter-mixed with occupation material [2003]. To the south (right-hand side) relatively sharp edges to the clay floor respected the position of the original stone furniture. Around the hearth, a thin primary ashy occupation deposit [2040], *c.*2cm, covered the clay floor.

A characteristic square hearth formed by four stone uprights was situated broadly in the centre of the floor (Fig. 6.34). The fill of the hearth was interesting in that it had two distinct layers of ash. A lower orange-red ash [2054], presumably relating to an earlier period of occupation, was separated by a thin, *c.*0.5cm, layer of yellow clay from a black upper deposit [2051] representing the ash from the final fire in the house (Fig. 6.35). A radiocarbon date of *3350–2620 cal BC (GU-12879)* was obtained from a cereal grain from ash layer [2051].

As seen within the majority of later phase houses at Skara Brae (Childe 1931a), directly to the left on entering House 1 were the remains of a rectangular box arrangement (Fig. 6.36). Three snapped upright stones were all that remained of the box (Fig. 6.36). This structure protruded into the house almost up against the western edge of the central hearth and would have effectively prohibited movement into the left-hand side of the house on entry. This is consistent with the layout of numerous late

Neolithic houses where the entrance is off-centered to the right of the hearth, thereby facilitating internal movement in an anti-clockwise direction around the hearth (Richards 1990; 2005b, 145–47). It also allowed light to filter into the right-hand side of the building (Richards 2005, 145–47; A. M. Jones 2012).

In the majority of later phase houses at Skara Brae, the right stone box 'beds' adjacent to the right-hand wall consistently seem part of a longer configuration running into the right-hand lower corner of the house. The same arrangement appears to have been present along the right-hand wall of House 1. This furniture is represented by several broken *in situ* uprights and packed slots projecting out from the wall, while the frontal position of the boxes is defined by the southern edge of the primary clay floor. For example, broken upright [2047] aligns with two further slots [2011] and [2013], to mark the position of the frontal divisional uprights, although slot [2013] may also be part of a stone 'box' arrangement at the rear of the house. A small 'D'-shaped box [2048] measuring 0.6 × 0.4m was set in the floor immediately to the right of the western entrance, adjacent to orthostat [2047]. The box contained a loose brown loamy fill [2049] but no artefacts were recovered.

On the left-hand side (north) of the house the main spread of the yellow clay floor seems to stop short of the suspected position of the inner wall face but there is no corresponding evidence for large stone boxes. Of course, this is the position of the second doorway and no furniture may have existed to obstruct its passage. Identification of the furniture present at the rear of the house is problematic. The stone packing [2013], already alluded to above, could relate to cut [2017] which had held a substantial orthostat, and together they form either a rear 'dresser' or stone box. Either of these options is a possibility because within Structure 8 at Barnhouse a stone 'dresser' was replaced by a stone box (Hill and Richards 2005).

Figure 6.34 Excavating the central hearth in House 1 (Siân Jones).

Figure 6.35 Section (west-facing) through House 1.

6.4.2 Secondary remodelling of Stonehall House 1

Because of the denuded condition of House 1 any structural modification incurred throughout the duration of occupation was indeterminable. Nonetheless, on the north (left-hand) side of the hearth a localised secondary yellow clay floor [2028] had been laid down over the ashy occupation deposit [2040]. That this area should be selected for re-flooring is of particular interest; initially it was considered to be some form of repair to the underlying clay floor (2003), but on excavation it became clear that the latter was in good condition beneath (Fig. 6.37). This suggests that the upper layer of clay had been deliberately deposited for other purposes. This apparent discontinuity was mirrored in the history of the central hearth where a thin, *c*.0.5cm, band of yellow clay [2053] divided the distinctive lower orange-red ash [2054] from a black ashy upper deposit [2051].

6.5 Living middens and flowing assemblages: the nature of midden at Stonehall Farm

One of the most exciting, frustrating and complicated excavation experiences of the project was the investigation of the middens at Stonehall Farm and Crossiecrown (Chapter 7). As the trowel cut through the soil, pottery sherds, stone and flint objects were occasionally revealed amidst soft bright red ash and thin charcoal-rich lenses. At other times brown, thick, homogeneous, organic midden was encountered, occasionally being wonderfully rich in material things. Indeed, the vast majority of material culture was derived from external midden contexts (Figs 6.38 and 11.2.8). Yet, attempting the stratigraphic unravelling of an Orcadian Neolithic midden through excavation is notoriously difficult and frustrating. For example, a layer within the midden that is being carefully unearthed and followed can suddenly appear to defy

stratigraphic logic and split into multiple lenses or simply disappear. John Hunter captures extremely well the difficulties and frustration of excavating a substantial Neolithic midden at Pool, Sandy:

Figure 6.36 The snapped stone uprights forming the rectangular box to the left of the entrance into House 1 (Siân Jones).

Figure 6.37 Successive layers of yellow clay flooring surrounded the central hearth (Colin Richards).

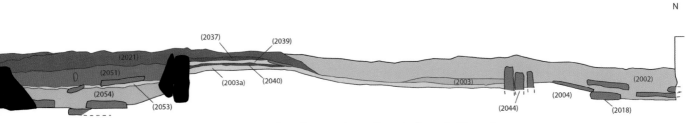

Figure 6.35 Section (west-facing) through House 1.

A major problem was encountered in the excavation of the Neolithic deposits, partly because of the number of layers, their narrowness and varied angle of deposition, but mostly as a result of their merged boundaries which made resolution virtually impossible. After much experimentation and test sectioning it was concluded that although major changes in the depositional sequence could be identified and excavated, the majority of the smaller individual lenses were inseparable in any practical sense. In effect the mound consisted of a vast series of interfaces presumably brought about by a relatively rapid rate of deposition in certain places and by a degree of merging when the sandy surfaces were originally exposed. For much of the mound single-context recording was not possible and other alternatives were considered.

(Hunter *et al.* 2007, 23).

It is instructive that the 'Wheeler' box method of excavation was employed at Pool in an attempt to tackle and understand the complexities of the deep midden deposits. Even then, attempting to excavate stratigraphically and negotiate dozens of dipping lenses running beneath thicker ash deposits was both time consuming and represented an impossibly demanding excavation experience (N. Card pers. comm.).

Similar frustrations were evident in attempting stratigraphic excavation at both Stonehall Farm and Crossiecrown (Chapter 7). The demanding task of digging the Stonehall Farm and Crossiecrown middens was evident in the blurred clarity of what was being excavated, as opposed to the virtual impossibility of unravelling it into discreet episodes of deposition or recording it in terms of individual events (cf. Hunter *et al.* 2007, 23–28).

At Stonehall Farm the midden constituting the settlement mound is extremely diverse, truly a meshwork of merging things and substances. The midden was clearly composed of discrete assemblages that fuse through a consistent but episodic process in the past of discarding materials and substances. This resulted in the interleaving of thick layers composed of what appeared homogeneous material juxtaposed with ephemeral and discontinuous tips and lenses (Fig. 6.39). Often, the layers incorporated identifiable objects such as Grooved ware sherds, flint and stone flakes and tools, however, the texture of soil and continuously changing colouration at the micro-scale constantly invoked a sense of loss, specifically the absence of organic remains which had literally dissolved in the acidic soils.

The midden to the east of Structure 1 was extensively examined and was carefully excavated in spits when the stratigraphy was too ephemeral and inconsistent

to follow. Contexts were assigned to layers as revealed and finds provenanced accordingly, although a generic context number was given to undifferentiated upper [800] and lower [809] midden layers. It was clear that large heaps of ash and organic waste, including faunal material, were present below and around Structure 1. Of this material, it was only to the east of Structure 1 that the midden was excavated down to the natural glacial till. The stratigraphy showed tip lines of material slipping down the sloping sides of pre-established mounds of midden as successive deposits of ash was sequentially dumped (Fig. 6.40). This had the effect of smoothing the topography of the established midden heaps (see Fig 6.41).

In the far eastern area of the trench (centrally positioned within the overall settlement mound) the lower midden was composed of a deep, homogeneous dark brown silty deposit [873] which as it was excavated was seen to contain numerous thin ashy lenses of variable thickness ranging from *c*.0.2–0.6cm. In reaching a compressed height of *c*.1.20m deep in places, this 'layer' represented material dumped onto the natural till and its accumulation over a considerable period of time. A radiocarbon date of *3310–2900 cal BC (GU-10322)* was obtained from birch charcoal in a sample *c*.0.20m above the natural till. Given the compaction of this midden over the last five thousand years it must have been considerably higher during the life of the village. To the southwest, the early midden was slightly different in composition containing more burnt bone and stone [874]. In the north–south and east–west sections of the eastern area of Trench B (Fig. 6.42), the profile of this large deposit of midden was extremely clear and could be seen to comprise two mounds. As the midden ran to the west, thicker layers of discernibly different ashy deposits were present reinforcing the view that the lower midden [873 and 874] was actually created through large numbers of depositional episodes; for instance, layers [896], [897] and [898] all seem to be thick dumps of different coloured ash within the main midden [873] (Figs 6.39 and 6.41).

To the northeast, further grey-brown ash [869] was piled over the northern summit of the lower midden [873] and flowed down to the southwest where it began to fill a hollow formed between two large rubbish heaps. Subsequent deposits of red-brown ash with decayed bone [868], black charcoal-rich ash [867], yellow-brown ashy silt [866] and red-brown ash [864] completely filled the hollow and higher mounds of ash and refuse began to emerge (Fig. 6.42). A radiocarbon date of *2880–2620 cal*

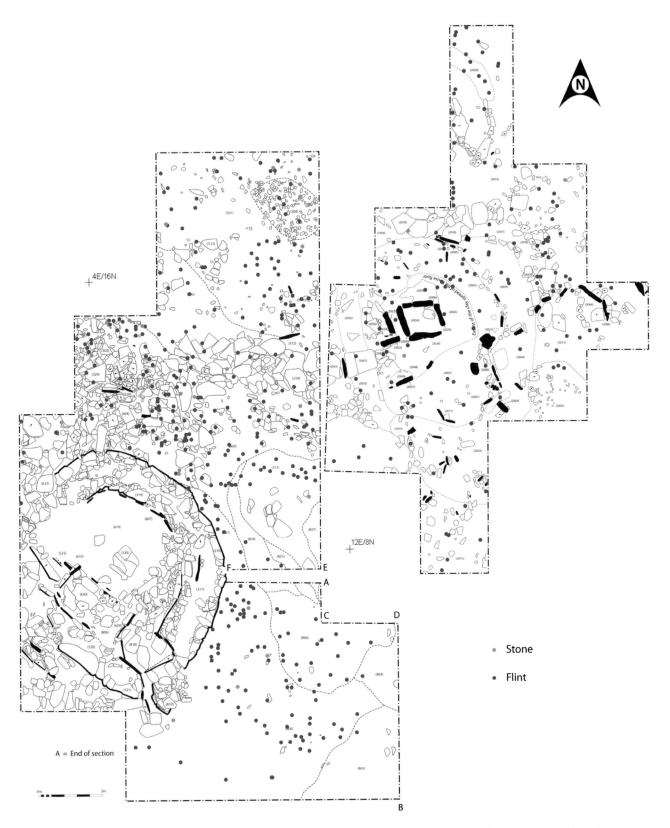

Figure 6.38 Distribution of worked stone and flint at Stonehall Farm (see Fig. 11.2.8 for the ceramic distribution).

Figure 6.39 Cleaning a colourful section of midden (section D–B) east of Structure 1 in Trench B at Stonehall Farm (Colin Richards).

BC *(GU-12876)* was obtained from a barley grain from the interface between layers [868] and [869].

The higher slopes of the various layers of ash running down from the larger midden heaps seen in the eastern sections (Fig. 6.42) are captured in the east–west section running up to the east wall of Structure 1 (Fig. 6.42). Here a series of thin layers, sloping down to the east and north, reveal the sequence of later material dumped on the pre-existing midden heaps [873]. The vital aspect of this section is that it clearly shows that the upper midden deposits were partially cut through to construct Structure 1 (see Fig. 6.42). Unfortunately, the exact level at which the midden is cut for Structure 1 was obscured through the cutting of a recent field drain [892]. The level at which Structure 1 is constructed is, however, visible and seems to be roughly at the top of the intermediate midden heaps [827]. It would seem that this probably provided a more compact surface for the erection of this unusual building.

The midden was also examined to the south of Trench B in a small 6m × 3m trench (Trench F – Fig. 5.3). Here, similar deposits were encountered to those present in the southern section of Trench B. The upper red ash [2050] ran across the entire trench, below which a spread of paving, represented by large flagstones covered the western area. The paving appeared sandwiched in the same midden material as no difference was observed between the upper and lower ash deposits which continued below the flagstones. Excavation was halted at a depth of *c*.0.3m, and the midden continued downwards. Apart from the paving, no structural evidence was present, however, a fine polished stone axe (SF 6410) was recovered from the lower midden deposit.

In assessing the midden deposits at Stonehall Farm we see clear differentiation in the matter being deposited, as identified in the contrasting large, highly-stratified eastern ash heaps (Fig. 6.40), and the heavy bone component of layer [505] adjacent to the pathway running up to House 1. Different depositional practices are afforded spatial definition as seen in the large spread of ash around the mounds of burnt stone [509, 523, 524 and 525], in the north and northeast of the trench. In contrast, the large ash heaps in the southeast seem to represent the accumulation of residues from (possibly different) hearths over a long period of time. As noted earlier, several midden layers, (*e.g.* [505] and [866]) contained large amounts of decayed animal bone as revealed by their yellow-brown 'dusty' appearance. Such a distinction shows clearly that segregation in the deposition of different material on and in the midden was occurring at Stonehall Farm. But was this segregation strategic, and were the processes of decay and the transformation of matter being managed within the actual structuring or stratigraphy of the midden?

Orcadian Neolithic middens are frequently referred to as if they are unitary entities (*e.g.* Clarke and Sharples 1990, 58–59). However, as is demonstrated at Stonehall Farm, in terms of composition and constitution, the midden was extremely heterogeneous. Equally, at Crossiecrown an identical midden structure was uncovered in Trench 1 (see Chapter 7). At Skara Brae, Childe (1931a, 24–28) stressed the variability of deposits labelled 'midden' drawing out a range of characteristics. Initially, an interesting sub-division is observed between a midden exhibiting 'the tenacity of a very tough clay' and a softer red-coloured midden which 'includes in varying proportions peat ash, dung, broken animal bones and shells, and sherds and other artifacts' (Childe 1931a, 24–25). Interestingly, these two middens are identified as maintaining a degree of spatial integrity with the former 'tough' material assuming a peripheral position around the village. The softer red-coloured midden was also recognised as heterogeneous; 'some layers are relatively rich in artifacts as well as food refuse and ash; in others, relics are sparse though broken bones and shells are plentiful; finally we encounter very red deposits, absolutely sterile of artifacts and containing few shells and fewer animal bones' notes Childe (1931a, 25).

Hence, late Neolithic middens could be understood in terms of both *bricolage* and processes of material transmutation, where a midden becomes an 'assemblage' comprising a palimpsest of different assemblages (see Bennett 2005). But clearly the edges blur, just as do

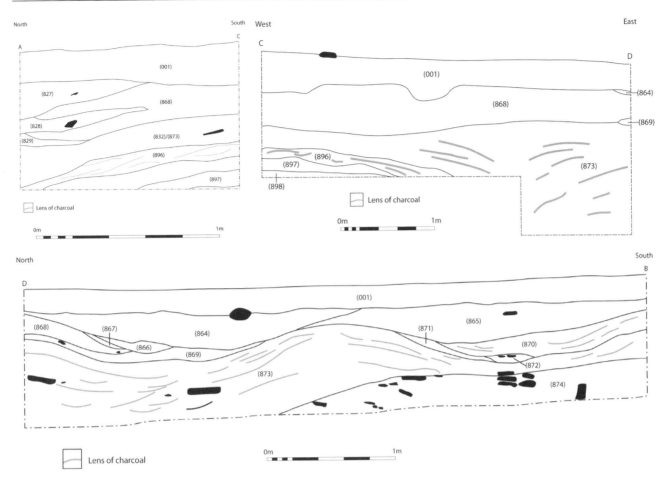

Figure 6.40 Sections through the Stonehall Farm midden east of Structure 1.

Figure 6.41 The conical profile of the midden heap can be clearly seen in the stratigraphy of the upper eastern section east of Structure 1.

East   West

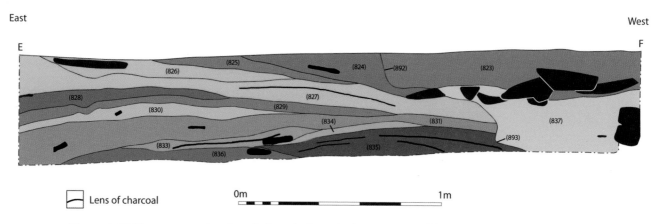

⌐ Lens of charcoal   0m   1m

Figure 6.42 East–west section (north facing) through the eastern midden running up to Structure 1.

the layers and lenses (cf. Hunter *et al.* 2007, 23). The emergence of the 'midden' is therefore dependant on consistent depositional practices and heterogeneity of substances. Such practices are clearly evident at Stonehall Farm where sequential deposition provides considerable structure to the midden, indeed, a sandwiching of deposits was clearly present in the upper midden (see Fig. 6.41). However, this assemblage could be said to become fused and rematerialised in both the processes of decay that alters its material state and the deployment of midden in other assemblages (*e.g.* wall core material and manure).

Undoubtedly middens are interesting entities. They accumulate as a consequence of things and substances becoming use-less, for instance, ash from burning turf (transforming) or sherds from a damaged pottery vessel (fracturing and fragmenting). These altered things are then redeposited, where they transmute and merge together on the midden heap. Hence, the composition of the midden is necessarily heterogeneous, a conglomeration of dislocated things, and yet homogeneous as a 'living' growing entity. In this respect middens are to a degree unintended 'assemblages' (cf. Bennett 2005), gathering things and substances together that were never necessarily projected by people to become associated. Indeed, a midden really 'is a curious substance' (Childe 1931a, 24), which could easily be understood and characterised as an interesting form of meshwork (*pace* Ingold 2011; Knappet 2011) where materials become not only entangled (cf. Hodder 2012) but actually transmute and physically merge together. As will become evident in the discussion below, the fluidity and instability of some of these things (see also Thomas 2013, 233), through the physical processes of decay, and the attrition and disturbance that they undergo, inevitably gives rise to new or altered forms of materiality. As Pollard (2004,

48) muses, this regime of transformation has tended to have negative connotations within archaeological discourse. However accepting that such affordances are unpredictable and ambiguous, the midden can be more positively portrayed as a 'living' thing capable of transforming itself; affecting an alternative physical resource of matter that can potentially be redeployed and function in new and multiple ways. Physical changes to the 'fabric' of a midden may occur through processes of decay; but as DeSilvey suggests 'decay reveals itself not (only) as erasure but as a process that can be generative of a different kind of knowledge' (2006, 323). If this is the case then how does this idea of a midden as 'living' matter with generative capacity affect the ontological status of 'rubbish' in the Orcadian Neolithic?

Before this is explored further there is another curious feature of decay as a process of the midden. Incorporation and accumulation, as a function of a midden, necessarily involves material dislocation (Pollard 2005). Now, whilst it is possible that such disarticulation from previous contexts 'may lead to other histories and other geographies' (DeSilvey 2006, 324), this will not be a uniform or general procedure. Undoubtedly, some things and substances will quickly abandon their physical constitution within the midden and effectively dissolve; other constituents are more robust and will remain in an identifiable form. For instance, a broken flint scraper or sherd of decorated pottery may be clearly visible in the rotting midden heap. Hence, amongst the midden certain things retain physical integrity whilst others dissolve and transmute into different matter that may bear little resemblance to deposited forms. This introduces an interesting divergence in the potential of middens as mnemonic devices because it will only be certain objects that maintain a recognisable form that can relate to particular events, times and places (cf. Pollard 2005, 110). Consequently, the 'curation' status of the midden as a place where materials associated with past events are merely stored is both inconsistent and partial.

When the settlement at Links of Noltland, Westray, was initially excavated, a substantial amount of domestic refuse was found in the Neolithic ploughsoil uncovered adjacent to the area of habitation. The presence of this material caused the excavators to suggest that 'one of the important functions of the community's midden was as a fertiliser on the fields' (Clarke and Sharples 1990, 73). More recently, this interpretation of midden being incorporated in Neolithic cultivated soils has been supported by micromorphological analysis (McKenna and Simpson 2011, 79). Prior to this, a combination of good preservation and keen interest in soil composition produced some extremely interesting results from the excavation project at the 3rd millennium cal BC settlement at Tofts Ness, Sanday (Dockrill *et al.* 2007). In seeing the site as marginal, clearly the management strategies of food production and soil productivity 'underpinned the viability for the economic survival of the site' (*ibid.*, 15). Here too, midden material was found to have been applied to an infield system, beyond the immediate settlement (*ibid.*, 34–39). Further evidence of midden-enhanced soils was also recovered from small-scale sampling of another Neolithic site at Bay of Stove, Sanday (Bond *et al.* 1995).

However, not only was midden found to have been employed to amend and enrich the infield soils at Tofts Ness, but 'Late Neolithic midden material… which extended beyond the area of immediate settlement, was also found to have been cultivated by ard' (*ibid.*, 17). The cultivation of midden material itself was not restricted to Bay of Stove, Links of Noltland or Tofts Ness. At the well-preserved 4th millennium cal BC settlement of Knap of Howar, Papa Westray, a large area of midden, nearly half a metre in thickness, was traced 20m south of the stone houses (Ritchie 1983). Anna Ritchie (1995, 23) considered that the midden was almost certainly spread across a wide area to enable its employment as bedding for cultivation.

Emerging from these observations is an appreciation of the practical generative capacity of the Orcadian Neolithic middens. The linkage between decayed and transformed matter, food production, and social reproduction is starkly revealed in the direct cultivation of midden. This symbiotic relationship is clearly multifaceted and incorporates a range of diverse elements that can be best understood as 'efficacious material configurations' (Bennett 2010, ix). Efficacy of midden assemblages not

only emerges in future uses, but crucially in its 'flowing' generative and transformatory qualities. This effect has been interpreted in another context as merely forming a fertility storage facility which becomes an important mechanism in the negotiation of status (Parker Pearson and Sharples 1999, 348). Ironically, in these terms the putrefaction and decay of substances translates not only into a fertility storage facility but a conspicuous medium of wealth (Thomas 2013, 233).

Perhaps one of the most interesting features of the late Neolithic middens is their apparently 'structural' character. At both Stonehall Farm and Crossiecrown (Chapter 7), the midden material provided the fabric of the settlement mounds, giving them an almost tell-like quality. Indeed, the deployment of midden material in such a structural capacity is a feature of a number of 3rd millennium cal BC settlements (*e.g.* Tofts Ness, Pool, Bay of Stove). Perhaps the most famous example of this phenomenon is Skara Brae, Mainland. Here, the all-encompassing nature of the midden allowed Childe to draw an analogy between the village and the human body where 'the so called midden stands to the huts and passages in the same relation as the flesh to the organs and veins of a living body' (1931a, 24). Such characterization enables a picture to be painted of people effectively living within a domed midden where the roofs protruded 'like pimples to break the smooth curve of the rubbish heaps outline' (*ibid.*, 28).

However, midden does not just constitute the fabric of the settlement mound. With the advent of stone being employed in the construction of houses during the late 4th and 3rd millennium cal BC comes the use of midden as wall-core material. For example, Anna Ritchie describes how at Knap of Howar, Papa Westray, 'cleared midden was used as wall-core to create a solid and weatherproof structure' (1983, 48). At Stonehall Farm, midden is certainly employed in the wall-core of House 1, moreover, Structure 1 is actually cut into the upper midden. A similar occurrence may have occurred at Skara Brae. In examining Hut 7, Childe ponders that 'since the base of this hut's casing wall lies four feet above the floor, it is not impossible that the foundations of this hut… were actually dug down… into a pre-existing rubbish heap upon the surface of which a casing wall would have been erected' (1931a, 10–11).

In the later Neolithic house, the practice of employing midden as wall core becomes exaggerated to almost monumental proportions. Here, the outer wall is effectively expanded to incorporate 'jackets' of midden contained by stone casing walls. Again, Childe details the presence of casing walls enclosing midden at Skara Brae, 'in most cases, indeed, when the hut was not directly backed up against another, it was surrounded by a regular platform of such material [midden], six or more feet wide, supported by a retaining wall of modest height' (1931a, 9).

Wrapping the house in midden also encourages an enhanced 'onion skin' form of construction as well as overall magnitude (see the later changes to the Red House in the following chapter). For example, Dockrill *et al.* (2007, 19–20) describe the outer walls of Structure 1 at Tofts Ness as having such an onion-skin construction. The presence of casing walls wrapping houses in the late Neolithic settlement of Pool prompts John Hunter to muse on their role. Similarities are noted between the onion-skin masonry of chambered cairns and houses, where it is accepted that such devices are not structural but 'may have been intentionally cosmetic in order to emphasise status, or draw attention to wealth by sheer size' (2007, 66). Here, the 'cumulative monumentality' (cf. Hedges 1983, 208) of late Neolithic houses can be re-phrased as accumulative monumentality, because as is argued here, wrapping the house in midden is a generative element of construction (Richards 2013a; 2013b). Significantly, when late Neolithic Orcadian houses are excavated large quantities of material culture are frequently recovered from their wall cores. Returning to Pool, Sanday, the description of Structure 8 is illustrative of this occurrence:

> Structure 8 was also circumscribed in whole or part, by a series of casing faces giving a wall thickness of up to 3m with the infills between successive skins containing assemblages of pottery sherds, flints and worked stone... Constructionally, these casing walls and their cores were stratigraphically of a single phase (unlike those at Skara Brae according to Childe); they have to be seen as being integral to an original design; and the assemblages have to be interpreted accordingly. While these assemblages exhibited no specific decorative or stylistic feature that marked them out as being 'special', the overall volume of material, particularly of pottery, was distinctive... the presence of a small polished adze in the main wall fill further supports the view that that the constructional process may have involved ritual elements.
>
> (Hunter *et al.*, 2007, 67).

Of course, the idea of 'ritual rubbish' redeposited in a range of contexts being associated with fertility is not new (*e.g.* Case 1969, 12–15). However, in thinking about midden as possessing vitality, it is not only a physical capacity for transmutation but also a generative capability that sheds further light on its deployment in late Neolithic Orkney.

Clarke and Sharples go further in promoting the potency and efficacy of midden material in claiming that at Skara Brae the 'creation of the midden heap is the first stage in the construction process' (1990, 58). Whilst the claim that midden comes before dwelling is difficult to sustain, it nonetheless may be possible to posit that it comes before late Neolithic dwelling. If the midden is multifaceted in being a material resource and a 'theatre' of memories, it is also a 'living assemblage' that enables the emergence of new assemblages intertwined with social reproduction. Through the interlacing and containment of midden by casing walls forming the fabric of the house wall, a vitality and regenerative capability is assumed by the house. That the midden assemblage is a transformational product of a range of other diverse assemblages, incorporating people, things and substances, enables its efficacy as strategically deployed in the fabric and maintenance of the house as a generative entity. Here the physical house could be understood as transcending the social relations realised in the daily and ritual practices of a *société à maisons* as an imagined entity. In this respect the deployment of midden, including known and recognisable objects, in the fabric of the house can be placed alongside other social strategies such as the re-use of hearth stones from earlier houses (Downes and Richards 2005). When thinking about the midden at Stonehall Farm, it should not be forgotten that the perpetuity of *sociétés à maisons* is not only manifest in the maintenance of the social relations of its membership but also in the ongoing vitality of things (see Joyce 2000). If identity and continuity are prime concerns of *sociétés à maisons* – the deployment of midden as a wrapping of the 'house' now manifest in the unified settlement – Ian Hodder's dictum that 'distributions of refuse on settlement sites thus give an insight into the location of the principal boundaries between "self" and "other"' (1990, 127), takes on greater significance.

6.6 Stonehall Farm: ancestral houses and settlement nucleation

Immersion within accumulating midden, as discussed above, is a material strategy accompanying the move towards nucleated settlement occurring towards the end of the 4th millennium cal BC. At Stonehall this development can be charted through time and space from a dispersed group of discrete house sites at the Knoll, Meadow and Farm, as described in the previous chapter, to their clustering at Stonehall Farm. Once nucleation occurs and the site is established as a unitary entity, the inhabitation of Stonehall Farm changes radically in character. In many ways Childe's (1931a, 24) characterization of Skara Brae as a single living organism could be equally applied to Stonehall Farm, especially in the various forms of attachment between discrete house units now situated within a few metres of one another. For example, the drainage network running through the settlement, because of its flagstone capping and merging flow of liquids provides a highly visual connection between dwellings and their inhabitants (Fig. 6.6). Significantly, the covering flagstones also create a convergence of different houses within the settlement (Fig. 6.5).

It can be argued that pathways between houses are not only made of stone but also of blood as social relations inevitably extend beyond individual households like tentacles to entangle the entire social unit. Of course, despite such visually prominent material emblems of unification, external marriage and the influx of affines from other groups would have been a necessity for social reproduction.

Following the theme of unification, the growing midden that consumes the dwellings creates a single settlement mound that maintains a physical presence today. Although participating in a process of fusion, the midden at Stonehall Farm is composed of things of the past and present that project into the future because it can be understood as a generative assemblage in a constant state of becoming. Combined with the structures the midden was also a highly visible material metaphor of the continuity of the *société à maisons* inhabiting and constituting Stonehall. In the following chapter we will follow this trajectory a step further in charting the history of the 4th, 3rd and 2nd millennium cal BC settlement of Crossiecrown.

CHAPTER SEVEN

The Settlement of Crossiecrown: the Grey and Red Houses

*Nick Card, Jane Downes, Colin Richards, Richard Jones, Adrian Challands,
Charles A. I. French and Antonia Thomas*

7.1 Settlement histories

Regardless of intention there is always a tendency to homogenise evidence in the quest of identifying broad trends in settlement patterns. As will be argued in Chapter 9, in Orkney there does seem to be a discernible trend towards conglomeration and the nucleation of houses through the latter 4th into the mid 3rd millennium cal BC. Significantly, however, some divergence is recognizable in the manifestation of this phenomenon. Undoubtedly, locality is an important component in the construction of identities in the Orcadian Neolithic (A. Jones 2005b; S. Jones and Richards 2005; Richards *et al.* 2013, 147–48). But again, the importance of 'place' and a sense of belonging in peoples' lives can be realized in a range of guises, just as proximity in *sociétés à maisons* can assume a number of manifestations (see papers in Carsten and Hugh-Jones 1995 and Macdonald 1987). Ultimately, ideas of proximity and the materialization of 'neighbourhoods' lies very much in the domain of discourses of social capital, and local histories of residence.

When Childe and Grant excavated the late Neolithic structures at Rinyo, Rousay, they immediately observed the structural remains to 'rest upon artificial deposits presumably accumulated before their erection' (1939, 7). This has become an increasingly consistent narrative of Neolithic settlement in Orkney (*e.g.* A. Ritchie 1983, 44–45; Hunter *et al.* 2007, Table 3.1), and clearly relates to extended settlement histories. At Rinyo, late Neolithic houses associated with Grooved ware were superimposed one upon another, demonstrating a consistent pattern of building, refurbishment, demolition and rebuilding,

leading to confusing stratigraphic sequences of floors and hearths as present in the five separate phases encountered beneath Chamber G (Childe and Grant 1947, 25–32). Moreover, a situation probably not so dissimilar to that witnessed at Stonehall (Chapters 5–6) existed at Rinyo with earlier habitation, represented by round-based bowl, being dispersed across a small area. Again, as at Stonehall, of this dispersed settlement pattern, one place at Rinyo, (areas G and K), provides the locus for the continuation and nucleation of 3rd millennium cal BC settlement.

A similar sequence may have occurred at Pool, Sanday, although the diversity of settlement trajectories on the island is instructive. At Tofts Ness (Dockrill *et al.* 2007) settlement coalescence in the 3rd millennium cal BC is accompanied by midden accumulation creating settlement mounds. The larger settlement at Pool follows a similar trajectory but on a larger scale. Finally, a shift in settlement during the early-middle 3rd millennium cal BC, at the Bay of Stove, resulted in a massive settlement mound building up to the east of the bay (Bond *et al.* 1995). The superimposed houses at Skara Brae would also seem to end up literally encased within 'a gigantic midden heap' (Childe 1931a, 24). Undoubtedly, a similar situation occurs at the newly discovered Neolithic settlement at Muckquoy, Redland, Mainland (see Chapter 9). All these examples involve the nucleation of a number of separate stone houses, and ultimately, as seen at Skara Brae, their physical conjunction. Accepting local diversity, this nucleation appears to represent the ultimate conclusion of Neolithic *sociétés à maisons* in Orkney.

However, a single 'house', Hut 8, stands apart from the settlement mound at Skara Brae, which architecturally is quite different. Indeed, in having a frontal 'porch' or annexe Hut 8 appears to conform to a surprisingly uniform development of habitation occurring at some of the late Neolithic 'villages' in the latter half of the 3rd millennium cal BC. This takes the form of the construction of double houses, facing one another, and as a form of dwelling interestingly extends beyond the shores of Orkney to embrace Shetland (Downes and Lamb 2000; Downes and Thomas 2014, 82). This phenomenon is discussed further in Chapter 9; however, here a detailed exploration of the settlement of Crossiecrown is undertaken because it provides a detailed local history of nucleated settlement, the accompanying midden mound, a double stone house configuration and a possible turf and timber early Bronze age building.

7.2 Discovery and excavation

Initially, a key part of the original *Cuween-Wideford Landscape Project* was to examine the range and density of early prehistoric settlement occurring within the Bay of Firth area of Mainland, Orkney. Obviously, the scale and scope expanded, but when the project began in 1994–95 the Stonehall sites had only recently come to light through the material brought into a museum open-evening by Mr Ronnie Flett. Also, the Wideford Hill 'flint field' recorded by Rendall (1931) had yet to be fully re-examined. Consequently, we possessed no real indication as to the density of occupation that once existed within the study area. If one were to take Colin Renfrew's (1979) social model as a guide, the expectation would be a concurrence between the three passage graves (Cuween Hill, Wideford Hill and Quanterness) and associated settlements. Even if this general scheme was appropriate, we knew from experience that the overall settlement pattern could be far more complex. For example, at the Bay of Stove, Sanday (Bond *et al.* 1995), a substantial spatial shift in habitation seemed to have occurred roughly halfway through the 3rd millennium cal BC. Moreover, if an association existed between chambered cairns and particular corporate groups, the nature and spatial organization of settlement may be considerably more diverse than a simple, one to one, settlement – tomb correspondence. Furthermore, rather than being a component of a normative material culture as understood by Piggott (1954), if the building of chambered cairns was not simply 'done' as a matter of course, but represented a manifestation of strategic practice, then a far more disjointed architectural, spatial and temporal picture could emerge, as indeed it does.

Some four years into the project, the Wideford Hill settlement (Chapter 2) represented the most easterly known Neolithic occupation within the Bay of Firth study area (Fig. 1.9). The large passage grave of Quanterness lies further to the east, occupying a position on the northern lower slopes of Wideford Hill. In assuming this location it is not actually visible from the Wideford Hill settlement and, in planning fieldwork, it was felt that other settlements further to the east may well relate to Quanterness. Consequently, fieldwalking was employed to examine the ground lying below and within sight of the passage grave. During this fieldwork, Mr Scott Harcus of Quanterness Farm, pointed us to a low amorphous mound in a field bordering the seashore, known locally as Crossiecrown, where his father had removed large amounts of building stone in the past (Fig. 7.1). Fortunately, the field was in the process of being ploughed and the area was instantly investigated. A dense scatter of flint and stone artefacts, including a barbed and tanged arrowhead and a variety of stone tools was discovered to cover the surface of the mound, which was *c.*40m in diameter.

A startlingly clear plot obtained by gradiometer survey of the area appeared to reveal the low mound to comprise a series of middens heaped up around possible structures (Fig. 7.2), much as was present at Stonehall Farm (Chapter 6). Given the chronological range of surface material, further investigation of Crossiecrown provided a rare opportunity to examine a Neolithic settlement that clearly continued into the 2nd millennium cal BC. Excavation began in 1998 when two trenches (Trenches 1 and 2) were opened to gauge the nature and condition of the site. Trench 1 revealed thick midden deposits rich in artefacts, particularly Grooved ware with upper-body applied decoration and scalloped rims (see Chapter 11.3). Initially, in Trench 2, part of a large sub-circular stone structure *c.*9m in diameter (the Red House) was exposed. This building had a central hearth around which were recesses in the internal wall faces, similar to examples of later Neolithic buildings at Barnhouse, Links of Noltland, Ness of Brodgar, Pool, Rinyo, Skara Brae and Tofts Ness.

In 1999, under the direction of Nick Card and Jane Downes, a further trench (Trench 3) was opened northeast of Trench 2 to explore the outer limits of the mound as revealed by geophysical survey. During the final 2000 season the original Trench 2 was reopened and expanded to the north and west. This allowed a more substantial investigation of the settlement mound and amalgamation of Trenches 2 and 3 (Fig. 7.3). The trench expansion led

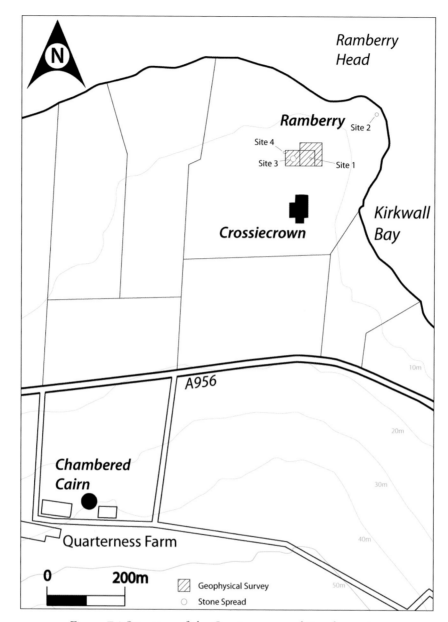

Figure 7.1 Situation of the Crossiecrown and Ramberry sites.

to the discovery of the fragmentary remains of a second building, the Grey House, which faced the Red House, and a possible early Bronze Age turf and timber building represented by a substantial hollow area.

As investigations commenced, it soon became evident that Crossiecrown had a long history of occupation running from the 4th to early 2nd millennium cal BC (see Chapter 10). Judging from the surface material collected by fieldwalking, this would appear to mirror the longevity of the recently discovered huge settlement mound at Muckquoy, Redland, Firth, Mainland (Chapter 9).

Given the presence of round-based pottery including

Unstan bowls, the founding and initial occupation of Crossiecrown began in the mid–late 4th millennium cal BC. This early period of occupation remained generally uninvestigated, apart from the identification of primary features either directly on or cut into the glacial till (Fig. 7.4). From this point onwards, occupation at Crossiecrown in stone-built houses involved a continuous sequence of construction and reconstruction. Because of the recycling of materials involved in this process, disappointingly, little evidence for earlier buildings remained apart from a series of disjointed sections of masonry, paving, spreads of rubble and midden deposits.

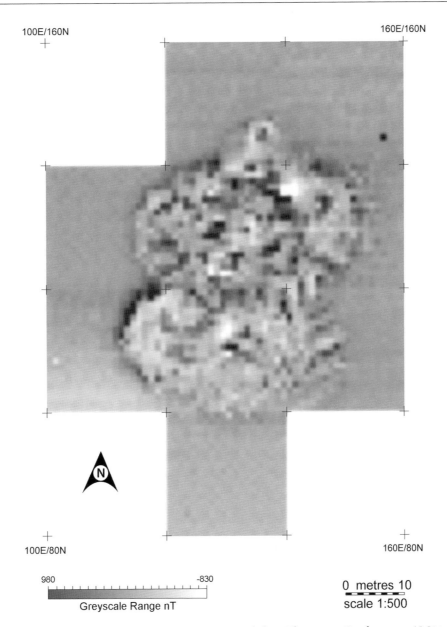

100E/160N   160E/160N

100E/80N   160E/80N

980   -830

Greyscale Range nT

0 metres 10

scale 1:500

Figure 7.2 Plot of the gradiometer survey of Crossiecrown, using a Philpot Electronics Gradiometer AM01; note the 'cloverleaf' shape of the high magnetic signature of midden deposits built up against the walls of a cluster of houses (Adrian Challands).

The most substantial and coherent structural evidence remaining at Crossiecrown; the Red and Grey Houses, relates to a later period of occupancy. The final phase of habitation is represented by a large 'hollow', probably the remains of a turf and timber structure located in the northern area of the expanded Trench 2.

Overall, a totally fluid and varied sequence of habitation can be recognized at Crossiecrown, however, particular 'phases' are apparent and in some instances do appear to concur with discontinuities in material culture. For example, the earliest occupation levels relate to mid–late

4th millennium cal BC activity and the use of Unstan bowls and plain round-bottomed pottery, whereas in later phases Grooved ware ceramics were in use. It remains to be seen whether such a sharp division exists between ceramic forms at Crossiecrown, as is claimed for Pool, Sanday (MacSween 1992; 2007), or whether such forms correspond with identifiable phases (see A. M. Jones 2012, 108–19). At a later time, probably early in the 3rd millennium cal BC, it is suggested that a cluster of four or five house structures were constructed and thick midden deposits accumulated around them. It is this midden that provides the main body

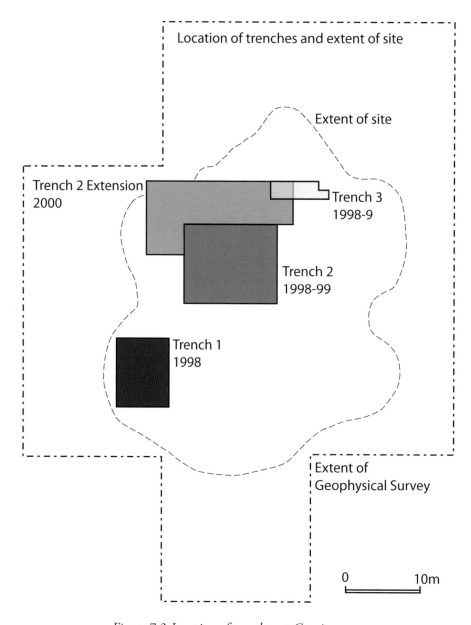

Figure 7.3 Location of trenches at Crossiecrown.

of the settlement mound. Subsequently, these houses were demolished and the materials of construction recycled; indeed, their presence is only known through the results of the gradiometer survey (Figure 7.2). Here, the highly magnetically-enhanced deposits that once built up around the outer group of houses are all that remains of a complete structural phase of the site. In other words we are seeing a 'ghost' image of a period of occupation at Crossiecrown that no longer exists.

The association of Grooved ware with the building of the Red and Grey Houses indicates they were erected during the first half of the 3rd millennium cal BC. Although

lacking a strong stratigraphic relationship, the Grey House would seem to have been constructed later than the Red House. When standing, the two houses faced one another to form a 'double house' unit. Subsequently, the Grey House fell into disrepair and became the outer 'yard' area to the Red House in much the same way as the Bronze Age double houses evolve in Shetland (Downes and Lamb 2000). Later activity is represented by an assortment of short stretches of masonry and truncated spreads of clay flooring associated with Grooved ware and Beaker pottery. The latter also relates to the curious hollow [213] in the northern area of the main trench (Trench 2) which is interpreted as the remains of a timber and turf structure, examples of which have been identified in Shetland at Sumburgh Airport (Downes, 2000, 121–22) and Kebister (Owen and Lowe 199, 255–57). Overall, settlement at Crossiecrown is dated as running into the early 2nd millennium cal BC.

7.3 The founding of Crossiecrown

Following the same trajectory as all the settlements discussed in the previous chapters, occupation at Crossiecrown was founded in the mid–late 4th millennium cal BC. Due to concentrating on a detailed examination of the Grey and Red Houses, evidence for the earliest activity at Crossiecrown is minimal but takes several forms. For instance, it is clear that, while small amounts of midden began to accumulate from the earliest period of occupation, it is not until very late in the 4th millennium cal BC that more substantial deposition occurred. This deep midden, forming the outer area of the settlement mound, was investigated in Trench 1. In contrast, in Trench 2 the earliest occupation was represented by the remains of paved areas [529] and [532] and a gulley or drain [526] cut into the glacial till (Fig. 7.4). Few of the features relating to this earlier period were revealed because the deposits were only excavated down to the lowest layers in two small and discrete cuttings in the southern part of Trench 2.

The areas of paving clearly represent initial levelling and the establishment of open areas related to the earliest dwellings at Crossiecrown. Some remnants of these early structural remains were present at different points across the excavated area. For example, an extant section of walling [566], later incorporated into an outer revetment wall [528] of the Grey House (Fig. 7.38), was clearly part of an earlier building. The presence of sherds of Unstan bowls (SFs 774 and 777) in deposits in the eastern recess of the Grey House clearly represents residual material incorporated into later deposits (Fig. 11.3.1). This is probably due to the spilling of redeposited midden, employed as wall core of the Grey House, when it collapsed or was demolished. The occurrence of similar Unstan ware sherds (*e.g.* SF 1042) together with round-based pottery (*e.g.* SFs 872, 882, 900, 997, 1002, 1083, 1124, 1129, 1140) in truncated midden deposits [471, 476, 515 and 517]) sealed beneath the Red House provides further evidence of the later 4th millennium cal BC occupation of Crossiecrown.

Identification of early Neolithic occupation places Crossiecrown in the broader context of the 4th

Figure 7.4 View of the curving early gulley or drain [526] cut into the glacial clay in the southern area of Trench 2 (Nick Card).

millennium cal BC settlement of the Bay of Firth area. Interestingly, the identification of classic Unstan bowl sherds provides some linkage between Crossiecrown and the nearby Wideford Hill and Brae of Smerquoy, and the more distant Knowes of Trotty settlement, as opposed to Stonehall where such pottery was entirely absent. The implications of the widespread early Neolithic settlement around the Bay of Firth and the various types of pottery in use will be explored further in Chapter 9.

The destruction or dismantling of early structures at Crossiecrown left discrete sections of walling and isolated spreads of rubble and midden (see also Fig. 7.2). On excavation the structural elements and deposits appeared fairly dislocated and extremely difficult to assign to any coherent architectural phases. This was due to their being either truncated or redeposited as foundation and levelling material for later structures. Because the lowest occupation deposits at Crossiecrown were generally unexcavated it is difficult to know whether there was an early, pre-stone period of timber architecture. Moreover, at Crossiecrown, the virtually complete demolition of buildings and the recycling of stone militates against the survival of earlier houses.

7.4 The middens at Crossiecrown: the southern (Trench 1) and north-eastern (Trench 3) areas

As discussed earlier, the gradiometer survey of Crossiecrown produced an image which appears to display an arrangement of individual circular structures (Fig. 7.2). Actually, the areas of high magnetic enhancement are not masonry but enriched midden material that

Figure 7.5 View of Trenches 1 and 2 looking to the north (Colin Richards).

originally was banked up against the house walls. But during the initial opening of trenches at Crossiecrown this was unknown and Trenches 1 and 3 were positioned in peripheral locations of the settlement mound in an attempt to define the limits of settlement and to examine the nature, depth and chronology of the Crossiecrown middens (Figs 7.3 and 7.5). In 2000, Trench 3 was incorporated into the larger Trench 2, but it will be included here as part of a broader investigation of the midden constituting the settlement mound.

7.4.1 Trench 1: the southern midden

As was hoped, the excavation of Trench 1 on the outer southern slope of the settlement mound (Fig. 7.5), exposed extensive spreads of ashy midden and a section of the wall of a roughly built structure sandwiched within the deposits (Figs 7.6 and 7.9). The stratigraphy of the midden was at one level fairly straightforward. Lying directly on the glacial till was a primary occupation layer of grey silt [058] with charcoal flecking and a few finds of Grooved ware pottery. This layer had a clearly defined interface with the underlying glacial clay suggesting a lack of buried ground surface; soil micromorphology suggests a programme of turf and soil removal across the whole site before occupation commenced. This primary deposit is interpreted as aggrading soil representing the truncated surface of the glacial till intermixed with midden or occupation material, essentially similar to the overlying midden [002] but less disturbed (see Chapter 16).

Above the basal layer was an extensive deposit, up to 0.4m thick, of sticky mottled red-brown midden [002] containing and being coloured by a high composition

of ash (Fig. 7.8). Unsurprisingly, soil micromorphology revealed that the midden contained much anthropogenic material, including fragments of partly decomposed plant remains, partly decomposed bone, and fragments of pottery (see Chapter 16.2). The majority of Grooved ware from the site was recovered from this relatively small area of midden where the remnants of over 130 vessels had been dumped (Fig. 7.7). The distribution of pottery was fairly evenly spread although particular 'dumps' are discernible, for instance, in the central northern area of the trench. The Grooved ware was of a broad range of sizes (*e.g.* large, medium and small), however, as Andrew M. Jones (Chapter 11) notes, this represents half the population of large and small vessels, but is only 37% of the total of medium vessels. Hence, there is a degree of depositional selection in what was discarded in the southern midden. Overall, the Grooved ware from the Trench 1 midden seems to represent, in some cases, the dumping of almost entire vessels, the sherds of which became scattered and in places partially abraded.

As discussed in section 6.5 of the previous chapter, the midden was a palimpsest of 'assemblages' merged into a unified body (a new assemblage) laid down in sequential depositional events. Stratigraphically, it was composed of multiple tip-lines, converging layers and broader spreads forming the midden mound. The tipping angle of layers sloped downwards from the north to south, vindicating the assumption that the entire settlement mound had built up through the dumping of organic waste and ash outwards from a group of centrally placed houses.

7.4.2 Structural remains in Trench 1

A partial circuit of badly constructed masonry [053] extended into the excavated area from the eastern baulk. This is clearly part of the outer walling of a ruined building, probably a later house structure (Fig. 7.9). Stratigraphically, the masonry appeared quite high in the sequence of accumulated midden deposits and extrapolating from the radiocarbon sequence from Trench 3 (Table 7.1) this would give a date of construction between *c.*2900–2600 cal BC. Although the structure was built on the midden [002], similar ashy material seems to have continued accumulating around its outer walls which gave the impression that it had been cut into a pre-existing midden. As only a small portion of the building ran into the trench it is difficult to comment further; no clay floor surface was recognized although a distinctive red-brown layer of burnt material [057] was present within the building (Fig. 7.9). Micromorphological

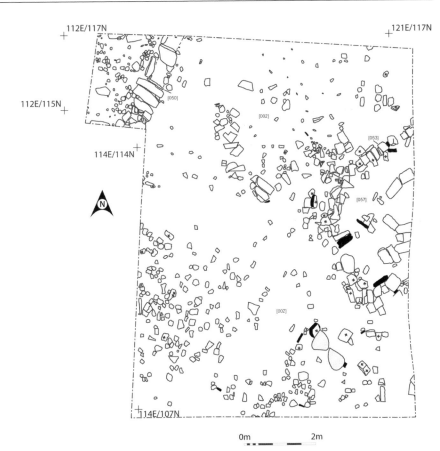

Figure 7.6 Plan of Trench 1 (spit 3).

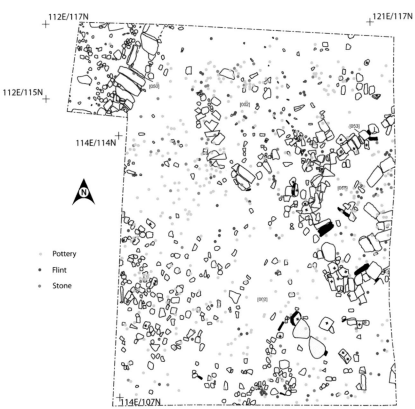

Figure 7.7 Distribution of worked stone (red), flint (blue), and pottery (yellow) in Trench 1.

Figure 7.8 View of the southern midden forming the settlement mound (Trench 1) from the south (Jane Downes).

Figure 7.9 Section across interior of Structure 1; note the red midden [057] within the building (Jane Downes).

Figure 7.10 Trench 3 from the west.

analysis of this layer revealed it to be constituted of re-deposited burnt soil. Hence, a hearth probably lies just beyond the limits of the trench.

In the northwest corner of the trench a short stretch of a drain [050] was uncovered (Fig. 7.6). The drain was well constructed with cover slabs, and was obviously contemporary with the latest occupation of Crossiecrown as it was cut through the upper midden.

7.4.3 Trench 3

Trench 3 was opened during the 1999 season to investigate the northeast area of the settlement mound (Figs 7.3 and 7.10). Excavation exposed a series of tips of ashy midden, which had been dumped directly on the glacial till that once again appeared to have been stripped of topsoil (Fig. 7.11). Directly over the midden a series of at least nine upright stones [205] were packed or jammed together to create an unusual surface or division between areas. An area of paving covered the midden to the north of the upright stones (Fig. 7.11). Once again, the thick midden was composed of mainly orangey-red-brown finely textured ashy layers, often incorporating lumps of charcoal in their makeup. In section, individual tip deposits were visible sloping gently downslope from west to east towards the edge of the mound (Fig. 7.12). Within the lower tips [210] a large amount of Grooved ware was present, the most remarkable being a substantial dump of sherds (Fig. 7.13), representing a single vessel (SFs 316, 343 and 380). The vessel was extremely large in being almost half a metre in height and profusely decorated by horizontal bands of finger impressed and plain cordons which alternate from the top to the base (Fig. 11.3.10)

The truncated northeast midden deposits remained up to half a metre in depth and extended across the eastern area of Trench 3. Although tip-lines with slight variation in colour were visible, there was no substantial divergence in the character of the midden to identify any changes in the nature of deposition through time. Equally, the composition and inclination of midden material [204] in the far northeast of the excavated area strongly resembled the extensive southern midden

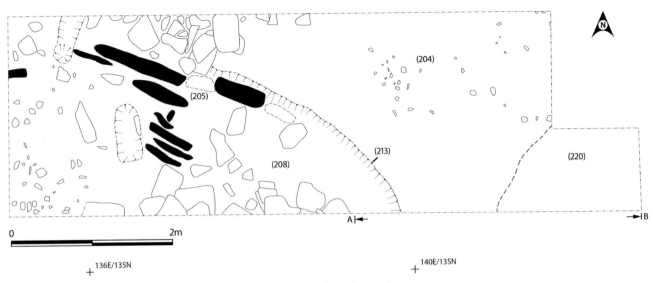

Figure 7.11 Plan of Trench 3.

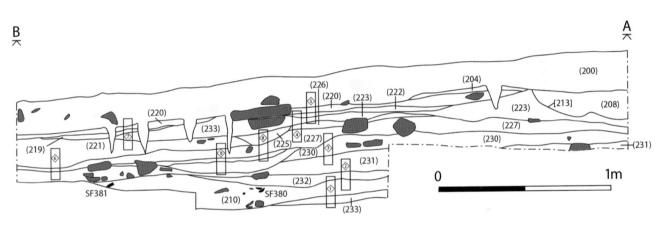

Figure 7.12 North-facing section through midden deposits in Trench 3.

Table 7.1 Radiocarbon dates through midden [204] in Trench 3.

Lab No	Material	Date	Position
GU-12482	Charcoal: *Conepodium majus*	2870–2490 cal BC	Upper midden
GU-12483	Charcoal: *Conepodium majus*	2880–2590 cal BC	Intermediate midden
GU-12484	Cereal: *Hordum vulgare*	3020–2880 cal BC	Lower midden
GU-12485	Charcoal: betula	3320–2910 cal BC	Lower midden

uncovered in Trench 1, and both areas included the deposition of substantial amounts of Grooved ware (Fig. 7.15). A series of radiocarbon dates were obtained from charred grain and charcoal through the midden in Trench 3 which indicated that deposition began late in the 4th millennium cal BC and ran through to the middle centuries of the 3rd millennium cal BC (Table 7.1).

7.5 The sequence of construction in Trench 2

The relationship between the Red and Grey Houses was always difficult to unravel stratigraphically. The Red House revealed substantial reconstruction and alteration and appeared to have a longer history of occupation. Both buildings conformed to late 4th–early 3rd millennium cal BC house architecture, comprising cruciform interior spaces formed by recessed areas in the inner wall faces.

Figure 7.13 Andrew Meirion Jones and Richard Jones excavating sherds of Grooved ware vessel (SFs 316, 343 and 380) in north-eastern midden deposit [210].

This is similar architecture to that identified elsewhere on Mainland, Orkney, at Barnhouse (Richards 2005) and early phases of Skara Brae (Childe 1931a; 1931b). The Grey House was discovered later in the excavation of Crossiecrown during the 2000 season, being partly sealed by deposits relating to the abandonment of the Red House. Deceptively, the Grey House was less well preserved than the Red House having been robbed of building materials making it appear more ruinous and therefore earlier. However, it would seem that for a long period of time the two buildings stood as a 'double house structure' with both entrances facing one another.

Although not unequivocal, reappraisal of the stratigraphic relationship between the two structures indicates the chronological primacy of the Red House. When the Grey House was constructed in front of the Red House, creating a double house arrangement, they were surrounded not only by substantial accumulation of midden material but also by the structural vestiges of the previous inhabitants of Crossiecrown. During excavation these relics of past settlement were extremely difficult to unravel either stratigraphically or as coherent structural entities and consequently we are left with a series of discrete structural components. What can be surmised is that these isolated structural components comprise the remains of a sequential pattern of building, demolition and rebuilding across the entire central area of settlement mound at Crossiecrown. Within the centre of Trench 2 the following succession of buildings and deposits can be recognized:

1. Earliest occupation of the site comprises a curving drain [526] and paving [529].
2. Several early buildings are represented by short sections of walling [160] and [402], foundation stones [134] and hearth [491] and surrounding ash spread [496]
3. Paving [193] was laid down, which incorporated stones [134] which acted as a foundation for the Grey House. A likely contemporary building is represented by the short section of walling [444] present in the southwest corner of the western area of Trench 2.
4. A general clay deposit *e.g.* [017], [133], [181], [528] was partially spread over paving [134] and [193] which provided a foundation for the northern outer wall of the Red House.
5. The Red House was constructed and a prolonged sequence of refurbishment and rebuilding ensues.
6. The Grey House was built and the outer casing wall [154] at the front of the Red House is demolished to facilitate the conjunction of the two buildings.
7. The Grey and Red Houses co-existed for a time during which substantial deposits of ashy midden [161] and [468] build up.
8. Further structures were built at this time as represented by the short section of wall [497].
9. The Grey House fell out of use and was levelled – this was followed by abandonment of the Red House.
10. An amorphous structure, interpreted as a turf and timber building, represented by the large sub-oval hollow [213], was constructed in the northeast area of Trench 2.

Little can be said of either the early organization of the settlement or the sequence of structures represented by various short stretches of masonry, associated features and the geophysical 'ghost' image of robbed structures surrounded by midden (Fig.7.2). It is only with the construction of the Red and Grey Houses that a more fine-grained narrative of occupation becomes possible. The practicalities of living at Crossiecrown, among the ruins, debris and decay of previous generations, are difficult to contemplate except through the lens of continuity. An idea of real 'phases' as expressing periods of occupation punctuated by the virtual demolition and rebuilding of an entire settlement has been criticized in relation to Skara Brae (cf. Richards 1991). However, the evidence from Crossiecrown throws new light on late Neolithic residential practices, which appear to frequently indulge in episodes of substantial if not total rebuilding.

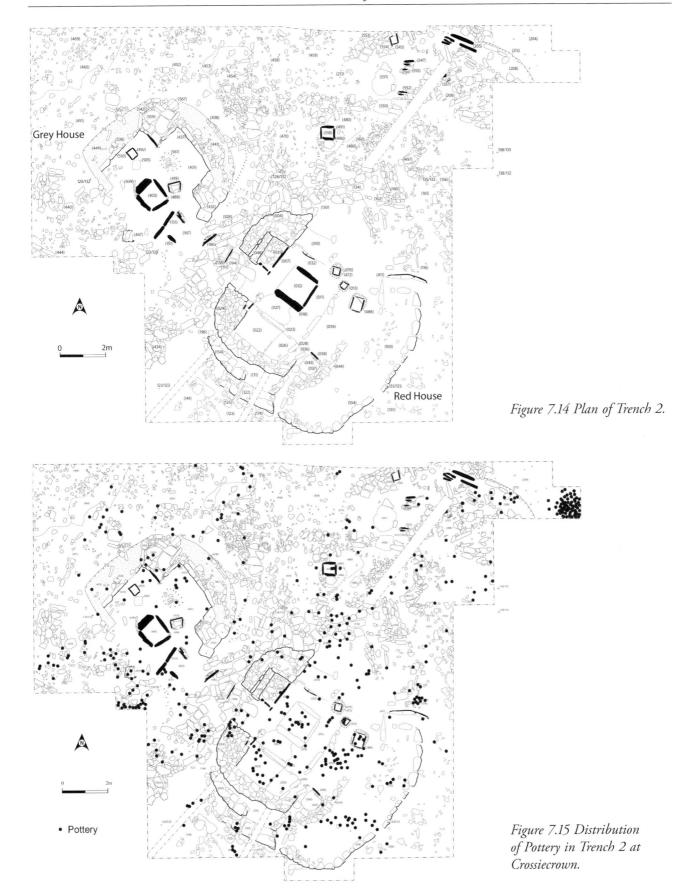

Figure 7.14 Plan of Trench 2.

• Pottery

Figure 7.15 Distribution of Pottery in Trench 2 at Crossiecrown.

Figure 7.16 Structure 1 at the Ness of Brodgar, shows the insertion of a wall changing the shape of the building from rectangular to sub-circular (Hugo Anderson-Whymark).

7.6 The Red House

The stone building, known as the Red House was partly uncovered in 1998 (Fig. 7.23), further defined in 1999, and its investigation was concluded in 2000. On excavation the structure (*c.*9m in diameter) appeared sub-circular in plan and displayed considerable disparity in style of construction. For example, sections of the outer wall showed divergent styles of masonry where parts of the building had been dismantled and rebuilt on a number of occasions.

Overall, the Red House has an interesting biography and enough remains of the primary architecture to identify that initially it possessed a cruciform spatial arrangement of recessed areas. Given the flush and exact internal masonry of the earliest wall sections, it is not unreasonable to ponder whether initially the Red House assumed a more elongated shape similar to that seen in House 2 at Barnhouse (Richards 2005, 129–156). Interestingly, if this is the case the subsequent modifications and remodelling of the Red House mirror those that occur in Structure 1 at the Ness of Brodgar (Fig. 7.16). Even if this was not the case, the quality of internal masonry, employment of red-coloured clay 'rendering' and presence of placed objects within the Red House indicates that this building possessed the special qualities of a 'big house' (see Chapters 6 and 9; Bradley

2005, 74–75; Richards 2013b), with enhanced ancestral significance and status.

When first uncovered, pink-red clay [008] was observed filling the joints of the dry-stone inner wall face and its presence was considered to merely constitute a form of clay bonding. On closer inspection the clay was seen to extend beyond the joints and in places partially covered surface areas of the inner wall-face. Even then the full significance of the discovery was unappreciated and it was only later realized that the red clay acted as a form of plaster. In Orkney, red clay is highly unusual with the majority of clay sources within the Bay of Firth coloured grey or yellow. The red colour could easily have been enhanced with a pigment created by haematite, several worked pieces of which were discovered at Crossiecrown (see Chapter 13.3). The main point to make is that originally this particular section of walling had its internal surface coloured red.

Through time the Red House underwent a series of alterations to its overall form involving the removal of wall sections and the addition of others. Given that it was built over spreads of rubble and midden, the possibility of subsidence contributing to architectural instability seems possible. The fact that the majority of rebuilding centres on the rear area of the house would seem to support the idea of structural failure, yet, given the similar structural history of Structure 1 at the Ness of Brodgar (Fig. 7.16), there are clearly broader social issues at play. Changes in the architecture of the Red House should also be put in the context of the associated Grey House which, accepting its poor condition, shows little evidence of reconstruction (Figs 7.14). However, there is clear evidence for the reuse of sections of walling from earlier buildings (see Fig. 7.38). Given the changes to practices that the addition of the Grey House would undoubtedly instigate, it is tempting to situate its construction within one of the phases of Red House refurbishment. The final reconstruction of the Red House involved the remodelling of the rear area and the addition of a new outer wall that acted as a form of 'jacket' effectively embracing and modifying the southern area of the house. Despite these changes to the outer wall of the Red House, its internal architecture seems to have remained fairly stable and unaltered, especially in the frontal area.

7.6.1 Construction, reconstruction and refurbishment of the Red House

The construction of the Red House followed the demolition and clearing of any earlier structures and the deposition of material in some areas to provide a level

Figure 7.17 View of the Red House showing the well-preserved wall in the northwest recess (Nick Card).

surface. These consisted of spreads of rubble, clay and midden material. In some areas, the normal practice of laying a thin skin of clay to create a smooth, level surface was implemented. A layer of pale grey clay, *c.*0.10m thick, acted as both a floor surface and foundation for the walls of the building. Together these deposits represented a fairly comprehensive effort to prepare a level and stable surface to facilitate the successful erection of the Red House.

The outer walls as preserved in the west and south clearly constitute part of the primary house, but even these display a degree of modification. Overall, the masonry in this area was regular and well constructed employing even-shaped sandstone blocks and slabs surviving up to three and four courses having a maximum height of *c.*0.30m (Fig. 7.17). The external wall face was curved, whereas internally the wall faces were exceptionally straight and flush with right-angled corners defining rectangular recesses. In a settlement context, this quality of masonry is comparable to that present in House 2 at Barnhouse and structures at the Ness of Brodgar.

At Crossiecrown, however, the outer walls attributed to the primary phases of the Red House display a degree of variability that must be attributed to subsequent reconstruction. For instance, a disparity occurs between the outer skins of masonry on either side of the entrance (Fig. 7.18). An additional skin of walling [004] faced the outer wall to the northeast of the entrance extending up to 0.5m in width. A partial 'ghost' impression of an equivalent outer masonry skin, together with small amounts of rubble, was recognized beyond the outer wall on the southwestern side of the entrance, indicating that it had been removed in this area. A degree of disturbance

Figure 7.18 Plan of modified Red House, showing different constuctional elements (red shows area of red-clay rendering).

Figure 7.19 The original casing wall [154] running around the west side of the Red House. To the right, a new casing wall [122] can be seen built against its face (Nick Card).

and impressions of stones was also noted running into and along the entrance passage. The removal of an entire skin of external masonry around the outer wall circuit on one side of the entrance and not the other is extremely curious, although it may have been removed to facilitate linkage with the Grey House. Even more curious is the width of the entrance passage, which in being over *c.*1.5m across (Figs 7.18 and 7.44), is highly unusual in the context of late Neolithic house architecture where the width of entrance passages rarely exceed a metre and more often are even narrower.

The walling on either side of the house entrance and along the west side appears primary, but unfortunately it had been removed in the east. An outer casing wall would have been essential for structural stability and insulation, and a stretch of masonry [154] serving this purpose

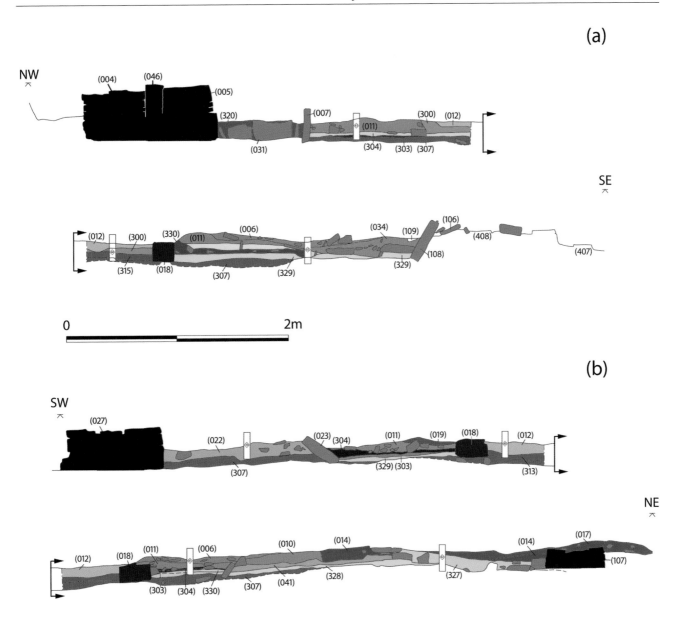

Figure 7.20 Southwest facing (a) and southeast facing (b) sections through the Red House (for location see Fig. 7.29).

was present further to the southwest (Fig. 7.19). In this area the basal core between the inner walling and outer casing wall was composed of clay, with overlying midden giving an overall wall thickness of *c*.1.5m. The apparently external position of an elevated entrance flagstone [138] and threshold upright [111] can also be understood in terms of the position of an outer casing wall, which is suggested to have been dismantled and removed to facilitate conjunction with the Grey House (Fig. 7.18).

Internally, the Red House saw much less structural modification and throughout its life maintained a generally cruciform spatial organization with recesses positioned

either side and to the rear of a large 'central' hearth [018]. Although one had been removed, the remaining three hearth stones clearly constituted a primary element of the house construction in having been laid directly on the underlying rubble and soil make-up [307] (see Fig. 7.34). The pale grey clay floor that also acted as a foundation for the outer walling was laid up against the hearth stones sealing them in place (Figs 7.20 and 7.21).

Unusually, the floors of the right and left recess were elevated *c*.0.15–0.20m above floor level by a thick layer of clay and small slabs, and each recess was delineated by a divisional orthostat (but see the shelf arrangement

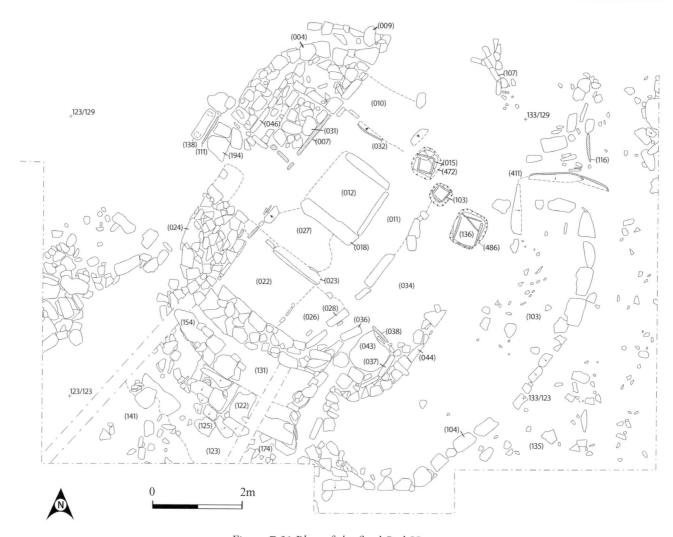

Figure 7.21 Plan of the final Red House.

in Structure 1, Stonehall Farm). There were indications that the right-hand recess had a split level floor with the front (northwest) being raised and the rear (southeast) at ground level. Whether this arrangement was mirrored in the left hand recess is difficult to establish due its ruinous condition. A polished stone axe (SF 63) had been deposited in the right-hand recess (Fig. 7.31), while a shaped stone ball (SF 428) was positioned adjacent to the divisional upright [023].

A smaller shelf-like recess was located directly on the left side of the entrance passage. The base of this recess was raised *c.*0.2m above floor level and was paved with flagstones. The elevation was achieved by depositing a thick layer of grey clay and rubble [320] upon which was laid a series of paving stones (Fig. 7.22). The 'shelf-recess' was bounded by a divisional orthostat. It was on the rear wall-face [005] of this shelf-recess that the pink-red clay had survived.

A small paved cell was present to the rear of the right-hand recess, being separated by a short length of walling [028] and [036]. As with the Grey House, entry into the cell involved crossing a threshold upright [038]. From the rear of the cell a drain ran out beneath the house wall and external casing wall (Fig. 7.23). A stone mortar (SF 85) was found *in situ* at the rear of the cell (Fig. 7.24).

Three small stone boxes [013], [015] and [136] were cut into the primary clay floor. In the fill [014] of one box [013] a deposit of cremated bone and burnt material was present. Here, it is worth mentioning that these boxes have been recognized as 'tanks' (Clarke and Sharples 1990, 60–64) or 'limpet boxes' (Childe 1931a, 17), however, significantly, they are also identical to small stone burial cists (Figs 7.25 and 7.26). Although no human bone was definitely present, at least some of the cremated bone was identifiable as animal (see Chapter

Figure 7.22 View of the shelf-like recess from the east when the Red House was first uncovered (Jane Downes).

Figure 7.23 Drain running out of cell in the Red House (Nick Card).

Figure 7.24 Stone mortar (SF 85) in situ at rear of the Red House Cell (Nick Card).

Figure 7.25 Small stone box [015] after the removal of its four uprights, box [013] and [136] can be seen in the background (Nick Card).

14). The presence of heather and Scots pine charcoal mixed with cremation deposits is consistent with fuel employed for 2nd millennium cal BC human cremations (see Chapter 15). Taken together, this evidence tends to support the interpretation of a 'non-human cremation deposit' being contained within the stone box.

Overall, it is difficult to tease out the complete sequence of refurbishment and reconstruction occurring within the Red House. Sub-circular cuts [113] and [463] in the floor at the rear of the house (Fig. 7.44) may relate to a demolished dresser structure. Certainly, stone-boxes [013], [015] and [136] (Figs 7.25 and 7.26), belong to the early occupation of the house. A small pit [139], situated southwest of the northern recess, appears to have been dug and backfilled with an ashy fill [140] during the earlier occupation of the house. Intriguingly, the central

hearth showed no signs of having been remodelled during the life-span of the house, and in both the Grey and Red Houses the 'central' hearths were situated unusually close to the entrances (Fig. 7.44).

One major alteration to the Red House was the building of a new rear wall [044], traces of which were discovered directly behind the right-hand cell (Fig. 7.18). Stratigraphically, it cut across the original wall-line which was represented by a short section of masonry [112]. At this time it seems likely that the cell was also modified. Although occupation material [304 and 303] had built up across the floor, at this time there seems to have been no attempt to refurbish the interior by laying a new clay floor.

The final remodelling of the Red House involved yet another episode of rebuilding the rear area. The constant alteration of this part of the house may have been a

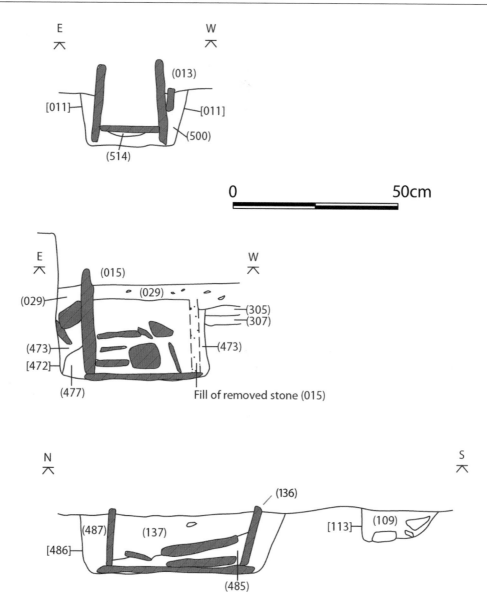

Figure 7.26 Sections through the three stone boxes [013], [015] and [136] in the Red House.

necessity due to subsidence and instability, especially as it was built over dumps of rubble and midden. This reconstruction entailed an enlargement of the building by the addition of a new external casing wall [122] built up against the outer face of the original casing wall [154], which had clearly collapsed and been removed in the west-northwest areas as it ran around towards the entrance (Fig. 7.21). This demolition probably concurs with the building of the Grey House. Towards the rear of the Red House, the thickened outer wall [044] attained a width of *c.*2m. Significantly, the wall displayed an entirely different construction technique in having a thick earth and midden core [047], with inner

and outer stone facing. The inner wall face survived only sporadically and its line was not entirely clear. In contrast, the outer wall-face was more clearly defined by a gently curving course of large stones (Figs 7.21 and 7.27). The construction of this section of the rear wall bears considerable resemblance to Structure 6, Links of Noltland, which also forms part of a 'double house' structure (Moore and Wilson 2011, 27). The final phase of occupation within the Red House was radiocarbon dated to *2460–2140 cal BC (GU-10319)* and *2480–2200 cal BC (GU-10318)* from charcoal within the lower hearth ash [315] and ash spread [012] respectively.

A line of orthostats [411] was present running through

Figure 7.27 Lesley McFadyen supervising the rear area of the remodelled Red House, the thickened outer wall with midden core is clearly visible (Colin Richards).

the thick outer wall in the eastern area. At first sight, this arrangement of orthostats is suggestive of it having been part of a secondary entrance into the eastern area of the Red House (Fig. 7.21). However, the position of an external orthostat, in line with the outer casing wall, effectively blocked access. This layout recalls a similar arrangement of orthostats forming a cell in Structure 1 at Stonehall Farm (Chapter 6). On excavation, the orthostats [411] were initially considered to have been set in the primary clay floor, whereas the rear blocking orthostat [116] appeared to be contemporary with the reconstructed outer wall. It was later decided that the clay layer was actually a thin secondary floor laid to accompany the reconstruction occurring at the rear of the Red House; therefore the orthostats would seem to form a secondary cell. This interpretation is supported by the presence of partial paving to the north of the orthostats. Unfortunately, the northern side of this feature was disturbed and any orthostats had been removed. It is possible that certain elements of this orthostatic arrangement date back to an early stage in the life of the Red House; however it was

clearly remodelled to form a cell at a later time. A surprising amount of artefacts were recovered from the floor surface between the orthostats (Fig. 7.30), adding more weight to the interpretation of a cell.

7.6.2 The Red House floors: a geochemical and geophysical investigation

One of the consistent features of Neolithic house building in Orkney is the employment of clay to create foundation platforms and floors. Sometimes, when prolonged occupation is present, a clear sandwich-like stratigraphy composed of thin yellow bands of clay separated by red-brown occupation lenses is evident. A further archaeological advantage of clay floors is their impervious qualities which can contain occupation sediments and prevent inter-surface contamination. Because these qualities lead to a high degree of stratigraphic integrity within houses, they provide ideal sealed contexts for geochemical and geophysical analysis to determine specific internal activity areas. After the encouraging results obtained from house floors at Barnhouse (Richards 2005b, 139), it was decided to undertake a more detailed analysis of the well preserved floor of the Red House (Jones *et al.* 2010). Surprisingly,

there was considerable variation in the colouring of the basal clay floor [329–30] as reflected in the heterogeneous descriptions, which led to the attribution of a number of different context numbers (*e.g.* [181] and [329]). Directly above the primary clay floor were remnants of several thin occupation layers, (*e.g.* [303] and [304]) over which a general and relatively uneven occupation deposit [011] had accumulated. This too displayed variability in colour, inclusions and so forth. The question is thus raised of whether such variability can be attributed to the effects of different activities, maintaining discrete spatial definition, occurring within the house interior.

Although occupation deposits had accumulated through time, generally it seems that the floor was kept relatively clean. The thicker upper deposit [011] relates to the final occupation and abandonment of the house. Unsurprisingly, in thin section (Table 7.2), a degree of bioturbation and mixing was noted within this upper layer. A similar mixing was also present in the upper hearth fill [012]. In contrast, the underlying black ash layer [315] was

Figure 7.28 The floor of the Red House with the sample square subdivision (Richard Jones).

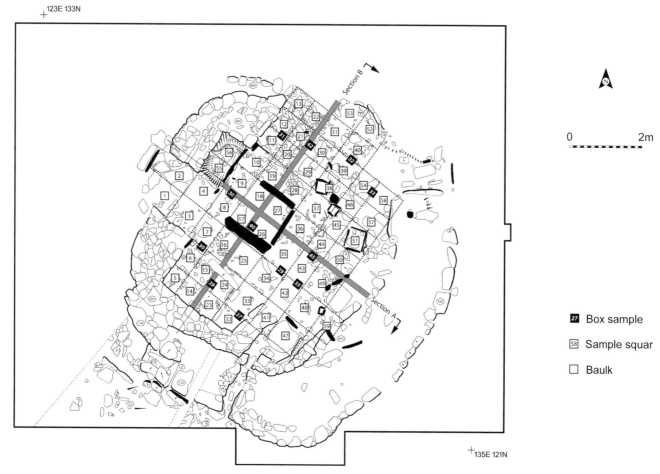

Figure 7.29 Plan showing the grid over the Red House; the sample squares from which soil samples were taken for multi-element analysis and the box samples for soil micromorphology are indicated.

Table 7.2 Summary of the soil micromorphology of the Red House floor.

Sample	Context	Description	Interpretation
27	303	Brown sandy clay loam with included ash and charcoal	Disturbed humic soil with midden ash and charcoal
29	303	Yellowish brown, massive to fine vughy sandy loam with charcoal and plant remains	Transition to glacial till substrate/primary floor layer [329]
30	304	Brown loam with zone of iron-impregnated, dark reddish-brown organic laminations at top	Finely bedded organic deposits representing floor levels, or possibly organic floor coverings. Main fabric of this sample is similar to sample 35
31	010	Yellowish-brown sandy clay loam with included organics, charcoal and burnt bone	Glacial till substrate with midden debris intermixed in recess
32	011	Five layers: disturbed iron-rich, dark reddish brown sandy loam over yellow-brown sandy clay loam, over dark brown charcoal-rich sandy clay over brown sandy clay loam	All soil material with some anthropogenic inclusions; either dumped and/or occupational build-up layers on a floor. Lower part of this sample similar to lower part (fabric/horizon 3) of 34, upper 42 and 45
33	041	Brown loam with blocky structure and charred organics and burnt bone	Mixed soil and midden debris. Similar to samples 33, upper 34, 35 and lower 42
34	011	Two fabrics/layers with distinct, irregular boundary between dark brown small blocky and intergrain channel structure. Loam over sandy loam in small aggregates with organic inclusions	Mixed soil/midden material over bioturbated humic soil. Upper part of this sample similar to samples 33, 35, upper 42 and 45; lower part of sample 34 similar to fabric/horizon 3 of sample 32
35	303	Dark brown subangular blocky loam with fine to coarse charcoal	Mixed humic soil and midden debris. This sample is similar to samples 33, upper 34, upper 42 and 45
41	011	Porous, pale/dark brown sandy loam in small aggregates with included organics, iron impregnation and iron hypo-coatings	Dumped, bioturbated soil; wet/dry conditions; much of organic component oxidized
42	012	Brown sandy silt loam with ash, charcoal and burnt bone over an iron impregnated, reddish brown, porous sandy clay loam with a subangular blocky ped structure	Dumped soil, midden and hearth material over deposited, clay and organic rich soil
43	329	Brown, dense/massive sandy clay strongly iron impregnated, reddish- brown sandy clay loam over yellowish-brown sandy clay loam with abundant iron nodules	Redeposited clay as floor around west side of hearth [018] over iron panned humic/midden-rich soil developed at upper surface of the glacial till substrate
44 (lower)	315–307	Yellowish brown sandy silt loam with abundant charcoal and burnt bone	Midden debris incorporated in surface of glacial till substrate; probably represents a floor surface
44 (middle)	315	Humic and charcoal-rich, dark brown over sandy loam with intergrain channel structure over 1cm thick lens of dark grey calcitic ash	Ash deposit directly on surface of glacial till substrate
44 (upper)	012	Humic and iron impregnated, reddish brown sandy silt loam	Dumped soil and midden material
	327	Iron impregnated, reddish brown sandy clay loam	Deposited, clay and organic-rich soil. Upper part of this sample is similar to samples 33, upper 34, 35 and 45
45	034	Well-developed, sub-angular blocky, dark-brown, humic/iron-rich sandy loam with included bone and charcoal	Midden material developed into structured soil since deposition

a product of the final fire within the hearth. Both upper and lower hearth fills provided samples for radiocarbon determinations which situates the final occupation of the Red House in the second half of the 3rd millennium cal BC (see Chapter 10). As the heart of the house, the central hearth is always going to be in operation and provides a focus for a range of tasks. The presence of 'dirty' ashy spreads ([303] and [304]) directly around the hearth was a product of extensive use, and resulted in the laying of a new surface of grey clay [330] to cover the worn and ashy floor.

Sampling for soil micromorphological analysis of the Red House floor area (Figs 7.28 and 7.29), produced a soil profile consisting of humified and bioturbated organic deposits, midden or occupation material that in places had accumulated directly on the glacial till substrate (Table 7.2). This suggests that the pre-house soil and earlier occupation deposits were removed in places, presumably as part of the construction process. There are, however, a number of different floor deposits present, and they occur at different stratigraphic *locales*

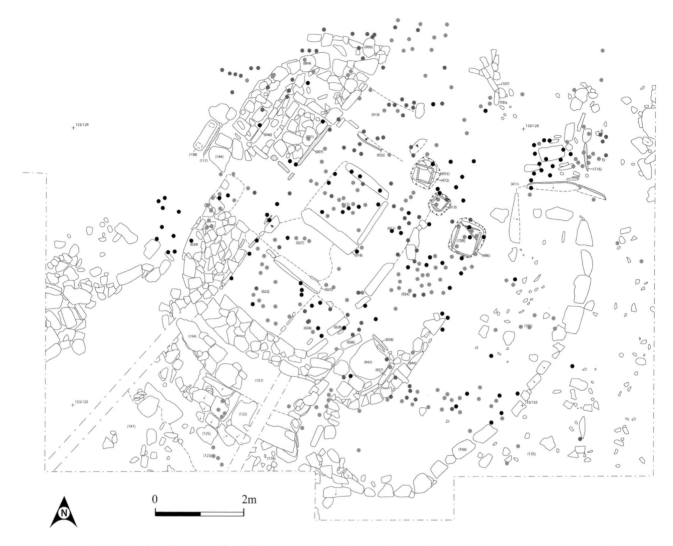

Figure 7.30 The distribution of flint (blue), stone (black), and Grooved ware (red) across the Red House floor.

within the Red House. Deposits of calcitic ash directly on the surface of the glacial till (in sample 44), indicate that in places the upper surface of the solid geology may have been a primary floor level. The general occupation spread [011] (in sample 32) also exhibits a series of five, discrete 1–2cm thick organic horizons which may represent a series of occupation trample zones. The lower floor [329] (in sample 43), a fine sandy clay material, was superimposed on *in situ* occupation – midden material, suggesting episodes of re-flooring after an initial period of occupation and/or midden accumulation. In the upper part of floor layer [304] (in sample 30), there was a superimposed series of finely-bedded organic deposits which again could represent either successive floor levels or, more interestingly, evidence of organic floor coverings. Thus, despite the shallow stratigraphy within

the Red House, there is clear evidence for floor surfaces composed of a variety of organic and mineral materials.

Although not plentiful, finds from the floor of the Red House included stone implements, Grooved ware, worked flint and burnt bone (Fig. 7.30). Most common among the stone implements were Skaill knives, stone discs and various cobble tools (Chapter 13). Of the stone tools (Fig. 7.30), the majority were found within occupation deposits in the left (northeast) of the house, four around the central hearth, one in the southern cell and five in the right (southwest) recess, including an igneous polished stone axe (SF 63) which was sitting on the clay surface [022] (Fig. 7.31). Two further stone tools came from the left (northeast) recess, five were buried in pits or boxes and two were recovered from the drain. From the right (southwest) recess and adjacent floor deposits were three pieces of worked pumice, and two pieces of haematite in contexts [025] and [026].

Some 30 pieces of worked flint were recorded in the interior of the house with a concentration around the hearth (Fig. 7.30). Analysis of the Grooved ware pottery indicates that the remains of large and medium vessels were present in the hearth deposits (Fig. 7.30), while both large and small vessels were found in close proximity to the hearth. In the small stone boxes there were sherds from a range of vessel sizes, although medium and small vessels seem to predominate. Unsurprisingly, given their assumed role for storage, sherds from large Grooved ware vessels were present in the recesses; however sherds from small vessels were also present.

In order to investigate the house floor in greater detail, including geophysical and geochemical analysis (Jones *et al.* 2010), a sampling strategy was adopted based upon a subdivision of the floor into a grid of 0.6m squares (Fig. 7.29). Soil samples were taken from up to five locations within each square; given the shallow depth of the floor deposits, some samples may represent an aggregate of adjacent Red House floor levels and indeed, encounter earlier floors. For reference purposes, samples of glacial till were taken from Cruan and Grimbister adjacent to the Stonehall settlement, and outside the chambered cairn at Crantit, St Ola (Ballin-Smith 2014). First, magnetic susceptibility (MS) and phosphate samples across the floor displayed high magnetic susceptibility within the hearth area (Fig. 7.32a) contrasting with high phosphate (Fig. 7.32b) occurring behind the hearth towards the rear of the house. Enhanced magnetic susceptibility was present elsewhere within the house often in the form of pockets, but the corresponding areas around the house and between its walls, associated with burnt debris

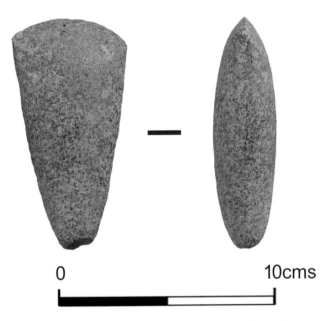

Figure 7.31 The polished stone axe (SF 63) from the right recess (Colin Richards).

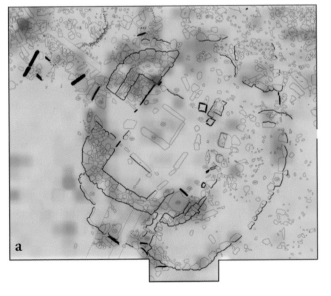

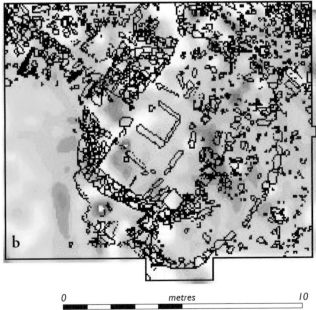

Figure 7.32 (a) magnetic susceptibility distribution across the Red House (blue to red palette corresponds to 10–450ms units), and (b) phosphate distribution across the Red House (white to dark brown corresponds to 0–10,000 µgkg⁻¹).

Table 7.3 Summary statistics for 13 selected elements and ranges in the reference material.

Element (oxide)	Element name	Mean	St. dev.	Median	Range	Range in reference material
FeO (%)	Iron	3.7	0.9	3.69	2.1–5.8%	2.8–5.8
CaO (%)	Calcium	0.7	0.5	0.53	0.18–2.62	0.41–0.75
MgO (%)	Magnesium	0.56	0.27	0.52	0.65–1.41	1.7–2.0
PO$_4$ (%)	Phosphorus	1.36	0.7	1.28	0.35–2.95	0.1–0.5
MnO (%)	Manganese	0.248*	0.175	0.20	0.04–0.77	0.018–0.15
Ba (ppm)	Barium	818	181	774	521–1243	549–608
Cu (ppm)	Copper	40	16	41	13–99	39–56
Sr (ppm)	Strontium	174	90	142	98–499	77–118
Zn (ppm)	Zinc	100	48	89	32–257	96–125
Co (ppm)	Cobalt	7.5	3.9	7	2–18	13–27
Ni (ppm)	Nickel	23.3	7.5	24	9–42	40–90
Pb (ppm)	Lead	12.8	2.5	12.7	8–19	24–48
Nd (ppm)	Neodymium	27	8	24	14–49	30–50

* Calculated without one anomalous value of 4.5% MnO

among the midden material, were less localized and more smeared. Like the magnetic susceptibility values, the phosphate concentration ranges were much the same within as outside the house. There were, however, marked phosphate concentrations behind the hearth and in the entrance area.

In the corresponding situations at Barnhouse where magnetic susceptibility and phosphate measurements were made within the interiors of Houses 1, 3, 6 and 10 (Downes and Richards 2005) and House 2 (Richards 2005b), there was a tendency for high phosphate to correlate with the main ash spreads and to the left-hand side of the hearths rather than behind the hearth as within the Red House at Crossiecrown. Magnetic susceptibility distributions within the houses at Barnhouse were also variable with little apparent correlation with the phosphate distributions.

The floor deposits within the Red House were also subjected to chemical analysis for thirty elements by ICP-OES, comprising (a) the central (or near central) sample within each square (59 samples) to give an overall view of the house floor, and (b) all five (sometimes four) samples within thirty squares (147 samples) to assess intra-square composition variation.

Thirteen elements exhibiting wide concentration ranges were identified, some of them showing high correlation (*e.g.* Al, K, Ca, P, Na, K, Zn, and especially Ca-Sr). Apart from Fe, Mn, Co, Ni and Pb, they exceeded the 'background' in concentration. The wide

ranges for Fe and Mn in the reference samples may not be surprising in view of a variety of natural effects and more particularly the frequent occurrence of iron nodules, pan and coatings observed in the soil thin-sections.

The spatial distribution patterns of many of these elements, some of which are illustrated in Fig. 7.33 a–h, are important because they appear to have anthropogenic significance and furthermore previous studies have identified a similarly informative suite of elements:

High concentration around the drain: Ca, P, Sr and Zn
High concentration at the entrance: P, Cu and Ba
Discrete raised concentrations, especially around the recess areas: Pb
High concentration close to the hearth – Ca and P – and on the edge of the hearth: Rb and Zr
High concentration over a wide area behind (*i.e.* east of) the hearth: Fe

The investigation of the floor deposits within the Red House identified a number of important points. First, soil micromorphology established a clear sequence of soil development, its deep truncation and floor construction on the upper surface of the glacial till (see Tables 7.2 and 16.5). During the life of the house there is a sequence of ash and occupation accumulation (or uncleared waste while the house was still occupied), stratigraphically punctuated by floor levels both within and on its upper surface. Finally, post-abandonment soil formed, which was disturbed by recent ploughing.

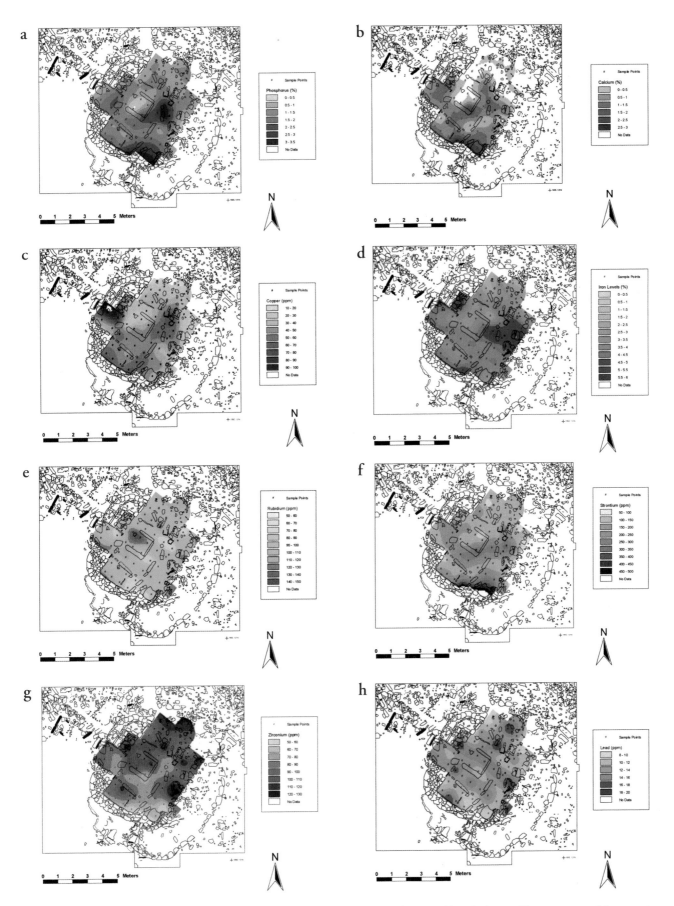

Figure 7.33 Distribution of (a) phosphorus, (b) calcium, (c) copper, (d) iron, (e) rubidium, (f) strontium, (g) zirconium and (h) lead across the interior of the Red House. P, Ca, Fe are expressed as % element oxide, the remainder as element ppm.

Figure 7.34 Excavating ash layers within the large Red House hearth, the underlying rubble make-up [307] is clearly visible below the ash (Jane Downes).

Second, there are apparently distinct distributions in the concentrations of several elements across the house, all of which have been recognized in previous studies as having anthropogenic significance. Third, as already mentioned, many of the locations of enhanced concentrations in these elements occur in spatially or functionally definable areas (*e.g.* hearth, recess, drain, *etc.*), and fourth, the extent to which enhanced concentrations in two or more elements coincide spatially is significant, while there are instances of individual elements that are capable of acting as independent, not correlated variables.

That leads onto the central issue of what the soil samples' compositions actually reflect. Could this be the activities undertaken on that floor surface, or a palimpsest of activities on more than one floor surface (*i.e.* the exposed floor surface and, say, one or two surfaces below) or a measure of both? The likelihood is that it is a measure of both, but the principal component to the observed signal comes from the exposed floor surface itself. Again, soil micromorphology plays a crucial role in resolving this issue. Despite bioturbation and soil pedogenesis as a result of secondary midden accumulations in the Red House, a succession of floor levels has been identified in thin-section, and, although these may be discrete spatial entities of survival, they definitively represent sustained occupation of the house. Whether the floor was partly or wholly covered with organic or plant material such as bracken and rushes (as in the Iron Age Oakbank Crannog on Loch Tay; Miller *et al.* 1998) is uncertain although there is a suggestion of organic covering of the floor on the clay surface [304]. If the floor were so 'carpeted', it could have absorbed,

albeit to varying extents, and possibly dispersed the by-products of activities taking place in well-defined areas with consequent alteration in the underlying soil's chemical composition.

Before turning to the main element distribution anomalies, some thought can be given to the notion of movement within the house. It has been noted that the entrances to House 2 at Barnhouse and Hut 7 at Skara Brae are asymmetric with respect to the buildings' axes (*e.g.* Richards 2005b; A. M. Jones 2012). This off-centre arrangement coupled with the houses' internal organization ensured that people entered into the right-hand side of the house, this side being more directly illuminated from the outside (Richards 2005, Fig. 5.26). The Red House at Crossiecrown follows this trend with the doorway being offset to the right of centre. Of course, this does not prohibit movement into the left-hand (north) side; it merely opens the right-hand area (south) to greater illumination and scrutiny on entry.

The first element anomaly to consider is the large one to the south of the hearth, which takes in the cell. This is registered by at least five elements – P being the most prominent, Ca, Sr, Zr and Zn the least (and probably Fe also). Centred on the drain and spreading to either side, its identity is probably generalized midden, composed perhaps of a mix of material including ash, charcoal, excrement and decomposed bone. At the rear of the house in the area behind the hearth lies the second anomaly. As in the previous anomaly, it is not expressed entirely uniformly: P, Ca and Sr parallel each other in direction (at an angle to the hearth peaking in the case of Ca on the hearth's southern corner) but not in intensity. They extend as far as the two boxes but no further. The trend of iron is somewhat different as it peaks at the position of the east wall. If it relates to the rake-out of ash from the hearth, then corresponding trends in P, Ca, Zn, Sr and Cu would be expected on the basis of the results of Wilson *et al.* (2005, Table 9), but this is not the case. In any event, to judge from the excavation evidence at other late Neolithic settlements such as Barnhouse (Richards 2005c, 105, Fig. 4.68), while in some houses there appears to be a left-hand preference for raking out the ashes from the hearth, this is not ubiquitous. Unfortunately, the chemical data has not shed light on the identity of the fuel(s) – peat, turf, wood or seaweed – giving rise to the ash (Jones *et al.* 2000, 45). The third anomaly is at the house entrance, evident in Ca, P and for Cu, it limits itself only to the northern part of the entrance.

The three main P anomalies are in the southwest of the house close to the drain and behind the hearth; the last two of these areas contain burnt organic material to judge from the high magnetic susceptibility and LoI values. There is marked P depletion within the central hearth. The low P and Ca values in the northern part of the house take on additional significance in view of the low to very low LoI values in that general area.

To the left on entering the house are significant anomalies in Zr, which lie in and around the hearth, directly behind the hearth as already mentioned, and also the north and northwest of the house (Fig. 7.33g). Only the Pb distribution shows anomalies in the same general area.

Examining how these observed anomalies relate to the artefact distributions, the stone tools reveal, as already mentioned, an activity focus in the left-hand (east) area of the house (Fig. 7.30). Here a P anomaly and associated high magnetic susceptibility and LoI values are evident extending from the hearth eastwards. For the corresponding flint distribution (Fig. 7.30) there is a concentration to the north of the hearth which seems to correlate with one of the Pb (Fig. 7.33h) and one of the Zr 'hot spots' (Fig. 7.33g).

The evidence from the Grooved ware pottery is more difficult to assess (Fig. 7.30). It might be assumed that large vessels are for storage and small-medium pots for food serving and cooking (see A. M. Jones and Richards 2005, 38–43), but this does not appear to be borne out in the Red House by depositional practices since large and medium-sized vessels seem to be present in the hearth deposits (Fig. 7.34), while both large and small vessels are found in close proximity to the hearth. Furthermore, in the small stone boxes there is a range of vessel sizes, although medium and small seem to predominate. Mainly large and small vessels occur in the recesses of the house. While the presence of large vessels does concur with a storage role this cannot be claimed for the small vessels considered to be for food serving. In sum, this points to the function of pottery *not* entirely correlating with vessel size, or rather the depositional context of different sized vessels. Little correspondence between elements and Grooved ware distribution is evident apart from the group of sherds situated behind the hearth, at the rear of the house which correlates with an anomaly in the iron distribution (Fig. 7.33d).

7.7 The Grey House

The building of the Grey House followed a similar sequence of events as is seen in house construction at many other Orcadian Neolithic settlements (Fig. 7.35).

Initially a layer of yellow-brown clay [431] was spread over an area to the north east of the Red House. This clay surface acted as both a stable level foundation for the walling and as an internal floor surface. During excavation the outer wall of the Grey House was found to be very ruinous but survived best in the eastern area where up to three courses of slightly slumped masonry defined the northeast recess and cell (Figs 7.36 and 7.40). To the north of the central hearth a line of stones, c.1.80m in overall length represented the back wall of the 'rear' recess. Elsewhere the wall had been generally robbed away, however its position could be traced either by the spread of wall core material [449] or by depressions where stones had been removed. Enough of the outer wall survived in the eastern area to determine part of the entrance which was orientated southeast and directly faced the Red House entrance. The Grey House entrance was defined by a low threshold slab [186] c.0.64m in length by 0.14m wide. Outside the entrance was a paved area of flagstones [193] (Fig. 7.37).

Behind the inner wall-face, a core composed of pale brown clay, extended the width of the outer wall to just over a metre in the eastern area. On the northwest side of the building, remnant wall core material of yellow-brown silty clay with suggestions of an outer wall-face were present allowing a rough estimate of the overall house diameter of c.8 m. Interestingly, an earlier extant wall [566], had been reused as an outer casing wall of the Grey House in the southeast area, which must have been an element of an earlier building (see Fig. 7.36).

Although only partially preserved, the internal architecture of the Grey House was similar to the Red House in being dominated by a large central fireplace [183] (see Figs 7.34 and 7.39). This was defined by four large slabs forming a slightly rectangular shape, c.1.50m by c.1.60m. On excavation it was evident that as with so many other Neolithic Orcadian houses the hearth constituted the primary element of construction. Once the hearth stones had been set in position in elongated slots, the primary clay floor [431] was laid over the cuts to lap against the hearth stones. The contents of the final fire were represented by an orange-grey ash c.0.15m deep (Fig. 7.39). Arranged around the west side of the hearth was a curious curved setting of three upright stones [439] that was probably associated with activities centred on the hearth (see Fig. 7.43).

Fortunately, the right-hand (northeast) recess was relatively well preserved and measured c.2.40m by c.1.20m. A polished stone tool (SF 654) of gneiss, shaped rather like a cushion macehead (described as a 'faceted and facially

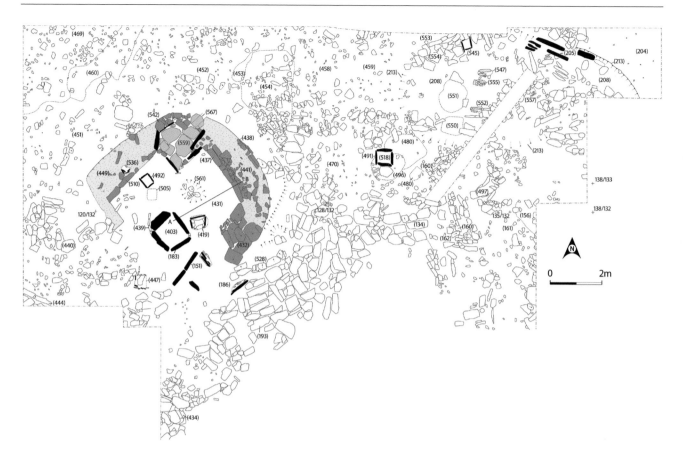

Figure 7.35 Plan of the Grey House and the northern area of Trench 2.

picked pebble' by Clarke in Chapter 13, but strongly resembling the 'cushion stones' currently discovered at the Ness of Brodgar), was found on the floor [431] of the recess (Fig. 7.40). The tool had been battered on each end, but interestingly had been placed in an equivalent position to the igneous polished stone axe (SF 63) deposited in the southwest recess in the Red House. To the left of the entrance, a rectangular orthostatic feature [151] formed the remnant of a piece of furniture, probably similar in form to that seen within House 1 at Stonehall Farm and Hut 7 at Skara Brae. A small well-constructed cell [542], *c.*1m square, with a paved floor [559] was positioned north of the east recess (Fig. 7.40). Definition of the cell in relation to the interior of the house was clearly of importance as, just as is seen in the Red House, a threshold upright was positioned at its entrance. A stone drain [567] ran out of the back of the cell and flowed beneath the exterior wall. Late in the life of the Grey House, the drain had been deliberately blocked. Incised decoration was present on one of the basal stones at the rear of the cell (Fig. 7.41)

Positioned around the hearth were three stone boxes, [419], [447], [492], each of which had been cut into the

clay floor (see Figs 7.35 and 742). A stone-lined box [419] was located directly east of the hearth, and measured 0.55m × 0.45m, and a second stone-lined box [447] of similar size, was located *c.*1m to the southwest of the hearth. The third box [492] was *c.*1.00m to the northwest of the hearth and measured *c.*0.45 by 0.35m. Also cut through the house floor were several pits, some of which judging by their shapes may have been the robbed-out remains of other stone boxes. For example, a square-shaped cut [505], measuring 0.40m × 0.33m, was almost certainly the remains of an earlier stone box whose uprights were removed. A more oval-shaped pit [536], measuring *c.*0.30m by 0.25m, contained small upright stones which may be remnant packing for an absent upright dresser-stone as it was centrally located in the wall of the rear recess. Finally, a larger pit [561] was positioned northeast of the hearth. Apart from the fills of these features and the central hearth, the clay forming the floor of the Grey House was not excavated, but after careful cleaning, its surface appeared to possess a sheen, a characteristic of clay floors which had seen prolonged periods of trampling and use.

The chronological relationship between the Grey

Figure 7.36 *The Grey House under excavation as seen from the northeast (Angus Mackintosh).*

Figure 7.37 *View of the Grey House from the west (Nick Card).*

Figure 7.38 *Paved area [193] south of the Grey House, the extant earlier wall [566] was incorporated in the outer casement wall (Nick Card).*

Figure 7.39 *View of sectioned central hearth in the Grey House (Angus Mackintosh).*

Figure 7.40 *Nick Card uncovering the polished gneiss tool (SF 654) deposited in the northeast recess of the Grey House (Jane Downes).*

Figure 7.41 *View of cell in northern area of the Grey House. Incised decoration is present on the stone to the left of the vertical scale (Nick Card).*

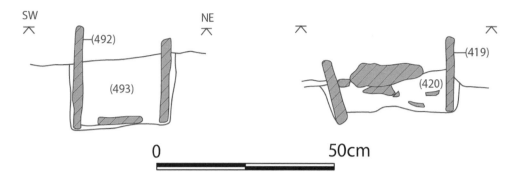

Figure 7.42 Sections of small stone boxes [419] and [492] in the Grey House.

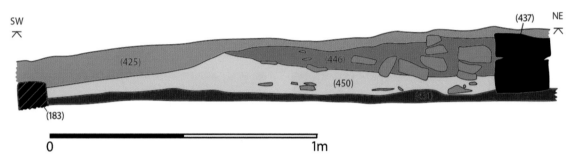

Figure 7.43 South-facing section through the eastern side of the Grey House (for location see Fig. 7.35).

House and the larger Red House was difficult to establish with any certainty. Although the paving [195] beyond the entrance to the Grey House became partially covered by a thin deposit of clay [017], which also acted as a foundation surface for the outer wall [004] of the Red House, there was no direct relationship between the flagstones [195] and the Grey House. A pedestal structure [138] which formed part of the entrance into the Red House was set into this material. The Grey House was positioned in such a way that the two entrances directly faced one another (Figs 7.14 and 7.44). This pairing of houses represents a similar inter-relationship to that seen between Structure 8 and 9 at Pool (Hunter *et al.* 2007, Ill. 3.15) and Structures 5 and 6 at Links of Noltland (Moore and Wilson 2011, Fig. 36). Moreover, it is more generally a feature of 2nd millennium cal BC dwellings in the Northern Isles (Downes and Thomas 2014). After a period of co-existence with the Red House, the Grey House fell out of use. At this time the walls of the Grey House were demolished or robbed out and midden material, mainly ash deposits derived from later activities at Crossiecrown, gradually accumulated over the levelled remains. It was this event that allowed the wall core (midden material pre-dating Grey House construction) to spill across part of the east recess.

7.8 The final occupation of Crossiecrown

In the second season of excavation at Crossiecrown, part of an oval shallow hollow [213] which had been dug into the top of the earlier midden [204] and partly lined by a series of orthostats [205] was revealed in Trench 3 (Figs 7.11. 7.45 and 7.46). The northwest extension to Trench 2 in 2000 revealed the full extent of this feature. Overall the hollow was sub-oval in plan and measured *c.*7m (E–W) × 4m (N–S) and was up to 0.3m deep. Part of the hollow was originally roughly paved as represented by several remnant flagstones. The orthostat lining did not continue all around the hollow, and in many instances the orthostats had been robbed out and their former presence was only indicated by a series of shallow hollows running along the edge of the cut. On the northwest side was a section of single-faced drystone walling [553,] and an associated small area of rough paving [554] and a stone box [545]. The remnants of another stone box [557] were set into the floor further to the east. Near the centre of the hollow were the remains of a stone setting supporting the stump of a broken orthostat. Parallel to this to the south were two similar features [555 and 552], though neither contained stone uprights on excavation. To the west and southwest of these features were large spreads of brightly coloured orange-red ash [550 and

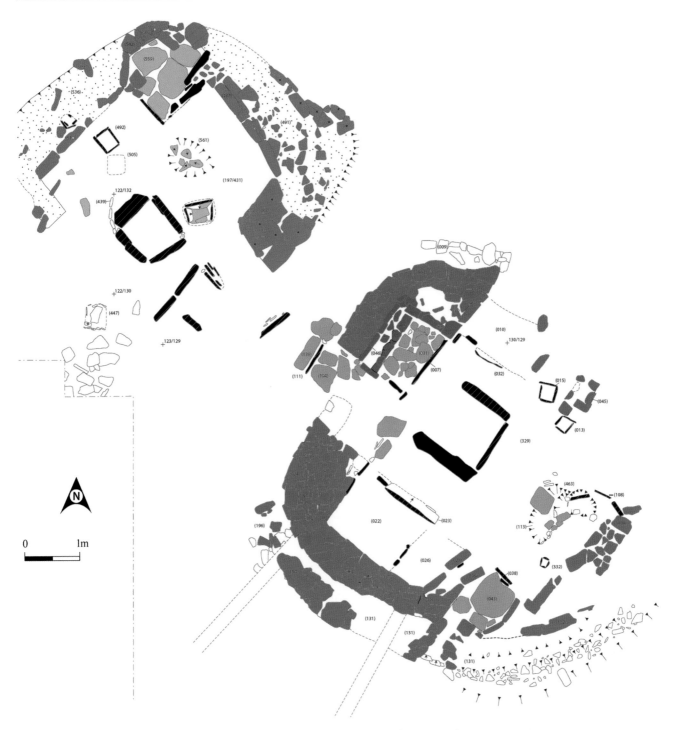

Figure 7.44 Plan of the Red (bottom) and Grey (top) Houses.

551]. Although unexcavated, this ash spread [551] was almost certainly directly related to a hearth.

Originally it was presumed that the hollow was some form of external activity area contemporary with the Grey and Red Houses, although the lack of any direct stratigraphical relationships could equally imply that this large feature post-dated the houses. It is now suggested that the oval could constitute the ruined remains of a structure of late 3rd–early 2nd millennium cal BC date. Certainly, occupation at Crossiecrown continued into the Early Bronze Age as demonstrated by the late radiocarbon date of *1960–1740 cal BC (GU-10327)* obtained from the

Figure 7.45 Hollow [213] under excavation, hearth [491] can be seen to the right (Nick Card).

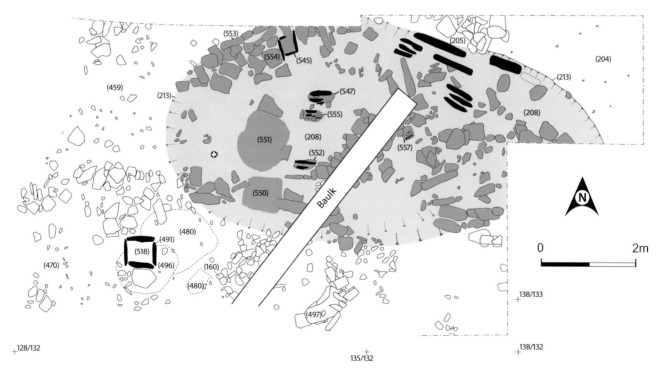

Figure 7.46 Plan of the northeast area of Trench 2, showing the extent and shape of the proposed timber and turf structure represented by hollow [213].

spread of ash associated with the hearth [491] (Figs 7.35, 7.45 and 7.47). On excavation this hearth appeared unrelated to any building, but given its high stratigraphic position it is possible that all structural remains had been robbed or destroyed by ploughing. Further indication of site longevity is provided by the presence of heavily ornamented late Grooved ware and Beaker pottery (Chapter 11.3).

The hollow [213] with associated late pottery represents one of the final elements of occupation at Crossiecrown. The presence of a posthole and the orthostatic settings is highly suggestive of internal roof support and furniture. Equally, inner paving and a compact clay layer would suggest a floor surface and the ash spreads almost certainly are related to a hearth which was not discovered or excavated. However, the lack of stone walling defining this area always caused interpretative problems, therefore, the possibility of this being a late Neolithic–early Bronze Age timber and turf building was not given serious consideration during its excavation. However, the presence of early Bronze Age timber buildings in Shetland at Sumburgh Airport (Downes and Lamb 2000) and Kebister (Owen and Lowe 1999), allowed a reconsideration of the Crossiecrown hollow. Armed with the knowledge that tree cover in the Northern Isles may have been greater than was previously suspected, together with the Shetland discoveries, we have greater confidence regarding the interpretation of the hollow constituting the remains of a timber and turf house structure (Fig. 7.46).

Eventually, the hollow became filled with stony occupation material [208], containing Beaker pottery (*e.g.* SF 229), that spread across and covered the paving. Prior to the abandonment of the site, the walls defining the northern and north-eastern sides of the Red House were entirely robbed out, as was the west side of the Grey House. Sherds of Beaker pottery (*e.g.* SF 51 and 150) and a possible short length of walling [020] across the interior of the Red House indicates later activity, probably contemporary with occupation associated with hollow [213].

7.7 Houses of colour: adornment, and strategies of identity and continuity

When excavations began at Crossiecrown, it was immediately noticed that the condition of some of the walling was excellent. The best preserved stretches of masonry were in the Red House (Fig. 7.22). As the inner wall-face of the elevated northern recess was

Figure 7.47 Detail of hearth [491] in the eastern area of Trench 2.

being uncovered, pink-red clay was noticed adhering to the masonry. Closer inspection revealed the clay to be remnants of rendering or plastering as opposed to a form of bonding (as was originally thought). In small patches, the coloured clay actually spread across the wall surface, and it was later discovered not to penetrate the masonry to any extent. Actually, a similar employment of clay had been noticed many years ago by Childe at Skara Brae:

> the outer wall of Hut 4 on the east at least is so well built that it must originally have been designed for exposure. Its bottom course is formed of slabs on edge.... and the whole surface has been puddled with blue clay over 6 inches thick (Childe 1931b, 40).

However, in this instance it was the outer, as opposed to the inner, masonry surface of Hut 4 that was rendered with blue clay.

Despite an absence of direct evidence, there has long been the suspicion that masonry could have been rendered or plastered during the Orcadian late Neolithic. For example, Bradley and Philips (2000, 110) pondered the possibility that the pick-dressing of stone within Maes Howe was to create a roughened surface to facilitate adhesion of plaster. The evidence from the Red House at Crossiecrown confirms the idea that walls were both rendered and coloured. To smooth and cover internal and external masonry with clay introduces interesting possibilities and allows a number of interpretative paths to be explored. The first considers the role of clay as a membrane or skin, which functions as a method of wrapping the house (see Richards 2013, 16–18). A function of wrapping as a form of containment intersects nicely with a suggestion of Andrew M. Jones (2002) regarding the analogous status of houses and pots. In this vein, the employment of a clay slip and applied plastic decoration to Grooved ware vessels, and clay rendering applied to house walls, may form part of wider 3rd millennium cal BC strategies of elevating surface over substance (Richards 2013, 149–83).

Just as with slip applied to Grooved ware, the application of clay rendering to the house also allows the potential of decoration and colour. The 'striking links' between the decorative components of Orcadian Grooved ware and passage grave art have been identified by Bradley (2009, 100-1), Can this observation be extended to houses? Orcadian Grooved ware vessels may be decorated both externally and internally, so taking this idea further the potential exists for the clay rendering of internal and external wall-faces of a house to function in an identical manner.

Certainly, it has been argued that the uniformity of decoration on the Grooved ware from Barnhouse was strategic in exhibiting a village identity (S. Jones and Richards 2005, 199–202). Not only were Skara Brae houses 'designed for exposure' (Childe 1931b, 40), the outer wall-face of chambered cairns were also intended to be seen (Davidson and Henshall 1989, 30). Different patterns of masonry have been observed in the outer wall-faces of stalled chambered cairns such as Unstan, Mainland, and Knowe of Yarso, Blackhammer Knowe of Ramsey and Midhowe, Rousay. This occurrence reveals that the outer walls of Neolithic buildings were a potential canvas and medium of discourse (cf. A. M. Jones 2005b). If houses formed part of this scheme, and were also decorated in some way, then clearly this comprised an additional strategy of identifying and 'naming' or identifying specific houses. Adorning the house interior would have also participated in this process of identification, but in a more intimate manner.

Another path to follow is the actual use and deployment of colour in late Neolithic Orkney. On a broader stage, the assemblage of monoliths comprising the Ring of Brodgar included different coloured lithologies (Downes *et al.* 2013, 105–107). This variability has been discussed in terms of gathering things and people within the competitive arena of monument construction. By implication therefore, the material constitution of the Ring of Brodgar merges particular lithologies, colours and social groups. Without expanding further, there is clearly a discourse of identification manifest in this context (cf. A. M. Jones 1999b; Jones and MacGregor 2002). A more intimate convergence of stone and colour also occurs in the interior of Structure 10, Ness

of Brodgar (Card and Thomas 2012, 120–21). This is suggested to enhance and emphasise specific parts of the house, and the different stones-colours indexically link different social groups involved in a 'communal activity' (*ibid.*).

The red clay applied to the inside of the Red House, forces a reconsideration of the role of materials and their colour in the architecture of late Neolithic Orcadian houses. For example, at the Ness of Brodgar, red and yellow sandstones were selectively quarried and then intensively pick-dressed in order to enhance and draw out the vibrancy of their colour. Although pick-dressing in this instance does not appear to have been to facilitate the adhesion of clay or plaster (Card and Thomas 2012, 120–21). Nonetheless, taken together, the identification of unprocessed pigment ores, grinding mortars for the preparation of 'paint', and *in situ* architectural stonework with extant pigment from the Ness of Brodgar, does suggest that internal walls may have been coloured.

Such rendering certainly occurs within the Red House and adhesion achieved through utilizing the crevices within the dry stone masonry. When uncovered by excavation, the Red House clay was of a pink-red colour. Naturally occurring clay of this colour is present within Orkney, albeit of restricted distribution. Alternatively, a 'firing' of clay can transform the appearance of more typical grey-yellow Orcadian clays to browns and reds as seen in the context of ceramic production.

Yet another potential strategy of colouration is seen in the small stone and whalebone mortars or 'paint pots' identified in Huts 1, 2, 3 and 7 at Skara Brae by Childe (1931a, 15–40). The excellent preservation at Skara Brae enabled the remnants of red and white pigment to be identified within several of the 'paint pots'. Polished lumps of haematite are seen as the potential source of red pigment (see Chapter 13.3), and a number were found at Crossiecrown, particularly in, or in the ploughsoil above, the Red House. Taken together, it would appear that ground haematite being added to the local yellow and grey clays was a favoured method of achieving a red colour for rendering.

Apart from Skara Brae, mortars or 'paint pots' are present at Barnhouse, Ness of Brodgar, Pool, Tofts Ness and Links of Noltland, all of which date to the 3rd millennium cal BC. A mortar or 'paint pot' (SF 85) was actually found *in situ* at Crossiecrown within the cell of the Red House (Fig. 7.24), perhaps giving some indication of one of the activities associated with liquid (and drainage) that occurs within house cells. Equally, haematite is also present in quantity at the majority of these sites. On the basis of this evidence it could be asserted that many later Neolithic houses were decorated with coloured rendering, and that dyes were created in house recesses.

However, for Childe rather than being employed as a means of colouring the house interior, 'the red and white pigments found in the small vessels... had doubtless been used for painting the body' (1931a, 144). Following on from this statement a further connection can be made between the colouring and adornment of houses and the human body. Significantly, given the general theme of this volume, such linkage has been pursued more widely in regard to *sociétés à maisons* (*e.g.* Waterson 1990), with specific reference to houses, ancestral bodies and particular historical conditions (*e.g.* Sissons 2010).

This brief discussion has taken us on a journey from wrapping and rendering the Red House, to the relationship between painting and adorning people, and named houses, as representing different social strategies to both maintain and differentiate relatively unstable corporate groups. For *sociétés à maisons*, the maintenance of identity and perpetuation of the 'house' during ever-shifting social circumstances is an essential condition (*ibid.*). The continuity and succession of 'houses' can be portrayed and materialized in a number of ways; in the context of 3rd millennium cal BC Orkney, it can be suggested that the reproduction of the physical house and its place was a prime mechanism. Yet, the contraction and fragmentation of the social group as represented by the Red and Grey Houses starkly reveals the changing and variable circumstances and fortunes of different Neolithic *sociétés à maisons* through time.

Due to the constant recycling of building material, a detailed picture of the expansion and contraction of occupation at Crossiecrown is difficult to trace. Judging from the spread of radiocarbon dates (Chapter 10) in conjunction with the range of ceramics and other forms of material culture, occupation of the site appears relatively continuous. Obviously, short duration breaks and other junctures may be difficult to discern but no major abandonment layers were observed within the excavated areas. A further characteristic of Crossiecrown is the lack of settlement shift.

Andrew M. Jones notes the continuity present within ceramic technology, again transcending 'stylistic' variability (Chapter 11; A. M. Jones 2012, 116–19). Such continuity in dwelling, as noted above, is almost certainly present at Muckquoy, Firth (see Chapter 9), and was observed at Pool, Sanday (Hunter *et al.* 2007). However, near the settlement of Pool, at the Bay of Stove, a clear settlement shift of over 200 metres occurred during the 3rd millennium cal BC (Bond *et al.* 1995). A similar situation may be present at Rinyo, Rousay, and Links of Noltland, Westray. A corollary of the inhabitation of a particular place, as seen at Crossiecrown, is the practice of demolishing dwellings and re-cycling the stone for new building projects. To live, wrapped in the stone of previous generations, is a potent material metaphor of continuity and connection.

Within the broader context of divergent settlement histories, Neolithic people appear to have occupied this place, on and off, for fifteen hundred years, an enormous length of time. Just as today we know the site as Crossiecrown, so during the Neolithic period this was a named and widely known place. As with a number of late Neolithic settlements, the inhabitants of the Red and Grey Houses lived among the detritus, and dwelled within the materials of their predecessors. Yet, at Crossiecrown they could claim a degree of longevity of place unmatched by many other social groups in Neolithic Orkney. With a degree of legitimacy, they could also declare that their 'name' had lived on over a huge expanse of time and could glance up towards the imposing passage grave of Quanterness to support such assertions, and it is to Quanterness and the mortuary monuments of the Bay of Firth that we now turn our attention.

CHAPTER EIGHT

Reorientating the Dead of Crossiecrown: Quanterness and Ramberry Head

Rebecca Crozier, Colin Richards, Judith Robertson† and Adrian Challands

Figure 8.1 View of Quanterness passage grave from Crossiecrown (Colin Richards).

8.1 The difficulty of Orcadian chambered cairns

Towards the end of the 4th millennium cal BC, when the inhabitants of Crossiecrown looked to the southwest, the familiar sight of the great passage grave of Quanterness greeted their eyes lying on the lower northern slopes of Wideford Hill (Fig. 8.1). In an ontological sense this must have been a reassuring sight, as its presence spoke of continuity, identity and connections. Continuity and identity existed in the knowledge that previous inhabitants of Crossiecrown, and perhaps other settlements in the Bay of Firth area, had built the monument and a number were actually resting within its dark interior. Connections were embedded in the very fabric and form of the monument, and the network of inter-relationships that enabled passage grave architecture to radiate well beyond the shores of Orkney. But was the great passage grave the sole component of an architecture of death? Could the ritual process of transformation from life to death involve greater complexity and different places? Finally, did all the inhabitants pass through the passage grave or was Quanterness involved in a broader meshwork of death?

Despite a recent reassessment of the chronology of the passage grave (Schulting *et al.* 2010), it is improbable that Quanterness would have been standing when Crossiecrown was founded nor during its initial occupation. This is an interesting corollary of the chronology of passage grave architecture in particular and Orcadian chambered cairns more generally. It affects not only Quanterness, but also the other passage graves of central Mainland, including Cuween Hill and Wideford Hill, which overlook the settlements of the Bay of Firth (see Figs 1.9 and 9.13). Consequently, when settlement began at Crossiecrown, Wideford Hill, Brae of Smerquoy, and Stonehall, the upper hill slopes were devoid of burial monuments. It would seem that only when the occupation of these sites became well established that the passage graves were built. This sequence of construction was not, however, all pervasive. For example, passage graves were not built overlooking the Bay of Firth settlements of Knowes of Trotty, Muckquoy or Saverock (Fig. 1.9).

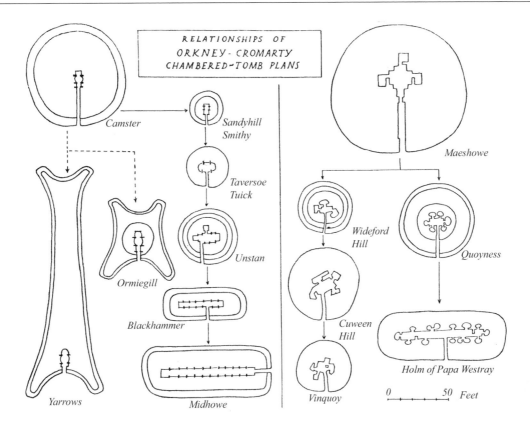

Figure 8.2 The typology of chambered cairns as constructed by Stuart Piggott (after Piggott 1954).

There are two main issues concerning the Orcadian chambered cairns which are brought into focus when considering monuments around the Bay of Firth. The first concerns the status of passage graves and their relationship with stalled cairns (Fig. 8.2). The second relates to the chronological relationship between passage graves and stalled cairns. Interestingly, there is no clear evidence that either form of architecture originated in Orkney. When Stuart Piggott classified the Orkney-Cromarty chambered 'tombs' into three typological groups – Yarrows, Camster and Maes Howe - the discourse was diffusionist and motivation was to help 'clarify the problem of the routes of colonization' (Piggott 1954, 234). Ironically, despite applying an underlying logic of cultural recognition in terms of architecture and spatial distribution, such *schema* failed to examine comparative landscape position or, in many instances, spatial distribution at a local level. As both passage graves and stalled cairns fall under the rubric of chambered cairns or 'tombs', we are left with substantial architectural (typological) differences apparent within chambered cairns of the same class of monument (*e.g.* Davidson and Henshall 1989). For Piggott, this was

unproblematic as the Maes Howe type passage graves belonged to a different cultural tradition, since 'there are no comparable monuments on the Scottish mainland… they can hardly be other than the products of some individual community coming to Orkney, probably by the western approaches' (1954, 245). The concentration of passage graves on Mainland, Orkney, was also noticed by Piggott who went so far as identifying Stromness as a point of entry (*ibid.*, 236).

Of course, this notion of colonization (see also Daniel and Powell 1949), along with futile questions concerning who was responsible for building the monuments, is now discredited. However, the presence of passage grave architecture along the western seaboard may relate to wider social strategies, particularly those concerned with the construction of relational identities, perhaps involving processes of mythologization (*e.g.* Richards 2013c, 276–80).

Because both stalled and passage grave architectural forms are identified as chambered cairns, a chronological disjunction between them has facilitated an evolutionary discourse (*e.g.* Renfrew 1979; Hedges 1984, 99–126). However, there seems little reason why, in terms of architecture, such entirely disparate monuments represent different ends of an evolutionary sequence (*contra* Renfrew 1979, 211). Apart from architectural divergence such a transformation is not necessarily supported by their chronological situation. As discussed in Chapter 2, the building of stalled chambered cairns was well under way by the mid-4th millennium cal BC (see also Chapter 10), while passage graves are being built and used slightly later. A recent re-assessment of the dating of Quanterness concludes that its contents date to the mid-late 4th millennium cal BC (Schulting *et al.* 2010). While this re-dating is worryingly early for Orcadian Neolithic evolutionary schemes (*e.g.* Renfrew 1979), it is not inconsistent with Irish passage grave chronologies (Scarre *et al.* 2003, O'Sullivan 2005; Bergh and Hensey 2013, 358). Consequently, there is little chronological support for an evolutionary scheme of replacing 'types'.

Accepting chronological disjunction between the building of the first stalled cairns and passage graves does not preclude their continued concurrent construction and use. A number of years ago, Niall Sharples (1985) inserted a degree of chronological control in his discussion of mortuary practices in relation to the different architecture of the Orcadian chambered cairns. Of pertinence here is the emphasis placed on the lengthening of the passage (through time), as an architectural adjunct of exaggerated physical and conceptual separation. This was to mitigate a supposed altering relationship between the living and the dead manifest in the construction of chambered cairns in new landscape positions, for instance, downhill and closer to the everyday domain of the living. The problem with this scheme when applied to the Bay of Firth is obvious. Although Quanterness is situated in a more downslope location (Fig. 8.1), the other two passage graves are upslope. In assuming this position they actually mimic the landscape placing of a number of stalled chambered cairns.

Here then we are faced with a conundrum. In the Bay of Firth area, the two passage graves on Cuween and Wideford Hills are built in a similar elevated position as is assumed by stalled cairns in other parts of Orkney. Consequently, in the Bay of Firth landscape, it seems as if either the different (typological) forms of chambered cairn architecture were interchangeable, or else an elevated position was required but that only passage grave architecture was appropriate. To confound the issue, there seems to be a confusing divergence in the contents of the chambered cairns, both in passage graves and stalled cairns. Equally, there appears to be little similarity or consistency within the contents of

either form of architecture. The question here then is whether the divergence in chambered cairn contents, and internal typological inconsistency, translates into a real difference in their role or related social practices. It is to the interpretation of passage grave deposits in the Bay of Firth that we will now turn to explore these issues further.

8.2 Rethinking mortuary practices occurring within the Bay of Firth

Possibly the sheer scale and substantial number of Orcadian chambered cairns (both stalled cairns and passage graves) compels a desire for suitably grandiose interpretations of the role they played in the presumed death rituals exercised within (and without) their confines. Always, considerations move beyond simple ossuaries, with interpretations encompassing visions of such structures as territorial markers (Renfrew 1979), monuments for ancestral worship (Sharples 1984; Barber 1997) or containers for select portions of society (Thomas 2000; Fowler 2005). The mobility of human remains, coupled with the disarticulated condition of many assemblages within the megaliths, has led to the development of theories of curation and circulation of bones across the landscape, with themes of transformation, manipulation and movement infusing the literature (*e.g.* Sharples 1985; Richards 1988; Thomas 2000).

Despite the large number of Neolithic chambered cairns identified in Orkney, few of them have yielded human remains, yet, even when conspicuously absent, the dead have occupied a central role in interpretation. Currently, the mortuary treatments identified as having been accorded to those manifest within the chambered cairns range from direct inhumation to secondary burial and exposure of the body to the elements (excarnation). However, the various interpretations are founded on evidence derived from only a few chambered cairns, reflecting both the limitations of the data and the variability in the contents of different sites.

A lack of real comprehension of the mortuary rites has evidently created challenges in understanding the nature of Orcadian chambered cairns. Such complications are perhaps compounded by a tendency to seek a homogeneous explanation for structures that are considered, based on key similarities in design, to serve the same role. An example of this may be observed in Reilly's (2003, 150) approach: a complex system of progressive disaggregation of the body across several stalled cairns on the southern hillslopes of Rousay. Perhaps one of the principal difficulties in accepting his elegant vision of the dissolution of the human body across the landscape lies in our inability to demonstrate the absolute contemporaneity of the chambered cairns. The fact that the mid-terrace cairn in Reilly's sequence, the Knowe of Lairo, was originally constructed with a tripartite-stalled chamber which is subsequently remodelled into 'passage grave' architecture within a horned cairn, does not appear to hinder such an interpretation. Nevertheless, accepting Reilly's hypothesis, Fowler (2010, 12) suggests this movement of bone is a mechanism for distributing the person throughout the landscape, with specific elements placed at higher points than others. These remains were therefore highly symbolic in their 'inalienable association' to their place of origin.

However, Reilly's intriguing interpretation is put to the test when applied to Quanterness. In a microcosm of what has been construed for the Rousay cairns, Reilly (2003, 150) proposes that within the passage grave the movement and disintegration of the body is confined to a single location. Fully or partly articulated corpses were placed in the main chamber until they became defleshed, at which point the larger bones were either removed or placed in the side cells. There are, however, a number of problems inherent in this interpretation. First, there was no discernible pattern within the Quanterness remains as was observable in the Rousay chambered cairns. Second, the different architecture of Quanterness could equally suggest an entirely different mortuary rite as it does a continuation, in microcosm, of the rites found in the stalled cairns. Third, the application of the interpretation to Quanterness ignores the temporal and spatial disparity between the monuments examined. However, while these concerns are equally important in their own right, collectively they point to an overarching issue that undermines such an interpretative discourse. Without a better understanding of the material, and specifically the human remains, how can we truly comprehend the activities associated with the passage grave?

Indeed, upon closer scrutiny, the foundations of many past and current interpretations of funerary practice in Orkney have depended on revisiting original excavation reports (*e.g.* Richards 1988; Fowler 2001, 142–45; Reilly 2003). Re-analysis of the human remains themselves has been largely neglected (although see Barber 1997; Lawrence 2006; 2013), a situation that has increasingly come under criticism (Beckett and Robb 2009, 57). Such apparent oversight arguably reflects the challenge presented by the uncompromising character of the material itself: disarticulated, mixed, fragmented and incomplete, with small sample sizes and a susceptibility to cultural and post-depositional biases (Wysocki and Whittle 2000, 591). Traditional osteological analyses are concerned with retrieving demographic information from skeletal populations. However, the absence of discrete skeletons within many of the Orcadian assemblages clearly precludes such investigations. Consequentially, this material has been considered unlikely to provide further evidence that might enhance our understanding of past populations.

This situation is not, however, insurmountable. In recent years, advances in the fields of forensic archaeology and taphonomy have furnished researchers with a new set of tools with which to approach less straightforward assemblages, such as those encountered in the Orcadian chambered cairns (*e.g.* Lawrence 2006; Crozier 2012; 2014). This chapter, therefore, presents new data derived from a recent taphonomic re-analysis of a number of assemblages (Crozier 2012; 2014), with a focus on the passage graves overlooking the Bay of Firth. This new data challenges current interpretations and forces a reconsideration of how we envisage the mortuary practices associated with the Orcadian chambered cairns.

8.2.1 Quanterness, Cuween and Wideford

As stated above, the Orcadian chambered cairns have tended to be seen as possessing homogeneity of function (*e.g.* Sharples 1985; Richards 1988). A cursory consideration of the various excavation reports clearly indicates that we have been too quick to seek a generalised interpretation for the associated deposits. A detailed re-examination of the passage graves, Quanterness, Wideford Hill and Cuween Hill, within the coastal zone of the Bay of Firth, serves to illustrate that for too long archaeologists have overlooked subtle, yet important variation in practice.

Colin Renfrew's excavations at Quanterness ran from 1972–1974 and revealed one of the best preserved of the Orcadian passage graves (Fig. 8.3), with four of its six side cells accessible and unblocked by rubble. This exploration led to the recovery of an unprecedented volume of human bone, in excess of 12,000 fragments according to their original analyst, Judson Chesterman (1979, 97). The conclusions drawn by Chesterman, from his original examination of the human remains has since had a profound impact on interpretations of the mortuary rites associated with similar structures (*e.g.* Hedges 1983; Richards 1988; Jones 1998; Thomas 2000; Fowler 2010).

Figure 8.3 The 1973 excavation trench running up the western side of Quanterness exposed the cairn material (reproduced by kind permission of Colin Renfrew and the University of Kent).

Figure 8.4 The upper bone spread running up to the entrance to the northern cell (reproduced by kind permission of Colin Renfrew and the University of Kent).

Despite being disarticulated, fragmented and in total disarray (Figs 8.4 and 8.5), Chesterman asserted that the 12,500 bone fragments from Quanterness were representative of a MNI (minimum number of individuals) of 157; one of the largest assemblages of human remains known for Neolithic Britain. Prior to this excavation, Orcadian passage graves had been found to range from containing no evidence of human remains, such as at Wideford Hill (Davidson and Henshall 1989, 169), up to 14 or 15 individuals at Quoyness, Sanday (Farrer 1870, 400; Wells 1952, 137). These figures were largely in line with numbers recovered from Neolithic chambered tombs in Southern England (Smith 2005, 2006; Smith and Brickley 2004, 2009). At Quanterness, Chesterman determined that both males and females were represented. Furthermore, nearly all ages were present with the only anomaly being an absence of infants younger than 3 months.

The condition of the human remains from Quanterness was explained in terms of a mortuary rite encapsulating excarnation and secondary burial practices. For example, Chesterman (1979, 101–102) envisioned a protracted ritual that was initiated with bodies being divested of flesh via exposure to the elements, or, due to an apparent absence of animal damage, possibly burial in

sand. Following the decay of soft tissue, the remains were then subjected to fire in what Chesterman refers to as a 'half-cremation', before being broken and finally brought to the cairn (Chesterman 1979, 102; Renfrew 1979, 158). Skulls and long bones were considered to be conspicuously absent. The parts most commonly found were often small bones: axis and atlas vertebrae and carpal and tarsal bones. This discrepancy in skeletal representation led Renfrew (1979, 167) to propose that bones were removed at a later time, a perspective that has seen considerable development in Neolithic studies (Fowler 2001, 2010; A. M. Jones 1998, 318; Richards 1988; Thomas 1988; Thomas 2000, 662).

Excavated by Charleson (1902), the passage grave of Cuween Hill is situated above cultivated land on a moorland hillside at 76 m OD (Fig. 8.6). At the base of the hill lie the settlement areas of Stonehall (Chapters 5 and 6). The passage grave is relatively small in having a diameter of 16.8m and a maximum height of about 2.6m (Davidson and Henshall 1989, 112). Actually, Cuween Hill is most often associated with the discovery of 24 dog skulls as opposed to human remains (Charleson 1902, 736). This proliferation of canine crania has been likened in significance to finds of sea eagle remains at Isbister, leading to suggestions of some form of totemism at these

Figure 8.5 The bone spread in the central chamber at Quanterness (reproduced by kind permission of Colin Renfrew and the University of Kent).

sites (A. M. Jones 1998; Hedges 2000, 158). Other bones including cattle, what is probably a small horse and birds were also present. Charleson also referenced bones of animals in the debris that was removed from the main chamber. This osseous material was described as being in a fragmentary state and beyond preservation (Charleson 1902, 733).

Prior to the availability of dating evidence, Renfrew hypothesised that Cuween Hill was probably constructed at a similar time to both Quanterness and nearby Wideford Hill, its simplicity in plan possibly suggesting that the more elevated pair were a little earlier (Renfrew 1979, 203). More recently, bones from three of the 24 dogs found in the tomb produced dates that cluster around the middle of the 3rd millennium BC (Sheridan 2005; Chapter 10; Table 8.1) and are assumed to represent later use of the passage grave (Schulting *et al.* 2010, 28).

With reference to the human remains, evidence for at least eight interments was identified. Located within the main chamber, accompanying the dog remains, were several human long bones and five human skulls, three of which 'crumbled away when touched' (Charleson 1902, 733). Within a recess of the west cell was another

Figure 8.6 Aerial view of Cuween Hill passage grave (Craig Taylor).

Lab No	Material	Date cal BC	Position
UB-6422	Human left femur	2150–1930	entrance passage
GU-12477	Dog humerus	2620–2460	chamber
GU-12478	Dog humerus	2580–2340	chamber
GU-12479	Dog humerus	2630–2460	chamber

skull; a seventh was in the centre of the south cell; the last was embedded in clay near the roof of the passage. During Charleson's excavation portions of human long bones 'showing evidence of cremation' were discovered close to the passage/chamber threshold (*ibid.*, 733–38). The skull embedded near the roof and the remains in the passage were thought to indicate a deliberate blocking (*ibid.*, 734). In 1888 the remains of a skeleton were found in the north part of the west cell. There is no further information regarding this occurrence and it is not clear if this refers to an articulated skeleton, a partial skeleton or bone fragments. Secondary interments were said to have been found at the west side of the cairn before 1901, but there was no further reference to the secondary interments within the report.

The human remains were originally examined by Professor Sir William Turner, who described five calvariae and portions of three femurs (*ibid.*, 737). Based on suture closure, he surmised that the cranial remains were from those in the 'later stage of life'. He thought two were probably male, but could not be certain. Other than details of various cranial measurements that were taken, Turner does not mention any other anomalies that would be of note, such as pathology or trauma.

Today, the stepped appearance of the Wideford Hill passage grave is a product of previous interventions by HM Office of Works (Kilbride-Jones 1973, 95; see Fig. 8.7). The burial chamber, with three large adjunct cells, is entered by a passage about 17.5 feet long. When Petrie excavated the cairn in 1849, he discovered three empty cells and a chamber semi-filled with stone rubble; the floor was devoid of artefacts (Kilbride-Jones 1973, 90; Davidson and Henshall 1989, 170). In terms of human remains, an absence of such evidence provides a stark contrast to the situations of Quanterness and Cuween Hill. In fact, the only remains discovered were animal bones and animal teeth recovered from what has been identified as the rubble fill of the central chamber. The rubble fill is suggested to be the result of debris being poured down through a square opening in the apex of the building, choking two-thirds of the chamber (Davidson and Henshall 1989, 170).

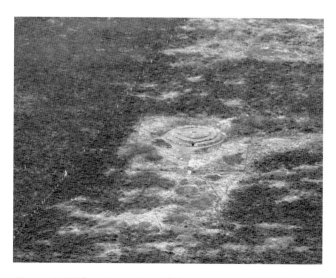

Figure 8.7 The orientation of the passage at Wideford Hill is roughly aligned on Cuween Hill passage grave to the west (Craig Taylor).

8.2.1.1 Whole bodies or partial remains? An osteological perspective

In approaching complex assemblages such as Quanterness, the first step is to deduce the minimum number of individuals represented by the commingled remains. Once the volume of material has been defined, it is then essential to explore how the individuals are represented; in other words, identifying which parts of the body (or bodies) are present or absent (Skeletal Element Representation or SER). This data is vital, as depositional practices may then be intimated according to the survival patterns of specific bone elements (Haglund *et al.* 1989, 993–94; Roksandic 2002; Saul and Saul 2002; Smith 2006). For example, the skeletal profile for identifying secondary burial activities is distinct from the profile indicating the interment of whole bodies. This approach is the premise behind much of the more recent research into the skeletal representation profiles of Neolithic mortuary sites in England (Smith 2005, 2006) and Ireland (Beckett and Robb 2009; Beckett 2011).

Evidently, in order to successfully distinguish patterns which are not indicative of 'normal' preservation and decay of human remains, it is first imperative to possess a detailed understanding of the 'normal' preservation pattern. This is the type of preservation encountered in bodies that have been interred whole and not suffered any further disturbance, such as occurs within a Christian inhumation cemetery. Much of the research concerning typical patterns of bodily decay and disarticulation

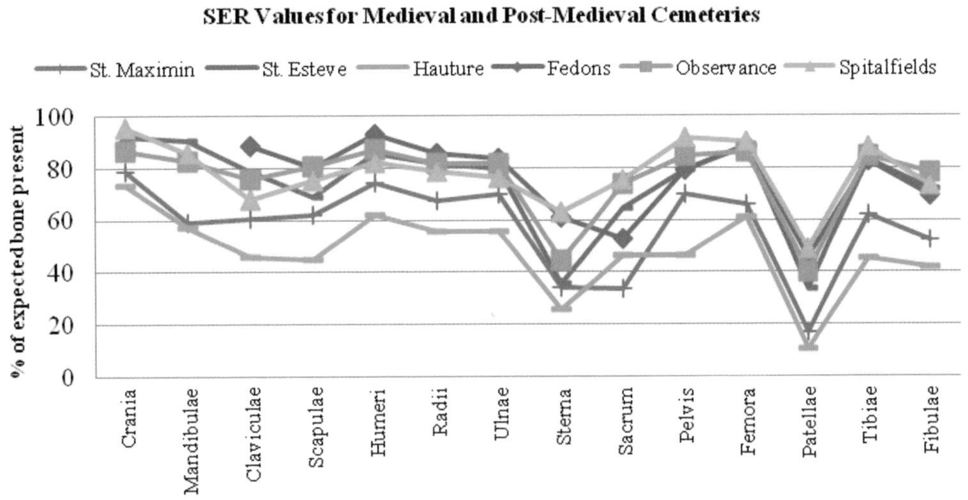

SER Values for Medieval and Post-Medieval Cemeteries

Figure 8.8 SER values observed for the whole sample (subadult and adult) (adapted from Bello and Andrews 2009, 3).

is contained within the forensic literature (*e.g.* Mant 1984; 1987; Janaway 1997; Gunn 2009, 12). However, investigation of the 'typical' patterns of preservation, but from an archaeological perspective, has been conducted by Bello and Andrews (2009). Their study utilised three medieval and three post-medieval Christian cemeteries from France and England. Within all six of these sites, interments involved complete corpses, without the intervention of practices that could result in the alteration or disappearance of selected portions of the skeleton. In this way, the patterns of preservation could be associated with natural taphonomic processes and therefore differences in the relative frequency of osseous remains in the assemblages were more likely to depend on the structural qualities of the bones (Bello and Andrews 2009, 9). All six sites were found to have very similar frequencies of skeletal parts represented (Fig. 8.8). Of further interest was the observation that representation frequencies between the French cemeteries (earthen burials) were very similar to Spitalfields (coffins within a crypt), intimating that human bones have a common macroscopic pattern of preservation, regardless of the characteristics of the site (Bello and Andrews 2009, 9). In broad terms, this pattern reflects higher frequencies for more robust and dense bones and lower frequencies for smaller and more cancellous (spongy) bones. It was therefore proffered that the comparison of the skeletal element representation of a collective burial, such as Quanterness, with the frequencies of human remains from these cemeteries could provide a new interpretive tool for the comprehension of this collective burial

formation (Bello and Andrews 2009, 9). Comparison of Neolithic SER (Skeletal Element Representation) to medieval and post-medieval SER has already been utilised in this way for other British (Smith 2005; Smith and Brickley 2009, 72) and Irish sites (Beckett and Robb 2009; Beckett 2011). According to studies by Bello and Andrews (2009, 3), SER values over 50% are considered to demonstrate good representation.

Defined as the act of depriving or divesting of flesh, excarnation may occur as the only stage of a mortuary ritual, or it may be the primary step, preceding a secondary rite. Many ethnographic examples of excarnation are recognised, a prominent example being the Sioux and the Cheyenne Indians of North America (Ubelaker and Willey 1978) who were known to expose the dead on platforms while the flesh decayed. Excarnation has also been recorded in Southern Taiwan as a means to speed up the de-fleshing of human remains, which have not sufficiently decayed, to allow progression of the mortuary ritual (Tsu 2000, 14).

One of the most frequently cited explanations for the discovery of human remains in a state of disarticulation and disorder, in the absence of evidence for deliberate or accidental disturbance, is of mortuary practices involving excarnation and/or secondary burial. However, with the advancement in understanding of various taphonomic agents (*e.g.* involvement of animals, differential decay of bones) identification of these funerary traditions is more cautious and considers more strands of evidence than simply the presence of disarticulation. Currently, the accepted archaeological indicators for exposed bodies are those outlined by Carr and Knüsel (1997, 170):

1. Animal gnawing on bones.
2. Scattered, isolated, fragmentary, weathered or splintered bones.
3. Disarticulated skeletons.
4. Incomplete skeletons lacking phalanges, a limb or other parts.

The recovery of a skeletal element representation profile lacking the smaller bones of the skeleton, for example, bones of the hands and feet, would logically suggest that the remains represent secondary burial *after* excarnation (Dowd 2002, 89; Dowd *et al.* 2006, 17). This is because the smaller bones are often overlooked when skeletal remains are being retrieved for interment elsewhere. Conversely, the discovery of scattered and isolated smaller bones, with an absence of the larger limb bones and skulls, would reasonably suggest the site of discovery was the *location* for the excarnation rite.

Secondary burial is defined by Metcalf and Huntington as 'the regular and socially sanctioned removal of the relics of some or all deceased persons from a place of temporary storage to a permanent resting place' (1991, 97). It is generally accepted that this movement of bone will occur after the flesh has decayed, with the time separating decomposition from final interment conceived and described as a liminal phase (Carr and Knüsel 1997, 167). As stated above, secondary burials tend to be identified by a predominance of long bones and crania in the skeletal element representation. The smaller bones, such as phalanges, patellae and vertebrae tend to be lost.

Confident assessment of secondary burial and excarnation on the basis of skeletal element representation alone is, however, too simplistic. This is because some disposal patterns may appear to be the result of secondary deposition when, in fact, they are the result of a primary disposal that has been modified by subsequent natural forces (Schroeder 2001, 82). For example, it has been established that the smaller bones of the hands and feet are often under-represented as they can be overlooked during excavation (Bello and Andrews 2009, 4), and the more delicate bones (such as the sternum and sacrum) may have already eroded. This phenomenon could create a similar profile to that of secondary burial deposition; predominantly crania and long bones. Research by Beckett and Robb (2009, 68) on human remains from the Irish Neolithic has highlighted similar problems. They argue that it is more reliable to look for an *over-representation* of the small fragile bones as this is more likely to reflect genuine patterning resulting from specific mortuary practices such as the removal of crania and long bones. Furthermore, it is suggested that as crania tend to survive

better than small or fragile bones, the curation or specific deposition of crania will be more likely to manifest as an imbalance between crania and major long bones (*ibid.*).

Thus, the taphonomic profile of an assemblage that has been excarnated and/or subjected to a secondary burial rite will involve consideration of more than the skeletal element representation. Assessment should also be mediated by the preservation patterns linked to the anatomical structure of human bones (Bello and Andrews 2006, 9). There may also be the presence of tool marks where the process of dismemberment is completed manually (Redfern 2008, 283; Beckett 2011, 403). Many researchers also attribute fragmentation in archaeological assemblages to secondary burial processes (Chesterman 1979, 107; Carr and Knüsel 1997, 170; Redfern 2008, 283; Beckett 2011, 403). However, Barber (1997) rightly cautions that none of the ethnographic examples of secondary burial practices, which involve the retention of human bone, ever involve the deliberate fragmentation of the remains. Fragmentation is often associated with burial rites which demand the obliteration of the individual, such as may be witnessed today during Tibetan Sky Burials (Pedersen 2013, 14).

Another hypothesis cited to explain the relative disorder of human remains within megalithic tombs is that of successive inhumation. This is defined as the continual deposition of complete bodies that are often displaced by the insertion of later interments (Beckett 2011, 402). Osteologically, this mortuary rite would be characterised by partial articulations and high/ proportional representation of skeletal elements: in other words, counts of human bones indicating that bodies decomposed *in situ* (*ibid.*), and similar patterns to that observed by Bello and Andrews (2009) would be expected (*e.g.* Richards 1988, Fig. 4.4).

8.2.1.2 Invisible Bones? Osteological Evidence from Quanterness

In order to reassess the burial practices, as represented by the human skeletal material within Quanterness, a detailed taphonomic analysis was required (Crozier 2012). The key aim of the investigation was to assess the remains for evidence that may account for their condition at the time of recovery, thereby generating new insights into the mortuary practices that may have occurred. As stated, the initial stage of examination was to assess how many individuals were represented by the volume of material present.

The resultant figures were found to be in disagreement with Chesterman's original estimate of 157 individuals,

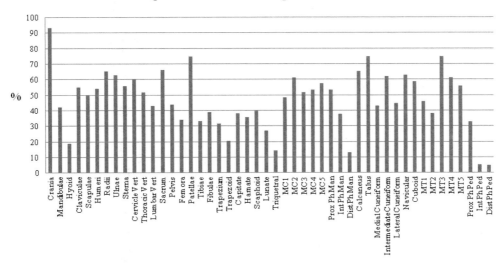

Figure 8.9 Skeletal element representation at Quanterness. This is calculated as the percentage of the MNI represented by the MNE.

with the reduced figure of 10,500 fragments actually representing a minimum of 59 individuals (Crozier 2012; 2014). Although this is a significant realignment of the original figures, it is not unprecedented. A similar reduction has previously been calculated by Lawrence (2006) for the human skeletal remains from the chambered cairn at Isbister. Additionally, it was found that all age ranges were represented, including the identification of infants under the age of 3 months. Infants of this age had previously been overlooked, most likely owing to their very small size. This original omission led to Quanterness being assigned a unique identity amongst the Orcadian chambered cairns; here, a section of the associated society was excluded from the seemingly collective monument (cf. Richards 1988). So much so that when infants of this age range are identified in the course of recent excavations, for example at Banks chambered cairn (Lee 2011), their discovery is seen as being noteworthy. Quanterness retains a unique quality in the volume of bone recovered, but the concept that this particular age range within society has been subjected to a differential mortuary treatment must now on current evidence be discarded.

The next stage in the analytical process was to determine which parts of the human skeleton were represented. As described above, this would provide direct evidence as to whether or not the remains indicated a mortuary rite of excarnation, secondary burial or direct inhumation. The Minimum Number of Elements (MNE) is the minimum number of a particular skeletal element necessary to account for the number of specimens representing that element (Lyman 2001, 102). The Skeletal Element Representation (SER) is then calculated as the proportion of an element present compared with what would be expected if the MNI is considered to represent whole skeletons.

Quanterness was found to possess a high level of skeletal representation (SER), with many representation values exceeding 50% (Fig. 8.9). Significantly, every bone of the skeleton was recorded as present, including the smaller and more delicate bones such as the distal phalanges and hyoid respectively. The presence of such material is not only an indication of the good general levels of preservation, but is also due to Renfrew's decision to sieve the Quanterness deposits, thereby maximising recovery. This representation is meaningful as it supports the hypothesis that whole bodies were interred. As intimated previously, funerary rites involving the relocation of human remains will inevitably result in the loss of the smaller bones of the hands and feet. Taking the 50% level as a threshold, the Quanterness crania, in particular, are very well represented. Skeletal elements of the upper body are better represented than the lower body. The clavicles are also in reasonable abundance, as are the scapulae. These patterns in the bone representation are, despite the temporal differences, of a similar pattern to that detailed by Bello and Andrews (2009, 3–5) for the medieval and post-medieval inhumation burials.

Generally speaking, the osteological investigation provides evidence that serves to undermine a hypothesis of excarnation at Quanterness. However, all is not entirely straightforward. It may be further observed that, due to their inherent structure, bones generally considered to be more susceptible to a low survivorship such as the sterna and sacrum, are also well represented (over 50%). Given the survival of these less dense and more fragile bones, it is curious that the femora display a noticeable under-representation (Fig. 8.9). Additionally, relative to the crania, the mandibulae, a more robust element considered to normally show good survivorship, also seems poorly represented. It may also be queried how Chesterman arrived at the conclusion that crania were underrepresented, when the results of this most recent study illustrate otherwise.

8.2.1.3 The Significance of Crania at Quanterness
When evaluating commingled and fragmented assemblages, such as those encountered for this study, one of the most common methods for quantifying the assemblage is to calculate the Number of Identified Specimens (NISP). The NISP is defined as the number of identified specimens in an assemblage (Lyman 2001, 100). A comparison of the NISP with the MNE (Minimum Number of Elements) will provide an indication of the intensity of fragmentation.

During evaluation of the Quanterness assemblage it became apparent that crania were particularly well represented. This observation was especially significant as it contradicted the previous perception that this element was extremely under-represented (Chesterman 1979, 102). Such fragmentation was the antithesis of the studies of Isbister, where Chesterman (1983) recorded that many of the crania were relatively complete. Data from the new taphonomic study provides a hypothesis for this occurrence. It is plausible that Chesterman's observation may have arisen due to the severe fragmentation of this particular element. This interpretation is verified by observing that the minimum number of 55 crania was represented by the NISP of over 670 fragments, a large ratio implying the Quanterness crania were indeed highly fragmented. However, even when fragmented, crania possess diagnostic elements, such as the petrous portion of the temporal bone (ear canal), allowing for easier recognition. It would seem that the Quanterness crania simply lacked the visual presence of Chesterman's comparative assemblage from Isbister (Hedges 1983), where many of the crania were relatively complete. Therefore, it can be advocated that the presence of

profoundly fragmented crania hindered the original analysis leading to an incorrect conclusion.

8.2.1.4 The Significance of Mandibles and Femora
The sacrum, sternum and hyoid are more fragile elements due to their lower bone density and shape. These elements are, therefore, traditionally accepted as having poorer levels of preservation relative to the rest of the skeleton (Bello and Andrews 2009). Good representation of these elements at Quanterness indicates there must have been favourable conditions for the survival of osseous material. Against this backdrop, the poorer representation of mandibles (relative to crania) and femora within this assemblage seems anomalous. An under-representation of long bones was noted in the original report (Renfrew 1979, 167). Both mandibles and femora, in particular, are usually expected to have much better survival rates due to their greater bone density and robustness (Bello and Andrews 2009, 4). Additionally, mandibles are considered to have good survivorship resulting from their association with the crania, and the crania have now been shown to be well represented. It would seem the apparent absence of these bones requires further explanation.

As demonstrated, the skeletal representation data is characteristic of the interment of whole bodies. Circulation and movement of human bone (Richards 1988; Thomas 2000; Fowler 2010) is one of the more prevalent interpretations of the partial nature of human remains within Neolithic burial contexts. Consequently, an obvious explanation for the negative presence of the mandibles and femora is their removal as part of such a process. Perceived under-representations of crania and femora at megalithic tombs in Ireland have been suggested to reflect a similar rite (Beckett and Robb 2009, 63; Becket 2011). Analogous patterns have also been observed for assemblages from southern Britain (Smith and Brickley 2009, 71). As with Quanterness, these southern British assemblages indicate good preservation of smaller and more delicate bones. Smith and Brickley (*ibid.*) have suggested three scenarios to explain this phenomenon:

1. The missing material never entered the monument. The bodies placed within the chambers were brought from a prior context elsewhere after the soft tissue had decayed, with some elements being left out either incidentally or through deliberate selection.
2. The missing elements were deliberately selected and removed from the chamber following the decomposition of the soft tissue.
3. The missing elements were removed in the course of more recent disturbance or unrecorded antiquarian activity.

Based solely on the information contained in the original excavation reports, these three scenarios are perfectly plausible. However, drawing on the new evidence from this most recent taphonomic study, a new, alternative hypothesis must be considered; it is arguable that the 'missing elements', following inhumation, *never left the tomb at all*. How does the evidence support this new hypothesis?

Comparison of the NISP to the MNE (Table 8.2) demonstrates considerable fracturing of both these elements (mandible and femur) at Quanterness. Accepting that severe fracturing reduces the capacity for identification, it can be suggested that this intensity of fragmentation therefore equates to destruction of the element. This extensive fragmentation would, therefore, be an *analytical*, rather than *actual*, absence (Lyman 1994, 379; Leach 2005, 61). In light of these observations, the apparent under-representation of mandibles and femora at Quanterness is argued to be the result of destruction, reflected in the large MNE to NISP ratios, rather than careful and deliberate removal as part of subsequent mortuary rites. The high levels of fragmentation have resulted in an obliteration of the more diagnostic parts of the elements utilised in the calculation of a MNE. The influence of severe fragmentation on interpretations of bone representation does not seem to have been considered for the human Neolithic assemblages where skeletal representation is investigated. In previous research, analysis has tended to focus upon discrepancies in representation between identifiable fragments. This observation highlights a potential pit-fall in deducing mortuary rites based on the skeletal representation. Therefore, whilst the MNE calculation has highlighted an anomaly in these particular elements, the explanation is not necessarily immediately evident.

At Quanterness the original analysis of the human remains indicated that skulls and long bones were conspicuously absent. The elements most commonly found were small bones: axis and atlas vertebrae and carpal and tarsal bones, thus prompting hypotheses that the 'missing' bones had been removed (Chesterman 1979, 102). However, subsequent studies into bone survivorship repeatedly demonstrate that, due to their greater density and therefore greater robustness, bones such as the axis and atlas are precisely the bones that are likely to survive (Mays 2002, 213). Undoubtedly, this combination of survivorship and the character of the Quanterness assemblage has ensured that Chesterman's observations have endured to influence broader interpretations of burial rites in Neolithic Orkney. However, as this

Table 8.2 Minimum number of elements and number of identified specimens for Quanterness (adapted from Crozier 2012).

Element	Minimum Number of Elements	Number of Identified Specimens
Crania	55	676
Femora	25	106
Mandibulae	40	153

new study has demonstrated, the formerly absent skulls and long bones are not missing, they are highly fragmented and, particularly in the case of the femora, this fragmentation has rendered them 'analytically invisible'. The under-representation is, in reality, an artefact of analytical technique, rather than by Neolithic design.

8.2.2 Differing Mortuary Practices? The evidence from Cuween Hill and Wideford Hill

One of the key criticisms of interpretations of the mortuary practices occurring in the Orcadian chambered cairns is the effort to identify a homogeneous burial rite for structures of architectural similarity (*e.g.* Richards 1988). It has been argued that the osteological evidence from Quanterness provides a more robust indication of, initially, direct inhumation. But does the evidence from the other Bay of Firth passage graves present a similar picture?

At Cuween Hill passage grave, the skeletal representation profile is conspicuously distinct. Absence of smaller bones, coupled with the presence of just five crania and two femurs, precludes support for a hypothesis indicating interment of whole bodies. Consisting of just seven bones, it is problematic to compare this assemblage to those consisting of hundreds, or in the case of Quanterness, thousands of bone fragments. The skeletal representation at Cuween Hill, with its predominance of long bones and crania, actually corresponds most to the taphonomic profile of secondary burial. Although it has been argued elsewhere (Crozier 2012; 2014) that Cuween Hill most probably contained more bone than has survived in the archive today, the difference in representation from Quanterness is striking. Other Orcadian chambered cairns are recognised as having a marked bias towards human skulls. One such example is the stalled cairn of the Knowe of Yarso, Rousay (Callander and Grant 1935). Within this stalled cairn were the remains of at least 29 individuals. The skulls were arranged around the walls of the inner compartment (see also Richards 1988, 49;

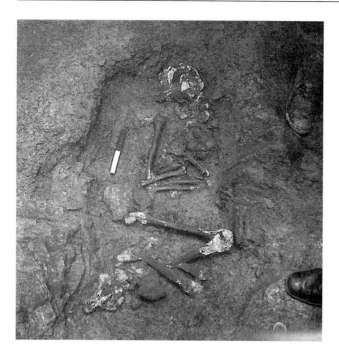

Figure 8.10 In the floor of the main chamber at Quanterness, below the main bone-spread, was a primary crouched inhumation in Pit A (reproduced by kind permission of Colin Renfrew and the Special Collections, University of Kent).

Figure 8.11 Unlike Pit A, Pit B at Quanterness was a nicely constructed stone cist with a well-fitting capstone (reproduced by kind permission of Colin Renfrew and the Special Collections, University of Kent).

Davidson and Henshall 1989, 140). Significantly, these crania all lacked their mandibles. These factors not only infer secondary manipulation of the remains, but also an ordering of the bones (Richards 1988, 46–49). Isbister also contained a large number of skulls that, like Yarso, had been grouped together (Hedges 1983). The find spots marked on Charleson's (1903) site plan do not suggest similar groupings of the Cuween Hill crania. However, evidence of significant peri-mortem trauma identified by Crozier (2012) affecting two of the Cuween Hill crania does imply something less straightforward than simple, direct inhumation and associated manner of death. The size of the assemblage, antiquarian disturbance and the knowledge that not all the bone present in this passage grave was recoverable, unfortunately obfuscate more confident interpretation of a secondary burial practice.

Turning next to Wideford Hill, an absence of human bone makes it impossible to be confident this passage grave ever contained any human bone at all. Suggesting bone simply has not survived would not make for a convincing argument, especially given the fact that animal bone was recovered from the rubble fill (see Kilbride-Jones 1973, 90). At Wideford Hill, we must say that either human bone was removed, in totality, prior

to the closing of this tomb, or it was never there in the first place.

8.2.3 New Interpretations

One of the most prevalent interpretations of mortuary practices associated with megalithic tombs is the involvement of secondary burial practices. This hypothesis is repeatedly expressed when considering disarticulated remains discovered in a 'chaotic' condition. New evidence generated by this latest taphonomic study evidently presents challenges to the existing interpretations of mortuary practices. The data derived from the skeletal representation at Quanterness presents a strong argument in favour of the deposition of *whole* bodies within the passage grave. This argument is established upon the observation that all bones of the skeleton were present, and with generally good (>50%) levels of representation overall. It should also be remembered that initial deposition of the dead within Quanterness took the form of crouched inhumations within Pit A (Fig. 8.10), decayed in Pit B (Figs 8.11 and 8.12) and, in all probability, in unexcavated Pit D (Renfrew 1979, 58–61).

Additional support for this interpretation is drawn

from consideration of the archaeological and ethnographic literature, which repeatedly cites the loss of smaller and more fragile bones in processes that involve the relocation of remains, with a concurrent over-representation of bones such as the long bones and crania (*e.g.* Metcalf and Huntington 1991, 97; Dowd *et al.* 2006, 17). Therefore, excarnation as the dominant burial rite at Quanterness (Chesterman 1979, 1983; Hedges 1983) is not supported by the osseous remains. It is acknowledged that the presence of smaller and more delicate bones of the body may, certainly, indicate a differential diagnosis whereby a corpse was wrapped or contained in some way, before being transferred to the monument (Graeber 1995, 262; Smith and Brickley 2009, 53). There are certainly historic accounts of whole bodies being buried temporarily before a final funerary rite (Taylor 2003, 92). However, there is a lack of artefactual evidence (Renfrew 1979), such as bone pins, to further develop such a hypothesis for the Orcadian remains.

Whilst the evidence from Quanterness is problematic for blanket interpretations involving the movement of human remains between places (*e.g.* Richards 1988; Fowler 2001, 2005; Thomas 2000), it still may retain some validity. Indeed, the presence of human remains in other, apparently non-funerary locations, such as Knap of Howar and Skara Brae, may actually imply that particular skeletal remains, or individuals, were imbued with greater significance and some exchange and movement took place between contexts. If this is occurring during the later 4th millennium cal BC, the circulation of human remains in Neolithic Orkney was more restricted and controlled than previously acknowledged.

It has been argued that the cellular spatial arrangement within passage graves such as Quanterness and Cuween Hill removes the public focal point from an area outside the entrance, to a private area situated at the heart of the monument (Richards 1988, 54). Furthermore, whereas the linearity of the stalled cairn makes the innermost chamber the ultimate goal (see Richards 1992), within the passage grave the central chamber becomes the focus of the monument, needing to be returned to in order to access different cells (Sharples 1985, 68; Richards 1988, 54).

A possible sequence of increasing capacity for bodies and accessibility for individuals suggested for the stalled cairns is not necessarily reflected in the development of the Orcadian passage graves. Passage lengths became increasingly elongated (see Sharples 1985), and consequently views into the interior became more restricted and fewer people could be accommodated inside sites such as Wideford Hill and Cuween Hill

Figure 8.12 After the capstone was removed from Pit B, the cist was seen to be built with sidestones but only decayed cranial fragments were present (although the stain of a decayed crouched inhumation was witnessed – see Renfrew 1979, 61), (reproduced by kind permission of Colin Renfrew and the Special Collections, University of Kent).

(Henshall 2004, 83; Noble 2006, 131). At the same time, platforms were incorporated into the architecture of passage graves, such as Maes Howe. While at other passage graves such as Quoyness and Pierowall Quarry, platforms were added (Sharples 1984), suggesting that attention was shifting to areas outside the monuments and gatherings at these locations were becoming larger in scale, with fewer individuals permitted access to the deposits inside (Richards 1988; Bradley 2006, 104; Noble 2006, 131). In short, the monuments were becoming more of a focal point within the social landscape, but what funerary rites might have been witnessed?

Reanalysis of the osseous remains demands a new interpretation of how we visualise the initial stage of mortuary practices at Quanterness. The relatively straightforward transport of a bundle of excarnated bones from the exterior of the passage grave into the interior no longer applies. It has now been established that whole, articulated bodies were placed within Quanterness. This simple fact has a significant bearing on our understanding of the practicalities involved in transferring a corpse from the outside world into the confines of the monument. The passage grave architecture transforms the journey of the deceased into a potentially arduous undertaking for the living. Where they exist, the entrance passages, assumed to be the point of entry (cf. Lynch 1973; Joanna Wright pers. comm.), are narrow and cramped, creating claustrophobic conduits with room for the passage of one individual at a time. Unfortunately, there is no evidence to inform on how the dead were manoeuvred inside the passage grave. It is possible a rope or matting may have been employed creating a more fluid movement of the deceased into the structure – without such assistance the incorporation of a body cannot have made for an elegant spectacle. If the process relied purely upon unassisted physical strength, the low heights of the passages demand the deceased and their 'handler' would have shared intimate space. Given these potential difficulties, it seems perplexing that the entrance passages should have been constructed in such a restrictive way. The heights of the ceilings within the interior of passage graves illustrate that more accommodating spaces were not a challenge to build. It may be conceived that this intentional distinction will have accentuated a sense of 'arriving', as the transition is made from the confines of the entrance passage into the comparatively more expansive space of the central chamber (see Richards 2000, 545–49). Another intriguing possibility is that bodies were deposited through the roof, and that the passage was not actually a conduit for human beings.

These observations permit some degree of cognizance of the more sensory and experiential aspect of the mortuary rites (Hamilakis 2002; Sofaer 2006, 22). At the passage grave, those responsible for the physical transition of the body from the world of the living to that of the dead were potentially surrounded by onlookers and other participants. With regard to a monument with a platform, such as Maes Howe, they may have felt a degree of separation from an audience. Potentially, they may have been aware of a small number of people waiting within the core of the mound. However, in contrast to the openness of the external world, if the passage was a means of access, the long crawl was accomplished alone and isolated from other people, most likely in darkness (see Richards 2000, 545–47).

When reconstructing mortuary rites, considerations of whether they occurred by day or night do not seem to be a prominent concern (cf. Bradley 1989). This may be very informative for gaining a greater understanding of the sensory aspect of these events for the individuals taking part. By day, the interior of the tombs are dark (Hedges 2000, 148). By night, the effect would have been total, heightening the senses. In modern times of light pollution, true darkness, such as would have been commonly experienced during the Neolithic, is difficult to attain. It could be envisioned, particularly if activities occurred at night that flames were used to assist when moving through these monuments. A quote from the essay, 'In Praise of Shadows', perhaps provides some illumination:

> I wonder if my readers know the colour of that 'darkness seen by candlelight'. It was different in quality from darkness on the road at night. It was a repletion, a pregnancy of tiny particles like fine ashes, each particle luminous as a rainbow. I blinked in spite of myself, as though to keep it out of my eyes.
>
> (Tanizaki 2001, 52)

In addition to this visual consideration, aroma must also have been a factor. Regarding the chambered cairn of Isbister, Hedges (2000, 148–49) refers to the stench of decay that would have been generated from animal remains. The air may indeed have had a stench of death and decay in the Orcadian chambered cairns, but from the new evidence presented, that stench would most certainly have come from decaying bodies. The smells associated with decaying corpses are considered repugnant today, but it must not be assumed that this was the case in prehistory. Whether such odours were considered polluting and abhorrent, or were simply associated with a period of transition and liminal time cannot be determined, but certainly they would have been experienced. Understandings of emotions and the feelings that might have been felt by people moving through the cairns may always be out of reach. Nevertheless, appreciation of the behaviour of a corpse allows the potential for a comprehension of what was faced by the living. However, this will always be from our own perspectives, our own attitudes, understandings and sensibilities to the physicality of the decay processes. Nevertheless, demonstrating that the individual retained their bodily integrity, at least until they were within the confines of the passage grave, intimates that certainly for understanding what was happening at Quanterness, a recognisable person disappeared into the heart of the mound, not a non-descript collection of bones.

Despite similarities in architecture, it is not possible to

be confident that Cuween Hill and Wideford Hill were used in a similar manner. In fact, given their proximity, is this really such a surprise? A subtle variation in practice would provide those associated with particular monuments their own identity, separating them from their neighbours. However, limitations exist to this suggestion. At Cuween Hill, the lack of dating evidence in relation to the initial use of the passage grave restricts more detailed interpretations and creates uncertainty over its coexistence and inter-relationship with Wideford Hill and Quanterness. The total absence of human remains within Wideford Hill is also problematic because we know the conditions were such to enable its survival.

While the frequency of human remains in settlement contexts accounts for a small proportion of the osseous material from the Orcadian Neolithic, they should not be overlooked. If such depositions were intentional and therefore a conscious act, this phenomenon would have implications for the perception that chambered cairns bound and constrained the remains of the dead. Thus, any action involving the movement of particular skeletal material between places could be imbued with an even more powerful significance. Whilst these 'alternative' deposits of human bone do occur in Orkney, for instance at Knap of Howar, they are much sparser than those reported from England, such as at Hambledon Hill (McKinley 2008, 504–505).

A detailed and systematic study of the human remains from Quanterness has provided evidence beyond what may be gleaned from re-examination of existing site reports. Although many have cast doubt upon the excarnation interpretation (Richards 1988, 46; Barber 1997; Reilly 2003; Lawrence 2006) it has still maintained a presence in the literature. The new study has unearthed evidence, from the osseous material itself, which clearly undermines the excarnation interpretation for Quanterness. In accepting that whole bodies were placed within this passage grave, the next consideration, naturally, is the arrangement and distinguishing of people once within the confines of the structure. Similarities in architectural design have led to an assumption that this reflects a shared cosmology and practice.

In the paradigm of archaeological investigation, the chambered cairns of Orkney were originally treated as artefacts; within this framework it was the architectural detail of chambered cairn construction which became the mechanism for their classification (Richards 1992, 63). It has now been demonstrated that this assumption has obfuscated a different narrative (see Chapters 1 and 9). The detail revealed, via taphonomic analysis, of the

representation of the individuals constrained within the confines of the structures, clearly indicates a lack of homogeneity in practice between sites. It is now time to develop our understanding of the chambered cairns not only from their architecture, but from direct evidence provided by the osseous remains within.

8.3 Changing narratives of death: mortuary architecture on Ramberry Head

The final interment in the Quanterness passage grave was an articulated single adult male estimated to be about 25 years of age (Renfrew 1979, 60). He was buried in the latter part of the 3rd millennium cal BC in an extended position within an elongated pit or depression cut through the main bone spread of the central chamber (Fig. 8.13). Yet, the radiocarbon dates and artefactual evidence from Crossiecrown demonstrates continued occupation into the early 2nd millennium cal BC (Chapter 10). Accepting a degree of association between the nearby passage grave and the settlement of Crossiecrown, there are several questions that require addressing. The first concerns the status of Quanterness as a receptacle for the dead of Crossiecrown. Given the potential length of occupation at Crossiecrown it is unlikely that all the dead were interred within Quanterness, although it has been suggested that the passage grave potentially contained a more substantial portion of a Neolithic community than usually considered (see Crozier 2012; 2014).

Despite the relatively high number of chambered cairns in Orkney, and the survival of burial deposits, the actualities of the mortuary process remain obscure. Movement of skeletal material has been suggested to form part of the transformatory process from life to death (*e.g.* Richards 1988; Reilly 2003), yet the above reanalysis of skeletal remains from Quanterness suggests the interment of complete bodies within the passage grave. We are left with an acknowledgement of variation, with different quantities of things, both artefactual and skeletal, being present in the Bay of Firth passage graves. This leads on to the possibility that the material contents of the passage graves were of less consequence than has been assumed. Here, the physical landscape presence of the passage grave could have been the most crucial aspect of such monumentality. Equally, the skeletal remains, whilst not of small value, may have been a remnant of alternative strategies concerning the dead, notions of ancestral presence and the nature of the materiality of a passage grave. For instance, the corpse undergoes processes of decay where the flesh rots and transmutes

Figure 8.13 The legs of the extended inhumation in Pit C cut into the upper bone spread layer within the central chamber of Quanterness (reproduced by kind permission of Colin Renfrew and the Special Collections, University of Kent).

into other forms of substance. Here, the stone passage grave could be envisaged as absorbing and incorporating 'flesh' through the decay of the identifiable person. Under such circumstances bodily decay is a generative process in which the person is absorbed into the very fabric of the passage grave, allowing a form of animation. Under such circumstances, we can understand a passage grave as possessing a form of agency as an embodiment of genealogical relations forming *sociétés à maisons*. In short, passage graves devour and consume the dead and their presence should be understood in terms of what they do as opposed to what they represent.

Nevertheless, the transformation of the corpse from a living person to an ancestral being, however that was articulated in relation to the materiality of the passage grave, involved a journey from the place of living to a place of death. Inevitably, rites of passage are articulated through spatial metaphors; consequently, the transference from one realm to another necessarily involves physical

transformation, displacement and separation. Of all the Neolithic settlements examined within the Bay of Firth area, only Crossiecrown could be identified as having a strong 'maritime' location. Under these conditions it is worth considering to what degree did the ocean feature in the practicalities of life and a cosmological rendering of the experienced world from the 4th to 2nd millennium cal BC? Furthermore, what influence did the ocean exert over the mortuary process, in terms of treatment of the corpse and its physical and metaphysical journey from life to death?

In 2005, a field on Ramberry Head, directly north of the site of Crossiecrown was ploughed for the first time in approximately 20 years (Figs 7.1 and 8.14). This field was 'improved' only in the 1940s and consequently has seen relatively little arable cultivation. During ploughing, Scott Harcus observed a series of soil-marks showing as sub-circular spreads of grey soil including concentrations of stone fragments, which on closer inspection took the appearance of two identifiable low mounds and a third denoted by a spread of 'grey' soil. In one case, several thin flagstones, together with burnt bone and pottery, had been brought to the surface by the plough (Fig. 8.15). All the indications were that these remains constituted a small 2nd millennium cal BC barrow cemetery and given its close proximity to Crossiecrown there was a requirement to investigate the site further. Specifically, one spread of surface material (Site 1) was selected for excavation.

8.3.1 Ramberry Head Ring Cairn (Site 1)

Site 1 appeared to have formed part of a cemetery of at least three small circular mounds. Subsequent gradiometer survey of this area (Fig. 8.16) indicated the presence of several magnetic anomalies, probably representing two further plough-damaged burial mounds, but Site 1 was selected for excavation as cremation deposits, pottery and stone tools were clearly visible on the field surface (Fig. 8.15).

Excavation demonstrated Site 1 to originally have assumed the form of a ring cairn (Fig. 8.17). The ploughsoil was remarkably shallow and when removed it was clear that the ring cairn had been built on a foundation spread of homogeneous orange-brown silty clay [002], which extended across the interior area. This primary layer assumed a very mottled appearance with visible patches of ash and white clay. Centrally, a stone setting had been built encircling a large horizontal slab (Fig. 8.18). The slab was not a quarried flagstone, as is

Figure 8.14 Ramberry Head from the southeast (Colin Richards).

Figure 8.15 At Ramberry Head, Site 1, deposits of cremated bone, pottery and stone artefacts were brought to the surface during ploughing in April, 2005 (Colin Richards).

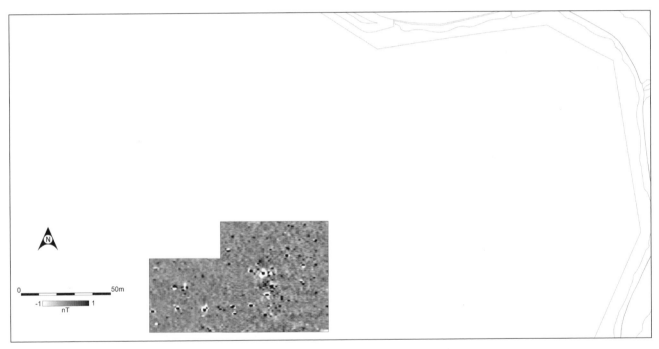

Figure 8.16 Gradiometer plot of survey undertaken over Sites 1 and 3 at Ramberry Head (ORCA).

frequently the case within cist structures, but was water-worn with rounded edges, being clearly derived from the seashore. The slab had been placed on a white clay foundation (Fig. 8.19). As no cuts were discovered around the water-worn slab it seems unlikely that a cist structure had actually been present. Instead, a rectangular setting of stone blocks [005] once entirely framed the central water-worn stone. While it is probable that these stones provided the base for higher courses, supporting a stone lid, no further structural evidence remained. It was upon

the water-worn stone that the human cremated bone had been placed, possibly contained within a pottery vessel. A radiocarbon date from the cremated bone produced a range of *1500–1310 cal BC (GU-20480)*.

Judging from the position of the cremated bone, it seems that the plough ran *c.*1cm above the upper surface of the basal water-worn stone. Amazingly, the majority of the cremation deposit and the square-shaped vessel with which it was associated (see Fig. 11.8.1), were simply turned over and deposited on the field surface

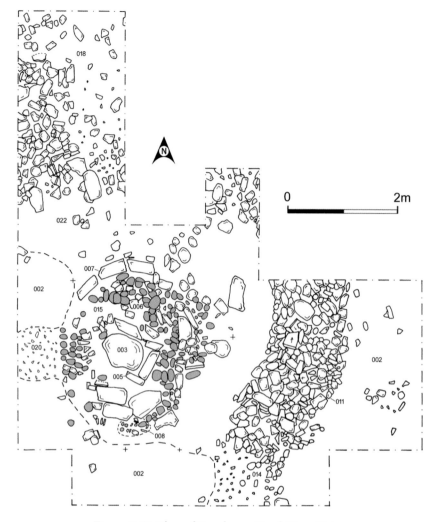

Figure 8.17 Plan of Ramberry Head Ring Cairn.

without significant damage (Fig. 8.15). The one point which is difficult to determine is whether the cremation had originally been placed within the vessel. Since the cremation deposit was not placed within a square cist it is interesting that it was buried within a square vessel, thereby creating a from of substitution. As is becoming increasingly realized more generally, the cremation deposit recovered from Site 1, Ramberry Head, included more than a single individual (see Chapter 14.1). Interestingly, it also included cremated bone of bird and cattle (see Chapter 14.1).

Encircling the cremation deposit and stone blocks was a laid surface composed mainly of similar sized beach pebbles. These had been set in the clay surface with great care and attention creating a beautiful arrangement; for example, to the west the pebbles had been set in perfectly aligned rows (Figs 8.18 and 8.32). Unfortunately, a number of the pebbles had been displaced through ploughing disturbance

but the remaining examples provided an unexpectedly intimate encounter with 2nd millennium cal BC aesthetics. Such aesthetics are in some ways anachronistic because the uncovering and exposure of the pebble setting was one of the most enjoyable tasks undertaken during excavation. A series of flagstones [007] created a well-defined outer paved curb to the central setting, *c.*2.5m in diameter, although the paving did appear to extend slightly in the northeast (see Figs 8.17 and 8.18).

A second crushed pottery vessel (SF 12) was positioned adjacent to the pebbles in the southwest area of the central setting (Fig. 8.20). Nearly all the pottery recovered from Site 1 was associated with the central setting (Fig. 8.21). Surrounding this setting was the open clay surface. As noted above, it had a mottled surface with patches of white degraded clay and discrete black spreads. Magnetic susceptibility survey over this surface showed little indication of burning (Fig. 8.22).

Figure 8.18 View of the Ring Cairn from the west; note the concentric ordering of beach pebbles and sandstone slabs wrapping the central water rounded slab (Adrian Challands).

Figure 8.19 Section view of the white clay foundation spread for the water-worn basal slab (Judith Robertson).

The central setting was further enclosed by a partial concentric stone bank [011], giving an overall diameter of c.8m to the site. The stone bank was best preserved in the eastern area (Fig. 8.23). This was because in this area the old ground surface was at a slightly lower level and, where it was a little more elevated to the south, the bank had been virtually removed. Although present to the north the bank had been considerably displaced. In constitution the bank was composed of pebbles, stone slabs, fragments and slithers of sandstone. Within the examined areas the bank seemed to maintain a stratigraphic sequence of sandstone slabs overlying a pebble core, however whether this sequence was consistently present throughout the now destroyed circuit is impossible to determine. In its northern circuit, a stone ard-point (SF 17) was incorporated in the fabric of the encircling bank (Fig. 8.24). These have been encountered in the kerbs of several Orcadian barrows and have been interpreted as items associating death with fertility (Downes 2009).

8.3.2 Ramberry Head passage structure (Site 2)

After ploughing, at the northeast corner of the field another sub-circular low mound of stone (Site 2) became visible (Figs 7.1 and 8.25). Today, Site 2 is only metres away from the c.2m high cliff edge and the sea. Initially, a trench measuring 4m × 4m was opened to examine the site but this was extended to a 10m × 7m after structural remains were encountered. This mound was excavated

Figure 8.20 Project geophysicist Adrian Challands excavates pottery from the central setting (Colin Richards).

on the assumption it represented the remains of another cairn similar to Site 1, but surprisingly directly beneath the ploughsoil a mass of stone work was encountered (Fig. 8.26). Although severely truncated by ploughing, once the initial collapsed and displaced material had been removed three constructional phases were identified.

The earliest identifiable phase of activity is represented by a c.4m curving length of walling [032], associated with a compact pebbles surface on its northeast side. The curved wall was built of chunky angular blocks which survived to two courses in height, c.0.24m, and had a dump of steeply tipping rubble, up to 0.8m wide, up

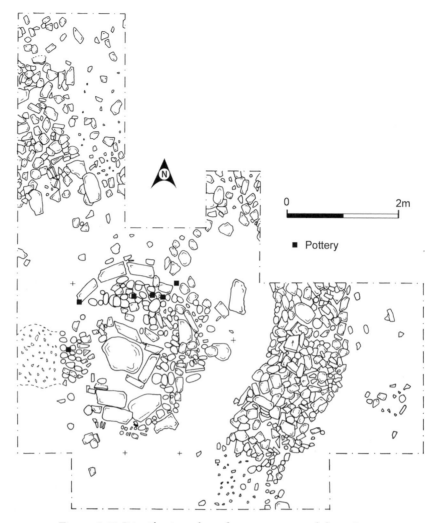

Figure 8.21 Distribution plan of pottery recovered from Site 1.

against and obscuring the southwest face. Subsequent structural phases reused this length of wall and rubble as the internal northeast side of a very unusual passage structure (Fig. 8.27).

The passage structure was clearly a secondary building. However, due to limited time it was not possible to investigate whether the primary structure, represented by the wall [032] possessed a similar architectural form. The passage structure was built on a mottled grey-brown old land surface, and had also been severely damaged by ploughing. Enough remained intact, however, to identify an intermittent masonry inner wall face [060] defining a sub-circular internal area. Apart from a short section of masonry [034] forming the southern side of the entrance passage, the outer wall facing was absent and a spread of rubble was all that remained to show the original wall thickness. Unsurprisingly, given its eventual name, the

most striking element of this building was its long entrance passage (Fig. 8.28). Due to the thickness of the outer wall, the passage measured nearly 3m in length and was partially paved with flagstones.

During excavation, it was considered that the passage had actually been lengthened during the life of the structure. This was on the basis of the presence of the inner faced wall being thickened and enhanced by the addition of another skin of walling [034] (see Fig. 8.27). Indeed, the entrance passage leading into the Ramberry Head passage structure could have been even longer since the building became extremely ruinous and truncated as it extended to the southeast (Fig. 8.28). Internally, a threshold stone was set in the floor of the passage adjacent to the inner wall face. Although ruinous, the architecture of the central chamber was unusual in assuming an oval shape.

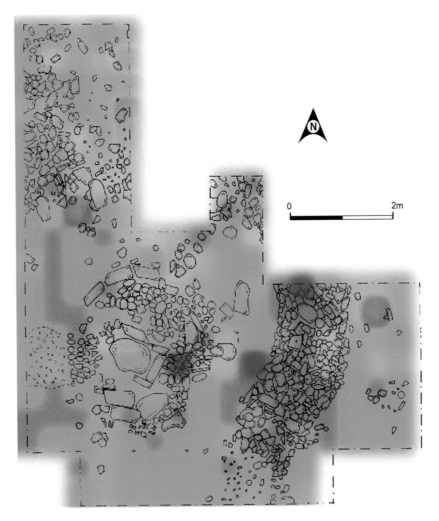

Figure 8.22 Magnetic susceptibility plot of Site 1; the blue to red colour gradation corresponds with low to high m.s. values (Adrian Challands).

Within the central chamber there was a limited area that had ephemeral traces of a floor surface located against the north face of wall, where it was partly protected by wall collapse and rubble. The possible floor [042] comprised a mottled compact grey clay surface with charcoal flecks. There was no indication of a hearth setting or any areas of *in situ* burning. Neither was there any evidence of collapsed stone furniture or slots cut into the clay floor surface. Consequently, when standing, the passage structure would have comprised a long passage leading to an oval central chamber. Associated with the floor was a small area of paving [064], composed of three small flagstones and a pivot stone positioned immediately inside the threshold stone. Several small sherds of pottery, probably of late Neolithic-Bronze date, were recovered from the floor deposit.

Figure 8.23 Site 1: view of the encircling stone bank where it was preserved in a hollow to the east, running concentric to the central setting (Colin Richards).

Figure 8.25 Adrian Challands stands centrally within the spread of stone (Site 2) brought to the surface by ploughing; note the close proximity of the site to the sea (Colin Richards).

Figure 8.24 Site1: ard-point (SF 17) incorporated in the encircling bank (Colin Richards).

Figure 8.26 Beneath the ploughsoil at Site 2 a mass of collapsed stonework was exposed in the original trench (Judith Robertson).

After the central chamber had collapsed and was little more than a pile of rubble, an arc of long stones [043] was laid on top of the debris (Fig. 8.30). Associated with this arc of stones was a stone ard-point (SF 30). There were no other deposits or features apparent that relate to this final activity. The site was 'sealed' by a more extensive layer of very compact degraded rubble and small stones that covered the entire structure.

8.4 Ramberry Head and architectures of the dead in the Bay of Firth

The bathymetry reconstruction model for sea level changes through the 4th and 3rd millennia cal BC in the Bay of Firth (Fig. 1.10) shows a tendency for the position of headlands and points to have remained fairly constant.

Consequently, the proximity of the sea to the Ramberry Head passage structure would have changed very little since it was initially constructed (Fig. 8.31). The passage structure is an unusual building and, while there can be no certainty that it performed a mortuary role, the absence of a hearth and internal stone furniture provides strong evidence that it did not serve as a dwelling. The inability to recover good evidence concerning the external appearance of the building does little to aid interpretation, but perhaps this lack of clarity may indicate a more cairn-like structure with less structural definition to its outer edge. Whilst the additional wall skin [034] added to the Ramberry Head passage structure may represent secondary reconstruction it is worth considering that concentric skins of masonry are a feature of passage grave construction. In this context,

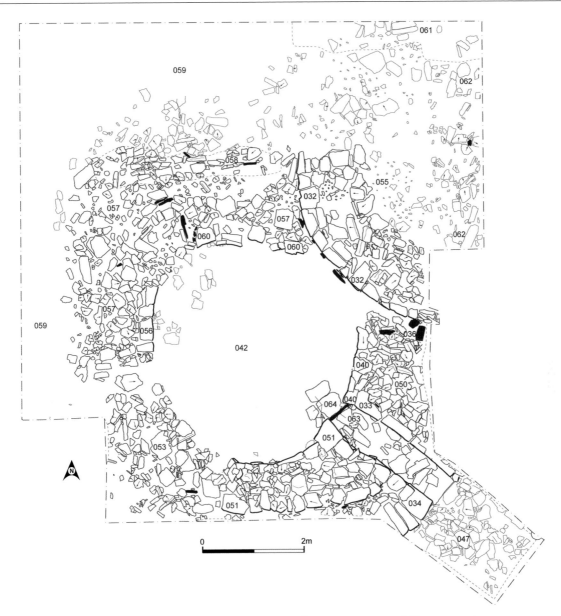

Figure 8.27 Plan of the Ramberry Head passage structure fully excavated.

concentric walls wrap around a central chamber; a building device which serves to create an extremely thick body to the cairn and a correspondingly long entrance passage.

Clearly, the Ramberry Head passage structure was not a passage grave of the same order as Quanterness, Wideford Hill or Cuween Hill, nonetheless its structural design with a central oval chamber would appear to owe more to this theme of architecture than that of the house. Equally, together with hillside locations, an exposed headland in close proximity to the ocean is a familiar haunt of Orcadian passage graves as opposed to settlement. Indeed, at the time of writing a newly

discovered passage grave at Swandro has been uncovered beneath the storm beach on the south coast of Rousay (S. Dockrill pers. comm.).

Apart from location (Fig. 8.31), the ocean is an important theme in the materiality of both the Ramberry Head sites we examined. At the centre of the ring cairn (Site 1) the sea-worn basal slab, upon which the cremation deposits had been placed, was clearly derived from the shore. This was surrounded and 'squared-off' by quarried slabs which in turn were wrapped by a jacket of sea-worn pebbles, nicely termed sea-stones by Hamilton *et al.* (2011, 179–80). Wrapping the sea-stones and providing an outer skin to the burial context was a curb of quarried slabs,

Figure 8.28 View from the southeast of the passage after it was first uncovered; notice the extremely shallow depth of ploughsoil covering the passage structure (Judith Robertson).

Figure 8.29 View of excavated passage structure from the southwest. The line of white clay extending the line of the west passage wall can be seen in the bottom of the picture (Judith Robertson).

land-stones (Fig. 8.32). Whilst aesthetics would seem to be influential in the creation of this architecture, the relational character and interplay within a burial context of materials derived from both the land and sea cannot be ignored. Indeed, as Bateson comments 'the symbolism of art – and about ritual perhaps – is not "about things" but "about relationships"' (1972, 139). Of course, it is also about 'things' in terms of what they do (*e.g.* Gell 1992; 1998) rather than simply represent. The deployment of different materials is magnified by the virtual absence of sea-rounded stone in the nearby settlement of Crossiecrown or passage grave of Quanterness. At one level, the deployment of materials from different sources evokes connections between different domains. Consequently, the juxtaposition of 'things' from different places, whilst creating both physical and metaphorical linkage between such domains, was also a product of people going to different *locales* and physically collecting stones. At another level, in the context of Ramberry Head Site 1, the juxtaposition of different materialities is

not merely the creation of representational architecture but the establishment of a form of *enchantment*. In this context enchantment is not effected totally through aesthetics or visual complexity (cf. Gell 1992), although such complexity is undoubtedly a feature of the material constitution of Ramberry Head Site 1 (Fig. 8.28).

Instead, we suggest that the enchantment of the central area of the ring cairn (Site 1) also lies in the networks in which sea-stone and land-stone form part. For instance, the sea-stones may be conceived as things which are formed through the processes of wave action and the abrasion of endless tides (Ingold 2011, 131), in other words their formation is a manifestation of the constant movement and character of the sea. For the inhabitants of Crossiecrown the sea would undoubtedly have been to some degree cosmologically rendered, simply because it constituted a different domain, a domain of different physical qualities to those of the land.

Few elements can be identified more powerfully as a living, vibrant thing than the ocean; it is always in motion and by nature is volatile and deceptive in character. The seas around Orkney can alternate from being calm and safe, to rough and threatening. When tranquil, the sea is like a blue skin of serenity, stretching mirror-like to the edge of the visible world. But in its anger the ocean has a darkness and fury of untold power that gradually dismantles the Orcadian coastline. At its kindest the sea acted as a benevolent resource providing a wealth of food and materials from its depths. However, when angry the ocean could also be cruel and murderous. Under these

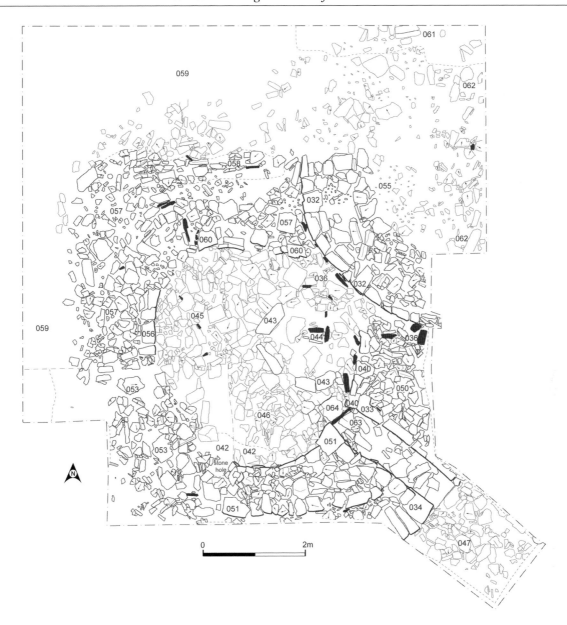

Figure 8.30 Plan of passage structure showing infill rubble and line of stones [043].

conditions it surely is the strongest of all barriers. Either way, we can have little doubt that the sea was an ever-present element of Neolithic and early Bronze Age life.

Consequently, things of the sea would have enjoyed considerable potency as material metaphors. Just as today, within a Neolithic Orcadian island world, the sea enables communication just as easily as it can define and enforce differences. As a conduit the sea may draw different realms together, through practical strategies of inter-island contact or cosmological themes of different domains and places of origin. Under such circumstance the imagery and materiality of Site 1 is not simply representative of an

equation of the dead of Crossiecrown being drawn into a different place through the medium of metaphorical extension. By laying the dead to rest (or not) within a context of elaborately laid and patterned sea-stones and land-stones, a form of magical efficacy (Gell 1992, 44–45) ensues whereby the stones exert a degree of enchantment on those performing mortuary ritual within a layered 'theatre of materiality'. It is also suspected that an even more complex array of materials was deployed at Ramberry Head Site 1 since the site was truncated to the extent that the majority of any protective mound or cairn material that would have sealed the interred remains no longer survived.

Figure 8.31 View of the passage structure (Site 2) under excavation. The photograph is taken from Site 1 and the sea clearly provides the broader context for both sites (Judith Robertson).

Apart from the other two probably similar sites (Site 3 and Site 4) identified along the slight ridge, a mere 200m away from the area of habitation at Crossiecrown (Fig. 7.1), just how extensive the distribution of Bronze Age burial mounds was along the coastal strip is difficult to know. Tumuli were stated to be 'comparatively rare in the parish' (Firth) by Fraser (1927, 53), but Wood notes the opening of several small mounds within Firth by an enthusiast 'imbued with the necessary courage' (1927, 57). In a similar coastal position to the burials at Ramberry, were four small mounds straddling the Grip of Wheeling stream on Finstown Market Green. Three of these were in a line, measuring *c.*7.5m centre to centre, and on opening contained two stone cists and two urns (*ibid.*).

A juxtaposition of these two realms (sea and land) is not restricted to the materiality and location of 2nd millennium cal BC burial monuments. As noted above, one of the common situations of Orcadian passage graves is adjacent to the seashore. Yet, at Crossiecrown it

seems as if the nature of death and journeys to another world became increasingly reoriented through the 3rd millennium cal BC. This is because the passage grave of Quanterness, regardless of complexities surrounding interment, is inland of Crossiecrown, as are Wideford Hill and Cuween Hill. Hence, a journey from the place of the living (Crossiecrown) to that of the dead (Quanterness) involved passage away from the ocean. Nor was any sea-stone mentioned as being a component of constructing the great passage grave (Renfrew 1979, 64–68). However, we possess little knowledge concerning either the geography of death rituals, or narratives surrounding the deposition of the physical remains and the spiritual destination of the dead. It seems quite likely that at times these 'domains' may converge, for instance, at particular places such as a passage grave. At others times these domains may diverge considerably creating a degree of fragmentation embracing different places in the 2nd millennium cal BC Orcadian world. Such differentiation is clearly expressed within the cremation process itself where the destruction of the body facilitates the freeing of spiritual essences (*e.g.* Downes 1999; Oestigaard 2000).

All that can be said with any confidence is that the variation in topographic locations of the Bay of Firth passage graves and later funerary architecture and mortuary practices indicates that different sites and places necessarily conjoin within the ritual process of the transformation of the living to the dead. Perhaps, in regard to the theme of this volume, a critical aspect is that at a later stage in the development of settlement within the Bay of Firth area the visibility of the dead through the medium of monumental constructions became extremely important. Once such a monumental discourse was established, any consistency in the treatment of the physical remains of the dead may have become less important. Of interest is the relational shift in the late 3rd–early 2nd millennium cal BC away from inward (inland) focused death ritual, to that which looks outwards (seaward) beyond Orkney. Significantly, this was also a time of social reorientation, both in terms of the decline of Neolithic *sociétés à maisons*, and a shift in relationships which now beckoned to the north, towards Shetland.

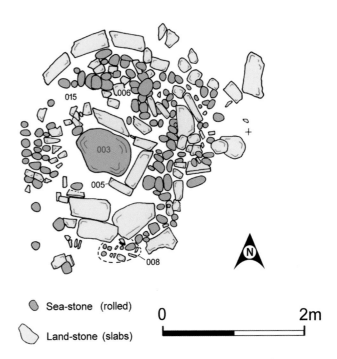

Sea-stone (rolled)

Land-stone (slabs)

0   2m

Figure 8.32 Plan showing the material complexity of the burial context at Ramberry Head Site 1.

CHAPTER NINE

Materializing Neolithic House Societies in Orkney: introducing Varme Dale and Muckquoy

Colin Richards, Jane Downes, Christopher Gee and Stephen Carter

9.1 The Bay of Firth

This volume describes the results of a long-term research project investigating the prehistoric settlement of Orkney from the 4th to 2nd millennia cal BC, within the Bay of Firth area of central Mainland (Figs 1.9 and 9.1). A number of settlements have been discovered and excavated as part of the project, all of which were founded in the early Neolithic period (*c.*3600–3200 cal BC). Although fieldwalking was undertaken, both independently (*e.g.* Cantley 2005) and as part of this project, surprisingly few traces of preceding Mesolithic occupation were discovered. The main site in close vicinity to the study area with a strong Mesolithic component is South Ettit (Rendall 1937), which lies further up the coast to the north of Muckquoy, Redlands (Fig. 1.9). Actually, the Wideford Hill site has a minor Mesolithic element comprising backed bladelets which form a small part of Rendall's (1931; 1934) surface collection, and the current excavated lithic assemblage (Chapter 12). Changing sea levels (Fig. 1.10a) may well have a bearing on the apparent absence of 5th and 6th millennia cal BC settlement, much of which may now be submerged within the bay. Certainly, isolated Mesolithic sites ranging from the 8th to early 4th millennium cal BC are known within Orkney (*e.g.* Wickham-Jones 1990; 1992; 2006; Wickham-Jones and Firth 2000; Cantley 2005; Lee and Woodward 2008; 2009; Kinnaird *et al.* 2011).

The Bay of Firth coastal zone came to be selected as a study area partly because it was clearly demarcated by a semi-circle of hills running from Wideford Hill in the east, to Cuween and Heddle Hills in the west. To the west, a narrow valley breaks through the hills at Binscarth before they rise again and run north towards Evie (Fig. 1.9). Travelling along the valley, towards the Bay of Firth from west Mainland, has been portrayed as passing from one world to another. For instance, Mackay (1905) describes how after moving through the inland terrain of the west Mainland bowl the sea suddenly and unexpectedly appears as the valley is traversed. In thinking of the hills acting as a barrier, when the weather is fine the rising slopes appear as a backdrop to the coastal zone, and when bathed in sunshine do not appear insurmountable. In all probability, during the Neolithic period, red deer would have been visible grazing on the upper slopes. However, just as the sea can be rough and foreboding so in bad weather the hill summits become shrouded in mist or heavy cloud and give all the appearances of belonging to a different realm and completely impassable.

It is worth pondering the effects this striking topography had on social identity and relationships between Bay of Firth communities in the 4th and 3rd millennia cal BC. In being located on the far side of the Rowamo Hill, the Knowes of Trotty settlement (Chapter 3) is physically close and yet may have seemed a world apart from the settlement of Muckquoy, Redland, which is situated a mere *c.*3km to the east (see Fig. 1.9). Similarly, the landscape position of Smerquoy (Chapter 4) is interesting in that although being set well back from the coastline it is deliberately situated looking west over the Bay of Firth (Fig. 4.44). If the settlement assumed a position just a few hundred metres further east it would possess an alternative aspect overlooking Kirkwall Bay and be part of

Figure 9.1 View of the Cuween-Wideford coastal zone from the north; the Holm of Grimbister occupies the foreground (Craig Taylor).

an entirely different topographic zone of central Mainland. Such a reorientation would not only provide Smerquoy with a different visual perspective, but also situate it within an alternative social arena that would include the inhabitants of the recently discovered 4th millennium cal BC settlement of Saverock which lies on the eastern lower slopes of Wideford Hill (Fig 1.9). Dwelling in particular landscape positions is not accidental but strategic and chosen for a number of reasons, some of which were practical, for instance, access to crucial resources such as water supplies (see Chapter 4). Equally, physical location may well translate into pragmatic concerns regarding placement within broader social geographies and access to particular social networks.

So, to what extent was the Cuween-Wideford landscape of the Bay of Firth conceived as a discrete spatial entity, physically and socially separated from the rest of Mainland, Orkney? And how did the people who occupied this fairly well-defined coastal zone relate to one another, and to those people who lived beyond the hills? With these questions in mind, and in relation to the issues raised by the discoveries reported in the previous chapters, it is now necessary to pull the different strands of evidence together and, drawing on specific ideas derived from Lévi-Strauss's concept of *sociétés à maisons*, situate the settlement histories unfolding in the Bay of Firth area within a broader Orcadian Neolithic social context.

9.2 The early Neolithic house and stalled chambered cairn as relational categories

In the introductory chapter, it was suggested that, in light of the nature of recent archaeological discoveries, some of the themes that constituted Lévi-Strauss' notion of *sociétés à maisons* provided a useful way of thinking through the new evidence derived from our project (and other excavations such as Ha'Breck, Green and Ness of Brodgar), in order to provide an alternative narrative of the Orcadian Neolithic. It will be recalled that one of the defining characteristic of *sociétés à maisons* is that relatedness predicated on practice as opposed to 'blood' relationships constitutes a social unit. That is not to declare the primacy of social over biological relationships, but to understand:

> how relatedness may be composed of various components – substances, feeding, living together, procreation, emotion – elements which are themselves not necessarily bounded entities but may overflow or contain parts of each other or take new forms.
>
> (Carsten 2000, 34)

Such networks of relatedness and identity are not necessarily restricted to human relationships but, as has become increasingly clear, embrace 'things' (and animals) within a more vital materialism (cf. Bennett 2010). These ideas are seductive because as the division between materials and people crumbles, so the possibility of realising the efficacy of materials and things increases. Such instability in distinctions between people and things necessarily translates into the allowance of broader categories of relatedness (Carsten 2000). For Lévi-Strauss the language of the 'house' and social relationships is one of kinship, hence position is recognized 'by gluing together real interests and mythical pedigrees' (1982, 187). Such mythical pedigrees are important in terms of social identity because they extend 'the experiences of the house beyond the immediacy of the here-and-now, strictly defined, into the wider space-time of the outside supernatural realm' (Helms 1998, 18). Consequently, there exists a heavy dependency on genealogy and origins, and it may be useful to think about genealogical pathways as networks which are fluid and exposed to reformulation. For this study, the interesting point is not the social legitimacy negotiated through genealogical discourse, but potential strategies of materialization as exposed in the presence and inclusion of 'things' within

Figure 9.2 Traditionally animals were transported by boat in Orkney (Orkney Photographic Archive).

its construction. Such a conjunction of people and things would allow material constructs such as the chambered cairn and house, and their specific components, to be actually inserted into genealogical sequences. In short, things may speak a thousand words in the construction of identities in relation to access to 'origins', place and status within *sociétés à maisons* (Helms 1998, 74–81).

It is now beyond question that the importance of origins has been generally overlooked in the British Neolithic mainly because of negative associations with culture-history avenues of enquiry (but see Whittle *et al.* 2007; Whittle *et al.* 2011). In such accounts, immigrants, routes of migration and the material correlates of such movement assumed analytical status within early discourses of the Scottish Neolithic (*e.g.* Childe 1940, 34; 1946, 24–25; Piggott 1954, 232–36; Atkinson 1962, 11–22). As noted above, a 5th and early 4th millennium cal BC Mesolithic presence in Orkney appears minimal. Consequently, people came to Orkney from elsewhere. As an archipelago and within a maritime context, a 'place' of origin would necessarily be 'across the sea' and assume great prominence within Neolithic cosmological frameworks (cf. Thomas 2001; Richards 2008). Of course, places of origin do not necessarily relate to actual locations from which 'founders' departed, but may fuse real places with mythical domains. Nonetheless, within an incipient Neolithic, social relationships, real or fictive, maintained or lapsed, almost certainly stretched web-like beyond Orcadian shores. This in turn provides an 'externalized' composition to genealogically situated identities, and an enhanced appreciation of external origins which at particular times, as a cosmological and social resource, came strikingly into focus. Such strategies may well account for the appearance of passage grave architecture or stone circles in Orkney towards the end of the 4th millennium cal BC (see Richards 2013c).

Unfortunately, even with the discoveries and research described in this volume, the very beginnings of the Orcadian Neolithic remain shrouded in mist and uncertainty. Clearly, domestic animals and cereals were introduced to Orkney, and, as was the custom until recently, transportation would have been by boat (Fig. 9.2). Once established, domestic animals and cereals provided the resources for increasing scales of subsistence production, alongside developing technologies of consumption (Schulting 2008). Specific human–animal–thing relations also established relational renderings of landscape and the land itself. In particular, the sociality of keeping cattle (and other animals), and their identification as 'social beings', may have established relationships extending into the

Figure 9.3 View of timber House 4, Trench A at Braes of Ha'Breck, Wyre (Antonia Thomas).

human realm (Thomas 2013, 404–10). The slaughter of large animals, as an act of sacrifice, has obvious ontological import (cf. Ray and Thomas 2003, 41), while subsequent feasts necessarily entwine 'others' and dramatically extend the scale of social interaction (*e.g.* Serjeantson 2006, 114–15; Schulting 2008). Moreover, it is also clear that technologies of consumption fuse social practices with discourses of competition. In short, the 4th millennium cal BC establishment of agriculture in Orkney initiated a fluid and unstable 'founder focused' regime, where social position and identity were initially grounded in broad-based collective strategies of material and agricultural production. This is the historical context, it is suggested, that produces altered social relationships, and concepts of identity, a process that can be best characterized as the emergence of Neolithic *sociétés à maisons* in Orkney.

For this narrative, the recognition of timber architecture and small domestic units at Wideford Hill in the middle of the 4th millennium cal BC marks the point of departure.

Figure 9.4 View of timber House 1, Trench C at Braes of Ha'Breck (Dan Lee).

These houses were initially circular buildings with a central scoop hearth and may have had small porch arrangements (see Fig. 2.7). A possible sub-rectangular wooden structure was also present at Wideford Hill (Fig. 2.18), a situation mirrored at Braes of Ha'Breck, Wyre (Thomas and Lee 2012) where at least two sub-rectangular timber structures were present (Figs 9.3 and 9.4). Similar architecture appears to be present at Green, Eday (Coles and Miles 2013), and in Chapter 4 it was noted that a probable sub-rectangular timber and turf structure has recently been discovered within Trench 2 at Smerquoy (Fig. 4.38).

Judging from the size of supporting posts utilized within the dwellings at Wideford Hill (Tables 2.1, 2.3 and 2.4), the life-span of timber houses was relatively short. Equally, the distribution and sequence of settlement at Wideford Hill, in conjunction with the overall lack of recut postholes, indicates that the buildings were replaced rather than refurbished. This leads on to the observation that timber houses participated in a spatially shifting settlement pattern with the replacement of buildings in a different location. Obviously, the process of decay inherent within timber houses materializes a temporal structure to early Neolithic sociality and dwelling. However, it is recognized that caution is required in translating such fluidity and transience in the materiality, duration and locality of dwelling directly into a scheme where social identity is principally constituted through strong kinship-based relations, as opposed to any emotional attachment to a specific houses or places.

Interestingly, the earliest Orcadian settlement evidence does to some extent now resemble residential characteristics of the early Neolithic in other parts of Scotland (Barclay 2003) and Ireland (Smyth 2014) where settlement is ephemeral at best. Indeed, it has been argued that early Neolithic timber house architecture in Ireland is representative of the formation of *sociétés à maisons* (Cooney 2003, 55; Smyth 2010, 28). The north of Scotland and the Western Isles are typical examples of 4th millennium cal BC lifeways where habitation is primarily represented by hearths, pits and postholes (*e.g.* Crone 1993; Armit 1996, 50–57; Branigan and Foster 2000; Murphy and Simpson 2003). However, from *c.*3700 cal BC there is another architectural element that features in each of these areas, including Orkney; the chambered cairn. For the majority of the Highlands and Islands chambered cairns provide the main form of evidence for early Neolithic occupation and consequently are necessarily elevated to a dominant interpretative role. This provisional situation was, however, fully recognized by Colin Renfrew, who mused that 'our only evidence for group membership at the earlier time is offered by the cairns themselves' (1979, 214).

Despite the early date for the establishment of stalled cairns in Orkney (see Chapter 10), Anna Ritchie concluded that 'the earliest settlers need not have been tomb-builders' (1990, 39), and paradoxically, she was both correct and incorrect. Accepting the existence of

relatively strong blood ties within social groups at this time, within the context of transient spatial and material forms of dwelling, as revealed for example, at Wideford Hill, Smerquoy, Ha'Breck and Green, the construction of social identities would still require a degree of fixidity in terms of place, ancestors and origins. Strategies to provide such social cohesion and sedimentation may have resulted in the impetus to build chambered cairns, and to build them in a manner resembling those from claimed origin areas and 'homeland'.

Many years ago, it was suggested the architecture of the stalled cairns represented a series of doorways which ultimately led to another world (Richards 1992; see also Robin 2008). Under these circumstances, the chambered cairns act as more of a conduit than a form of container as had been envisaged by Renfrew (1979, 170–72). If the primary role of the stalled cairn was to provide a sanctioned and controlled point of access or contact between two realms and allow passage between them, certain places in the earliest Neolithic Orcadian landscape may have been more appropriate than others, especially if origin-places were essential to claimed social identity and status differentiation. Under such circumstances, the themes governing chambered cairn location could be very different, and bear no necessary relation to notions of territoriality or access to particular resources (*contra* Renfrew 1973; Chapman 1981 – but see Chapman 2003). For instance, seashore locations may be important because they marked traditional places where founders were claimed to have first landed in Orkney. Alternate locations could be ascendant and relate to ancestral domains and elevated 'other worlds' (Chapter 3; Reilly 2003). As it turns out, this precisely parallels the variation present in landscape settings of early stalled chambered cairns (Fig. 9.5).

This alternative narrative also goes some way to accounting for the broad absence or relatively small numbers of human skeletal material within the stalled cairns, and the divergent arrangements of skulls and long bones (*e.g.* Richards 1988; Reilly 2003) seemingly attesting to idiosyncratic and inconsistent mortuary ritual (see Chapter 8). The nature of ancestry within this schema is one concerned with origins, descent and the question of journeying or passage from primordial sources. Importantly, 'in this context ancestral beings are conceptualized not as emerging from the house but as *preceding* the house – that is, as existing or originating separate from the house and as "coming to" the house from a cosmological setting that was originally somewhere outside it, implying a spatial component as basic to the

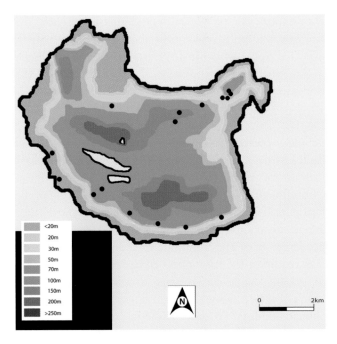

Figure 9.6 Knap of Howar from the air; the primary House 1 is seen as a substantially larger dwelling (Craig Taylor).

Figure 9.5 Distribution of stalled chambered cairns in Rousay, Orkney (after Davidson and Henshall 1989).

identification' (Helms 1998, 38). In short, in the early to middle centuries of the 4th millennium cal BC, it was the stalled cairns in their various landscape settings that provided externalized ontological security within a fluid and transient regime of dwelling (cf. Whittle 1988, 85; Carey 2012, 41). They also performed a role as conduits between different worlds or realms.

As we saw in Chapter 2, in the latter quarter of the 4th millennium cal BC (see also Chapter 10), timber houses were being replaced by stone houses, and the nature of dwelling in Orkney became transformed. Until this time stone, as a building material, had been restricted to chambered cairn construction. Within the new dwellings, not only was the materiality of chambered cairns replicated in the house, but the house assumed the architecture of a stalled cairn. Some stone-built houses, for example, House 3 at Stonehall Meadow, the Smerquoy Hoose, and those at Knowes of Trotty and Knap of Howar, Papa Westray, reveal very clearly that the architecture of the house was influenced directly by the imagery of the stalled cairn. The employment of opposed orthostats projecting from the inner wall-face to provide divisions or compartments is the very characteristic of chambered cairn architecture which led to the term *stalled* (Callander and Grant 1934, 326). Interestingly, the employment of orthostatic sub-division was not a unitary development of house architecture. Judging

from Wideford Hill Stonehouse 1, which was built in quick succession over a timber house, the architecture of the house is not initially heavily reliant on orthostatic divisions.

With the advent of stone houses, the materiality and architecture of house and tomb now merge. Moreover, as opposed to the shifting building pattern of timber houses, stone houses tend to be sedimented in one place. A notion of the house as characterized by transience and renewal is replaced by strategies concerned with maintenance, refurbishment and reconstruction. Continuity and place now appear as dominant discourses of dwelling, together with a fusion of house and chambered cairn, where death is internalized and the dead dwell together with the living (cf. Hodder 1990, 292). We claim that this shift in the materiality and architecture of dwelling materialized the emergence of Neolithic *sociétés à maisons* in Orkney. From this point on, the continuity of *sociétés à maisons* is to a degree articulated through the treatment of stone-built houses.

For example, houses at Knowes of Trotty (Chapter 3) and Stonehall Meadow (Chapter 5) were built to incorporate the materials of primary or earlier houses. Here, the masonry of preceding inhabitation was incorporated in the fabric of the later house. A similar process of re-use has been noted for hearth stones, perhaps the most potent symbol of house and household identity in the past and present (see Downes and Richards 2005, 125–26). Although the evidence is currently slight, a related process of incorporation and re-incorporation may well involve the deployment of decorated stones (see Chapter 4). Of course, a sequence of prolonged construction and reconstruction, as revealed at Knowes of Trotty and on Stonehall Knoll, almost certainly belies the constant re-use of building materials. Perhaps most revealing is the desire at this time, where possible, to maintain and refurbish the house as is well illustrated by the ongoing struggle against structural failure in House 3 on Stonehall Knoll. After building the house on an elevated cross-slope, remedial actions were initiated by the employment of a series of upright slabs wedged against the western inner wall-face concluding with the building of a completely new inner wall-face (Figs 5.28 and 5.29).

Taken together these changes in residential practices seem to promote themes of longevity, permanence and place. Continuity and endurance, appears to be the principle characteristics embodied by the transformation from timber to stone architecture in early Neolithic house construction. If it is accepted that the change from timber to stone house construction represents a strategic decision to replicate stalled cairn architecture, then the first stone houses, as exemplified by sites such as Knap of Howar (Fig. 9.6) are effectively houses of the dead and a material language of 'genealogy'. This is a complete reversal of the idea that the builders of stalled cairns were 'in utilizing the architecture of the house… drawing on a particularly potent metaphor' (Richards 1992, 67). While this transformation in dwelling relates to attempts to materially realign the relationship between social units (households) with cosmological realms, it also appears to emphasise vertical genealogical relations of descent and sediment ancestral narratives with particular places in the context of everyday practice. But of course

appearances can be deceptive and this is precisely the strategic manipulation of material metaphors that may be expected to occur within an embryonic *société à maisons*.

Another interesting way of thinking about the transition from timber to stone house architecture is as an act of 'hardening' (Bloch 1995, 214; Fowler 2004, 110–11). This is not simply a mechanism of binding people together, but of fixing potentially disparate and fluid identities to specific materials and place. Moreover, just as the relationships of which the 'house' is an embodiment become 'hardened', so the materiality of the house itself becomes an instrument of endurance. These are not abstract metaphors but practical strategies as the procurement of building stone itself is a labour-intensive task requiring the labour and co-operation of a number of people. As Julian Thomas insightfully comments, 'the collective labour of construction can represent "house-building" in more than one sense: it can bring a new community into being' (2013, 291). Collective labour is also grounded in historical conditions and agricultural production provides the principal context for its mobilization, which at this time comprises both arable cultivation and animal husbandry.

9.3 An agrarian early Neolithic: cereal production and Varme Dale, Rendall, Mainland

In contrast to the main forms of subsistence in the 3rd millennium cal BC which seem to be dominated by animal husbandry, cereal production maintains a very high profile within settlement contexts of the earliest Orcadian Neolithic. As discussed in earlier chapters, cereals and a range of evidence for cereal processing have been found in substantial quantities in 4th millennium cal BC settlements in the Bay of Firth area and beyond (*e.g.* Ha'Breck, Wyre). For example, charred grain was present within posthole [034] and the hearth of Timber structure 1 at Wideford Hill (Chapters 2 and 15). However, it is the massive deposit of *c.*6000 charred barley grains from posthole/pit [044] from 'Timber structure 3' that really emphasizes the level and importance of cereal within subsistence regimes.

Here, it is worth recounting the find of a substantial quantity of burnt grain, which is comparable to that found in House 3, Braes of Ha'Breck (Antonia Thomas pers. comm.), sealed beneath a 2nd millennium cal BC barrow at Varme Dale, Rendall. Varme Dale barrow cemetery lies at the periphery of the study area on the southern slopes of Gorseness Hill, above the Bay of Isbister which faces the Bay of Firth (Figs 1.9 and 9.7).

Figure 9.7 Varme Dale barrow excavations from the northwest, the burnt layers can be seen to the right running around the outside of the mound. Wideford Hill is visible in the background (Jane Downes).

Excavation of one of the barrows (Mound 2) within this cemetery was undertaken in 1998 by Jane Downes as part of *The Orkney Barrows Project*. The mound had been constructed over a series of burnt deposits, which are likely to be directly related to early Neolithic settlement. Traces of the burnt deposits were also located in Trench 2b (Figs 9.7 and 9.8) indicating that the early Neolithic area of habitation was of considerably greater extent, but that it survived best where sealed beneath the later barrows.

Soil micromorphological analysis indicated that the burnt sediments were deposited on a bare soil surface, from which the topsoil had been stripped, suggesting either deliberate removal of the topsoil or considerable erosion. There was no indication that the deposits had been burnt *in situ*. On the glacial clay a thin sooty soil [2042] was overlain by a thick deposit of baked clay [2041]. This in turn was overlain by a layer of ashy soil [2027], which was interspersed with stone blocks and slabs [2028], most of which showed clear signs of burning. Overlying this was a 0.12m layer of grey clay [2024], comprising the topsoil that had developed over the Neolithic deposits, and which was in turn sealed by the barrow. On the exterior of the mound, to the west, the spread of ash and burnt stones, a 'sooty' soil

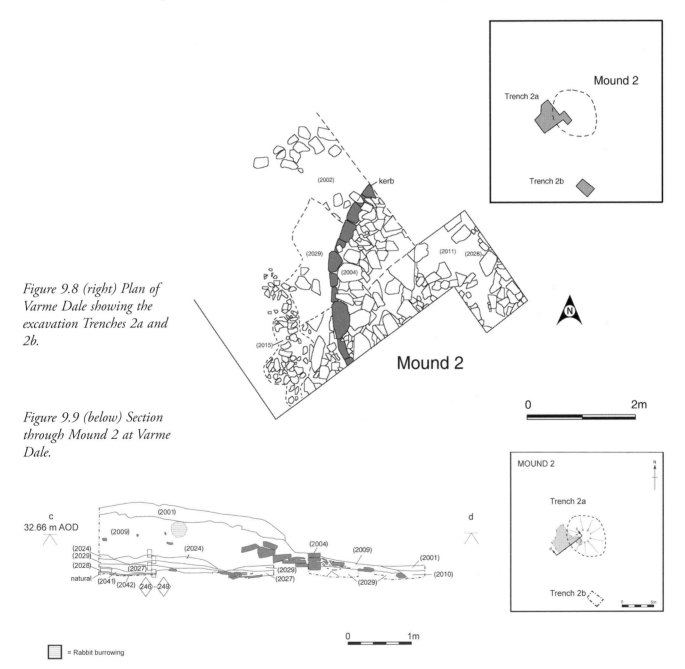

Figure 9.8 (right) Plan of Varme Dale showing the excavation Trenches 2a and 2b.

Figure 9.9 (below) Section through Mound 2 at Varme Dale.

[2022] and dark burnt material [2034], extended beyond and underlay part of the kerb. The charcoal from four samples across the range of early Neolithic contexts was almost entirely *Salix* (willow) with only one, immeasurable fragment of *Corylus* (hazel). Contexts [2041] and [2027], of which the latter overlay the former, both contained *Salix sp* (willow) charcoal which produced radiocarbon dates of *3770–3620 cal BC (GU-10629)* and *3770–3630 cal BC (GU-10628)* respectively. Taken together, these dates make Varme Dale the earliest occurrence of both Neolithic settlement and cereals yet discovered in Orkney (see Chapter 10.4.2).

The charred seeds from the early Neolithic deposits sealed beneath Mound 2 at Varme Dale produced a remarkable assemblage testifying to the possibility of a very early date for the introduction of cereals into Orkney (see Table 15.9). Examples of cereals included 2-grained einkorn wheat (*triticum monococcum*) and naked barley (*hordeum distichum/vulgare* var. *nudum*), together with linseed (*linum* sp.) and hazel nut (*corylus* sp.) (see Chapter 15.6). From these results naked barley can be identified as the dominant crop, followed by einkorn wheat. Of interest is the possible presence of low levels of rye (*secale cereale*) and oat (*avena* sp.); curiously no seeds of wild species were recovered.

Given the amount of cereals present within the small samples taken, the potential total amount accumulated within deposits at Varme Dale is extraordinary. For example, the quantity of grain in the black lens of silt [2022] was such that it was clearly visible during excavation. Equally, as these deposits below the actual barrow were observed running into all sections (Fig. 9.9), it can be inferred that there remain substantial amounts of grain still sealed beneath Mound 2. It should also be noted that the presence of einkorn wheat is unusual in an assemblage from prehistoric Scotland, and the quantities of cereal grains found at Varme Dale, Wideford Hill and Braes of Ha'Breck find comparison with similar deposits at early Neolithic timber 'halls' outside Orkney, such as Balbridie (Fairweather and Ralston 1993).

It appears that the deposits sealed by the barrow accrued in a low pile over a relatively short time period. Although these deposits only partially survive beyond the protection of the barrow, it is likely that they represent spreads of debris associated with habitation of a very similar nature to the timber architecture of Wideford Hill, and Braes of Ha'Breck (see below). In addition, the substantial stonework that forms the kerb of the barrow (Fig. 9.10) could derive from an unidentified nearby stone-built early Neolithic house. In this vein, it will

be recalled that the positioning of a barrow cemetery at the location of an early Neolithic settlement, and the incorporation of the materials from the earlier settlement into the fabric of the barrow are paralleled by the findings at the Knowes of Trotty (Chapter 3).

That cereal production continues as a substantial component of subsistence after the transformation in dwelling from timber to stone houses is revealed by the large quantities of charred barley present at Stonehall Meadow and the stone phases of Braes of Ha'Breck. Substantial amounts of charred barley grain were present in midden material incorporated as part of the wall core of House 2, and pit [3074] within House 3 at Stonehall Meadow. More recently, vast quantities of charred barley were recovered from areas of burning on the floor of House 3 at Braes of Ha'Breck, Wyre (Thomas and Lee 2012) (Fig. 9.11).

Apart from the charred naked barley from the midden (Dickson 1984, 115), a large quern was present within the inner compartment of House 1 at Knap of Howar. Querns are also present in the porch of the Smerquoy Hoose (Fig. 4.31) and at the field edge above the Smerquoy Hoose (Fig. 4.43), and it is suggested that in total these early to middle 4th millennium cal BC agrarian practices relate to new forms of collective labour and the realigning of 'kinship' relations within the evolving Neolithic *sociétés à maisons* in Orkney.

9.4 Move closer: settlement nucleation and the raising of the 'big house' at the turn of the 4th millennium cal BC

In the wide variety of ethnographic contexts (*e.g.* Errington 1989; Waterson 1990; Sissons 2010) there is much diversity in a correspondence between *sociétés à maisons* and houses as material constructs (see Carsten and Hugh-Jones 1995, 49–53). In this section the anatomy of late 4th and 3rd millennium cal Orcadian settlement will be explored within a narrative embracing the material expressions of developing *sociétés à maisons*.

In the architecture of Knap of Howar, Papa Westray, Green, Eday (Miles 2011, 8), Knowes of Trotty (Chapter 3) and probably at Wideford Hill, Mainland, we see a trajectory of single house expansion into double house units. Precisely the same occurs at Stonehall Meadow where House 3 is built against the northern wall of House 2 (Fig. 5.35). At Braes of Ha'Breck (Fig. 9.12) and Brae of Smerquoy (Fig. 4.29), house enlargement is achieved differently by the addition of a longitudinal structural element. In both instances, however, the house is expanded into a larger unit building. A slightly different form of expansion may be present at Howe, Stromness, Mainland (Carter *et al.* 1984; Ballin Smith 1994, 14), where two buildings initially interpreted as a stalled cairn and mortuary house, due to the presence of hearths, can be confidently re-interpreted as early Neolithic houses facing one another (see Davidson and Henshall 1989, 52; Carey 2012, 15–16).

At Braes of Ha'Breck Wyre (Thomas and Lee 2012), Pool, Sanday (Hunter 2007, 28–32), Smerquoy and Stonehall, Mainland, another facet of settlement emerges in the latter centuries of the 4th millennium cal BC with the beginnings of conglomeration. Through the extensive investigations at Stonehall at least three discrete areas of habitation were recognised, each represented by stone-built houses that were positioned 50m–100m apart. Although the early occupation of Stonehall Farm was not thoroughly investigated, both Stonehall Knoll and Stonehall Meadow revealed lengthy periods of occupation at particular places. Such maintenance of place translates into continuity of

the house through lengthy processes of reconstruction and rebuilding at both locations. In each case, parts of earlier structures were incorporated into the new, or the

Figure 9.10 Varme Dahl: the burnt deposits containing charred grain ran beneath the barrow. Substantial blocks of 'building stone' can be seen forming the barrow kerb (Jane Downes).

Figure 9.11 House 3 at Braes of Ha'Breck, Wyre showing the large spread of burnt barley grains at the rear of the house (Antonia Thomas).

Figure 9.12 House 3 at Braes of Ha'Breck was elongated and doubled in size by the addition of House 5 (Antonia Thomas).

Figure 9.13 Planning in House 3 at Stonehall Meadow, Cuween Hill Passage grave is visible high up on the hillside (Siân Jones).

material of earlier structures was re-used to create the new. Either way, two strategies are evident; the first involves material expressions of household continuity articulating vertical relations emphasising place and descent. The second is manifest in the architectural divergence of houses at Stonehall Knoll and Meadow. Architectural distinction creates visible differences expressing discrete and separate social identities in the face of converging residence patterns.

The desire to accrue social capital through spatial proximity (cf. Musterd 2003, 639) may well have accelerated the evolution of Neolithic *sociétés à maisons* in Orkney. Yet, the heterogeneity of dwelling described above reveals the tensions manifest in residential strategies to gain access to resources. However, simply living together as neighbours does not necessarily secure admission into social networks, nor creates inclusive communities (*e.g.*

Arthurson 2002: Nast and Blokland 2014). Indeed, there is nothing 'equalitarian' about the trend towards house conglomeration evident in the latter centuries of the 4th millennium cal BC (*contra* Childe 1946, 32) because intra-house and inter-house rivalries and competition are inevitable within the fluidity of social relations within *sociétés à maisons* (Gillespie 2000a, 10). *Sociétés à maisons* are intrinsically unstable social entities both internally and externally (cf. Carsten and Hugh-Jones 1995, 8–9). For example, the evanescent social relations manifest in the 'house' are subsumed within the collective strategies linked to reproduction and continuity (cf. Helms 2007, 502). Yet, the relationships forged within face-to-face situations of everyday practices provide the character and cohesion of the corporate group. Consequently, *sociétés à maisons* are potentially highly competitive entities both internally and externally (Beck 2007, 6). Ironically, intergroup competition, in particular, may provide the necessary conditions under which *sociétés à maisons* thrive and transform themselves. As Gillespie notes, 'within-house and between-house rivalries may intensify, and house statuses may fluctuate due to unstable economic or political factors, as new sources of wealth become available or interactions with other societies change the local dynamics' (2000a, 10).

The stone-built house is considered an essential feature of Neolithic *sociétés à maisons* in Orkney. This significance is multifaceted and ranges from the labour expended in construction to the materiality and architecture of the house. The material house is also an emblem of its inhabitants. Its embellishment, visual appearance and spatial position are potential strategies of competitive practice between people and households in the quest to maintain or enhance social position within the local community or neighbourhood. If changes in subsistence can be identified as providing the altered conditions necessary for the establishment of *société à maisons*, they can also feature in strategies of status enhancement.

As we saw in Chapter 5, such inequality is manifest in the landscape position of the houses at Stonehall. For example, living in an elevated position on Stonehall Knoll, despite the many structural problems attached to building houses on an elevated slope, was clearly socially rewarding. Apart from the obvious advantages of assuming a prominent topographic position in terms of visual access and surveillance in relation to neighbouring houses, the importance of the vertical axis becomes increasingly obvious when the Cuween passage grave is built higher upslope (Fig. 9.13).

Significantly, topography was also a consideration in regard to the organization of dwelling at Braes of Ha'Breck. Although more ruinous and truncated due to a higher position, Houses 1 and 2 assumed an elevated aspect, originally overlooking the other dwellings (*e.g.* Houses 3, 4 and 5) within the settlement complex (Farrell *et al.* 2014, Fig. 4). Little is known of the earliest inhabitation of Crossiecrown, but geophysical survey at Smerquoy indicates that as it was built on the lower slopes of Wideford Hill, the Smerquoy Hoose was overlooked by, and in turn overlooks, other buildings, some of which are currently under investigation (Figs 4.3 and 4.38). The Knowes of Trotty house is positioned high on the hillside and other magnetic anomalies detected downslope during geophysical surveys may well represent further houses (Fig. 3.2).

Through time, Neolithic house architecture begins to change in Orkney and the rigid 'stalled' character

Figure 9.14 Northern view of the late 4th millennium cal BC house structure at Green, Eday, showing the highly curved inner wall-faces and small projecting divisional orthostats (Diana Coles).

of interior space diminishes. Instead of strong internal divisions created by substantial lateral orthostats, 'softer' segregation of space is achieved through greater curvature of the internal wall-face. The meeting of curved stretches of walling created a 'pinching' effect to delineate internal compartments. Such pinching is evident in the architecture of House 3 on Stonehall Knoll (Figs 5.21 and 5.22), and is also present in the house structure at Green, Eday, where curved internal wall faces create recess-like spaces which are weakly defined by small projecting orthostats (Fig. 9.14). One consequence of this opening up of the house interior, and absence of substantial projecting orthostats, is the creation of side recesses formed as part of the actual fabric of the building. It is this architectural trajectory that potentially leads to the sub-circular houses with developed recesses ('beds') of the late 4th and early 3rd millennia cal BC. Another feature of this change is a disengagement of the material house with the architecture of the stalled cairn, and in this act we see a move towards a new fluidity of practices and relations within the household. Furthermore, the architectural cleavage between house and stalled cairn necessarily concurs with a weakening of traditional discourses of descent, allowing a metamorphosis in house architecture which relates to new material strategies and avenues of constructing identity.

Within the last two centuries of the 4th millennium cal BC, the settlement of Barnhouse was founded adjacent to the Loch of Harray, in west Mainland, Orkney (Fig. 9.15). Continuing the trend towards conglomeration discussed above, Barnhouse can best be described as a nucleated settlement in the sense of a gathering of houses around

Figure 9.15 Barnhouse from the air (Jane Downes).

a central open area and dominant 'big house'; House 2 (Richards 2005b). Indeed, the degree of nucleation has led to the settlement being characterized as a 'village', and the increasing conglomeration of houses occurred in tandem with an architectural shift to smaller circular buildings with internal stone furniture arranged according to cruciform principles of order (Richards 1990; Parker Pearson and Richards 1995; Downes and Richards 2005, 57–60). Accompanying these changes is the appearance of Grooved ware pottery, which with its flat base and expanded range of sizes must relate to different practices and forms of presentation and display. Because of the large-scale excavations at Barnhouse, the organization of houses and households was explored in detail and appears to be arranged according to centre–periphery spatial principles (A. M. Jones and Richards 2005, 49–52). This form of spatial order also embraces social differences according to proximity and distance from a 'centre'.

In short, two concentric rings of houses respectively using differently manufactured Grooved ware (stone and shell temper) emerge as partially discrete entities, constructing identities through divergent social practice

(Jones 2002; 2005; A. M. Jones and Richards 2005). Here then we see a hierarchy of identities based on centre–periphery distinctions being dissolved in certain contexts to the level of the individual house. There can be little doubt that settlements like Barnhouse embody the apogee of Neolithic *sociétés à maisons* in Orkney. Despite houses and their inhabitants being enmeshed in fluid and unstable social relationships, the Barnhouse *société à maisons* constituted and outwardly portrayed itself as a coherent, permanent, unified community through material signifiers. Grooved ware manufacture may have varied according to individual houses and households, but its decoration was highly formalized and restricted to a small range of designs, which also extended to employment within activities occurring at the nearby Stones of Stenness (Fig. 9.16). This material strategy, which was visually prominent and aimed at wider audiences, materialized a fabricated image of a *société à maisons* in which internal differentiation (and competition) appears to be rendered redundant.

Concurrently, group identity began to be articulated by, and condensed within, a single 'big-house' (cf. Bradley

2005, 65–80; 2013). Apart from being a substantially larger building, House 2 at Barnhouse draws on earlier house architecture by employing masonry piers in the same manner as divisional orthostats in earlier houses, for example at Stonehall Meadow, Knowes of Trotty, Smerquoy, Knap of Howar and Braes of Ha'Breck (compare Fig 9.12 with Fig. 9.17). In appropriating and re-presenting this architecture, House 2 offers the imagery of the past in the present, a house that embodies and makes tangible the continuity and substance of the Barnhouse *société à maisons* (Richards 2013b, 82). Consequently, it is unsurprising that burial occurred within House 2 (Richards 2005b, 137–38), and the sophisticated masonry replicates that seen within prominent passage graves such as Maes Howe and Howe of Howe. Through the presence of the dead, descent and ancestry combine to create a material discourse of continuity. Given the status of House 2 as a material embodiment of the *société à maisons* and its continuity, it is equally unsurprising that within its confines ritual objects were created and as 'heirlooms' buried within the floor (Richards 2005b; Joyce 2000).

Figure 9.16 Grooved ware from the Stones of Stenness and Barnhouse displays identical decoration (© Crown Copyright reproduced courtesy of Historic Scotland).

Figure 9.17 House 2 at Barnhouse from the southwest (Colin Richards).

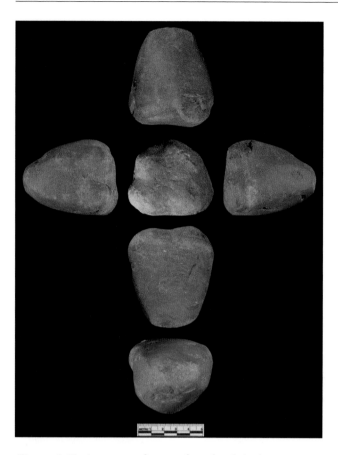

Figure 9.18 An unusual ground and polished camptonite object with knobs collected by Christopher Gee from surface material overlying a newly discovered late Neolithic settlement at Bookan, Sandwick, Mainland (Hugo Anderson-Whymark).

Indeed, the 3rd millennium cal BC marks the appearance of a range of beautifully fashioned and finished objects, including, carved stone balls, highly polished maceheads and ground stone objects of unusual form (see Figs 9.18 and 13.5), many of which are recovered from settlement contexts. A significant aspect of these things is their distinction, for example, many of the ground stone objects from Skara Brea (Childe 1931a, plates XXXVII–XLI) remain unparalleled at other villages, despite the substantial number of excavations that have taken place since the 1930s. Even maceheads, which fall into standardized forms (*e.g.* Orkney pestle, cushion, ovoid), remain exclusive due to their distinctive colouring and banding (*e.g.* Figs 4.34, 9.24 and 9.35).

Interestingly, at another level within the Barnhouse community, individual kin identities were maintained by divergent practices and differently constructed houses. The continuity of individual houses and their

occupants at Barnhouse was achieved by a range of material strategies, such as re-deploying hearth stones extracted from earlier houses in those newly constructed (*e.g.* Downes and Richards 2005, 125–26). Also, houses were rebuilt on the same site, for example House 5 at Barnhouse was re-stablished at least four times (*ibid.*, 69–82), re-using materials from the older buildings. This re-use of stone was merely a maintenance of tradition, materializing the old in the new as seen in constructional sequences at Crossiecrown, Knowes of Trotty, Stonehall and Smerquoy. This strategy can also be extended to include the redeployment of decorated stones within the fabric of new buildings, for instance as seen in the Smerquoy Hoose and several buildings at the Ness of Brodgar (Antonia Thomas pers. comm.).

With the form of house conglomeration that we see at Barnhouse comes the accruement and utilization of middens on a scale unseen before in the Orcadian Neolithic (see discussion in Chapter 6). Such changes to dwelling, however, were not restricted solely to Barnhouse but also occurred elsewhere in Orkney (see Fig. 9.2). Nevertheless, there is a substantial divergence between Barnhouse and other settlements or villages. No round-based ceramics or earlier structures were located at Barnhouse (although there may have been a shift in settlement location north along the Loch of Harray), whereas, in virtually every late Neolithic settlement, including the Ness of Brodgar, there is considerable temporal depth to the occupation of a single place, in most cases running from the last three centuries of the 4th millennium cal BC. This is precisely what occurs at Stonehall within the Bay of Firth study area, where houses follow a similar trajectory towards nucleation at Stonehall Farm (Chapter 6). Excavations were limited at Stonehall Farm because of the extent of settlement, mainly due to the clustering of houses and build up of extensive midden material. Nonetheless, two discrete small circular structures, together with clear evidence for another, attest to the almost centripetal nature of habitation occurring at Stonehall Farm. Although a different order of settlement than that seen at Barnhouse, dwellings at Stonehall Farm also nucleate around a 'big house', except in this case the house is not physically large. Structure 1, Stonehall Farm appears to have originally been a dwelling that is transformed into a special building by virtue of replacing the hearth with a burial cist (Fig. 6.24). In much the same way as Barnhouse House 2, Structure 1 resonates with themes of death and the past; it also is a place for depositing and keeping fine objects and heirlooms (Figs 6.16, 6.17 and 6.28).

As at Stonehall, Wideford Hill, Smerquoy and Knowes

of Trotty, stone buildings at Crossiecrown would appear to be founded within the last three hundred years of the 4th millennium cal BC. However, Crossiecrown represents a settlement that seems to be obsessed with the continual recycling of materials, particularly building stone. Consequently, the trajectory of conglomeration towards nucleation is no longer directly visible as represented by extant houses. The gradiometer geophysical survey, which detects magnetically enhanced material such as midden, discovered the ghost image of an earlier form of settlement organization (Fig. 7.2). The enhanced midden material appears to have been deposited against house walls and consequently ringed discrete houses. Early Skara Brae (phase 1–2) is yet another Mainland settlement that reveals conglomerating circular houses at this time, which nucleate around an earlier manifestation of Hut 7 (see Childe 1931, 38; Clarke 1976). Like the 'big houses' present at other sites, Hut 7 incorporates the dead in the form of two women buried within a cist beneath its western wall (Childe 1931, 140–42). Hut 7 is also profusely decorated which tends to concentrate around the point of burial (see Richards 1991; A. Thomas pers. comm.).

Further settlements displaying the nucleation of houses at the end of the 4th millennium cal BC are present in the Outer Isles. Within the excavated area at Pool, Sanday, a number of houses were built in close proximity to one another between phases 2.3–3.1 (Hunter *et al.* 2007, 34–40). One building at Pool, Structure 8 'the largest Neolithic structure represented on the site' (*ibid.*, 40), was enhanced during the 3rd millennium cal BC and may well conform to the 'big house' status afforded to House 2 at Barnhouse, Hut 7 at Skara Brae and Structure 1 at Stonehall. Further confirmation of this role comes from the presence of a decorated orthostat extending the house entrance (*ibid.*, 41). Current investigations at the Links of Noltland, Westray, seem to be uncovering another late Neolithic settlement having numerous small houses, *e.g.* Structures 7 and 9, nucleating around a large 'big house' numbered yet again Structure 8 (Moore and Wilson 2011, 19–23).

This trajectory of settlement towards nucleation at the end of the 4th millennium cal BC was suggested above to represent the apogee of Neolithic *sociétés à maisons* in Orkney. Virtually every known Orcadian early 3rd millennium cal BC settlement displays a similar spatial organization of smaller circular houses clustering around a special structure, a 'big house'. This residential trend reaches its zenith at Barnhouse with the construction of Structure 8 (Hill and Richards

2005). The 'big houses' in the 3rd millennium cal BC settlements can be recognized as a materialization of *sociétés à maisons* in terms of a physical embodiment of descent and continuity of the 'house' coalescing in a monumental construct. Significantly, it may even have been experienced as an animated, living thing (cf. Waterson 1990). Consequently, to enter these buildings would enable access to another world, an ancestral realm (much like the stalled cairns, and by implication early Neolithic stone houses) where past, present and future fuse. However, broader questions must be asked at this point; first, why are the Neolithic *sociétés à maisons* in Orkney following a similar trend towards the congregation of smaller physical houses around 'big houses'? Second, why are social strategies being enacted to ensure that people are predominantly and obsessively constructing identities in relation to communities dwelling in such closely assembled settlement units?

9.5 Going back to our roots: mythologization and externalizing late Neolithic Orcadian identities

At precisely the time that the process of conglomeration appears to accelerate, external relationships and contacts beyond Orkney emerge in sharp focus. At some time during the late 4th millennium cal BC passage grave architecture becomes established in Orkney. In some respects, given that pre-existing stalled cairns are widely distributed across Orkney (Fig. 9.6), the appearance of passage graves is curious. A clue may come from the completely different geographic distribution of stalled cairns to passage graves, the latter of which run out to the west and include the Outer Hebrides, and eastern and western Ireland. Interestingly, the Orcadian passage graves initially tend to be treated in the same way as stalled cairns in terms of landscape location and their role in the mortuary process (see Chapter 8).

The building of Orcadian passage graves is consistent with construction processes seen elsewhere along the western seaboard. Basically, the central and side chambers are erected with fine corbelled masonry to create spaces with excessively high roofs. Then the chambers are wrapped by rings of masonry and the cavities filled with stone, or, in the case of Maes Howe clay and earth (Childe 1956). The length of the passage is determined by the size and thickness of the cairn. The main difference between Orcadian passage graves and similar monuments further to the west is an absence of a kerb or peristalith. This is a surprising omission since it appears to be such an important element of Hebridean and Irish passage grave

Figure 9.19 Kerb running around Cairn S, Loughcrew, Ireland (Colin Richards).

Figure 9.20 Peristalith at Reineval, Sout Uist (Vicki Cummings).

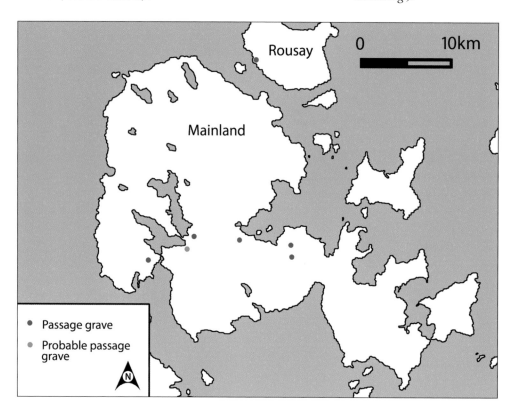

Figure 9.21 Distribution of passage graves in Mainland, Orkney.

architecture (Fig. 9.19). Moreover, in a number of places, for instance, the Boyne Valley, Ireland, the kerb provides a medium of display for a range of megalithic art (*e.g.* Shee Twohig 1981; O'Kelly 1982, 152–85; O'Sullivan 1993; Robin 2010). Similarly, the kerb at Newgrange comprises a number of different lithologies (Stout and Stout 2008, 8–12). Within Hebridean passage grave architecture, the kerb is exaggerated in taking the form of a peristalith, basically a ring of monoliths set within or around the cairn (see Cummings and Richards 2013). In some instances, such as Dun Bharpa, Barra and Reineval, South Uist, the peristalith monoliths are over two metres in height (Fig.

9.20). It is these two components of the western passage graves, the kerb or peristalith and the passage grave cairn, which are separated in the late Neolithic Orcadian context to create two entirely different monumental forms: the stone circle and passage grave.

While passage graves are built across Orkney, there is an obvious clustering in west-central Mainland (Fig. 9.21). Although this distribution has in the past been recognised as a cemetery (Daniel and Powell 1949, 178), such a characterization is misleading due to the topographic situation of the monuments. Instead, the large number appears to be more a consequence of a network of local groups on Mainland, appropriating and manipulating a form of funerary architecture derived from the west. This social strategy reaches a zenith in the massive labour investment involved in the construction of the extraordinary Maes Howe passage grave. In this burst of megalithic construction it is an externalized monumental view of ancestry, as manifest in the 'imported' passage grave that is reproduced within the Orcadian context. This is not merely a materialization of 'origin' claims outwith Orkney, but more the appropriation and reconstitution of ancestral 'others' as part of a strategy of mythologization (see Friedman 1992; Richards 2013c). In this context, mythologization may be understood as a reforging of 'other' people's pasts (in this case looking towards the west) as part of a quest by late Neolithic Orcadian *sociétés à maisons* to create exotic ancestral origin myths. This social strategy, in the context of constructing Orcadian identities, has been argued to have dramatic consequence in terms of monumental construction in the very areas of appropriation, such as the Outer Hebrides (see Richards 2013c, 276–80).

Once 'extracted' from the architecture of the western passage grave, the kerb or peristalith becomes transformed into the stone circle. In line with arguments concerning the status of the 'big house' as a material manifestation of the *sociétés à maisons*, it is as a method of monumentally wrapping such architecture that the stone circle makes its first appearance in Orkney early in the 3rd millennium cal BC (Richards 2013b; Griffiths and Richards 2013). The stone circle wrapping a 'big house', or certainly a manifestation of a 'big house' within the Stones of Stenness (Fig. 9.22), is a deployment of monoliths not unlike the peristalith wrapping the Hebridean passage grave (Fig 9.20). In this way, the Stones of Stenness can be seen as an extension of Barnhouse village and a material objectification of a *société à maisons* through a truly monumental embellishment of the 'big house'.

9.6 The gathering of late Neolithic *sociétés à maisons* in Orkney

If Neolithic communities in Orkney were now claiming, in a more forceful and conspicuous manner, fabulous and distant origins through extended ancestral links beyond the Northern Isles, then external social networks were becoming increasingly vital. The elevation of distant relationships, and a desire to materialize them through things, is not just confined to monumental architecture and its construction. From the beginning of the 3rd millennium cal BC, a number of 'exotic' materials appear

Figure 9.22 The Stones of Stenness (Colin Richards).

in settlement assemblages, for instance, shiny black pitchstone from Arran (Middleton 2005, 295), 'foreign' rocks utilized in the manufacture of axes (R. Ritchie 1992, 214; M. Edmonds pers. comm.) and maceheads (Fig. 9.24).

The pursuit of ancestral claims beyond Orkney appears to be part of a series of parallel strategies which revolve around inter-group competition. Here, different corporate groups were engaging in competitive practices at a series of different levels, one of which is through the ability to accrue resources and mobilize relationships to participate in a burst of monumental construction that occurs between *c.*3000–2600 cal BC. Such competitive practices are mainly played out in a public arena and perhaps the epitome of this social strategy is the construction of the stone circle at the Ring of Brodgar (Fig. 9.23).

The stone circle within the Ring of Brodgar is composite in the sense that it is composed of different types of rock (see Downes *et al.* 2013, 105–107). Each rock type came from a different quarry and place (Richards *et al.* 2013). Here we can follow Andrew M. Jones' (2005b) argument concerning the construction of identity of specific social groups through their relationship to 'place' as materialized through stone. Consequently, the

Figure 9.23 The great Ring of Brodgar (Craig Taylor).

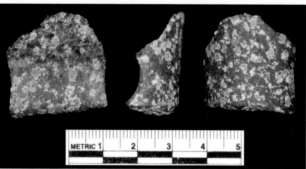

Figure 9.24 Macehead fragment (Orkney pestle) collected from the fieldsurface adjacent to the Stones of Stenness by Christopher Gee. The rock is an alkaline porphyritic rock not present in Orkney but probably derived from a glacial erratic from Scandinavia (John Brown pers. comm.). Interestingly, the erratic is likely to derive from the northern isles, for example Westray (Hugo Anderson-Whymark).

gradual accumulation of monoliths within the Ring of Brodgar can be characterized as a form of gathering and materializing different social groups, or *société à maisons* within the competitive arena of monument construction. In this light, the process of stone circle construction is a planting of *sociétés à maisons* in specific order within the circle. Consequently, the Ring of Brodgar can be identified as nothing more than a monumental discourse, a language of the house, which presents and 'projects an outward facade of unity, one that masks…. underlying tensions and conflicting loyalties' (Gillespie 2000a, 8).

A similar projection may underlie the building and

gathering of 'big houses' at the Ness of Brodgar (Card 2010; Card and Thomas 2012). It has been suggested that the architecture and morphology of the Ring of Brodgar participate in a structured south-westerly journey along the Brodgar isthmus (Downes *et al.* 2013, 91–94). The journey ends at the Ness of Brodgar where at least seven 'big houses' are assembled (Fig. 9.25). If the structures at the Ness of Brodgar are equivalents or analogues of the 'big houses' located within the different settlements, and material extensions of various *sociétés à maisons*, then the same social strategies are being deployed as seen in the different stones dragged and set up in the great Ring of Brodgar (Downes *et al.* 2013). Equally, under these circumstances it should come as no surprise that just as special objects, or heirlooms, are present within the 'big house' in a settlement context, they are also present in the gathering of 'big houses' at the Ness of Brodgar (Nick Card pers. comm.).

In the latter centuries of the first half of the 3rd millennium cal BC, the descent-based 'language of *sociétés à maisons*' takes on a more material inflection in the enlargement and reconstruction of ancient chambered cairns. Selected local funerary monuments, solely stalled cairns, are re-appropriated and transformed into massive long cairns. Some are merely enlarged by adding new skins of masonry and horn-works, as seen at Point of Cott, Westray (Barber 1997), while others have both horns added and chambers modified as occurs at Knowe of Lairo,

Figure 9.25 The gathering of 'big houses' at the Ness of Brodgar (Adam Stanford – Aerial Cam).

Rousay (Grant and Wilson 1943). Finally, 'new' horned cairns such as Vestra Fiold, Mainland, and probably Staneyhill, Mainland, are erected. However, the 'box-like' technique of construction employed is not enduring, and the monumentality is clearly predicated on an immediacy embodied in a 'surface over substance' regime (Barber 1997, 63; Richards *et al.* 2013, 174–83).

9.7 The fusion and fragmentation of *sociétés à maisons* towards the end of the Neolithic

Surely these highly visible material strategies are a consequence of the competitive, fluid and unstable nature of the *sociétés à maisons*, and the imperative of claimed descent and genealogical linkage to founding ancestors. In late Neolithic Orkney, the increasing structural volatility of social relations translates into even greater emphasis on signalling social cohesion.

Of all the Orcadian Neolithic settlements, Skara Brae probably remains the most well-known example and is part of the designated World Heritage Site (Fig. 9.26). The fortuitous engulfment of the settlement by sand has led to a degree of preservation unseen elsewhere. When looking down into the house interiors now devoid of inhabitants,

Figure 9.26 Aerial view of Skara Brae (Craig Taylor).

Figure 9.27 Looking into Hut 1 at Skara Brae (Colin Richards).

Figure 9.28 Structure 8 at Barnhouse overlies part of the earlier village.

the size and scale of the buildings is quite striking (Fig. 9.27). Indeed, the character of house architecture in the later Neolithic is a move towards larger internal areas. This is seen at Barnhouse with the construction of Structure 8, which stands as a single 'monument' built over the remains of the preceding village (Figure 9.28). On a less monumental scale, the same stratigraphic superimposition occurs at Skara Brae and to a more limited extent at Rinyo, Rousay (Childe and Grant 1939; 1947). At a practical level, the physical enlargement of the late Neolithic house could be construed as an architectural response to a growth in the size of the household. But what effect did the enlargement of the household have on the social relations comprising the *société à maisons*?

It is suggested here that the increase in magnitude of the household dwelling beneath a single roof initiates fault lines through the broader community or village. In the face of growing internalized 'discreteness' and consequently the promotion of more kin-based social relations, the process of conglomeration that has been traced through the late 4th into the early 3rd millennium cal BC, now enters its final stages. In describing Skara Brae, Childe states that 'the dwellings… were not isolated buildings', but 'the seven domestic structures referred to periods III and IV were autonomous members of a larger organic unit, interconnected by stone roofed passages' (1931, 19). In this situation, individual houses become physically conjoined to one another, a strategy deployed to project an image of increasing unity and cohesion (Fig 9.29). The necessity for a 'big house' remains in the form of Hut 7, but this building is no longer a separate entity but also becomes physically attached by virtue of a linking passage. Such a conjunction is clearly symbolically problematic or 'dangerous', and requires dual sanction by virtue of a series of thresholds, many of which are embellished by incised art along the access passage B (Richards 1991; A. Thomas pers. comm.). Running parallel with this move towards the fusion and unification of dwellings is the enlarging and greater material wrapping of individual houses. This is achieved through constructing an encircling casing wall running concentrically around the house. At Skara Brae the gap between the original house wall and the outer casing wall is filled with midden, over 2m in thickness (see Childe 1931, 9; Chapter 6). Consequently, within the late Neolithic settlements as houses become physically closer together, they paradoxically become more separated through a process of extensive wrapping.

Although an image of greater social cohesion is being projected through spatial changes in dwelling, it is significant that individual houses are becoming more discrete by being additionally wrapped by midden within casing walls. Significantly, at precisely this time monument construction ceases. The diminishing of large monument building projects perhaps portrays the degree of fragmentation and decline of *sociétés à maisons* and an inability to organise large labour forces or even act in unison as a collective.

Strangely, within late 3rd millennium cal BC Orkney, any transition to a 'Chalcolithic' as represented by the introduction of metalwork and Beaker pottery or burials (see Allen *et al.* 2012) is difficult to discern. Judging from the evidence from Crossiecrown even though Beaker-like ceramics (*e.g.* SFs 51 and 150) appear in the latter period of occupation they still comprise a small component of a primarily Grooved ware assemblage (Jones 2012, 116–19; Chapter 11). A similar minor Beaker component is present at Rinyo, Rousay (Childe and Grant 1939, 26) and other late Neolithic settlements. If a re-orientation of social relationships is discernible in the latter centuries of the 3rd millennium cal BC, it involves a more visible shift to the north towards Shetland.

As the end of the 3rd millennium cal BC approaches, a disjunction occurs in the trajectory of settlement nucleation and the appearance of closer social interaction. Moreover, for the first time during the Neolithic period in Orkney, a change occurs in dwelling which interestingly appears to run parallel with developments that are also occurring in Shetland (cf. Øvrevik 1990, 146–47; Downes and Thomas 2014). For example, Crossiecrown exhibits a long history of inhabitation, involving a variety of stone houses, organized in a number of different

configurations (*e.g.* Fig. 7.2). Ultimately, as occupation at Crossiecrown runs into the 2nd millennium cal BC, this once substantial settlement diminishes in size to just two dwellings: the Grey and Red Houses (Fig. 7.44). The Crossiecrown pairing of houses, positioned face to face is replicated in an almost identical manner at a number of settlements (Fig. 9.30). Apart from those illustrated in Figure 9.30, additional examples may include Houses 8 and 9 at Pool, Sanday (Hunter *et al.* 2007, illus 3.15) and Houses 1 and 6 at Barnhouse (Fig. 9.31). If the latter are included, then the possibility exists that the origin of the early Bronze Age 'double house' actually extends back to the beginning of the 3rd millennium cal BC.

The supposed disastrous end of Skara Brae was expressed in emotive terms by Gordon Childe:

> What was this catastrophe? Its effect was to leave the huts exposed to the infiltration of sand but otherwise the fixtures of the interior were undisturbed. There is no trace of hostile violence. The huts had not been pillaged nor the valuables hidded in them carried off..... It is, therefore, more reasonable to think of a natural agency, namely a hurricane from the north-west, perhaps coinciding with a high tide... At the same time the sand dunes might be set in motion, and people, so poorly equipped as our villagers, could only find refuge from this foe on higher ground
>
> (Childe 1931, 64).

In later publications this disaster was substantially embellished:

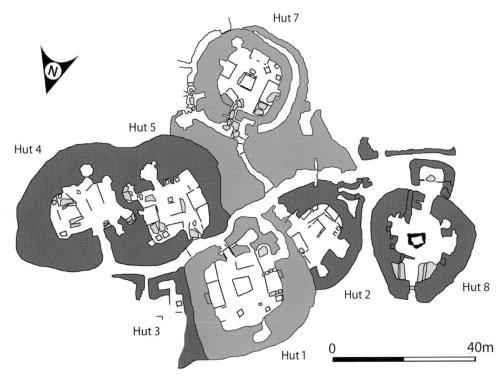

Figure 9.29 Plan of the later configuration of houses at Skara Brae. By this time the majority of houses are physically attached to one another. Even here a constructional sequence is visible; the latest houses are coloured darker grey (after Childe 1931).

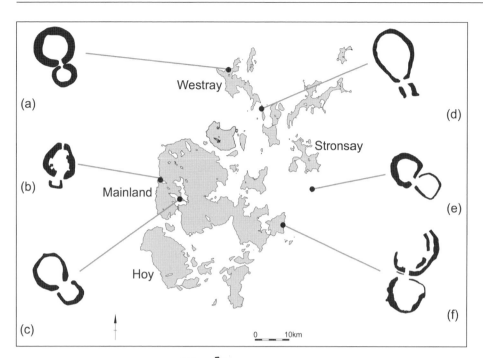

Figure 9.30 Orcadian double houses span the 3rd and 2nd millennium cal bc: (a) Links of Noltland; (b) Skara Brae; (c) Wasbister; (d) Holm of Farray; (e) Auskerry; (f) Skaill, Deerness.

Figure 9.31 'Double' houses 1 and 6 at Barnhouse.

It was eventually overwhelmed by a sudden catastrophe. The inhabitants of the huts were forced to flee their homes, abandoning in the store rooms and on the floor many treasured possessions, fashioned with great labour and ingenuity. One woman in her haste to squeeze through the narrow door of her home (No 7) broke her necklace and left a stream of beads behind as she scampered up the passage (Childe 1933, 7).

The difference between a catastrophe, abandonment or transformation is quite difficult to discern archaeologically. Certainly, Childe's vivid portrait of disaster subsequently caused him numerous interpretative problems (Richards 1995). It also seems quite probable that Hut 8 at Skara Brae, rather than being a constituent of the main settlement, represents a single dwelling, with an added porch-like structure attached to its front, built alongside a decaying settlement (see Downes and Thomas 2014, 82–84). In contrast to Crossiecrown, Skara Brae Hut 8 lies adjacent to the main settlement mound in much the same way as occurs at Links of Noltland. Both displacement and dislocation appear to betray the fragmentation of the Neolithic *sociétés à maisons* in Orkney. However, a more mixed and disjointed picture actually emerges with the continuation of particular nucleated villages apparently running concurrently with settlements now reduced in scale and comprising double houses, as evident at Crossiecrown. One example of a long-running nucleated village was discovered recently at Muckquoy, Redland, to the west of the Bay of Firth (Figs 1.9 and 9.32).

Figure 9.32 Location of Muckquoy, Redland, Mainland, Orkney.

9.8 Muckquoy, Redland, Mainland

A surface scatter of flint and stone artefacts at Muckquoy, Redland, was initially recognized in 2006 by the farmer, the late Mr Eoin Scott, who was at that time chair of the 'Friends of the Orkney Archaeological Trust'. The site, situated adjacent to the Finstown–Evie road (Fig. 9.32), takes the form of a low mound in the southwest corner of the field (Fig. 9.33). The field was subsequently

walked in the spring of 2006 by Martin Carruthers and James Moore of Orkney College, University of the Highlands and Islands, together with local volunteers. After the field was ploughed once again in 2011, a second phase of fieldwalking was undertaken by Dan Lee of ORCA. A total surface collection on a five metre grid was undertaken by Colin Richards, Mairi Robertson and members of the Orkney Archaeological Society in May

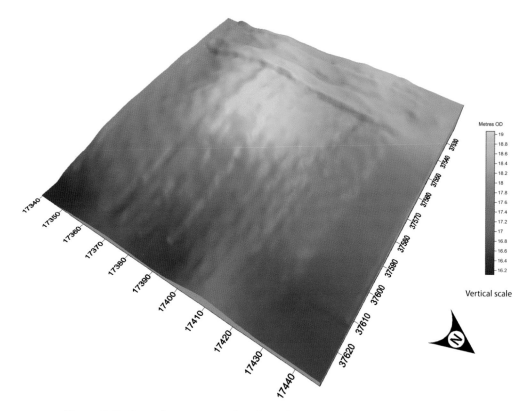

Figure 9.33 Immediate topography of Muckquoy, Redland (Mark Littlewood).

2013, and the field surface was examined once again by Christopher Gee in 2014–15.

Judging from the size of the mound, Muckquoy was clearly a substantial settlement situated on relatively level ground on the western coastal plain of the Bay of Firth. It is sheltered from westerly winds by a continuous ridge of hills, running north–south, comprising the hills of Cuffie, Burrien and Rowamo (Fig. 1.9). In occupying this location Muckquoy lies directly 3km west of the Knowes of Trotty (see Chapter 3), yet, situated on the other side of the hill, appears to exist almost in a different world.

The archaeological material from fieldwalking included burnt bone, pottery, stone and flint tools. The assemblage was chronologically diverse, for example, 4th millennium cal BC occupation was demonstrated by an Unstan bowl rim sherd and a leaf-shaped arrowhead recovered in 2008. That the inhabitation of the settlement continued into the 3rd and 2nd millennia cal BC was apparent from numerous sherds of Grooved ware (Fig. 11.10.3), Bronze Age ceramics, and a broken macehead (Fig. 9.35) collected from the field surface. Just as at Crossiecrown, several substantial pieces of polished haematite were also collected during fieldwalking (Fig. 9.36).

The main concentration of surface material coincided

with the mound and given the chronological range of artefacts present it was supposed that a settlement of similar nature and longevity to Crossiecrown lay beneath the ploughsoil. However, when the geophysical plot was revealed, not only were circular house structures visible but the site was seen to be far more extensive than had been envisaged. Of particular interest, and totally unexpected, was the bounded nature of the settlement (Fig. 9.37). Boundaries around late Neolithic–early Bronze Age settlements had not been previously identified in Orkney. One example of such an enclosure occurs at the Ness of Brodgar which is delineated by substantial stone walls of beautifully faced masonry (Fig. 9.38). This, however, was considered to be a unique feature of this extraordinary site. The possibility of an enclosure had been considered at Barnhouse but due to extensive ploughing little survived beyond the area of occupation. More recently a boundary has also been revealed by geophysical survey to surround the late Neolithic settlement at Rinyo, Rousay (J. Downes pers. comm.).

The gradiometer plot (Fig. 9.37) clearly shows the substantial boundary that encloses the entire Muckquoy settlement, indeed, the results of the survey are so clear that the enclosure could be seen to cut through an

Figure 9.34 View of Muckquoy from the east during geophysical survey (Colin Richards).

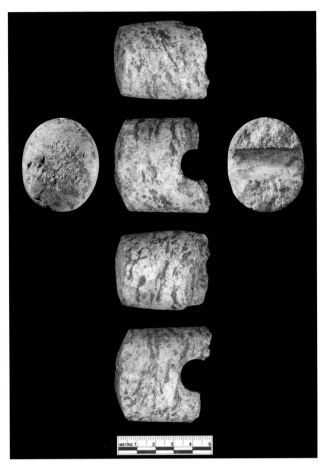

Figure 9.35 Fragment of a gneiss pestle macehead recovered from fieldwalking (Hugo Anderson-Whymark).

earlier structure in its northwest circuit. The nature of the enclosure remained uncertain; for example, was it composed of a stone wall against which midden may have accumulated or a ditch, or both? Consequently, it was decided to excavate a small trial trench across the enclosure in May 2013 (Fig. 9.37: red). The trench was positioned in order to expose a section of the enclosure as it ran around from the southwest towards a possible entrance. Removal of the topsoil revealed a mottled old ground surface which in places appeared to contain ash material [006]. Towards the northeast of the trench this layer gave way to yellow-orange glacial till. On further investigation the supposed old ground surface [006] was found to be a truncated surface of extensive midden deposits radiating from the settlement mound. The midden at this point reached a depth of over a metre and was typically composed of extensive ash deposits tipping down away from the settlement mound (Fig. 9.39).

To everyone's astonishment, when the topsoil was removed, rather than stone walling, the boundary that had showed so clearly on the geophysical plot was actually an amalgam of at least five small concentrically organized slots (Fig. 9.40). Each slot was fairly consistent in size having a width of *c*.0.20m–0.30m, and depth of *c*.0.24m–0.30m (Figs 9.39 and 9.41). The bases of the slots were consistently flat with rounded corners. Despite having the appearance of palisade or 'fence' trenches, the bases of only two postholes were detected in slots [005] (Fig. 9.42) and [040]. Although difficult to determine, there was no evidence to suggest that they represented a chronological sequence as all the slots had been dug from the same stratigraphic level into the upper midden deposits. Consequently, the slots are likely to

Figure 9.36 Polished haematite recovered from fieldwalking (Christopher Gee).

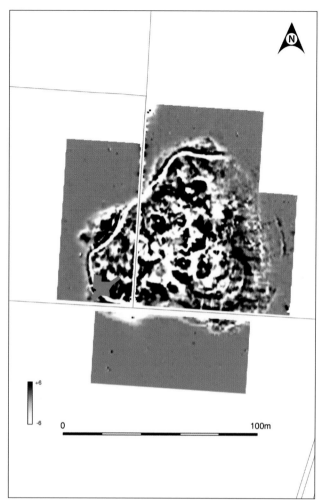

Figure 9.37 Gradiometer survey of Muckquoy, Redland. Excavation trench marked in red. (Christopher Gee and James Moore).

Figure 9.38 The south-eastern stone wall bounding the Ness of Brodgar (Colin Richards)

be contemporary features which belong to a late phase in the life of the Muckquoy settlement, on stratigraphic grounds probably dating to the early 2nd millennium cal BC.

At least two of the concentric slots [040 and 042] appeared to have been cut by a broad shallow ditch having a width of at least one metre (Figs 9.39 and 9.40). The top of the 'ditch' was truncated by ploughing so it is difficult to estimate its original depth, but in all probability it was always fairly shallow. Its base had a split level rounded profile and was filled with three silty loam layers of slightly different shades of mid-red-brown [031, 002 and 001] (Fig. 9.39). It is possible that rather than being a ditch, this was the amalgamated upper cuts of a 'double' slot with the respective bases of the pair of slots [040] and [042] being visible at a lower level. Taken together, difficult though these

features are to interpret, they obviously held some arrangement of upright barrier, presumably timber or some form of wickerwork fencing, although the small number of postholes in the base of the slots (Fig. 9.42), together with the lack of any stone packing, is slightly problematic for such an interpretation.

Overall, the small excavation at Muckquoy was interesting for several reasons. First, the depth of midden running from the settlement mound was of great surprise, despite the trench being located on level ground that was a considerable distance away from any noticeable slope (Fig. 9.39). Hence, Muckquoy is a massive Neolithic settlement mound of greater proportions than either Skara Brae or Ness of Brodgar. Second, quite late in the life of the settlement, probably sometime in the 2nd millennium cal BC it becomes a bounded entity. Although the form of enclosure is uncertain it is bedded in at least five concentric slots that, judging from the gradiometer plot (Fig. 9.37), encircle the entire site.

It seems that the material bounding of 'communities' does reach its zenith in the 2nd millennium cal BC. This is shown by the wrapping of the main village of Muckquoy by a palisade or a circuit of fencing. A similar strategy may be deployed in a number of different villages, such as the enclosure recently discovered at Rinyo, Rousay. However, how this process of self-definition relates to the wider distribution and density of settlement is far from clear. Further geophysical survey around the main mound at Muckquoy by Christopher Gee disclosed an extraordinary array of settlement locations (Fig. 9.43); some on the basis of reported flint scatters are clearly of 4th–3rd millennium cal BC date. If we are witnessing

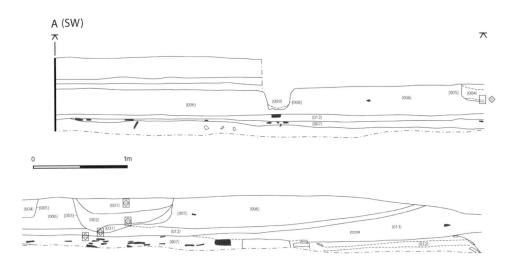

Figure 9.39 South-facing section through the peripheral midden at Muckquoy.

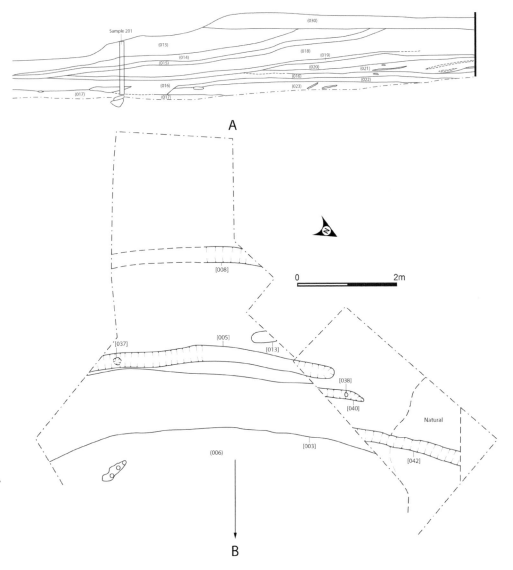

Figure 9.40 Plan of 'ditch' [003] and slots [005], [008], [013], [040] and [042] at Muckquoy.

Figure 9.41 Boundary slot [005] cutting upper midden deposits [002] (Colin Richards).

a process of household nucleation embodying the final social strategies of Neolithic *sociétés à maisons* in Orkney, then the gradiometer survey may well have detected a relic landscape of more dispersed dwellings that had been abandoned by the 2nd millennium cal BC.

9.9 Conclusion: Neolithic house societies in Orkney

The above description of Muckquoy, a substantial Neolithic settlement with a long history running from the 4th to 2nd millennium cal BC, which becomes wrapped towards the end of its life marks the conclusion of this account of Neolithic *sociétés à maisons* in Orkney. From transient, shifting timber settlements, such as Wideford Hill, we have traced a process of conglomeration that results in nucleated settlements of substantial magnitude. There is no claim here for this being a teleological process, nor a consistent development encapsulating all Neolithic communities and settlements; instead we are merely witnessing the highly varied material and social consequences of day-to-day strategies of people facing an ever changing Neolithic world. Ultimately, two broad trajectories can be recognized as Orcadian *sociétés à maisons* become fractured and fragmented in the later 3rd millennium cal BC. First, a form of devolution occurs in density and population of specific settlements as represented by the double houses (Fig. 9.31). Second, larger nucleated settlements, such as Muckquoy, reach an extreme of self definition by resorting to enclosure as a material strategy of wrapping disparate 'identities' in an attempt to exhibit unified communities.

This chapter has attempted to draw multiple strands of evidence together, mainly derived from the Bay

Figure 9.42 The base of posthole [037] showing in the base of slot [005] (Colin Richards).

of Firth study area, to provide an account of the development of communities in Orkney over a *c.*1500 year period from the 4th to 2nd millennia cal BC. This narrative has been informed by some of the ideas constituting Lévi-Strauss's (1982, 1987) conception of *sociétés à maisons*. In our account, *sociétés à maisons* are seen not as social type but as social process appearing under very specific social and (pre)historical conditions (cf. Sissons 2010). It is suggested that the introduction of agriculture into the Northern Isles provided the material conditions and social practices which required and brought into being broader-based social units. Interestingly, what begins as an Orcadian social Neolithic world possessing a combined subsistence base of domesticated cereals and animals seems to change in the 3rd millennium cal BC to one based primarily on animal husbandry. Accompanying this change a clear trajectory towards nucleated settlements surrounded and fused by massive middens is discernible.

In this volume a large number of excavations have served to provide details of 4th, 3rd and 2nd millennia cal BC settlement that have transformed the way the Orcadian Neolithic is understood. Perhaps one of the most interesting aspects to be derived from examining the Orcadian Neolithic within the context of developing *sociétés à maisons* is the exposure of the tensions, fault-lines and conflict underlying the extraordinary accomplishments of this early farming society. Stone-built 'monumental' domestic architecture certainly evolved in Neolithic Orkney, but this was not a result of a general Neolithic teleology. Instead, it was the product of highly competitive localised conditions, where different 'houses' competed for social status and elevated position. Subsequent building of the great monuments of the 3rd millennium cal BC provided a highly visual arena of this inter-house competition. However, ultimately it was the desire and requirement to portray disparate social groups as unified and cohesive communities, and to construct identity in terms of claimed descent, that served to create the Orcadian Neolithic. It was also these very social strategies and conditions that led to its eventual demise.

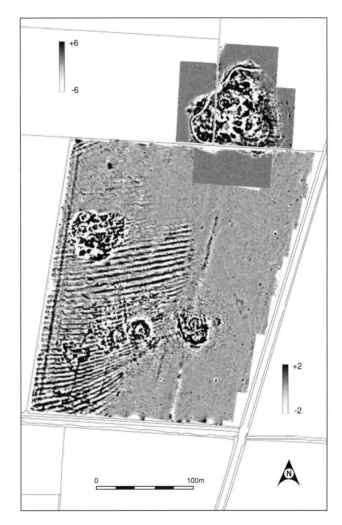

Figure 9.43 Gradiometer survey of area around Muckquoy, Redland, undertaken by Christopher Gee and Georgie Ritchie.

CHAPTER TEN

Beside the Ocean of Time: a chronology of Neolithic burial monuments and houses in Orkney

Seren Griffiths

The provision of stone-built Neolithic settlements is perhaps the most important characteristic which separates Orkney from other areas of Britain.

(Richards 1993a, 206)

10.1 Introduction

This chapter provides an assessment of radiocarbon chronological data from early Neolithic houses and cairns in Orkney. The available evidence from sites within the Bay of Firth study area is examined in detail (see Figs 1.6 and 10.1). The model also calculates chronologies estimates associated with the use of Neolithic burial monuments, and early Neolithic houses, which form the basis for some observations about the timing of the early Neolithic in Orkney.

The 'Neolithic' first appears in Orkney in the 4th millennium cal BC, with sites including chambered cairns and houses, and the 3rd millennium cal BC sees the addition of henge monuments, stone circles and standing stones. In 2005, the chronological currency of the Neolithic in Orkney was defined as spanning the mid-4th millennium to *c.*2000 cal BC. This very broad chronology is traditionally divided into an 'early' Neolithic and 'late' Neolithic, and the two phases are regarded as overlapping, with a transition period generally considered to have occurred around 3000 cal BC (*e.g.* Card 2005, 47). The earlier Neolithic in Orkney is associated with round-based bowl pottery (including 'Unstan' ware; Hunter and MacSween 1991) and Orkney-Cromarty cairns, while the later Neolithic is notable for the presence of Grooved ware and 'Maes Howe type' passage graves. This very broad

material culture phasing drew upon studies including Henshall's (1963) framework for chambered cairn types, and Renfrew's (1979) model of social evolution from territory based, 'Unstan' bowl-using, segmentary societies, to centralised, Grooved ware-using chiefdoms (see Chapter 1). The scientific chronological evidence includes the then ground-breaking results from the use of radiocarbon dates to examine Neolithic sites in Orkney during the 1970s (Renfrew *et al.* 1976; Renfrew 1979).

Several 'tipping points' or disjunctures in the interpretation of Neolithic material culture on the islands can be suggested. In all these developments, chronological understandings – including the recognition that different types of evidence represented Neolithic activity – have been key to challenging our perceptions of the nature of society on Orkney at this time. Integral to these changes in interpretation have been shifts in what archaeologists have 'expected' for Neolithic settlements in Orkney (Downes and Richards 2000). These disjunctures included V. G. Childe's (1931b) work at Skara Brae, with the subsequent recognition of the site as Neolithic demonstrating the potential scale of Neolithic settlement sites on the islands and prompting a series of influential excavations. The eventual realization that the stone-built stalled houses at the Knap of Howar were of early Neolithic date (Ritchie 1983) contributed to a model of isolated, early Neolithic Orkney settlement (Richards 1993a; Barclay 1996). Equally important was the excavation of the Barnhouse structures (Richards 2005c), which led to a fundamental reassessment of the relationships between monuments and occupation (*e.g.* Richards 2000), a theme of enquiry that

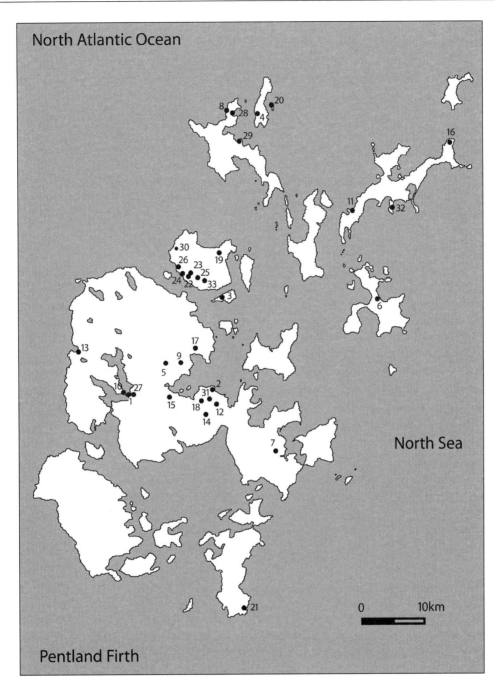

Figure 10.1 Map of Neolithic sites in Orkney with radiocarbon dates mentioned in the text, or shown in the model in Fig. 10.2.1. Barnhouse; 2. Crossiecrown; 3. Ha'Breck; 4. Knap of Howar; 5. Knowes of Trotty; 6. Links House; 7. Long Howe; 8. Links of Noltland; 9. Muckquoy; 10. Ness of Brodgar; 11. Pool; 12. Saverock; 13. Skara Brae; 14. Smerquoy; 15. Stonehall; 16. Tofts Ness; 17. Varme Dale; 18. Wideford Hill; 19. Rinyo; 20. Holm of Papa Westray North; 21. Isbister; 22. Knowe of Lairo; 23. Knowe of Ramsay; 24. Knowe of Rowiegar; 25. Knowe of Yarso; 26. Midhowe; 27. Maes Howe; 28. Pierowall Quarry; 29. Point of Cott; 30. Quandale; 31. Quanterness; 32. Quoyness; 33. Taversoe Tuick.

very much continues with fieldwork at the Ness of Brodgar. In recent years another important theme concerning early Neolithic habitation has emerged in the recognition of 4th millennium cal BC wooden post-built structures, initially at Wideford Hill (Chapter 2), and subsequently at Smerquoy (Chapter 4; see below) on Mainland, Ha'Breck, on Wyre (Lee and Thomas 2011; Farrell *et al.* 2014; see below), and Green on Eday (Coles and Miles 2013).

The importance of non-stone built evidence in the early Neolithic of Orkney is relevant to recent work at two other sites. At Varme Dale (see Chapter 9), Evie, Mainland, a series of burnt deposits underlying a Bronze Age mound containing charred cereal remains were dated to the earlier 4th millennium cal BC (see discussion below). At Links House on Stronsay, 4th millennium cal BC radiocarbon dates have been produced from a pit on the site of much earlier Mesolithic activity.

With the exception of these two examples, which are discussed in detail below, the majority of 4th millennium cal BC radiocarbon dates from archaeological sites in Orkney derive from Neolithic chambered cairns and houses. An analysis of the chronological evidence associated with stone circles from Orkney is given in Griffiths and Richards (2013). A mid-5th millennium radiocarbon result has been produced on an oak timber from Cummi Ness, Bay of Ireland, Mainland. The timber may have been anthropogenically modified (Timpany 2014), but cannot be associated with occupation activity and is not discussed further here.

The majority of the non-chambered cairn structures discussed here are termed 'houses', reflecting the theme of this volume, however it is noted that the range of activity associated with these structures might have included domestic as well as other functions, and a formal distinction between domestic and other contexts is probably inappropriate (Brück 2008; Sharples 2000). As part of the discussion below, architectural forms of Neolithic Orkney houses are defined here as:

- Stalled early Neolithic houses such as the Knap of Howar and Smerquoy (see Chapter 4),
- Apparently early Neolithic timber structures including rectilinear structures as at Ha'Breck and circular structures as at Wideford Hill (see Chapter 2).
- Compartmentalized houses with 'pinched' walls, and without substantial orthostatic division, as at Stonehall Knoll (see Chapter 5),
- Sub-square houses as at Skara Brae, and Structure 8 at Barnhouse, a structure at Crossiecown and at Stonehall Farm (see Chapter 5 and Chapter 7),
- Small circular houses as found at Barnhouse,
- Double cruciform houses as found at Barnhouse,
- 'Atypical' constructions.

Results from a number of chambered cairns are discussed, which include Henshall's 'Orkney-Cromarty' group. This group of chambered cairns has been further sub-divided into 'tripartite' chambers (where orthostats are employed to create three compartments accessed from a passage; see the Knowe of Lairo below), 'stalled'

chambers which comprise the majority of the 'Orkney-Cromarty' chambered cairns discussed here (with more compartments than tripartite cairns), and 'Bookan' chambers (with two to five compartments arranged around a central space and roofed at a low level). Other variants include horned cairns, where drystone walling 'horns' are projected from the 'front' of cairns (such as at the Point of Cott discussed below). The majority of chambered cairns known from Orkney comprise 'Orkney-Cromarty-type' structures, with Davidson and Henshall (1989) able to list 59 examples.

Radiocarbon measurements have been produced from a number of passage graves ('Maes Howe-type' structures). These monuments comprise high-roofed, rectangular chambers accessed by a passage and covered by a round mound. Within passage graves, cells radiate off the main chamber, with six present at Quanterness and Quoyness, and four at Wideford Hill and Cuween (all discussed below). While these passage graves are referred to here as 'Maes Howe types', Maes Howe itself is in many ways unusual – in its scale, execution, and the use of orthostats within the central chamber (Richards 1996b, 196; 2000; Renfrew *et al.* 1976, 198; Davidson and Henshall 1989, 46–51). Davidson and Henshall (1989) list twelve passage graves, to which can be added a recent discovery at Swandro on Rousay (Steve Dockrill pers. comm.).

A synthetic discussion and catalogue of the chambered cairns of Orkney is provided by Davidson and Henshall (1989), with a more recent review of many of the sites discussed here provided by Schulting *et al.* (2010). Davidson and Henshall (1989, 87) emphasised the early presence of Orkney-Cromarty cairns and their similarities to chambered cairns of Caithness. Renfrew *et al.* (1976; Renfrew 1979) proposed that Maes Howe-type passage graves post-dated Orkney-Cromarty structures, but that activity at several Orkney-Cromarty sites, such as the Knowe of Yarso, went on for some period of time. Renfrew *et al.* (1976, 200) also suggested a period of overlap between 'Unstan' ware (cf. Hunter and MacSween 1991) and Grooved ware occurred in Orkney between 3300 cal BC and 3000 cal BC, with the first Maes Howe-type passage graves – including Cuween and Wideford Hill – constructed in this period. Within the Maes Howe-type group, Renfrew (1979, 210) developed a model informed by radiocarbon results, which placed Quanterness and Quoyness as earlier monuments, with Maes Howe itself being a later development.

This chapter builds on the recent analysis of Schulting *et al.* (2010), and includes results from the *Cuween-*

Wideford Landscape Project, and other recently available data to review the chronology of Neolithic house and chambered cairn sites in Orkney.

10.2 Method

The approach taken here applies a Bayesian statistical model to the available data associated with early Neolithic stalled and timber houses, and chambered cairns from Orkney. Data selection and modelling techniques are detailed below and in Table 10.1. Bayesian modelling provides a means of counteracting the statistical scatter that is inherent in an assemblage of radiocarbon (or other scientific dating) measurements. It provides a means of incorporating archaeological information about the relative ordering of dated events, or relationships between dated samples, to constrain scientific chronological data. Bayesian chronological modelling has been applied in archaeology for over 20 years (*e.g.* Buck *et al.* 1991; 1992; 1996; Bronk Ramsey 1995; 1998; 2001; 2009). Bayesian modelling can make use of 'informative' understandings about the relationships between dated samples, for example from stratigraphy, and can include less 'informative' archaeological understandings, for example using the concept of an archaeological site phase to relate activity (Bayliss *et al.* 2007). Recent applications to Neolithic studies in Britain and Ireland have included Bayliss and Whittle (2007), Whittle *et al.* (2011), and Schulting *et al.* (2010; 2012). Several of the models presented here are adapted or derive from the analysis presented by Schulting *et al.* (2010).

Results have been calibrated and Bayesian modelling applied using OxCal v4.2 (Bronk Ramsey 1995; 1998; 2001; 2009). Results have been calibrated using the original error terms, rather than those recommended by Ashmore *et al.* (2000; cf. Schulting *et al.* 2010; Bayliss *et al.* 2011).

The majority of the results in Table 10.1 have been calibrated with the internationally agreed IntCal13 atmospheric calibration curve (Reimer *et al.* 2013), though several of measurements on marine species have been calibrated with the internationally agreed marine calibration curve (Reimer *et al.* 2013). A revised, local radiocarbon reservoir offset **has been applied**. This reservoir offset reflects new approaches to calculating uncertainty and the error term means that previous local radiocarbon reservoir effects calculated from measurements at Skara Brae (Ascough *et al.* 2007) are statistically indistinguishable. A few measurements on samples from Holm of Papa Westray North have been calibrated with a mix of terrestrial and marine calibration curves, reflecting differences in diet of these organisms. These cases are discussed in further detail below.

Many of the radiocarbon results presented here only have stable carbon values produced to correct for fractionation as part of radiocarbon measurement. In the case of accelerator mass spectrometry measurement these values tend not to be suitable for dietary reconstruction. Other indicative stable isotopes, such as nitrogen and sulphur are not available. Any appropriate offsets are consequently difficult to reconstruct robustly, and the picture is further complicated by the evidence for enrichment in stable carbon values, perhaps as a result of terrestrial plant signals (Jones *et al.* 2012). Additional difficulty in interpreting the importance of marine reservoirs in the northen Isles is emphasised by the evidence from Neolithic Shetland for the strategic consumption over short periods of marine resources (Montgomery *et al.* 2013, 1070), which in turn dovetails with archaeological evidence from Orkney (for example from the Knap of Howar; Ritchie 1983) for the use of marine resources at least as part of the subsistence repertoire.

Date ranges in the table have been quoted using the intercept method (Stuiver and Reimer 1986), with end points rounded out by 10 years where the error terms are 25 years or greater, and by 5 years when they are less than 25 years (Millard 2014). The probability distributions shown in the figures were calibrated using the probability method of calibration (Stuiver and Reimer 1993). Output from the Bayesian chronological modelling is by convention given in the text in italics. Commands from the OxCal v4 program are cited in `Inconsolata` font to differentiate them from archaeological terms. The overall model structure is shown in Fig. 10.2. The OxCal v4 commands and brackets define the model structure.

Model sub-sections for house sites in the Bay of Firth are shown in Fig. 10.3–10.4, other early Neolithic house sites from Orkney in Fig. 10.5–10.6, and stalled (Orkney-Cromarty) cairns in Fig. 10.7–10.9. Passage graves (Maes Howe-type) sites are shown in model sub-sections in Fig. 10.10–10.11. A model for the Orcadian passage graves (Maes Howe-type) results is shown in Fig. 10.12.

10.2.1 Data selection and treatment

The analysis presented here uses published radiocarbon dates from Neolithic timber and stone-built stalled houses and chambered cairns from Orkney, and results

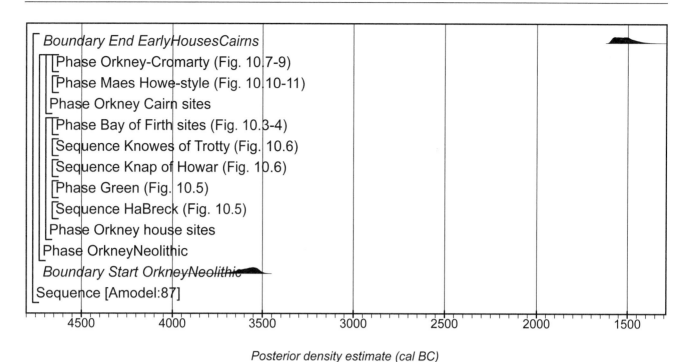

Figure 10.2 The model structure for the analysis of radiocarbon dates from Neolithic houses from the Bay of Firth landscape project, early Neolithic houses from across Orkney, and Neolithic cairns from Orkney (see main text for data selection). Subsections of the model are shown in the following figures as indicated. The large square brackets down the left hand side along with the OxCal keywords define the model, which is described in the text. An estimate for the start of Neolithic activity associated with these sites has been produced (Start OrkneyNeolithic), this and other posterior density estimates calculated in the model are described in Table 10.2.

from sites in the Bay of Firth project area (see chapters in this volume), the Knowes of Trotty (Chapter 3), Mainland, and from Green, Eday and Ha'Breck, Wyre (D. Garrow pers. comm. 2014). This analysis is intended to provide an estimate for the start of the earliest Neolithic activity on Orkney from house and chambered cairn sites. The later Neolithic house sites at Skara Brae, Pool, Barnhouse, Links of Noltland, and Ness of Brodgar are about to be massively updated as part of the *Times of Their Lives* project by Alasdair Whittle and Alex Bayliss, so these, and the later Neolithic evidence from Tofts Ness, are not included in the modelling here. Sites were included in the model presented here if they produced results with calibrated ranges in part in the 4th millennium cal BC, thus for example the results from chambered graves on Rousay at Quandale (GrA-19988 3600±50 BP 2140–1780 cal BC 95% confidence; GrA-19989 3660±50 BP 2200–1890 cal BC 95% confidence), Taversoe Tuick (GrA-21734 3580±60 BP 2140–1750 cal BC 95% confidence), and Blackhammer (UB-6419 3520±34 BP 1950–1740 cal BC 95% confidence) were not

included in the model. The results from the chambered cairn at Crantit (Ballin-Smith 1999), and Cuween Hill are also too late, though the latter site is discussed below with reference to house sites in the Bay of Firth.

10.2.2 The sites

While many of the burial monuments have been known and investigated at least since the 19th century, the evidence for domestic structures has changed significantly in recent years. In the mid-1980s Kinnes (1985; see also Barclay 1996) was able to note only one early Neolithic house site at the Knap of Howar. The change in the pattern of evidence for Neolithic houses in Orkney has in part derived from research within the Bay of Firth landscape (this volume), which has resulted in an archaeological sample of settlement evidence from Crossiecrown, Knowes of Trotty, Wideford Hill, the Stonehall sites, and Smerquoy, all of which have produced radiocarbon results. The less visible nature of house structures in contrast to burial monuments may have contributed to their omission from

Knap of Howar, HY4805180, Bay of Firth, Orkney Mainland: Stalled house – house 2; Stalled house – house 1

Laboratory Number	Dated sample	Parent context	Radiocarbon result (BP)	δ13C δ15N C:N	Calibrated date range (cal BC; 95% confidence unless otherwise stated)
OxA-16475	Sheep bone	A sheep bone from layer 9/14, primary midden redeposited within the wall-core of house 1, stalled house. *Termini post quos* for the construction of house 1	4603±39	-21.7 / 7.5 / 3.2	3510–3130
OxA-16476	Sheep/goat bone	A sheep/goat scapula from layer 16, primary midden sealed below the wall of house 1, stalled house. *Terminus post quos* for the construction of house 1	4458±39	-20.1 / 7.6 / 3.2	3350–2930
OxA-16477	Sheep/goat bone	A sheep or goat humerus from, passage B, layer 4, a secondary floor deposit in house 2, stalled house, at the entrance to the passage linking the two houses, sealed by blocking material and thus providing a *terminus post quem* for the blocking material and end of use of house 2.	4420±39	-21.2 / 6.3 / 3.2	3330–2910
OxA-16478	Cattle bone	A cattle metatarsal from layer 7, a secondary floor deposit of house 2. Dates activity associated with house 2	4510±39	-21.7 / 6.4 / 3.2	3370–3030
OxA-16479	Sheep/goat bone	A sheep or goat second phalanx from layer 12, a primary floor deposit of house 2. Dates activity associated with house 2	4552±39	-20.8 / 4.2 / 3.2	3490–3100
OxA-16480	Sheep bone	A sheep foetus metatarsal from trench III, layer 3, secondary midden some 20 m south of house 1. Dates Neolithic activity on the site	4633±41	-20.0 / 8.0 / 3.2	3520–3340
OxA-16481	Sheep/goat bone	A sheep or goat left calcaneum from trench V, layer 2, secondary midden outside house 2. Dates Neolithic activity on the site	4443±39	-21.5 / 6.1 / 3.2	3340–2920
OxA-17778	Pig bone	A pig humerus distal fragment from trench III, layer 4, primary midden some 20 m south of house 1. Replaces OxA-9760 (Sheridan and Higham 2007, 225). Dates Neolithic activity on the site	4673±31	-19.7 / 7.3 / 3.2	3630–3360
SRR-344	Mixed animal bone	Animal bone from a secondary midden A/III/3 of period II in Trench III outside the south wall of a house. Not included in the model because of the uncertainty the dated sample could include material of a range of ages	4451±70	-21.1	3370–2900
SRR-345	Mixed animal bone	Animal bone from house 1 refuse in floor deposit B/I/2 of period II. Not included in the model because of the uncertainty the dated sample could include material of a range of ages	4348±75	-20.7	3330–2870
SRR-346	Mixed animal bone	Animal bone from refuse in secondary floor C/I/4 in the passage of House 1a. Not included in the model because of the uncertainty the dated sample could include material of a range of ages	4532±70	-21.2	3500–3010
SRR-347	Mixed animal bone	Animal bone from primary midden D/I/9 in the wall core of house 1, period 1; from same context as a fresh sample dated as SRR-452 (4080±70 BP). The two measurements are very different, and it is unclear if this measurement represents some kind of offset, a measurement outlier, or evidence of much earlier activity on the site. Not included in the model because of the uncertainty the dated sample could include material of a range of ages	5706±85	-22.2	4730–4350
SRR-348	Mixed animal bone	Animal bone from E/II/3, secondary midden of Period II in trench II outside south wall of house. Not included in the model because of the uncertainty the dated sample could include material of a range of ages	4765±70	-21.9	3700–3360
SRR-349	Mixed animal bone	Animal bone from the primary midden F/II/11 in trench II period 1. Not included in the model because of the uncertainty the dated sample could include material of a range of ages	4422±70	-22	3360–2890

Table 10.1 Results from sites from the Bay of Firth landscape study area, early Neolithic stone-built stalled houses and timber structures from across Orkney, and from cairns across Orkney included in the model shown in Fig. 10.2. Details of the 'types' of structure and burial monument are included along with details of the individual samples. Continued pp. 260–271.

Laboratory Number	Dated sample	Parent context	Radiocarbon result (BP)	δ13C δ15N C:N	Calibrated date range (cal BC; 95% confidence unless otherwise stated)
SRR-352	Mixed animal bone	Animal bone from primary midden D/I/9 in the wall core of House 1, period 1; from same context as a sample dated as SRR-347 (5706±85 BP), see note above	4081±65	-23.1	2880–2470
Birm-813	Mixed animal bone	Midden filling wall of house 2 (lower midden). Not included in the model because of the uncertainty the dated sample could include material of a range of ages	4270±100	-23.1	3270–2580
Birm-814	Mixed animal bone	House 2, floor deposit, in the secondary floor of period II. Not included in the model because of the uncertainty the dated sample could include material of a range of ages	4690±130	-19.1	3710–3030
Birm-815	Mixed animal bone	Animal bone from the lower midden in trench IV of period I. Not included in the model because of the uncertainty the dated sample could include material of a range of ages	4250±130	-19.1	3340–2480
Birm-816	Mixed animal bone	Animal bone from the lower midden of period I in trench V. Not included in the model because of the uncertainty the dated sample could include material of a range of ages	4770±180	-19.4	3970–3020
Birm-817	Soil	Organic soil buried at the base of test-pit 16. Not included in the model because of the uncertainty of the association of the sample with any archaeological 'event'	4830±100	-25.2	3900–3370

Knowes of Trotty, HY342174, Bay of Firth, Orkney Mainland: Stalled house

Laboratory Number	Dated sample	Parent context	Radiocarbon result (BP)	δ13C δ15N C:N	Calibrated date range (cal BC; 95% confidence unless otherwise stated)
SUERC-18233	*Betula* sp. charcoal	Hearth 082. This hearth has been attributed to phase 3, associated with fragments of walling overlying the apparently ruinous original building. Stone-built hearth 215 is sealed over by the time of the use of this hearth. Dates the firing of hearth 082	4495±35	-27.2	3360–3020
SUERC-18234	Unidentified charred rhizome	Phase 2 lower layer of stone-built hearth 215. Dates the firing of stone-built hearth 215. Stratigraphically post-dates fire pit 220	4405±35	-26.5	3270–2910
SUERC-18235	*Betula* sp. charcoal	Phase 1 pit 282, underlying walling	4570±35	-26.5	3500–3110
SUERC-18239	*Betula* sp. charcoal	Phase 2 from a scoop, 302, indicating *in situ* burning on south side of stone-built hearth, underlies small scoop 294 subsequently dug	4490±35	-26.2	3360–3020
SUERC-18240	*Calluna* sp. charcoal	Phase 2 deposit 220, within scoop 294, later than scoop 302 south of hearth 215. This measurement is too early for its stratigraphic position in the model, and has not been included as an active element in the model presented here	4405±35	-27.3	3270–2910
SUERC-18241	*Betula* sp. charcoal	Phase 2 fill of fire scoop 302, underlies small scoop 294 subsequently dug	4485±35	-25.8	3360–3020
SUERC-18242	*Betula* sp. charcoal	Phase 2 debris spread 311 in east entranceway/porch	4475±35	-27.3	3350–3020
SUERC-18243	Unidentified wood charcoal	Phase 2 hearth rake out 331, overlies hearth deposit 340. Unidentified nature of sample could mean that there is an inbuilt 'old wood' offset, which would make this a *terminus post quem* for the firing of the hearth. However, this result is not notably older than others from phase 2. It has been included in the model as a *terminus post quem*	4490±35	-25.4	3360–3020
SUERC-18244	*Calluna* sp. charcoal	Phase 2 hearth rake out 340. Deposit 340 is overlain by 331	4525±30	-26.4	3370–3090

Stonehall Knoll, HY366126, Bay of Firth, Orkney Mainland: Compartmentalized house – house 3

Laboratory Number	Dated sample	Parent context	Radiocarbon result (BP)	δ13C δ15N C:N	Calibrated date range (cal BC; 95% confidence unless otherwise stated)
AA-51370	*Salix* sp. charcoal	Occupation (4041) of secondary floor in house 3. Sample found in a thin layer of burnt material and ash tramped into a secondary layer of clay floor. The pottery from this house was round-based bowl. The sample potentially represents material from earlier activity redeposited in the secondary occupation deposit. Not included as an active parameter in the model	4510±40	-26.3	3370–3020
AA-51380	*Betula* sp. charcoal	Occupation (4041) of secondary floor in house 3. Sample found in a thin layer of burnt material and ash tramped into a secondary layer of clay floor. The pottery from this house was round-based bowl. The sample potentially represents material from earlier activity redeposited in the secondary occupation deposit. Not included as an active parameter in the model	4250±40	-26.5	2920–2710

Laboratory Number	Dated sample	Parent context	Radiocarbon result (BP)	δ13C δ15N C:N	Calibrated date range (cal BC; 95% confidence unless otherwise stated)
AA-51379	Betula sp. charcoal	Occupation (4041) of secondary floor in house 3. Sample found in a thin layer of burnt material and ash tramped into a secondary layer of clay floor. The pottery from this house was round-based bowl. The sample is the latest of three radiocarbon measurements in the secondary occupation deposit. It may therefore provide an estimate for the timing of this secondary occupation	4010±40	-25.4	2630–2460
AA-51385	Salix sp. charcoal	Charcoal fill (1028) of pit in east area of trench. This result is not included in the model.	1610±35	-25.3	Cal AD 380–550
Stoneball Meadow, HY366126, Bay of Firth, Orkney Mainland: Stalled house – house 3					
AA-51386	Hordeum vulgare var nudum charred grain	Lower fill 3075 of pit in outer compartment of house 3	4475±45	-25.7	3360–3010
AA-51382	Betula sp. charcoal	Occupation deposit 3050 around hearth in inner compartment of house 3	4485±40	-25.6	3360–3020
AA-51383	Salix sp. charcoal	Upper ash fill 3068 of hearth 3070 house 3	4455±40	-25.6	3360–2930
AA-51375	Hordeum vulgare charred grain	Lower ash fill 3069 of hearth 3070 house 3	4435±40	-24.1	3340–2920
AA-51384	Hordeum vulgare var nudum charred grain	Ash spread 029 from hearth, trench A. Occupation activity not stratigraphically related with the stalled house, or associated with diagnostic material culture	4500±40	-22.4	3370–3020
AA-51374	Hordeum vulgare charred grain	Hearth fill 019 trench A. Occupation activity not stratigraphically related with the stalled house, or associated with diagnostic material culture	4550±40	-22.6	3490–3090
Stoneball Farm, HY366126, Bay of Firth, Orkney Mainland: Sub-square house (late Barnhouse-style house) – house 1; 'Atypical' structure – structure 1					
SUERC-5790	Hordeum vulgare var nudum charred grain	Lower midden deposit (809)	4500±40	-24	3370–3020
AA-51376	Betula sp. charcoal	Lower midden deposit (809)	4395±40	-24.9	3270–2900
SUERC-5789	Hordeum vulgare charred grain	Upper midden deposit (800)	4170±35	-24.1	2890–2620
AA-51371	Betula sp. charcoal	Fill (816) of clay bowl [815] in structure 1	4495±40	-25.4	3360–3020
AA-51387	Betula sp. charcoal	Lower cist fill (631) structure 1	4485±55	-24.5	3370–2930
SUERC-5792	Indeterminate charred cereal grain	Upper ash fill (2051) of house 1	4480±40	-21.8	3360–3020
SUERC-5791	Hordeum vulgare var nudum charred grain	Midden deposit (2015) adjacent to house 1	4340±40	-22.5	3090–2890
Wideford Hill, HY4090I2II, Bay of Firth, Orkney Mainland: Timber structures – structure 1 (circular) and structure 3 (probably circular with a central scoop hearth, subsequently modified into rectangular timber structure); Compartmentalized house – house 1					
SUERC-4868	Corylus avellana charcoal	Primary ash fill of hearth scoop (115) from timber structure 1	4495±35	-25.5	3360–3020
SUERC-4867	Betula sp. charcoal	Intermediate ash fill of hearth scoop (89) from timber structure 1	4455±35	-26.5	3340–2940
SUERC-4863	Corylus avellana charcoal	Upper mixed fill of hearth scoop (68) from timber structure 1	4530±35	-25.5	3370–3090
SUERC-4862	Hordeum vulgare var nudum charred grain	Basal fill (054) of posthole [053] from timber structure 3	4645±40	-24.7	3630–3350

Table 10.1 Results from sites from the Bay of Firth landscape study area, early Neolithic stone-built stalled houses and timber structures from across Orkney, and from cairns across Orkney included in the model shown in Fig. 10.2. Details of the 'types' of structure and burial monument are included along with details of the individual samples. Continued pp. 262–271.

Laboratory Number	Dated sample	Parent context	Radiocarbon result (BP)	δ13C δ15N C:N	Calibrated date range (cal BC; 95% confidence unless otherwise stated)
SUERC-4869	*Hordeum vulgare var nudum* charred grain	Old land surface (128) beneath rammed surface (002)	4545±40	-22.8	3490–3090
SUERC-4860	*Hordeum vulgare var nudum* charred grain	Old land surface (128) beneath rammed surface (002)	4525±35	-23.9	3370–3090
SUERC-4859	*Hordeum* charred grain	Spread of ashy material 003 on rammed stone surface 002	4580±40	-22.4	3500–3120
SUERC-4870	*Hordeum vulgare var nudum* charred grain	Spread of ash (148) in centre of house 1	4450±35	-22.4	3340–2930
SUERC-4861	*Hordeum vulgare var nudum* charred grain	Rammed stone surface (002)	4555±35	-24.9	3490–3100
Crossiecrown, HY42137, Bay of Firth, Orkney Mainland: Sub-square house (late Barnhouse-style house) – house 1					
AA-51373 (GU-10319)	*Salix* sp. charcoal	Ash deposit (315) surrounding hearth [018]	3830±40	-26.9	2470–2140
AA-51372 (GU-10318)	*Prunus* cf *padus* charcoal	Ash deposit (012) surrounding hearth [018]	3895±40	-26.6	2480–2210
AA-51381 (GU-10319)	*Hordeum vulgare var nudum* charred grain	Clay and ash deposit (480) associated with collapse deposit (003) of house 1, stratigraphically later than hearth [018]	3535±40	-22.2	1980–1740
SUERC-4857	*Hordeum vulgare* charred grain	Lower midden deposit. Uncertain association with structures	4315±35	-22.8	3020–2880
SUERC-4858	*Betula* sp. charcoal	Lower midden deposit. Uncertain association with structures	4405±35	-26.5	3270–2910
SUERC-4853	*Conopodium majus* charcoal	Intermediate midden deposit. Uncertain association with structures	4155±40	-27.1	2890–2580
SUERC-4852	*Conopodium majus* charcoal	Upper midden deposit. Uncertain association with structures	4100±35	-26.7	2870–2500
Smerquoy, HY40501109, Bay of Firth, Orkney Mainland: Stalled house					
SUERC-49682	Salicaceae charcoal	Lower occupation deposit (22)	4518±29	-26.5	3360–3090
SUERC-49938	*Hordeum* sp. grain	Fill (45) of small pit at rear of house	3637±32	-23.2	2140–1910
SUERC-49687	Ericaceae charcoal		3533±29	-27	1950–1760
SUERC-49684	*Betula* sp. charcoal	Foundation deposit (15) beneath outer skin of wall	4527±29	-26.2	3370–3090
SUERC-49683	Cereal grain x1, Poaceae grain x1		4546±29	-21.7	3370–3100
SUERC-49685	Hulled *Hordeum* sp. grain x1, Cereal grain x1	Upper occupation deposit (27) in house	3651±29	-23.8	2140–1940
SUERC-49686	Ericaceae charcoal		3689±27	-26.1	2200–1980
Ha'Breck, HY374025933, Wyre: Linear timber house – house 1, house 2, house 3, house 4; Stalled house – house 2, house 3, house 5					
SUERC-34506	*Hordeum* sp. charred grain	Deposit (436) from stalled stone house 2, material used to pack around the outside of the hearthstones	4550±30	-22.7	3370–3100
SUERC-34503	*Crataegus* sp. charcoal	Deposit (676) from timber house 4	4530±30	-24.5	3370–3090
SUERC-34505	*Corylus avellana* nutshel	Midden deposit (139) in trench A, overlying house 3	4510±30	-28.4	3360–3090
SUERC-34504	*Hordeum* sp. charred grain	Blocking deposit (197) in house 3	4470±30	-22.3	3350–3020
SUERC-35990	*Hordeum* sp. charred grain	Pit fill (528) in centre of timber house 1, sealed by hearth of house 2	4425±30	-25 (assumed)	3320–2920

Laboratory Number	Dated sample	Parent context	Radiocarbon result (BP)	δ¹³C δ¹⁵N C:N	Calibrated date range (cal BC; 95% confidence unless otherwise stated)
SUERC-37959	*Betula* sp. roundwood charcoal	Primary fill stone quarry	4690±35	−24.8	3630–3360
SUERC-37960	*Hordeum* sp. (hulled) charred grain	Midden deposit associated with Grooved ware	3780±35	−22	2300–2050
OxA-29154	*Salicaceae* roundwood charcoal	Preconstruction landsurface, under stalled stone house 3	4662±33	−26.1	3630–3360
OxA-28983	*Salicaceae* roundwood charcoal		4640±32	−26.8	3520–3350
OxA-28861	*Hordeum* (naked) sp. charred grains	Burned deposit associated with the end of primary occupation in stalled stone house 3	4474±30	−22.7	3350–3020
OxA-28862	*Hordeum* (naked) sp. charred grains	South hearth from secondary occupation in stalled stone house 3	4444±30	−23.4	3340–2940
OxA-28863	*Hordeum* (naked) sp. charred grains	Blocking deposit in stalled stone house 3	4448±30	−22.7	3340–3010

Green, HY569289, Eday: Stalled house, with possible later portable material culture (Grooved ware and maceheads) maybe similar to Barnhouse circular structure (though site not published at time of writing) – house 1

Laboratory Number	Dated sample	Parent context	Radiocarbon result (BP)	δ¹³C δ¹⁵N C:N	Calibrated date range
OxA-28984	*Calluna* sp. charred twig	Posthole fill in ?timber structure	4676±32	−26.3	3630–3360
OxA-29155	*Hordeum* sp. (naked) charred grains	Lower hearth fill (290) in stalled stone house 1	4489±32	−22.8	3360–3020
OxA-28454	*Hordeum* sp. grains	Upper hearth fill (116) in stalled stone house1	4472±31	−21.3	3350–3020
OxA-28864	*Hordeum/Triticum* charred cereal grains	Midden context (214) post-dating stalled stone house 1	4463±30	−23.5	3340–3020

Quanterness, HY4177l292, Bay of Firth, Orkney Mainland: Passage grave (****showing the original error terms and the revised error terms from Ashmore et al. (2000))

Laboratory Number	Dated sample	Parent context	Radiocarbon result (BP)	δ¹³C δ¹⁵N C:N	Calibrated date range
Q-1294****	Organic soil	Area ZB, III, stratigraphic. layer 1 from the chamber. Described as immediately on bedrock, cut in places by pits/cists. Grid square N3 (from plan Renfrew 1976, 51, fig, 19).	4590±75 (original) 4590±110 (revised)	–	3630–3090
SRR-754****	Human right and left tibia	Pit A, stratigraphic layer 2. Cut into bedrock pre-dates main bone-spread. Crouched inhumation. Area ZB, II, layer 26, small finds no. 308-01, -02, -03 and 307-01.	4360±50 (original) 4360±110 (revised)	–	Weighted mean (original error terms): 4291±25 (T'=4.6; T'5%=7.8; df=3)
Pta-1626****	Human humerus	Pit A, stratigraphic layer 2. Same individual as SRR-754, small finds no. 316.	4300±60 (original) 4300±110 (revised)	–	2920–2880
Q-1479****	Human right and left femur	Pit A, stratigraphic layer 2. Same individual as SRR-754, small finds no. 311-10, 310-01.	4170±75 (original) 4170±110 (revised)	–	
SUERC-24001 (GU-18421)	Human cranium	Layer 26, pit A, stratigraphic layer 2. Same as SRR-754, Pta-1626, Q-1476.	4280±35	−21.3 12.4 3.6	

Table 10.1 Results from sites from the Bay of Firth landscape study area, early Neolithic stone-built stalled houses and timber structures from across Orkney, and from cairns across Orkney included in the model shown in Fig. 10.2. Details of the 'types' of structure and burial monument are included along with details of the individual samples. Continued pp. 264–271.

Laboratory Number	Dated sample	Parent context	Radiocarbon result (BP)	δ13C δ15N C:N	Calibrated date range (cal BC; 95% confidence unless otherwise stated)
Q-1363****	Human left femur	Main chamber, stratigraphic layer 3. Main bone spread. Described by Renfrew (1976, 70) as ZB, area II, layer 22, small find no. 156-01.	4540±110 (original) 4540±155 (revised)	–	3630–2910
Q-1451****	Human left femur	Main chamber, stratigraphic layer 3. Main bone spread. Described by Renfrew (1976, 70) as ZB, area III, layer 62, small find no. 1321-02, 03 and -04.	4110±100 (original) 4110±140 (revised)	–	2910–2460
Pta-1606****	Human left radius	Pit C, stratigraphic layer 5. Inhumation in shallow pit dug into main burial layer. Area ZB, V, layer 158, small find no. 4590-02.	4130±60 (original) 4130±110 (revised)	–	2890–2490
Q-1480****	Human left tibia	Pit C, stratigraphic layer 5. Same individual as Pta-1606, small find no. 4606-01 and -02.	3905±70 (original) 3905±110 (revised)	–	df=1 T=0.2(5% 3.8) (3883±44)
SRR-755****	Human right femur	Pit C, stratigraphic layer 5. Same individual as Pta-1606, small find no. 4602.	3870±55 (original) 3870±110 (revised)	-19.9 –	2480–2200
SUERC-24000 (GU-18420)	Human phalanx, hand	Layer 23, zone II, stratigraphic layer 1. Cat. ID. 3023.04, lay directly on bedrock	4440±35	-20.4 11.4 3.3	3340–2920
SUERC-24012 (GU-18429)	Human cranium (0-6 months)	Layer 71, zone III, stratigraphic layer. Cat. ID. 1393.06, lay directly on bedrock	4610±35	-21.5 10.5 3.2	3500–3340
SUERC-24002 (GU-18422)	Human femur	Layer 26, pit A, stratigraphic layer. Cat. ID. 311.02, crouched inhumation in pit, same as SRR-754, Pta-1626, Q-1476	4510±35	-20.2 11.5 3.4	3370–3090
SUERC-23998 (GU-18418)	Human right clavicle (14-19 years)	Layer 22, zone II, stratigraphic layer 3. Cat. ID. 164.09, from main bone spread	4585±35	-20.3 9.7 3.3	3500–3130
SUERC-23999 (GU-18419)	Human right clavicle	Layer 22, zone II, stratigraphic layer 3. Cat ID. 221.04, from main bone spread	4555±35	-20.5 10.6 3.3	3490–3100
SUERC-24009 (GU-18426)	Human right clavicle	Layer 6, zone III, stratigraphic layer 3. Cat. ID. 1121.02, from main bone spread	4430±35	-20.3 11.5 3.4	3330–2920
SUERC-23993 (GU-18416)	Human right clavicle	Layer 21, zone II, stratigraphic layer 4. Cat. ID. 189.13, from main bone spread	4490±35	-20.5 11.2 3.4	3360–3020
SUERC-23997 (GU-18417)	Human right clavicle	Layer 21, zone II, stratigraphic layer 4. Cat. ID. 199.17, from main bone spread	4395±35	-20.5 10.7 3.4	3270–2910
SUERC-24003 (GU-18423)	Human left clavicle	Layer 57, zone III, stratigraphic layer 4. Cat. ID. 1084.02, from main bone spread	4570±35	-20.6 10.3 3.2	3500–3110

Laboratory Number	Dated sample	Parent context	Radiocarbon result (BP)	δ13C / δ15N / C:N	Calibrated date range (cal BC; 95% confidence unless otherwise stated)
SUERC-24007 (GU-18424)	Human right ulna	Layer 60, zone III, stratigraphic layer 4. Cat. ID. 1264, from main bone spread	4255±35	-20.8 / 11.3 / 3.2	2920–2770
SUERC-24008 (GU-18425)	Human sacrum (3-6 years)	Layer 60A, zone III, stratigraphic layer 4. Cat. ID. 1263.03, from main bone spread	4095±35	-21.0 / 11.4 / 3.2	2870–2490
SUERC-24010 (GU-18427)	Human left ulna (9-12 years)	Layer 63, zone III, stratigraphic layer 4. Cat. ID. 1175.01, from main bone spread	4415±35	-20.7 / 10.9 / 3.3	3320–2910
SUERC-24011 (GU-18428)	Human right clavicle	Layer 64, zone III, stratigraphic layer 4. Cat. ID. 4009.19, from main bone spread	4510±35	-20.6 / 10.2 / 3.3	3370–3090
SUERC-24013 (GU-18430)	Human metacarpal	Layer 102, zone IV, stratigraphic layer 4. Cat. ID. 1579.2, from main bone spread	4500±35	-20.2 / 12.1 / 3.2	3360–3020
SUERC-24017 (GU-18431)	Human calcaneous	Layer 102, zone IV, stratigraphic layer 4. Cat. ID. 1587.01, from main bone spread	4480±35	-20.2 / 10.9 / 3.2	3360–3020
SUERC-24018 (GU-18432)	Human right fibula	Layer 150, zone V, stratigraphic layer 5a. Cat. ID. 4513.04, stonefall from chamber decay and latest burials; after deposition of main bone spread	4360±35	-21.3 / 11.4 / 3.3	3090–2900
SUERC-24019 (GU-18433)	Human left tibia (9-12 years)	Layer 151, zone V, stratigraphic layer 5a. Cat. ID. 4542, stonefall from chamber decay and latest burials; after deposition of main bone spread	4580±35	-19.8 / 10.7 / 3.2	3500–3120
SUERC-24020 (GU-18434)	Human sacrum	Layer 155, pit C stratigraphic layer 5b. Cat. ID. 4574.04, inhumation in shallow pit dug into main bone spread	4375±35	-20.1 / 11 / 3.2	3100–2900
SUERC-24021 (GU-18435)	Human femur (14-19 years)	Layer 158, pit C, stratigraphic layer 5b. Cat. ID. 4580.08, inhumation in shallow pit dug into main bone spread	4465±35	-20.1 / 11.3 / 3.3	3350–3010

Holm of Papa Westray North, HY50445228, Papa Westray: Stalled cairn

Laboratory Number	Dated sample	Parent context	Radiocarbon result (BP)	δ13C / δ15N / C:N	Calibrated date range (cal BC; 95% confidence unless otherwise stated)
GrA-25636	Human phalange	Human sub-adult phalange (HPWN 1) from cell 3(W), context 1; calibrated with a mixed terrestrial/marine curve and local offset (see main text). Slightly elevated δ13C (possible small input marine protein, maximum c15% Schulting and Richards (2009, 69), they use 16% (2009, 70)).	4715±40	-19.6 / 11.3 / 3.2	3620–3320
GrA-25638	Human right femur	Human adult right femur (HPWN 1158) from cell 5, context 4; calibrated with a mixed terrestrial/marine curve and local offset (see main text). Slightly elevated δ13C (possible small input marine protein, maximum c15% Schulting and Richards (2009, 69), they use 13% (2009, 70)).	4690±40	-19.9 / 10.4 / 2.9	3610–3190
GrA-25637	Human phalange	Human adult right femur HPWN 664, from cell 3(E), context 1; calibrated with a mixed terrestrial/marine curve and local offset (see main text). Probably terrestrial (but Schulting and Richards (2009, 70) apply a 2% marine contribution).	4640±40	-20.8 / 10 / 3.0	3520–3130
GU-2068	Human bone	Human bone from a primary burial in the innermost compartment 4	4430±60	-19.4 / –	3360–2900

Table 10.1 Results from sites from the Bay of Firth landscape study area, early Neolithic stone-built stalled houses and timber structures from across Orkney, and from cairns across Orkney included in the model shown in Fig. 10.2. Details of the 'types' of structure and burial monument are included along with details of the individual samples. Continued pp. 266–271.

Laboratory Number	Dated sample	Parent context	Radiocarbon result (BP)	δ13C δ15N C:N	Calibrated date range (cal BC; 95% confidence unless otherwise stated)
GU-2067	Human bone	Human bone from the deliberate filling of the end-cell 5	4395±60	-19 / —	3340–2890
OxA-17780	Otter bone	An otter bone from trench I, compartment 5 layer 2 the second highest of four levels of filling of the end-cell 5. Replaces OxA-9871 (Sheridan and Higham 2007, 225); calibrated with marine curve and local offset (see main text)	4331±32	-10.5 / 16.8 / 3.2	2670–2280
OxA-16472	Sheep metatarsal	A young sheep metatarsal from trench IV layer 1(2), midden adjacent to the kerb of the back of the cairn containing Grooved ware and Beaker. Cold season marine component. Replaces OxA-9834 (Sheridan 2006, 202-3); calibrated with a mixed terrestrial/marine curve and local offset (see main text)	4352±39	-15.3 / 10.6 / 3.3	3000–2480
OxA-17779	Sheep vertebra	A sheep bone from trench I, compartment 5 layer 3, the second lowest of four levels of filling of the end-cell 5 (Sheridan and Higham 2007, 225). ?Cold season marine component; calibrated with a mixed terrestrial/marine curve and local offset (see main text)	4167±31	-19.8 / 7.1 / 3.3	2860–2250
OxA-16473	Deer antler	A single piece of red deer antler from a secondary deposit (trench V, layer 1) associated with demolition of the tomb facade in the forecourt of the chambered tomb. Replaces OxA-9752 (Sheridan 2006, 202-3)	4127±39	-21.7 / 5.9 / 3.2	2880–2570
OxA-16474	Sheep metatarsal	A single sheep metatarsal from a primary floor deposit (trench V, layer 2) in the forecourt of the chambered tomb and contemporary with its use. Replaces OxA-9753 (Sheridan 2006, 202-3). ?Cold season marine component; calibrated with a mixed terrestrial/marine curve and local offset (see main text)	4113±40	-20.1 / 7.0 / 3.2	2830–2160
OxA-17782	Deer astralagus	A red deer astralagus from trench IV layer 1(1), midden adjacent to the kerb of the back of the cairn containing Grooved ware and Beaker. Replaces OxA-9872 (Sheridan and Higham 2007, 225)	4111±32	-21.8 / 7.1 / 3.2	2870–2570
OxA-17781	Deer astralagus	A red deer astralagus from trench IV layer 1(1), midden adjacent to the kerb of the back of the cairn containing Grooved ware and Beaker. Replaces OxA-9872 (Sheridan and Higham 2007, 225)	4075±30	-21.6 / 7.1 / 3.3	2860–2490
GU-2069	Sheep bone	Sheep bone from the deliberate filling of the entrance passage of the cairn. ?Cold season marine component; calibrated with a mixed terrestrial/marine curve and local offset (see main text)	4070±60	-19.3 / —	2790–2070
OxA-16471	Deer bone	A red deer bone from trench I, compartment 5, layer 1, the uppermost filling of the end-cell 5. Replaces OxA-9832 (Sheridan 2006, 202-3).	4046±38	-21.8 / 7.4 / 3.3	2840–2470
Point of Cott, HY4654746, Westray: Stalled cairn – later transformed into horned cairn					
UtC-1658	Human bone	Skeleton B, from Compartment 3	4680±50	-20.8 / —	3640–3350
UtC-1660	Human bone	Skeleton E, compartment 2 of floor deposit	4680±50	-20.9 / —	3640–3350
GU-2936	Human bone	Skeleton C, from compartment 3	4390±60	-21.2 / —	3340–2890
UtC-1663	Bulk faunal bone	Sheep, vole and bird bone in the lower level of the chamber (54)	4380±90	-22.6 / —	3360–2870
GU-2940	Human bone	Skeleton I, from compartments 1 and 2, in the floor deposit	4360±50	-22.3 / —	3270–2890
UtC-1661	Human bone	Skeleton F, compartment 3 floor deposit	4300±50	-20.7 / —	3030–2870
AA-11697	Human bone	Infant burial (54) in compartment 1	4505±60	-20.1 / —	3490–3010

Laboratory Number	Dated sample	Parent context	Radiocarbon result (BP)	δ13C δ15N C:N	Calibrated date range (cal BC; 95% confidence unless otherwise stated)
AA-11698	Human bone	Infant burial in the north end of the collapsed cairn matrix	4585±85	-19.6 / –	3630–3020
GU-2934	Human bone	Skeleton A, from compartment 3	4250±90	-21.8 / –	3090–2580
GU-2941	Sheep bone	Sheep bone, lower level of passage blocking (157)	4110±50	-22.2 / –	2880–2490
GU-2942	Bulk faunal bone sample	Cattle, sheep and bird bone from the chamber roof collapse (54)	3670±70	-20.3 / –	2280–1880
GU-2945	Bird bone	Bird bone (106) in compartment 4	3610±100	-20.7 / –	2280–1690
UtC-1659	Human bone	Skeleton D from compartment 1	4600±50	-20.8 / –	3520–3120
UtC-1664	Bulk faunal bone sample	Dog and cattle bone from the passage fill (sample 4770)	3870±80	-20.2 / –	2570–2060
UtC-1665	Otter bones	Otter bones behind the wall face at the passage north end (66); calibrated with marine curve and local offset (see main text)	4040±50	-12.7 / –	2320–1870
Pierowall, HY43894905, Westray: Passage grave					
GU-1582	Cattle bone	A single cattle bone in a wall supporting platform (layer 21) over a demolished chambered cairn (Sharples 1984)	4140±60	-20 / –	2900–2490
GU-1583	Cattle bone	Cattle bone in a secondary occupation (layer 10) of a small structure built over demolished cairn	4140±60	-20 / –	2900–2490
GU-1584	Cattle bone	Cattle bone in secondary occupation (layer 10) of a small structure over demolished cairn (Sharples 1984)	4030±65	-20 / –	2870–2400
GU-1585	Ovicaprid bone	Sheep/ goat bone in a translocated shillet layer (layer 71) used to construct a platform against the round cairn (Sharples 1984)	4045±140	-20.8 / –	2920–2150
GU-1586	Ovicaprid bone	Sheep/ goat bone in the collapse (layer 22) of the revetment of the chambered cairn (Sharples 1984)	4330±110	-20 / –	3360–2630
GU-1587	Cattle bone	Cattle bone in the collapse (layer 22) of the revetment of the chambered cairn (Sharples 1984)	4065±90	-21.8 / –	2890–2340
GU-1588	Ovicaprid bone	Sheep/ goat bone in the collapse (layer 20) of the revetment of the chambered cairn (Sharples 1984)	4105±120	-21.5 / –	2920–2310
Isbister, ND47048449, South Ronaldsay: Stalled cairn					
GU-1178	Human bone	Human bone from a foundation deposit (IS76SF72) (Renfrew et al. 1983)	4240±100	-20.2 / –	3100–2500
GU-1179	Human bone	Human bone from a foundation deposit (IS76SF73) (Renfrew et al. 1983)	4435±55	-19.6 / –	3350–2910
GU-1180	Human bone	Human bone from a floor deposit (IS76SF74) in stall 4 (Renfrew et al. 1983)	4410±90	-20.5 / –	3370–2880
GU-1181	Human bone	Human bone from a floor deposit (IS76SF75) in stall 4 (Renfrew et al. 1983)	4420±130	-19.5 / –	3500–2700

Table 10.1 Results from sites from the Bay of Firth landscape study area, early Neolithic stone-built stalled houses and timber structures from across Orkney, and from cairns across Orkney included in the model shown in Fig. 10.2. Details of the 'types' of structure and burial monument are included along with details of the individual samples. Continued pp. 268–271.

Laboratory Number	Dated sample	Parent context	$\delta^{13}C$ $\delta^{15}N$ C:N	Radiocarbon result (BP)	Calibrated date range (cal BC; 95% confidence unless otherwise stated)
GU-1182	Human bone	Human bone from a deposit below shelf in tomb (Renfrew et al. 1983)	-20.2	4475±80	df=1, T=1.1; T'5%=3.8
Q-3013	Human bone		–	4375±50	4403±43 / 3330–2900
Q-3016	Human bone	Human bone from a deposit in cell 3 (Renfrew et al. 1983) (IS76SF79)	–	4360±55	df=1; T'5=0.2; T'5%=3.8
GU-1185	Human bone		-20.8	4405±95	4371±48 / 3270–2890
GU-1187	Human bone	Intrusive burial (IS76SF82) in fill behind hornwork	-20	3250±55	1650–1410
GU-1183	Human bone	Human bone from a deposit (IS76SF77) under shelf in stall 5	-19.4	3920±80	3856±43
Q-3014	Human bone		–	3830±50	df=1 T=0.9(5% 3.8) / 2470–2150
GU-1184	Human bone	Human bone from a deposit (IS76SF78) in cell 3	-19.5	4375±90	4292±47
Q-3015	Human bone		–	4260±55	T=1.2(5% 3.8) / 3020–2870
Q-3017	Human bone	Human bone from a stone infill (IS76SF80) of chamber	–	4030±50	4033±45
GU-1186	Human bone		-19.8	4045±100	df=1 T=0.0(5% 3.8) / 2840–2460
Q-3018	Animal bone	Animal bone from back-fill (IS76SF83) behind hornwork	–	4285±45	4275±35
GU-1190	Animal bone		-20.7	4260±55	df=1 T=0.1(5% 3.8) / 2920–2870
UB-6552	Left ulna from white-tailed sea eagle	Fragment of left ulna from white-tailed sea eagle reportedly found in a 'foundation deposit' (L12) sealed under the floor of stall 5	-14.1	4017±38	2630–2460
UB-6553	Long bone from white-tailed sea eagle	Long bone from white-tailed sea eagle reportedly found in a 'foundation deposit' (L12) sealed under the floor of stall 5	-15.6	4072±39	2860–2480
MAMS-14922 (S-EVA 24028)	Human rib ISB 1		-19.2	4517±18	3355–3100
MAMS-14923 (S-EVA 24029)	Human long bone ISB 2		-20.2	4427±19	3265–2970
MAMS-14924 (S-EVA-24030)	Human femur ISB 3		-19.7	4483±19	3340–3090
MAMS-14925	Human tarsal or carpal ISB 4		-20.2	4490±18	3340–3090
OxA-25626	Human cranium IS(7210)	ST3, juvenile c2–4 years (Lawrence and Lee-Thrope 2012).	-20.7 / 12.0 / 3.3	4507±39	4463±27 (T'=2.4; T'5%=3.8; df=1) / 3340–3020
OxA-25627			–	4425±36	
OxA-25623	Human cranium IS(2783)	ST4, adult male, perimotem penetrating cranial trauma.	-19.7 / 11.9 / 3.2	4516±37	3370–3090

Laboratory Number	Dated sample	Parent context	Radiocarbon result (BP)	δ13C δ15N C:N	Calibrated date range (cal BC; 95% confidence unless otherwise stated)
OxA-25624	Human cranium IS(7015)	ST4, adult, sex not identified.	4420±36	-20.5 11.9 3.3	3330–2910
OxA-25578	Human cranium IS(1958)	SC3, adult male with clear case of multiple myeloma.	4416±32	-20.8 12.3 3.3	3320–2920
OxA-25625	Human cranium IS(7209)	SC3, juvenile c2 years. Lawrence and Lee-Thorpe (2012) suggest pathology indicates possible scurvy	4467±36	-20.9 12.4 3.3	3350–3010
OxA-25622	Human cranium IS(2642)	SC1-2/ST1-2. Highest nitrogen values for the skulls analysed in (Lawrence 2006) from this site, suggested as indication of dietary stress (Lawrence and Lee-Thorpe 2012).	3915±34	-20.2 3.0 3.3	2490–2290
OxA-25628	Human cranium IS(7284)	SC1-2/ST1-2, young adult female, with perimortem cranial trauma.	4456±36	-21.2 11.2 2.4	3350–2940
OxA-25579	Human cranium IS(1972)	North horn cist, adult female, with perimortem blunt force cranial trauma.	3255±29	-19.2 12.8 3.2	1620–1450
Knowe of Rowiegar, HY37332978, Rousay:Stalled cairn					
Q-1221	*Bos* sp. tibia and radius	Cattle bone from stalled cairn	4305±50	– –	3080–2870
Q-1227	Red deer demur, tibia, and humerus	Deer bone from stalled cairn	4005±60	– –	2840–2340
UB-6420	Ovicaprid cranium	Sheep skull fragment from 'level above human bones', in same level as human skull fragment dated by UB-6421	4435±36	-22.4 –	3340–2920
UB-6421	Human cranium	Human skull fragment from 'level above human bones'; in same level as sheep skull fragment dated by UB-6420	4515±37	-21.5 –	3370–3090
SUERC-39631 (GU-26856)	Human right humerus (90047H1)	Adult ?female human skeletal remains from cairn	4605±35	-20.5 10.4	3500–3340
SUERC-39632 (GU-26857)	Human right humerus (90029H2)	Adult male human skeletal remains from cairn	4355±35	-20.2 10.8	3090–2890
SUERC-39636 (GU-26858)	Human right humerus (15084H3)	Adult ?female human skeletal remains from cairn	4540±35	-19.5 10.3	3370–3090
SUERC-39637 (GU-26859)	Human right humerus (90072H4)	Juvenile c 2 years human skeletal remains from cairn	4555±35	-20.9 11.2	3490–3100
SUERC-30638 (GU-26860)	Human right humerus (90075H5)	Adult ?female human skeletal remains from cairn	4470±35	-20.8 10.8	3350–3020
SUERC-39639 (GU-26861)	Human right humerus (90075H6)	Adult ?female human skeletal remains from cairn	4455±35	-20.3 11.1	3340–2940
SUERC-39640 (GU-26862)	Human right humerus (16319H7)	Juvenile c 7 years human skeletal remains from cairn	4545±35	-19.9 9.8	3370–3100

Table 10.1 Results from sites from the Bay of Firth landscape study area, early Neolithic stone-built stalled houses and timber structures from across Orkney, and from cairns across Orkney included in the model shown in Fig. 10.2. Details of the 'types' of structure and burial monument are included along with details of the individual samples. Continued pp. 270–271.

Laboratory Number	Dated sample	Parent context	Radiocarbon result (BP)	δ13C δ15N C:N	Calibrated date range (cal BC; 95% confidence unless otherwise stated)
SUERC-39641 (GU-26863)	Human skull (90085S1)	Juvenile c 5 years human skeletal remains from cairn	4510±35	-20.8 10.8	3370–3090
SUERC-39642 (GU-26864)	Human skull (90060S2)	Juvenile c 2–3 years human skeletal remains from cairn	4555±35	-20.8 11.5	3490–3100
SUERC-39646 (GU-26865)	Human skull (90070S3)	Adult ?male human skeletal remains from cairn	4525±35	-20.9 10.8	3370–3090
SUERC-30647 (GU-26866)	Human skull (90066S4)	Adult ?male human skeletal remains from cairn	4545±35	-20.5 11.2	3370–3100
SUERC-39648 (GU-26867)	Human skull (90068S5)	Adult male human skeletal remains from cairn	4575±35	-20.6 10.8	3500–3120
SUERC-39649 (GU-26868)	Human skull (90071S6)	Adult male human skeletal remains from cairn	4475±35	-19.9 10.5	3350–3020
SUERC-39650 (GU-26869)	Human skull (90057S8)	Adult ?male human skeletal remains from cairn	4560±35	-20.4 11.6	3490–3100
SUERC-39651 (GU-26870)	Human skull (90058S9)	Adult ?female human skeletal remains from cairn	4475±35	-20.3 10.2	3350–3020
SUERC-39652 (GU-26971)	Human skull (90035S10)	Adult male human skeletal remains from cairn	4570±35	-20.4 11.1	3500–3110
SUERC-39656 (GU-26872)	Human skull (90063S11)	Adult male human skeletal remains from cairn	4290±35	-19.5 10.5	2930–2870
SUERC-39657 (GU-26873)	Human skull (90064S12)	Adult male human skeletal remains from cairn	4500±35	-20.5 11.1	3360–3020
SUERC-39658 (GU-26874)	Human skull (90065S13)	Adult ?male human skeletal remains from cairn	4515±35	-19.7 10.6	3370–3090
SUERC-39659 (GU-26875)	Human skull (1498lS14)	Young adult male human skeletal remains from cairn	4665±35	-20.3 10.5	3630–3360
SUERC-39660 (GU-26876)	Human skull (000x1S15)	Adult male human skeletal remains from cairn	4495±35	-20.7 11.2	3360–3020
SUERC-39661 (GU-26877)	Human skull (90057aS15)	Juvenile c 8–9 years human skeletal remains from cairn	4320±35	20.5 10.1	3020–2880

Knowes of Ramsay, HY40042800, Rousay: Stalled cairn

Laboratory Number	Dated sample	Parent context	Radiocarbon result (BP)	δ13C δ15N C:N	Calibrated date range (cal BC; 95% confidence unless otherwise stated)
Q-1222	*Bos* sp. metacarpal, tibia, ulna, and tibia	Animal bone from stalled cairn	4010±60	–	2840–2340
Q-1223	Animal ribs, including cattle	Animal bone from stalled cairn	4340±65	–	3270–2870
Q-1224	Humerus, metacarpal, and radius of red deer	Deer bone from stalled cairn	4300±60	–	3090–2770

Knowe of Yarso, HY40482795, Rousay: Stalled cairn

Laboratory Number	Dated sample	Parent context	Radiocarbon result (BP)	δ13C δ15N C:N	Calibrated date range (cal BC; 95% confidence unless otherwise stated)
Q-1225	Three tibia, probably of red deer	Deer bone from chambered tomb	4225±60	–	2920–2630
SUERC-45838 (GU-30088)	Human adult male skull 14662	Human skeletal remains from cairn	4500±35	-20.2 10.2	3360–3020

Laboratory Number	Dated sample	Parent context	Radiocarbon result (BP)	δ13C δ15N C:N	Calibrated date range (cal BC; 95% confidence unless otherwise stated)
Knowe of Lairo, HY39882796, Rousay: Stalled cairn					
SUERC-45833 (GU-30086)	Human adult male skull 24761	Human skeletal remains from cairn	4537±34	-20.8 11.2	3370–3090
Midhowe, HY37223048, Rousay: Stalled cairn					
SUERC-46400 (GU-30636)	Human adult male skull 25898	Human skeletal remains from cairn	4700±30	-20.5 10.3	3630–3370
SUERC-46401 (GU-30637)	Human late teens male skull 25899	Human skeletal remains from cairn	4531±28	-20.6 10.3	3370–3100
Quoyness, HY67663779, Sanday: Passage grave					
SRR-752	Human tibia	Human tibia from the chamber	4190±50	-20.5 –	2910–2620
SRR-753	Human bone	A single human bone from the chamber	4270±50	-19.1 –	3010–2710
MAMS-14921 (S-EVAA-24027)	Human rib QUO1	Human skeletal remains from cairn	4487±18	-19.9	3340–3090
Maes Howe, HY31821277, Stenness, Orkney Mainland: Passage grave					
Q-1482	Silty peat	North trench, basal organic material above bedrock, duplicate with SRR-505	3970±70	–	Weighted mean= 4060±48 BP (T'=3.0; T'5%=3.8; df=1)
SRR-505	Silty peat	North trench, basal organic material above bedrock, duplicate with Q-1482	4135±65	-29.9	2860–2480
SRR-504	Silty peat	North trench, lower organic layer of two on inner slope of ditch, 0.85 m below ground level	3660±45	-28.8	2200–1920
SRR-791	Peat	North trench, from layer beneath bank	5090±60	-27.8	4040–3710
Q-1481	Silty peat	South trench, layer 9K, basal organic material, duplicate with SRR-524	3765±70	–	Statistically inconsistent (T'=14.0; T'5%=3.8; df=1)
SRR-524	Silty peat	Sample 8A. South trench, layer 9K, basal organic material, duplicate with Q-1481	3445±50	-29.8	
SRR-523	Silty peat	Sample 7A. South trench, layer 9f/h, above sample 8A	1020±45	–	Cal AD 900–1150
SRR-522	Silty peat	Sample 6A. South trench, layer 9d, above sample 7A	1685±45	-29.8	Cal AD 240–430
SRR-521	Silty peat	Sample 5A. South trench, layer 9a, above sample 6A	1235±45	-29.7	Cal AD 660–900

Table 10.1 Results from sites from the Bay of Firth landscape study area, early Neolithic stone-built stalled houses and timber structures from across Orkney, and from cairns across Orkney included in the model shown in Fig. 10.2. Details of the 'types' of structure and burial monument are included along with details of the individual samples, continued.

Parameter name	Estimates	Figure showing model	Posterior density estimate (95% probability unless otherwise stated)
Start OrkneyNeolithic	Boundary parameter estimating the start of Neolithic activity associated with the use of stalled and timber houses across the islands, all house sites from the Bay of Firth, and cairns from across the islands	10.2	3730–3480
End EarlyHousesCairns	Boundary parameter estimating the end of activity from sites shown in the model	10.2	1610–1400
Start Stonehall Meadow	Boundary parameter estimating the start of activity associated with Stonehall Meadow stalled house	10.3	3490–3040
End Stonehall Meadow	Boundary parameter estimating the end of activity associated with Stonehall Meadow stalled house	10.3	3330–2750
SUERC-5792	Radiocarbon date associated with occupation in Stonehall Farm late Neolithic Barnhouse sub-square style house 1	10.3	3340–3020
FirstCrossiecrownHouse	First parameter estimating the first dated event associated with Crossiecrown House late Neolithic Barnhouse sub-square style house 1	10.3	2480–2270
LastCrossiecrownHouse	Boundary parameter estimating the last dated event associated with Crossiecrown House late Neolithic Barnhouse sub-square style house 1	10.3	2430–2140
FirstTimberStructure1	First parameter estimating the first dated event associated with Wideford timber structure 1	10.4	3360–3140
LastTimberStructure1	Last parameter estimating the first dated event associated with Wideford timber structure 1	10.4	3350–3130
SUERC-4862	Radiocarbon date from the posthole of Wideford timber structure 3	10.4	3500–3130
SUERC-4859	Radiocarbon dates associated with the occupation within Wideford compartmentalized house 1	10.4	3340–3090
SUERC-4870			3340–3020
Start SM13	Boundary parameter estimating the start of the early activity from midden deposits under the Smerquoy stalled house	10.4	3460–3120
Construct SM13	Date parameter estimating the construction of Smerquoy stalled house and erection of pecked rock art panel	10.4	3360–3100
Start SM13 Late	Boundary parameter estimating the start of the later phase of activity in Smerquoy stalled house	10.4	2470–1970
End SM13	Boundary parameter estimating the end of the later phase of activity in Smerquoy stalled house	10.4	1970–1600
FirstBayOfFirthHouse	First parameter estimating the first dated event associated with activity from Neolithic houses in the Cuween-Wideford landscape project	10.4	3600–3310
LastBayOfFirthHouse	Last parameter estimating the last dated event associated with activity from Neolithic houses in the Cuween-Wideford landscape project	10.4	1920–1530
FirstHouse3	First parameter estimating the first dated event associated occupation from stalled Ha'Breck house 3	10.5	3350–3250
LastHouse3	Last parameter estimating the last dated event associated with stalled Ha'Breck house 3	10.5	3240–3020
SUERC-34503	Radiocarbon date associated with occupation of timber Ha'Breck house 4	10.5	3360–3100
SUERC-35090	Radiocarbon date associated with occupation of timber Ha'Breck house 1	10.5	3330–2920
OxA-28984	Radiocarbon date associated with occupation of timber ?structure at Green	10.5	3530–3360
FirstGreenStalledHouse	First parameter estimating the first dated event associated with occupation from stalled house at Green	10.5	3360–3150
LastGreenStalledHouse	Last parameter estimating the last dated event associated with occupation from stalled house at Green	10.5	3330–3050
ConstructHouse1	Date parameter estimating the construction of stalled house 1, Knap of Howar	10.6	3350–2950
FirstHouse2_KH	First parameter estimating the first dated event associated with occupation from stalled house 2, Knap of Howar	10.6	3490–3140
LastHouse2_KH	Last parameter estimating the last dated event associated with occupation from stalled house 2, Knap of Howar	10.6	3340–2970
Start Knowes of'Trotty	Boundary parameter estimating the start of activity associated with the Knowes of Trotty stalled house	10.6	3340–3120
End Knowes of Trotty	Boundary parameter estimating the end of activity associated with the Knowes of Trotty stalled house	10.6	3270–2860
Start Phase2	Boundary parameter estimating the start of occupation associated with the use Knowes of'Trotty stalled house	10.6	3280–3110

Parameter name	Estimates	Figure showing model	Posterior density estimate (95% probability unless otherwise stated)
Start Holm of Papa Westray North	Boundary parameter estimating the start of activity associated with the primary use of Papa Westray North	10.7	3610–3370
End Holm of Papa Westray North	Boundary parameter estimating the end of activity associated with the primary use of Papa Westray North	10.7	2580–2080
Start Point of Cott human burial	Boundary parameter estimating the start of activity associated with the use of Point of Cott for burial	10.8	3620–3390
End Point of Cott human burial	Boundary parameter estimating the end of activity associated with the use of Point of Cott for burial	10.8	3010–2670
Start Isbister	Boundary parameter estimating the start of activity associated with the use of Isbister for burial	10.8	3490–3230
End Isbister	Boundary parameter estimating the end of activity associated with the use of Isbister for burial	10.8	2460–2190
Start Knowe of Rowiegar	Boundary parameter estimating the start of activity associated with the use of Knowe of Rowiegar for burial	10.9	3500–3360
End Knowe of Rowiegar	Boundary parameter estimating the end of activity associated with the use of Knowe of Rowiegar for burial	10.9	3010–2840
First Knowes of Ramsey	First parameter estimating the first dated event associated the use of the Knowes of Ramsey	10.9	3100–2690
Last Knowes of Ramsey	Last parameter estimating the last dated event associated the use of the Knowes of Ramsey	10.9	2860–22340
SUERC-45838_GU-30088	Radiocarbon date associated with the use of the Knowe of Yarso	10.9	3360–3090
Q-1225	Radiocarbon date associated with the use of the Knowe of Yarso	10.9	2930–2580
SUERC-45833_GU-30086	Radiocarbon date associated with the use of the Knowe of Lairo	10.9	3370–3100
SUERC-46400_GU-30636	Radiocarbon date associated with the use of Midhowe	10.9	3630–3370
SUERC-46401_GU-30637	Radiocarbon date associated with the use of Midhowe	10.9	3370–3100
Start main use Quanterness	Boundary parameter estimating the start of activity associated with the use of Quanterness for burial	10.10	3560–3340
End main use Quanterness	Boundary parameter estimating the end of activity associated with the use of Quanterness for burial	10.10	2570–2280
Start Pierowall Quarry	Boundary parameter estimating the start of later activity associated with Pierowall *Terminus ante quem* for construction passage grave	10.11	3120–2600
FirstQuoyness	First parameter estimating the first dated event associated with the use of the Quoyness	10.11	3340–3090
LastQuoyness	Last parameter estimating the last dated event associated with the use of the Quoyness	10.11	2900–2620
ConstructMaesHoweEarthwork	Date parameter estimating the construction of Maes Howe earthwork	10.12	3870–2600
FirstStalledHouse	First parameter estimating the first dated event associated with the stone-built stalled houses on Orkney	10.13	3520–3290
FirstTimberStructure	First parameter estimating the first dated event associated with a Neolithic timber structure on Orkney	10.13	3520–3360
FirstHouseSite	First parameter estimating the first dated event associated with a timber or stone-built early Neolithic house on Orkney	10.5–6	3640–3440
FirstOrkney Cromarty	First parameter estimating the first dated event associated with an Orkney-Cromarty cairn on Orkney (calculated with the Phase Orkney-Cromarty; shown in Fig. 10.16)	10.7–9	3640–3440
FirstMaesHoweStyle	First parameter estimating the first dated event associated with a Maes Howe-style cairn on Orkney (calculated with the Phase MAes Howe-style; shown in Fig. 10.16)	10.10–11	3590–3340

Table 10.2 Key posterior density estimates from the model shown in Fig. 10.2 and its subsections, the model shown in Fig. 10.12, and the calculations shown in Fig. 10.13.

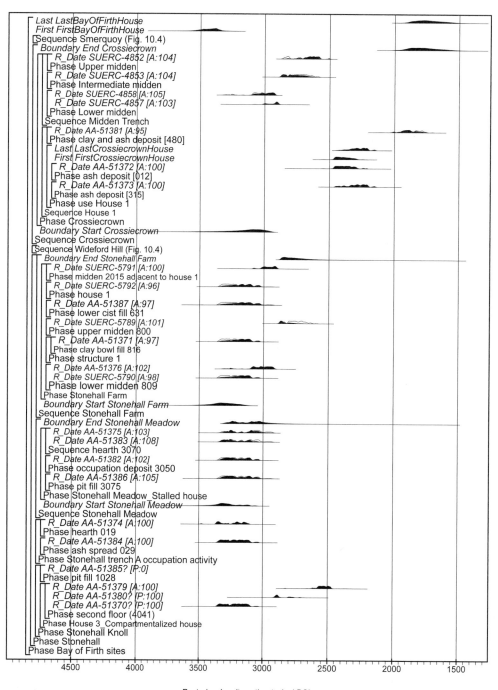

Figure 10.3 The first part of the Bay of Firth component of the model (see also Fig. 10.4). The overall model structure is shown in Fig.10.2. For each radiocarbon result included in the model as an active likelihood two ranges have been plotted. The ranges in outline represent the calibrated radiocarbon results, the solid distributions represent the posterior density estimates – the outputs from the Bayesian statistical model illustrated in the figure. Results not included in the model as active likelihoods are indicated in the figures with a '?' after the laboratory code; for example for the result AA-51380 shown here is not included in the model for reasons described in the text.

antiquarian work. It has also meant that the interpretation and chronological evidence for these sites has changed rapidly over the last 40 years.

For each site included in the model, a brief introduction is provided to the archaeology, the radiocarbon data selected for inclusion, and the modelling approach.

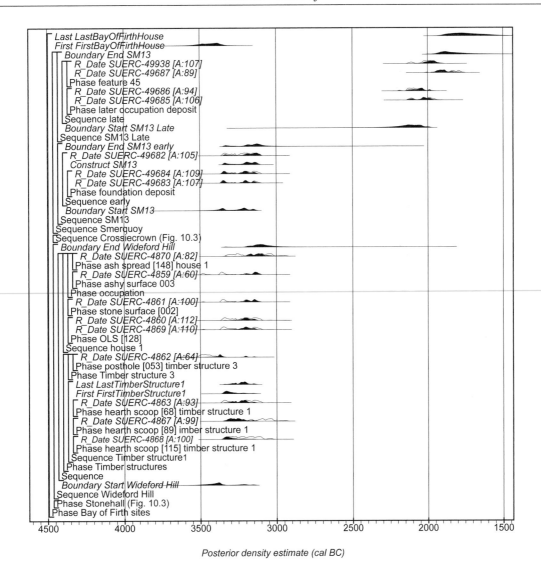

Figure 10.4 The second part of the Bay of Firth component of the model (see also Fig. 10.3).

Consideration of the model outputs and the wider context is made in section 10.3.

10.2.3 Radiocarbon dates from the Bay of Firth sites

The density and diversity of Neolithic structures and occupation evidence from Stonehall, and at nearby Wideford Hill and Smerquoy, has significant implications for understandings of Neolithic Orkney (see Chapters 2, 4 and 5). The Bay of Firth component of the model is shown in Fig. 10.3–10.4. The density of occupation in this area has its own implications for producing robust chronologies of sites. Evidence for re-use of stone-built structures – as demonstrated at Smerquoy – means that sites with limited radiocarbon measurements may not sample the full duration of activity. The density

of occupation also emphasises the importance of the associations of dated samples with archaeological events of interest. For several sites around the Bay of Firth, dated samples came from contexts – for example secondary floor deposits from House 3 from Stonehall Knoll – which might have included material redeposited from earlier activity.

Stonehall Knoll, Mainland (see Chapter 5)

Radiocarbon dates were produced on samples associated with 'compartmentalized' House 3, from Stonehall Knoll. Three radiocarbon measurements were produced on samples from a thin layer of burnt material and ash trampled into a secondary clay floor of House 3. The floor had seen several episodes of patching, mending and re-levelling. The radiocarbon samples from this horizon

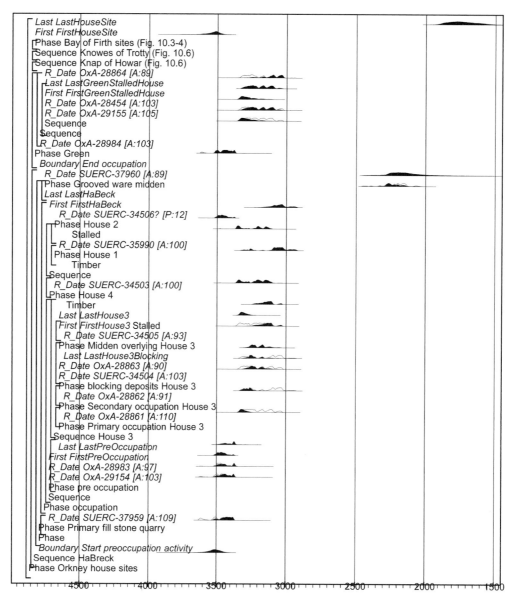

Figure 10.5 *The first part of the early Neolithic Orkney house component of the model (see also Fig. 10.6). The overall model structures is shown in Fig. 10.2.*

are of very different ages, suggesting at least some of this material could have been redeposited. The two earlier results (AA-51370 and AA-51380) have not been included as active likelihoods in the model presented here; the latest result from this deposit (AA-51379) may provide an estimate for the timing of secondary occupation within House 3, but could equally represent redeposited material. Another result from this trench (AA-51385) derives from a sample from pit fill [1028], which represents much later activity again, and has not been included as an active likelihood in the model.

Stonehall Meadow, Mainland (see Chapter 5)
Four results were produced from House 3, a stone-built stalled early Neolithic structure, at Stonehall Meadow. The results were all produced on samples associated with the occupation of House 3, from a pit in the outer compartment of the house (AA-51386), from two stratified hearth deposits (AA-51383 from an upper deposit, AA-51375 from the lower deposit), and from an occupation deposit from around the hearth in the house inner compartment (AA-51382). Results from the hearth deposit [3070] are modelled reflecting the stratigraphic

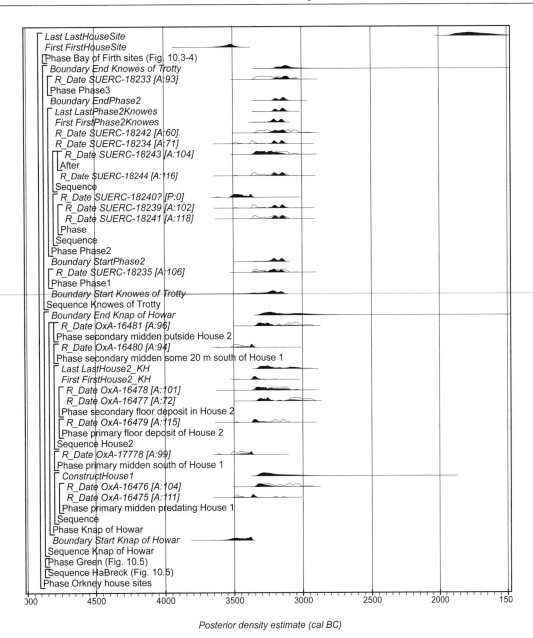

Figure 10.6 *The second part of the early Neolithic house component of the model (see Fig. 10.5 and its caption).*

sequential relationship between the parent contexts. These and the other results from Stonehall Meadow stalled house are presented as representing a phase of archaeological activity.

From trench A at Stonehall Meadow, two radiocarbon measurements (AA-51374 and AA-51384) were produced on samples from a hearth and an ash spread which were statistically consistent and could therefore be of the same actual age (T'=0.8; T'5%=3.8; df=1; Ward and Wilson 1978). It is not clear if the hearth was associated with the occupation of House 3, or any of the other Neolithic

occupation activity in the vicinity. These results have been included in a phase of Neolithic activity, but have not been associated with any particular structure.

Stonehall Farm, Mainland (see Chapter 5)
Several styles of Neolithic structure were excavated at Stonehall Farm, some of which were superimposed on midden deposits. Radiocarbon dates were produced in association with 'atypical' Structure 1 and sub-square House 1. Two statistically consistent measurements (AA-51376 and SUERC-5790; T'=3.4; T'5%=3.8; df=1)

were produced on samples from a lower part of the midden deposit that underlay Structure 1. From an upper midden deposit a sample was recovered for measurement SUERC-5789. Stratigraphically later than the lower midden deposits, a result was produced on a charcoal sample from the clay bowl which was associated with the use of Structure 1 (AA-51371). A radiocarbon date (AA-51387) on birch charcoal from a cist dug into the floor of the structure was also produced.

A sequential model reflecting the stratigraphic relationships between the parent deposits from the midden underlying Structure 1, the clay bowl associated with the use of Structure 1, and the later cist has poor overall agreement (model not shown). The nature of the deposits means that some of these results could have been produced on redeposited material. The results have been included in a less informative Phase model for Neolithic activity on the site.

A single result (SUERC-5792) from an ash-rich fill of sub-square House 1 might have a more robust association with occupation activity of this house, and this result is statistically consistent with a result (SUERC-5791) from a midden adjacent to House 1 (T'=0.8; T'5%=3.8; df=1). These results have been included in the model as representing a phase of Neolithic activity at Stonehall Farm.

Wideford Hill, Mainland (see Chapter 2)

At Wideford Hill, radiocarbon dates were produced from circular Timber structures 1 and 2, and an apparently rectilinear Timber structure 3, which were stratigraphically earlier than Stonehouse 1 (which stratigraphically overlay Timber structure 2). Results from circular Timber structures 1 and 2 are statistically consistent (SUERC-4868, SUERC-4867, SUERC-4863; T'=2.3; T'5%=6.0; df=2). Three radiocarbon measurements were produced on samples from a sequence of superimposed hearth deposits from Timber structure 1. These results have been modelled to reflect the stratigraphic sequence of these samples. A single result (SUERC-4862) from Timber structure 3 is older than the results from Timber structures 1 and 2.

Stonehouse 1 is here classified as a 'compartmentalized'-type house, and is associated with a stratigraphic sequence of radiocarbon samples. These derived from the old land surface [128] underlying the structure, a rammed surface deposited over this old land surface [002], and deposits [148] and [003] associated with occupation activity within the structure. The results from Stonehouse 1 have been modelled to reflect the stratigraphic sequence between

the radiocarbon samples' parent deposits. In the model shown here, the results from the timber structures are all presented as belonging to a phase of activity that pre-dates Stonehouse 1, which reflects site phasing, and is based upon the stratigraphic relationship between Timber structure 2 and Stonehouse 1.

Crossiecrown, Mainland (see Chapter 7)

At Crossiecrown, radiocarbon samples were recovered in association with occupation of the Red House (House 1 – a later Neolithic sub-square structure), from a clay and ash deposit [480] associated with the collapse of the Red House, and from midden deposits. Results associated with its occupation (AA-51373 and AA-51372) are statistically consistent (T'=1.3; T'5%=3.8; df=1). The interval between the sample of radiocarbon dates associated with the use of the structure, and the date from the deposit associated with the structure's collapse (AA-51381) indicates that this structure could have had a long and punctuated use-life history, which is poorly understood. Samples (SUERC-4857, SUERC-4858, SUERC-4853, SUERC-4852) from a sequence of deposits from the south midden excavated in Trench 3 were also radiocarbon dated. Two results from a lower midden deposit (SUERC-4857 and SUERC-4858) are statistically consistent (T'=3.3; T'5%=3.8; df=1), and the midden results have been modelled to reflect the Sequence of stratigraphic relationships of the radiocarbon samples parent deposits. These results cannot be directly associated with the use of the Red House, or other occupation evidence on the site.

The results from the midden deposits are considerably earlier than those associated with the Red House, and confirm the earlier occupation of the site. All these results have been included in a Phase model.

Smerquoy, Mainland (see Chapter 4)

Radiocarbon samples were submitted from two phases of activity associated with the use of the Smerquoy Hoose. Following production of radiocarbon dates it became apparent that the later occupation activity was significantly younger than the construction and initial use of the structure. Additional evidence for the complex history of occupation at Smerquoy was apparent from the repositioning of the central stone-built hearth. Extensive sampling for plant macrofossils for radiocarbon measurements did not produce any suitable material from the central hearth, so the timing of this reorientation cannot be established with any certainty. However, from the radiocarbon chronology associated with the occupation horizons alone, it is clear that the structure was the focus of activity – though probably intermittently – for a considerable period of time.

Importantly, while the Smerquoy Hoose has earlier Neolithic stalled architecture, a panel set into the walling near the entrance has rock art decoration showing a pecked horned spiral motif previously associated with later Neolithic sites. The position of this panel low in the wall-coursing indicates that it must have been executed prior to the construction of the stalled stone house (see Chapter 4).

Two statistically consistent results (SUERC-49683 and SUERC-49684; T'=0.2; T'5%=3.8; df=1) from foundation deposits predating the stone walling at Smerquoy provide *termini post quos* for the construction of the Smerquoy Hoose (which is estimated by the parameter *ConstructionSM13*), and the erection of the rock art panel in the walling. Initial occupation is sampled only by one result (SUERC-49682; another measurement failed due to a yield of insufficient carbon). The chronology of the stratigraphically later occupation is measured by results from an occupation horizon (SUERC-49685 and SUERC-49686) and a stratigraphically later pit (SUERC-49687 and SUERC-49938). The results on the later occupation horizon are statistically consistent (T'=0.9; T'5%=3.8; df=1), though the two results from the later pit are statistically inconsistent (T'=5.8; T'5%=3.8; df=1), and indicate that the later activity was of some duration. The results are presented in the model reflecting the stratigraphic sequence – pre-stone house foundation deposits, early occupation, later occupation and stratigraphically later negative features – from the site.

10.2.4 Radiocarbon dates from other early Neolithic stalled house and timber sites

Knowes of Trotty, Mainland (see Chapter 3)
Radiocarbon samples from the Knowes of Trotty stone-built stalled house were related to a sequence of deposits associated with phases of activity in the early Neolithic structure. From phase 1, SUERC-18235 was produced on shortlife charcoal recovered from a pit underlying the house walling. This result provides a stratigraphic *terminus post quem* for the construction of the house. From phase 2, deposits associated with the use of hearths (SUERC-18242, SUERC-18243, SUERC-18244, SUERC-18241 SUERC-18239) including stone-built hearth [215] (SUERC-18234), and floor/occupation deposits (SUERC-18240), within the stalled house

produced radiocarbon samples. Of the radiocarbon results, SUERC-18240 is too early for its stratigraphic position within the model presented here, and this result has not been included as an active likelihood. Later, phase 3 activity within the stalled structure is represented by SUERC-18233, which was produced on a sample from a hearth [082] that had a raised location within the northern part of the house. This result is interpreted as representing the latest use of the structure, with the stratigraphically-earlier stone-built hearth [215] sealed over by this time. One of the results (SUERC-18243) was produced on unidentified charcoal, which therefore could include an 'old wood' offset, is included in the model as a *terminus post quem*.

The model for the Knowes of Trotty stalled house uses the sequential phases of activity pre-dating the stone structure, and associated with use of the structure as its basis. Estimates for the start of different archaeological phases of activity associated with the stalled house (*Start Knowes of Trotty, StartPhase2, EndPhase2, End Knowes of Trotty*) are produced from the model.

The Knap of Howar, Papa Westray
The Knap of Howar is located adjacent to the sea shore on the west coast of Papa Westray. The site was first excavated in 1929, but it was not until Anna Ritchie's work (1983) that the two stone-built stalled houses were recognised as being of Neolithic date. The two structures are conjoined by a connected passageway, and House 1 was probably constructed prior to House 2 (Ritchie 1990a, 42). House 1 was divided into two areas by a stone stall; within the first compartment was a stone bench, while in the second were a quern, hearth and wall recess. House 2 was divided into three compartments. The inner compartment included several wall recesses, and the middle included a hearth. At least two phases of activity are associated with House 2, as evidenced by the blocking of the door into this structure.

The structures at the Knap of Howar represent the 'classic' early Neolithic Orkney stalled rectilinear house, with walls formed from midden core material and stone facing (see Chapter 1). The walls have rounded corners internally and externally, and the internal space is divided by paired orthostats. Material culture recovered included flint, animal bones (including fish), pottery and polished stone axes. The pottery was defined as forming four categories, with some 13 Unstan ware bowls, simple bowls, bowls with cordons, and miscellaneous sherds represented (Henshall 1983, 70). The assemblage also included sherds with similarities to Grooved ware (*ibid.*, 72).

Two groups of radiocarbon measurements were produced. Results on samples of mixed animal bone (Birm-813–816; SRR3449; SRR-352) and a result on 'soil' (Birm-817) have not been included in the model presented here. More recently, a series of short-life, single entity measurements on samples identified to species level were produced (Sheridan and Higham 2006). Two results (OxA-16475 and OxA-16476) on midden material from under House 1 provide stratigraphic *termini post quos* for the construction of the structure, an estimate for which is provided by the *ConstructHouse1* Date parameter. Radiocarbon results (OxA-16477, OxA-16478 and OxA-16479) from samples from a stratigraphic sequence through the primary and secondary floor deposits from House 2 are interpreted here as dating occupation activity associated with this structure (see discussion below). Other radiocarbon measurements on single entity bone samples from midden deposits from the site are associated with Neolithic occupation (OxA-16480, OxA-16481 and OxA-17778). As well as the stratigraphic relationships described above through the floor deposits of House 2, and a Sequence model to provide an estimate for the construction of House 1, the results from the site are modelled as if they represent a related Phase of activity associated with the Neolithic use of the site.

Ha'Breck, Wyre

Excavations at Ha'Breck, Wyre have revealed a series of early Neolithic stone-built stalled structures, early Neolithic rectilinear timber structures, a stone quarry, and later activity which includes midden deposits associated with Grooved ware. Five structures have been excavated at the site (Lee and Thomas 2011; Farrell *et al.* 2014), linear timber structures are represented by House 1 and House 4. Stone-built earlier Neolithic stalled houses were represented by House 2, House 3 and House 5. Radiocarbon results from the site were produced as part of the recent *Stepping Stones* AHRC-funded project directed by Duncan Garrow and Fraser Sturt, and post-excavation analysis is ongoing.

The Ha'Breck early Neolithic structures show evidence of transition from timber to stone architecture, with houses rebuilt on the same footprint, and with stratigraphically later stone structures rebuilt adjacent to timber ones (Farrell *et al.* 2014). The excavators suggest that several of the buildings were used for a relatively limited period of time, with the corner timber posts comprising House 4 removed as the structure was decommissioned. This can be contrasted with the apparent longevity of occupation

associated with stone-built stalled House 3 immediately to the west of House 4. Stone-built House 3 included wooden central posts, and occupation went on for long enough to necessitate the replacement of these posts four or five times (Farrell *et al.* 2014).

A single radiocarbon measurement each was produced from a context from timber House 1 (SUERC-35990) and from a context from timber House 4 (SUERC-34503). Samples from a sequence of deposits from House 3 exist, including statistically consistent measurements from a pre-occupation deposit underlying this building (OxA-29154 and OxA-28983; T'=0.2; T'5%=3.8; df=1), and deposits from within House 3. A stratigraphic sequence from the occupation of House 3 comprises 'primary occupation' (from which a sample for OxA-28861 was recovered), 'secondary occupation' (from which a sample for OxA-28862 was recovered), and closure or blocking deposits (from which statistically consistent measurements SUERC-34504 and OxA-28863; T'=0.3; T'5%=3.8; df=1) were produced. Stratigraphically later than this again was a midden deposit overlying House 3, from which a sample for SUERC-34505 was recovered.

Stalled stone House 2 is stratigraphically later than timber House 1. However, the result from House 2 (SUERC-34506) is earlier than that from House 1 (SUERC-35990), and when modelled reflecting this stratigraphic sequence of the results have poor agreement (model not shown). Too few measurements exist from these structures to explore their chronology in any detail; for the purposes of the model shown here, the earlier result (SUERC-34506) from House 2 has not been included as an active likelihood on the grounds that it may represent redeposited material. Neither of these measurements can be demonstrated to represent really robust estimates for the use House 2 or House 1.

In addition to the measurements from these structures, a single result (SUERC-37959) was produced on a charcoal sample from the stone quarry, and a single result was produced on a sample from a 'Grooved ware midden' on the site (SUERC-37960).

The results from the pre-occupation deposit under House 3, the sequence of results through the structure, and the result from the midden over this structure have been modelled to reflect the stratigraphic sequence. The rest of the results from Ha'Breck are presented as representing a phase of archaeological activity on the site. The presence of the much later result (SUERC-37960) associated with Grooved ware activity on the site indicates that occupation at Ha'Breck might have had considerable longevity and complexity.

Green, Eday

Excavation at Green, Eday, revealed Neolithic occupation (Coles and Miles 2013), and post-excavation analysis is ongoing. A stalled stone-built early Neolithic structure is present on the site. Finds from the site included later Neolithic material culture (Grooved ware and maceheads). Radiocarbon results from the site were produced as part of the recent *Stepping Stones* AHRC-funded project.

Four radiocarbon dates exist from Green. OxA-29155 and OxA-28454 were produced on samples from superimposed hearth deposits in stalled stone-built House 1. OxA-28864 was produced on a sample from a midden deposit (214) stratigraphically later than House 1. OxA-28984 was produced on a sample from a posthole that may be associated with the use of a timber structure, The stratigraphic sequence of relationships between the hearth deposits in House 1 and the overlying midden context has been used in the model presented here. OxA-28984 is included in the model as part of the phase of Neolithic activity.

10.2.5 Radiocarbon dates from Orkney-Cromarty cairns

Holm of Papa Westray North, Papa Westray

Holm of Papa Westray North is a stalled early Neolithic chambered cairn, with a long history of use. The site is close to the coast, on the north of Papa Westray, at *c*.5m OD (Davidson and Henshall 1989). The cairn was rectangular, measuring 11.8m by 6.3m. Interventions at the site were recorded in 1849 and 1854, though prior to this, the site had been robbed (Ritchie 2009). Modern excavation at the site occurred in 1982–83, and revealed a stalled cairn, with a series of phases of activity. The monument comprised a forecourt, an entrance passage, and a chamber that was divided into four compartments by orthostats. At the end of the chamber was a small cell (cell 5). The primary phase of the monument comprised a round cairn and cell 5. In phase 2, the structure was elaborated to form a rectangular cairn and passageway. After some period of use, cell 5 was filled in and the entrance blocked. In phase 4, the chamber and passage appear to have been deliberately infilled.

A range of material culture was recovered from the cairn, including round-based plain bowl pottery (including flanged-rim bowls), Grooved ware (with both incised and applied decoration), as well as human remains from individual stalled compartments. Finds other than human skeletal remains were nearly all recovered from the central area and the east side of compartments

1–3. The skeletal remains were disarticulated, and perhaps moved around as part of the use of the cairn, with elements from different compartments refitting (Ritchie 2009, 30). Sheep, bird, otter, rodent and fish bones, limpet shells, and a deer antler were recovered from within the chamber, and may represent a range of taphonomic processes. Faunal remains in the chamber might indicate that it was open for a period of time after its initial use (Ritchie 2009). Beaker pottery was recovered from contexts outside the cairn.

Radiocarbon measurements were produced on samples of human bones from cell 3 (context 1 – GrA-25636 and GrA-25638), from cell 5 (GrA-25638, and from the stratigraphically later infilling of cell 5 GU-2067, OxA-17779, and OxA-17780), from compartment 4 (GU-2068), and from the midden deposit which contained Grooved ware and Beaker pottery (OxA-16472 and OxA-17781) adjacent to the kerb of the back of the cairn. From a primary floor deposit in the forecourt a sample of red deer bone was dated (OxA-17782).

From the later modification of the monument, OxA-16473 was produced on a sample from the demolition of the grave facade in the forecourt, OxA-16471 was produced on a sample from the final fill of cell 5, and a measurement (GU-2069) was produced on a sample from the deliberate infilling of the entrance passage (Ritchie 2009, 22). Initial modelling of the results from Holm of Papa Westray North making use of the published stratigraphic relationships between the samples' parent deposits indicated that human skeletal remains may have been redeposited. Results are modelled here as a Phase of activity associated with the use of the site (Schulting *et al.* 2010, 27). Separate estimates for the First and Last dated events associated with results from within the cairn and from the midden have been calculated.

The model presented here makes use of the estimates for marine contributions to the diets of three humans represented at the cairn (Schulting and Richards 2009, 69; a 16% marine contribution for GrA-25636, a 2% marine contribution for GrA-25637 and a 13% contribution for GrA-25638). The uncertainty associated with this portion of the dietary contribution has been applied as ±10, which in this case is an arbitrary figure. The local radiocarbon marine reservoir has been applied as 24±67, as described above.

Work by Balasse and Tresset (2009) indicated a marine contribution to the diet of some sheep/goat remains from the site, including that the individual dated by OxA-17779 consumed marine fodder in winter seasons (Balasse and Tresset 2009, 81). For measurements OxA-17779, OxA-16474 and GU-2069 a marine diet fraction of 30±50% has been applied to reflect a cold season contribution, or possible cold season contribution, of marine resources with the local marine reservoir offset. This reflects an estimate that one third of the dietary contribution might be derived from marine resources during the winter and early spring. Results on several young sheep metatarsal bones (OxA-16472, OxA-16474 and GU-2069) indicate greater marine contributions. For these young sheep samples, a marine dietary contribution is increased to 50±50% to reflect the greater proportional effect over these individuals' short lifespans, with a five month gestation period (*ibid.*, 77). In light of recent work indicating strategic, small-scale marine contributions to Neolithic diets on Shetland (Montgomery *et al.* 2013), further work examining the nature of these contributions would be welcome.

A measurement on an otter bone (OxA-17780) has been calibrated using the marine curve and the local reservoir value. The radiocarbon results on vole bones from the site (OxA-18665 4054±28 BP 2840–2480 cal BC 95% confidence; OxA-18666 4089±29 BP 2860–2500 cal BC 95% confidence) are not included in the analysis as the radiocarbon ages and nature of the samples mean that they are likely to be intrusive.

Point of Cott, Westray

Point of Cott, Westray, is a stalled horned cairn, with a chamber divided into four compartments. The site was first excavated in 1935 (Henshall 1963), and was subsequently excavated in 1984–85 in response to coastal erosion (Barber 1997). The monument was initially constructed as a stone-built stalled chamber with surrounding cairn. Drystone walls were then extended at the front of the chamber to give the monument a trapezoidal or horned appearance. The horn on the south west of the monument had been destroyed by coastal erosion prior to investigation by Calder in the 1930s (Henshall 1963). The minimum length of the cairn was estimated to be over 30m, with the southern façade 16m wide. The surviving hornwork was 6m long. In the chamber, the fourth, terminal compartment was subdivided by a slab along the longitudinal cairn axis (Barber 1997). At the north of the monument, two infant inhumations were recovered, representing stratigraphically later burials than activity associated with the cairn construction.

Pre-cairn deposits produced animal bones and lithics that were identified by Finlay (1997) as later Mesolithic and probably redeposited. The cairn produced human

skeletal remains, animal bone and pottery. Whale ivory beads were recovered from compartments 3 and 4 of the chamber. The pottery assemblage comprises 65 sherds, the majority of which derived from five vessels, three of these with flanged rims and round bases, and two with flat rims (MacSween 1997). Sherds from some of these vessels were found distributed between different chambers and the passage. Two sherds from secondary contexts possibly represent incised Grooved ware.

Fifteen radiocarbon dates were produced on human skeletal remains and faunal remains from the stalled cairn compartments. Samples on bulk bone and bird bone are not included in the model shown here. A result on an otter bone has been calibrated with the marine calibration curve and local offset (see above). This otter bone was recovered from behind the wall face of the north of the passage.

Results produced on human bone have been modelled as representing a Phase of use of the cairn for burial. These results are constrained to be earlier than both the one measurement on single entity animal bone from the passage blocking (GU-2941), and the result on the otter bone (UtC-1665), which is much later and cannot be associated with the initial activity at the site. Because the bulk faunal samples have been excluded from the model, and the sheep bone (GU-2941) and the otter bone (UtC-1665) have not been included in the main Phase of the model, this Phase only includes results on human remains. The result (AA-11698) on an infant burial from the collapsed matrix of the cairn at the northern end of the chamber is in keeping with the other results from human remains from the chamber.

Isbister, South Ronaldsay

The stone-built stalled cairn at Isbister, South Ronaldsay, is located on cliffs, with impressive views of the sea, and a commanding position in the landscape. The monument takes the form of an oval cairn, with a stalled central passage perpendicular to the entrance passage. The longer axis of the mound is currently some 31.5m, though the eastern side of the monument has been damaged by erosion, and the mound was probably originally circular. The central passage is divided into five compartments by four sets of orthostats (Davidson and Henshall 1989, 126). From the central passage, three side cells project and the termini of the main chamber are divided into compartments. These terminal compartments included stone shelves set within them, though any deposits on these had been disturbed prior to excavation in 1958. Isbister has had a complex history of investigation.

Published excavations include those in 1958, work by the then landowner in 1976, 1978, 1982–83 (Hedges 1983), and those sponsored by the local council in the late 1980s (Davidson and Henshall 1989). The characteristics of the site have led to it being classed a 'hybrid', including both a stalled chamber and side cells (cf. Schulting *et al.* 2010).

From the central chamber an assemblage of disarticulated human skeletal remains, animal bones, charcoal and an Unstan bowl was recovered from the site (Schulting *et al.* 2010, 26). Human and animal bones, including bones of the white-tailed sea eagle, were recovered from below the floor slab in the south end compartment. This deposit was interpreted as a foundation deposit associated with the monument construction. From the forecourt on the east side of the entrance passage three stone axes, a macehead, knife and jet button were recovered. After a period of use, the chamber appears to have been deliberately decommissioned and sealed. A much later cist was inserted into the cairn mound, and another later cist into the north horn of the cairn.

Thirty-two radiocarbon measurements have been produced on the human and animal bone assemblage from the site (Renfrew *et al.* 1983; Schulting *et al.* 2010: Lawrence and Lee-Thorp 2012); these results include repeat measurements on the same bone samples (Renfrew *et al.* 1983). The recently published results (MAMS-14922, MAMS-14923, MAMS-14924, MAMS-14925) reported in Sheridan *et al.* (2012, 202) are included in the model, as are the results (OxA-25626, OxA-25627, OxA-25623, OxA-25624, OxA-25578, OxA-25625, OxA-25622, OxA-25628, OxA-25579) reported in Lawrence and Lee-Thorp (2012, 203). Weighted means are taken prior to calibration on statistically consistent repeat measurements on the same individuals (GU1182 and Q-3013; GU-1186 and Q-3017; OxA-25626 and OxA-25627; GU-1183 and Q-3014).

As extensively discussed by Schulting *et al.* (2010), modelling the results from Isbister according to their reported stratigraphic association produces a model which has poor agreement (model not shown). For example, two results from the 'foundation deposit' (UB-6552 and UB-6553) are much later than measurements on samples from deposits in the stalls, and are of similar age to results from the cairn infilling (GU-1186 and Q-3017). This tension between the results and recorded stratigraphy could indicate that material within the grave had been mixed and redeposited. The sea eagle bones clearly do not relate to the site 'foundation deposit' (Schulting *et al.* 2010, 26).

The results from the main chamber are all included in a Phase of activity that is earlier than the results from stratigraphically later cists. The results on the sea eagle bones (UB-6552 and UB-6553) and the repeat measurements on the same unidentified animal bone (Q-3018 and GU-1190) have not been included in the model as active likelihoods. By excluding these results, the earlier Phase from the model estimates the currency of human burial at the site.

Knowe of Rowiegar, Rousay
The Knowe of Rowiegar, Rousay, is a stone-built stalled cairn, located at 6m OD on the south west shore of Rousay. The first recorded excavation of the site was in 1937 by Walter Grant (Davidson and Henshall 1989, 136-8) where it was found that the central part of the chamber of the long stalled cairn had been subsequently modified to form a souterrain. In its original form, the main chamber probably comprised 12 stalled compartments (Davidson and Henshall 1989). Unbonded walling was added to the northwest and southeast ends of the cairn at some point. There is evidence for Iron Age occupation on top of the cairn and to its east.

Material culture included sherds of Unstan ware (Kinnes 1985), scrapers of chert and flint, a flint knife recovered from the fourth compartment, and flint flakes. Human remains were recovered from within the chamber, along with cattle and sheep bones, and the wings of a gannet (Davidson and Henshall 1989).

Radiocarbon dates were produced over a considerable period of time on samples recovered from the site (Renfrew *et al.* 1976; Sheridan 2005b; Curtis and Hutchison 2013). Samples of human bone and faunal remains all appear to derive from the use of the monument (cf. Davidson and Henshall 1989, 87), and results have been modelled in a single Phase. One result (Q-1227) had poor agreement with this model in initial runs. This result is later than others from the site and this has not been included as an active parameter in the model presented here.

Knowe of Ramsay, Rousay
The Knowe of Ramsay, Rousay, is a stone-built stalled cairn (Callander and Grant 1936), at 55m OD, immediately to the west of the Knowe of Yarso, and to the immediate north east and overlooking the Knowe of Lairo. The site was excavated in 1935, though it had been subject to robbing prior to this (Callander and Grant 1936; Henshall 1963). The chambered cairn was rectangular in plan, and some 34.4m long by 8.2m wide.

The chamber had been divided into 14 compartments by pairs of transverse slabs. A small stone cist was found near the southwest corner of the fifth compartment from the entrance. Finds included six small sherds of pottery, a scraper and five pieces of flint or chert, human bones and numerous animal bones.

Three radiocarbon results on animal bone samples from the site have been produced (Renfrew *et al.* 1976); of these the nature of the animal species used for measurement (Q-1223) is unclear, and this result has not been included as an active parameter in the model. The Knowe of Ramsay results have been presented in a Phase model (cf. Davidson and Henshall 1989, 87). As with other sites discussed here, the animal bone may not be associated with the earliest use of the site as a mortuary monument, and an estimate from the site for the First dated event might better provide a *terminus ante quem* for its construction and initial use (see discussion below).

Knowe of Yarso, Rousay

The Knowe of Yarso is a stone-built stalled cairn, located on the south coast of Rousey (100m OD). Prior to excavation, the rectangular mound was *c.*19m by 9.7m. The monument included a central passage divided into three side compartments, and a terminal compartment (Callander and Grant 1935). The site was investigated in 1934, and finds recovered included human remains from the passage and chamber, though most of these were recovered from the inner compartments, where skulls had been arranged along the base of the walls (Richards 1988, 49; Davidson andHenshall 1989). The faunal assemblage included deer, sheep and dog bones. Food Vessel and Beaker pottery, flint arrowheads and other worked flints were also recovered.

Two radiocarbon dates were produced from the site, on a deer sample (Q-1225; Renfrew *et al.* 1976) and a sample of human skeletal remains (SUERC-45838; Curtis and Hutchison 2013). The results are presented as representing a Phase of archaeological activity (cf. Davidson and Henshall 1989, 87). As with other sites detailed here, the animal bone is considerably later than the sample of human bone.

Knowe of Lairo, Rousay

The Knowe of Lairo, is an extraordinary stone-built, long horned cairn, which was excavated in 1936 (Grant and Wilson 1943). The site had been robbed and disturbed prior to excavation (Henshall 1963; Davidson and Henshall 1989). The cairn is located on the edge of a terrace at 15m OD, below the hillside which is the location of the Knowes of Ramsay and the Knowe of Yarso (Davidson and Henshall 1989, 132).

The monument was roughly trapezoidal, and the cairn survived to a height of 3.2m at the east end above the chamber. It is *c.*17m wide at the east end, 9m at the west, and some 45.7m in length from the start of the passage entrance to the west end of the mound. The inner chamber was divided by orthostats creating a tripartite plan. However subsequently a line of masonry blocked the third compartment, and ran along the side of the first two compartments (Davidson and Henshall 1989). Within this masonry skin were four recesses at varying heights, two of which were two-storeyed. Material recovered from the cairn includes a ground stone axe and two sherds representing wall or base sherds from round bowl pottery. A single result on human bone from the Knowe of Lario (Curtis and Hutchison 2013) provides and indication of the date of the later use of the monument.

Midhowe, Rousay

The stone-built stalled cairn at Midhowe, Rousay, was excavated by Callander and Grant in the early 1930s. The site is located on the south westcoast of Rousay, at 10m OD. Before excavation the mound survived to *c.*2.7m high. The cairn was of rectangular plan, and measured *c.*32.5m long by *c.*13 m wide (see Callander and Grant 1934). The chamber was divided into 12 compartments, with the terminal compartment subdivided by transverse slabs. Low shelves or benches ran along the northeast side of the chamber in compartments five to eleven. Human remains were recovered on these shelves, with more material deposited below the bench, and on the floor of the chamber.

At the northwest of the cairn, evidence for subsequent modification took the form of a passage from the end of the cairn to the chamber, while a cist-like tank in the north end of the cairn also indicated remodelling of the site (Davidson and Henshall 1989). The chamber was blocked with collapsed material from the roof. Stratigraphically later than the roof collapse were the remains of two inhumations. Also after the initial cairn construction, two walls were constructed that abutted the northeast corner and southeast corners of the monument.

Faunal remains recovered from the site included cow, sheep, and fish bones, red deer bones and antler, and limpet shells. Finds included a flint knife, and 'Unstan' bowl pottery (Callander and Grant 1934; Kinnes 1985). Two results (Curtis and Hutchison 2013) were produced on human bone probably from two different individuals from Midhowe, and are presented as part of a Phase of activity associated with the use of the structure.

10.2.6 Radiocarbon dates from passage graves

Quanterness, Mainland

Quanterness, which was discussed extensively in Chapter 8, comprises a large circular mound, and survived to *c.*31m diameter and a height of *c.*3.4m (Davidson and Henshall 1989). A stone-built passage led to a rectangular central chamber, from which six side cells radiate. The cells were roughly rectangular, though the three southern cells had concave bowed outer walls. An Iron Age house was built on the east side of the monument. Early 19th century exploration of the site is reported (Barry 1805), but it remained predominantly undisturbed until the systematic excavation by Renfrew (Renfrew *et al.* 1976; Renfrew 1979).

A sequence of five 'strata' was identified in the central chamber, with a similar sequence in the southwest cell. The site produced a large Grooved ware pottery assemblage representing at least 34 vessels, a small quantity of flint and stone, and faunal remains. Human remains were recovered from the main chamber (80% of which was excavated), from one cell and from the innermost part of the passage, the majority of which was disarticulated. The nature of the assemblage was interpreted as resulting from excarnation (Chesterman 1979). Schulting *et al.* (2010, 9) reassessed the human skeletal remains, and as well as revising the size of the population represented, emphasised that the assemblage does not show weathering or alteration, and includes small skeletal elements which are not usually present in an assemblage if subject to secondary burial.

Twenty radiocarbon dates were recently reported from the site (Schulting *et al.* 2010) in addition to the nine older results that existed for the site. Dated samples include human remains from a variety of contexts within the cairn – including contexts that are related stratigraphically – and a single sample on 'organic soil'. Several measurements were made on samples that are thought – on archaeological grounds – to represent the same skeletons. Schulting *et al.* (2010, 16) note a tension between the reported stratigraphic association of the parent contexts and the radiocarbon measurements, and suggest that post-depositional disturbance has limited the stratigraphic integrity of the sequence. The model presented here adapts that of Schulting *et al.* (2010) using the original error terms, with results from the site presented within a Phase of activity associated

with the use of the cairn for burial. A weighted mean is taken prior to calibration of results from a single articulated inhumation burial in pit C (statistically consistent Q-1480 and SRR-755; T'=0.2; T'5%=3.8; df=1). Another original result (Pta-1606) which was thought to also date the inhumation in pit C, and two more recent results (SUERC-24020 and SUERC-24021) from pit C produced much earlier measurements, and are included in the model as estimates for the dates of death of other individuals. A weighted mean is taken prior to calibration of statistically consistent results (SRR-754; Pta-1626; SUERC-24001; Q-1479; T'=4.6; T'5%=7.8; df=3) on skeletal remains from pit A. The output from the model provides a currency for the use of the site for burial.

Pierowall, Westray

Excavation at Pierowall, Westray, in 1981 occurred when quarrying revealed the remains of a chambered cairn and later activity. The site is located at 20m OD, above the west side of the Bay of Pierowall, Westray. The monument comprised a *c.*18m diameter cairn defined by two circular stone revetments, and a central passage. The two revetments were not bonded, though the excavator suggests that there was no significant interval between the construction of these structures (Sharples 1984, 82). The cairn is notable for producing three large decorated stones, one of which may have served as a lintel from the passage. After the initial construction of the site it was significantly altered, with the cairn levelled and paved over, and a small rectangular structure constructed adjacent to the location of the cairn. This structure was associated with a significant quantity of flint-working debris, and pottery including some sherds of Grooved ware. Subsequently a large early Iron Age roundhouse was constructed at the site.

A large quantity of disarticulated human bone was recovered in the cairn rubble, potentially representing material cleared out of the chamber as the cairn was levelled. These had been dumped in association with a large quantity of limpet shells. Animal bones were recovered from the later structures, and from the fill behind the outer cairn wall face.

Radiocarbon results were produced on samples of cattle and ovicaprid bone from deposits from the collapsed cairn revetment, and two later phases of occupation over the demolished cairn. Results from the site have been modelled to represent a Phase of activity associated with the collapsed cairn revetment, and then two sequential phases of later occupation reflecting the stratigraphic relationships between the radiocarbon samples' parent contexts. The extant radiocarbon data cannot demonstrably be associated with the earliest phases of use of the passage grave. The estimate for the start of the radiocarbon dated activity is probably best understood as a *terminus ante quem* for start of the use of the site for burial activity.

Quoyness, Sanday

The passage grave at Quoyness, Sanday, was investigated by Farrer and Petrie in 1867, and re-excavated by Childe (Childe 1952; Davidson and Henshall 1989). The site is located on the shore on the south side of Sanday. The monument includes a rectangular chamber, passage, cairn and surrounding platform. The mound was defined by two retaining walls, and recorded as *c.*20.5m by *c.*17m in plan, and surviving to 4m high. Six cells radiated from the central chamber. These were irregular in plan, and of variable size. The platform appeared to mask the mouth of the passage and was associated with material culture including Grooved ware, two Skaill knives, limpet shells, animal bone and two deer antler tines. The site has two decorated stone panels in the southern side of the chamber (Bradley 1998a).

From inside the passage, human remains (many of which were removed by Farrer), animal bone, and a few sherds of Grooved ware pottery were recovered (Childe 1952, 135). Three radiocarbon dates have been produced on human remains from Quoyness. The results show differences in ages, with MAMS-14921 (Sheridan *et al.* 2012) representing an individual who died earlier than the other two measurements. The results have been presented as representing a Phase of activity associated with use of the site for burial.

Maes Howe, Mainland

Maes Howe passage grave is located near the southeast end of the Loch of Harray at 20m OD, in proximity to Barnhouse, the Ness of Brodgar, and the Stones of Stenness and Ring of Brodgar. The site was excavated in 1861 by Farrer, by Childe in 1954–55 (Childe 1956), and the ditch and bank by Renfrew (Renfrew *et al.* 1976). More recent excavations by Richards in 1991–92 located the drain from an earlier building running out beneath the front platform, and a standing stone socket at the rear of the passage grave (Challands *et al.* 2005). Further investigations of the 'bank' and ditch revealed the former to have actually been a standing wall during the 3rd millennium cal BC (*ibid.*, 234–7). Material culture recovered from the chamber and cells

included human remains and animal bones, which are now lost. The site comprises a large earth mound, a stone-built central passage, square chamber, and three cells. A passage leads into a square chamber, which is defined at the corners by orthostats. Prior to excavation in 1861, the mound was between 28 to 30m diameter, and some 11m high (Davidson and Henshall 1989). Initially, the mound was described by a ditch and stone wall, the earliest construction of which was probably contemporary with the mound (see Childe 1956; Challands *et al.* 2005).

Renfrew's investigation of the ditch was explicitly designed to recover radiocarbon samples (Renfrew *et al.* 1976). Nine radiocarbon measurements were produced on samples of 'peat' or 'silty peat' through the ditch fills, and from underlying the passage grave bank (Renfrew *et al.* 1976; Renfrew 1979). The majority of the results come from the southern trench. These measurements were all produced by radiometric dating (rather than accelerator mass spectrometry), so the samples probably represent an 'averaged' radiocarbon content from the peat horizon. If the peat or silty peat sediment predominantly reflects the *in situ* products of plant humus decay, these measurements could provide robust estimates for the age of these horizons. Two results (Q-1482 and SRR-505) from the basal organic fill of the ditch from the north trench are statistically consistent, and probably provide the most robust results for the start of infilling the ditch, and *termini ante quos* for the excavation of the ditch. Renfrew *et al.* (1976) also produced a radiocarbon result (SRR-791) from peat underlying the bank, which was interpreted as the ground surface prior to the construction of the monument.

In the model presented here results from under the bank and ditch fill are included in a Sequence model (Fig. 10.12). An estimate (*ConstructMaesHoweEarthwork*) for the construction of the monument has been calculated to occur sometime after the peat (SRR-791) formed on the old ground surface underlying the bank, and before the ditches began infilling (sampled by Q-1482 and SRR-505 modelled using the R_Combine function); this is a slightly different treatment of the data than presented in Griffiths and Richards (2013).

Two results (Q-1481; SRR-524) from the basal organic deposit from the south trench are statistically inconsistent, and given the nature of the material we cannot present a very robust understanding of when infilling in this area began; these results have not been included in the model. The next result (SRR-523) in the ditch sequence is much younger than those overlying it, and has not been included in the model. The estimate (*ConstructMaesHoweEarthwork*; *3870–2600 cal BC 95% probability*; or *3730–2840 cal BC 68% probability*; Fig. 10.12) for the construction of the monument is necessarily imprecise.

10.3 Results and discussion

The overall model presented here includes results from Neolithic sites excavated in the *Cuween-Wideford Landscape Project*, early Neolithic timber and stalled houses from across Orkney, and Neolithic burial cairns with results from the 4th millennium. These sites have been analysed using the models outlined above, and as shown in Fig. 10.2. The model has good overall agreement between the prior information and the radiocarbon dates (A_{model}=87%). Using evidence from early Neolithic stalled stone houses and timber structures, and from chambered cairns, the Neolithic in Orkney began in *3730–3480 cal BC (95% probability)*, most probably in *3630–3510 cal BC (68% probability; Start OrkneyNeolithic*; Fig. 10.2; Table 10.3). The end of activity represented at these sites is estimated to have occurred in *1610–1400 cal BC (95% probability*; or *1530–1430 cal BC 68% probability; End EarlyHousesCairns*; Fig. 10.2); the sample presented here includes results from later phases of activity at several sites.

From the different site-specific elements of the models, a series of posterior density estimates for the first dated events associated with different types of site is presented in Table 10.2. Activity associated with the use of Neolithic timber houses in Orkney is estimated to have begun in *3520–3360 cal BC (95% probability*; or *3520–3480 cal BC 16% probability* or *3470–3390 cal BC 51% probability; FirstTimberStructure*; Fig. 10.13). The first estimate for the activity associated with a Neolithic stalled house suggests this occurred in *3520–3290 cal BC (95% probable*; or *3390–3310 cal BC 68% probable; FirstStalledHouse*; Fig. 10.13). The first activity associated with an Orkney-Cromarty chambered cairn is estimated to have occurred in *3640–3440 cal BC (95% probability*; or *3570–3470 cal BC 68% probability; FirstOrkney Cromarty*; Fig. 10.7–10.9). The first estimate for activity associated with a passage grave occurred in *3590–3340 cal BC (95% probability*; or *3510–3470 cal BC 14% probability* or *3450–3360 cal BC 55% probability; FirstMaesHoweStyle*; Fig. 10.10–10.11). An estimate for the first activity on 'house' sites, though not necessarily directly associated with structures, is

3640–3440 cal BC (95% probability; or *3570–3480 cal BC 68% probability; FirstHouseSite*; Fig. 10.5–10.6) (see discussion below).

There are a number of limitations associated with the available data presented in the model here. In many cases numbers of radiocarbon dates from individual sites are limited, and often without a good understanding of sample taphonomy or association. In these cases, this model cannot be used to estimate robustly the dates of the archaeological events of interest, such as the construction of a cairn or house. In several cases, due to the excavation techniques applied to a site, the use of the site in prehistory, or because of the preservation conditions at the site, dated samples are only associated with what probably represents later phases of activity, rather than the earliest use of sites. This appears to have been the case with several cairn sites. While in these cases the modelled estimates for the *end* of activity might be accurate, such models may under-estimate the antiquity of the earliest activity at these sites, and fail to sample the full duration of activity at these sites.

10.3.1 Neolithic settlement in the Bay of Firth

The density of occupation around Wideford Hill, and the apparent longevity of activity associated with different forms of house structures in this area is significant. People were repeatedly drawn to dwell on the lower hillsides overlooking the Bay of Firth, and to the eastern slopes of Wideford Hill if recent fieldwalking discoveries at Saverock by Christopher Gee represents settlement (see Fig. 1.6). These people also produced a range of styles of 'domestic' architecture. While the vertical stratigraphy of these sites does not appear to be comparable to, for example, that present at Skara Brae, the Ness of Brodgar or Muckquoy (Chapter 9), the density of structures in plan and the associated midden deposits demonstrate that this was a desirable or favoured location, and remained so for many years.

Using posterior density estimates produced from the model shown in Fig. 10.2, it is possible to estimate the duration of activity associated with different house structures from the Bay of Firth (Fig. 10.3–10.4). The first Neolithic house in the Bay of Firth probably dates to *3590–3310 cal BC (95% probability*; or *3500–3360 cal BC 68% probability; FirstBayOfFirthHouse*; Fig. 10.3–10.4), an estimate that derives from the parameter associated with the use of timber structure 3, Wideford Hill. The last dated event associated with houses included in the model here from the Bay of Firth dates

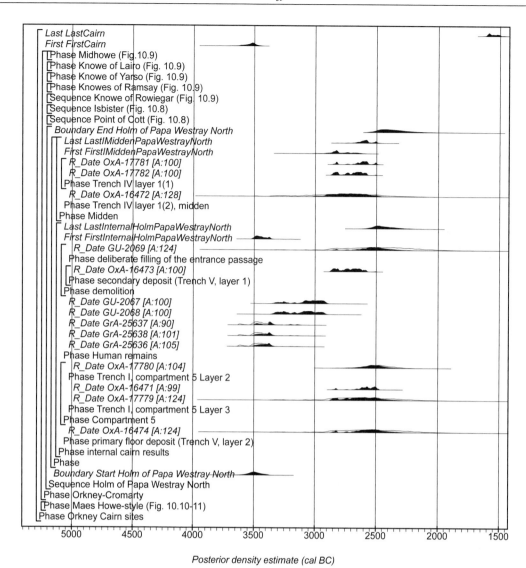

Figure 10.7 The first part of the Orkney-Cromarty cairn component of the model (see also Fig. 10.8 and Fig. 10.9). The overall model structures is shown in Fig. 10.2.

to *1920–1530 cal BC (95% probability; or 1880–1660 cal BC 68% probability; LastBayOfFirth*; Fig. 10.3–10.4).

Activity at house structures in the Bay of Firth, shown in Fig. 10.3–10.4 went on for *1460–1960 years (95% probability; or 1550–1800 years 68% probability; DurationBayOfFirthHouse*; no figure). This occupation might be regarded as sampling the whole of the duration of the Orcadian Neolithic, and beyond, and within this range we have a very limited understanding of the timing and tempo of house-lives, a picture that holds true for the rest of Orkney. As Schulting *et al.* (2010) noted, despite the density of Neolithic evidence we still have a relatively impoverished understanding of the development of occupation, both in the earliest regional Neolithic, and into the later regional Neolithic.

Timber Neolithic structures are only known from a few locations on Orkney. Of these, the full extent of some structures has not been uncovered (for example at Wideford), while some sites such as Brae of Smerquoy (Chapter 4) are still being excavated, and at others, such as at Green and Wideford Timber Structure 3, a very limited number of radiocarbon results has been produced. The identification of wooden post-built and discrete 'Neolithic' pit deposits (as might have been sampled at Links House, see below) is an important development in the understanding of different early Neolithic social practices. The impression that a *balanced* sample of the evidence from Neolithic of Orkney is available (Barclay 1996, 61) is not substantiated if it is accepted that a proportion of the earliest evidence is

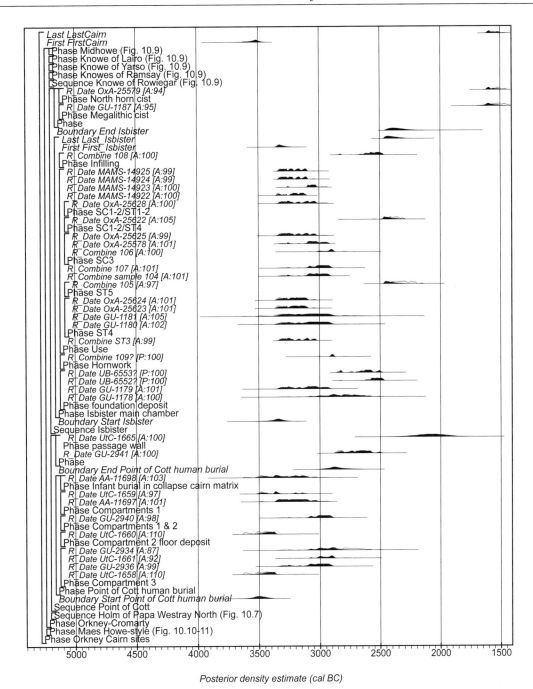

Figure 10.8 The second part of the Orkney-Cromarty cairn component of the model (see also Fig. 10.7 and Fig. 10.9). The overall model structures is shown in Fig. 10.2.

represented not by stone architecture, but by earthfast features.

At Wideford Hill, a result (SUERC-4862) on Timber Structure 3 is significantly earlier than the statistically consistent results on Timber Structure 1 (SUERC-4868, SUERC-4867, SUERC-4863 T'=2.3; T'5%=6.0; df=2). How representative this result is remains to be seen as dating material was not recovered for the full extent of

the structure. Moreover, Timber Structure 3 probably represents a palimpsest of postholes from at least two structures (see Chapter 2). Habitation at Green, Eday, produced an even earlier result (OxA-28984) from a timber structure, however, once again it is poorly understood in terms of its representativeness of activity associated with timber structures on the site. Evidence from two timber structures from Ha'Breck

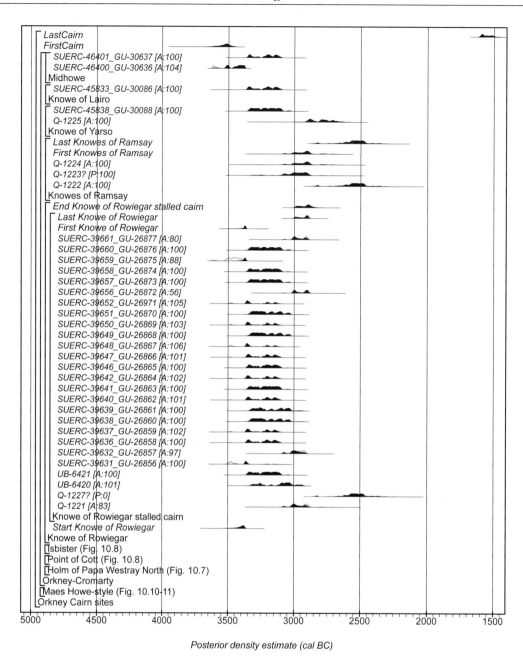

Posterior density estimate (cal BC)

Figure 10.9 The third part of the Orkney-Cromarty cairn component of the model (see also Fig. 10.7 and Fig. 10.9). The overall model structures is shown in Fig. 10.2.

(SUERC-35990 and SUERC-34503) suggests that these could have continued to be used on this site in the 33rd–32nd centuries cal BC, a pattern of later use of wooden architecture in Orkney which might be supported by the estimate for the end of activity associated with Timber Structure 1 on Wideford Hill.

Posterior density estimates from stone-built houses with stalled architecture suggest that the earliest evidence for these structures in Orkney occurs in the second half

of the 4th millennium cal BC. At Green, Knap of Howar House 2, and Ha'Breck House 3, it is possible that the structures were constructed before *c*.3300 cal BC. At a number of sites (Smerquoy phase 1, Stonehall Meadow, and the Knowes of Trotty), stone-built stalled houses could also have been constructed around this time, but the posteriors are insufficiently precise to allow a more detailed chronology. Activity associated with Stonehall Meadow stalled house began in *3490–3040 cal BC (95%*

probability; or *3390–3230 cal BC 60% probability; Start Stonehall Meadow;* Fig. 10.3). At Smerquoy, the earliest results were produced on midden deposits underlying the stone stalled house, from *3460–3120 cal BC (95% probability;* or *3390–3330 cal BC 24% probability* or *3260–3140 cal BC 44% probability; Start SM13;* Fig. 10.4). At the Knowes of Trotty the earliest activity, again associated with occupation evidence under the stone structure, in this case a pit, is dated to *3340–3120 cal BC (95% probability;* or *3280–3130 cal BC 68% probability; Start Knowes of Trotty;* Fig. 10.6). The phase of the site associated with occupation within the structure is dated to *3280–3110 cal BC (94% probability;* or *3230–3130 cal BC 68% probability; StartPhase2;* Fig. 10.6).

From the model presented here, it is more probable that the posterior density estimate associated with the first use of House 2 at the Knap of Howar occurred before the estimate produced here for the construction of House 1 at the Knap of Howar. The phasing of the Knap of Howar structures suggested that House 1 was built earlier than House 2 (Ritchie 1983, 52), but that the passage linking the two structures was an integral part of the design, and therefore that there could be little chronological gap in the construction. The earlier estimates for the earliest activity associated with House 2 (Fig. 10.6) could derive from earlier midden material redeposited on the floor of House 2 perhaps as part of the occupation. Alternatively it might be that subsequent to the house abandonment primary midden material was redeposited within the houses where walls had collapsed (cf. Ritchie 1983, 53). If we accept that the houses represented a relatively closely timed construction, the later estimate for the construction of House 1 might be most appropriate for both the structures.

The estimate for the start of phase 2 at the Knowes of Trotty, which is suggested as an estimate for the construction of the stalled stone house, appears later than much of the other estimates from the construction of stone-built stalled houses with the exception perhaps of the Smerquoy Hoose (Fig. 10.13). As noted above, however, occupation evidence underlying this structure indicates that the stone-built phase was not the earliest activity on this site.

The Smerquoy Hoose, with stone-built stalled architecture, has a relatively imprecise estimate for its construction. Within this rather bimodal distribution, it is possible that the construction could be associated either with an earlier 33rd century BC phase of activity, which would be akin to the timing of the first activity associated with the use of House 2 at the Knap of

Howar (though see discussion above). Alternatively, the later part of this estimate could be in keeping with the estimate for the start of phase 2 activity at the Knowes of Trotty associated with the construction of the stone-built stalled structure. We cannot revise the estimate for the Smerquoy Hoose further at the current time, and as discussed here, both the Knowes of Trotty estimates and the evidence from the Knap of Howar may include caveats in their interpretation.

Perhaps one of the most interesting aspects of the chronology of stone-built stalled houses is the evidence for later occupation at Smerquoy (Chapter 4). Here, radiocarbon dates revealed a much later phase of activity within the stone structure (at a higher level, and associated with discrete negative features) which began in *2470–1970 cal BC (95% probability;* or *2200–2020 cal BC 68% probability; Start SM13 Late;* Fig. 10.4), and ended in *1970–1600 cal BC (95% probability;* or *1940–1770 cal BC 68% probability; End SM13;* Fig. 10.4). These results emphasise that the Smerquoy Hoose would probably have been evident as a stone structure, or ruined feature, for a significant time after its first construction in the early Neolithic.

From the evidence presented here, it appears that both timber structures and stone-built stalled houses were constructed in Orkney in the second half of the 4th millennium cal BC. The radiocarbon date from Green is notable in potentially being earlier than the other timber structures, though there are insufficient results from this site to be able to assess whether this result is representative of the chronology of the earliest structures. At Ha'Breck, the available chronological evidence appears to suggest that timber structures could have been in use at the same time as stalled houses, though again here the small numbers of radiocarbon dates from timber structures introduces a degree of uncertainty.

Sub-square structures have been identified at Crossiecrown (Chapter 7) and Stonehall Farm House 1 (Chapter 6). Similar forms of structure may also represented by some of the activity at the Ness of Brodgar, Structure 1 at Tofts Ness, and possibly Structure 8 at the Links of Noltland. Evidence from Stonehall Farm House 1 (SUERC-5792) could be consistent with the start of this activity in the second half of the 4th millennium cal BC. However, the statistically consistent results from the Red House (House 1) at Crossiecrown (AA=51373; AA-51372; T'=1.3; T'5%=3.8; df=1) are much later, associated with activity in the middle of the 3rd millennium cal BC.

The very limited evidence associated with compartmentalized stone houses from the Bay of Firth (Stonehall Knoll House 3 and Wideford Hill Stonehouse 1) again cannot reveal chronological patterns in the use of such structures. It is of note that the structures at Stonehall Knoll and Wideford Hill, while in close geographical proximity, appear to represent activity of significantly different ages, though the association of samples from Stonehall Knoll may suggest that the chronology of this structure at least is not robustly understood. Equally, this is the third structure erected on the knoll and stratigraphically earlier postholes are present (see Chapter 5). Though the results from Wideford Hill appear to be more internally consistent, the small numbers of well-associated samples limit our understanding of the development of the site.

More convincing parallels with the use of Structure 1 at Stonehall Farm (AA-51371) may be found with the use of the atypical Structure 8 at Barnhouse. The result from Stonehall Farm (AA-51371) is statistically consistent with the three results from Structure 8 at Barnhouse (OxA-3763 4360±60 BP 3310–2880 cal BC 95% confidence; OxA-3764 4400±65 BP 3350–2890 cal BC 95% confidence; OxA-3765 4475±65 BP 3370–2910 cal BC 95% confidence; T'=4.2; T'5%=7.8; df=3). Later architectural changes witnessed in the Bay of Firth therefore appear to have been part of a series of developments across Mainland, Orkney. The 'atypical' 'Grobust' structure at the Links of Noltland appears to have been in use much later (GU-1692 3850±65 BP 2480–2130 cal BC 95% confidence; GU-1695 3750±100 BP 2470–1890 cal BC 95% confidence).

The discussion here emphasises one of the issues in assessing very limited data associated with types of houses, meaning that it is impossible to differentiate whether site types change over time and space – or both – or whether evidence from some areas is regionally atypical or more common. Arguably, tendencies to produce typologies risk abstracting narratives of change that might have represented hyper-local regional stories, as part of variable traditions across Orkney (Barclay 1996).

What is apparent from this discussion is that while the spectacular evidence from the Ness of Brodgar and Skara Brae demonstrates a very specific type of later Neolithic occupation, the Bay of Firth includes evidence for diverse and enduring occupation in a relatively circumscribed area. This exercise emphasises that while there has been considerable research dedicated to producing relative and scientific chronologies for Neolithic sites (*e.g.* Renfrew 1979; Ritchie 1990a, 51–52), the number of structures with sufficient, well-associated radiocarbon dates to

estimate key archaeological events are few. The evidence for significantly later activity within the Smerquoy Hoose indicates that at least some of the stone-built structures in this area were returned to. Re-use of structures, together with a limited radiocarbon sample, could account for the apparent variability in age of activity associated with different forms of house architecture. As noted in a different context by Richards (2005c, 2), we are still in the situation where the 'type' of site provides the dominant archaeological narrative, rather than having achieved a chronological framework that is sufficiently robust to allow emphasis on local trajectories of change, traditions or practices.

The reuse of Smerquoy, and the density of occupation activity in the Bay of Firth over a considerable period of time suggest that while the deep vertical deposits of midden apparent from other Neolithic sites on Mainland, for example at Skara Brae and the Ness of Brodgar, are not apparent here, space – or perhaps better *place* – was at a premium. Over a very long period people returned here, constructed and perhaps reused a range of house types.

10.3.2 Chambered cairns

From the model developed here, a number of interesting aspects of the data for chambered cairns are apparent. An overall estimate for the first dated event associated with Orkney-Cromarty cairns is *3640–3440 cal BC (95%* probability; or *3570–3470 cal BC 68% probability; FirstOrkney Cromarty*; Fig. 10.16). Though the overall sample size is limited, the estimates for the start of activity associated with stalled cairns from the Point of Cott (*3620–3390 cal BC 95% probability;* or *3550–3440 cal BC 68% probability; Start Point of Cott Human burial;* Fig. 10.14) and the Holm of Papa Westray North (*3610–3370 cal BC 95% probability;* or *3550–3430 cal BC 68% probability; Start Holm of Papa Westray North*; Fig. 10.14) are similar. This might indicate that these two sites provide the best currently available estimates for activity associated with Orkney-Cromarty cairns across the archipelago. Alternatively, the proximity of these sites could indicate a highly local tradition and timing associated with cairn building on Papa Westray and Westray. The current evidence for the main phases of these sites (see Table 10.2), indicates that each one, and most probably both, came into use in the second half of the 36th–first three quarters of the 35th centuries cal BC.

The evidence we have indicates that activity at the Knowe of Rowiegar began in *3500–3360 cal BC (95%*

probability), most probably in *3420–3360 cal BC (68% probability; Start Knowe of Rowiegar;* Fig. 10.14). It is highly probable (*92%*) that the start estimated for activity at the Knowe of Rowiegar (*Start Knowe of Rowiegar;* Fig. 10.14) occurred after the start of activity at the Point of Cott (*Start Point of Cott Human burial;* Fig. 10.14), and highly probable (*88%*) that activity at Rowiegar also occurred after activity began at the Holm of Papa Westray North (*Start Holm of Papa Westray North;* Fig. 10.14). The temporal and spatial similarities between the estimates for the start of the human bone assemblage of the Point of Cott and the Holm of Papa Westray suggest that these could have been related processes.

The rest of the data associated with the use of Orkney-Cromarty chambered cairns shows marked variability in the timing of activity. It is notable that at many of the chambered cairns, as at the Knowe of Ramsay and Knowe of Yarso, Rousay, results produced on animal bone indicate much later activity, which might be indicative of reuse, or that the monuments were open for some time, rather than providing estimates for the primary construction and use of the monuments (cf. Schulting *et al.* 2010). At the Holm of Papa Westray North, where more radiocarbon dates exist than for the Knowe of Ramsay, Knowe of Yarso, Knowe of Lairo and Midhowe, animal bone samples represent activity later than the oldest human remains at the site. The duration of the primary phase of use of these sites, or their subsequent reuse, cannot be established because of the relatively limited numbers of samples from these structures. Recent results produced from Rowiegar suggest that at least some stalled cairns might have been the focus of considerable later activity; at Rowiegar activity appears to have gone on for *360–560 years (95% probability; 370–500 years 68% probability; DurationRowiegar;* no figure). Unfortunately, considerable disturbance at the site prior to its excavation means that a more precise chronology of the site cannot be achieved (Curtis and Hutchison 2013). Of the different forms of Orkney-Cromarty cairns, no 'Bookan'-type sites (a very nebulous category) have produced radiocarbon dates for this sample, and only one 'tripartite' cairn, the Knowe of Lairo, is represented, and this site saw considerable reconstruction. From the available data, this small sample means that we cannot identify evidence for chronological development in these supposed 'types' of structure.

Of the chronological samples from passage graves, Quanterness is interesting in providing a posterior density estimate that is precise, and importantly earlier than any other estimate for the start of activity at such a site

on Orkney, with the possible exception of Maes Howe. The start of activity at Quanterness is here estimated as occurring in *3560–3340 cal BC (95% probability; or 3450–3350 cal BC 61% probability; Start main use Quanterness;* Fig. 10.10). The estimate for the first dated event associated with the main phase of use of the Quanterness passage grave is significantly earlier than the next reasonably precisely dated estimates for activity associated with passage graves from the islands, at Quoyness (*3340–3090 cal BC 95% probability or 3330–3210 cal BC 48% probability,* or *3180–3150 10% probability,* or *3130–3100 10% probability; First Quoyness;* Fig. 10.11), and Pierowall Quarry (*3120–2600 cal BC 95% probability; or 2940–2680 cal BC 68% probability; Start Pierowall Quarry;* Fig. 10.11). The results from Pierowall are best understood as *termini ante quos* for construction of the use of the first monument, and it is unclear how representative of the duration of use the available data from Quoyness are. The chronology of Maes Howe could be consistent with the early range from Quanterness, but this estimate is so imprecise as to make comparison with other passage graves of limited use.

For Quanterness, Schulting *et al.* (2010, 18; Table 10.2) noted the inconsistency of the recorded stratigraphy of parent units with the age of radiocarbon samples from these units. They note the potential for considerable longevity of practice at Quanterness, which they suggest makes the site one of the longer-lived funerary monuments in Neolithic Britain (Schulting *et al.* 2010, 29). Cooney *et al.* (2011, 657) have noted the limited evidence from passage grave sites that can be presented as associated with the *use* of these structures.

For Ireland, as well as the Mound of the Hostages at Tara, Knowth (Cooney *et al.* 2011), and the recent results commissioned from Carrowmore (Berg and Hensey 2013), Cooney *et al.* (2011, 657) suggest that results from Newgrange (GrN-5462-C 4425±45 BP 3340–2910 cal BC 95% confidence; GrN-5463 4415±40 BP 3330–2910 cal BC 95% confidence), from Carrowmore 51 (Ua-11581 4625±60 BP 3630–3120 cal BC 95% confidence) and from Carrowmore 56 (Ua-10735 4495±80 BP 3500–2910 cal BC 95% confidence; Ua-10736 4525±80 BP 3510–2920 cal BC 95% confidence; Ua-10737 4620±70 BP 3630–3100 cal BC 95% confidence; Ua-4487 4395±65 BP 3340–2890 cal BC 95% confidence; Ua-4488 4480±75 BP 3490–2910 cal BC 95% confidence) may date the use of Irish passage grave examples. In addition, Schulting *et al.* (2012) present recent results produced on skeletal remains from Millin Bay and Ballynattay, sites which they define as having passage-grave affiliations. These results are not discussed here.

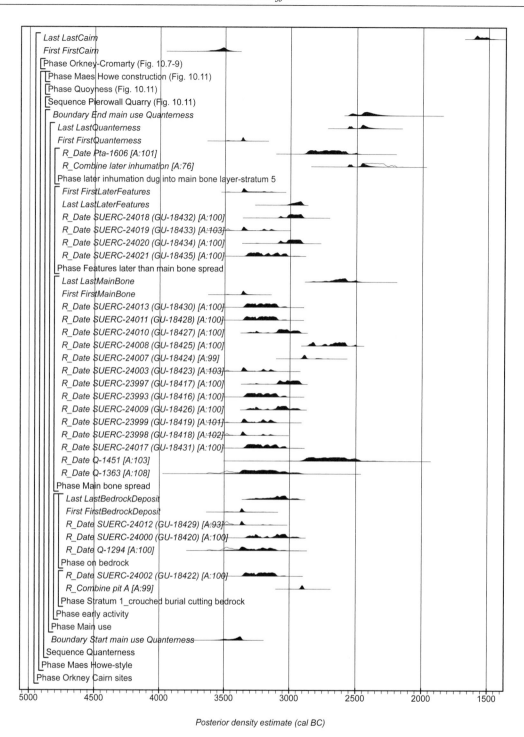

Figure 10.10 The first part of the passage grave (Maes Howe-type) component of the model (see also Fig. 10.11). The overall model structures is shown in Fig. 10.2.

The models for the Mound of the Hostages at Tara (Cooney *et al.* 2011, 651, Fig. 12.47), the Carrowmore recent results (Berg and Hensey 2013), and the model for the construction of Bryn Celli Ddu (Burrow 2010) have been reprogrammed in OxCal v4.2, and calculated using IntCal13 (Reimer *et al.* 2013), and key posterior density estimates from these models are shown in Fig. 10.15. The shortlife results from Carrowmore 56, which may be associated with the use of the structure (Cooney *et al.* 2011, 657) have been analysed using a Phase model

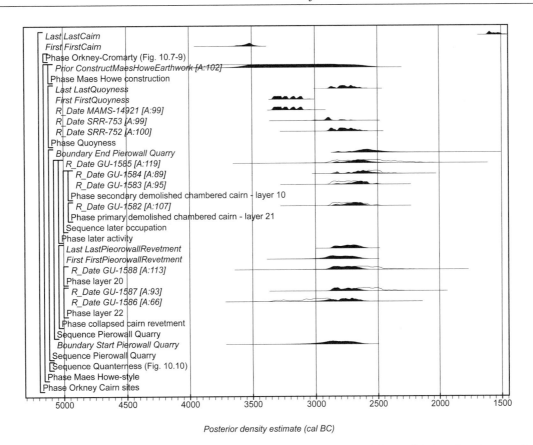

Figure 10.11 *The second part of the passage grave (Maes Howe-type) component of the model (see also Fig. 10.10). The overall model structures is shown in Fig. 10.2.*

defined by Boundary parameters shown in Fig. 10.15 (model not shown). A result from Bryn yr Hen Bobl on human bone (OxA-12742 4441±34 BP 3340–2920 cal BC 95% confidence) produced by Rick Schulting and cited in Burrow (2010) may date the use of this monument.

Comparison of the Quanterness posteriors with the recently published Carrowmore results (Bergh and Hensey 2013), demonstrates that Quanterness is not out of keeping with these County Sligo sites. It is highly probable (*98% probable*) that the estimate for the start of activity at Carrowmore 3 (*Start Carrowmore3*; Fig. 10.15) occurred before the estimate for the start of activity at Quanterness (*Start main use Quanterness*; Fig. 10.15). These results could be consistent with a suggestion (*e.g.* Sheridan 2014; Schulting *et al.* 2010, 39–41) that the design of the Orcadian passage graves had been influenced by, or even copied from, passage graves in Ireland, as part of a strategy of competitive conspicuous consumption by their builders (see also Richards 2013c). Importantly for the discussion here, results shown in Fig. 10.15 emphasise, as the stratigraphy suggests, that the

estimate from Pierowall probably under-samples early activity associated with the passage grave. The evidence from Quoyness is less clear, as the estimate for the first dated activity at this site (*FirstQuoyness*) could be in keeping with other evidence for passage grave use. This estimate is earlier than that for the construction of the monument at Bryn Celli Ddu (*construction of grave*; Fig. 10.15).

Later again are the results produced on animal bones from Cuween Hill, a passage grave overlooking the Bay of Firth (Chapter 8). The excavation of this site in 1888 (Charleson 1902) recovered numerous animal bones from the main chamber, and human and animal bones from the side cells. A lower fill in the main chamber contained human and dog bones, including 24 dog skulls. Three statistically consistent radiocarbon dates (SUERC-4847 4010±35 BP 2620–2460 cal BC 95% confidence; SUERC-4848 3965±40 BP 2580–2340 cal BC 95% confidence; SUERC-4849 4025±40 BP 2840–2460 cal BC; T'=1.2; T'5%=6.0; df=2; Fig. 10.15) on dog bones recovered from the lower fill of the chamber are probably *termini ante quos* for the construction of the monument.

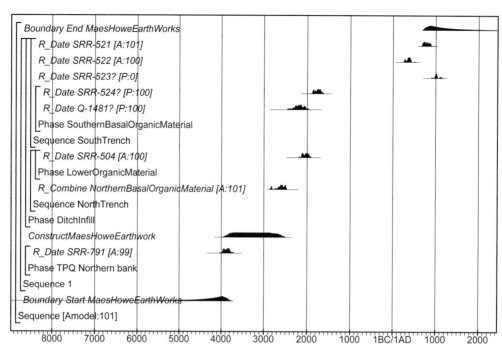

Figure 10.12 A model for radiocarbon results from Maes Howe sampled by Renfrew (et al. 1976). For each radiocarbon result included in the model as an active likelihood two ranges have been plotted. The ranges in outline represent the calibrated radiocarbon results, the solid distributions represent the posterior density estimates – the outputs from the Bayesian statistical model illustrated in the figure. Results not included in the model as active likelihoods are indicated in the figures with a '?' after the laboratory code. An estimate for the construction of the earthwork has been produced from the model.

A human femur (UB-6422 3668±36 BP 2200–1940 cal BC 95% confidence) from the entrance passage post-dates the use of the chamber stratigraphically, and is chronologically significantly later again. These results have not been included in the analysis here, because of the data selection criteria outlined above.

Comparison of the calibrated radiocarbon results from Cuween Hill with the results for the *end* of activity at Quanterness demonstrate that the activity represented by the Cuween samples probably pre-dated the last evidence from Quanterness (Fig. 10.15). Indeed, the end of activity at Quanterness (*2570–2280 cal BC 95% probability; or 2550–2510 cal BC 11% probability or 2470–2280 cal BC 57% probability; End main use Quanterness;* Fig. 10.10) could well be part of the same traditions sampled by the available radiocarbon results from Cuween. It could therefore be that rather than the activity at Quanterness representing very long, continuous rites, the later evidence from the site represents subsequent revisitation as part of a different series of traditions, which was related to the deposition of the dog-rich lower fill of the main chamber at Cuween as part of allied secondary activity at passage

graves in the Bay of Firth. Given the evidence for much earlier activity at Quanterness it seems that the activity as represented by the radiocarbon samples from Cuween are not associated with its primary use.

10.4 Other evidence for early Neolithic activity

10.4.1 Varme Dale early cereals

Two Bronze Age barrows, which form part of the cemetery at Varme Dale (see Chapter 9), Evie, Mainland (Fig. 1.6), were excavated as part of *Orkney Barrows Project* directed by Jane Downes. Mound 2 had been constructed over a series of burnt deposits (Downes pers. comm. 2014). *Salix* sp. charcoal samples from two of these deposits (contexts [2041 and 2027]) produced statistically consistent radiocarbon results (AA-53158 4875±45 BP 3750–3530 cal BC 95% confidence; AA-53157 4890±40 BP 3760–3630 cal BC 95% confidence; T'=0.1; T'5%=3.8; df=1; Fig. 10.13). A weighted mean taken prior to calibration using the intercept method produces the calibrated range of 3710–3630 cal BC (95% confidence) or 3700–3640 (68% confidence;

Fig. 10.13). Both these contexts produced significant quantities and ranges of species of charred cereals for early Neolithic Orkney (cf. Bishop *et al.* 2009, 63–65). Context [2027] (AA-53157) produced around 100 grains, including wheat and barley identified to various levels, and individual grains of rye, oat, and three grains of flax. Similar quantities and species were recovered from context [2041].

These burnt deposits may reflect a single archaeological burning 'event', which occurred before a topsoil formed, and subsequently was sealed by the barrow. While the grains themselves were not used for the radiocarbon measurements, the nature of the deposits, and the consistency of the measurements suggest these results might be robust estimates for the age of the cereal assemblage.

10.4.2 Late Mesolithic presence? Links House, Stronsay

There is a paucity of evidence for Mesolithic activity in Orkney, and the region has been regarded as having little potential for Mesolithic archaeology (Ritchie and Ritchie 1981). Largely because of the perceived limited evidence for such activity, Mesolithic material culture has been suggested to have been present on 'Neolithic sites' as 'the survival of old-fashioned ideas' (Ritchie 1995, 20). Surface collection in the last 15 years has located Mesolithic material (Wickham-Jones and Firth 2000; Cantley 2005; Richards 2005a, 11–14), and a review of the available Orkney evidence has occurred (Saville 2000), while microliths were recovered from the body of a Bronze Age mound at Long Howe, Tankerness (Wickham Jones and Downes 2007). A charred hazel nutshell from the mound at Long Howe produced a radiocarbon date (SUERC-15587 7900±35 BP 7030–6640 cal BC 95% confidence), but this cannot be robustly associated with diagnostic Mesolithic activity.

The limited evidence from across the islands can be contrasted with the recent work at Links House, Stronsay. The site is located on the east side of Stronsay, a couple of hundred meters west of the coast at Mill Bay. Work at the site was targeted on a discrete lithic scatter, and excavation occurred in response to ongoing threat from ploughing. A series of test pits and trenches excavated over several seasons recovered a large Mesolithic lithic assemblage in association with groups of negative features, including timber structures (Lee and Woodman 2009a). The lithic assemblage is blade based, utilising small beach and till flint nodules. A range of lithics – points, obliquely blunted points, awls, microliths, blades,

backed blades, and tanged points – has been recovered, which led the excavators to suggest that the site was the focus of activity from the early Mesolithic (indicated by the presence of tanged points) to the Mesolithic-Neolithic transition (Lee and Woodward 2009a, 32). However, the excavators are at pains to note that this activity was probably not continuous (Lee pers. comm. 2014) and post-excavation activity is on-going. A series of early radiocarbon results from the site are in keeping with that from Long Howe, while three others represent much later activity.

The later results from the site comprise three statistically consistent (T'=0.9; T'5%=6.0; df=2) radiocarbon dates (SUERC-24023 5080±35 BP 3970–3780 cal BC 95% confidence; SUERC-24027 5110±35 BP 3980–3790 cal BC 95% confidence; SUERC-24028 5065±35 BP 3970–3770 cal BC 95% confidence; Fig. 10.13), which were produced on *Salix* sp. charcoal from a pit associated with group 1 features. A weighted mean taken prior to calibration using the intercept method produces the calibrated range of 3970–3790 cal BC (95% confidence) or 3960–3800 (68% confidence; Fig. 10.13).

Links House represents an important development in Orcadian prehistoric studies, as it demonstrates the survival of discrete negative features associated with extensive early prehistoric activity. The nature of this early 4th millennium cal BC activity is far from clear, as diagnostic Mesolithic or Neolithic material culture has not been identified from the feature. The chronology of the earlier results from the site also raises an interesting set of implications for the start of the Neolithic in Orkney.

10.4.3 The evidence for the earliest Neolithic in Orkney

The dates from Varme Dale probably represent the earliest diagnostic Neolithic evidence that is currently available from Orkney (Fig. 10.16). It is *100% probable* that the weighted mean on the two Varme Dale results occurred before the estimate for the first event associated with other first Neolithic settlement evidence (*FirstHouseSite*). It is *100% probable* that the first event associated with the use of chambered cairns (*FirstOrkney Cromarty*) occurred after the first event associated with the Varme Dale results. The earliest evidence from structures (*FirstTimberStructure* and *FirstStalledHouse*) occur later than the first occupation at these sites (*FirstHouseSite*; Fig. 10.16); it is *90% probable* the *FirstHouseSite* occurred before *FirstTimberStructure*. It is *96% probable* that *FirstHouseSite* occurred before *FirstStalledHouse*.

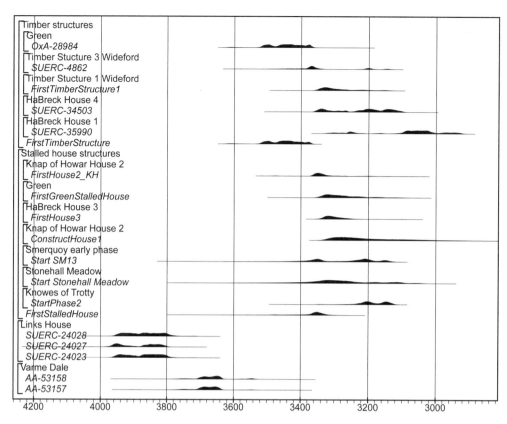

Figure 10.13 Posterior density estimates associated with early Neolithic timber structures and stone-built stalled houses from Wideford Hill, Ha'Breck, the Knap of Howar, Smerquoy, Stonehall Meadow and the Knowes of Trotty calculated in the model sub-sections shown in Fig. 10.3–6. Calibrated radiocarbon dates from the later activity from Links House, and the results from Varme Dale are also shown; these results are given in the text.

At the same time, we are unable probabilistically to order the first estimates for the use of Orkney-Cromarty cairns and the first evidence of any form of activity from settlement sites; it is *51% probable* that *FirstHouseSite* occurred before *FirstOrkney Cromarty* (Fig. 10.16). The evidence from all the activity at settlement sites and from Orkney-Cromarty cairns suggest that this activity could have occurred over a closely related timeframe.

In several cases detailed here, as at Green and Ha'Breck, the earliest radiocarbon dates from the site do not derive from the structures. At other sites, such as the Knowes of Trotty, and at the Knap of Howar House 1, evidence for early Neolithic structures built on top of midden deposits indicates that these did not represent the earliest occupation activity on the sites. At these sites therefore the nature of the earliest occupation activity is poorly understood, and the earliest Neolithic occupation evidence on such sites might pre-date activity indicated from radiocarbon dates from these structures.

The differences between the current estimate for the start of the Orkney Neolithic derived from the analysis presented here (parameter *Start OrkneyNeolithic*; Fig. 10.2) and the weighted mean of the three later results from Links House is estimated as *80–380 years (95% probability)* or *180–320 years (68% probability; LinksHouse_Neolithic*; Fig. 10.17). The estimate for the difference between the weighted mean associated with the Varme Dale cereals and the first evidence for timber structures (*FirstTimberStructure*; Fig. 10.13) is *120–330 years (95% probability;* or *170–280 years 68% probability; VarmeDale_Structure*; Fig. 10.17). The difference between the earliest evidence from house sites with evidence of structures (*FirstHouseSite*; Fig. 10.3–10.6) and the Varme Dale weighted mean is *20–240 years (95% probability)* most probably or *100–200 years (68% probability; VarmeDale_Settlement*; Fig. 10.17). These estimates may suggest how much the model presented here for early Neolithic houses and cairns under-estimates the antiquity of the earliest Orkney Neolithic.

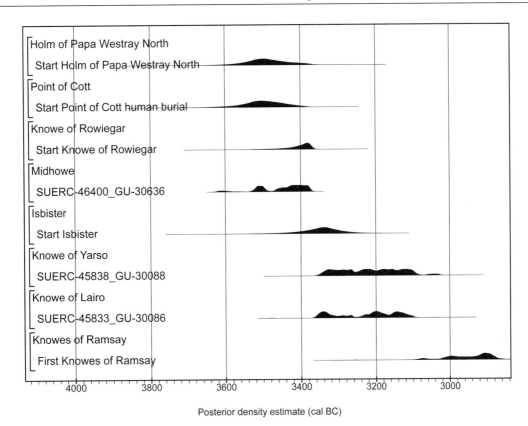

Figure 10.14 Posterior density estimates associated with start of activity from early Neolithic Orkney-Cromarty cairns at Holm of Papa Westray North, Point of Cott, Knowe of Rowiegar, Midhowe, Isbister, the Knowe of Yarso, the Knowe of Lairo and the Knowes of Ramsay. These posterior density estimates have been calculated in the model sub-sections shown in Fig. 10.7–9.

In early Neolithic Orkney, domesticated plant (and possibly animal) resources therefore may have predated the current evidence for the first appearance of timber structures and stone-built stalled houses. Such a scenario would have implications for the nature of the role of early domesticates in the first appearance of Neolithic lifeways in Orkney (cf. Cooney *et al.* 2011). It is possible that in Orkney cereals were part of the introduction of domesticates as a component of the transportation of portable Neolithic material culture and lifeways (see for example, Sheridan 2014), as well as perhaps timber structures and practices which involved digging earthfast features. This would have included the introduction of domesticated animals, and resurrects arguments about the introduction of animal resources to Orkney and the movement of human populations (Sharples 2000, 112).

The late dates from the pit feature at Links House could also support such a scenario. The late dates from Links House appear to represent people living much later on at a 'Mesolithic' site, and engaged in activities including the digging of small pits. In other parts of the country, such activity would be more in keeping with early 'Neolithic' traditions. In this scenario the presence of late dates at Links House might actually represent activity associated with novel Neolithic lifeways, but without, in this context, diagnostic early Neolithic material culture. The tantalising evidence from Links House might therefore support the view that emphasis on both stone-built 'early' and 'late' Neolithic structures may not quite acknowledge the full range of 4th millennium practices in Orkney. Excluding the uncertain nature of the Links Howe activity, the presence of late 5th or 4th millennium Mesolithic populations on Orkney does not currently appear substantiated by the available chronological evidence. While evidence from Links House (Lee pers. comm. 2014), and suggestions from Long Howe, indicate the presence of much earlier Mesolithic groups, this leaves open the possibility that if the early 4th millennium presence at Links House represents Neolithic activity, the Orkney Isles represented a landscape 'empty at least of human settlement' (Ritchie 1990a, 37).

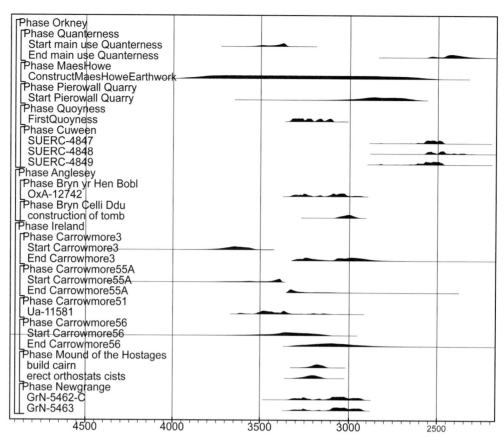

Posterior density estimate/calibrated radiocarbon date (cal BC)

Figure 10.15. Posterior density estimates associated with passage graves from Quanterness, Maes Howe, Pierowall and Quoyness calculated in the model subsections shown in Fig. 10.9–10. Posterior density estimates from Carrowmore 3 (Berg and Hensey 2013, Carrowmore 55A (Berg and Hensey 2013), the Mound of the Hostages (Cooney et al. 2011), Bryn Celli Ddu (Burrow 2010) have been recalculated from models cited in the text. Boundary parameter estimates for the start and end of activity associated with the use of Carrowmore 56 have been calculated from results described in the text (Ua-10735; Ua-10736; Ua-10737; Ua-4487; Ua-4488), modelled in a Phase (model not shown).

The wider context of the early Neolithic in Scotland has been most recently outlined by Whittle *et al.* (2011, 808–33). As with the current case in Orkney, this sample is necessarily contingent on the history of research and practice in the study region, defined by the authors as a 'grab' sample of data from Scotland south of the Great Glen. In this sample, an estimate for the start of Neolithic activity is provided by the modelling of radiocarbon dates associated with northern carinated bowls, cereals and ground stone axes, and results from Neolithic monuments (long barrows, rectilinear mortuary enclosures, chambered cairns, non-megalithic round mounds and linear constructions) and rectilinear timber halls (Whittle *et al.* 2011, 822).

This analysis suggests that the Neolithic in southern Scotland began in *3835–3760 cal BC (95% probability; 3815–3535 cal BC 68% probability; start S Scotland;* Whittle *et al.* 2011, 822), while the early Neolithic of north-east Scotland is estimated to have begun in *3950–3765 cal BC (95% probability; 3865–3780 cal BC 68% probability; start NE Scotland;* Whittle *et al.* 2011, 824; Fig. 10.16). The distributions in Fig. 10.16 emphasise a potential connection between the timing of the activity at Links House and the start of the Neolithic in mainland Scotland. The Links House results could be closely chronologically related to the timing of the start of Neolithic practices in mainland Scotland, but are earlier than the available evidence for Neolithic activity in Orkney.

Importantly for the Orkney discussion presented here,

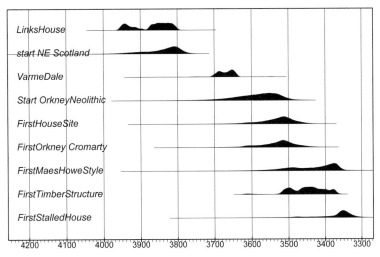

Posterior density estimate/calibrated radiocarbon date (cal BC)

Figure 10.16 A comparison of posterior density estimates calculated in the model shown in Fig. 10.2 (FirstMaesHoweStyle; FirstOrkney Cromarty; Start OrkneyNeolithic). Estimates for the first dated event associated with timber structures (FirstTimberStructure) and a stone-built stalled houses (FirstStalledHouse) from Neolithic Orkney calculated in Fig. 10.13 are also shown. The distributions shown for Varme Dale (VarmeDale) and Links House (LinksHouse) are weighted means of the radiocarbon dates from these sites taken prior to calibration; these results are described in the text. A posterior density estimate for the start of Neolithic activity in the north east Mainland Scotland from Whittle et al. (2011, 824; Start NE Scotland) is also shown.

long barrows and timber halls in Scotland appear to have been relatively short-lived, ending in the first half of the 37th century cal BC (Whittle *et al.* 2011, 833). If the earliest Neolithic activity in Orkney included relatively short-lived sites such as timber structures, pits and early midden or burnt deposits, the currently available evidence might well under-sample and under-estimate the timing of this activity. The similarities of the estimates for the start of the Neolithic in northeast Scotland and the latest activity at Links House, leaves open the possibility that the timing of the earliest Orcadian Neolithic might be much more in keeping with changes and processes happening, most probably in the 39th or 38th centuries cal BC, on the nearby Scottish mainland.

10.5 Conclusion

Limited evidence for Mesolithic presence (though see Wickham-Jones 1994, Fig. 47, 74; Lee and Woodward 2009a) has arguably meant that, for Orkney, one of the 'great leaps forward', 'revolutions', or 'climaxes' (Renfrew 1990, 248) in prehistory has been shifted from the Mesolithic-Neolithic transition to the 'revolution' from early Neolithic activity to later Neolithic activity. Arguably, the imposition of dramatic revolutions in the archaeological

record, which might not be demonstrated by chronological evidence, promotes the quest for 'moments' of transition (cf. Schulting 2000; Brophy 2004), which might not usefully add to the discourse. The sequential development from groups with relatively limited early Neolithic things to groups with lots of conspicuous later Neolithic things, has been glossed in terms of developments in 'complexity' (Richards 2005c, 37), with evidence for superimposition of Grooved ware over round-based early Neolithic pottery at Pool, on Sanday (MacSween 1992; Hunter *et al.* 2007), and Rinyo, on Rousay (Childe 1952, 136), perhaps appearing to underline a directional change (*e.g.* Renfrew 1979, 206).

Discussions emphasising other parts of Britain (Sheridan 2010; Thomas 2008; 2013; Whittle *et al.* 2011) have centred on the role of robust chronologies as the means to readdress what otherwise had appeared as 'synchronous' changes in material culture and types of site, and contribute more nuanced, regionally-specific narratives. Currently the available chronological evidence from Orkney does not allow this kind of precision. A degree of restraint should perhaps be encouraged (cf. Richards 1998; Card 2005), both because the scientific chronology outlined here is necessarily provisional, and because simplistic linear models of change across a highly

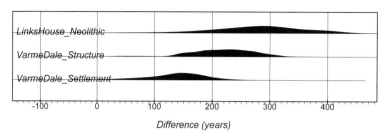

Figure 10.17 A comparison of posterior density estimates calculated in the model shown in Fig. 10.2 (FirstMaesHoweStyle; FirstOrkney Cromarty; Start OrkneyNeolithic). Estimates for the first dated event associated with timber structures (FirstTimberStructure) and a stone-built stalled houses (FirstStalledHouse) from Neolithic Orkney calculated in Fig. 10.13 are also shown. The distributions shown for Varme Dale (VarmeDale) and Links House (LinksHouse) are weighted means of the radiocarbon dates from these sites taken prior to calibration; these results are described in the text. A posterior density estimate for the start of Neolithic activity in the north east Mainland Scotland from Whittle et al. (2011, 824; Start NE Scotland) is also shown.

divergent island archipelago may be inappropriate (cf. Richards 1998).

The nature of the Orkney material record (Parker Pearson and Richards 1994; Cummings and Pannett 2005) offers a continual challenge to differentiate between exceptional processes, people, places and times, and the exceptional preservation of these remains. This said, the spatial scale and concentration of evidence for Neolithic activity over relatively small areas, for example in the Bay of Firth, mean that it is appealing to argue that quite distinct processes and emphases were being played out. Taken together, we are presented with a record, which while perhaps not quite distinctly different from other parts of Britain, for example in the emphasis on the manipulation and use of midden deposits (for example Beamish 2009; Allen 2005), is markedly regional. This is not to argue for insularity or distinction from mainland Scotland, as evidenced from similarities in stalled cairns in Caithness (Davidson and Henshall 1989), but could suggest a unique set of processes (see Richards 2013c)

which still require contextualizing with reference to wider changes occurring in mainland Britain and Ireland, and in terms of different rates of timing and tempo across Orkney in the Neolithic.

Inherent in the early–late Neolithic chrono-typological schemes which until recently have been employed might also contribute to a latent emphasis on disjuncture in the types of lifeways that are envisaged. Within the 'early' Neolithic complex of round-based ceramics, Orkney-Cromarty cairns and stalled houses, and the 'later' Neolithic Grooved ware and passage graves, it might be increasingly more appropriate to recognise '...some tombs [and houses] exhibiting features from both styles of architecture' (Card 2005, 47), not least for example in the recently identified inscribed 'horned spiral' stone from the Smerquoy Hoose. The evidence presented here might not be sufficient to present a simple chronological pattern for development and change in Neolithic Orkney, but it might also indicate a distinct set of traditions which are not well served by frameworks of 'late' or 'early' 'Neolithics'.

CHAPTER ELEVEN

Prehistoric Pottery from Sites within the Bay of Firth: Stonehall, Crossiecrown, Wideford Hill, Brae of Smerquoy, Muckquoy, Ramberry and Knowes of Trotty

Andrew Meirion Jones, Richard Jones, Gemma Tully, Lara Maritan, Anna Mukherjee, Richard Evershed, Ann MacSween, Colin Richards and Roy Towers

11.1 Introduction

Andrew Meirion Jones and Richard Jones

This substantial chapter presents the pottery derived from excavations within the Cuween-Wideford Project and associated fieldwork undertaken between 1994 and 2013. During the first phase of research, between 1994 and 2003, the Neolithic settlements at Stonehall (Chapters 5 and 6), Crossiecrown (Chapter 7) and Wideford Hill (Chapter 2) were excavated, producing ceramic assemblages of variable size which are presented in 11.2, 11.3 and 11.4 respectively. Stonehall is a multi-period site with spatially discrete components; Stonehall Knoll, Meadow and Farm. As a conglomerated settlement, Stonehall was founded in the mid to late 4th millennium cal BC, and displays a sequence running from early Neolithic neutral/plain round-based bowls dating to *c*.3300–3000 cal BC, through to a large Grooved ware component associated with the late Neolithic nucleated settlement at Stonehall Farm (some 2000 sherds in total). Crossiecrown is likewise a multi-period settlement, with a sequence that includes small components of early Neolithic neutral/plain round-based bowls and Unstan Ware, much Grooved Ware (associated with the main periods of occupation including the Red and Grey Houses) and ending with small numbers of Beaker vessels (>2000 sherds in total). At this site the earliest dates are from the midden deposits – *c*.3000–2800 cal. BC – and

habitation continues through to the latest settlement at *c*.1900 cal. BC. In some senses Wideford Hill dating to the mid–late 4th millennium cal BC has the simplest assemblage being composed entirely of early Neolithic neutral/plain bowls and Unstan Ware (an estimated 318 vessels in total).

This initial phase of work deliberately combined study of the pottery with programmes of clay materials prospection, experimental work and petrographic analysis. Such a holistic approach was adopted to provide a necessary background for interpreting some of the more technical aspects of pottery production at all three sites. The prospection and experimental work was also designed to challenge some of the traditional, often well-entrenched views about pottery making, to offer fresh viewpoints on the 'life cycle' of vessels. Finally, our work included an educational aspect, encouraging students participating in the project to consider the excavated pottery from several viewpoints. Section 11.5 is based on Jones and Brown's (2000) account of that prospection and experimental work, and the following section, 11.6, is devoted to a detailed petrographic study undertaken in Glasgow in 2000 by Lara Maritan of selected pottery from Stonehall and Crossiecrown. This report supplements the petrographic data presented by other authors elsewhere in this chapter and by David Williams (1976; 1979; 1982). Maritan also experimented with using the measurement of magnetic susceptibility of sherds as a means of determining non-destructively and quickly whether they contained magmatic inclusions. In 2004 it fortunately became possible to include Stonehall, Crossiecrown and Wideford Hill in a large study of organic residues extracted from British Neolithic pottery, particularly Grooved ware, which was carried out by Anna Mukherjee and Richard Evershed at Bristol (Mukherjee *et al.* 2008). Their results are reported in section 11.7.

The final component of this chapter presents the pottery from a number of other sites that have formed part of the overall project. These pottery assemblages are small but welcome in giving either time depth or extending the project's spatial range. The excavations in 2005 of two small, adjacent sites at Ramberry Head, very close to Crossiecrown (see Chapter 8), yielded a small pottery assemblage (see Section 11.8). Investigations at Smerquoy (Chapter 4), not far from and probably contemporary with Wideford, and pick-up survey and excavation at Muckquoy, Redland, in 2013 produced pottery which is included in section 11.9. Finally, the pottery found at the Knowes of Trotty, which was introduced in Chapter 3, is reported in section 11.10. Section 11.11 provides a synthesis of the pottery from the Bay of Firth sites.

Collectively, these assemblages offer a unique opportunity to investigate the role and function of pottery at several settlement locations within a *single* well-defined area of Mainland Orkney: as a function of time from the early Neolithic to the early Bronze Age, and on an inter-site comparative basis. These assemblages allow a fresh look at several issues that are still central to Neolithic pottery studies in Orkney, if not beyond, for instance, the transition from round-based bowls characteristic of the earlier Neolithic to flat-based pottery, the chronological development of the latter and its relationship with Beaker pottery, and the relationship between settlement and mortuary pottery. Finally, until now, the picture of Orcadian Grooved ware has been largely constructed on the basis of finds from sites spatially well distributed across the Islands of Orkney from Skara Brae to those more recently published such as Barnhouse, Pool and Links of Noltland. In the process of comparing aspects of pot shape and decoration at these sites, similarities and contrasts have been noted and explanations proposed. But this task of exploring variation in shape and decorative motif can now be extended beyond intra-site analysis to inter-site

comparisons at a regional level. For example, can we infer communication between contemporary settlements in the Bay of Firth area on the basis of similar decorative Grooved ware motifs? Is there any sense of a Bay of Firth style Grooved ware, that of a repertoire of shared motifs?

For Grooved ware, on which so much has been written (*e.g.* Cleal and MacSween 1999; Thomas 1999, 113–25; A. M. Jones 2005a), the starting point for this chapter draws on the recent work in Orkney which emphasises that the attributes of vessel shape, function, decoration and fabric reflect the complex combination of 'signatures': the personal (in the form of the potter and later the user), the household, the group of households and the community. These signatures in turn reflect identity, on the one hand the sense of shared identity, on the other the sense of individual identity and thus of difference, for instance, Thomas' (1997, 117) 'objectification of difference'. As MacSween (in press) notes, 'at any one time, ideas were being exchanged, absorbed and translated. Local communities being introduced to Grooved ware could choose to ignore it, adopt it, or modify it'.

Study of the pottery reported here has proceeded along similar lines to the extent that the main features of each site assemblage can be suitably compared. But beyond that, the approaches taken at Stonehall, Crossiecrown and Wideford Hill reflect the demands of each assemblage as much as the priorities that the two authors have identified. A further common starting point is that as the traditional labels such as 'Grooved ware' and 'Beaker' are no longer rigid categories, so the alternative of viewing Neolithic-early Bronze Age pottery as the products of a pottery 'tradition', each one carrying a set of recognisable attributes, becomes more attractive and realistic. One of those attributes is technology which should be considered as a series of socially motivated practices within a spectrum of technological choices (*e.g.* A. M. Jones 2007, 122-40). As illustrated in the analysis of the Crossiecrown assemblage (section 11.3), each pottery 'tradition' may best be viewed as the manifestation of an evolving series of technological choices. In the reports that follow, the technological characteristics of pottery will generally be given primacy over prescriptive descriptions of ceramic traditions as a means of alleviating or side-stepping the fixed and bounded categories of traditional analyses. As regards Smerquoy and Muckuoy where excavations are currently on-going, the reports on the pottery are at the 'work in progress' level.

11.2 Stonehall

Richard Jones

11.2.1 Introduction

The three loci at Stonehall produced plentiful pottery. On the Knoll and in the Meadow it is essentially of early Neolithic type, consistently comprising undecorated round-based vessels and no decorated Unstan ware. At Stonehall Farm it is predominantly late Neolithic Grooved ware, which is present in greater amount than the combined assemblage on the Knoll and in the Meadow.

The pottery is fragmentary since much of it was recovered in midden and related deposits; there are no whole pots and only a few instances of sherds found together that formed part of, but no more than half, a vessel. As for their condition, there are examples of large, well-fired sherds, as well as many small friable fragments and others that are highly abraded. Macroscopically, the fabric can be described as medium coarse to coarse in the sense that inclusions are usually visible, common to abundant in quantity and poorly sorted. There are examples of fine-textured clay with few small inclusions visible to the naked eye – the clay balls are the best example – but much more commonly there are clays of varying texture containing rock inclusions ranging considerably in frequency, size and colour. Fine white mica is commonly visible.

11.2.2 Methodology

Study of the pottery proceeded in several stages. Basic recording, largely carried out by David Sneddon, was followed by identification of the diagnostic sherds for further examination. As with the Crossiecrown and Wideford Hill assemblages, all sherds were laid out according to context to look for associations, a process which helped build up groups of sherds, each group forming potentially a single vessel; in ten such cases (six from the Knoll (Trench C) and four from the Meadow (Trench Z)) they were sent to the National Museum in Edinburgh where Belén Cobo del Arco was able to undertake partial restoration. Sherds from the three loci were then selected for petrographic and organic residue analyses (sections 11.6 and 11.7 respectively).

Assessment of the fabric proved difficult to make on visual grounds for the reasons which have just been alluded to, exacerbated by the frequent lack of a fresh break on the sherds. In this situation of an apparent continuum of fabric appearance, it proved preferable to combine the routinely determined description of fabric in terms of its macroscopically visible attributes of general appearance, texture and colour with the fuller, more objective petrographic descriptions as presented in section 11.6. The estimations of inclusion density which were part of that petrographic study are included in this section (Fig. 11.2.7). The correspondence between the respective definitions of fabric at the macro and micro levels was uneven across the assemblage as a whole. At Stonehall Meadow (Trench A) fabric categories were somewhat more discernible macroscopically than usual and a few individual sherds with visually distinctive characteristics were present, yet these categories did not necessarily translate into petrographically distinct groupings.

The chemical and mineralogical compositions of some pottery and clays found near Stonehall are reported in section 11.5. Using a Thermo-Niton XL3 hand-held X-ray fluorescence instrument, non-destructive analyses were made of a small number of sherds from Stonehall Farm (Trench B) with a view to differentiating chemically the fabric and residue compositions. Exploratory non-destructive analyses of the clay balls by FTIR used a A2 Technologies Exoscan instrument to try and determine their thermal history (Rein, Higgins and Leung 2011).

11.2.3 Characterisation of the assemblage

The pottery is presented according to its findspot and chronological attribution. Here it is worth mentioning that the Stonehall Farm assemblage is dominated by Grooved ware. Yet, radiocarbon dates from Structure 1 and the underlying midden (see Chapters 6 and 10) suggest that initially this site is contemporary with both Stonehall Knoll and Meadow. It is argued that only from the turn of the 3rd millennium cal BC that Stonehall Farm becomes the main focus of settlement. Equally, it is from this point that the midden begins to build up giving rise to the broad settlement mound.

11.2.3.1 Stonehall Knoll (Trench C)

There were 405 individual small find entries recovered from Stonehall Knoll, making up *c.*1500 sherds of different sizes, and a total weight of *c.*9.1 kg. With the exception of one clay ball fragment (SF 8039 in [4006]), all were sherds.

Distribution and associations

The main concentration of pottery occurs in the downslope midden (Fig. 5.32b). More specifically, the pottery is found in contexts as follows:

Table 11.2.1 Associations of sherds on Stonehall Knoll.

Associated with House	Context	SF
	400	**870**, 871, 876, 919
	402	1758
	403	2842
	419	1673
	427	1622
	428	1546, 1800
	431	1549, 1570, 1580b
	1002	**2300**
	1008	**2303, 2360, 2384, 2314**, 2491, 2499
	1017	**2430**
	1018	**2436**
3	4009	8040, 8042, 8052, 8058, 8061, 8065
3	4032	8014

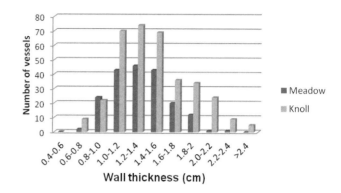

Figure 11.2.1 Wall thickness (cm) in all sherds from Stonehall Knoll and Meadow.

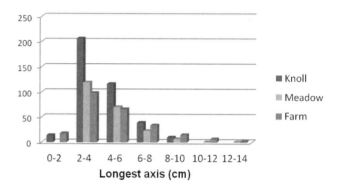

Figure 11.2.2 Longest axis (cm) in all sherds from Stonehall Knoll, Meadow and Farm.

- Mainly Period 3 associated midden but some Period 2 midden [427, 428 and 431] and Structures [429 and 430] (4.6 kg)
- Spreads forming [1001] and [1008] in Period 3 associated midden, and Layer [1058] (3.4 kg)
- Layer context [4006] in Period 2 House 3

Several individual small finds comprised more than ten sherds, and they tended to concentrate in the contexts listed in Table 11.2.1 with the larger vessels being highlighted in bold (Table 11.2.1).

It is notable the way the larger pots concentrate in the higher midden/occupation debris spread of [1017] which runs downslope to the east. Association rates are high: 91 out of 194 Small Finds (*i.e.* 47%) in the [400] context series have associations, in the [1000] series 74 out of 155 (48%), and in the [4000] series 27 out of 48 (56%). There is a particular series of associations among small finds *within* the [400] series (SF 1549 [431] with SF 1551 [431], SF 1706 [450], SF 1749 [428] and SF 1622 [427]), and *between* the [400] and [1000] context series (SF 2322 [1002] with SF 2344 [1012], SF 915 [400], SF 942 [400], SF 1803 [453], SF 938 [400], SF 1748 [446], SF 2372 [1002], SF 2493 [1068], SF 2345 [1012], SF 2374 [1008], SF 2499 [1008], SF 1673 [419], SF 1676 [419]. However, most of the associations occur *within* a context and concern only three or four sherds. There appear to be very few cases of associations between widely spatially separated contexts.

Wall thickness

The overall distribution of wall thickness at the Knoll shows a broad peak in the 1.0–1.6cm range with a slow tail to higher values (Fig. 11.2.1). Within that distribution there may be distinctions, for example between the pottery in the [400] and [1000] context series; the former has a bimodal distribution, one in the 1.0–1.6cm range joined by one of presumably larger vessels at 1.8–2.2cm.

Sherd size

As judged by longest axis, the most common sherd size is 2–4cm, followed by the 4–6cm range (Fig. 11.2.2). Such a distribution of sizes, which in outline is also observed elsewhere at Stonehall, reflects a breakage pattern of vessels which have been deposited as refuse in midden or spread and then probably trampled, irrespective of vessel size.

Diagnostic sherds

1. Rims

There is significant variation among the rim shapes from different vessels, and even some variation within a given vessel, a point which should caution in favour of a simple classification. The main observation to be made

Table 11.2.2 Rims from Stonehall Knoll, those in italics are illustrated in Fig. 11.2.5.

SF (context)	Description	Wall thickness (cm)	Rim diameter (cm)
852 [400]	Three conjoining sherds of flat plain rim. Abraded; sooting and residue on exterior; medium coarse fabric, occasional large, angular inclusions.	1.2	18
870 [400]	Flat everted rim and body sherds; slight sooting along axis of upper part of rim; abraded; medium coarse fabric, occasional large inclusions. Cf. Wideford SF 579 and 870	1.9	35
875 [400]	Round plain rim; sooted exterior; fine fabric with several mainly dark inclusions not exceeding 0.2cm in size. Cf. Knap of Howar period I: 1-8.	0.7	
1562 [431]	Inward sloping	1.4	30
1622 [427]	Round plain	1.8	
1749 [428]	Flat plain	1.1	24
1801 [428]	Flat plain rim. Heavy sooting on exterior and rim. Abraded interior, Medium coarse fabric, several large inclusions.	1.3	20
2303 [1008]	Flat plain	2	
2308 [1008]	Inward sloping rim with internal lip; fire scorching running along rim axis; some sooting on exterior; poorly finished exterior surface. Coarse fabric.	2.1	23
2310 [1008]	Flat plain rim. Abraded; no sooting. Coarse, oxidised fabric. Knap of Howar Period II: ?70.	1.2	12
2314 [1008]	Almost half of neutral bowl with plain round rim. Some sooting on upper exterior and rim top; abraded interior. Very prominent angular siltstone inclusions on interior surface; some residue in lower interior.	1.7	16
2321 [1002]	Inward sloping rim. Thick sooting on exterior and rim. Coarse fabric, frequent large inclusions.	1.6	22
2340 [1017]	(Almost) flat plain rim. Sooting on exterior and on rim top. Abraded interior. Coarse fabric, frequent large inclusions.	1.8	
2358 [1001]	Flat top, everted lip	*1.6*	34
2360 [1008]	Large section of neutral bowl with broad inward sloping rim. Abraded exterior; prominent sooting on outer rim top and upper exterior; crudely finished; residue in lower interior. Coarse fabric. Cf. Wideford SF 579 and 815	1.8	30
2373 [1008]	Round plain rim; sooting on exterior, rim top and extending to upper interior. Medium fabric, frequent large dark inclusions. Cf. Knap of Howar Period II: 69	1.4	22
2378 [?]	Small everted rim; sooted; residue on exterior and rim top; abraded. Fine fabric.	0.9	18
2384 [1008]	Round plain	2.2	28
2430 [1017]	Flat plain	1.8	
2801 [1008]	Medium sized inward sloping rim of large vessel with internal lip. Almost no sooting on exterior or rim; distinct striation marks on successfully smoothed exterior; abraded interior. Fine fabric with occasional siltstone inclusions.	*1.5*	31
2802 [1008]	Round plain	0.8	
2838 [1058]	Inward sloping	1.2	21
2874 [1058]	Broad flat plain rim. Slight sooting on exterior. Medium coarse fabric with occasional large angular inclusions.	2.0	26
2878 [1058]	Inward sloping	1.2	22
2895 [1002]	Flat plain rim. Sooting in and out; coarsely finished fabric. Coarse chunky fabric.	1.2	25
8064 [1058]	Flat with external lip, heavily sooted on exterior and most of rim top. Like U6, smoothing marks on exterior. Medium coarse fabric.	1.0	24
Unstrat. 6	Medium-size flat everted rim, heavily sooted on exterior and along of axis of part of rim; abraded interior; few finishing/smoothing marks on exterior. Coarse fabric.	1.7	28

from Table 11.2.2 is that the most common rim shapes are Plain and Inward Sloping, that is with interior bevel, and their associated variants. The Inward Sloping rim is unusual at the Wideford Hill settlement.

In Figure 11.2.3, the 20–24cm rim diameter range is the mode, followed by 24–28cm and 28–32cm. This gives the impression of two overlapping size distributions, one perhaps at 20–24cm, and the other at 28–32cm. A plot of rim diameter against wall thickness reveals a continuous spectrum of vessel sizes, blurring any distinction between small, medium and large vessels, and furthermore, there is no apparent correlation between

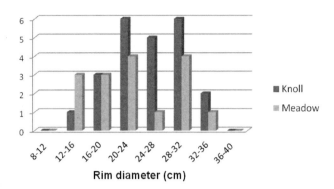

Figure 11.2.3 Rim diameter (cm) in all sherds from Stonehall Knoll and Meadow.

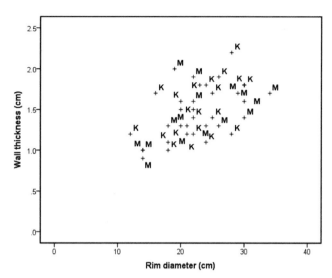

Figure 11.2.4 Plot of rim diameter against wall thickness for rims at Stonehall Knoll (K) and Stonehall Meadow (M).

rim shape and vessel size. When the corresponding data from Stonehall Meadow is added, the picture improves in that some correlation between rim diameter and wall thickness becomes visible (Fig. 11.2.4).

Rounded bases

A number of single sherds having a combination of distinct curvature and larger than average thickness were identified as likely base sherds (*e.g.* SFs 823, 1606, 1622, 1820, 2304, 2356, 2366, 2372, 2430, 4.1, 4.2). In the case of multiple sherds bearing these same two features the identification was much more confident than in the corresponding case with single sherds (*e.g.* SFs 1603, 2300, 2314, 2343, 2360, 2384, 2426, 842 and 8026). Although the thickness of the bases was typically 2cm or more, one exception was SF 2314 representing the single vessel with a complete profile, (see Fig. 11.2.5). The experience here is salutary as the thickness increases from the rim (1.5cm) to the start of the base (1.8cm) and then decreases to nearer 1.5cm at the base itself.

Decoration

Apart from one sherd with a possible stab design (SF U2) and another, SF 8025, with a possible raised knob or lug, there are no instances of decoration. SF 8025 is problematic, however, as it can be alternatively interpreted as a badly formed base which in turn would suggest a later Neolithic date.

Abrasion

A majority of sherds have abraded surfaces which vary considerably in their extent. Spatial or other patterning of the abrasion is not evident.

Construction and surface treatment

There are no definite examples that show construction detail. Smoothing of the outer surface is quite common and certainly more frequent than burnishing, of which there are only a few instances (*e.g.* SFs 1680, 1760, 2801 and 8032).

Use wear

Sooting occurs on both the exterior surface of vessels, particularly towards the rim (SFs 826, 822, 870, 888, 1599, 1624, 2314, 2321, 2496, 2497, 8040, 1736, 1008, 8055, 8064, 8069, 8127, U4, U6), and the interior surface (SFs 870, 913, 915, 947, 1599, 1606, 1727, 2300, 2338, 2349, 2430b, 2899, 2901, 8047, 8053, 8055, 8069, 8131, 4.3). An example of a vessel with light sooting on the top 5cm of the exterior is SF 2314 which has a complete profile. Two vessels (SFs 870 and 2308) are notable in having a fire scorch line running along the rim axis. Carbonised residue is present on the exterior surface of sherds (SFs 852, 2373, 2401, 80310. However, as expected, residue is more frequent on the interior surface of sherds.

Fabric

Macroscopically, the fabric, which in general resembles that from elsewhere at Stonehall, can be classed as coarse. There is some correlation between texture and sherd thickness, as many of the thicker sherds appear to have a coarser texture. Distinctive or unusual fabrics are few: SF 1855 has a fine fabric, as does the clay ball fragment (SF 8039). A few sherds, including SF 905, appear to

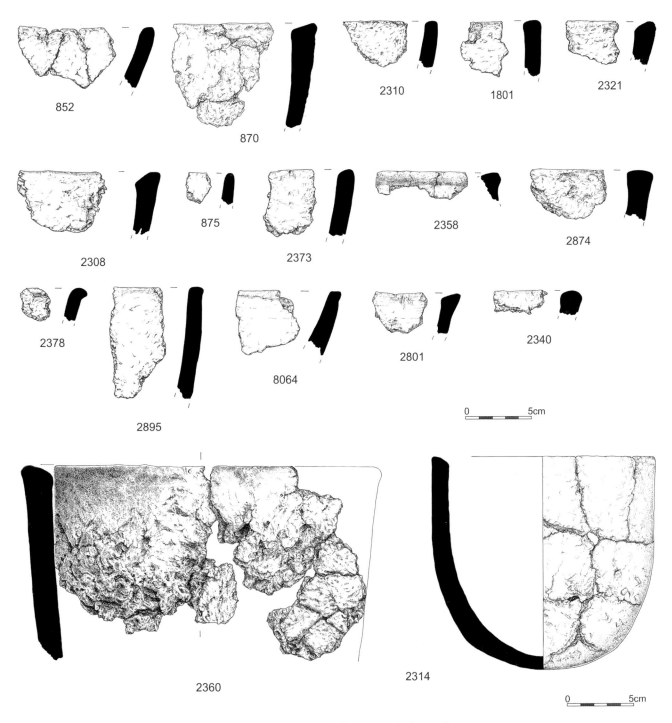

Figure 11.2.5 Sherds from Stonehall Knoll.

the eye to have a shelly fabric. As the petrographic study in section 11.6 shows, there is one predominant group containing sandstone and siltstone as major inclusion types; weathered igneous rock fragments are also present in two samples, one of which may also contain shell although this was not identified in the petrographic study

(Table 11.2.3). The distribution of inclusions according to their quantity lies in the 20–60% range (Fig. 11.2.6).

11.2.3.2 Stonehall Meadow (Trenches A and Z)
The two trenches at Stonehall Meadow, respectively excavated at the beginning and end of the project's

Table 11.2.3 Petrographic groups in pottery from Stonehall Knoll.

Petrographic group	SF No.
Sedimentary	819, 906, 911, 914, 917, 936, 1533, 1537, 1603, 1622, 1655, 1673, 1699, 1708, 1709, 1725, 1726, 1742, 2343, 2360, 2384, 2430, 2499, 2877
Igneous + Sedimentary	836 (with shell?), 848, 1230

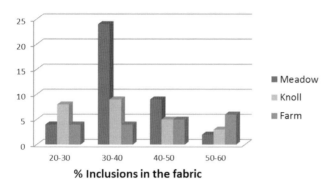

Figure 11.2.6 Percentage of the fabric made up by inclusions in all sherds from Stonehall Knoll, Meadow and Farm, based on data from Table 11.6.1.

Table 11.2.4 Associations of individual sherds from Stonehall Meadow (Trench A) (* indicates SFs each with more than ten individual sherds).

Context	SF
2	25, ?65, 85
2	31, 68, 86 and 94
2	67, 75, 1206
2	20, 21, 27
2 and 27	1207, 1276
4, 2	28, 61, 1221
34, 54	1242, 1251
2, 4, 29	14*, 49, 44, 1229, 1216
4, 3	29, 168*, 169*
2, 30, 34	1227, 1230*, 1237*
2, 30	56, 1240
2	64*, 1203, 1238
2, 27	1257, 1268, 1282
27	1258, 1269, 1263
27	1273, 1279

duration, are spatially separated by the ditch that runs through the site (see Fig. 5.3). As explained in Chapter 5, they form a coherent unit of earlier Neolithic date and thus are considered together in this section. There are about 125 Small Finds of pottery in Trench A (400 sherds in all), eight of which comprise more than ten sherds, weighing *c*.3.25 kg, and the corresponding figures for Trench Z are 111 Small Finds, 26 of them having more than ten sherds (*c*.820 sherds in total) weighing 10.5 kg. Arising directly from these figures, it is apparent that Trench Z sherds are larger in size and less abraded than those in Trench A, an observation that is directly attributable to the poor state of preservation of the deposits and structural remains in the latter due to the agricultural activity in the field.

Distribution and Associations
Within the broad spatial distribution of sherds in Trench A (Fig. 5.50c) associations are found, occurring mostly within the ash midden [2] and between [002], [027], [030] and [034] (Table 11.2.4).

In Trench Z sherds concentrate on the one hand to the south, less to the north, on entry into the house (from the east) and on the other at the back of the house (Fig. 5.49c). Dominant sherd groups are SFs 7064, 7094, 7101, 7160, 7177 and 7202, each with more than thirty

sherds, and of these SFs 7101 and 7177 go together (Table 11.2.5). Furthermore, there are no less than 24 Small Finds each with more than ten sherds (SFs 7047, 7049, 7064, 7065, 7093, 7096, 7101, 7102, 7107, 7112, 7119, 7123, 7128, 7134, 7141, 7143, 7144, 7145, 7146, 7151, 7160, 7177, 7200 and 7202). But despite this welcome situation of several concentrated deposits of pottery, it proved very difficult to make substantial joins (with the notable exception of SF 7064) and thereby restore much of the shape.

Wall thickness
Collectively, the wall thickness distribution in Trench A (Fig. 11.2.1) shows a clear peak at 1–1.2cm but with a long tail at greater thickness, not exceeding 2cm. There is nothing less than 0.8cm thickness. As discussed below, it was possible to isolate macroscopically two broad, overlapping fabric groups: coarse and medium-coarse. For the latter fabric group the majority lie in the 1–1.2cm thickness range, while the coarser fabrics have a wider range of thickness. In Trench Z the mode, which lies between 1.2 and 1.6cm, is significantly higher than those

Table 11.2.5 Associations of individual sherds from Stonehall Meadow (Trench Z).

Location	Context	SF No.	Comment
Front of house	3003, 3039	7097, 7154, 7185, 7091	
	3003, 3008, 3017, 3039	7143, 7126, 7119, 7093, 7142, 7118, 7165, 7066, ?7144, 7032	Large group
	3003	7177, 7044, 7101	Distinctive siltstone inclusions in SF 7177
	3003	7096, 7103, ?7060	
Back of the house	3031	7094, 7123	SF 7094 is probably one vessel despite variation, for example in rim fragments: one decorated fragment joining an undecorated rim
	3003, 3041, 3050	7105, 7106, 7169	Possible link with SF 7094
	3001, 3051	7151, 7161, 7156	Possible link with SF 7094
	3003	7128, 7140	
	3003, 3041? 3048, 3050	7111, 7194, 7191, 7189, 7110	
	3039	7112, 7145	

in Trenches A and C. The thickness values, showing a sharp drop between the 1.4–1.6 and 1.6–1.8cm ranges (Fig. 11.2.1), hints at a complex, composite distribution.

Sherd size
Using the values obtained for the *largest* sherd in each Small Find in Trench A, irrespective of the number of sherds in the Small Find, there is a peak in the 2–4cm range with a fair proportion in the 4–6cm range. The high end of the distribution is made up of the large sherds belonging to the eight Small Finds with multiple sherds, but overall the sherds in this trench have been subject to deposition giving rise to smaller sizes than is the case in Trenches C and Z; this may be due to greater trampling as well to the general condition of the house already alluded to. 47% of sherds in Trench Z have a longest axis in the 2–4cm range, falling to 37% in the 4–6cm range, the corresponding figures for Trench A being 68% and 21% and 54% and 30% for Trench C.

Diagnostic sherds
1. Rims
Although only nine in number in Trench A, the rims can be assigned to the shape categories identified in Trench C, albeit with the same caveat that the categories are not 'watertight' (Fig.11.2.7a, b; Table 11.2.6). The presence of an everted lip on the broad rim in SF 1227 and SF 1237 is indicative of Unstan ware, yet in the absence of the lip they would be placed in the Flat Plain group. In Trench Z the 28 rims are typologically quite diverse but not greatly dissimilar to those in Trench A (Table 11.2.6). Combining the rims from both trenches, the thickness

varies quite widely with the 1.0–1.2cm range being the mode, and at least two vessel sizes are hinted in the rim diameter distribution (Fig. 11.2.3).

2. Bases
To the four round bases in Trench Z (SFs 7032, 7045, 7064c and 7156) with their wall thickness ranging up to 2.3cm (SF 7032) and five probable bases (SFs 7038, 7123, 7128, 7177 and 7198) are two likely round bases (SFs 66 and 168) in Trench A. From that same trench there are a few sherds close to the base because they thicken significantly, in the case of SF 1232 from 1.1 to 1.6cm. There is notable curvature in SFs 48, 56, 63, 86, 94, 168, 1231, 1242, and 1257.

3. Decoration
The single decorated sherd in Trench A, SF 42, with a circular finger impression, has possible counterparts in Trench Z: SF 7047 and SF 7094b (the finger impression giving a dimpling effect). Faint incision or impression marks are evident on SFs 7047, 7065, 7140 and 7154, but these are unlikely to be deliberate decoration. There is a bore hole in SF 7172 and a possible one on SF 7111. The presence of Grooved ware in Trench Z, albeit in very small amount, is indicated by the occurrence on SF 7151 of a 1cm wide band on the surface where a raised band was probably attached; SFs 7118 and 7184 also exhibit slight evidence for a raised band.

Abrasion
This is common, more so in Trench A than Trench Z; in the former only 18 out of 126 SFs (14%) have no or slight abrasion, while the corresponding figure for the

Table 11.2.6 Pottery from Stonehall Meadow, Trenches A and Z, (illustrated rims appear in italics).

SF [context]	Description	Thickness (cm)	Rim diameter (cm)
Trench A			
42 [002]	Body sherd with finger impressed dimple (clay pressured downwards) on sooted exterior; inner surface largely abraded. Grey core; medium coarse fabric, few angular inclusions.		
43 [002]	Inward sloping rim	1.7	34
44 [002]	Inward sloping rim; some sooting on exterior towards but not on the rim. Oxidised interior. Coarse fabric, large dark angular inclusions	1.4	22
86a–c [002]	Round bases of small vessels; smoothed exterior; no residue or sooting; coarse dark fabric, plentiful large dark inclusions. Flat Plain rim	1.4	30
95 [002]	Flat plain rim with interior lip; sooting on exterior, rim top and interior of body sherd; dark core. Coarse fabric, very large dark angular inclusions and sandstone fragments.	1.5	24
168 [003]	Three round bases from two vessels. Illustrated base has coarse dark fabric with angular inclusions, well fired; some abrasion; smoothing marks on interior and exterior. Slight sooting on exterior.		
1227 [002]	Inward sloping and everted rim; some resemblance with Wideford SF 203 and 428. Some sooting on exterior of sherd and on rim. Dark coarse fabric, mainly small dark inclusions.	2.0	
1237a [034]	Thick everted rim with well-formed ridge on exterior lip. Sooted in and out, Dark coarse fabric, medium sized dark inclusions; slight striation marks on rim top.	2.0	30
1237b [034]	Large b/s, not from the same pot as 1237a; some pitting on exterior surface from burnt out organic inclusions; sooting on interior only. Coarse fabric, frequent large mainly dark inclusions. Raised horizontal band on (upper) body.		
Trench Z			
7030 [3008]	Small plain inward sloping rim; some sooting in and out; dark core. Coarse fabric, frequent dark angular inclusions.	0.7	
7045 [3005]	Flat top rim, slight exterior lip	1.4	
7047 [3003]	Rim with exterior lip, sloping inward	1.5	
7055 [3003]	Thin, inward sloping rim of small vessel; cf. Knap of Howar Period II; body has sooting in and out; carbonised residue in interior; crudely finished exterior with some visible smoothing marks. Coarse fabric, frequent large inclusions.	0.7	18
7064a [3031]	Flat top, club-like rim; some resemblance with Wideford SF 636 and 682.	2.0	30
7064c [3031]	Three conjoining base sherds; carbonised residue on much of interior; almost no sooting on exterior; oxidised core. Coarse fabric, frequent dark angular inclusions.		
7064d [3031]	Plain with exterior lip	1.5	36
7093a [3008]	Flat top, club like rim	1.6	36
7093b [3008]	Flat top, club-like rim; heavy sooting on interior of body, less so on rim and exterior; coarse fabric with medium-sized inclusions.	1.9	22
7094a [3031]	Flat top, club-like rim ; heavy sooting on exterior and outer half of rim top; dark core; coarse fabric, frequent dark angular inclusions.	2.0	30
7094b [3031]	Flat top rim with two small dimples just below it	1.7	
7104 [3003]	Round plain, slightly everted rim ; sooting on exterior and carbonised residue in interior; rim clean; dark core; medium coarse fabric.	0.9	14
7111 [3048]	Flat broad plain rim; very slight interior bevel.	1.5	20
7118 [3003]	Inward sloping with interior and exterior lips	1.3	
7123 [3031]	Broad flat, slight inward sloping rim. Dimple immediately below exterior rim cf *7094b* and *42* (Trench A). Sooted exterior and outer half of rim top, but not interior; much carbonised residue in interior. Coarse fabric, frequent mainly dark inclusions.	1.9	
7133 [3003]	Inward sloping, slightly everted rim; sooting in and out; dark core. Fine fabric, occasional large dark inclusions. Abraded interior.	1.3	
7141 [3039]	Broad, inward sloping rim; sooting throughout, especially on exterior abraded interior; medium coarse fabric, frequent medium sized mainly dark inclusions.	1.5	30
7146 [3030]	Flat top rim	1.3	26
7154 [3003]	Inward sloping rim with exterior lip; cf. Knapp of Howar Period I: 67a. No sooting, oxidised in and out; crudely finished exterior with some visible striations marks. Distinct fine orange fabric, occasional large inclusions.	0.9	14
7186 [3050]	Plain round rim	1.1	22
7196 [3030]	Flat top rim, inward lip slightly everted	1.7	29

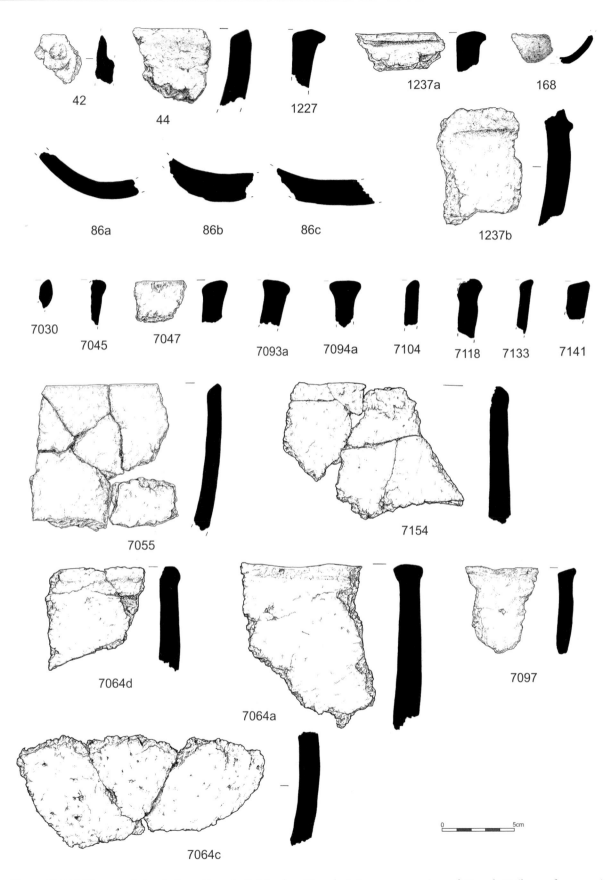

Figure 11.2.7 Illustrated sherds from Stonehall Meadow Trench A (top two rows), and Trench Z (lower four rows).

Table 11.2.7 Sherds with carbonised residue and/or sooting from Stonehall Meadow.

Position on vessel	SF No.
Interior	Trench A: 20, 25, 30, 35, 38, 48, 49, 53, 61, 65, 85, 95, 137, 168, 1201, 1203, 1206, 1207, 1210, 1216, 1229, 1236, 1237 (rim sherd) 1244, 1250, 1261, 1262, 1263, 1265, 1270, 1273, 1276, 1277, 1279, 1280, 2257 Trench Z: 7003, 7027, 7033, 7038, 7055, 7064, 7065, 7093, 7094, 7095, 7100, 7101, 7104, 7105, 7106, 7107, 7111, 7112, 7118, 7123, 7126, 7128, 7133, 7134, 7141, 7142, 7143, 7144, 7145, 7150, 7151, 7160, 7161, 7162, 7165, 7169, 7173, 7185, 7189, 7191, 7197, 7198, 7200
Exterior	Trench A: 14, 17, 21, 38, 42, 43, 44, 67, 86, 95, 1227, 1237 (body sherd), 1253, 1261, 1262 Trench Z: 7018, 7020, 7033, 7040, 7082, 7093, 7156, 7161, 7186, 7196, 7111, 7124, 7148

latter is 38% (42 out of 110 SFs). No trends in the spatial or other patterning of abrasion are discernible.

Construction and surface treatment

SF 50 has a groove for a coil, and SF 56 has slight ridge where two coils have possibly joined. Potters finger marks are apparent on the rim of SF 1237. The surface has been smoothed if not actually burnished on SFs 37, 50, 64, 66, 94, 137, 168, 1229, 1236, 1255 and 1276. In Trench Z there are smoothing marks on SFs 7055 (grass?), 7091 (straw or grass) and 7162. Forming marks are evident on SF 7140, and finger drag marks on SF 7095. Construction detail is apparent on some of the rims (*e.g.* SFs 7064, 7097 and 7133 – see Table 11.2.6).

Use/wear

Carbonised residue and/or sooting are prominent on the interior surfaces (Table 11.2.7).

That the sherds with use/wear distribute themselves across Trench Z points to a functional similarity of the vessels across the excavated part of the house. On only two sherds (SFs 7033 and 7111) is the carbonised residue on both the interior and exterior.

Fabric

In Trench A the fabric is typically grey brown but it is generally darker coloured in Trench Z owing to the frequency of burnt pottery within the House 3. While fabric texture varies in the former, it appears to do so in a less continuous fashion than in the pottery elsewhere. Classifying the Trench A fabrics on the basis of macroscopic examination into medium coarse and coarse categories and acknowledging that these categories would overlap, it was noted that the coarser sherds (*c.*60 examples) have greater wall thickness than the medium coarse ones (*c.*37). A further distinctive feature of the fabrics is the way fabric appearance and composition is not uniform: hand-specimen examination

revealed several singletons or groups with the following characteristics:

- *Dense hard 'chunky'*: SFs 37, 53, 66, 67, 71, 94, 95, 1206, 1209, 1210, 1227, 1232, 1237, 1264, 1266, 2257
- *Porous, straw?*: SFs 28, 1238
- *Fine chalky*: SF 34
- *Orange*: SFs 64, 1255
- *Soft, friable*: SFs 27, 30, 145, 1205, 1239, 1240, 1244, 1262
- *Fibrous*: SF 1236
- *Voids*: SF 1276

By contrast, the situation in Trench Z appears different. Apart from some dense fabrics (SFs 7040, 7082, 7137 and 7154) and the group of sherds (SFs 7044, 7101 and especially SF 7177) displaying the feature of large siltstone inclusions, smoothed onto the exterior surface, there is a relative absence of macroscopically identifiable unusual fabrics. But whether this observation is a reflection of different activities occurring near the entrance to the house (*i.e.* Trench A) as opposed to its centre (Trench Z) is entirely speculative.

Petrographically, the two main fabric groups are evenly represented (Table 11.2.8), in striking contrast to the situation in Trench C (Table 11.2.3). Also notable is the narrower distribution of inclusions in the sherds from the Meadow – 30–40% – by comparison with elsewhere (Fig. 11.2.16).

The weathered Igneous + Sedimentary group is better represented than the Sedimentary group (Table 11.2.8), as is the case in Stonehall Meadow (Trench A), but in marked contrast with the situation at Stonehall Farm. The two groups seem to distribute spatially between the three main concentrations mentioned above. It is noted with interest that the three sherds belonging to SF 7128 cut across the two groups. The distribution of inclusions in the pottery from the Meadow has already been noted.

11.2.3.3 Stonehall Farm: Trenches B, E and F

The pottery finds from Trench B are the most numerous

Table 11.2.8 Petrographic groups in pottery from Stonehall Meadow (Trenches A and Z).

Petrographic group	SF No. (Trench A)	SF No. (Trench Z)
Sedimentary	1200 (2 samples), 1209, 1242, 1243, 1261, 1263 and 1268	7064 (2 samples), 7093, 7119, 7128 (2 samples), 7134, 7148, 7203
Igneous (weathered) + Sedimentary	25, 29, 94, 126, 160, 1200, 1210, 1230, 1248, 1275, 1282	7047, 7064, 7094, 7107, 7112, 7118, 7123, 7128, 7144, 7145, 7181, 7185, 7189, 7200

at the site (370 Small Find entries, no more than 1100 sherds, weight 16.2 kg), the large majority of them coming from the large midden deposits. Treated here together with Trench B are the sherds from Trench E which are less numerous (some 34 Small Finds, weight *c*.1.15 kg). In Trench F there are 13 Small Finds representing *c*.50 sherds weighing *c*.0.48 kg. Besides the sherds, there are some fragments of unfired clay and several clay balls.

All the pottery from Stonehall Farm is fragmentary: there are no whole pots, and the opportunity for pot restoration was minimal. While the pottery in Trenches E and F appears to be all Grooved ware, that is flat-based vessels, probably, but more specifically, cylindrical and bucket-like jars, the same may not apply to Trench B. Here examination of the deep stratigraphy of the midden confirms the presence of an early phase but the absence of pottery in the relevant contexts of that early phase [829–836, 873, 874, 897–898] prevents identification of any potential round-based pottery. However, the pottery evidence is ambiguous: the sherds found at the lowest levels could be either round-based or Grooved ware. Throughout Stonehall Farm decorated vessels are in a clear minority. Sherd size and condition vary significantly as described below.

Associations and distribution
TRENCHES B AND E

The distribution of pottery in Trenches B and E is shown in Fig. 11.2.8. As may be expected, associations within the midden contexts are common (about 35), but each of them is generally limited to two or three sherds. Associations occur within the upper midden context [800] as they also do within the lower [809] midden, but there are also instances of links between these contexts, for example, SF 6125 [800] with SF 6041 [809] which hint at some measure of mixing within this large midden. Within House 1 numerous associations each involving three or four vessels were identified particularly in and between contexts [2002] and [2021]. Again, as expected, larger-sized sherds are found in the midden than in the structures (Fig. 11.2.2).

Clay balls

Roughly twenty in number, they are a feature mainly of the reddish clayey/ashy occupation [301/501] and related midden deposits [305/505] rather than the main midden [829-836 and 864-869]; as such, they belong to the later phase of settlement. From their descriptions (Table 11.2.9) and illustrations (Fig. 11.2.9) a feature of many of them is their amygdaloid or spindle-whorl shape.

Half a fired, well-made, clay bead (SF 2195) of fine pale clay was recovered from the upper midden deposits [303] north of Structure 1. A few clay fragments, possibly architectural and probably unfired were also found in the upper middens. Finally, there were a number of clay lumps of amorphous shape, which were probably unfired.

Although none of the balls shows indications of sooting or having been fired, exploratory Fourier-transform Infra-Red analysis of a few of them, including SF 683, indicated that they had been exposed to moderate heat, that is, over 100°C.

Wall thickness

Wall thickness (Fig. 11.2.10) is commonly in the 1–1.2 and 1.4–1.6cm ranges, but the corresponding situation for the fine fabric sherds (*c*.40 sherds, see section on Fabric below) is somewhat different: peaks in the 0.8–1 and 1.2–1.4cm ranges indicate a tendency for the smaller-sized vessels to be in the finer fabric.

Diagnostic sherds
Rims (Fig. 11.2.12)

Among the forty or so rims there is variation in their shape but not as much as at Stonehall Knoll and Meadow. A few uncertain identifications occur among either sherds whose possible rim is heavily abraded or body sherds having what looks like an abraded rim but may well be a tenon. Some rims, for example SF 6310, are best presented as decorated sherds (below).

The large majority of rims are plain, rounded (*e.g.* SFs 300, 2016b, 2036, 6043, 6159, 6231, 6280, 6285, 6291, 6351, 6365 and 6432). These are not dissimilar to, but not as varied as equivalents at Crossiecrown (section 11.3)

Figure 11.2.8 The distribution of pottery from Stonehall Farm (Trenches B and E).

Table 11.2.9 *Clay balls from the Farm (Trench B); see Fig. 11.2.9 for those illustrated.*

SF (context)	Description
652b [301]	Complete clay ball, amygdaloid shaped, ?fired but abraded. Greyish exterior, probable fine fabric.
683 [301]	Fragments of two halves of one or more balls; fine orange clay.
719 [303]	Possible fragments, but small and abraded. Orange, soft fabric.
2004 [301]	Half clay ball in fine fabric.
2049 [501]	Well preserved, complete ball with amygdaloid shape. Made from two halves luted together, orange fabric. Weathered and slightly abraded.
2075 [503]	Fragment in pale orange-brown fine fabric.
2089 [503]	Almost complete; appears as if two halves have been luted together. Possible finger marks; surface crudely smoothed. Usual pale colour: on broken edge a few inclusions are visible indicating it is coarser than other clay balls.
2104 [503]	Fragment, in fine light orange fabric, very similar to 2105a.
2105a [501]	Fragment, amygdaloid shaped.
2112 [528]	Fragment.
2122 [501]	Fragment in soft sandy fabric, low fired.
2123 [501]	Oblong-shaped fragment. Porous pale fabric with ?straw, many voids. Stands apart from other clay balls, if indeed it is a ball.
2126 [501]	Possible fragment, with nearly flat surface.
2149 [503]	Quarter clay ball fragment, amygdaloid shaped. Few inclusions in fine pale grey orange fabric. Abraded.
2172 [?]	Fragment. Probable natural darkening on exterior.
2198 [503]	Similar to 2199; flat base.
2199 [501]	Three quarter clay ball; only small portion broken off; usual orange fine fabric. Smoothed exterior, except one portion which may have been a base.
2200 [501]	Similar to 2198 and 2199 in having a base, but smaller in size. Soft light orange fine fabric. Some abrasion.
2253 (Ditch)	Half clay ball with probable flattened base.
2503–2505 [600–608]	Small fragments of probable clay ball.
2594 [612]	Two very small fragments of probable clay ball.

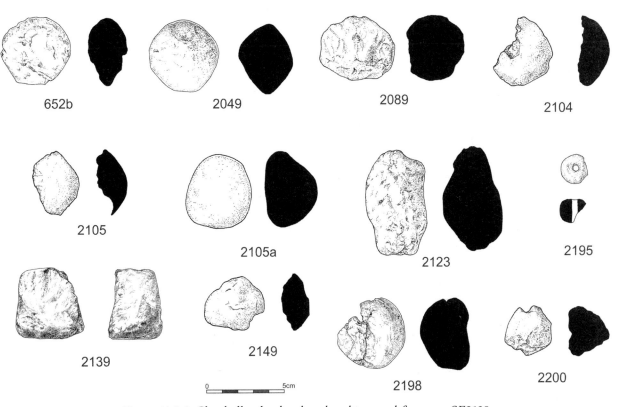

652b   2049   2089   2104

2105   2105a   2123   2195

2139   2149   2198   2200

0   5cm

Figure 11.2.9 Clay balls, clay bead and architectural fragment SF2139.

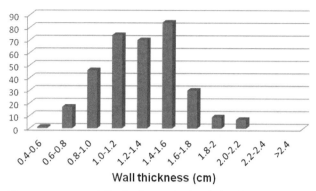

Figure 11.2.10 Wall thickness (cm) of sherds at Stonehall Farm (Trenches B, E and F).

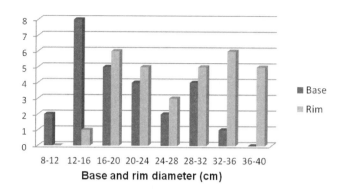

Figure 11.2.11 Rim and base diameters (cm) at Stonehall Farm (Trenches B, E and F).

and Barnhouse (A. M. Jones 2005a, Fig. 11.6 top row 4 and 5 in from the left). A few examples have everted rims (SF 6432 and SF 2255), while SF 2145 and SF 6058 have inward sloping rims, and SF 2210 a flat top. There are at least three with an inner shelf, presumably for holding a pot-lid (*e.g.* SFs 6231 and 6263 in Trench B and possibly SF 4080 in Trench E), and there is a single scallop rim (SF 6288). Notable are the decorated rims, with either incision or raised band (Table 11.2.10).

Notwithstanding the small number of rims for which measurements were feasible, the distribution of diameters (Fig. 11.2.11) indicates a group in the 16–24cm range and a much broader, possibly bimodal group at 28–40cm. Rim diameter shows poor correlation with sherd thickness, indeed the latter variable changes little over a wide range of vessel volume.

Bases

Over thirty bases, some of them more confidently identified than others, have been recognised. Where it has been possible to classify the bases, those of the *flat plain* (BP) type with walls going vertically up or at a slight angle are predominant (*e.g.* SFs 372, 639b, 2254, 4124, 6024b, 6024c, 6101, 6154, 6198, 6238, 6247, 6260, 6283, 6415). Flat bases with *foot ring* (BF) (equivalent to footed bases at Crossiecrown) are also present (*e.g.* SFs 24, 302, 329, 2027, 2029, 6036b, 6037a and 6039), and a majority of them have walls at a distinct angle to the base (see Fig. 11.2.13). There seem to be several bases of intermediate type, such as SFs 6024b and 6328, and others which are not amenable to classification because of the small sherd size (SFs 6271 and 6308). The decorated base (SF 6181) is described in the next section. Overall, the bases, comparable to those at Crossiecrown, are less variable in shape than, for example, at Pool (MacSween

2007, Ill. 8.1.7, 9 and 11).

It is notable how many bases are in poor crumbly condition. The distribution of their diameters in Fig. 11.2.11 suggests two modes, one in the range 12–16cm (or 12–18cm), followed by a smaller one at 28–32cm. Since almost all the illustrated bases indicate the flaring of the vessel profile it can be supposed that these two size groups correlate with the 16–24cm and 28–40cm rim diameter ranges respectively. No bases with mat impressions were found. Table 11.2.11 describes the bases illustrated in Fig. 11.2.13.

Decoration

Trenches B and E

The relative frequency of decorated sherds varied across the structures and midden at Stonehall Farm, reaching nearly 20% in the upper midden [800], upper-intermediate midden in Trench E (the midden was not fully excavated in this area), and in the clayey material above slabs in Trench E [822] and [838].

The two main types of decoration are incision and application, as is the case at Crossiecrown, followed by the very minor one of impression. These types are set out in Table 11.2.12 according to the schemes outlined at Crossiecrown, Barnhouse (A. M. Jones 2005a, 264), Pool (MacSween 2007, Ill. 8.1.10 and 81.14) and Links of Noltland (Sheridan 1999, Ill. 12.6).

Incision most commonly occurs as single or multiple forms (Incision type I at Crossiecrown; Sheridan type 3) and notably on the interior of the vessel below the rim. Examples are given in Table 11.2.13 and illustrated in Fig. 11.2.12. These incised sherds occur in a wide chronological range of contexts within the midden.

Table 11.2.10 Decorated and other pottery from Stonehall Farm (Trench B); see Fig 11.2.12.

SF (context)	Description
3.7 unstratified	Plain narrow rim sherd with two horizontal incised lines on the exterior and interior; the latter protrusion is too small to be regarded as a ledge. Very coarse evenly oxidised fired fabric with rock fragments (40%). Diameter 25cm.
652a [301]	Small sherd (longest axis 3.5cm) with finely executed linear grooves and circular depression. Coarse fabric with large inclusions. Well smoothed exterior.
2030 [501]	Body sherd with horizontal raised bands. Sooted exterior but not interior. See text. Coarse, frequent sandstone and siltstone inclusions.
2117–18 [501]	Two body sherds probably from the same vessel with horizontal raised bands and partial diagonal band. Much sooting on exterior; abraded interior surface.
2684 [641]	Pointed rim (c.5mm) of large vessel with several circular depressions – four large (0.5cm diameter) and one smaller – and two stab marks on the rim interior. Below them is an incised parallel to the rim. Exterior decoration consists of two parallel cordons with regular vertical incisions. Sooted exterior. Pale, fine fabric.
6043 [812]	Plain rim with two incised horizontal lines on exterior. Some abrasion. At least one other parallel (6248). No sooting. Fine, orange fabric. Diameter 38cm.
6150 [809]	Multiple body sherds from a single vessel with horizontal and diagonal raised cordons. Thick chunky fabric, very coarse, large dark inclusions up to 0.6cm. Sooting on the exterior as well as interior, except at the plain rounded rim.
6159 [809]	Plain round rim; oxidised; no sooting; incised horizontal line and applied band below interior rim; fine light colour fabric.
6181 [846]	Two small base sherds with narrow v-shaped incised lines on exterior. Dense dark fabric, few inclusions.
6196 [800]	Pointed rim decorated on interior. Pale fabric, moderate frequency of large angular inclusions up to 0.5cm. Well sooted exterior up to rim. Diameter 36cm.
6197b [809]	Two horizontal incised lines on inside of rim, interrupted by circular depression and raised knob on the rim. Exterior plain and slightly abraded. Fine light grey fabric, no sooting. Diameter 22cm.
6231 [804]	Large body sherd with large raised cordon which has multiple thick, diagonal incisions. Horizontal cordon, 5cm long, applied 1cm below (plain round) rim (diameter 32cm) on vessel's *interior*. Crudely smoothed interior. Medium coarse inclusions of varying colour and size. Joins SF 6261.
6249 [814]	Body sherd with raised cordon and three circular depressions, one of them deep. Some incision beside the raised cordon. Coarse pale fabric with occasional large inclusions; sooted on exterior; heavily abraded interior.
6258 [809]	Two conjoining body sherds with prominent raised cordon which several vertical incisions. Fabric is yellowish coloured and coarse fabric, but the raised cordon is of notably finer clay.
6280 [809]	Three sherds, two of them conjoining with two broad deep horizontal impression on interior. Pale almost yellow coarse fabric, rather friable. Sooted exterior up to rim, no sooting on interior. Not illustrated.
6288 [800]	One large body sherd and conjoining likely scallop rim fragment. Yellow coarse fabric with occasional large inclusions up to 1.2cm. No sooting or residue. Crudely shaped vessel, poorly smoothed exterior; some abrasion. Rim diameter 40cm. Wall thickening of body sherd indicates proximity to base in which case the height of the vessel may be no more than c.7cm.
6310 [838]	Three conjoining rim sherds. Plain rim (0.7cm) but for distinct raised 'knob' lying directly above depressed hole on the interior. Below the hole are two prominent, incised horizontal, almost parallel lines. Distinctive pale fine fabric with grey core; no sooting; smoothed interior surface, contrasting with crude exterior.
6351 [822]	Two conjoining sherds with pointed rim; raised horizontal and raised diagonal band; heavily sooted exterior with residue; interior has no sooting apart from slight trace 9cm below rim; coarse fabric, frequent angular inclusions up to 0.5cm.
6379 [800]	Plain rim (0.4 cm thick) with shallow groove 0.5cm below it on interior. No sooting. Abraded. 20cm diameter. Not illustrated.

Application of cordons is the most frequent type. Some of them are definitely applied, while others which are somewhat less frequent have been raised by the potter. The distinction between the two is not absolute; there are sometimes lines made by the potter above and below a cordon to accentuate that cordon: those impressed lines may be formed by either a finger to create a groove or light application of a tool to incise/impress. Again, the distinctions between these possibilities are not absolute, nor should they be expected to be.

There are some fifty four examples with *applied or raised decoration*. A majority have an *applied* cordon. This was usually made of a finer clay than the body and was applied after the pot dried; the frequency of finds of cordon fragments points to the relative ease with which the cordon became detached from the body (see Towers and Card 2014). A good example of a distinct separate layer having been added to the surface of the pot, and then being manipulated into shape is SF 2030.

A smaller proportion has a *raised* cordon which

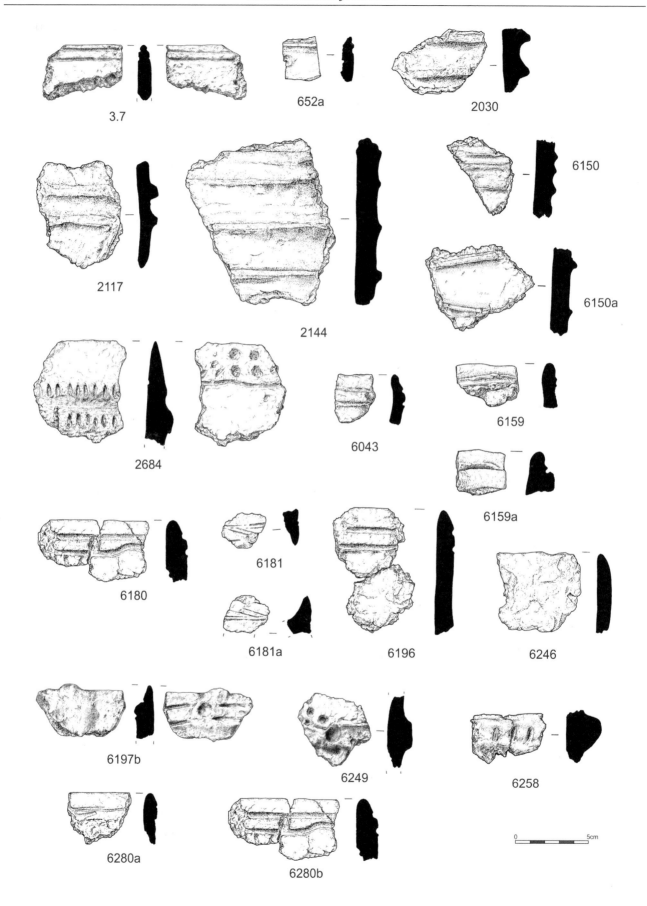

3.7

652a

2030

2117

2144

6150

6150a

2684

6043

6159

6159a

6180

6181

6181a

6196

6246

6197b

6249

6258

6280a

6280b

0 5cm

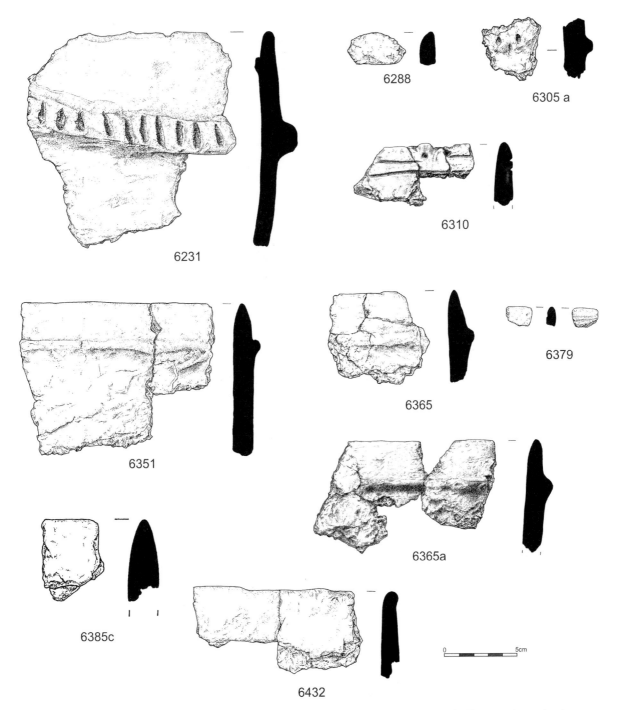

Figure 11.2.12 (above and opposite) Decorated and other pottery from Stonehall Farm (Trench B).

is usually accompanied by *grooves* above and below (*e.g.* SFs 652a, 6196 and 6280). Examples belonging to this category appear to be distributed throughout the midden. The decorative repertoire in this general category is limited to the few types indicated in Table 11.2.13: straight lines, wavy or zig-zag lines and slashes. One example (SF 6365) has an applied band at the rim,

and another is unusual in having a possible groove on the rim (SF 6379). One sherd (SF 6263) has a raised band on the interior, probably for a stone-lid.

Impressed decoration is restricted to a few sherds (SF 652a (groove with impressed hole); SF 6249 (dots impressed); SF 6197b (two horizontal incised lines on inside of rim, interrupted by circular depression and raised

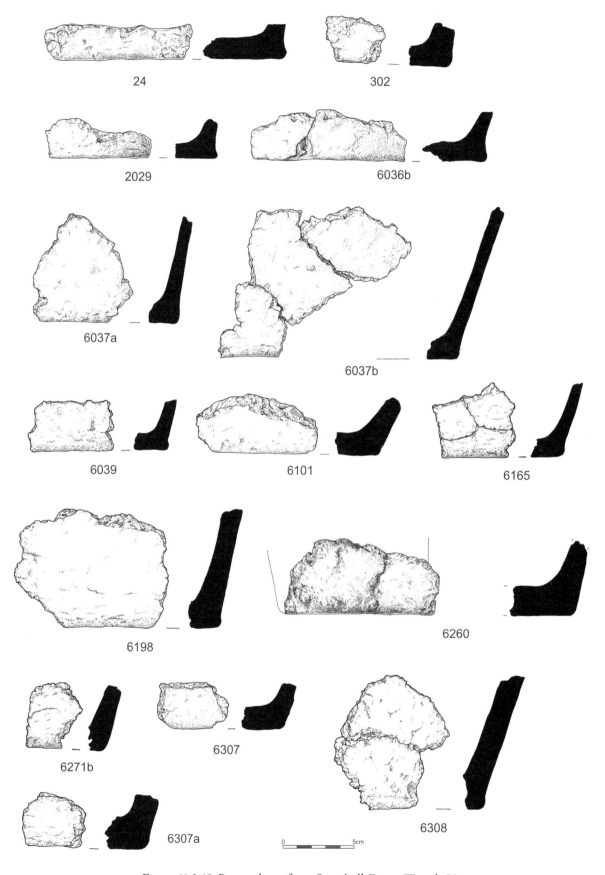

Figure 11.2.13 Pottery bases from Stonehall Farm (Trench B).

Table 11.2.11 Description of bases from Stonehall Farm (Trench B bases); see Fig. 11.2.13.

SF (context)	Description
24 [001]	BF; small area of sooting on exterior but not interior. Orange to grey rather coarse fabric.
302 [301]	BF; coarse friable fabric with heterogeneous large (cm long) sandstone inclusions and several dark inclusions. Sooting on base and exterior wall. Diameter 16cm.
2029 [501]	BF; visible coil added around the base; pale orange to grey coloured fabric with some angular sandstone. Hint of sooting at exterior base. Diameter 10cm.
6036a, b [800]	BP; pale orange fine fabric with occasional sandstone and siltstone fragments up to 0.8cm. No sooting; slight (brown) concretion on interior. Diameter 14cm.
6037 [800]	2 bases (BF) in dark coarse fabric with frequent dark angular inclusions up to 1cm. Prominent residue in interior; sooted exterior. Diameter 14cm.
6039 [800]	BF, crudely smoothed exterior; sooted exterior but not interior; similar fabric to SF 603b. Diameter 16cm.
6101 [800]	Large BP; light coloured exterior with no sooting, grey core; coarse fabric with sandstone; grey concentrated concretion in the interior of base gives way to dark core above. Diameter *c.*26cm.
6165 [800]	Probable BF due to slight flare from added coil. Sooting in and out; hard coarse fabric. Diameter *c.*14cm.
6198 [809]	Large body sherd extending to BP. Coarse with frequent small dark and sometimes light inclusions; sooting on exterior base and 1 cm above base; sooting/residue on interior stops 2cm before base, almost like SF 6308. Diameter 22cm.
6260 [809]	Two large conjoining sherds of BP. Coarse light coloured fabric with common rock fragments up to 0.5cm. Slight sooting on exterior base; notable sooting and residue on interior wall immediately above the base. Diameter 34cm.
6307a [838]	Thick (1.7cm) BP; chunky coarse fabric with angular siltstone up to 0.8cm. Sooted on interior and exterior. Diameter 18cm.
6308 [800]	Large thick-walled body sherd extending to base (?)BF. Coarse fabric with frequent angular siltstone and igneous fragments up to 0.8cm. Sooting on interior but stops approximately where the two body sherds join; lower sherds is almost free of sooting/residue. Cf. SF 6198. Diameter *c.*20cm.

Table 11.2.12 Decorative types in Grooved ware from Stonehall Farm (Trenches B, E and F).

Type	Description	Overall frequency	Elaboration	Elaboration frequency	Illustrated examples in italics
Incised		Less common	a. Straight lines b. Wavy or zig-zag c. Slashes		a. 6152 b. 6268 c. *6231, 6258, 6261, 6305*
Applied	1. Applied cordon 2. Raised cordon	More common	a. Straight lines b. Wavy or lozenge c. Slashes	a. Most common b. Occasional c. Rare	1. *6231, 6365* 2. *6196, 6280* a. 6152 b. 2112, *2117*, 2210, *6150* c. 6458
Impressed		Rare			6249

Table 11.2.13 Incised decoration on Grooved ware from Stonehall Farm.

SF (context) (in italics if illustrated)	Comment
251 [303]	Possible horizontal linear incisions
323 [305]	Raised band with linear incision
686 [303]	One linear groove
2610 [614]	Light surface treatment with piece of wood or twig (Sheridan type 6)
2685 [001]	Angled. Visible nail incisions (Sheridan type 6)
6159 [809]	Below rim on interior
6181 [846]	Two fragments, one on base, angled; cf. Sheridan type 14; cf. Pool 3536B (MacSween 2007, Ill 8.1.11)
6187 [809]	V-shaped (Sheridan type 6)
6196 [800]	Below rim on interior
6197b [809]	Two horizontal incised lines on inside of rim, interrupted by circular impression and raised notch on the rim
6246 [838]	Below rim on interior
6300 [800]	Parallel incised lines
6307 [838]	Parallel incised lines
6310 [838]	Two incised lines with impressed hole on rim
6344 [822]	Parallel incised lines

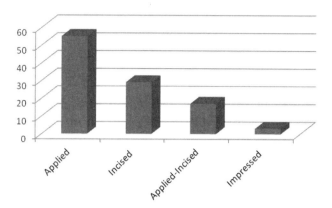

Figure. 11.2.14 Distribution of decoration types at Stonehall Farm (Trenches B, E and F).

knob on the rim) and SF 6310 (two parallel incised lines on interior and depressed hole on rim). One example (SF 6249) has clear parallels at Barnhouse (A. M. Jones 2005a, Fig. 3.24 I; Fig. 11.9; SFs 4273, 3934).

Looking at the distribution of decoration schemes in Trenches B, E and F (Fig. 11.2.14); there is a preponderance of applied decoration in the 300 and 500–600 context series, while in the 800 series there is proportionately more incised decoration. Comparing the frequency of applied and incised decoration according to sherd thickness, no significant difference is found, that is, both types of decoration encompass all sizes of vessel.

Abrasion

An estimated 80–85% of the sherds in Trench B showed signs of abrasion, the proportion in Trench E and F being more than 90%. In Trench B no particular trends in either the occurrence or extent of abrasion were detectable either between or within the main context series. Abrasion commonly affects both exterior and interior to the same extent, yet there are some good examples of notably abraded *interiors* (the exterior being only slightly abraded – *e.g.* SFs 254, 652a, 640, 2014, 2016a, 2017, 2118, 2150, 2533, 2542, 2569, 4080 and 6269). Correspondingly some exteriors occur that are much more abraded than the interior (*e.g.* SFs 235, 251, 324, 2543, 2571 and 6354).

Use wear

In Trench B, 30–35% have some indication of a darkened/burnt area on the interior or exterior surface (or both) that can be called sooting. There is no apparent distinction in this frequency across this trench. A smaller number of sherds (20 %) have a residue, concretion and/

or carbonised residue (CR), indicating more directly their connection with a cooking/food preparation activity. In Trenches E–F the corresponding figures are approximately the same.

Of the 25% of sherds in Trench B with residue, concretion/carbonised residue, in 49 cases it is on the interior and 32 cases on the exterior; in a few cases, such as SFs 539 and 6328, it is on both surfaces. For Trenches E and F, the corresponding figures are the reverse of Trench B: 4 (interior) and 10 (exterior) cases. All scenaria are found in the *amount* of residue: slight through to SFs 324, 639a, 2211, 2256, 2571, 2686b, 2617, 6062, 6198, 6342, 6356, 6368, 6305 which all have heavy residue. Observations on the *location* of residue include:

*   SF 72 residue on interior edge of base
*   SF 639b dark residue on base interior but lighter residue on inner wall
*   SF 723 white ?calcareous concretion in interior
*   SF 2255 residue on interior base
*   SF 2571 residue on interior near rim
*   SF 2686 residue on lower part of interior
*   SF 6024b residue exterior near base but not on bottom
*   SF 6198 residue a few cm above interior of base

Sherds with residue and sooting appear across the spectrum of vessel sizes. Exploratory analysis with pXRF of a few sherds indicated that the residue was significantly richer in phosphorus and calcium than the body, but whether this was simply due to the sherds' proximity to decayed bone in the midden was not resolved.

Technique

The evidence for manufacture is modest in Trench B. Some twenty sherds have some kind of construction mark:

*   Good examples of grooves for coil: SFs 2252, 2254, 6206
*   Tenon: SFs 2251, 2252, 6320, 609
*   Groove: SFs 609, 724, 2150, 2251, 2252, 2254, 6037, 6039, 6206
*   Coil around base: SFs 6260, 6065, 2029.
*   Smoothing out of coils: SF 724 smoothing marks in and out, SFs 6206 and 6320. SF 725 depression in and out where coils have joined.
*   SF 6024c shows wall thickening with marked striation from fingers working in the vertical sense, *i.e.* up down, rather than the horizontal. These striations are not coils.
*   No grass impression on base, but SF 358 has what looks like grass smoothing marks on the exterior. Grass impression on interior of one body sherd of SF 2211.

Detail

*   Coil construction: SFs 351, 672, 2571 and 2625b
*   Depression in and out where coils have joined: SF 725
*   Coil added round the base making it BF. Several signs

of the way this coil has been worked: SF 2029.

- Small groove on interior: SF 2152
- Tenon goes with groove of SFs 2251 and 2252
- Formation/construct markings on interior, and thickening of base at one end: SF 2096.

Surface treatment

Smoothing of the surface is the most common treatment exhibited by 34 sherds. Sometimes this smoothing is crude (*e.g.* SFs 2089, 2107b, 2605, 6077, 6092, 6118 and 6288), and occasionally the smoothing is the same in and out. One vessel (SF 358) has been smoothed perhaps with grass. Another vessel, represented by SF 2569 is good example where smoothing of the exterior has protected that surface, whereas the unsmoothed interior has abraded badly. Very few sherds possess burnish marks (*e.g.* SF 282). Finger marks are evident on a number of sherds (*e.g.* SFs 2089, 6024c, 6099, 62552 and 639b).

The issue of *slip* is problematic. Initial recording of the assemblage, which isolated some twenty examples (SFs 302, 724, 2016a, 2018, 2031, 2087, 6355, 6356, 6077, 6079, 6116, 6257, 6261, 6269, 6291, 6322, 6354, 2203, 2251 and 2542), would suggest the process of slipping was not common. It is significant that, first, it is most apparent on a darkened surface (on a lighter interior) where the effects of the firing and/or use have accentuated the presence of a thin fine surface layer. In a few cases the supposed slip appears on a dark surface showing 'crazing', which is probably due to heat (*e.g.* SFs 6261, 6269 and 6322). One vessel has a slip that looks as if it was created by function (*e.g.* SF 2018). Second, slip is apparent on some sherds with applied bands/cordons (*e.g.* SFs 6291 and 2087). On two joining sherds (SF 2501), there is an applied band whose position the potter has outlined with incised lines. It is noticeable that the area above the band is not only darkened but also slipped (with a brush?), perhaps to aid the binding of the applied band. Overall, the impression gained is that at Stonehall Farm slipping was not regularly part of the potter's finishing process, and yet some potters probably appreciated its purpose and used it; for example SF 302 is an example of apparent slipping in and out.

Fabric

Initial macroscopic study of the pottery recovered from Stonehall Farm indicated a remarkably wide range of fabrics. A clear majority can be classed as having a coarse fabric, and within this broad category there is at the visual level apparently a whole spectrum of shape,

size and frequency of inclusions. Efforts to subdivide the coarse category into meaningful subgroups proved too subjective to be useful. Nevertheless some visually distinctive or unusual fabrics were noted:

- Coarse pale fabric characterised by yellowish sandstone inclusions, commonly encountered in the context '6000' series in Trench B. This fabric may be the product of poor firing with the decaying sandstone fragments giving rise to the yellowish effect but this would not accord with the observation that it is often yet not consistently well fired.
- Voids left by ?straw (SFs 2107a, 654, 4175 and 4122)
- Soft, often pale and powdery: encountered among the clay balls and sherds (SFs 670, 2603, 6230, 6058, 6067 and 6272)
- Shell (SFs 2016a and 6407)
- 'Chunky' with dark siltstone inclusions (SFs 2543, 6024c, 6326, 6431, 6352 and 4194)

The identification of shell temper proved problematic. Unlike at Crossiecrown or Barnhouse where the void left by the shell fragment is visible either to the eye or in thin section (A. M. Jones 2005a, 277: Fabric C), this has *not* been the case at Stonehall. While the number of instances of shell in the pottery at Stonehall may have been underestimated, it is confidently asserted that shell was not a common ingredient in this pottery.

Fine-textured pottery at Stonehall is not absent. About forty small finds of pottery and almost all the clay balls are in what can be regarded as fine or semi-fine fabric, albeit varying widely in colour and appearance. Since this fine-textured pottery comprises relatively small-sized fragments (by comparison with the coarser pottery), its overall frequency in the Stonehall Farm assemblage is probably less than the 10% which is calculated on the basis of individual small find counts of fine vs coarse. In any case, this same pottery tends to correlate, albeit subjectively, with smaller vessel size, as judged by the attribute of wall thickness.

The pottery in Trench E shows an apparent similar range of fabric appearance as that in Trench B, but macroscopically there seems to be a greater preponderance in the former trench of paler and finer-textured colours. This is potentially interesting.

Thin section examination

The results drawn from section 11.6 for Trenches B, E and F are summarised in Table 11.2.14 and Fig. 11.2.15. Bearing in mind the subjective nature of the selection criteria for thin sectioning, four observations can be made:

- A contrast is apparent between on the one hand the 300 and 500–600 contexts, and on the other hand the 800 contexts in Trench B: those in the former have a slight predominance of the sedimentary fabric, while those in the latter have a clear predominance of the igneous+sedimentary fabric.
- There is an apparent predominance of the igneous+sedimentary fabric in Trenches E–F.
- The igneous fragments, which are all found together with one or more of the sedimentary inclusions (sandstone, siltstone and mudstone), are *all* camptonite, and in nine cases out of fourteen this camptonite is weathered to very weathered.
- Regarding the sedimentary inclusions, the Trench B samples are notably poor in sandstone by comparison with the situation in the other trenches.
- There is a wide distribution in inclusion sizes (Fig. 11.2.16) with the mode lying in the 40–50% range which is higher than the corresponding figure for the EN (Knoll and Meadow) pottery.

Colour and other characteristics

In view of the variability in the appearance of the fabrics across the site, little has been gained from estimating its colour. Nevertheless, two comments can be made; first, the pottery at Stonehall Farm has a colour range that

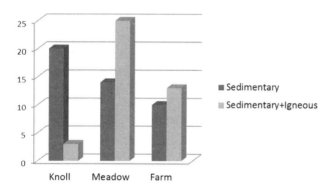

Figure 11.2.15 Distribution of the Sedimentary and Igneous+Sedimentary fabric groups identified at Stonehall Knoll, Meadow and Farm.

overlaps with those of the pottery from other parts of the site and thus no chronological trend is apparent. Second, there is a discernible difference in colour between the pottery *en masse* at Stonehall and the assemblages, for instance, from respectively Barnhouse and Crossiecrown that the writer has seen. Colours at Stonehall tend to encompass the range within light reddish brown (Munsell 5YR 6/4 to 7.5YR 6/4), while at Barnhouse it is more orange (reddish yellow 7.5YR 6/6 to brownish-yellow 10YR 6/6) and at Crossiecrown it is commonly lighter in chroma (*e.g.* yellow 10YR 7/6 to 8.6). This is a broad, somewhat subjective yet comforting observation, simply reflecting the contrasts in colour between the clays used at each of the sites rather than differences in firing conditions or practices. The majority of the pottery at Stonehall Farm is moderately well fired, not hard but not crumbly. But needless to say, hardness covers a wide spectrum and there are some examples of hard solid fabrics and at the other end of the scale crumbly, friable fabrics.

11.2.4 Discussion

The pottery assemblage at Stonehall presents a snapshot view of pottery production and use over a period of nearly 500 years at the settlement. Viewed in this light and despite the large number of sherds – nearly 4,000 – recovered in varying size and condition, the scale of production was small, probably a few hundred pots. Nevertheless, the assemblage is important for the main reason of its time depth. Within the relatively short life time of the settlement, as determined by the C14 dating programme (Chapter 10), not only does the nature and form of house architecture progress from 'classic' early Neolithic to late Neolithic but the pottery closely parallels that transition: early Neolithic round-based pots to Grooved ware typical of the late Neolithic. Second, these two crude chronological labels, early and late Neolithic, appear to conflate at Stonehall; although insufficient of the settlement has been excavated to determine whether

Table 11.2.14 Petrographic data for pottery from Stonehall Farm (Trenches B, E and F).

Examination	Sedimentary	Igneous + Sedimentary
Detailed examination	*Tr B*: 236, 652, 2009, 2014, 2017, 2044, 2048, 2120, 2134(×2), 2150 *Tr F*: 6398	*Tr B*: 271cw, 253c, 345w, 351cw, 375w, 2074w, 2107cw, 2156w, 2253c *Tr E*: 4114c, 4122c, 4124c–cw, 4127c *Tr F*: 6392 cw
Summary examination	*Tr B*: 327, 2016, 6242	*Tr B* 6076, 6077, 6090, 6116, 6217, 6288
Total	14	20

it was either occupied on a continuous basis, albeit with 'settlement drift' taking place, or abandoned and later re-settled. However, the excavation record gives no obvious hint of the latter scenario. The corresponding pottery seems to tell the same story of an apparently seamless transition from one tradition to another. Third, the early tradition is confined to undecorated pottery; there is no decorated Unstan ware, as is present at Wideford Hill, Crossiecrown, Knowes of Trotty and Brae of Smerquoy. An attractive feature of the assemblage is that the round-based and Grooved ware traditions are equally represented at the site, making it sufficiently large to be amenable to meaningful morphological, decorative, spatial and fabric analysis. On the other hand, the decorative repertory in the Grooved ware is limited, and much of the pottery, both early and late, is fragmentary, making identification of pot groups and complete profiles very difficult. Although much of the decorated Grooved ware was in the form of applied cordons, many of them were found detached from the body, and as a result the proportion of Grooved ware that was decorated has probably been under-estimated.

Turning to a more detailed assessment, the round-based pottery evidence points to Stonehall Knoll and Meadow being occupied in the mid–late 4th millennium cal BC. Taking into account the 3rd millennium cal BC C[14] dates (see Chapter 10), the presence of later pottery on Stonehall Knoll is possible, but the (near) absence of decorated pottery there suggests its quantity is very limited. The occurrence of a very small amount of Grooved ware in Trench A should not cause surprise in view of its proximity to the main locus of late Neolithic activity at Stonehall Farm.

Superficially, the pottery at Stonehall Knoll and Meadow is morphologically similar, consisting of plain, undecorated round-based bowls. Their size forms a continuum as judged by (body) sherd thickness and to a lesser extent rim diameter, and yet there are certain trends within these two measurement sets which suggest that vessel size categories can be defined, if only loosely. The distribution of sherd thickness at Stonehall Meadow Trench A reveals a mode at 1.2–1.4cm among the coarser fabrics and one at 1.0–1.2cm among the less coarse fabrics, while at Stonehall Meadow Trench Z this occurs at a larger size – 1.2–1.6cm; jointly they make up the distribution seen in Fig. 11.2.1. At least two vessel sizes are hinted in the rim diameter distribution (Fig. 11.2.3). As for sherd size, the explanation of the smaller size in Trench A was made above in terms of the poor preservation there due to (recent) agricultural activity

in the field, but an alternative is that activities at the entrance of the house led to trampling of the pottery, contrasting with the situation within House 3 where the pottery was found on the paved floor.

On Stonehall Knoll there is a large peak in sherd thickness at 1.0–1.4cm and a smaller one at 1.8–2.0cm, a wide range of rim diameters (Fig. 11.2.3), and poor correlation between rim diameter and sherd thickness (Fig. 11.2.4). Collectively, this data suggests that small to large size vessels were made at Stonehall Knoll and Meadow, but there can be no attempt (or even implicit need) to create particular size categories. Smaller vessels appear more commonly in the less coarse fabrics. Stonehall Knoll seems to have a greater preponderance of large-sized vessels; this interesting contrast with the situation at Stonehall Meadow extends to the location of deposition, with the pottery at the latter being for most part *within* the houses (particularly House 3 Trench Z), while at the former it concentrates *outside* the houses in the adjacent midden(s).

Turning to Stonehall Farm (Trench B) where the largest concentration of pottery was found, notably in the midden adjacent to Structure 1, it is possible, even likely, that this midden in view of its size encompasses the lifetime of Structure 1 as well as earlier phases of the settlement. But, unfortunately, examination of the pottery does not illuminate this issue because of the similarity in general appearance between undecorated Grooved ware and round-based vessels and the lack of sherds securely attributable to contexts of respectively early and late phases. Even sherd thickness cannot be safely employed as a diagnostic of either earlier or later phase pottery.

Overall, pottery production at Stonehall appears modest in scale, conservative in execution in the sense that decoration is limited in frequency and elaborate in neither style nor content. Nevertheless, the potters were undoubtedly competent at their craft, and the decorative motifs they used in the later period find parallels at contemporary sites such as Crossiecrown, Barnhouse, Ness of Brodgar and Links of Noltland. But at the same time there are on the one hand contrasts, applied cordons, for example, being much preferred than at Barnhouse where incision was more common (A. M. Jones 2005a, 264). On the other hand, a measure of individuality seems to be evident among some of the decorated rims (*e.g.* SFs 6197b and 6310 in Fig. 11.2.12). In the course of probably other activities beyond their settlement, potters were aware of the availability of different clays in the vicinity, these ranging from naturally coarse clays to naturally finer clays, like that at Cruan today, and those observed in the clay balls from Stonehall Farm. They worked the naturally coarse clays, only occasionally or rarely finding the need to deliberately temper the finer clays with sandstone, grog, and less frequently igneous rock fragments (see Fig. 11.2.15 below).

Initial examination of the Stonehall assemblage as a whole does point to a certain randomness in the nature of the pottery's fabric, yet there are indications that there was some level of empirical understanding that the larger vessels benefited from employing a coarser fabric. Having said that, the experimental work reported in section 11.5 consistently indicated that tempering *per se* neither markedly improved the tensile properties of the clay nor was it a straightforward technical task. Moreover, it seems most unlikely that those pots containing igneous rock fragments performed better when employed on the hearth than those containing the quartz-rich sandstone/siltstone fragments because the igneous rock fragments were not present in sufficient quantity to make any discernible difference in thermal shock resistance.

There are now two issues to reconcile. On the one hand, we believe the potters drew on the supplies of clay brought to the site for a broad range of purposes, including preparing clay floors and insulating buildings, as well as pottery making. This would favour the argument that the potters were not exercising choice in what clays they used for pottery making; instead purely practical considerations were uppermost in their minds: the clay was primarily for building purposes and what was left over from those tasks was adequate for the potters to use. The properties of much of that clay were undemanding, although a case could be made for the selection of a finer quality clay for the floor; in principle, the clays could have been obtained anywhere, but for logistical reasons preferably from sources as close to the site as possible. The boulder clay which is present around the site would have been workable if the large fragments were removed. Moreover, the marshy conditions that occur today in the depression 50m NW of the settlement (see Fig. 5.4) could have been exploited for the natural puddling process taking place, giving clay fractions of contrasting quality.

On the other hand, the petrographic data indicates that the potters at Stonehall were deliberately using clays from different locations within, say, a two mile radius of the site and that this tradition continued over the lifetime of the site affecting production of both the round-based vessels and Grooved ware. Some clays were collected from deposits that naturally contained weathered igneous

rock. Whether the potter was aware that that clay naturally contained fragments of such rock was in some way advantageous for pottery making is unlikely. Rather it argues that it was the *location* of the clay that was significant. We suggest that no reconciliation of the two opposing scenaria is necessary as *both* of them were operating. Although potters may have been aware of the hard dark rock appearing in the igneous dykes, there are no indications from the excavations that they exploited that rock for working it into a shape, as was the case of the blanks for possible stone balls found at Barnhouse for example (Clarke 2005, 327, 332–33).

Pottery making, one of many craft activities practiced at Stonehall but probably not a primary one, was combined with other domestic activities. The social dimension of pottery-making as proposed by A.M. Jones (*e.g.* 2000, 130) may be observed at Stonehall in the form of at least some potters adopting particular recipes. Significantly, this feature is shared in both the round-based vessel and Grooved ware traditions. Classifying these recipes at their simplest level, that is Sedimentary based and Igneous-Sedimentary fabrics (Maritan's Groups alpha and beta respectively, section 11.6), there is a measure of spatial and diachronic patterning across the settlement: a contrast between the dominance of the Sedimentary fabric in the early pottery on the Knoll and the greater frequency of the Sedimentary+Igneous fabric in the later pottery at the Farm (in Trench B), and a further contrast between the situation on the Knoll and the apparent predominance of the Sedimentary+Igneous fabric in the Meadow (Trenches A and Z) (Fig. 11.2.15). Two other features about Stonehall Farm Trench B require emphasis; one is the variation in the relative proportions of the two fabrics *within* the pottery in Trench B. The other is the appearance, observed macroscopically among some twenty sherds, of unusual fabrics: (a) relict straw-like inclusions in a few sherds and one clay ball, (b) fine, soft and almost powdery fabric common among the clay balls, and (c) a hard chunky fabric.

Within the Sedimentary fabric group are the very common and frequent sandstone and siltstone inclusions, but there are two other classes of inclusion that might be expected and deserve comment. First is shell which, for example, features in some of the pottery at Crossiecrown, Wideford Hill and Barnhouse. Although its presence at Stonehall cannot be excluded, it has not been confidently identified either in thin section or macroscopically (apart from one or two examples) as or as a platy void following the shell's dissolution or combustion. This apparent lack of shell is important because it strengthens the view that little or no pottery at Stonehall was deliberately tempered; were shell to be present in the fabric would imply tempering, whether as crushed or calcined shell. The absence of first shell as part of a recipe and second fish residues in the pottery (see section 11.7) is perhaps significant given that the inhabitants of Stonehall were surely familiar with the sea and sea shore which lay less than a mile from the settlement. Lacking also is the presence of grog in the pottery, there being only a handful of examples in Grooved ware. As Maritan has indicated (section11.6), such a low occurrence must point to accidental presence rather than deliberate addition. Leaving the issue of shell aside, the practices of clay preparation at Stonehall were generally comparable to those elsewhere in the Cuween-Wideford Plain, but in comparison with Barnhouse (A. M. Jones 2005a) were unsophisticated.

The tendency for the later Neolithic pottery to have a greater quantity of inclusions than the earlier pottery has already been commented on. But there is also a trend in the size of inclusions; the earlier pottery shows a unimodal distribution with a long tail and a mode at 2–6mm which is rather similar to that of the clays from the Stonehall vicinity (Fig. 11.2.16), contrasting with the later Neolithic pottery's possible bimodal distribution. This later pottery tends to have larger inclusions, some of which may have been added.

11.2.5 Pottery traditions at Stonehall

More important is the relationship between the two traditions at Stonehall. Morphologically, the round-based pottery comes in different sizes. On Stonehall Knoll there are proportionately more large-sized vessels than at the Meadow (Fig. 11.2.1). Within the Stonehall Meadow assemblage there are distinctions: Trench A has more small-sized vessels and these tend to be in a finer fabric than the larger vessels, while in Trench Z medium to large size vessels predominate. The size of Grooved ware vessels also varies and in a continuous fashion to judge by the distribution of wall thickness (Fig. 11.2.10). Using the ranges loosely defining medium and large sizes at Crossiecrown (1–1.2 and >1.3cm respectively), it is apparent that these two sizes predominate at Stonehall, the former being numerically more common perhaps for two reasons: it was easier to make and it had greater functional convenience as a cooking pot. The larger-sized vessels were also used for cooking and no doubt for storage as well, as is proposed at Crossiecrown. Among the finer fabric vessels, some are small sized,

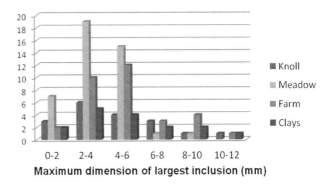

Figure 11.2.16 Distribution of sizes (in mm) of the maximum dimension of the largest inclusion observed in the thin sections of clays, early Neolithic pottery (Knoll and Meadow) and late Neolithic pottery (Farm).

as in Stonehall Meadow (Trench A), more of them are medium sized. Pots were broken before they were thrown onto the middens at Stonehall Knoll and Farm because there were fragments of different pots one on top of the other.

Drawing on the experience of the experimental pottery making (section 11.5), one of the more striking contrasts between the respective attempts at making round-based and flat-based vessels was the time factor. While the basic making of the former series could be completed in one operation with the aid of moulds, a medium-size flat-based vessel needed a day or so to dry between each series of coils and could easily have taken several weeks to complete. In both cases, the pots would probably have needed several more weeks to dry sufficiently for firing. Although several pots could be under construction at any one time, it seems unlikely that this would be a large-scale activity and all the more likely that it should be considered a small scale, even seasonal one. But the more general important point is that while fabric analysis has pointed to *common materials* for both pottery classes, conceptual differences lie behind the classes' *forming methods*.

These conceptual differences can be explored further. First, there is a hint that the mind set or attitude invoked in forming the vessel altered: to judge from such detail as the rims, for example, greater variation occurs in the earlier than the later pottery, as if pottery shape was rather more personalised, less regimented than it was later. This is a trend, not an absolute. One explanation could be that the early phase potters were few in number and they operated relatively independently of each other, while later on there were more potters and they communicated and shared ideas more. However, little evidence is available to support this: the population of Stonehall Farm does not appear suddenly to have expanded during the Grooved ware period, thereby increasing the number of potters.

The second difference moves to the steps intermediate between forming and firing the vessel, namely treating and decorating the surface. Leaving aside burnishing or polishing, the limited evidence for which suggests it was happening in both early and later phases, there is one obvious difference and that is the (total) lack of decoration in the early phase and its relative frequency later on when greater emphasis was placed on the social significance of how the pottery was viewed from *without*. It was Grooved ware's *external* features – its general appearance and decoration - which were important. The sense of difference extended *beyond* Stonehall as the pottery tradition of pottery during the early Neolithic took a different path to the contemporary one at Wideford Hill, where Unstan ware with all its manifestations of decoration was being produced, and to a lesser extent at Brae of Smerquoy where the common round-based vessels are joined by some Unstan ware bowls. This serves to emphasise the individuality and separateness of 4th millennium cal BC communities on Orkney. In fact, there is as much variation in the earlier Neolithic pottery within Stonehall as between that and the nearby Wideford Hill assemblage.

Some further comments on the experiments reported in 11.5 can be mentioned here. First, burnishing was an essential step in reducing the replica pots' porosity and improving their appearance. A small smooth pebble consistently proved to be the best tool for this purpose. It was nevertheless the case that even after burnishing the replica pots had a significantly more sandy, less smooth surface feel than the Neolithic pottery. Furthermore, the burnishing process left visible markings on the experimental pottery, but ironically it was much less evident on the Neolithic pottery; instead the surface was at least smoothed, if not polished. Either the burnishing was not sufficiently accomplished in the experimental pots to remove the 'hackly' surface feel, or there was an additional step – perhaps the application of an oil/fat to the surface – that the Neolithic potter used to improve the pots' finish. Alternatively, this contrast may be a reflection of the Neolithic pot's surface being smoothed as a result of use as a cooking pot or even the way it had abraded after discard.

Second, the view that the firing was a communal small-scale operation, not domestic, as has been argued at Barnhouse (A. M. Jones 2005a, 34f), remains plausible and indeed is not inconsistent with a potential firing area at Stonehall. Located some 30m away from the main locus of settlement at Stonehall Farm was a high magnetic susceptibility burnt area (Trench D: Figs 5.3 and 11.5.7c) without any evident associated structural remains. The experimental firings at Stonehall, all based on the use of a bonfire and far from exhaustive in either scope or design, nevertheless highlighted the effectiveness of seaweed as a fuel, the importance of a pre-firing step, and the variable quality of the products according to their position within the bonfire. But it should now be acknowledged that several elements in the firing process, ranging from the firing structure, its location, the fuel or fuels used, the length and frequency of firing, varied in space and time. Important evidence here comes from the Knowes of Trotty (section 11.10 and Chapter 3.4) where not only was a firing structure found, akin to a kiln but without an underlying pit or separation of fuel from pots, dating to the earlier Neolithic phase, but it was located in the yard immediately adjacent to the house (Chapter 3, Fig. 3.18). This firing structure, perhaps holding around ten vessels and roughly half the size of Harrison and Appleby's experimental 'kiln' (Harrison 2008), was fuelled with peat and turves. To the potters, who would probably not have been adventurous in their firing techniques, neither the simple 'kiln' nor the bonfire held a functional advantage; the decision to use one or the other was less a matter of choice and more of habit or tradition. The potters knew and accepted that a given firing produced unique products and that the same firing routine could give different products, as Livingstone Smith (2001) has observed in present-day (non-kiln) firings at locations in West Africa.

This hypothesis, questioning whether a structure like that at Knowes of Trotty would give superior quality products, appears to be in accord with the excavation evidence that the pottery was not highly fired, and yet it may conflict with results of a different kind from another site, Pool, Sanday (Hunter *et al.* 2007). Here, Spencer and Sanderson (2012) have shown that the high-temperature thermoluminescence signal from pottery belonging to the full Neolithic sequence (Periods 1.1 to 3.1) changed in a manner suggesting that the earlier pottery was better fired. It remains to be seen whether this had more to do with more plentiful fuel than the nature of firing structure in the earlier periods. At Stonehall it may only have been when environmental or other circumstances changed that potters adapted to a different fuel or firing location. The absence of any pots with repair holes may suggest that so long as the pot survived the firing, which pre-supposes that some did not, the pot was a functioning vessel. Some pots, although probably poorly fired (< 600°C), would have still been serviceable, indeed their subsequent use on the hearth may have provided repeated 'bakings'. In identifying in the course of this discussion the range of variables involved in the firing process, further experimental work could usefully be carried out, including elucidating the comparative performance of 'kiln' and bonfire and how to achieve a greater economy of fuel than has been possible thus far. An open mind on this matter of variation of firing over time and space is called for at present, recognising that further direct archaeological evidence of firing structures on Orkney or beyond is likely to be very limited, as explained in Chapter 3 and in 11.10.3.

We can now tackle the issue of the extent of overlap between the two traditions, distinguished as we have just argued on the basis of technique of manufacture and decoration. The starting position is an acceptance that the first appearance of Grooved ware corresponds to changing practices *within* society. It can be assumed to have been a slow transition in which some houses within the settlement were adopting the new tradition, while others retained the old. In the archaeological record this transition manifests itself as a palimpsest effect, yet once it was completed it was final. This is significant because whereas the transition from round to flat-based vessels has been observed to occur in many Neolithic societies, rarely is it final; round-based vessels may disappear from the repertory of shapes, only to reoccur later on as the need arises. The intriguing difficulty here is that that change was *not* apparently triggered by a new agricultural regime: the results of organic residue analysis seem confidently to assert no significant change in the food types consumed as reflected in residues in the round-based and Grooved ware pottery (see section 11.7), and the botanical evidence (Chapter 15) points to continuity in the cultivated crops.

Instead a whole host of other factors are likely to be in operation. The suggested development of *société à maisons* in Orkney clearly involved changing practices and material strategies of group identity which influenced the form of house architecture and the use of space within the house (see Chapter 9). Among many possible manifestations of these factors is one already alluded to, that there was a need for Grooved ware to be self-supporting and visible: the vessels had to stand alone, they were perhaps more visible within the house, and their shape, size and decoration assumed more significance than previously

(cf. Clarke and Sharples 1990, 60–64). This suggestion implicitly situates and integrates processes of ritual and domestic activities within the 'house'. One measure of support for this suggestion comes from the observation of greater uniformity in details such as the vessel rim.

In connection with domestic activities it is relevant to turn to the clay balls which are a feature of the later Neolithic midden at Stonehall Farm in Trench B (although one was encountered in Trench C in [4006]); a few were found complete but more were in fragmentary form. Their notable and common features are a distinctly fine orange-grey clay, soft almost chalky to the touch, and a bi-conical shape made from two halves, *c.*4cm maximum diameter and *c.*5cm height (complete ball). They constitute the best and unequivocal evidence for the use of a fine clay at the site. Their condition ranges from unfired to lightly fired, perhaps from proximity to a hearth, to more fully fired. Their functions could be various; that they represent 'playing' with clay seems unlikely in view of their apparently deliberate two-part manufacture. Their lack of a central perforation rules out that they were spindle whorls. They are twice the size of spherical clay balls found at Pool (Phase 2.2) which MacSween (2007, 294, Ill. 8.16) has suggested could have formed part of a game or had some connection with pottery production.

Other clay balls of similar size have been recovered from Links of Noltland and Ness of Brodgar (Graeme Wilson and Roy Towers pers. comms.). Andrew Appleby's suggestion (pers. comm.) that the potter prepared the balls and kept them moist under a cloth for later use in decoration accords well with the applied cordons on Grooved ware being consistently made of a fine clay but such a function should not require the two-part manufacture. Looking beyond Orkney, Atalay and Harstof (2005, 188f, Fig. 8.3) proposed that the clay balls found in the recent excavations at Çatalhöyük were closely connected with cooking, serving as a type of grill. Such a scenario would mean that the balls would be well-baked, they probably broke easily and had a short lifetime. That the Stonehall examples are mostly unfired or low fired need not be problematic; they look as if they had been freshly made but for some reason they were never used and instead found their way onto the midden. The 'used' clay balls have simply not survived.

An alternative and perhaps more realistic view would see the two halves acting as temporary feet for hot vessels recently removed from the hearth and placed on the floor. This tentative link between the clay balls, Grooved ware and the hearth conveniently draws in the use wear evidence: a third of the sherds at Stonehall Farm in Trench B display some indication of sooting on the exterior or interior surface or both, and a quarter have some form of residue, more often on the interior than on the exterior. Furthermore, the particular location of that residue, ranging from the interior edge of the base to the interior close to the rim, hints at a variety of cooking operations, from boiling with/without a lid, baking to grilling. A new phase of experimental work could usefully explore this topic by resolving which of those operations are most relevant.

On the links between Stonehall and its environs within the Bay of Firth, the pottery evidence suggests they were limited but directed, to judge from the comparable finds at other sites. In the early Neolithic there was a definable connection between Stonehall and Brae of Smerquoy in that plain round-based vessels were made at both settlements, but such a link was apparently absent in the case of Stonehall and Wideford Hill. For the later Neolithic and bearing in mind the relative lack of chronological contemporaneity between Stonehall and Crossiecrown, it is remarkable that there is but one sherd with scallop rim at Stonehall, a decorative feature so characteristic of Grooved ware at Crossiecrown, Links of Noltland and Ness of Brodgar. Mention has already been made of the decorative feature of SF 6249 from Stonehall Farm (Trench B), also encountered at Barnhouse, and more generally there was an awareness at Stonehall of decorative motifs that had currency throughout Orkney. The impression gained is that while Stonehall naturally belonged to the network of communities on Orkney, implying it had contacts and communications going well beyond the Bay of Firth, it was probably not a major member of that network; it was somewhat outside.

To the evidence for function on the basis of GC-MS analysis reported in section 11.7, the following additional comments can be made: ruminant dairy fats are numerically the most common in both early and later Neolithic phases at Stonehall, yet there is a distinctly greater frequency of mixtures of fats in the Grooved ware than in the early Neolithic round-based bowls. Fish residues are absent. No distinctions can be made, nor may be expected, in the contents of the early Neolithic bowls according to findspot at Stonehall Knoll and Meadow. There is no apparent correlation between content and vessel size (based on sherd thickness). The highest concentration of extracted lipid (>500 μg/g) appears among sherds from Stonehall Knoll and Meadow, and finally it is noted that many of the sherds with greatest wall thickness (>2.0cm) have the lowest extracted lipid yield.

11.3 Crossiecrown

Andrew Meirion Jones

11.3.1. Introduction

The Neolithic settlement site at Crossiecrown represents a unique opportunity in terms of Orcadian prehistory to examine long-term changes in pottery sequence and ceramic technology. Neolithic settlement sites with deep stratified pottery sequences have been excavated previously, at Pool (Hunter *et al.* 2007; Hunter and MacSween 1991) and Rinyo (Childe and Grant 1939, 1947). However the sequence is either broken, as at Pool, and does not include the late Neolithic/early Bronze Age transition, or it has been called into question as at Rinyo (Clarke 1983).

The presence at Crossiecrown of small quantities of stratified Unstan ware and Beaker pottery, along with a major assemblage of Grooved ware, allows us to confirm the veracity of the pottery sequence discussed by both Childe and Grant (1939; 1947) and Renfrew (1979). More importantly it enables us to examine in detail the changes in ceramic technology during the full sequence of the Orcadian Neolithic.

To this end, the Crossiecrown section of this chapter is directed towards two main aims:

- The primary aim is to characterise the pottery assemblage from the Neolithic and early Bronze Age site of Crossiecrown, Orkney.
- The secondary aim is to understand the changes in ceramic technology that occur within a pottery sequence that begins with early Neolithic Unstan ware and ends with the production of late Neolithic/early Bronze Age Beaker pottery. In order to define and characterise these changes in ceramic technology a series of attributes of the pottery were recorded, which included construction technique and base and rim morphology. Macroscopic analysis of pottery sherds was undertaken alongside a petrological analysis of Unstan ware, Grooved ware and Beaker. The methodology and results of this analysis are detailed below (sections headed *characterisation of assemblage*, *technological analysis of pottery* and *petrological analysis*).

In terms of organisation most sections of the report are divided by the traditional classification of 'Unstan ware', 'Grooved ware' and 'Beaker'. It is important at this juncture to point out that this merely serves as a heuristic device as a means of organising the report and providing the reader with an understanding of the ceramic sequence. As discussed elsewhere (Jones 2007), we need to consider ceramic technologies as a series of socially motivated practices within a spectrum of technological choices. As such the hard and fast distinctions between, say, Grooved ware and Beaker are less rigid, and, as illustrated in this analysis of the Crossiecrown assemblage, we are best viewing each pottery 'tradition' as the manifestation of an evolving series of technological choices. In the report that follows, the technological characteristics of pottery will be given primacy over prescriptive descriptions of ceramic traditions, as a means of alleviating or side-stepping the fixed and bounded categories of traditional analyses.

In addition to examining the changes in pottery sequence, an analysis of the major spatial patterns of the large Grooved ware assemblage is key to understanding the social practices associated with pottery use and deposition, and also the occupation and abandonment of the settlement site itself.

11.3.2. *General comments on assemblage*

This section provides a brief overview of the three major pottery traditions present at Crossiecrown and discusses the parallels between the Crossiecrown assemblage and ceramics from other Orcadian sites, as well as further afield. In undertaking such an exercise it is wise to sound a note of caution. As noted elsewhere (Jones 1997; 2002), it is problematic to treat pottery assemblages as static markers of cultural tradition (see also S. Jones and Richards 2000; 2005). Instead we need to understand that pottery is produced, used and deposited in relation to a complex and dynamic set of social practices. As the analysis of the Grooved ware assemblage at Barnhouse demonstrated, Grooved ware vessels of different sizes from the same site are produced quite differently and have quite distinct life histories or biographies (Jones 1997; 2000; 2002). Notwithstanding this, the comparison of pottery assemblages, especially within Orkney, is a useful exercise which enables us to consider the degree of contact between sites and the role of pottery as a means of expressing community identity (Jones 2000).

11.3.2.1 *Unstan ware*

The Unstan ware assemblage at Crossiecrown is relatively small. The major unequivocal sherds of Unstan ware are SFs 774 and 777 (Pot group 1, [446]) which come from redeposited midden material in the recess of the Grey House. The characteristic features are the carination and the cross-hatched diagonal incisions above this (Fig. 11.3.1). The pot from which these sherds are derived is a medium size bowl which is paralleled at most of the

main sites where Unstan ware occurs including Unstan (Davidson and Henshall 1989), Isbister (Hedges 1983), Knap of Howar (Ritchie 1983) and Wideford Hill (Chapter 2; Chapter 11.4). The sherds from Crossiecrown are slightly coarser and thicker than some of the examples from Knap of Howar, but by comparison with the more complete assemblage from Wideford Hill the sherds fall well within the range of sizes from settlement sites.

In addition, another decorated sherd is the rim SF 1042 (Pot group 3, [515]) which came from midden deposits beneath the collapse of the Red House. This sherd is decorated with a series of linear impressions below the rim, and in appearance is paralleled with some of the plain bowls bearing minimal decoration from Knap of Howar, Unstan and Isbister (Davidson and Henshall 1989; Hedges 1983; Ritchie 1983). A number of very definite early Neolithic rim forms are evident, again likely to be from plain bowls, including SFs 1124, 1129, 1140 (Pot group 3, [517]) from midden layers beneath the collapse of the Red House. The rim from this group of sherds is characteristically club shaped. Furthermore, SF 1083 (Pot group 1, [515]) from the same midden context as SF 1042, has a characteristic T-shaped rim found in a number of plain bowl assemblages (*e.g.* Davidson and Henshall 1989: Calf of Eday, bowl 9; Isbister, bowls 15, 33; Taversoe Tuick, bowl 4, 20).

Further to this, a small number of sherds exhibit a pronounced curvature and thickness suggesting that they are from round-based vessels. These include SFs 872, 882 (Pot group 2, [471]) from the collapse beneath the Red House; SF 1002 (Pot group 1, [476]) and SFs 900 and 997 (Pot group 2, [476]) from midden deposits beneath the Red House.

All the sherds from early Neolithic vessels are derived from fairly discrete contexts and are either found in the layers interfacing the Red and Grey Houses, or within the redeposited/collapsed wall-core material of the Grey House. As expected, while these are securely stratified, they are subject to a degree of mixing as these deposits also include sherds from unequivocal Grooved ware vessels.

11.3.2.2 *Grooved ware*

The clearest parallels for the Grooved ware from Crossiecrown come from Pool, Sanday and the Links of Noltland, Westray (and Ness of Brodgar, R. Towers pers. com.). The resemblances between these are striking. Just as scalloped rims with applied decoration are a component of the Pool, phase 3 assemblage and the Links of Noltland assemblage (*e.g.* MacSween 1992, figure 19.2; Sheridan 1999; Fig. 12.4, 2–4) so too are they a component of the Crossiecrown assemblage (see list below). The rims at Crossiecrown are, however, noticeably larger and more massive than those at Pool and Links of Noltland. There is likewise a resemblance between SF 1481 with two applied cordons near the rim, one with stab impressions and a vessel from the Links of Noltland (Sheridan 1999; Fig. 12.4, 1). Indeed, slash or stab impressions are a feature of both Crossiecrown and Links of Noltland (see Sheridan 1999; Fig. 12.6, 12–14). Lozenge motifs, both incised and applied, seem to predominate at Crossiecrown. Three of the vessels with incised lozenge motifs are identical; SF 150 (pot group 1, [003]), SFs 152, 154 (pot group 4, [006]) and SF 256, [987] (pot group 1, [142]). All of these vessels bear a striking resemblance to a pot from Pool, phase 2 (MacSween 1992; Fig. 19.1).

A further feature of the Crossiecrown Grooved ware is of note. This is the unusual internal decoration on the base of SFs 316, 380, 343 (pot group 2, [210]). The vessel is decorated with an applied cruciform, one segment of which is decorated with applied pellets which are finger-tip impressed. This base decoration bears a superficial resemblance to a pot from Links of Noltland (Sheridan 1999; Fig. 12.7), however the latter vessel has incised rather than applied decoration and has far more sparse external decoration than the Crossiecrown example. What is noticeable is the resemblance in decoration between each of these three late assemblages. It has been suggested elsewhere that during the later phases of the Orcadian late Neolithic, Grooved ware decoration is less of a marker of specific settlements and instead converges to reflect a wider Orcadian sense of identity (Jones 2000). This would seem to be borne out by this brief comparison of these assemblages from three distinct locations within Orkney.

11.3.2.3 Beaker
Like the Unstan ware assemblage, the Beaker assemblage from Crossiecrown is also relatively small. However, it is critically important as it represents some of the few unequivocal Beaker sherds from Orcadian Neolithic settlement sites. Nevertheless despite the presence of 'classic Beaker' sherds, a greater number of sherds diverge from the standard Beaker repertoire and, as argued below, represent an evolution and experimentalism within the existing Grooved ware tradition.

Probably the best examples of a Beaker are sherds SF 229 (Pot group 1, [208]) from the stony occupation material filling the probable timber structure in the

northern area of Trench 2. These represent a rim and shoulder from a pot decorated with twisted-cord impressions. The rim is rounded with an external cordon and is decorated with two parallel horizontal twisted-cord impressions with an infill of short vertical twisted-cord impressions. The shoulder has three parallel horizontal twisted-cord impressions. Beneath the third of these is a series of diagonal twisted-cord impressions. These sherds are paralleled in many Beaker assemblages to the south, but probably the best parallel for these sherds in terms of technique is the Beaker vessel from Rinyo (Childe and Grant 1939, 1947).

11.3.3 Methodology
The ceramic assemblage from Crossiecrown was analysed on a context by context basis. This involved, just had been previously done for the Barnhouse assemblage, laying out the individual sherds in the spatial positions and contexts in which they were excavated. This allowed a clear assessment of the similarity or difference of groups of sherds with different find numbers. The aim in doing this was not only to understand the spatial patterning of the site, but to assess the number of vessels in the assemblage. In those parts of the site where a single context prevailed (such as Trench 1) sherds were analysed by individual spit and were grouped using the site grid. Accordingly, sherds of different small find number are grouped as 'pot groups' by context. Pot groups are defined by concordances in fabric, wall thickness and diagnostic features such as rim or base morphology and decoration. This allows for a clear and accurate assessment of the numbers of *vessels* of each pottery class in the assemblage.

11.3.4. Characterisation of assemblage

11.3.4.1 Unstan ware
The total number of Unstan ware/early Neolithic vessels was 18.

Only 18 early Neolithic or Unstan ware vessels, represented by individual pot groups, were recovered at Crossiecrown. Although difficult from this small sample to determine the overall demography of the assemblage, it is notable that most of the diagnostic sherds appear to be from plain as opposed to decorated vessels (only two decorated vessels are present, *e.g.* SF 774 – Fig. 11.3.1). This pattern mirrors that at the Knap of Howar where plain vessels appear to predominate. In terms of the composition of the assemblage, there seems little to distinguish the vessels in terms of size and tempering strategy. Unlike the tempering of Grooved ware there are no obvious distinctions in terms of frequency or type of temper in small or large vessels. However this may be due to the fairly small size of the sample.

Rim sherds

A number of rim forms are produced; these include T-shaped and club-shaped rims, flattened rims with exterior lips or inversions, rounded rims with exterior lips and rounded and bevelled rims. Finally pointed rims also occur, one on a vessel with an external lug. Due to the small number of early Neolithic vessels from Crossiecrown there are few examples of these rim forms, and it is consequently difficult to determine their frequency in the assemblage overall. Rim diameters are likewise sparse, there being just four measurements on early Neolithic rims. The two T-shaped rims are 22cm and 27cm; one flattened and inverted rim also produced a rim diameter of 22cm, while a pointed rim gave a diameter of 18cm. Based on just four measurements this gives a very general picture that pointed rims are from neutral bowls, while the T-shaped and flattened rims are on larger open bowls (Table 11.3.1).

Base Sherds

A series of sherds have a pronounced thickening of the base, suggesting they come from round-based vessels. A number of sherds are tapered or flattened towards the base by incorporating elements of late Neolithic base technology such as the addition of internal coils of clay to thicken and strengthen the interior (Table 11.3.2).

Decoration

Decoration is sparse on early Neolithic vessels at Crossiecrown. The only examples being on SFs 774, 777 (pot group 1, [446]) which is a series of diagonal incisions above a classic Unstan ware carination (Fig.11.3.1). The other example is SF 1042 (pot group 7, [515]) which is on a rim sherd (Fig.11.3.3a), which consists of three stab impressions just below the rim from a rounded edge tool. In addition sherds from one vessel, SFs 1055, 1093 (pot group 1, [493]), is lugged with a small pellet of clay and another sherd, SF 1072 (pot group 2, [517]), has a plain cordon.

Unusual characteristics

Furthermore, one rim sherd, SF 1072 (pot group 1, [517]) is perforated. The perforation is made through wet clay, and is evidently an intentional component of the pot design, probably a suspension hole.

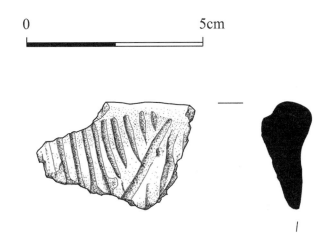

Figure 11.3.1 Unstan ware sherd SF 774 from context [445], Trench 2 at Crossiecrown.

Table 11.3.1 Early Neolithic rim forms.

Rim form	SF No.	Pot group	Context	Rim diameter (cm)
T-shaped rims	1008	-	-	22
	1083	5	515	27
Club-shaped rims	1124, 1129, 1140	3	517	
Flat rim with exterior lip	1072	2	517	
Flat rim, inverted	671	1	001	22
	1042 (Fig. 11.3.3)	7	515	
Rounded, external lip	1099	1	144	
Rounded, bevelled	1072	1	517	
Pointed or tapered rims	887, 973, 992	2	481	
	1055, 1093 (Fig. 11.3.3)	1	493	18

Table 11.3.2 Characteristics of round-based vessels.

Base details	SF No.	Pot group	Context
Thickening base	939, 949	8	003
Thickening base	872, 882	2	471
Thickening base	1002	1	476
Thickening base	900, 997	2	476
Thickening base	917, 950	2	480
Tapering base	782, 813, 1123, 1138	2	446
Tapering base	1156	3	450

Table 11.3.3 Round-based vessel sherds showing sooting.

Rim or base	SF No.	Pot group	Context	Description
Rim		5	515	Soot and residue
Rim		7	515	Soot and residue
Rim		2	481	Soot near Rim
Rim		1	493	Soot and residue
Rim		3	517	Soot and residue
Base		2	471	Residue
Base		1	476	Soot
Base		1	480	Soot

Surface Treatment

All the identifiable early Neolithic or Unstan ware sherds were smoothed, however a few seem to have been both smoothed and burnished. These include SF 872, 882 (pot group 2, [471]), SF 1002 (pot group 1, [476]), SF 1042 (pot group 7, [515]) and SFs 1124, 1129, 1140 (pot group 3, [517]).

Tempering Strategy

There are no obvious patterns to note in the tempering strategy amongst the early Neolithic sherds. Most sherds are tempered with between 10–40% angular rocks; only one sherd differs, SF 1099 (pot group 1, [144]), which is tempered with 5% rounded rock. A few sherds are tempered with a mixture of shell and rock. These are usually of a sparser frequency than the rock-tempered sherds, with between 1–20% shell and typically 5% rock. There is little difference between the temper in rim and base sherds, and no obvious distinction between larger and smaller vessels.

Use-wear

A number of the rims and bases exhibit evidence of use in the form of sooting. Interestingly the evidence for use crosses most rim types and soot is found on smaller and larger vessels, suggesting little discernible difference in use. The evidence for use on the base suggests the suspension of the vessels above the fire during cooking (see Table 11.3.3).

11.3.4.2 Grooved ware

Numbering 337 vessels by individual pot groups, the Grooved ware assemblage from Crossiecrown is both complex and extensive. The Grooved ware mainly comes from the Red House, but is also found in the Grey House and in the large midden spread in Trench 1. The assemblage seems to broadly conform to the pattern observed at Barnhouse (Jones 1997; 2002; A. M. Jones and Richards 2003, 38–43) and Links of

Noltland (Sheridan 1999), with at least three main sizes of vessel: large, medium and small. These vessel sizes also relate to vessel form, with larger vessels tending to be more upright bucket-shaped, smaller vessels more splayed or open shapes, and medium size vessels either bucket or open-shaped. At Barnhouse a clear difference in tempering strategy was evident in vessels of different size; although this broadly holds for Crossiecrown, the tempering strategy is a lot less clear-cut. Furthermore, like Barnhouse, there are distinct forms of decoration on vessels of different size, although we often observe scaled-down/scaled-up versions of decorative motifs or designs found on vessels of different size.

Following the presentation below of the features of Grooved ware vessels, there is discussion of the specific characteristics of large, medium and small-sized vessels. In determining the size of vessels particular attention is paid to wall thickness/width as a crude index of vessel size (see Jones 1997; 2002; A. M. Jones and Richards 2003; Fig. 3.18).

Rim sherds

A number of distinctive rim forms occur amongst the Grooved ware assemblage. These include bevelled, pointed, rounded, scalloped and flat rims. Flat rims have a number of additional features such as evertions and internal lips or steps.

Most of the rims (nine) are grouped in the 1.3–1.5cm range, and an equal number (nine) are 1–1.2cm wall thickness. A minority (four) are on small vessels with a wall thickness of less than 1cm. This suggests that bevelled rims are especially appropriate on vessels of medium to large size, with a very small number produced on small vessels. Nevertheless, bevelled rims representing twenty four vessels are the most frequent rim form and it is important to note that they are appropriate for vessels across all size ranges. Rim diameters vary from 10cm–43cm (Fig. 11.3.2), in other words across the entire size range.

Table 11.3.4 Bevelled rims (Fig. 11.3.3).

SF No.	Pottery group	Context	Wall thickness (cm)	Rim diameter (cm)
1232	88	002	0.6	10
1429,1503	10	002	1.5	26
1366, 1412, 1499, 1609	13	002	1.4	
1381, 1459	23	002	0.7	16
1440, 1481, 1505	24	002	1.4	38
1269, 1293	34	002	1.3	
1308, 1203, 1252, 1477	46	002	1.2	23
1387, 1508	51	002	1.3	
1208, 1209, 1254, 1257, 1358, 1525	53	002	1.5	
1284, 1215	59	002	1.2	22
1261, 1262, 1213, 1258, 1256, 1426	62	002	1.4	
1106, 1298, 1296, 1406, 1270	67	002	0.8	23
1483, 1278, 1385	75 and 76	002	1.0	
1281, 1323, 1282, 1531, 1590, 1612 (Fig. 11.3.3), 1389	83	002	1.5	36
1547 (Fig. 11.3.3), 1596, 1560	84	002	1.4	30
1324 (Fig. 11.3.3), 1319, 1533	92	002	0.7	
1454, 1565, 1388	104	002	1.0	25
1356	113	002	1.0	
1540, 1539, 1601, 1449	117	002	1.5	23–6
517, 500, 60	2	026	1.0	18
278	2	033	1.2	20
1106	1	484	1.0	
316, 380, 343	2	210	1.3	43
991	2	175	1.0	

Table 11.3.5 Pointed rims (Fig. 11.3.3).

SF No.	Pottery group	Context	Wall thickness (cm)	Rim diameter (cm)
1434, 1607	11	002	0.7	
1403	16/17	002	0.7	
1526	58	002	0.7	
1579, 1581	78	002	1.4	
1310, 1313, 1349, 1379, 1439, 1541, 1577	87	002	1	
1316, 1346, 1347	109	002	0.7	
1321 (Fig. 11.3.3), 1553	90	002	1	
1233	91	002	1.2	
1598 (Fig. 11.3.3)	94	002	0.6	10
1380, 1552, 1578, 1603	95	002	0.7	
1291, 1442, 1237, 1240, 1584, 1315, 1207, 1206, 1247	98	002	1.4	
1550, 1468, 1292,	103	002	0.9	
1452, 1465	108	002	1	
150 (Fig. 11.3.5)	1	003	1	19
944	7	003	1	
SF A	6	006	1.4	24+
693, 700, 723, 733, 998	1	145	1.8	
831	3	464	1.2–1.5	

Table 11.3.6 Rounded rims (Fig. 11.3.3).

Type	SF No.	Pottery group	Context	Wall thickness (cm)	Rim diameter (cm)
Rounded	1030, 1050, 1242, 1244, 1423, 1473, 1611	15	002	1.2	
Rounded	1196 (Fig. 11.3.3), 1235, 1236, 1307, 1417, 1519, 1613	33	002	1	
Rounded	1253	47	002	0.7	
Rounded	1490	48	002	0.6	
Rounded	1285, 1306, 1509	56	002	1	
Rounded	1401, 1286, 1204, 1201, 1250	63	002	1.3	
Rounded	1580 (Fig. 11.3.3)	79	002	1	
Rounded	1536, 1309, 1314, 1597, 1534, 1606	97	002	1.2	
Rounded	1438, 1604	105	002	1	
Rounded	1602, 1576, 1436, 1485	121	002	0.9	
Rounded	No SF number	4	001	1	
Rounded	51, 55	1	019/021	0.7	
Rounded	232, 264	1	025	1	
Rounded	449, 440, 456	1	034	1	
Rounded	64	4	034	2	
Rounded	476, 441, 436	7	034	1	
Rounded	68 (Fig.11.3.3), 72	1	041	1	
Rounded	185, 248, 76, 249, 254, 250, 253, 246	1	047	1	
Rounded	929	2	144	0.6	
Rounded	808, 823	1	451	0.5	
Rounded	831	4	464	1.5	
Rounded	271, 277	1	135	1	
Rounded, everted rim	1529, 1304, 1251, 1530	45	002	0.8	
Rounded, everted rim	533	6	034	0.7	14
Rounded, everted rim	161, 524	3	103	0.8	14
Rounded rim, internal lip	703, 714, 748, 758, 805, 904	2	180	1.3	
Rounded, inverted rim	537, 151, 152	1	006	1.3	

Pointed rims are produced on a minimum of 17 vessels across the size range. There are a relatively high number of small vessels (seven) with wall thickness below 1cm, and almost equal numbers of large (five) vessels of 1.3cm or greater and medium-size (six) vessels with wall widths of 1–1.2cm. It would seem that pointed rims are especially appropriate forms for small vessels. Rim diameters range from 10 to 24cm.

Rounded rims, representing 27 vessels, appear to be the major rim form produced at Crossiecrown. They are produced on vessels of a range of different sizes. There are only a few large vessels (five) of wall thickness 1.3–2cm, while there are more small vessels (nine) of wall thickness less than 1cm. The majority of vessels (fifteen) are medium-size vessels of 1–1.2cm wall thickness. It would seem that this particular rim form is especially appropriate for medium-size vessels. Some vessels appear to have rounded everted or rounded inverted or lipped rims. Notably

rounded, everted rims are all made on small vessels, while inverted rims are made on medium and large vessels. Both measured rounded rims are 14cm in diameter.

Scalloped rims (Fig. 11.3.3: SF 1443 and scallop and incision) constitute one of the more remarkable elements of Grooved ware technology. Almost all the scallops are added to the top of the rim to produce a wavy, 'pie-crust' effect. Many of them are decorated internally with a thumbnail or stab impression. Scallops seem to be produced on vessels of different sizes, of which six vessels are represented from the recovered sherds. Three vessels are grouped in the range from 1.3–3.6cm, two vessels in the 1–1.1cm size range, and a single vessel is below 1cm in wall thickness. Again this seems to broadly reflect the demography of vessels of different size range across the site. However it is notable that scallop rims seem to be used on some of the most spectacular Grooved ware vessels, including some of the largest vessels in the assemblage.

Table 11.3.7 Scalloped rims (Fig. 11.3.3).

SF No.	Pottery group	Context	Wall thickness (cm)
325	2	169	0.6
1191, 1259, 1239, 1238, 1308, 1294, 1518, 1214, 1066, 1398, 1290, 1466, 1218, 1418, 1230, 1453, 1363	41	002	2–3.6
1467, 1528, 1260, 1480, 1524, 1443 (Fig. 11.3.3), 1520	61	002	1.7–2
1280	80	002	1
1328, 1326, 1325, 1025, 1327, 1227, 1224	82	002	1.1
1413, 1419, 1435, 1570, 1335, 1334, 1523, 1501, 1476, 1573	124	002	1.3

Table 11.3.8 Flat rims (Fig. 11.3.3).

Type	SF No.	Pottery group	Context	Wall thickness (cm)	Rim diameter (cm)
Flat rim	1481	25	002	1.7	
Flat, everted rim	1040, 1050, 1067, 1068, 1086, 1096	3	127	1–1.2	
Flat, everted rim	1267, 1516	9	002	0.8	
Flat, everted rim	1302	38	002	1	20–22
Flat, everted rim	1433, 1197, 1472, 1470, 1374, 1248 (Fig. 11.3.2a), 1428,	66	002	1.6	32
Flat, everted rim	1029, 1054	4	515	1	
Flat, internal step rim	218	1	137	1.2	
Flat, inverted slope	999	9	145	1	
Flat, inverted, interior lip	665. 1017	3	145	1	
Flat, inverted, stepped	695, 795, 1012	6	145	1	22
Flat rim, slight inversion	833	2	006	1	13
Flat rim, slight inversion	810, 814	2	451	0.8	20

However they are also found on one of the smallest and finest vessels.

The flat-rimmed vessels are essentially further divided into rims with an everted profile, and rims with an inverted profile or internal step. Only two large vessels of wall thickness greater than 1.3cm and two small vessels of less than 1cm wall thickness are produced with flat rims. The majority of flat-rimmed vessels (seven) seem to be produced on medium-size vessels between 1 and 1.2cm wall thickness. Rim diameters of flat rims range from 13 to 32cm, and represent a minimum of 9 vessels.

Synopsis of Grooved ware rims

There is an extensive range of rim sizes amongst the Grooved ware assemblage. Where a wall thickness could be measured to establish vessel size there are eight large vessels, ten medium-size vessels and six small vessels. The large vessels have rim diameters in the range 23–43cm, medium vessels 13–25cm, and 10–20cm.

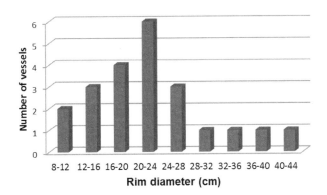

Figure 11.3.2 Grooved ware rim sizes.

Base Sherds

There are a total of 65 bases, all of them flat sherds, however there are a variety of different forming techniques including footed, rounded interior and rounded interior, squared exterior bases. It is also worth drawing a distinction between bases with upright walls (rising at 90 degrees from the base) with those with walls rising at 45 degrees as this provides an insight into the overall shape of the vessel.

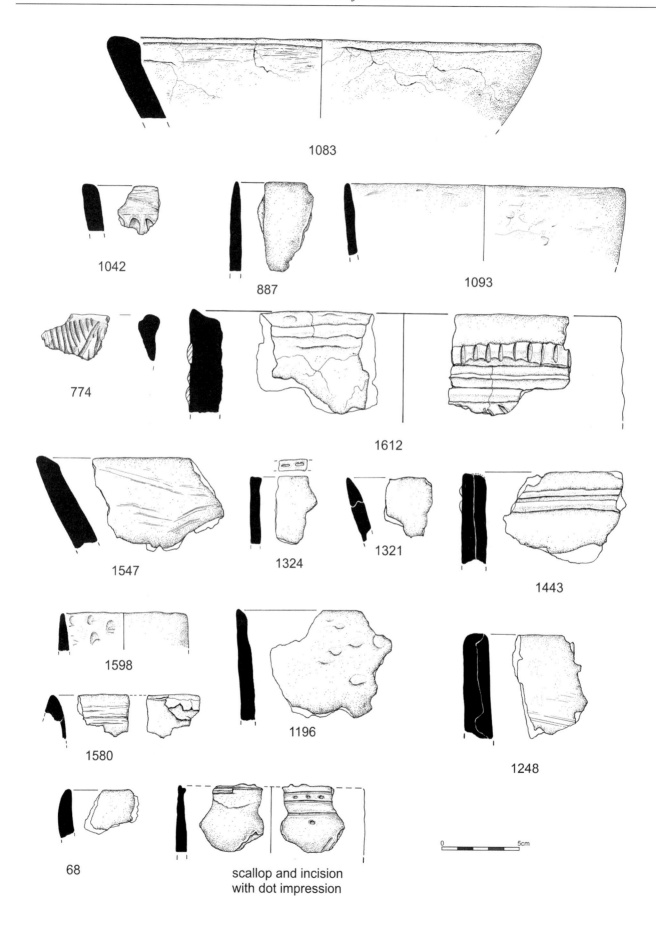

1083

1042

887

1093

774

1612

1547

1324

1321

1443

1598

1196

1580

1248

68

scallop and incision
with dot impression

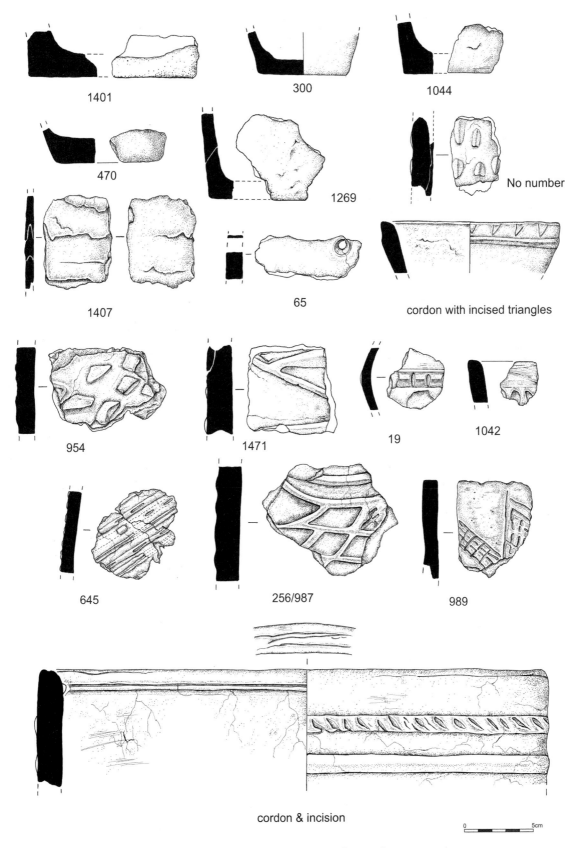

1401

300

1044

470

1269

No number

1407

65

cordon with incised triangles

954

1471

19

1042

645

256/987

989

cordon & incision

0   5cm

Figure 11.3.3 (above and opposite) Grooved ware from Crossiecrown.

Table 11.3.9 Flat bases.

SF No.	Pottery group	Context	Base thickness (cm)	Wall thickness (cm)	Base diameter (cm)	Rim type
68, 72	1	041	1.8	1		Rounded
831	4	464	2	1.5		Rounded
232, 264	1	025		1		Rounded
1529, 1304, 1251, 1530	45	002		0.8		Rounded, everted
1191, 1259, 1239, 1238, 1308, 1294, 1518, 1214, 1066, 1398, 1290, 1466, 1218, 1418, 1230, 1453, 1363	41	002	2	2–3.6		Scalloped
1328, 1326, 1325, 1025, 1327, 1227, 1224	82	002		1.1		Scalloped
517, 500, 60	2	026		1		Bevelled
1452, 1465	108	002		1		Pointed
1347, 1316, 1346	109	002		0.7	13	Pointed
1422, 1432, 1504	1	002	2.8	1.6		
1331, 1407, 1420, 1425, 1450, 1464	22	002	1.5	0.7	16	
1283	69	002				
1393, 1566, 1311	99	002		1		
1500, 1555, 1355	127	002		0.6	10	
No SF number	1	001	1.8	1		
53, 223	1	026	1.3	1		
181, 348, 538, 612, 834, 839	4	103		1		
224	1	109	2.2	1		
4000	1	110		1.5–2		
1044, 1046, 1049, 1051, 1085	1	127	1.7	0.8–1.2		
603, 642, 644, 651, 657	1	129	1.3	0.7		
346	2	173		1		
1158	2	450	0.7			
920, 939	4	490	1.2	0.8		
933	5	490	1.5	1.3		
1348, 1318	110	002	1.5	1		
No SF number	5	001	1.7	1		

Table 11.3.10 Footed bases.

SF No.	Pottery group	Context	Base diameter (cm)	Base thickness (cm)	Wall thickness (cm)	Rim diameter (cm)	Rim type
150 (Fig. 11.3.3)	1	003	11	1.7	1	19	Pointed
1536, 1309, 314, 1597, 1534, 1606	97	002	30–32		1.2		Rounded
1538, 1542, 1228	114	002			1		
1575, 1448, 1568, 1511, 1549,	129	002			0.7		
462	1	220			0.7		
1510, 1212	57	002	8		0.6		
298, 300 (Fig. 11.3.3)	1	147	16	1.7	1		
368	1	173		1	0.8		
83, 84	1	027	10	0.9	0.7		

Table 11.3.11 Bases with rounded interiors and/or square exteriors.

SF No.	Pottery group	Context	Base diameter (cm)	Base thickness (cm)	Wall thickness (cm)	Rim diameter (cm)	Rim type	Exterior
161, 524	3	103			0.8	14	Rounded, everted	
693, 700, 723, 733, 998	1	145		2	1.8			
712, 781, 1132	1	436	22	2.1	1			
934, 945, 948, 956	2	490		1.5				
65	1	033		2.5	1.5–2			
339	1	117		2				
870, 880	3	144		1.7				
732, 736	4	145		1.7				
407, 564	1	303		1.2	0.8			
305	4	025	8	1.2	0.7			Squared
256, 987	1	142	11	2	1.2			Squared
297, 304, 307, 308, 314	1	123	20		1			Squared
283	3	033	14	1	1			

Table 11.3.12 Bases with angled walls at 45 degree angle to base.

SF No.	Pottery group	Context	Base diameter (cm)	Base thickness (cm)	Wall thickness (cm)	Rim diameter (cm)	Rim type
1352, 1234, 1535	96	002			1.4		
1300	40	002	10		0.9		
414, 411, 425, 415	2	022	16	1.4	1		
55, 51	1	019/021	9	1	0.7		Rounded
1253	47	002			0.7		Rounded
1429, 1503	10	002	13		1.5	26	Bevelled
1381, 1459	23	002	11		0.7	16	Bevelled

Table 11.3.13 Bases with angled walls at 90 degree angle to base.

SF No.	Pottery group	Context	Base diameter (cm)	Base thickness (cm)	Wall thickness (cm)	Rim diameter (cm)	Rim type	Interior
316 (Fig. 11.3.4), 380, 343	2	210	30	2.2	1.3	43	Bevelled	Decorated base
1278, 1424, 1522	119	002			1			
1598	94	002	10–11		0.6	10	Pointed	
1269, 1293	34	002			1.3		Bevelled	
1196, 1235, 1236, 1307, 1417, 1519, 1613	33	002			1		Rounded	
1401 (Fig. 11.3.3), 1286, 1204, 1201, 1250	63	002			1.3		Rounded	

Synopsis of Grooved ware bases

There is an extensive range of base sizes amongst the Grooved ware assemblage. Where a wall thickness could be measured to establish vessel size there are twelve large vessels, 26 medium-size vessels and 18 small vessels. In terms of base diameters the large vessels range in base diameter from 26–30cm (based on only two measurements), medium vessels range in size from 11–30cm (based on seven measurements), while small vessels range from 9–16cm (based on twelve measurements). Most base forms, such as the rounded interior bases and those with walls angled at 45 or 90 degrees to the base, are made on vessels across a range of sizes. However, footed bases seem to be preferentially produced on medium- and small-size vessels.

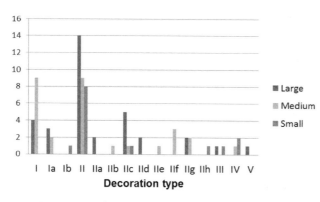

Figure 11.3.4 Decoration types for Grooved ware.

Decoration

There are 74 decorated vessels from Crossiecrown, representing 21.8% of the Grooved ware assemblage. Three main decorative techniques are employed: incision, application and impression (Fig. 11.3.4). The first two techniques are used in the main, with just a small number of sherds exhibiting impressed techniques. The basic decorative motifs are incised horizontal grooves (often multiple parallel grooves), or applied cordons. The predominant impressed motif is stab-and-drag and thumbnail. As with the production of rim and base forms, many decorative motifs or schemes occur on vessels of all sizes. In terms of the three basic decorative techniques, incision is found mainly on large and medium vessels with seven large vessels, eleven medium-size vessels and one small vessel being incised. Application is found on large, medium and small vessels; with 26 large vessels, 18 medium and 10 small vessels decorated with applied cordons or clay pellets. Impression is rare as a stand-alone technique and only one large, one medium and two small vessels are decorated by impressed techniques alone. The major technique at Crossiecrown appears to be application, with plain applied cordons predominating.

In considering Grooved ware decoration, it is helpful to consider the decoration of the vessel as a series of choices (Richards and Thomas 1984; Richards 1993b; Jones 2002): whether to decorate or not; choice of dominant decorative technique; overall complexity of design; additions to overall design. All of these occur as a series of stepwise choices in decorating a vessel. These choices can be classified as a series from simple to complex (see examples in Fig. 11.3.3):

Incision

I.   Single or multiple incision (Fig. 11.3.3 SF 1443)
Ia: Complex incised lozenge design (Fig 11.3.5)
Ib: Incision plus dot impression (Fig. 11.3.3 scallop and incision)

Application

II.   Single or multiple cordons
IIa: Cordon with incision in centre of cordon (Fig 11.3.3 SF 645)
IIb: Pinched or 'pin-tucked' cordons.
IIc: Alternating plain/decorated cordon designs with either thumbnail, lenticular or diagonal stab impressions (Fig. 11.3.3 SF 1612)
IId: Complex lozenge/'fish-net' design in cordons (Fig. 11.3.3 SFs 954, 1471)
IIe: Cordons plus incised triangles (Fig. 11.3.3 SF 256/987)
IIf: Cordons plus rosettes or impressed pellets of clay.
IIg: Cordons plus incision (Fig. 11.3.3 SF 19)
IIh: Cordon plus incision plus dot impression (Fig. 11.3.3 SF scallop and incision)
IIi: Rosettes/pellets of clay (Fig. 11.3.10)

Impression

IV: Vertical stab-and-drag motif up vessel wall (Fig. 11.3.3 no number)
V: Impressed zig-zag design (Fig. 11.3.3 SF 1042)

The relative frequency of the decorative types defined above can be seen in Figure. 11.3.4. A number of points need to be drawn out here. Overall, most of the plain cordoned vessels are large, a number of more complex cordon designs are produced on large vessels, but where cordons are combined with other motifs such as rosettes or incisions they are generally produced on medium-size vessels. There are few small decorated vessels, but those that are decorated tend to bear the most complex designs, either incised motifs with the addition of dot impressions or cordons, incision and dot impression, or on one occasion a rosette. Likewise the stab-and-drag motifs seem to be found on small vessels. This broad pattern of simple decoration on large vessels and more complex decoration on smaller vessels is paralleled at Barnhouse. However it is worth pointing out that at Crossiecrown applied decoration seems to predominate, and many complex designs incorporating applied cordons mainly appear on large and medium-size vessels.

Lozenge motifs seem to characterise Crossiecrown. Notably many of the incised lozenge designs are found on large vessels. It is also notable that applied cordons are used to produce lozenge or fishnet designs and these are also found on large vessels. The overall visual effect of incised or applied lozenge patterns seems to be similar. At least three of the vessels with incised lozenge motifs are identical; SF 150 (pot group 1, [003]), SFs 152, 154 (pot group 4, [006] – see Fig. 11.3.5) and SFs 256, 987 (pot group 1, [142]). Quite possibly these are made by the same potter or group of potters.

Unusual characteristics

Two vessels have evidence for repair. SF 65 (pot group 1, [033]) is a large vessel with a repair hole drilled close to the rim. SF 465 (pot group 2, [459]) has an unfinished repair hole, in the form of a drilled hole which does not go through the entire width of the sherd.

Surface Treatment

Of the 285 vessels where some form of surface treatment could be detected 50.5% of these (144 vessels) were simply smoothed. Smoothing was detected on vessels of all sizes. This suggests that smoothing was a standard finishing procedure in the production of Grooved ware vessels at Crossiecrown. However other forms of surface treatment were also detected including burnishing, slipping, wiping and finally very fine smoothing. Of the burnished vessels two were large, eleven were medium size and thirteen were small. This suggests that burnishing was a preferential surface treatment for medium and small vessels. Of the slipped vessels 41 were large, 40 were medium and seven were small, signifying that slipping was a preferential surface treatment for medium and large vessels. Wiping of vessels seems to be executed across all size ranges, with three large, four medium and three small vessels being wiped. The two cases of very fine smoothing were both on small vessels.

One vessel, (SFs 340, 378, 383, 389, 571, 573, 578, 760 – pot group 2 [129]) has a woven mat impression on two base sherds, suggesting that, as at Barnhouse, mats were used to stabilise vessels during the manufacture process. The high incidence of smoothing as a finishing technique means that in many cases the evidence of primary production, such as mat impressions, is likely to be removed.

Tempering Strategy

Overall there are four main basic fabric types produced in the Grooved ware assemblage at Crossiecrown:

    A. rock temper (either angular or rounded)
    B. shell temper (usually visible as platy voids)
    C. rock and shell
    D. fabrics with no visible inclusions.

Section 11.6 has demonstrated the presence of several tempers in type A; sedimentary rock fragments are common, followed by rocks of magmatic origin, especially camptonite and monchiquite (see discussion in *Analysis of petrological thin-sections*). Those fabrics that are tempered are further divided by the percentage of temper included; rock temper ranges from 1–5%, 10%,

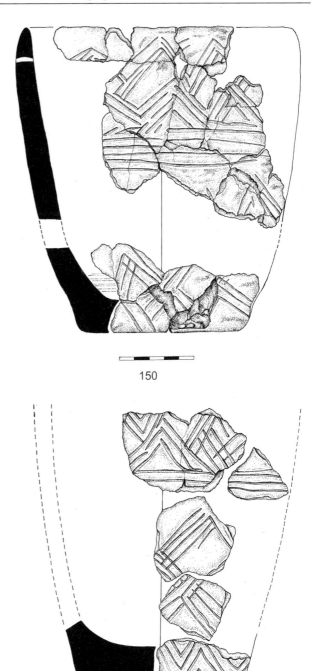

150

152, 154

Figure 11.3.5 Grooved ware SFs 150, 152 and 154 at Crossiecrown.

20%, 30%, 40% and up to 50%; shell temper ranges from 5%, 10–15%, 20%, 30%, up to 40%; rock and shell ranges from 5%, 10%, 20% up to 30%.

As can be seen, the use of temper is variable (Fig.11.3.6).

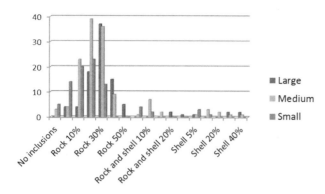

Figure 11.3.6 Grooved ware fabrics in large-, medium- and small-size vessels.

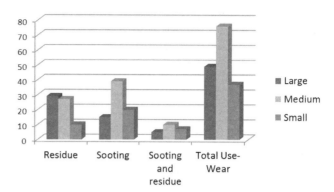

Figure 11.3.7 Grooved ware use wear and vessel size.

Small vessels tend to have low percentages of temper or no visible inclusions, medium vessels have between 10% and 30%, while large vessels tend to have high percentages of temper. There are larger numbers of vessels tempered with rock than with shell or rock and shell, and greater numbers of large vessels are rock tempered, while a greater number of medium and small vessels are tempered with shell or rock and shell. However the decision to temper with either rock, shell or rock and shell does not appear to be determined by vessel size.

Use Wear

Use-wear is investigated alongside a series of factors including wall thickness, fabric, rim and base morphology and surface treatment. There are 66 vessels with evidence for residue, 77 for sooting and 23 for both residue and sooting, representing just under half (48.9%) of the assemblage. exhibited evidence for some form of use-wear. Examining the incidence of use-wear in relation to vessel size (Figs 11.3.6 and 11.3.7) at a simplified level seems to indicate that the majority of vessels with evidence for sooting, residue or both are medium size, with a high number of large vessels and lower number of small vessels. This would seem to suggest that large and medium-size vessels are more often used for cooking. Considering the distinction between vessels with evidence for residue and sooting, we begin to see differences in the frequency of vessels of certain size. The number of large vessels with evidence for residue is more than double that for sooting, while the numbers of medium and small vessels are more or less equal for both. It would seem that large vessels are more often used for the sort of sustained high temperature cooking that produces charred residue.

The overall distinction between large, medium and small vessels is borne out when use-wear and fabric are

examined. Here the picture seems to suggest that rock-tempered fabrics dominate the assemblage. 90% of the vessels with evidence for use-wear are rock tempered, while shell tempered fabrics occupy 4% and rock and shell 6% of the total. Furthermore, fabrics with a high frequency (20% or over) of temper, whether rock or rock and shell, appear to predominate, occurring in 62.5% of the assemblage.

In terms of surface treatment a similar pattern emerges. As noted above, burnishing seems to predominate on medium and small vessels, while slipping predominates on large and medium vessels; thus the distinction between burnishing and slipping provides a broad understanding of size range. A simple tabulation of numbers of burnished and slipped vessels indicates that only seventeen burnished vessels exhibit evidence for use-wear, while 52 slipped vessels do so. From the analysis of vessel size and fabric it seems that greater numbers of large and medium vessels are utilised in cooking, and of these larger numbers are slipped than burnished. While burnished vessels do appear around the hearth, burnishing may have been used preferentially in vessels used for other tasks.

All forms of rim morphology are found on vessels exhibiting evidence for use-wear. Of these rounded rims (thirteen) and flat rims (eight) appear to predominate, bevelled (seven), pointed (seven) and scalloped (four) rims also occur, with just one stepped rim. Where residue can be observed around the rim, both are bevelled rims on large vessels.

Of a total of thirty bases with evidence for use wear, twelve have residue suggesting high temperature cooking of substances within the vessel, and the rest for sooting. This is typically around the sides of bases suggesting they have been placed in the hearth. Although no specific base morphology predominates, it is notable that there are six footed bases. Given their relatively small numbers in the assemblage as a whole (nine in total), it would seem that footed bases might be produced specifically for cooking vessels.

Summary of Crossiecrown Grooved ware

Certain features of Grooved Ware are best considered as a continuum, the frequency of temper used, the wall thickness of vessels of different size, the degree of surface treatment and level of decoration all being cases in point. The classification of vessels into large, medium and small is therefore not cut and dried and we should expect to see blurring at the edges of these categories. What is especially notable is that features which are found on vessels of one size may be scaled up or down for use on vessels of different sizes. A rough definition of the characteristics of vessels of each size is therefore offered below.

Large Vessels can be characterised by the following series of attributes:

- Wall thickness of 1.3cm or more.
- Rim diameter of 23–43cm, Base diameter of 26–30cm.
- Tempered with 20% or greater frequency of rock, rock and shell or shell.
- Will tend to have bevelled or scalloped rims, although all other rim forms are possible.
- Will tend to be smoothed or slipped.
- Are most likely to be decorated with applied cordons or incisions. Many bear single applied cordons, although a number have complex alternating plain/decorated cordon patterns or complex lozenge designs executed in cordon or incised lines.
- Are likely to be used in cooking, and are likely to have residue.

Medium Vessels

- Wall thickness of 1–1.2cm.
- Rim diameter of 13–25cm, base diameter of 11–30cm.
- Tempered with between 5–10% rock, rock and shell or shell.

- Will tend to have flat or rounded rims, although all other rim forms are possible.
- Will tend to be smoothed and may be slipped and/or burnished.
- Are likely to be decorated with multiple incisions or applied cordons. Many bear complex applied cordon patterns such as pinched cordons, cordons and rosettes, and cordons plus incisions. They may also have complex incised lozenge designs.
- Are likely to be used in cooking and have a high incidence of both sooting and residue.

Small Vessels

- Wall thickness of 0.5–0.9cm.
- Rim diameter of 10–20cm, Base diameter of 9–16cm.
- Tempered with low frequencies of rock, rock and shell or shell. Rock and shell and shell may be found more frequently. May also be untempered.
- Will tend to have pointed or rounded rims, although all other rim forms are possible.
- Will tend to have footed bases, although other base forms are possible.
- Will tend to be smoothed and may be burnished.
- Are unlikely to be decorated, but when decorated often bear the most fine and complex design schemes, often incorporating dot or small rosette motifs or stab and drag impressions.
- Are less likely to be used in cooking, although a high number of vessels with footed bases are used.

It is also useful to consider the demography of vessels from the site in its entirety. In total there are 90 large vessels, 130 medium-size vessels and 85 small vessels. This makes a total of 305 vessels. This figure is smaller than the overall total of Grooved ware vessels, as it was not possible to accurately determine size in all cases.

11.3.4.3 Beaker

The Crossiecrown Beaker assemblage numbers 18 vessels represented by individual pot groups.

Table 11.3.14 List of Beaker rim forms.

SF No.	Pottery group	Context	Rim diameter (cm)	Form	Description
989	1	507	13	Beaded	
228, 230	4	022		Beaded	
1399	93	002		Beaded	
938, 1180	2	507		Rounded	Out-turned rim
229	4	208		Rounded	External cordon
441, 446	4	309		Rounded inverted	
447, 467, 468, 470, 479	2	309	27	Pointed, notched	

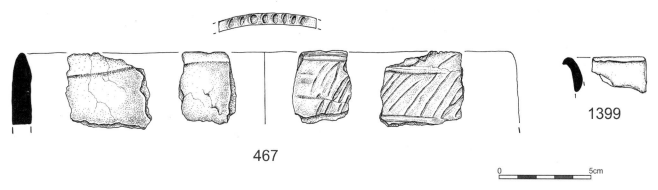

Figure 11.3.8 Beaker rims SF 467 and SF 1399 from Crossiecrown.

Rim sherds

A fairly restricted set of rim forms are produced, mainly beaded or rounded. One rim has a small external cordon just below the rim, another rim, from a vessel which appears to be transitional between Beaker and Grooved ware, is notched. Many of the rims are characteristically out-turned or have a pronounced inward turn (Table 11.3.14).

There are only two rim diameters available for measurement. These indicate a fairly extensive range of diameters from 13 to 27 cm. It is impossible to determine the spread of rim diameters from this sample, but on the basis of the distribution of rim and body sherd widths it would seem that most of the vessels are at the lower end of this range.

All of the base sherds attributable to Beaker vessels are flat and footed and have a characteristic outward curve. They include:

- SFs 83, 84, pot group 1, [027]
- SF 504, pot group 3, [022]
- SFs 411, 414, 415, 425, pot group 2, [022]
- SFs 169, 219, pot group 1, [022]

One of these bases, SF 504 (pot group 3, [022]), has a foot ring, or coil of clay, placed externally to stabilise the vessel. One vessel represented by SFs 444, 487, 434, (pot group 1, [309]), has a pronounced S-shaped shoulder.

Decoration

The major diagnostic feature of Beaker decoration at Crossiecrown is the use of either twisted-cord or comb impressions as decorative techniques (Tables 11.3.15 and 11.3.16). However we also observe incision and other forms of impressed decoration as techniques. The majority of the decoration is found in two specific zones of the Beaker, below the rim or on the belly or shoulder. Decoration generally consists of a series of simple horizontal or vertical impressions, although we do observe more complex infill patterns.

Surface Treatment

All of the identifiable Beaker sherds were smoothed, however a few seem to have been both smoothed and burnished. All the identified Beaker base sherds were burnished, while one vessel SFs 17, 19, 165, 241, pot group 5, context [003] was also burnished.

Tempering Strategy

Overall most of the Beaker sherds are tempered with angular rock, from 10 to 40% frequency. A few sherds are also tempered with shell. Shell is added to rock as with SF 229, pot group 4, context [208], which has 20% angular rock with 5% frequency of platy voids (decayed shell), and SFs 447, 467 (Fig. 11.3.8), 468, 470, 479, pot group 2, context [309], which has 10% angular rock and 20–30% shell. Shell may also be found as the main constituent of temper, as with SFs 83, 84, pot group 1, context [027], which has 30% frequency of platy voids. A number of sherds are also untempered, including SFs 434, 444, 487, pot group 1, context [309], SF 1399, pot group 93, context [002] (Fig. 11.3.8). There seems to be some relationship between vessel size and tempering strategy. All Beaker sherds are between 0.5 and 1 cm in width. Vessels with a width of 0.5-0.7 are either untempered, shell tempered or tempered with a low frequency of rock. Vessels between 0.8 and 1 cm tend to be tempered with rock of greater frequencies. Based on the small number of Beaker sherds, this interpretation is necessarily provisional.

Use-Wear

Use-wear in the form of sooting and residue was detected on a few of the identified Beaker sherds (Table 11.3.17).

Table 11.3.15 Beaker sherds with evidence of twisted-cord impressions.

SF No.	Pot group	Context	Description
1605, 1457, 1512, 1437, 1390	125	002	Vertical twisted-cord impressions.
291	1	029	Vertical twisted-cord impression, possibly near to rim.
514	5	011	A series of horizontal twisted-cord impressions around the belly of the vessel.
169, 219	1	022	Faint cord impressions.
431	5	034	Twisted-cord impressions in horizontal bands.
229	4	208	Decorated rim has two horizontal cord impressions with diagonal infill executed in twisted-cord. The body of the vessel has three horizontal twisted-cord impressions with a series of twisted-cord diagonals below.

Table 11.3.16 Beaker sherds with comb impression, incision and other impressed decoration.

SF No.	Pottery group	Context	Method	Description
989	1	507	comb impression	On rim a lozenge pattern executed by comb with comb infill.
1587	139	003	incision	A faint incised vertical chevron pattern.
447, 467, 468, 470, 479	2	003	incision	A series of diagonal incisions across body of sherd, cut by a horizontal incision.
17, 19, 165, 241	5	003	impressed	A line of vertical lenticular impressions on shoulder of vessel.

Table 11.3.17 Sooting and residue on Beaker sherds.

SF No.	Pottery group	Context	Area of vessel	Type
1605, 1457, 1512, 1437, 1390	125	022		sooting
17, 19, 165, 241	5	003		residue
514	5	011		residue
434, 444, 487	1	309		sooting
983, 1180	2	507	rim	sooting
411, 414, 415, 425	2	022	base	sooting

Notably, use-wear is evident on rim, base and shoulder sherds. It is also evident on both undecorated and decorated sherds. The presence of soot on the *side of the base* of one vessel (SFs 411, 414, 415 and 425) suggests it was placed into the fire during heating or cooking.

11.3.5 Petrological Analysis of Pottery Sequence

Analysis of petrological thin-sections

The major objective of the petrological analysis was to compare the tempering strategy across the assemblage from the early Neolithic Unstan ware to Grooved ware and Beaker (Tables 11.3.18, 11.3.19 and 11.3.20). The relative numbers of each pottery class examined in thin section reflects their overall frequency in the assemblage. The major point that emerges from this analysis is the degree of similarity in tempering strategies from Unstan ware to Beaker. The presence of the igneous rock

monchiquite in thin-sections from all pottery classes is striking and suggests continuity of practice, and a long-term attachment to specific rock sources in the surrounding environment. The same geological source is exploited across all classes of material.

Comparison of this rock with a suite of thin sections obtained from the British Geological Survey (Edinburgh), and with samples taken in the field by the author confirm that this particular igneous rock comes from a swarm of igneous dykes outcropping in the Bay of Firth (Fig. 11.6.13 and also section 11.6.3) (Mykura 1976, 96–99). Despite the continuity in use of specific rock sources, there are subtle differences in tempering practice from one pottery class to another. The early Neolithic Unstan ware sections have a notably lower frequency of monchiquite than the two other classes of pottery, with minute quantities of monchiquite. Further, the sandstone in the sections is rounded. Both of these features suggest that the temper

Table 11.3.18 Unstan ware petrology.

SF No.	Context	Description
1042	515	10% coarse sub-angular sandstone 1–2mm across; 1% platy voids (shell), 0.5mm across; 1% angular and rounded monchiquite, 0.5–0.8mm across.
1083	515	10% coarse sub-angular sandstone, 1% platy voids (shell), 0.5mm across; 1% angular and rounded monchiquite, <1mm across.
1093	493	Coarse rounded sandstone 2-3mm across; 1% mudstone 0.5–1mm across; 1% monchiquite, <1mm across; and mudstone. Quartz and mica present in clay matrix.

Table 11.3.19 Grooved ware petrology.

SF No.	Context	Description
191	025	10% rounded coarse sandstone 102mm across; 2% platy voids (shell), 0.5mm across
199	025	10% rounded coarse sandstone, 1–2mm across
256	142	30% angular coarse sandstone 1–2mm across; 10% monchiquite <1mm across
300		Angular coarse sandstone 1–3mm across; 10% angular monchiquite 1–2mm across; 5% large pieces of angular quartz, 1–2mm across
317	025	10% platy voids (shell) 1–2mm across
340	173	10% angular mudstone 1–2mm across; angular coarse sandstone 1–2mm across
407		10% rounded coarse sandstone 1–3mm across
433	309	30% well crushed angular monchiquite, <1mm across
887	481	10% angular monchiquite 1–2mm across; micaceous clay matrix
896	484	30% angular coarse sandstone 3–5mm across, 5% rounded quartz, <1mm across (see also Table 11.6.3)
899	490	5% angular monchiquite <1mm across, 10% angular coarse sandstone 3–5mm across.
950	480	20% angular coarse sandstone 2–4mm across, 5% platy voids (shell) <1mm across.
964	487	30% angular monchiquite 1–2mm across, nb separate thin section of SF 964 shows frequent diabase (Table 11.6.3)
1075	002	30% angular coarse sandstone 3–5mm across, 2% angular mudstone *c.*1mm across; 2% platy voids (shell), <1mm across
1191	002	30% monchiquite 1–2mm across and angular coarse sandstone 1–3mm across
1192	002	30% sub-angular coarse sandstone 3–5mm across, 5% monchiquite, 1–2mm across
1194	002	30% sub-angular coarse sandstone 3–5mm across, 5% angular monchiquite, 1–2mm across
1224	002	30% angular monchiquite 1–2mm across
1231	002	10% angular mudstone 3–5mm, angular coarse sandstone, 1–2mm across; 1% platy voids (shell), <1mm across
1242	002	30% angular monchiquite, angular mudstone, angular coarse sandstone, possible angular camptonite?, all 2–4mm across. Well mixed.
1248		10% angular monchiquite, 2–4mm across
1309	434	5% rounded coarse sandstone 1–2mm across; 5% platy voids (shell), <1mm across
1407	002	30% angular coarse sandstone, 3–5mm across; 10% angular monchiquite, 1–2mm across
No SF No	001	30% angular monchiquite, 1–3mm across; angular coarse sandstone, 1–2mm across

Table 11.3.20 Beaker petrology.

SF No.	Context	Description
229	208	30% angular monchiquite 1–2mm across; Micaceous clay matrix.
467	309	5% coarse angular sandstone, 1–2mm, 5% angular mudstone, 1–2mm across; 10% angular monchiquite 1–3mm across.

within these sections is either a component of boulder clay or is obtained from clay weathered from the dyke source. It suggests a selection less of temper for the clay, more of suitable clay sources with attendant temper components. By contrast the Grooved ware and Beaker thin-sections have high quantities of angular sedimentary and igneous rock which suggests that these components were deliberately added to the clay. This is highlighted by the differences in the treatment of monchiquite in the Grooved ware and Beaker thin-sections. In the former monchiquite is well crushed and angular, whereas in the two Beaker thin-sections it is poorly crushed and angular. For both classes of pottery monchiquite may have been specifically selected and treated as a temper, while the manner of its use perhaps varied from one period to another.

11.3.6 Technological Analysis of Pottery Sequence

One of the major aims of the analysis of the Crossiecrown assemblage was to understand the evolution of pottery technology in Neolithic Orkney. To this end a series of characteristics such as manufacture technique, rim and base morphology and decorative technique and design was recorded. Here I want to assess the similarities and differences in these attributes across the assemblage as a whole as a means of understanding changes in pottery technology.

Changes in manufacture: One of the striking points to emerge from the analysis of manufacture is the consistent use of coil and mortice and tenon techniques across the entire assemblage from Unstan ware to Beaker.

Changes in rim technology: Bevelled rims and pointed rims are sparse elements of the Unstan ware assemblage, yet these emerge as major components of the Grooved ware assemblage. They are again elements in the Beaker assemblage.

Changes in base technology: One of the major changes we might observe is from round base to flat. This change is more subtle than we might first realise. A number of vessels in the Unstan ware assemblage exhibit bases which are tapered or flattened near the base which include SFs 138, 782, 813, 1123 (pot group 2, [446]) and SF 1156 (pot group 3, [450]). These bases incorporate elements of late Neolithic base technology such as the addition of internal coils of clay to thicken and strengthen the interior. The use of internal coils of clay as a stabilising technique predominates in the Grooved ware assemblage. This technique effectively evolves into the rounded interior bases of the Grooved ware tradition (see above for list of these bases) and is also evident in some of the basic flat bases such as SF 933 (pot group 5, [490]). Developments in the flat base Grooved ware tradition are also evident in the Beaker tradition. Footed bases are produced particularly on smaller Grooved ware vessels, and it is footed or splayed outward-curving bases that emerge in the Beaker tradition, again produced on relatively small vessels.

Changes in decoration and design: There is little apparent similarity between the Unstan ware and Grooved ware decorative repertoire apart from the use of incision and impression as decorative techniques. Similarities do arise between the Grooved ware and Beaker repertoire, for instance, the use of multiple incisions or multiple cord impressions, but also in the use of incision in the Beaker assemblage. Most striking is the similarity in design between the Grooved ware vessels with lozenge and triangle motifs, such as SF 150 (pot group 1, [003]), SFs 152, 154 (pot group 4, [006]) and SFs 256, 987 (pot group 1, [142]). These designs are similar to the decoration of Beaker vessels like SF 989 (pot group 1, [507]) decorated on the rim with a lozenge pattern executed by comb with comb infill.

Changes in function: based upon the lipid analysis (Chapter 11.7), there seems little apparent change in the functional use of pots, based on the formal categories Grooved ware and Beaker. Both Grooved ware and Beaker samples produced similar lipid components on analysis indicating evidence for ruminant dairy and ruminant adipose fats. Despite this similarity in use, on a small sample of five Grooved ware sherds and one Beaker sherd there does appear to be some slight distinction between the two, with Grooved ware being utilised for adipose fat and ruminant dairy fat, while the Beaker sample is only utilised for ruminant dairy fat. On the basis of these results the evidence could be argued a number of ways; we can see both a distinction and an overlap between Grooved ware and Beaker, with the evidence for ruminant dairy fats in both Grooved ware *and* Beaker possibly indicating a growing predominance in the use of dairy products towards the end of the Grooved ware sequence and the beginning of Beaker use.

As noted above, we need to view these changes, along with the changes in tempering strategy discussed above, as an evolving series of socially motivated technological choices. It is important to consider why it is that specific choices in technology are made, and how these relate to wider social practices. Key changes occur from the early Neolithic to late Neolithic in the differentiation of the pottery repertoire and in the development of the use of temper in the production of vessels of differing size. A further major change towards the end of the late Neolithic is the adoption of a new decorative technique (comb and cord impression) mainly for the production of small fine vessels (Beakers). Overall, we can see changes in the capacity and variety of the ceramic repertoire from the early Neolithic to the end of the late Neolithic.

Figure 11.3.9 Pot spread (SFs 316, 380 and 343) in the northern midden at Crossiecrown (Colin Richards).

Grooved ware, marking an expansion in the variety and capacity of vessels, quite likely related to new strategies of storage (Jones 1999) and to settlement nucleation and the concomitant change in social relations (Jones 2002, 163–64). The production of small fine vessels (*i.e.* Beakers) towards the end of the late Neolithic also marks a change in social relations, or at least underlines the importance of display and novelty in the social relations surrounding serving and eating food and drink. Given their size, Beakers are likely to have replaced, or have been used alongside, the finer Grooved ware vessels, most likely used for serving and consuming food (Jones 2002, 132). This point is underlined by the overlap in the use of Grooved ware and Beakers, from the evidence of the GC-MS analysis, pointing to a degree of continuity in the Grooved ware/Beaker repertoire towards the end of the late Neolithic and the beginning of the early Bronze Age.

To conclude this section it is emphasised that we are not simply viewing each class of pottery as the manifestation of 'culture groups'; instead, as we have seen with the analysis of tempering practices, base technologies, decorative schemes/designs and function based on GC-MS analysis, change is subtle and there is marked continuity of practice.

11.3.7 Biographical analysis of SF 316

The sherds of a complete Grooved ware vessel SFs 316, 380, 343 (pot group 2, context [210]) were found in a midden at the east end of Trench 3 (Figs 7.13 and 11.3.9). The excavated sherds constitute most of the vessel. Here I want to describe this remarkable vessel, its context and outline its biography or life-history. I believe a full description of this vessel will be illuminating for the

discussion of spatial analysis and depositional practices below.

Description of SFs 316, 380, 343:
Dimensions: the vessel is bucket shaped and has an approximate total height of 42cm (Fig. 11.3.10). Its base has a base diameter of 30cm, and its rim has a diameter of 43cm. It tapers from 1cm wall thickness at the rim to 1.5cm at the base, with an average mid-point measurement of 1.3cm; the base thickness is 2.2cm. It is tempered with 40% frequency of angular rock of between 2–5mm.

Method of manufacture: the breakage pattern indicates that the vessel was ring built. This technique culminates in a mortice-and-tenon style of join between rings in the horizontal section. Rings of clay are added and flattened into 'straps' of clay as they are worked. Each ring is smoothed and joined to the preceding one in a downward smoothing motion. There are no apparent vertical joins that would indicate straightforward slab production.

Rim and base morphology: it has a bevelled rim with a series of thumbnails just below the rim interior. It has a flat base with an internal decoration of applied cordons in a cross shape. This creates four equal segments, one of which is infilled with applied pellets of clay impressed with a finger-tip.

Surface Treatment: heavily slipped internally and externally. This slip appears to cover the internal 'shell' of the pot. The slipped surface is finger and grass smoothed; the grass smoothing is clear of the base interior.

Decoration: both applied and impressed techniques. Horizontal bands of finger-impressed and plain cordons alternate from top to base of pot. These begin around 2cm from the rim, with very little gap between bands of decoration. This is partially caused by smoothing down each cordon. Impressions are made with a left hand using the thumb.

Use-wear: notably there is little evidence of use-wear on the inside of the vessel. The upper 6cm from the rim down appears discoloured but this is fire scorching, not sooting. There is no evidence of heat treatment on the exterior or interior of the base. Some sherds show a little evidence of internal residue.

Function based on GC-MS analysis: the absence of use-wear resonates with the lipid analysis (Chapter 11.7) of a sherd from this vessel (sampled from midway up the vessel wall) which indicates low lipid content; the contents were so low that individual lipid components could not be distinguished. This is remarkable when compared with the strong lipid concentrations from much of the rest of the Grooved ware assemblage.

Context of deposition: almost the entire vessel was placed in midden downhill from the main site (total number of sherds in pot group: 188). Above the pot debris two hammerstones were deposited.

The above detail enables a life history for the vessel to be reconstructed. After procuring the clay and temper, the production of the vessel began with the base, which was reinforced with an internal pad of clay. The walls of the pot were produced by making straps or rings of clay, each of which were added onto the next from the base upwards and smoothed down. Once finished, the pot was slipped in a heavy slurry of clay. It was placed in the slip rim downwards. After this, and once leather hard, the pot could be decorated. Decoration of the rim was executed from the rim downwards by a finger-tip. Then a series of applied cordons were placed around the vessel and smoothed down. Alternate cordons were decorated using the thumb of the left hand as the pot was turned with the right hand. At some stage in the production process a cruciform pattern of applied cordons was added to the interior of the base. At least one segment was infilled with pellets of clay which were further decorated with a finger-tip (and likely the alternating segment of the base interior).

The pot was bonfire fired in an inverted position, as ash built up around the exterior of the vessel and the interior was also fire scorched. After this the use-life of the vessel seems to have been short. Based on GC-MS analysis and use-wear analysis, there is little evidence of use, although it was probably used once. Its base was smashed and with half the base missing it was thrown downhill into midden deposits and deliberately smashed by two people using hammerstones.

There are three possible alternatives for the use of this vessel:

A. It may have been made for a single event and then smashed.
B. Given the absence of half the base this vessel may have been smashed during use.
C. It may have been used as a storage vessel which had come to the end of its use-life.

In view of the elaborate production and equally deliberate destruction of the vessel, interpretations A and C seem the most likely. As I have argued elsewhere (Jones 2002, 146), large Grooved ware vessels are likely to have been made infrequently. Some vessels are so large

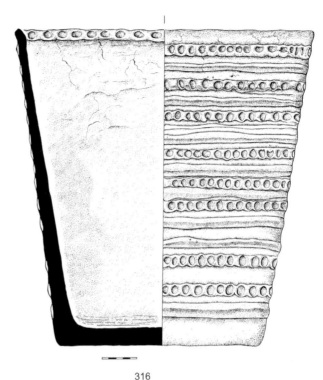

316

316

Figure 11.3.10 The Grooved ware vessel (SFs 316, 380 and 343), from the midden in Trench 3 (see also Fig. 7.11).

they effectively function as furniture in house alcoves. Moving vessels of this size would be hazardous. They are most likely to be broken up and deposited on the abandonment of the house, possibly on the death of specific members of the household. At Crossiecrown large vessels also seem to be used more regularly for cooking, although we can see little evidence of use for this vessel, suggesting it was made and used for a specialised and specific event. On balance, the writer favours scenario A which together with the deposition of the vessel away from the main settlement area on the edge of the midden suggests deliberate and prescribed treatment of certain categories of vessels.

11.3.8 *Spatial and Chronological Analysis*

To begin with I want to discuss the stratigraphic integrity of Unstan ware and Beaker vessels, before considering the spatial distribution of Grooved ware.

Unstan ware is found in a fairly discrete set of contexts, in association with both the Grey and Red Houses; these include contexts [517, 515, 493, 481, 480, 471, 476, 450 and 446]. These sherds appear to be residual and associated with the collapse or destruction of the outer wall of the Grey House. There is obviously some mixing as a few sherds of Unstan ware are found in topsoil [001] and upper level contexts, such as [003]. Some contexts, such as [471 and 476] are evidently related to the rubble or collapse beneath the Red House, likely to relate to earlier midden contexts *e.g.* [481]. Contexts [517] and [515] are associated with early occupation layers/contexts in the Red House, but may, in some cases, relate to mixing with the earlier occupation layers. It is notable that unequivocal sherds of Grooved ware are also obtained from context [515] suggesting a degree of mixing.

The clearest stratigraphic contexts for Unstan ware ([450 and 446]), both from a recess [437] within the Grey House. This is especially striking since one of the most unequivocal 'Unstan' sherds from a decorated carinated bowl, SFs 774 (Fig. 11.3.1), 777 (pot group 1, [446]) is derived from this context. However, these sherds are clearly redeposited 'midden' wall-core material that spilled across the internal area of the Grey House on its collapse.

Beaker vessels are likewise found in relatively few contexts. A number are in upper contexts, such as [003], [022] and [034]. One sherd comes from the midden spread [002] in Trench 1. Another comes from stratified contexts in the hollow [208] that is suggested to be the remains of a late timber structure at Crossiecrown (see Chapter 7). Crucially at least two come from contexts within the Red House ([309 and 507]). Context [309] is the fill of a cut [312] into the floor and the sherds deposited in this context are from an incised Beaker (vessel SFs 447, 467, 468, 470, 479 – pot group 2, [309]), from an undecorated shouldered vessel SFs 444,

487, 434 (pot group 1, [309]) and a rounded inverted Beaker rim, SFs 441, 446 (pot group 4, [309]). Context [507] is a layer in the interior of the Red House. The sherd from this context, SF 989 (pot group 1, [507]) is an unequivocal Beaker having both a beaded rim and a lozenge pattern executed by comb with comb infill. Both of these deposits indicate that Beaker vessels are utilised in the later phases of the occupation of Red House.

This impression is underlined by the series of vessels from the midden spread in Trench 1. These include the beaded rim SF 1399 (pot group 93, [002]), SFs 1605, 1457, 1512, 1437, 1390 (pot group 125, [002]) decorated with vertical twisted-cord and SF 1587 (pot group 139, [002]) which has an incised chevron pattern. These sherds were intermixed with Grooved ware material from the midden spread suggesting a degree of contemporaneity. Probably the most unequivocal Beaker vessel is derived from deposits within the 'hollow' (see Figs 7.44 and 7.45) associated with a series of uprights in the northern area of the site; SF 229 (pot group 4, [208]) from this context has both a rim and body decorated with twisted-cord. Again it is derived from a context mixed with Grooved ware. It seems from these series of contextual associations that Beaker vessels are associated with the final occupation of the house and may have been used alongside Grooved ware.

Turning to the spatial distribution of Grooved ware from Crossiecrown, we will consider the distribution of vessels within the interior of the Red House, and then evaluate the nature of the deposits in the series of midden spreads in Trench 1. It is important to draw out the nature of the deposits in relation to the life history of the Red House, and the Crossiecrown settlement in general. A series of well-stratified deposits are located in the interior of this building. Careful spatial analysis of the pottery from these contexts (see above for discussion of methodology) allows us to consider the spatial patterning of Grooved ware vessels within the house. It is notable that most of the vessels located in the hearth deposits were sherds from large Grooved ware vessels. These include SF 459 (pot group 1, [315]), SF 461 (pot group 1, [300]), SFs 400, 401 (pot group 2, [300]) and SFs 458, 567 (pot group 1, [012]). Along with these four large vessels a medium-size vessel SF 592 (pot group 1, [424]) was also deposited in the hearth. In between the hearth [183] in the northwest corner of the trench and orthostat [151] a series of vessels was deposited. A small vessel SF 340 (pot group 1, [170]) was found in the cut for orthostat [151], while a large vessel, SF 384 (pot group 1, [187] and a small vessel, SFs 1103, 1102 (pot group 1, [197]) was also found next to this orthostat.

A series of vessels is found deposited within orthostatic arrangements. In the northeast of the Red House an orthostatic structure, or stone box, contained two vessels: a large vessel, SF 352 (pot group 1, [169], and a small and extremely finely decorated vessel, SF 352 (pot group 2, [169]). A medium vessel, SF 367 (pot group 1, [179]) was located in the lower fill of stone box [116]. In the upper fill two medium vessels, SF 346 (pot group 2, [173]) and SF 359 (pot group 3, [173]), one large vessel, SFs 302, 362, 350 (pot group 4, [173]) and one small vessel, SF 368 (pot group 1, [173]) were also deposited. A further orthostatic box [136] had a medium-size vessel, SF 218 (pot group 1, [137]) deposited within it. A further small vessel, SF 1667 (pot group 1, [105]), was deposited in the west recess of the Red House. In the north recess, a large vessel, SF 846 (pot group 1, [327]) was deposited. In the entrance another large vessel, SFs 853, 852 (pot group 1, [405]) was deposited. A series of vessels were present in the lower fill of the Red House drain [147]. These include two medium-size vessels, SFs 300, 298 (pot group 1) and SF 729 (pot group 2), and a large vessel SF 322 (pot group 3). Most other vessels within the Red House are in a series of compact occupation layers (*e.g.* [313, 314 and 106]). These contexts include a medium-size vessel and a small vessel. Context [106] constitutes a rubble patch with a curious deposit of fired clay which, judging from the angular shapes and worked nature of the clay, may be the remains of a hearth lining or clay oven. Four medium-size vessel vessels are also found in the wall core [196, 175 and 158] of the Red House.

To sum up, large and medium vessels seem to be deposited in the hearth deposits, while both large and small vessels are found in close proximity to the hearth. In the small stone boxes we observe the full continuum of vessels, although medium and small vessels seem to predominate here. The recesses of the house seem to be home mainly to large and small vessels. This is interesting since this pattern is more complex than the spatial distribution of vessels in the early phases at Barnhouse (Jones 1997; 2002, 134, 145–47; A. M. Jones and Richards 2003) where medium and small vessels were generally clustered around the hearth, and large vessels in 'box-beds' and recesses. That large vessels are notably found in hearth deposits at Crossiecrown may reflect the changing use of large vessels. In the later phases at Barnhouse, Structure 8, large vessels were used for cooking rather than storage. As the use-wear analysis for Crossiecrown noted many large vessels are used in high-temperature cooking, suggesting that this was a major role for large vessels at Crossiecrown. The finds of small vessels, often finely decorated as with SF 352 (pot

group 2, [169]), in stone boxes is again different from the majority of houses at Barnhouse where they were found around the hearth. There is a higher frequency of small vessels than at Barnhouse, again reflecting a changing role for these vessels, possibly as more common individual serving vessels, stored in stone boxes while out of use.

Given the nature of the site and the relatively high number of vessels from the house, it is important to consider what the deposition of vessels in this context might reveal about the occupation and abandonment of the Red House. The level of preservation of vessels within the house is good, and a number of vessel deposits are represented by high numbers of sherds. In addition many of these deposits are relatively unabraded and are represented by a number of base sherds. All of these factors indicate that these deposits were not simply overlooked or abraded sherds resulting from accidental loss during the routine clearing of the house. Rather, I believe that these series of factors indicate that the pots within the Red House are likely to represent deliberate abandonment deposits which have remained sealed within the house after the process of decommissioning. This point is underlined by the observation that large and small vessels seem to be over-represented in house deposits, while medium vessels are proportionally under-represented, again indicating the selectivity involved in the deposition of vessels within houses. Again this observation has parallels with Barnhouse where large and small vessels were preferentially associated with the house and settlement.

Significantly, a number of well-preserved vessels also occur in upper level contexts associated with the abandonment of the Red House, which include SF 150 (pot group 1, [003] and SF 152, 154 (pot group 4, [006]), both represented by 25 and 33 sherds respectively. I believe that the high number of sherds in these deposits likewise suggests deliberate deposition into the upper level of abandonment deposits. Similar deliberate depositional processes are indicated by the high number of preserved sherds in the houses at Barnhouse (Jones 1997; Jones 2005a, 270). The deposits of entire preserved vessels at Skara Brae also suggest that vessels were deliberately left in abandoned houses. It is also attested at Rinyo where entire vessels remained in house alcoves. Likewise artefacts and human burials were deposited into the abandoned houses at Skara Brae. Although the date of these deposits is open to question, it is nevertheless worth noting that abandoned settlements were foci for deposition. Originally the floor deposits were construed by Childe (1931a) as refuse and ordure and taken to indicate the poor state of hygiene of the inhabitants. However, I believe we need to recognise the practice of depositing artefacts both at floor level within abandoned houses and the practice of depositing artefacts within the upper layers of abandoned settlements. Furthermore we need to think differently about these deposits. Before expanding on this point I want to compare the Crossiecrown house deposits with those in the midden.

The midden in Trench 1 contains over 131 vessels, over a third of the entire Grooved ware assemblage. Of these, 43 are large, 48 medium-size and 40 small. This represents around half the population of large and small vessels, but is only 37% of the total of medium vessels. This suggests that certain categories of vessel are more appropriate for deposition in these particular midden deposits than others. The practice of formal deposition within prescribed midden deposits was also attested at Barnhouse (Jones 2002, 143; A. M. Jones and Richards 2003). Although they are remarkably well preserved these midden deposits differ from the deposits in the Red House. The high level of refitting and concordance and the number of sherds deposited in the midden context suggest that here too largely complete vessels were deposited. However, the sherds in the midden deposits differ substantially in terms of abrasion and fragmentation.

The sherds within the Red House are remarkably unabraded given their use and deposition within the building, while vessels in the midden deposits suffer from a high degree of abrasion. More importantly while the sherds in the Red House are in discrete locations, the sherds in the midden deposits are scattered across far greater areas. To some extent this pattern might be expected as one set of sherds is preserved in the stone architecture of the house, while the others are in loose midden deposits. However I believe that we are not simply observing the deposition of single 'orphan' sherds in each of these cases. Instead it is argued that more or less complete vessels are being deposited. The level of concordance within the midden deposits suggests that the midden contained almost entire vessels that had been scattered, whilst the Red House contained entire vessels deposited *in situ*. At this juncture it is important to recall the deposition of SFs 316, 380, 343 in the midden deposits [210]. Again we observe the deposition of a complete vessel *in situ* within the midden, in this case with little apparent evidence of disturbance. It is also worth noting where both the midden [002] and the midden [210] are located in relation to the settlement. They are both located on the edge of the settlement. Indeed SF 316 was discovered while investigating the outer extent of midden. Again this pattern of deposition

of large vessels at the edge of the settlement is mirrored at Barnhouse (A. M. Jones and Richards 2003).

11.3.9 Discussion

Three aspects of the Crossiecrown pottery assemblage need to be underlined:

There are important changes in ceramic technology in the Crossiecrown assemblage. We can observe continuities both in production technology and tempering practice from the early Neolithic to late Neolithic. Most importantly, it is possible to observe continuities between Grooved ware and Beaker in terms of tempering strategy, production technology, decorative scheme and function. One of the most striking points to arise from the analysis of the Grooved ware assemblage is the significance of large and small vessels, both of which appear more predominant than at comparable sites such as Barnhouse. It is evident that large vessels are not solely used for storage, but are also large cooking vessels. This is underlined by the evidence from GC-MS analysis which indicates that Grooved ware vessels of all sizes had similar contents – ruminant dairy fats. Here we see a marked difference from the situation at Barnhouse where ruminant dairy fats were only detected in medium-size vessels. Based on a comparison with Barnhouse, this suggests a change in consumption practices over the course of the late Neolithic, from small-scale household-based consumption at the beginning of the late Neolithic to large-scale communal consumption towards the end of the period. Concomitant with this is the rise in numbers of small vessels. At Barnhouse it was suggested that small vessels were shared between people, whereas at Crossiecrown the numbers of small vessels and their high incidence in the Red House suggest they are far more common, possibly owned/used individually. This is important since in terms of size Beaker vessels seem to fit most closely within the size range of small vessels, and it is suggested they were utilised in tandem with, or as an addition to, the repertoire of small vessels at Crossiecrown. They effectively 'slotted in' as another element of the fine ware component of the assemblage.

It is evident from the analysis of both the house and the midden deposits that the deposition of vessels in these contexts is not accidental or expedient but associated with clear cultural rules. Large vessels appear to be preferentially placed at the edge of the settlement. There seems to be less of a clearly demarcated depositional area for medium-size vessels. Similarly large and small vessels are preferentially placed in the final abandonment deposits within Red House. It is important that the deposits of material culture within late Neolithic settlements are recognised for what they are: the final deposits left within the house prior to abandonment or decommission. The practice of closing down or sealing deposits within abandoned houses is well attested across Neolithic Europe (*e.g.* Stevanovic 1996). It is also a practice that continues well into the Bronze Age both in the Northern Isles and further afield (Nowakowski 2001). This is a process that Nowakowski (2001, 139) describes as 'planned abandonment', and often results from the closure of the house upon the death of a member of the family. The life cycle of houses is therefore intimately bound up with the life cycle of the people who occupy the house. The close relationship between the developmental cycle of the house and the person has long been studied by anthropologists (Parker-Pearson and Richards 1993; Carsten and Hugh-Jones 1995; Waterson 1995). If the association between the house and the person is accepted, then we also need to reconsider the deposits found in the upper abandonment levels of settlements. Rather than treating them as simple refuse areas, we should instead realise that deposition into the top of abandoned houses is a powerful mnemonic act.

It is clear that the use of specific resources was closely tied to the occupation of Crossiecrown. Given this it is interesting to note that a number of vessels from Quanterness passage grave were tempered with monchiquite, suggesting a close link between the inhabitants of settlement and cairn (Williams 1979; 1982). While the manner of tempering pottery was an identity marker so too was the decoration of pots. The clearest indicator of this is the prevalence of lozenge motifs as a style which seems to mark out Crossiecrown from other settlements. Like other late Neolithic settlements certain aspects of Grooved ware decoration appear distinctive. However the similarity of other elements, such as the scalloped rim, to settlements like Ness of Brodgar, Pool, and Links of Noltland suggests that in keeping with other settlements at the end of the late Neolithic decoration may have become less of a means of expressing communal identity (Jones 2000; 2002, 165) and more a means of expressing a holistic sense of identity between settlements.

11.4 Pottery from Wideford Hill

Andrew Meirion Jones and Gemma Tully

11.4.1 Introduction and general comments on the assemblage

The Wideford Hill pottery assemblage is interesting in being a large domestic Unstan ware assemblage associated in part with timber structures (Fig. 11.4.1). In terms of

the size of the assemblage it is only rivalled by Orcadian settlement sites such as Ha'Breck, Wyre (Lee and Thomas 2011) and Loch Olabhat, N. Uist (Armit 1992). As such it provides the opportunity of defining the character and composition of the pottery assemblage from an early Neolithic settlement; in effect this is what an early Neolithic Orcadian pottery assemblage 'looks like'.

There are a total of 318 vessels from secure contexts, over four times greater in quantity than the estimated 78 vessels from the contemporary settlement at the Knap of Howar (Henshall 1983, 69) and at least ten times greater than most chambered cairn assemblages. In defining the categories of pottery at Wideford Hill the terms open bowls and neutral bowls are used (after Cleal 1992) to define shape, while the term Unstan ware is used to describe the particular form of carinated bowls peculiar to Northern Scotland. These shape-based terms are preferred over 'plain' bowls or 'undecorated' bowls (as used by Henshall (1983) for Knap of Howar) as many of the neutral bowl forms are neither plain nor undecorated, while many of the open Unstan forms are both plain and undecorated. The Wideford Hill assemblage comprises a mixture of both neutral bowls and 'classic' open Unstan bowls. Of the latter a coarser component of the assemblage is decorated with finger or thumbnail decoration and often fired in an oxidising atmosphere. These can be defined against a finer component decorated with incision or stab-and-drag and often fired in a reducing atmosphere. There are 53 'classic' Unstan vessels, of which thirteen are coarse vessels decorated with finger or thumbnail impressions. In addition to this there are nine undecorated Unstan vessels. The remainder are bowls decorated with the stab-and-drag or incised motifs typical of Unstan ware. There is a clear ratio of 5: 1 decorated to undecorated vessels, indicating that decoration is a significant feature of the Unstan ware tradition.

The neutral bowl component consists of fourteen decorated vessels and a further six undecorated neutral bowls, together pointing to a 2:1 ratio of decorated and undecorated vessels. Overall the ratio of Unstan vessels to neutral bowls in the assemblage is 2.5:1, emphasising the significance of the open bowl form in the early Neolithic ceramic tradition of Orkney. This is interesting since the neutral bowl form at the Knap of Howar dominated the assemblage with a ratio of neutral bowls to Unstan forms of 5:1 (based on figures in Henshall 1983, 69–71). At the Knap of Howar, Unstan forms were both low in number and of a fairly small size prompting Henshall to consider the functional differences between the Knap of Howar Unstan ware assemblage and that from contemporary chambered cairns (Henshall 1983, 72). In terms of size, the Wideford Hill vessels are mostly unlike the Knap of Howar assemblage and compare better with vessels from chambered cairn contexts. The Wideford assemblage stands out from Crossiecrown, Stonehall and Knowes of Trotty, where at Crossiecrown there is one unequivocal 'classic' Unstan rim sherd from the earliest phase, a similar paucity at Smerquoy, whereas at Stonehall the assemblage was dominated by neutral bowl forms, with no Unstan vessels evident.

At this point it is useful to compare the Wideford Hill assemblage with other pottery assemblages. One of the decorative components that stands out from the Wideford Hill assemblage is the use of finger and thumbnail decoration around the upper collar of the vessel (see below for full list of vessels exhibiting this feature). In terms of technique this involves a deep lenticular impression probably executed by impressing the thumbnail into damp clay. Comparable vessels can be found in a series of chambered cairns including Midhowe (vessel 2) and Unstan (vessels 15 and 30). The decorative technique, though not the form, of Calf of Eday vessel 19 is not dissimilar. In terms of the execution of thumb/fingernail on the vessel surface, there are also resemblances to Isbister vessels 5 and 6 (based on Davidson and Henshall's 1989 classification of finds from the Orkney chambered cairns) and to Knap of Howar vessel 79 (Henshall 1983, 67).

Another characteristic decorative technique at Wideford Hill is the use of stab-and-drag (see below). This is often used to produce herringbone pattern. There are a few vessels from chambered cairns that compare with this, including Taversoe Tuick (vessel 1), Unstan (vessels 6 and 11) and Isbister (vessel 15). There is also a close comparison in terms of technique and execution with Knap of Howar vessel 39 (Henshall 1983, 64). It is notable that like the Knap of Howar vessel, the execution of stab-and-drag motifs on vessels at Wideford Hill is fine (with the exception of SF 293) and it therefore seems to stand out from the coarser stab-and-drag technique of vessels from chambered cairn contexts.

A number of chambered cairns have deposits of undecorated Unstan vessels very like those from Wideford Hill, including Knowe of Rowiegar (vessel 2), Calf of Eday (vessel 8), Isbister (vessel 11), Taversoe Tuick (vessel 17) and Unstan (vessels 16 and 17) (as above, based on Davidson and Henshall 1989). The greater body of decorated Unstan vessels from Wideford Hill are decorated with incision, either incised herringbone pattern or incised horizontal, vertical and diagonal motifs. In this they compare with most Orcadian Unstan

assemblages. The combined use of horizontal and vertical incision compares with Midhowe vessel 1.

The neutral bowl forms are best compared with vessels from the Knap of Howar, in particular vessel 26 with its series of rounded impressions on the upper rim compares with the series of vessels with thumbnail impressions on their upper rims: SF 581 (pot group 75, [002]), SFs 233, 994 (pot group 22, [002]), SFs 201, 439 (pot group 24, [002]), SF 995 (pot group 7, [002]), SF 523 (pot group 1, [016]), SF 20 (pot group 2, [004]), SF 912 (pot group 1, [031]) and SF 538 (pot group 18, [029]). In addition the neutral bowl forms bear similarities with those from Stonehall Knoll and Stonehall Meadow, in particular the everted rims on SF 2360, SF 870 and the rolled rims on SFs 2373, 2314 and 1801 at Stonehall Knoll.

In terms of rim morphology, most neutral bowls have exterior or interior lips and are best compared with some of the neutral bowls from Isbister (vessel 28), Knowe of Craie (vessel 2) (Davidson and Henshall 1989), or Knap of Howar (vessel 64) (Henshall 1983, 66). They also compare with some of the neutral bowl forms from Stonehall Meadow and Stonehall Knoll.

11.4.2 Methodology

The ceramic assemblage from Wideford Hill was analysed on a context by context basis. As with Crossiecrown, this involved laying out the individual sherds in the spatial positions and contexts in which they were excavated. This procedure enabled a clear assessment of the similarity or difference of groups of sherds with different find numbers. The aim in doing this was not only to understand the spatial patterning of the site but also to assess the number of vessels in the assemblage. In those parts of the site where a single context prevailed sherds were analysed using the site grid. Accordingly, sherds of different small find number are grouped as 'pot groups' by context. Pot groups are defined by concordances in fabric, wall thickness and diagnostic features such as rim or base morphology and decoration. This allows for a clearer and more accurate assessment of the numbers of vessels in the assemblage.

11.4.3 Characterisation of the assemblage
11.4.3.1 Rim Sherds
A variety of rim forms are produced at Wideford Hill (Fig.11.4.1). These include bevelled, club-shaped, flat, flat and everted or inverted, flat with an interior and exterior lip, rounded, rounded and everted and rounded with an external or internal lip.

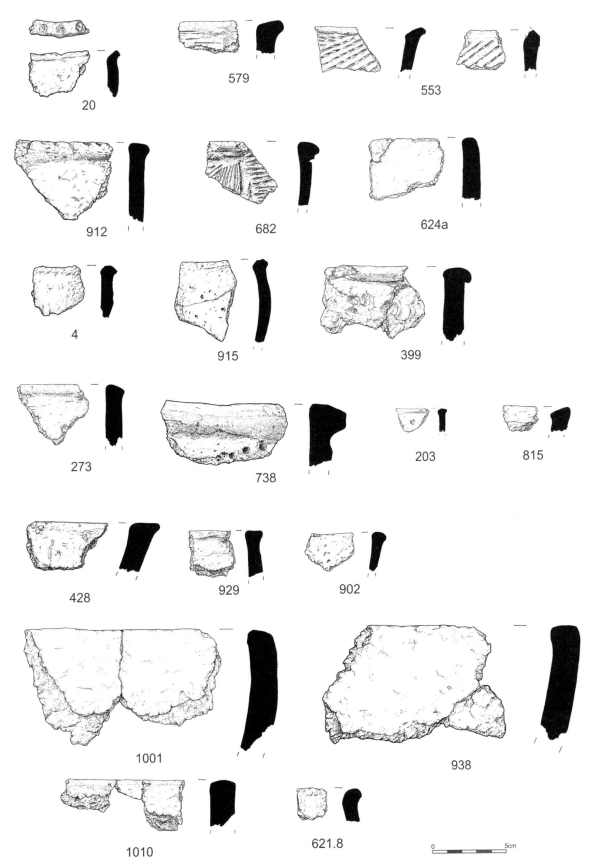

Figure 11.4.1 Pottery from Wideford Hill. Continues pp. 360–361.

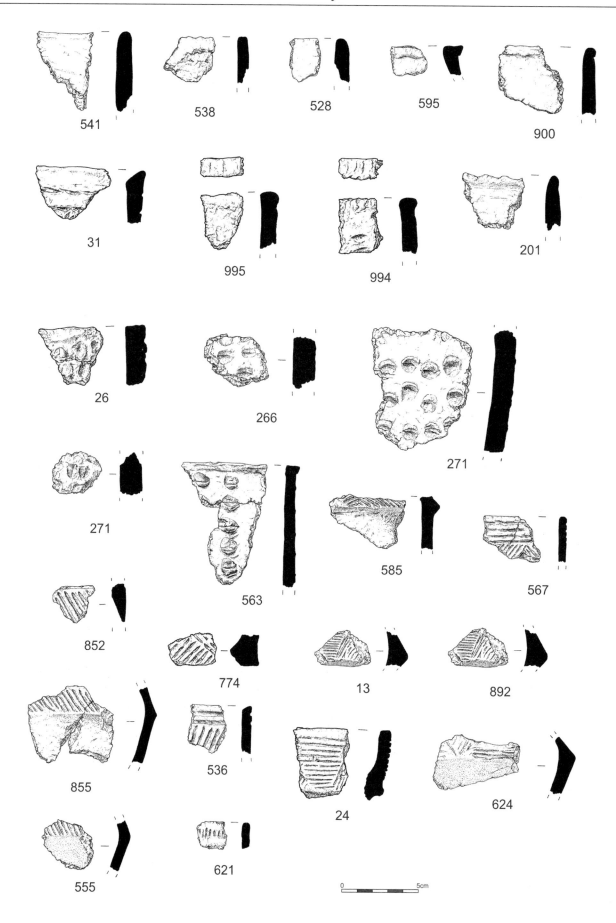

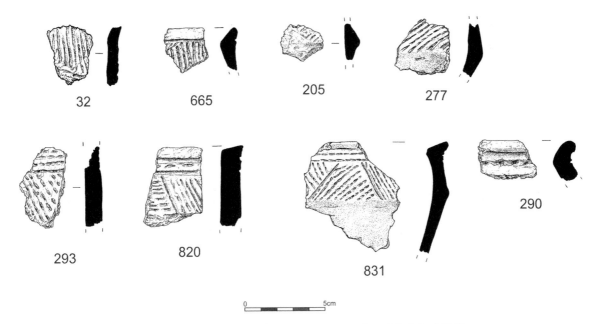

Figure 11.4.1 (above and opposite) Pottery from Wideford Hill.

Table 11.4.1 Bevelled rims.

SF No.	Pottery group	Context	Rim thickness (cm)	Rim diameter (cm)	Description
20	2	002	0.9	16–18	Thumbnail impressions on upper rim
809	6	002	1.1		
579	11	002	1	20	Series of incisions on upper rim
284	155	002	0.8	8	
553	5	029	0.7	14–16	Stab-and-drag herringbone pattern between rim and carination.
913	21	031	1	16	
609	26	031	0.8		

Bevelled rims

Bevelled rims are produced on seven vessels of a variety of sizes (Table 11.4.1). The rim diameters suggest that most of the vessels are small vessels with a rim diameter of around 16cm, and one tiny vessel of 8cm (one of the smallest in the assemblage) and one larger vessel having an upper range of 20cm. Notably the range of vessel sizes broadly conforms to differences in rim thickness, with the smallest vessel 0.8cm in thickness, the largest 1cm in thickness. Importantly it appears that bevelled rims are appropriate for 'classic' Unstan vessels, and also for vessels with decorated upper rims.

Representing three different vessels, all three club-shaped rims are produced on Unstan bowls. Two of these, SFs 682 and 686 are clearly small Unstan vessels whose small rim thickness indicates they are also fine-wares. SF 682 has 'classic' Unstan herringbone decoration, while the larger vessel SF 912 is decorated

on the upper rim. Flat rims appear to be produced on nine vessels of a variety of sizes, with rim thickness of 0.5–1.2cm. It was only possible to measure three flat rims for their rim diameters. As with other rim forms, 16cm seems to be the average (representing two small vessels), while another vessel was slightly larger with a rim diameter of 20–22cm. Five vessels were decorated and each of these is a 'classic' Unstan vessel. Three of these, SFs 462, 552 and 536 are finer vessels all decorated by incision, while SF 25 is a coarser vessel decorated by thumbnail impressions above the carination. Finally, one vessel, SF 523 has thumbnail impressions on the upper rim.

A number of flat everted/inverted rims, representing 10 vessels, are obviously from 'classic' Unstan vessels including SFs 629, 820 and 290, 810. The few rim diameters indicate that they are appropriate for both small vessels (14, 16cm) and larger vessels 18–20cm.

Table 11.4.2 Club-shaped and flat, flat everted and inverted rims.

Shape	SF No.	Pottery group	Context	Rim thickness (cm)	Rim diameter (cm)	Description
Club	912	1	031	1	22–24	Thumbnail impressions on upper rim
Club	682	1	057	0.5		Alternating panels of horizontal incised lines and diagonal stab motifs bounded by horizontal lines near rim
Club	686	12	057	0.6	16	Plain Unstan vessel
Flat	816	130	002	1.2	16–18	
Flat	462	167	002	0.5		Incised herringbone pattern
Flat	25	176	002	1		Thumbnail impressions running diagonally across surface.
Flat	523	1	016	0.9		Thumbnail impressions on upper rim
Flat	552	1	024	0.7		Three incised lines
Flat	536	4	029	0.8		Two incised lines below rim, series of diagonal incisions below. Fragment of herringbone pattern?
Flat	537	8	029	0.8		
Flat	624	29	031	1	20–22	
Flat	3		001	1	16	
Flat everted	290, 810	5	002	1.2	16	Two lines of stab marks below the rim
Flat everted	449	86	002	0.6		
Flat everted	292	87	002	1		
Flat everted	463	100	002			
Flat everted	435	119	002	0.7	14	
Flat everted	800	162	002	0.9		
Flat everted	4		001	0.6		
Flat everted	915	4	031	0.9	18–20	
Flat everted	629	5	031	1		Shoulder 2cm below rim (probable Unstan vessel)
Flat inverted	820	1	095	1		Horizontal incised lines framing stab-and-drag motifs. Below this opposed herringbone pattern of stab-and-drag and incised lines.

Rims with interior and exterior lips, representing 18 vessels (Table 11.4.3), appear to be produced on two groups of vessels; either very large neutral bowls or small 'classic' Unstan vessels. A series of rim diameters indicates that the majority of these rims are made on large vessels, mainly plain neutral bowls or vessels with minimal decoration, such as SF 788 (pot group 20, [002]) which has four stab impressions just below the rim and stands as one of the largest vessels in the entire assemblage with a rim diameter of 32–36cm. There are seven vessels with a diameter of 20cm or above, three of small/medium size between 16–18cm diameters and two small vessels of 14–16cm rim diameters. There are a number of vessels which are small fine Unstan vessels including SFs 652, 664, 665 and 902. SF 831 is evidently a small/medium-size Unstan vessel.

Taking all the rounded rims together (Table 11.4.4), the notable point is that they are mostly produced on small vessels. The suite of rim diameters has a fairly narrow range from 6–8cm and up to 18–20cm, suggesting that only small and medium size vessels have rounded rims. Notably, rounded rim vessels appear to be mainly small fine vessels with a range from 6–8 up to 16cm. Groups of vessels are mainly defined by rim form. Rounded everted rims constitute a clear group all of which have finger or thumb nail impressions on the upper rim. Lipped rims have both incision and thumbnail decoration near the rim. A large number of 'classic' Unstan vessels have rounded rims, such as SFs 528, 205, 24, 618, 619, 620, 621 and SFs 420, 423, 591. Amongst the group of rounded rim vessels at least nine are very fine vessels (with rim widths from 0.6–0.8cm), and three slightly larger vessels (rim widths 1–1.1cm).

Summary of rim types
As noted above, a variety of rim forms are produced at Wideford Hill. Treating the rims as a group, their diameters range from 6cm to 36cm (Fig. 11.4.2); there are a few vessels with a very small rim diameter (6–12cm), and most vessels seem to cluster in the 14–18cm range, with a clear distinction between vessels of 14–16cm and 16–18cm. These too will be relatively small vessels. There

Table 11.4.3 Flat, lipped rims.

SF No.	Pottery group	Context	Rim thickness (cm)	Rim diameter (cm)	Description
399	3	002		14–16	
273	10	002	1.1	24	
220, 486	18	002	0.8		
788	20	002	1.6	32–36	Four stab impressions near rim
787	21	002	0.6		Two zones of thumbnail impressions. Four fine fingernail impressions into upper rim
203	23	002	0.6	20–24	
815	25	002	1.1		
26	93	002	1.2	26–28	
319	97	002	1		
428	2	009	1.2	24–26	
831	2	031	0.7	16–18	Three horizontal lines of stab motifs. Below this are herringbone pattern of stab motifs bordered by incised lines
929	3	031	1	18	
828	6	031	0.8	16–18	
902	33	031	0.4	14	Small plain Unstan vessel
1001	41	031	2		Large plain bowl
652, 664, 665	6	057	0.5		Stab-and-drag running vertically at carination. Alternating incision and stab-and-drag near rim
938	5	104	1.5	26–28	Large plain bowl
1010	1	139	1.6	24–26	

Table 11.4.4 Rounded rims.

Type	SF No.	Pottery group	Context	Rim thickness (cm)	Rim diameter (cm)	Description
Rounded rim	205	14	002	0.6		Three stab impressions on carination. Incised line and series of diagonal stab impressions below
Rounded rim	24	16	002	0.6	16	Eleven horizontal incised lines with incised herringbone diagonals either side
Rounded rim	289	138	002	0.6	6–8	
Rounded rim	618, 619, 620, 621	1	013	0.6		Three horizontal incisions with incised herringbone pattern below
Rounded rim	420, 423, 591	1	015	0.8		Horizontal stab-and-drag below rim
Rounded rim	556	1	029	1	16	
Rounded rim	541	2	029	1	16	
Rounded rim	538	18	029	0.8		Thumbnail impressions on upper rim
Rounded rim	528	27	031	0.7		Shallow incisions which continue below the carination
Rounded rim	643	14	057	1.1		
Rounded rim	758	19	057	0.6		
Rounded rim	981	1	128	0.6	12	
Rounded external lipped rim	580, 595	9	002	0.8		Vertical incisions on carination, horizontal incisions on rim
Rounded external lipped rim	900	4	031	1		
Rounded internal lipped rim	31	3	004	1	18–20	Two horizontal lines of stab-and-drag
Rounded everted	995	7	002	0.9		Thumbnail impressions on upper rim
Rounded everted	223, 994	22	002	1		Fingernail impressions on rim edge and upper rim
Rounded everted	201, 439	24	002	1.1	16	Thumbnail impressions on upper rim
Rounded everted	581	75	002	0.9		Fingernail impressions on upper rim

are a number of medium-sized vessels of 18–24cm rim diameter range, which likewise cluster into vessels of 18–20cm, 20–22cm and 22–24cm, with the greatest number at the top of this range. Finally there are truly large vessels of 24cm+ diameter, most in the range 24–28cm, with two groups of 24–26cm and 26–28cm, and finally there is one monstrous neutral bowl with a rim diameter of 32–36cm.

Rounded rims appear to be produced on small and medium vessels exclusively. A large number of these are 'classic' Unstan vessels. Flat everted rims are likewise mainly on small or medium vessels of 'classic' Unstan type. Flat rims are mainly in the small to medium-size range with a few produced on 'classic' Unstan vessels. Club-shaped rims are all on small Unstan vessels. Flat-lipped rims are often produced on large plain bowls, but are also produced on small Unstan vessels. Similarly, bevelled rims appear to be appropriate for a range of vessels from tiny Unstan vessels to medium/large plain bowls.

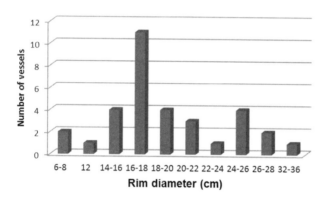

Figure 11.4.2 Rim diameter ranges in Wideford Hill pottery.

11.4.3.2 Decoration
We can distinguish between decoration on the *body* of the vessel above the carination and decoration on the *upper rim*. Both of these zones are important areas for decoration, and in some cases they serve to distinguish between 'classic' Unstan bowls which tend to be decorated above the carination and neutral bowl forms which have sparse decoration, usually around the upper body or rim area.

Decoration on the body (Fig. 11.4.1)
There are a total of 50 vessels with decoration on the upper body (either above the carination or below the rim). Of these 44 vessels are 'classic' Unstan bowls. The remaining six are neutral bowl forms. Let us begin by looking at the nature of decoration on the Unstan bowls. The decoration of Unstan bowls involves two main techniques: impression and incision. Impression may be either stab-and-drag impressions or finger or thumbnail impressions. The assemblage can be primarily divided by the use of these two main techniques. There is a group of bowls with finger or thumbnail, mainly medium or large-sized with a coarse fabric and appearance which largely remains unburnished. There are a total of 13 vessels with this kind of decoration (Table 11.4.5).

There is a variety of sizes of vessels decorated with thumb or fingernail impressions. Although their wall thickness suggests medium-size vessels, from the few rim diameters it appears that small and large vessels are also decorated using this technique. Most of the vessels have a fairly haphazard decoration above the carination, although SF 585 (pot group 17, [002]) has a more complex

Table 11.4.5 Vessels with finger or thumbnail impressions.

SF No.	Pottery group	Context	Wall thickness (cm)	Description
26	93	002	1.2	Flat, lipped rim with diameter 26–28cm
504	37	002	1.1	
301	27	002	0.7	
596	42	002	1	
226, 271, 777, 814	12	002	1.1–1.4	
276, 449	126	002	1	
399	3	002	1.2–3	Flat, lipped rim with diameter 14–16cm
260, 288	104	002	1	
233, 994	22	002	1	Rounded, everted rim
563	13	029	1.2	
25	176	002	1	Flat rim
585	17	002	0.9	
788	21	002	0.6	Flat, lipped rim with diameter 24cm

decorative motif of thumbnail impressions framed by fingernail impressions.

Vessels with incised or stab and drag motifs
These decorative techniques are used to produce the herringbone or cross-hatched pattern above the carination of 'classic' Unstan bowls (Table 11.4.6). It is likely that incisions and stab and drag impressions are executed with the same kind of tool either used as a means of cutting into the clay (incision) or punctuating it with the point (stab-and-drag). These techniques are used to create a variety of different designs:

1. *Incision only*
   1a. Incisions in herringbone pattern (6 vessels)
   1b. Diagonal incisions
   1c. Incised horizontals with incised diagonals below
   1d. Incised horizontals with incised herringbone pattern below
   1e. Alternating panels of horizontal incisions and diagonal incisions
   1f. Vertical incisions
   1g. Incised horizontals with vertical incisions below

2. *Stab-and-drag only*
   2a. Horizontal stab-and-drag motifs
   2b. Vertical stab-and-drag motifs
   2c. Diagonal stab-and-drag motifs
   2d. Stab-and-drag motifs in herringbone pattern
   2e. Stab-and-drag in chevron pattern

3. *Mixture of stab-and-drag and incision*

At least three decorated vessels are neutral bowl forms rather than Unstan ware (Table 11.4.7). These have a variety of decorative motifs which includes incision but also another decorative technique: the application of clay cordons.

Both 'classic' Unstan vessels and neutral bowl forms have decorated rims (Table 11.4.8). Again stab-and-drag, incision and thumbnail impressions are the major decorative techniques. The decoration on Unstan and neutral bowl forms will be analysed separately.

Analysis of decorated rims
There is a clear distinction in terms of vessels with decorated rims between those with and those without further decoration on the body. This distinction clearly defines decoration on 'classic' Unstan and neutral bowl forms: Unstan vessels have additional decoration on the body above the carination; neutral bowl forms have little or no decoration on the body. The decorative motifs on Unstan vessels often relate and refer to the decoration on the body. A number of vessels have vertical incisions

near the carination and *horizontal or diagonal* motifs near the rim. Likewise those Unstan vessels decorated with thumbnail motifs on the body have *fingernail* impressions around the rim.

Neutral bowl forms have decoration around the upper rim only (see Table 11.4.8). These too refer to the general repertoire of motifs found in Unstan vessels (thumbnail, incision and stab-and-drag motifs prevail). Notably, there seems to be little correlation between rim morphology and decoration amongst either the Unstan vessels or neutral bowl forms.

11.4.3.3 Undecorated Unstan vessels
In addition to the decorated Unstan ware there are a number of 'classic' Unstan ware vessels that remain undecorated (Table 11.4.9).

The undecorated Unstan bowls fall into two main groups: small and medium forms, with one large vessel, SF 755, also occurring (Table 11.4.9). Almost all of them are completely reduced (apart from SF 898) and only one has evidence for use wear (SF 460) which suggests that first undecorated forms are deliberately produced to have a reduced surface appearance, and second, counter to expectation, undecorated vessels do not appear to be used for cooking; on the basis of this small sample they are more likely to be used for serving food.

11.4.4 Surface Treatment
Of the 288 vessels for which surface treatment could be recorded, 207 (72%) were smoothed and 81 (28%) were burnished. Of those that were burnished 35 vessels received both smoothing and burnishing, while seven were Unstan bowls burnished below the carination. Of the burnished vessels nineteen were decorated, four of these were only decorated in the rim area and all were large neutral bowl forms. Three undecorated Unstan bowls were also burnished.

An examination of the spread of rim diameters for burnished and smoothed vessels indicates that burnished vessels are mainly small and medium-sized, with some extremely large vessels being burnished. By comparison smoothed vessels are mainly small or medium with very few large vessels being simply smoothed.

11.4.5 Firing profiles
The firing profiles of the Wideford pottery assemblage are notable for their regularity and uniformity. Unlike later Neolithic Grooved ware from Orkney which has

Table 11.4.6 Vessels with incised or stab-and-drag motifs.

Motif	Type	SF No.	Pottery group	Context	Wall thickness (cm)	Description
Incised		552	19	002	0.8	Flat rim decorated with three horizontal incisions which is likely to be an Unstan rim
Incised	1a	567	1	033	0.6	
Incised	1a	462	167	002	0.5	Flat rim
Incised	1a	852	7	031	0.6	
Incised	1a	774	85	002		
Incised	1a	13	8	002	1	
Incised	1a	892	------	013	0.8	
Incised	1b	390	28	002	0.7	
Incised	1b	534, 555	3	029	1	
Incised	1b	785	26	002	0.5	
Incised	1b	528	27	031	0.7	Vessel has diagonal incisions continuing below the carination, rounded rim
Incised	1c	536	4	029	0.6	Vessel with horizontal incisions and incised diagonals, flat rim
Incised	1d	618, 619, 620, 621	1	013	0.6	Vessel with horizontals incisions and incised herringbone pattern, rounded rim
Incised	1d	831	2	031	0.7	Vessel with horizontals incisions and incised herringbone pattern. Flat, lipped rim with diameter 16–18cm
Incised	1e	24	16	002	0.6	Vessel with alternating panels of horizontal and diagonal incisions. Rounded rim with diameter 16cm
Incised	1f	580, 595	9	002	0.6–0.8	Vessel with vertical incisions, rounded rim
Incised	1g	624	30	031	0.6	Vessel with horizontal incisions and vertical incisions
Incised	1g	32	1	003	0.6	Vessels with horizontal incisions and vertical incisions
Stab-and-drag	2a	31	3	004	1	Vessel with horizontal stab-and-drag motifs, rounded, lipped rim with diameter 18–20cm
Stab-and-drag	2a	420, 423, 591	1	015	0.8	Vessel with horizontal stab-and-drag motifs, rounded rim
Stab-and-drag	2b	652, 664, 665	6	057	0.8	Vessel with vertical stab-and-drag motifs, flat, lipped rim
Stab-and-drag	2b	205	14	002	0.6	Vessel with vertical stab-and-drag motifs, rounded rim
Stab-and-drag	2c	277	2	002	1.1	Vessel with diagonal stab-and-drag motifs
Stab-and-drag	2c	534	6	029	0.7	Vessel with diagonal stab-and-drag motifs
Stab-and-drag	2d	553	5	029	0.7	Vessel with stab-and-drag in herringbone pattern, bevelled rim with diameter 14–16cm
Stab-and-drag	2d	293	13	002	1.1	Vessel with stab-and-drag in herringbone pattern
Stab-and-drag	2d	624	2	031	0.7	Vessel with stab-and-drag in herringbone pattern, flat, lipped rim with diameter 16–18cm
Stab-and-drag	2e	914, 921	37	031	0.7	Vessel with stab-and-drag chevron motifs just above the carination
Stab-and-drag with incised	3	682	1	057	0.5	Vessel with alternating stab-and-drag and incised motifs, club-shaped rim
Stab-and-drag with incised	3	820	1	095	1	Vessel with alternating stab-and-drag and incised motifs, flat inverted rim
Stab-and-drag with incised	3	831	2	031	0.7	Vessel with alternating stab-and-drag and incised motifs, flat, lipped rim with diameter 16–18cm

very mixed firing profiles it was notable when analysing the Wideford assemblage that a high number of vessels exhibit either fully reduced or oxidised profiles or crisp firing profiles with clear distinctions between oxidised and reduced zones. Of the entire assemblage the firing profiles were recorded for 322 vessels (Table 11.4.10).

The high number of vessels with either completely reduced profiles or oxidised exteriors and reduced

Table 11.4.7 Other decorated vessels.

SF No.	Pottery group	Context	Wall thickness (cm)	Description
989	152	002	1	Two thin vertical cordons
634, 672, 887	2	057	1.8	Three horizontal incisions aligned on a suspension hole
583	19	002	0.8	Six horizontal incisions
941, 947, 951	4	104	0.7	Single shallow incision (attribution to either Unstan or neutral bowl form is equivocal

Table 11.4.8 Decoration on the upper rim.

Vessel type	SF No.	Pottery group	Context	Wall thickness (cm)	Rim	Description
Unstan	652, 664, 665	6	057	0.8	Flat, lipped	Vertical stab-and-drag at carination. Alternating incision and stab-and-drag near rim
Unstan	580, 595	9	002	0.6–0.8	Rounded, lipped	Vertical incisions at carination. Horizontal incisions on rim
Unstan	205	14	002	0.6	Rounded	Three vertical stab impressions on carination. Incised line and series of diagonal stab impressions
Unstan	788	21	002	0.6	Flat, lipped – diameter 24cm	Two zones of thumbnail impressions. Four fine fingernail impressions on upper rim
Unstan	233, 994	22	002	1	Rounded, everted	Thumbnail impressions on body. Fingernail impressions on upper rim, thumbnail on rim edge
Neutral bowl	290, 810	5	002	1–1.2	Flat, everted	Series of stab motifs 1.1cm below rim, another line 0.5cm below
Neutral bowl	788	20	002	1.6	Flat, lipped rim with diameter 32–36cm	Four stab impressions near rim.
Neutral bowl	579	11	002	1	Bevelled rim with diameter 20cm	Series of incisions on rim
Neutral bowl	581	75	002	0.9		
Neutral bowl	233, 994	22	002	1	Rounded, everted rim	Fingernail impressions on upper rim
Neutral bowl	201, 439	24	002	1.1	Rounded, everted rim with diameter 16cm	Thumbnail impressions on upper rim
Neutral bowl	995	7	002	0.9	Rounded, everted rim with diameter 18cm	Thumbnail impressions on upper rim
Neutral bowl	523	1	016	0.9	Flat rim	Thumbnail impressions on upper rim
Neutral bowl	20	2	004	1	Bevelled rim with diameter 16–18cm	Thumbnail impressions on upper rim
Neutral bowl	912	1	031	1	Club-shaped rim with diameter 22–24cm	Thumbnail impressions on upper rim
Neutral bowl	538	18	029	0.8	Rounded rim	Thumbnail impressions on upper rim

interiors suggests that the firing of pottery was controlled, quite possibly to achieve a specific surface appearance. The comparable numbers of reduced and oxidised vessels suggests the control of oxygen levels during firing; this is particularly true for the reduced vessels whose high numbers indicate this is not a matter of positioning during firing but of the intentional control of oxygen supply. The high numbers of vessels with oxidised exteriors and reduced interiors suggest that these vessels at least were upright during firing. There is no obvious correlation between firing profile and wall thickness, fabric or decoration.

Table 11.4.9 Undecorated Unstan vessels.

SF No.	Pottery group	Context	Wall thickness (cm)	Rim type and diameter
987	184	002	1	
460	175	002	1	
249	179	002	1	
902	33	031	0.4	Flat, lipped rim with diameter 14cm
837	40	031	1	
898	31	031	1	
636	12	057	0.6	Club-shaped rim with diameter 16cm
755	11	057	1.4	
958	1	089	0.6	

Table 11.4.10 Firing profile of Wideford Hill pottery assemblage.

Firing profile	Number of vessels
Complete reduction	44
Complete reduction	129
Mixed oxidation	13
Oxidised interior	14
Oxidised exterior (reduced interior)	119

11.4.6 Use-Wear

A total of 119 vessels exhibit evidence for use-wear in the form of either internal residue or exterior sooting. An examination of the range of wall thickness against use-wear indicates that the entire range of vessel sizes is utilised for cooking and food preparation activities, as vessels with wall thickness from as small as 0.4cm wall thickness and up to 2cm are used for cooking.

A comparatively small number of vessels that exhibit evidence of use-wear are also decorated. There are only nine decorated vessels. All of these are Unstan vessels; four of these are decorated with thumb or fingernail impressions, the rest with incision or stab-and-drag motifs. Given the low number of decorated vessels exhibiting signs of use-wear it seems likely that decorated vessels tend not to be used for cooking and food preparation. However, it is curious that many of the vessels with decoration around the rim exhibit use-wear evidence, and this is especially true of the group of neutral bowl forms decorated with thumbnail around the rim (see above) and for large vessels such as SF 788 (pot group 20, context 2). A number of Unstan vessels decorated around the rim also exhibit evidence for use-wear including SFs 652, 664, 665 (pot group 6, [057]), SFs 580, 595 (pot group 9, [002]), SFs 233, 994 (pot group 22, [002]) and SF 788 (pot group 21, [002]). This may indicate that vessels with decorated rims are marked out or specifically categorised for food

preparation and cooking. Sooting is apparent around the carination on two vessels, while sooting is found near the rim on nine vessels. This pattern of sooting suggests that vessels are placed directly in the fire during cooking/food preparation.

11.4.7 Evidence for function on the basis of organic residue analysis

Six neutral vessels and three Unstan vessels were analysed for their lipid content (see section 11.7). The results were remarkable as they did not distinguish between the contents of the two types of vessels; both contained ruminant dairy fats. This may be interpreted in a number of ways: either the apparent differences in form and decoration bear no relationship to Neolithic categories of use, or the vessels are used differently (*e.g.* cooking, serving) for the same contents. Given the apparent differences in form within the assemblage, the latter interpretation is preferred. This is underlined by the slight differences in use-wear discussed above, where undecorated vessels tend to exhibit more evidence for sooting than decorated vessels. However, it is apparent from both the use-wear and GC-MS analysis that there are strong overlaps in function and contents.

11.4.8 Evidence for repair or suspension holes

Four vessels exhibit evidence for repair or suspension holes (Table 11.4.11). Three of these vessels are decorated (one Unstan vessel and two decorated neutral bowls). This suggests that the repair of decorated vessels may be of significance. It is likely that most of these holes were produced during the life of the vessel and were not intended from the outset. In fact SF 439 exhibits evidence of having been drilled through, and that sherd and SFs 219, 860 both show evidence of wear around the hole indicating binding of a repair.

Table 11.4.11 Evidence for repair or suspension holes.

SF No.	Pottery group	Context	Description
774	85	002	Incised herringbone pattern. Hole drilled through sherd at carination
634, 672, 887	2	057	Three horizontal incised lines. Incised lines coincident with suspension hole
201, 439	24	002	Rounded everted rim with diameter 16cm. Thumbnail impression on upper rim. Hole drilled 2.5cm below rim of SF 249. Wear traces of binding internally
219, 860	124	002	Repair hole, traces of wear at edges.

11.4.9 Tempering strategy

Overall there are four basic fabric types produced in the Wideford pottery assemblage:

A. rock temper (either angular or rounded)
B. shell temper (usually visible as platy voids)
C. rock and shell
D. fabrics with no visible inclusions.

Those fabrics that are tempered are further divided by the percentage of temper included; rock temper ranges from 1–2%, 3%, 5%, 7%, 10% and up to 30%; shell temper ranges from 1–2%, 3%, 5%, up to 7–10%; rock and shell ranges from 1–2%, 3%, 5%, 7%, 10% and up to 20%. As can be seen from Fig. 11.4.3, the use of temper is variable. As a basic rule of thumb, small vessels (wall thickness 0.4-0.8cm) tend to have low percentages of temper or no visible inclusions and are characterised by the use of low percentages of shell or rock. Medium vessels (wall thickness 0.9–1.1cm) have between 1 and 10% and are characterised by low percentages of shell, rock and rock and shell. Larger vessels (1.2cm–2.3cm) tend not to be tempered with shell and are more often tempered with rock or rock and shell in both lower and higher percentages. The decision to temper with either rock, shell or rock and shell appears to be partly determined by vessel size (Table 11.4.12).

11.4.9.1 Analysis of petrological thin-sections

All the tempering material used in the Wideford Hill assemblage was locally available. Key components of the temper are the igneous dyke materials bostonite, camptonite and monchiquite. All three of these rocks outcrop at the Bay of Firth. It is worth commenting on the character of tempering material within the Wideford thin-sections. The material is uniformly small and often rounded or rolled, suggesting that much of it may have been present in the clay sources. This observation is confirmed by the presence of feldspars, weathering products of igneous rock, of which clay is the final product. It is our contention that the potters at Wideford Hill were exploiting clay deposits local to

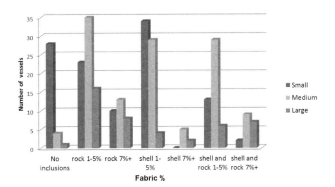

Figure 11.4.3 Wideford pottery fabrics and vessel size.

specific dyke sources. Andrew M. Jones has observed weathered clay at a number of the Bay of Firth dykes. The tempering material would therefore be less a matter of addition to pure clays, and more by-products of using weathered clay from igneous sources. This suggests that the differentiation in temper that we observe in other periods of Orcadian prehistory may have been less of a preoccupation during the early Neolithic.

Analysis of the links between the macro-scale classification of pottery and petrology across different contexts within the site produced no conclusive patterns. Intra-site clay resources and temper vary between different contexts and pottery forms; similarly vessel size and fabric, and vessel size and context provided no correlations (Tully 2004). As the huge diversity in production strategy extends to individual contexts, this suggests that even within households there is no clear temper or clay preference.

Although pottery composition is not necessarily constant over time, especially in long periods of occupation, as clays can vary depending on the area of extraction even within the same clay bed, it is perhaps unsurprising that the Wideford Hill fabric assemblage is so varied. However, this stands in marked contrast to later Neolithic Grooved ware where clear differentiation in the use of temper from different household contexts can be observed (Jones 2000; 2005). Since some of the samples from Wideford Hill

Table 11.4.12 Catalogue of petrological samples.

SF No.	Context	Description
295	002	5% coarse sub-angular sandstone 1–2mm across, 1% angular and rounded camptonite, 0.5–0.8mm across. 1% angular Plagioclase feldspar, 0.5mm across
236	002	10% angular and rounded monchiquite, 0.5–1mm across
856	002	1% coarse sub-angular sandstone 1–2mm across, 5% angular and rounded monchiquite, 0.5–0.8mm across
268	002	2% coarse sub-angular sandstone 1–2mm across, 1% platy voids (shell) 1–2mm across
457	002	5% well crushed monchiquite (angular and rounded) 0.5mm across, 1% angular and rounded camptonite, 0.5mm across
979	002	1–2% angular and rounded monchiquite, 0.5–0.8mm across
980	002	1% coarse sub-angular sandstone 1–2mm across, 1% platy voids (shell) 1–2mm across, 1% rounded monchiquite, 0.5mm across
484	002	1% coarse sub-angular sandstone 1–2mm across, 1% platy voids (shell), 1–2mm across, 1% angular plagioclase feldspar 0.8–1mm across
344	002	×2 thin-sections: 5% coarse sub-angular sandstone 1–2mm across, 2% angular and rounded camptonite, 1–2mm across
888	002	5% angular and rounded monchiquite 0.5–0.8mm across, 2% angular and rounded fine grained mudstone 0.8–1mm across
460	002	1% coarse sub-angular sandstone 1–2mm across, 2% angular and rounded fine grained mudstone 1–2mm across, 1% angular microcline feldspar around 0.4–0.5mm across
249	002	7% angular and rounded monchiquite, 1–2mm across. 1% rounded quartz 0.3–0.5mm across
571	002	5% angular and rounded monchiquite, 1–2mm across, 1% angular microcline feldspar around 0.4–0.5mm across
484	002	1% angular and rounded monchiquite, 0.5–0.8mm across
869	002	2% coarse sub-angular sandstone 1–2mm across, 2% angular and rounded camptonite, 1–2mm across, 1% angular and rounded fine grained mudstone 0.5–1mm across
259	002	5% angular and rounded fine grained mudstone 0.8–1mm across, 1% rounded quartz, 0.3–0.5mm across, 2% angular and rounded monchiquite, 0.8–1mm across
462	002	Very coarse clay matrix. 1% rounded quartz, 0.3–0.5mm across, 2% angular and rounded fine grained mudstone 0.8–1mm across
18	002	1% coarse sub-angular sandstone 1–2mm across, 2% angular and rounded camptonite, 1–2mm across, 2% angular and rounded fine grained mudstone 0.5–1mm across
457	002	1% coarse sub-angular sandstone 1–2mm across, 2% angular and rounded camptonite, 1–2mm across, 2% angular and rounded fine grained mudstone 0.5–1mm across
488	002	10% angular and rounded camptonite, 1–2mm across
979	002	5% angular and rounded monchiquite, 1–2mm across, 1% angular microcline feldspar around 0.4–0.5mm across
969	002	2% angular and rounded fine grained mudstone 0.8–1mm across, 5% angular and rounded monchiquite, 0.8–1mm across
875	002	5% platy voids (shell), 1–2mm across, 1% angular and rounded monchiquite, 0.5–1mm across, 1% angular and rounded fine grained mudstone 0.8–1mm across
980	002	Darker clay matrix. 1% coarse sub-angular sandstone 1–2mm across, 1% angular and rounded fine grained mudstone 1–2mm across, 1% angular and rounded bostonite, 0.8–1mm across
857	002	10% angular and rounded camptonite, 1–2mm across, 1% angular and rounded fine grained mudstone 0.8–1mm across
326	002	1% coarse sub-angular sandstone 1–2mm across, 1% angular and rounded fine grained mudstone 1–2mm across
988	002	5% angular and rounded monchiquite, 1–2mm across, 1% angular and rounded fine grained mudstone 0.8–1mm across, 5% platy voids (shell), 1–2mm across
885	002	5% angular and rounded monchiquite, 1–2mm across, 1% rounded fine grained mudstone 0.8–1mm across
798	002	2% rounded quartz, 0.5–1mm across, 1% angular plagioclase feldspar 0.5–0.8mm across, 1% angular and rounded fine grained mudstone 0.8–1mm across, 1% platy voids (shell), 0.5–1mm across
451	002	5% rounded quartz, 0.5–1mm across, 2% angular and rounded fine grained mudstone 0.8–1mm across, 1% platy voids (shell), 0.5–1mm across
25	009	10% angular and rounded monchiquite, 1–2mm across
533	029	2% coarse sub-angular sandstone 1–2mm across, 2% angular and rounded fine grained mudstone 0.8–1mm across, 1% platy voids (shell), 0.5–1mm across
840	031	1% coarse sub-angular sandstone 1–2mm across, 5% angular and rounded fine grained mudstone 1–2mm across, 1% angular microcline feldspar around 0.4–0.5mm across
897	031	10% angular and rounded monchiquite, 1–4mm across; 5% angular and rounded monchiquite, 1–2mm across, 2% rounded fine grained mudstone 0.8–1mm across

Table 11.4.12 Catalogue of petrological samples, continued.

SF No.	Context	Description
517	031	2% angular and rounded fine grained mudstone 0.8–1mm across, 1% platy voids (shell), 0.5–1mm across, 1% angular plagioclase feldspar around 0.5–0.8mm across
919	031	5% well crushed angular monchiquite, 0.5–0.8mm across
597	031	1% coarse sub-angular sandstone 1–2mm across, 1% rounded quartz, 0.4–0.5mm across
1001	031	1/3: 1% coarse sub-angular sandstone 1–2mm across, 1% rounded quartz, 0.4–0.5mm across, 1% rounded monchiquite, 1–2mm across. 2/3: 1% coarse sub-angular sandstone 1–2mm across, 1% rounded quartz, 0.4–0.5mm across, 2% platy voids (shell) 1–2mm across. 3/3: 1% coarse sub-angular sandstone 1–2mm across.
900	031	5% angular and rounded monchiquite, 1–2mm across, 2% rounded fine grained mudstone 0.8–1mm across
530	031	5% angular and rounded monchiquite, 1–2mm across, 2% rounded fine grained mudstone 0.8–1mm across, 1% platy voids (shell) 0.5–1mm across
601	031	5% angular and rounded monchiquite, 1–2mm across
877	057	5% coarse sub-angular sandstone, 2–4mm across, 2% angular fine grained mudstone, 2–4mm across, 1% angular plagioclase feldspar around 0.5–0.8mm across
660	057	1% coarse sub-angular sandstone, 1–2mm across, 1% angular and rounded fine grained mudstone, 1–2mm across, 1% angular camptonite, 1–2mm across, 1% platy voids (shell), 0.5–1mm across
758	057	5% angular and rounded monchiquite, 1–2mm across, 2% fine grained mudstone 0.8–1mm across
936	104	10% angular and rounded monchiquite, 1–2mm across
970	109	×2 thin-sections: 1% coarse sub-angular sandstone, 1–2mm across, 1% angular plagioclase feldspar around 0.5–0.8mm across.
1011	139	5% coarse sub-angular sandstone, 2–4mm across. Laminated clay possibly indicating a lack of mixing
SF C S2	001	Pure clay matrix. 1% platy voids (shell) 0.4–0.5mm across
No SF	006	1% coarse sub-angular sandstone, 1–2mm across, 1% rounded fine-grained mudstone, 1–2mm

came from the same phase, at least some fabric grouping would be expected if there were a formalised procedure for fabric type. Petrological analysis of the contemporary early Neolithic settlement assemblage at the Knap of Howar, although identifying the pottery as locally made, also found no correlation between fabric and finished product (Williams 1983).

Even from the rammed stone working area [002] the abundant pottery finds still reveal extensive temper and fabric variation. This implies that the potters brought their individually obtained clay and temper resources to a focal place. Here they may have shared the mixture of the locally available resources to craft a homogeneous Unstan ware assemblage.

11.4.10 Spatial analysis of pottery from different contexts

11.4.10.1 Pottery associated with Timber structure 1
Only one vessel was found in context in Timber structure 1:

- SF 955 comprises six undecorated body sherds with a wall thickness of 0.7cm which are completely reduced and the outer surface is smoothed. There is evidence of internal residue. The sherd came from context [068], a burnt charcoal-rich layer within the central scoop hearth.

11.4.10.2 Pottery associated with Timber structure 3 and associated midden
Two decorated vessels were associated with Structure 3. Both came from the fill of the postholes that make up the outer wall of the structure.

- SF 552, from the fill of posthole 25 ([24]), is the rim of a decorated Unstan vessel. It is a fine flat rim (0.7cm wall thickness) decorated with three incised horizontal lines. The vessel is oxidised on the exterior and smoothed, and exhibits evidence of residue internally. It is tempered with 7–10% rock.
- SF 567 comes from the fill of posthole 41 ([33]) and is a fine (0.6cm wall thickness) decorated carination with part of the vessel body. It is completely reduced, smoothed and burnished and decorated with incision in herringbone pattern above the carination. It is tempered with 1% shell.

In addition, a midden spread is associated with Structure 3. Three vessels come from this deposit ([128]).

- SF 981 comprises two fine (0.6cm wall thickness) undecorated rounded rims sherds, completely reduced and are smoothed externally. There is evidence of sooting around the rim exterior. The rim diameter of the vessel is 12cm. The vessel is tempered with 3% rock.

- SF 983 is one fine (0.6cm wall thickness) body sherd. It is completely reduced and smoothed externally. It is tempered with 1% rock.
- SFs 976, 977 comprise 6 base sherds. Completely reduced and tempered with 15% rock.

Although these are labelled as distinct vessels, given the uniformity in firing and tempering practice, it is not inconceivable that they constitute fragments from a single plain vessel. None of these sherds seems to relate to those deposited in the posthole fills of Timber structure 3.

11.4.10.3 Pottery associated with Stonehouse 1

Six vessels come from the upper floor of Stonehouse 1 ([104]):

- SFs 934, 946, 949, 971 comprise 41 base sherds with a basal thickness of 1.4–2cm. The vessel has an oxidised exterior and is smoothed. There is evidence of residue in the interior. The vessel is tempered with 30% angular rock.
- SFs 954, 963 comprise 3 body sherds of 1.2cm wall thickness. The vessel is smoothed and there is evidence of internal residue. It is tempered with 10–15% shell.
- SFs 952, 953 comprise 1 base and 2 body sherds of 0.9cm wall thickness. The vessel is completely reduced and smoothed externally. There is evidence of internal residue. It is tempered with 3% shell.
- SFs 941, 947, 951 comprise 3 body sherds of 0.7cm wall thickness. The vessel has an oxidised exterior. It is tempered with 1–2% rock. It is decorated with shallow incisions.
- SF 938 comprises 1 rim of 1.5cm rim thickness. It is completely reduced and smoothed externally. There is sooting near the rim exterior. The rim is flat with an interior lip and has a rim diameter of 26–28cm. It constitutes the rim from a large plain bowl.
- SF 970 comprises 1 body sherd of 1cm wall thickness. It is completely reduced and is smoothed externally. It is tempered with 10% angular rock.

Two vessels come from the fill of a cut in the north of Stonehouse 1:

- SF 1010 comprises 3 rims and 16 body sherds of 1.6cm wall thickness. The vessel is completely reduced and smoothed externally. It has sooting near the rim. It is tempered with 5% rounded rock. It has a flat rim with a lipped interior and exterior overhang. It has a rim diameter of 24–26cm.
- SF 1011 comprises 1 body sherd of 1cm wall thickness with an oxidised exterior and reduced interior. It is tempered with 5% rounded rock.

Given the large numbers of vessels from the associated working platform, Stonehouse 1 has to be judged to be relatively clean of pottery deposits. The deposits from [104] and [139] must be viewed as final occupation deposits. In many ways they are very like the deposits found in the internal occupation layer at Knap of Howar (Henshall in Ritchie 1983, 54). The substantial nature of deposits like SFs 934, 946, 949, 971 with 41 base sherds and SF 1010 with 3 rims and 16 body sherds is indicative of a low level of disturbance. There are a variety of vessels here, and notably most of them exhibit evidence for cooking in the form of sooting and residue suggesting their use within the house. The deposition of final occupation deposits, often consisting of large deposits of base sherds, in houses mirrors similar deposits at the nearby Neolithic site at Crossiecrown as well as other sites, such as Skara Brae and Barnhouse.

In addition one vessel was deposited amongst the wall core material [051]:

- SF 577 comprises 30 base sherds of 1.7cm basal thickness. The vessel is oxidised on the exterior, reduced interior and is smoothed. It is tempered by 20% angular rock.

This too looks like an undisturbed possible foundation deposit. The practice of depositing vessels within the wall core of houses occurs at the late Neolithic sites of Barnhouse and Skara Brae.

11.4.10.4 Associated 'working platform'

The bulk of the deposits come from the rammed stone pavement or working platform [002] adjacent to Stonehouse 1. There are a total of 303 vessel groups from this context with an additional eight from topsoil contexts just above this area. There are a number of layers of activity within this area, with probable successive layers of cobbling. An analysis of pots from these layers yields little indication of any major changes in style. However, it is notable that only one vessel decorated with thumbnail impressions comes from context [029], beneath [002], as against the large numbers from [002] itself, suggesting a possible increase in the use of this decorative motif later in the history of the site. Both neutral bowls and decorated Unstan bowls are deposited intermixed in this area.

The nature of this area is suggestive of a working or activity area immediately to the east of Stonehouse 1 (but see section 11.11). Areas such as this have been found at late Neolithic settlements such as Barnhouse and Skara Brae. At both settlements there were defined areas for the production of artefacts. At Skara Brae this was a built structure (Hut 8), and at Barnhouse it was a central space used for, amongst other things, the production and firing of pottery. At Wideford Hill there are no obvious zones of burning suggesting the firing of pottery in this area. Unlike the deposits from the similar area at Barnhouse the pots from this area are not wasters. Instead they are more likely to have been produced, used and subsequently deposited in this area. However, the deposits are relatively clean and do not have the character of midden. Nevertheless the discrepancy in numbers and the character of pottery in Stonehouse 1 against the large numbers of pots from the rammed stone area suggest that this was a defined location for either pottery production or the deposition of pots. If we compare the character of pots from this area with Stonehouse 1, it is notable that there are no Unstan vessels from within the house.

Given the argument that the deposits within Stonehouse 1 are final occupation deposits sealed within the house upon abandonment it seems likely that during use the interior of Stonehouse 1 was kept relatively clean. In this case the deposits on the cobbled platform adjacent to Stonehouse 1 are likely to represent material cleared out of the house during its occupation. It is interesting that this material is relatively 'clean' and not intermixed with other midden debris suggesting the possible categorisation of different types of refuse.

11.4.11 Discussion

The discussion falls into two parts: the 'shape' and character of the assemblage from Wideford Hill, and the significance of that assemblage in a wider Orcadian context. As noted in the introduction, the Wideford Hill assemblage can be divided into two major pottery forms: open bowls of 'classic' Unstan ware and neutral bowl forms with a deeper profile. The ratio of open bowl forms to neutral bowls is 4:1 indicating the predominance of open bowl forms of Unstan type. It is important at this point to summarise the differences and similarities between the two pottery forms in order to gain an idea of contrasting use and function.

11.4.11.1 Characterising Unstan ware

In total there are 53 diagnostic carinated Unstan vessels in the Wideford Hill assemblage. These can be broadly divided into a decorated and undecorated component with a ratio of 5:1 decorated to undecorated vessels. This indicates that decoration is a significant feature of the Unstan ware tradition. Of the decorated component there is also a broad division based on technique with thirteen vessels decorated with finger or thumbnail impressions, and the remaining 31 by incision or stab-and-drag.

Vessels can be divided into three major sizes based on wall thickness: small (wall thickness 0.4–0.8cm), medium (0.9–1.1cm) and large (wall thickness 1.2–2.3cm). Undecorated vessels are mainly medium-size or small. It is interesting to find a size distinction between vessels decorated with finger or thumbnail decoration and those decorated with other motifs. The former tend to be large (four vessels) or medium size (six vessels). Only three were small vessels. Of the latter the majority are small (23 vessels) or medium (8 vessels), and there are no large vessels. This indicates that there is a larger coarser component of the assemblage decorated with finger or thumbnail decoration and a finer and smaller component decorated with incision or stab-and-drag, often in the 'classic' herringbone style. Undecorated vessels also fall into this size range.

Large numbers of Unstan vessels are fired in a reducing atmosphere to produce a darker finish. However, many of the large finger or thumbnail decorated forms are produced in oxidising atmospheres giving them a redder appearance. In terms of use it is evident that very small numbers (only nine vessels) exhibit such evidence. However, some of those vessels decorated around the upper rim area may be used in cooking or food preparation. Overall it seems that most Unstan vessels are not used for cooking, and are instead more likely to be specialised serving vessels.

11.4.11.2 Characterising neutral bowl forms

It is important to contrast the use of Unstan ware with the use of neutral bowl forms. There are a total of 21 diagnostic neutral bowls. There is a ratio of around 2:1 decorated to undecorated forms (fourteen decorated, six undecorated), again indicating the significance of decoration within the assemblage as a whole. In terms of size the majority of decorated forms are small (six vessels) or medium (five vessels), with only three large vessels. For undecorated forms the majority are large (three vessels) or medium (two vessels) with only one small vessel, indicating a slight dichotomy in size dependent on decoration. Decoration on neutral bowl forms can be divided between decoration on the upper body (three vessels), or around the upper rim area (eleven vessels). Decoration on the upper body is mainly with incision or in one case vertical cordons. Those vessels decorated on the upper rim are mainly decorated by thumbnail impressions.

In terms of surface treatment there seems to be a slight indication that large neutral bowl forms are preferentially burnished. Since only nine Unstan vessels could be unequivocally associated with evidence for use-wear, it seems likely that large numbers of neutral bowls are associated with use-wear. It is difficult to be certain about this since the profile and attribution of many sherds was difficult to ascertain. However, it seems likely that there is a greater amount of evidence for sooting and residue amongst the neutral bowl component of the assemblage, especially given that much of the evidence for use-wear came from large and medium vessels. Most of the neutral bowls are large or medium in size.

11.4.11.3 Similarities and differences between neutral bowls and Unstan ware

It is critical that both the shallow open Unstan forms and the deep neutral bowl forms are viewed as components of the same tradition (Jones 2000), albeit often used in contrasting ways and contexts. There are obviously key differences in morphology which may relate to contrasting function, as argued above, although it is evident that the use of both pottery forms is complex with evidence for use-wear on both. Nevertheless there are morphological elements found in both forms; for example, the shouldered form of Unstan ware is echoed in the high shoulder of one neutral bowl form, SF 629 (pot group 5, [031]). There are also clear continuities in terms of decoration. The finger and thumbnail motif found on 'classic' Unstan forms predominated in the neutral bowl assemblage, mainly used around the upper rim. Similarly incision was used to decorate both Unstan and neutral bowl forms. It is also important to note that in both forms it is the upper area of the vessel that is reserved for decoration. A variety of rim forms are found both on Unstan and neutral bowl forms including bevelled, flat, flat everted/inverted and flat lipped. This again suggests continuity between the two forms.

11.4.11.4 Wideford, Unstan ware and the Orcadian Early Neolithic

One of the key points to emerge from the analysis of the Wideford assemblage is the predominance of Unstan ware. This is in marked contrast to the Knap of Howar where Unstan ware was a relatively minor component of the assemblage (but see Ha'Breck – Thomas and Lee 2012). There has been a tendency to view Unstan ware as more closely related to mortuary contexts, while plain neutral bowls are more closely related to domestic assemblages (see Henshall 1983; Jones 2000). Given the variety of Unstan forms and their relationship to neutral bowls at Wideford Hill this broad-brush view can no longer be sustained. This point is reinforced by

the presence of Unstan forms at the nearby settlement of Crossiecrown (although the small quantities do not suggest a predominance of Unstan forms at this settlement). Indeed it is notable that neutral bowls are found in a number of chambered cairn contexts, such as Isbister, Knowe of Craie, Sandyhill Smithy, Knowe of Rowiegar, Calf of Eday Long, Taversoe Tuick and Unstan (Davidson and Henshall 1989, 66–76). By comparison with Wideford Hill, the relative quantity of Unstan ware to neutral bowl forms in these chambered cairn contexts may be a clear reflection of the relative numbers of each form in a typical assemblage. It may be that the mixed neutral and Unstan bowls in chambered cairns provide an accurate picture of a 'typical' early Neolithic assemblage.

How do these vessels compare with those from chambered cairn contexts? There are clear overlaps in decorative technique as discussed in the introduction, as well as overlaps in the size of vessels from the Wideford assemblage and those in chambered cairn contexts. As Fig. 11.4.2 indicates, the majority of rims are less than 20cm in diameter, while a minority are greater than this with an upper scale of 26–28cm for Unstan rims. Although some vessels in chambered cairn contexts are of this size (for example Kierfea Hill 1 and 2, Bigland Round 1, Sandyhill Smithy 1, Blackhammer 1, Midhowe 1, Calf of Eday 1–3, Isbister 1–8, Taversoe Tuick 1 and 6 and Unstan 1, 12, 15 and 16), there are a large number with rim diameters exceeding 28cm. The larger vessels from Calf of Eday, Isbister and Unstan have rim diameters between 32 and 40cm. Like the assemblage from the Knap of Howar, the Unstan ware from Wideford Hill tends to be finer in size and finish than those vessels from chambered cairn contexts (Henshall 1983a for similar observation).

Although the neutral bowls clearly overlap in size with Unstan vessels with an upper range of 32cm, the neutral bowls from Wideford Hill are larger than any from chambered cairn contexts. These differences in the size of vessels in different contexts suggest that the while the neutral bowls on settlement sites are used for cooking and preparation, this function is less well defined in chambered cairn contexts. Here specialised serving vessels – Unstan ware – predominate, and these are produced for large-scale communal feasting in the context of mortuary rituals (see Jones 2000). That vessels are clearly categorised by depositional context is evinced by the dump of material on the rammed stone pavement at Wideford Hill. The predominance of large neutral bowls in the Wideford settlement is paralleled at Stonehall (see Chapter 11.2).

A clear point to emerge from the excavation at Wideford Hill is the fact that Unstan ware is produced at the earliest phases of the sites occupation and continues to be used until the final phases. It is found in the postholes of structure 3 and is also associated in large quantities with the rammed stone pavement related to the occupation of Stonehouse 1. If we assume that the timber posthole structures from Wideford Hill represent some of the earliest Neolithic settlement in Orkney, then we have to assume that Unstan ware is not a later evolution from a plain ware. In fact it is produced at an early stage of the occupation of the islands. If we further assume low-level population movement between Mainland Scotland and Orkney, it is interesting to note that Unstan ware is found on the Scottish Mainland in regions such as Caithness (see Davidson and Henshall 1991 for discussion of Caithness sites) and as far south as Aberdeenshire (Alexander 1997), while it is also a significant ceramic form in the Western Isles (Armit 1992).

Unstan ware is an important component of the ceramic repertoire of the Neolithic of Northern and Western Scotland. A key question remains: is this a ceramic form indigenous to Orkney or does its relationship to other ceramics in the Western Isles and mainland Scotland suggest that it was one component in a network of interactions? The available radiocarbon dates for the Western Isles and Caithness (Armit 1992; Ashmore 2000a) are indistinguishable from the available dates within Orkney, suggesting a continuous network of interaction across a large region rather than a simple wave of advance or diffusion. That Unstan ware is a component of a shared tradition emerges clearly from the analysis of the Wideford Hill assemblage. It has been noted elsewhere that Unstan ware decoration and production is not a medium for social differentiation (Jones 2005b). The Wideford Hill assemblage is decoratively identical to vessels from chambered cairn and domestic contexts in Orkney. Furthermore as our analysis of the petrology has shown, unlike later Neolithic tempering practices, there is no clear differentiation in the use of temper. It appears that the pottery is used to signal membership of a wider cultural group, rather than to define membership of a specific settlement. At the regional and inter-regional level the use of Unstan ware is an important feature of shared cultural practices.

11.5 Potters' raw materials in the Cuween-Wideford area: prospection and experimental and replication studies

Richard Jones

11.5.1 Introduction

This section forms a natural background or accompaniment to the accounts of the pottery finds from the three sites, Stonehall, Crossiecrown and Wideford Hill. It describes work that took place at an early stage of the Cuween-Wideford project, most of it on Orkney itself, and it represents the deliberate attempt from the project's outset to take a holistic approach to the pottery finds; simply put, to place information gained about the location of potters raw materials within the present-day Bay of Firth landscape, to investigate their potting properties, to establish a *chaîne opèratoire* in replicating early and late Neolithic pottery, and to carry out experimental firings. The work was carried out Bill Brown and Richard Jones. This combined information could serve as a source of experience as well as a framework of knowledge and data, both of which would aid interpretation of the Neolithic pottery. Furthermore, as Jones and Brown (2000) noted in their account of this work, the approach could not itself directly resolve archaeological questions, rather its value lay first in challenging often well-entrenched views about pottery making, and second in encouraging the view that pottery study is not an end in itself; it should offer fresh viewpoints on pottery's 'life cycle'.

Two final introductory remarks should be made, first that the work described here had a pedagogic element – students were closely involved in it during the field seasons in 1994 and 1995 – and second it was hoped to be relevant to those working at other Neolithic sites on Orkney (and beyond) as well as present-day professional potters on Orkney who continue to take an interest in early prehistoric pottery by replicating Neolithic and later pottery (Appleby 2011; Harrison 2008).

11.5.2 Prospection

Prospection for raw materials formed the first step in the experimental programme, and much of it was focused around Stonehall, before the sites at Crossiecrown and Wideford Hill had been discovered. It was recognised at the outset that the Bay of Firth coastal plain, like most of Orkney, was rich in surficial deposits of boulder clay, glacial till. It was also appreciated that, in the near absence of a traditional ceramic tradition on the Islands during the last millennium and the almost complete

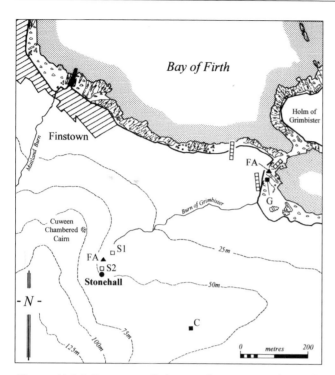

Figure 11.5.1 Location of clays and igneous rock in the Stonehall-Grimbister area: clays (S and S1 Stonehall, C Cruan and G Grimbister), the Grimbister and Maitlands Burns along which clay prospection took place; FA the experimental firing areas at Stonehall and Grimbister beach, and the parallel lines representing the dyke occurrences of igneous rock.

lack of evidence or documentation on the materials or methods of indigenous pottery making on the Islands, local knowledge about clays was confined to its use, both in antiquity as well as today, in a building context as a simple coating/insulating material.

11.5.2.1 Clays

The strategy adopted for clay prospection was:

1. to exploit the natural sections offered by the burns (principally the Maitland and Grimbister burns, Fig. 11.5.1) or ditches within a 1 km radius of the site that drained into the Bay of Firth, and any exposures along the beach below the site. To the north of the bay Coubister and Redlands (where building clay sources are known) were also examined. As a comparative exercise, the same approach was also adopted on the southern shores of the Loch of Harry close to Barnhouse and on the southern side of the Bay of Skaill immediately west of Skara Brae. Any clay-like material observed in the section (but at least 50cm below ground surface) was tested on the spot for plasticity and workability; if promising it was sampled (not less than 0.5kg) and its position recorded and if necessary photographed. Some thirty samples were collected in this way (see Site archive).

2. to exploit local knowledge of clay sources in the district used within living memory for building or other purposes. Such sources were sampled in the same way.

Table 11.5.1 Characteristics of clays from Stonehall and environs.

Location (Fig. 11.5.1)	Working and firing properties
Stonehall 1: frequently waterlogged area 50m north of site	gritty with some organic material. Colour when dry: 5Y 6/1 grey. Relative lack of plasticity; on levigation quality was not greatly improved
Stonehall 2: from the ditch between trenches A and Z	coarse, large fragments of sandstone present; 5Y 7/1 when dry; fires to reddish yellow 7/8
Grimbister beach, discovered in the course of preparing a firing area on the beach; 0.5m below surface, few m in length	grey, plastic, easily worked – quite varied properties within the deposit; maybe a small alluvial deposit; fires to dark reddish grey 4/2
Cruan: a known source of building clay below Cruan farm from a drainage trench	light grey in colour (2.5Y 4.4 olive brown when dry), quite plastic; works and fires well; fires to reddish yellow 6/8

Table 11.5.2 Comparison of the compositions of the clays and Neolithic pottery.

Composition	Clays	Neolithic pottery
Mineralogical	All clays: *Major:* Quartz, Feldspar, *Minor:* mica, chlorite/kaolin	Grooved ware: *Major:* quartz, feldspar. *Minor:* mica
Petrographic	See section 11.6.3	See section 11.6
Chemical	SiO_2 50–65%, Al_2O_3 10–15%, Fe_2O_3 3–8%, MgO 1.5–3.5%, K_2O 1.5–2.5%, CaO <0.5%, MnO <0.04%	EN deep bowls: SiO_2 50–65%, Al_2O_3 11–16%, Fe_2O_3 5–10%, MgO 3.5–4.8%, K_2O 3–4%, CaO <0.6%, MnO 0.18–0.22%, 0.74%

The main observations made in the course of clay prospection were first, how silty much of the material was, second, how variable their textures often were within a 1m section, and third that whereas some of the clays, for instance that at Cruan, were part of large exposures, others for instance at Grimbister were found as a pocket or lens. Not unexpectedly, there was little concept of a large *and* uniform clay deposit. Within a couple of days' fieldwalking it became possible to spot potentially promising clay: orange-brown layer with orange and dark flecks. Following their collection, some of the more promising clays, whose locations are marked on Fig. 11.5.1, were tested further for their working properties by using them (at Stonehall Farm) to construct simple shapes. At the end of the excavation season, all the clays were tested more rigorously for both working and firing properties in the laboratory at Glasgow in the following way: a simple classification of texture and gross impurities present, determination of colour, formation of briquettes or small slabs, observation of their condition following drying for 48 hours, and firing at temperatures 600–900°C for 3 to 8 hours. A majority of the clays collected were poor because they were too silty, giving an orange sandy and porous fabric on firing. The remaining few clays with superior properties (Table 11.5.1) merited characterisation mineralogically (by X-ray diffraction), petrographically and chemically (Table 11.5.2).

Clay characterisation
All the clays in Table 11.5.1 together with five sherds from Stonehall Farm Trench B (SF 253, 236, 325, 345, 375) were analysed mineralogically and chemically (Table 11.5.2). Quartz was the major component, followed by feldspar. The clay mineral content was low, but was apparently higher in the Grimbister and Stonehall clays than in the Cruan clay which was finer textured and had the best working properties. Mica was more common in Grimbister and Skaill Bay clay than in the others. Chemically, the clays had on average more silica than the (EN) pottery due to the greater quantity of free quartz in the former, but lower iron and magnesium and much lower manganese. The explanation of the difference in iron (and manganese) contents should be related to iron leaching from the clay, a process accelerated by peat acids, and to the deposition of iron oxides enriched in manganese oxides in the pottery following burial. As expected, what differences there are in the chemical composition of the pottery seem not to be significant. The general picture is one of broad overlapping ranges of composition among the clays and the pottery, the

variation among the clay compositions having less to do with its source and much more with its texture.

11.5.2.2 Igneous rock
Several dykes of igneous rock occurring in the Bay of Firth area (Fig. 11.6.3) were located in the course of walking along the beach. A small one (probably camptonite) was discovered in this way on the beach at Grimbister, only 20m away from the clay referred to in Table 11.5.1 (Fig. 11.5.1). Recognising the existence of additional dykes, probably small and previously unrecorded dykes, led Andrew Jones and Lorna Sharpe to use a proton magnetometer to relocate successfully (in 1996) some outcrops at the western end of the bay, including that at Benzarioth (Fig. 11.6.3).

Some of the dyke material was crushed for the experimental work and later thin sectioned. As the programme of petrographic analysis progressed, more reliance was placed on the large collection of specimens of igneous rock held by BGS in Edinburgh (see section 11.6).

11.5.3 Replication experiments

1. Forming the shape
The experiments in 1995 and 1997 aimed to explore the techniques needed to form two series of ware: one round-based and broadly resembling Unstan ware, the other flat based resembling Grooved ware. Variations of coil building were employed to form all the pottery. The working properties of all the clays sampled in Orkney were assessed using a commercial terracotta clay to provide a comparison. The experimental pots were fairly small, ranging from 10 to 30cm (height and diameter). Although some of the clays (particularly from Grimbister and Cruan) were relatively free of large impurities and appeared to be very plastic and workable at first appraisal, the 'shearing' effect of the silt in prolonged working made the clay flabby and fluid in handling. The effect of this was to make the walls of the forms sag if any attempt was made to build up the height quickly. It was found that after building 4–5cm of wall it was necessary to allow the clay to dry and stiffen considerably before continuing to extend the wall height.

Round-based ware
In building round-based forms, mainly between 15 and 25cm, it quickly became apparent that these could not be formed without a former of some kind and a variety of 'moulds' were used to form the curved bases and support the vertical walls of the vessels. A hollow scooped out

Figure 11.5.2 Reconstruction of a round-based vessel, using a hollow scooped in the ground.

Figure 11.5.3 Constructing a flat-based vessel using ribbon-shaped coils.

of the earth and made smooth with a Skaill knife and a beach pebble could be used to define the shape of the base; in practice a variety of plastic tubs were filled with earth and the formers made in them. A coiled disc of clay was then placed into this hollow and pressed firmly into shape (Fig. 11.5.2). The edge was trimmed roughly and a short vertical or angled wall added to the edge. The internal surface of the form was then smoothed. As long as the vertical extension to the wall was kept fairly short (*c.*5cm or less), the pot could be completed in one session. The earth helped to absorb some of the moisture from the clay and the pot could be removed from the former, trimmed and burnished after as little as half an hour. With more time available more effective and pleasing moulds could have been made from dry or fired clay. Most of the round-based forms were made from the relatively smooth Cruan clay without any additions of tempering material, or with relatively small amounts of sand or calcined shell. There did not appear to be any appreciable difference in the handling quality of the clay or in the ease of maintaining a consistent shape.

Flat-based ware

A wide range of flat-based forms were constructed, ranging in size from 5 to 30cm in height. The usual method was to form a base first and then to add a succession of rolled out coils to build up the walls. To help speed up production, the use of a simple mould proved useful, and a 'turntable' in the form of a sandstone slab made the task of building much easier. However, it proved extremely difficult to maintain any control of the form if too many coils were added at once, although using a bat-and-anvil technique did help to consolidate the walls and to keep them reasonably straight. If the vessel was intended to be more than 5–8cm high, the clay had to be left to dry out for a period after two or

three coils (approx. 3–4cm) had been added. Using a ribbon-shaped rather than a round coil was helpful, but even by this means it was not possible to add more than 4–5cm. at a time without distortion (Fig. 11.5.3).

Different tempering materials were tried, including rock, (sandstone and camptonite) calcined shell and sand, with a variety of results as well as reactions from the potters. Additions of sandstone and camptonite, ground to a grain size of 1–1.5mm and mixed *c.*20% w.w. with Grimbister clay, gave handling difficulties, especially in forming coils (Durning 1997). Further additions of water to help the coils hold together resulted in a weakening in the structure of the pot wall. Shell, crushed to *c.*1mm, had less effect on the clay, possibly due to the shape of the particles. Camptonite, crushed *c.* 5–10mm appeared to make it marginally easier to build the clay wall higher, possibly because of the stones' jagged shape. In all cases the clay had to be worked very thoroughly to consolidate the tempering material and to work it into the core of the vessel walls. This tended to be a lengthy process and was never fully achieved in the experiments.

The clay proved to be slow in drying, sometimes taking a full day to stiffen enough to add further coils. In the natural course of events it seems likely that vessel making would have been a protracted business, perhaps taking a week or more, and considerably longer in damp weather.

Burnishing was routinely carried out on the dried vessels, using a pebble or other small tool. It was consistently both successful and necessary. The silty nature of the clays, and the impurities present in all of them, made for a fairly rough surface if left untreated. Several experiments were made levigating the Grimbister and Cruan clays to give a finer fraction that could be used as a slip. The process of levigation was achieved but application of the resultant slip was much less successful. Our evidence indicates slipping was not commonly employed on the pottery at Stonehall (see section 11.2), nor did slipping feature in Steven Harrison and Andrew Appleby's Orkney Grooved ware experiment (http://www.pcrg.org.uk/Articles/Orkneys.htm). A variety of incised or impressed decoration was used on the surface of the pottery, using small pieces of stick or stones (cf. plate 29 in Harrison and Appleby's experiments). In some cases decorative coils were also added to the pieces.

Regarding post-firing treatment, in common with practices observed elsewhere, for instance in making Hebridean Crogans (Craggan ware) in the last century (Cheape 1992–93, 121), pouring milk into the freshly-fired pot had the effect of reducing significantly its porosity. A short, rather than a long, exposure to milk was found to be most efficacious in giving a stable, 'waxy' finish to the surface.

2. Firing

The design of the experiments was kept simple and in cognisance of experimental firings done elsewhere in Scotland on prehistoric pottery. For instance, Woods (1983) working on Skye used peat fuel in a bonfire reaching a maximum temperature range of 800–920°C after 116 minutes. At Pool, Sanday, MacSween (1990) reports on a bonfire 'clamped' with turves fired with peat for six hours. In Andrew Appleby's experiment in Skaill Bay the firing was initiated with wood followed by a layer of peat dross and cow dung on top. A similar cocktail of fuels was used in Harrison and Appleby's more recent experiments which involved a circular turf-walled kiln c.0.9m high (Harrison 2008; see also section 11.10 and Chapter 3 this volume) with a peat dome covered by damp seaweed; the fuel requirement was high: c.450kg. On firing the pots whose volumes ranged from c.2 to 35 litres, the temperature rose rapidly to 835°C then dropped to below 400°C, and rose again when the peat ignited to just over 1000°C; the complete sequence was nearly 40 hours. The survival rate was 70%, the coarser fabrics surviving best.

Besides answering several direct technical questions, it was hoped our experiments would shed light on whether the firing could be carried out on a range of scales, and what part weather conditions might play in the success or otherwise of firing. Two contrasting locations were selected, one on the beach at Grimbister close to the source of clay, the other in a natural hollow between the Stonehall sites and Stonehall croft (Fig. 11.5.1). Drying the pots before firing was essential; they were all preheated over hot ashes (Fig. 11.5.4a) and sometimes also had handfuls of burning straw placed inside them to heat them up as much as possible before subjecting

them to the sudden heat rise of the firing itself. The firing site at Stonehall was defined with a ring of stones or sandstone flags and a grate of flagstones was laid to raise the pottery up above the ash deposits since the lowermost layer of pots appeared to be under-fired when ash had built up. Monitoring the temperature was accomplished with two thermocouples placed 10 and 25cm above ground level, and with Buller's Bars in a range between nos 1 and 14 (c.600–950°C) (Fig. 11.5.4b).

Peat was excluded as a fuel in part because the deposits immediately adjacent to the Stonehall settlement would probably have been too wet to provide useful, compact turves, leaving the potential of the following fuels to be considered: wood, either felled trees or driftwood, barley straw, hay, animal dung, heather and seaweed. In the event, most of them were rejected as either being too precious and wasteful (wood and dung) or they burnt too rapidly (straw, heather and brushwood). Attention was thus turned to the potential of seaweed, such a function having been documented by Fleming (1923, 205) who mentions its use (together with dry whin) in pottery firing on Tiree. In the event, seaweed, which it is noted was found in two contexts at the site of Stonehall itself (see section 11.6.2), proved to be a very effective fuel in the forms of bladderwrack and kelp.

At the start of Firings 1, 4 and 5 (see Table 11.5.3), dry seaweed was used, but as the firing progressed more and more damp seaweed was added to the bonfire. The layer of damp material was very effective in sealing the surface of the fire and containing the flames and heat. It was noticeable that the seaweed firings were very much easier to stoke than those in which wood or brushwood were used. Being able to approach the fire more closely allowed either any gaps in the fuel or any pots which had become exposed to be covered more easily. In the firings reaching the highest temperatures (e.g. Stonehall 5) the ash which had formed under the pots had begun to 'sinter' into a fairly solid mass.

Descriptions of firings are summarised in Table 11.5.3. The pots made for the firings ranged in size from 10cm height and diameter up to 30cm diameter (Fig.11.5.5b, c). At least three people attended each firing, some monitoring progress, others constantly checking the draught holes and preparing the next batch of fuel. At the end of the firing, the ash was raked away before the cooled pots were removed. The pots survived the firing well irrespective of whether the clays had been tempered or not. The pots' variegated surface and smudged carbon was immediately striking. Looking at the results in Table 11.5.3, wood, straw and brushwood burnt as expected very rapidly in Firing 2,

Figure 11.5.4 Preheating a Grooved ware-type vessel at Stonehall (a), prepared firing area with Central 'grate' and Buller's bar (b).

the temperature reaching a plateau of 500–600°C after an hour (Fig. 11.5.6); the differential temperature within the fire was small. But the situation was quite different in the short duration Firing 3: the lower thermocouple recording a slow rise in temperature up to 430°C, the upper one revealing two peaks following addition of dried seaweed at 38 and 60 minutes giving maximum temperatures of 808° and 700°C respectively. The same general pattern was found in Firing 5 which was maintained for over five hours. In Firing 1 it took nearly four hours for the lower part of the fire to reach the temperature of the upper part (500°C).

At the end of the experiments and having removed the surface debris of ash and broken pot, the firing areas were surveyed to determine whether there was a residual magnetic signature. Whereas there was an

Figure 11.5.5 (a) Stonehall firing 4 (Table 11.5.4); damp seaweed has been added to the top and soon the replaces the burnt seaweed within the main fire which has turned to ash; (b) raking out the ash after the firing; (c) close-up of pots (and Bullers bar) after firing; note the variegated surface on most of the pots.

insignificant change in magnetic susceptibility over the Grimbister site, interpreted as the result of its location on the sandy beach, the corresponding results

Table 11.5.3 Firings at Stonehall 1997.

Firing/fuel	Approx. number of pots	Size of fire	Weather conditions	Temperature (°C)	Thermo-bars	Results
1. 6 (bin-liner) bags of dry seaweed	10	1m diam.	Windy, dry	780 (550)	No. 6 bent	Medium-sized firing. Quite good, well-fired results
2. Wood, dry straw, brushwood *etc.*	20	1.5m diam.	Calm, fairly dry	640 (490)	No. 2 bending	Larger scale firing, using materials other than seaweed. Difficult to stoke because of high level of radiated heat. Pots rather underfired.
3. Dry seaweed, dry cow dung, some straw	5–6	0.5m diam.	Windy, dry	808	No. 2 bent	Small-scale firing. Difficult to keep all pots covered by the fire, but results surprisingly even and well-fired
4. 10–12 bags dry and part-dried seaweed	20	1.5m diam.	Light wind, fairly dry	780 (420)	No. 2 bent	Larger-scale seaweed firing. Ash build-up greater than in the calmer wind conditions. Fair results.
5. 5–6 bags seaweed; dry and part-dried seaweed	6–8	1m diam.	strong wind	No readings available but probably >900	No. 9 bent	Main thermocouple became victim of exploding sandstone. Well-fired pots. Ash left after firing showed signs of sintering.

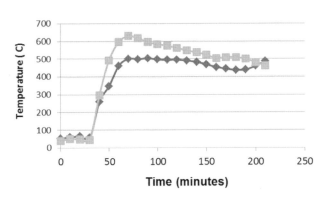

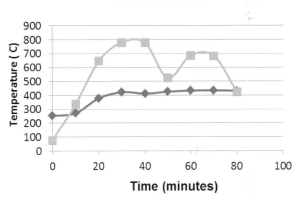

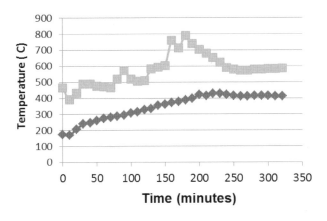

Figure 11.5.6 Characteristics of Firings 2, 3 and 4 at Stonehall using two thermocouples. Temperature measurements in Stonehall Firings 3 and 4 were recorded 40 minutes after the start of the fire.

at Stonehall were encouraging. Not only was there a thermoremanent magnetic anomaly resulting from the firing but it correlated with that observed in Trench D (Fig. 11.5.7a). On the other hand, the corresponding magnetic susceptibility readings showed a more localised area of magnetic enhancement (only 10% of readings above 150 m.s. units) than in Trench D (Fig.11.5.7b).

The results of this section are further discussed above in section 11.2.

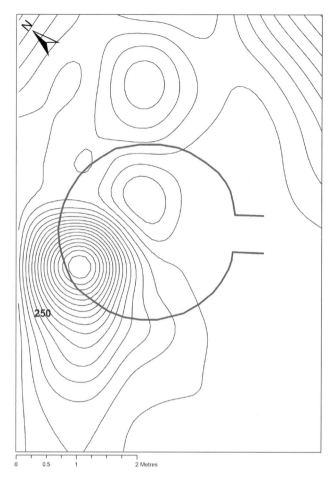

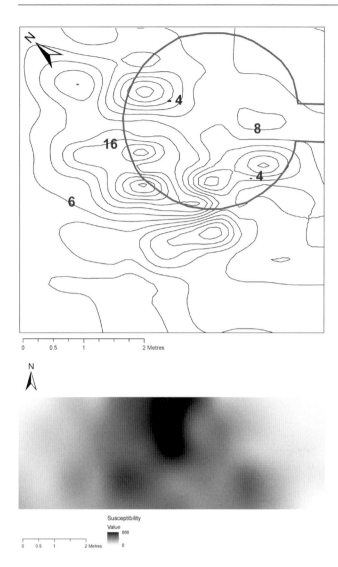

Figure 11.5.7 Magnetic (top left) and magnetic susceptibility (right) plots at the experimental firing area at Stonehall (a), Magnetic and magnetic susceptibility plots at Trench D at Stonehall (b).

11.6 Petrographic analyses: Stonehall and Crossiecrown

Lara Maritan

The pottery examined in thin section was classified according to minero-petrographic composition, abundance and frequency of the main inclusions using the scheme developed by Whitbread (1995, Appendix 3).

11.6.1 Stonehall

The sherds were selected from six main areas (Trenches A, B, C, E, F and Z), representing early (Round-based ware) and late Neolithic (Grooved ware) production. Under the polarising microscope, the samples show a groundmass of black, brown to light brown colours, often presenting one side or the core darker than the remainder. This colour distribution reflects heterogeneous firing conditions or

is due to direct contact with fire during the use of the ceramic objects. The brightest areas are often optically active, presenting generally a sub-parallel thin striated birefringent fabric (b-fabric). Only some of the samples show a preferential orientation of the groundmass, voids and elongated inclusions, parallel to the external walls.

The porosity is variable especially in quantity and sometimes difficult to estimate because of damage to the ceramic during thin sectioning, so that pores can be larger and new planar voids and fracture occur, thereby changing the original porosity. Concerning the shapes of the pores, most of the samples exhibit vughs and planar voids, which reach dimensions up to some millimetres. The inclusions are always present in abundant or very abundant quantity (generally more than 20%, up to 50% for some samples). Their grain-size frequency distribution is either continuous or iatal and the grain size goes from a few microns up to some mm. Generally the mm inclusions are represented by fragments of sedimentary (sandstone, siltstone and mudstone) and magmatic rocks, often more or less strongly weathered, while the small ones (silt- and fine sand-sized) are composed of single crystals (quartz, white mica, plagioclase, K-feldspar, biotite, opaque minerals, brown amphibole, pyroxene). All studied samples contain the minerals just mentioned in different quantities as well as the sedimentary rock fragments, while only in some of them do the magmatic rock inclusions also occur. On the basis of the petrographic characteristics of the large rock inclusions, the pottery has been divided into two main groups.

Group alpha

All the samples contain inclusions of quartz, sandstone, siltstone, claystone (mudstone), opaque minerals, white mica, biotite, and occasionally amorphous concentration features (acf), K-feldspar and plagioclase, occurring in different quantities and dimensions in the various potsherds (Table 11.6.1).

Sandstone occurs in large fragments, ranging between some hundreds of microns to millimetre, generally with angular, sub-angular and sometimes sub-rounded shapes. They show either a fine or coarse-grained texture, with variation in grain size also within the same fragment. They are formed from abundant quartz and subordinate plagioclase, K-feldspar, white mica, opaque minerals and a clay matrix, particularly scarce in the coarser-grained fragments, but more abundant in the sub-rounded and rounded geometry. Siltstone fragments occurring with medium and large dimensions (hundreds of microns) are formed of abundant clay matrix and silt-sized inclusions of quartz, white mica, subordinate plagioclase, K-feldspar and opaque minerals. Sometimes the white mica flakes are slightly oriented, determining an anisotropic structure. Mudstone fragments occur in these ceramics with medium dimensions, generally less than 1mm either with angular or with well-rounded shape. They are composed predominantly of clay minerals and very few or rare silt-sized inclusions of quartz, white mica plates and opaque minerals. In some fragments it is also possible to see the passage from a coarser lithology to a finer one due to variation in grain size. All the sedimentary rock inclusions occurring in these ceramic derive from a clastic sedimentary sequence, in which the coarser (sandstone) and the finer (mudstone) lithotypes represent the end members.

This large group of samples is quite heterogeneous in terms of the absolute and relative abundance of the inclusions. Two main situations can be identified in

which large fragments of sedimentary rock are either predominant (Fig.11.6.1a) or practically absent or very scarce (Fig.11.6.1b), respectively.

Interestingly, one sample (SF 6398) also contains a large fragment of grog (Fig. 11.6.1c). This special type of temper was distinguished from the other argillaceous inclusions occurring in this ceramic group (mudstone and fine siltstone), since, in addition to the characteristic angular shape, large size (5mm) and occurrence of shrinkage rims (Whitbread 1986; Cuomo di Caprio and Vaughan 1993), it contains large inclusions of sedimentary rocks (siltstone and very fine sandstone) which cannot occur in the mudstone in Orkney since they are contemporaneous. The chemical composition of the matrix of this inclusion (major elements determined by SEM-EDAX on a small area) is comparable with that of the groundmass of the pottery, suggesting that the grog came from a clay material very similar to that used to produce the sherd in question.

Group beta

Apart from the sedimentary rock fragments and the minerals, comparable with those occurring in the samples of group alpha, these sherds also contain large inclusions of subangular to well-rounded magmatic rocks (Table 11.6.2). Three main petrographic types have been recognised:

Type 1 Camptonite: the fragments occurring in the pottery represent essentially the groundmass of the magmatic rock, characterised by a holocrystalline and porphyritic structure (Fig. 11.6.1d). The groundmass is microlite bearing, and composed of sub-euhedral crystals of plagioclase (albite) and euhedral brown amphibole (kaersutite). Small rare crystals of euhedral pyroxene (augite) and opaque minerals and sometimes serpentinised minerals, after probably olivine and/or amphibole, are also present. In some samples altered camptonite also occurs (type 1w).

Type 2 Dolerite: the fragments are holocrystalline, showing a continuous grain-size distribution and coarse grain size. The labradorite laths of plagioclase and the small euhedral opaque minerals are embedded in the pyroxene crystals (augite) in the typical sub-ophitic texture (Fig. 11.6.1e). Although the fragments present in the pottery are quite small and give only a partial view of what the original rock would be, the texture and structure indicate that the inclusions can be defined as dolerite. This type of inclusion occurs in only two samples (SFs 1230 and 848).

Table 11.6.1 The main inclusions of the samples of Group α at Stonehall.

Inclusions: QTZ quartz; PL plagioclase; FLD K-feldspar; OP opaque minerals; AMP amphibole; MS muscovite; ACF amorphous concentration features; BT biotite. Frequency: XXXX predominant; XXX dominant; XX frequent; X common; ++ few; + very few; - rare; -- very rare (according to Whitbread 1995).

SF [context]	Trench	Inclusion quantity	Sandstone	Siltstone	Mudstone	Grog	QTZ	PL	FLD	OP	AMP	MS	ACF	BT
1200 [002]	A	20%	+	+	++		XXX	-	+	++		+	+	--
1209 [030]	A	30%	X	XXX	+		++					--	+	
1242 [034]	A	40%	XXX	++	+		X	--		+		-		
1243 [034]	A	30%	XXX	++			XX	+		--		--		
1261 [027]	A	30%	XXX	X			XX	--		++		-		
1263 [027]	A	30%		XX	XX		XX	--		++		--	-	
1268 [027]	A	30%	XXX	XX	X		++	--		++		++	+	
236 [303]	B	40%	X	XXX			X	--	--	+		++	+	--
652 [301]	B	30%	X				XXX	--		+		+	+	
2009 [301]	B	50%	+	XX	XX		XXX	--				-		
2014 [307]	B	30%	X				XXXX			++			++	
2017 [301]	B	40%		XXX			XX	--	--	+		+	+	
2044 [507]	B	20%	++	X	X		XX			-		-	++	
2048 [501]	B	20%	+	X			XXX			+		-	X	
2120 [519]	B	30%	X	XXX			XX	--				-		
2134 (2)[519]	B	10%	XXX				XXX							
2134 (1)[519]	B	20%	XX	++			XXX					-	++	
2150 [501]	B	50%	++	XX	XX		XX	--		-		--		
819 [400]	C	40%	XX	X	++		XX	-		+		+	-	--
906 [400]	C	30%	XX	XX	++		X	--		-		+	+	--
911 [400]	C	30%	X	X	XX		X	+		++		+	X	
917 [400]	C	40%	XXX	X	++		X	-	-	+		++	+	-
936 [400]	C	20%	X	XX	X		X			+		++	-	--
1533 [428]	C	20%		X			XXXX			+		+		
1537 [428]	C	30%		XXXX			XX	--		++		+	+	
1603 [427]	C	30%	X	XX			XXX			+		--	+	
1622 [427]	C	30%	+	XXX	X		XX	--		+		+	+	--
1655 [442]	C	20%	XXX				XXX			+				
1673 [419]	C	30%	-	XXX			XX	--				-		
1699 [464]	C	20%	X	X			XXX		--	++		-	X	--
1708	C	20%	XX		X		XX			X		-	++	--
1725 [428]	C	30%	XX	X	X		XXX			+		-	X	
1726 [428]	C	30%		XXX	++		XXX	--	--	+		+	+	
1742 [433]	C	20%		X	XXX		XX			+		+	+	
2343 [1012]	C	50%	XX	X	X		X	-	-	+		+	-	--
2360 [1008]	C	50%	X	XX	X		X	--		+		+	++	
2384 [1008]	C	50%	XX	XX	X		X		--	+		+	++	
2430 [1017]	C	40%	XXX	XX			++	--		-		-	++	--
2499 (4) [1008]	C	20%	XX	XX	X		X			+		+	X	-
2499 (3) [1008]	C	20%	X	XX	X		X			+		+	X	-
2499 (2) [1008]	C	30%	XXX		++		X					-	X	-
2499 (1) [1008]	C	30%	XX	X	X		X					+	++	-
2499 [1008]	C	30%	X	XXX	X		++			++		--	++	
6398 [2050]	F	30%		XX	XX	X	X			++		+	X	
7064 (2)[3031]	Z	30%	X	X	++		X				-	-	++	
7093 [3031]	Z	30%	XX	XX	+		XX	--		+		-	++	
7119 [3003]	Z	40%	XX	XX	X		X			+	-	+	+	
7128 (2) [3003]	Z	30%	X	X	XX		X			++		++		
7134 [3003]	Z	30%	XXX	X	++		XX		--	++		+	-	
7148 [3050]	Z	30%	XX	XX	X		XX	--		+	--	+	+	--
7203 [3012]	Z	20%	XX		++		XXX	--		+		X		-

Table 11.6.2 The main inclusions of the samples of Group β at Stonehall.
Inclusions: QTZ quartz; PL plagioclase; FLD K-feldspar; OP opaque minerals; AMP amphibole; MS muscovite; ACF amorphous concentration features; BT biotite; PX pyroxene; Magmatic rocks: C camptonite, Cw weathered camptonite; D dolerite, Dw weathered dolerite; W magmatic inclusions strongly weathered. Frequency: XXXX predominant; XXX dominant; XX frequent; X common; ++ few; + very few; - rare; -- very rare.

SF [context]	Trench	Inclusion quantity	Sandstone	Siltstone	Mudstone	Magmatic rocks		QTZ	PL	FLD	OP	AMP	MS	ACF	BT	PX
25 [004]	A	30%	++	X	XX	XX	W	X			+	-		-	-	
29 [004]	A	50%	XX	++	XXX	X	W	X			++	--	--		--	
94 [002]	A	30%	XX	X	+	X	C, W	X	-	-	-	+		--		
126 [002]	A	20%	-	-	XX	XX	W	X	+	+	+					
160 [016]	A	30%	+		XXX	XX	C, W	++	+	-		--				
1200 (1) [002]	A	30%	++		+X	-	W	XXX	+	--	X		-		+	--
1210 [030]	A	30%	XX	XXX	++	++	W	X	--		+	--	+			
1230 [028]	A	20%	++	X	X	XX	D, W	XX	+	-	+	--	-	+	--	--
1248 [019]	A	40%	XX	XX		XXX	C, W	++			+		--			
1275 [027]	A	50%	XX	XXX	+	++	W	++	--	--	++	-	-	--		
1282 [027]	A	30%	+			XXX	W	XX	-	-	X		--	+		
253 [301]	B	50%	XXX	X	--	X	C	X	-		-		++		++	
271 [303]	B	40%	++			XXX	Cw, W	XX	+		+		-		-	
345 [303]	B	50%	XXX	++		--	W	XX	--	--	--	--	+		-	
351 [303]	B	40%	XX	++		+	Cw, W	XX	--	--	-		+			
375 [303]	B	50%	X	XX	++	+	W	XX	-		--	-	+		--	
2074 [503]	B	50%	+			XXXX	W	+			+		--		-	
2107 [501]	B	30%	++			XXX	C, W	X					+			
2156 [503]	B	40%	X	X	++	XX	W	XX	--	--			--			
836 [400]	C	40%	X	++	+	XX	Cw, W	XX	--	--	+		-		--	++
848 [400]	C	40%	X			XXX	Dw, W	XX	-	-	-		+	-		--
2877 [1058]	C	30%	++	X	XXX	+	C	++			++		--	++		
4114 [2002]	E	40%	++		++	XXX	C	XXX	--		+	--	++		-	
4122 [2021]	E	40%	X	++		XXX	C	XX	--		-	-			--	
4124 [2002]	E	40%			-	XXXX	C-Cw	X			-	+	--			
4127 [2002]	E	40%	X	++		XXX	C	XX			++	-	+	-		
6392 [2050]	F	50%				XXX	C, W	XX			+	-	++			
7047 [3003]	Z	30%	X			XXX	C, W	XX	--		+	-	++			
7064 (1) [3031]	Z	30%	XXX	XX	X	+	W	X			-	+				
7094 [3031]	Z	30%		X		XXX	Cw, W	XX		--	+	+	+			-
7107 [3003]	Z	40%	X	++	++	XX	Cw, W	XX	--		+	++	+			
7112 [3039]	Z	40%	++	X	++	XX	C, W	XX	--	--	+	++	-			
7118 [3003]	Z	40%	XX	X	++	+	(W)	XX	--		+	+	++			
7123 [3031]	Z	40%	X	X		XX	Cw, W	XX			++	++	+			-
7128 (1) [3003]	Z	30%	X	X	X	X	W	X	--	--	+		++			
7144 [3039]	Z	30%	++	XX	++	XX	W	XX	--		++					
7145 [3039]	Z	40%	X	X		XXX	Cw, W	XX	--	--	+	-	-			
7181 [3003]	Z	30%	X	XX	XX	X	W	++			++		--		+	
7185 [3039]	Z	30%	XX	XX	X	+	W	X	--		+	++	+			
7189 [3050]	Z	30%	XX	XX	XX	++	W	X	--		--		+			
7200 [3050]	Z	40%	XX	XX		XX	W	X	--		++	--	+			

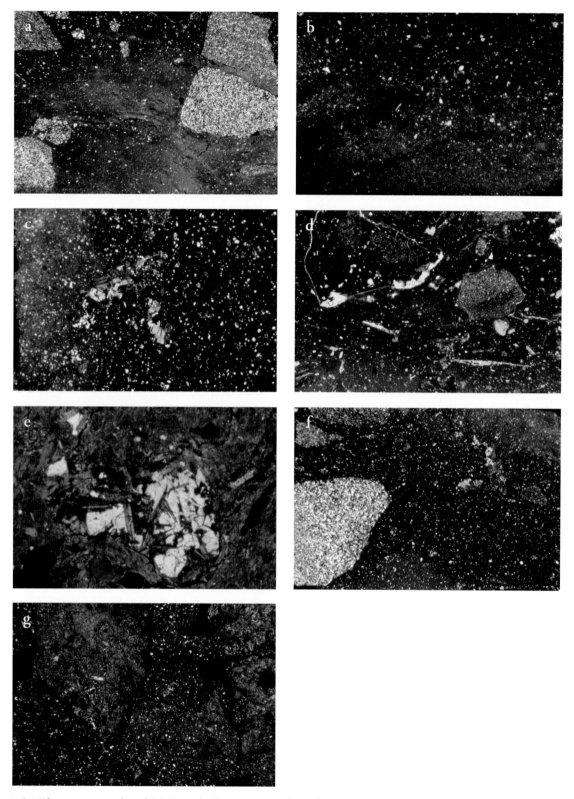

Figure 11.6.1 Photomicrographs of (a) Stonehall group α with predominant sedimentary inclusions (SF 2430, 6.3×), (b) Stonehall group α, with scarce sedimentary inclusions (SF 1533, 10×), (c) grog fragment (Stonehall SF 6398, 6.3×), (d) camptonite inclusion (Stonehall SF 94, 10×), (e) dolerite inclusion (Stonehall SF 1230, 20×), (f) Stonehall group β with scarce magmatic inclusions (SF 94, 6.3×), (g) Stonehall group β with abundant magmatic inclusions (SF 6392, 6.3×). All images are with cross polars.

Type W Weathered: in this type are grouped all the magmatic fragments which are strongly weathered such that their mineralogical composition and texture are not at all recognisable. In some cases these inclusions show relicts of minerals and a ghost magmatic texture which suggest a volcanic or sub-volcanic origin. Since the inclusions of magmatic rock are present in varying quantities, as in group alpha, two different cases can be identified. In the first case, the magmatic inclusions are often weathered, of small dimensions, scarce and are associated with abundant fragments of sedimentary rocks (Fig. 11.6.1f). Most of the samples studied, however, belong to the second case characterised by the presence of abundant magmatic inclusions and of more or less numerous sedimentary fragments (Fig. 11.6.1g).

11.6.2 Crossiecrown

The sherds studied here were selected from three main areas of the excavation: Trenches 1 and 2 (Red House), all of Neolithic date. The samples show similar characteristics for the groundmass, which present black to light brown colours, often arranged in a sandwich-type structure or with one side darker than the other, as a result of uneven firing conditions or direct contact with the fire. The porosity is quite variable in terms of quantity of voids, their shape (generally vughs) and dimensions which reach many millimetres in size.

Regarding the inclusions, they occur in abundant quantity, ranging from more than 20% to 60%, showing continuous or iatal grain-size distribution. They reach many millimetres in size and exhibit angular to well-rounded shapes. The samples contain, in different quantity, crystals of quartz, plates of white mica and biotite, plagioclase, opaque minerals and sometimes also K-feldspar, brown amphibole, pyroxene and olivine (Table 11.6.3). They are also characterized by the presence of large rock inclusions. On the basis of the typology of these lithic fragments and of their occurrence in the pottery, seven different groups have been defined.

Group A: the pottery is characterized by the presence of inclusions of *sedimentary clastic rocks*, sandstone, siltstone and mudstone, associated with the minerals already mentioned (Fig. 11.6.2a). These large rock fragments show angular to well-rounded shapes and dimensions reaching many millimetres. Sandstone occurs with fragments generally angular and subangular in shape, but occasionally also sub-rounded. They are either fine or coarse grained, often showing variation in grain size within the same fragment, and formed of predominant grains of quartz

and subordinate plagioclase, K-feldspar, white mica and opaque minerals. Siltstone occurs in fragments of different shape often with sub-rounded and rounded geometry. The fragments are composed of more or less abundant clay matrix and silty inclusions of quartz, white mica, subordinate plagioclase, K-feldspar and opaque minerals. Sometimes the white mica is slightly oriented so that the structure is anisotropic. Mudstone fragments occur in these ceramics with either angular or well-rounded shape. They are composed predominantly of clay materials containing very few or rare inclusions of silt-sized quartz, white mica flakes and opaque minerals. In some of these sedimentary fragments it is also possible to see the passage from a coarser lithology to a finer one, due to variation in grain size of grains. They belong to a sedimentary sequence, formed from fine- and coarse-grained rocks and the whole transition typology between the end members.

Group B: the characteristic of this group is the presence of angular and sub-angular fragments of *camptonite* (Fig. 11.6.2b), associated with sedimentary rock fragments, apart from the minerals already mentioned; some fragments of weathered rock of magmatic origin are also present. The camptonite inclusions represent essentially the groundmass of the lamprophyric rocks. The texture is clearly microlite bearing, and the groundmass is composed of subeuhedral crystals of albite, euhedral amphibole (kaersutite), rare crystals of pyroxene and opaque minerals. Some camptonite fragments are weathered but are still recognizable, especially for their texture. One sample (SF 346 (1)) also includes a fragment of grog, easily distinguished from other argillaceous inclusions because it contains a fragment of camptonite.

Group C: two sherds are characterized by the occurrence of abundant fragments of *dolerite* (Fig. 11.6.2c), associated with small and few inclusions of sandstone and siltstone. The magmatic inclusions have millimetric dimensions and angular to sub-rounded shape. They have a holocrystalline and coarse-grained structure, with a continuous grain-size distribution. Their texture is typically sub-hophitic, where laths of labradorite and some small opaque minerals are embedded in large crystals of augite. Some strongly weathered crystals of olivine are also present.

Group D: the pottery of this group contains large and abundant sub-angular to sub-rounded fragments of *monchiquite* (Fig. 11.6.2d), sandstone, siltstone, mudstone, weathered magmatic rock and the other cited minerals. The monchiquite is holocrystalline and porphyritic; euhedral crystals of olivine, often strongly

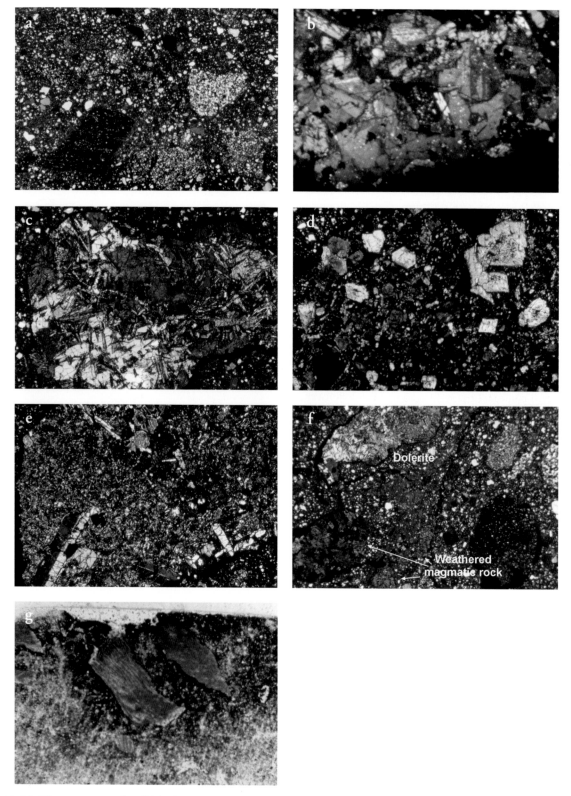

Figure 11.6.2 Photomicrographs of (a) Crossiecrown group A (SF 983, 8×), characterized by the presence of large sandstone and siltstone inclusions, (b) camptonite inclusion (SF 346₍₁₎, 32×), (c) dolerite inclusion (SF 466(4), 15×), (d) monchiquite inclusion (SF 400, 15×), (e) basalt inclusion (SF 362, 10×), (f) Crossiecrown group G (SF 466₍₄₎, 6.3×) with inclusions of camptonite, dolerite, monchiquite and strongly weathered magmatic rock are associated together, (g) shell in Quanterness 187 (courtesy David Williams). All images are with cross polars.

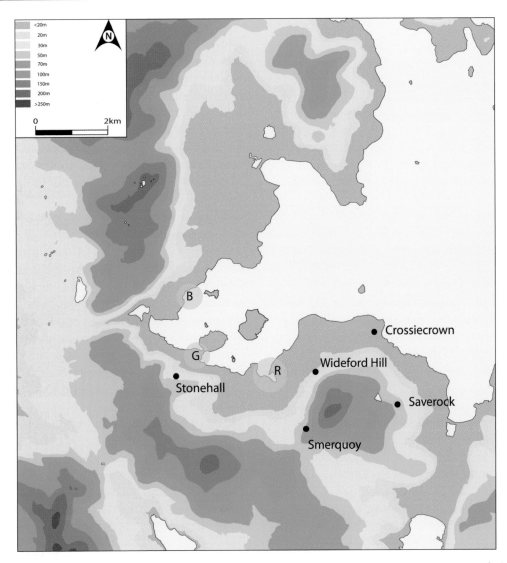

Figure 11.6.3 Location of dykes in the Bay of Firth area (based on Mykura 1976, Fig. 25). B= Benziaroth (olivine basalt); G= Grimbister (camptonite); R= Rennibister (camptonite and monchiquite).

altered, lie on a microlite-bearing groundmass, showing an intersertal texture. The groundmass is composed of small crystals of pyroxene and opaque minerals.

Group E contains a single sample characterized by the presence of large angular and sub-angular inclusions of *basalt* (Fig. 11.6.2e). The magmatic fragments show the typical hypocrystalline porphyritic texture. Phenocrystals of strongly altered euhedral olivine and some laths of labradorite are present in the intersertal microlite-bearing groundmass of plagioclase, altered pyroxene and glass. It is interesting to note that this sherd does not contain any sedimentary fragments; quartz is present in scarce quantity, while crystals of plagioclase and amphibole are common.

Group F: large and small fragments of *strongly weathered magmatic rock*, present in predominant or scarce quantity

in the different samples, characterize this group. Their mineralogical composition and texture are not completely recognizable, but some relics of minerals and especially of the original texture indicate a sub-volcanic origin for them. In this group, they are associated with inclusions of sedimentary rocks, apart from the already mentioned minerals.

Group G: this group is composed of six samples, five of them coming from a single pot. Their petrographic composition suggests that the large rock inclusions are not similarly represented in each sherd; millimetric fragments sub-angular and sub-rounded in shape of *camptonite, dolerite, monchiquite* and *strongly weathered magmatic rock* occur, associated with inclusions of sandstone siltstone and mudstone, apart from the generic minerals (Fig. 11.6.2f).

Further petrographic data for Crossiecrown appears in section 11.3.

11.6.3. Discussion

Boulder clay containing lithic inclusions of sedimentary rocks accounts for the majority of the pottery at both sites. The nature of these sedimentary rock fragments is not informative in terms of origin. In fact most of the rock outcrops in Orkney are composed of Old Red Sandstone, the sedimentary sequence of which has been divided in different stratigraphic units on the basis of their fossil content (Mykura 1976; AA.VV. 1978; Flett 1898; Fannin 1970). But, since the sedimentary fragments present in the pottery do not contain any fossil remains, it is impossible to define to which stratigraphic unit they belong. Moreover, the Old Red Sandstone outcrops throughout the whole Orkney archipelago, so the presence of these rock types in the pottery cannot indicate an unequivocal source area of the raw materials. In the area surrounding Stonehall many outcrops of Stromness Flags (western) and Rousay Flags (eastern) are present.

The clays collected from the vicinity of Stonehall for the experimental work described in section 11.5 were found to be very variable because of the different content of large sedimentary rock inclusions, sometimes very abundant and sometimes scarce. This characteristic is related to the nature of the sampled material having a natural variation in particle size. Some of these fired clays are comparable in terms of texture and composition with the pottery, in particular for the occurrence, size and shape of the large sedimentary rock fragments, indicating that these inclusions occurring in the pottery represent the natural lithic content of the original clay material.

Turning to the inclusions of magmatic rocks, such rocks are well known in Orkney. There are more than 200 lamprophyric dykes, intruded in late Carboniferous-Permian Age (Baxter and Mitchell 1984; Halliday *et al.* 1975; Brown, 1975; Mykura 1976; Rock 1983) which have been mapped and studied by the British Geological Survey (BGS) in Edinburgh since the end of the 19th century (Fig. 11.6.3). The camptonite recognised in the pottery belongs to this magmatic activity, while the dolerite is referable to Middle Old Red Sandstone age intrusions (Mykura 1976). The existence of a substantial thin-section collection of these dykes and intrusive bodies in the BGS collection in Edinburgh was very important in the present work for comparative purposes. As a result, some dykes and magmatic bodies were found to have the same textural, structural and mineralogical characteristics as the magmatic inclusions present in the pottery.

Camptonite in the pottery from both Stonehall and Crossiecrown is analogous in terms of composition and structure. It seems to be very similar to the dykes at Rennibister, North Gaulton, Holms of Stromness on Mainland and some of those on Rousay (Table 11.6.4). It is significant that the camptonite in dykes occurring in the area of Rennibister are very similar to each other so that the camptonite inclusions present in the pottery could come from one or more dykes in that area. On the basis of these petrographic considerations the source area of the raw material can be identified as the vicinity of Stonehall and Crossiecrown, indicating that the sherds containing the camptonite inclusions represent local production. The dolerite in a single sample at Stonehall and in weathered form in another sample is interesting in the way it closely resembles that outcropping at Deerness (Table 11.6.4) in southeast Mainland, Orkney. But before supposing that these one or two samples are imports, it is necessary to bear in mind that our picture of all the occurrences of outcrops of dolerite or other types is incomplete. Many may not be visible today owing to either sea level change or burial under peat since the Neolithic. In the case of the few samples at Crossiecrown containing dolerite (Group G), the situation is more straightforward since the dolerite is associated with other magmatic inclusions which are of local origin. As concerns the monchiquite found in the pottery of Crossiecrown, it seems to be very similar to some dykes located either on Mainland, at Finstown, Kirkwall, Holm of Houton and Burn of Grelen, or in South Ronaldsay. The basalt, less common than the lamprophiric rocks on the archipelago, is very similar to that outcropping northeast of Finstown and the Bay of Firth. Therefore, both monchiquite and basalt, as well as camptonite, have been found to be available in the area surrounding the site of Crossiecrown. Concerning the strongly weathered fragments of magmatic origin, their source cannot be defined since they do not show any characteristics helpful in the identification of the original type of rock and hence its location.

A preliminary distinction can be made about the abundance, shape and status of the magmatic rock fragments in the pottery. The small and often weathered magmatic inclusions present in small quantity can be considered a natural component of the clay material used, as are the sedimentary fragments. In fact, from a geological point of view the moraine-like clay occurring in Orkney would be expected to contain these types of rocks since they are exposed in the archipelago. But since the outcrops of minor intrusions are small, the magmatic fragments are present in the boulder clay in only limited quantity. For this reason, these

SF	Context (Trench)	Group	Inclusion quantity	Sandstone	Siltstone	Mudstone	Magmatic rocks	Grog	QTZ	PL	FLD	OP	AMP	MS	ACF	BT	PX	OL
218	137 (2)	B	30%		++	+	XX, C, W		X					+	-	--		
346 (1)	173 (2)	B	50%	XX	++		X, C, W	X	XX	++		+	+	+	-	-		
346 (2)	173 (2)	B	50%	XX	X		X, C		XX	+	--	++	+	+		--		
346 (3)	173 (2)	B	50%	XX	X		X, C, W		XX	+		-	+	+		--		
362	173 (2)	E	60%				XXXX, B, W		+	X			X	--				
400	300 (2)	D	60%	X			XXX, W, M		XX			++		--		++	++	
440	34(2)	B	10%	XX			XX, C, W		XX					--		-	-	
466 (1)	Sq. 27	G	40%	X	X		XXX, C-Cw, M-Mw		X	-	-	+	--	+		--	-	
466 (2)	Sq. 27	G	60%	X	++		XXX, C-Cw, Mw		X	--		--		--		--	--	-
466 (3)	Sq. 27	G	60%	X	++		XXXX, C-Cw, D, Mw		++	--		--		--		--		
466 (4)	Sq. 27	G	50%	XX	X	++	XX, C, D, Mw, W		X	-	--	+	--	-	+	--	--	-
466 (5)	Sq. 27	G	50%	XX	++	+	XXX, Mw, W		X	-		+	--	-	+	-		
479	309 (2)	B	30%	X	X	X	++, C		XX	--		??		+	+			
868	Tr. 2	A	40%	XX	XX	++			XX	-	--	-		++	+	-		-
896	484 (2) ext.	A	50%	XX	X				XXX	-	--	--						
915	Tr. 2 ext.	C	40%	-	-		XXXX, D-Dw		XX	-		--				--	--	
934	490 (2) ext.	G	40%	XX	XX	++	X, Cw, M		XX	--				-	+	-	-	
964	487 (2) ext.	C	50%		+		XXXX, D		X			--		-		--		
983	507 (2) ext.	A	50%	XX	XX	+	XX, Mw		XX	-		+		+		-		
987	142 (2)	D	40%	XX	X	++	XXX, W		XX			+		--				
1036 1228?	2 (2)	F	30%	XX	++	X	XXX, W		+					--		-		
1072	517 (2)	F	60%	X	++		XXX, W		XX	--	-			--		-		
1086	127 (2) ext.	A	60%	XX	XXX				XX	-	-	--		-		-		
1487 (1)	Tr. 1	B	50%	XX	X	+	XX, Cw		XX	-	-	--		-		-		
1487 (2)	Tr. 1	B	50%	X	XX	+	XX, Cw		XX	-		--		+		-		
1381	2 (1)	B	30%	+	+	-	XXX, C-Cw, W		XXX	-	--	--		-			-	
No number	Tr. 1	D	60%	XX	+	-	XX, M-Mw		XX	--	--	+	-	-		-	+	
No number	Tr. 1	D	60%	X	X		XX, M-Mw		XX	--	--	+	-	-		-	++	
64	34 (2)	F	30%	XX	XXX		++		++	--	--	-		+	+	-	-	
1436	2 (1)	A	50%	++	XXX				X	--	-	+		-	-	-		
60	26 (2)	F	50%	XX	X		XX, W		X	--	-	+		-		-	-	
1410	Tr. 1	A	60%	-	XXXX	-			X	--	-	+	--	+		--	--	
1433 (1)	2 (1)	A	60%	XX	XXX	+			XX	--	-	+		+		-	-	
1433 (2)	Tr. 1	A	60%	XX	XX				XX	--	-	-	--	+		--	--	

Table 11.6.3 The main inclusions in the pottery at Crossiecrown. Inclusions: QTZ quartz; PL plagioclase; FLD K-feldspar; OP opaque minerals; AMP amphibole; MS muscovite; ACF amorphous concentration features; BT biotite; PX pyroxene; Magmatic rocks: C camptonite, Cw weathered camptonite; D diabase, Dw weathered diabase; M monchiquite, Mw weathered monchiquite; B basalt, W magmatic inclusions strongly weathered. Frequency: XXXX predominant; XXX dominant; XX frequent; X common; ++ few; + very few; - rare; -- very rare.

Table 11.6.4 BGS thin-sections similar to camptonite, dolerite, monchiquite and basalt recognised in the pottery at Stonehall and Crossiecrown and their locations on Orkney.

BGS thin-section	Magmatic type	Findspot
15194	Camptonite	Rennibister Firth, West Burn
15195	Camptonite	Rennibister Shore, 1.2m dyke
15212	Camptonite	Rennibister dyke in Burn
15214	Camptonite	Rennibister Burn, centre
15218	Camptonite	Rennibister
15243	Camptonite	Holms of Stromness
15260	Camptonite	North Gaulton
26573	Camptonite	North of Brough of Biggin, Sandwick
26653	Camptonite	Geo of Skaill, Rousay
27437	Camptonite	Rousay
50141	Camptonite	Rennibister, 3km SW of Finstown
15160	Dolerite	Ayre, Deerness
115168	Dolerite	Mermaids Castle, Deerness
26998	Dolerite	East of Skea
27001	Dolerite	SE of Stonehall on coast
15189	Monchiquite	Peerie sea, Kirkwall
15297	Monchiquite	Skaill, Dyke II Rousay
25824	Monchiquite	S side of Barent Head, south Ronaldsay
25835	Monchiquite	SE of Hesta Head, South Ronaldsay
25924	Monchiquite	270* SW of Knowe, in Burn of Grelen
25976	Monchiquite	SW of Trig Pt. On Holm of Houton, Orphir
26325	Monchiquite	Cliff 300 yds E of Rinebir, Hoxa, South Ronaldsay
26990	Monchiquite	Coast 625 yds E4°N of Biggin, SE of Finstown
26991	Monchiquite	Coast 480 yds E43°N of Biggin, SE of Finstown
27407	Monchiquite	Shore 1000 NW of Geo of Rottenloch South Walls
27445	Monchiquite	Duncan Geo
15221	Basalt	Binniquoy Firth below Boathouse, W dyke
15232	Basalt	Binni, Scarva Taing, Firth
26987	Basalt	Benziaroth, NE of Finstown

small and/or scarce inclusions, whether sub-angular or sub-rounded in shape, would not have been added by the potter. However, the situation regarding the large magmatic fragments contained in all the other samples may be different. Here a good case in point are the two samples at Crossiecrown with large but different rock types (Group G) coming from different locations in the same area. This seems to be the only instance in which rock fragments could have been deliberately added by the potter. Their shapes, which are not always angular, hint that the temper was not taken directly from the dykes, which were in any case very hard to break, but was perhaps collected from the gravel derived from the alteration of magmatic rocks.

The rare occurrence of grog in the pottery may not be significant, being perhaps accidentally included in the preparation of the paste. No shell has been identified either as voids or as observed by Williams (1979) at Quanterness (Fig. 11.6.2g).

In summary, the pottery from Stonehall and Crossiecrown can be divided into two groups:

- pottery produced using a boulder clay as found naturally,
- pottery produced using boulder clay naturally rich magmatic inclusions or, exceptionally, tempered with camptonite or dolerite.

Both these groups are encountered in round-based ware and Grooved ware. Finally, it is worth noting the presence in some of the pottery of secondary orange-coloured phosphate-rich minerals (probably mitridatite). These could form a useful focus for further study since their occurrence has implications for environmental conditions of burial.

11.7 Organic residue analysis of the early Neolithic and Grooved ware pottery from Stonehall, Crossiecrown and Wideford Hill

Anna Mukherjee and Richard P. Evershed

11.7.1 Introduction

We report here the results of organic residue analysis of pottery from Stonehall, Crossiecrown and Wideford Hill which was carried out at the Organic Geochemistry Unit (OGU), a subdivision of the Bristol Biogeochemistry Research Centre at the University of Bristol as part of a wider enquiry into animal husbandry, food processing and consumption in British prehistory (Mukherjee *et al.* 2007; Mukherjee *et al.* in press). This programme of analysis, which included Grooved ware from Skara Brae and Links of Noltland on Orkney (Mukherjee *et al.* 2008, 2061, Table 1), considered a range of pottery classes in addition to Grooved ware – Peterborough, Unstan, Impressed and Beaker Wares – from findspots, most of them in southern England.

This study has employed the well-known techniques of Gas chromatography (GC) and GC-mass spectrometry (GC-MS) to analyse the lipid residues. But recourse has also been made to compound-specific stable isotope analysis *via* GC-combustion-isotope ratio MS (GC-C-IRMS) to allow greater specificity in relating lipids to individual animal species. Thus $\delta^{13}C$ values of fatty acids provide the basis for distinguishing between ruminant (*e.g.* sheep/goat and cattle) and porcine (pig) adipose fats (Evershed *et al.* 1997; Mottram *et al.* 1999) and also between ruminant adipose fats and ruminant dairy fats (Dudd and Evershed 1998), thereby providing a means to address some key questions such as the earliest evidence for dairying in prehistoric Britain (Copley *et al.* 2003). Compound-specific $\delta^{13}C$ values are readily determined for fatty acids (analysed as FAMEs) deriving from archaeological artefacts by GC-C-IRMS. Although the detection of degraded animal fat is straightforward, the identification of the species of origin is complicated by diagenetic alteration and inherent similarities between animal fats. However, due to subtle differences in the way that different animals assimilate their diet the $\delta^{13}C$ values of the major fatty acids ($C_{16:0}$ and $C_{18:0}$) are sufficiently distinct to allow differentiation between the fats of the major domesticates.

Representative examples at the three sites of early and late Neolithic and early Bronze Age pottery, all in the form of sherds were selected (by Richard Jones) for analysis, some of which had surface residue (Table 11.7.1). The sherds were screened using high temperature GC

(HTGC) in order to determine the presence or absence of organic residues. Where residues were detected, further analyses comprising HTGC and GC-MS were performed. If degraded animal fats were observed, compound specific stable carbon isotope analyses were used to measure the $\delta^{13}C$ values of the major fatty acids ($C_{16:0}$ and $C_{18:0}$), and from these data a ruminant or non-ruminant origin could be assigned.

11.7.2 Materials and methods

Lipid analyses were performed using established protocols which are described in more detail by Mukherjee *et al.* (2008). Approximately 2g of the sample were taken and the surface cleaned using a modelling drill to remove any exogenous lipids such as soil or finger lipids due to handling. The sample was ground in a pestle and mortar to a fine powder and accurately weighed. Lipids were extracted using a mixture of chloroform and methanol (10 ml, 2:1 v/v). A portion of the resultant total lipid extract (TLE) was then derivatised by silylation using *N,O-bis*(trimethylsilyl)trifluoroacetamide (BSTFA) containing 1% trimethylchlorosilane. The TLE were saponified, and fatty acid methyl ester (FAME) derivatives were prepared for analysis by GC, GC-MS and GC-C-IRMS.

11.7.3 Results

11.7.3.1 Stonehall (Table 11.7.2)

Of the early Neolithic (EN) and Grooved ware (GW) sherds, 86% and 87% respectively contained detectable lipid residues. One early Neolithic sherd (29), contained only free fatty acids and sixteen were identified as degraded animal fats with five of these containing mid-chain ketones. Thirteen of the fifteen Grooved ware sherds had lipid compositions consistent with degraded animal fats characterised by a distribution of free fatty acids, mono-, di- and triacylglycerols (TAGs). Four residues were highly degraded consisting of only free fatty acids. Mid-chain ketones were observed in four extracts, which are known, through laboratory degradation experiments, to be formed through the heating of fatty acids at high temperature (> 300°C) in the presence of clay minerals (Evershed *et al.* 1995; Raven *et al.* 1997). They may have been produced during the 'cooking' of animal fats.

11.7.3.2 Crossiecrown (Table 11.7.2)

All the Grooved ware extracts were identified as degraded animal fats characterised by a distribution of free fatty

Table 11.7.1 Early Neolithic and Grooved ware sherds and surface (S) residues from Stonehall, Crossiecrown and Wideford Hill.

Site	SF
Stonehall	*Knoll*: 859, 1571, 1800, 1300, 2303, 2430, 2499, 26281, 8065
	Meadow: 29, 168, 269, 1230, 1571 (Tr A); 7055, 7064, 7094, 7118, 7119, 7123, 7145, 7154 (Tr Z)
	Farm: 393, 2016, 2107b, 2134, 2150, 2625, 6077, 6260, 6261, 6305, 6306, 6433, 4114, 4124
Crossiecrown (all Grooved ware except where indicated (U Unstan; B Beaker)	19, 150, 316, 808, 899, 937, 938, 1042, 1459, 740 (U), 229 (B), 989 (B), 1093 (B)
Wideford Hill	6, 13, 286, 290, 399, 567, 636, 912, 915, 995

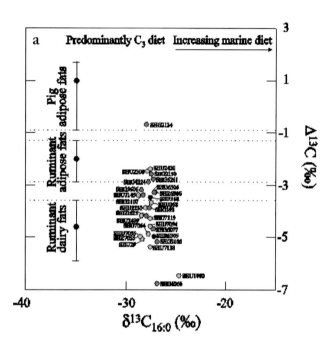

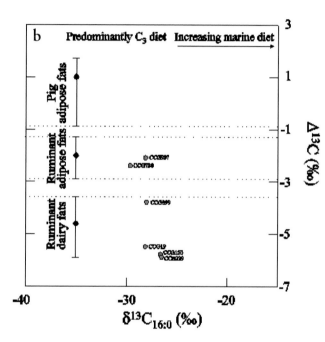

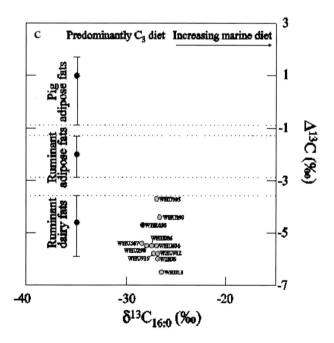

Figure 11.7.1 Plot of $\Delta^{13}C$ against $\delta^{13}C_{16:0}$ values for (a) Grooved Ware (red) and Early Neolithic (yellow) sherds and surface residues (black) from Stonehall, (b) the Grooved Ware (red) and Beaker Ware (green) sherds from Crossiecrown, and (c) Unstan Ware absorbed (yellow) and surface residues (black) from sherds from Wideford. The ranges for the modern reference fats are plotted to the left of the plots.

acids, mono-, di- and triacylglycerols, although two of these were highly degraded containing only free fatty acids. Mid-chain ketones were observed in four vessels. Ketones observed in high abundance in some vessels (*e.g.* 1042) indicate that fatty acids present in low abundance or no longer observed in the TLE (*e.g.* $C_{14:0}$) were once a component of the lipid residue present in the vessel. The two Beaker Ware sherds containing significant concentrations of lipid were also identified as degraded animal fats, one of which also contained mid-chain ketones.

Table 11.7.2 Lipid assignments for Early Neolithic and Grooved Ware from Stonehall, Crossiecrown and Wideford Hill based on TLEs, TAGs, $\delta^{13}C$ and $\Delta^{13}C$ values

	Ruminant dairy	Mixed ruminant adipose/dairy	Mixed porcine/ ruminant	Animal fat	Ruminant adipose	Ruminant adipose and/or dairy
Early Neolithic	Stonehall 29, 168, 168S, 1230, 7055, 7055S, 7064, 7094, 7118, 7119, 1800, 2499 Wideford 6, 13, 286, 290, 399, 567, 636, 636S, 912, 915, 995S	Stonehall 7145		Stonehall 29S, 169, 859, 2300, 2430S, 2436, 2681, 2681S, 8065	Stonehall 2300S, 2430	Stonehall 7094S, 7118S Wideford 6, 912S, 995S
Grooved ware	Stonehall 393, 262, 607, 6260, 6305S Crossiecrown 19, 150, 899	Stonehall 210, 6306S	Stonehall 213, 6261	Stonehall 630 Crossiecrown 19S, 1042, 1042S	Stonehall 4124 Crossiecrown 808, 937, 938, 938S	
Beaker	Crossiecrown 229					Crossiecrown 1093

11.7.3.3 Wideford Hill (Table 11.7.2)

The Unstan Ware sherds were all identified as degraded animal fats. They also contained mid-chain ketones.

11.7.4 Stable carbon isotope analysis

Distributions of triacylglycerol (TAG) preserved in ancient fats can provide evidence complementary to the compound-specific $\delta^{13}C$ values which are presented below. At all three sites there were residues exhibiting wide TAG distributions characteristic of ruminant diary fats, and others with narrower TAG distributions which may be of ruminant adipose origin or, more likely, degraded ruminant dairy fats.

Compound specific-carbon isotope analysis consisted of the determination of the $\delta^{13}C$ values for the $C_{16:0}$ and $C_{18:0}$ fatty acids. Data obtained for modern reference animal fats from species known to have been the major domesticates exploited in British prehistory are grouped within ellipses, onto which the data for archaeological pottery have been overlaid. The $\delta^{13}C$ values for the $C_{18:0}$ fatty acid are more depleted in ruminant milk fats than in ruminant adipose fats thus enabling the distinction between milk fat and adipose fat in ruminants (Dudd and Evershed 1998; Copley *et al.* 2003). The less depleted $\delta^{13}C$ values for the $C_{16:0}$ and $C_{18:0}$ fatty acids in non-ruminant fats compared to those in ruminants are believed to be due to differences in diet, physiology and in the metabolic and biochemical processes involved in the formation of body fats in ruminant and non-ruminant animals. The stable isotope data are presented here by calculating the difference between the $\delta^{13}C$ values for the two major fatty acids – $\Delta^{13}C$ value = $\delta^{13}C_{18:0}$ – $\delta^{13}C_{16:0}$ – which is plotted against $\delta^{13}C_{16:0}$ values.

11.7.5 Summary

The residues extracted from the *Stonehall* potsherds were well preserved with 86 % containing lipid concentrations considered to be significant. The mean lipid content was higher for Unstan ware vessels than for Grooved ware vessels. All of the extracts were identified as degraded animal fats and a few vessels had been heated sufficiently for mid-chain ketones to be formed. Almost 50 % of the extracts contained intact triacylglycerols (TAGs). Of the Grooved ware extracts analysed by GC-C-IRMS six were identified as ruminant dairy fats, one as ruminant adipose fat, three as mixtures of ruminant adipose and dairy fats and three as mixtures of porcine and ruminant fats. Eleven of the early Neolithic extracts were identified as ruminant dairy fats, one as a ruminant adipose fat and one as mixed ruminant adipose and dairy fats.

Three quarters of the *Crossiecrown* potsherds were found to contain significant lipid concentrations. The mean lipid concentration was higher for the Grooved ware than the Beakers, and the Unstan ware sherd contained only trace amounts of lipid. As at Stonehall, all the extracts were identified as degraded animal fats and a few vessels had been heated sufficiently for mid chain ketones to be formed. Over 50 % of the extracts contained intact TAGs. From the analysis of extracts by GC-C-IRMS one Beaker and three Grooved ware samples were identified as ruminant dairy fats and two other Grooved ware samples with ruminant adipose fats. From their TAG distributions, a further Grooved ware and Beaker ware sherd were identified as ruminant fats, although they did not contain sufficient concentrations of lipid for stable isotope analysis. These results from both Stonehall and Crossiecrown harmonise with the identification of faunal remains at the two sites (see Chapter 14).

The preservation of the extracts from the *Wideford Hill* Unstan ware sherds was exceptional with all ten sherds and all four surface residues containing significant quantities of lipid, all fourteen extracts also exhibited intact TAGs. In each case the lipid residues were identified as degraded animal fats; mid-chain ketones were observed in all the sherd extracts but interestingly were absent from the surface residue extracts. This can perhaps be explained by the fact that the ketonic decarboxylation of fatty acids is catalysed by metal oxides present in clay (Evershed *et al.* 1995), although mid-chain ketones have been observed in other surface residues. GC-C-IRMS analysis of ten extracts from Unstan ware and one surface residue extract showed they were all derived from ruminant dairy fats. The three surface residues, for which $\delta^{13}C$ values were not obtained, had TAG distributions indicative of either ruminant adipose fats or degraded ruminant dairy fat, however, since the vessels from which they derived seemed to have been used solely for the processing of dairy fats it is likely that these represent dairy fats which have been less well preserved as they were not protected by the clay matrix of the vessel. The apparent absence of indicators of a marine component reflected in any of the residues at the three sites is in accord with the strong evidence arising from recent findings showing that marine products were of little overall importance to the Neolithic farmers of the northeast Atlantic archipelagos (Cramp *et al.* 2014).

11.8 Ramberry Head

Richard Jones

11.8.1 Introduction

A little over 1kg of pottery was recovered from the Bronze Age funerary monument (Site 1) and passage structure (Site 2) at Ramberry Head, the large majority from the former. The small assemblage is dominated by SF 12 found adjacent to the pebbles in the south-west area of

the central setting (see Figs 8.20 and 8.21) and by the square- or rectangular-shaped vessel (SF 21) which was found on the field surface and within the pebbles on the north side of the central flagstone setting (Figs 8.15 and 8.21). Nearly all the pottery from Site 1 (fifteen Small Finds) was associated with the central setting (context [015]). SFs 9, 10, 11, 13, 21 and 22 came from the soil matrix of the pebble setting, and SFs 5, 8, 23 and 26 from the soil matrix of the flagstone kerb (Fig. 8.21). There were only four pottery Small Finds from Site 2.

The interest of this assemblage lies in the presence of the square-shaped vessel (SF 21), the Beaker rim and body sherd (SF 36) and several rims in SF 12. Regarding the square-shaped vessel, much of it was present on the surface of the field having been turned up by the plough. Given this occurrence it was remarkably well preserved and was clearly associated with cremated human bone. The one point which is more difficult to assess is whether the cremation had originally been placed within the vessel. Since the cremation deposit was not placed within a square cist it does seem probable that it was buried within or beneath the square vessel, thereby creating an interesting substitution (see Chapter 8).

11.8.2 Description

No more than ten vessels are represented in this assemblage, which is otherwise composed largely of small undiagnostic sherds in poor condition. This pottery, which was poorly made and fired, is light in weight. Indicators of construction are absent, and the surface was smoothed but not burnished.

The feature sherds are as follows:

- SF 8 Plain flat rim (1.1cm thickness, maximum dimension 3.2cm and weight 10g). Abraded exterior; some residue on rim and top of interior. The sherd is too small to estimate diameter and is not illustrated.
- SF 11 Two conjoining flat top rims (1.0cm thickness, maximum dimension 3.9cm and weight 13g) displaying no curvature; perhaps this is another square shaped vessel. Slight sooting on rim and top of interior (not illustrated).
- SF 12 comprises eighteen sherds and numerous small fragments, forming at least three vessels to judge from the evidence of the rims (Fig. 11.8.1):

a. Two conjoining plain, slightly inward-sloping narrow (*c.*1.0cm) thickness rims (Fig. 11.8.1, c and b) having a diameter of 18cm. The fabric is reddish fine-textured with frequent small inclusions; smoothed interior, heavily abraded exterior, overall crudely made and no sooting even on other body sherds. The body tapers toward the rim.

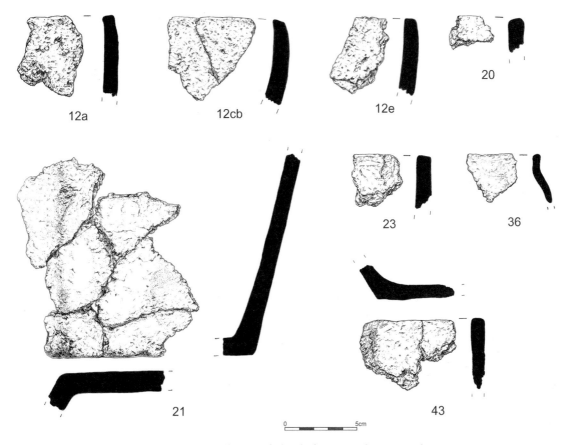

Figure 11.8.1 Illustrated sherds from Ramberry Head.

b. Abraded rim from a different pot but of similar fabric. Possible traces of residue on interior of sherd (Fig. 11.8.1, e).

c. Abraded rim sherd, probably not from same pot as (a) but of similar fabric. The vessel has a rim diameter of *c*.14cm.

- SF 20 Plain rim sherd, 1.2cm in thickness, having a coarse dark fabric with frequent small inclusions, poorly sorted. No sooting is visible and the diameter is too small to estimate (Fig. 11.8.1).

- SF 21 Comprises 24 sherds and numerous small fragments totalling 0.44kg in weight. Six joining sherds and three associated sherds make up part of a square or rectangular-shaped vessel which stands apart due to its shape as well as its fabric. In colour it has a reddish exterior (5YR 4/4 reddish brown), darker core and brownish red interior (10YR 4/3 brown), compared with the colour range at Crossiecrown which is typically 7.5YR 5/3 brown to 7.5YR 5/6 yellowish brown. The quite distinctive firing signature of the square-shaped vessel is surprisingly consistent. Interestingly, this vessel was undecorated.

Sherds from a second vessel were incorporated in SF 21. This vessel is more fragmentary and has a different, more uniform and darker fabric.

- SF 23 Rim sherd of a slightly possible straight-sided pot with exterior sooting, a thickness of *c*.1cm and a carinated effect 2cm below the rim. Some abrasion is present and the fabric is coarse with moderate dark angular inclusions (Fig. 11.8.1).

- SF 36 Thin-walled Beaker rim of a vessel *c*.20cm in diameter. It is of a well-fired, coarse dark fabric, with frequent small inclusions, occasional larger inclusions to 0.4cm (Fig. 11.8.1).

- SF 43 Two conjoining flat top rims of a crudely constructed possible square vessel. Smoothed and slighted sooted exterior and the interior is abraded. Overall, light in weight (26g), the vessel has a coarse dark fabric with frequent small inclusions up to 0.2cm (Fig. 11.8.1).

Petrographic analysis
- SF 5 Dense dark fabric, very coarse, 60% inclusion quantity. Remarkable is the predominance of rounded (weathered) camptonite (up to 5mm in length), with minor free quartz and very minor sandstone.

- SF 10 Frequent, mostly small (up to 0.1mm) quartz distributed throughout the clay matrix. Two large igneous (?camptonite) inclusions, *c*.5 × 4mm, one of which is very weathered and frequent small (1mm) rounded ?camptonite inclusions. One large siltstone (5mm largest dimension) and one sandstone (2mm) fragment.

- SF 12 An unusual looking fabric comprising fine orange-red inclusions distributed evenly throughout the light-coloured clay matrix, which are likely to include camptonite due to the shape and colour of crystals.
- SF 13 Dark fabric is dominated by frequent igneous fragments, probably camptonite, mostly sub-rounded typically 1mm but at least one fragment is 4mm in size. Common very small quartz.
- SF 21 Dark fabric with predominance of (weathered) ?camptonite, the larger fragments in the 2–4mm range. 40% inclusion quantity. Frequent very small quartz; Sandstone is minor (1mm in size) and no siltstone.
- SF 24 Red-brown fabric with much free quartz (unlike all the other samples) up to 0.2mm apart from one large (1mm) rounded quartz crystal. The main feature are the igneous rock fragments, probably camptonite, from 1 to 3mm in size. Some sandstone typically 1.5mm long. No siltstone. Overall, 50% inclusion quantity.

11.8.3 Commentary

The interest of this small assemblage lies in the presence of the square or rectangular-sided pot in SF 21 and the Beaker (SF 36). Vessels of the former type are not unknown on Orkney and furthermore they need not be restricted to the early Bronze Age to judge from an example from Phase 3.1 (late Neolithic) at Pool (MacSween 2007, 302: 3539, Ill. 8.1.11), and one at Windwick (M. Carruthers pers. comm.) which is of supposed early Iron Age date, much later than Ramberry Head itself, and has a steatite-rich fabric. The square shape however is more at home in late Bronze Age-early Iron Age Shetland where it appears at Sumburgh Airport as Jar type 5 with a narrow cordon along the corner of the rim (Downes and Lamb 2000, 49, Fig. 20: 4.1, 4.3). Such morphology is also present at Jarlshof, probably as a ceramic skeuomorph of steatite, and at Old Scatness. But there the similarity ends, at Ramberry Head the undecorated square-shaped vessel (SF 21) should be seen to be of local inspiration; its association with the bone is noted (Appendix 14.1).

Apart from SF 12, there is some consistency about the fabric composition, suggesting a single source, probably local in view of the presence of igneous rock such as camptonite, most of which is weathered. Sandstone is present, but in contrast to the situation at Crossiecrown, siltstone is rare. SF 12 deserves further investigation; like the other samples examined, it contains igneous inclusions but it stands alone by virtue of its unusual coloured fabric as well as the presence of possible steatite.

11.9 Brae of Smerquoy and Muckquoy, Redland

Roy Towers and Richard Jones

11.9.1 Brae of Smerquoy

Some 140 sherds, a clay ball and several fragments from the excavation of Trenches 1 and 2 in May 2013 have been examined. They represent a minimum of 60 vessels with a total weight of 1.33kg. There were a number of diagnostic sherds which are described in Table 11.9.1.

11.9.1.1 Discussion

Small body sherds make up the majority of this assemblage. Their characteristics are notable abrasion, a greater preponderance of an oxidised rather than a reduced core; 15% of the sherds have visible residue, generally on the interior surface. Only one base has been recorded. The fabric is usually coarse, with rock fragments whose frequency, shape and size vary considerably: many of these fragments are rounded, while others are more angular and range in size up to 7mm; frequency does not appear to exceed 30–40%. Other inclusions are small, round and light-coloured, suggestive of a clay source close to running water. Voids are visible in a few sherds, in a few cases probably resulting from organic material. There are few sherds in a fine, reddish fabric. Smoothing of the exterior surface is evident in a few cases, and in one case the marks may be from burnishing. The pottery is somewhat lighter in colour than at Wideford Hill. The modal wall thickness is 1–1.2cm (Fig. 11.9.2), contrasting with the clear bimodal distribution at Wideford (0.6–0.8cm and 1–1.2cm).

The rims are of interest for their range of shape: plain, flat, rounded and with an interior bevel. None of these features is particularly distinctive and all of them, and in particular the flat and interior bevel varieties, have a lengthy currency in prehistory. They are, however, frequently found in the earlier to middle Neolithic period. Parallels are perhaps closer to Stonehall Meadow (SF 7104, Fig. 11.2.9b) than to Wideford Hill, with most of the Brae of Smerquoy rim sherds being consistent with an early Neolithic date. The decoration on SF 24, which so closely resembles SF 595 at Wideford Hill, and the presence of a small round base (SF 117) further supports the early Neolithic date. On the other hand, there is as yet no immediate parallel for the very small plain rim, SF 226. The identification of two possible straight-sided pots, one of them with a rim (SF 241), the other being SF 39a, is consistent with the later Neolithic phase (see Chapters 4 and 10).

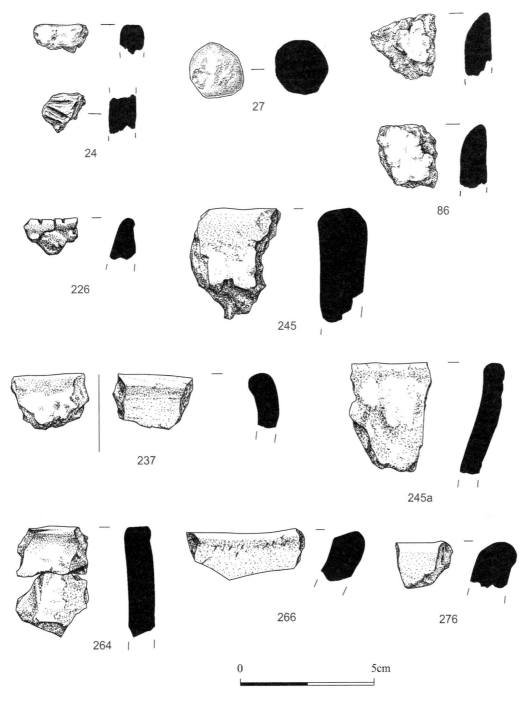

Figure 11.9.1 Illustrated sherds from Brae of Smerquoy.

11.9.2 Muckquoy, Redland

11.9.2.1 Assemblage 1 (Trench 1)

Assemblage 1 is made up of some 212 sherds which weigh, in all, 5.45kg. It is predominantly Grooved ware of later Neolithic date, as evidenced by fabrics, rim forms and, in particular, applied cordons of various sorts. It is not unusual to find in assemblages of this sort that there has been a degree of mixing and two sherds may indicate this. The very small unstratified fragment SF 28 may be Medieval or later and SF 26 [033], although morphologically undiagnostic, has a fabric which may hint at an earlier date than the late Neolithic (Table 11.9.2; Fig. 11.9.3).

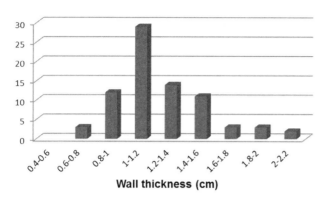

Figure 11.9.2 Distribution of sherd thickness (cm) at Brae of Smerquoy.

11.9.2.2 Assemblage 2 (Fieldwalking survey)
Assemblage 2 comprised 91 sherds from the *fieldwalking survey*, weighing 0.92kg (Table 11.9.2). Those with asterisk are illustrated in Fig. 11.9.3.

11.9.2.3 Discussion
Like Assemblage 1, this assemblage appears to be later Neolithic, characterised by Grooved ware. Where it occurs, decoration in the form of cordons, often applied, is common, sometimes with incision (*e.g.* 10/20, 20/40), groove (no number) or stab mark (*e.g.* SFs 15, 19, 30) is common. Such decoration is paralleled at least in concept if not in execution at neighbouring Stonehall

Table 11.9.1 Sherds from Brae of Smerquoy.

SF No.	Context	Description
24a	001	Flat rim fragment of neutral bowl, maximum dimension 2cm, thickness 1cm, weight 1.1g. It parallels two rims at Stonehall Knoll: 2384 and 2874. Coarse with dark angular inclusions.
24b	001	Decorated sherd, maximum dimension 1.5cm, thickness 1cm, weight 1.5g, reduced core. It has three stabs, similar to Wideford Hill (SF 664) in colour and shape and SF 595 which has similar stabs on the rim (Fig. 11.4.1). Coarse with some dark angular inclusions.
27	078	Clay ball, not perfectly round, probably not fired, oxidised fine clay; maximum dimension 2.1cm and weight 6.2g.
39a	001	Fragment of straight-sided pot, thick walled (1.6cm), with visible curvature on interior but not possible to estimate diameter. Maximum dimension 4.5cm, weight 23g. Evenly fired; coarse, moderately frequent large rock fragments up to 7mm.
66	016	Two conjoining body sherds, partly reduced with unusual untempered fabric; maximum dimension 4.8cm, thickness 1.4cm and weight 26g. The curvature suggests a vessel with diameter 38-40cm. Unevenly fired; few small rounded inclusions.
86	007	Two probably conjoining rims; abraded exterior, reduced core, sooting on interior and exterior. Coarse with dark angular inclusions.
117	007	Fragment of probable round base, residue spread unevenly in interior, oxidised exterior; maximum dimension 4.3cm, thickness 1.3cm and weight 18g. Fabric has frequent small white rounded inclusions and sparse rock fragments.
226	Unstrat	Two small conjoining rim fragments. Marked tapering of rim, thickness ranging from 0.8 to 0.3cm at the pointed rim. Stabs on the top of the rim and possible incision just below rim on exterior; exterior surface is slightly sooted; fabric is friable, evenly fired, abraded. Maximum dimension 2.1cm; weight 3g.
237	201	Rim sherd. The rim is rounded and appears thickened in comparison with the wall. The wall also curves inwards immediately from the rim, suggesting a bowl shape. The exterior surface is smoothed and the interior surface is sooted while the fabric is relatively fine clay with a few, probably natural, rock inclusions. The sherd is oxidised throughout and is fired medium. Maximum dimension 2.8cm, thickness is 1.1cm at rim top, 9mm at wall and weight 6g.
241	205	Plain rim of straight-sided vessel of *c.*9cm diameter; rounded top of rim is rounded with a very slight bevel which may have been caused by use-wear on the interior side of the rim. Maximum dimension 4.6cm, thickness 9mm, weight 11g; abraded and hard, reduced fired; no residue. Rock fragments present in the fabric are predominantly rounded.
245	201	Flat top rim, maximum dimension 4cm, thickness 1.7cm, weight 21g; smoothed surfaces, minor abrasion; oxidised firing; residue on interior and on rim; low proportion of rock fragments, mainly rounded. One rim sherd from a substantial vessel. The sherd has a flattened top and the fabric is sandy clay with sparse rock fragments visible which are predominantly rounded. It is oxidised throughout, is fired hard and surfaces have been smoothed. The interior surface is sooted and sherd thickness is 16mm while weight is 22g and the longest axis is 40mm.
264	201	Rim sherd and body sherd from a single vessel. The rim, differing from SF 237 and SF 245, is flat and both surfaces are smoothed while the fabric is coarse sandy clay with *c.*30% dark grits. The rim sherd is 26 mm on its longest axis and weighs 5g while wall thickness is 10mm. Both sherds are reduced.
266	201	Pointed rim with distinct interior bevel; rim has maximum thickness of 1.3cm and diameter of 16cm; maximum dimension is 4.3cm and weight 12g. Smoothed surfaces but slight abrasion, no residue; evenly fired and hard, fine sandy fabric with a few black grits.
276	201	Plain rounded rim but with slight inclination to the interior; maximum dimension 2.1cm, thickness 1.3cm and weight 5g. Smoothed surfaces. Friable, evenly fired fabric showing some abrasion; slight sooting on the interior.

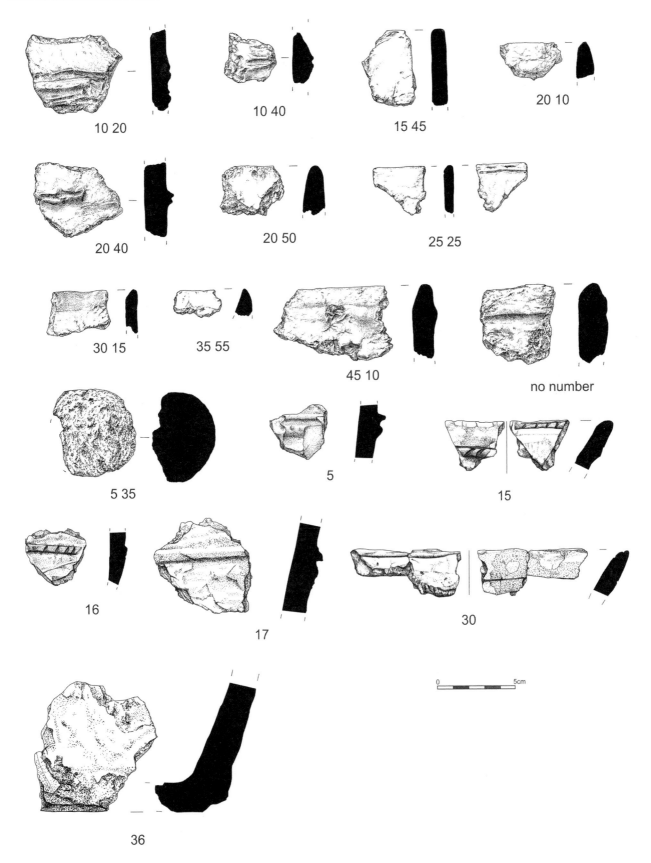

Figure 11.9.3 Illustrated sherds and clay ball from Muckquoy, Redland.

Table 11.9.2 Sherds from fieldwalking at Muckquoy.

SF No. Fieldwalking co-ords	Context	Description
07	030	Two rims, six body sherds and three fragments from one vessel. The rims are abraded and plain. The sherds are oxidised with exterior sooting. Thickness is 7mm and weight is 21g.
14	023	Two base sherds and fourteen body sherds from one vessel and one base sherd from what is probably a separate vessel. The two similar sherds are flat, have slightly angled walls and are very slightly footed. They have oxidised surfaces, smoothed on the exterior and reduced cores. All sherds are rock tempered (*c.*30%), fired soft and thickness is 1.4cm. Weight is 128g. The separate base has a curved rather than footed exterior profile but is otherwise similar to the other two. It has a single oblique incised line running upwards from the base on the exterior but it is not clear whether this is accidental or decorative. Weight 15g.
15	033	One rim sherd, from the same vessel as SF 16 (above). The rim is pointed and two incised parallel lines have created a cordon on the interior surface at the top of the rim. The cordon has then been decorated with the same oblique stab marks as SF 16. The exterior surface is sooted and 1.7cm below the top of the rim a low, horizontal cordon has been decorated with the same oblique stabs. Two detached crumbs of cordon are also present. The sherd is tempered as SF 16; weight 10g, thickness 9mm.
16	033	One body sherd from a fine vessel decorated with a low, horizontal applied cordon which has oblique stab marks with a fine point at regular intervals. What may be a very low, plain applied cordon is placed at an angle above and probably conjoins the applied/incised cordon. The sherd is rock tempered (*c.*30–50%) and has a reduced core with oxidised surfaces. Weight 13g, thickness 1.0cm.
17	033	One large, heavily rock tempered (*c.*50%) body sherd with plain horizontal cordon which has been pinched-up or at least finished in that manner. The cordon has then been underscored by an implement. The sherd is fired hard, is oxidised throughout; weight 55g, thickness 1.9cm. One small body sherd with a low, plain applied cordon. The exterior surface is sooted with fine horizontal smoothing marks. The sherd is rock tempered (*c.*30%) and has been fired soft and is incompletely oxidised. Weight 9g, thickness 1.2cm.
18	033	One small body sherd with a low, plain applied cordon. The exterior surface is sooted with fine horizontal smoothing marks. The sherd is rock tempered (*c.*30%) and has been fired soft and is incompletely oxidised. Weight 9g, thickness 1.2cm.
19	033	One decorated rim from a fine grooved ware vessel. The sherd is pointed and two parallel horizontal lines at the very top of the interior surface create a cordon which is then slashed at a slight angle and which is sooted. The exterior surface is also sooted with a low applied cordon 1.7cm below the top of the rim. The cordon is emphasised at its top by a horizontal incised line and the cordon itself is filled with stab marks made with a fine point. The overall scheme of decoration is lost due to the small size of the sherd. It is rock tempered (*c.*30%) and is reduced throughout. Weight 4g, thickness 7mm (at cordon).
21	018	Three small, abraded sherds, one of which is a pointed rim from a small vessel. Sandy clay fired soft; weight 4g, thickness 6mm.
30	023	Three rim sherds from two vessels. Two of the sherds join and have an estimated diameter of 16.0cm. The rims are pointed and have an internal bevel which is decorated by two parallel incised lines. The 'cordon' thus formed is 6mm wide and has small stab marks applied from the right-hand side and some 12mm apart. The sherds are oxidised and the exterior is sooted and may be slipped. The larger sherd has a single parallel line incised 20 mm below the rim on the exterior. The sherds are rock tempered (50%) with angular fragments up to 7 mm. Weight is 20g. Thickness is 1.2cm. The third sherd is broken, although probably similar to the above, and consists largely of the interior section of a rim with a single incised horizontal line. It is oxidised and weighs 3g. All sherds are late Neolithic Grooved ware.
35	017	This small find number contains sherds from three vessels. *Vessel One* consists of seven body sherds and four other sherds which may belong to it. It is rock tempered and has been slipped and burnished on the exterior. Three of the sherds also have on the exterior a low, plain applied cordon. The sherds are abraded and are fired soft with oxidised surfaces and a reduced core. The surfaces, where present, are orange. Weight 98g, thickness 1.3cm. *Vessel Two* consists of forty-one body sherds and four fragments. They are from a large vessel sooted on the interior and exterior. The surfaces are smoothed and two sherds, broken just above the base, suggest that the base was flat and that the walls sloped outwards. The sherds are rock tempered and fired differentially. Weight 592g, thickness 1.1cm. *Vessel Three* consists of five body sherds and two fragments. Four of the sherds have applied cordons grooved lengthwise and the sherds are tempered with small black grits. The sherds are incompletely oxidised and are friable. Weight 75g, thickness 9–14mm.
36 & 37	017	These two small find numbers are taken together as they contain one large vessel. SF 36 consists of fifty substantial sherds and eleven fragments. Four of the sherds are bases and two conjoin. There is thick exterior sooting and a few small patches of interior sooting. The sherds are heavily rock tempered (50% plus) and are incompletely oxidised. The vessel is coarsely made with no evidence of decoration. There are no rims present but many of the sherds give excellent evidence of N-shaped coil joins, as do those in SF 37 below. Weight 2339g, thickness 1.8cm. SF 37 consists of two pointed rims, twenty-seven body sherds and two base sherds. The description of the vessel is otherwise as for SF 36 above. Thickness 1.8–2.0cm, weight 1829g.

SF No. Fieldwalking co-ords	Context	Description
102	017	Rim sherd and decorated sherd from one vessel. The rim is pointed and finely made and the body sherd has a low, plain applied cordon. The sherds are oxidised throughout and the small fragments of rock visible in the matrix may be natural to the clay. They are probably from the same vessel as SF 104. Weight 6g, thickness 1.0cm.
103	017	Seven sherds and one fragment from one vessel. All are body sherds with smoothed exterior surface, except for the fragment which is a small, detached plain cordon. One body sherd also has a low, plain, applied cordon. The sherds have oxidised surfaces and a reduced core. Rock tempered (*c*.20%) and with a thickness of 1.3cm. Weight is 66g. Late Neolithic
104	017	One small body sherd with a plain applied cordon. The sherd is rock tempered (*c*.30%) and is fired soft. It has oxidised surfaces and a reduced core. Weight 5g, thickness is 9mm.
00/30		Probable flat base, maximum dimension 2.8cm, thickness 1.3cm, weight 6.6g; very similar to 35/45 but very abraded.
00/35		Body sherd with 2cm long applied cordon; maximum dimension 3.9cm, thickness 1.5cm, weight 20g. Coarse fabric, reduced; dark interior.
05/35*		Clay ball in coarse (40%) fabric with similar inclusions as those in the pottery, 5.1cm diameter, 100g weight. Its size, shape and fabric contrast with the clay balls found at Stonehall Farm (section 11.2). Partly oxidised.
10/20*		Body sherd with applied cordon decorated with parallel incisions; dark residue on exterior, but sherd is overall oxidised; unusual interior surface with pale concretion; maximum dimension 5.9cm, thickness 1.4cm away from the band; weight 44g.
10/40*		Body sherd with cordon decorated with applied grooved incision, similar to 20/40; maximum dimension 3.3cm, thickness 1.3cm away from the cordon, weight 10g. Oxidised; medium coarse fabric (15%). Fabric has medium scatter of small rounded inclusions.
10/45		Everted rim (24cm diameter) with slight residue on the exterior. A thin applied cordon is placed immediately (and unusually so) below the rim.
20/10*		Plain rim, 8cm diameter, maximum dimension 3.9cm; thickness up to 1.0cm, weight 8.5g. Light sooting on exterior continues to rim and to 0.5cm below rim on the interior. Medium coarse.
20/35		Tiny flat base fragment with some vertical wall, maximum dimension 1.8cm, thickness 1.1cm and weight 2g; slightly sooted exterior base, interior is oxidised. Medium coarse with small inclusions.
20/40*		Body sherd with applied cordon decorated with single, perhaps step-like incision; maximum dimension 5.9cm, 1.4cm thick, weight 36g; exterior oxidised, dark core, some darkening on interior but otherwise oxidised. Very coarse with round and angular dark inclusions. Abraded interior.
20/50*		Twelve sherds, 100g in weight, of which the largest (illustrated) has slight curvature, dark residue on the interior, oxidised exterior and coarse fabric; rim 1.5 maximum dimension, 1.6 thickness, 15cm radius, oxidised, coarse with angular inclusions (40%).
20/55		Possible flat base fragment, thickening out at edge; maximum dimension 3.8cm, thickness 1.3cm and weight 21g; exterior and interior are oxidised.
25/25*		Rounded rim (28cm diameter), on the interior of which are two small horizontal stabs and below them a single incised line; oxidised in and out; fabric like 30/15 is less coarse than the norm; maximum dimension 3.8cm, thickness 0.7cm, weight 6.5g.
30/15*		Everted rim, with dark band of sooting on exterior and on rim itself but not the interior; maximum dimension 3.6cm, thickness 0.9cm, weight 25g. Notable is the way the dark band ends abruptly 1cm below the rim forming a straight line as if painted. Two body sherds, one with dark exterior and clear curvature. Largely oxidised core. Fabric has few visible inclusions.
35/00		Small fragment of rounded plain rim of small ?bowl, maximum dimension 2.3cm, thickness 0.7cm and weight 2g.
35/45		Possible flat base, interior uniformly dark but it is not residue; maximum dimension 4.2cm, thickness 1.2cm and weight 13g; exterior is oxidised, coarse fabric heavily reduced.
35/55*		Very small straight rim, maximum dimension 2.9cm, thickness 0.9cm and weight 4g. Partially reduced; smoothed surfaces. Medium coarse fabric with dark rounded inclusions.
45/10*		Large flat rim 36cm diameter, remnants of a ridge (not applied band) in orange fine clay against dark coarse fabric; heavily reduced; residue in and out; shallow bevel on interior consists of separate layer of clay which was not reduced; incised line on the rim. Maximum dimension 7cm, 1.1cm thickness at rim increasing to 1.6cm below, weight 7g. Coarse (30%) with mainly dark angular inclusions. Body sherd with applied cordon on dark exterior; core only partly reduced and interior not reduced; interior surface is abraded; maximum dimension 3.8cm, thickness 1.5cm and weight 4g.
55/40		Curved fragment of a clay ball? Maximum dimension 2.3cm, thickness 1.3cm and weight 2.3g.
No number		Large everted rim (>38 cm diameter) with applied cordon close below it and possibly another one below that; maximum dimension 5.2cm and weight 44g. Exterior is dark, rim and interior are oxidised; coarse fabric with dark angular and other sub-rounded inclusions; the sherd is notably thick walled (2cm).

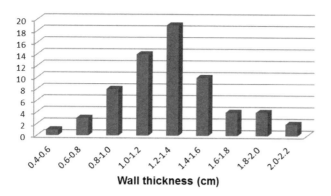

Figure 11.9.4 Distribution of sherd thickness (cm) at Muckquoy, Redland.

Farm (Table 11.2.12), Crossiecrown (SF 19, Fig. 11.3.3a, b) and Barnhouse (*e.g.* Downes and Richards 2005, Fig. 4.17). The rims, on the other hand, overlapping in shape with those elsewhere in the Bay of Firth, seem to be less diagnostic of the later Neolithic; they include the remarkably plain shape of 15/45. Fig. 11.9.4 shows a broad distribution of wall thickness with a mode at 1.2–1.4cm and a small tail in the 1.8–2.0cm range; this is a simpler distribution than that for the later Neolithic pottery at Stonehall Farm (Fig. 11.2.10).

Sherds from grid squares 30/15 and 20/10 are interesting for their sooting pattern: the abrupt demarcation between the exterior, the rim and the interior of these two sherds points to the use of a lid placed not on top of the vessel but a few centimetres below it while they were sitting on the hearth.

11.10 Knowes of Trotty

Ann MacSween, Colin Richards and Roy Towers

11.10.1 The assemblage

Ceramic material from the Knowes of Trotty comprises some 276 sherds from 66 vessels. The sherd count includes 154 fragments which is indicative of the fragmentary and crumbly nature of the assemblage. Most of the sherds are small body sherds. None of the sherds is decorated and while the surfaces of some sherds are smoothed there was no evidence for any other surface finish such as combing or burnishing.

Several rim forms are present, including plain (SF 32 [008]), flat (SF 309 [311], SF 301 [210], SF 253 [282], SF 137 [057]) or interior bevelled (SF 6 [057], SF 285 [308], SF 308 [347], SF 219 [224], SF 263 [263], SF 281 [263]) forms (Fig. 11.10.1). Unfortunately, due to their

small size it was not possible to reconstruct a profile for any of the vessels, or to determine the diameter of any of the rims. One rim sherd, (SF 6), from context [057] has an internal bevel and an apparently thickened exterior lip. The sherd is not Beaker, or even 'rusticated' Beaker, and while bevelled rims are present in many Grooved ware assemblages (*e.g.* A. M. Jones 2005a), a thickened, external lip is less usual. This rim form is more consistent with Unstan ware types (see section 11.8.2 below). Flat bases are represented by one definite (SF 266) and a second more ambiguous example (SF 303). These two are clearly derived from different vessels.

Where manufacturing technique can be determined the vessels are coil-constructed (with diagonal junctions). None of the vessels is decorated. Smoothing of the surface with a wet hand finish is common. The clay most commonly used was fine, although sandy clay was also used, and 10–30% of rock fragments were common, sometimes probably natural to the clay. Organics (evidenced by voids) were noted in some sherds.

As none of the sherds is diagnostic, it is not possible to suggest a definite date for the assemblage from the ceramic evidence alone. However, given the minimal number of flat base sherds, presence of well-fired vessels and the inclusion of rim forms that are similar to those from Smerquoy, and other 4th millennium cal BC sites in the Bay of Firth area, the assemblage is not inconsistent with that date.

In terms of the ceramic assemblage, a degree of longevity of habitation at Knowes of Trotty is evidenced by the presence of one or two flat-based vessels. Regarding fabric and quality of firing, these would fall happily into the Grooved ware tradition and be consistent with the duration of occupation demonstrated by architectural changes to the Knowes of Trotty dwelling (see Chapter 3). There are two contextual features of the assemblage that require further comment.

The first is the small sherd size and the overall poor and abraded condition of the pottery. Given that excavation was confined largely to the structural remains and wider external areas were not examined, the main component of the ceramic assemblage was derived from within the different phases of house construction. Under these circumstances the pottery recovered is not inconsistent with that recovered from other 4th millennium cal BC stone house structures, for example, at Wideford Hill (Chapter 2) or Smerquoy (Chapter 4). The latter excavation was also mainly restricted to the Smerquoy Hoose resulting in the recovery of a similar assemblage of small and fragmentary sherds. However, investigations at Wideford Hill did

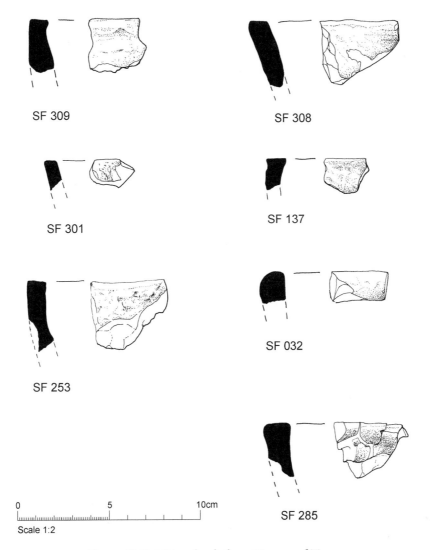

SF 309

SF 308

SF 301

SF 137

SF 253

SF 032

SF 285

0   5   10cm
Scale 1:2

Figure 11.10.1 Rim sherds from Knowes of Trotty.

include a sizable area beyond the stone dwelling to the east of Stonehouse 1. Here a large rammed stone surface [002] was examined which was clearly the context of a range of 'domestic' activities. From the surface, and incorporated within the rammed stone area a substantial assemblage of Unstan ware and round-based pottery of a broader range of size and condition was recovered (Fig. 2.34b). Equally, on Stonehall Knoll (Chapter 5) the largest amount of round-based pottery was derived from outside Houses 2 and 3 in ash and midden deposits running downslope to the east (Fig. 5.32b). Consequently, the condition and size of the Knowes of Trotty ceramic assemblage is consistent with that obtained from other 4th millennium stone houses.

In terms of ceramics, the second feature which makes the Knowes of Trotty excavations of significance is the suggested kiln or firing area. A number of sherds were recovered from the firing area, and consequently, the conditions of the ceramics from contexts associated with this feature are worth further attention. The area of the kiln is described as being partly characterised by reddened clay and stones indicative of burning (see discussion in Chapter 3). A number of the sherds from the relevant contexts also show signs of reddening, but under magnification many of them exhibit striking evidence of illuviation by iron minerals. Sherds such as SFs 228, 263 and 281, all from context [263], are noticeably red in colour and have either 'veins' of oxidised material on their surfaces or present within the core of the sherd. In addition, one sherd, (SF 284), again from the same context [263], is reddened and has carbonised organic material still visible in the sherd core, suggesting a low firing temperature.

Of course, the absorption of iron minerals by the sherds in the firing area may well have resulted from the same natural formation processes which led to iron-panning on other areas of the site. However, it is equally possible that the clay source used for these sherds was iron-rich clay, perhaps derived from a location nearby. Iron compounds in clay react to the firing atmosphere (Orton, Tyers and Vince 2003, 133), and in oxidising conditions, which might be present if the firing process was undertaken using a bonfire or open firing, the iron compounds will usually be changed to ferric oxide (Fe_2O_3) which produces a red colour in the clay.

Obviously, this process could indicate the type of firing undertaken at the site, but it is equally likely in this case that the oxidised minerals are present in the pottery as a result of the influx of water from the higher ground above, carrying iron minerals through the area of the kiln. The soil micromorphology report (McKenzie 2007) mentions the presence of small fragments of bone in the hearth of the nearby built structure which exhibit a dull reddish colour indicative of iron impregnation. Discrete layers of the same hearth contain relatively frequent iron-rich nodules, and the iron-panning nearby indicates a natural long-term process. The micromorphological report also describes iron-impregnated plant matter visible in a thin section taken from the kiln area (*ibid.*). Evidence in the archaeological conservation literature confirms that iron oxide may deposit within a porous clay body as iron compounds do in the soil (Cronyn and Robertson 1990, 146). It is at least likely, therefore, that the reddened appearance of these sherds under magnification is a direct result of the post-deposition processes described above and does not necessarily indicate the nature of the firing process or the clay used in vessel formation (see Chapter 3 for a more detailed discussion).

The majority of sherds from the kiln area of the Knowes of Trotty excavation can be considered to be low-fired. Hence, it could be argued that to call the firing area a kiln is a misnomer. Analysis of Sample 275 from context [263] within the kiln area indicates heating in the temperature range of up to and around 400°C (McKenzie 2007). This is a very low temperature for the pottery firing, even within a bonfire. Here it should not be forgotten that the purpose of drying and firing clay is to change the minerals of which the vessel is formed from clay into ceramic, and the relevant and necessary chemical and physical transformation occurs at around 600°C (Rice 2005, 90–93; Orton, Tyers and Vince 2003, 126).

Interestingly, a similar situation appears to have existed in the central area at Barnhouse, which chronologically is not so far removed. Although lacking the structural composition of the Knowes of Trotty firing structure, a range of evidence, including reddened pottery, burnt clay, substantial amounts of 'cramp' and ash deposits were interpreted as the remnants of firing Grooved ware (A. M. Jones and Richards 2003). Certainly, low temperature manufacture was manifest in the poorly-fired condition of Grooved ware at Barnhouse.

11.10.2 Examination of sherd SF 6, context [057] at the Knowes of Trotty

The detailed examination of a rim sherd (SF 6) with exterior lip and interior bevel (Fig.3.7) was undertaken to draw out additional information which may inform the understanding of the wider assemblage (Fig. 11.10.1). Rim sherd SF 6 is 35mm on its longest axis and weighs 14g. The sherd is abraded and much of the exterior and interior surface has been lost; what surface remains is soft orange in colour and has been smoothed. The fabric is coarse, sandy clay which is micaceous and also has small, rounded black rock fragments. It is fired hard and, although the uncovered matrix is light-grey in colour, magnification shows elements of oxidation throughout the body of the sherd. It has probably been fired in a relatively oxidised atmosphere. Examination of the core fabric by magnification shows a tiny piece of carbonised roundwood which appears to be embedded in the clay matrix. There are no traces of decoration.

Initial examination suggested tentatively that the sherd may be from the rim of a small, undecorated food vessel, alternatively it may be a rim from an 'Unstan' or round-bottomed vessel, either of the classic collared design or of the deeper-profiled 'neutral' bowl type. The very large Unstan ware assemblage from Wideford Hill (see above) is a good point of assessment. Although comparison cannot be done physically, Jones and Tully (section 11.4) raise a number of relevant points which can be considered. Clearly, the form of the sherd could indicate Unstan ware. The interior surface is gouged and pitted, which is partly due to the trowel but the major part of the damage appears to be use-wear. It is noted above (section 11.4.11) that Unstan ware vessels of all classes appear to have been used in the preparation or serving of food, and the damage may be the result of repeated scouring and cleaning. There are no indications of sooting so the vessel may well have been indeed used for the serving of food.

The fabric of sherd SF 6 is of particular interest in being coarse clay with small rock inclusions, which are mostly rounded and almost certainly are part of the natural clay rather than any deliberately introduced temper. Jones and Tully (see above) indicate that one of the Wideford Hill fabrics is much like this and make the interesting point that the potters operating at this settlement seem to have used weathered clay from local sources which were probably associated with igneous dykes. They seem to have been content to use this naturally mixed clay/rock material rather than seeking out additional rock to deliberately prepare and include. This same process probably accounts for the rounded nature of the small rock inclusions in Knowes of Trotty sherd SF 6 and, when taken together with its hard, well-fired constitution, may indicate an early Neolithic date.

The context [057] of the Knowes of Trotty sherd SF 6 is within the wall core of the house structure confirming a likely 4th millennium cal BC date, and consequently a strong probability that it is part of an Unstan ware or round-based vessel. However, the most important point in this discussion is the nature of the fabric, which is also consistent with this designation.

The sherd SF 6 was compared with two of the undeniably Unstan ware rims from Ha'Breck, Wyre (Context [302] SF 31 and Context [225] SF 83). The Wyre rims are much finer and have carefully executed incised design, one on the collar and the other on the rim. The interesting point is that they also have a fabric which appears composed of weathered clay with naturally rounded rock inclusions. Obviously, they are from different clay sources, but they reinforce the point that the Wideford Hill potters employed similar types of weathered/igneous clay sources to those on Wyre, and similarly felt no need to crush fresh rock for added inclusions.

11.10.3 Conclusion

Overall, the pottery assemblage from the Knowes of Trotty has proved to be fairly chronologically indeterminate, although it is not inconsistent with a 4th–early 3rd millennium cal BC date. Nonetheless, its examination has led to a further consideration of firing and the question of whether a firing structure is present, and if so, of what type. It is suggested that the remains of a firing structure may indeed be present and that it could be a pit-structure (see Chapter 3). Gosselain (1992) and Livingstone Smith's (2001) reservations on the usefulness of maximum firing temperatures and the assumed links

between hard and soft-fired sherds and kiln and open firings are instructive and, it is suggested, should be borne in mind by pottery specialists.

Finally, it seems evident that only a further excavation of the firing structure and the surrounding area is likely to resolve the question of its identity. While there is a large array of comparative material to consider from Roman and Medieval kilns, the excavators of early prehistoric 'kilns' tread a lonely and largely unexplored path. Orton, Tyers and Vince (2003, 130) suggest a continuous section drawn across the structure and its infill from front to back, a section through the kiln at right angles to the flue (if identifiable) and careful consideration of the stratigraphy in the flue. There is, as they comment, far too little information on the structure of very early kilns or burnings, for any scrap of information to be lost.

11.11 Bay of Firth pottery: a conclusion

Andrew Meirion Jones

11.11.1 Introduction

The purpose of this final discussion of the major pottery assemblages at Crossiecrown, Stonehall and Wideford, as well as the smaller assemblages from Ramberry Head, Brae of Smerquoy, Muckquoy and Knowes of Trotty, is to reflect on the similarities and differences in craft production activities relating to pottery within the Bay of Firth region, as well as Orkney more generally. In addition we will consider some of the social practices associated with pottery. Importantly, the time depth of many of the settlements excavated provide a fantastic opportunity to observe changes in craft production over a considerable period of time; taken as a whole the Bay of Firth settlements and their pottery assemblages provide a complete sequence for the Orcadian Neolithic. The central aim is to place the Bay of Firth pottery assemblages, and their associated practices, in context. This concluding discussion will focus on five main aspects of pottery production and associated activities:

- Deposition and Representativeness
- Ceramic sequences
- Resource procurement
- Decoration and form
- Ceramic repertoire and use.

11.11.2 Deposition and representativeness

An important aspect of the pottery assemblage that has been overlooked in the previous site reports is the representativeness of the distinct assemblages: are the pottery assemblages representative of domestic assemblages, and what are the depositional processes that led to the formation of each assemblage? This concluding discussion will review the issue of formation processes and representativeness, a key issue when dealing with settlement assemblages (Schiffer 1976). The discussion below will not seek to reconstruct life histories for individual classes of vessels (*e.g.* Schiffer 1972; La Motta 2012), but it will consider aspects of their biographies, such as resource procurement and use.

More important at this juncture is to assess the character of the deposits from the various excavated sites. Beginning with the earlier Neolithic sites, the pottery at Wideford Hill was associated with a series of timber structures, probable houses. The numbers of ceramics from each of these structures was quite small and probably relates to breakage and loss of ceramics utilised in each of the houses; they therefore represent occupation assemblages. This is also likely to be true of the small assemblage from Brae of Smerquoy and Crossiecrown. The major component from Wideford Hill derived from the Stonehouse 1, and its associated rammed stone [002] 'working floor'. There were relatively few vessels associated with Stonehouse 1, and this can probably be taken as representative of a household assemblage. More striking is the sheer amount of pottery associated with the rammed stone surface [002] associated with Stonehouse 1. To what extent can this assemblage be treated as a residue of production activities? There was no sign of any wasters amongst the assemblage, and no evidence for firing on the site, though the surface was packed with cobbles, suggesting a floor surface possibly for working on.

Alternatively, the rammed stone assemblage might be regarded as midden dumped on this surface, though the usual thick deposits associated with midden were absent. Notably, midden deposits were possibly associated with Timber structure 3 at Wideford Hill, though very few sherds were associated with this deposit. The assemblage associated with the 'working floor' at Wideford Hill is problematic given that it comprises the greatest quantity of pottery on this site. Does it represent deliberate deposition associated with the final stages of occupation. Given the numbers of sherds associated with this deposit it seems probable that these are communal deposits of sherds retrieved from across the site. If we question the relationship between this deposit and the occupation assemblages at Wideford Hill, we begin to see that Wideford Hill occupation assemblages represent a far more modest number of pots, much more in

line with sites such as Knap of Howar (Ritchie 1983). Before turning to the late Neolithic assemblages, the significance of Knowes of Trotty can be highlighted, less for its small assemblage which comprises little that is typologically diagnostic, apart from a single Unstan ware rim (Fig. 3.7), and more for its firing structure (Chapter 3.4; Fig. 3.18); at a stroke, this feature at Knowes of Trotty effectively transforms the indirect evidence for production such as that at Wideford Hill just mentioned, as well, for the later Neolithic, as at Barnhouse and Stonehall (see discussion in 11.2.4).

For the late Neolithic assemblages we observe a more complex picture. At Crossiecrown a group of larger vessels were likely to be associated with occupation deposits, particularly those around hearth, in context [300], of the Red House. As argued in the Crossiecrown section above, the excellent levels of preservation and high number of sherds from several vessels suggest that these comprise part of abandonment deposits deliberately left *in situ* after the occupation of the house was discontinued. Notably, abandonment deposits of this kind are a common feature of Neolithic settlements across Europe (see contributors to Hofmann and Smyth 2013). Thick midden deposits were also associated with the Red and Grey Houses at Crossiecrown, and the sherds of Grooved ware and Beaker associated with these may have derived from the occupation of the Red House or a later structure. In addition a number of vessels were derived from upper contexts overlying the Red House, again many of these were quite well preserved. These deposits cannot be regarded as occupation material and must relate to abandonment deposits inserted into the upper layers of the Red House at some (indeterminate) period after occupation. As argued in the Crossiecrown section above, it would appear that certain categories of vessels, the large and small size vessels are preferentially deposited in these upper abandonment deposits, while just over one third of medium size vessels were found in these upper deposits. This suggests deliberate practices of curation followed by deposition.

The situation at Stonehall differs, and here it seems more probable that the pottery assemblages associated with the Farm (Trenches B, E and F) were related to occupation deposits, on the basis of their contextual association and far more fragmentary nature as compared with Crossiecrown.

11.11.3 Ceramic sequences

As indicated above, the Bay of Firth settlements provide a complete sequence of the Orcadian Neolithic. Along with this, we can also observe a complete sequence of pottery production over the course of the Orcadian Neolithic. A single site – Crossiecrown – allows us to outline the basic sequence, with a shift from Unstan ware to Grooved ware and then to Beaker pottery forms. Indeed, such a sequence was predicted by the radiocarbon analysis of Renfrew (1979), though not empirically verified by him.

We can refine the beginning of the sequence by looking at the composition of the Wideford Hill assemblage, composed of contemporaneous neutral bowl and Unstan ware forms, with a 2.5:1 ratio of Unstan ware to neutral bowl forms. Crossiecrown and Smerquoy also had a mixture of neutral bowl and Unstan ware forms. It would appear that, at the very beginning of the Orcadian Neolithic sequence, mixed assemblages of pottery were produced, and were in use together, with potential functional differences in the two pottery forms. This pattern is also paralleled elsewhere in Orkney at the site of Knap of Howar (Ritchie 1983). Interestingly, the Stonehall assemblages were only composed of neutral bowl forms. It is possible that we observe a shift over time from open and decorated Unstan Ware forms to neutral and plain bowls. Arguably, these taller and thick-based neutral bowl forms eventually gave way to straight sides and flat-bottomed vase forms: Grooved ware (Jones 2012, 116–18).

The Grooved ware at Crossiecrown and Stonehall comprised a range of sizes: large; medium and small, with lesser numbers of small and large size vessels and greater numbers of medium size vessels. The same pattern of size frequencies is observed at Barnhouse (Jones 1997; 2002; 2005a) and Links of Noltland (Sheridan 1999). As Hunter and MacSween (1991) observed in the pottery sequence at Pool, we see a shift in terms of decoration from incised decoration to applied decoration. While this shift in decorative treatment is upheld at Crossiecrown we also need to remember that these shifts are the result of changing craft practices, and associated patterns of consumption. Incised decoration is generally found on small and medium size vessels, while applied decoration is found on larger vessels. On the basis of GC/MS work on the Barnhouse Grooved ware assemblage (Jones 1997; 2002; 2005a; Jones *et al.* 2005), vessels of differing size are used for different contents. The shift from incised to applied decoration is not simply stylistic or typological, it also relates to changing patterns of vessel production and use.

Decoratively, the two major Grooved ware assemblages in the Bay of Firth region, Crossiecrown and Stonehall, differ. Again this is a pattern that can be observed at a number of Late Neolithic settlements across Orkney where each settlement produces Grooved ware with its own distinctive decorative style; this is true in particular of the earlier incised Grooved ware. Towards the end of the Grooved ware sequence, associated with applied decoration, we begin to see a convergence of decorative styles. Notably, the Crossiecrown Grooved ware bore a resemblance to the Grooved ware from Pool, Sanday and Links of Noltland, Westray.

Finally, at the end of the Neolithic sequence we begin to see a new form of flat bottomed pottery decorated with a new decorative technique, the use of twisted-cord impressions: Beakers. Small numbers of Beaker sherds were found in the upper contexts at Crossiecrown. As noted above, these Beaker sherds have possible decorative parallels to the Beaker vessel from Rinyo, Rousay, and to Beaker pottery in Northeast Scotland. However, on the basis of the small number of Beaker sherds from Crossiecrown it is difficult to draw clear conclusions in terms of stylistic or typological parallels.

11.11.4 Resource procurement

Petrographic analysis of all assemblages has enabled us to build up a detailed picture of changing practices of resource procurement and use. In terms of procurement there seems to be a remarkable focus on, and continual procurement of, monchiquite. Monchiquite is an igneous rock that outcrops in dyke form and is part of a suite of igneous dykes that extrude through the sedimentary geology of the islands (Mykura 1976); a group of these igneous dykes outcrop on the shore of the Bay of Firth between Rennibister and Finstown. Based on prospection and petrographic analysis conducted as part of the project (see section 11.5), and by the present author as part of his doctoral research, we can state with certainty that the monchiquite dyke utilised by Neolithic potters in the settlements documented here, is part of this group. Furthermore, monchiquite was identified in several of the sherds from Crossiecrown (section 11.6), with camptonite also commonly present (Table 11.6.3).

Monchiquite is present as temper in pottery from Wideford Hill and Crossiecrown, though not at Stonehall and Smerquoy. Monchiquite is not the only rock source occurring as temper (there is also evidence for the use of sedimentary sources), however it is interesting that for the earlier ceramics at Wideford Hill and Crossiecrown we observe the common use of the same rock source. The use of this rock source also continues to the later Grooved ware and Beaker phases at Crossiecrown. In these later phases we observe an expanded repertoire of rock sources being utilised, with the addition of camptonite and the increased use of sedimentary rocks such as mudstone and sandstone as temper.

We are also able to observe changing practices of resource procurement through petrographic analysis, as we see more rounded lithic inclusions in early ceramic thin-sections, suggesting that temper was a component of the clay used for pottery production. This contrasts with the sharp angularity and size of the lithic inclusions in Grooved ware thin-sections, suggesting these components had been deliberately added to the clay. Yet further changes could be seen in the thin-sections produced on the Beaker assemblage from Crossiecrown. Here the lithic inclusions were of very small size, in contrast to those found in thin-sections from earlier ceramic types; this suggests a greater degree of crushing of lithic sources for temper prior to inclusion in the clay for pot production.

Continuities are observed in the consistent use of monchiquite as a source for temper at a few of the settlement sites. The use of this common source in a series of early Neolithic assemblages raises the possibility of resource sharing amongst broadly contemporary settlement sites. However, interestingly we also see continuity in the use of this particular igneous rock source into the late Neolithic at Crossiecrown, suggesting that this particular source held long-term connections and significance for those living in this part of Neolithic Orkney.

It is possible to consider the use of monchiquite at Crossiecrown in several ways. As previously argued for the Grooved ware settlement at Barnhouse, the use of resources for pottery temper may be restricted at household or settlement level (A. M. Jones 1997; 2000; 2002). In this light we might view the use of monchiquite as particularly distinctive to Crossiecrown, although, as just noted, camptonite features as well.

The distinctiveness of the use of monchiquite as a tempering agent over long periods of time also leads us to consider the longevity and place-specificity of this rock source, and its appearance in pottery from a number of sites in the Bay of Firth region; in that sense the monchiquite dyke in the Bay of Firth accrues significance over time as an ancestral source of rock for pottery production.

This makes the mixture of tempers utilised in the Grooved ware deposited within Quanterness passage grave all the more remarkable, as while monchiquite is present it is not the only temper utilised in the Quanterness pottery (see Williams 1979). At Quanterness 'just under half of the twenty-nine vessels examined contained dyke material: camptonite, bostonite, monchiquite and olivine-basalt' (Williams 1982, 11). As Williams notes, dykes of monchiquite and camptonite occur in the locality of Quanterness (within a two mile radius), but not bostonite and olivine-basalt. This underlines the variety of probable sources of the pots deposited at Quanterness and the likely kinship (or other) connections associated with the population of people buried at Quanterness (A. M. Jones 1997; 2002); these will have included immediately local people, such as those from Crossiecrown, as well as those from more distant locations in Orkney, such as Barnhouse.

To sum up, there are a series of distinguishing characteristics relating to resource procurement for pottery production at the Bay of Firth Neolithic settlement sites. We can note strong continuity, and also distinctive change (see Jones 2012, 100–119). Continuities occur in the particular sources utilised for pottery production, while changes occur in the manner of their use.

11.11.5 Decoration and form

The theme of continuity and change characterised resource procurement at the Bay of Firth Neolithic settlements. It is also a feature of decoration and form. Change can be observed in the forming of the pots over time, with rounded bases being produced to begin with at Wideford Hill, Crossiecrown and Smerquoy. We observe a period of experimentation around 3300 cal BC at Stonehall with changes in the height and thickness of pots, and experiments with forming flatter bases. At Crossiecrown, through much of the later Neolithic and with the production of Beaker pottery, flat bases have become the norm. However, there were also long periods of repetition and continuity. Round bases were produced for several hundred years at Wideford, Smerquoy and Crossiecrown. We then see a marked change in the form of pots with the development of flat bases c.3300 cal BC at Stonehall as taller neutral bowl forms were produced. We also observe a period of experimentation with the earliest Grooved ware forms at Crossiecrown, with base forms with rounded interiors and footed exteriors and rounded interiors with squared-off exteriors. Both these forms are suggestive of a forming technique familiar with round-based vessels, with the addition of a technique for stabilising the exterior of vessels, such as the use of footing or squaring. As above, we can observe continuity and change occurring hand in hand.

Probably the most marked changes occur in pottery decoration. The earliest bowl forms were either plain or the Unstan ware forms were decorated above the carination with impressed decoration. A quite different set of decorative techniques appear after 3300 cal BC, and with the development of Grooved ware forms: incised decoration on the earliest Grooved ware at Crossiecrown and Stonehall, followed by the increasing use of applied decoration. The Grooved ware assemblages at both sites also included a small number of vessels decorated by impressed decoration. Impressed decorative techniques also occur in the Beaker pottery found at Crossiecrown.

Commonalities can be seen in the decoration of the earliest Unstan ware forms, with little obvious difference in the decorative style of pots from Wideford Hill, Crossiecrown and Smerquoy. Notably, much of the Unstan ware repertoire across Orkney appears similar in terms of decoration (Jones 2005b). This stands in contrast to the Grooved ware assemblages at Crossiecrown and Stonehall which both differ quite markedly in decorative style.

It is possible that, as with resource procurement, we are observing a trend in which communities begin with strong shared links in terms of decoration. Eventually this gives way to greater differentiation around 3300 cal BC with the earliest Grooved ware assemblages. These early Grooved ware assemblages appear to be decorated with a distinctive settlement-specific decorative scheme. This specificity and differentiation breaks down towards the end of the Grooved ware sequence, and we begin to observe commonalities in decorative scheme (Jones 2000). Potentially, these changing decorative traditions may relate to changing kinship links and community ties.

11.11.6 Ceramic repertoire and use

Once again, we observe marked continuity in the contents of vessels determined on the basis of GC-C-IRMS analysis. Dairy and adipose fats from ruminants dominated all assemblages, and these were detected in pots from early Neolithic and late Neolithic contexts at all sites (Wideford Hill, Stonehall and Crossiecrown). There were some small differences in the greater concentration of lipids in early Neolithic pots versus late Neolithic pots, possibly reflecting intensity of use or manner of use.

Taking a long view of changing ceramic traditions it is possible to see changes in the repertoire or composition of assemblages over time. Beginning with Unstan ware and neutral bowls, ceramic assemblages appear to be composed of two contemporaneous forms, potentially reflecting different functions such as cooking and serving. While on the face of it later Neolithic settlements are

dominated by a single vessel form, flat-based, bucket-shaped Grooved ware, in fact by the later Neolithic ceramic assemblages become more diverse with three different sizes of Grooved ware vessel being produced. On the basis of the work at Barnhouse (A. M. Jones 1997; 2002; 2005a), these different vessel sizes almost certainly relate to differing functions, including storage, cooking and serving. However, analysis of the composition of the Crossiecrown Grooved ware assemblage suggests that there were a slightly greater number of larger vessels. In addition, GC-C-IRMS analysis suggests these larger vessels had similar contents to small and medium size vessels.

Changing ceramic forms therefore relate to changing functions, and changes in the social practices surrounding food use. In particular in the later Neolithic, food storage in large Grooved ware vessel emerges as a significant change in economic and culinary practices (Jones 1999a). However, the evidence from Crossiecrown raises the possibility that large vessels were also used in a similar fashion to small and medium size vessels; in this case it is possible to think of these changes in ceramic repertoire not only as changes in economic practices, but as changes in food provisioning capacity. As noted above from the GC-C-IRMS analysis, the contents of vessels remain largely unchanged over the course of the Neolithic. Instead, what appears to change is the scale and capacity of food consumption. These changes in ceramic repertoires are unlikely to be accidental, but must also relate to changing social practices, potentially associated with shifting patterns of residence, and community and kinship ties.

11.11.7 Conclusion

Analysis of the set of pottery assemblages from the Neolithic settlements of the Bay of Firth region allow us to observe over the long term a series of changing practices associated with pottery. As discussed above, when looking at changing repertoires of use it is evident that differing, but contemporaneous, forms – neutral bowls and Unstan ware – give way to a suite of vessels with similar forms but differing scales: the large, medium and small size Grooved ware vessels. Coupled with this, continuities and changes were also noted in resource procurement, with the continued use of monchiquite as a source for pottery temper, and a changing mode of use, from non-treatment of temper in the early Neolithic to the crushing of temper prior to its use in the late Neolithic, followed by more extreme crushing of temper at the end of the Neolithic sequence. Alongside this, we also observe an expansion in the use of temper, with a greater variety of sources being used during the late Neolithic period.

Similar themes of differentiation and change were drawn out in the discussion of decoration, where we initially see a strong degree of similarity in pottery decoration in the early Neolithic, followed by decorative schemes distinctive to particular settlements at the beginning of the late Neolithic; these are in turn followed by a return to a common mode of decoration in later Grooved ware assemblages.

It is unhelpful to consider these changes simply as the result of unmotivated evolutionary or stylistic change. Instead it is important to consider these changes alongside the flux and flow of changing patterns of settlement – discussed in further detail elsewhere in this volume. The changing scale and capacity of vessels will relate to changing social obligations, and the use of food sharing in these. Likewise the changes in temper use will relate to the requirement to produce vessels of greater capacity and scale, while changes in decoration will relate to changing patterns of connection and association (whether of kinship or other social relationships). Alongside these, the continuities in practice – such as the continued use of particular resources – will also relate to the need to maintain social ties. In each of these cases continuity and change relate to the changing fortunes of the settlements and their inhabitants. Finally, it is because of their close association with settlements, that by the late Neolithic we see pottery being deliberately deposited in houses remains after settlements were abandoned.

CHAPTER TWELVE

Flaked Lithic Artefacts from Neolithic Sites around the Bay of Firth: Wideford Hill, Knowes of Trotty, Brae of Smerquoy, Stonehall, Crossiecrown and Ramberry

Hugo Anderson-Whymark, Richard Chatterton, Mark Edmonds
and Caroline Wickham-Jones

12.1 Introduction

The excavations undertaken around the Bay of Firth between 1994 and 2013 recovered 2744 flaked artefacts weighing 5.912kg. The majority of sites yielded comparatively small assemblages of less than a few hundred flints, but Stonehall Farm and Crossiecrown each produced nearly one thousand artefacts (Tables 12.1 and 12.2). The flaked lithic assemblages include a small number of residual Mesolithic artefacts, but the greater part of the material described here is contemporary with the early and late Neolithic structures excavated on the respective sites. In addition, a limited early Bronze Age assemblage was recovered from Crossiecrown. This chapter explores the range of raw materials employed, reduction techniques and artefact types, and, where context information was available, assemblage composition and patterns of deposition will be considered.

12.2 Methodology

This report has been prepared by Hugo Anderson-Whymark and Mark Edmonds, but over the life of the project many individuals have contributed to this analysis. Richard Chatterton produced catalogues for the greater part of the Wideford Hill, Stonehall and Crossiecrown assemblages, leaving many useful notes and summaries. He also selected artefacts for pen and ink illustration (undertaken by Matt Brudenell). Caroline Wickham-Jones catalogued the Knowes of Trotty

assemblage, producing a report that is summarised below. In spring 2014 Hugo Anderson-Whymark catalogued the remaining assemblages and comprehensively reviewed existing catalogues against the artefacts to ensure consistent terminology was employed.

Detailed records were made of raw material, edge-damage and condition (*e.g.* cortication, burning and breakage). Artefacts were measured using callipers with an accuracy of ±0.1mm, following methods defined by Saville (1980), and each artefact was weighed on scales accurate to ±0.2g. Artefact colour was visually distinguished under a bright daylight light box and described using hue and modifier (*e.g.* mid orangey-brown). In the absence of a cortical surface that allows artefacts to be more accurately sourced, flint raw materials are described as 'unclassified flint'. A copy of the full catalogue has been deposited with the archive.

Artefacts have been classified on the basis of technological and typological attributes. Many standard typological descriptions employed in Britain are not applicable to Orcadian assemblages, although often applied, and classifications of scrapers and knives in particular mask diversity in Orcadian assemblages. A typology specifically for Orkney is currently in development and the diverse range of knife forms presented in this report represents a first step towards the development of a meaningful classification for several different artefact categories. Scrapers were classified according to the position of the retouched edge (*e.g.*

Table 12.1 Summary struck lithic assemblage quantified by number and weight.

Artefact type	Wideford Hill		Smerquoy		Knowes of Trotty		Stonehall Knoll		Stonehall Meadow		Stonehall Farm		Crossiecrown		Ramberry		Total No.	Total Wt (g)
	No.	Wt (g)	No.	Wt (g)	No.	Wt (g)	No.	Wt (g)	No.	Wt (g)	No.	Wt (g)	No.	Wt (g)	No.	Wt (g)		
Flake/blade	71	83.3	33	55.4	6	3.6	117	115	65	92.5	350	692.2	208	318.9	1	5	851	1365.7
Bipolar flake/blade	42	77.9	22	77	9	13.2	83	140.7	52	116.8	171	391.9	284	559.3			663	1376.8
Irregular waste	13	25.9	5	11.5	2	2.1	23	54.3	17	36.3	77	199.9	46	86.7	1	15.6	184	432.3
Chip	47	6.0	4	0.4	11	0.9	67	10.7	29	2.5	136	14.7	68	11.4	3	1.3	365	47.8
Crested blade	1	0.8									2	9.3					3	10.1
Flake from ground implement	2	1.5							2	0.8	6	13.9	3	3.7			13	19.9
Trimming flake, Levallois style											1	0.9					1	0.9
Tested nodule/bashed lump	2	20.4									3	48.7	3	26.7			8	95.8
Split pebble (bipolar)	7	41.9	2	11.2	1	5.1	2	10.4	3	21.7	12	66.7	17	91.6			44	248.5
Bipolar core	9	34.3	3	7.3	3	7.9	17	39.9	11	35.8	40	241	28	97			111	463.2
Platform core	3	18.7					1	3.1	1	5.2	6	68.3	1	2.4			12	97.7
Scraper	30	104.7	4	12.2	3	4.4	22	86	17	72.9	58	219.7	112	338.6			246	838.5
Knife	7	50.5	2	17.7			3	32.6	5	17.6	56	230.4	20	83			93	431.8
Arrowhead	1	1.6	1	1.8							3	9.4	5	13.3			10	26.1
Piercer											1	1.4	1	1			2	2.4
Edge retouched flake	1	4.2	2	3.3	1	2.3	2	4.6	2	3.6	13	28.4	14	57.4			35	103.8
Fabricator											1	0.7	1	4.7			2	5.4
Notched flake	1	1.9															3	6
Truncated flake/blade	1	0.8									2	4.1					1	0.8
Misc. retouch													1	9.3			1	9.3
Unclass. retouched flake tool	1	0.3					2	1.4	3	4.5	11	13.4	5	9.2			22	28.8
Unworked pebble	11	23.2	1	7.3			3	37.6	12	17.3	14	70.4	30	142.3			71	298.1
Burnt unworked flint											1	0.5	2	1.9			3	2.4
Grand total	250	497.9	79	205.1	36	39.5	342	536.3	219	427.5	964	2325.8	849	1858.4	5	21.9	2744	5912.3

Table 12.2 Summary lithic assemblages shown as percentages of site total.

Artefact type	Wideford Hill		Smerquoy		Knowes of Trotty		Stonehall Knoll		Stonehall Meadow		Stonehall Farm		Crossiecrown		Ramberry		Total No.	Total %
	No.	%	No.	%	No.	%	No.	%	No.	%	No.	%	No.	%	No.	%		
Flake/blade	71	28.4%	33	41.8%	6	16.7%	117	34.2%	65	29.7%	350	36.3%	208	24.5%	1	20.0%	851	30.9%
Bipolar flake/blade	42	16.8%	22	27.8%	9	25.0%	83	24.3%	52	23.7%	171	17.7%	284	33.5%			663	24.2%
Irregular waste	13	5.2%	5	6.3%	2	5.6%	23	6.7%	17	7.8%	77	8.0%	46	5.4%	1	20.0%	184	6.7%
Chip	47	18.8%	4	5.1%	11	30.6%	67	19.6%	29	13.2%	136	14.1%	68	8.0%	3	60.0%	365	13.3%
Crested blade	1	0.4%									2	0.2%					3	0.1%
Flake from ground implement	2	0.8%							2	0.9%	6	0.6%	3	0.4%			13	0.5%
Trimming flake, Levallois style											1	0.1%					1	0.0%
Split pebble (bipolar)	7	2.8%	2	2.5%	1	2.8%	2	0.6%	3	1.4%	12	1.3%	17	2.0%			44	1.6%
Tested nodule/bashed lump	2	0.8%									3	0.3%	3	0.4%			8	0.3%
Bipolar core	9	3.6%	3	3.8%	3	8.3%	17	5.0%	11	5.0%	40	4.1%	28	3.3%			111	4.0%
Platform core	3	1.2%					1	0.3%	1	0.5%	6	0.6%	1	0.1%			12	0.4%
Scraper	30	12.0%	4	5.1%	3	8.3%	22	6.4%	17	7.8%	58	5.9%	112	13.2%			246	8.9%
Knife	7	2.8%	2	2.5%			3	0.9%	5	2.3%	56	5.8%	20	2.4%			93	3.4%
Edge retouched flake	1	0.4%	2	2.5%	1	2.8%	2	0.6%	2	0.9%	13	1.3%	14	1.6%			35	1.3%
Fabricator											1	0.1%	1	0.1%			2	0.1%
Piercer											1	0.1%	1	0.1%			2	0.1%
Arrowhead	1	0.4%	1	1.3%							3	0.3%	5	0.6%			10	0.4%
Notched flake	1	0.4%									2	0.2%					3	0.1%
Truncated flake/blade	1	0.4%															1	0.0%
Misc. retouch													1	0.1%			1	0.0%
Unclass. retouched flake tool	1	0.4%					2	0.6%	3	1.4%	11	1.1%	5	0.6%			22	0.8%
Burnt unworked flint											1	0.1%	2	0.2%			3	0.1%
Unworked pebble	11	4.4%	1	1.3%			3	0.9%	12	5.5%	14	1.5%	30	3.5%			71	2.6%
Grand total	250	100%	79	100%	36	100%	342	100%	219	100%	964	100%	849	100%	5	100%	2744	100%
Total burnt artefacts*	29	15.1%	6	8.1%	3	12.0%	14	5.1%	29	16.3%	105	12.9%	84	11.2%			270	11.7%
Total broken artefacts*	64	33.3%	18	24.3%	9	36.0%	79	29.0%	70	39.3%	296	36.4%	200	26.7%			736	31.9%
Total retouched tools*	42	21.9%	9	12.2%	4	16%	29	10.7%	27	15.2%	144	17.7%	159	21.2%			414	18.0%

* Totals and percentages exclude chips, burnt unworked flint and unworked pebbles.

end scraper or side scraper), but during the course of the analysis it became clear that this mode of classification masks significant technological and morphological differences, most notably a distinctive late Neolithic form, defined as the '*Stonehall Farm type*' (see definition below).

12.3 Condition

The flaked lithic artefacts from the Bay of Firth sites are typically in fresh condition, with only a few pieces, mostly from topsoil, exhibiting any traces of post-depositional edge-damage. This indicates that the vast majority of artefacts from archaeological contexts, including midden deposits, were subject to little or no trampling or disturbance before being sealed in an archaeological deposit. A small number of exceptionally water-worn flakes were recovered and these have been interpreted as pieces of raw material imported from beach deposits; they provide evidence of flint knapping on the shore, but in which period is unclear.

The greater part of the lithic assemblage was free from surface cortication, although a few pieces exhibited a light to moderate white surface. As the true colour of these flints was unclear they have been excluded from discussions of colour.

12.4 Artefact recovery

The vast majority of the flaked lithic artefacts were recovered from hand excavation, with additional pieces retrieved from the residues of environmental samples. A good level of artefact recovery appears to have been achieved with some small chips identified, but as dry sieving was not undertaken some smaller artefacts may have been missed.

The recovery of artefacts from topsoil was very variable between sites, depending on the method employed for removal. At Crossiecrown and Stonehall where topsoil was removed by hand, 56.4% and 20.9% of the respective total assemblages were recovered from topsoil contexts, whereas at Wideford Hill topsoil was removed by mechanical excavator and only three flints (*c*.1% of the assemblage) were recovered. At Wideford Hill, artefacts from the topsoil are clearly under-represented as this site was originally identified from an artefact scatter located by Robert Rendall in the 1930s (Rendall 1931; 1934). Lithics from the topsoil represent a valuable but frequently overlooked resource that can complement and enhance narratives provided by stratified assemblages.

In particular, it is worth noting that many of the Mesolithic artefacts were recovered from topsoil, adding significantly to the narrative for this period. Moreover, at Crossiecrown despite the presence of *in situ* deposits dating from the early Neolithic and early Bronze Age, the only diagnostic artefacts were retrieved from topsoil.

12.5 Raw materials

The flaked stone artefacts are almost exclusively manufactured from flint (98.3%), but chert, quartz, quartzite and rhyolite were also used as raw materials (Table 12.3). These materials are all readily available in different parts of Orkney. Flint, quartz and quartzite is present in glacial till deposits on the east coast of Mainland, most notably Deerness, and many of the Northern and Southern Islands, but it is most easily obtained from beach deposits in the same regions, in the form of sub-rounded, water-worn, beach pebbles. Quartz and quartzite, often of reasonable flaking quality, is frequently found in the same locations as flint, so the dominance of flint in the archaeological assemblages indicates preferential selection.

Excluding non cortical 'unclassified flint' that cannot be sourced, the archaeological assemblage is overwhelmingly dominated by flint derived from beach deposits. A small number of flints exhibit comparatively unabraded cortical surfaces indicating the raw material for these pieces was obtained directly from the glacial till or from beach deposits shortly after it had eroded from the till. The dimensions of split pebbles indicate the working of pieces of raw material with maximum dimensions ranging from 14mm to 40mm, and the vast majority of flint artefacts fall within this size range. Forty-nine flints (2.1% of the assemblage excluding chips) have a maximum dimension that exceeds 40mm, indicating that larger pieces were available as a raw material; the largest flint is a beach pebble flake from Stonehall Farm that measures 95.5mm. It is, however, notable that the largest flints at each site often include non- or partly-cortical flakes and tools (19 of the 49 flint over 40mm were retouched tools) that are likely to have been imported rather than produced on site. Flints of distinctively coloured raw materials (typically opaque greys, mottled greys, reds, orange reds, browns and orange browns), many of which are retouched tools, were also probably imported as 'blanks' or finished artefacts via networks of trade or exchange (Tables 12.4 and 12.5). For example, only ten artefacts of one particularly distinctive dark reddish brown flint with beige inclusions and grey mottling were recorded, but five artefacts of this flint were knives and three were scrapers. The source of these larger and/or distinctively coloured raw materials is open to debate, but it is probable that they were obtained in the Orkney Archipelago. Although not common in Orkney Mainland, large nodules of grey and vivid orange-brown/brownish red flint have been found in Sanday and North Ronaldsay by one of the authors (HAW) as part of an ongoing lithic raw materials project and other Northern Isles not yet visited may possess a similar resource (*e.g.* Papa Westray and Stronsay). On the island of Stroma, to the south of Orkney, flint nodules of '8–10 inches' that weigh 'several pounds' have also been reported in glacial deposits (Peach 1860). The possibility that flint was imported from more distant sources (*e.g.* Den of Boddam or further afield) cannot be entirely excluded, but considering the plentiful local resource of good quality flint there is no practical necessity to import flint from these distant resources.

The chert and rhyolite present in the assemblage can be obtained from west Mainland: black chert of variable quality is present in the Lower Stromness Flagstone, for example at Netherton to the west of Stromness, while rhyolite is available from an igneous intrusion and nearby beach deposits in the Bay of Navershaw, east of Stromness. It is unclear if the rhyolite was intentionally flaked as the sub-conchoidal fracture many have been initiated by other use activities (*e.g.* by use as a hammerstone), but the limited use of the black chert is notable as this raw material is common in the late phase flaked stone assemblage from Skara Brae. All four pieces of black chert from the Bay of Firth excavations were recovered from Crossiecrown and these comprise two scrapers that are likely to have been imported as finished tools, a bipolar core and a flake. Arran pitchstone is notably absent from all of the assemblages under consideration.

Used artefacts also provided a source of raw material and 56 flints (2.4% of the assemblage, excluding chips) were re-worked from tools, including scrapers, knives and polished tools (Table 12.6). The majority of these tools were re-worked by bipolar percussion, with bipolar flakes most commonly struck transversely across the former artefact producing a narrow flake. At Crossiecrown, two end scrapers were manufactured from fragmentary polished implements, one of which was a fine knife that had been ground and polished on both faces.

The raw materials from the sites around the Bay of Firth were reduced using a variety of knapping techniques, all of which exploit the strong conchoidal fracture properties of the raw materials. The variable shape (*e.g.* angular and rounded pebbles) and small size of much of the raw material present a number of challenges to the knapper and the reduction techniques presented below represent methods employed in the assemblages under discussion. The use of these techniques varied between sites and some reduction strategies were only employed in specific periods. An overview is presented in this section and detail can be found in the descriptions of the assemblage from each site.

12.6 Techniques

12.6.1 Bipolar and anvil reduction

Bipolar reduction was a strong feature of all of the assemblages under consideration, but it was particularly dominant in assemblages dating from the early Neolithic (*e.g.* Wideford Hill, Stonehall Knoll and Stonehall Meadow). The assemblage from Crossiecrown also raises the possibility that bipolar reduction was the dominant technique in the Bronze Age, but in the absence of unmixed assemblages and given the presence of early Neolithic activity on site, this cannot be asserted with any degree of confidence.

The bipolar technique involves the reduction of a piece of raw material against an anvil, such as a beach cobble, by direct percussion with a hammerstone (see facially pecked pebbles and hammerstones in the Coarse Stone, Chapter 13). The raw material is held directly against the anvil, often with its long axis uppermost, and the hammerstone is used to deliver a blow to the upper surface inducing conchoidal fracture between the point of percussion on the upper surface and the part of the raw material in contact with the anvil. The delivery of a hammerstone blow of adequate force is critical to the success of the technique; a successful first strike can neatly split a pebble in half; however, if the blow is too gentle, incipient cones may be formed that hinder subsequent removals, whereas a hard blow can result in uncontrolled shattering. Bipolar 'orange-segment' flakes are often the result of an overzealous blow, but these are notably rare in the assemblage. Once split, pebbles were commonly reduced by repeated bipolar blows until the core, which often has a cortical back, is too narrow to reduce any further. As the core is worked, a shattered and crushed core edge commonly develops. In some instances, where blade removals are desired, the narrow edge of the core was orientated towards the knapper and thin slivers were removed. The latter technique was commonly used to re-work scrapers and knives. In a few instances, small flakes were removed from the upper and/or lower surfaces of the bipolar core to create a sharp ridge that could be accurately struck, but this appears to be relatively uncommon.

Table 12.3 Raw materials by site, excluding chips and unworked pebbles.

Raw material	Wideford Hill No.	%	Smerquoy No.	%	Knowes of Trotty No.	%	Stonehall Knoll No.	%	Stonehall Meadow No.	%	Stonehall Farm No.	%	Crossiecrown No.	%	Ramberry No.	%	Total No.	Total %
Unclassified flint	89	46.4%	39	52.7%	17	68.0%	137	50.4%	99	55.6%	497	61.1%	316	42.1%	1	50.0%	1195	51.8%
Beach pebble flint	84	43.8%	32	43.2%	8	32.0%	125	46.0%	72	40.4%	272	33.4%	395	52.6%	1	50.0%	989	42.9%
Glacial till flint	7	3.6%	3	4.1%			4	1.5%	5	2.8%	39	4.8%	26	3.5%			84	3.6%
Milky quartz	12	6.3%							1	0.6%	4	0.5%	6	0.8%			23	1.0%
Beach pebble quartzite									1	0.6%			3	0.4%			4	0.2%
Black chert													4	0.5%			4	0.2%
Unclassified chert?											2	0.2%					2	0.1%
Rhyolite							6	2.2%					1	0.1%			7	0.3%
Grand Total	192	100%	74	100.0%	25	100%	272	100%	178	100%	814	100%	751	100%	2	100%	2308	100%

Table 12.4 The colour of struck flints from selected sites.

Colour	Wideford Hill No	%	Smerquoy No	%	Knowes of Trotty No	%	Stonehall Knoll No	%	Stonehall Meadow No	%	Stonehall Farm No	%	Crossiecrown No	%	Total No.*	Total %
Mid grey	38	25.7%	16	24.2%	7	31.8%	44	17.8%	26	18.6%	163	23.6%	171	26.7%	465	23.8%
Mid orangey brown	27	18.2%	15	22.7%	4	18.2%	41	16.6%	31	22.1%	104	15.0%	97	15.2%	319	16.3%
Light grey	16	10.8%	10	15.2%	4	18.2%	27	10.9%	16	11.4%	86	12.4%	107	16.7%	266	13.6%
Mid yellowish brown	7	4.7%	4	6.1%		0.0%	40	16.2%	10	7.1%	63	9.1%	36	5.6%	160	8.2%
Mid orangey red	6	4.1%	5	7.6%	4	18.2%	22	8.9%	5	3.6%	45	6.5%	44	6.9%	131	6.7%
Light brown	14	9.5%	3	4.5%		0.0%	16	6.5%	9	6.4%	47	6.8%	36	5.6%	125	6.4%
Light yellowish brown	4	2.7%	3	4.5%		0.0%	25	10.1%	14	10.0%	35	5.1%	24	3.8%	105	5.4%
Mid brown	13	8.8%	1	1.5%	1	4.5%	1	0.4%	11	7.9%	26	3.8%	32	5.0%	85	4.3%
Dark grey	9	6.1%	2	3.0%		0.0%	6	2.4%	4	2.9%	34	4.9%	29	4.5%	84	4.3%
Mixed light cream and mid orange brown	3	2.0%	4	6.1%	1	4.5%	8	3.2%	2	1.4%	16	2.3%	18	2.8%	52	2.7%
Light yellowish white (cream)	2	1.4%		0.0%		0.0%	1	0.4%	3	2.1%	8	1.2%	11	1.7%	25	1.3%
Light yellow		0.0%		0.0%		0.0%	2	0.8%		0.0%	14	2.0%	2	0.3%	18	0.9%
Mid grey with small light grey inclusions		0.0%				0.0%	1	0.4%	2	1.4%	7	1.0%	7	1.1%	17	0.9%
Mid orange	1	0.7%						0.0%		0.0%	4	0.6%	11	1.7%	16	0.8%
Mid brownish red	1	0.7%					1	0.4%		0.0%	6	0.9%	2	0.3%	10	0.5%
Mottled dark brownish red with beige inclusions and mid grey	1	0.7%					1	0.4%		0.0%	7	1.0%		0.0%	9	0.5%
Light grey with white cherry inclusions		0.0%						0.0%	1	0.7%	5	0.7%	2	0.3%	8	0.4%
White		0.0%	1	1.5%			2	0.8%		0.0%	2	0.3%	1	0.2%	6	0.3%
Mid yellowish orange		0.0%	2	3.0%	1	4.5%		0.0%		0.0%	2	0.3%		0.0%	5	0.3%
Dark brown	2	1.4%		0.0%		0.0%	2	0.8%		0.0%	1	0.1%		0.0%	5	0.3%
Other (20 colour variations)	4	2.7%		0.0%		0.0%	7	2.8%	6	4.3%	17	2.5%	10	1.6%	44	2.3%
Grand Total	148	100%	66	100%	22	100%	247	100%	140	100%	692	100%	640	100%	1955	100%

* Totals exclude unworked pebbles, chips, burnt pieces and corticated pieces. Ramberry excluded due to low artefact count.

Table 12.5 Colour by key artefact type. Artefacts from all sites combined.

Colour	Flake/core		Scraper		Knife		Other flake tool		Arrowhead		Total No.	Total %
	No.	%	No.	%	No.	%	No.	%	No.	%		
Mid grey	419	22.6%	55	26.1%	15	18.1%	12	23.5%	2	22.2%	503	22.8%
Mid orangey brown	319	17.2%	33	15.6%	10	12.0%	11	21.6%	1	11.1%	374	16.9%
Light grey	266	14.4%	26	12.3%	9	10.8%	5	9.8%	1	11.1%	307	13.9%
Mid yellowish brown	153	8.3%	14	6.6%	8	9.6%	4	7.8%			179	8.1%
Light yellowish brown	139	7.5%	11	5.2%	4	4.8%	1	2.0%	1	11.1%	156	7.1%
Mid orangey red	128	6.9%	11	5.2%	6	7.2%	4	7.8%	1	11.1%	150	6.8%
Light brown	115	6.2%	11	5.2%	4	4.8%	3	5.9%	1	11.1%	134	6.1%
Mid brown	72	3.9%	6	2.8%	3	3.6%	5	9.8%			86	3.9%
Dark grey	73	3.9%	7	3.3%	5	6.0%			1	11.1%	86	3.9%
Mixed light cream and mid orange brown	45	2.4%	5	2.4%	1	1.2%	2	3.9%	1	11.1%	54	2.4%
Light yellowish white (cream)	23	1.2%	1	0.5%	1	1.2%	1	2.0%			26	1.2%
Light yellow	22	1.2%	2	0.9%	1	1.2%					25	1.1%
Mid orange	11	0.6%	6	2.8%							17	0.8%
Mid grey with small light grey inclusions	8	0.4%	7	3.3%	2	2.4%					17	0.8%
Mottled grey flint (various shades)	4	0.2%	3	1.4%	5	6.0%	2	3.9%			14	0.6%
Mid brownish red	6	0.3%	3	1.4%	1	1.2%					10	0.5%
White	8	0.4%	2	0.9%							10	0.5%
Mottled dark brownish red with beige inclusions and mid grey	3	0.2%	1	0.5%	5	6.0%					9	0.4%
Light grey with white cherry inclusions	6	0.3%	1	0.5%	1	1.2%					8	0.4%
Other (15 colour variations)	33	1.8%	6	2.8%	2	2.4%	1	2.0%			42	1.9%
Grand Total	1853	100%	211	100%	83	100%	51	100%	9	100%	2207	100.0%

* Totals exclude unworked pebbles, chips, burnt pieces and corticated pieces. Bold figures denote colours more common as artefacts than as flakes/cores.

Table 12.6 Classification of reworked artefacts.

Original artefact type	Reworked artefact type*	Wideford Hill	Smerquoy	Stonehall Knoll	Stonehall Meadow	Stonehall Farm	Crossiecrown	Grand Total
End scraper	Flake	1						1
	Bipolar flake			1		2		3
	Bipolar flake core			1	1	1		3
Side scraper	Flake						1	1
	Bipolar flake						1	1
	Bipolar flake core						1	1
	Piercer						1	1
Unclass. scraper	Flake		1					1
	Bipolar flake	2		1	1	3	2	9
	Bipolar flake core	1	1		1			3
Ground implement	Flake from ground implement	2			2	6	3	13
Flake from a ground implement	Bipolar flake	1						1
	End scraper						1	1
Polished knife	End scraper						1	1
Cortex backed knife	Bipolar flake core					1		1
Unclass. fragmentary knife	Flake					1		1
	Bipolar flake				1	1		2
Unclass. retouched flake tool	Bipolar flake	1		1		9	1	12
Grand Total		8	2	4	6	24	12	56

* This classification is used in Tables 12.1 and 12.2, and subsequent site specific tables.

Bipolar flakes, when complete, commonly exhibit a primary bulb of percussion from the blow with the hammerstone and a smaller distal bulb that results from contact with the anvil. The bulbs are often diffuse or flat and ripples are commonly seen radiating from both bulbs, although those from the hammerstone blow are usually most apparent. Bipolar reduction is a particularly effective method of working small rounded pieces of raw material, such as well worn beach cobbles, that do not possess <90° angles required for flaking. The technique also allows flakes the same length of the raw material to be struck, maximising flake size from small pieces of raw material. Small split pebbles and cortical flakes were often reasonably thick and were frequently modified into tools, such as scrapers.

For the purpose of this report the term '*anvil percussion*' is used to describe a similar knapping process to bipolar percussion, whereby a core is held against an anvil when struck, but in this technique the anvil only provides support and flake is solely detached by the hammerstone struck (*i.e.* the bipolar rebound from the anvil plays no part in detachment of the flake). In many instances, these anvil percussion flakes will be detached within bipolar reduction strategies, however, as they lack the distal bulb from percussion against an anvil they are classed as flakes/blades.

12.6.2 Platform reduction

Platform struck lithics were present in all assemblages, but were more common in late Neolithic assemblages, such as Stonehall Farm. In its simplest form, platform reduction can entail the removal of a flake by striking a flat, even cortical, surface positioned at *c*.90° to the core face. In most instances, however, flakes were struck from simple platforms created by the removal of one or two flakes. Platform-edge abrasion, which can ensure an accurately positioned removal by shaping the platform edge with a series of small scars, was only observed on Mesolithic artefacts; the absence of this technique from Neolithic flints is notable. The presence of clear hertizan cones indicate that the majority of flakes were struck using a hard hammer percussor, but a small number of artefacts exhibited slight lips at the point of percussion which may indicate the use of a soft hammer, such as a bone baton. No core rejuvenation flakes were present, indicating that when a platform was exhausted the core was either rotated to allow further working (resulting in a multi-platform core) or it was abandoned.

Platform reduction allows considerable control over the form of the flake product as removals can be carefully positioned, and typically result in blanks that are broader and thicker than those produced by bipolar percussion. Many of these flakes were utilised without adaptation, but others were retouched into scrapers, knives and edge retouched flakes.

12.6.3 Levallois and variant Levallois prepared platform reduction

Classic late Neolithic 'Levallois' reduction involves the careful preparation of a small discoidal core with a domed upper surface from which a single Levallois flake is struck from a finely facetted platform. Only two flints from Stonehall Farm – a core trimming flake and a chisel arrowhead manufactured on a Levallois flake – attest to the use of this reduction technique. The occurrence of a chisel arrowhead manufactured on a Levallois flake may, however, indicate that Levallois reduction was only employed to manufacture selected artefact types. Late Neolithic Levallois reduction techniques exhibit a broad geographic spread across Britain, first appearing in association with Impressed wares in Scotland and Peterborough wares in England but continuing into the 3rd millennium cal BC with Grooved ware associations (Edmonds 1995).

Although classic Levallois reduction was uncommon, a distinctive variant of Levallois reduction, most readily identified by the presence of a finely facetted butt, was observed in the late Neolithic structures at Stonehall Farm and Crossiecrown; residual examples were also recorded at Stonehall Knoll and the Brae of Smerquoy. No cores or debitage relating to this reduction technique were present and considering that 12 of 31 facetted butt artefacts are retouched tools (two knives, eight scrapers, a petit tranchet arrowhead and an unclassifiable fragmentary flaked tool) it is probable that this specialised manufacturing technique was undertaken at another location.

Aspects of the reduction strategy can be reconstructed from the artefacts recovered. Firstly, it is clear that a core face was prepared by the removal of three parallel flakes, possibly with additional removals from the sides and distal end of the core. A strong striking platform was then established by removing two adjacent flakes from the ridges created by the three removals forming the face. The platform was then facetted, creating clearly isolated 'noses' in the middle and at both sides of the platform. The middle flake was then removed, probably by hard hammer percussion, and if correctly struck a broad double-ridged flake/scraper blank was removed. Flakes were then removed from each side of the cores:

these are typically narrower than the central flakes, but make good blanks for knives. The core could then be re-facetted and further removals made, indicating that this is likely to represent a repetitive reduction strategy. This technique is not entirely dissimilar to a 'Levallois-like' technique from Stoneyhill, Peterhead, Aberdeenshire, but the unusual crested and lateral blades argued to form part of that reduction sequence are not part of the Orcadian reduction technique that we have seen thus far (Ballin 2011).

12.7 Wideford Hill

Excavations at Wideford Hill in 2002 and 2003 yielded 224 flaked artefacts of flint and 15 of milky quartz (Table 12.7). In addition, nine small unworked pebbles of flint and two of milky quartz were recovered. The largest quartz and flint pebbles (16.7g and 4.5g, respectively) may have been imported as raw materials, but the other unworked pebbles are too small to knap and may represent natural occurrences from the local glacial till.

The lithic assemblage is exclusively early Neolithic, with the notable exception of four residual artefacts that date from the later Mesolithic. The latter comprise an obliquely truncated blade (Fig. 12.1.1), which would be classed as an obliquely blunted point if the bulbar end had been removed, two bladelets and a unifacial crested bladelet. These artefacts are readily distinguished from the Neolithic flintwork as they exhibit punctiform butts, fine abrasion on their platform edges and clearly derive from a blade-orientated industry.

The Neolithic assemblage is dominated by bipolar reduction, but a reasonable component of platform reduction was also observed. The latter flakes typically exhibit plain platforms and were stuck using both hard and soft hammer percussors without preparation of the platform edge. All stages of core reduction are present in the assemblage, including unworked raw materials, split pebbles that could be reduced further or modified into tools and 12 exhausted cores (*e.g.* Figs 12.1.2 and 12.1.3). The presence of numerous chips (flakes with a maximum dimension of 10mm or less) demonstrate that flint knapping was undertaken and a concentration of 19 chips on the rammed stone surface [002] indicates either *in situ* knapping or the dumping of knapping waste. Three retouch chips were noted, indicating the production of simple flake tools, such as scrapers or knives, while two refitting flakes from a polished implement (from rammed surface [002] and adjacent drain fill [022]) indicate the reduction or re-working of

Table 12.7 The struck lithic assemblage from Wideford Hill by artefact type and raw material.

Artefact type	Beach pebble flint		Glacial till flint		Unclassified flint		Milky quartz		Total No.	Total %
	No.	%	No.	%	No.	%	No.	%		
Flake	17	18.7%	3	42.9%	37	27.4%	4	23.5%	61	24.4%
Blade-like flake	1	1.1%			1	0.7%			2	0.8%
Bladelet	3	3.3%			5	3.7%			8	3.2%
Bipolar flake	25	27.5%			16	11.9%			41	16.4%
Bipolar blade	1	1.1%				0.0%			1	0.4%
Chip	6	6.6%			38	28.1%	3	17.6%	47	18.8%
Irregular waste	5	5.5%	2	28.6%	6	4.4%			13	5.2%
Crested blade					1	0.7%			1	0.4%
Flake from ground implement					2	1.5%			2	0.8%
Tested nodule/bashed lump							2	11.8%	2	0.8%
Split pebble (bipolar)	1	1.1%					6	35.3%	7	2.8%
Single platform flake core	1	1.1%			1	0.7%			2	0.8%
Multiplatform flake core	1	1.1%				0.0%			1	0.4%
Bipolar flake core	6	6.6%	1	14.3%	1	0.7%			8	3.2%
Bipolar blade core					1	0.7%			1	0.4%
Unworked pebble	1	1.1%			8	5.9%	2	11.8%	11	4.4%
Leaf arrowhead (kite-shaped)					1	0.7%			1	0.4%
End scraper	10	11.0%			5	3.7%			15	6.0%
Side scraper	1	1.1%	1	14.3%	3	2.2%			5	2.0%
Double-side scraper	1	1.1%							1	0.4%
End and side scraper	3	3.3%			1	0.7%			4	1.6%
End and side scraper (D-shaped)	2	2.2%							2	0.8%
Disc scraper					1	0.7%			1	0.4%
Other scraper	1	1.1%				0.0%			1	0.4%
Unclassifiable scraper					1	0.7%			1	0.4%
Single-edged knife	1	1.1%							1	0.4%
Cortex-backed knife	3	3.3%							3	1.2%
Plano-convex knife					1	0.7%			1	0.4%
Plano-convex knife (two phase retouch)					1	0.7%			1	0.4%
Symmetric pointed knife (narrow)					1	0.7%			1	0.4%
Edge retouched flake	1	1.1%				0.0%			1	0.4%
Notched flake					1	0.7%			1	0.4%
Truncated flake/blade (microlith)					1	0.7%			1	0.4%
Unclassifiable retouched flake tool					1	0.7%			1	0.4%
Grand Total	91	100%	7	100%	135	100%	17	100%	250	100%

other tools. In addition to artefacts manufactured on site, many of the larger flakes and tools appear to have been imported as finished artefacts or blanks of distinctive raw materials. These include the largest six flints that range from 36mm to 44mm in length (four knives, an end and side scraper, a flake of glacial flint and a piece of glacial flint irregular waste).

Retouched tools are particularly numerous, forming 21.9% of the assemblage excluding chips, but comprise a limited range of tools. The total is overwhelmingly dominated by 30 scrapers (Figs 12.1.4–12.1.7), with only seven knives (Figs 12.1.8–12.1.11) and single examples of an edge retouched flake, notched flake, kite-shaped leaf arrowhead (Fig. 12.1.12); one retouched flake tool was not classifiable. The scrapers are predominately manufactured on bipolar flakes (eight on cortical bipolar flakes) and all have dimensions between 15mm and 25mm, with the exception of two large examples (Figs 12.1.4 and 12.1.5). Four scrapers exhibit invasive scars on their ventral surfaces and three of these scrapers exhibit spurs on

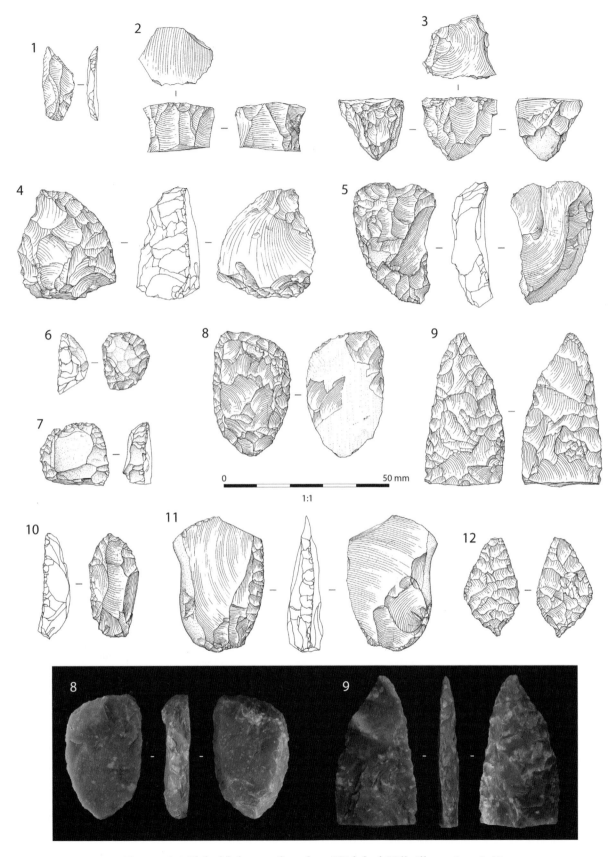

Figure 12.1 Flaked lithic artefacts from Wideford Hill. Illustrations 1–12.

the corner of the scraping edge (rammed stone surface [002] SFs 225, 304, 325 and context [005] SF 63, see Figs 12.1.1 and 12.1.4). The seven knives comprise four simple forms (three cortex backed, see Fig. 12.1.11, one single edge), a narrow symmetric pointed form (Fig. 12.1.10) and two fine plano-convex knives. The finest plano-convex knife (Fig. 12.8) exhibits low angle, fully invasive flaking across its ventral surface, with a bi-convex D-shaped form created by the application of semi-abrupt retouch around the artefact's perimeter. The flat 'plano' surface has been formed by invasive flaking that has been ground and polished. Several fine plano-convex knives from Orkney exhibit 'two phases' of retouch on the ventral surface, including examples from Braes of Ha'Breck, Wyre, Ness of Brodgar, Mainland and the Sourin Valley, Rousay. This pattern of retouch may be the product of intentional design, but equally it may result from the re-working or re-sharpening of large fine knives over their use-life. The chronology of this knife has yet to be defined, but securely stratified examples have only been found on early Neolithic sites. The second plano-convex knife (Fig. 12.1.9) is broken but exhibits many technological similarities to the former example, although it lacks the secondary semi-abrupt retouch around its perimeter. The dorsal surface exhibits fully invasive retouch and the 'plano' surface has been flaked flat, although not polished. The knife, although broken, appears to have been of an elongated bi-convex D-shaped form.

12.8 Knowes of Trotty

Thirty-five flint artefacts weighing 39.4g were recovered from Trench B and two chips weighing 0.1g were recovered from Trench F. Flint artefacts were retrieved in small numbers from various archaeological contexts, with the majority relating to the Neolithic structure in Trench B (Tables 12.8 and 12.9). The cortex, where present, was beach worn indicating that raw material was obtained from beach deposits in the form of small sub-rounded pebbles.

The majority, if not all, of the lithic assemblage was produced by bipolar reduction. On-site flint knapping is attested to by the presence of a split pebble, three small exhausted bipolar cores and eleven chips. Three chips from hearth deposit [082] probably originate from the same core. Despite the limited size of the assemblage, four retouched artefacts were recovered indicating tools form a significant component of the assemblage (*c*.16%, excluding chips). The tools comprise three scrapers and

an edge-retouched bipolar flake, but two of the scrapers are broken and none of the tools are intrinsically datable. Five of the artefacts were burnt, of which three were from context [238], and eleven were broken.

This is a small assemblage likely to result from the knapping of local flint. It comprises material from both the manufacture and use of flint tools, but the small number of pieces suggests that lithic waste was not allowed to accumulate in the Neolithic structure in any quantity.

12.9 Brae of Smerquoy

A small assemblage of 78 struck flints and one unworked flint pebble was recovered from excavations at the Brae of Smerquoy in 2013 (Table 12.10). The greater part of the lithic assemblage dates from the early Neolithic and was recovered from stratified deposits associated with the stone structure, but some late Neolithic activity is indicated by the presence of a petit tranchet derivative arrowhead and a flake with a facetted butt in the topsoil and a late phase deposit [007], respectively. These lithics concur with the presence of a broken polished macehead (SF 29) from clay blocking the Smerquoy Hoose entrance and the late Neolithic radiocarbon dates from pits cut into internal upper occupation deposits (see Chapter 10). Given the limited nature of the excavations, particularly of the associated occupation deposits, caution should be exercised before using artefact densities or assemblage size as a reliable basis for comparison with other sites.

The vast majority of flakes were produced by bipolar or anvil reduction techniques. Only 13 flints were platform struck, with 12 examples struck from plain platforms and one from a dihedral platform. Platform-edges were not prepared and no core rejuvenation flakes were present. The majority of artefacts were of small proportions with only four flints exceeding 40mm; the largest artefact is a plano-convex knife measuring 60.3mm.

Nine retouched artefacts are present, representing 12.2% of the assemblage, excluding chips. These artefacts comprise a plano-convex knife, a single edge knife, two edge retouched flakes (one of which is slightly denticulated), four scrapers, and a petit tranchet derivative arrowhead (see Figs 12.2.13–12.2.17). The scrapers are of small proportions with maximum dimensions between 17.6mm and 22.8mm. Two of the scrapers were manufactured on bipolar flakes (one of which was a cortical flake), while one was manufactured on a soft hammer platform struck flake and the other was on an indeterminate blank. The platform struck scraper was recovered from topsoil and is of late

Table 12.8 The struck lithic assemblage from Knowes of Trotty by artefact type and raw material.

Artefact type	Beach pebble flint No.	%	Unclassified flint No.	%	Total No.	Total %
Flake	2	25.0%	4	14.3%	6	16.7%
Bipolar flake	4	50.0%	5	17.9%	9	25.0%
Chip			11	39.3%	11	30.6%
Irregular waste			2	7.1%	2	5.6%
Split pebble (bipolar)	1	12.5%			1	2.8%
Bipolar flake core	1	12.5%	2	7.1%	3	8.3%
Side scraper			1	3.6%	1	2.8%
Unclassifiable scraper			2	7.1%	2	5.6%
Edge retouched flake			1	3.6%	1	2.8%
Grand Total	8	100%	28	100%	36	100%

Table 12.9 The flint assemblage from the Knowes of Trotty by trench, context and artefact type.

Artefact type	6	8	80	82	99	121	130	220	224	238	249	293	311	312	323	Trench F 99	Grand Total
Flake	1	1		1				1			1				1		6
Bipolar flake	1	2				1	1	2		2							9
Bipolar flake core	1									2							3
Chip	1	1		3				1		3						2	11
Split pebble			1														1
Irregular waste											1	1					2
Edge retouched flake														1			1
Side scraper	1																1
Unclassifiable scraper	1												1				2
Grand Total	6	4	1	3	1	1	1	3	1	7	2	1	1	1	1	2	36

Table 12.10 The struck lithic assemblage from the Brae of Smerquoy by artefact type and raw material.

Artefact type	Beach pebble flint No.	%	Glacial till flint No.	%	Unclassified flint No.	%	Milky quartz No.	%	Total No.	Total %
Flake	10	31.3%	2	66.7%	20	46.5%			32	40.5%
Bladelet	1	3.1%							1	1.3%
Bipolar flake	12	37.5%	1	33.3%	8	18.6%			21	26.6%
Bipolar blade	1	3.1%							1	1.3%
Chip					4	9.3%			4	5.1%
Irregular waste	1	3.1%			4	9.3%			5	6.3%
Split pebble (bipolar)	2	6.3%							2	2.5%
Bipolar flake core	1	3.1%			2	4.7%			3	3.8%
Unworked pebble							1	100%	1	1.3%
Petit tranchet derivative arrowhead					1	2.3%			1	1.3%
End scraper	2	6.3%							2	2.5%
Side scraper	1	3.1%							1	1.3%
End and side scraper					1	2.3%			1	1.3%
Single-edged knife	1	3.1%							1	1.3%
Plano-convex knife (two phase retouch)					1	2.3%			1	1.3%
Edge retouched flake					2	4.7%			2	2.5%
Grand Total	32	100%	3	100%	43	100%	1	100%	79	100%

Figure 12.2 Flaked lithic artefacts from the Brae of Smerquoy. Illustrations 13–17.

Neolithic date. The plano-convex knife is comparatively crudely manufactured and may represent an unfinished blank, but exhibits a flat invasively flaked 'plano' surface and two phases of retouch on its dorsal surface (Fig. 12.2.13). The earliest retouch on the dorsal surface is fully invasive, while the secondary retouch is semi-abrupt and forms an asymmetric point with one straight side and one convex side. The other edge is a rough cortical surface, indicating the artefact was manufactured from flint from the glacial till. This knife can be paralleled with examples from Wideford Hill, considered above.

12.10 Stonehall Knoll

Excavations at Stonehall Knoll (Trench C) recovered 339 struck lithic artefacts, one unworked 34.3g pebble of glacial till flint that was probably imported as raw material and two unworked quartz pebbles (Table 12.11). The vast majority of these artefacts derive from early Neolithic occupation, but a few pieces of flintwork from the topsoil and late deposits date from the late Neolithic. The diagnostic late Neolithic artefacts comprise an end

scraper and a flake that exhibit facetted butts (topsoil [400] and rubble [1021]) and a 'Stonehall Farm type' end scraper with invasive scars on its ventral surface (rubble [427]; see Fig. 12.3.28).

Like other early Neolithic assemblages, the vast majority of lithics were produced by bipolar or anvil percussion (see Fig. 12.3.18). Only 23 flakes were platform struck and the majority of these removals were from plain (18 examples) or cortical platforms (4 examples); only one dihedral platform was recorded. The dominance of bipolar reduction is further demonstrated through the presence of 17 bipolar cores and only one single platform core (see Figs 12.3.19–12.3.21). The cores, which weigh between 4.5g and 12g, are fully exhausted and their presence alongside 67 chips indicate that flint knapping debitage represents an important component of the assemblage. Moreover, the presence of ten definite and possible retouch chips indicates the production of simple flake tools. The lithics at Stonehall Knoll are typically of small proportions with only the unworked flint pebble, a flint knife and a piece of rhyolite measuring more than 40mm.

Twenty-nine retouched tools were recovered from

Table 12.11 The struck lithic assemblage from Stonehall Knoll by artefact type and raw material.

Artefact type	Beach pebble flint		Glacial till flint		Unclassified flint		Milky quartz		Rhyolite		Total No.	Total %
	No.	%	No.	%	No.	%	No.	%	No.	%		
Flake	33	25.0%	1	20.0%	77	39.5%			3	50.0%	114	33.3%
Bladelet	1	0.8%			2	1.0%					3	0.9%
Bipolar flake	48	36.4%	1	20.0%	28	14.4%			1	16.7%	78	22.8%
Bipolar blade	2	1.5%			3	1.5%					5	1.5%
Chip	7	5.3%			58	29.7%	2	50.0%			67	19.6%
Irregular waste	10	7.6%			11	5.6%			2	33.3%	23	6.7%
Split pebble (bipolar)	2	1.5%									2	0.6%
Single platform flake core	1	0.8%									1	0.3%
Bipolar flake core	9	6.8%			8	4.1%					17	5.0%
Unworked pebble			1	20.0%			2	50.0%			3	0.9%
End scraper	12	9.1%	1	20.0%	2	1.0%					15	4.4%
Side scraper					4	2.1%					4	1.2%
Double-end scraper	1	0.8%									1	0.3%
End and side scraper	1	0.8%									1	0.3%
Disc scraper	1	0.8%									1	0.3%
Cortex-backed knife	1	0.8%			1	0.5%					2	0.6%
Other knife			1	20.0%							1	0.3%
Edge retouched flake	2	1.5%									2	0.6%
Unclassifiable retouched flake tool	1	0.8%			1	0.5%					2	0.6%
Grand Total	132	100%	5	100%	195	100%	4	100%	6	100%	342	100%

the excavations, but these represent only 10.7% of the assemblage excluding chips; the lowest proportion of tools for any of the excavated sites. The range of flint tools is also limited, with 22 scrapers, 3 knives, 2 flakes with slight abrupt retouch and 2 broken unclassifiable flake tools. Twenty of the scrapers were on bipolar flakes (see Figs 12.3.22–12.3.26), of which 15 were cortical flake blanks (see Figs 12.3.22–12.3.24), and with the exception of one kite-shaped form (and excluding the later 'Stonehall Farm type' end scraper mentioned above) the scrapers were of rounded or oval forms, lacking spurs. The scrapers are typically of small proportions ranging in size from 15.4mm to 25.7mm, with the exception of two larger examples with maximum dimensions of 32.9mm and 39.2mm respectively (Figs 12.3.25–12.3.26). The knives comprise two simple cortex backed forms and a simple edge retouched knife manufactured on an irregular tabular piece of glacial till measuring 56.2mm long by 44.4mm wide and 13mm thick.

12.11 Stonehall Meadow

Excavations at Stonehall Meadow (Trenches A and Z) yielded a small assemblage comparable to Stonehall Knoll,

Brae of Smerquoy and Wideford Hill. In total, 207 struck lithic artefacts were recovered along with one beach pebble flint that was probably imported as raw material; 11 small milky quartz pebbles probably derive from local glacial till deposits and are of no significance (Table 12.12). The lithics form a coherent early Neolithic assemblage with the exception of a possibly late Neolithic 'Stonehall Farm type' end scraper from a ditch that bisects the site and a blade, a bladelet and a blade-like flake that derive from a blade-orientated industry, probably of Mesolithic date. The blade and the blade-like flake exhibit slight platform edge abrasion and lipped bulbar scars consistent with soft hammer percussion; the butt on the bladelet is missing. The blade-like flake exhibits dorsal blade scars that indicate it was stuck from an opposed platform blade core.

As with Stonehall Knoll, the majority of the struck lithics were produced by bipolar or anvil reduction (see Fig. 12.4.29). Only eight flakes and one edge retouched flake were struck from platform cores; all exhibit plain platforms. The presence of eleven bipolar cores and one single platform flake core (Fig. 12.4.30) further confirms the prevalence of bipolar reduction and combined with the presence of many chips and pieces of irregular waste indicates the presence of flint knapping debitage in the

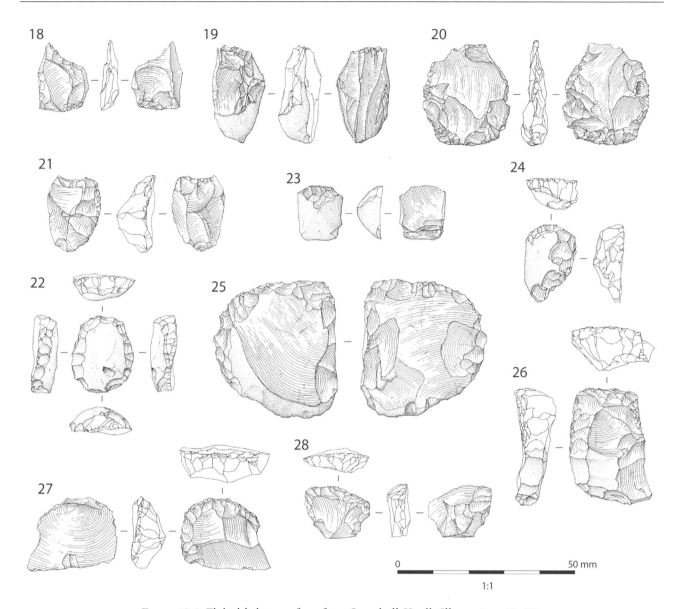

Figure 12.3 Flaked lithic artefacts from Stonehall Knoll. Illustrations 18–28.

assemblage. The lithics are typically of small proportions with only five artefacts exceeding 40mm; the largest artefact is a bipolar flake measuring 45.8mm.

Twenty-seven retouched artefacts were present, forming 15.2% of the assemblage excluding chips, but only a limited range of artefacts were recovered. Scrapers were the most common retouched tool (17 examples), followed by knives (5 examples) and minimally edge retouched flakes (2 examples); three fragmentary flake tools were unclassifiable. Nine of the scrapers were manufactured on bipolar flakes and one was manufactured on a bipolar core (Fig. 12.4.31); excluding the late Neolithic example from the ditch, none of the scrapers were definitively

manufactured on platform struck flakes. Four scrapers were manufactured on cortical bipolar flakes and a further six scrapers were manufactured on partly cortical flakes. The majority of scrapers were sub-circular in outline with maximum dimensions of 17.6mm to 33.8mm (with the exception of one well used scraper measuring 42.8mm long that was recovered as an unstratified find). One scraper exhibited spurs on the left and right corners of the scraping edge, the latter enhanced by a slight removal on the ventral surface (orthostat cut [3057], fill [3058], SF 7187). Only one other scraper exhibited a spur (topsoil, SF 1304) and another exhibited limited removals on its ventral surface (context [3031], SF 7098). The presence of

Table 12.12 The struck lithic assemblage from Stonehall Meadow by artefact type and raw material.

Artefact type	Beach pebble flint		Glacial till flint		Unclassified flint		Milky quartz		Beach pebble quartzite		Total No.	Total %
	No.	%	No.	%	No.	%	No.	%	No.	%		
Flake	18	24.3%	1	20.0%	43	33.9%					62	28.3%
Blade-like flake			1	20.0%							1	0.5%
Blade					1	0.8%					1	0.5%
Bladelet					1	0.8%					1	0.5%
Bipolar flake	27	36.5%	1	20.0%	20	15.7%					48	21.9%
Bipolar blade					3	2.4%					3	1.4%
Bipolar 'orange-segment' flake									1	100%	1	0.5%
Chip	1	1.4%			28	22.0%					29	13.2%
Irregular waste	7	9.5%			9	7.1%	1	8.3%			17	7.8%
Flake from ground implement					2	1.6%					2	0.9%
Split pebble (bipolar)	3	4.1%									3	1.4%
Single platform flake core					1	0.8%					1	0.5%
Bipolar flake core	6	8.1%			4	3.1%					10	4.6%
Bipolar blade core	1	1.4%									1	0.5%
Unworked pebble	1	1.4%					11	91.7%			12	5.5%
End scraper	6	8.1%			5	3.9%					11	5.0%
Side scraper	2	2.7%	1	20.0%	1	0.8%					4	1.8%
End and side scraper					1	0.8%					1	0.5%
Disc scraper			1	20.0%							1	0.5%
Cortex-backed knife	1	1.4%									1	0.5%
Plano-convex knife					1	0.8%					1	0.5%
Symmetric pointed knife (narrow)					1	0.8%					1	0.5%
Other knife					1	0.8%					1	0.5%
Unclassifiable fragmentary knife					1	0.8%					1	0.5%
Edge retouched flake					2	1.6%					2	0.9%
Unclassifiable retouched flake tool	1	1.4%			2	1.6%					3	1.4%
Grand Total	74	100%	5	100%	127	100%	12	100%	1	100%	219	100%

spurs and ventral scars may be significant as these features are not present in the Stonehall Knoll assemblage, but are common in late Neolithic assemblages (*e.g.* Stonehall Farm and Ness of Brodgar). The knives recovered comprise the tip of a narrow symmetrical form, a cortex backed form, a sub-rectangular form with rotor retouch (other knife), a crude plano-convex form and an unclassifiable fragment. The plano-convex knife is a poor example of the type as fully invasive flaking is confined to only one part of the dorsal surface (Fig. 12.4.32). The artefact may originally have been a bi-convex D-shape, but the distal end is broken and the edge is damaged by use or the application of irregular retouch (context [034], SF 1241).

12.12 Stonehall Farm

The excavations at Stonehall Farm (Trenches B, E and F) yielded a substantial assemblage of 949 struck flints, one piece of burnt unworked flint and 14 unworked pebbles (Tables 12.13 and 12.14). The latter comprise six flint pebbles that were probably imported as raw materials and eight small quartz pebbles that probably originate from the local glacial till and are of no consequence. The lithic assemblage includes both early and late Neolithic flintwork, however, detailed phasing was not available during the analysis and it has only been possible to identify late Neolithic contexts when diagnostic artefacts and/or technological attributes are present. This is not entirely satisfactory as it is not possible to clearly define assemblages and technological differences relating to specific structures present in the trench. The description of this assemblage is therefore generic, but includes contextual information, where available. Two crested blades, probably dating from the Mesolithic were recovered from topsoil.

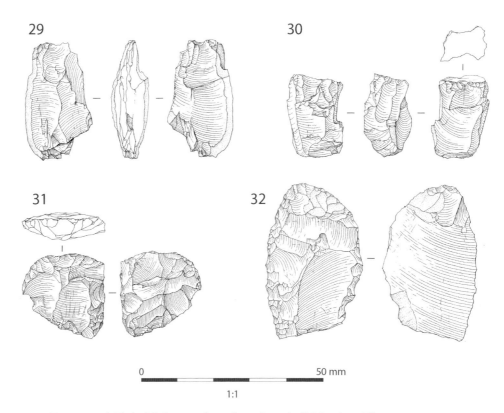

Figure 12.4 Flaked lithic artefacts from Stonehall Meadow. Illustrations 29–32.

12.12.1 Flakes and cores

Bipolar percussion was the most common reduction method, as demonstrated by the presence of numerous bipolar and anvil struck flakes (see Figs 12.5.33–12.5.35), 12 split pebbles and 40 bipolar cores (see Figs 12.5.36–12.5.41). Platform reduction was, however, more frequently observed in this assemblage compared to Stonehall Knoll and Meadow. Plain or dihedral platforms were recorded on 61 flakes and 23 retouched tools; 3 single platform (see Fig. 12.5.42) and 3 multi-platform flake cores were also recorded. Platform reduction was, however, almost entirely absent from Trench E, with the notable exception of the upper midden deposit [200]); this possibly reflects the presence of earlier Neolithic structures in this area. The presence of numerous cores and chips indicate that bipolar and platform flint knapping was probably undertaken on site; this is further supported by the identification of a refit between two bipolar flakes from upper midden contexts [800] and [822]. Nineteen chips and four small flakes can be classified as retouch chips, indicating the production or maintenance of simple edge-retouched tools, such as scrapers or knives.

Levallois and Levallois-variant prepared core reduction strategies also form a small but significant element of the assemblage. Classic Levallois discoidal core reduction is attested by the presence of a chisel arrowhead manufactured on a Levallois flake (Tr. E, Upper midden [2002], SF 4021; (see Fig. 12.6.63) and a preparation flake from the upper face of a discoidal core (Tr. B, context [303], SF 701). A distinctive unidirectional variation on Levallois reduction technique was, however, more commonly identified. This technique, which was commonly employed to produce blanks for scrapers and knives, is most readily identified by the presence of fine facetted butts. Facetted butts were recorded on 21 flints from Trenches B and E (Table 12.15). No Levallois or Levallois-style cores were present in the assemblage, raising the possibility that production occurred off site, possibly as a specialised industry.

As with other sites, the vast majority of artefacts measured less than 40mm. Only 27 artefacts (3.3% of the assemblage, excluding chips) have a maximum dimension over 40mm; the largest being a beach pebble flake measuring 95.5mm.

Table 12.13 The struck lithic assemblage from Stonehall Farm by artefact type and raw material.

Artefact type	Beach pebble flint		Glacial till flint		Unclassified flint		Milky quartz		Unclassified chert		Total No.	Total %
	No.	%	No.	%	No.	%	No.	%	No.	%		
Flake	92	32.4%	18	46.2%	223	35.6%	1	8.3%	1	50.0%	335	34.8%
Blade-like flake	1	0.4%	2	5.1%	4	0.6%					7	0.7%
Blade	1	0.4%	1	2.6%	1	0.2%					3	0.3%
Bladelet					6	1.0%					6	0.6%
Bipolar flake	77	27.1%	3	7.7%	79	12.6%					159	16.5%
Bipolar blade	3	1.1%			9	1.4%					12	1.2%
Chip	6	2.1%			130	20.7%					136	14.1%
Irregular waste	21	7.4%	5	12.8%	51	8.1%					77	8.0%
Crested blade					2	0.3%					2	0.2%
Trimming flake, Levallois style					1	0.2%					1	0.1%
Flake from ground implement					5	0.8%					5	0.5%
Tested nodule/bashed lump	1	0.4%	2	5.1%							3	0.3%
Split pebble (bipolar)	9	3.2%					3	25.0%			12	1.2%
Single platform flake core	3	1.1%									3	0.3%
Multiplatform flake core	1	0.4%			2	0.3%					3	0.3%
Bipolar flake core	23	8.1%	2	5.1%	13	2.1%					38	3.9%
Bipolar blade core					2	0.3%					2	0.2%
Unworked pebble	6	2.1%					8	66.7%			14	1.5%
Chisel arrowhead	1	0.4%			2*	0.3%					3	0.3%
End scraper	12	4.2%	2	5.1%	26	4.2%					40	4.1%
Side scraper	4	1.4%			4	0.6%					8	0.8%
End and side scraper			1	2.6%	4	0.6%					5	0.5%
Unclassifiable scraper	1	0.4%			4	0.6%					5	0.5%
Single-edged knife	6	2.1%			13	2.1%					19	2.0%
Cortex-backed knife	8	2.8%	2	5.1%	1	0.2%			1	50.0%	12	1.2%
Flake knife with limited edge retouch			1	2.6%	1	0.2%					2	0.2%
Rod-shaped knife					1	0.2%					1	0.1%
Symmetric pointed knife (narrow)					3	0.5%					3	0.3%
Asymmetric pointed knife	1	0.4%			2	0.3%					3	0.3%
Knife/scraper combination tool					2	0.3%					2	0.2%
Other knife					1	0.2%					1	0.1%
Unclassifiable fragmentary knife	1	0.4%			12	1.9%					13	1.3%
Edge retouched flake	4	1.4%			9	1.4%					13	1.3%
Notched flake					2	0.3%					2	0.2%
Piercer					1	0.2%					1	0.1%
Fabricator					1	0.2%					1	0.1%
Unclassifiable retouched flake tool	1	0.4%			10	1.6%					11	1.1%
Burnt unworked flint	1	0.4%									1	0.1%
Grand Total	284	100%	39	100%	627	100%	12	100%	2	100%	964	100%

* One manufactured on a Levallois flake blank.

12.12.2 Retouched tools

In total, 144 retouched tools were recovered, representing 17.7% of the assemblage, excluding chips. Scrapers represent the most common tool type (58 examples: Figs 12.5.43–12.5.50), although knives occur in almost equal numbers (56 examples: Figs 12.5.51–12.5.61). The range of other tools is limited, comprising flakes with minimal edge-retouch (11 examples: Fig. 12.5.62), three chisel arrowheads (Figs 12.6.63–12.6.65), two notched flakes, a piercer and the tip of a fabricator (strike-a-light); eleven fragmentary retouched flake tools were not classifiable. The scrapers can be divided into three broad

Table 12.14 The lithic assemblage from Stonehall Farm by Trench.

Artefact type	Trench B	Trench E	Trench F	Grand Total
Flake	264	62	8	334
Blade-like flake	5	2		7
Blade	3			3
Bladelet	5	1		6
Bipolar flake	110	41	8	159
Bipolar blade	8	4		12
Chip	109	26	1	136
Irregular waste	56	20	1	77
Crested blade	1	1		2
Trimming flake, Levallois style	1			1
Flake from ground implement	5	1		6
Tested nodule/bashed lump	3			3
Split pebble	10	2		12
Single platform flake core	3			3
Multiplatform flake core	3			3
Bipolar blade core	1	1		2
Bipolar flake core	34	4		38
Natural	13	1		14
Chisel arrowhead	2	1		3
Fabricator		1		1
End scraper	31	7	2	40
Side scraper	5	3		8
End and side scraper	3	2		5
Unclassifiable scraper	5			5
Cortex-backed knife	11	1		12
Single-edged knife	15	4		19
Flake knife with limited edge retouch	1	1		2
Symmetric pointed knife (narrow)	2		1	3
Asymmetric pointed knife	3			3
Rod-shaped knife	1			1
Other knife	1			1
Unclassifiable fragmentary knife	9	4		13
Knife/scraper combination tool	1	1		2
Edge retouched flake	9	4		13
Piercer		1		1
Notched flake		1	1	2
Unclassifiable retouched flake tool	10	1		11
Burnt unworked flint	1			1
Grand Total	**744**	**198**	**22**	**964**

* contexts: 400 and 1021. ** contexts: topsoil, 303, 305, 503, 510, 519, 643, 619, 800 and 806. † contexts: 2002 and 2015.

Table 12.15 Flints with facetted butts from Stonehall Knoll and Stonehall Farm.

	Stonehall Knoll	Stonehall Farm		Grand Total
Artefact type	*Tr. C**	*Tr. B***	*Tr. E†*	
Flake	1	10	1	12
Blade-like flake			1	1
Flake from ground implement		1		1
End scraper	1	5	1	7
Knife/scraper combination tool		1		1
Unclassifiable retouched flake tool		1		1
Grand Total	**2**	**17**	**4**	**23**

groups. The first group comprises 18 end or side scrapers with a convex retouched scraping edge on an otherwise unmodified flake. Where identifiable, these scrapers were manufactured on bipolar flakes, and in one case on a bipolar core; three of the flakes were cortical. These scrapers are comparable to the early Neolithic examples from Stonehall Knoll and Meadow and were recovered from topsoil and contexts [303], [614], [751], [800], [814], [2002], [2015] and [2050], of which context [809] is lower midden.

The second group of 34 scrapers are a distinctive 'Stonehall Farm' type that are symmetric, of squat proportions, with a regular convex scraping edge and straight, frequently retouched sides that taper towards a squared base (essentially they resemble a cupcake in cross-section). This group includes four examples manufactured on bipolar flakes, but these scrapers are more commonly manufactured from flakes with plain of dihedral butts struck from platform cores (6 examples) or facetted butts struck from Levallois-variant cores (6 examples); the base on other examples has been formed by a break. Spurs are common on the left and/or right distal corners of the scraping edges (14 examples) and invasive scars were frequently noted on the ventral surface of the scraper (17 examples); on ten scrapers the ventral removal helped form the spur. These scrapers were recovered from topsoil and midden contexts [303], [304], [510], [612], [643], [800], [809], [813], [822], [2002] and [2015]. A number of examples were recovered from floor contexts [619], [806], 858], and the fill [643] of the stone box in Structure 1. Another example came from the fill [2034] of a stone box in House 1.

This form of scraper and the presence of spurs and ventral scars can be directly paralleled in the lithic assemblage from the Ness of Brodgar, but more remarkably, parallels can noted between scrapers of an unusual and distinctive raw material present on both sites (a mottled dark brownish red flint with mottled beige inclusions, SF 2614, 6155 and 6374). The remaining group of scrapers are not readily classified as they are either fragmentary or atypical, for example an end and side scraper that may have been manufactured on a knife.

As noted above, knives are a common feature of the Stonehall Farm assemblage, however, most are comparatively simple unspecialised forms that exhibit retouch on only one edge, such as cortex backed knives (Figs 12.5.51 and 12.5.52) and single edge knives (Fig. 12.5.53). The narrow symmetric pointed knives (Fig. 12.5.54), asymmetric pointed knives (Fig. 12.5.55) and the rod-shaped knife (Fig. 12.5.56) are recognisable forms

that can be paralleled in other Neolithic assemblages, including the Ness of Brodgar. With the possible exception of one burnt and broken fragment (context [300], SF 207; Fig. 12.5.61), finely finished knives are notably absent from the Stonehall Farm assemblage. In relation to the overall assemblage, a large proportion of the knives are broken (27 of 56), but few are burnt (4).

The three arrowheads recovered are all classifiable as late Neolithic transverse chisel types. A particularly fine example manufactured on a Levallois flake (Tr. E, upper midden [2002], SF 4021; Fig. 12.6.63) survives as a burnt and broken fragment. The second chisel arrowhead is a comparatively simple form transversely manufactured on a partly cortical flake from a beach pebble by the application of semi-abrupt retouch along both sides and limited retouch on the ventral surface (Structure 1, upper floor/occupation [619], SF 6401; Fig. 12.6.64). The final example exhibits a slightly asymmetric butt but was reasonably well manufactured by the application of slightly invasive bifacial retouch along both sides. The blade edge, rather unusually, is formed by semi-abrupt retouch (topsoil, SF 2680; Fig. 12.6.65).

In addition to the complete tools, six flakes struck from polished stone implements were recovered. One flake exhibits a convex surface and may have been struck from close to the blade edge of a polished flint axe-head (context [800], SF 6078), but the other examples only possess limited areas of polish and it is unclear what form of artefact they were struck from.

12.12.3 Contextual analysis

The lithic assemblage from Stonehall Farm includes elements that can be paralleled in the early Neolithic assemblages at Stonehall Knoll, Stonehall Meadow and beyond, such as scrapers manufactured on bipolar blanks and certain knife forms. That said, the presence of artefacts manufactured from Levallois and Levallois-like cores including chisel arrowheads and distinctive 'Stonehall Farm type' scraper forms demonstrate that a good proportion of the assemblage dates from the late Neolithic. Some of these diagnostic late Neolithic artefacts derive from deposits relating to Structure 1. For example, two distinctive 'Stonehall Farm type' scrapers, a cortex backed knife and 14 bipolar and platform struck flakes and chips from the stone box deposit [643], and various artefacts noted above were recovered from floor and occupation deposits (*e.g.* [619] and [858]). However, at the time of writing in the absence of additional phasing information it is not possible to determine if a

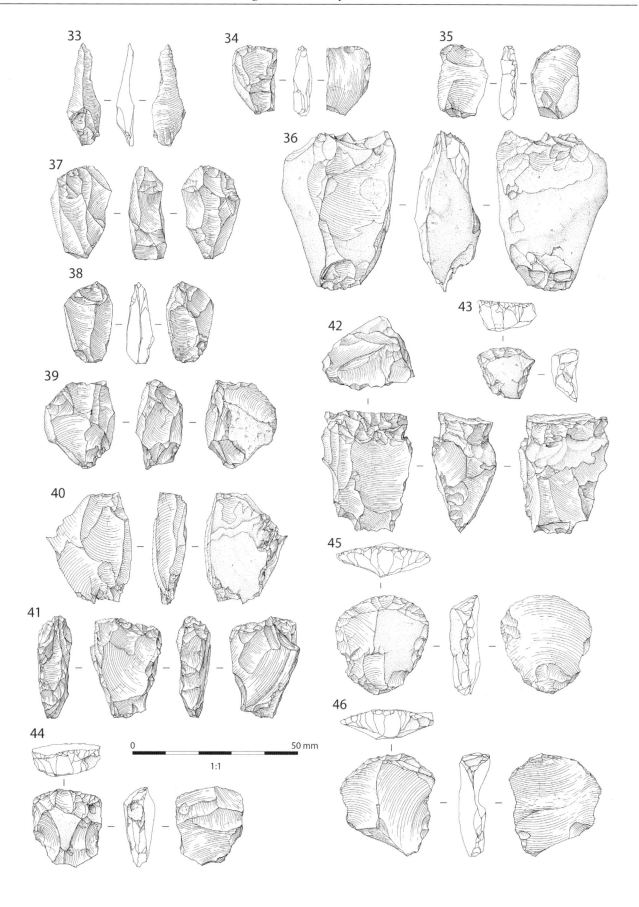

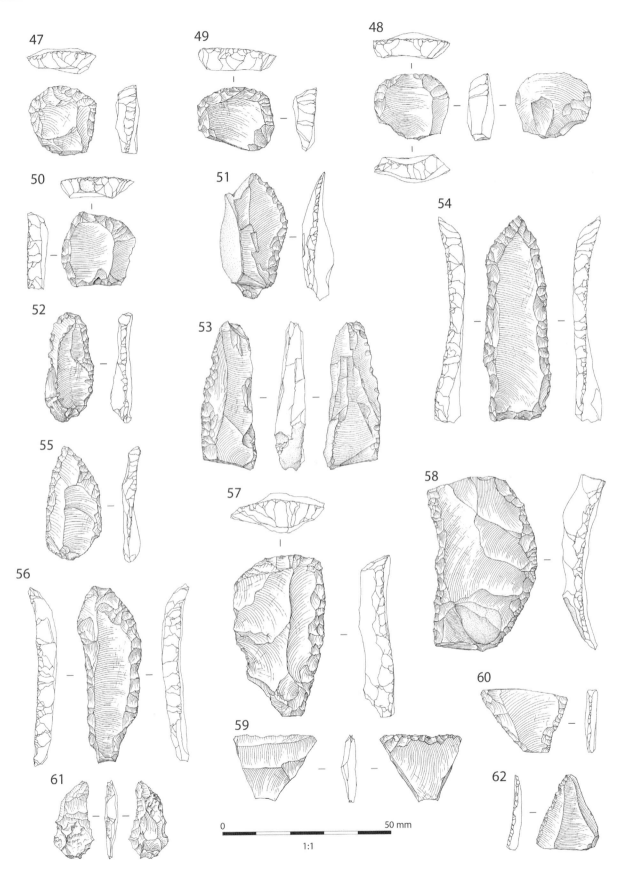

Figure 12.5 Flaked lithic artefacts from Stonehall Farm. Illustrations 33–62.

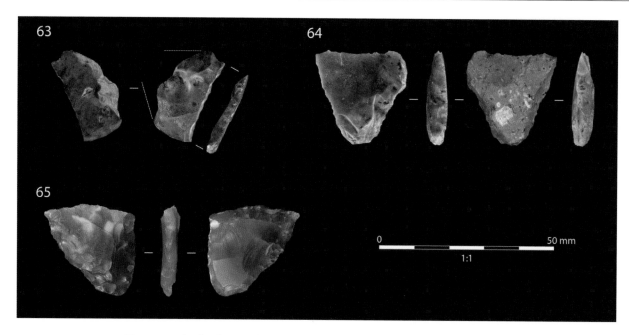

Figure 12.6 Chisel arrowheads from Stonehall Farm. Illustrations 63–65.

clearer distinction can be made between early and late Neolithic assemblages at Stonehall Farm.

12.13 Crossiecrown

Excavations at Crossiecrown yielded a substantial assemblage of 817 flaked lithics, 30 unworked pebbles and 2 pieces of burnt unworked flint (Table 12.16). Flint is the most common raw material, but this assemblage is notable for the presence of several artefacts of milky quartz, quartzite and black chert. The presence of two scrapers, a bipolar core and a flake of black chert is of particular significance as this material was not present in any other assemblage from sites examined around the Bay of Firth, yet represents a significant raw material in the late phases of Skara Brae on west Mainland. The presence of 23 imported but unworked flint beach pebble flints, weighing 1.2g–15.5g with maximum dimensions of 13.3mm–33.5mm, indicate that significant quantities of raw material were imported to the site. Five of the larger flint pebbles, weighing 5.7g–15.5g with maximum dimensions of 23.8–33.5mm, were recovered from an occupation deposit [010] in the recess of the Red House and one further pebble (2.2g with maximum dimension of 21.2mm) was recovered from the fill of an orthostat lined feature within the Red House [173].

The assemblage from Crossiecrown presents several analytical challenges. Over half of the assemblage was recovered from topsoil, and deposits dating to the early Neolithic, late Neolithic and early Bronze Age were all present. The lithic assemblage from the topsoil is clearly a palimpsest, a quality reflected in the presence of a leaf arrowhead and a tanged arrowhead, and it is likely that residual artefacts are present throughout the assemblage. A broad descriptive account is therefore presented below before detailed consideration of phased deposits.

12.13.1 Flakes and cores

Bipolar reduction is the dominant technique in the Crossiecrown assemblage, with many other flakes probably resulting from anvil reduction. All aspects of bipolar reduction are present, including 16 split flint beach pebbles, with maximum dimensions of 13.9g–39.5g, that could have been further reduced or modified into tools and 28 exhausted bipolar cores (Figs 12.7.66 and 12.7.67). Platform struck flakes are remarkable scarce and only one small single platform flake core was present. Facetted butts are also uncommon with only five examples present: a minimally facetted butt on a symmetric pointed knife (Red House construction layer [307], SF 496; Fig. 12.7.74) and four flakes (two from topsoil, Phase 4/5 middens [130] and [468].

12.13.2 Retouched tools

Retouched tools were exceptionally common with 159 recorded, representing 21.2% of the assemblage

Table 12.16: The struck lithic assemblage from Crossiecrown by artefact type and raw material.

Artefact type	Beach pebble flint		Glacial till flint		Unclassified flint		Milky quartz		Beach pebble quartzite		Black chert		Rhyolite		Total No.	Total %
	No.	%	No.	%	No.	%	No.	%	No.	%	No.	%	No.	%		
Flake	69	16.2%	10	38.5%	117	31.2%	2	14.3%			1	25.0%			199	23.4%
Blade-like flake					2	0.5%									2	0.2%
Blade					1	0.3%									1	0.1%
Bladelet	3	0.7%			3	0.8%									6	0.7%
Bipolar flake	191	44.9%	4	15.4%	73	19.5%	2	14.3%	2	50.0%					272	32.0%
Bipolar blade	3	0.7%			8	2.1%									11	1.3%
Bipolar 'orange-segment' flake							1	7.1%							1	0.1%
Chip	7	1.6%			59	15.7%	2	14.3%							68	8.0%
Irregular waste	22	5.2%	3	11.5%	20	5.3%							1	100%	46	5.4%
Flake from ground implement	1	0.2%			2	0.5%									3	0.4%
Tested nodule/bashed lump	1	0.2%			1	0.3%			1	25.0%					3	0.4%
Split pebble (bipolar)	16	3.8%					1	7.1%							17	2.0%
Single platform flake core					1	0.3%									1	0.1%
Bipolar flake core	20	4.7%			7	1.9%									27	3.2%
Bipolar blade core											1	25.0%			1	0.1%
Unworked pebble	23	5.4%					6	42.9%	1	25.0%					30	3.5%
Leaf arrowhead					1	0.3%									1	0.1%
Triangular arrowhead					2	0.5%									2	0.2%
B+T arrowhead (Ballyclare a)	1	0.2%			1	0.3%									2	0.2%
End scraper	30	7.1%	2	7.7%	26	6.9%					2	50.0%			60	7.1%
Side scraper	14	3.3%	3	11.5%	12	3.2%									29	3.4%
Double-end scraper	1	0.2%			1	0.3%									2	0.2%
Double-side scraper					1	0.3%									1	0.1%
End and side scraper	3	0.7%			8	2.1%									11	1.3%
End and side scraper (D-shaped)	1	0.2%			1	0.3%									2	0.2%
Disc scraper					1	0.3%									1	0.1%
Unclassifiable scraper	2	0.5%			4	1.1%									6	0.7%
Single-edged knife	1	0.2%	1	3.8%	2	0.5%									4	0.5%
Cortex-backed knife	8	1.9%	1	3.8%	2	0.5%									11	1.3%
Symmetric pointed knife (broad)					1	0.3%									1	0.1%
Symmetric pointed knife (narrow)					2	0.5%									2	0.2%
Asymmetric pointed knife					1	0.3%									1	0.1%
Unclassifiable fragmentary knife					1	0.3%									1	0.1%
Edge retouched flake	5	1.2%	2	7.7%	7	1.9%									14	1.6%
Piercer	1	0.2%													1	0.1%
Fabricator					1	0.3%									1	0.1%
Unclassifiable retouched flake tool					5	1.3%									5	0.6%
Misc. retouch					1	0.3%									1	0.1%
Burnt unworked flint	2	0.5%													2	0.2%
Grand Total	425	100%	26	100%	375	100%	14	100%	4	100%	4	100%	1	100%	849	100%

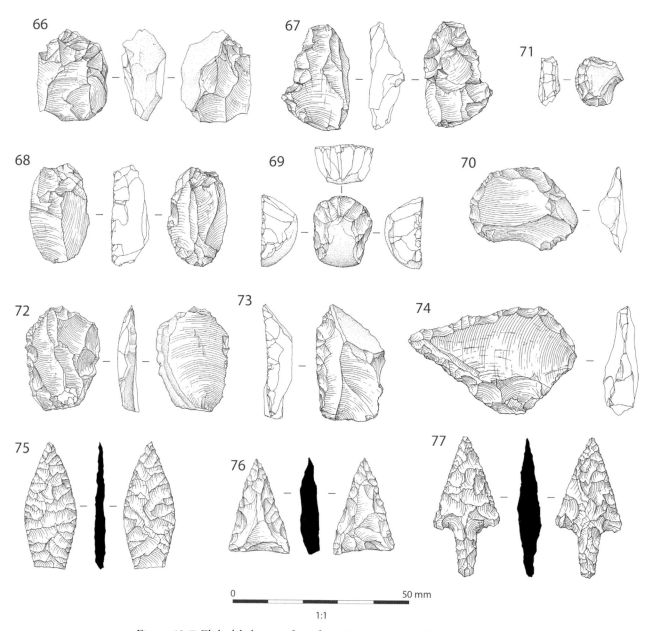

Figure 12.7 Flaked lithic artefacts from Crossiecrown. Illustrations 66–77.

excluding chips. Scrapers overwhelmingly dominate the tool assemblage (112 examples: Figs 12.7.68–12.7.71), but knives (20 examples: Figs 12.7.72–12.7.74), simple edge-retouched flakes (14 examples), arrowheads (5 examples: Figs 12.7.75–12.7.77; Figs 12.8.75–12.8.79), a well used rod-shaped fabricator (strike-a-light) and a piercer were also recorded. The arrowheads comprise a broken but exceptionally finely worked early Neolithic leaf-shaped arrowhead (Figs 12.7.75; Fig. 12.8.75), two triangular arrowheads that may represent blanks for barbed and tanged arrowheads (Fig. 12.7.76; Figs 12.8.76 and 12.8.78) and two early Bronze Age tanged arrowheads

of Green's (1980) Ballyclare type 'a' (Fig. 12.7.77; Figs 12.8.77 and 12.8.79).

The scrapers vary in form, but a few distinct types are present. The vast majority appear to have been manufactured on bipolar flakes by the application of convex retouched scraping edge on one side or end (Figs 12.7.68 and 12.7.70). Seven 'Stonehall Farm type' scrapers were noted, three of which exhibit spurs at on the left and/or right corner of the scraping edge and five exhibit scars on their ventral surface (Figs 12.9.80–12.9.6). These scrapers were recovered from topsoil (3 examples), an occupation layer in the Red House [011], a wall core of the Red

House [110], a phase 4/5 midden [180], and an occupation layer in the Grey House [450]. However, in contrast to Stonehall Farm, spurs (10 examples) and ventral scars (8 examples) were also present on more amorphous scraper forms. Two scrapers from the topsoil are finely retouched, possibly pressure flaked, and may represent early Bronze Age thumbnail forms (*e.g.* Fig. 12.7.69).

The knives from Crossiecrown are dominated by simple cortex backed and single edge forms (see Figs 12.7.72 and 12.7.73). Only four flake knives of refined forms were present. These comprise: two narrow symmetrical knives (topsoil and LN/EBA midden [002], SF 1031), a large broad symmetrical point knife manufactured from a distinctive orangey red flint (Red House construction layer [307], SF 496; Fig. 12.7.74) and an asymmetric pointed knife (topsoil). These knife forms are not closely datable, but the broad symmetric pointed knife exhibits a facetted butt and probably dates from the late Neolithic; parallels for this form can also be found at the Ness of Brodgar. Also notable is a fragmentary high quality knife of translucent mid orange brown flint, recovered from the topsoil. This has bifacial polish and was reworked into an end scraper; the original size and form of the implement is unclear. In addition, two of four flakes from polished artefacts were possibly struck from polished knives (topsoil and phase 4/5 midden [180]); none appeared to be from axe/adze-heads.

12.13.3 Stratigraphic discussion

The greater part of the assemblage was retrieved from topsoil but through the presence of diagnostic artefacts it is possible to demonstrate the presence of early Neolithic, late Neolithic and early Bronze Age flintwork. The unstratified 'debitage' component of the assemblage cannot be closely dated, but the dominance of bipolar reduction is notable as securely stratified early Neolithic assemblages, such as Wideford Hill, tend to have a higher prevalence of bipolar working. However, a measure of caution is needed here as bipolar working may be a feature of the early Bronze Age.

The stratified assemblage is presented by phase in Tables 12.17 and 12.18. Given the presence of sherds of Unstan Bowl, the 'early Neolithic' material in the Grey House (Phase 3 and 3a) is clearly redeposited and yielded a small and inconsequential assemblage without artefacts of note. The presence of a large broad symmetric pointed knife in the construction deposits for the Red House (Phase 4) is potentially significant as parallels for this artefact can be found at the Ness of Brodgar, but its stratigraphic position

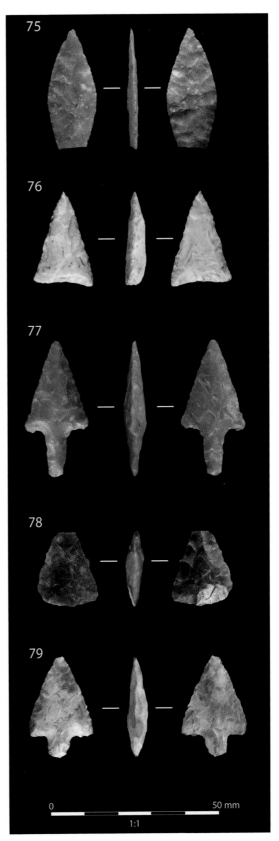

Figure 12.8 Arrowheads from Crossiecrown. Illustrations 75–79.

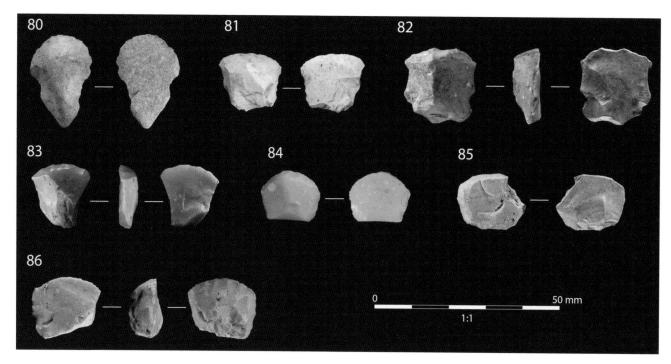

Figure 12.9 The 'Stonehall Farm-type' scrapers from Crossiecrown. Illustrations 80–86.

Table 12.17 The struck lithic assemblage from Crossiecrown Trench 1 by phase.

Flint category	LN/EBA Midden	6. Modern	Grand Total
Flake	18	51	69
Blade-like flake		1	1
Bladelet		4	4
Bipolar flake	33	76	109
Bipolar blade	2	2	4
Chip	2	32	34
Irregular waste	3	7	10
Flake from ground implement		1	1
Split pebble	3		3
Tested nodule/bashed lump		1	1
Bipolar flake core	3	9	12
Leaf arrowhead		1	1
End scraper	6	24	30
Side scraper	5	9	14
End and side scraper		5	5
Double-end scraper	1		1
Unclassifiable scraper		3	3
Cortex-backed knife	2	3	5
Single-edged knife	1		1
Symmetric pointed knife (narrow)	1	1	2
Piercer		1	1
Edge retouched flake	3	2	5
Unclassifiable retouched flake tool		1	1
Natural	3	10	13
Grand Total	**86**	**244**	**330**

only provides a *terminus ante quem* for manufacture and use. The occupation deposits in the Red House, which date from the second half of the 3rd millennium BC, yielded 61 flints including a broad range of flakes, cores and tools. Notably, the assemblage from the occupation deposits is broadly comparable to the assemblage recovered from the site as a whole. Levels of burning and breakage are, however, lower than the middens. The presence of a small cache of beach pebbles within a deposit in a niche [010] can be paralleled with the collection of much larger split nodules found at Barnhouse (Hill and Richards 2005, 171; Middleton 2005). No securely stratified early Bronze Age deposits were identified and the only intrinsically datable early Bronze Age artefacts were recovered from topsoil. It is, however, notable that a large number of Bronze Age stone bars and two ard points were recovered from midden deposits attributed to Phase 4/5 and Phase 5 (see Chapter 13). It is therefore likely that some of the flintwork in these phases also dates from the early Bronze Age, although it is not possible to distinguish this material from the Neolithic assemblage.

12.14 Ramberry

Excavations at Ramberry recovered five flaked flints. These comprise three chips, a flake and a piece of irregular waste (Table 12.19). The latter derives from

Table 12.18 *The struck lithic assemblage from Crossiecrown Trenches 2 and 3 by phase.*

Flint category	3. Grey house occupation	3a. Pre-red house	4. Red house: construction	4. Red house: use	4/5. contemporary with or post Red house	5. Post red house	LN?	6. Modern	Unphased	Grand Total
Flake	4	5	3	26	23	23	2	42	2	130
Blade-like flake			1							1
Bladelet					1			1		2
Blade								1		1
Bipolar flake	6	4	6	13	34	20		80		163
Bipolar blade		2	1	1	1			2		7
Bipolar 'orange-segment' flake				1						1
Chip	1			3	6	2		21	1	34
Irregular waste	4				4	5		23		36
Flake from ground implement					1			1		2
Split pebble	2				1	4		7		14
Tested nodule/bashed lump						1		1		2
Single platform flake core						1				1
Bipolar blade core								1		1
Bipolar flake core		1	1	1	2	4		5	1	15
Triangular arrowhead								2		2
B+T arrowhead (Ballyclare a)								2		2
Disc scraper								1		1
End scraper	1	2	3	2	4	3		15		30
Side scraper		1		4	2	3		5		15
Double-end scraper					1					1
Double-side scraper								1		1
End and side scraper					1	2		3		6
End and side scraper (D-shaped)								2		2
Unclassifiable scraper			1	1				1		3
Cortex-backed knife		1		1	2	2				6
Single-edged knife			1	1				1		3
Symmetric pointed knife (broad)						1				1
Asymmetric pointed knife								1		1
Unclassifiable fragmentary knife					1					1
Fabricator								1		1
Edge retouched flake				1	2	2	1	3		9
Misc. retouch								1		1
Unclassifiable retouched flake tool				1		1		2		4
Unworked pebble				6	5	3		3		17
Burnt unworked flint	1							1		2
Grand Total	19	16	17	61	91	77	3	231	4	519

Table 12.19 The struck lithic assemblage from Ramberry by artefact type and raw material.

Artefact type	Beach pebble flint		Unclassified flint		Total No.	Total %
	No.	%	No.	%		
Flake			1	25.0%	1	20.0%
Chip			3	75.0%	3	60.0%
Irregular waste	1	100%			1	20.0%
Grand Total	1	100%	4	100%	5	100%

a beach pebble. The flake (Trench 2, context [030] exhibits a plain butt indicating that it was struck from a platform core, but this reduction technique is not intrinsically datable. An early Bronze Age barbed and tanged arrowhead is reported to have been found in the same field as the excavation trenches (Nick Card pers. comm.), but this artefact was not available for analysis.

12.15 Discussion

The flaked lithic assemblage recovered from the excavations around the Bay of Firth provides a valuable opportunity to consider broad chronological changes in lithic technology in Orkney and patterns of contact within and beyond the archipelago. The ten residual Mesolithic artefacts from Wideford Hill, Stonehall Farm and Stonehall Meadow are of particular note as these add to the corpus of Mesolithic findspots in Orkney and potentially indicate that a low density scatter of Mesolithic artefacts may be present across much of Firth parish (Saville 2000). The artefacts are of little intrinsic interest, with the exception of an obliquely truncated blade, but the technological attributes identified on these flints are consistent with blade-orientated reduction from single and opposed platform blade cores. Blade production appears to have been initiated by the preparation and removal of a crested blade and subsequent blades appear to have been struck from a well abraded platform edge using a soft hammer percussor. These platform reduction techniques are characteristic of Mesolithic industries across much of Britain and while this may indicate long distance movement by hunters and gatherers, the technology is very persistent with a wide geographic and chronological spread.

In the absence of well dated, securely stratified, assemblages it is challenging to consider specific aspects of mobility and the temporality of occupation in Mesolithic Orkney. It is, however, notable that the predominantly bipolar reduction strategies of the early Neolithic represent a distinctly different technology to that of the Mesolithic artefacts recovered. Bipolar

reduction was also the dominant Neolithic flint working technique in the Hebrides (*e.g.* An Doirlinn, Pirie in prep.); a region that shares many common features with Orkney including funerary monuments and Unstan ware ceramics. From the current assemblages it is not yet possible to determine if this change in technique coincides with the arrival of other Neolithic practices and the appearance of domesticated animals and pottery; we have arguably yet to see the (well dated) earliest phases of the period anywhere on the archipelago. However, ongoing analysis of lithics from structures dating to the early 4th millennium cal BC at Links House, Stronsay may help to shed light on this question (Woodward 2008; Lee and Woodward 2009b).

The early Neolithic assemblages from Wideford Hill, Brae of Smerquoy, Stonehall Meadow and Stonehall Knoll are broadly comparable in technology, range of artefacts and types of raw materials present. As noted above, cores and flakes from the bipolar reduction of beach pebbles dominate the assemblage, with only a limited number of artefacts from platform reduction, the latter predominantly from single platform cores with plain platforms and unprepared platform edges. Retouched tools are relatively numerous on these sites, with scrapers representing by far the most common artefact. Each of the early Neolithic assemblages provides good evidence that small flint pebbles were imported whole or as split pebbles from beaches *c.*15–20km to the east of Mainland in Deerness or from more distant islands. The composition of each assemblage demonstrates complete core reduction sequences and the production of simple flake tools. In addition, a small number of flakes and tools, particularly knives, appear to have been imported to the site as blanks or finished artefacts. These artefacts are frequently among the largest in the assemblage and often manufactured from distinctive colours, including opaque orange red and orange brown. The source of these flints is probably within the archipelago, possibly the Northern Isles; ongoing fieldwork by two of the authors (HAW and ME) may refine the source of these raw materials. Plano-convex knives represent a notable feature of the early Neolithic assemblages, with two examples on imported materials found at Wideford Hill and another at the Brae of Smerquoy; a further possible fragmentary example was found at Stonehall Meadow. The two finest examples, both from Wideford Hill, were produced by a skilled knapper and display a level of expertise that is considerably higher than the rest of the flintwork. The other examples are of poorer workmanship, although they are manufactured on large flakes and follow a similar template. Ground and polished flint implements were not common in the early Neolithic assemblages and the only identifiable forms were partly polished knives; the presence of polish on the flat 'plano' surface of a plano-convex knife and two further refitting flakes probably struck from a fine knife from Wideford Hill are notable.

Stonehall Farm and Crossiecrown produced the bulk of the late Neolithic material reported here, with only a few residual artefacts recovered from other sites. The reduction strategies are broadly comparable to the early Neolithic, being dominated by bipolar reduction with limited platform reduction, but Levallois and Levallois variant techniques represent a significant addition to the knapping repertoire. The date at which Levallois techniques were first used in Orkney is unclear, but they derive from a widespread British flint working tradition first associated with Impressed wares/Peterborough wares. The Levallois variant technique most commonly used in the assemblages under consideration is peculiar to Orkney, although the technique shares some affinities with a 'Levallois-like' technique defined at Stoneyhill, Aberdeenshire (Ballin 2011). In Orkney, this Levallois variant technique is commonly used to produce blanks for scrapers from the central part of the core and blanks for knives from the left and right lateral flakes.

As with the early Neolithic, small beach pebbles were most frequently worked. A small cache of these pebbles was located in Structure 1 at Stonehall Farm and complete bipolar and platform knapping sequences were identified in this raw material, including retouch chips from the production of simple flake tools. However, only a limited number of flakes and tools produced by Levallois and Levallois variant reduction techniques are present, indicating that these were probably produced at another location. A number of large flakes, scrapers and knives, often of distinctive raw materials, are also likely to have been imported as finished tools or blanks; the latter includes scrapers of black chert probably from west Mainland, Orkney.

Retouched tools formed a significant component of the Stonehall Farm and late Neolithic phase contexts

at Crossiecrown, the range of forms dominated by scrapers, knives and simple edge retouched flakes. Unusually, at Stonehall Farm knives were almost as common as scrapers, but this pattern was not repeated at Crossiecrown where scrapers considerably outnumbered knives. These scrapers include a number of simple flake forms that are comparable to early Neolithic assemblages, but one distinctive type was only found in late Neolithic contexts. This has been termed the 'Stonehall Farm type' on account of its stratigraphic secure, well dated, associations. The form is also present in Grooved ware associated contexts at the Ness of Brodgar and examples manufactured from the same unusual raw materials have been identified at both sites. The vast majority of knives are simple forms manufactured on flakes that are comparable to examples found in early Neolithic assemblages. Plano-convex knives are notably absent from late Neolithic contexts, and no elaborate (including polished) forms were recovered from secure contexts.

Taken together, the Bay of Firth assemblages display a number of trends and characteristics that are worthy of note. To begin with, they give the lie to the often voiced assumption that Orkney was bereft of good, workable stone and that what there was tended to be worked with relatively low levels of skill. As with any assemblage, there is considerable variety here, both in terms of raw material selection and in technological choices. But it would be a caricature to describe this material in such dismissive terms. In fact, the material described here often reflects care in the selection of stone, even linking specific colours to particular artefact categories. Whether or not these links (*e.g.* between red/mottled flint and fine knives) was all about the colour, or was also linked to the relative sizes of parent nodules remains to be seen, but colour does seem to have been fastened upon and influential in the selection of material for different kinds of implement.

Of course, we are dealing here with material that has been brought to each site, most likely from beach or till deposits identified and visited at various locations across the archipelago. Some may have been obtained by various forms of direct procurement, others through varied transactions, from barter to more formal moments of exchange. Individual settlements did not stand in isolation, and it is likely that interaction at various scales, from the neighbourhood communities of the bay to wider networks of communication were mediated, to some degree, by the movement of stone and of artefacts themselves. Ongoing work on the character and distribution of nodules across the archipelago may yet help us to determine the scales over which different materials circulated. Even at this stage, we should certainly allow that materials might have been both 'local' and 'travelled', a potential evident at Skara Brae, where flint was worked alongside dark cherts of varied quality that are likely to have been found relatively close at hand. There, and no doubt in many other settings, stone flowed in a number of different ways and at a number of different scales.

It is also worth noting that whilst bipolar working is a commonplace, particularly in earlier material, it makes little sense to cast this as an unskilled response to small and intractable nodules. On the contrary, bipolar and anvil working requires considerable skill, and the pattern of flaking evidenced on all sites suggests that this was exercised to make the most of the material to hand, often with specific products in mind. The same is no less true of more specialised forms of reduction that are more apparent in later Neolithic contexts, among them Levallois-like core working and the concerted faceting of flake platforms. In short, much of the stoneworking reflected in these assemblages was highly structured, with systematic choices made throughout the various stages of different *chaînes opératoires*.

Another general point concerns the overall size of assemblages. On most sites, our topsoil finds say as much about the *longue durée* of activity in particular locales as they do about tools and tasks during the lifetimes of the excavated structures. And when we confine ourselves to those structures, the assemblage sizes are relatively small. This is interesting in its own right. On the one hand, it may reflect a general attitude towards good flint, a respect for stone that was paid by making as much of particular nodules as possible. This may well have been the case, but another possibility is that we are only seeing part of the picture. By prospecting for particular kinds of structure, principally those defined by stone walls, we necessarily focus in upon very particular kinds of dwelling. As noted elsewhere in this volume, this means that we may be missing other elements of the contemporary (and/ or earlier) settled environment, where structures were built in other materials such as timber. But there is a more basic problem here, at least so far as stonework is concerned. Because our 'windows' onto these sites are so closely tied to recognised structures, it remains possible, perhaps likely, that we are missing part of our picture. There is no *a priori* reason to suppose that all activities involving stone working took place within buildings nor even in their immediate environs. Equally, the deposition/discard of material might have also been at a scale beyond the limits of our trenches, something that the current sample does not allow us to explore. Here, it is worth noting the disparity between the highest density of surface flints and the main area of structural remains at Barnhouse (Richards 2005a, 17–21). A widening of focus, to consider stoneworking and the biographies of artefacts at a landscape scale, must be a priority for future research. Some, at least, of these questions are currently being explored as part of a review of all prehistoric Orcadian stone tool assemblages (by Hugo Anderson-Whymark, Mark Edmonds and Ann Clarke). The scale offered by that work will hopefully allow us to place the Bay of Firth material in that all important landscape context.

CHAPTER THIRTEEN

The Coarse Stone from Neolithic Sites around the Bay of Firth: Stonehall, Wideford Hill, Crossiecrown, Knowes of Trotty and Brae of Smerquoy

Ann Clarke

13.1 Stonehall

Throughout the three areas of Neolithic settlement examined at Stonehall, cobble tools of various types were in continuous use. Certainly within the excavated areas, Skaill knives do not appear to have been made or used, despite their common use at the nearby sites of Wideford Hill, Smerquoy and Crossiecrown. Neither do stone discs occur in any great quantity, again showing contrasts with the other sites within the Cuween-Wideford area. Significantly, these patterns of use are maintained between the early and late Neolithic occupation of the site revealing a certain consistency of stone tool production and the practices to which they relate (Fig. 13.1).

One notable difference between the early and later phases is the singular use of smoothers, grinding stones and grinding slabs in the earlier Neolithic at Stonehall Knoll and Stonehall Meadow. These items were found in both internal and external deposits and the concentration on the Knoll must indicate a manufacturing base within and around House 3. In contrast the Stonehall Farm late Neolithic settlement mound did not produce this array of tools. This disparity is most likely a chronological feature as accumulated evidence from Early Neolithic sites indicates an emphasis on the use of stone tools for grinding during this period in contrast to the lack of such tools in the later Neolithic phases (see below).

The unusual Structure 1 at Stonehall Farm is notable for its 'cleanliness' as the only stone tools found here were the cache in the cavity below the flagstone [645] (see Fig. 6.17). This collection of a fine quartz axe, a Knap of Howar grinder, and four fine knapping hammers together with the products of flint knapping clearly represents a special deposit. Another Knap of Howar grinder was found in the wall core deposits of this structure.

13.1.1 Artefact types

Axes (Total =10)

From Stonehall there are five complete axes, four broken across the width and one possible rough-out. Two of the axes are fine miniature examples (SFs 87 and 6410), the former made of micaceous mudstone and the latter a grey volcanic rock. Both are of a similar size and each has been ground all over to shape. The other small axe (SF 7035) is made of siltstone and a fresh break indicates it would originally have been a very light grey colour. It is quite stubby in form and given the multiple grinding facets on one face it was most likely reground from a larger axe fragment. Another fine piece is the quartz axe (SF 2658), which is part of the cache of objects in the floor of Structure 1, Stonehall Farm (see below). This unusual axe has been formed by flaking and grinding. Rough pecking and/or flaking is present on the butt end and sides whilst the blade end, though carefully ground, has a blunt, rounded edge; interestingly, this feature of deliberate blade blunting is shared with the other four known quartz axes in Orkney (Clarke 2011). The other complete axe (SF 2678) is also made of the grey volcanic rock and has been ground all over to a near polish. Some pecking

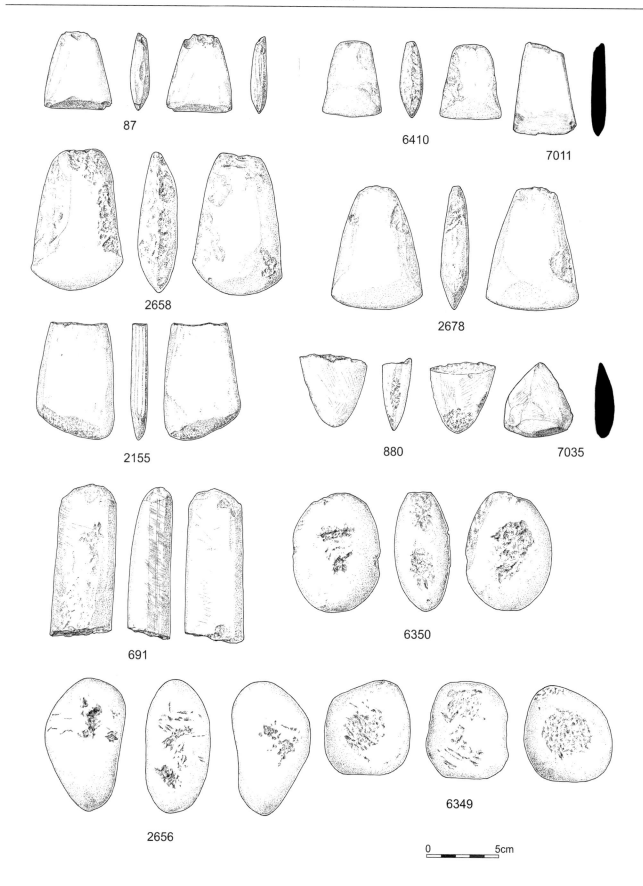

87

6410

7011

2658

2678

2155

880

7035

691

6350

2656

6349

0   5cm

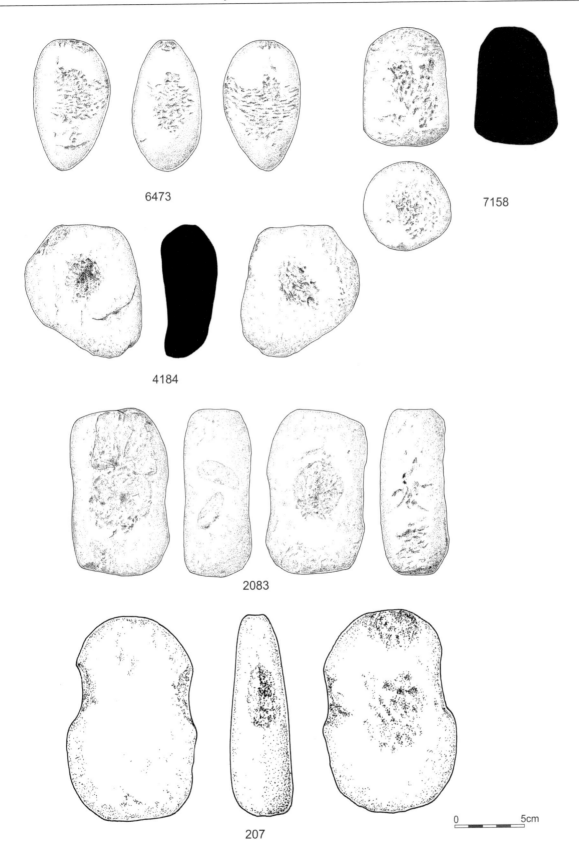

6473

7158

4184

2083

207

0   5cm

Figure 13.1 Worked stone from Stonehall. Continues p. 448.

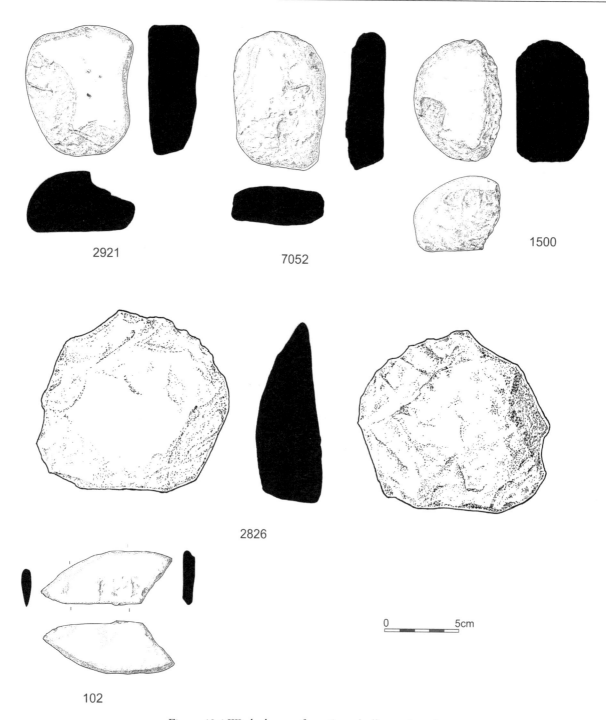

Figure 13.1 Worked stone from Stonehall, continued.

down the sides and associated friction polish indicate that this axe would originally been hafted though the lack of damage on the finely-ground blade would suggest that it was not used for heavy work. Of the broken axes (SFs 7011, 2155, 880, 691) the latter is the most interesting since it is the butt-end of a chisel-like axe, for instance, it is narrower than a regular axe with straighter sides and

a thick cross-section. The unusual grey-coloured banding of this fine-grained micaceous sandstone was clearly selected as appropriate for this axe. A finely shaped axe of micaceous siltstone (SF 7011) is broken at the butt end. Finally, there is a possible axe rough-out (SF 1511) which is really just a lump of volcanic rock which has been roughly flaked to a curved blade end and thick butt

Table 13.1 Artefact types from the excavated trenches at Stonehall (Headings are trench letters followed by: Interior = I; Exterior = E; Wall = W; TS = Topsoil; T = Total).

	AI	AE	CI	CW	CE	BI	BW	BE	EE	FE	Z	TS	T
Axe				1		1		2		1	2	3	10
Faceted cobble	1		1					2				1	5
Facially pecked cobble		1	2		1	3			2		1	3	13
Faceted & Facially pecked cobble		1				1		2			2		6
Plain hammerstone			2		1			1				2	6
?Polisher											1		1
Smoother		1	3	1	1						1	1	8
Grinding slab			1		1								2
Grinding stone			1		1							1	3
Knap of Howar grinder						1	1						2
Ground stone knife		1							1				2
Stone disc									1		2	2	5
Flaked cobble					1						1		2
Flakes	1	1	1	3	2			1					9
Total	2	5	11	2	9	8	1	10	2	1	10	13	74

without any subsequent grinding or polishing. Present evidence suggest that this raw material only occurs in archaeological deposits in artefactual form such as axes or stone balls, for example, at Barnhouse (Clarke 2005a) and Braes of Ha'Breck.

The axes are scattered across the site and only one, the quartz axe (SF 2658), is associated directly with a structure being deliberately deposited with other artefacts in the cavity below the flagstone [645] in Structure 1. The rough-out (SF 1511) was associated with the wall collapse of House 2 on Stonehall Knoll so its original circumstances of deposition are not clear. The rest of the axes are not associated with structures being found either in the topsoil of Stonehall Farm (Trench B) and Stonehall Knoll (Trench C) (SFs 2155, 691, 880) in positions outwith the structures, or else in a midden (SF 6410). There is also an unstratified axe from Stonehall Farm (SF 2678) and one from the topsoil at Stonehall Meadow. The latter was directly over an area of red midden [002], which is associated with a working area (identified in Trench A) beyond the entrance of House 3.

Cobble Tools (Total = 31)
These tools have been divided into four main types on the basis of the patterns of use wear left on the surface. They comprise facially pecked cobbles (Total = 13); faceted cobbles (Total = 5); faceted and facially pecked cobbles (Total = 6); and plain hammerstones (Total =

6). These tool types have been discussed in more detail elsewhere (Clarke 2006) and none of the cobble tools from Stonehall show any deviation from the norm.

Of interest is the cache of stone tools found deposited beneath the large slab [645] in Structure 1, Stonehall Farm, which amongst other types included one faceted and facially pecked hammerstone (SF 6350) and three facially pecked hammerstones (SFs 2656, 6349; 6473). These are in fact the nicest and most well-formed of all the cobble tools on site; they retain a hard rolled cortex indicating that they were collected on the beach. They also have a fresh appearance in comparison to many of the other tools presumably because they have been protected from the elements in the underlying cavity. They have been heavily used in comparison to other cobble tools on the site and the traces of linear pecking on the faces of three of the cobbles (SFs 6349, 6350, 6473) indicate their use as hammerstones in flint knapping particularly using the bipolar technique.

Indeed most of the cobble tools were most probably used in flint knapping given the number of cobbles with pecking on the faces. Other functions such as the processing of a soft, possibly vegetable, matter may be indicated by SF 1666 which has a discolouration on the narrow facet as if from the substance being worked. Other cobbles bear quite heavy circular indentations (SFs 4184, 2083) on opposite faces which may be from their use as an anvil whilst on another large cobble tool

(SF 207) the heavily pecked indentations on the sides are most probably notches for hafting. A pestle-like form (SF 7158) with pecking in the centre of the rounded end facet looks like it may have been used in a stirring and grinding motion in a mortar.

There is an additional quartz pebble (SF 7195) which appears to have been used for rubbing/polishing on each flat face. A further 66 cobbles were collected on-site which had no signs of wear. These are catalogued but not included in Table 13.1.

Ground stones (Total = 15)

The assemblage breaks down into: Smoothers (Total=8), Grinding stones (Total = 3), Grinding slabs (Total= 2) and Knap of Howar grinders (Total = 2). The smoothers all have single faces which have been worn flat and smooth. In most cases the original cobble face has been worn either lightly, for example, SF 1744, or else more heavily with defined edges (SF 7052). Three of the smoothers have been made on split cobbles whereby the broken face becomes the working face and is very flat and smooth (SFs 2921, 1500). These tools were most probably used by rubbing the worked face on a flat surface. Striations are visible on only one fragment indicating that the material being worked was soft; a possibility may be the preparation and softening of cured or dried hides.

The grinding stones differ from the smoothers because they appear to be the base stones upon which a substance was worked. They are fragments of flat, circular cobbles with faces which have been worn smooth, either flat or concave, and which have some pecking in the centre to provide purchase for the substance being worked. Both grinding slabs are large blocks of stone but one (SF 2881) may have a similar function to the grinding stones (see above) since it bears a face worn to a smooth concave profile with pecking in its centre. The other slab bears a different wear pattern (SF 2807) having a band of smoothing, 45mm wide, running down the length of one face. The slight concavity in the profile and the striations running down the length suggest it may be for grinding axes or possibly bone tools too.

Two artefacts resemble a particular type of grinder which was first found during excavations at the Knap of Howar (Ritchie 1983) and subsequently found at Pool (Clarke 2007a) and Tofts Ness (Clarke 2007b). Their characteristics are a domed upper face with a flat base usually with pecking over the upper surface and in the centre of the lower flat face. One piece, SF 2657, from the cavity below the flagstone [642] set in the floor of Structure 1 at Stonehall Farm, is most similar to a Knap

of Howar grinder though the flat base bears a shallow, pecked groove as well as a spread of pecking. The other, SF 6141, was recovered from the wall core of Structure 1 (thus predates its construction) and has been used for smoothing and grinding although the worked face is irregular in cross-section.

With the exception of the Knap of Howar grinders, which are both from Stonehall Farm, the greater majority of the other three tool types are present on Stonehall Knoll. These include six of the smoothers, the two grinding slabs and two of the grinding stones. Another grinding stone was from the topsoil of Stonehall Farm (Trench E) and single smoothers from Stonehall Meadow (Trenches A and Z). The interior of House 3 on Stonehall Knoll had three smoothers, a grinding stone and the banded grinding slab indicating the probable use of the structure for processing and manufacturing activities.

Ground stone knives (Total = 2)

The two ground stone knives are made of flat pebbles of micaceous siltstone. One (SF 702) has simply been ground bifacially to form a sharp edge. Striations are visible along this edge as well as a red discolouration which may be a stain from the substance being worked. The other knife (SF 102) is more carefully shaped with grinding and narrow facets along the back edge. The working end is pointed and ground sharp. A damaged end which was re-ground over the break indicates that the tool was carefully curated.

Stone discs (Total = 5)

The stone discs are all simple tabular pieces of sandstone chipped around the edge to shape a sub-circular outline. They are 100mm–170mm in diameter and are thus at the smaller end of the size range of stone discs from other Neolithic sites such as Pool (Clarke 2007a).

Flaked cobbles (Total = 2)

The two flaked cobbles have had their edges modified by flaking. A tabular form (SF 2826) has been bifacially flaked around most of the perimeter to form a long chopping edge whilst the other (SF 7001) has been flaked all over one face leaving a rough edge.

Flakes (Total = 9)

The flakes are all simple primary flakes of black micaceous sandstone. Most look as though they are simple spalls from larger slabs or else from hammerstones. None look as though they can be classed as Skaill knives as they do not appear to have been deliberately manufactured as part of a flaking industry. Of course, this does not preclude their being used for similar practices, *e.g.* butchery.

13.2 Wideford Hill

A total of 145 pieces of stone were collected on site, just under half of which were simply cobble fragments and spalls from the working area (Table 13.2). The stone tool assemblage is comprised of a variety of forms and is dominated by cobble tools, ground stone, Skaill knives and axes.

Cobble tools of various types are the most common tools in the assemblage. A range of use wear traces including pecking, grinding and faceting are evident on the cobbles indicating the different uses to which the cobbles were put (Table 13.3). Some of the smaller faceted hammerstones and facially pecked cobbles were most likely to have been used as knapping hammerstones associated with the production of the flaked lithic assemblage (Clarke 2006). The group of six pounder/grinders is of interest as these particular tools are more common to Bronze Age and Iron Age sites in Scotland.

However, two of the group bear close comparison with the pounder/grinders from Knap of Howar, both in their size, smoothly ground facets, and the presence of a patch of pecking in the centre of one worn face (SFs 3, 43) (Ritchie 1983, fig 18). The other four pounder/grinders from Wideford Hill have similar wear patterns to those above but bear additional heavy damage over the original smooth facets (*e.g.* SFs 13, 510) in the form of heavy flaking and it would appear that these tools were re-used as heavy duty hammerstones after their original use as grinders.

A large flaked hammerstone is of interest (SF 1009). It has been used for heavy work in such a fashion as to leave both ends with heavy bifacial flake damage. Its use as an anvil is indicated by the presence of two characteristic patches of pecking, one linear and the other circular in plan on one face.

There are just two stone discs and these are barely passable examples of the type. One is a fragment of laminated sandstone that has been roughly bifacially flaked to shape. The other is a fragment of a flat cobble that has been bifacially flaked to form a rough curved edge.

Table 13.2 Wideford Hill: coarse artefacts and context type.

	Over Stonehouse 1 (105)	Work area (rammed stone surface)	Stonehouse 1	Pre-Stonehouse 1	Timber structure 3	Unstratified
Flaked stone bar	1					
Cobble tools		35	2	1		1
Stone disc		2				
Skaill knife		10				
Axe		5				
?Grinding stone				1		
Ground stone		2	1			
Ground edge tool		2	1			1
Edge tool		1	2			
Finger tool		1				
Countersunk pebble		1				
Knap of Howar grinder		1				
Stone ball			1			
Flaked hammerstone			1			
Ground and polished quartz cobble			1			
Pumice		1				
Flaked quartz		1	1			
Total artefacts	1	61	10	2	0	2
Unused cobbles		3				
Cobble frags		27	1	3	3	
Spalls		29				

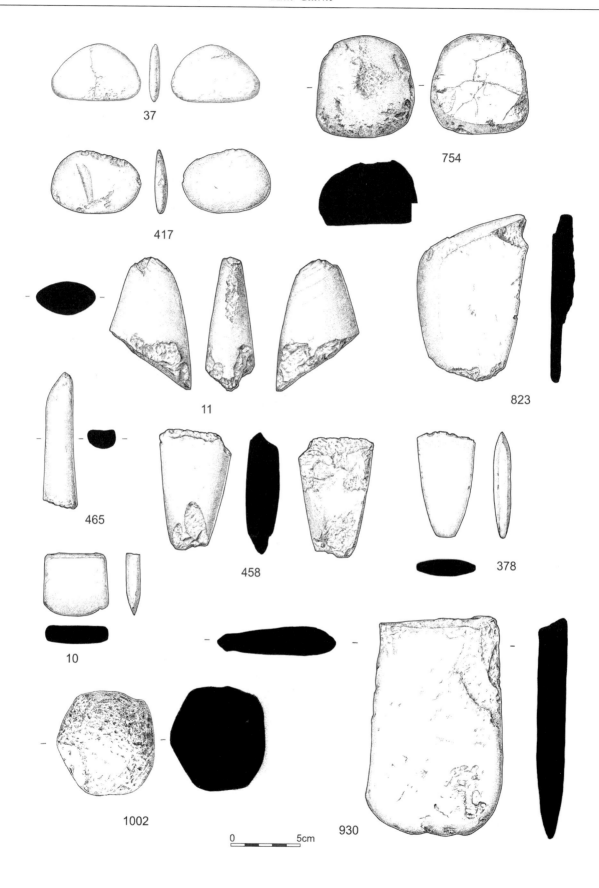

37

417

754

11

823

465

458

378

10

1002

930

0   5cm

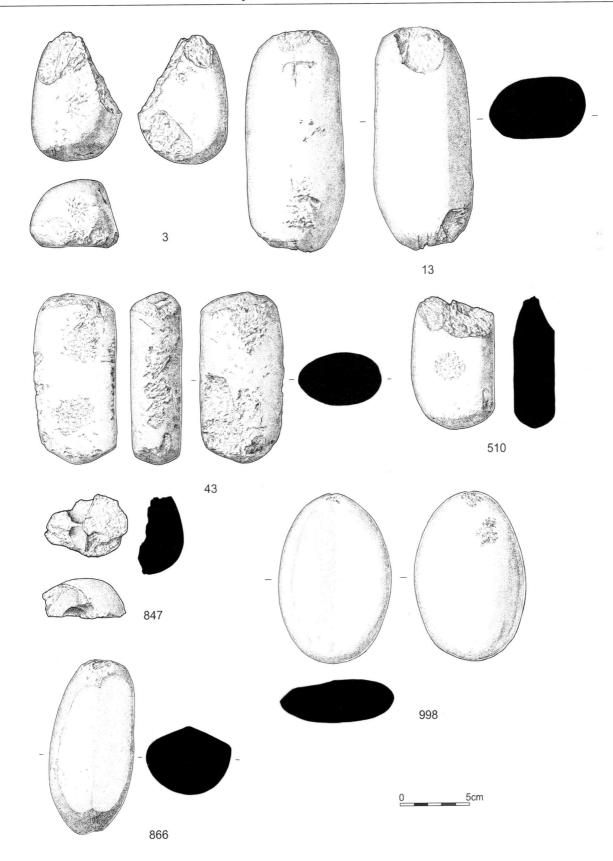

Figure 13.2 Worked Stone from Wideford Hill.

The ten Skaill knives have clear detachment marks where the flake was deliberately removed from the parent cobble (Clarke 2006). They differ from those pieces from the site defined as spalls (Table 13.2) since these have no detachment marks and are less regular in form and were most likely detached from the cobble by heat damage. The Skaill knives are primary, occasionally secondary, flakes of micaceous sandstone. None of the Skaill knives have been modified by the retouching of an edge and neither are there any clear traces of use wear on the edge of the flake in the form of breakage, flaking or rounding.

A fragment of a small counter-sunk pebble (SF 847) bears two steep-sided hollows, each with a smooth interior, worn onto opposite faces with just 4mm separating them. Although a countersunk pebble of a similar thickness was found at Knap of Howar (Ritchie 1983, fig. 17, SF 216), the hollows are formed in a very different way to the example from Wideford Hill being shallow and pecked to shape.

Evidence for grinding on the tools dominates the non-cobble tool part of the assemblage and in most cases the grinding has developed on the surface of the tool whilst it was used. However, one tool (SF 866) of a very unusual and distinctive form may have been shaped deliberately prior to use. It is an oval cobble of fine-grained micaceous sandstone and one face has been entirely re-shaped by grinding to form two very smooth, flat faces that have been worn at an angle to each other and which form a rounded longitudinal bevel where they meet. The tool is very symmetrical in form and it was most likely shaped prior to use though for an unknown purpose. It is doubtful whether the surface of this cobble would have been altered in such a symmetrical fashion if it had been worn solely by the use of the tool.

Another very finely shaped piece is the flat cobble of quartz (SF 998) that has been shaped to form fine, highly polished bevels down both faces of one long side. Further alteration to this cobble includes a highly polished face with visible striations and a shallow, wide channel running the length of the cobble again highly polished and with striations. The bevelled edge resembles the blade end of an axe, but its location down a long side and the concave area of smoothing suggests that this cobble has been formed through use rather than in order to shape it deliberately. The putative grinding stone (SF 964) is simply a large, flat sandstone cobble, since broken, with traces of light grinding and possible pecking. The lack of significant wear traces would indicate that the stone was not in heavy use as a grinder or anvil.

The four ground edge tools are thin, flat pebbles. On one (SF 37) light unifacial grinding on part of one edge has formed a light bevel with heavy striations that follow the curve of another edge. Two of the other ground edge tools bear no striations though parts of the edge appear to have been ground to a sharp edge. A further putative ground edge tool has only light traces of wear. Two other tools (SFs 307, 823 have simply been ground on the edges to concave or convex profiles. The Knap of Howar grinder (SF 754) is typical of its type both in size and form. Here a cobble has been broken to form a flat face, which has subsequently been worn flat by grinding. Unidirectional striations are present on this worn face together with the characteristic patch of light pecking in the centre.

The three 'edge tools' are also simple flat pebbles of black micaceous sandstone that bear light flaking along parts of an edge as if having been used in a light 'chopper' fashion. In this manner the flaking damage along the edge would have been caused incidentally through the use of the tool rather than as deliberate flaking in order to modify the edge. One tool (SF 417) has light unidirectional striations on one face indicating that the edge would have been used in a back and forth 'slicing' action though the working edge would be considered too blunt to function as a knife. The finger tool (SF 465) is a simple narrow pebble with some pecking on one end.

The five axes all from the rammed stone surface [002], are varied in form and represent various levels of manufacturing stages and finish. One (SF 11) is a probable axe roughout. It is a broken cobble of banded mudstone with some pecking on the narrow end and side to form a facet and some flaking on a broken edge, which may be an attempt to thin the blank. Banded mudstone was also employed for an axe (SF 578) of which just the butt survived; some reflaking or flake damage was present on the butt end. Another axe (SF 458) of fine-grained sandstone is larger than SF 378 and is damaged on the butt and blade ends. Less care has been taken in the manufacture of this axe since one of the faces has been more finely ground and polished than the other which is flatter and ground over a rougher face; this may be an unfinished axe or, more likely, there was no need to polish one face either because it was not intended to be shown or the method of hafting required one rough face. The other two axes are more finely shaped and finished, in particular the chisel axe (SF 10) of siltstone which though just a fragment displays regular parallel sides and has been finely finished by grinding and polishing. The other fine axe (SF 378) of siltstone has a narrow butt splaying out to a wide curved blade and is finely ground and polished all over.

One very heavily worked piece is the stone ball (SF 1002). This is a rounded cobble that has had its entire original cortical surface worn away by pecking. It appears to have been shaped by turning the cobble constantly whilst pecking with the tool. There are occasional patches of grinding over some of the pecked areas. The ball is not completely round; rather it has a broad band of faceting around the middle, a rounded facet on one face and four facets on the opposite face that form a rough cone.

The flaked stone bar (SF 930) is just a single example of the type. Made on a tabular slab of micaceous sandstone, it has been flaked around the perimeter to shape a tapering rectangle with a curved end and a fine asymmetrical, elliptical cross-section. Some notching on the thicker side at the break indicates that this stone bar was originally hafted. The whole tool is much abraded from exposure to the elements and this has formed a very smooth surface.

Context and Function

Most of the stone artefacts (80%) were found in the rammed stone working area [002] east of Stonehouse 1. There would appear to be no significant differences between the types of tools found in the working area and those found outwith it (Table 13.2) and consequently neither chronological nor functional differences can be inferred between the different contexts. Within the working area there appear to be a few distinctive episodes of deposition. Within a general plot of worked stone on the rammed stone surface (Fig. 2.34a) interesting depositional difference are present. For instance, the smaller cobble tools form a general scatter right across the area and this is in contrast to the group of five pounder/grinders that are found in a spread to the west of the working area. Not only do all the pounder/grinders from the site appear here, but they are also the dominant cobble tool form in the group. To the east of this grouping is a concentration of the four hammerstone flakes as well as the two ground-edge tools, a single edge tool, an axe, and the finely shaped ground stone. Further to the east another concentration is found, this time of four Skaill knives, three cobble tools and the countersunk pebble.

Though the numbers are small, the fact that the groupings are composed of specific tool forms – pounder/grinders; hammerstone flakes and edge tools; and Skaill knives – makes it most likely that these reflect distinctive events on the rammed stone working area.

Either these are the locations for specific activities or they were discrete dumps from processing activities that were carried out elsewhere and brought to the area to consolidate the rammed stone floor. Another factor to consider is the significant number of broken stones, including cobble fragments and spalls, which have been incorporated in the working area (Table 13.2). Only a small percentage of these are fragments of cobble tools, and the rest are spalls or pieces of unused cobbles, some of which may be a result of heat damage to sandstone cobbles. It is hard to escape the conclusion that cobbles were deliberately broken up in order to provide material to consolidate this external working area.

In general, the stone tools from the working area are in good condition, however, the axes, pounder/grinders and stone discs are the most fragmented tool groups. Some of the pounder/grinders have been heavily flaked over the original ground ends and perhaps the damage had formed when they were used to break up the cobbles in order to provide the material to stabilise the working area. The fragmented axes and stone discs and the scattered nature of their distribution suggest that these were brought in and broken up to be dumped and incorporated with the cobble fragments in the working area. In contrast, the smaller cobble tools such as the faceted and/or facially pecked hammerstones and the tools with grinding tend to be complete specimens and this may indicate that these tools were actually used on the working area itself. In this respect the group of Skaill knives and the group of edge tools could possibly indicate the processing of soft substances, perhaps butchering (Clarke 1989). As has been mentioned before, several of the hammerstones may have been used as flint knapping tools and a plot of these with the flints (Fig. 2.34a and c) shows that both types have a similar wide scatter though no particular concentrations of activity. A distribution map of the flints, by type, may help to clarify how these tools were used on the working area (see Chapter 12).

Not very many tools are associated with Stonehouse 1 itself though it is of interest that three of the most interesting stone artefacts come from here. Both the finely shaped and polished quartz cobble (SF 998) and the flaked hammerstone (SF 1009) are from [159] the fill of a channel running under the length of the Stonehouse 1 west wall core. The stone ball (SF 1002) is from the upper floor of Stonehouse 1 together with a putative ground edge tool fragment.

The only tool that can confidently be assigned a Bronze Age date is the flaked stone bar which comes from [105] overlying Stonehouse 1. These artefacts come from domestic Bronze Age contexts at Tofts Ness, Bu and Skaill (Clarke 2006) and recent excavations at Bronze Age barrows such as Linga Fiold have also demonstrated the presence of these flaked stone bars in funerary contexts (*ibid.*). What is perhaps surprising is that only one such tool was found at Wideford Hill. Flaked stone bars often occur in quite large numbers, especially when associated with structures. Instead, this single example of may have been discarded due to breakage within the field it was being used in and this may in turn imply that the early Neolithic stone-built house at Wideford Hill had become incorporated within a Bronze Age field system.

Orcadian Context

The stone assemblage from Wideford Hill shares some similar characteristics with the other early Neolithic assemblages from Orkney, specifically the dominance of cobble tools in the assemblage and the small number, if even present, of Skaill knives and stone discs (Table 13.4). This is in contrast to the later Neolithic stone assemblages such as at Pool and Skara Brae where Skaill knives occur in their hundreds and large stone discs are frequent (Clarke 1996). The evidence from these stone tool assemblages would indicate that there were particular storage and food processing activities that differed

Table 13.4 Stone assemblages from Orcadian 4th millennium cal bc sites (BH Barnhouse; SH Stonehall; WH Wideford Hill; KOH Knap of Howar).

	BH	WH	SH	KOH
Cobble tools	67	39	31	15
Stone discs	-	2	5	-
Skaill knives	9	10	9	6
Knap of Howar grinders	-	1	2	3
Facially ground (smoothers)	14	-	8	-
Side ground cobbles	3	2	-	-
Ground edge/knife/spatulate	3	2	2	-
Finger tool	7	1	-	-
Other ground stone	1	1	-	-
Grinding stone	-	1	3	-
Grinding slab	2	-	2	-
Quern	-	-	-	2
Axes	11	4	8	1
Maceheads	4	-	-	-
Knap of Howar borers	-	-	-	6
Stone balls	6	1	-	-
Multi-hollowed stones	6	-	-	-
Counter-sunk pebbles	-	1	-	1

between these periods and this is most likely linked to the changes in ceramic form (see Jones 1999a; 2002).

With regard to the other tool types the assemblage from Wideford Hill bears the closest similarity with the other early Neolithic Orcadian sites in the Bay of Firth area, such as Knowes of Trotty, Smerquoy and Stonehall. Interestingly, it also has similarities with Barnhouse (Clarke 2005a). At some of these sites the proportion of stone tools that has been used for, or altered by, grinding is significant (Table 13.4). An instance of bifacial grinding along long edges occurs on SF 6015, a sandstone slab from Barnhouse which, though not producing an artefact of such regular form as the quartz piece from Wideford Hill, is the nearest comparison available from anywhere in the Northern Isles. Artefacts of quartz with polish are also present at Barnhouse.

A stone ball from Wideford Hill is of similar proportions to those from Barnhouse, averaging 70mm–80mm in dimensions with a flattened base. The ball from Wideford Hill was made of grey micaceous sandstone whilst those from Barnhouse were of a grey volcanic rock, a material seemingly reserved for the manufacture of stone balls and axes. Similar contexts of deposition for this artefact form are also noticed at these sites. At Barnhouse two of the stone balls were from features just external to the wall and entrance of Structure 8 whilst one was from the floor of House 4. At Wideford Hill the stone ball is associated with the occupation of Stonehouse 1.

The assemblage from Knap of Howar is different in its lack of ground stone though the six distinctive borers from this site would indicate a specific activity being carried out here (and see Smerquoy below). These early Neolithic sites most likely shared the same basic processing activities that made use of cobble tools and Skaill knives whilst specific manufacturing activities involving grinding varied between sites. At some late Neolithic sites there are single finds of, for example, Knap of Howar borers and Knap of Howar grinders (Pool, Tofts, Links of Noltland, Crossiecrown) and the occasional finger tool or spatulate piece but in general there is little evidence for grinding or ground stones in the later Neolithic assemblages (Clarke 2006).

The chisel axe, though broken, is similar in dimensions to the butt end of a chisel axe from Stonehall, and one from surface collection at Muckquoy, though at the former it was found associated with late Neolithic material. A surviving blade end of an axe from Barnhouse (SF 3025) also has similar width and thickness dimensions.

13.3 Crossiecrown

Earliest Occupation

The few artefacts from this phase are all from the levelling material and early midden layers. They are undiagnostic of any particular period and comprise a few Skaill knives, chipped slabs and a stone disc and two plain hammerstones.

The Red House period

The most varied stone assemblage from Crossiecrown comes from the Red House (Fig. 7.30b; Table 13.5). As well as numerous Skaill knives, stone discs and cobble tools there are also some single examples of other artefact types such as a stone mortar, an axe, a Knap of Howar grinder and a sculpted stone. The Skaill knives and stone discs are found in every type of context, particularly the construction and wall core layers as well as a significant number from floor and hearth contexts. Of note is that six of the total seven stone discs with heat damage are from the floor and hearth contexts of the Red House suggesting that cooking was carried out in this area and this is further supported by the association of two stone discs with a deposit of pottery in pit [463]. Other significant artefact deposits are the igneous speckled axe (SF 63) (Fig. 7.31), and two facially pecked cobbles from the southern recess, the former from the floor and the hammerstones from an ashy deposit. The mortar (SF 85) was found in the right-hand cell (Fig. 7.24) and the sculpted pieces on the floor.

The Grey House period

As well as having the same artefact types as the earliest occupation, and clearly overlapping with the late occupation of the Red House, this period also includes three other different types of cobble tool, a smoother and a flaked stone bar. The smoother is of an undeveloped type consisting simply of a cobble with a lightly worn cortical face. The flaked stone bar is of a standard size and shape but the rounding of the sides suggests that it may have been utilised in a different way to the rest of this type – perhaps in a construction context. The artefacts are found variously associated with the midden, construction and collapse of buildings of this period, though of note are three tools: a metamorphic faceted cobble; a facially pecked cobble; and a faceted and facially pecked cobble (see Fig, 7.40), all found in the east recess [437] of the Grey House.

Post-Red and Grey House period

The assemblage from the final period of occupation at Crossiecrown, which judging from the radiocarbon dates runs into the early Bronze Age, has been divided into several context types: the midden over the Red House; the hollow [213] (Table 13.6) representing a late house structure; the rubble; and the later soil deposits to determine whether there were any differences in the context of deposition (Table 13.7). There is a significant change in the composition of artefact types during this phase with the introduction of flaked blanks: flaked stone

Table 13.5 Distribution of stone artefacts in the Red House at Crossiecrown.

	Construction	Wall core	Drain	Loam around orthostat	Midden	Layer	Floor	Hearth	Cell 35	N recess	S recess	Pits	Box
Skaill knives	3	8	1	6			9	2		2	2	1	3
Stone discs	1		1	3			5	2				2	
Facially pecked cobble					1	1	1				2	1	
Faceted and facially pecked		1											
Plain hammerstones				2								1	
Ground stone					1								
Mortar									1				
Knap of Howar grinder				1									
Sculpted stone							1						
Axe												1	
Chipped slab							1						

Table 13.6 Distribution of stone artefacts in the post-Red House occupation of Crossiecrown.

Artefact type	H1 midden	Hollow	Rubble	Soil
Skaill knives	18	5	9	9
Faceted cobbles	2	0	1	0
Facially pecked cobble	0	0	2	1
Faceted and facially pecked	1	3	1	0
Plain hammerstone	2	2	1	0
Smoothers	1	1	0	0
Necked hammerstone	0	1	0	0
Ground stone	0	1	0	0
Flaked stone bars	3	1	5	2
Flaked cobble	0	0	1	0
Ard point	0	1	0	0
Axes	1	0	0	0
Flakes	1	1	0	0
Chipped slab	1	0	0	0

Table 13.7 Distribution of stone artefacts in the later occupation of Crossiecrown.

Artefact type	Phase 5	T2 external layers and topsoil	T1 Upper midden and topsoil	T3 midden and topsoil
Skaill knives	41	58	40	9
Stone discs	0	3	10	0
Faceted cobbles	3	2	1	1
Facially pecked cobble	3	3	1	0
Faceted and facially pecked	5	1	1	1
Plain hammerstone	5	7	5	1
Smoothers	2	5	4	0
Necked hammerstone	1	2	1	0
Ground stone	1	1	1	0
Flaked stone bars	11	4	6	1
Flaked cobble	1	1	5	1
Ard point	1	1	0	0
Axes	1	0	1	0
Sculpted stone	0	1	0	0
Flakes	2	4	1	1
Chipped slab	1	0	4	0

bars; ard points and flaked cobbles. Also appearing at this time are stone flakes, necked hammerstones and the developed forms of smoothers made on split cobbles. Stone discs are lacking in these deposits whilst Skaill knives and cobble tools remain common. There are no obvious differences in artefact deposition between the different contexts, with the deposits over the Red House having a similar assemblage to those in external contexts.

Middens

Although the Trench 1 upper middens, Trench 2 external layers and the middens of Trench 3 are difficult to relate stratigraphically, the evidence from the stone tools would suggest that these contexts are relatively late in date. Equally, they almost certainly post-date the main occupation of the Red House and this is derived from comparison with the upper midden stone tools (Table 13.6). There are clear similarities in the composition of the assemblages from the different areas most notably in the presence of a combination flaked stone bars, ard points or flaked cobbles in all areas. Necked hammerstones and smoothers from the middens are also present at this later time.

Summary

The Crossiecrown stone assemblage indicates two main periods of use which concord with the Neolithic dwellings

and the Bronze Age artefacts found stratigraphically above the occupation of the Red House and in the middens and external layers elsewhere on the site (Fig. 13.3).

As well as Skaill knives, stone discs and various cobble tools, the Red House contains artefact types clearly associated with late Neolithic occupation. The Knap of Howar grinder, named after the early Neolithic site at which it was first identified (see above), has since appeared at other sites in later Neolithic contexts such as Pool and Tofts Ness as well as Crossiecrown. Their earlier presence at Stonehall and Wideford Hill indicates a late 4th–early 3rd millennium cal BC date for occupation at Crossiecrown (confirmed by radiocarbon dates). The mortar too is common to the late Neolithic, *e.g.* at Skara Brae, Barnhouse and Pool. The sculpted piece is still a relatively unusual artefact to find (see Fig. 13.4) though such three-dimensional pieces are most probably indicative of a late Grooved ware date as supported by the presence of the spiked objects from the latest Neolithic phases at Pool (Clarke 2006; 2007a).

The artefacts which are traditionally linked specifically with the Bronze Age are the flaked stone bars, ard points and flaked cobbles. Here, it must be noted that although single objects from late Neolithic contexts have previously

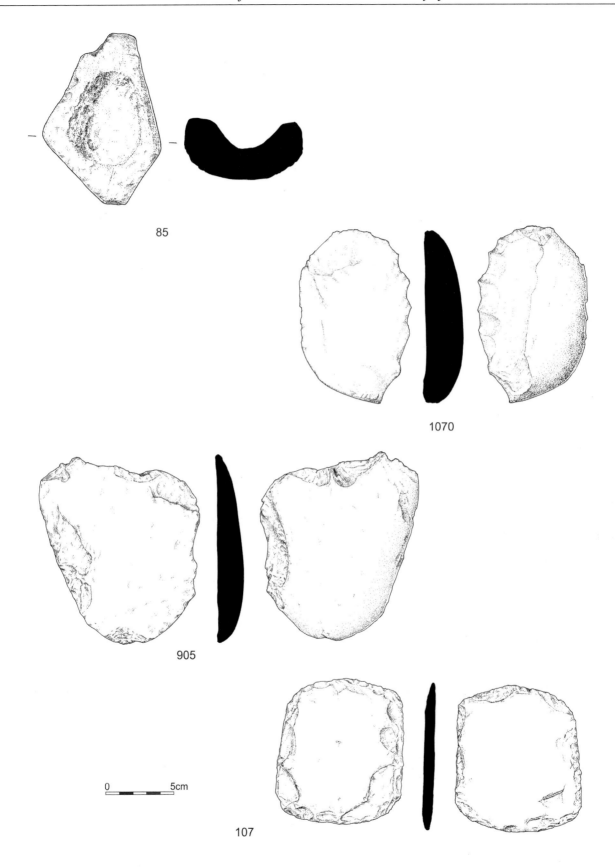

85

1070

905

0   5cm

107

Figure 13.3 Worked stone from Crossiecrown. Continued pp. 460–462.

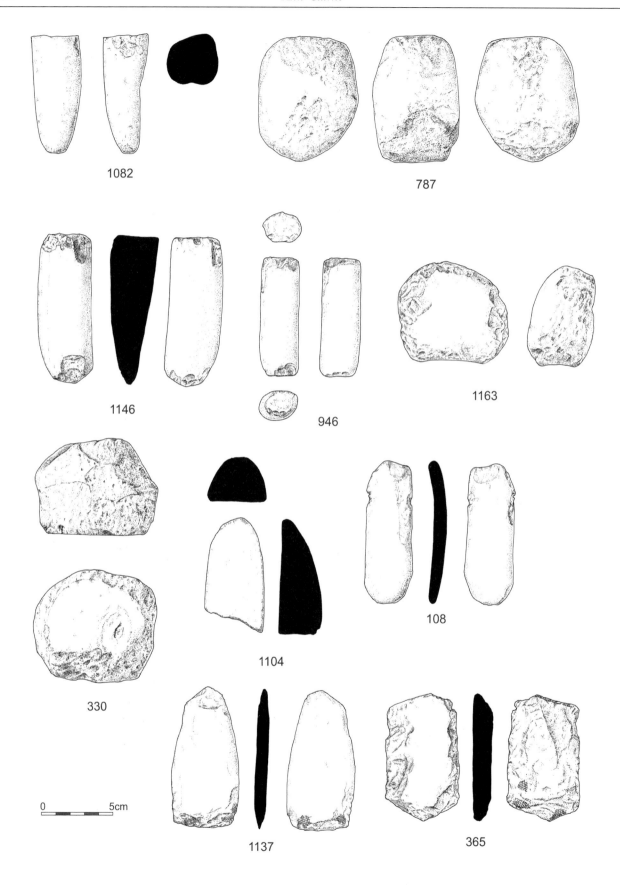

1082

787

1146

946

1163

330

1104

108

1137

365

0   5cm

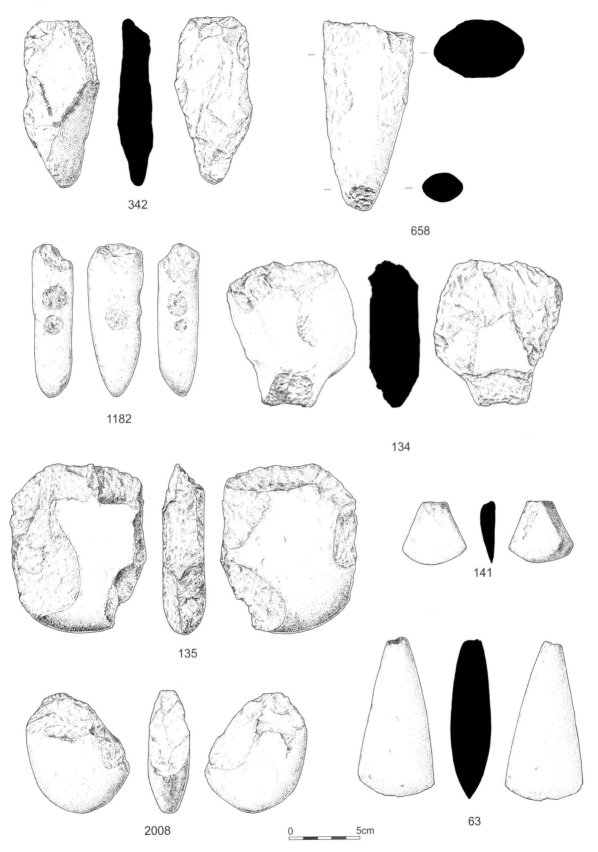

342

658

1182

134

135

141

2008

0   5cm

63

Figure 13.3 Worked stone from Crossiecrown, continued.

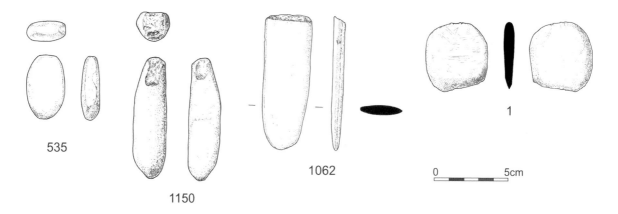

Figure 13.3 Worked stone from Crossiecrown, continued.

been termed as flaked stone bars or flaked cobbles, for example, at Pool (Clarke 2007a) and Links of Noltland (Clarke 2006), (and at Crossiecrown itself there is a possible flaked stone bar from the Grey House period), they tend to be of a smaller size or of a more irregular manufacture than those more numerous and standardised artefact forms from the Bronze Age which clearly constitute an 'industry'. All three of these tool types were found in the Bronze Age phases of Tofts Ness, Sanday, and Skaill, (east) Mainland. Flaked stone bars and ard points are also common to funerary deposits of this period being found around the kerbs of several burial mounds in Orkney (Clarke 2006), particularly Linga Fiold (Downes forthcoming) and Quoyscottie (Hedges 1977). Other tools which may be late Neolithic or Early Bronze Age in date are the necked hammerstones and smoothers since, with the exception of one lightly worn smoother, the rest of these tools appear in the post-Red House deposits and in the external layers associated with stone artefacts of the Bronze Age.

The continued use of some tool types from the Neolithic through to the Bronze Age is common too. In particular, Skaill knives, stone discs and the various forms of cobble tools have a long period of use and the evidence from Tofts Ness and now supported by that from Crossiecrown indicates that where these tools are used in the early 3rd millennium cal BC they continue to be used in later 3rd and early 2nd millennia cal BC phases of the same site (Clarke 2006).

Artefact types

Skaill Knives (Total = 211)

Skaill knives form the greater part (60%) of the assemblage. These simple flake tools have been dealt with in great detail elsewhere (Clarke 1989; 2006). Suffice it to say that the assemblage of Skaill knives from Crossiecrown bears similar characteristics to other large assemblages. It is comprised mainly of primary flakes from cobbles of micaceous sandstone and in most cases the original flake edge has been kept for the work. There is retouch on the edges of just three flakes (SFs 2030, 1070, 905) usually in an irregular fashion to thin an edge. A large percentage of the flakes, 22%, bore edge damage in the form of flaking, rounding or denticulation indicating that these flakes were damaged through use. In summary the Skaill knives are tools which are quickly and easily made from an accessible resource of beach cobbles. Some experimental use of these flakes has pointed to their facility as butchering tools as not only were they able to be used as knives and choppers but the edge damage patterns on the experimental knives were very similar to those left on the prehistoric tools (Clarke 1989). The evidence from some sites such as Skaill Bay shows close physical associations between Skaill knives and butchering waste, in this case deer and whale bones (Richards *et al.* forthcoming).

Stone discs (Total = 30), Chipped slabs (Total = 8)

The stone discs are made of the finely laminated black micaceous sandstone, some in cobble form and the rest as slabs. They have been flaked around the edge to form a sub-circular outline or in six cases a distinctive oval outline. There are four discs which have a distinctive straight edge (SFs 455, 321, 544, 2005); on two pieces the natural straight cobble edge remains unflaked whilst on the other two discs the straight edge has been caused by breakage prior to flaking.

The discs vary in size between 70mm to 300mm in diameter reflecting closely the size range for the stone discs from the Neolithic phases at Pool, Sanday. Another feature of these discs is the presence of a red discolouration around the edges caused by heat, or alternatively, a black, sooty deposit located around the perimeter. At Crossiecrown seven discs had been affected by heat in this way indicating their use as pot lids whilst the pot was over a fire.

The chipped slabs are also made on cobbles or slabs of the black micaceous sandstone but they are more irregular in form and thicker than the stone discs. One (SF 107) has been shaped to a quadrilateral form whilst another (SF 174) is a tear-drop form.

Cobble tools (Total = 67)

As with the Stonehall assemblage (see section 13.1), the cobble tools from Crossiecrown will be dealt with only summarily. An additional cobble tool type has been recognised at Crossiecrown giving five main tool types: facially-pecked cobbles (Total = 14); faceted cobbles (Total = 11); faceted and facially-pecked cobbles (Total = 12); plain hammerstones (Total = 26); necked hammerstones (Total = 4).

The necked hammerstones are an unusual form of cobble tool. They are formed from elongated cobbles which have been broken across the width. The broken face has subsequently been used as a platform from which flakes have been removed but only from a fifth to a half of the total perimeter. The reason for this flaking is not known; in no case does it alter the outline of the platform significantly and neither does it alter the profile of the tool by making the flaked end significantly narrower so it appears unlikely that this flaking was to enable the tool to be hafted. However, a facet which has been ground down one side of SF 1206 may indeed be to facilitate hafting. The opposite ends of these tools have been worked to rough facets (SFs 946, 1082) or flaked through use (SF 1146).

The most likely function for many of the rest of the cobble tools must have been as flint knapping hammerstones (SF 787) or else as grinders (SF 8) especially where a face has been worn smooth too (SF 1163). A further 66 cobbles were collected on site but bore no obvious traces of use wear.

Smoothers (Total = 12) and Knap of Howar grinder (Total = 1)

The smoothers are similar in form to those from Stonehall. Seven of them are made on whole cobbles utilising the original flat face. On two of these, striations are visible running across the width of the tool. On SF 1076 the face has been worn flat and smooth as well as single ground facets on the end and side. The other five

smoothers have been made on split cobbles with the fractured face forming the working surface (*e.g.* SF 1104).

The Knap of Howar grinder (SF 330) has been affected by weathering, most likely indicating a degree of residuality, and the original cobble surface of the upper face has been destroyed. The base, however, is flat and smooth with a spread of pecking in the centre and to one side. The presence of this tool, the currency of which seems to run from the mid 4th–early 3rd millennium cal BC, in conjunction with the 'Unstan ware' sherd may provide additional evidence for an earlier Neolithic settlement component at Crossiecrown.

Flaked stone bars (Total = 23)

These flaked stone bars conform to the general pattern of characteristics identified on those tools from other sites (Clarke 2006). They are made on slabs or flat cobbles of black micaceous sandstone and have been flaked around the edges to shape. Most of the flaked stone bars are broken but the indications are that they tend to be longer and narrower than the flaked stone bars from Tofts Ness (Clarke 2007b).

There are no traces of notching, pecking or friction wear on the sides of these tools to indicate that they may have been hafted in a particular manner but this information may have been lost because of the high breakage component. The exception (SF 108) has some flaking on either side towards the butt end which could have facilitated hafting. Wear traces in the form of smoothing and rounding on the working end are present on a few pieces (*e.g.* SFs 1137, 365, 342).

Ard points (T=2)

The surviving working tip of an ard point (SF 658) was found in the external layers of Trench 2. The wear traces are obscured by abrasion but there is some light flaking from the tip as if through use. Another possible ard point is made on a cobble (SF 1182). The butt end has been squared by flaking and the opposite end makes use of a natural pointed end. On either side a pair of deep circular hollows have been pecked and there are single patches on the faces presumably to facilitate hafting. Such notching is unusual on ard points though it has been observed on several examples from the Bronze Age Shetland sites of Sumburgh (Downes and Lamb 2000) and Catpund (Ballin Smith 2005).

Flaked cobbles (Total = 8)

These cobbles have been flaked around the perimeter to form a chopper-like edge. They all vary in the amount and location of flaking, for instance, SF 134 has been flaked over most of one face and then along part of one edge on the opposite face, and SF 135 has been bifacially flaked around most of the perimeter. A quartz cobble (SF 2006) has been flaked over other wear traces, which suggests it was a re-used faceted and facially-pecked cobble. Despite the prepared chopper edge there are no wear traces to suggest these cobbles were used at all, as opposed to the flaked cobbles from Bronze Age Tofts Ness which were quite heavily rounded over the chopping edge (Clarke 2007b).

Axes (Total = 3)

A finely-shaped axe of a speckled igneous rock was found in the southern recess of the Red House (SF 63). It has been ground all over to shape and the blade end is asymmetrically curved. The sides bear pecking most likely to facilitate hafting. A miniature axe of volcanic rock (SF 141) has been shaped by grinding. It is asymmetrical in cross-section as one side remains in its original thick pebble edge. A possible unfinished axe or roughly-shaped piece comes from the rubble infill of the Red House. It has been made on a split quartz cobble and flaked to shape. The blade is not sharp but obtuse in angle and there are traces of polishing over the flake scars.

Ground stone (Total = 4)

This group comprises four pebbles of fine-grained micaceous sandstone which have been shaped by grinding in different ways. Two tools were most likely ground through use; SF 1150 is a ground-end tool with small flakes around the edge of the ground area and SF 535 has a narrow flat facet ground on one end and down a side. The other two pieces have been ground deliberately to shape and in these cases (SFs 1 and 1062) an acute blade-like edge has been formed by grinding.

Sculpted stone (Total = 2)

The most obvious sculpted stone was found on the floor of the Red House (SF 532). It is a block of coarse-grained sandstone shaped by a series of grooves. A flat face has been formed which is most probably the base. On one face three deep grooves have been channelled diagonally across the surface and on the opposite face a larger groove has been channelled diagonally from top to bottom. This piece is asymmetrical in form. The grooved form of decoration has not been observed before on other sculpted objects which tend to be decorated with knobs or spikes (Clarke 2006). Another sculpted stone (SF 184) from the floor [006] of the Red House utilized an unusual concave-based natural triangular-shaped

stone (Fig. 13.4). The form had been enhanced through use on the concave edge, possibly as a shaft-smoother.

The final sculpted piece is much less obvious as it appears to have been heavily damaged by heat or weathering. This rough-looking lump (SF 687) may have had three knobs made on it originally but these are not clear and it is difficult to determine whether it is an intentionally sculpted piece or not.

Mortar (Total = 1)

The mortar (SF 85) is a classic Neolithic form being made on a block of sandstone, diamond-shaped in plan. A round-based hollow, oval in plan has been pecked into one face and the interior has subsequently been smoothed through use.

Flakes (Total = 10) and Core (Total = 1)

The flakes are distinguished from the Skaill knives because they are larger, thicker, usually secondary and present a more irregular edge. The core is a large cobble from which irregular flakes have been removed from multiple platforms. Given the irregularity of the flakes it is unlikely that they were produced deliberately – either for the flake or to shape a blank. They just seem to have been produced incidentally during the reduction of a core, however, this process in itself suggests the manufacture of an as yet unknown object.

Comparison of worked stone with other Orcadian sites

There are few similarities between the stone assemblages of Stonehall, Wideford Hill and Crossiecrown. Crossiecrown has a standard late Neolithic Grooved ware assemblage of numerous Skaill knives and stone discs and cobble tools as seen at Skara Brae, Mainland, Links of Noltland, Westray and Pool, Sanday, as well as the individual objects such as the Knap of Howar grinder, the mortar and the sculpted piece. In contrast, Stonehall does not have the Skaill knives, nor the large numbers of stone discs though Knap of Howar grinders are present in late 4th millennium cal BC contexts (e.g. Stonehall Farm, Structure 1). One point of similarity is in the presence of smoothers at both sites though their circumstances of deposition are quite different. At Stonehall they were in use during the earlier Neolithic and were clearly linked with the grinding slabs and stones as part of a processing area. In contrast, at Crossiecrown the smoothers are not associated with structures but instead occur in external layers in association with artefacts of a Bronze Age date.

The Stonehall assemblage is much more similar to that

of Barnhouse most notably in the lack of Skaill knives and stone discs, though Stonehall does not have the greater variety of tool types which is present at Barnhouse. There is an emphasis on the use of grinding stones at both sites most particularly in the use of smoothers (the Barnhouse stone report refers to these tools as Facially Ground Cobbles) though the wear patterns are slightly different with several of the smoothers at Barnhouse having a slightly skewed profile whilst others have a light gloss on the working face. Neither of these wear patterns were present on the smoothers from Stonehall. A chisel-shaped axe was found at Barnhouse and the field surface at Muckquoy (see Chapter 9) as well as Stonehall.

The Crossiecrown assemblage is similar to other late Neolithic sites such as Pool (Clarke 2007a), Tofts Ness (Clarke 2007b), Links of Noltland (Clarke 2006; McLaren 2011) and Skara Brae (Childe 1931a; Clarke 2006). The presence of flaked stone bars, ard points and flaked cobbles in the external middens indicates the continuation of occupation well into the 2nd millennium cal BC. At Tofts Ness, the Bronze Age levels were clearly marked by the introduction of these tool types whilst Skaill knives, stone discs and various types of cobble tool continued in use from the Neolithic as they do at Crossiecrown.

One unusual aspect of the Crossiecrown assemblage is the presence of the flakes, core and necked hammerstones. Such artefacts have only been noted before at the site of Links of Noltland, Westray where they are present across the site. Up until the recent excavations there has been no phasing to help in dating these tools but Links of Noltland has traces of habitation dating from the late Neolithic to the early Bronze Age (Moore and Wilson 2011). At Crossiecrown the necked hammerstones are found in the external contexts associated with the Bronze Age stone tools but it is not clear whether these can be dated as late as the Bronze Age or whether they are indeed of a late Neolithic/early Bronze Age date.

13.4 The Knowes of Trotty

A total of 19 stone artefacts were found during excavation of the Neolithic house in Trench B at the Knowes of Trotty (Table 13.9) including a finely ground axe of micaceous siltstone, two Knap of Howar grinders, two sharpening stones, an anvil, three stone discs (two putative), several cobble tools, a ground stone tool and three structural slabs. Several other stone finds were collected but these were mainly spalls or thin slabs which were produced naturally through weathering or breakage and they are not included in this report.

Figure 13.4 The sculpted stone (SF 184) from the floor of the Red House (Nick Card).

Table 13.8. Knowes of Trotty stone artefacts and context type.

	Structure	External working area	Unstratified
Axe		1	
Knap of Howar grinder	1	1	
Sharpening stone	2		
Anvil	1		
Stone disc	3		
Structural slab	3		
Cobble tool		5	1
Ground stone		1	

The artefacts

The broken axe (SF 280) has a curved butt with a finely ground facet and one side is ground to a square cross-section whilst the opposite side is rounded, however, they are of a similar dimensions (Fig. 3.19). This axe was found in the external working floor [263] to the east of the house.

There are two Knap of Howar grinders (Fig. 3.21), one of which (SF 135) has been very finely worn. The base of this tool is extremely smooth and polished and slightly convex in section with the characteristic spread of pecking in the centre of the face. The domed upper face is pecked over the surface. Its dimensions of 69mm long and 49mm thick make this amongst the smallest of this tool type to be found so far in Orkney though the grinders from Wideford Hill and Stonehall are of similar dimensions. The other grinder (SF 299) is of a less classic form but it has a fractured face forming the working face. There is no pitting in the centre of this worn face and neither has the domed face been pecked to shape. However, there is some flaking from the flat face down one side that has altered the outline of the original cobble. This grinder is rather more elongated in shape than the more usually circular tools.

Two sharpening stones are of interest. Both are made from slab fragments of micaceous siltstone. One (SF 88) has a single narrow U-shaped groove worn on one face and the other stone (SF 53) has smoothly worn sides with some striations that could have been made by a metal or flint edge (Fig. 13.5). On this latter piece there is also a shallow but wide concavity worn along the length of the stone. The wear on these tools resembles that which is found on used pumice (*e.g.* Barnhouse) and it is possible that the light, soft rock was selected for similar work, such as smoothing, burnishing or bone working, in the absence of pumice which would have been available from some parts of the Orcadian seashore. In this respect a rounded lump of vesicular volcanic rock (SF 286) that was found in the working area [301], may have been used for some kind of smoothing or rubbing; though there were no obvious wear traces on this tool, some grey staining or concretions on the flat face may indicate that some substance was being processed using this as a tool. A cuboid block of stone (SF 67) has been used as an anvil; on two faces there are areas of coarse pecking as if from a large hammer.

A number of cobble tools were found, including two plain hammerstones; a faceted and facially pecked cobble and a hammerstone flake all of which were undistinguished in terms of wear traces. Two additional fragments (SFs 259 and 151) conjoined to form an elongated pebble but weathering had destroyed any obvious wear traces. There were also three possible stone discs (SFs 53, 57, 168), all of which are fragments. The discs are from the house structure, and as these have little evidence for deliberate shaping they could just be natural fragments of flagstone of which there were quite a number in Trench B.

A fragment of a possible ground stone tool (SF 284) was found in the working area [311]. This thin pebble of black micaceous siltstone appears to have been ground unifacially to create a sharp edge. However, not much of this tool survives to determine the extent of alteration.

Finally there were three slabs that may be structural. Two (SFs 25 and 144) are fragments of flagstone that have traces of chipping around a surviving edge to form a concave and convex edge. The other (SF 306) is an unworked, rectangular slab of fossiliferous flagstone which was found on the floor of the structure and may have been used as some kind of base or rest for another object.

Context

The stone tools from the Neolithic house in Trench B include a Knap of Howar grinder from the collapse and decay of the structure after the first phase of use [121]. The other grinder was from the external working area [308]. The sharpening/smoothing stone (SF 53) was found together with two possible stone discs in [122], the material into which wall [101] was built. The other sharpening stone was found in a part of the west wall of the building which was disturbed through stone robbing. Finally, the anvil and the other putative stone disc were from the uppermost turf and topsoil layers [06/08].

The assemblage of stone artefacts from the external working area differed from those from the rest of the site by its dominance of cobble tools. An axe and a Knap of Howar grinder were also recovered. The tools were mainly in a fragmentary and abraded condition and the conjoining pebble fragments indicate a degree of mixing of the deposits. Stone artefacts from the rammed stone working area [002] at Wideford Hill were similarly damaged and they may have been used and deposited in the same way as at Knowes of Trotty.

The evidence from the stone tools is typical of an early Neolithic site based around the structure and external working floor – this is demonstrated by the dominance of cobble tools, presence of ground stone, the absence of flake tools such as Skaill knives, the small ground stone axe and, to a certain extent, the Knap of Howar grinders. Such an assemblage is characteristic of sites from the earlier Neolithic such as Wideford Hill, Knap of Howar, Stonehall Meadow and Stonehall Knoll (see also Clarke 2006).

It should not be forgotten that the Knowes of Trotty excavations covered Bronze Age burial mounds. In this context, a complete axe was recovered from Bronze Age burial contexts in Trench F (SF 15). This axe has been ground all over to form a squared butt with faceted sides and an asymmetrically curved blade end. In respect of shape and size this axe is almost identical to that from Mousland, Stromness (Downes 1994, 145, and see Clarke 2011 for other examples of axes in Bronze Age contexts). The axe is usually considered a Neolithic form, especially numerous in deposits from the earlier Neolithic. At present it is uncertain how it may have functioned in Bronze Age ritual; perhaps it was made in the Neolithic, held as an heirloom (see Chapter 9) and reused in the

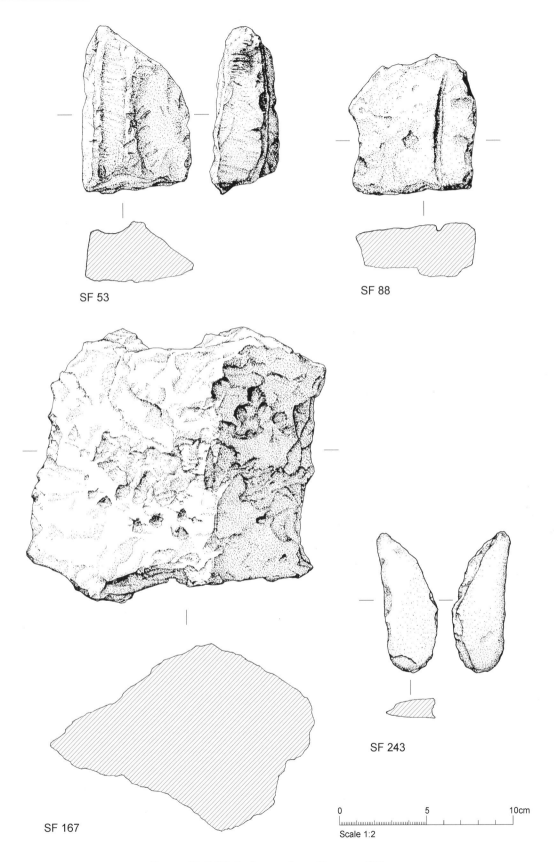

SF 53

SF 88

SF 167

SF 243

0   5   10cm

Scale 1:2

Figure 13.5 Worked stone from Knowes of Trotty.

Table 13.9 Stone tools from Smerquoy excavation 2013.

	Trench 1	Trench 2	FW
Skaill knives	6	13	
Anvils	4	1	
Axe		1	1
Macehead	1		
Flaked hammerstones	4		
Plain hammerstones	3		1
Faceted cobbles	1		1
Faceted cobble/polisher	1		
Facially pecked cobbles	2		
Smoother	1		
Polisher	1		
Knap of Howar Grinder	1		1
Ground end tool	2		1
Ground end tool blank	3		
Chopper edge tool	1		
Incised? pebble	1		
Opposed hollowed stone			1
Stone Disc	1	2	
Worn pumice	1	1	
Flaked stone bars	1		1
Total	35	18	7

2nd millennium cal BC. Given the close proximity of the early Neolithic settlement it is possible that it could have been rediscovered centuries later, however, the similarities to the axe from Mousland may indicate that axes were indeed being manufactured and used in the Bronze Age, perhaps confined to mortuary ritual.

13.5 Brae of Smerquoy

The overall settlement complex at Braes of Smerquoy is a subject of on-going fieldwork, and although with 'incomplete' post-excavation work, the fieldwalking and excavation assemblages recovered up to 2013 can be nonetheless compared with those from the other sites in this volume. During 2013, the bulk of fieldwork concerned Trench 1 and concentrated on the interior and very immediate environs of a single structure known as the Smerquoy Hoose. The second trench (Trench 2) lies further upslope and judging from recent fieldwork (July 2014) can be recognised as representing an earlier timber component of the settlement complex.

A wide range of stone tools were found at Smerquoy despite the small size of the excavated area (Table 13.9). Skaill knives, cobbles tools, and stone discs were present as well as a number of pieces of ground stone, a polissoir

and anvils. The stone structure had double the number of tools from Trench 2 and these included all the cobble tools found that year as well as the range of ground-end tools and anvils.

Although most of the stone tools came from the Smerquoy Hoose, the fact that the upper layers relate to a secondary period of occupation apparently occurring several hundred years after the initial inhabitation (see Chapter 10) means chronological clarity is an issue. For example, the presence of a flaked stone bar (SF 712, [002]) as well as one found during fieldwalking (FW 19) confirms subsequent activity dating to the Bronze Age in the immediate area. Whether this activity merely involved working the soils with the stone mattocks or deposition within the ruined Smerquoy Hoose, or more substantial nearby Bronze Age occupation is not known at present (a flaked stone bar was also found at Wideford Hill raising the same issues – see above). Nor is it known just how many of the other cobble tools could be linked with this later activity rather than the Neolithic occupation of the structure. There is some indication that the house was filled with later Neolithic material just prior to a fragment of a cushion macehead made of gneiss (SF 29) being buried in clay fill that sealed the northwest entrance.

There are three ground-end tools with a series of complex wear patterns, two of which (SFs 303 and 304) were found together at the base of pit [312] (see Fig. 4.21). A third was unstratified being recovered from ploughsoil (Fig. 13.6). The most common and noticeable feature is the rounded ground facets that have been worn on one or both ends of the pebbles. These pieces have also then been used as borers leaving light undeveloped wear patterns around the tool tip from grinding and twisting the pebble to depths of between 9mm and 13mm. On one piece (SF 304) both ends have been used in this manner whilst the other two pieces differ slightly: on SF 303 the end opposite the ground borer end bears distinctive angled facets on either side of the ground angled end as well as a sharp ridge formed by bifacial grinding down one side; the unstratified piece (Fig. 13.6) bears ground facets on opposite faces at the other end – on one side two facets form a distinctive ridge with striations running along the length of the pebble. A further three unused pebbles were identified as probable blanks for use as ground-end tools because of their size and shape. There are two Knap of Howar grinders; the unstratified piece is a classic example of its type (Fig. 13.7); the other (SF 36) is less heavily ground on the lower face and with no central pecked dimple, yet appears to have been pecked to shape a domed upper face.

Figure 13.6 Unstratified ground end 'finger' stone tool from Trench 1, Smerquoy (Christopher Gee).

Figure 13.7 Unstratified 'Knap of Howar' grinder from Trench 1, Smerquoy (Christopher Gee).

Other notable artefacts are the five anvils with traces of linear indentations pecked in one or two patches on the surface of a cobble. These were most likely used as anvils for the reduction of flint nodules using the bipolar technique.

The two axes are small and made from sedimentary rock. The axe collected during fieldwalking (A8) is damaged and burnt but still retains ground facets down both sides (Fig. 13.8). The other from Trench 2 (SF 285) appears unfinished as it is simply a flat triangular pebble with traces of grinding down both sides and along part of blade, none of which are quite heavy enough to considerably alter the profile of the edges. The presence of a block of medium to coarse-grained sandstone in Trench 1 with traces of use as a polissoir indicates that axes were ground to shape in the immediate vicinity.

13.5.1 Comparisons

The assemblage from Smerquoy, though small, shows clear similarities to those from other early Neolithic sites with respect to the presence of ground-end tools (Barnhouse and Baes of Ha'Breck), Knap of Howar grinders (Knap of Howar, Wideford Hill, Stonehall, Knowes of Trotty, Braes of Ha'Breck and Crossiecrown), a polissoir/grinding stone (Barnhouse, Braes of Ha'Breck and Stonehall) and small ground and faceted axes (Braes of Ha'Breck, Knowes of Trotty, Wideford Hill and Stonehall). In particular, the recent excavations at the Braes of Ha'Breck, Wyre (Lee and Thomas 2012; Farrell

Figure 13.8 Broken sandstone axe recovered from fieldwalking in 2010 (Christopher Gee).

et al. in press), have produced a much larger assemblage of stone tools but essentially similar in composition to that from Smerquoy, particularly with regard to the ground-end tools/Knap of Howar borers. Hopefully, future work on both these sites will be able to explore the use of these tools and perhaps compare them to the use of the ground edge or spatulate type tools occurring at other Neolithic sites.

Table 13.10 Ramberry Head: stone artefacts by site.

	Site 1	Site 2
Plain hammerstone	2	2
Pounder/grinder	-	2
Faceted cobble	1	-
Smoother	-	1
Skaill knife	1	1
Ard point	1	1
Incised slab	-	1
Notched slab	-	1
Pumice	3	-
Flint	5	1

13.6 Ramberry Head

Site 1

The stone assemblage from Ramberry Head burial cairn (Site 1) is small but varied and includes coarse stone, flint and pumice (Fig. 13.9; Table 13.10). The cobble tools are simple forms, worn by pecking, flaking and faceting. The Skaill knife bears some light traces of use wear. The ard point is a fine specimen with a squared butt and pointed working end (SF 17; Fig. 13.9). It was flaked from a larger block of black micaceous sandstone; there was no additional surface pecking to shape or strengthen the tool, which is sometimes present on other tools of this type. Wear traces that are visible over one face indicate that this ard point had been used prior to deposition.

Only two pieces of pumice had traces of wear and this was simply in the form of lightly worn faces. The flints from the site were undistinguished; just chunks or small inner flakes, one of which appeared burnt. A small barbed-and tanged arrowhead of mottled grey and white flint was found on the surface some 22m to the east of the trench.

Context

The three pieces of pumice were all from the primary layer [002]. The faceted cobble was incorporated into the cobble (sea-stone) setting [006] around the cist slab and another plain hammerstone came from [009] adjacent to this cobble setting and it is possible that it too was originally part of it. The ard point formed part of the outer ring of stones [017] encircling the central setting, as did the Skaill knife [018] and a small flint flake [014]. The remaining three pieces of flint and a plain hammerstone were unstratified. The barbed-and-tanged point cannot be directly associated with this ring cairn.

Site 2

Cobble tools were the most common stone artefacts including two plain hammerstones, two small pounder/grinders and one possible smoother. This latter tool made use of a long, spatulate-shaped pebble and may have been used lightly on one end as a smoother. The single Skaill knife appears to have light traces of use wear along the distal end. The ard point (SF 30; Fig. 13.9) is similar in manufacture and shape to the example from Site 1, but this one has not been used.

The incised slab (SF 46; Fig. 13.9) bears groups of around four scratches set in parallel lines with one group forming a possible chequerboard pattern. The slab is damaged at one end and appears to have truncated a possible notch. A single flint flake exhibits a prepared flat platform.

Context

There is nothing of special interest to say about the context of these tools. Most of them (the two pounder/grinders, Skaill knife, incised slab, notched slab and flint flake) came from the ploughsoil or the degraded rubble [031] directly underneath. The two plain hammerstones and possible smoother came from the rubble dumps of the earlier phases.

The ard point has perhaps the most interesting context being placed along with the arc of large stones [043] in the centre of the rubble-filled structure.

Discussion

The stone assemblage from Site 1, though small, is quite varied for a 2nd millennium cal BC funerary context in Orkney. More usually the stone tools form discrete assemblages of particular artefact types. Thus, flaked stone bars and ard points are most often associated with the kerbs, or occasionally the mound material of the burial cairns whilst other types of stone tools including cobble tools are less common and when present, for example, at Linga Fiold, are usually associated with activity in areas around and beyond the cairns themselves (Clarke 2006, 105). At Linga Fiold too, there was an indication that the cobble tools did not have the wear traces typical of those used for processing in domestic settings and instead these cobbles were most likely used to shape the construction slabs (*ibid.*, 107).

At Ramberry Head Site 1 the ard point could be interpreted as having been deliberately placed in or on the encircling stones in an imitation of burial cairn kerb deposits.

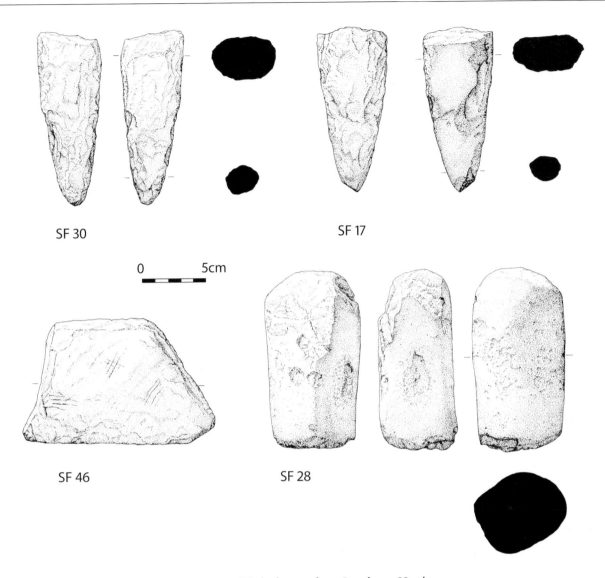

SF 30

SF 17

0   5cm

SF 46

SF 28

Figure 13.9 Worked stone from Ramberry Head.

The means of deposition of the other stone artefacts is less clear, particularly since they appear to have derived from a 'domestic' occupation rather than as a result of activity associated with the funerary rites. Certainly, at least two of the cobble tools have been redeposited in the cobble setting, but the presence of flint, pumice and the Skaill knife is less easy to interpret and it may be that they are derived from an earlier, perhaps Neolithic, occupation deposit.

The small stone assemblage from Site 2 can also be interpreted as being from a 'domestic' occupation of the Neolithic to Bronze Age though the notched slab and incised slab are rather at odds with any prehistoric period. The ard point most definitely has a Bronze Age date and its deposition over the arc of stones within the structure is reminiscent of placing such tools on the kerbs of burial cairns (see above).

The proximity of these sites to Crossiecrown is of interest. It is probable that the Grey and Red Houses were occupied late into the 3rd millennium cal BC, while stone assemblages from the middens and soils of the final occupation dated to the 2nd millennium cal BC (Chapter 10) exhibited a clear change in composition with the introduction of flaked stone bars, flaked cobbles, ard points and a developed form of smoother made on split cobbles. Skaill knives and cobble tools of various forms continued in use from earlier periods. It is with the latest 2nd millennium cal BC period of occupation at Crossiecrown that the Ramberry head stone assemblage is consistent. This is also matched to some extent by the late 3rd–early 2nd millennium cal BC component of the Muckquoy

Figure 13.10 Cobble tool from 2013 fieldwalking at Muckquoy, Redland (Hugo Anderson-Whymark).

fieldwalking assemblage (see Chapter 9) which also includes some nice examples of cobble tools (Fig. 13.10).

13.7 Conclusion

The rich assemblages of stone tools from each of the above sites demonstrate that stone was used for tools in a variety of activities. In the early Neolithic stone was employed in a number of ways linked to grinding – polissoirs to grind and shape the axes; flat cobble smoothers; Knap of Howar grinders with their distinctively-shaped forms and wear traces; Knap of Howar borers and ground-end tools which were clearly used to make perforations in an as yet unknown material; ground-edge or spatulate tools with an emphasis on shaping an acute edge; as well as a range of miscellaneous ground stone pieces. There is growing evidence from the recent excavations that some element of specialism exists within these site assemblages. For example, at Stonehall there are distinctive cobble smoothers; at Wideford Hill there are pounder/grinders; and at Smerquoy there are the ground end tools.

During the later Neolithic the use of grinding seems to decline. Whether this reflects a difference in manufacturing activities, or locations, or that other materials were used for tools is not yet understood. A more limited range of stone tools came into use including Skaill knives which most likely are indicative of butchering. Large assemblages of these flakes are associated with midden deposits at Crossiecrown, Pool, Skara Brae and Links of Noltland. Stone discs are also linked to middens at the above sites and also intimately associated with the hearth at Crossiecrown (see Chapter 7).

The Pumice from Stonehall and Crossiecrown

Ann Clarke

13.1.1 Description

The pumice from each site is of the usual type found on prehistoric sites in the Northern Isles: a brown-grey in colour with small vesicles. Just one piece, from Stonehall (SF 2088) has large vesicles, which form an open, honeycombed appearance (Fig. 13.1.1). Although there were no definite signs of wear on this particular piece it is likely that pumice of this texture was used for extremely coarse work.

The pumice must have been deliberately collected from the beach where it was washed up in strands of seaweed, and then brought to the site for use. At Crossiecrown most of the pumice pieces show signs of having been used though the wear patterns are not standardised enough to suggest that generally it was used for specific tasks. Overall, the wear is light, comprising a single worn face (SF 480) with a slightly skewed, concave or convex profile and these pieces may have been used for preparing soft materials such as leather or smoothing the curved surface of unfired pottery (Barrowman 2000). Just one piece (SF 480) has remnant grooves around the faces and these are U-shaped, about 5mm deep and 8mm wide at the top suggesting the shaping and smoothing of narrow cylindrical objects such as bone points or narrow wooden shafts. Another piece from Stonehall has a distinctive wear pattern (SF 7132) and this has a deep concave profile worn on one face.

Most of the pumice from Crossiecrown was found in the upper midden/ occupation deposits (Table 13.1.1)

Figure 13.1.1 Pumice SF 2088 from Stonehall (Richard Jones).

and a further three pieces were from the north recess and floor deposits of the Red House. At Stonehall there were no significant deposits of pumice.

Other Neolithic pumice assemblages from Orkney are similar in composition to that of Crossiecrown. At Barnhouse (Clarke 2005b) and Pool (A Smith pers. comm.) those pieces with simple worn faces are the dominant form. Both sites had grooved pieces and at Barnhouse, with the exception of two pieces with narrower, shallower grooves, the remainder fall within the size range of those on the Crossiecrown piece (SF 480).

Table 13.1.1 Crossiecrown pumice by context.

Phase	Context	Pumice total
Topsoil	001	1
Upper midden/occupation	002	11
4 – N recess	10	1
4 - Floor deposit	11	2
		15

Table 13.1.2 Stonehall pumice by context.

Trench	Description	Context	Pumice total
A	External midden	002	1
	Platform clay	16	1
B	Occupation layer	301	1
	External midden	503	3
C	Wall collapse in H3	3033	1
			7

The Black Stone Bead from Structure 1, Stonehall Farm

Alison Sheridan

Subsequent to the hearth being replaced by a cist in the centre of Structure 1 at Stonehall Farm (Figs 6.8 and 6.9), a number of 'special' objects were buried within the upper floor deposits [519]. One of these objects was a chunky disc-shaped black bead (SF 2520; Fig. 13.2.1).

The bead of blackish stone is approximately circular in plan with straight to slightly bowed sides. It has an hourglass-shaped perforation that is roughly central on one face and slightly eccentric on the other, the drill having entered the bead at a slight angle on this side. The rotation of the drill has left circular ridges in the borehole. The surfaces are smooth and have been polished to a low sheen. External diameter 26.2–27.5mm; perforation diameter *c*.3.4mm at centre, 5.7mm and 6.4mm respectively at outer edges; thickness 10.3mm. There is ancient chipping to the edge of the bead on both of its flat sides, and one ancient shallow chip scar at the edge of the perforation on one side, but there are no obvious signs of use-wear to the perforation, and the bead may not have been worn or used (or at least suspended on a cord) for very long. There are a few short, shallow, multi-directional striations on each of the flat surfaces, which probably relate to the initial shaping of the bead through grinding.

The stone used to manufacture the bead is a fairly soft laminar material, slightly warm to the touch, and this led the excavators to speculate whether it was jet. The bead has a 'stony' texture rather than the fine-grained woody texture that is often visible macro- or microscopically in jet and its laminar structure is similarly not a characteristic of that material. The fact that it has a low to negligible zirconium content and a relatively high iron content (as revealed through non-destructive compositional analysis using X-ray fluorescence spectrometry (XRF) confirms the non-jet identification; such a compositional signature is more characteristic of materials in the cannel coal to shale 'family' of rocks. There are no deposits of cannel coal as such in Orkney, but Jurassic deposits of oil shales and cannel coals are known from Caithness and Sutherland (*e.g.* the Brora oil shales). However, it is suspected that this bead does *not* represent an exotic import to Orkney; there is nothing in its simplicity of shape to link this bead to the Neolithic beads found on mainland Scotland, some of which are known to have travelled considerable distances (Sheridan and Davis 2002), Several types of black stone are known to outcrop in Orkney, and among these the carbon-rich, finely laminated Devonian siltstones and mudstones would seem to offer the most plausible candidates for the raw material.

Beads of various substances – but principally of bone and marine ivory – are known from Neolithic contexts in Orkney, from both domestic (*e.g.* Skara Brae) and funerary contexts (*e.g.* Isbister). Four chunky black stone beads from Skara Brae were previously analyzed (by Mary Davis, using XRF) and, like the Stonehall bead, were similarly demonstrated not to be of jet.

0   50 mm

1:1

Figure 13.2.1 The black stone bead from Structure 1, Stonehall Farm (Hugo Anderson-Whymark).

The Haematite and Related Iron-rich Materials

Effie Photos-Jones, Arlene Isbister and Richard Jones

13.3.1 Introduction

We present here the small but interesting assemblage of 21 objects of haematite and other iron-rich materials, 21 objects found at Crossiecrown and a few more at Stonehall. Unfortunately, more recent objects, including a knobbed-shaped artefact, discovered during fieldwalking at Muckquoy, are not included. The aim is to describe the finds, characterise them mineralogically and chemically and to assess their suitability and evidence for use as pigments. The potential sources of these materials on Orkney are also reviewed. Whereas some of the finds from Crossiecrown were recognised on first examination as likely to be haematite or goethite, there were several cases at both sites that were more difficult to identify macroscopically; chemical analysis proved helpful in identifying specimens whose iron content was too low to be classed as a ferruginous material, but at Crossiecrown that still left a few specimens, some of which were surface finds, that could be classified as bog iron or even iron slag. For this reason the finds at Crossiecrown are labelled neutrally as iron-rich products (IP). Some terminology is introduced below.

Isbister (2000) has set the scene by outlining the early published evidence of haematite on Orkney, mainly from Skara Brae, its use as a pigment and its possible mystical and medicinal roles. Having examined various finds and using both haematite from Creekland Bay, Hoy and mined Cumbrian haematite, she reported the results of pigment/paint producing experiments, including the effects of temperature on the colour (see also Isbister 2009 with colour illustrations). Exploring how the fine faceted surfaces were created, it emerged that surfaces had produced an abundance of highly coloured pigment/paint, in sharp contrast to their very dark surface appearance which would also have no adhering pigment. While such surfaces may have had secondary uses, such as polishing leather (Clarke and Maguire 1989, 25; Ritchie 1995, 18), Isbister's experiments demonstrated that they were primarily used for their quality pigment,

and she argued that the significant process that modified the raw material and created the artefact should not be overlooked (Isbister 2000, 192).

13.3.2 Terminology

Haematite: ferric iron oxide mineral, Fe_2O_3, includes a very hard and fine-grained crystalline variety, mainly coloured black, steel-blue or purplish-grey in the field, that may give a bright or sub-metallic lustre (specular iron ore), particularly when polished or worked for pigment. It gives a red streak.

Goethite: hydrated ferric iron oxide, $FeOH$, is an iron mineral that can be very similar in appearance to haematite but is duller and browner and gives a yellow-brown streak.

Red ochre: is a 'pigment' name for the soft earthy forms of iron-rich materials that are generally mixed with clays. It does not have to be natural.

Iron pan: concentration of ferric iron oxy-hydroxides found in soil and usually of natural origin.

Iron seepages: iron-rich spring-water with deposits of ferric iron oxy-hydroxides formed by oxidation (bacterially mediated) of ferrous iron in solution. Deposits are usually reddish-brown.

Limonite: earthy poorly crystallised or amorphous ferric iron oxy-hydroxide that is essentially goethite with molecular water, $FeOH.nH_2O$.

Bog iron: an impure iron deposit that develops in bogs, consisting mainly of hydrated iron oxides.

13.3.3 Methodology

All the material was examined by eye and magnifier. The presence of metallic iron was tested with a simple magnet. EPJ streak tested thirteen samples on a porcelain plate to reveal colours ranging from pale yellow to deep red as a means of differentiating between haematite and other iron-rich minerals. A sample of crystalline haematite from the mine at Muirkirk in

Figure 13.3.1 The wet abrasion method demonstrated on a white quartzite stone showing micronised pigment production from the surfaces of a nodule of crystalline haematite from Bay of Creekland, Hoy. In the process the nodule is very finely striated, faceted and polished (Copyright: Arlene Isbister).

southern Scotland was used as a standard for the typical deep red streak of haematite.

Many of the finds were analysed mineralogically by powder X-ray diffraction (XRD) (Phillips 1050/35 instrument (Department of Geology, Glasgow University) with vertical goniometer and a Co Kα Fe-filtered radiation source; scanning speed 1° 2θ/min; scan range 0–60° 2θ) and for semi-quantitative elemental composition by portable X-ray fluorescence (pXRF) with a Niton XL3t instrument. The samples selected for XRD consisted of ground powder packed into a cavity in a ceramic mount. Simple heating experiments were carried out to confirm conversion of hydrated ferric iron minerals to haematite.

To develop experiments, Arlene Isbister utilised her sizable collections of haematite and goethite from the Florence Mine at Egremont, Cumbria (*e.g.* kidney and pencil ore, massive compact and botryoidal haematite and specularite) and sources from Bay of Creekland (*e.g.* black, steely and purplish-grey lumps and nodules, some botryoidal). Examining and working the raw material in both its 'pure' whole state and the form it was most likely found in, *i.e.* as weathered beach finds, expanded knowledge of the material and enabled development of previous experiments. Preliminary comparisons in shape, size, colour and surface texture were drawn between the finds and the unmodified and experimental material. Wet and dry streak tests of the finds were taken on white quartzite pebbles.

Wet Abrasion Method

Experimental context

Some preliminary painting experiments were carried out: small fragments were crushed to powder, a few drops of water were added and the paint was applied by brush to either experimental brickettes made of modern red clay or pots made and fired at Stonehall (see Chapter 11.5). Alternatively, pigments were prepared using a technique that removed a fine layer of pigment particles from the nodule face. This was achieved by rubbing down a nodule's face in a drop of water on a hard stone that had the added advantage of dispersing the pigment and binding it to any mineral 'impurities' which produced a tacky paint or a pigmented stone surface; the presence of an organic binder was found to be superfluous (Isbister 2000, 193).

The *wet abrasion method* reduces the pigment particle size and creates a finer more cohesive paint; in the process the hard haematite nodule is lightly faceted and polished, and often marked with the finest striations, producing the same use-wear as observed on many of the finds. This is evidently a very economical and resourceful means for the Neolithic inhabitant to acquire quality polychromatic pigment materials, particularly over an extended period; an abraded nodule is easily stored, can produce various rich colours, is portable and unlike the former method is very unlikely to be gone after one session (Isbister 2000, 194). The comparison is not unlike the long use obtained from a water colour pan (when only the small amount required is made up at a time), and the crushing up of that same pan and using it quickly and crudely. Some other *wet abrasion method* experiments were carried out using haematite with gum/resin binders; and sample dry and aquarelle crayon tests on stone were taken (see Fig. 13.3.1).

Historical context

Traditionally, artists employed the age-old technique of muller and grinding slab to create their pigments which is largely similar in effect to the above *wet abrasion method*. The stone muller and slab reduced the pigment material to a state of fineness and optimized pigment dispersion in a binder or medium. (Mortar and pestle was only required for the initial breaking up of very hard materials.) The technique is recommended by early writers for obtaining the highest quality pigment and colours. The main process involved moving and rotating by hand, a muller (cone-shaped porphyry or a pebble stone sliced in half to provide a flat smooth surface) on pulverized pigment, wetted with water, across a stone grinding slab. This was done for lengthy

Table 13.3.1 Haematite and related iron-rich materials at Crossiecrown. Continued p. 478.

IP (SF)	Location (coordinates)	Context	XRD ID (%Fe content determined by pXRF)	Description	Streak
1	Topsoil	001	Haematite/quartz (>50)	Nodule of black haematite with bright lustre. Near all surfaces have been rounded and worked smooth with deep and fine striations visible on all surfaces. Upper slim facet and orthogonal facet show metallic lustre through much use. Similarly shaped and sized nodule observed at Creekland Bay (CB). Max. dimension 3cm. (Figs 13.3.3b, c)	Pale red (cf IP6), but deep red in wet streak test
1 bis	Tr 1	001	(>50)	Amorphous brown lumps of bog iron	Not tested
2 (221)	House 1	026	Goethite/quartz (>50)	Roughly rhomboid lump of black iron ore, goethite, massive in form and with compact crystalline structure; two surfaces have been roughly smoothed. Similarly shaped and sized nodule at CB; 8×6.5×4cm. Fig. 13.3.3a	Dark yellow
3	Midden area close to House 1	122	Goethite/quartz (>50)	Large black heavy lump of iron ore crudely worked/smoothed on two orthogonal surfaces; max. dimension 10.5cm. Fig. 13.3.3a	Dark yellow but changed to deep red on heating to 600°C for 2 hours
4	(113/106)	001	Haematite/quartz (>50)	Dull, purple-grey reddish lump of compact crystalline haematite with two orthogonal surfaces rubbed down flat/smooth and another rubbed. Similarly shaped and sized nodule observed at CB. 4.5×3×2.7cm.	Bright deep red like Muirkirk standard
4 bis	(113/106)	001	Haematite/quartz (>60)	Fragment of dark haematite with two smoothed facets parallel to each, one of them with striations, and two other facets; max. dimension 3cm, thickness 1.6cm; Fig. 13.3.3d (>60)	Bright deep red like Muirkirk standard
5	Midden area by House 1 (121/108)	002	Haematite (>50)	Fragment of black botryoidal haematite with lustrous shiny appearance. Four surfaces rubbed down; the underside and long orthogonal side surface worked extensively flat/smooth, showing fine striations. 4.5×3.5; max. thickness 1.3cm. Figs 13.3.3b, c	Deep red
6 (189)	Feature NE of House 1	025	(8)	Rounded weathered nodule with large fresh black crystals visible in the broken section; 7×5×4cm	Grey; but crushing with muller on slab gives mid to dark brownish colour suggestive of the presence of manganese as well as iron oxides (although XRF indicated <0.5% Mn).
7	(119/109)	001	Haematite (>50)	Thin rectangular fragment of black botryoidal haematite which joins 5 above has one well smoothed surface; 3×2×0.5cm	Not tested
8	Plough soil (118/109)	001	(>50)	Sandstone ?sea pebble with remains of black hematite vein (now only 2mm thick) which has been rubbed down to give an excellent smoother; similar size piece forming haematite veinlet on half sandstone pebble observed at CB. 3×2×2.8cm Fig. 13.3.3d	Pale red, but yellow on wet streak
9	Tr 1 spit 1	002	(>50)	Rectangular, rhomboid of fibrous 'pencil ore' of dark grey haematite, with longest surfaces and point partially rubbed down. Top and front stained red; side and underside stained brown. 2×1.7×1cm; Fig. 13.3.3b	
10	(118/106)	topsoil	Quartz/goethite, feldspar (>50%)	Amorphous lump of iron-rich material; max. dimension 8cm; Fig. 13.3.3d	
11 (766)	Tr 2 ext.	454	Not analysed	Nodule of black haematite with botryoidal exterior; other main surface has been rubbed down very smooth; very similar pieces observed at CB; max. dimension 3cm; thickness 1cm; Figs 13.3.3b, c	
12	(113.6/104)	topsoil	(4)	Amorphous fragments of iron-rich material	
13	Tr 3	Topsoil	Not analysed (>50)	Dark dense pebble with one smoothed surface; max. dimension 4cm and max. thickness 2cm	
14 (550)	2	001	Goethite, pyrite/quartz (>50)	Roughly rounded, dense and heavy fragment; weathered rusty looking brown surface. Bog iron? Fig. 13.3.3d. One surface 4cm long has probably been deliberately smoothed; max. dimension 6cm	
15	(120/112)	002	Feldspar, clay/quartz, dolomite, siderite, kaolin, haematite (10% Fe, 1% Ti)	Small powdery lumps of bog iron. Acceptable as a pigment.	

Table 13.3.1 Haematite and related iron-rich materials at Crossiecrown, continued.

IP (SF)	Location (coordinates)	Context	XRD ID (%Fe content determined by pXRF)	Description	Streak
16 (570)	Tr 2	003	(>50)	Amorphous grey-brown lump with metallic feel on outer smoothed surface; 3×2.5×1cm	
17 (643)	Tr 2	425	(45)	Roughly rectangular shaped lump of iron-rich material, metallic feel (but not magnetic), coarse surfaces; 6×3×2cm	
18 (676)	Tr 2 ext	142	(>50)	Lump of black haematite with two worked smoothed surfaces, orthogonal to each other; one surface with visible striations from use; max. dimension 3cm; Fig. 13.3.3b	
19 (735)	Tr 2 ext	001	(>50)	Amorphous black fragment with smoothed outer surface; iron slag? but not magnetic. Max. dimension 4cm	
20 (765)	Tr 2 ext	145	(30??)	Amorphous, brown, dense fragment, metallic feel but not magnetic; max. dimension 4cm	
21 (817)	Tr 2 ext	458	(10)	Small amorphous fragment of orange iron-rich sandstone; max. dimension 1.5cm	

periods of time until the desired finely-ground material was achieved (Mayer 1991, 188). The technique was first detailed by Cennino Cennini, a 14th century painter and an authority on the painting techniques of the day. To obtain rich or translucent reds, purples and oranges, he ground the purest and hardest 'crystalline' haematite forms, and in particular 'specular iron-ore', the same type he used for making burnishers and not the amorphous earthy varieties. Cennini reports:

> Pound this stone in a bronze mortar at first, because if you broke it up on your porphyry slab you might crack it. And when you have got it pounded, put on the slab as much of it as you want to work up, and grind it with clear water; and the more you work it up, the better and more perfect color it becomes.

(Thompson 1933, 25)

It would appear that the Crossiecrown inhabitants did not have to use their mortar to crush their haematite. They could use a technique more suited to their needs and means which combined the two-step process described by Cennini, into an innovative one-step process which could also transform the haematite into finely ground, highly coloured and optimally dispersed pigment material; it was possibly similar in quality and colour to the historic technique still used by fine artists today.

13.3.4 Results

13.3.4.1 Crossiecrown

The descriptions and identifications are given in Table 13.3.1; Fig. 13.3.2 shows the results of the streak tests. The assemblage includes very hard and heavy, crystalline haematite and goethite, some in botryoidal forms and largely coloured black and grey, rather than the more common red and yellow ochres. Most of the finds were assessed as potential pigments and many displayed evidence of such production. The striking characteristic of many of these lumps, such as **IP1, 5, 11** and **18** (Figs 13.3.3a–c) among others, is the presence of one or more very finely striated and polished faceted surfaces that, on close inspection, reveal clear evidence of pigment-producing modification and *wet abrasion method* techniques. Streak tests, experimental work and observations on the majority of wear-facet surfaces indicate that various saturations of red, orange, purple and yellow pigment material could have been produced.

Of the samples analysed mineralogically five were identified as haematite (**IP1, IP4bis, IP5**) or likely to be haematite (**IP4, IP7**); they would probably be joined by **IP8, IP9, IP11, IP18** on the basis of elemental composition and appearance. The rest were goethite (**IP2, IP3**) or goethite as the major constituent with quartz and pyrite as the minor ones (**IP14**). Amorphous non-crystalline ferruginous constituents are likely to be present in **IP15** having a dark brown colour and, uniquely among the finds examples analysed chemically, a notable titanium content; only **IP15** had a weak magnetism, all the rest had none.

Two main varieties of crystalline haematite predominate: a purplish-grey type (**IP4, IP4bis**) and a shiny-black type (**IP1, IP5, IP7, IP11**). Judging from the XRD results, **IP4bis** has considerably more crystallinity than either **IP1** or **IP5**, which would appear to correlate with Cennini's description that the purest mineral form of haematite has the outward 'colour of purple or turnsole' (*ibid.*, 25). **IP9**, unique in the group, is an example of 'needle' or 'pencil ore'. Many pieces from Bay of Creekland are similar to the finds in shape (rhombohedral crystal habit), streak, size, colour and surface texture. Not only does this imply a 'potential' source for the finds but it can also reveal the amount of pigment use that finds were put to. Several unmodified pieces were employed in experiments.

Weathering can affect the surface appearance of primary iron oxides such as haematite. For example, both the finds and the unmodified lumps show similarities in their surface weathering, unlike the pristine material sourced from Florence Mine. However, working the Hoy material for pigment, using the wet abrasion method, dramatically changed tarnished surfaces into 'specular' (metallic or sub-metallic) or lightly sparkling faceted surfaces. Several unmodified pieces were cracked open with a hammer and it was notable how their glittery grey and purplish inner surfaces matched the outward appearances of the high ore-grade Cumbrian material. Working with haematite from the Middle Stone Age of southern Africa, Ian Watts also reports that weathering can change the surface of the mineral giving a highly oxidized patina and dark brown surface appearance, but a fresh surface exposure of highly crystalline haematite would reveal a steely-grey, iron-black or blue grey colour (Watts 1998, 279).

There appears to be no difference in how the two main varieties of haematite were modified; none have been fashioned to any particular form, which is the same for nearly all other haematite finds from local sites (Isbister 2000, 192). Many feature rubbed flat and smooth-faceted surfaces from prolonged pigment production use, most likely from the earlier described *wet abrasion method* (*e.g.* **IP4, IP4bis, IP5, IP7, IP8**). However, it is worth noting that it might be easy to presume that the naturally shiny-black type has been 'overtly' polished due to some other secondary use, when, more than likely, its high polish is only inherent to its type. After all, these finds, which are particularly hard, have 'polish' across even unworked surfaces *i.e.* not only on the facetted faces and can be observed on **IP11**. The purplish grey type is much duller in comparison, yet the pieces show the same worked surfaces. This suggests, and is supported by shiny black pieces from Bay of Creekland, that variability in raw material or haematite type need not imply a different mode of use (Watts 1998, 415).

The colour of haematite pigment varies greatly depending on its particle size. When the hardest, crystalline haematite is broken down and pulverised, the colour of the particles (coarse to fine), go from silver-

Figure 13.3.2 Streak test on ceramic plate of samples (top row) left to right: M=Muirkirk standard, Crossiecrown IP1, IP2, IP3, IP4, IP5; (bottom row): IP6, IP7, IP8, IP10, IP14, IP5, IP21.

Figure 13.3.3a Crossiecrown haematite IP3 and IP2.

Figure 13.3.3b Crossiecrown haematite: top row IP1, 5, 9; lower row IP 11, 18.

Figure 13.3.3c Crossiecrown haematite IP1, 5 and 11 showing very finely striated and polished faceted surfaces that, on close inspection, reveal clear evidence of pigment-producing modification and wet abrasion method techniques.

Figure 13.3.3d Crossiecrown haematite: top IP8, 10; bottom IP4bis, IP14.

grey, to near black to dark brown to brown-red to red. As indicated by Cennini (Thompson 1933), the quality of grinding, dispersion of pigment to water (or binder), and crystallinity and mineral impurities all affect whether haematite materials can produce rich colours, such as deep reds, purples and oranges. The brightest colours are achieved when the purest haematite is in its finest red form, or approximately 3 microns and finer in particle size. Its characteristic red or orange-red colour is then displayed as the smaller grains scatter red light (Bowles *et al.* 2011, 247).

Pigment prepared from **IP7** was an effective paint on a pottery surface: the paint layer was stable and had a deep rich red colour. By striking contrast, **IP21**, having a soft orange texture, was able to give a streak with ease to either stone or pot but it was fugitive; when applied as a paint the colour was weak and, on drying, rubbed off (Fig. 13.3.4). In her experiments, Isbister (2000) found that alternate facets on a single nodule could produce different colours, and, for example, the distinctive facet on **IP1**, similar to that on examples from Skara Brae, could have been created when the nodule was pulled along a carved stone groove, infilling the area with wet pigment. Those varieties slightly less hard than **IP1**, such as the purple-grey type, might also have been used similarly on a grooved pot.

IP5 and **IP7** jigsaw together, forming one of the largest haematite finds that has been heavily modified. Breakage more than likely occurred due to the thinning effects of prolonged use. It is estimated, from unmodified similar pieces, that the front and back have been rubbed down extensively using the *wet abrasion method*, the longest side of **IP5** by possibly at least a centimetre. Striations on each surface side vary and all are almost imperceptible to the naked eye; with magnifier they are most pronounced on the underside and least so on the botryoidal surface. Experiments show that the hardest of black haematite (Mohs scale 7–7.5) such as this requires wet abrasion on the hardest and coarsest of sandstones to produce any quantity of pigment. During one session, much wet, fine red pigment would have been produced, opaque or transparent, thin or viscous depending on the liquid used as well as the weight and time applied by the maker. The resulting surface facet would have been further striated and polished; however in one short session, due to the particular hardness of the material, little obvious modification would have occurred to its face. The earlier comparison to the prolonged use that a water colour pan gives serves correct in this context, because even the very small and well-worn rubbed haematite nodule would be perfectly proficient at producing finely micronized pigment for various applications.

Several pieces, particularly **IP9** and **IP4bis**, show possible use as 'crayons' *i.e.* that a small pointed area has been overtly rubbed or directly applied on stone as dry or aquarelle crayoned marks. **IP4bis** is also the only find with scored striations from rubbing, on one of its well smoothed surfaces. Experiments show that this may indicate the nodule face was rubbed down for pigment, partially wetted, scratching its face in the process; or it is possible the same technique was applied to a vertical, flat stone surface, such as a wall as it created aquarelle painted areas. Both finds show that they could have lightly scored and eloquently 'crayoned' and 'painted' a design on a vertical stone surface which supports Arlene Isbister's previous suggestion regarding how the now fragmented and faintly incised wall designs from Skara Brae (and indeed other similar Orcadian megalithic art) were originally produced (Isbister 2000, 194; Bradley *et al.* 2001, 54, 65).

Further experiments have shown that the *wet abrasion method* achieves brighter and more saturated colours and even finer pigment material when employing viscous binders or mediums instead of water which has delivered some interesting results. Equally, the finest nodule surfaces are created when these viscous media (such as gum or resin) are employed. This cushions the grinding process while simultaneously binding the pigment, allowing finer pigment particles to scatter creating rich or highly saturated orange-red pigment material (Isbister 2009). However, it is important to note there are other variables which can affect the overt smoothness of a facet, such as surface texture of the sandstone and the pressure applied to the process. For example, rubbing down the very hardest haematite materials in water can give a similar surface facet to one created by a viscous material; but with plain water, in most applications, a brighter colour is not achieved.

The *wet abrasion method* was also employed to explore pigment colour and optimal saturation that was potentially exploited from the finds. Preliminary experiments specifically using gum of turpentine from pine resin had some unexpected results. Two experimental test pieces were each rubbed down in gummy turpentine and the material was thinly smeared on fragments of white glazed pottery to test colour saturation and brightness. One produced a highly saturated pure orange saffron colour and the other a translucent deep crimson or blood red. Their vividness, particularly that of the orange was unexpected as was the

Figure 13.3.4 (Modern) pot made of Orcadian clay showing painted decoration using haematite (left band) and iron-rich sandstone (right band) after firing at 500°C for 3 hours.

sparkling shimmer the colours emitted when placed in direct sunlight. The same shimmer was absent in other light, including artificial light. Water-soluble tree gum, a traditional water colour binder, was also used which produced satisfactory matt colours, brighter than those rubbed down in water but without the translucency and sparkle of the water-resistant turpentine.

In the above context, gum of turpentine may only appear as an artist material but it may be relevant that pine sap and its associated products have a longer history as a powerful antibacterial in Britain.[1] Similarly haematite is also a healing agent for the body and some medicinal and symbolic associations have been previously discussed (Isbister 2000, 194–95; 2009). It is feasible that they were employed together not only for artistic reasons but for medicinal ones too. After all, both agents have physiological properties that stop bleeding and they share a potent symbolism still referred to today: the sap or resin, the tree's blood (Stross 1997, 177–86) and haematite the Earth's blood, when mixed together and applied to a wound may have provided a powerful healing concoction. Equally, the highly saturated 'crystalline' colour applied to the skin or any other surface may have held a highly sensory presence. We return to this issue in the Discussion section.

Some years ago, Arlene Isbister observed various orange-red pigment materials from the William Watt Skara Brae collection at the Orkney Museum, one of which could tentatively be said to look similar to a hardened resinous material mixed with finely ground haematite. However no analysis of these materials has yet

Table 13.3.2 Iron-rich materials at Stonehall.

SF	Trench	Context	Provisional ID (%Fe content determined by pXRF)
6434	B	521	Roughly shaped fragment of iron-rich material, dark grey and dense; max. dimension 4cm (30)
8013	C	4004	Small fragment of orange iron-rich sandstone; max. dimension 2cm; (5).

been reported and whether the piece does or does not contain resin of course would not imply it was not used with pigments at Crossiecrown or Skara Brae. George Petrie appears to describe a similar hard resinous material when he refers to a large 'mass' of red haematite pigment 'resembling a brick in form' (Petrie 1867, 210).

13.3.4.2 Stonehall

At Stonehall the situation is different as there are no examples of black crystalline haematite (Table 13.3.2). **SF634** from the Farm site (Trench B) with an iron content of 30% may be impure goethite or alternatively a fragment of haematite that was partly worked, discarded and then heavily weathered. The other finds are small orange fragments of sandstone with a low but varying iron content. At least a dozen small finds (especially in Trench C (the Knoll) and Trench Z (the Meadow)) were initially labelled as ochre but subsequent examination indicated they were fragments of sandstone with a few percent of iron. Usually soft in texture, they streaked well but were wholly inadequate as pigments for painting.

13.3.5 Sources of haematite and related iron ores on Orkney

These mainly occur on Hoy at locations in the northern part of the island such as the Bay of Creekland (haematite, limonite and goethite: Mykura 1976, 119; Wilson *et al.* 1935, 151–52). There, veins are associated with a west-north-west fault, which can be traced inland and were worked by the Carron Company around 1765, in the field above the cliff, or near the Kirk, as reported by Low and Fleming (MacGregor *et al.* 1920, 216–17). Although it was available in great quantities (Low 1879, 4), apparently the economic venture was not a success, largely because the veins were not of workable breadth, however a quantity of ore raised was sufficient to be detailed as 'Orkney Ore' in published iron ores used at Carron in 1768 (Wilson *et al.* 1935, 152).

As already mentioned, Isbister (2000, 193) found at the Bay of Creekland quantities of haematite along the sandy shoreline, the majority of which was probably drawn in by the sea's undertow, from the eroded lining joints in the fractured seaward beds. However she also located on the rocky foreshore other pieces, in particular a palm-sized piece of black, botryoidal haematite (*c.* 9 × 7 cm) wedged between the large sandstone rocks, which, by its shape, looked to have 'grown' *in situ* (see Fig. 13.3.5). It was apparent that a very black glossy shine had formed on its upper surface where water percolated.

There are other occurrences on Hoy at the Candle or Burn of the Sale, lying close by the major Bring fault line (red-stained soils with minute crystals of haematite and goethite: Wilson *et al.* 1935, 151–52; Heddle 1901, 90; at Lead Geo (bog iron ore (with psilomelane): Heddle 1901, 109; MacGregor *et al.* 1920, 216–17) and in the south as at the east shore of Aith Hope (red haematite specimens: Heddle 1901, 89–90). Occurrences of haematite, not *in situ* but as lumps usually on the beach, on Mainland have recently been discovered by Christopher Gee at Redland north of Finstown (see now Fig. 9.36), which in terms of proximity is most relevant to this study, and around Deer Sound (at Deerness, Comely, and near the Hall of Tankerness) (John Brown, pers. comm.).

Better understanding of the geology of the known sources combined with these new discoveries on Mainland may help us map the bigger picture of the whereabouts of even small quantities of these iron ores, sources that were sought across Orkney during the Neolithic. According to geological research, it would appear that haematite can form as either a product of volcanic activity, forming precipitates during submarine volcanism, or subaqueous deposition of material from volcanic vents; and also abundantly as sublimates in the clefts of volcanic cones and in cavities of lava streams. Equally relevant is the apparent association between the fine-grained, platy habit of haematite and its formation in hydrothermal conditions (Bowles *et al.* 2011, 249–51; Geikie 1882, 67–68, 598–99).

Clearly, this work in Orkney would require further study, but for now it is interesting to note that where Orkney's geological vents are located (Mykura 1976, 97, 103–104), which are often associated with principal folds and fault systems (Wilson *et al.* 1935, 8, 13; Mykura 1976, 10), there appears to be a correlation with the known haematite sources or some significant archeological finds of haematite. Of the eight or so vent area locations reported by Mykura and Wilson nearly all appear to be so associated. For example, of the above-mentioned Hoy sources, the north-west area behind the Bay of Creekland hosts a cluster of five volcanic orifices: three vents and two volcanic plugs. Another vent is just north of the Candle of the Sale and the remaining other two on Hoy are close by the reported haematite at Aith Hope in the south-east. Of the three vents on South Ronaldsay, two are a few miles from Isbister chambered tomb, where a unique shiny black haematite axe head was found as part of a hoard (Ritchie 1995, 54); the outcropping of haematite found recently in east Mainland by Deer Sound and by St Peter's Bay is well within the vicinity of the west coast Deerness vent. The Harra Ebb, near Yesnaby on Mainland's west coast, has six small crypto-vents and, although no haematite has been reported there, it cannot be ignored that Skara Brae is only a few miles north along the coast line where Childe and Paterson (1928, 268) report its presence and Isbister (2004; see also Callander 1930, 99) estimates around fifty pieces from the early and 1970s excavations. In addition Childe (1931, 137) and Callendar (1930, 99) acknowledged the presence of haematite nodules in the Old Red Sandstone on Mainland and presumed its collection by the villagers; this is possibly similarly to how AI found nodules, including an (*in situ*) specimen at the Bay of Creekland.

Finally, one other vent is recorded, in association with a monchiquite dyke, on the shore of the Bay of Firth at Rennibister (Wilson *et al.* 1935, 180) that is but a mile or so from our assemblage of iron minerals at Crossiecrown. It is particularly significant in terms of this study as it associates the area with particular geological activities, including possible hydrothermal conditions that might have contributed to the formation of high-grade haematite and goethite deposits in the Bay of Firth area; it also provides a possible new context for the recent discovery of haematite at Redland.

13.3.6 Discussion

The pieces of haematite/goethite at Crossiecrown constitute an exceptional assemblage that is unique among recently excavated sites on Orkney. A wide-ranging assemblage such as this is unusual and demonstrates evidence for some of the techniques once used to prepare pigment, for example the earlier described *wet abrasion method*, and as such exhibits archaeological potential for further practical application and interpretation. The corresponding finds at Stonehall are much more limited.

It seems likely that samples of Orcadian haematite

Figure 13.3.5 Palm-sized specimen of shiny, black, botryoidal haematite (c.9 × 7 cm) found in situ between the sandstone boulders at Bay of Creekland on Hoy (Copyright: Arlene Isbister).

may be easily confused with well-crystallised dark goethite which resembles but is not hematite. The iron nodules rich in goethite should not be under-estimated as a source of red pigment, although to what extent they produced a 'desirable red' requires further investigation. The colouring matter found in the paint pots of stone and whale bone at Skara Brae was shown by analysis to consist of powdered haematite (Childe 1931, 137) but it is not possible to say whether the powder was either ground up haematite or goethite which had been heated and converted irreversibly to haematite. Heating to a temperature of *c.*250°C in a domestic hearth for a few hours would be sufficient for the reaction to take place (Gualtieri and Venturelli 1999).

Turning to the known sources of iron minerals on Orkney, Hoy features strongly in the literature in part because the ores there comprising haematite in association with limonite and goethite have been exploited in recent times. There is furthermore frequent reference in Table 13.3.1 to visual similarity between individual pieces at Crossiecrown and those found (by AI) at the Bay of Creekland on Hoy. But in the light of recent discoveries mentioned above (including the Bay of Firth's association with possibly the only geological vent on central Mainland that might have contributed to the deposition of iron minerals in the area), its occurrence in the form of lumps on the NW side of the Bay of Firth, if confirmed by further prospection, is highly significant because it offers a potential near-local source. To take that argument a step further, the relatively high frequency of haematite finds at Crossiecrown may signify the presence of outcrops close to the site whose weathering has yielded lumps that have accumulated near the coast. There are as well other local ferruginous materials such as bog iron, inferior in quality to haematite or goethite, which may have been noticed either *in situ* or as lumps owing to their colour. Both the size of **IP3** and the indications of the first working of its surfaces are suggestive that this was a large lump found perhaps in the course of walking or travelling near the settlement.

The contrast with the comparable situation elsewhere is striking: no haematite at Wideford Hill or Knap of Howar has been reported; Barnhouse yielded a single fragment (Clarke 2005a, 327), as did Pool in phase 3.1 (Clarke 2007, 387–88). On the other hand, at Rinyo lumps of polished and striated haematite were found in chambers A and D (Childe and Grant 1939, 29), and the haematite axe head from Isbister and quantities from Skara Brae are mentioned above.

Nevertheless, it would appear that even during Neolithic times Hoy's iron ore deposits would have been plentiful, given the island's prolific geological past and associated iron ore veins, and was probably collected as described above. However, along with other likely Mainland sources including the west Mainland coast, by Skara Brae and Deerness in the east, there is in principle little reason to doubt, given the new indications, that the inhabitants of Crossiecrown did not have access to a considerable amount of iron ore minerals on the shores of the Bay of Firth and in their wider locality.

Further experimental work is called for. The shape of nodules and their facets' surface texture are fashioned not only by the wet medium employed to grind down the pigment material but also by the surface qualities of the 'grindstone'. Likewise stone surfaces become smoothed from repetition of the described techniques. The stone mortar excavated from Crossiecrown and selected cobble stones (see Chapter 13.3) might be examined for associated use-wear, bearing in mind that wet pigment production techniques need not leave staining on grindstones. Pigment preparation techniques should be explored in light of further examination of the material and in association with finds from other sites. And finally, in relation to the role

that stones played in traditional medicine in the Scottish Highlands and Islands (Beith 2004, 144–46), it is possible that haematite could have been regarded as a magical stone having curative properties, as already alluded to in the section above on Crossiecrown. Writing in the 16th century and relying heavily on ancient sources, Agricola believed that was the case: 'Haematite is so-called either because it is the color of blood, as Galen rightly believes, following Theophrastus; because it stops the flow of blood; or because, having been ground on a wet whetstone, it imitates a bloody juice' (Bandy and Bandy 2004, 86), and furthermore 'Physicians use haematite since it dries and is astringent. The powder, after the mineral is completely pulverized in a mortar, reduces roughness of the eyelids, a disease the Greeks call τράχωμα, when mixed with egg and smeared on the inflamed lid. If mixed with water it stops bleeding from an open vein. It is beneficial in the treatment of all ulcers. The powder reduces all fleshy growths' (*ibid.*, 88). Returning to a Scottish context, two related points may be added; first the role of the blacksmith as someone traditionally endowed with magical and healing powers and second the link between him and the raw materials he sought. The blacksmiths who worked the early bloomery iron furnaces in Scotland and Ireland were accustomed to searching for bog iron ore; the precursors of these crude ores were the iron seepages whose colour in streams or springs would have been a dramatic bright red (Photos-Jones and Hall 2011). The symbolic association of this natural material with human blood would have been clear enough.

Note

1. For example, several early 19th-century doctors revived this antibacterial medicine with much success which is reported to have had prior long use in Britain and Ireland. They prescribed spirit or oil of turpentine, taken internally, and were successful in treating, to name but a few conditions: childbed and typhus fevers and chronic rheumatism and dysentery; topically they cured extensive scalds and burns (Spratt 1830, 29–31); whereas its resin was used in the composition of medicinal plasters and its raw form, pine sap, was then used as ointments and plasters by farriers (*ibid.*, 17 and 19).

CHAPTER FOURTEEN

The Animal Remains from Stonehall and Crossiecrown

Catherine Smith and Julie A. Roberts

14.1 Stonehall

14.1.1 Introduction and Methods

An assemblage of cremated animal bones and teeth was recovered during the excavation of the Neolithic site at Stonehall, Orkney. The bones were in a particularly poor state of preservation and only those fragments which had been burned or completely calcined had survived burial conditions. The teeth seem to have survived rather better than the bones, probably due to their higher mineral component. Of the bones which were recovered, only a very small proportion of the fragments could be identified: out of a total weight of 12.1kg, only a very few grams of material were recognisable.

All fragments from Stonehall were assessed. The unidentifiable (mainly calcined) bone material was classified as Indeterminate Mammal. Tooth fragments from the larger species were classified as either cattle (cf. Cattle, Large Ungulate or if very small or decomposed, Ungulate). There was a possibility that some of these tooth fragments might have come from red deer, since this species is known to have been present in Orkney during the Neolithic period, but as there were no definite identifications of deer teeth it is probable that all large tooth fragments from Stonehall did in fact come from cattle. Far fewer fragments were positively identified as Sheep/goat, (cf. Sheep/goat or Small Ungulate). This last category can include Roe Deer, but as in the case of the larger deer species there were no positive identifications.

14.1.2 Quantification of the fragments

All fragments classified as Indeterminate Mammal were quantified by abundance and given a coding indicating the number of fragments (an abundance of + indicates a quantity of from 1–10 fragments, ++ indicates 11–20 fragments, *etc.*). This method was adopted since it was clear that the material had become more fragmentary since excavation and counting fragments would therefore be meaningless. Full spreadsheets containing the identifications and weights of bone recovered are available in the site archive.

14.1.3 Results

The numbers of bones and teeth identified according to the criteria above are shown in Table 14.1. It should be noted that since most of the teeth had fragmented into their component parts, a 'minimum number' system has been used to record the number of teeth recorded in this table. The full fragment description is given in the archive spreadsheet. For the purpose of the summary, it should be noted that under unfavourable burial conditions, herbivore molars usually break down into their component parts. Each molar contains two infoldings of enamel and dentine in the tooth crown, known as infundibula, which help to give the teeth their characteristic selenodont form (Hillson 1986, 19).

Since the infundibula are surrounded by a column of enamel, and tooth enamel is harder and more resistant to decomposition than dentine, the infundibula, along with the outer enamel shell of the tooth, are often the only recognisable parts remaining. At Stonehall, most of the molars have broken down in this way, while the remainder of the tooth has not been preserved. For the purposes of estimating the minimum numbers of teeth present at each find spot, it has been assumed that each molar has two infundibula and any loose outer enamel

Table 14.1 Bone and teeth identification from Stonehall.

Trench	A (Stonehall Meadow)		B (Stonehall Farm)		BW (Stonehall Farm)		C (Stonehall Knoll)		E (Stonehall Farm)		Total	
Species	Bone	Teeth	Bone	Teeth	Bone	Teeth	Bone	Teeth	Bone	Teeth	Bone	Teeth
Cattle			4	112		1				60	4	173
cf Cattle			5	8		1			2		7	9
LU			2	3					3		5	3
S/G		1	3	2							3	3
cf S/G				*					1		1	
SU		1										1
Ungulate				1					1		1	1
Pig										1		1
Bird			3						1		4	
IM	!		!		!		!		!		!	
Total	!	2	17	126	!	2	!		8	61	25	191

Key: LU = large ungulate; S/G = sheep/goat; SU = small ungulate; IM = indeterminate mammal; * = tooth enamel fragments only; ! = present but not enumerated

has been discounted. In the case of the lower third molar, there is also a smaller infundibulum associated with the fifth cusp of the tooth. If recognised, these have been discounted. As regards the other types of teeth, herbivore incisors break down to a characteristic enamel shell, which has been used in the estimation of minimum numbers of teeth. Recognisable premolar shells have also been counted.

It is clear from the table that the most abundant species recovered from Stonehall is cattle. However, there has probably been a taphonomic bias in recovery. Cattle teeth are larger than those from sheep and thus fragments from this species are more easily recognisable than those from sheep. It is therefore not possible to state for certain whether cattle were the most numerous animals at the site in the Neolithic period, only that their teeth survived more readily than those from other species. While sheep (or less likely, goats) were present at Stonehall, they were represented only by three bones and a minimum number of three teeth. One molar tooth from a pig was the sole evidence of this species.

Three bird rib fragments recovered from Stonehall Farm (Trench B) could not be assigned to any particular species. The bones were unburnt and are probably intrusive. At the Neolithic site at Barnhouse (King, 2005) preservation of animal bone was also very poor and the range of species recovered was, as at Stonehall, limited to the three major domesticates, cattle, sheep/goat and pig.

Skeletal elements recovered at Stonehall Farm tended to be fragments of the smaller bones of the carcass, such as the tarsals (calcaneum, astragalus, os malleolare) although fragments of vertebral centra were also noted. Two conjoining fragments of a right distal cattle femur recovered from midden [605], (SF 2581) may possibly bear butchery marks. In this specimen, there appear to be three v-shaped cut marks on the lateral condyle, although it is by no means certain that these are man-made. While this femur was apparently from an adult animal, since the epiphysis was fused, not all of the animals at Stonehall were adult when killed. There was some evidence that some animals died while still immature: a large ungulate (probably cattle) unfused vertebral epiphysis was recovered from Stonehall Farm [809], (SF 6250).

Further evidence from Stonehall Farm of young cattle was provided by the presence of deciduous molars, most commonly the lower third deciduous molar (e.g. Trench B [303], [503], [3011] and Trench E [2015]). The lower third permanent molar also provides some guide to the age at death. The fifth cusp of this tooth comes into wear at approximately five years of age in modern cattle. In some of the better preserved third molars from Stonehall Farm it was apparent that the fifth cusp was unworn, indicating a date of death prior to maturity (e.g. Trench B, Spit 3 [605], SFs 2576 and 2500; [814], SF 6193; Trench E, [2002]). Other individuals were present in which the fifth cusp had come into wear and thus represented adults (e.g. Trench B [301]; Trench E [2015] SF 4160).

For sheep/goats there was much less evidence of the age at death since the teeth were few in number and in a very fragmentary condition. However, at Stonehall Farm an unfused proximal epiphysis from a sheep/goat femur was indicative of an immature animal (Trench B [809]). The single pig molar from Trench E ([2002], SF 4227) appeared to be unworn, indicating an animal that had not reached full maturity.

As regards the distribution of animal bones over the site, no clear pattern emerges. Bones and teeth are scattered across the site, occurring in all trenches, although they are more numerous in the late Neolithic, upper layers at Stonehall Farm (Trenches B and E) than in the early Neolithic Stonehall Meadow (Trench A) and Stonehall Knoll (Trench C).

The absence of bones from species other than large domesticated animals at Stonehall is not surprising given the poorly preserved, cremated condition of the material. However the probable absence of wild species, particularly red deer, should be noted, since the species' presence on Orkney from the Neolithic to the Iron Age is well attested. Several bones from the late Neolithic site at Crossiecrown probably originated from red deer, although unfortunately the faunal assemblage consisted of small cremated fragments in a similar state of preservation to those from Barnhouse.

At Neolithic Knap of Howar on Papa Westray, there was evidence, in this case from a substantial animal bone assemblage, that domesticated cattle, sheep and pigs had all been kept, providing the bulk of the meat consumed there, while wild deer contributed only a small proportion to the diet (Noddle 1983, 92–100). However, for other sites of comparable date on the Scottish mainland, the animal bone evidence is more sparse, due, as at Barnhouse and Crossiecrown, to the poor condition of the surviving material. For example at Claish, near Callander, only a few cremated fragments were identified. However, these also indicated that that cattle and pigs were reared and the diet supplemented by the meat of red deer (Smith 2002).

14.2 Crossiecrown

14.2.1 Preservation

Two sample bags of burnt bone (SF 14), from the fill [014] of stone box [013] in the Red House, weighing 48.55g in total were examined by the human remains analyst. The size of the fragments ranged from <2mm to 33mm, with the majority measuring <15mm. Overall, the condition of the bone was poor, and post-depositional erosion had resulted in a powdery surface texture. The predominant colour of the fragments was white, indicating that the

organic component of the bone had been completely combusted. This generally occurs at temperatures in excess of 700°C (Holden *et al.* 1995), although other factors such as the duration of burning and oxygen circulation are involved. A further sample from Trenches 1 and 2 was submitted to the animal remains analyst (Table 14.2).

14.2.2 Species and Elements Represented

None of the fragments in the fill of the stone box [14] (SF 14) were identifiable as human bone. A minimum number of one animal was represented within [14], the species of which was unknown. Recognisable elements included fragments of vertebra, rib, cranium and two unfused epiphyses. The presence of the epiphyses indicated that the animal was immature. There was no evidence of skinning or cut marks on the bones that might indicate butchery.

Significantly, blue/green discolouration was evident on one fragment of vertebra. This type of staining has been frequently observed in the past, in cremation deposits from Orkney (Roberts 1995). It has been suggested that the colour is caused by copper body adornments that have melted during the cremation process (McKinley 1993), or by the presence and reaction of trace elements and minerals in the soil or pyre material (A. Hall, pers. comm.). The same type of discolouration has also been observed on the remains of modern animals that have been incinerated in a furnace, which suggests that a more probable cause might be a reaction between the bone and soft tissue itself and the heat. There was no evidence of skinning or cut marks on the bones from either within the stone box or the remainder of the deposits that might indicate butchery.

The identified fragments from all deposits other than within [14] are listed in Table 14.2. Only bags containing identifiable material were fully recorded. Abbreviations and abundances are similar to those used for the Stonehall material.

Due to the poor preservation, degree of fragmentation and the distortion and shrinkage caused by exposure to heat, it was not possible to be certain of the species to which some of the bones belonged. In particular, several fragments which may originate from red deer could not be identified with confidence. These are mainly fragments of phalanges (toe bones) and one carpal, an *os magnum* (SF 28). This latter specimen is calcined and very shrunken, and the extent to which it has lost mass cannot be determined with certainty. Shrinkage and

Table 14.2 Bone identification from Crossiecrown.

Trench	Spit	Context	SF	Easting	Northing	Species	Bone	Details
2		001				LU	vertebra	lateral process; calcined
2		001				IM		5 calcined fragments
1	S2	002		115	112	SU	rib	shaft; calcined
1	S2	002		115	112	IM		++ calcined fragments
	S2	002		117	115	Cattle	sesamoid	pisiform; from carpal row
	S2	002		117	115	IM		+ calcined fragments
1	S2	002		116	113	Ungulate	tooth	+ enamel fragments
1	S2	002		116	113	IM		++ enamel fragments
1	S2	002		117	112	Cattle	os malleolare	entire; calcined
1	S2	002		117	112	IM		++ calcined fragments
1	S3	002		117	114	SU	vertebra	dorsal fragment; calcined
1	S3	002		117	114	IM		++ calcined fragments
1	S2	002		119	115	Sheep/goat	R astragalus	proximal; calcined
1	S2	002		119	115	IM		+ calcined fragments
2	S2	002		120	113	Cattle/deer	1st phalange	proximal; calcined
2	S2	002		120	113			+ calcined fragments
	S3	002		120	115	Cattle/deer	1st phalange	distal fragment; calcined
	S3	002		120	115	IM		++ calcined fragments
	S3	002		121	112	Sheep/goat	femur	proximal epiphysis only; calcined
	S3	002		121	112	IM		+ calcined fragments
2	S3	003	28			cf. Red deer	carpal	R magnum; calcined
2	S3	003		120	115	cf. Red deer	1st phalange	distal fragment; calcined

subsequent loss of organic material in bones exposed to a high temperature has been shown experimentally to amount to a loss of up to 5% of the size and as much as 50% of the weight of a cremated bone (von den Driesch 1976, 3). Thus the carpal from Crossiecrown, although agreeing in morphology with a comparable specimen from modern red deer, has possibly shrunk so much in size it is now only slightly larger than that from a modern sheep.

It is unfortunate that it has not been possible to identify the species of the animals at Crossiecrown with a greater degree of certainty. Cattle and sheep or goats both appear to have been kept at the site, as they were at Stonehall and Barnhouse. Pigs were absent from the Crossiecrown assemblage, but this is not surprising, given the fragmentary nature and relatively small size of the sample. Most importantly, however, red deer may have been hunted and their carcasses brought back to the site.

The Human Remains from Ramberry Head

David Lawrence

14.1.1 Introduction

In April 2005, ploughing disturbed archaeological deposits in a field at Ramberry Head, near the foot of Wideford Hill to the west of Kirkwall in Orkney (see Fig. 8.15). These deposits included a quantity of burned bone and unusually angular pottery of a type sometimes associated with Bronze Age cremation burials (see Chapter 8.3.1).

Bone was confirmed as being human and a subsequent investigation of the discovery site was undertaken by the Orkney Archaeological Trust, in association with both the then Geophysics Department of Orkney College and Colin Richards of Manchester University. Excavation as part of this project led to the recording of a stone-built setting of cobbles around a central flagstone with an outer peripheral bank, where burned bone had been deposited in antiquity. Some 26 contexts were recorded at the site and a number of small-finds and soil samples containing calcined bone were recovered (see Table 14.1.1).

14.1.2 Method

Ten bulk soil samples (Table 14.1.2) were taken to retrieve carbonized environmental remains, bone and artefactual evidence by water flotation. The burned bone was collected from the residue and flot. After sorting, all the burned bone (Table 14.1.3) was passed through nested sieves of 10mm, 4mm and 2mm gauge to examine fragment size distribution. The bone fraction less than 2mm in diameter was negligible and all bone under 4mm diameter was found to be unidentifiable. The fragments over 4mm were examined and recorded individually.

Each fragment was identified as precisely as possible and was measured along its major axes. Fissure patterns were recorded using the recommendations of Buikstra and Ubelaker (1994) and colour measured by comparison with a Munsell soil colour chart. Two fragments from sample 14 were subjected to a histological examination – one midshaft femur fragment and one cranial fragment.

The prepared thin sections were examined at ×100 under transmitted light, both with and without polarization.

14.1.3 Results

14.1.3.1 Quantity of bone recovered, fragment size and colour

A total of 561.7g of bone fragments was recovered (154.4g >10mm, 10mm >333.9g >4mm, 4mm >73.4g, the quantity below 2mm in diameter was negligible). This is similar to the bone weight recovered from the Bronze Age cremations at Linga Fiold and Mousland (Wiggins in Moore and Wilson 1995; Dickson *et al.* 1994) and would represent between 25 and 30% of the total expected to result from the cremation of a single adult female (McKinley 1993). The average maximum dimension (of the fragments over 4mm) was only about 10mm with few fragments reaching this size in two or more dimensions; and their mean weight was only 0.3g; 1435 fragments were over 4mm in diameter and about 1200 fragments between 2 and 4mm. It was rare for any fragment to retain a significant part of the original bone diameter. The largest fragment was a 32mm long rib shaft only 6mm across; maximum weight was 4.1g. This maximum fragment size is much smaller than from bone found at Knowes of Trotty (Roberts 2004) or that recorded by McKinley from modern cremations (McKinley 1993, 284) for example. The macroscopic fracture patterns appeared to follow fissures developed during cremation.

Several general guidelines have been proposed for the interpretation of colour and fissure patterns observable in cremated bone (*e.g.* Mays 1998; Shipman *et al.* 1984). These variables relate to complex interactions between the original condition of the bone, temperature, oxygen availability and cremation time, all of which may vary between different skeletal elements and may not remain constant during the cremation process, not least because

Table 14.1.1 Contexts that produced burnt bone or that were bulk sampled for flotation.

Context	Description	Sample nos	Small find nos
001	Ploughsoil	14	27
002	Widespread silty clay layer	10	
003*	Central flagstone*		2*
004	Fill of slot near 003 (lost orthostat?)	8, 9	
014	(peripheral?) Bank around deposits	13	
015	Inner cobble layer around 003	7, 12	19
018	N section of peripheral bank	5, 6	
023	Area within 015, with pot and bone	11	

*   Note that the burnt stone recovered as SF 02 was recorded as being 'above [003]' and that context [003] will, albeit improperly, be used here for simplicity.

Table 14.1.2 Samples processed as part of this study.

Context	Sample	Volume	% context	Contents
001	14	6l	1	Pot, bone, frequent roots, 30% stone
002	10	4l	5	No finds, moderate roots, 25% stone
004	8	5l	20	Burnt clay, frequent roots, 40% stone
014	9	5l	10	No finds, frequent roots, 20% stone
014	13	5l	5	No finds, frequent roots, 20% stone
015	7	5l	25	Pot, bone, frequent roots, 20% stone
015	12	4l	5	Bone, frequent roots, 25% stone
018	5	5l	?	Carbonised plant remains, some roots, 20% stone
018	6	3l	?	Carbonized plant remains, freq roots, 15% stone
023	11	3l	100	Bone, freq roots, 35% stone

Table 14.1.3 Finds recovered during processing.

Context	Bags of bone	Bone fragments	Weight of bone	Other finds
001	7	1330 (>4mm)	451.7g (>4mm)	Pottery
002	0	0	0	None
003	1	55 (>4mm)	28.7g (>4mm)	None
004	0	0	0	Burnt clay
014	0	0	0	None
015	3	16 (>4mm)	2.7g (>4mm)	Pottery
018	0	0	0	None
023	1	34 (>4mm)	4.4g (abraded)	None

of human intervention. Interpretation is not therefore necessarily as straightforward as might initially appear (Lyman 2001). The colour was almost uniformly white in this material (varying from Munsell 2.5Y8/0 to 10YR8/1) with rare occurrences of light grey (2.5Y7/0) and pale yellowish brown (10YR5/4) patches on predominantly white fragments.

During cremation, bone loses its organic components as well as associated soft tissue and is likely to become distorted (*e.g.* Correia 1997; Shipman *et al.* 1984). Bone may shrink by up to 30% transversely so that observations based on size criteria must be considered cautiously. This shrinkage is related to the temperature of cremation and is believed to occur progressively between 700 and 900°C. Removal of the water and organic constituents of the bone account for most of this and combine with stresses developing in the heated soft tissues to cause stresses in the bone that result in fissuring, cracking and splintering. Fragmentation tends to occur most markedly in compact bone because trabeculae develop specifically to endure stress. The fracture pattern of cremated bone relates to its condition when originally exposed to fire. 'Green' or flesh-covered bone develops curved and transverse fissures and irregular longitudinal splits, possibly with warping and twisting, whereas dry bones typically develop only minor surface cracking and longitudinal splits.

It is likely that the material recovered from this site became finely broken at the end of cremation, perhaps intentionally when first recovered but more likely as a result of collection whilst the bone was still hot (making it fragile) or as the result of quenching of the pyre with water and consequent sudden temperature changes (McKinley 1993). The discovery of the site during ploughing indicates another potential factor: bones in the cultivation zone are subject to blunt force modification, leading to simple breaks and splintering even in fresh bone, which is compounded by trampling (by people or grazing animals) and being run over by heavy machinery (Haglund *et al.* 2002). The bone assemblage from context [023] exhibited slightly different characteristics to the rest. Much, though not all of the bone from the context showed evidence of abrasion and all fragments recovered from this context were rather small. It is likely that the limited quantity of bone from [023] had been trampled or otherwise disturbed more than that from the other contexts. Even the finer material from contexts [015], [003] and [001] in contrast appeared largely sharp edged, which may reflect less post-depositional disturbance. Haglund *et al.* (2002) noted that scattering of bone occurred up to 32m (×14m) from a primary burial site in a cultivated field that had been cultivated to a depth estimated as 7–10 inches (*sic*). Such displacement is predominantly in the direction of tillage, with associated fragmentation occurring to a degree inversely related to bone robusticity. Modern ploughs may use reversible blades so that the direction of working can be in alternating directions and buried bone may therefore become more widely scattered; similar dispersal can result from harrowing.

14.1.3.2 Bone identification: Anatomical parts, age, sex and minimum number of individuals

By weight, 75.2% of all bone was identified, with varying degrees of precision. Many fragments, although probably human were of insufficient completeness to demonstrate diagnostic features. Sometimes only a tentative identification was possible, allowing for uncertainty of element, age or species. The recognizable fragments were predominantly human in origin, although one anterior shaft fragment from the metacarpal of probable *Bos sp.* (probably *B. taurus* – domestic cattle) and a fragment of bird ulna were found as well as several rib fragments

likely to be animal. A moderate number of fragments were tentatively identified as diaphyses from human metatarsals, metacarpals or phalanges but could possibly be from seal, pig, sheep or other medium-sized animals.

Diagnostic criteria are more readily identifiable in larger fragments and so identification to anatomical element in this material was poor. Note that because many fragments could not be precisely identified, any comparisons between the quantities present from the different anatomical areas, such as upper and lower limb, are virtually meaningless as any data is swamped by the unidentifiable fraction. A greater identifiability of lower limb fragments was due partly to their greater relative robustness. The relative paucity of recovery of the axial skeleton likely to be due to the thinness of cortical bone in this anatomical area and greater fragmentation during or after cremation. The proportion of bone recorded as unidentified from Ramberry (Table 14.1.4) is comparable to that from the Knowes of Trotty (Table 14.1.5); the overall weight of bone recovered from each site was also approximately the same and this suggests that the formation processes of the deposits and recovery methods prior to deposition were similar, as might be expected. Difference between the two sites is the result of the greater identification of longbone fragments as specific to upper or lower limbs at Knowes of Trotty; it can be seen that the overall limb weights are similar when the uncertain limb fraction is included.

The identified human bone was derived from all areas of the body (see Tables 14.1.4 and 14.1.5) in proportions that are not unlikely for either random or attempted total collection. It may be noted that the number of fragments appears disproportionate (a large number of cranium fragments in particular) but this reflects identifiability and is not an indication of element proportions in the assemblage (*e.g.* McKinley 2004). Unfortunately, fragmentation was such that most parts could not provide information on sex, age or stature. Although epiphyseal fragments were present, they were rarely associated with a diaphysis and no unfused metaphyseal surfaces were recognized.

The number of individuals present in a deposit of cremated bone is estimated from duplicated anatomical elements and from parts that could not consistently derive from a single individual. Such diagnosis is not necessarily related to the quantity of bone recovered. Cist 56 at the Knowes of Trotty for example contained elements of three individuals with a total weight of only 6g (Roberts 2004), compared with the maximum weight of bone recorded from the modern cremation of

Table 14.1.4 Overall identification of skeletal areas.

Bone	Weight	% Ramberry	% Trotty	% (modern)
Unidentified	121g	24.8	25.6	0
Cranium	60.5g	12.4	23.1	18.2
Axial	49.1g	10.1	5.4	23.1
Upper Limb	11.7g	2.4	15.1	20.6
Lower Limb	54.3g	11.1	30.6	38
Other Flatbone	12.3g	2.5	N/a	N/a
Other Longbone	167.9g	34.4	N/a	N/a
Total Appendicular	233.9g	47.9	45.7	58.6

Table 14.1.5 Age range equivalents for descriptive terms used.

Descriptive Term	Age Range in Years (Roberts 2004)	Age Range in Years (Buikstra and Ubelaker 1994)
Infant	0–3	0–3
Child	3.1–11	3–12
Adolescent	11.1–18	12–20
Young Adult	18.1–30	20–35
Middle Adult	30.1–45	35–50
Mature Adult	45+	50+

a single adult male of over 3000g (McKinley 1993) or the 2063g recovered from a less calcined cremation at Ratho (McSweeney 1995).

No duplicate finds of anatomical parts or incompatible elements were made that might indicate more than one individual being represented in the bone from Ramberry. All elements were of a size that would be consistent with coming from just one fully grown gracile individual. Most fragments are similar both in colour and condition, which suggests uniform cremation and processing throughout. It is assumed here that fragments identified belong to the same skeleton as the remainder of the identifiable bone. A small number of fragments were noted that were chalky white in colour and these tended to have some minor surface abrasion, which suggests that they were already present on the site when the cremation occurred. It is likely that the pyre site had been used previously and had retained some residual dry, fragmented or cremated bone.

Skeletal attribution of age is based on morphological features, which could not be observed in this sample. The bones appeared to be fully formed but no evidence for epiphyseal fusion or otherwise was observed. Several fragments from the cranial vault were recognized that demonstrated that the coronal, sagittal, lambdoid and temporal sutures were at least partly open; indeed there was no evidence of any of them being closed at all. This

suggests that the individual was a juvenile or young adult at death but that can only be a tentative assertion since suture closure is highly variable between individuals (Acsádi and Nemeskéri 1970, 115–21).

The only fragment giving qualitative information on secondary sexual characteristics was a piece of the superior orbital margin of a left frontal. This had a moderately sharp edge, suggesting that the individual represented may have been female or juvenile.

The metric method suggested by Gejvall (1963) was not entirely appropriate in this case because it was impossible to positively identify the locations to be measured. The definition of sexual dimorphism is problematic in past cultures practicing cremation, where many criteria are often not observable and norms cannot be satisfactorily determined. Any such interpretation here is based on analogies with samples that may be inappropriate. The greatest longbone cortical thickness was 6mm, which lies in the overlap between male and female distributions for femora. All the cranial measurements were low, even for a female (in the bottom 5% expected), only one being greater than 3.7mm. Although this is not a satisfactory set of criteria, the measurements are consistent with the individual having been female or an older juvenile. It is possible that cranial thickness was affected by disease but there was no evidence to support this and it is most likely that the cranium simply lies at the lower end of the distribution of adult bone thickness. The cranial fragments follow the size distribution expected for an adult female (Gejvall 1963). One fragment was found to be 4.3mm thick but the cranial thickness averaged only 3.05mm.

Histological examination of a polished thin transverse section of midshaft femur was undertaken using transmitted light. In cremated bone there is some shrinkage, fracturing and warping to which the bone has been subjected, resulting in microfissures that were observed; fine structures were difficult to distinguish. The bone examined showed no evidence of osteon fragments but only of complete osteons. This may be indicative of youth but could be the result of difficulty in getting a sufficiently clear thin section. Several different methods at ageing were attempted (Ahlqvist and Damsten 1969; Kerley and Ubelaker 1978; Hummel and Schutkowski 1993) but none could be satisfactorily applied because of limitations from the sample (size and diagenesis) and probable systematic errors (*e.g.* applying factors to allow for field of view, assumptions regarding bone shrinkage, allowing for fissures in the fragments). The density and size of osteons and Haversian canals all gave typical values for human tissue. The histological results were inconclusive and it was considered undesirable to destroy further fragments in attempting to produce clearer slides but the general appearance of the thin sections was consistent with a healthy young adult or older juvenile.

No evidence of non-metric traits – developmental, genetic or behaviourally-determined features – or symptoms of pathology or trauma were observed. This is not unexpected with the degree of fragmentation in this assemblage and does not imply the absence of such features during life.

14.1.3.3 Evidence of pyre technology and cremation ritual

Cremation conditions can be inferred through consideration of the discoloration and fissuring of the bone fragments and the presence of pyre elements such as artefacts or charcoal. Colour of bone is closely related to temperature and redox conditions within the pyre, gross fissuring of bone relates to its initial condition (fresh or dry); ash and charcoal can demonstrate the presence of fuel materials or votive offerings. Identifying any systematic variations of discoloration in or between skeletal elements can suggest the posture of the cadaver during cremation or the relationship of the pyre to the body.

It is probably not exceptional for burned bone to become deposited away from the core of the interment: similar observations have for example been made at Mousland and Knowe 1, Quoyscottie (Downes 1994; Hedges 1977). Whether this has any particular significance remains undetermined, but it could merely be incidental.

The bone fragments recovered throughout the site were almost uniformly white, which broadly suggests a cremation temperature greater than 700°C with adequate oxygenation. A very small number of fragments displayed minor localized patches of light grey and yellowish brown, implying a localized area of lower temperature or decreased oxygen availability during cremation. These were probably indicative of small localised areas of different conditions existing rarely within the pyre, possibly implying stirring of the ashes but generally uniform heating and complete combustion throughout the cadaver (McKinley 2006, 84). Such stirring of the pyre would be consistent with the fine fragmentation observed.

Microscopically, there were numerous fine cracks in the two prepared thin sections, especially near the periosteal surface, that were attributed to the stresses from cremation and associated combustion products or expansion of gases. It was found that polarization of the source light did not produce any birefringence and this suggests that all the collagen had been lost from the bone, probably due to cremation.

The vitrified mineral material known as 'cramp' was found fused to a small number of bone fragments: this was also identified in association with the Bronze Age cremations at Linga Fiold, Orkney (Newton in Moore and Wilson 1995) and Cnip, Lewis (Close-Brooks 1995). This vitrification suggests that a high temperature was achieved locally in the pyre, though not necessarily on the occasion that the majority of bone recovered was cremated, since it is likely that the pyre site had been reused.

The occurrence of fragments of burned clay with rounded stone inclusions may reflect the ground surface used for the pyre. That some burned clay was recovered adhering to cremated bone may suggest both that the pyre site had been reused and that the surface had been refreshed since the bare bone and unfired clay must have been in intimate contact at some point for this fusion to occur.

The presence of animal bone is not unusual in cremated deposits and could be related either to offerings or feasting (McKinley 2006, 84). It is interesting that the two most identifiable animal bone fragments come from totally different animals (bird ulna and cattle metacarpal) but neither is from an element considered important for food, although animal rib and longbone fragments were also identified. It is possible that meat-bearing bones were present but that the degree of fragmentation was too great to be certain of species. Usefully, although the majority of animal bone was recovered from context [001] (ploughsoil), some was from context [003], associated with a flagstone surface, which suggests association of animal remains with the cremation. An estimated 16% of Bronze Age cremation deposits have been recorded that included animal bone and it has been pointed out that faunal remains were probably inefficiently collected too (McKinley 1997).

Overall, it would seem that the cremation had adequate fuel and took place on a surface with good air circulation to achieve high temperatures and complete combustion. Perhaps curiously, no evidence of charcoal was recovered, unlike the cremation burials at Queenafjold, Mousland or Quoyscottie (Ritchie and Ritchie 1974; Downes 1994; Hedges 1977). Pottery fragments were recovered from the site (see Chapters 8.3 and 11) and it is likely that the bone remains were deposited in association with the square-shaped pottery vessel.

14.1.4 Conclusions

The age, sex and number of individuals represented in the assemblage could not be determined with any confidence because the study material consists of commingled incomplete and fragmentary remains. The material is consistent with the remains of a single older juvenile or a young adult female. A small quantity of bone may have derived from earlier cremations performed on the same pyre site. The greater part of cremated bone recovered was from the layer described as 'ploughsoil' and, although it is consistent with the stratified material, it cannot conclusively be demonstrated that the separate fragments derive from the same individual.

The presence of a small number of eroded chalky white fragments may be due to differential combustion but is probably best explained by reuse of a pyre site and collection of fragments residual from earlier activity. This may then imply an accepted location for cremation activity that was distinct from deposition. The greater abrasion of the cremated bone from context [023]

over other contexts may imply that the cobble surface remained open for some time or that the material used in construction had been taken from another site related to cremation or burial.

The apparent absence of charcoal from bone-containing contexts suggests that the bone was either collected with great care or was cleaned to remove extraneous material; it is possible that it was the result of incidental sorting during collection or deposition and that the carbonised material has since been lost. The small fragment size of the bone suggests that it may have been intentionally broken after cremation or collected before cooling, although plough disturbance may be a further contributory factor.

The quantity of bone collected from Ramberry (561.7g) may be considered typical for ancient cremations (*e.g.* Wahl 2008; McKinley 2006, 85–86), McKinley 2008 – notably it is similar to the 633g from Linga Fiold (Moore and Wilson 1995) and the 407g from cist 059 at the Knowes of Trotty (Roberts 2004)). This would be about 30% of the expected total cremated bone weight from an adult female. Such partial deposition seems to be common in cremation burials and could potentially relate to token deposition or selective recovery. The presence of parts of all skeletal elements in this assemblage suggests that no deliberate selection occurred and neither is the deposit a mere token burial. Natural taphonomic processes can probably be dismissed as a major cause of bone loss in this case because the fragments recovered are predominantly of good surface condition. The small fragment size suggests that it is possible that fine fragments were lost during any processing in antiquity. The most likely explanation is incomplete collection from the pyre site prior to deposition and this might itself be related to the method of collection employed and how much tending of the funeral pyre was done. McKinley (2000) has noted, for example, that it required some 4 hours to collect the complete skeletal remains by hand from a sheep cremation but that raking could be of great assistance: such factors would be expected to lead to limited collection.

It seems most likely that the burial usage of the monument at Ramberry was for a single older juvenile or young adult female whose body had been efficiently and completely cremated in association with mixed animal remains.

CHAPTER FIFTEEN

Bay of Firth Environments from the 2nd to 4th Millennium BC: the evidence from Stonehall, Wideford Hill, Crossiecrown, Knowes of Trotty, Varme Dale and Brae of Smerquoy

Jennifer Miller, Susan Ramsay, Diane Alldritt and Joanna Bending

15.1 Introduction: The botanical remains from Stonehall, Wideford Hill and Crossiecrown

The information presented here comes from the results of botanical analysis of samples from four settlement sites within the Bay of Firth area on Mainland, Orkney, namely Stonehall, Wideford Hill, Crossiecrown and Knowes of Trotty. The results are recorded and discussed individually for each site (sections 15.2–15.6), and then compared and contrasted within a global overview of the study area as a whole (section 15.9).

15.1.1 Methodology

The samples prepared for botanical analysis were all from free-draining contexts in which uncarbonised archaeological plant remains were unlikely to have been preserved. Consequently, samples intended for archaeobotanical analyses were processed using standard flotation procedures, with the resultant flots and retents dried. For Knowes of Trotty, bulk environmental samples were processed by ORCA using a Siraf-style water flotation system (French 1971) fitted with a 1mm internal mesh and an external sieve stack consisting of 1mm and 300 micron sizes.

Subsequent examination and preliminary identification was undertaken using a binocular microscope with independent cold light source, at variable magnifications of between ×4 and ×45. Following this, the morphological characteristics of charcoal were observed at ×200 using the reflected light of a Zenith metam P-1 metallurgical microscope. Identification of seeds was initially by reference to the texts of Beijerinck (1947) and the extensive reference collection of Glasgow University. Charcoal was identified using the text and photographs in Schweingruber (1990). Vascular plant nomenclature follows Stace (1997) other than cereals, which follow the genetic classification of Zohary and Hopf (2000). In the tables of results all macrofossils are seeds unless otherwise specified. Latin plant names and their English equivalents are given within those tables of results, but for ease of comprehension, all plant names are given in English within the text.

15.2 Stonehall

Jennifer Miller and Susan Ramsay

15.2.1 Stonehall Meadow (Trench A)

The contexts analysed from the ruined Early Neolithic structure and midden deposits uncovered at Stonehall Meadow Trench A produced a varied selection of charcoal taxa with birch, hazel, heather family, cherry type and willow all represented (Table 15.1). A significant number of carbonised cereal grains were recovered from Trench A contexts associated with the hearth deposits sampled in 2001 (contexts [019] and [029]). From these deposits AMS radiocarbon dates of 3497–3470 cal BC and 3360–3080 cal BC respectively (see Chapter 18), confirmed the early Neolithic provenance of these remains. Naked (six-row) barley predominated with only one grain of hulled (six-row) barley identified. However, the majority of the grain was identifiable only to barley

Table 15.1 The botanical evidence from Stonehall Meadow (Trench A).

Stonehall Trench A	Site Code	SH'94	SH'94	SH'94	SH'94	SH'01	SH'01	SH'01
	Context	?	2	4	34	12	19	29
Matrix								
Total carb veg		10ml	5ml	15ml	5ml	<5ml	10ml	15ml
Modern veg		-	-	-	-	+	+	+
Charcoal	**Common Name**							
Betula	birch			18 (2.9g)				2 (<0.05g)
Corylus	hazel	19 (0.2g)			1 (0.7g)			
Ericaceae	heather family						3 (<0.05g)	>20 (<0.05g)
Prunoideae	cherry type		1 (0.75g)					
Salix	willow			2 (0.1g)				1 (<0.05g)
Indet		1 (<0.05g)						
Cereals (c)								
Hordeum vulgare var *nudum*	naked six-row barley							15
Hordeum vulgare var *vulgare*	hulled six-row barley							1
Hordeum vulgare sl	barley						10	18
indet cereals							2	19
Macrofossils (c)								
Carex sp	sedge							3
monocot rhizomes	grass/sedge rhizomes						9 (0.2g)	>20 (<0.05g)
Rumex sp	dock							1
Misc								
bone								+ (<0.05g)

For Tables 15.1–15.7: + rare, +++++ abundant, (c) carbonised

or indeterminate cereal and so the proportions of naked to hulled barley may not be as clear-cut as appears from the identifiable grain. The only other significant botanical finds in these contexts were taxa indicative of the utilisation of turf. The carbonised underground rhizomes of grasses or sedges were present as were occasional seeds of grassland types such as sedges and docks. Of particular note is context [029] which produced the greatest concentration of cereal remains as well as evidence for turf and heather family stems. This combination of plant taxa is often indicative of some form of cereal processing being undertaken and will be discussed more fully later.

15.2.2 Stonehall Meadow (Trench Z)

Trench Z was positioned adjacent to Trench A, in an area which had been less disturbed by agriculture. It produced evidence of two degraded structures, which were considered to represent three phases of construction (Table 15.2.).

An early phase of construction (Phase 1, House 1) was represented by just two contexts ([3016] and [3039]), which produced evidence of only birch and hazel charcoal. This is not enough information from which to draw any significant conclusions although the fact that each context contained only one type of charcoal may suggest a structural origin for the fragments identified.

Phase 2 (House 2) was also represented by only two contexts ([3038] and [3085/3086]) both connected with the northern wall of the structure. The material in these contexts was thought to have represented midden used to infill the core of the wall. However, it is possible that some of this midden material may have derived from the burning of earlier structural features since large fragments of birch, hazel and willow charcoal were present, all types associated with wattlework constructions. Nevertheless, it is not possible to rule out midden deposits as the source of this charcoal as all these types could also have been used for fuel. The significant number of indeterminate cereal grains also recovered from Building B confirms that at least some of the wall core material was formed from domestic midden material.

Table 15.2 The botanical evidence from Stonehall Meadow (Trench Z).

Stonehall Trench Z	Site Code	SH'00	SH'00	SH'00	SH'00	SH'00	SH'00	SH'00	SH'00	SH'00	SH'00	SH'00	SH'00
	Context	3003	3004	3016	3031	3038	3039	3050 (+SF)	3058	3068	3069	3075	Wall core
Matrix													
Total carb veg		5ml	20ml	10ml	20ml	10ml	10ml	50ml	15ml	100ml	5ml	30ml	300ml
Modern veg		+++	-	-	-	-	-	++	-	++	++	+	+
Charcoal	**Common Name**												
Betula	birch		17 (5.4g)	20 (1.4g)	1 (6.8g)	9 (1.4g)		29 (3.7g)	23 (1.35g)	13 (0.35g)		7 (0.3g)	12 (2.25g)
Corylus	hazel		6 (0.55g)				1 (0.7g)						1 (0.15g)
Ericaceae	heather family							5 (0.1g)		1 (<0.05g)	6 (<0.05g)		
Rosaceae	rose family									1 (<0.05g)			
Salix	willow	1 (<0.05g)	7 (0.7g)		14 (3.4g)			1 (0.05g)		1 (0.1g)		6 (0.2g)	7 (1.45g)
indet								3 (0.1g)		1 (0.15g)			
burnt peat/soil								+		+++ (6.0g)		2 (<0.05g)	
Cereals (c)													
Hordeum vulgare var *nudum*	naked six-row barley									5		22	
Hordeum vulgare sl	barley										3	47	
cf *Hordeum vulgare sl*	cf barley											39	
indet cereals		2						1		5	2	62	23
Macrofossils (c)													
Carex hostiana	tawny sedge									1			
Carex viridula sl	yellow sedge									1			
Empetrum nigrum	crowberry									3			
Rumex sp	dock										4		
Misc													
bone										+ (0.55g)	+ (<0.05g)		
mineralised stems/ rhizomes								++ (3.4g)		>30 (1.5g)			

Phase 3 (House 3), the final phase of construction in this area, was represented by five contexts, four of which were similar ([3050], [3068], [3069], [3075]), while the fifth [3058], was significantly different from the rest. Context [3058] represented the fill of a cut (3057), which contained packing stones, and broken orthostats which were considered evidence for the portioning of this structure into two rooms. The fact that context 3058 contained solely birch charcoal and no other carbonised remains suggests that it originated from a single birch post or support used in connection with the orthostats to divide up the internal space. A similar conjunction of posts and orthostats to form internal divisions is present at Knap of Howar, Papa Westray (Ritchie 1983). Charcoal from context [3050], an occupation layer, was AMS radiocarbon

dated to 3350–3080 cal BC. In addition, AMS dating of context [3075] produced a similar date, of 3360–3010 cal BC. This is good evidence towards the undisturbed nature of these deposits.

The remaining contexts from House 3 all contained evidence of cereals grains and general domestic occupation debris. The upper fill [3068] and lower fill [3069] of the hearth [3070] both contained evidence of barley which was further identifiable to the naked form of the grain in the upper fill [3068]. AMS radiocarbon dates within the range of 3340–3010 cal BC were obtained for these fills, putting the final occupation of this structure into the early Neolithic period. The upper fill [3068] of the hearth was also notable because of the greater diversity of charcoal taxa, in addition to strong evidence (in the form of grass/sedge rhizomes and burnt soil/peat) for the burning of turves. The fill [3075] of pit [3074] situated near a box-type structure at the side entrance from House 3 to House 2 produced the greatest quantities of cereal grains recovered from any of the Stonehall samples. The majority of these grains were identifiable to barley or *cf* barley with a proportion well enough preserved to enable them to be classified as the naked form of this cereal. The fact that charcoal was also recovered from this context may suggest that it was the dumped result of a domestic cooking accident but it would seem more likely that it represents the fill of a grain storage pit which had been accidentally or intentionally burned.

15.2.3 Stonehall Farm (Trench B)

Stonehall Farm Trench B was interpreted during excavation as part of a substantial late Neolithic settlement containing at least one structure in addition to deep midden deposits. The contexts examined included representative samples from both the midden and the central cist feature within Structure 1 (Table 15.3).

The midden contexts examined from this trench had a generally similar plant taxon composition. A lower midden deposit [809] was AMS radiocarbon dated to 3110–2900 cal BC. Heather family charcoal was present in most of the samples although the quantities of identifiable charcoal were generally very low. The only other charcoal taxa identified from this trench were birch and willow. Carbonised plant macrofossils commonly encountered included a wide variety of sedges and grasses, which, together with the abundance of heather type charcoal, and material identified as either burnt soil or peat, suggest that turf cut from damp heathland locations was the primary source of fuel during this occupation.

One of the most interesting features uncovered by this trench was a stone cist located in the centre of Structure 1. Two contexts were examined from this feature: context [631], which represented general fill of the cist, and context [542] which was a layer of highly, decayed bone, not calcined, which lay just below the capstone. Cist fill [631] was AMS radiocarbon dated to 3360–3010 cal BC. Both contexts contained large quantities of bone, and, although only a little heather family charcoal was recovered, there were numerous macrofossils recovered from plants of grassland or heathland. This suggests that any burning, which had occurred in conjunction with the cist deposit, had relied heavily on turf for fuel.

East of the central cist feature a raised circular clay bowl [815] was examined. Context 816 represented the ashy fill of this feature. The plant macrofossil evidence from this feature was in stark contrast to that from the rest of Trench B in that it contained only birch charcoal and no other identifiable plant remains. Much of the birch charcoal was found as large fragments, which was also unusual for Stonehall as a whole. AMS radiocarbon dating of the charcoal from [816] gave a date for the upper fill of the clay bowl to 3360–3080 cal BC.

15.2.4. Stonehall Farm (Trenches D and E)

The Trench E results are shown in Table 15.4. Trench E is actually the north-easterly extension of Trench B. The results obtained from Trench E contexts are essentially similar to those of Trench B with stems from members of the heather family and seeds of damp heathland habitats predominating. As in Trench B evidence for cereals is slight although grains identifiable as barley are present. The only charcoal other than heather family recovered was from context [2015], and was identified as birch. This indicates the utilisation of the natural, albeit probably sparse, local scrub woodland, whether for fuel or construction purposes.

Context [2051] represented the lower fill of a hearth, which had apparently had two distinct phases of use, with the upper and lower fills separated by a thin clay layer. There are no remains of charcoal and only a few turf indicators. The most notable feature of this context is the high concentration of burnt bone found within it.

The results from Trench D are shown in Table 15.4. Only one context [701] was examined from Trench D, although several individual samples were studied from it. During excavation, Trench D, which revealed no occupation deposits, just scorched glacial till, was interpreted as a small area of firing, either a hearth or a fire for baking pots. Carbonised plant remains were relatively abundant although the charcoal recovered was very poorly preserved. However, the assemblage of carbonised plant macrofossils was well enough preserved to indicate the same utilisation of damp heathy turf as the primary source of fuel, as was also suggested for Trenches B and E.

15.2.5 Stonehall Knoll (Trench C)

The results for Stonehall Knoll are shown in Table 15.5. The excavators interpreted the features from this trench as the remains of a sequence of structures built on the top of a natural knoll overlooking the other areas of settlement.

Table 15.3 The botanical evidence from Stonehall Farm (Trench B). Continues p. 500.

Stonehall Trench B	Common Name	SH'94	SH'95	SH'97	SH'95	SH'95	SH'97	SH'97	SH'99	SH'97	SH'99	SH'99	SH'99	SH'99	SH'99
Context		301	509	520	528	542	612	631	631	643	809	816	864	866	873
Matrix															
Total carb veg		15ml	10ml	<5ml	250ml	10ml	<5ml	5ml	<5ml	-	15ml	100ml	10ml	20ml	50ml
Modern veg		-	-	+	+	+	-	+	++	-	-	+	++	+	+
Charcoal															
Betula	birch										10 (1.0g)	55 (13.15g)			
Coniferales	conifer	15 (0.3g)													
Ericaceae stems	heather family		17 (0.05g)		7 (0.05g)	++ (0.05g)		+ (0.15g)	+					+ (<0.05g)	15 (0.15g)
Picea / Larix	spruce/larch	5 (0.25g)													
Salix	willow						1 (<0.05g)								
indet					2 (<0.05g)										
burnt soil/peat			+		+		+								
Cereals (c)															
Hordeum vulgare sl	barley		1												
indet cereal	cereal		1			1									
Macrofossils (c)															
Aphanes sp	parsley-piert													1	1
cf *Bromus* sp	brome			1											
Bryophyte stems	moss				+	+	+								
Calluna vulgaris leafy shoot	heather						1								
Carex echinata	star sedge														1
Carex hostiana	tawny sedge					6	2						5	7	21
Carex nigra	common sedge													1	1
Carex panicea	carnation sedge				3	3							3	2	11
Carex rostrata	bottle sedge						4							5	
Carex viridula sl	yellow sedge					3		1		3			1		6
Carex sp	sedge					1	4	1					2		3
Danthonia decumbens	heath-grass					3		1	1				26	4	16
Danthonia decumbens cleistogenes	heath-grass					++									
dicot stems			+	3	+					+					
Epilobium sp	willowherb			1											
Isolepis setacea	bristle club-rush						3	1					10	15	22

Table 15.3 The botanical evidence from Stonehall Farm (Trench B), continued.

Stonehall Trench B	Site Code	SH'94	SH'95	SH'97	SH'95	SH'95	SH'97	SH'97	SH'99	SH'97	SH'99	SH'99	SH'99	SH'99	SH'99
Leontodon autumnalis/hispidus	autumn/rough hawkbit														1
monocot rhizomes			++		+		++	++	+	++			++	++	++
Montia fontana	blinks					1							2		12
Persicaria maculosa	redshank		2												
Plantago lanceolata	ribwort plantain					1							1	4	3
Poa sp	meadow-grass						1			1					
Poaceae	grass														3
Poaceae stems	grass		+	+	+		++	+	+	+			++	+	+
Potentilla cf *erecta*	cf tormentil						2							1	
Potentilla sp	cinquefoil					2							1		8
cf *Potentilla* sp	cf cinquefoil						1								
Ranunculus flammula	lesser spearwort												1		3
Ranunculus repens	creeping buttercup		1			1									3
Ranunculus cf *repens*	cf creeping buttercup														3
Ranunculus sp	buttercup							1							1
Rumex acetosella	sheep's sorrel								1						
Rumex sp	dock												1	1	2
Scirpus sp	club rush		1												
Stachys sp	woundwort									1					
Stellaria/Cerastium	chickweed/mouse-ear														
Urtica dioica	nettle														
Misc															
bone			3 (0.2g)		+ (3.8g)	+ (11.9g)	++ (40.2g)	+ (3.6g)	++ (42.0g)	+ (3.8g)	+ (0.2g)	++ (3.3g)	+ (5.3g)	++ (8.1g)	++ (67.7g)

Table 15.4. The botanical evidence from Stonehall Farm (Trenches D and E).

Stonehall Trenches D & E	Site Code	SH'97	SH'99	SH'99	SH'99	SH'99
	Context	701	2015	2036	2040	2051
	Trench	D	E	E	E	E
Matrix						
Total carb veg		3500ml	10ml	5ml	5ml	10ml
Modern veg		+	++	-	+	+
Charcoal	**Common Name**					
Betula	birch		11 (0.35g)			
Ericaceae stems	heather family	+ (0.15g)	++ (0.45g)	+ (<0.05g)	28 (0.05g)	
burnt peat/soil		++				
Cereals (c)						
Hordeum vulgare var *nudum*	naked six-row barley	1				
Hordeum vulgare sl	barley		2			
indet cereals	cereal	3	1			1
Macrofossils (c)						
Ajuga reptans	bugle	2				
Bryophyte stems	moss		+			
Carex disticha	brown sedge	2				
Carex hostiana	tawny sedge	2				3
Carex nigra	common sedge		1	3		1
Carex panicea	carnation sedge		2	1		
Carex viridula sl	yellow sedge	1				
Cerastium fontanum/glomeratum	common/sticky mouse-ear	5				
Chenopodium album	fat hen	2				
Chenopodium rubrum	red goosefoot	23				
Danthonia decumbens	heath-grass		2	6		5
dicot stems			+			
Empetrum nigrum	crowberry	6				
Isolepis setacea	bristle club-rush		1	2		
monocot rhizomes		++	+	+	11 (<0.05g)	+
Montia fontana	blinks			7		4
Plantago lanceolata	ribwort plantain	6				1
Poa trivialis	rough meadow-grass	1				
Poa sp	meadow-grass	7				
Poaceae	grass			1		
Poaceae stems	grass	++	+	+		+
Ranunculus flammula	lesser spearwort		1			
Ranunculus repens	creeping buttercup	6				
Ranunculus cf repens	*cf* creeping buttercup	1				
Ranunculus sp	buttercup	1				
Rumex acetosella	sheep's sorrel	2				
Rumex sp	dock	11		1		
Scirpus sp	club rush	1				
Stachys sylvatica	hedge woundwort	1				
Stellaria media	chickweed	1				
Stellaria/Cerastium	chickweed/mouse-ear	1	1			
Vicia sp	vetch	2				
Misc						
bone			++ (7.7g)	++ (8.4g)	++ (3.5g)	++ (26.25g)
mineralised stems/rhizomes					++ (1.2g)	

Table 15.5 Botanical evidence from Stonehall Knoll (Trench C).

Stonehall Trench C	Site Code	SH'95	SH'95	SH'95	SH'97	SH'97	SH'97	SH'97	SH'97	SH'97	SH'97	SH'97	SH'97	SH'00
	Context	402	427	433	408	1003	1008	1022	1028	1042	1051	1052	1053	4041 (+SF)
Matrix														
Total carb veg		1000ml	10ml	20ml	10ml	4000ml	1500ml	200ml	6000ml	200ml	100ml	500ml	<5ml	15ml
Modern veg		++	-	-	-	+	+	+	+	+	+	+	+	+
Charcoal	**Common Name**													
Betula	birch		4 (0.05g)	1 (0.55g)			8 (0.35g)	7 (0.9g)		1 (<0.05g)				43 (3.95g)
Ericaceae stems	heather family						7 (0.2g)	7 (0.2g)	1 (0.1g)		1 (<0.05g)			
Maloideae	apple type						1 (0.1g)							
Salix	willow	20 (2.5g)	6 (0.1g)		1 (0.6g)	65 (42.05g)	3 (0.25g)	1 (<0.05g)	90 (46.2g)	5 (0.9g)	24 (3.35g)	30 (5.0g)	3 (<0.05g)	1 (0.2g)
indet				8 (0.6g)			25 (2.65g)			2 (<0.05g)			+ (<0.05g)	
burnt peat/ soil						++	++	+	+	+				
Macrofossils (c)														
buds indet.						4								
Chenopodium rubrum	red goosefoot						6							
Fucoid seaweed	brown seaweed						15 (0.15g)	++ (2.8g)						
monocot rhizomes			+	+			+							
Misc														
bone									+	+ (0.3g)				+ (0.1g)

The carbonised plant assemblage from Trench C is totally different to that from Stonehall Farm, in that tree taxa charcoal is abundant but indicators of peat or turves are extremely rare. It appears that the carbonised plant macrofossils assemblages from Stonehall Knoll contexts suggest two distinct provenances. One group contained large quantities of charcoal, almost exclusively willow roundwood or a mixture of willow and birch. Much of the willow roundwood had been cut when the branches were between 7–12 years of age, suggesting that these are the carbonised remains of willow poles and smaller withies, which had formed the bulk of a large wicker structure that had been destroyed by fire. The birch branches present in some of the contexts may have been used as additional upright supports within the structure. Charcoal from three samples from context [4041] gave a range of AMS radiocarbon dates covering around a thousand years, from the mid-3rd millennium cal BC to the mid-4th millennium cal BC. However, this is not thought to reflect 1000 years of occupation. Charcoal from context [1028] was also AMS radiocarbon dated, and yielded a date of cal AD 350–370 which related to the final small stone structures built on the knoll (Fig. 15.5).

In contrast to the structural origin suggested for the contexts outlined above, the carbonised assemblages from the second group tend to be indicative of mixed hearth deposits, including heather type, birch, willow and rowan type charcoal. Contexts [1008] and [1022] also contained numerous fragments of carbonised seaweed, which was presumably also burnt as fuel. It is possible to speculate that seaweed was burnt for a particular reason in these hearth deposits, perhaps having burning properties suited to some activity other than general domestic cooking, since cereals were not associated with them.

No cereal grains were recovered from any of the Stonehall Knoll contexts and there was very little evidence for the use of turf as fuel. This is in contrast to the findings from many of the other trench locations, and this fact, together with the presence of seaweed and a greater diversity of charcoal taxa, suggests perhaps that this area of the site is different to the others. It may have had a different use, or may relate to a separate, probably earlier, period of occupation.

15.3 Crossiecrown

Jennifer Miller and Susan Ramsay

15.3.1 Trench 1

Contexts from Trench 1 represented what was considered during excavation to be midden deposits that were rich in artefacts of late Neolithic/Early Bronze Age date. Unfortunately, only very scarce plant remains possibly indicative of the burning of turf and birch for fuel was recorded from the Trench 1 deposits (Table 15.6).

15.3.2 Trench 2

Trench 2 contexts are primarily from features within the Red House and include hearth and general occupation deposits in addition to the contents of several stone boxes. Contexts within a second house structure, the Grey House, which faced the Red House, were also examined. The carbonised plant assemblages identified from the Trench 2 contexts are generally dominated by finds of heather family charcoal and grass/sedge rhizomes with occasional seeds of grassland and heathland herbs. As for much of the rest of the site, this indicates that turf, cut from either grassland or heather heath, was the major source of fuel for the inhabitants of the structures uncovered at Crossiecrown.

Of particular note are the contexts examined from hearth deposits and from two of the stone boxes. Grey House hearth contexts ([403] and [409]) contained birch, hazel, willow and heather type charcoal but carbonised seeds were scarce and mainly sedges. No cereal grains were recovered from either of these hearth contexts although burnt bone fragments were relatively common. It may be that this hearth was used more for cooking meat than for cereal-based food preparation but this is based on a very limited set of results.

Three contexts ([012], [300] and [315]) from the Red House hearth differed from the more general occupation deposits in containing a much greater diversity of charcoal types including birch, hazel, heather family, blackthorn type, *cf* bird cherry and spruce/larch. This assemblage suggests that the inhabitants were utilising the locally available woodland for fuel but supplementing this supply with spruce/larch driftwood collected from the shore. An AMS radiocarbon date from [012] gave a range of 2460–

2190 cal BC, and a statistically similar date of 2480–2270 cal BC was obtained from context [315] (see Chapter 10).

Four stone boxes were excavated within the Red House and the contents of two of them (fill [014] from box [013] and fill [029] from box [015]) were examined for carbonised plant macrofossils. Although fill [029] contained only trace amounts of heather family charcoal, fill [014] contained a large quantity of bone, some trace amounts of heather charcoal and, more significantly, Scots pine charcoal. This appears to be strong evidence for the presence of a cremation deposit within box [013]. The combination of Scots pine charcoal with that from the heather family has been noted elsewhere on Orkney in connection with cremation deposits and its importance will be discussed later.

One of the most interesting contexts from Trench 2 was context [480], which was described during excavation as a dump of compact clay and ash sealed by context [003], the rubble and collapse signifying the abandonment of the site. Context [480] contained very large numbers of carbonised cereal grains with naked barley predominating over hulled barley in a ratio of approximately 6:1. Of the less well-preserved cereal grains it was still possible to categorise many of them as either barley or *cf* barley and there was no indication that any other cereal type was present within the context. Although grain was abundant there was only a trace amount of chaff present. This, together with a lack of carbonised crop weeds within the sample, suggests that this was the remains of an already processed crop, which had been lost during an accident either during storage or just prior to being prepared for cooking. The presence of heathy turf indicators within this context would tend to favour the latter explanation with the grains perhaps catching fire during a final parching process prior to grinding. AMS radiocarbon dating of naked barley gave a date range of 1960–1740 cal BC for this context.

15.3.3 Trench 3

Trench 3 contained midden material into which a large shallow hollow had been dug and then lined with stone. Elaborate Grooved ware pottery from this trench suggests an early Bronze Age date. The three contexts analysed from this trench all contained very similar carbonised plant remains. Charcoal was mainly from the heather family with a smaller amount of willow also present. The carbonised macrofossils identified were mainly sedges and grasses, including a large number of grass/sedge underground rhizomes. These findings suggest that

Table 15.6 Botanical evidence from Crossiecrown.

Crossiecrown	Common Name	CC'98	CC'98	CC'99	CC'99	CC'99	CC'98	CC'99	CC'99	CC'99	CC'99	CC'99	CC'99	CC'99	CC'98	CC'99	CC'99	CC'99	CC'99	CC'99
Site Code / Trench		1	1	2	2	2	2	2	2	2	2	2	2	2	2	2	2	2	2	2
Context		051	058	010	011	012	014	017	021	022	026	027	029	031	033	033	034	036	041	102
Other Description		Midden	Midden		Floor	Hearth House 1	Stone Box						Stone Box							
Matrix																				
Total carb veg		<5ml	<5ml	20ml	20ml	175ml	30ml	<5ml	<5ml	60ml	30ml	50ml	10ml	10ml	5ml	15ml	60ml	10ml	40ml	5ml
Modern veg		+	+	++	++	+	+	++	++	++	+	++	+	+	+	++	++	+	++	+
Charcoal																				
Alnus	alder																			
Betula	birch		4 (<0.05g)	3 (0.05g)													3 (<0.05g)	2 (<0.05g)	2 (<0.05g)	1 (0.05g)
Coniferales	conifer					4 (<0.05g)														
Corylus	hazel																			
Ericaceae	heather type		1 (<0.05g)	42 (0.05g)	>100 (0.3g)	>200 (1.95g)	10 (0.2g)	3 (<0.05g)		>150 (0.7g)	>50 (0.2g)	>50 (0.35g)	8 (<0.05g)	7 (<0.05g)	8 (0.2g)	>20 (0.1g)	>100 (0.6g)	>30 (0.1g)	>150 (1.15g)	11 (0.05g)
Picea / Larix	spruce / larch					12 (<0.05g)									1 (0.05g)					
Pinus sylvestris type	Scot's pine type						5 (<0.05g)													
Prunus cf padus	cf bird cherry					7 (0.05g)														
Prunus spinosa type	blackthorn type																			
Quercus	oak									2 (<0.05g)						1 (<0.05g)	1 (<0.05g)	1 (<0.05g)		
Salix	willow			1 (<0.05g)												2 (<0.05g)				
indet																				3 (0.1g)
	burnt peat/soil					++														
Cereals (c)																				
Hordeum vulgare var nudum	naked six-row barley																			
Hordeum vulgare var vulgare	hulled six-row barley																			
Hordeum vulgare sl	barley									1							1			
Hordeum vulgare rachis internode	barley chaff																		1	
cf Hordeum vulgare	cf barley																			

		1	2										
Indet cereals	indet cereals												
Macrofossils (c)													
Aphanes sp	parsley-piert												
Betula pendula / pubescens	silver / downy birch												
Bromus sp	brome												
Calluna vulgaris flower / capsules	heather												
Carex disticha	brown sedge								1				
Carex hostiana	tawny sedge												
Carex nigra	common sedge												
Carex panicea	cf carnation sedge												1
Carex viridula sl	yellow sedge					13		4	1		2			1
Carex sp	sedge					2			1				
Cyperaceae indet	sedge familiy					2							
Danthonia decumbens	heath grass	2			4	27		6	1			2	
Isolepis setacea	bristle club-rush												
monocot rhizomes / stems	grass / sedge rhizomes	+	5 (0.3g)	4 (<0.05g)	11 (0.2g)	>100 (3.15g)	25 (0.5g)	>50 (0.55g)	12 (<0.05g)	+	>20 (0.3g)	>50 (0.7g)	>20 (0.15g)	>25 (0.5g)
Montia fontana	blinks								1				
Plantago lanceolata	ribwort plantain	1											
Poaceae stems	grass	1		1					2				
Poaceae	grass		1										
Potentilla sp	cinquefoil					1							
Rumex sp	dock		1										
Scirpus / Schoenoplectus	club-rush					7		4			1		
Sorbus aucuparia	rowan												
Misc													
bone			+ (0.3g)		++ (48.55g)	+ (<0.05g)		+ (<0.05g)			+ (<0.05g)		+ (<0.05g)	+ (0.15g)

grassy and perhaps heathy turf formed a large proportion of the fuel being utilised at this time. In general, the archaeobotanical findings from Trench 3 are indicative of midden material from a domestic context.

15.4 Wideford Hill

Jennifer Miller and Susan Ramsay

15.4.1 Timber structure 1

Five posthole fills within Timber structure 1 were analysed for carbonised botanical remains. Evidence was very slight, but included a little charcoal and occasional carbonised cereals, indicating domestic occupation rather than an industrial workspace. Most of the small quantity of charcoal recovered was birch, but hazel and willow were also recorded. These taxa are suitable for the fabrication of woven panels as well as fuel, and the charcoal recovered from the postholes could be residual from either the wooden structure itself or from the occupation within it. The few cereals recovered were generally in very poor condition, but four from context [035] (posthole [34]) were identifiable as six-row barley (Table 15.7).

The central hearth in Timber structure 1 contained three fills ([115], [089], [068]). Carbonised plant remains from all three of the hearth fills were consistent, including charcoal mainly of birch and hazel. Context [089] also contained scant evidence of heather family twigs. Carbonised cereal grains and calcined bone were recorded from the hearth fills, further concurring with the implied domestic status of this structure. Identifiable cereals were primarily barley, of which the naked six-row type was recorded regularly. This concurs with a Neolithic date for this structure.

15.4.2 Timber structure 2

The fill [162] of posthole [161] was examined for carbonised plant remains. This posthole was from a series of five, comprising Timber Structure 2, although the fill examined was almost devoid of plant material containing only a single, tiny fragment of birch charcoal.

15.4.3 Timber structure 3

Eleven posthole fills were examined for botanical remains. It is suggested that the easterly group of postholes (including [058], [060], [065]) might relate to a different building, possibly of rectangular construction. Unfortunately the scant carbonised remains contained within the fills of those three features were synonymous with residual occupation scatter only, and could not aid in the interpretation of the interrelationship of the postholes.

The carbonised assemblage within the other posthole fills examined from Timber structure 3 included moderately large quantities of charcoal, primarily of birch, but with hazel and willow also recorded in significant amounts. Contexts [033] and [045] were notable in containing large quantities of cereal grains. Context [045], in particular, contained nearly 6000 cereal grains and may possibly represent the deposition of a single burning accident. Although a few grains of wheat were recorded from this posthole fill, all of the other identifiable grain was barley, including a sizeable percentage of the naked type.

15.4.4 Midden associated with the early timber structures

A layer of ashy soil and burnt stone [128], sealed below the rammed stone surface [002] associated with Stonehouse 1, is interpreted as midden or occupation material that had possibly accumulated during the occupation of the early timber structures. The carbonised remains from [128] would concur with this hypothesis, and the relatively large quantities of both charcoal and cereals would suggest that these are remains from hearth or midden deposits. In common with the contexts examined from the timber structures, charcoal is of birch and hazel, and the identifiable percentage of the cereal assemblage is six-row barley, including many naked grains. Clay layer [029] and cobble surface [031] below the rammed stone working surface [002] also contained carbonised botanical material concurrent with general occupation detritus on the old land surface sealed below the stonework.

15.4.5 Stonehouse 1

The lowest internal occupation surface of the Stonehouse 1 was built over timber Structure 2. The ashy soil layer [127], representing the interface of the occupation floors of these two buildings, produced very little carbonised material. In contrast, the upper floor layer [104] of Stonehouse 1 contained significant quantities of charcoal, with birch and hazel again predominant, as well as a few grains of six-row barley. The upper fill of hearth [152] also produced barley grains, some of which were of the naked variety.

15.4.6 Work area associated with Stonehouse 1

A spread of variably sized stones had been laid to the east of Stonehouse 1 to make a compacted, level surface area.

Table 15.7 Botanical evidence from Wideford Hill Continues p. 508.

Wideford	Common Name	002	021	023	024	027	029	031	033	035	043	045	048	051	054	059	061	066
Context	Description	compact outside? surface	silty/loam fill of drain 020	sticky red-black burnt soil	fill of posthole 025	fill of posthole 026	clay below cobble spread	line of burnt cobbles	fill of posthole 041	fill of posthole 034	fill of posthole 042	fill of cut 044	fill of posthole 047	fill of drain/ditch 106	basal fill posthole 053	Fill of 058	Fill of 060	Fill of 066
Matrix																		
Total Carb veg		80ml	10ml	5ml	10ml	30ml	10ml	110ml	10ml	<5ml	<2.5ml	340ml	10ml	10ml	15ml	<2.5ml	5ml	5ml
Modern veg		+	+++	-	-	+	-	-	++	+	+	-	++	-	+	+	+	+
Charcoal																		
Betula	birch	40 (4.65g)	2 (1.2g)		6 (3.3g)	28 (4.45g)	5 (0.45g)	45 (14.9g)	1 (0.1g)	4 (<0.05g)	2 (0.15g)	25 (11.6g)	2 (<0.05g)	1 (1.4g)	3 (<0.05g)	–		1 (<0.05g)
Corylus	hazel	9 (1.1g)				7 (0.5g)		5 (0.5g)				6 (1.4g)	1 (<0.05g)		7 (0.05g)			
Ericales	heather family		8 (<0.05g)															
Salix	willow	9 (3.2g)						1 (0.2g)		1 (<0.05g)			1 (0.05g)					
	peat/cinder	1 (0.1g)																
	Indet cinder	3 (0.6g)			5 (0.15g)	4 (0.15g)												
	Indet bark			1 (0.55g)														
Cereals																		
Hordeum vulgare var *nudum*	naked six-row barley					1			37			1499	9		19			
Hordeum vulgare cf var *nudum*	cf naked six-row barley	2	1						2									
Hordeum vulgare sl	six-row barley	3				10		1	56	4		1265	7		17	2	2	1
cf *Hordeum vulgare sl*	cf six-row barley								44			360						
Triticum sp	wheat											15						
	Indet cereal	5	4			5			118		2	3030	19		22			
Carb seeds																		
Rumex sp	docks								1									
Stellaria sp	stitchwort																	
Misc																		
	Bone																	
	Burnt clay																	

Table 15.7 Botanical evidence from Wideford Hill, continued.

Wideford	002	021	023	024	027	029	031	033	035	043	045	048	051	054
Context	067	068	072	084	089	099	104	114	115	126	127	128	148	162
Description	irregular oval cut	upper fill of 067	fill of posthole 071	fill of posthole 085	charcoal layer, base of 067	fill of posthole 098	upper floor House 1, nr hearth	fill of posthole 113	ash layer in hearth 067	fill of posthole 125	primary floor layer House 1	primary OLS below 002	ash spread in centre of House 1	fill of posthole 161
Matrix														
Total Carb veg	10ml	250ml	<5ml	10ml	130ml	30ml	35ml	5ml	5ml	10ml	<5ml	70ml	<5ml	<2.5ml
Modern veg	-	+	++	-	+	+	++	-	++	+	++	+	++	+
Charcoal — Common Name														
Betula — birch	8 (0.3g)	10 (1.2g)		17 (0.7g)	23 (3.1g)	13 (0.8g)	28 (2.35g)	5 (<0.05g)	14 (0.4g)	18 (0.55g)	1 (<0.05g)	30 (4.05g)		1 (<0.05g)
Corylus — hazel		11 (1.1g)			33 (2.75g)	4 (0.3g)	2 (0.05g)		5 (0.4)	6 (0.5g)		9 (2.2g)		
Ericales — heather family					1 (0.05g)									
Salix — willow						4 (0.45g)	3 (0.1g)							
peat/cinder														
Indet cinder	2 (0.25g)			3 (0.1g)	14 (0.8g)		2 (0.45g)	14 (0.6g)				1 (0.3g)		
Indet bark							1 (<0.05g)							
Cereals														
Hordeum vulgare var nudum — naked six-row barley		30			3	7			3	11		53	5	
Hordeum vulgare cf var nudum — cf naked six-row barley		2						2		2				
Hordeum vulgare sl — six-row barley		6			6	5	2		4	5	1	84	6	
cf *Hordeum vulgare sl* — cf six-row barley									2	4		50	3	
Triticum sp — wheat														
Indet cereal — indet cereal		15	1		6	14			4	14		118	10	
Carb seeds														
Rumex sp — docks										3		2		
Stellaria sp — stitchwort										2				
Misc														
Bone					3 (0.4g)			2 (<0.05g)						
Burnt clay														

Layers of ash and silt containing charcoal interlaced the stones, indicating that the stone surface had been added to regularly. The charcoal examined from samples within [002] included the same mix of birch, hazel and willow that has been recorded over much of the site. A few cereals, including six-row barley, were also recorded. This assemblage is indicative of general occupation detritus, including structural elements and/or hearth waste. Samples from a gully and drain also contained general domestic debris, but in small quantities only. These remains may have been redeposited from occupation events anywhere on the site.

15.5 Knowes of Trotty

Diane Alldritt

A total of 111 bulk environmental sample flots ('GBA' *sensu* Dobney *et al.* 1992) from the early Neolithic house at Knowes of Trotty, Harray, Orkney, were fully examined for carbonised plant macrofossils and charcoal. Only the 67 samples containing significant quantities of charred plant remains from secure contexts are tabulated here (see Table 15.8). Environmental samples have been analysed from three distinctive phases of occupation at the early Neolithic house, encompassing primary phases including floor surfaces and ashy spreads (phase 1), occupation layers, hearth-related fills and external areas (phase 2), and later structural layers, hearth fills and final abandonment (phase 3). In some cases contexts could only be assigned broadly to phase, such as the fills of hearth [215] in phase 2–3, but are included here due to the archaeological significance of this feature.

The carbonised plant remains from the early deposits at Knowes of Trotty included cereal grains, weed seeds, wood charcoal and large amounts of rhizomes and other heathy grassland turf indicators. This material adds further to the growing body of data for the early Neolithic period in Orkney, providing economic and environmental evidence reflecting the types of activity taking place within an early domestic structure and showing marked uniformity with other similar sites such as Stonehall (see above).

The flots produced varied amounts of carbonised plant material with the smallest containing <2.5ml of charred detritus, generally consisting of small fragments of degraded and crushed wood charcoal. Larger flots produced from 5ml up to 210ml of charred plant remains, consisting mainly of well-preserved wood charcoal, heather family stems, rhizomes, and small amounts of cereal grain. Heather and rhizomes were

particularly abundant from scoop hearth [220] in Phase 2, with lower amounts present throughout the remaining Phase 2 samples and from Phases 1 and 3. Other categories of plant material consisted of weed seed macrofossils, peaking in Phases 2 and 2/3, with fewer found in Phase 3. Occasionally samples were completely sterile of carbonised material, and these have been omitted from this analysis.

15.5.1 Phase 1: house construction and early internal features

Nine samples from Phase 1 produced carbonised plant remains, with wood charcoal the main category of material recorded. Fills [282], [283] and [289] from pit [286] produced a large concentration of well-preserved *Betula* (birch) charcoal, indicating a possible fire-pit with material burnt *in situ* or a dumped deposit of fuel waste from a nearby hearth. The condition of the material suggested it had not been moved very far (a fragment of birch from [282] was radiocarbon dated to 3500–3460 cal BC at 95.4% probability – SUERC 18239). Clay surface [224] and layer [324] near the hearth also produced birch, suggesting some spillage or sweeping out of fuel waste from the hearth becoming compacted into the floor layers. Interestingly, [204] an infill against wall [203] contained five grains of nicely preserved *Hordeum vulgare* var. *nudum* (naked six row barley), indicating drying or cooking of grain occurring in the building, with these grains probably swept from the hearth and surviving trampling by becoming lodged in the wall.

15.5.2 Phase 1-2: ashy layer

A single sample from ashy layer [293] contained only one highly degraded indeterminate cereal grain and a single rhizome. This material is probably trace remains from nearby burning and not particularly relevant.

15.5.3 Phase 2: alterations to the house, building of hearth [215], internal occupation surfaces and external features

A total of 27 samples and one charcoal small find produced carbonised material assigned to Phase 2. This phase was marked by the construction of oblong hearth [215], with an associated build-up of floors and occupation surfaces, together with the use of a messy external area.

Phase 2 showed a peak in fuel use with large amounts of wood charcoal, mainly birch with smaller amounts of

Table 15.8 Botanical evidence for Knowes of Trotty (phased).

Knowes of Trotty Summary: PHASE	P1	P1/2	P2	P2/3	P3	External
Total No. of Samples (Volume (Litres))	9 (105.5)	1 (15)	28 (392)	7 (58)	15 (155)	7 (76.5)
Cereal Grain						
Naked Barley	5	0	0	1	0	0
Barley	0	0	9	0	6	2
Total Cereal Grain:	5	0	9	1	6	2
Charcoal						
Birch	30 (12.53g)	0	52 (22.41g)	2 (0.16g)	16 (2.02g)	12 (24.94g)
Hazel	0	0	2 (0.46g)	0	1 (0.02g)	2 (1.71g)
Cherry Type	0	0	0	0	2 (0.1g)	0
Total Charcoal:	30 (12.53g)	0	54 (22.87g)	2 (0.16g)	19 (2.14g)	14 (26.65g)
Wild Resources						
Ericaceae stems	0	0	2500+ (125.19g)	0	11 (0.02g)	0
Rhizomes	2 (0.39g)	1 (0.15g)	216 (14.51g)	5 (0.18g)	1 (0.08g)	0
Weed Ecology:						
Weeds of agriculture	0	0	0	2 (1sp.)	3 (2sp.)	0
Turf and grassland weeds	0	0	69 (4sp.)	21 (8sp.)	8 (5sp.)	0

Corylus (hazel) recorded from the ashy clay floor layers and other occupation surfaces. This suggested a large amount of burning taking place within the house, with the waste becoming trampled, crushed and compacted into the floor, particularly in [218], [219], [271] and [290] (birch charcoal from [271] was radiocarbon dated to 3350–3080 cal BC at 95.4% probability – SUERC 18239). Some attempts were obviously made at sweeping the building out at various points, as evidenced from ashy build-up layers [311] and [320], but this appears to have only made it as far as the porch entrance area.

Evidence for the use of heathy or grassy turf for fuel or construction purposes, in the form of rhizomes and heather family stems, was present in low numbers in a few of the samples, including [183] and [271]. In marked contrast to this general scatter of burnt material, deposit [220] the fill of rounded pit [294], produced a highly abundant quantity of heather stems, rhizomes, and weed macrofossils from grassy and damp heathland environments. This feature was probably a fire-pit or scoop hearth, with the fuel remains still *in situ*. No charcoal was found in this deposit suggesting turf was the main source of fuel, perhaps for processes such as cereal grain drying requiring long smoldering heat, rather than high temperatures. Two *Hordeum vulgare* sl. (barley)

grains were also found in [220], indicating possible cereal drying or cooking waste. The material from [220] skews the weight for weight comparison data in favour of turf fuel, but it must be remembered that wood charcoal was found in varied amounts in nearly every sample from Phase 2, and largely spread by trampling and sweeping, so its importance as the probable main fuel source for hearth [215] should not be eclipsed by a single *in situ* deposit.

Carbonised cereal grain was found in small amounts from six contexts, from floor and occupation deposits, [099], [183], [217], from hearth scoop fill [220], and also in the entrance area [323] and from [337] near hearth [215]. All the grain was quite degraded, probably from being trampled into floors and occupation surfaces, and could only be identified as *Hordeum vulgare* sl. (barley). This evidence suggested grain drying taking place within the house, or cooking waste, with ashes from hearth area [215] regularly cleaned out.

15.5.4 Phase 2/3: fills from hearth [215] and floor layers

Seven samples broadly phased to Phase 2/3 produced small trace amounts of carbonised plant material, with single specimens of birch charcoal from floor layer [149] and clay and stone area [119] and no wood charcoal from the final fills of hearth [215]. Interestingly, [119] contained a single naked barley grain, as with [204] from Phase 1; the survival of this well-preserved grain was probably chance due to it becoming lodged in a stony layer and escaping some of the more trampled areas.

Hearth fills [234] and [236] produced trace burnt plant remains which indicated probable use of turf as fuel for the final burning activity taking place. The turf was probably burnt down to a mixture of ashy waste and blackened soil as few actual rhizome fragments, and no heather stems, were found. Interestingly, the weed flora was more informative with the specimens indicating rough grassy turf and damp heathland ecologies, the majority being found in the lower two fills [235] and [236] of the hearth. Only trace quantities of grassland weeds were present in the top fill [233], and these possibly could have trickled down and become charred, from organic material (such as straw) being dumped on top of the hearth to dampen it down, as suggested by the soil analysis, but little macrofossil evidence for this has survived.

15.5.5 Phase 3: abandonment and renovation, hearth [082]

Thirteen samples and one charcoal small were assigned to Phase 3, with central hearth [215] deliberately sealed over, a period of abandonment and collapse, followed by construction of a smaller house in the north part of the old building with a new smaller sub-rectangular hearth [082] constructed in the NW corner.

Small amounts of charcoal were found, with birch the main fuel waste recorded in hearth fill [082] and clay hollow [157], along with occasional finds of hazel and Prunoideae (cherry type) charcoal also found, perhaps suggesting a more opportunist use of whatever wood was available. Hearth [082] was radiocarbon dated to 3360–3080 BC at 95.4% probability (SUERC 18233). Heather family stems and various weeds of grassland from [082] and [157] indicated turf was probably still being cut for fuel. Barley cereal grain was found in small amounts in [082], tipped layer [121] and [157] but none of this could be further attributed to type, with indeterminate grain in clay layer [152].

The samples from Phase 3 indicated there was still burning activity going on, involving similar fuels as earlier, and probably also a degree of cereal processing, but the activity is very much scaled back compared to the previous habitation (Figs 15.1–15.3)

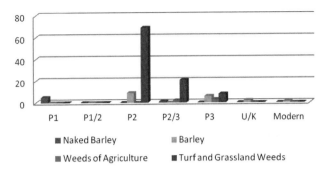

Figure 15.1 Comparison of cereals present in different phases at Knowes of Trotty (U/K= Unknown).

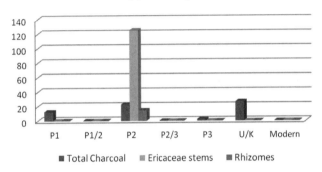

Figure 15.2 Comparison of fuel types present in different phases at Knowes of Trotty.

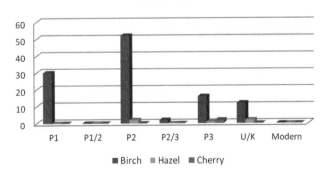

Figure 15.3 Comparison of charcoal present in different phases at Knowes of Trotty.

15.5.6 Phase Unknown: external work areas, porch/entrance

Seven samples could not be firmly phased, and these produced a small amount of cereal grain and some charcoal, possibly swept out of the structure from various burning activities, *e.g.* charcoal from the porch [312], but perhaps also indicating some work activity requiring fuel taking place in the external areas, such as [258]. Two barley cereal grains were found in brash deposit [316], but are probably not that significant as they could have originated during any of the three phases. External work areas [258] and [276] produced some nicely preserved hazel and birch charcoal in quite large 'chunks' up to 2–3cm in size, indicating some possible *in situ* burning activity occurring here.

15.6 Varme Dale

Joanna Bending

Mound 2 of a Bronze Age barrow cemetery at Varme Dale was excavated as part of the *Orkney Barrow Project* (see Chapter 9). The discovery of large quantities of charred cereals was totally unexpected and together with Smerquoy will be further investigated as part of a new project into the earliest Neolithic in the Northern isles. However, a provisional presentation and discussion of the botanical remains will be offered here. The information derived from the identification of the charred seeds from the early Neolithic layers sealed by mound 2 at Varme Dale was most remarkable. Charred seeds were recovered from five samples, presented in Table 15.9.

Overall, the material was fairly well preserved, with some distortion of uncertain origin (*i.e.* wrinkling of surface of grain). The positive identifications of 2-grained einkorn wheat (*triticum monococcum*), naked barley (*hordeum distichum/vulgare* var. *nudum*), linseed (*linum* sp.) and hazel nut (*corylus* sp.) were made. Naked barley was the dominant crop (3 out of 5 samples and 56% of all crop items – see Table 15.9), followed by einkorn wheat (2 out of 5 samples and 40% of all crop items). The possible presence of low levels of rye (*secale cereale*) and oat (*avena* sp.) were also noted. One glume base was recovered, which could not be identified beyond the genus *triticum*. Charcoal and/or bark were present in four of the five samples, at low levels in all. No seeds of wild species were recovered.

It is worth going into a little more detail regarding the contexts of this unusual series of deposits. The density of grain in one particular black lens of silt [2022] was such that it was observable in the field and a small bag sample was taken of this deposit (sample 227). All samples were wet sieved in the laboratory and therefore the minimal amount of chaff found should be representative of what was present. The other four samples which yielded grain

were general bulk samples of varying sizes, none of which were more than 10 litres and sample 224 only 5 litres. As only a small part of this series of deposits was excavated and a smaller part sampled, and the deposits could be seen clearly to extend into all sections revealed in Trench 2a cutting the barrow, it could be inferred that there is substantial amount of grain sealed under this barrow perhaps comparable with the quantities of charred barley found at the early Neolithic settlement Braes of Ha'Breck, Wyre (Lee and Thomas 2011).

There is some exclusivity in the location of wheat and barley; samples 215 [2018] and 227 [2022] contain 97% and 96% barley to 1% and 2% wheat respectively. Context [2018] was a discrete area of burnt stone and ash outside the kerb of the barrow (Fig. 9.9) and [2022] was a patch of black silt. Wheat dominated sample 241 [2027/8] and 244 [2041] by 94% wheat to 6% barley and 67% wheat to 29% barley respectively. Although it is not possible to be certain on the level of evidence available, it is possible to infer that processing of barley and wheat was being undertaken separately.

The possible presence of low levels of rye (*Secale cereale*) and oat (*Avena* sp.) were also noted. Little chaff and charcoal (of small twigs) were present, and no seeds of wild species were recovered. The presence of einkorn wheat is unusual in an assemblage from prehistoric Scotland, and dating of the grains themselves is desirable to confirm this early date. Although it should be noted that *Salix* charcoal from one of the contexts [2041] that contained *T. monocoum* and one [2027] that contained *Triticum* were the source of the two existing dates, and these contexts were both well sealed beneath the buried ground surface [2024].

15.7 Brae of Smerquoy

Mark Robinson and Dana Challinor

As Brae of Smerquoy has revealed itself to constitute a large early Neolithic settlement complex, investigations are still ongoing. Consequently, only a brief and provisional statement can be made concerning the identified charred plant remains recovered from contexts within the Smerquoy Hoose.

Sixty-five bulk samples for charred plant remains, monoliths and pollen spot samples were taken during the 2013 excavation season that concentrated on investigating the Smerquoy Hoose (Chapter 4). Bulk samples were processed at ORCA using a Siraf-style water flotation system (French 1971) fitted with a 1mm internal mesh and an external sieve stack consisting of 1mm and 300 micron sizes.

Table 15.9 Botanical evidence from Varme Dale.

Sample Number	215	224	227	241	244
Context	2018	2027	2022	2027/2028	2041
fraction sorted	¼	½	½	1	¼
charcoal volume (ml)	<0.5	0.5	0	0	<0.5
T. monococcum 2 grained (grain)		1		9	9
T. cf. *monococcum* 2 grained (grain)				8	6
T. monococcum/dicoccum (grain)		4		15	9
Glume wheat (grain) indet.		1			
Triticum (grain) 'wrinkled'		22		13	57
Triticum (grain) indet.	1	19	3	6	8
Triticum glume base		1			
Hordeum distichum/vulgare var. *nudum* (grain)	20	30	5	1	18
Hordeum distichum/vulgare var. *nudum* 'straight' (grain)	2				
Hordeum distichum/vulgare var. *nudum* cf. 'straight' (grain)	1		1		
Hordeum distichum/vulgare cf. var. *nudum* (grain)	42	25	54	1	9
Hordeum distichum/vulgare (grain)					
Hordeum (grain) indet.	51	9	70	1	12
Triticum/Hordeum (grain)	2				3
Cereal (grain) indet.		11	1		
cf. *Secale cereale* (grain)		1	1		1
cf. *Avena* sp. (grain)		1			
Linum sp.		3			1
Corylus sp. (nut shell)					Frag.

Frag.: categories present but too small an amount to be accurately quantified;
cf.: compares with;
var.: variety;
indet.: indeterminate.

The preliminary identification of samples reported here was primarily for radiocarbon dating was undertaken by Mark Robinson and Dana Challinor. Hulled *Hordeum* sp. cereal grains from contexts [022], [027], and [045] were identified, along with indeterminate cereal grains from contexts [015], [027], and [045]. Ericaceae charcoal was identified from context [045] and [027]. *Betula* sp. charcoal was identified from context [015], and Salicaceae charcoal from context [022]. Contexts [022] and [027] represented superimposed occupation deposits within the stalled house, while context [015] comprised foundation material beneath the outer wall-skin of the Smerquoy Hoose. Context [045] represented the fill of a small pit at the rear of the structure.

Cereal grains occur in many interior contexts of the Smerquoy Hoose and although full identification and analysis remains to be undertaken there is clear evidence for a strong cereal content to subsistence strategies in the 33rd and 32nd centuries cal BC at Brae of Smerquoy. Given the large spread of burned cereal in the rear compartment of House 3 at Ha'Breck (Thomas and Lee 2012), the burnt floor surface behind the hearth in the inner compartment of the Smerquoy Hoose assumes greater significance. Certainly the possibility remains that cereals were dried and processed in the rear areas of houses.

15.8 Discussion

15.8.1 Stonehall

The early Neolithic contexts from Stonehall contain a much greater diversity of wood charcoal types than those from the later Neolithic period. This implies that more woodland was available for exploitation during this early period, with those timber resources being depleted over the following centuries until they were scarce in the area.

At this point, wood may have been utilised for specific purposes rather than simply domestic fuel. Evidence for this 'saving' of wood for particular purposes may be seen in the carbonised assemblage from the clay 'bowl' [815] in Structure 1 at Stonehall Farm, which was exclusively composed of birch charcoal, with no evidence of the turf that was ubiquitous elsewhere.

Another example of selection of a fuel for a specific purpose is seen in a few of the hearth deposits from the early Neolithic contexts on Stonehall Knoll in which fragments of carbonised brown seaweed were found. Seaweed was not found in any other contexts at Stonehall, which suggests that a particular activity, perhaps unrelated to everyday domestic cooking, may have been undertaken using these hearths.

As the Neolithic progressed there is additional evidence for the increasing scarcity of woodland resources and the apparent growing reliance on turf for fuel at Stonehall, a situation mirroring that at the contemporary village of Barnhouse (Hinton 2005). Much of the carbonised material considered to be the remains of burnt turves was relatively minerogenic in nature and contained rhizomes of grasses or sedges in addition to numerous sedge nutlets. This implies cutting or stripping of turves from damp grassland habitats as well as from more peaty, heathland areas. The botanical results from Stonehall show that the inhabitants were burning these turves as their primary source of fuel by the later Neolithic.

The heather-type charcoal identified from many of the samples represents burning of collected 'above ground' heather stems as well as the incidental burning of subterranean heather stems when heathland turves were used as fuel. The carbonised heather type remains from this site indicate utilisation of this taxon as fuel, but other uses, such as thatching, bedding and flooring cannot be ruled out prior to burning as fuel.

Evidence for the use of wood in a structural context was most clearly seen in the early Neolithic remains excavated on Stonehall Knoll (Trench C). Significant quantities of large fragments of willow roundwood were recovered from contexts in this trench. In general these branches were between 7–12 years old, the age range within which willow is harvested to provide poles and smaller withies for the construction of wattle-work panels. Consequently, these charcoal fragments are considered to be the remains of wattle structures destroyed by fire during the earlier phases of occupation at Stonehall.

Evidence for food remains at Stonehall is exclusively in the form of carbonised cereal grains, with barley being the only cereal type identified from the site. The significant number of cereal grains recovered from Pit [3074] (Fill [3075]) in House 3 at Stonehall Meadow suggests that storage of grain in pits occurred at Stonehall and that, furthermore, the grain was cleaned prior to storage as no weed seeds or chaff were recovered from this context. Of particular note is the predominance of naked barley over the hulled type within the assemblage.

15.8.2 Crossiecrown

Although the carbonised remains recovered from the Grey House hearths were scarce there is a suggestion of less reliance on turf as the major fuel source in this earlier structure than for the later Red House, where heather turf dominates the hearth assemblages and driftwood was also used. This provides further evidence for the general decline in the availability of woodland resources on Orkney as the Neolithic period progressed.

None of the hearth features contained any carbonised cereal grain. This absence suggests that the processing of grain occurred elsewhere, or that these buildings were later used for a purpose other than domestic occupation.

It is possible to speculate on the possibility that the stone box [015] contained a cremation deposit because of the large quantity of fragmentary burnt bone and trace amounts of heather and pine charcoal. A similar assemblage was recorded from the Bronze Age cist at Crantit, Mainland, Orkney by these authors (Ramsay in Ballin-Smith 2014, 59, 60, 74). Pine wood, either from local sources or driftwood, may have been collected and then stockpiled especially for use in cremation rituals in order to give the high temperatures required for the funeral pyre. The rarity of charcoal, or carbonised plant remains of any sort, in these types of cremation deposits may be attributable to the necessity of burning fuel until it has turned to ash, in order to maximise the energy obtained from this scarce resource.

The presence of very small fragments of spruce/larch charcoal is a clear indication of the use of driftwood as a fuel resource by the inhabitants of Crossiecrown. Due to the small size and flaked nature of the charcoal fragments it was impossible to be confident in the anatomical separation of these two closely similar genera. However, neither spruce nor larch is native to Scotland, and the original wood is most likely to have come from North American driftwood, although in the case of spruce, timber could also have originated in southern Scandinavia. The later contexts from Crossiecrown, which represent the early Bronze Age, suggest even greater reliance on turf as fuel, indicating that woodland was a very scarce resource by this time.

Context [480], a cereal dump, gave the best indication of cereal crops for Crossiecrown, with more than 2500 cereal grains recovered. Identifiable grains of naked and hulled barley were present in a ratio of approx 6:1. It also appears to be a cleaned crop as weed seeds are very scarce and so may indicate that this grain was lost either during storage or during drying prior to grinding.

15.8.3 Wideford Hill

The charcoal assemblages from the three timber structures and Stonehouse 1 were essentially very similar. There was no significant difference in terms of species content between contexts representing structural remains and those ascribed to midden or hearth deposits. This suggests that the same, locally available scrub woodland resources were being utilised for both construction and domestic hearth fuel. This fact would further imply that this site is occupied before the local woodland declined sufficiently to necessitate the burning of heathland resources, turves, driftwood or seaweed as fuel, or the utilisation of stone and driftwood for construction. It is not possible to state whether the continuity of charcoal types observed between the earlier Timber structures 1–3 and later Stonehouse 1 is a real phenomenon, due to the continued availability of local resources, or whether it indicates the reuse of timbers from the abandoned structures for fuel. However, both scenarios may be true, as the floor in the later house seals a void from a posthole relating to the earlier Timber structure 2, which was deemed during excavation to have rotted *in situ*. One interesting fact to emerge from the botanical analyses at Wideford Hill is the total absence of any coniferous charcoal that would reflect the utilisation of driftwood. Considering that Timber structures 1–3 are of wooden construction, this implies that local deciduous woodland resources including birch, hazel and willow were sufficiently abundant at this time for there to be no need to use coniferous driftwood for building or fuel for domestic hearths.

The cereal assemblage from the earlier Timber structures 1–3 and later Stonehouse 1 indicate that six-row barley was the dominant cereal grown and consumed at this site throughout the period of occupation of these structures. At least a significant part of the arable cultivation practiced here concerned the growing of the naked variety of six-row barley.

One posthole fill [045] from Timber structure 3 at Wideford Hill was unique to the site in having wheat in the grain assemblage. However, out of the more than 5800 grains recorded, only 15 grains of wheat (not specifically identifiable) were recorded, compared to more than 3000 barley grains, almost half of them of the naked variety. Six-row barley has always been the main cereal type grown in Scotland, with the emphasis on the naked and hulled varieties changing over time. In this case, it is most likely that the wheat grains represent accidental cultivation of wheat as a 'weed' within the barley crop. The very noticeable lack of carbonised seeds of arable weeds associated with the cereal grains suggests that the grains are from completely cleaned crop assemblages. The reasons for incorporation of the cereals within each of the posthole fills probably vary, with low numbers possibly resulting from background occupation scatter and larger numbers perhaps coming from fire waste or redeposited midden material. However, generally speaking, none of the fills are suggestive of crop processing accidents such as gleaning or parching. The scarcity of weed seeds at Wideford Hill is noticeable, and may be related to the fact that turf was not being used as fuel at this site.

15.8.4 Knowes of Trotty

Radiocarbon dating suggested occupation at Knowes of Trotty spans about 500 years, from approximately 3500–3000 cal BC. Indeed, comparison of the plant remains from Knowes of Trotty with material from Stonehall reveals very similar practices in crop regimes and fuel use. It may be possible to identify a particular signature in the archaeobotanical record characterized by the dominance of naked barley in certain early Neolithic assemblages, followed by a later resurgence in the use of this type of cereal in the Mid-Iron Age (Alldritt 2013). These patterns may be reflective of the types of sites being more recently analysed and published, with the use of naked barley possibly more widespread in later periods on the Scottish Mainland than previously thought (S. Ramsay pers. comm.), but could also reflect social changes such as the necessity to increase food yields to meet the needs of feasting or population increase. Whilst hulled barley agriculture may have been steered more toward brewing and probably also animal fodder during the later Iron Age, naked barley grown on heavily fertilized land could have provided an efficient source of food production throughout various points in prehistory.

Evidence from Phase 1 indicated the main use of birch as fuel, suggesting light open areas of scrub, perhaps with birch growing on wetter areas of carr such as the edges of damp heathland. Birch burns well, although its heat is short-lived, and would have been a good source of domestic fuel (Gale and Cutler 2000, 50). Birch trees were also believed to ward off evil spirits so perhaps a fire entirely composed of birch could be seen as bringing good luck (Grigson 1958). A significant amount of the birch charcoal came from the fills of pit [286] indicating this was probably the location of an early hearth or dumping area for hearth waste. A small number of rhizomes from Phase 1 provided a tentative suggestion for turf also being cut as fuel in this early phase.

Fuel use peaked in Phase 2, largely based around the main period of use of hearth [215], scoop hearth [220] and the clearing out, scattering and general trampling of burnt waste across the occupation surfaces. Birch continued to be the main source of woodland fuel, with a small amount of hazel found, probably originating from hearth [215] and being trampled and crushed across the floor layers (Fig. 15.2). A greater volume of sample was analysed from Phase 2 than from Phase 1, so it is possible the birch peak is slightly inflated, nevertheless birch was found throughout a significant number of samples from Phase 2, whilst largely concentrated in fire-pit [286] in Phase 1. A large concentration of grassy and heathland indicator species from [220] indicated turf was the main source of fuel in this smaller hearth, perhaps for small-scale drying of cereal grain, away to the side of the main hearth. A small amount of burnt turf material was incorporated into the floor deposits, and probably represented a general scatter of trampled material. Dickson and Dickson (2000, 53) suggested turves would be used to keep the fire in at night, and unlikely to be the main source of fuel, due to the difficulty in drying them out and the high sediment content. At Knowes of Trotty there appears to have been a plentiful supply of birch for the main hearth during Phases 1 and 2, so turf was possibly used as a supplement for the smaller hearth places or for purposes requiring different levels or controls of heat.

By Phase 3 there was a marked drop in the quantities of charcoal and turf indicators when compared weight for weight with earlier phases (Fig. 15.3), possibly as a result of the scaling back of activity and general abandonment during this period. Hearth place [082] suggested birch continued to be used as fuel, but there was a general broadening out to include cherry type and more hazel. Grassland weeds from Phase 3 could suggest straw being burnt as fuel or thrown onto hearth places to seal them off, particularly in hollow [157].

Cereal grain from Phase 1 indicated cultivation of barley, with naked six row barley the only type

identified. The survival of cereal grain here was quite rare and largely dependent upon context [204] offering some protection from the general trampling and messy accumulation of ashy waste occurring across the floor surfaces and elsewhere. Low recovery of barley grain seems fairly typical from within early domestic houses in Orkney, and the Knowes of Trotty house follows this pattern. Cultivation of barley continued into Phases 2 and 3 although largely due to the types of context much of it was too poorly preserved to identify further than simply 'barley'. A single grain broadly phased to 2/3 was found to be the naked type, and as with [204] probably offered some protection from trampling within stony layer [119]. Barley grains found within scoop hearth [220] suggested drying or cooking of grain over a slow burning turf fire. A very small number of weeds of agricultural land were present within Phase 2/3 and in Phase 3, probably arriving at the site with locally grown cereal grain, but in too small amounts to propose anything further about the type of arable land under cultivation.

15.9 Comparative discussion of Crossiecrown, Knowes of Trotty, Stonehall and Wideford Hill

Jennifer Miller, Susan Ramsay and Diane Alldritt

15.9.1 Native woodland resources and driftwood

It appears from the archaeobotanical analyses undertaken at the three sites, that there has been a significant change in the availability of native woodland resources during the period of occupation of these sites. The earliest Neolithic occupants appeared to have access to a wide range of woodland types. Although birch, hazel and willow are by far the commonest tree types present there is evidence for a variety of lesser, and perhaps more 'shrubby' types to have been available for use. These include several of the cherry types as well as rowan.

As the Neolithic progressed the availability of trees for construction and/or fuel is reduced (cf. Farrell *et al.* in press). Evidence for wood charcoal in hearths and other domestic deposits declines and it is suggested that wood was being kept for specific purposes other than everyday domestic fuel. The clay 'bowl', excavated in Structure 1 at Stonehall Farm had a fill that was made up solely of birch charcoal, much of it in large pieces. This was in stark contrast to other contexts that contained domestic hearth waste, where a mixture of tiny fragments of wood charcoal mixed with burnt heather and turf was the standard carbonised assemblage. It was suggested previously that wood might have been kept for burning during processes in which a high temperature was required. It would be difficult to maintain high temperatures with peat or turves, which tend to burn slowly and with few flames. Birch wood, on the other hand, contains resins that would produce a hot flame during combustion (Edlin 1973), a property that would probably have been highly valued.

It would appear that by the Bronze Age very little wood was available in the Bay of Firth area, either for construction or burning. The later contexts from Crossiecrown, which represent the early Bronze Age, show a high reliance on turf as fuel, indicating that by now woodland was a very scarce resource. This correlates well with a substantial decline in woodland cover from the early Neolithic period onwards noted by Bunting (1994) in the pollen record of west Mainland, Orkney. Pollen analysis has also indicated that the mounds at the Bronze Age cemetery at Linga Fiold were constructed over a pastoral landscape (Bunting *et al.* 2001). With regard to the pollen assemblage (see Appendix 15.1), we also observe evidence for an open, agricultural landscape recorded in sediments from a mire, adjacent to Stonehall, in the Cuween-Wideford study area by around 2000 BC.

The possible cremation deposit from the site at Crossiecrown contains small fragments of Scots Pine as the only evidence for wood making up the pyre material. Much of the pyre material appears to have been heather which would not have burned in any sustained manner and is thought to have been used only because nothing else was available rather than through choice. The Scots Pine charcoal may have come from sources on the island, although its native status on Orkney is disputed by some authors, but is more likely to have been collected as driftwood from the coast. Evidence for the collection and utilisation of driftwood is indisputable from some of the contexts examined from the Bay of Firth study area since they contain fragments of larch/spruce charcoal. As neither of these tree types is native to Scotland, or even the British Isles, the most likely geographical source is the eastern seaboard of North America or, in the case of spruce, from southern Scandinavia (Dickson 1992).

Both spruce and larch charcoal have been identified from many archaeological sites in the Northern Isles, including Papa Stour (Dickson 1992) and Knap of Howar (Dickson 1983) and have been interpreted as North American driftwood. The straight trunks of both of these conifer types would have rendered the wood highly valuable for use in construction in a regional landscape where the native trees are reduced to twisted, stunted shrubs by the exposed conditions.

15.9.2 Other natural resources: turf, peat and seaweed

Turf and Peat

There appears to be a significant and increasing reliance on the utilisation of turf for fuel as the Neolithic progressed. As previously discussed, the inhabitants of Orkney were significantly depleting the local woodland resources as early as the beginning of the Neolithic Period. By the Bronze Age, Orkney was virtually treeless and so the inhabitants had to turn to other sources of fuels.

Peat was commonly used in the Highlands and Islands of Scotland as fuel, particularly in areas where woodland had been cleared and blanket peat had formed in its place. Peat is often found in a carbonised form from archaeological sites in Orkney. However, very little evidence of carbonised peat was found from the three settlements. Instead, it appears that the local inhabitants were using turves cut from minerogenic heathland or grassland soils rather from true peats. There is little, if any, evidence for the burnt amorphous organic 'lumps' that are characteristic of burning of true moss or sedge peat. However, many contexts, particularly those of later Neolithic or early Bronze Age date, contained archaeobotanical evidence for the use of minerogenic turves. These included significant quantities of heather underground stems, grass/sedge rhizomes and also large numbers of seeds of heathland and grassland plants. These seeds suggest that the turf had been cut from damp, but not very wet habitats, with a wide variety of sedges as well as heath-grass commonly found.

This increasing reliance on turf for fuel, in addition to peat, is also seen at many early sites in the Northern Isles including Skara Brae (Dickson and Dickson 2000), Howe (Dickson 1994), the Biggins (Dickson 1999) and Knap of Howar (Dickson 1983). At these sites the emphasis on the use of turf was determined by the age of the site and the availability of other fuel resources. For example, turf was not deemed to have been the primary fuel at Skara Brae, but at that site woodland and driftwood were prolific enough to use in preference to turf. In contrast, turf was used as the pyre fuel at the Bronze Age cemetery at Linga Fiold (Bunting *et al.* 2001), probably as a result of necessity rather than choice. However, turf has often been valued in its own right as the fuel of choice for use in drying cereal grain and other situations requiring a fuel that burns with a slow, steady heat (Dickson 1998). In the case of cereal drying, this phenomenon is less likely to result in the grain itself catching fire. However, when wood is scarce, turf can become the main source of everyday domestic fuel for cooking and warmth, with turf from roofing material and byre waste also able to be reused for fuel (Fenton 1978).

The heather twigs recovered from contexts thought to contain the remains of burnt turf were the thick, twisted stems/roots characteristic of the parts of heather that have grown underground. However, many contexts also contained significant quantities of thinner, straighter heather stems, which are more liable to have been from above ground growth. This indicates that people were collecting heather stems for use in the settlements. The heather may have been collected primarily for fuel or perhaps as thatching, flooring or bedding material which was subsequently burned for fuel when no longer required for its original purpose.

Seaweed

Evidence for the burning of seaweed was recovered from only two contexts from the entire Bay of Firth study area. These contexts were from Stonehall and were associated with hearth deposits on the knoll. However, although the seaweed was limited in distribution, there was a significant amount in each context with context [1022] containing at least 2.8g. Significantly, these hearth deposits were unusual in containing no carbonised cereal grains. This suggests that a process, other than cooking, was taking place using these hearths towards the end of their active lives. This might be confirmed by the presence of some flint flakes that were also associated with these same contexts.

Seaweed is rich in minerals, particularly iodides, resulting in its use throughout history in many industrial processes *e.g.* soap and glass production. It also has an important role as a soil fertiliser in areas where other organic resources are scarce (Fenton 1978). There is a growing catalogue of sites in the Northern Isles in which carbonised seaweed has now been identified *e.g.* Howe (Dickson 1994). It is possible to speculate that the inhabitants of Stonehall were also using seaweed for a specific purpose that relied on its particular chemical composition rather than just as an additional fuel resource.

15.9.3 Cereals and other foods

At all four sites investigated during this study the dominant cereal type was naked barley, although some hulled barley was identified from both Stonehall and Crossiecrown. This is in contrast to the carbonised cereals recovered from Wideford Hill where none of the grains in the barley assemblage were recognisable as the hulled

variety. A similar situation exists for Knowes of Trotty, although a little caution is necessary due to the degraded and trampled condition of the barley from within the house. As hulled barley is usually more identifiable in archaeobotanical terms than the naked form, it would appear that the absence of hulled barley from Knowes of Trotty and Wideford Hill is a real phenomenon rather than an artefact of differential preservation. This situation is mirrored at the contemporaneous Neolithic site of Knap of Howar, where Camilla Dickson concluded that it was probable that the entire cereal assemblage was naked barley (Dickson 1983).

Further afield on Shetland recent work at Firths Voe, Delting, produced trace amounts of hulled six-row barley from house deposits dated from the early to middle Neolithic period, with the scarcity of remains suggesting the structure was regularly swept clean (Alldritt in prep.). Recent re-evaluation of the structural remains and radiocarbon dating at Ness of Gruting, Shetland, where a very large cache of naked barley was discovered, has suggested broadly early Bronze Age origins rather than Neolithic (Sheridan 2012, 17). This may prove to be a similar story at Hill of Crooksetter, Delting, which also produced large quantities of naked barley, possibly late Neolithic–early Bronze Age in date, but awaiting final radiocarbon phasing (Alldritt 2012). As further work is radiocarbon dated and published it may be possible to more closely dissect the regional rise and fall of naked to hulled barley ratios throughout prehistory.

Naked barley is commonly recorded from sites from Orkney dating to the Neolithic period, *e.g.* Skara Brae (Dickson and Dickson 2000), Isbister (Lynch 1983), Barnhouse (Hinton 2005) and Knap of Howar (Dickson 1983), but the popularity of this cereal variety declined in the Bronze Age gradually being replaced by the hulled type which could be stored more easily due to the protective outer hulls of the grain (van der Veen 1992). This phenomenon occurred throughout Scotland, although naked barley remained the cereal of choice in scattered areas for an extended period. Alldritt (2003) then observes a short resurgence of the naked type of barley in the Iron Age in the Northern Isles, and this may relate to a change in agricultural practice or population influx.

An interesting find was the presence of a few grains of wheat in the cereal assemblage from the site at Wideford Hill. Many areas of Scotland are not conducive to the growing of wheat because satisfactory yields cannot be guaranteed due to the vagaries of the weather. As a result, wheat has frequently been imported or traded in

Scotland, and is often associated with sites of apparent 'high status' or 'ritual significance', such as Claish (Miller and Ramsay 2002) and Balbridie (Fairweather and Ralston 1993). This has happened throughout history, although trade or high status is not thought to be a likely explanation for the wheat grains of Neolithic age found at Wideford Hill. Evidence of bread wheat was recorded at Skara Brae for the Neolithic period (Dickson and Dickson, 2000) where it was considered to represent the remnants of a locally grown crop. Wheat pollen was also observed within Neolithic sediments at Knap of Howar (Whittington 1983), suggesting further that wheat was able to be cultivated, at least on a small scale, on Orkney at this time. Nevertheless, it is not possible to rule out the importation or exchange of wheat at Wideford Hill, although its relative scarcity suggests this occurrence is unlikely. Furthermore, the low ratio of wheat compared to barley is not indicative of maslin cultivation or the growth of wheat as a crop in its own right.

At Wideford Hill the quantities of wheat recorded are so low that they probably came from plants growing as contaminants within the main crop of six-row barley. Crop weeds *per se* were generally rare within the three sites studied in this area, but especially so at Wideford Hill. This could suggest that the grain on this site in particular came from almost cleaned crops or those threshed free from handpicked ears of naked barley. Evidence of turf and heather within the cereal assemblages on the later sites may be due to parching accidents or similar such events, although the possibility of accidental conflagration of stored crop products on any or all of these sites cannot be ruled out.

Palaeoenvironmental Investigation of a Peat Core from Stonehall

Susan Ramsay, Stephanie Leigh-Johnson and Rupert Housley

15.1.1 Introduction and methodology

As part of the investigations into the archaeology of the Cuween-Wideford area on Mainland, Orkney, it was recognised that it was important to be able to place the on-site archaeological and environmental evidence recovered into a wider landscape perspective. This could be achieved through pollen analysis of a suitable sediment core from an area in close proximity to the archaeological sites being investigated. In September 1997 Rupert Housley visited the area, identifying and coring two sites, at Stonehall and Cuween Hill, which had palaeoenvironmental potential. In 1999–2000 preliminary analysis of the pollen and macrofossil content of these sites was undertaken by Stephanie Leigh-Johnson as the dissertation element of her BSc degree (Johnson 2000). The following report concentrates only on the site at Stonehall and incorporates the original plant macrofossil study undertaken (*ibid*), a re-analysis of the pollen by Susan Ramsay and two radiocarbon dates which were not available to Leigh-Jones for her dissertation.

Coring

A peat core was taken from a small area of mire (see Fig. 5.4; NGR HY366126), located in a natural depression near the site of Stonehall. A profile of the peat depth present within the mire was determined in order to identify the most

suitable location from which to extract the longest possible core (Fig. 15.1.1). A large diameter Russian peat corer was used to take two peat cores: one extending to a depth of 88cm and a second extending to a depth of 98cm. The longer core was chosen for all subsequent investigations, which included pollen and plant macrofossil analyses in addition to AMS radiocarbon dating.

Sampling procedure

Prior to any destructive sampling occurring, the peat core was visually assessed by Leigh-Johnson for any obvious stratigraphic changes contained within it. However, no such changes were visible. The core appeared to be a homogeneous, highly organic peat. The remains of aquatic and semi-aquatic plants were visible within the core and will be discussed later. Twelve samples, each covering a depth of 1cm and approximately $2cm^3$ in volume, were removed from the core for further analyses. The samples were prepared for pollen analysis using the standard techniques outlined in Moore, Webb and Collinson (1991). Hydrofluoric acid treatment was required on some of the samples (17–18cm, 49–50cm, 73–74cm, 81–82cm, 89–90cm), which were found to contain a significant mineral component. The concentrated pollen samples were stained with safranin, dehydrated with tertiary butyl alcohol and mounted in silicone oil prior to preparation of microscope slides. Plant macrofossils were recovered from these samples during the pollen preparation procedure. These were collected on a 120μm sieve directly after sodium hydroxide digestion and prior to acetolysis treatment being undertaken.

Pollen counting and identification

Preliminary pollen counting of these samples was undertaken by Leigh-Johnson in April 2000 but the counts on which this report is based were undertaken on the same samples by Susan Ramsay in March 2003. At least 300 identifiable pollen grains (excluding Cyperaceae and aquatics) were counted from each level wherever

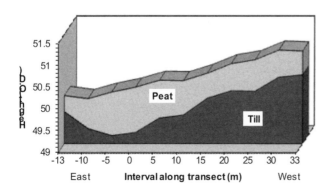

Figure 15.1.1 Stonehall peat profile.

possible but when this was not feasible two complete slides were counted instead. Counting was undertaken using an Olympus CH30 microscope at ×400 magnification, with ×1000 for critical determinations. Identification of pollen grains was by reference to Moore *et al.* (1991) and Punt (1976–91). All critical determinations were checked against the University of Glasgow reference collection. Pollen nomenclature follows Moore *et al.* (1991) apart from Ranunculaceae and Polygonaceae where further determination was carried out using the Northwest European Pollen Flora keys. The category 'Coryloid' is used for grains that may be either *Corylus* (hazel) or *Myrica* (bog myrtle), although in this study it is thought that the majority of grains will have originated from *Corylus* (hazel). Cereal-type pollen grains were distinguished from other Poaceae by having a grain size >37µm and an annulus diameter of >8µm. Measurements of cereal pollen grain size and annulus diameter were made and compared with the cereal categories identified by Andersen (1979) and Dickson (1988) to provide a greater degree of information regarding potential cereal crops that may have been growing in the area at various points in time. Vascular plant nomenclature follows Stace (1997). Broken, crumpled, corroded and otherwise unidentifiable pollen grains were recorded during the counts to give information on the general state of pollen preservation. Microscopic charcoal particles >10µm were counted on the pollen slides and assigned to the size categories suggested by Tipping (1995), *i.e.* with a longest axis length of 10–25µm, 26–50µm, 51–75µm and >75µm.

Plant macrofossils

Plant macrofossil remains recovered during pollen preparation were separated and identified by Leigh-Johnson using a binocular dissecting microscope at variable magnifications of ×4–×45. Very small seeds and translucent vegetative remains were mounted on slides in glycerine jelly for examination at magnifications of ×100 and ×400. The same sample depths used for pollen analysis were also subjected to plant macrofossil analysis. Seeds and vegetative remains were recorded using a scale of 1–5 where 1 represented trace quantities and 5 represented very abundant quantities. Identification of vascular plant remains was facilitated by the Glasgow University reference collection and with Beijerinck (1947). Identification of *Potamogeton* seeds to species was aided by reference to Preston (1995). Vascular plant nomenclature follows Stace (1997). Mosses were identified by reference to Watson (1981), Crum and Anderson (1981) and the considerable help of Prof. J. H. Dickson of Glasgow University.

Pollen and plant macrofossil diagram production

Individual pollen taxa were expressed as a percentage of a total land pollen (TLP) sum that excluded Cyperaceae, aquatics and spores. Cyperaceae were excluded from the pollen sum due to such an extremely high local presence in some levels that they masked the fluctuations in other taxa. Taxa excluded from the pollen sum were expressed as a percentage of a sum comprising all identified pollen grains and spores (TPS). Charcoal counts were also presented as percentages of the total pollen sum (TPS). The pollen diagram (Fig. 15.1.3) was produced using the TILIA and TILIA.GRAPH computer programs (Grimm 1991) and shows all taxa identified. To facilitate interpretation, the pollen diagram has been divided into three vegetation assemblage zones (SH-1 to SH-3), which are described in Table 15.1.2.

Vegetative remains and seeds were recorded on a 5-point scale of relative abundance to enable a corresponding macrofossil diagram (Fig. 15.1.4) to be produced for comparison with the pollen diagram. The macrofossil diagram is divided into the same three vegetation assemblage zones (SH-1 to SH-3) as the pollen diagram.

15.1.2 Results

Radiocarbon dates

Two radiocarbon dates were obtained from the Stonehall peat core to aid with the interpretation of the vegetation history of this area and to enable comparison with the botanical results obtained from the archaeological excavations at Stonehall, Crossiecrown and Wideford Hill. The results of the radiocarbon dating program are shown in Table 15.1.1 and a time-depth plot for the Stonehall peat core is shown in Fig. 15.1.2.

Pollen and macrofossil diagrams

The results from the pollen analysis are shown in Fig. 15.1.3 and the corresponding macrofossils analysis is shown in Fig. 15.1.4. The boundaries of the vegetation assemblage zones are the same in both diagrams to enable direct comparison between the two.

Local vegetation assemblage zones

The pollen and plant macrofossil diagrams were divided into three local vegetation assemblage zones. The boundaries of these zones were defined as the depths at which significant vegetation changes occurred within the

Table 15.1.1 Radiocarbon dates.

Lab Code	Peat Depth	Uncalibrated radiocarbon date	Calibrated date (1σ)	Calibrated date (2σ)
GU-10324	50–51 cm	2845 ± 40 BP	1050–920 cal BC	1130–900 cal BC
GU-10323	95–96 cm	3475 ± 35 BP	1880–1730 cal BC	1890–1680 cal BC

pollen and/or plant macrofossil profiles. Within each zone the vegetation remained relatively constant. The details of the environmental changes noted within these vegetation zones are discussed below. A summary of the depths and age ranges of the zones are given in Table 15.1.2, together with a brief summary of the significant events in the vegetation history of the area associated with each zone.

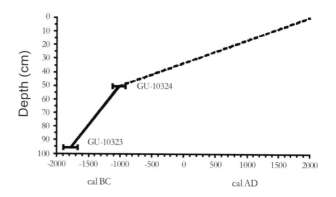

Figure 15.1.2 Time-depth plot.

Zone SH-1 (85–98cm)

This zone is characterised by high percentages of *Myriophyllum alterniflorum* (alternate water milfoil) pollen and relatively low amounts of Cyperaceae (sedge) pollen in comparison to those seen in the zone above (SH-2). It would appear that the hollow was filled with water during this period and was actually a small, shallow pond or lake. This is confirmed by the presence of seeds of *Potamogeton cf polygonifolius* (bog pondweed), characteristic of shallow ponds on acid soils, and oospores of the aquatic alga *Chara*. The mosses present within this zone (*Drepanocladus cf aduncus* and *Fontinalis antipyretica*) are both characteristic of very wet or often truly aquatic habitats.

The area surrounding this pond appears to have been open grassland and heather heathland with very little woodland growing in the vicinity. There are a considerable number of agricultural indicator pollen types within this zone. The most significant of these are *Plantago lanceolata* (ribwort plantain), *Plantago major* (greater plantain) and *Ranunculus acris* (meadow buttercup) group, but there are lesser quantities of a wide variety of other 'weedy' types. The majority of these types are characteristic of pastoral agriculture which, taken together with the absence of cereal pollen from this zone, may suggest that any cereal cultivation was being undertaken some distance from the site at Stonehall. A charcoal peak at the base of this zone may be another indicator of intensive human activity in this area, although it is not possible to tell if this charcoal resulted from domestic fires or the burning of standing vegetation such as heather heathland. This zone dates approximately to the period 1600–1900 cal BC.

Zone SH-2 (29–85cm)

The most characteristic feature of this zone is the overwhelming dominance of Cyperaceae (sedge) pollen, which must have been growing on the site rather than just being a component of the regional vegetation. A reduction in aquatic taxa, particularly *Myriophyllum alterniflorum* (alternate water milfoil), suggests that the open water of the pond was gradually reducing, as a result of hydroseral succession, becoming a wet fen-mire type habitat. This change in habitat from truly aquatic pond to drier fen-mire is also mirrored by the change in the dominant mosses found on-site *i.e.* the aquatic types *Drepanocladus cf aduncus* and *Fontinalis antipyretica* being replaced by *Calliergon cf giganteum*, a species characteristic of wet fens.

Within the more regional environment there seems to have been a minor reduction in heathland and a corresponding slight increase in woodland taxa. As the percentages of Poaceae (grass) and agricultural indicators remain relatively unchanged within this zone in comparison with zone SH-1, it would appear that the increase in pollen of woodland taxa was caused by trees colonising areas of heathland. This might have been a result of an amelioration in climate or a change in agricultural practice away from utilising heathland in a way which maintained its species composition *e.g.* by burning, to one in which trees could recolonise

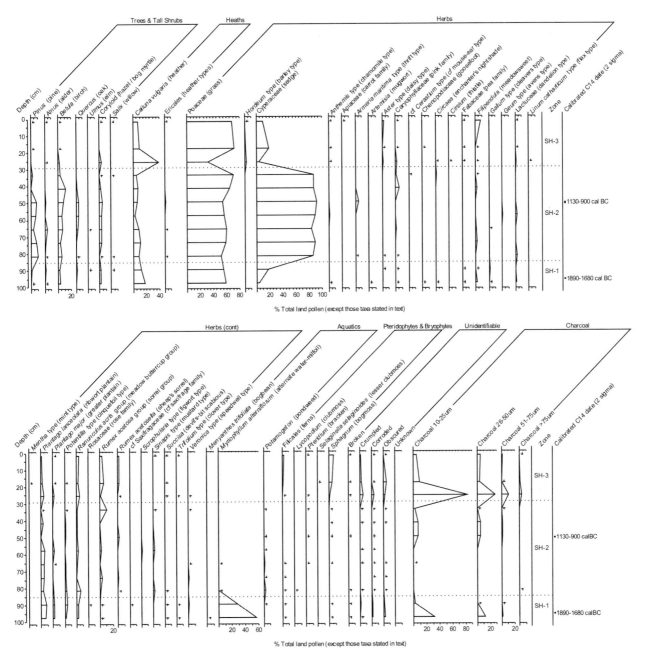

Figure 15.1.3 Stonehall pollen diagram.

these areas. Although several tree taxa show an increase within this zone, *Pinus* (pine) and *Betula* (birch) seem to have been most abundant. This would correlate with the renewed growth of trees on former heathland sites, as both these taxa readily invade heather-dominated heath when drying of the heathland surface occurs or when grazing or burning pressure is reduced. This zone dates approximately to the period 1600 cal BC–cal AD 200.

Zone SH-3 (0–29cm)

The most noticeable change in the vegetation within this uppermost zone is the sudden and dramatic decline in pollen of Cyperaceae (sedge) which had been the most abundant pollen type throughout zone SH-2, accounting for more than 90% of the total pollen rain landing on the site during this period. However, at the beginning of SH-3 Cyperaceae (sedge) pollen declines to less than 20% of the total pollen sum. This suggests a change in the local vegetation growing on the mire surface itself.

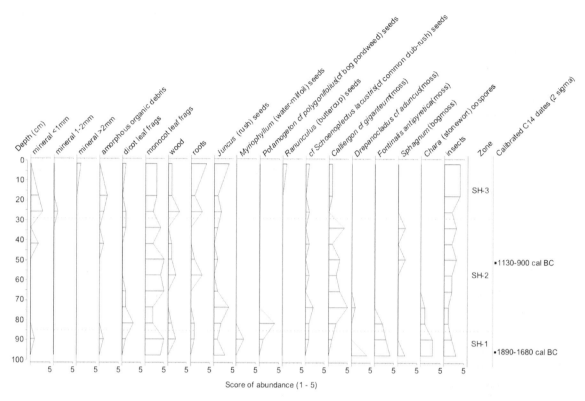

Figure 15.1.4 Stonehall macrofossil diagram.

The pollen diagram shows an increase in *Calluna vulgaris* (heather) pollen at this time but no *Calluna vulgaris* (heather) macrofossils were recovered from the sediment in this, or any other, zone. Therefore, it seems unlikely that Cyperaceae (sedge) was replaced by *Calluna vulgaris* (heather) as the dominant on-site vegetation.

No other major pollen taxa appear to increase during this period but the macrofossil diagram shows that *Juncus* (rush) became more prevalent. *Juncus* (rush) pollen does not preserve in sediments and so is, therefore, invisible to the technique of pollen analysis. It is likely that the mire surface became colonised by *Juncus* (rush) at the expense of the Cyperaceae (sedge), but that this significant change in the dominant plant taxon can only be argued through negative pollen evidence. Toward the top of this zone there is an increase in the pollen of *Filipendula* (meadowsweet), a plant often associated with fens and marshes, and it would appear that this is evidence for on-site growth within a marshy environment.

The increase in *Calluna vulgaris* (heather) pollen is a 'real' event but it would appear that this heather was colonising an area outwith the local habitat of the mire. The pollen diagram records a decline in the pollen of trees and shrubs between zones SH-2 and SH-3. It appears that any small areas of woodland present in the

vicinity of Stonehall were finally felled towards the end of zone SH-2 and by the beginning of zone SH-3 the landscape was more or less treeless, as it still is today. It would seem likely that the areas cleared of trees may then have been recolonised by heathland, hence the rise in pollen of *Calluna vulgaris* (heather).

The beginning of zone SH-3 is notable for a sudden peak in microscopic charcoal, particularly the smaller size fractions. This suggests that the charcoal had been wind-blown onto the site rather than representing on-site burning of vegetation. Since no macroscopic charcoal was noted in this, or any other, zone, it is likely that the onsite vegetation was never burnt. As the peak in charcoal corresponds with the heathland maximum, it is possible that this correlation points to the burning of regional heather heathland as the source of the microscopic charcoal recorded on the pollen slides.

This zone is also characterised by the presence of *Hordeum* (barley) type pollen, the first time cereals are seen in the pollen diagram. The diversity of agricultural weed taxa also increases within this zone, with *Ranunculus* (buttercups), *Rumex* (sorrels) and *Plantago* spp (plantains) particularly prevalent. This suggests that arable agriculture was being practiced throughout the last two millennia in fields very close to the site at Stonehall.

Table 15.1.2 Summary of vegetation zones.

Depth	Zone	Approximate date	Vegetation characteristics
0–29 cm	SH-3	Cal AD 200–present	Grassland and heather heathland dominate. Woodland more or less absent. *Hordeum*-type (barley type) pollen consistently present. Coring locality was a wet mire.
29–85 cm	SH-2	1600 cal BC–cal AD 200	Grassland dominates. Woodland at its most significant. Very high values for Cyperaceae (sedge). Coring locality was a very wet, sedge-dominated fen.
85–98 cm	SH-1	1600–1900 cal BC	Grassland dominates with highest values of *Plantago lanceolata* (ribwort plantain). Woodland very scarce. High values for pollen and macrofossils of aquatic types. Coring locality was a shallow lake.

15.1.3 Discussion

On-site vegetation history

It is clear from the analyses undertaken that the on-site vegetation has undergone significant changes throughout the last 4000 years, the time period during which sediment accumulation has taken place. The site was initially fully aquatic, probably a shallow pond, dominated by *Myriophyllum alterniflorum* (alternate water-milfoil) and *Potamogeton polygonifolius* (bog pondweed) but with a number of aquatic mosses also present. This aquatic phase may have persisted for a few hundred years before the pond began to show signs of infilling with plant material and silts by about 1500 cal BC. This change in habitat may have followed on from a period of climatic change but, more likely, was a result of the natural process of hydroseral succession. The vegetation changed from aquatic to that associated with a marshland habitat. The on-site vegetation was dominated by Cyperaceae (sedges) and the moss *Calliergon cf giganteum*, whilst the previously dominant aquatic taxa had completely disappeared. Further changes in the local vegetation occurred around cal AD 200 when it appears that there was a massive shift in the dominant on-site vegetation, with Cyperaceae (sedges) probably being largely replaced by *Juncus* (rushes). The reason for this is not clear but may be related to changing agricultural practices on the surrounding slopes. This, in turn, may have led to changes in the nutrient status of any inflowing water. The macrofossil diagram certainly shows an increase in the mineral input to the site, probably as a result of intensification of arable agriculture on the surrounding slopes leading to increased hillwash into this low-lying area.

Native Woodland

The evidence for the native woodland of this area is mainly seen in zone SH-2 of the pollen diagram. *Betula* (birch), Coryloid (probably hazel), and *Alnus* (alder) are present in the pollen profile and are all known to have been growing in Orkney at this time. *Pinus* (pine) also has a significant presence in the pollen profile. It has been argued by some authors (*e.g.* Keatinge and Dickson 1979) that the appearance of pine pollen in diagrams from Orkney is due to long-distance transport of grains on the wind, probably from mainland Scotland. However, Bunting (1994) is of the opinion that the pine pollen seen in Orkney sediments is evidence for pine growing on these islands, particularly in the more sheltered eastern areas of Mainland Orkney. The percentages of pine seen at Stonehall are such that it is considered likely they are representative of a pine presence on Orkney rather than from a distant source. There is also a small but significant record for *Quercus* (oak) in zone SH-2 with values of around 5% of the total land pollen consistently present. Again, much has been said in the literature about tree pollen arriving in Orkney on the wind, but this consistent record of *Quercus* (oak) from the Stonehall pollen diagram is more suggestive of very local patches of *Quercus* (oak) growing nearby, possibly in more sheltered pockets. The fact that *Quercus* (oak) declines in the pollen diagram at a similar time to *Betula* (birch), and *Corylus* (hazel), which are always considered to be native taxa, provides a further indication that all these tree types are native to the island. Bunting (1994) also considers it likely that *Quercus* (oak) is native to Orkney and regards the pollen percentages of *c.*5% that she recorded at Quoyloo Meadow to be evidence of this.

By the beginning of the 1st millennium AD woodland indicators have all but disappeared from the pollen profile of Stonehall. It is probable that the last remnants of the remaining native woodland had been removed by the local inhabitants to provide fuel and building material. Regeneration of woodland was probably prevented by grazing animals, whose numbers would have increased along with the increasing human population in the area. From that point until the present day, the landscape of Orkney has remained essentially treeless, with the only surviving area of native woodland colonising a small valley at Berriedale on the island of Hoy (Dickson and Dickson 2000).

Human impact on the landscape

It is clear from the pollen diagram that major human influences on the surrounding vegetation of Stonehall had already occurred prior to the beginning of the pollen record at this site. The lowermost levels of the pollen diagram show an open agricultural landscape, almost devoid of trees, with strong evidence for pastoral agriculture being practiced. The lack of pollen from trees and shrubs indicates that the inhabitants of this area may have had to travel some distance to collect wood for fuel or building and, in fact, might have only had access to driftwood and heather as sources of wood fuel. However, if the inhabitants were practicing some form of woodland management, *e.g.* coppicing of hazel or willow, then it would be possible for there to be very little evidence for woodland in the pollen record but for there to have been a regenerating supply of wood available for use. Another source of fuel would have been peats from heathland or other areas of mire. However, the peat deposits from the Stonehall site itself were probably never utilised for fuel as the site is too wet to provide useful, compact turves.

Although there is no clear evidence for arable crops during the earliest phase of the pollen diagram, this does not rule out the possibility that arable agriculture was being practiced in the Stonehall area. Indeed, the significant quantities of carbonised grain, mainly naked six-row barley, from the archaeological excavation at Stonehall confirm the local inhabitants were consumers, as well as producers, of grain in the Neolithic period. Cereals are generally self-fertile and release only very small quantities of pollen into the atmosphere. In addition, the pollen grains themselves are very large and do not travel far on the wind. Therefore, if the site chosen for pollen analysis is upwind of any cereal growing area and/or more than a few tens of metres distant from it, cereal pollen may be all but absent from the profile. Cereal pollen, in the form of *Hordeum* type (barley type), is seen in the profile from approximately cal AD 200 onwards. This may indicate intensification of arable production or perhaps a shift in the areas of land used for cereal growing.

Charcoal peaks are seen in the pollen diagram in both zones SH-1 (1600–1900 cal BC) and SH-3 (cal AD 200–present) with charcoal particles in the smallest size category predominating. This indicates charcoal from an off-site source, either domestic fires or perhaps burning of heathland. Either way, it appears to provide correlating evidence for the presence of significant occupation in the vicinity of Stonehall during these periods. Pollen evidence for heathland is particularly strong at the beginning of zone SH-3 around cal AD 200 and correlates particularly well with the strong charcoal signal that also occurs at this point. This might point to the charcoal signal containing a significant component that is the result of heathland burning. Although it is possible for the heathland fires to have had a natural origin it is more likely that they were started deliberately by the local inhabitants, either to clear ground or to regenerate heather plants to provide better grazing.

The intervening period, represented by zone SH-2 (1600 cal BC–cal AD 200), appears to show a decline in the effects of human impact of the vegetation of the local area. Woodland types recover somewhat and the pollen of agricultural weeds shows a significant decline. This, combined with very low levels of charcoal particles throughout most of zone SH-2, suggests that human occupation in the vicinity of Stonehall declined significantly during this period. Whether this is representative of a general population decline in Orkney during this time or perhaps, more likely, is evidence for a shift away from the Stonehall area to other locations, is impossible to tell from the information recorded here.

15.1.4 Conclusion

The study of both pollen and plant macrofossils from the mire site at Stonehall has produced a picture of the local and more regional environment of this part of Mainland Orkney during the past 4000 years. It is clear the people who lived near Stonehall throughout this period inhabited an open landscape with relatively little access to woodland resources. They farmed extensively, in the earlier period concentrating on pastoral agriculture, but in the last two millennia there was a change to more arable agriculture with the growing of barley in particular. They deliberately modified their landscape by felling trees, growing crops and burning heathland but also indirectly through the effects of their grazing animals and by soil erosion from farming.

CHAPTER SIXTEEN

The Micromorphological Analysis of Soils and Site Contexts at Stonehall and Crossiecrown

Charles French

16.1 Stonehall

16.1.1 Introduction

Ten soil profiles associated with the excavations were described and sampled, as well as a series of six hearth profiles. In addition, a series of seven exploratory test pits were excavated and recorded in the immediate vicinity of the site. A series of 27 sample blocks were taken for micromorphological analysis (after Murphy 1986; Bullock *et al.* 1985) in 1994. Of these, four profiles were taken from the east-facing north–south section face of Trench B (1–4), one profile (5) from the modern ditch cutting adjacent to Trench A, one profile (6) taken from the drainage channel cut on the downslope/eastern edge

of Trench A, and six profiles from hearth areas occurring in most trenches and within structures. The main profile descriptions are given in Table 16.1.

In addition, a series of seven test pits were hand dug on the lower half of the slope immediately above Trenches A (Fig. 5.47) and B (Fig. 6.4), and to either side of Trench C (Fig. 5.5). These were intended to indicate the presence and preservation of any palaeosols, and to assess the potential for further micromorphological and possible palynological work.

Most of the test pits on the slope indicated that there was only a shallow depth (<25cm) of turf and topsoil present resting directly on the subsoil. The area of

Table 16.1 Profile descriptions at Stonehall.

Profile	Depth (cm)	Description
1. Farm (Tr B): Outside Structure 1	0–20	Turf and structure-less dark brown silt loam
	20–42+	Midden material: silt loam matrix with high charcoal component; exhibits alternating lenses of dark-brown, brown and reddish-brown coloured material
2. Farm (Tr B)	0–19	Turf and dark brown structure-less silt loam
	19–36	Mottled yellow/greyish brown silt loam with occasional charcoal flecks
3. Farm (Tr B)	0–18	Turf and dark brown structure-less silt loam
	18–32	Pale greyish brown silt loam
4. Meadow: in modern ditch between Trenches Z and A	0–12	Turf and dark brown structureless silt loam
	12–32	Pale greyish brown silt loam
	32–50	Reddish/purplish brown silt loam
	50+	Very pale yellowish brown silt with gravel and sandstone flagstones
5. Meadow: immediately east of Trench A	0–12	Turf and dark brown structureless silt loam
	12–32	Pale greyish brown silt loam
	32–50	Dark brown silt loam
	50+	Till subsoil

pasture immediately upslope of Trenches A and B was once cultivated, as indicated by the presence of a relict, narrow 'ridge and furrow' system running perpendicular to the slope. This system may well be a product of spade agriculture and be more akin to 'lazy bed' cultivation. Whatever its origin and date, it has led to erosion of the original soil profile, soil creep downslope and accumulation on the uphill side of the cross-slope modern drainage ditch. This additional soil accumulation was observed in profile 5.

Once the slope begins to steepen and there is a change to rough, heather-covered pasture upslope, the soil profile changes dramatically. It becomes a very shallow (<40cm) podzol, which is prone to erosion and peat growth. In addition, there are three areas of deeper peat growth which occur in small, natural basins on the slope. They contain a minimum of 1m accumulation of peat, with a present-day ground water table only about 50cm below the ground surface.

16.1.2 Micromorphological analyses

A series of 27 samples from 12 profiles were sampled and analysed. The sample locations were chosen to represent different contexts both within and outside structures on the site. Throughout, the profiles are not deeply buried and the upper one-third is essentially the modern colluvial ploughsoil and therefore subject to considerable mixing processes. The profiles are described briefly below and in Tables 16.1, 16.2 and 16.3, with the more detailed descriptions found in the site archive.

Profile 1

DESCRIPTION

Profile 1 was taken from near the north-west corner of Trench B and comprised the modern ploughsoil and midden deposit [607] (see Fig. 16.1). The topsoil (sample 1/1) is a very fine sandy clay loam, dominated by very fine quartz sand and dusty or impure clay. In addition, there is a sizeable component of very fine sand-size fragments of pure clay with strong birefringence and also amorphous iron reddened zones of soil fabric. The soil is porous, with large intrapedal channels defining the blocky ped structure of the profile, and smaller interpedal vughs.

Organic matter is common and is present mainly as finely comminuted to amorphous fragments and amorphous staining of the groundmass (Fig. 16.2a). In addition, there are two large pieces of charred plant remains and occasional plant tissue fragments, partially decomposed but with some of the cell structure still visible. The plant remains are mainly impregnated with amorphous iron, and often appear as pseudomorphs within the groundmass. There are also a few fragments of phosphatised decaying bone scattered throughout the sample (Fig. 16.2b). Other features present within the profile include sesquioxide nodules and quite a few larger stone and pebble inclusions, but these are mainly restricted to the top half of the profile.

The transition to the underlying horizon is characterised by a distinct but undulating boundary dividing the topsoil and underlying fabrics. Small inclusions of both

Table 16.2 Summary of the main micromorphological features of profiles 1–6.

Profile	Description	Interpretation
1	Dark brown, very fine sandy clay loam, sub-angular blocky to vughy; abundant charcoal, plant remains, bone and burnt bone fragments, fine pottery sherds, ash	Midden material in humic soil; possibly dumped material; all subsequently mixed, oxidised; more recent structural development; very similar to Profile 5
2	Very dark brown sandy clay loam, weak sub-angular blocky to vughy, heterogeneous; with abundant organic and anthropogenic material increasing with depth	Midden material in humic soil; subject to oxidation; possibly occupation material accumulating in structure on a ? floor surface
3	Two fabrics in heterogeneous mix; 75% calcitic ash and 25% humic sandy loam soil; with abundant organic and anthropogenic material	Poorly mixed ash and soil; possibly dumped and/or colluvial slumping downslope
4	Dark reddish brown very fine sandy clay loam, weakly developed sub- blocky with vughy/pellety microstructure; abundant organic and anthropogenic material increasing with depth; ash in middle of profile	Midden material and humic soil; some dumping of ash from hearths; all mixed, oxidised; more recent structural development; possibly occupation material accumulating on a ?floor surface; very similar to profile 1
5	Greyish/yellowish brown sandy loam, weak intergrain channel structure with pellety microstructure; zone of calcitic ash in middle and base of profile; very abundant fine charcoal	Humic soil and ash; possibly dumped and/or result of colluvial slumping; all bioturbated by soil fauna

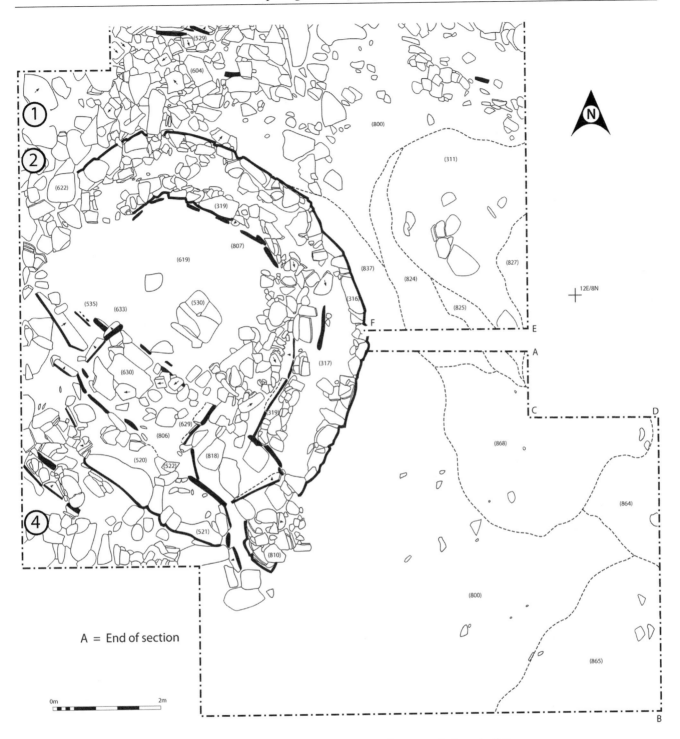

Figure 16.1 Location of profiles in respect to Structure 1, Stonehall Farm.

groundmasses have been moved up and down across the boundary, which gives it a heterogeneous appearance. The fabric in sample 1/2 is distinctive and different from the topsoil. It exhibits a vughy and striated appearance, and the few channels present are partially or totally infilled with 'pellety' groundmass material. It is dominated by calcitic ash and very fine sand layers alternating with degraded organic matter, often with cell structure visible and bone fragments present. The clay component is restricted mainly to the same pure clay fragments (or papules) present in the groundmass that are present in the topsoil, and as some dusty clay coatings in voids within the groundmass.

In sample 1/3 there is an abrupt change to a more homogeneous, porous, less striated, more ash-dominated and more organic groundmass. Porosity is about 20%, with common sub-angular to sub-rounded vughs. About halfway down the sample, there is a discrete lens of fine bone and pottery fragments about 10mm thick. Organic matter comprises the second most common component of the sample after the ash, consisting mainly of finely comminuted to amorphous black organic remains and larger decaying plant remains with still-visible cell structure, along with some phytoliths. The degraded bone is mainly restricted to the lens in the middle of the sample, though there are some small bone fragments scattered throughout the profile. In addition to this lens, other notable features included a few aggregates and streaks of burnt soil.

Interpretation

This profile represents a midden deposit dominated by calcitic ash and comminuted organic matter with a modern ploughsoil above. Post-depositional oxidation, slight acidification and mixing processes have been affecting this profile since its accumulation began.

The topsoil is well-mixed with a 'pellety' or excremental fabric in some of the channels which is a result of worm activity and bioturbation. The large pebble and stone inclusions in the top half of the profile are probably a result of recent ploughing and agricultural activities. The high ash component of the groundmass must derive from fires and/or hearth activity, so the profile may well represent periods of cleaning out and dumping of material from a hearth or cooking area. In addition, chemical changes have affected the profile since deposition, primarily oxidation and slight acidification. The bone fragments exhibit degradation, as does the cell structure of the plant remains, and many of them have been largely replaced by amorphous iron, impure clay, or other secondary materials. The striated appearance in sample 1/2, on the other hand, may be a result of within-soil intercalation of impure clay resulting from soil disturbance in the past and/or localised colluviation (hillwash erosion).

Sample 3 exhibits some of the features of sample 1/2 above, such as the high ash and organic content, but has a different textural appearance. Indeed, the more homogeneous, less striated appearance of this part of the profile is probably due to greater mixing of the materials before deposition, or that the profile represents fewer overall episodes of dumping. The discrete lens of bone and pottery probably represents a single episode of dumping.

All three samples in profile 1 share some of the same groundmass characteristics, especially in terms of the clay content. The fragments of pure clay that are found all the way through the profile probably result from the weathering of the underlying till substrate. There are also a few voids with very thin linings of clay which are suggestive of post-depositional disturbance, possibly associated with recent agricultural activities and/or hillwash.

Profile 2

Description

Profile 2 was taken from the northwest corner of Trench B through the modern ploughsoil and midden deposits situated on an area of stone rubble, probably representing building collapse [302]. Sample 2/1 and the upper part of sample 2/2 make up the topsoil component of the profile. It is also a very fine sandy clay loam, dominated by small quartz grains and unoriented dusty or impure clays. There is a minor component of highly birefringent pure clay fragments present in the groundmass of the profile. It exhibits a blocky ped structure with large interpedal channels and smaller intrapedal channels and vughs.

There is a high organic component including finely comminuted to amorphous black organics in the groundmass (Fig. 16.2c). In addition, there are some partly decomposed and amorphous iron impregnated plant remains, forming plant pseudomorphs in the groundmass. There are a few fragments of phosphatised and decaying bone, and a few larger fragments of charcoal. Some of the plants have a 'halo' of iron oxide staining forming around them, and there is general organic staining of the entire groundmass. Other features include some pellety excremental infilling of channel and void space, some stone and pottery fragments scattered throughout the profile, and some small sesquioxide nodules.

The lower half of sample 2/2 exhibits a spongy to vughy structure, with an almost complete absence of channels and a greater number of separate and interconnected vughs. There is a much higher percentage of anthropogenically introduced materials in this part of the profile than in sample profile 1, including organic matter, bone and calcitic ash. The organic component takes on much more importance, accounting for about half of the overall groundmass, while the sandy clay loam fabric and ash comprise the remaining half. The organic components include degraded bone fragments, fragments of charcoal and other charred organics, amorphous iron impregnated plant remains, and amorphous to finely comminuted organics in the groundmass. In addition, there are a few fragments of burnt soil within the groundmass. Other features include some secondary iron impregnation of plant pseudomorphs and amorphous iron rings around voids. There are some excremental earthworm pellets infilling void and channel space, and a few fragments of pottery. Overall, this sample exhibits many of the same components and features to the midden section of sample profile 1, but without the striated appearance.

The upper part of sample 2/3 (Fig. 16.2c) is similar to the above sample but has a much higher overall concentration of organic matter, charcoal and bone, mostly in larger fragments. Bone makes up about 30% of the total groundmass, with fine amorphous and iron impregnated organic remains making up about 35–40% of the groundmass. The remaining 30–35% is the same very fine sandy clay loam fabric as occurs in the other samples, with two large pottery fragments also included.

The bulk of sample 2/3 is a weakly striated sandy clay loam fabric with calcitic ash, exhibiting a weakly blocky to vughy structure. It contains a lower organic component than the above samples, but it is still high at about 40% and is comprised of finely comminuted to amorphous black organics, decaying bone fragments and larger iron-stained black plant and charcoal remains. There is also a small component of fresh charcoal fragments. Other features include a few small fragments of burnt soil, general amorphous iron impregnation of much of the groundmass along with specific areas of impregnation of the organics, phosphatic reduction of the bone fragments, some pottery fragments, and a general dark organic staining to much of the groundmass. There are a few highly birefringent clay fragments in the groundmass and a few very thin dusty clay coatings of some of the vughs and voids. There are some pellety excremental features, although this is not as pronounced as in other samples.

INTERPRETATION

Like sample profile 1, this profile represents a very fine sandy clay loam soil which has been subjected to varying soil formation processes overlying layers of anthropogenically introduced material containing charcoal, ash, bone and pottery.

Many of the same processes affecting profile 1 have been at work in profile 2. There is evidence of bioturbation, in the form of earthworm pellets and partially infilled earthworm channels. The deposits in this profile are much more homogeneous and well-mixed than those of

profile 1. This could be either a result of more thorough mixing by the soil fauna, or possibly a difference in the way the material was dumped in the first place. In addition, the very vughy nature of the soil suggests that there had been a much greater organic component present in the past. This is undoubtedly associated with oxidation and soil faunal mixing processes, with which the general impregnation with amorphous iron is also associated.

Profile 3
DESCRIPTION
Profile 3 was taken at the section through midden [868]. Only the lower half of the profile was sampled and was found to consist of two fabrics. The main fabric was a calcitic ash (75%) with the secondary fabric being a dark brown very fine sandy loam (25%). These fabrics were in irregular zones in a heterogeneous mix with fine anthropogenic material.

INTERPRETATION
This profile appears to be a poorly mixed fabric comprised of ash from hearths and humic soil containing fine midden debris. It could represent the dumping of settlement related material, and as it is located at the base of the slope, it could also have resulted from localized colluvial slumping. This would explain the poorly mixed aspect of the fabric.

Profile 4
DESCRIPTION
This profile represents an off-site soil profile and was taken from a modern drainage ditch, immediately west of Trench A, which cuts the deposits directly beyond the entranceway into House 3 in Trench Z. Upslope of this profile, overlying Trench Z, 'ridge and furrow' agricultural practices have led to some soil creep and erosion, the results of which were visible in this profile as soil accumulation.

Sample 4/1 is a very fine sandy clay loam dominated by very fine quartz sand, clay and amorphous calcium carbonate. Clay is present as fragments of pure clay and impure or dusty clay infills in the groundmass. It is very well mixed and bioturbated, high in secondary amorphous iron impregnation of the groundmass and plant remains, with excremental pellets present and a low (<10%) organic component (Fig. 16.2d). There are some finely comminuted to amorphous black organics, and a minor component of partly decomposed plant remains with still-visible cell structure. There are common (15%) very large pebble and stone inclusions in the upper 5cm of the sample, but the underlying 7cm is stone-free. Structure becomes better developed with depth and in the bottom quarter exhibits well-developed blocky peds. Through the middle part of the sample, the structure appears more granular or crumbly, with large amounts of vughs and void space. Channels are partly accommodated and define the blocky ped structure. There are common vughs and many interconnected packing voids of larger size.

Sample 4/2 is a very fine sandy clay loam with a component of amorphous calcium carbonate, exhibiting a weakly developed blocky ped structure defined by interpedal channels and a lower porosity than sample 4/1. About 5–10% of the sample is comprised of large stone and pebble inclusions distributed throughout the slide. Other features include some very thin, laminated, dusty clay coatings around vughs, a component of pure clay fragments in the groundmass and some clay nodules within the groundmass, as well as some iron-phosphatic infills of voids (Fig. 16.2e).

There is more diversity to the organic remains in this slide, although the total percentage of organics is not much higher than that of sample 4/1. This includes finely comminuted, black, amophous organic material, some amorphous iron-replaced plant pseudomorphs, a few larger fragments of charcoal and excremental pellets.

Sample 4/3 contains a very substantial pebble and stone component, up to 30% of the total material in the slide. The structure of the groundmass is generally denser and more homogeneous than the previous two samples with about 20% porosity. There are a few weakly developed blocky peds, although the overall structure is weakly vughy to spongy. Towards the base of the sample, there is a ratio of about 50:50 fine pebbles to void space, with almost no groundmass present.

The percentage of very fine sand increases in this profile. There is a high component of highly birefringent clay fragments, and a smaller component of dusty unoriented clay and calcium carbonate. The organic component is also similar to sample 4/2, with finely comminuted black organics, often iron replaced, and a higher component of larger charcoal fragments. Other features include some very thin dusty clay coatings of the voids, lots of excremental pellets infilling pore space and within the groundmass, and a few sesquioxide nodules.

Finally, sample 4/4 exhibits a very disturbed and unoriented appearance. The structure is much more open than above, with some moderately developed blocky peds and a vughy/spongy appearance. Large stone and pebble fragments make up about 10% of the total

material in this slide. The groundmass is mainly a very fine sand, with a sizeable component of dusty organic stained clay. There is a higher percentage of organics and amorphous iron, with the overall fabric stained by amorphous organic matter and iron. In addition, there are a few large fragments of charcoal, a minor component of decomposing carbonised plant remains with the cell structure still visible, a few smaller amorphous black fragments, and iron-replaced, comminuted organics and iron 'halos' around plant pseudomorphs. Other features include pellety void infills, some clay nodules, a few very small bone fragments, some dirty clay coatings at the edge of void spaces and a very few, very small fragments of brilliant crimson-red burnt soil.

INTERPRETATION

Profile 4 is an iron-dominated very fine sandy clay loam soil which also contains some anthropogenically derived elements. The base of the profile appears to have reached *in situ* archaeological levels of anthropogenic debris.

First, the soils and sediments in this sample seem to have undergone many of the same post-depositional processes as affected profiles 1 and 2. There is plenty of evidence of earthworm activity, bioturbation, secondary iron and organic staining, and the incorporation of relatively minor amounts of anthropogenic debris. The stone rubble component in samples 4/1, 4/3 and 4/4 is almost certainly derived from the collapse of the two house structures immediately upslope.

The base of sample 4/3 exhibits a fine gravel lens with almost no soil component. This may be the result of washing-out of the fines through an erosional episode. Indeed, the general increase in fine sand down profile is suggestive of the flushing through and depletion of the fine component. This could be associated with leaching down-profile and lateral flushing downslope which could be in turn associated with disturbance of the hillslope, and processes such as clearance, podzolisation/acidification and peat formation. In particular, the relatively high laminated and non-laminated dusty clay component present throughout the profile, but particularly marked in sample 4/2, is indicative of within-soil mass movement of fines. This suggests that there was a fine hillwash-derived component to this soil at this mid-slope position prior to later peat formation.

Profile 5
DESCRIPTION
Profile 5 which was taken just downslope and to the northeast of Trench A has a representative off-site profile.

Table 16.3 Summary of the main features of the Stonehall hearth sequences.

Profile	Description	Interpretation
Knoll (Tr C) House 3 midden [1008/403]	Stone over sandy clay loam over ash	Collapsed structure and eroded soil accumulated on hearth rake-out
Knoll (Tr C) House 3 hearth [4028]	Fine stone and sandy loam soil over ash and soil, developed on surface that has been subject to heat and inclusion of urine	Collapsed structure over hearth on floor; possible previous use as animal byre
Trench Z scoop hearth [3068–69]	Ash and charcoal over reddened surface of clay loam deposit on reddened ash and fine charcoal	Hearth rake-out over raised hearth made up of re-deposited subsoil material over primary hearth deposits

It consists of a greyish to dark brown sandy loam with an intergrain channel structure and pellety microstructure intermixed with significant quantities of calcitic ash and abundant very fine charcoal. The ash concentrates towards the middle and the base of the profile.

INTERPRETATION

Despite the off-site location, the general fabric is very similar to that observed in Profile 3, and may have the same origin, either as dumped occupation material and/ or resulting from some downslope colluvial slumping of settlement debris after the site went out of use. The whole profile has been severely mixed by the soil fauna, but has subsequently begun to develop some structure with stability.

16.1.3 Conclusions

All five soil profiles examined micromorphologically are very fine sandy clay loam to sandy loam soils which exhibit greater or lesser degrees of structural development, bioturbation and the inclusion of greater/ lesser amounts of organic and anthropogenic debris and colluvial fine material.

Modern ploughing of the site is responsible for some of the mixing, oxidation and secondary processes observed in all profiles, as well as the general reworking of all deposits by the soil fauna. Consequently, actual floor surfaces were not readily identified, although the anthropogenic deposits accumulating at the base of Profiles 2 and 4 may represent the primary accumulations of domestic refuse on a floor surface. What is clear is that there are large amounts of occupation debris present, with evidence for faunal mixing and oxidation affecting the degree of organic preservation and slight acidification affecting the preservation of the bone remains in particular. The latter process is probably associated with the post-Neolithic, thin peat formation on the adjacent slopes, the weakly acidic glacial till subsoil and lateral

flushing leading to leaching and acidification of the profile. In addition, the whole slope has been affected by colluvial processes prior to peat formation, although this has not been on a great scale or very severe, and possibly caused some soil slumping and disturbance downslope.

16.1.4 Hearth and hearth-related sequences

Stonehall Knoll (Tr C) House 3 midden [1008/403]

DESCRIPTION

There are two horizons evident in this sample. The upper 4–5cm is composed of large stone fragments (<3cm) within a sandy clay loam soil fabric dominated by impure or dusty clay infills and strong impregnation with amorphous sesquioxides. This exhibits a gradual transition to alternating fine laminae of calcitic ash with included fine charcoal and amorphous iron-replaced and carbonised organic matter in the lower half of the slide (Fig. 16.2f).

INTERPRETATION

The abundant stone fragments could represent fragments of collapsed wall and/or foundation material. The abundant impure clay infills of the fabric could possibly suggest some very localised erosional input to this abandoned structure.

This post-depositional material has accumulated on a mixture of soil, ash, organic matter and fine charcoal, probably representing hearth rake-out and/or episodes of organic and soil accumulation. Both units have been subject to soil faunal mixing.

Stonehall Knoll (Trench C) House 3 hearth [4028]

DESCRIPTION

A *c.*3cm zone of fine stone fragments with an horizontal orientation overlies *c.*4.5cm of very organic fine sandy loam which has accumulated on a *c.*6cm horizon composed of a mixture of fine sandy loam soil, ash and very fine charcoal. The base of the profile exhibits strong amorphous iron reddening and discontinuous iron-phosphatic infills of the void space.

INTERPRETATION

As for hearth context [1008], this profile appears to represent post-depositional structural collapse and soil accumulation within a structure, that has accumulated on hearth rake-out material. But in this case, the basal reddened zone with amorphous iron and phosphatic enrichment is suggestive of a floor surface which has been subject to alternate heating and drying out, as well as the probable presence of animal urine. Very tentatively what is being seen is a structure that is first used as a byre and then a hearth is made, then abandoned.

Stonehall Meadow (Tr Z) scoop hearth [3068/9]

DESCRIPTION

This sample contained a series of eight units, from top to bottom, as follows:

1. ash, fine charcoal and irregular aggregates of reddened/burnt soil fabric (Fig. 16.2g).
2. fine charcoal.
3. zone of amorphous iron and organic impregnation on the upper surface of unit 4.
4. a clay loam with reticulate striated aspect.
5. mixture of clay loam and ash.
6. mixture of clay loam, ash and abundant fine charcoal.
7. ash and fine charcoal with common iron-phosphatic formation and fine aggregates of clay loam soil fabric in the void space (Fig 16.2h).
8. fine lens of ash.
9. ash and fine charcoal, with the upper contact reddened by strong impregnation with amorphous iron.

INTERPRETATION

The two levels of strong impregnation with amorphous iron (units 3 and 7) would suggest that these may represent floor surfaces where the combination of heat and drying in association with *in situ* fires has occurred. Between and above these two levels was an accumulation of ash and charcoal representing hearth rake-out. In addition, there was also a zone (units 4 and 5) of clay loam soil material which is unlike that found in any other context except in the upper surface of the underlying solid geology (see off-site profile 5 above). Therefore, this re-deposited substrate material would appear to have been used to create a raised hearth area.

16.1.5 Conclusions

From the analysis of these hearth and hearth-related sequences, considerable accumulations of ash, with

and without the addition of fine organic midden and possible structural collapse debris was accumulating in these structures. Whether these occur during the contemporary use of the structures, or associated with the post-abandonment use of the structures is not clear from this evidence alone. There are several instances of *in situ* floor surfaces which have been subject to heat and drying associated with hearths and in one instance, a hearth pad was actually constructed from re-deposited substrate material.

16.2 Crossiecrown

16.2.1 General introduction

As at Stonehall, although the structural remains were truncated the internal floor deposits and external midden layers at Crossiecrown displayed a degree of integrity. Consequently, together with detailed sampling for geochemical analysis (see section 7.6.2 and Table 7.2), some 27 block samples were taken from the Red and Grey Houses for micromorphological analysis following the methodology of Murphy (1986) and the descriptive terminology of Bullock *et al.* (1985; Fig. 7.29).

16.2.2 Trench 1

Three sample blocks were initially taken for micromorphological assessment through the main midden/soil sequence in Trench 1 of the 1998 excavations. Each exhibited six different horizons, which are described below and in Table 16.4.

SAMPLE 15

This sample comprised three horizons. Horizon 1 forms the upper 4.5cm of the sample and horizon 3 the basal 5cm, with a 2cm thick band in the middle that comprises horizon 2. The fabric of horizons 1 and 3 is very similar, and horizon 2 represents a layer with a high proportion of burnt soil and amorphous iron impregnation.

The structure of horizon 1 is complex, consisting of a vughy to spongy structure with some granular aspects and channels that are partly to almost completely infilled with a 'pellety' or excremental fabric derived from earthworm activity. It is a poorly sorted, very fine sandy clay loam, with a significant proportion of fine amorphous organic matter and general organic staining of the groundmass. Other organic remains present in the sample include carbonised but partially decomposed plant remains with some of the cell structure still visible, phytoliths and a few small pieces of bone exhibiting internal degradation. A small

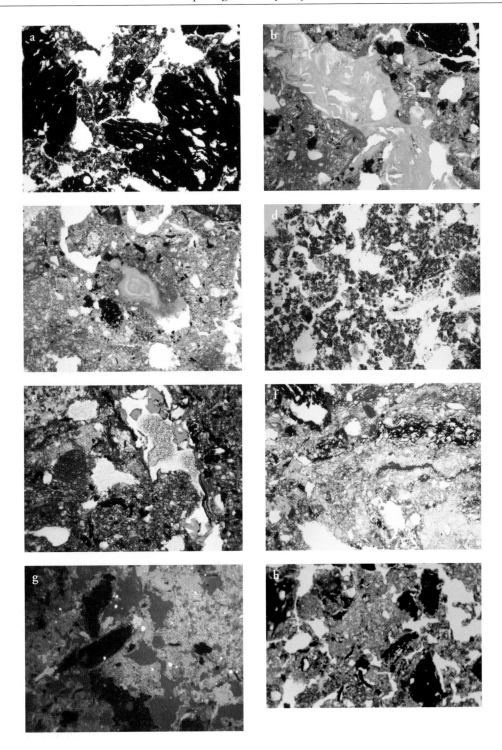

Fig. 16.2 Stonehall photomicrographs (frame width = 4.5mm; plane polarized light) of (a) charcoal and amorphous iron/organic material, SHF/00: Profile 1, sample 1, (b) phosphatised bone, SHF/94: Profile 1, sample 2, (c) ash, charcoal, bone fragments and phosphatic accretions, SHF/94: Profile 2, sample 3, (d) excremental/pellety fabric, SHF94: Profile 5, sample 1 base, (e) coprolitic/phosphatic material, SHF/97: Profile 5, sample 1/2, (f) alternating fine ash and charcoal lenses, SHF/97: 1008/403, (g) burnt soil hearth deposit with ash and charcoal, SHF/01: 3068/9, upper and (h) ash, fine charcoal iron-phosphate formations, sample context 3068/9.

Table 16.4 Summary of the micromorphological descriptions and interpretations for samples 15–17, Crossiecrown Trench 1, 1998.

Sample	Horizon	Description	Interpretation
15	1	Vughy very fine sandy clay loam with calcitic ash, fine charcoal, bone and secondary iron impregnation	Humin A with much midden debris
15	2	50% similar fabric to horizon 1 above; 50% burnt soil; very strong amorphous iron impregnation	Humin A with midden debris and ?dumped burnt soil
15	3	Vughy very fine sandy clay loam with calcitic ash, amorphous and fine charcoal, bone fragments and phytoliths, and secondary iron impregnation	Humic A soil with greater frequency of midden material
16	4	Similar to horizon 3	
17	5	Similar to horizons 3 and 4	
17	6	Fine vughy very fine sandy clay loam amorphous iron and calcium carbonate, minor charcoal, bone and pottery fragments	Surface of glacial till substrate with fine midden debris suggesting it is a floor surface and pre-site soil has been deliberately removed

proportion of the clay is in the form of pure fragments of clay, whereas the majority is non-laminated and dusty. There is considerable secondary iron impregnation of the groundmass. There is also a relatively minor but consistent presence of calcitic ash throughout. The fabric of horizon 2 is similar in structure and composition to horizon 1, but 50% of the total groundmass is composed of fragments of burnt soil. There is pronounced amorphous iron impregnation of the whole horizon.

Horizon 3 is similar to horizon 1 except that it is slightly more compacted and there is a slightly higher proportion of anthropogenically introduced fragments of bone, pottery and burnt soil. There is also common amorphous organic staining and amorphous iron staining of the whole groundmass, along with included calcitic ash.

SAMPLE 16
Sample 16 (Fig. 16.3a) consists of one fabric (horizon 4), which has more or less the same fabric and appearance as horizon 3 above. It is slightly more densely packed with more void spaces left by plant and bone pseudomorphs rather than open vughs or channels. The groundmass is a very fine sandy clay loam, with a varied organic component comprising finely comminuted to amorphous organic matter, many fragments of partly decomposed plant remains with some of the cell structure still visible, several pieces of partly decomposed bone, and one or two pottery fragments. There is also a higher percentage of amorphous calcium carbonate within the groundmass.

SAMPLE 17
Sample 17 is comprised of an upper (horizon 5) and a lower horizon (6). The division between them is a distinct boundary that cuts diagonally across the lower

half to one-third of the slide. It appears that this cut represents the truncation of the upper surface of the *in situ* geological substrate or glacial till. The fabric of horizon 5 is very similar to horizons 3 and 4, with a few more included fragments of pottery and bone. Horizon 6, or the upper surface of the glacial till, is slightly more dense, contains a higher percentage of very fine quartz sand, exhibits a depleted or leached appearance and has a much lower proportion of organic matter.

16.2.2.1 Discussion
The whole profile is a very fine sandy clay loam becoming a very fine sandy loam at its base. Essentially, the profile exhibits the following sequence of pedogenesis from the base to the modern ground surface:

1. an *in situ* glacial till substrate which possibly exhibits a truncated upper surface;
2. aggrading soil material containing much anthropogenically-derived material which has accumulated either during the use of the site or as a post-abandonment feature as horizons 3, 4 and 5;
3. a single event of dumping of burnt soil material as horizon 2 (between horizons 2 and 4);
4. an upper, organic A horizon with much included anthropogenic debris (horizon 1);
5. the modern ploughsoil.

The soil profile exhibits much evidence of anthropogenic influence. It is midden-like, although evidence of deliberate and sequential dumping is only visible in one instance in horizon 2. The re-deposited burnt soil was probably associated with a hearth located elsewhere, and for some reason this material was discarded here.

Horizons 1 to 5 have contained a much greater organic component in the past and have been subject

Table 16.5 Summary of the micromorphological descriptions and interpretations for Crossiecrown Trench 2, 1999.

Sample	Horizon	Description	Interpretation
27	303	Brown sandy clay loam with included ash and charcoal	Disturbed humic soil with midden ash and charcoal
29	303	Yellowish brown, massive to fine vughy sandy loam with charcoal and plant remains	Transition to glacial till substrate
35	303	Dark brown subangular blocky loam with fine to coarse charcoal	Mixed humic soil and midden debris
		(sample 35 is similar to sample 33, upper 34, upper 42 and 45)	
30	304	Brown loam with zone of iron-impregnated, dark reddish brown organic laminations at top	Compressed, dumped organic debris or floor levels on mixed humic soil/midden horizon
		(main fabric of sample 30 is similar to sample 35)	
31	010	Yellowish brown sandy clay loam with included organics, charcoal and bone	Glacial till substrate with midden debris intermixed
32	011	5 layers: disturbed iron-rich, dark reddish brown sandy loam over yellowish brown sandy clay loam over brown sandy clay loam over dark brown charcoal-rich sandy clay loam over brown sandy clay loam	All soil material with some anthropogenic inclusions; either dumped and/or occupational build-up layers on a floor
		(lower part of sample 32 is similar to lower part [fabric/horizon 3] of 34, upper 42 and 45)	
34	011	2 fabrics/layers with distinct, irregular boundary between: dark brown small blocky and intergrain channel structure, loam over sandy loam in small aggregates with organic inclusions	Mixed soil/midden material over bioturbated humic soil

to much soil mixing and oxidation processes, and more recent agricultural activities. All of these horizons exhibit evidence of reworking by the soil fauna, oxidation and changing soil moisture conditions. Horizon 6 probably represents the part of the profile that is relatively undisturbed, but nonetheless does contain some fine organic material as a result of soil mixing processes. The apparent cut line defining its upper surface probably represents a deliberate truncation of the substrate's upper surface. The evident internal degradation of bone throughout the profile suggests that there has been some slight acidification of the whole profile. This was undoubtedly associated with the presence of the underlying glacial till substrate and in this case is similar to both the deposits at Stonehall and Barnhouse (French 2005).

16.2.3 Trench 2

A series of 14 samples was taken from 11 contexts in Trench 2. All of the samples were taken through the soil and midden deposits associated with the Red House (House 1). There are many similarities with the samples analysed from Trench 1, and essentially the same stratigraphy is also recorded in Trench 2. But greater

detail is evident from the samples in this trench for the make-up of possible floor levels and the deposits accumulating on them. The main contexts analysed are described below briefly and are summarised in Table 16.5.

Context [303]

Three samples (27, 29 and 35) were taken through the midden deposit beneath the Red House. The upper sample (27) comprised a brown sandy clay loam with a vughy (or porous) microstructure and irregular zones of included ash and charcoal as well as charred plant remains, diatoms, phytoliths, very fine and amorphous organic matter and fragments of burnt bone (Fig. 16.3b). There was also general impregnation of the whole fabric with secondary amorphous iron, and the occurrence of dusty (or impure) clay coatings and infillings of voids. This very organic soil has been subject to some kind of mechanical mixing and disturbance, such as the dumping of both midden and soil material, later digging over and/or ploughing of the soil, illuviation of fine material down profile, bioturbation and oxidation. Thus this is a mixed humic soil and midden material deposit.

Sample 29 is a yellowish brown, dense to fine vughy and intergrain channel structured, sandy loam with included charcoal and charred plant remains. It contained similar organic, amorphous iron and clay components to sample 27 above. This suggests some faunal mixing and wetting and drying cycles of this deposit which is acting as the transition to the underlying glacial till substrate.

Sample 35 is a dark brown loam with a well-developed subangular blocky ped structure with micro- and macro-charcoal, amorphous organic matter, amorphous iron impregnation and some dusty clay coatings and infillings. This sample is a well-structured humic soil which contains midden-derived organic, and mainly charcoal, debris. The well-developed structure suggests that this well-mixed soil and midden debris is now acting as the B horizon of the present day soil profile.

Context [304]

Sample 30 was taken from a rubble layer under floor deposits of the Red House (House 1). It is a relatively non-porous loam with a distinctive zone of dense, amorphous iron impregnated and laminated organic material at the top with many included fine (<2mm), sub-rounded fragments of bone (Fig. 16.3c). The underlying fabric is similar to the mixed midden and humic soil material of sample 35.

Context [010]

Sample 31 is a yellowish brown sandy clay loam with included organics, charcoal and bone which exhibits an inter-grain channel structure and many sesquioxide nodules in its lower part. It is a very similar fabric to sample 29 from context [303], or the _in situ_ glacial till substrate. In this case it has a certain amount of fine midden-derived material incorporated in it through faunal mixing processes and is again the transition zone between the midden and the underlying geological substrate.

Context [011]

Four separate samples were taken through context [011].

Sample 32 exhibits five micro-layers, each of 1–2cm in thickness, which are composed of sandy clay loam soil material containing variable amounts of anthropogenic-derived debris. In each case, these thin horizons could represent either deliberately dumped material and/or occupational build-up layers on a floor. None of the horizontal and vertical micro-cracking normally suggestive of _in situ_ floors (Matthews _et al._ 1997) is visible, but these could have been destroyed by subsequent bioturbation and wetting and drying cycles.

Sample 34 is comprised of two distinct horizons: an upper intergrain channel structured, bioturbated, dark brown humic soil (similar to samples 33, 35 and lower part of 42) above a massive to fine vughy, brown sandy loam with much included charcoal (similar to fabric/horizon 3 of sample 32), and dusty clay infills in its lower part (Fig. 16.3d). This is again a mixed humic soil and midden deposit overlying a bioturbated, charcoal-rich sandy loam soil, all probably indicative of midden and soil material that has been reworked by the soil fauna and perhaps even by subsequent recent agricultural activities.

Sample 41 is a pale/dark brown, porous sandy loam in small, irregular aggregates. This fabric is suggestive of a very bioturbated soil which has seen much of its organic content removed through oxidation. It has also suffered much alternate wetting and drying conditions leading to iron impregnation and the formation of hypo-coatings of amorphous iron.

The lowermost part of sample 44 also exhibits what is believed to be part of context [011]. In this case, the material is a yellowish brown sandy silt loam dominated by charcoal and bone fragments. The soil material exhibits the same characteristics as the transition zone to the glacial till substrate that has been observed before, but in this case contains a substantial amount of humic matter, charcoal and bone fragments incorporated within it. This appears to be a floor surface that is on the surface of the glacial till substrate, and this is seen in the context/sample 44 described below.

Contexts [012] and [315]

The upper part of sample 44, or the floor context [012], is a humic and iron impregnated, reddish brown sandy silt loam (Fig. 16.3e). The lower part of sample 44 is a dark brown humic and charcoal-rich sandy loam with an intergrain channel structure which overlies a 1cm thick lens of grey calcitic ash (context [315]). This whole sequence has accumulated on the surface of the glacial till substrate. Here, it appears that the surface of the _in situ_ subsoil is acting as the floor surface. On this is a deposit of hearth-derived ash with a mixture of humic soil and midden material accumulating above it, all presumably by deliberate dumping. The fine channel structure of the dumped soil/midden material has probably developed subsequently.

Contexts [012] and [327]

The upper part of sample 42, or floor context [012], is a sandy silty loam containing much settlement debris (_e.g._ ash, charcoal and burnt bone). This is developed on context [327] (clay deposits behind north recess in

House 1) in the lower part of sample 42 which is an iron-impregnated, reddish brown, porous sandy clay loam with a subangular blocky ped structure. The upper horizon is very similar to samples 33, upper 34, 35 and 45. This sequence represents midden debris accumulating over a clay-rich deposit which formerly contained a much greater organic component and has been subject to much wetting and drying and consequent oxidation. This sequence appears to represent midden material accumulating on an organic clay-rich floor deposit.

CONTEXT [329]

This context in sample 43 was identified as a clay floor deposit with amorphous iron-impregnated fine bone fragments incorporated around the west side of the hearth [018]. In thin section it comprises three fabrics in three horizons, as follows: a massive, brown fine sandy clay over a reddish-brown sandy clay loam with an intergrain channel structure and abundant fine charcoal over a yellowish-brown sandy loam with abundant iron nodules. Here, there is a fine sandy clay deposit apparently deliberately laid on a humic/midden-rich soil which in turn has either accumulated on or has been dumped upon the *in situ* glacial till substrate. As this fine sandy clay fabric (Fig. 16.3f) is not characteristic of the natural soil profile on site, it is reasonable to assume that this is brought from elsewhere in the vicinity to the site, and was used to create a new floor surface over the midden material that was accumulating on the subsoil or first floor surface.

CONTEXT [034]

Sample 45 is a dark brown, humic and iron rich sandy loam with included charcoal and bone which exhibits a loose subangular blocky structure with a bioturbated microstructure. This mixture of midden and soil material has developed a structure since deposition. It is similar to samples 33, upper 34, 35 and lower 42.

CONTEXT [041]

Sample 33 is a brown loam with a sub-angular blocky structure and included charred organics, calcitic ash and bone fragments. It is similar mixture of humic soil and midden material which has undergone subsequent structural development that is exhibited in sample 45/context [034] (above), as well as samples 33, upper 34, 35 and lower 42.

CONTEXT [022]

Sample 39 is a brown fine sandy loam with common humified organic matter and fine charcoal similar to

the middle horizon of sample 43 (above), although it is marked by an approximately horizontal zone of amorphous iron and phosphatised, partly-degraded bone (Fig. 16.3g). This suggests that there is amended soil present that is receiving fragmentary faunal remains that are weathering *in situ* and then receiving more soil/midden dumped material above.

16.2.4 Trench 3

16.2.4.1 Introduction
A series of nine block samples were taken from context [028] and one sample block from context [026] in Trench 3 (Table 16.6). This trench was located towards the northeastern edge of the site (Fig. 7.3) and revealed a series of midden deposits and an orthostatic structure.

16.2.4.2 Descriptions
CONTEXT [028]
The thin sections taken through this context (samples 1–6, 8 and 9) reveal a very similar sequence to that already seen and described in Trench 2. Namely, this is a humic soil and midden debris accumulating directly on the surface of the glacial till substrate, often subject to very strong bioturbation effects (Fig. 16.3h).

CONTEXT [026]
In context 26, a relatively non-porous and compacted humic loam with common fine charcoal fragments was used as the core infill of wall 024. Thus fine soil material was used in house construction as wall core make-up and would certainly act as a good insulator from the elements.

16.2.4.3 Discussion of floor and deposit types
There are a series of main types of deposition that are repeatedly occurring in thin section from the archaeological sequences recovered in Trenches 1 to 3. These are as follows:

HUMIC SOILS WITH MIDDEN MATERIAL ON THE *IN SITU* GLACIAL TILL SUBSOIL
(*E.G.* CONTEXT [303] IN SAMPLES 27, 29 AND 35)
The nature of the midden material is quite consistent, although the anthropogenically derived inclusions vary from sample to sample. Essentially, the midden matrix is dark brown, humic fine sandy clay loam to loam to fine sandy loam. The high organic component, exhibiting often considerable oxidation and replacement with amorphous iron, with varying admixtures of calcitic

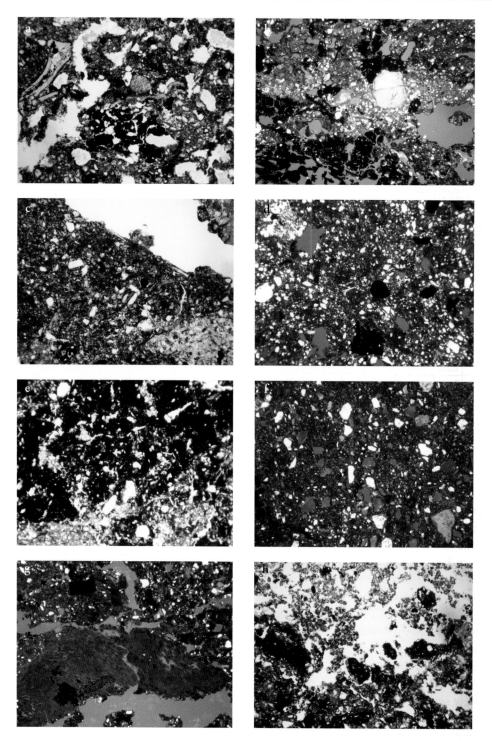

Fig. 16.3 Crossiecrown photomicrographs (frame width = 4.5mm; plane polarized light) of (a) intermixed topsoil and midden material, sample 16, (b) mixture of soil and midden material including charcoal, humified peat and ash, Trench 2, sample 27, (c) stained fine sandy/silt loam, Trench 2, context [304], sample 30, (d) sandy (clay) loam fabric with dusty clay infills and fine charcoal, Trench 2, context [011], sample 34, (e) humic/amorphous iron stained fine sandy/silt loam, Trench 2, context [315], upper sample 44, (f) clay-rich fine sand or the geological till, Trench 2, context [329], lower sample 43, (g) lens of degraded, sub-rounded, fine bone fragments in fine sandy loam, Trench 2, context [022], sample 39, and (h) bioturbated fabric over dense midden material, Trench 3, context [028], S8.

Table 16.6 Summary of the micromorphological descriptions and interpretations for Crossiecrown Trench 3, 1999.

Sample	Horizon	Description	Interpretation
1	28	Homogeneous, iron/humic rich, reddish brown sandy/silt loam with included organics and charcoal, and intergrain channel structure	Mixed humic soil and midden material
2	28	Homogeneous, iron/humic rich, reddish brown sandy clay loam with included organics and charcoal, and intergrain channel structure	Mixed humic soil and midden material
3	28	Upper fabric: as above over lower fabric: yellowish brown, dense to vughy sandy clay loam	As above over glacial till substrate
4	28	Reddish brown organic sandy loam similar to samples 1–3 above with amorphous zones of iron impregnation	Mixed humic soil and midden material
5	28	Dark brown, subangular blocky, sandy loam with/without iron impregnation and variety of midden material (similar to sample 45)	Humic soil and midden material that has undergone subsequent pedogenesis
(6)	28	(data missing)	
8	28	2 layers: dark brown sandy silt loam with abundant charcoal (essentially similar to samples 1–4)	Humic soil material and midden debris
		over yellowish brown sandy loam	over glacial till substrate
9	28	Dark to reddish brown silty clay loam with large blocky structure and intrusive yellowish brown humic sandy loam	Humic soil and midden material and intrusive, redeposited (?) glacial till fabric
	36	Iron/humic rich, brown sandy loam with vughy to intergrain channel structure	Humic soil and midden debris
26	025/131/132 (section 27)	Pale brown, dense, homogeneous loam	Compacted soil material in wall core buttressing 122 and wall 024

ash, phytoliths, macro- and micro-charcoal, plant tissue remains, and burnt and unburnt bone all reflect human settlement debris. The fabric has been thoroughly mixed by the soil fauna, and possibly even by more recent ploughing. The development of varying types and degrees of soil structure that is evident probably reflects post-depositional and more recent soil pedogenesis as this deposit effectively becomes the modern B horizon beneath the present day ploughsoil.

In all cases, the midden-rich soil occurs on the glacial till substrate. The relatively distinct upper contact of the *in situ* subsoil strongly suggests that the pre-site soil has first been deliberately truncated and largely removed prior to the construction of the structures on the site.

FLOOR SURFACE ON THE UPPER SURFACE OF THE GLACIAL TILL SUBSTRATE
(*E.G.* CONTEXTS [011] AND [315] IN BASE OF SAMPLE 44)
In this particular case in sample 44, there is a 1cm thick deposit of calcitic ash occurring directly on the surface of the glacial till substrate. This serves to confirm that the pre-site soil was truncated. The ash may either be

dumped or spread from a hearth, but this cannot be ascertained from the thin section. It is suggested that the upper surface of the truncated *in situ* subsoil may be acting as the actual floor surface with the ash possibly accumulating during the use of the structure.

Above the ash material there is a greater thickness of humic midden material which has probably accumulated on the ash/till floor surface after the structure went out of use.

DELIBERATELY-LAID FINE SANDY CLAY FLOOR ON HUMIC MIDDEN MATERIAL ON THE GLACIAL TILL SUBSTRATE
(*E.G.* CONTEXT [329] IN SAMPLE 43)
In sample 43, there is a fine sandy clay deposit on top of iron-impregnated humic soil/midden material which has accumulated directly on the glacial till substrate. In this case, the clay may represent an attempt to create a new and cleaner surface by sealing off the accumulating midden debris on the initial floor surface. The strong iron impregnation of the humic soil/midden material may have been a secondary consequence of the deposition of the relatively impermeable clay above and the poorly

draining till beneath. Another example of a redeposited fine sandy clay deposit occurred around the west side of the central hearth 018, which was believed to be a floor.

Floor levels of horizontally bedded and compacted organic matter
(e.g. upper context [304] in sample 30)

There are finely bedded organic deposits which occur on the midden soil deposits at the top of sample 30. They could indicate organic bedding and compacted material or just organic material being dumped/laid on the midden, or they could represent an attempt to create a surface on thin deposits of aggrading midden material by laying down reeds or rushes as a floor covering, for example.

Sequential fine floor deposits
(e.g. context [011] in sample 32)

In sample 32, there is a series of five horizons super-imposed on each other through a thickness of <6cm with each horizon thickness in the range of 1–2cm. There are distinct and level contacts between the individual deposits which suggest that they may well represent floor deposits rather than just dumped lenses of midden-type debris and soil.

16.2.5 Conclusions

Despite the shallow stratigraphy of this prehistoric occupation site, there is clear evidence for the making of floors or surfaces using a variety of readily available materials. In addition, there was the ubiquitous accumulation of midden deposits on these floors, and in a few cases an attempt was made to create secondary floor surfaces on these pre-existing floor and midden/occupation deposit sequences.

In summary, initially some floors may have been clean and fresh, hard-packed silty clay to sandy loam surfaces. These were made by truncating and removing the whole of the pre-site soil profile to reveal the underlying glacial till substrate. But midden material soon accumulated on these earthen floor surfaces and fine elements of this midden material became reworked into the upper surface of the glacial till substrate. Sometimes, attempts were made to create new surfaces using either calcitic ash or fine sandy clay. Most of the post-floor sequence deposits involve the accumulation of humic soil and midden material derived from the fine debris of human living. The proximity of many of these sequences to the modern ground surface inevitably means that there is a fair degree of post-depositional mixing of later deposits, but it confirms that these settlement and midden areas were subsequently highly sought after for arable activities. These soils were effectively amended and enhanced, making an excellent nutrient-rich tilth for a good crop growth (cf. Simpson 1997, 1998; Guttman *et al.* 2004). In some cases these midden deposits are capped by a second floor level, also composed of either clay, ash or possibly even deliberately laid layers of organic matter.

Since these micromorphological studies at Stonehall Farm and Crossiecrown were completed, there have been a number of important geoarchaeological studies of floors and 'dark earth' type deposits from some of the prehistoric sites in Orkney. Intensive studies of Tofts Ness on Sanday (Simpson 1998; Simpson *et al.* 2006), Skara Bare (Simpson *et al.* 2006), the Links of Noltland on Westray (Hamlet 2014) and the Knowes of Trotty (see Chapter 3; McKenzie 2007), for example, have also shown that settlement-derived 'dark earth' type highly organic midden deposits have been used as wall in-fills, floor preparation or foundation layers and subsequently for arable agricultural activities as fertiliser and to create organic topsoil, and is not just found in midden dumps. These complementary studies have demonstrated the extreme importance of managing settlement rubbish as a midden in the later Neolithic period, and utilising that same material for a whole variety of uses in and around the settlement and subsequently for providing sustainable arable soils through later prehistoric times.

Bibliography

Acsádi, G. Y. and Nemeskéri, J. 1970. *History of Human Life Span and Mortality.* Budapest: Akadémiai Kiaidó.

Ahlqvist, J. and Damsten, O. 1969. A modification of Kerley's method for microscopic determination of age in human bone. *Journal of Forensic Sciences* 14, 205–212.

Alexander, D. 1997. Excavation of pits containing decorated Neolithic pottery and early lithic material of possible Mesolithic date at Spurryhillock, Stonehaven, Aberdeenshire. *Proceedings of the Society of Antiquaries of Scotland* 127, 17–27.

Alldritt, D. M. 2003. *Economy and Environment in the First Millennium AD in Northern Scotland and the Northern Isles.* Unpublished PhD Thesis, University of Glasgow.

Alldritt, D. M. 2012. Carbonised plant remains and charcoal from Hill of Crooksetter, Delting, Shetland. Projects 246 and 248. Unpublished specialist report for ORCA.

Alldritt, D. M. 2013. Carbonised plant remains and charcoal from Mine Howe, Tankerness, Orkney. Unpublished specialist report for ORCA.

Allen, M. J., Gardiner, J. and Sheridan, A. (eds) 2012. *Is There a British Chalcolithic? People, Place and Polity in the late 3rd Millennium.* Oxford: Prehistoric Society Research Paper 4/Oxbow Books.

Allen, T. 2005. Excavations at the Eton rowing course 1996–97. The Neolithic middens. Unpublished report. Oxford: Oxford Archaeology.

Andersen, S. T. 1979. Identification of wild grass and cereal pollen. *Danmarks Geologiske Undersøgelse* Årbog 1978: 69–92.

Appleby, A. 2011. Grooved Ware Firing at Fursbreck Pottery. *Orkney Archaeological Society Newsletter.* Newsletter 6 Autumn 2011.

Armit, I. 1992. The Hebridean Neolithic. In N. Sharples and A. Sheridan (eds) *Vessels for the Ancestors.* Edinburgh: Edinburgh University Press, 307–21.

Armit, I. 1996. *The Archaeology of Skye and the Western Isles.* Edinburgh: Edinburgh University Press.

Armit, I. 2003. The Drowners: permanence and transience in the Hebridean Neolithic. In I. Armit, E. Murphy, E. Nelis and D. Simpson (eds) *Neolithic Settlement in Ireland and Western Britain.* Oxford: Oxbow books, 93–100.

Arthurson, K. 2002. Creating inclusive communities through balancing social mix. *Urban Policy and Research* 20(3), 245–61.

Ascough, P., Cook, G., Dugmore A. and Scott, E. 2007. The North Atlantic marine reservoir effect in the Early Holocene: implications for defining and understanding MRE values. *Nuclear Instruments and Methods in Physics Research B* 259, 438–47.

Ashmore, P. 1996. *Neolithic and Bronze Age Scotland.* London: Batsford/Historic Scotland.

Ashmore, P. 1998a. A list of Historic Scotland archaeological radiocarbon dates. *Discovery and excavation in Scotland,* 125–28.

Ashmore, P. 1998b. Radiocarbon dates for settlements, tombs and ceremonial sites with Grooved ware in Scotland. In A. Gibson and D. Simpson (eds) *Prehistoric Ritual and Religion.* Stroud; Sutton, 139–47.

Ashmore, P. 1999. Radiocarbon dating: avoiding errors by avoiding mixed samples. *Antiquity* 73, 124–30.

Ashmore, P. 2000a. Dating the Neolithic in Orkney. In A. Ritchie (ed.) *Neolithic Orkney in its European Context.* Cambridge: McDonald Institute Monographs, 299–308.

Ashmore, P. 2000b. *Dating News, November 22nd, 2000.* Edinburgh: Historic Scotland.

Ashmore, P. 2005. Dating Barnhouse, in C. Richards (ed.) *Dwelling Among the Monuments: the Neolithic village of Barnhouse, Maeshowe passage grave and surrounding monuments at Stenness, Orkney.* Cambridge: McDonald Institute Monographs, 385–88.

Ashmore, P., Cook, G. and Harkness, D. 2000. A radiocarbon database for Scottish archaeological samples. *Radiocarbon* 42, 41–48.

Atalay, S. and Harstof, C. 2005. Foodways at Çatalhöyük. In I. Hodder (ed.) *Çatalhöyük Perspectives* 6. Cambridge: McDonald Institute Monographs, 109–24.

Atkinson, R. J. C. 1962. Fishermen and farmers. In S. Piggott (ed.) *The Prehistoric Peoples of Scotland.* London: Routledge and Kegan Paul, 1–38.

Balasse, M. and A. Tresset. 2009. A key to the adaptation of Neolithic husbandry in the Orkneys: contributions of seaweed to the sheep diet at Holm of Papa Westray, revealed through the stable isotope analysis (δ^{13}C and δ^{18}O) of teeth. In A. Ritchie (ed.) *On the Fringe of Neolithic Europe: Excavation of a Chambered Cairn on the Holm of Papa Westray, Orkney.* Edinburgh; Society of Antiquaries of Scotland, 74–83.

Ballin, T. B. 2011. The Levallois-like approach of Late Neolithic Britain: a discussion based on finds from the Stonehill Project, Aberdeenshire. In A. Saville (ed.) *Flint and Stone in the Neolithic Period.* Oxford: Neolithic Studies Group Seminar Papers 11/Oxbow Books 37–61.

Ballin Smith, B. (ed.) 1994. *Howe, Four Millennia of Orkney Prehistory,* Edinburgh: Society of Antiquaries of Scotland Monograph Series 9.

Ballin Smith, B. 1999. Crantit (Kirkwall and St Ola parish). *Discovery and Excavation in Scotland 1999,* 67.

Ballin Smith, B. 2005. Catpund: a prehistoric house in Shetland. *Scottish Archaeology Internet Report 7*.

Ballin Smith, B. 2014. *Between Tomb And Cist: the funerary monuments of Crantit, Kewing and Nether Onston, Orkney.* Kirkwall: The Orcadian Press.

Bandy, M. C. and Bandy, J. A. 2004. *Agricola, Georgius (2004). De natura fossilium (Textbook of mineralogy).* Translation from the first Latin edition of 1546. Mineola, N.Y.: Dover Publications.

Barber, J. 1997. *The Excavation of a Stalled Cairn at the Point of Cott, Westray, Orkney.* Edinburgh: Scottish Trust for Archaeological Research Monograph 1.

Barclay, G. 1996. Neolithic buildings in Scotland. In J. Thomas and T. Darvill (eds) *Neolithic Houses in North-West Europe and Beyond.* Oxford: Oxbow, 61–76.

Barclay, G. 2000. Between Orkney and Wessex: the Search for the Regional Neolithics of Britain. In A. Ritchie (ed.) *Neolithic Orkney in its European Context.* Cambridge: McDonald Institute for Archaeological Research, 275–85.

Barclay, G. 2003. Neolithic settlement in the lowlands of Scotland: a preliminary survey. In I. Armit, E. Murphy, E. Nelis and D. Simpson (eds) *Neolithic Settlement in Ireland and Western Britain.* Oxford: Oxbow books, 71–83.

Barrowman, C. 2000. Use of pumice. In J. Downes and R. Lamb (eds) *Prehistoric Houses at Sumburgh in Shetland.* Oxford: Oxbow, 109–10.

Barry, G. 1805. *History of the Orkney Islands.* Edinburgh: D. Willison.

Barth, F. 1987. *Cosmologies in the Making, a Generative Approach to Cultural Variation in Inner New Guinea.* Cambridge: Cambridge University Press.

Bates, M. R., Nayling, N., Bates, R., Dawson, S., Huws, D. and Wickham-Jone, C. 2013. A multi-disciplinary approach to the archaeological investigation of a bedrock-dominated shallow-marine landscape: an example from the Bay of Firth, Orkney, UK. *International Journal of Nautical Archaeology* 42(1), 24–43.

Bateson, G. 1972. *Steps to an Ecology of Mind.* Chicago: Chicago University Press.

Baxter, A. N. and Mitchell, J. G. 1984. Camptonite-Monchiquite dyke swarms of Northern Scotland; Age relationships and their implications. *Scottish Journal of Geology* 20, 297–308.

Bayliss, A. and Whittle, A. 2007. Histories of the dead: building chronologies for five southern British long barrows. *Cambridge Archaeological Journal* 17(1), Supplement.

Bayliss, A., Bronk Ramsey, C., van der Plicht, J. and Whittle, A. 2007. Bradshaw and Bayes: towards a timetable for the Neolithic. *Cambridge Archaeological Journal* 17(1), Supplement, 1–28.

Bayliss, A., Healy, F., Whittle, A. and Cooney, G. 2011. Neolithic narratives: British and Irish enclosures in their timescapes. In A. Whittle, F. Healy and A. Bayliss (eds) *Gathering time. Dating the early Neolithic enclosures of southern Britain and Ireland.* Oxford: Oxbow Books, 682–847.

Bayliss, A. and O'Sullivan, M. 2013. Interpreting chronologies for the Mound of the Hostages, Tara and its contemporary contexts in Neolithic and Bronze Age Ireland. In M. O'Sullivan, C. Scarre and M. Doyle (eds) *Tara – from the Past to the Future. Towards a new research agenda.* Dublin: Wordwell, 26–104.

Beamish, M. 2009. Island visits: Neolithic and Bronze Age activity on the Trent valley floor. Excavations at Egginton and Willington, Derbyshire, 1998–1999. *Derby Archaeological Journal* 129, 17–172.

Beck, R. A. 2007. The durable house: material, metaphor and structure, *The Durable House: house society models in archaeology.* Carbondale: Centre for Archaeological Investigations, 3–24.

Beckett, J. 2011. Interactions with the dead: a taphonomic analysis of burial practices in three megalithic tombs in County Clare, Ireland. *European Journal of Archaeology,* 14, 394–418.

Beckett, J. and Robb, J. 2006. Neolithic burial taphonomy, ritual, and interpretation in Britain and Ireland: a review. In R. Gowland and C. J. Knüsel (eds) *Social Aarchaeology of Funerary Remains.* Oxford: Oxbow Books, 57–80.

Beijerinck, W. 1947. *Zadenatlas der Nederlandsche Flora.* Wageningen: Veenman and Zonen.

Beith, M. 2004. *Healing Threads.* Edinburgh: Birlinn.

Bello, S. and Andrews, P. 2006. The intrinsic pattern of preservation of human skeletons and its influence on the interpretation of funerary behaviours. In R. Gowland and C. J. Knüsel (eds) *Social Archaeology of Funerary Remains.* Oxford: Oxbow Books, 16–29.

Bennett, J. 2005. The agency of assemblages and the North American blackout. *Public Culture* 17(3), 445–65.

Bennett, J. 2010. *Vibrant Matter: a political ecology of things.* Durham (NC): Duke University Press.

Bergh, S. and Hensey, R. 2013. Unpicking the chronology of Carrowmore. *Oxford Journal of Archaeology* 32(4), 343–66.

Binford, L. R. 1981. *Bones: ancient men and modern myths.* New York: Academic Press.

Bishop, R., Church, M. and Rowley-Conwy, P. 2009. Cereals, fruits and nuts in the Scottish Neolithic. *Proceedings of the Society of Antiquaries of Scotland* 139, 47–103.

Bond, J. M. 1994a. *Change and Continuity in an island system: the Palaeoeconomy of Sanday, Orkney.* Unpublished PhD thesis University of Bradford.

Bond, J. M. 1994b. The faunal and botanical remains at Tofts Ness, Sanday, Orkney: an integrated study of a buried Orcadian landscape. In R. Luff, and P. Rowley-Conwy (eds) '*Whither Environmental Archaeology?*' Oxford: Oxbow Monograph 38, 128–31.

Bourdieu, P. 1984. *Distinction: a social critique of the judgement of taste.* Cambridge (MA): Harvard University Press.

Bowles, J. F. W., Howie, R. A, Vaughan, D. V and Zussman, J. 2011. *Rock Forming Minerals, Vol. 5A, Non silicates: Oxides, Hydroxides and Sulphides,* Deer, Howie and Zussman series, second edition. London: The Geological Society.

Bradley, R. 1984. *The Social Foundations of Prehistoric Britain.* Harlow: Longmans.

Bradley, R. 1997. *Rock Art and the Prehistory of Europe: signing the land.* London: Routledge.

Bradley, R. 1998a. Incised motifs in the passage-graves at Quoyness and Cuween, Orkney. *Antiquity* 72, 387–90.

Bradley, R. 1998b. *The Significance of Monuments*. London: Routledge.

Bradley, R. 1989. Darkness and light in the design of megalithic tombs. *Oxford Journal of Archaeology* 8(3), 251–59.

Bradley, R. 2002. *The Past in Prehistoric Societies*. London: Routledge.

Bradley, R. 2005. Domestication, sedentism, property and time: materiality and the beginnings of agriculture in northern Europe. In E. DeMarrais, C. Gosden and C. Renfrew (eds) *Rethinking Materiality: the engagement of mind with the material world*. Cambridge: McDonald Institute Monographs, 107–115.

Bradley, R. 2006. Ritual and ceremony in the prehistoric landscape. In P. Greenwood, D. Perring and P. Rowsome (eds) *From Ice Age to Essex. A history of the people and landscape of east London*. Museum of London, London, 55.

Bradley, R. 2009. *Image and Audience: rethinking prehistoric art*. Oxford: Oxford University Press.

Bradley, R., Philips, T., Richards, C. and Webb, M. 2000. Decorating the houses of the dead: incised and pecked motifs in Orcadian chambered tombs. *Cambridge Archaeological Journal*, 11(1), 45–67.

Branigan, K. and Foster, P. 1995. *Barra, Archaeological Research on Ben Tangaval*. Sheffield Environmental and Archaeological Research Campaign in the Hebrides 1. Sheffield: Sheffield Academic Press.

Branigan, K. and P. Foster. 2000. *From Barra to Berneray – Archaeological Survey and Excavation in the Southern Isles of the Outer Hebrides*. Sheffield: Sheffield Academic Press.

Brock, F., Lee, S. Housley, R. and Bronk Ramsey, C. 2011. Variation in the radiocarbon age of different fractions of peat: a case study from Ahrenshöft, northern Germany. *Quaternary Geochronology* 6, 505–55.

Bronk Ramsey, C. 1995. Radiocarbon calibration and analysis of stratigraphy: the OxCal program. *Radiocarbon* 37(2), 425–30.

Bronk Ramsey, C. 1998. Probability and dating. *Radiocarbon* 40(1), 461–74.

Bronk Ramsey, C. 2001. Development of the radiocarbon calibration program OxCal. *Radiocarbon* 43(2A), 355–63.

Bronk Ramsey, C. 2009. Bayesian analysis of radiocarbon dates. *Radiocarbon* 51 (1), 337–60.

Brophy, K. 2004. The searchers: the quest for causewayed enclosures in the Irish Sea area. In V. Cummings and C. Fowler (eds) *The Neolithic of the Irish Sea. Materiality and traditions of practice*. Oxford: Oxbow, 37–45.

Brown J. F. 1975. Potassium-argon evidence of a Permian age for the camptonite dykes: Orkney. *Scottish Journal of Geology* 11, 259–262.

Bryce, T. H. 1931. An account of the Skara Brae skeletons and their probable affinities. In V. G. Childe, *Skara Brae, A Pictish Village in Orkney*. London: Kegan Paul, Trench, Trubner and Co.

Brück, J. 2008. The architecture of routine life. In J. Pollard (ed.) *Prehistoric Britain*. Oxford; Blackwell, 248–67.

Buck, C., W. Cavanagh and C. Litton. 1996. *Bayesian Approach to Interpreting Archaeological Data*. Chichester: John Wiley and Sons.

Buck, C., Litton, C. and Smith, A. 1992. Calibration of radiocarbon results pertaining to related archaeological events. *Journal of Archaeological Science* 19, 487–512.

Buck, C., Kenworthy, J., Litton, C. and Smith, A. 1991. Combining archaeological and radiocarbon information; a Bayesian approach to calibration. *Antiquity* 65, 808–21.

Buikstra, J. E. and Ubelaker, D. H. (eds) 1994. *Standards for Data Collection from Human Skeletal Remains*. Arkansas: Arkansas Archaeological Survey Research Series 44.

Bullock, P., Fedoroff, N., Jongerius,, Stoops, G. and Tursina, T. 1985. *Handbook of Thin Section Description*, Wolverhampton: Waine Research.

Bunting, M. J. 1994. Vegitation history of Orkney, Scotland: pollen records from two small basins in west Mainland. *New Phytologist* 128, 771–92.

Bunting, M. J. 1996. Holocene vegetation and environment of Orkney. In A. M. Hall (ed.) *The Quaternary of Orkney: field guide*. Cambridge: Quaternary Research Association, 20–29.

Bunting, M. J., Tipping, R. and Downes, J. 2001. 'Anthropogenic' pollen assemblages from a Bronze Age cemetery at Linga Fiold, West Mainland, Orkney. *Journal of Archaeological Science* 28, 487–500.

Burrow, S. 2010. Bryn Celli Ddu passage tomb, Anglesey: alignment, construction, date and ritual. *Proceedings of the Prehistoric Society* 76, 249–70.

Buteux, S. 1997. *Settlements at Skaill, Deerness, Orkney*. Oxford: British Archaeological Report 260.

Calder, C. S. T. 1937. A Neolithic double-chambered cairn of the stalled type and later structures on the Calf of Eday, Orkney. *Proceedings of the Society of Antiquaries of Scotland* 71, 115–54.

Callander, J. G. 1931. Notes of (1) certain prehistoric relics from Orkney and (2) Skara Brae, its culture and its period. *Proceedings of the Society of Antiquaries of Scotland* 65, 78–114.

Callander, J. G. and Grant, W. G. 1934. A long stalled chambered cairn or mausoleum (Rousay type) near Midhowe, Rousay, Orkney. *Proceedings of the Society of Antiquaries of Scotland* 68, 320–50.

Callander, J. G. and Grant, W. G. 1935. A stalled cairn at Knowe of Yarso. *Proceedings of the Society of Antiquaries of Scotland* 69, 325–51.

Callander, J. G. and Grant, W. G. 1936. A stalled cairn at Knowe of Ramsay. *Proceedings of the Society of Antiquaries of Scotland* 70, 407–19.

Cantley, M. 2005. Mesolithic Orkney Fieldwalking Project. *Discovery and Excavation in Scotland* 5, 96–97.

Card, N. 2005. Part 2. Resource assessment. History of prehistoric research. In J. Downes, S. Foster and C. Wickham-Jones (eds) *The Heart of Neolithic Orkney World Heritage Site Research Agenda*. Edinburgh: Historic Scotland, 40–46.

Card, N. 2010. Neolithic temples of the Northern Isles: stunning new discoveries in Orkney. *Current Archaeology* 241, 12–19.

Card, N. and Thomas, A. 2012. Painting a picture of Neolithic Orkney: decorated stonework from the Ness of Brodgar. In A. Cochrane and A. M. Jones (eds) *Visualizing the Neolithic*. Oxford: Oxbow Books, 111–24.

Carey, G. 2012. *The Domestic Architecture of Early Neolithic Orkney in a Wider Interpretative Context: Some Implications of Recent Discoveries*. Unpublished MA thesis. Kirkwall: University of Highlands and Island.

Carr, G. C. and Knüsel, C. J. 1997. The ritual framework of excarnation by exposure as the mortuary practice of the early and middle Iron Ages of central southern Britain. In A. Gwilt and C. Haselgrove (eds) *Reconstructing Iron Age Societies. New approaches to the British Iron Age*. Oxford: Oxbow Books, 167–74.

Carsten, J. 2000. Introduction: cultures of relatedness. In J. Carsten (ed.), *Cultures of Relatedness*. Cambridge: Cambridge University Press, 1–36.

Carsten, J. and Hugh-Jones, S. 1995. *About the House*. Cambridge: Cambridge University Press.

Carter, S., Haigh, D., Neil, N. and Smith, B. 1984. Interim report on the structures at Howe, Stromness, Orkney. *Glasgow Archaeological Journal* 11, 61–73.

Case, H. J. 1969. Settlement patterns in the north Irish Neolithic. *Ulster Journal of Archaeology* 32, 3–27.

Challands, A., Edmonds, M. and Richards, C. 2005a. Beyond the village: Barnhouse Odin and the Stones of Stenness. In C. Richards (ed.) *Dwelling Among the Monuments: the Neolithic village of Barnhouse, Maeshowe passage grave and surrounding monuments at Stenness, Orkney*. Cambridge: McDonald Research Monograph, 205–28.

Challands, A., Muir, T. and Richards, C. 2005b. The great passage grave of Maeshowe. In C. Richards (ed.) *Dwelling Among the Monuments: the Neolithic village of Barnhouse, Maeshowe passage grave and surrounding monuments at Stenness, Orkney*. Cambridge: McDonald Research Monograph, 229–48.

Chapman, R. W. 1981. The emergence of formal disposal areas and the 'problem' of megalithic tombs in prehistoric Europe. In R. W. Chapman, I. Kinnes and K. Randborg (eds) *The Archaeology of Death*. Cambridge: Cambridge University Press, 71–81.

Chapman, R. W. 2003. Death, society and archaeology: the social dimensions of mortuary practices. *Mortality* 8(3), 305–12.

Charleson, M. M. 1902. Notice of a chambered cairn in the parish of Firth, Orkney. *Proceedings of the Society of Antiquaries of Scotland* 36, 733–38.

Charleson, M. M. 1903. *Account of the Excavation of a Chambered Cairn in the Parish of Firth, Orkney*. Stromness: W. Rendall.

Cheape, H. 1992–93. Crogans and Barvas Ware: handmade pottery in the Hebrides. *Scottish Studies* 31, 109–28.

Chesterman, J. T. 1979. Investigation of the human bones from Quanterness. In C. Renfrew (ed.) *Investigations in Orkney*. London: Thames and Hudson, 97–111.

Chesterman, J. T. 1983. The human skeletal remains. In J. W. Hedges (ed.) *Isbister. A Chambered Tomb in Orkney*. Oxford: British Archaeological Report 115, 114–24.

Childe, V. G. and Paterson, J. W. 1929. Provisional report on the excavations at Skara Brae, and on finds from the 1927 and 1928 campaigns. *Proceedings of the Society of Antiquaries of Scotland* 63, 225–80.

Childe, V. G. 1930. Operations at Skara Brae during 1929. *Proceedings of the Society of Antiquaries of Scotland* 64, 158–91.

Childe, V. G. 1931a. *Skara Brae, a Pictish Village in Orkney*. London: Kegan Paul, Trench, Trubner and Co.

Childe, V. G. 1931b. Final report on the operations at Skara Brae. *Proceedings of the Society of Antiquaries of Scotland* 65, 27–77.

Childe, V. G. 1933. *Ancient Dwellings at Skara Brae*. Edinburgh: HMSO.

Childe V.G. 1939. The Orient and Europe. *American Journal of Archaeology* 43(1), 10–26.

Childe, V. G. 1940. *Prehistoric Communities of the British Isles*. London and Edinburgh: W and R Chambers.

Childe, V. G. 1942. The chambered cairns of Rousay. *Antiquaries Journal* 22(2), 139–42.

Childe, V. G. 1946. *Scotland without the Scots*. London: Methuen.

Childe, V. G. 1947. *History*. London: Cobbett Press.

Childe, V. G. 1952. Re-excavation of the chambered cairn of Quoyness, Sanday, on behalf of the Ministry of Works in 1951–2. *Proceedings of the Society of Antiquaries of Scotland* 86, 155–72.

Childe, V. G. 1956. Maes Howe. *Proceedings of the Society of Antiquaries of Scotland* 88, 155–72.

Childe, V. G. and Grant, W. G. 1939. A Stone Age settlement at the Braes of Rinyo, Rousay, Orkney. *Proceedings of the Society of Antiquaries of Scotland* 73, 6–31.

Childe, V. G and Grant, W. G. 1947. A Stone Age settlement at the Braes of Rinyo, Rousay, Orkney (second report). *Proceedings of the Society of Antiquaries of Scotland* 81, 16–42.

Childe, V. G. and Patterson, J. W. 1929. Provisional report on the excavations at Skara Brae. *Proceedings of the Society of Antiquaries* 63, 225–80.

Clarke, A. 1989. The Skaill knife as a butchering tool. *Lithics* 10, 16–27.

Clarke, A. 1996. *Observations of Social Change in Prehistoric Orkney and Shetland based on a Study of the Types and Context of Coarse Stone Artifacts*. Unpublished MPhil Dissertation, University of Glasgow.

Clarke, A. 2005a. The Stone Tool Assemblage. In C. Richards (ed.) *Dwelling Among the Monuments: the Neolithic village of Barnhouse, Maeshowe passage grave and surrounding monuments at Stenness, Orkney*. Cambridge: McDonald Institute Monographs, 323–334.

Clarke, A. 2005b. The pumice from Barnhouse, in C. Richards (ed.) *Dwelling Among the Monuments: the Neolithic village of Barnhouse, Maeshowe passage grave and surrounding monuments at Stenness, Orkney*. Cambridge: McDonald Institute Monographs, 335–38.

Clarke, A. 2006 *Stone Tools and the Prehistory of the Northern Isles*. Oxford: British Archaeological Report 406.

Clarke, A. 2007a. Coarse stone. In J. Hunter, J. M. Bond and A. N. Smith (eds) *Investigations in Sanday, Orkney: a multi-*

period settlement from Neolithic to Late Norse times. Kirkwall: The Orcadian, 353–88.

Clarke, A. 2007b. Coarse stone. In S. J. Dockrill, J. M. Bond, A. N. Smith and R. A. Nicholson (eds), 2007. *Tofts Ness, Sanday: an island landscape through 3000 years of prehistory.* Kirkwall: The Orcadian, 292–315.

Clarke, A. 2011. Does size matter? Stone axes from Orkney: their style and deposition. In V. Davis and M. Edmonds (eds) *Stone Axe Studies 3.* Oxford: Oxbow Books, 309–22.

Clarke, D. V. 1976. *The Neolithic Village at Skara Brae, Orkney, Excavations 1972–3, An Interim Report.* Edinburgh: HMSO.

Clarke, D. V. 1983. Rinyo and the Orcadian Neolithic. In A. O'Connor and D. V. Clarke (eds) *From the Stone Age to the 'Forty-Five', Studies presented to R. B. K. Stevenson.* Edinburgh: Edinburgh University Press, 45–56.

Clarke, D. V. and Sharples, N. 1990. Settlements and subsistence in the third millennium BC. In C. Renfrew (ed.) *The Prehistory of Orkney.* Edinburgh: Edinburgh University Press, 54–82.

Clarke, D. V. and Maguire, P. 1989. *Skara Brae: Northern Europe's best preserved prehistoric village.* Edinburgh: Historic Scotland.

Cleal, J. R. 1992. The Neolithic and Beaker Pottery. In C. Gingell (ed.) *The Marlborough Downs: a Later Bronze Age Landscape and its Origins.* Devizes: Wiltshire Archaeological and Natural History Society. Monograph 1, 61–70.

Cleal, R. and MacSween, A. (eds) 1999. *Grooved Ware in Britain and Ireland.* Oxford: Oxbow Books.

Close-Brooks, J. 1995. Excavations of a cairn at Cnip, Uig, Isle of Lewis, *Proceedings of the Society of Antiquaries of Scotland* 125, 253–77.

Cochrane, A. and Jones, A. M. 2012. Visualising the Neolithic: an introduction. In A. Cochrane and A. M. Jones (eds) *Visualizing the Neolithic.* Oxford: Oxbow Books, 1–14.

Coles, D. and Miles, M. 2013. The Neolithic settlement at Green Farm. *Orkney Archaeological Society Newsletter* 9, 3–8.

Coles, D., Miles, M. and Walkling, T. 2010. A pecked stone from a settlement site at Green, Isle of Eday, Orkney. *Past* 65, 15.

Cooney, G. 2003. Rooted or routed: landscapes of Neolithic settlement in Ireland. In I. Armit, E. Murphy, E. Nelis and D. Simpson (eds), *Neolithic Settlement in Ireland and Western Britain.* Oxford: Oxbow Books, 47–55.

Cooney, G., Bayliss, A., Healy, F. Whittle, A., Danaher, E., Cagney, L., Mallory, J. Smyth, J., Kador, T. and O'Sullivan, M. 2011. Ireland. In A. Whittle, F. Healy and A. Bayliss (eds) *Gathering Time: dating the early Neolithic enclosures of southern Britain and Ireland.* Oxford: Oxbow Books 562–669.

Copley, M. S., Berstan, R., Dudd, S. N., Docherty, G., Mukherjee, A. J., Straker, V., Payne, S. and Evershed, R. P. 2003. Direct chemical evidence for widespread dairying in prehistoric Britain. *Proceedings of the National Academy of the United States of America* 100, 1524–1529.

Correia, P. M. 1997. Fire modification of bone: a review of the literature. In W. D. Haglund and M. H. Sorg (eds) *Forensic Taphonomy: the post-mortem fate of human remains,* 275–94.

Cramp, L. J. E., Jones, J., Sheridan, A., Smyth, J., Whelton, H., Mulville, J., and Evershed, R. P. 2014. Immediate replacement of fishing with dairying by the earliest farmers of the northeast Atlantic archipelagos. *Proceedings of the Royal Society B – Biological Sciences* 281(1780), [20132372].

Crone, A. 1993. Excavation and survey of sub-peat features of Neolithic, Bronze and Iron Age date at Bharpa Carinish, North Uist, Scotland. *Proceedings of the Prehistoric Society* 59, 361–82.

Cronyn, J. M. and Robertson, W. S. 1990. *The Elements of Archaeological Conservation.* London: Routlegde.

Crozier, R. 2012. *A Taphonomic Approach to the Re-analysis of the Human Remains from the Neolithic Chamber Tomb of Quanterness, Orkney.* Unpublished PhD thesis, Queen's University Belfast.

Crozier, R. 2014. Exceptional or conventional? Social identity within the chamber tomb of Quanterness, Orkney. In V. G. Ginn, R. A. Enlander and R. Crozier (eds) *Exploring Prehistoric Identity in Northwest Europe. Our construct or theirs.* Oxford: Oxbow Books, 165–80.

Crum, H. A. and Anderson, L. E. 1981. *Mosses of Eastern North America.* New York: Columbia University Press.

Cummings, V. and Pannett, A. 2005. *Set in Stone: New approaches to Neolithic monuments in Scotland.* Oxford: Oxbow Books.

Cummings, V. and Harris, O. 2011. Animals, people and places: the continuity of hunting and gathering practices across the Mesolithic–Neolithic transition in Britain. *European Journal of Archaeology* 14(3), 361–82.

Cummings, V. and Richards, C. 2013. The peristalith and the context of Calanais: transformational architecture in the Hebridean early Neolithic. In C. Richards (ed.) *Building the Great Stone Circles of the North.* Oxford: Windgather Press, 186–200.

Cuomo Di Caprio, N. and Vaughan, S. J. 1993. An experimental study in distinguishing grog (chamotte) from argillaceous inclusions in ceramic thin sections. *Archaeomaterials* 7, 21–40.

Curtis, N. and Hutchinson, M. 2013. Radiocarbon dates for human remains from chambered cairns along the south and south-west coast of the island of Rousay, Orkney. *Discovery and Excavation in Scotland* 14, 212–13.

Daniel, G. E. 1950. *The Prehistoric Chambered Tombs of England and Wales.* Cambridge: Cambridge University Press.

Daniel, G. E. and Powell, T. G. E. 1949. The distribution and date of the passage graves of the British Isles. *Proceedings of the Prehistoric Society* 15, 169–87.

Davidson, D. A. and Jones, R. L. 1990. The environment of Orkney. In C. Renfrew (ed.) *The Prehistory of Orkney.* Edinburgh: Edinburgh University Press, 10–35.

Davidson, J. L. and Henshall, A. S. 1989. *The Chambered Cairns of Orkney.* Edinburgh: Edinburgh University Press.

Davidson, J. L. and Henshall, A. 1991. *The Chambered Cairns of Caithness.* Edinburgh: Edinburgh University Press.

Davidson, D. A. and Jones D. L. 1985. The environment of Orkney. In C. Renfrew (ed.) *The Prehistory of Orkney BC 4000–1000 AD.* Edinburgh: Edinburgh University Press, 10–35.

Davis, S. J. 1987. *The Archaeology of Animals*. London: Batsford.

Deboer, W. 1997. Ceremonial centers from the Cayapas (Esmereldas, Ecuador) to Chillicothe (Ohio, USA). *Cambridge Archaeological Journal* 7, 225–53.

DeSilvey, C. 2006. Observed decay: telling stories with mutable things. *Journal of Material Culture* 11(3), 318–38.

Dickson, C. A. 1983. Macroscopic plant remains from Knap of Howar, Orkney. In A. Ritchie (ed.) Excavation of a Neolithic Farmstead at Knap of Howar, Papa Westray, Orkney. *Proceedings of the Society of Antiquaries of Scotland* 113, 114–15.

Dickson, C. A. 1988. Distinguishing cereal from wild grass pollen: some limitations. *Circaea* 5, 67–71.

Dickson, C. A. 1994. Plant remains. In B. Ballin Smith (ed.) *Howe: Four Millennia of Orkney Prehistory Excavations 1978–82*. Edinburgh: Society of Antiquaries of Scotland Monograph 9, 125–39.

Dickson, C. A. 1998. Past uses of turf in the Northern Isles. In C. M. Milles and G. Coles (eds) *Life on the Edge: human settlement and marginality*. Oxford: Oxbow Books, 105–109.

Dickson, C. A. 1999. The plant remains. In B. E. Crawford and B. Ballin Smith (eds) *The Biggings Papa Stour, Shetland: the history and archaeology of a royal Norwegian farm*. Edinburgh: Society of Antiquaries of Scotland Monograph Series 15, 104–18.

Dickson, C. A. and Dickson, J. H. 2000. *Plants and People in Ancient Scotland*. Stroud: Tempus Publishing.

Dickson, C.A., Downes, J., McKinley, J. I. and Hinton, P. 1994. The contents of the cist in J. Downes (ed.) Excavation of a Bronze Age burial at Mousland, Stromness, Orkney. *Proceedings of the Society of Antiquaries of Scotland* 124, 146–47.

Dickson, J. H. 1992. North American driftwood, especially *Picea* (spruce), from archaeological sites in the Hebrides and Northern Isles of Scotland. In J. P. Pals, J. Buurman and M. van der Veen (eds) *Festschrift for Professor van Zeist. Review of Palaeobotany and Palynology* 73, 49–56.

Dickson, N. 1990. *An Island Shore: the life and work of Robert Rendall*. Kirkwall: Orkney Press.

Dobney, K., Hall, A. R., Kenward, H. K. and Milles, A. 1992. A working classification of samples types for environmental archaeology. *Circaea* 9, 24–26.

Dockrill, S. J., Bond, J. M., Smith, A. N. and Nicholson, R. A. (eds) 2007. *Tofts Ness, Sanday: an island landscape through 3000 years of prehistory*. Kirkwall: The Orcadian.

Dowd, M. A. 2002. Kilgreany, Co. Waterford: biography of a cave. *Journal of Irish Archaeology* 11, 77–97.

Dowd, M., Fibiger, L. and Lynch, L. G. 2006. The human remains from Irish Caves Project. *Archaeology Ireland* 20(3), 16–19.

Downes, J. 1994. Excavation of a Bronze Age burial at Mousland, Stromness, Orkney. *Proceedings of the Society of Antiquaries of Scotland* 124, 141–54.

Downes, J. 1995. *Linga Fold, Sandwick, Orkney; excavation of a Bronze Age barrow cemetery*. Glasgow: GUARD report 59.2.

Downes, J. 1999. Cremation: a spectacle and a journey. In J. Downes and T. Pollard (eds) *The Loved Body's Corruption. Archaeological Contributions to the Study of Human Mortality*. Glasgow: Cruithne Press, 19–29.

Downes, J. 2000. Architecture, spatial organization and material culture. In J. Downes and R. Lamb (eds) *Prehistoric Houses at Sumburgh in Shetland*. Oxford: Oxbow Books, 117–28.

Downes, J. 2009. The construction of barrows in Bronze Age Orkney – an 'assuagement of guilt'? In M. J. Allen, N. Sharples and T. O'Connor (eds) *Land and People: papers in memory of John G. Evans*. Oxford: Prehistoric Society Research Paper 2/Oxbow Books, 126–35.

Downes, J. in prep. *Bronze Age Burial Rites in Orkney. The Excavation of Linga Fiold and other Orkney Barrows and Cists*. Oxford: Oxbow Books. '

Downes, J. and Richards, R. 2000. Excavating the Neolithic and Early Bronze Age of Orkney: recognition and interpretation in the field. In A. Ritchie (ed.) *Neolithic Orkney in its European Context*. Cambridge: McDonald Institute Monograph, 159–68.

Downes, J. and Lamb, R. 2000. *Sumburgh Airport: the archaeology of later prehistoric houses in Shetland*. Oxford: Oxbow Monograph.

Downes, J. and Richards, C. 2005. The dwellings at Barnhouse. In C. Richards (ed.) *Dwelling Among the Monuments: the Neolithic village of Barnhouse, Maeshowe passage grave and surrounding monuments at Stenness, Orkney*. Cambridge: McDonald Institute Monographs, 57–128.

Downes, J., Richards, C., Brown, J., Cresswell, A. J., Ellen, R., Davies, A. D., Hall, A., McCulloch, R., Sanderson, D. C. W. and Simpson, I. A. 2013. Investigating the great Ring of Brodgar, Orkney. In C. Richards (ed.) *Building the Great Stone Circles of the North*. Oxford: Windgather Press, 90–118.

Downes, J. and Thomas, A. 2014. Where mythical space lies: land ownership versus land use in the northern Bronze Age. In M. Relaki and D Catapoti (eds) *Land Matters: Analytical limitations and potential in archaeological studies of land ownership*. London: Routledge, 70–92.

Dudd, S. N. and Evershed, R. P. 1998. Direct demonstration of milk as an element of archaeological economies. *Science* 282, 1478–1481.

Edlin, H. 1973. *Woodland Crafts of Britain*. Newton Abbot: David and Charles.

Edmonds, M. R. 1995. *Stone Tools and Society: working stone in Neolithic and Bronze Age Britain*. London: Batsford.

Edwards, K. 1996. A Mesolithic of the Western and Northern Isles of Scotland? Evidence from pollen and charcoal. In T. Pollard and A. Morrison (eds) *The Early Prehistory of Scotland*. Edinburgh: Edinburgh University Press, 23–38.

Edwards, K. and Mithen, S. 1995. The colonization of the Hebridean islands of western Scotland: evidence from the palynological and archaeological records. *World Archaeology* 26(3), 348–65.

Eliade, M. 1959. *The Sacred and the Profane, the nature of Religion*, New York (NY): Harcourt Bruce.

Errington, S. 1989. *Meaning and Power in a Southeast Asian Realm*. Princetown: Princetown University Press.

Evans, J. G. and Vaughan, M. 1983. The molluscs from Knap of Howar. In A. Ritchie, Excavations of a Neolithic farmstead at Knap of Howar, Papa Westray, Orkney. *Proceedings of the Society of Antiquaries of Scotland* 113, 106–14.

Evershed, R. P., Stott, A. W., Raven, A., Dudd, S. N., Charters, S. and Leyden, A. 1995. Formation of long-chain ketones in ancient-pottery vessels by pyrolysis of acyl lipids. *Tetrahedron Letters* 36, 8875–8878.

Evershed, R. P., Mottram, H. R., Dudd, S. N., Charters, S., Stott, A. W., Gibson, A. M., Conner, A., Blinkhorn, P. W. and Reeves, V. 1997. New criteria for the identification of animal fats preserved in archaeological pottery. *Naturwissenschaften* 84, 402–406.

Fairweather, A. D. and Ralston, I. B. M. 1993. The Neolithic timber hall at Balbridie, Grampian Region, Scotland: the building, the Date, the Plant Macrofossils. *Antiquity* 67, 313–23.

Fannin, N. G. T. 1970. The sedimentary environment of the Old Red Sandstone of Western Orkney. Unpublished PhD thesis, University of Reading.

Farrell, M., Bunting, M. J., Lee, D. H. J. and Thomas, A. 2014. Neolithic settlement at the woodlands edge: palynological data and timber architecture in Orkney, Scotland. *Journal of Archaeological Science* 51, 225–36.

Farrer, J. 1870. Note of excavations in Sanday, one of the North Isles of Orkney. *Proceedings of the Society of Antiquaries of Scotland* 7, 398–401

Fenton, A. 1978. *The Northern Isles: Orkney and Shetland.* Edinburgh: John Donald.

Fieller, N. R. J. and Turner, A. 1982. Number estimation in vertebrae samples. *Journal of Archaeological Science* 9, 49–62.

Finlayson, B. 2004. The use of stone tools in Mesolithic Scotland: function, value, decision–making, and landscape. In A. Saville (ed.) *Mesolithic Scotland and its Neighbours.* Edinburgh: Society of Antiquaries of Scotland, 221–28.

Finlay, N. 1997. The lithic assemblage. In J. Barber, *The Excavation of a Stalled Cairn at the Point of Cott, Westray, Orkney.* Edinburgh: Scottish Trust for Archaeological Research Monograph 1, 30–34.

Finlayson, B. and Edwards, K. J. 1997. The Mesolithic. In K. J. Edwards and I. B. M. Ralston (eds) *Scotland: environment and archaeology, 8000 BC–AD 1000.* Chichester: John Wiley and Sons, 109–25.

Fleet, A. J. 1976. Cramp from the Stones of Stenness, Orkney. In J. N. G. Ritchie (ed.) The Stones of Stenness, Orkney. *Proceedings of the Society of Antiquaries of Scotland* 107, 46–48.

Fleming, J. A. 1923. *Scottish Pottery.* Glasgow: Maclehose, Jackson and Co.

Flett, J. S. 1898. The Old Red Sandstone of the Orkney. *Transactions of the Royal Society of Edinburgh* 39, 313–319.

Fowler, C. 2001. Personhood and social relations in the British Neolithic with a study from the Isle of Man. *Journal of Material Culture* 6, 137–63.

Fowler, C. 2004. *The Archaeology of Personhood.* London: Routledge.

Fowler, C. 2005. Identity politics. personhood, kinship, gender and power in Neolithic and Early Bronze Age Britain. In E. C. Casella and C. Fowler, C. (eds) *The Archaeology of Plural and Changing Identities.* New York: Kluwer Academic/Plenum Publishers, 109–34.

Fowler, C. 2010. Pattern and diversity in the Early Neolithic

Mortuary practices of Britain and Ireland: contextualising the treatment of the dead. *Documenta Praehistorica* 41, 1–22.

Fox, J. J. 1993. *Inside Austronesian Houses: perspectives on domestic designs for living.* Canberra: Australian National University.

Fraser, J. 1927. The antiquities of Firth parish. *Proceedings of the Orkney Antiquarian Society* 5, 51–56.

Friedman, J. 1992. Myth, history and political identity. *Cultural Anthropology* 7(2), 194–210.

French, C. A. I. 2005. Soil analysis at Barnhouse and Maeshowe. In C. Richards (ed.) *Dwelling Among the Monuments: the Neolithic village of Barnhouse, Maeshowe passage grave and surrounding monuments at Stenness, Orkney.* Cambridge: McDonald Institute Monographs, 371–380.

French, D. H. 1971. An experiment in water sieving. *Anatolian Studies* 21, 59–64.

Gale, R. and Cutler, D. 2000. *Plants In Archaeology: Identification Manual of Artefacts of Plant Origin from Europe and the Mediterranean.* London: Westbury.

Garnham, T. 2004. *Lines on the Landscape, Circles from the Sky: monuments of Neolithic Orkney.* Stroud: Tempus.

Garrow, D., Raven, J. and Richards, C. 2005. The anatomy of the megalithic space. In C. Richards (ed.) *Dwelling Among the Monuments: the Neolithic village of Barnhouse, Maeshowe passage grave and surrounding monuments at Stenness, Orkney.* Cambridge: Cambridge University Press, 249–60.

Geikie, A. 1882. *Text Book of Geology (Book 2).* London: Macmillan and Co.

Gejvall, N. G. 1963. Cremations. In D. Brothwell and E. Higgs (eds) *Science in Archaeology.* London: Thames and Hudson, 379–90.

Gell, A. 1992. The technology of enchantment and the enchantment of technology. In J. Coote and A. Shelton, (eds) *Anthropology, Art and Aesthetics.* Oxford: Clarendon Press, 40–66.

Gell, A. 1998. *Art and Agency: an anthropological theory.* Oxford: Clarendon Press.

Gibson, A. M. 2002. *Prehistoric Pottery in Britain and Ireland.* Stroud: Tempus.

Gibson, A. M. and Woods, A. 1997. *Prehistoric Pottery for the Archaeologist.* London: Leicester University Press.

Gillespie, S. D. 2000a. Beyond kinship. In R. A. Joyce and S. D. Gillespie (eds) *Beyond Kinship: social and material reproduction in house societies.* Philadelphia: University of Pennsylvania Press, 1–21.

Gillespie, S. D. 2000b. Levi Strauss: *Maison and société à maisons.* In R. A. Joyce and S. D. Gillespie (eds) *Beyond kinship: social and material reproduction in house societies.* Philadelphia: University of Pennsylvania Press, 22–52.

Gosselain, O. P. 1992. The bonfire of the enquiries. Pottery firing temperatures: what for? *Journal of Archaeological Science* 19, 243–59.

Graeber, D. 1995. Dancing with corpses reconsidered: an interpretation of famadihana (in Arivonimamo, Madagascar). *American Ethnologist* 22, 258–78.

Grant, W. G. and Wilson, D. 1943. The Knowe of Lairo, Rousay, Orkney. *Proceedings of the Society of Antiquaries of Scotland* 77, 17–26.

Green, H. S. 1980. *The Flint Arrowheads of the British Isles: a detailed study of material from England and Wales with comparanda from Scotland and Ireland*. Oxford: British Archaeological Report 75(i).

Griffiths, S. 2011. Chronological modelling of the Mesolithic–Neolithic transition in the north and midlands of England and Wales. Unpublished PhD thesis, Cardiff University.

Griffiths, S. 2014a. Points in time: the chronology of rod microliths. *Oxford Archaeology Journal* 33(3), 221–43.

Griffiths, S. 2014b. A Bayesian radiocarbon chronology of the early Neolithic of Yorkshire and Humberside. *Archaeology Journal* 171, 2–29.

Griffiths, S. 2014c. Simulation and outputs: simple chronological modelling of archaeological activity. *Radiocarbon*, 52(2), 871–76.

Griffiths, S. and Richards, C. 2013. A time for stone circles, a time for new people. In C. Richards (ed.) *Building the Great Stone Circles of the North*. Oxford: Windgather Press, 281–91.

Grigson, G. 1958. *The Englishman's Flora*. Manchester: Phoenix House.

Grimm, E. 1991. *Tilia and Tilliagraph*. Chicago: Illinois State Museum.

Gualtieri, A. F. and Venturelli, P. 1999. *In situ* study of the goethite-hematite phase transformation by real time synchrotron powder diffraction. *American Mineralogist* 84, 895–904.

Gunn, A. 2009. *Essential Forensic Biology*. Chichester: John Wiley and Sons.

Guttman, E. B. A., Dockrill, S. J. and Simpson, I. A. 2004. Arable agriculture in prehistory: new evidence from soils in the Northern Isles. *Proceedings of the Society of Antiquaries of Scotland* 134, 53–64.

Habermehl, K. H. 1985. *Altersbestimmung bei wild und pelzieren*. Hamburg: Paul Parey.

Haglund, W. D., Connor, M. and Scott, D. D. 2002. The effect of cultivation on buried human remains. In W. D. Haglund and M. H. Sorg (eds) *Advances in Forensic Taphonomy: method, theory and archaeological perspectives*. Boca Raton: CRC Press, 133–50.

Hamilakis, Y. 2012. Archaeologies of the senses. In T. Insoll (ed.) *The Oxford Handbook of the Archaeology of Ritual and Religion*. Oxford: Oxford University Press, 208–25.

Hamilton, S., Seager Thomas, M. and Whitehouse, R. 2011. Say it with stone: constructing with stones on Easter Island. *World Archaeology* 43(2), 167–90.

Hamlet, L. E. 2014. *Anthropic sediments on the Scottish North Atlantic Seaboard: Nature, Versatility and Value of a Midden*. Unpublished PhD, University of Stirling

Harrison, S. 2008. An experimental prehistoric pottery firing at Harray, Orkney. *Antiquity* 82(317) n. p. http://www.antiquty.ac.uk/projgall/harrison/.

Hawkes, C. and Hawkes, J. 1943. *Prehistoric Britain*. Harmondsworth: Pelican Books.

Heddle, M. F. 1901. *The Mineralogy of Scotland, edited by J. G. Goodchild*, Vols I and II. Edinburgh: David Douglas.

Hedges, J. 1975. Archaeology within a County Planning Department – Essex. In R. T. Rowley and M. Breakell (eds)

Planning and the Historic Environment. Oxford: Oxford University Department for External Studies, 29–49.

Hedges, J. 1983. *Isbister: a Chambered Tomb in Orkney*. Oxford: British Archaeological Report 115.

Hedges, J. 1984. *Tomb of the Eagles: a window on stone age tribal Britain*. London: John Murray.

Hedges, M. E. 1977. The excavation of the Knowes of Quoyscottie, Orkney: a cemetery of the first millennium BC. *Proceedings of the Society of Antiquaries of Scotland* 108, 133–55.

Helms, M. 1998. *Access to Origins: affines, ancestors and aristocrats*. Austin: University of Texas Press.

Helms, M. 2007. House life. In R. A. Beck (ed.) *The Durable House: house society models in archaeology*. Carbondale: Centre for Archaeological Investigations, 487–504.

Henshall, A. S. 1963. *The Chambered Tombs of Scotland (vol. 1)*. Edinburgh: Edinburgh University Press.

Henshall, A. S. 1972. *The Chambered Tombs of Scotland (vol. 2)*. Edinburgh: Edinburgh University Press.

Henshall, A. S. 1983. The Neolithic pottery from Easterton of Roseisle, Moray. In A. O'Connor and D.V. Clarke (eds) *From the Stone Age to the 'Forty–Five*, Edinburgh: John Donald, 19–44.

Henshall, A. S. 2004. Scottish passage graves: some confusions and conclusions. In A. Gibson and A. Sheridan (eds) *From Sickles to Circles*. Stroud: Tempus, 78–91.

Hey, G. and Robinson, M. 2011. Neolithic communities in the Thames Valley: the creation of new worlds. In A. Morigi, D. Schreve, D. White, G. Hey, P. Garwood, M. Robinson, A. Barcley and P. Bradley (eds) *The Thames through Time: the archaeology of the Gravel terraces of the Upper and Middle Thames. Early Prehistory to 1500 BC* Thames valley Monograph 32. Oxford: Oxford Archaeology, 221–58.

Hill, J. and Richards, C. 2005. Monumentality at Barnhouse. In C. Richards (ed.) *Dwelling Among the Monuments: the Neolithic village of Barnhouse, Maeshowe passage grave and surrounding monuments at Stenness, Orkney*. Cambridge: McDonald Institute Monographs, 157–94.

Hillson, S. 1986. *Teeth*. Cambridge: Cambridge University Press.

Hinton, P. 2005. The charred plant remains from Barnhouse and Maeshowe. In C. Richards (ed.) *Dwelling Among the Monuments: the Neolithic village of Barnhouse, Maeshowe passage grave and surrounding monuments at Stenness, Orkney*. Cambridge: McDonald Institute Monographs, 339–58.

Hodder, I. 1984. Burials, houses, women and men in the European Neolithic. In D. Miller and C. Tilley (eds) *Ideology, Power and Prehistory*. Cambridge: Cambridge University Press, 51–68.

Hodder, I. 1990. *The Domestication of Europe, Structure and Contingency in Neolithic Society*. Oxford: Blackwell.

Hodder, I. 2012. *Entanglement: an archaeology of the relationships between humans and things*. Oxford: Wiley-Blackwell.

Hofmann, D. and Smyth, J. 2013. *Tracking the Neolithic House in Europe. Sedentism, Architecture, and Practice*. New York: Springer.

Holden, J. L., Phakey, P. P. and Clement, J. G. 1995. Scanning Electron Microscope observations of heat-treated human bone. *Forensic Science International* 74, 29–45.

Hoskins, J. 1998. *Biographical Objects: how things tell the stories of peoples' lives.* London: Routledge.

Howell, S. 1995. The Lio house: building, category, idea, value. In J. Carsten and S. Hugh-Jones (eds) *About the House: Levi-Strauss and beyond.* Cambridge: Cambridge University Press, 149–69.

Hummel, S. and Schutkowski, H. 1993. Approaches to the histological age determination of cremated human remains. In G. Grupe and A. N. Garland (eds) *Histology of Ancient Human Bone: methods and diagnosis.* London: Springer, 111–23.

Hunter, J. R. 2000. Pool, Sanday and a sequence for the Orcadian Neolithic. In A. Ritchie (ed.) *Neolithic Orkney in its European context.* Cambridge: McDonald Institute Monographs, 117–25.

Hunter, J. and MacSween, A. 1991. A sequence for the Orcadian Neolithic. *Antiquity* 65, 911–14.

Hunter, J., Bond J. M. and Smith, A. N. 2007. *Investigations in Sanday, Orkney: a multi-period settlement from Neolithic to Late Norse times.* Kirkwall: The Orcadian.

Ingold, T. 2000. *The Perception of the Environment: essays in livelihood, dwelling and skill.* London: Routledge.

Ingold, T. 2011. *Being Alive: essays on movement, knowledge and description.* London: Routledge.

Isbister, A. 2000. Burnished hematite and pigment production, A. Ritchie (ed.) *Neolithic Orkney in its European Context.* Cambridge: McDonald Monograph, 191–95.

Isbister, A. 2004. *Pigment Resources.* Unpublished report commissioned by the Skara Brae project, National Museums of Scotland.

Isbister, A. 2009. Pigment resources report: excavations at Sand, Applecross, 2000. In K. Hardy and C. Wickham-Jones (eds) *Mesolithic and Later Sites around the Inner Sound, Scotland: the work of the Scotland's First Settlers project 1998–2004.* Scottish Archaeological Internet Report 31: Section 3.8.

Janaway, R. C. 1996. The decay of buried human remains and their associated materials. In J. Hunter, C. A. Roberts and A. Martin, (eds) *Studies in Crime: An introduction to forensic archaeology.* London: Routledge, 58–85.

Johnson, S.-L. 2000. *An Investigation into the Effects of the Inhabitants of the Prehistoric Site of Stonehall on their Environment.* Unpublished BSc thesis, University of Glasgow.

Jones, A. M. 1997. *A Biography of Ceramics: food and culture in Late Neolithic Orkney.* Unpublished PhD thesis, University of Glasgow.

Jones, A. M. 1998. Where eagles dare: landscape, animals and the Neolithic of Orkney. *Journal of Material Culture* 3, 301–24.

Jones, A. M. 1999a. The World on a plate: ceramics, food technology and cosmology in Neolithic Orkney. *World Archaeology* 31(1), 55–78.

Jones, A. M. 1999b. Local colour: megalithic architecture and colour symbolism in Neolithic Arran. *Oxford Journal of Archaeology* 18(4), 339–50.

Jones, A. M. 2000. Life after Death: monuments, material culture and social change in Neolithic Orkney. In A. Ritchie (ed.) *Neolithic Orkney in its European Context.* Cambridge: McDonald Institute Monographs 127–38.

Jones, A. M. 2002. *Archaeological Theory and Scientific Practice.* Cambridge: Cambridge University Press.

Jones, A. M. 2005a. The Grooved ware from Barnhouse. In C. Richards (ed.) *Dwelling Among the Monuments: the Neolithic village of Barnhouse, Maeshowe passage grave and surrounding monuments at Stenness, Orkney.* Cambridge: McDonald Institute Monographs, 261–82.

Jones, A. M. 2005b. Natural histories and social identities in Neolithic Orkney. In E. Casella and C. Fowler (eds) *The Archaeology of Plural Identities.* New York: Kluwer/Plenum.

Jones, A. M. 2007. *Memory and Material Culture.* Cambridge: Cambridge University Press.

Jones, A. M. 2012. *Prehistoric Materialities: becoming material in prehistoric Britain and Ireland.* Oxford: Oxford University Press.

Jones, A. M. and MacGregor, G. (eds) 2002. *Colouring the Past: the significance of colour in archaeological research.* London: Bloomsbury Academic.

Jones, A. M. and Richards, C. 2003. Animals into ancestors: domestication, food and identity in late Neolithic Orkney. In M. Parker Pearson (ed.) *Food, Culture and Identity in the Neolithic and Early Bronze Age*, Oxford: British Archaeological Report 1117, 45–52.

Jones. A. M., Cole, W. J. and Jones, R. E. 2005. The results of residue analysis using GC-MS on the Barnhouse Grooved ware assemblage. In C. Richards (ed) *Dwelling Amongst the Monuments: Excavations at Barnhouse and Maes Howe, Orkney.* Cambridge: McDonald Institute Monographs, 283–92.

Jones, D. M. (ed.) 2004. *Human Bones from Archaeological Sites: Guidelines for producing assessment documents and analytical reports.* CfA Guidelines, English Heritage in association with the British Association for Biological Anthropology and Osteoarchaeology.

Jones, J., Mulville, J., McGill, R. and Evershed, R. 2012. Palaoenvironmental modelling of $\delta^{13}C$ and $\delta^{15}N$ values in the North Atlantic Islands: understanding past marine resource use. *Rapid Communications in Mass Spectrometry* 26, 2399–406.

Jones, R. E. and Brown, B. 2000. Neolithic pottery–making on Orkney: a new look. In A. Ritchie (ed.) *Neolithic Orkney in its European Context.* Cambridge: McDonald Institute Monograph, 169–84.

Jones, R. E., Challands, A., French, C., Card, N., Downes, J. and Richards, C. 2010. Exploring the location and function of a late Neolithic house at Crossiecrown, Orkney by geophysical, geochemical and soil Micromorphological methods. *Archaeological Prospection* 17(1), 29–47.

Jones, S. 1997. *The Archaeology of Ethnicity.* London: Routledge.

Jones, S. and Richards, C. 2000. Neolithic cultures in Orkney: classification and interpretation. In A. Ritchie (ed.) *Neolithic Orkney in its European Context.* Cambridge: McDonald Institute Monographs, 101–106.

Jones, S. and Richards, C. 2005. The villagers of Barnhouse. In C. Richards (ed.) *Dwelling Among the Monuments: the Neolithic village of Barnhouse, Maeshowe passage grave and surrounding monuments at Stenness, Orkney.* Cambridge, McDonald Research Monograph, 195–204.

Joyce, R. A. 2000. Heirlooms and houses: materiality and social memory. In R. A. Joyce and S. D. Gillespie (eds) *Beyond Kinship: social and material reproduction in house societies*. Philadelphia: University of Pennsylvania Press, 189–212.

Keatinge, T. H. and Dickson, J. H. 1979. Mid–Flandrian changes in vegetation on Mainland Orkney. *New Phytologist* 82, 585–612.

Kerley, E. R. and Ubelaker, D. H. 1978. Revisions in the microscopic method of estimating age at death in human cortical bone. *American Journal of Physical Anthropology* 46, 545–46.

Kilbride–Jones, H. E. 1973. On some aspects of Neolithic building techniques in Orkney. *Acta Praehistorica et Archaeologica* 4, 75–96.

Kinnaird, T. C., Sanderson, D. C. W. and Woodward, N. L. 2011. Applying luminescence methods to geoarchaeology: a case study from Stronsay, Orkney. *Earth and Environmental Science Transactions of the Royal Society of Edinburgh* 102(3), 191–200.

Kinnes, I. 1985. Circumstance not context: the Neolithic of Scotland as seen from the outside. *Proceedings of the Society of Antiquaries of Scotland* 115, 15–57.

King, S. E. 2005. Barnhouse faunal remains. In C. Richards (ed.) *Dwelling Among the Monuments: the Neolithic village of Barnhouse, Maeshowe passage grave and surrounding monuments at Stenness, Orkney*. Cambridge: McDonald Institute Monograph, 367–70.

Kirch, P. V. 2000. Temples as 'Holy Houses': the transformation of ritual architecture in traditional Polynesian societies. In R. A. Joyce and S. Gillespie (eds) *Beyond Kinship: social and material reproduction in house societies*. Philadelphia: University of Pennsylvania Press, 74–102.

Kovacik, J. J. 1999. Memory and pueblo space. In J. Brück and M. Goodman (eds) *Making Places in the Prehistoric World*. London: UCL Press, 160–77.

Knappett, C. 2011. Networks of objects, meshworks of things. In T. Ingold (ed.) *Redrawing Anthropology: materials, movements, lines*. Farnham: Ashgate, 45–64.

Kuper, A. 1982. Lineage theory: a critical retrospect. *Annual Review of Anthropology* 11, 71–95.

La Motta, V. M. 2012 Behavioural archaeology. In I. Hodder (ed.) *Archaeological Theory Today* (2nd edn). Cambridge: Polity, 62–92

Lanting, J. N. and Brindley, A. L. 2001. Dating of cremated bones. *Radiocarbon* 43(2), 249–54.

Lawrence, D. 2006. Neolithic mortuary practice in Orkney. *Proceedings of the Society of Antiquaries of Scotland* 136, 47–60.

Lawrence, D. and Lee-Thorp, J. 2012. New radiocarbon dates from Isbister, Orkney. *Discovery and Excavation in Scotland* 13, 203.

Leach, S. 2005. Heads, shoulders, knees and toes: human skeletal remains from Raven Scar Cave in the Yorkshire Dales. In S. R. Zakrzewski and M. Clegg, (eds) *Proceedings of the Fifth Annual Conference of the British Association of Biological Anthropology and Osteoarchaeology*. Oxford: Archaeopress, 59–68.

Lee, D. 2011. *Banks Chambered Tomb, South Ronaldsay*. Kirkwall: ORKA.

Lee, D. and Thomas, A. 2011. *Braes of Ha'Breck, Wyre, Orkney: excavation 2011*. Unpublished ORCA Report 270.

Lee, D. and Woodward, N. 2008. *Links House, Stronsay, Orkney: excavations (Phase II)*. Unpublished ORCA Report 203.

Lee, D. and Woodward, N. 2009a. *Links House, Stronsay, Orkney: excavations (Phase III)*. Unpublished ORCA Report 213.

Lee, D. and Woodward, N. 2009b. Links House, Stronsay, Orkney (Stronsay parish), excavation. *Discovery Excavation Scotland*, new series 10, 141.

Lee, S. and Bronk Ramsey, C. 2012. Development and application of the trapezoidal models for archaeological chronologies. *Radiocarbon* 51(1), 107–22.

Lévi-Strauss, C. 1982. *The Way of the Masks*, (trans. S. Modelski). Seattle and London: University of Washington Press.

Lévi-Strauss, C. 1987. *Anthropology and Myth: lectures 1951–1982*. Oxford: Blackwell.

Lin, N. 1999. Building a network theory of social capital. *Connections* 22(1), 28–51.

Livingstone Smith, A. 2001. Bonfire II: the return of pottery firing temperatures. *Journal of Archaeological Science* 28, 991–1003

Low, G. 1879. *A Tour Through the Islands of Orkney and Schetland: Containing Hints Relative to Their Ancient, Modern, and Natural History Collected in 1774*. J. Anderson, ed. Kirkwall: William Peace & Son.

Lyman, R. L. 2001. *Vertebrate Taphonomy*. Cambridge: Cambridge University Press.

Lynch, A. 1983. The seed remains. In J. W. Hedges (ed.) *Isbister: A Chambered Tomb in Orkney*. Oxford: British Archaeological Report 115, 171–6.

Lynch, F. 1973. The use of the passage in certain passage graves as a means of communication rather than access. In G. Daniel and P. Kjaerum (eds) *Megalithic Graves and Ritual: papers presented at the III Atlantic colloquium, Moesgård 1969*. Copenhagen: Jutland Archaeological Society Publications XI, 147–62.

Macdonald, C. (ed.) 1987. *De la hutte au palaise: sociétés 'à maisons' en Asie du Sud–est insulaire*. Paris: Editions du CNRS.

MacGregor, M., Lee, G. W. and Wilson, G. V. 1920. *Special Reports on the Mineral Resources of Great Britain* XI, Iron ores of Scotland. Memoirs of the Geological Survey of Scotland. Edinburgh: HMSO.

Mackay, W. 1905. The Oyce of Firth. In M. M. Charleson (ed.) *Orcadian Papers, being the selections from the Proceedings of the Orkney Natural History Society* 1887–1904. Stromness, 25–31.

MacSween, A. 1992. Orcadian Grooved Ware. In N. Sharples and A. Sheridan (eds) *Vessels for the Ancestors*. Edinburgh: Edinburgh University Press, 259–71.

MacSween, A. 1995. Grooved ware in Scotland: aspects of decoration. In I. Kinnes and G. Varndell (eds) *Unbaked Urns of Rudely Shape*. Oxford: Oxbow Monograph 55, 41–48.

MacSween, A. 1997. The pottery. In J. Barber (ed.) *The

Excavation of a Stalled Cairn at the Point of Cott, Westray, Orkney. Edinburgh; Scottish Trust for Archaeological Research, 27–29.

MacSween, A. 2007. The pottery. In J. Hunter with J. M. Bond and Andrea N. Smith (eds) *Investigations in Sanday, Orkney: a multi-period settlement from Neolithic to Late Norse times.* Kirkwall: The Orcadian Ltd, 287–345.

MacSween, A. in press. Regional and local identities in the later Neolithic of Scotland as reflected in the ceramic record. In L. Campbell, L., N. Hall and A. D. Wright (eds) *Roots of Nationhood: the archaeology and history of Scotland.* Springer.

Mant, A. K. (ed.) 1984. *Taylor's Principles and Practice of Medical Jurisprudence.* Edinburgh and New York: Churchill Livingstone.

Mant, A. K. 1987. Knowledge acquired from post-war exhumations. In A. Boddington, A. N. Garland and R. C. Janaway (eds) *Death, Decay and Reconstruction: approaches to archaeology and forensic science.* Manchester: Manchester University Press.

Maritan, L. and Mazzoli, C. 2004. Phosphates in archaeological finds: implications for environmental conditions of burial. *Archaeometry* 46, 673–683.

Marshall, Y. 2000. Transformations of Nuu-chah-nulth houses. In R. A. Joyce and S. D. Gillespie (eds) *Beyond Kinship: social and material reproduction in house societies.* Philadelphia: University of Pennsylvania Press, 73–102.

Marwick, E. W. 1975. *The Folklore of Orkney and Shetland.* London: Batsford.

Marwick, H. 1929. Skerrabrae. *Proceedings of the Orkney Antiquarian Society* 7, 17–26.

Masters, L. 1997. The excavation and restoration of the Camster Long chambered cairn, Caithness, Highland, 1967–80. *Proceedings of the Society of Antiquaries of Scotland* 127, 123–83.

Matthews, W., French, C. Lawrence, T., Cutler, D. and Jones, M. K. 1997. Microstratigraphic traces of site formation process and human activities. *World Archaeology* 29, 281–308.

Mayer, R. M. 1991. *The Artists Handbook of Materials and Techniques.* London: Faber and Faber.

Mayewski, P. A., Buckland, P. C., Edwards, K. J., Meeker, L. D. and O'Brien, S. 1996. Climate change events as seen in the Greenland Ice Core (GISP2). In T. Pollard and A. Morrison (eds) *The Early Prehistory of Scotland.* Edinburgh: Edinburgh University Press, 74–84.

Mays, S. 1998. *The Archaeology of Human Bones.* London: Routledge.

Mays, S. 2000. Asymmetry in metacarpal cortical bone in a collection of British post–Medieval skeletons. *Journal of Archaeological Science* 29, 435–41.

McCormick, F. and Buckland, P. C. 1997. The vertebrate fauna. In K. J. Edwards and I. B. M. Ralston (eds) *Scotland: environment and archaeology 8000 BC–AD 1000.* London: Wiley and Sons, 83–103.

McKenna, L. E. and Simpson, I. A. 2011. Thin section micromorphology of anthrosols (Area 1) . In H. Moore and G. Wilson (eds) *Shifting Sands: Links of Noltland, Westray:*

interim report on Neolithic and Bronze Age excavations, 2007–09. Edinburgh: Historic Scotland Archaeology Report 4, 77–89.

McKenzie, J. 2007. Manuring practices in Scotland: deep anthropogenic soils and the historical record. In B. Ballin Smith, S. Taylor and G. Williams (eds) *West Over Sea: Studies In Scandinavian Sea-Borne Expansion And Settlement Before 1300.* Leiden: Brill (Northern World Series), 401–417.

McKinley, J. I. 1993. Bone fragment size and weights of bone from modern british cremations and the implications for the interpretation of archaeological cremations. *International Journal of Osteoarchaeology* 3, 283–87.

McKinley, J. I. 1997. Bronze Age barrows and funerary rites and rituals of cremation *Proceedings of the Prehistoric Society* 63, 129–45.

McKinley, J. I. 2000. The analysis of cremated bone. In M. Cox and S. Mays (eds) *Human Osteology in Archaeology and Forensic Science.* London: Greenwich Medical Media, 403–21.

McKinley, J. I. 2004. Compiling an inventory: cremated human bone. In M. Brickley and J. I. McKinley (eds) *Guidelines to the Standards for Recording Human Remains.* British Association for Biological Anthropology and Osteoarchaeology, IFA Paper 7, 9–13.

McKinley, J. I. 2006. Cremation ... the cheap option? In R. Gowland and C. Knüsel (eds) *Social Archaeology of Funerary Remains.* Oxford: Oxbow Books, 81–88.

McKinley, J. I. 2008. Human remains. In R. Mercer and F. Healey (eds) *Hambledon Hill, Dorset, England: excavations and survey of a Neolithic monument complex and its surrounding landscape.* London: English Heritage Archaeological Report.

McLaren, D. 2011. The course stone. In H. Moore and G. Wilson (eds) *Shifting Sands: Links of Noltland Westray, interim report on Neolithic and Bronze Age excavations, 2007–09.* Edinburgh: Historic Scotland Archaeology Report 4, 99–103.

McSweeney, K. 1995. Report on Cremated Bone. In Smith, A. N. 1995. The excavation of a Neolithic, Bronze Age and early historic features near Ratho Edinburgh. *Proceeding of the Society of Antiquaries of Scotland* 125, 69–138.

Megaw, J. V. S. and D. D. A. Simpson. 1979. *Introduction to British Prehistory.* Leicester: Leicester University Press.

Melton, N. D. and Nicholson, R. A. 2007. A late Mesolithic–Early Neolithic midden at West Voe, Sumburgh, Shetland. In N. Milner, O. E. Craig and G. N. Bailey (eds) *Shell Middens in Atlantic Europe.* Oxford: Oxbow Books, 94–100.

Meskell, L. M. and Renfrew, C. 2000. From social to cognitive archaeology: an interview with Colin Renfrew. *Journal of Social Archaeology* 1(1), 13–34.

Metcalf, P. and Huntington, R. 1991. *Celebrations of Death. The Anthropology of Mortuary Ritual.* Cambridge: Cambridge University Press.

Middleton, R. 2005. The Barnhouse lithic assemblage. In C. Richards (ed.) *Dwelling Among the Monuments: the Neolithic village of Barnhouse, Maeshowe passage grave and surrounding monuments at Stenness, Orkney.* Cambridge: McDonald Institute Monograph, 293–322.

Miles, M. J. 2010. Green, Eday, Orkney. *Discovery and Excavation* 11, 119–20.

Miles, M. J. 2011. *A fourth season of excavation on a Neolithic settlement site at Green, Isle of Eday.* Unpublished report BEVARS.

Millard, A. 2014. Conventions for reporting radiocarbon determinations. *Radiocarbon* 56(2), 555–59.

Miller, J. and S. Ramsay. 2002. Plant macrofossils. In G. J. Barclay, K. Brophy and G. MacGregor, Claish, Stirling: an early Neolithic structure in its context. *Proceedings of the Society of Antiquaries of Scotland* 132, 90–96.

Miller, J., Dickson, J. H. and Dixon, T. N. 1998. Unusual food plants from Oakbank Crannog, Loch Tay, Scottish Highlands: cloudberry, opium poppy and spelt wheat. *Antiquity* 72, 805–11.

Montgomery, J., Beaumont, J., Jay, M., Keefe, K., Gledhill, A., Cook, G., Dockrill, S. and Melton, N. 2013. Strategic and sporadic marine consumption at the onset of the Neolithic: increasing temporal and resolution in the isotope evidence. *Antiquity* 87, 106–72.

Mook, W. and Waterbolk, H. 1985. *Handbook for Archaeologists. No 3. Radiocarbon Dating.* Strasbourg: European Science Foundation.

Moore, H. and Wilson, G. 1995. Two Orcadian Cist burials: excavations at Midskaill, Egilsay, and Linga Fiold, Sandwick. *Proceedings of the Society of Antiquaries of Scotland* 125, 237–51.

Moore, H. and Wilson, G. (eds) 2011. *Shifting Sands: Links of Noltland Westray, interim report on Neolithic and Bronze Age excavations, 2007–09.* Edinburgh: Historic Scotland Archaeology Report 4.

Moore, P. D., Webb, J. A. and Collinson, M. E. 1991. *Pollen Analysis* (2nd edn). Oxford: Blackwell Scientific Publications.

Mottram, H. R., Dudd, S. N., Lawrence, G. J., Stott, A. W. and Evershed, R. P. 1999. New chromatographic, mass spectrometric and stable isotope approaches to the classification of degraded animal fats preserved in archaeological pottery. *Journal of Chromatography* A 833, 209–221.

Mukherjee, A. J., Copley, M. S., Berstan, R., Clark, K. A. and Evershed, R. P. 2005. Interpretation of δ13C values of fatty acids in relation to animal husbandry, food processing and consumption in prehistory. In J. Mulville and A. K. Outram (eds) *The Zooarchaeology of Fats, Oils, Milk and Dairying.* Oxford: Oxbow Books, 77–93.

Mukherjee. A. J., Berstan, R., Copley, M. S., Gibson, A. M. and Evershed, R. P. 2007. Compound-specific stable carbon isotopic detection of pig product processing in British Late Neolithic pottery. *Antiquity* 81, 743–54.

Mukherjee, A. J., Gibson, A. M. and Evershed, R. P. 2008. Trends in pig product processing at British Neolithic Grooved Ware sites traced through organic residues in potsherds. *Journal of Archaeological Science* 35, 2059–73.

Murphy, C. P. 1986. *Preparation of Soils and Sediments in Thin Section.* Berkhamsted: AB Academic.

Murphy, E. and Simpson, D. 2003. Neolithic Northton: a review of the evidence. In I. Armit, E. Murphy, E. Neils and D. Simpson (eds) *Neolithic Settlement in Ireland and Western Britain.* Oxford: Oxbow Books, 101–11.

Musterd, S. 2003. Segregation and integration: a contested relationship. *Journal of Ethnic and Migrations Studies* 29(4), 623–41.

Mykura, W. 1976. *British Regional Geology: Orkney and Shetland.* Edinburgh: HMSO.

Myres, A. 1989. Reliable and maintainable technological strategies in the Mesolithic of mainland Britain. In R. Torrence (ed.) *Time, Energy and Stone Tools.* Cambridge: Cambridge University Press, 78–90.

Nature Conservancy Council. 1978. *Orkney: Localities of geological and geomorphological importance.* Newbury.

Nast, J. and Blokland, T. 2014. Social mix revisited: neighbourhood institutions as setting for boundary work and social capital. *Sociology* 48, 482–99.

Noble, G. 2006a. *Neolithic Scotland. Timber, Stone, Earth and Fire*, Edinburgh University Press.

Noble, G. 2006b. Tree architecture: building monuments from the forest. *Journal of Iberian Archaeology* 8, 54–72.

Noddle, B. A. 1983. Animal bone from Knap of Howar, in A. Ritchie, Excavation of a Neolithic farmstead at Knap of Howar, Papa Westray, Orkney. *Proceedings of the Society of Antiquaries of Scotland* 113, 92–100.

Nowakowski, J. A. 2001. Leaving home in the Cornish Bronze Age: insights into planned abandonment processes. In J. Brück (ed.) *Bronze Age Landscapes: tradition and transformation.* Oxford: Oxbow Books, 139–48.

Oestigaard, T. 2000. *The Deceased's Life Rituals in Nepal: present cremation burials for the interpretations of the Past.* Oxford: British Archaeological Report S853.

O'Kelly, C. 1982. Corpus of Newgrange art. In M. J. O'Kelly (ed.) *Newgrange: archaeology, art and legend.* London: Thames and Hudson, 146–85.

Ortner, D. J. 2003. *Identification of Pathological Conditions in Human Skeletal Remains* (2nd edn). London: Academic Press.

Orton, C., Tyres P. and Vince, A. 2003. *Pottery in Archaeology.* Chicago: Chicago University Press.

O'Sullivan, M. 1993. *Megalithic Art in Ireland.* Dublin: Country House.

O'Sullivan, M. 2005. *The Mound of Hostages, Tara.* Dublin: Wordwell.

Øvrevik, S. 1990. The second millennium BC and after. In C. Renfrew (ed.) *The Prehistory of Orkney.* Edinburgh: Edinburgh University Press, 131–49.

Owen, O. and Lowe, C. 1999. *Kebister, the four-thousand-year-old story of one Shetland township.* Edinburgh: Society of Antiquaries of Scotland Monograph 14.

Parker-Pearson, M. 2004. Island prehistories: a view of Orkney from South Uist. In J. Cherry, C. Scarre and S. Shennan (eds) *Explaining social change: studies in honour of Colin Renfrew.* Cambridge: McDonald Institute Monographs, 127–40.

Parker-Pearson, M. and Richards, C. 1994. *Architecture and Order: approaches to social space.* London: Routledge.

Parker-Pearson, M. and Sharples, N. M. 1999. *Between Land and Sea: excavations at Dun Vulan, South Uist.* Sheffield: Sheffield Academic Press.

Peach, C. W. 1860. On the chalk flints of the Island of Stroma, and vicinity of John o' Groat's in the County of Caithness. *Proceedings of the Royal Physical Society of Edinburgh* 2, 159–61.

Pedersen, P. D. 2013. Forensic medicine – seen through the eyes of a social anthropologist. *Scandinavian Journal of Forensic Science* 19(1), 13–15.

Petrie, G. 1860. Notice of a barrow at Huntisgarth in the parish of Harray, recently opened. *Proceedings of the Society of Antiquaries of Scotland* 3, 195.

Petrie, G. 1867. Notice of ruins of ancient dwellings at Skara Brae, Bay of Skaill in the parish of Sandwick, Orkney, recently excavated. *Proceedings of the Society of Antiquaries of Scotland* 7, 201–19.

Philips, T. 2002. *Landscapes of the living, landscapes of the dead: the location of the chambered cairns of northern Scotland.* Oxford: British Archaeological Report 328.

Philips, T. 2003. Seascapes and landscapes in Orkney and northern Scotland. *World Archaeology* 35(3), 371–84.

Photos-Jones, E. and Hall, A. J. 2011. 'Harvesting' the ore: the use of iron seepages in the early bloomer furnaces in Ireland. In I. Turbanti-Memmi (ed.) *Proc. 37th International Symposium of Archaeometry.* Springer Verlag, 631–36.

Piggott, S. 1954. *Neolithic Cultures of the British Isles.* Cambridge: Cambridge University Press.

Pollard, J. 2004. The art of decay and the transformation of substance. In C. Renfrew, E. DeMarrais and C. Gosden (eds) *Substance, Memory, Display: archaeology and art.* Cambridge: McDonald Institute Monographs, 47–62.

Pollard, J. 2005. Memory, monuments and middens in the Neolithic landscape. In G. Brown, D. Field and D. McOmish (eds) *The Avebury Landscape: aspects of the field archaeology of the Marlborough Downs.* Oxford: Oxbow, 103–14.

Preston, C. D. 1995. *Pondweeds of Great Britain and Ireland (BSBI Handbook 8).* London: Botanical Society of the British Isles.

Punt, W. 1976–1991. *The Northwest European Pollen Flora* (vols 1–6). Amsterdam: Elsevier.

Rackham, J. 1994. *Animal Bones.* London: British Museum Press.

Ray, K. and Thomas, J. 2003. In the kinship of cows: the social centrality of cattle in the earlier Neolithic of southern Britain. In M. Parker Pearson (ed.) *Food, Culture and Identity in the Neolithic and Early Bronze Age.* Oxford: British Archaeological reports S1117, 37–44.

Raven, A. M., van Bergen, P. F., Stott, A. W., Dudd, S. N. and Evershed, R. P. 1997. Formation of long-chain ketones in archaeological pottery vessels by pyrolysis of acyl lipids. *Journal of Analytical and Applied Pyrolysis* 40–1, 267–285.

Redfern, R. 2008. New evidence for Iron Age secondary burial practice and bone modification from Gussage All Saints and Maiden Castle (Dorset, England). *Oxford Journal of Archaeology* 27, 283–301.

Reilly, S. 2003. Processing the dead in Neolithic Orkney. *Oxford Journal of Archaeology* 22, 133–54.

Reimer, P. J., Bayliss, A., Beck, J. W., Blackwell, P. G., Bronk Ramsey, C., Grootes, P. M. Guilderson, T. P., Haflidason, H.,

Hajdas, I., Hattž, C., Heaton, T. J., Hoffmann, D., Hogg, A. G., Hughen, K. A., Kaiser, K. F., Kromer, B., Manning, S. W., Niu, M., Reimer, R. W., Richards, D. A., Scott, E. M., Southon, J. R., Staff, R. A. Turney, C. S. M. and van der Plicht, J. 2013. IntCal13 and Marine13 Radiocarbon Age Calibration Curves 0–50,000 Years cal BP. *Radiocarbon,* 55(4), 1869–87.

Rein, A., Higgins, F. and Leung, P. T. 2011. Art Application Note 301, http://www.polytec.com/fileadmin/user_uploads/ Solutions/Spektroskopie/Documents/Art_App_301.pdf.

Reinhard, K. J. and Fink, T. M. 1994. Cremation in Southwestern North America: aspects of taphonomy that affect palaeopathological analysis. *Journal of Archaeological Science* 21, 597–605.

Rendall, R. 1931. Notes on a collection of flints from Wideford Hill. *Proceedings of the Orkney Antiquarian Society* 9, 21–24.

Rendall, R. 1934. Further notes on an Orkney flint field. *Proceedings of the Orkney Antiquarian Society* 12, 19–25.

Rendall, R. 1937. The South Ettit flint industries. *Proceedings of the Orkney Antiquarian Society* 14, 45–56.

Renfrew, C. 1973. *Before Civilization: the radiocarbon revolution and prehistoric Europe.* London: Jonathan Cape.

Renfrew, C. 1979. *Investigations in Orkney.* London: Thames and Hudson.

Renfrew, C. 1985. *The Prehistory of Orkney.* Edinburgh: Edinburgh University Press.

Renfrew, C. 1990. Epilogue. In C. Renfrew (ed.) *The Prehistory of Orkney* (2nd edn). Edinburgh: Edinburgh University Press, 243–61.

Renfrew, C., Harkness, D. and Switsur, R. 1976. Quanterness, radiocarbon and the Orkney cairns. *Antiquity* 50, 194–204.

Renfrew, C., Stenhouse, M. and Switsur, R. 1983. The radiocarbon determinations. In J. Hedges (ed.) *Isbister: A Chambered Tomb in Orkney.* Oxford; British Archaeological Report 115, 61–71.

Rice, P. M. 2005. *Pottery Analysis: a sourcebook.* Chicago: University of Chicago Press.

Richards, C. 1988. Altered images: a re-examination of Neolithic mortuary practices in Orkney. In J. Barrett and I. Kinnes (eds) *The Archaeology of Context in the Neolithic and Bronze Age.* Sheffield: University of Sheffield, 42–56.

Richards, C. 1990. The late Neolithic House in Orkney. In R. Samson (ed.) *The Social Archaeology of Houses.* Edinburgh: Edinburgh University Press, 111–24.

Richards, C. 1991. Skara Brae: revisiting a Neolithic village in Orkney. In W. S. Hanson and E. A. Slater (eds) *Scottish Archaeology: new perceptions,* Aberdeen University Press, Aberdeen, 24–43.

Richards, C. 1992. Doorways to another world, the Orkney-Cromarty chambered tombs. In N. Sharples and A. Sheridan (eds) *Vessels for the Ancestors, Essays on the Neolithic of Britain and Ireland.* Edinburgh: Edinburgh University Press, 62–76.

Richards, C. 1993a. *An Archaeological Study of Neolithic Orkney: Architecture, Order and Social Classification.* Unpublished PhD thesis: University of Glasgow.

Richards, C. 1993b. Contextual analysis of the Grooved Ware at Balfarg. In G. Barclay and C. J. Russel-White, Excavations in the ceremonial complex of the fourth to second millennium BC at Balfarg/Balbirnie, Glenrothes, Fife, *Proceedings of the Society of Antiquaries of Scotland* 123, 185–92.

Richards, C. 1995. V. G. Childe at Skara Brae and Rinyo: research and redemption. In P. Gathercole, T. Irving and G. Melleuish (eds) *Childe and Australia.* Brisbane: University of Queensland Press, 118–27.

Richards, C. 1996a. Henges and water, towards an elemental understanding of monumentality and landscape in late Neolithic Britain. *Journal of Material Culture* 1(3), 313–36.

Richards, C. 1996b. Monuments as landscape: creating the centre of the world in late Neolithic Orkney. *World Archaeology* 28, 190–208.

Richards, C. 1998. Centralizing tendencies: social evolution in Neolithic Orkney. In M. Edmonds and C. Richards (eds) *Understanding the Neolithic of Northwest Europe.* Glasgow: Cruithne Press, 516–32.

Richards, C. 2000. Monumental choreography: architecture and spatial representation in late Neolithic Orkney. In J. Thomas (ed.) *Interpretive Archaeology: a reader.* London: Routledge, 541–60.

Richards, C. 2005a. The Neolithic settlement of Orkney. In C. Richards (ed.) *Dwelling Among the Monuments: the Neolithic village of Barnhouse, Maeshowe passage grave and surrounding monuments at Stenness, Orkney.* Cambridge: McDonald Institute Monograph, 7–22.

Richards, C. 2005b. The ceremonial House 2. In C. Richards (ed.) *Dwelling Among the Monuments: the Neolithic village of Barnhouse, Maeshowe passage grave and surrounding monuments at Stenness, Orkney.* Cambridge: McDonald Institute Monograph, 129–56.

Richards, C. (ed.) 2005c. *Dwelling Among the Monuments: the Neolithic village of Barnhouse, Maeshowe passage grave and surrounding monuments at Stenness, Orkney.* Cambridge: McDonald Institute Monograph.

Richards, C. 2008. The substance of Polynesian voyaging. *World Archaeology* 40(2), 206–23.

Richards, C. (ed.) 2013. *Building the Great Stone Circles of the North.* Oxford: Windgather Press.

Richards, C. 2013a. Interpreting stone circles. In C. Richards (ed.) *Building the Great Stone Circles of the North.* Oxford: Windgather Press, 2–30.

Richards, C. 2013b. Wrapping the hearth; constructing house societies and the tall Stones of Stenness. In C. Richards (ed.) *Building the Great Stone Circles of the North.* Oxford: Windgather Press, 64–89.

Richards, C. 2013c. The sanctity of crags: mythopraxis, transformation and the Calanais low circles. In C. Richards (ed.) *Building the Great Stone Circles of the North.* Oxford: Windgather Press, 254–80.

Richards, C. and Thomas, J. 1984. Ritual activity and structured deposition in later Neolithic Wessex. In R. Bradley and J. Gardiner (eds) *Neolithic Studies.* Oxford: British Archaeological Report 133, 189–218.

Richards, C., Clarke, A., Ingrem, C. and Mulville, J. forthcoming. Over the wall: a late Neolithic butchery site at Skaill Bay, Mainland, Orkney. *Proceedings of the Society of Antiquaries of Scotland.*

Richards, C., Brown, J., Jones, S., Hall, A. and Muir, T. 2013. Monumental risk: megalithic quarrying at Staneyhill and Vestra Fiold, Mainland, Orkney. In C. Richards (ed.) *Building the Great Stone Circles of the North.* Oxford: Windgather Press, 119–48.

Richards, M. P. and Schulting, R. 2006. Touch not the fish: the Mesolithic–Neolithic change of diet and its significance. *Antiquity* 80, 444–56.

Ritchie, A. 1983. Excavations of a Neolithic farmstead at Knap of Howar, Papa Westray, Orkney. *Proceedings of the Society of Antiquaries of Scotland* 113, 40–121.

Ritchie, A. 1990a. The first settlers. In C. Renfrew (ed.) *The Prehistory of Orkney.* Edinburgh: Edinburgh University Press, 36–53.

Ritchie, A. 1990b. Orkney in the Pictish kingdom. In C. Renfrew (ed.) *The Prehistory of Orkney.* Edinburgh: Edinburgh University Press, 183–204.

Ritchie, A. 1995. *Prehistoric Orkney.* London: Batsford/Historic Scotland.

Ritchie, A. 2009. *On the Fringe of Neolithic Europe: excavation of a chambered cairn on the Holm of Papa Westray, Orkney.* Edinburgh: Society of Antiquaries of Scotland Monograph.

Ritchie, A. and Ritchie, G. 1974. Excavation of a barrow at Queenafjold, Twatt, Orkney. *Proceedings of the Society of Antiquaries of Scotland* 105, 33–40.

Ritchie, A. and Ritchie, G. 1981. *Scotland, Archaeology and Early History.* London; Thames and Hudson.

Ritchie, J. N. G. 1976. The Stones of Stenness, Orkney. *Proceedings of the Society of Antiquaries of Scotland* 107, 1–60.

Ritchie, R. 1992. Stone axeheads and cushion maceheads from Orkney and Shetland: some similarities and contrasts. In N. Sharples and A. Sheridan (eds) *Vessels for the Ancestors, Essays on the Neolithic of Britain and Ireland.* Edinburgh: Edinburgh University Press, 213–20.

Roberts, C. and Manchester, K. 1995. *The Archaeology of Disease* (2nd edn). Stroud: Alan Sutton.

Roberts, J. A. 1995. The taphonomy of cremated human remains: an experimental study of the fragmentation of bone from the bronze age cremation cemetery at Linga Fold, Orkney. Unpublished MSc dissertation, University of Sheffield.

Roberts, J. A. 2003. *The Cremated Remains from a Bronze Age Mortuary Site, Loth Road, Sanday, Orkney.* GUARD Project 1587, report for Orkney Archaeological Trust.

Roberts, J. A. 2004. *Cremated Remains from Knowes of Trotty, Harray, Orkney.* GUARD Project 1367, report for Orkney Archaeological Trust.

Robertson, J. and Woodward, N. 2007. Excavation at Long Howe, Tankerness, Orkney. Unpublished Structures Report, Kirkwall: ORCA.

Robin, G. 2008. *Neolithic Passage Tomb Art Around the Irish Sea: iconography and spatial association.* PhD thesis, University of Nantes.

Robin, G. 2010. Spatial structures and symbolic systems in Irish and British passage tombs: the organization of architectural elements, parietal carved signs and funerary deposits. *Cambridge Archaeological Journal* 20(3), 373–418.

Rock, N. M. S. 1983. *The Permo-Carboniferous Camptonite-monchiquite Dyke-suite of the Scottish Highlands: Distribution, field and petrological aspects*. HMSO Institute of Geological Sciences, Report 82/14.

Roksandic, M. 2002. Position of skeletal remains as a key to understanding mortuary behavior. In W. D. Haglund and M. H. Sorg (eds) *Advances in Forensic Taphonomy. Method, Theory and Archaeological Perspectives*. New York: CRC Press.

Russell, N., Cook, G., Ascough, P. and Dugmore, A. 2011. Examining the inherent variability in ΔR: new methods of presenting ΔR values and implications for MRE studies. *Radiocarbon* 53(2), 277–88.

Saul, J. M. and Saul, F. P. 2002. Forensics, archaeology, and taphonomy: the symbiotic relationship. In W. D. Haglund and M. H. Sorg (eds) *Advances in Forensic Taphonomy. Method, Theory and Archaeological Perspectives*. New York: CRC Press.

Saville, A. 1980. On the measurement of struck flakes and flake tools. *Lithics* 1, 16–20.

Saville, A. 2000. Orkney and Scotland before the Neolithic period. In A. Ritchie (ed.) *Neolithic Orkney in its European Context*. Cambridge: McDonald Institute Monograph, 91–100.

Scarre, C., Arias, P., Burenhult, G., Fano, M., Oosterbeek, L., Schulting, R., Sheridan A. and Whittle, A. 2003. Megalithic chronologies. In G. Burenhult (ed.) *Stones and Bones: formal disposal of the dead in Atlantic Europe during the Mesolithic–Neolithic interface 6000–3000 BC*. Oxford: British Archaeological Report S1201, 65–114.

Schiffer, M. 1972. Archaeological context and systemic context. *American Antiquity* 37, 156–65.

Schiffer, M. 1976. *Behavioural Archaeology*. New York: Academic Press.

Schneider, D. M. 1965. Some muddles in the models: or, how the system really works. In M. Banton (ed.) *The relevance of models for Social Anthropology*. London: Tavistock Press, 25–85.

Schneider, D. M. 1984. *A Critique of the Study of Kinship*. Ann Arbor: University of Michigan Press.

Schroeder, S. 2001. Secondary disposal of the dead: cross-cultural codes. *World Cultures* 12: 77–93.

Schulting, R. 2000. New AMS dates from the Lambourn long barrow and the question of the earliest Neolithic in southern England: repacking the Neolithic package? *Oxford Journal of Archaeology* 19(1), 25–35.

Schulting, R. 2004. An Irish Sea change: some implications for the Mesolithic–Neolithic transition. In V. Cummings and C. Fowler (eds) *The Neolithic of the Irish Sea: materiality and traditions of practice*. Oxford: Oxbow Books, 22–28.

Schulting, R. 2008. Foodways and social ecologies: early Mesolithic to Early Bronze Age. In J. Pollard (ed.) *Prehistoric Britain*. London: Blackwell, 90–120.

Schulting, R. and Richards, M. 2009. Radiocarbon dates and stable isotope values on human remains. In A. Ritchie (ed.) *On the Fringe of Neolithic Europe: excavation of a chambered cairn on the Holm of Papa Westray, Orkney*. Edinburgh: Society of Antiquaries of Scotland Monograph, 66–74.

Schulting, R., Murphy, E., Jones, C. and Warren, G. 2012. New dates from the north and a proposed chronology for Irish court tombs. *Proceedings of the Royal Irish Academy* 112C, 1–60.

Schulting, R., Sheridan, A., Crozier, R. and Murphy, E. 2010. Revisiting Quanterness: new AMS dates and stable isotope data from an Orcadian chambered tomb. *Proceedings of the Society of Antiquaries of Scotland* 140, 1–50.

Schultz, M. 2001. Paleohistopathology of bone: a new approach to the study of ancient diseases. *Yearbook of Physical Anthropology* 44, 106–47.

Schweingruber, F. H. 1990. *Anatomy of European Woods*. Berne and Stuttgart: Paul Haupt.

Scott, W. L. 1950. Eilean an Tighe; a pottery workshop of the 2nd millennium BC. *Proceedings of the Society of Antiquaries of Scotland* 85, 1–37.

Serjeantson, D. 2006. Food or feast at Neolithic Runnymeade? In D. Serjeantson and D. Field (eds) *Animals in the Neolithic of Britain and Europe*. Oxford: Oxbow Books, 113–34.

Sharples, N. 1984. Excavations at Pierowall Quarry, Westray, Orkney. *Proceedings of the Society of Antiquaries of Scotland* 114: 75–125.

Sharples, N. 1985. Individual and community, the changing role of megaliths in the Orcadian Neolithic. *Proceedings of the Prehistoric Society* 51, 59–74.

Sharples, N. 1992. Aspects of regionalisation in the Scottish Neolithic. In N. Sharples and A. Sheridan (eds) *Vessels for the Ancestors: essays on the Neolithic of Britain and Ireland*. Edinburgh: Edinburgh University Press, 322–31.

Sharples, N. 2000. Antlers and Orcadian rituals: an ambiguous role for Red Deer in the Neolithic. In A. Ritchie (ed.) *Neolithic Orkney in its European Context*. Cambridge: McDonald Institute Monograph, 107–16.

Shee Twohig, E. 1981. *The Megalithic Art of Western Europe*. Oxford: Clarendon.

Sheridan, A. 1999. Grooved Ware from the Links of Noltland, Westray, Orkney. In R. Cleal and A. MacSween (eds) *Grooved Ware in Britain and Ireland*. Oxford: Oxbow Books, 112–24.

Sheridan, A. 2000. Achnacreebeg and its French connections: viva the 'auld aliiance'. In J. C. Henderson (ed.) *The Prehistory and Early History of Atlantic Europe*. Oxford: British Archaeological Report S861, 1–16.

Sheridan, A. 2003. French connections I: spreading the marmite thinly. In I. Armit, I. Murphy, E. Nelis and D. Simpson (eds) *Neolithic Settlement in Ireland and Western Britain*. Oxford: Oxbow Books, 3–17.

Sheridan, A. 2005a. Cuween, Cuween-Wideford project. *Discovery and excavation in Scotland* 6, 177.

Sheridan, A. 2005b. The National Museums of Scotland Radiocarbon dating programmes: results obtained during 2004/2005. *Discovery and Excavation in Scotland* 6, 182–3.

Sheridan, A. 2010. The Neolithization of Britain and Ireland: the 'big picture'. In B. Finlayson and G. Warren (eds) *Landscapes in Transition*. Oxford; Oxbow Books, 89–105.

Sheridan, A. 2012. Neolithic Shetland: a view from the 'mainland'. In D. L. Mahler (ed.) *The Border of Farming and Cultural Markers.* Copenhagen: National Museum of Denmark, 6–31.

Sheridan, A. 2014. Little and large: the miniature 'carved stone ball' beads from the eastern passage tomb under the main mound at Knowth, Ireland, and their broader significance. In R.-M. Arbogast and A. Greffier-Richard (eds) *Entre archéologie et écologie, une préhistoire de tous les milieux. Mélanges offerts à Pierre Pétrequin.* Besançon: Presses universitaires de Franche-Comté, 303–314.

Sheridan, A. and Davis, M. 2002. Investigating jet and jet-like artefacts from prehistoric Scotland: the National Museums of Scotland project. *Antiquity* 76, 812–25.

Sheridan, A. J., Goldberg, M., Blackwell, A., Mahler, D., Richards, M., Duffy, P., Gibson, A., Macniven, A. and Caldwell, D. 2012. Radiocarbon dates associated with the Scottish History and Archaeology Department, National Museums Scotland 2011/12. *Discovery and Excavation in Scotland* 13, 200–202.

Sheridan, A. and Higham, T. 2006. The redating of some Scottish specimens by the Oxford Radiocarbon Accelerator (ORAU). *Discovery and Excavation in Scotland 2006*, 202–204.

Sheridan, A. and Higham, T. 2007. The redating of some Scottish specimens by the Oxford Radiocarbon Accelerator (ORAU): results received during 2007. *Discovery and Excavation in Scotland 2007*, 225.

Shipman, P., Foster, G. and Schoeninger, M. 1984. Burnt bones and teeth: an experimental study of colour, morphology, crystal structure and shrinkage. *Journal of Archaeological Science* 11, 307–25.

Simpson, D. and Ransom, R. 1992. Maceheads and the Orcadian Neolithic. In N. Sharples and A. Sheridan (eds) *Vessels for the Ancestors, essays on the Neolithic of Britain and Ireland.* Edinburgh: Edinburgh University Press, 221–43.

Simpson, I. A. 1997. Relict properties of anthropogenic deep top soils as indicators of infield land management in Marwick, West Mainland, Orkney. *Journal of Archaeological Science* 24, 365–80.

Simpson, I. A. 1998. Early land management at Tofts Ness, Sanday, Orkney: the evidence of thin section micromorphology. In C. M. Mills and G. Coles (eds) *Life on the Edge: human settlement and marginality.* Oxford: Oxbow Books Monograph 100, 91–98.

Simpson, I. A. and Dockrill, S. J. 1996. Early cultivated soils at Tofts Ness, Sanday, Orkney. In A. M. Hall (ed.) *The Quaternary of Orkney: Field guide.* Cambridge: Quaternary Research Association, 130–44.

Simpson, I. A., Vesteinsson, O., Adderley, W. P. and McGovern, T. H. 2003. Fuel resource utilisation in landscapes of settlement. *Journal of Archaeological Science* 30, 1401–20

Simpson, I. A., Guttmann, E. B., Cluett, J. and Shepherd, A. 2006. Characterising anthropic sediments in north European Neolithic settlements: an assessment from Skara Brae, Orkney. *Geoarchaeology* 21, 221–35.

Sissons, J. 2010. Building a house society: the reorganization of Maori communities around meeting houses. *Journal of the Royal Anthropological Society* (NS) 16, 372–86.

Smith, A. 2001. Bonfire II: The return of pottery firing temperatures. *Journal of Archaeological Science* 28, 991–1003.

Smith, C. and Hodgson, G. W. I. 1994. Animal bone report. In B. Ballin Smith (ed.) *Howe: four millennia of Orkney prehistory.* Edinburgh: Society of Antiquaries of Scotland Monograph 9, 139–53.

Smith, C. 2002. *The Mammal Bone from Claish, Callander.* Archive report for Stirling University/First Farmers Project.

Smith, M. 2005. 'Picking up the pieces': an investigation of Cotswold-Severn funerary practices via re-analysis of human skeletal material from selected monuments. Unpublished PhD thesis, University of Birmingham.

Smith, M. 2006. Bones chewed by canids as evidence for human excarnation: a British case study. *Antiquity* 80, 671–85.

Smith, M. and Brickley, M. 2004. Analysis and interpretation of flint toolmarks found on bones from West Tump long barrow, Gloucestershire. *International Journal of Osteoarchaeology* 14, 18–33.

Smith, M. and Brickley, M. 2009. *People of the Long Barrows. Life, Death and Burial in the Earlier Neolithic.* Stroud: History Press.

Smyth, J. 2010. The house and group identity in the Irish Neolithic. *Proceedings of the Royal Irish Academy* 111C, 1–31.

Smyth, J. 2014. *Settlement in the Irish Neolithic. New Discoveries at the Edge of Europe.* Oxford: Prehistoric Society Research Papers 6/Oxbow Books.

Sofaer, J. R. 2006. *The Body as Material Culture,* Cambridge, Cambridge University Press.

Spence, T. F. 1968. The anatomical study of cremated bone fragments from archaeological sites. *Proceedings of the Prehistoric Society* 33, 70–83.

Spencer, J. Q. G. and Sanderson, D. C. W. 2012. Decline in firing technology or poorer fuel resources? High–temperature thermoluminescence (HTTL) archaeothermometry of Neolithic ceramics from Pool, Sanday, Orkney. *Journal of Archaeological Science* 39, 3542–52.

Spratt, G. 1830. *Flora Medica: containing coloured delineations of the various medicinal plants admitted into the London and Dublin pharmacopoeias* (vol. 2). London: Callow and Wilson.

Stace, C. 1997. *New Flora of the British Isles* (2nd edn). Cambridge: Cambridge University Press.

Stevanovic, M. 1996. The age of clay: the social dynamics of house destruction. *Journal of Anthropological Archaeology* 16, 334–95.

Stevens, C. J. and Fuller, D. Q. 2012. Did Neolithic farming fail? The case for a Bronze Age agricultural revolution in the British Isles. *Antiquity* 86, 707–22.

Stout, G. and Stout, M. 2008. *Newgrange.* Cork: Cork University Press.

Stross, B. 1997. Mesoamerican copal resins: Austin, University of Texas at Austin. *U Mut Maya* VI, 177–186.

Stuiver, M. and Reimer, P. 1993. Extended ^{14}C data base and revised CALIB 3.0 ^{14}C age calibration program. *Radiocarbon* 35(1), 215–30.

Stuiver, M. and Reimer, P. 1986. A computer program for radiocarbon age calculation. *Radiocarbon* 28, 1022–30.

Stuiver, M. and Braziunas, T. 1993. Modelling atmospheric

^{14}C influences and ^{14}C ages of marine samples to 10000 BC. *Radiocarbon* 35(1), 137–91.

Sturt, F. 2005. Fishing for meaning: lived space and the early Neolithic of Orkney. In V. Cummings and A. Pannet (eds) *Set in Stone: new approaches to Neolithic monuments in Scotland*. Oxford: Oxbow.

Tanizaki, J. 2001. *In Praise of Shadows*. London: Vintage.

Taylor, T. 2003. *The Buried Soul. How Humans Invented Death*. London: Fourth Estate.

Thomas, A. 2008. Braes of Ha'Breck, Wyre: excavation. *Discovery and Excavation in Scotland* 9, 131–32.

Thomas, A. and Lee, D. 2012. Orkneys first farmers: early Neolithic settlement on Wyre. *Current Archaeology* 268, 12–19.

Thomas, J. 1988. Neolithic explanations revisited: the Mesolithic–Neolithic transition in Britain and southern Scandinavia, *Proceedings of the Prehistoric Society* 54, 59–66.

Thomas, J. 1991. *Rethinking the Neolithic*. Cambridge: Cambridge University Press.

Thomas, J. 1995. Neolithic houses in mainland Britain and Ireland – a skeptical view. In T. Darvill and J. Thomas (eds) *Neolithic Houses in Northwest Europe and Beyond*. Oxford: Oxbow Monograph 57, 1–12.

Thomas, J. 1997. The materiality of the Mesolithic–Neolithic transition in Britain. *Analecta Praehistorica Leidensia* 29, 57–64.

Thomas, J. 1999. *Understanding the Neolithic*. London: Routledge.

Thomas, J. 2000. Death, identity and the body in Neolithic Britain. *Journal of the Royal Anthropological Institute* 6, 603–17.

Thomas, J. 2001. Archaeologies of place and landscape. In I. Hodder (ed.) *Archaeological Theory Today*. Cambridge and Oxford: Polity Press.

Thomas, J. 2008. The Mesolithic–Neolithic transition in Britain. In J. Pollard (ed.) *Prehistoric Britain*. Oxford: Blackwell Publishing, 58–89.

Thomas, J. 2010. The return of the Rinyo-Clacton folk? The cultural significance of the Grooved Ware complex in later Neolithic Britain. *Cambridge Archaeological Journal* 20, 1–15.

Thomas, J. 2013. *The Birth of Neolithic Britain: an interpretive account*. Oxford: Oxford University Press.

Thomas, T. 2001. The social practice of colonization: re-thinking prehistoric Polynesian migration. *People and Culture in Oceania* 17, 27–46.

Thompson, D. V. Jr. 1933. *The Craftsman's Handbook 'Il Libro dell' Arte' by Cennino d'A. Cennini*. New Haven: Yale University Press.

Timpany, S. 2014. Preliminary investigation of a 'worked' wooden plank, submerged forest and intertidal peats at Cummi Ness, Bay of Ireland, Orkney. *The Current. Newsletter of the Island and Coast Archaeology Interest Group* 2(1), 12–13.

Tipping, R. 1995. Holocene evolution of a lowland Scottish landscape: Kirkpatrick Fleming. Part II, regional vegetation and land-use change. *Holocene* 5(1), 83–96.

Towers, R. and Card, N. 2014–15. Technological adaptation in Grooved ware pottery from the Ness of Brodgar, Orkney, or how to make your cordons stick. *Scottish Archaeological Journal* 36–7, 51–63.

Traill, W. and Kirkness, W. 1937. Howar, prehistoric structure on Papa Westray, Orkney. *Proceedings of the Society of Antiquaries of Scotland* 61, 309–21.

Tsu, T. Y. 2000. Toothless ancestors, felicitous descendants: the rite of secondary burial in south Taiwan. *Asian Folklore Studies* 59, 1–22.

Tully, G. 2004. *Ceramics and Identity: a petrological examination of the Early Neolithic settlement site at Wideford Hill, Orkney*. Unpublished BA dissertation, University of Southampton.

Ubelaker, D. H. 1999. *Human Skeletal Remains Excavation, Analysis, Interpretation* (3rd edn). Washington: Taraxacum.

Ubelaker, D. H. and Willey, P. 1978. Complexity in Arikara mortuary practice. *Plains Anthropologist* 23, 69–74.

van der Veen, M. 1992. *Crop Husbandry Regimes*. Sheffield: Sheffield Archaeological Monograph 3.

von den Driesch, A. 1976. *A Guide to the Measurement of Animal Bones from Archaeological Sites*. Peabody Museum Bulletin 1, Harvard: Harvard University.

Wahl, J. 2008. Investigations on Pre–Roman and Roman Cremation Remains from Southwestern Germany: Results, Potentialities and Limits. In Schmidt, C. W. and Symes, S. A. (eds) *The Analysis of Burned Human Remains*. London, Academic Press, 145–61.

Walker, P. L., Miller, K. W. P. and Richman, R. 2008. Time, temperature and oxygen availability: an experimental study of the effects of environmental conditions on the color and organic content of cremated bone. In C. W. Schmidt and S. A. Symes (eds) *The Analysis of Burned Human Remains*. London, Academic Press, SA, 128–35.

Ward, G. and Wilson, S. 1978. Procedures for comparing and combining radiocarbon age determinations: a critique. *Archaeometry* 20, 19–31.

Warren, S. H., Piggott, S., Clark, J. G. D., Burkitt, M. C., Godwin, H. and Godwin, M. E. 1936. Archaeology of the submerged land-surface of the Essex coast. *Proceedings of the Prehistoric Society* 2, 178–210.

Waterson, R. 1990. *The Living House*. London: Thames and Hudson.

Waterson, R. 1995. Houses and hierarchies in island Southeast Asia. In J. Carsten and S. Hugh–Jones (eds) *About the House*. Cambridge: Cambridge University Press, 47–68.

Waterson, R. 2000. House, place and memory in Tana Toraja (Indonesia). In R. A. Joyce and S. D. Gillespie (eds) *Beyond Kinship: social and material reproduction in house societies*. Philadelphia: University of Pennsylvania Press, 177–88.

Watson, E. V. 1981. *British Mosses and Liverworts* (3rd edn). Cambridge: Cambridge University Press.

Watts, I. 1998. *The Origin of Symbolic Culture: the Middle Stone Age of Southern Africa and Khoisan Ethnography*. Unpublished PhD thesis, University of London.

Wells, C. 1960. A study of cremations. *Antiquity* 34, 29–37.

Wells, L. H. 1952. Note on the human skeletal fragments at Quoyness. *Proceedings of the Society of Antiquaries of Scotland* 86, 137–38.

Whitbread, I. K. 1986. The characterisation of argillaceous inclusions in ceramic thin sections. *Archaeometry* 28, 79–89.

Whitbread, I. K. 1995. *Greek Transport Amphorae: A petrological and archaeological study*. British School at Athens, Fitch Laboratory Occasional Paper 4.

Whittaker, D. 2000. Ageing from the dentition. In M. Cox and S. Mays (eds) *Human Osteology: in archaeology and forensic science*. London: Greenwich Medical Media, 83–99.

Whittington, G. 1983. Palynological studies from Knap of Howar, Papa Westray, Orkney, 1975. In A. Ritchie, Excavation of a Neolithic Farmstead at Knap of Howar, Papa Westray, Orkney. *Proceedings of the Society of Antiquaries of Scotland* 113, 116–17.

Whittle, A. 1988. *Problems in Neolithic Archaeology*. Cambridge: Cambridge University Press

Whittle, A. 1996. *Europe in the Neolithic: the creation of new worlds*. Cambridge: Cambridge University Press.

Whittle, A. 2000. Bringing plants into the taskscape. In A. Fairbairn (ed.) *Plants in Neolithic Britain and Beyond*. Oxford: Oxbow Books, 1–7.

Whittle, A., Barclay, A. Bayliss, A., McFadyen, L., Schulting, R. and Wysocki, M. 2007. Building for the dead: events, processes and changing world views from the thirty-eighth to the thirty-fourth centuries cal. BC in southern Britain. *Cambridge Archaeological Journal* 17(1), 123–47.

Whittle, A., Healy, F. and Bayliss, A. 2011. *Gathering Time: dating the early Neolithic enclosures of southern Britain and Ireland*. Oxford: Oxbow.

Wickham-Jones, C. R. 1981. Flaked stone technology in northern Britain. *Scottish Archaeological Forum* 11, 36–42.

Wickham-Jones, C. R. 1990. Orkney Islands: survey of Mesolithic sites. *Discovery and Excavation in Scotland 1990*, 44.

Wickham-Jones, C. R. 1992. Fieldwork to investigate the location of the tanged flint point from Millfield, Stronsay. *Lithics* 13, 40–51.

Wickham-Jones, C. R. 1994. *Scotlands First Settlers*. London: Batsford.

Wickham-Jones, C. R. 1997. The flaked stone. In L. Masters, The excavation and restoration of the Camster Long chambered cairn, Caithness, Highland, 1967–80. *Proceedings of the Antiquaries of Scotland* 127, 160–71.

Wickham-Jones, C. R. 2006. *Between the Wind and the Water: World Heritage Orkney*. Macclesfield: Windgather Press.

Wickham-Jones, C. R. and Dalland, M. 1998. A small Mesolithic site at Fife Ness, Fife, Scotland. *Internet Archaeology* 1998.

Wickham-Jones, C. and Downes, J. 2007. Long Howe, Orkney (St Andrews and Deerness parish), excavation. *Discovery and Excavation in Scotland* 8, 147.

Wickham-Jones, C. R. and Firth, C. R. 2000. Mesolithic settlement of Northern Scotland: first results of fieldwork in Caithness and Orkney. In R. Young (ed.) *Mesolithic Lifeways: current research from Britain and Ireland*. Leicester: Leicester Archaeology Monograph 7, 119–32.

Wickham-Jones, C. R., Dawson, S. and Dawson, A. 2008. Rising tide: sea-level survey. *Discovery and Excavation in Scotland* 9, 133–34.

Williams, D. F. 1976. Petrological analysis of pottery. In J. N. G. Ritchie, The Stones of Stenness, Orkney. *Proceedings of the Society of Antiquaries of Scotland* 107, 45–46.

Williams, D. F. 1979. Petrological analysis of pottery. In C. Renfrew, *Investigations in Orkney*. London: Society of Antiquaries of London, 94–96.

Williams, D. F. 1982. Aspects of Prehistoric pottery-making in Orkney. In I. Freestone, C. Johns and T. Potter (eds) *Current Research in Ceramics, Thin-section Studies*. London: British Museum Occasional paper 32, 9–13.

Williams, D. F. 1983. Petrological analysis of pottery and stone axe. Appendix 1 in A. Ritchie (ed) Excavations of a Neolithic farmstead at Knap of Howar, Papa Westray, Orkney. *Proceedings of the Society of Antiquaries of Scotland* 113, 88–90.

Wilson, C. A., Davidson, D. A. and Cresser, M. S. 2005. An evaluation of multi-element analysis of historic soil contamination to differentiate space use and former function in and around abandoned farms. *Holocene* 15, 1094–99.

Wilson, C. A., Davidson, D. A. and Cresser, M. S. 2008. Multi-element soil analysis: an assessment of its potential as an aid to archaeological interpretation. *Journal of Archaeological Science* 35, 2–24.

Wilson, G. V., Edwards, W., Knox, J., Jones, R. C. B. and Stephens, J. V. 1935. *The Geology of the Orkneys*, Memoirs of the Geological Survey of Great Britain. Edinburgh: HMSO.

Wood, A. 1927. Supplementary notes on Firth Parish. *Proceedings of the Orkney Antiquarian Society* 5, 57.

Woods, W. J. 1983. *Analysis of Soils from the Carrier Mills Archaeological District: Human adaptation in the Salines Valley County, Illinois,* Centre for Archaeological Investigations 2, 1382–407.

Woodward, J. 1951. The Scottish seaweed research association. *Journal of the Marine Biological Association of the United Kingdom* 29, 719–25.

Woodward, N. 2008. Links House, Orkney (Stronsay parish), fieldwalking, geophysics and excavation. *Discovery Excavation Scotland*, new series 9, 137.

Wysocki, M. and Whittle, A. 2000. Diversity, lifestyles and rites: new biological and archaeological evidence from British Earlier Neolithic mortuary assemblages. *Antiquity* 74, 591–601.

Zohary, D. and Hopf, M. 2000. *Domestication of Plants in the Old World* (3rd edn). Oxford: Oxford University Press.

Zvelebil, M. 2003. People behind the the lithics. Social life and social conditions of Mesolithic communities in temperate Europe. In L. Bevan and J. Moore (eds) *Peopling the Mesolithic in a Northern Environment*. Oxford: British Archaeological Report 1157, 1–26.

Index

Numbers in *italics* denote pages with illustrations

agriculture 1, 5, 14, 31, 40, 85, 90, 125, 227, 230, 252, 331, 340, 515, 517, 518, 522, 524, 525, 526, 528, 529, 542
  historic/modern 310, 327, 496, 520, 531, 537, 538
  pastoral/animal husbandry 522, 526, 220, 227, 230, 252, 393
Allt Chrysal, Bara, possible pottery 'kiln' 57–8
ancestors/ancestral significance 13, 61–2, 63, 64, 145, 173, 195, 198, 211–2, 228–30, 237, 239, 241, 243
animals
  introduced domesticates (esp. cattle) 226–7, *226*, 252, 299, 442
  husbandry 220, 227, 230, 252, 393
  slaughter 227
  see also bone, animal
art 14, 194, 240; *see also* stone, decorated
ashes/ashy deposits 22, 23, 25, 27, 30, 31, *32–3*, 35, 36, 38, 47, 51, 52, 53, 54, 65, 82, 94, 96, 100, 101, 106, 107, 109, 110, 111, 117, 121, 122, 131, 139, 150, 152, 154, 156, 166, 168, 170, 178, 181–2, 184, 186, *186*, 187, 193, 232, 249, 277, 278, 310, 336, 379, 457, 503, 509, 510, 511, 530, 531, 533, 534, 537, 538, 539, 541, 542
  red 14, 60, 66, 79, 82, 83, 85, 92, *95*, 100, 101, 106, 109, 111, *117*, 118, 119, 120, 150, 190–1, 516

Barnhouse 10, 13, 16, 23, 30, 36, 60, 85, 128, 139, 143–4, 145, 146, 150, 161, 170, 172, 173, 180, 184, 186, 194, 199, 235–9, *236–7*, 241, 244, *244*, 245, 248, 254, 256, 258, 286, 292, 304, 315, 325, 326, 327, 328, 329, 330, 332, 333, 355, 356, 372–3, 400, 406, 408, 409, 410, 411, 440, 449, 456, 458, 465, 466, 469, 473, 484, 487, 488, 514, 518, 537
Barnhouse–Meashowe Project 10
Bay of Firth 9–10, *9–10*, *12*, 13, 14, 15, 62, 64, 65, 90, 91, *91*, 92, 161, 165, 173, 195, 196, 197, 198, 207, 211, 218–23, 224–5, *225*, 230, 238, 246, 248, 252, 254, 258, 275, 287–8, 291, 296, 302, 304, 332, 349, 365, 375, *389*, 400, 407, 410, 411, 413, 416, 417, 436, 441, 443, 444, 456, 483, 484, 495, 517, 518
  bathymetry *11*, 218
Bay of Stove, Sanday 128, 157, 160, 161, 195
bead 246
  amber 41
  black stone 143, 146, *146*, 474, *474*
  clay 315, *315*
  whale ivory 282, 483

'big house' 143–6, 172, 232, 236–9, 241, 242, *243*, 244
birch 4, 502, 515, 516, 517, 523, 525
  charcoal 23, 30, 38, 47, 48, 52, 54, 109, 140, 144, 152, 169, 278, 495, 496, 497, 498, 503, 506, 509, 510, 511, 512, 513, 514, 515–7
boat 5, 226, *226*
bone and antler, animal 266, 131, 152, 154, 176–7, 201, 202, 208, 214, 259–60, 268, 270, 279–80, 282, 283, 284, 285, 295, 485–8, 493–4, 538, 539, 541
  bird 201, 214, 266, 267, 281, 282, 283, 486, 491, 494
  burnt/cremated 23, 48, 52, 60, 176–7, 182, 212, 213–4, *213*, 232, 406, 487–8, 491, 498, 503, 506, 537, 538, 541
    bird 214, 491
    cattle 214, 487, 491
    pig 487, 491
    red deer 487, 488
    ?sheep 491, 494
  butchery 109, 126, 451, 455, 462, 472, 486, 487
    cattle 201, 214, 259, 267, 269, 270, 283, 284, 285, 485, 486, 488
  decayed 120, 131, 142, 154, 166, 498, 528, 529, 530, 531, 533, 534, 536
  deer 266, 269, 270, 281, 284, 286, 462, 487, 491, 494
  dog 200–2, 267, 284, 295, 296
  fish 279, 281, 284
  otter 281, 282
  pig 486, 487, 488
  red deer 224, 266, 269, 281, 284, 285, 485, 487, 488
  sheep and/or goat 138, 216–7, 259, 269, 281, 282, 283, 284, 285, 485, 486–7, 488, 491, 494
  white-tailed sea eagle 200, 268, 283
bone, human *see* human bone *and* mortuary practices
'box-bed' 105, 117, *118*, 143, 150, 355
Brae of Smirquoy, St Ola 15, 62, 64–90, *66–87*, 91, 196, 224, 225, 237, 258
  excavation 65–6
  fieldwalking 14, 65, *66*, 89, 468
  flint and stone artefacts 421, 424–6, *426*, 442, 443, 445, 456, 468–70, *469*, 470, 472
  geophysical survey 14, 65–6, *66*, 84, 89, 235
  hoose (house) 14, 30, 33, 35, 39, 40, 43, 44, 46, 48, 60, 63, 66–83, *67–84*, 229, 232, 233, 235, 238, 239, 256, 278–9, 290, 292, *298*, 424, 468, 512–3
  charred plant remains 89, 232, 278

Brae of Smirquoy *continued*
    decorated stone *15*, 66, 69–70, *70*, 73, *76*, 85–9, *87*, 238, 279, 302
    drainage system/hydrology 66, 67, *69*, 71, 75–6, 77–9, *78–9*, 80–1, *83*
    entrance and passage 69–70, *69–71*, 71, 73, 279, 424, 468
    flooring and foundations (clay and flagstone) 67–8, 69, 70, *71*, 73, 76, *76*, 77, 79, 80–1, 83, *84*, 85, *87*, 279, 513
    hearth 71, *71*, 72, 73, *73*, *76*, 77, 79–80, *80*, 82, 89, 278, 513
    internal features/division of space 66, 68, 70–1, *71*, 104, 126
    orthostats 66, 67, 69, 70, 71, *71*, 76, 81, 82, 83, 237
    later occupation/features 79–82, *81*, 99
    pits 73–6, *74–6*, 77, 80, 513
    post/stakeholes 72, 73, 75, 76
    secondary features 71–2, *72–3*
    stone box 82
    threshold stone 69, 70
    walling 66, 68, *69*, 82, 103, 104, 279
  midden 66, 68, 83
  other features 83–5, *84–7*
    fireplace 85
    timber structure 84–5, *85*, 87, 89, 96, 103, 228, 255, 288
  plant remains 512–3
  pottery 65, 73, 65, 304, 327, 332, 358, 398–400, *399*, 404, 407, 408, 409, 410
  radiocarbon dates 262, 272, *274–5*, 278–9, 290–1, *298*, 424
  red ash 14, 82
  stone/flint tools 65, 66, 73, 75, 76, 82, *82*, 83, *83*, 89, *89*, 125
  topographic setting 65, *65*
Bronze Age, early
  barrow/funerary monument 13, 41, 61, *144*, 212–3, *213*, 222, 296, 396, 468, 511, 514, 517
    building 13, 162, 163, 164, 165, 170, 190–2, *192*, 354, 457, 462, 503
    burial 60, 62, 137, 466
    cremation 60, 489–94
    grave goods 13, 41, 137
  'double house' 164, 161, 164, 170, 178, 245, *245*, 246
  lithics 12, 161, 413, 416, 417, 436, 437, 438, *438*, 439, 440, 442, 451, 455–6, 458, 462, 463, 464, 465, 466, 470, 471–2
  mound 256, 297
  pottery 14, 57, 248, 304, 332, 352, 393, 396, 398, 503
  settlement/occupation 12, 13, 61, 191, *192*, 248, 357, 468, 503, 514, 517, 178
    timber houses 4, 161, 162, 193
Bronze Age, late
  'bangle' 14

Caithness 1, *2*, 6, 17, 256, 302, 375, 474
cereals 226, 252, 299, 300, *512*, 513

charred/carbonised 23, 27, 30, 89, 150, 230, 232, *233*, 256, 297, 495, 496, 497, 502, 506, 510, 514, 526
  2-grain einkorn wheat 232, 297, 512
  linseed/flax 232, 297, 512
  barley 496, 497, 498, 503, 511, 512, 514, 516, 518, 519
  hulled 495–6, 503, 506, 514, 515, 518
  naked (six-row) 23, 30, 36, 116, *117*, 120, 125, 146, 154, 169, 230, 232, 297, 495–6, 497, 498, 503, 506, 509, 510, 511, 514, 515, 516, 518, 526
  chaff 503, 512, 514
  oat 232, 297, 513
  rye 232, 297, 512
  wheat (einkorn) 506, 512, 515, 518–9
cultivation/production 120, 230–2
drying/processing of 54, 109, 110, 121, 125, 126, 230, 496, 503, 509, 510, 511, 513, 514, 515, 516, 517–8
pollen 522, 524
chambered cairn 4–6, 8, 17, 39, 40, 60, 62, 63, 64, 97, 145, 158, 161, 194, 197–213, 220, 222, 229, 242–3, 254–8, 357
  chronology, radiocarbon dating and typology 197–8, *197*, 211, 254–8, *258*, *273*– 281–7, 292–3, *294–5*, 297–302, *298–301*
  human remains 198, 199–211, *200–1*, *203*, *205*, *208*, 228, 263–71, 272, 281, 282, 283, 284, 285, 286, 288–9, 292, 293, 295–6, *299*
  on Rousay 194, 198–9, 207, *229*, 243, 256, 2588, 283–4, 293
  Orkney-Cromarty 4, 6, 40, 197, *197*, 254, 256, *288–90*, 292–3, *294–5*, 297–302, *298–301*
  passage grave 8, 9, 11, 63, 65, 85, 92, 196–23, *196–7*, *200–3*, *205*, *208–9*, *212*, 239–53, *240*, 254
    art 194, 240
    Cuween Hill 9, 11, 91, 92, *92*, 161, 196, 198, 199, 200–2, *201–2*, 219, 222, *234*, 235, 256, 258, 295–6
    Eday Manse 88
    Holm of Papa Westray South 88
    Howe of Howe 237
    Irish 86, 198, 239, 240, *240*, 293–5, *300*
    lack of kerb or peristalith in Orcadian examples 239–41
    Maes Howe 60, 63, 193, 197, 209, 210, 237, 239, 241, 256, 263, 271, 273, 286–7, 293, *294*, *296*
    Quanterness 12, 92, 161, 195, 196, *196*, 198, 199–201, 202–12, *200–1*, *205*, 207–12, *208–9*, *212*, 219, 220, 222, 256, 263, 273, 285, 293, *294–5*, 295–6, *300*, 357, 392, 410
    Quoyness, Sanday 200, 209, 256, 271, 273, 275, 286, 293, 295, *294–5*, *300*
    Pierowall Quarry, Westray 87, 88, *88*, 209, 267, 273, 285–6, 286, 293, *294–5*, 295, *300*
    Swandro, Rousay 219, 256
    Wideford Hill 161, 196, 198, 199, 201, 202, *202*, 196, 198, 199–201, 202, *202*, 207, 208–9, 211, 219, 222, 256
    spatial relationship with settlements 198, 211, 254
  pottery 333, 357, 358, 374
  radiocarbon dates from 256, 258, 269, 270, 271, 283–7, 292–6, *294–5*, 297–302, *299–300*

relationship with early Neolithic house 40, 64, 88–9, 98, *98*, 145, 225–30, 233, 234, 254–5

stalled 5, 6, 16, 40, 64, 194, 197–9, 239, 242–3, 256

    Calf of Eday Long 98, *98*, 333, 374

    Holm of Papa Westray North 257, 265, 273, 281–2, *288–90*, 292, 293, *299*

    Isbister 205, 206, 267, 273, 282–3, *288–9*, *299*, 333, 358, 374, 474, 484

    Knowe of Lairo, Rousay 243, 256, 271, 273, 283, 284, *288–90*, 293, *299*

    Knowes of Ramsay, Rousay 270, 283–4, *288–90*, 293, *299*

    Knowe of Rowiegar, Rousay 269, 273, 283, *288–90*, 292–3, *299*, 374

    Knowe of Yarso, Rousay 5, 207–8, 256, 270, 273, 283, 284, *288–90*, 293, *299*

    Midhowe, Rousay 271, 273, 284–5, *288–90*, 293, *299*, 374

    Point of Cott, Westray 242–3, 256, 266, 273, 282, *288–90*, 292, 293, *299*

    Staneyhill 243

    Unstan 333, 374

    Vestra Fiold 243

charcoal 18, 23, 27, 30, 33, 38, 47, 48, 52, 53, 54, 56, 80, 82, 85, 94, 116, 120, 121, 139, 140, 144, 151, 152, 166, 169, 177, 178, 217, 232, 278, 371, 494, 495–526, 512, *512*, 524, *524*, 526, 530, 531, 532, 533, 534, 537, 538, 539, 541

    birch 23, 30, 38, 47, 48, 52, 54, 109, 140, 144, 152, 169, 278, 495, 496, 497, 498, 503, 506, 509, 510, 511, 512, 513, 514, 515–7

    blackthorn type 503

    cherry type 495, 503, 510, 511, 516

    grasses/sedges (rhizomes/nutlets) 54, 496, 498, 501–2, 503, 505, 509, 510, 511, 514, 516, 517

    hazel/hazelnut 23, 38, 232, 297, 495, 496, 503, 506, 509, 510, 512, 515, 516

    heather/heather family 54, 109, 177, 495, 498, 502, 503, 506, 509, 510, 511, 513, 514, 516–7, 518, 526

    pine 38, 481, 484, 514, 523, 525

    rowan 109, 502, 516

    Scots pine 177, 503, 504, 517

    seaweed 109, 111, 379–81, *380*, 502

    spruce/larch 503, 514, 517

    willow 23, 38, 94, 109, 232, 297, 495, 496, 498, 502, 503, 506, 509, 512, 513, 514, 515, 516, 526

Childe, Gordon 5–6, 7, 16, 34, 143, 154, 156, 157, 159, 160, 193, 194–5, 244, 246, 254, 286, 355, 483

clay 17, 23, 38, 46, 52–3, 58, 60, 66, 71, 85, *165*, 166, 173, 195, 231, 315, 350, 370, 376–7, 390, 407; *see also* soil micromorphology

    ball 305, 308, 315, *317*, 325, 328, 331–2, 398, 399, *401*

    bead 315

    burnt/baked/fired 54, 55, 231, 355, 390, 404, 493

    flooring/spreads/surfaces within structures 67, 73, 81, 98, 99, 100, 101, 119, 120–1, 167, 378, 498 *see also* individual sites

pellets 335, 344, 352, 353

sourcing and prospection 305, 326, 327–9, 350, 353, 357, 365, 369–71, 375–8, *376*, 390, 398, 406, 407, 409, 411

unfired 315

use in wall coloration 12, 172–3, *174*, 176, 193, 194, 195

use in walling/construction 30, *35*, 44, 108, 148, 149, 173, 175, 187, 202, 239, 278, 424, 503

colluvium *see* soil, hillwash

colonization, Neolithic 5–6, 17, 197, 226, *see also* agriculture *and* animals, introduced domesticates

cosmology 62, 63, 145, 211, 212, 220, 221, 226, 228, 230

Crossiecrown 12, 15, 62, 91, 128, 151, 152, 159, 160–95 *162–80*, *182–3*, *185–6*, *188–93*, 196, 220–2, 235, 238, 239, 245, 256, 258, 291, 303, 372, 471

    animal bones 487–88

    clay flooring 164, 541–2

    'double house' 161, 164, 170, 178, 245, *245*, 246

    drainage system/hydrology 165, *165*, 168, 170

    excavation 12, 161–2

    fieldwalking 162

    flint and stone artefacts 12, 161, 162, *167*, 173, 176, *177*, 182, *182*, 187, *189*, 194–5, 413, 416, 417, 421, 436–40, *438–40*, 443, 445, 456, 457–65, *459–62*, *465*, 470, 472, 473

    geophysical survey 12, 130, 161, *163*, 164, 170, 239

    'Grey House' 135, 144, 162, 164, 165, 169–70, *171*, 173, 174, 175, 177, 178, 187–190, *188–91*, 191, 193, 195, 245, 303, 333, 336, 354, 408, 439, 457–8, 462, 471, 503, 514, 534

        decorated stone 188, *189*

        drainage system/hydrology 188

        entrance 187, 188, 190

        flooring and foundations (clay and flagstones) 187, 188, 190

        hearth 177, 187, 188, *189*, 503, 514

        internal features/division of space 187–8

        orthostats 188, 190, 193

        paved area 187, 188, *189*, 190

        pit 188

        stone box 188, *190*, 503

        threshold stone 188

        walling 165, 170, 187

    haematite 173, 183, 194, 195, 248, 475, 477–82, *479–80*, 483–4

    hollow/turf and timber building (early Bronze Age) 13, 162, 163, 164, 165, 170, 190–2, *192*, 354, 457, 462, 503

        flooring (clay and flagstones) 193

        hearth 193 *192–3*

        paving 190, 193

        possible internal features 193

        posthole 193

        stone box 190

        walling 190, 193

    midden 128, 152, 154, 157, 161, 162, 163–4, 165–8, *168–70*, 173, 175, 178, 182, 186, 190, 194, 239, 278, 303, 333, 336, *352*, 353, 354, 356, 408, 436, 439, 440, 457, 458, 471, 473, 503, 534–42

Crossiecrown *continued*
  other structural remains 163–4, 165, 166–9, *167*, 170, 173
  paving 165, 168, 170
  plant remains 485, 503–6, 514–5, 516–7, 518
  pottery 161, 163, 164, 165, 166, *167*, 168, 169, *170–1*, 182,
    182, 183, 187, 193, 245, 303–4, 305, 315, 318, 325,
    326, 327, 328, 332–57, *335*, *339–41*, *344–6*, *348*, *352*,
    353, 374, 375, 387–92, *388*, 393–5, *394*, 400, 407,
    408–12, 457
  radiocarbon dates 169, 178, 191–2, 195, 211, 262, 272,
    274–5, 278, 291, 303, 457, 503
  red ash 190–1
  'Red House' 12, 135, 144, 158, 162, 163, 164, 165, 169–79
    171, *173–9*, 188, 190, *191*, 191, 193, 195, 245, 278, 291,
    303, 333, 336, 354–5, 387, 408, 436, 438–9, 440,
    457–8, 462, 464, 471, 503, 514, 534, 537–9
    activities 186–7
    as 'big house' 172
    cremated bone 176–7, 514, 517
    drainage system/hydrology 176, *177*, 182, 355
    ?'dresser' 177, 188
    entrance 174, 179, 186, 190
      flooring and foundations (clay and flagstones) 164,
        170, 173, 175, 176, 177, 179–87, 457, 464, 538, 539
    hearth 161, 175, 177, 181, 183, 186–7, *186*, 354, 355,
      457, 503, 514
    internal features/division of space 175–6, *176*
      orthostats 175, 176, 178–9, 354, 355, 356, 436, 538
    magnetic susceptibility 183–4, *183*, 187
    phosphates 183, *183*
    placed deposits 172, 457
    radiocarbon dates 178, 181
    red clay 'render' 172–3, *174*, 176, 193, 194, 195
    stone box 176–7, *177–8*, 182, 183, 186, 187, 355, 487,
      503, 514
    structural history 173–9, *173–6*
    threshold stone 177
    walling 170, 173–6, *173*, 177, 178–9, *179*, 193
  relationship with Quanterness passage grave 211
  soil micromorphology/chemistry 166–7, 179, *180*, 183–7,
    185, 534–542, *541*
  Stucture 1 *168*
culture-history 5, 6–7, 39, 226
Cuween Hill 9, 91, 92, 102, 224
  passage grave 11, 91, 92, *92*, 161, 196, 198, 199, 200–2,
    200–2, *201*, 207–8, 209, 211, 219, 222, *234*, 235, 256,
    258, 295–6
  peat core 520
Cuween-Wideford Landscape Project 10, 15, 161, 256–7, 303, 375

decoration
  of body 195
  of houses 13, 14, 172, *174*, 176, 193–5, 239
  of pottery 304, 308, 311, 318–24, 327–8, 331, 333–5, 344,
    344, 347–8, 351, 352, 354, 357–8, 361, 362, 364–7,
    371–4, 375, 379, 400, 404, 409–11, 412

  of stone *15*, 66, 69–70, *70*, 73, *76*, 85–9, *87*, 188, *189*, 229,
    238, 279, 239, 285, 286, 302 457, 458, 464, *465470*
diatoms 52, 60, 537
diet 110, 126, 257, 281–2, 393, 395, 487, *see also* staple isotopes
    and pottery, organic residues
'double house' 30, 161, 164, 170, 178, 245, *246*, 252
dresser 45, 46, 69, 70, 112, 116, 138, 143, 145, 148, 216, 217
driftwood
    as construction material 38, 379, 515
    as fuel 503, 514, 515, 526

fieldwalking 12, 14, 15, 17, 18, 65, *66*, 161, 162, 224, 247–8,
    253, 287, 377, 402–3, 404, 468, 469, 472, 475
Flett, Ronnie 10, 92, 111, 122, 128–9, 161
flint artefacts *see* lithics
food production, processing, preparation and serving 54, 72,
    73, 77, 79, 109, 126, 157, 187, 226–7, 324, 331, 332, 336,
    346–7, 349, 352, 353, 355, 356, 365, 368, 372, 373, 374,
    393, 406, 498, 411, 457, 502, 503, 509, 510, 514, 515, 516,
    518, 530
    feasting 227, 374, 493, 515
fuel 58, 109, 111, 177, 379, 498, 502–3, 506, 509, *511*, 514,
    515–9, 526
    driftwood 503, 514, 515, 526
    for pyres 517
    heather 109, 379, 506, 510, *511*, 514, 516, 517, 518, 526
    peat 51, 52, 53, 54, 56, 60, 330, 379, 502, 517–8, 526
    seaweed 109, 111, 186, 330, 379–81, *380*, 502, 514, 515, 518
    turf 52, 54, 56, 109, 121, 126, 156, 330, 496, 498, 502,
      503–4, 510, *511*, 514–5, 516, 517–8

genealogy 226, 230, 243
geology 1
    boulder clay 46, 61, 328, 350, 375, 390
    glacial till 43, 44, 45, 49, 67, 96, 101, 103, 130, 132, 162,
      165, 166, 168, 181, 182, 183, 184, 249, 375, 416, 421, 426,
      427, 429, 431, 437, 533, 536, 537, 538, 539, 541, 542
geophysical survey 10 *see also* individual sites
gold objects 13, 41
grave good, Early Bronze Age/'Wessex' 13, 41, 137
Green, Eday 15, 40, 62, 69, 85, 87, *88*, 89, 90, 96, 225, 228,
    232, 235, *235*, 255, 258, 263, 272, *276–7*, 281, 288, 289,
    290, 291, 298

Ha'Breck (Braes of), Wyre 15, 26, 30, 39, 40, 61, 62, 69, 82, *82*,
    89, 90, 96, 118, *120*, 125, 225, 227–8, *227*, 230, 232, 233,
    233–4, 235, 237, 255, 256, 258, 262, 272, 280, 289–90,
    291, 298, *298*, 357, 374, 407, 424, 449, 469, 512, 513
haematite 14, 173, 183, 194, 195, 248, *249*, 475–84, *476*,
    479–81, 483–4 *483*
    as pigment (inc. experiment) 173, 183, 194, 195, 475,
      476–84, *479*, *481*
    Creekland Bay source 475, 476, *476*, 479, 482, *483*, 483,
      484
hazel 23, 38, 232, 297, 495
hazelnut 232, 297, 512

hearth *see* individual sites

heath/heathland 54, 498, 503, 509, 510, 511, 514, 515, 516, 517, 522, 523, 524, 525, 526

heather 23, 54, 121, 379, 518, 522

    as fuel 109, 379, 506, 510, 511, 514, 515–6, 517, 518, 526

    charcoal 54, 109, 177, 495, 498, 502, 503, 506, 509, 510, 511, 513, 514, 516–7, 518, 526

    charred 23, 54, 121, 496, 502, 503, 506, 509, 519

    pollen 522, 523, 524

    possible roofing/flooring/bedding 23, 514, 518

heirloom 146, 237, 238, 242

Hill of Heddle/Heddle Hills 9, 91, 92, 224

house 7, 8, 14

    as monumental/ceremonial structure 64, 158, 253

    'big' 143–6, 172, 232, 236–9, 241, 242, *243*, 244

    dating and chronology 254–81, *274–7, 287–92, 297–2, 298*, 301–2

    decoration 13, 14, 172–3, *174*, 176, 193–5, 239

    'double' 164, 161, 164, 170, 178, 245, *245*, 246

    early Neolithic stone 4, 13, 14, 15, 16–7, 40, 46, 60–3, 64, 90, 128, 232–3, 235; *see also* individual sites

    internal division/orthostats/'stalled 4, 30, 34, 44, 46, 47, 50, 51, 53, 54, 61, 66, 67, 69, 71, *71*, 76, 81, 82, 83, 94, 96, 99, 100, *100*, 101–4, 105, 109, 112–8, 120, 122, 124, 126, 135, 136, *137*, 138, 142, 149, 150, 175, 176, 178–9, 188, 190, 193, 219, 235, *235*, 237, 256, 279, 281, 282, 284, 286, 354–5, 428, 436, 490, 497, 539; *see also individual sites*

    late Neolithic 4, 8, 14, 15 23, 126, 134–6, 143–4, 145, 148, 150, 160, 174, 193, 194, 244, 299

    life cycle 356–7

    materiality of 8, 13–4, 38, 39, 40, 90, 228, 229–30, 235

    of the dead/ancestors 38–40, 64, 229–30, 233

    relationship with stalled and chambered cairns 40, 64, 88–9, 98, *98*, 145, 225–30, 233, 234, 254–5

    society (*sociéte à maisons*) 7–8, 14, 15, 31, 40, 60, 63, 64, 89, 90, 111, 124–5, 127, 145, 146, 158, 159, 160, 195, 212, 225–30, 232–4, 331

    superimposition/succession 25–8, 38, 129, 131, 160, 195, 228–30, 232–8, *233*, 244, 277–8, 280, 281

    timber 4, 5, 14, 15, 16, 18, 40, 64, 161, 162, 193, 228, 229, 254–5, 257, 280, 287, 301, *301*; *see also* Brae of Smerquoy, Crossiecrown, Stonehouse Knoll *and* Wideford Hill

    wrapping of 158, 193–4, 195, *215*, 219, 241, 244

Hoy 1, *3*, 62, *63*, 475, 429, 482, 483, 484, 526

human bone/remains 137, 142, 143, 145, 176, 355, 487, 489–94

    from chambered cairns 198, 199–211, *200–1, 203, 205, 208*, 228, 263–71, 272, 281, 282, 283, 284, 285, 286, 288–9, 292, 293, 295–6, *299*

    cremated/cremation 41, 145, 176, 177, 212, 213, *213*, 223, 396, 487, 489–94, 514, 517

        pyre technology and ritual 493–4, 517

    within domain of the living 145, 211, 237

hydrology/drainage systems 31, 34–5, *34–5*, 59, 62, 63, 66, 67, *69*, 71, 75–6, 77–81, *78–9*, 100, 105, 131–4, *134*, 159, 165, 176, 188, 195

Iron Age 4, 487, 515, 518

    Knowe of Rowiegar 283

    Oakbank Crannog 186

    objects 14, 398, 451

    Pierowall Quarry, Westray 285

    Quanterness 285

jet objects 13, 283

kinship/kinship structures 7–8, 125, 226, 228, 232, 410, 411–2; *see also* social/group kin identity/status

Knap of Howar, Papa Westray 4–5, *5*, 6, 16, 17, 30, 38, 40, 44, 46, 48, 50, 54, 62, 66, 67–8, 69, 76, 79, 80, 90, 125, 103, 104, 110, 111, 126, 157, 209, 211, 229, *229*, 230, 232, 237, 254, 256, 257, 258, 259, 272, *276–7*, 279–80, 290–1, 298, *298*, 333, 334, 357, 358, 372, 374, 408, 409, 454, 456, 466, 468, 469, 484, 487, 497, 517, 518, 519

Knowes of Trotty barrow cemetery 13, *14*, 41, *42, 44*, 60–1, *61–3*, 466, 491

    human bone 491–2

    Mound 1 structure 61, *62–3*

    geophysical survey 13, 41, *43*, 60, 235

Knowes of Trotty house 13, *14*, 41–63, *42–53, 59, 63*, 66, 67, 69, 77, 80, 118, 196, 224, 229, 230, 232, 235, 238, 239, 258, 298, 358, 515–6

    associated structures 41, 48, 54–5, *55*

    'box-bed' 105

    burnt bone 48, 52, 406

    burnt clay 54

    drainage system/hydrology 59, 62

    dresser 50

    entrance/porch 41, 46, 48, *50*, 50, 51, 53, 510, 511

    excavation 41

    flint and stone tools 53, 54, 55, *56, 58*, 58, 424, 456, 465–8, *467*, 469

    floor (clay and flagstone) 47–8, 50, 52–3, 54–5, 58–9, 139, 279, 509, 510, 511, 516

    hearth 41, 47–8, *47*, 48–9, 50, 51–2, *51–2*, 54, 56, 58, 59, 60, 61, 279, 406, 424, 509–10, 511, 516

    internal features/division of space 46, 50, 51, 54, 61, 126

    orthostats 44, *46*, 47, 48, 50, 51, 53, 54, 237

    midden 58, 60

    occupation deposits 52–3, 516

    phase 2 rebuilding 48–54, *49–53*, 291, 509–11, 516

    phase 3 final refurbishment 58–60, *59*, 279, 509–11, 516

    pit 48, *48*, 279, 510, 516

    plant remains 495, 509–11, *511*, 515–6, 518

    porch 53–5, *53*

    post/stakehole 48, 50

    pottery 44, *47*, 48, 53, 54, 55, 57–8, 165, 304, 327, 404–7, *405*, 408

    pottery 'kiln' 55, *56–7*, 56–8, 330, 405, 407

    radiocarbon dating 47, 48, 52, 54, 60, 260, 272, *276–7*, 279, 290–1, 298, *298*, 509, 510, 511, 515

    soil micromorphology 406, 511

    stone box 60

Knowes of Trotty house *continued*
  threshold stone 45, 46
  walling 41, 44, *46*, 48, 49–50, 53, 54, 58–60, 103, 465
Knowes of Trotty, other investigations 60–1, *61*, 542

Lévi–Strauss, Claude 7, 8, 14, 40, 225–6, 252
  personnes morales (corporate group) 8
  société à maisons (house society) 7–8, 14, 15, 31, 40, 60, 63,
    64, 89, 90, 111, 124–5, 127, 145, 146, 158, 159, 160, 195,
    212, 225–30, 232–4, 331
limpet 143, 176, 281, 284, 285, 286
Linga Fiold 456, 462, 470, 489, 493, 494, 517
Links of Noltland, Westray 16, 85, 128, 157, 161, 178, 190, 194,
  195, 239, 246, *246*, 258, 291, 292, 304, 318, 327, 331, 332,
  333–4, 336, 357, 393, 456, 462, 464, 465, 472, 542
Links House, Stronsay 256, 288, 297, 298, 299, 300, 301,
  301–2, 318, 393, 442
  late Mesolithic activity 297, *298*, 299, 422, 456
lithics, 413–44, *423*, *426*, *428*, 430, *434–6*, *438–40*, 445–84,
  446–8, *452–3*, *459–62*, 465, 467, *469*, *471–2*, *473–4*, *476*,
  479–81, *483*
  anvil 79, 449, 451, 454, 465, 466, 468, 469
    percussion 417–20, 424, 426, 427, 430, 436, 444
  ard-point 215, 218, *218*, 440, *461*, 462, 463, 458, 465,
    470, 471, *471*
  arrowhead 17, 284, 422, 428
    barbed and tanged 12, 161, 438, *438*, 442, 470
    chisel/transverse 421, 430, 431, 432, 433, *436*
    leaf-shaped 248, 432, 436, 437, 438 *438*
    petit tranchet 421
    petit tranchet derivative 421, 424, 425
    tanged 436, 438–9, *438–9*
    triangular 437, 438, *438*
  axe polished/ground/roughout 14, 18, 55, *56*, 65, 73, 76,
    118, 126, 137, *139*, 146, 154, 176, 182, *183*, 188, 241, 279,
    283, 284, 300, 433, 439, 443, 445–9, *446*, 450, 451,
    452, 454–5, 456, 457, *463*, 464, 465, 466, 467, *468*,
    469, 470, 472, 483, 484
  ball 176, 238, 328, 449, *453*, 455, 456,
  bar 440, *452*, 455–6, 457, 458–62, *460*, 463, 465, 468,
    470, 471, 472
  bead 143, 146, *146*, 474, *474*
  chipped slab 457, 462–3
  chisel/chisel axe 146, 448, 454, 456, 465
  cobble tools 73, 137, 182, 445, 449–50, *446–8*, 451–2,
    455–6, 457–8, 462, 463, 464, 65, 466, 468, 470, 471,
    472, *472*
    flaked 109, 450, 451, 458, *460–1*, 462, 463–4, 465,
      471, 472
    ground 451, 454
    pecked 451, 457, 463, 466, 470
  core 421, 426, 427, 430, 436, 440, 442, 464, *430*, 465
    Levallois type and flakes 421, 430, 433, 443, 444
  ?cushion macehead/stone 187–8, *189*, 468
  disc 58, 182, 450, 451, 455, 456, 457, 458, 462–3, 464–5,
    466, 468, 472

early Bronze Age 413, 416, 417, 436, 438, 439, 440, 442,
  451, 455–6, 458, 462, 463, 464, 465, 468, 471–2
fabricator 431, 438
flint artefacts 10–11, 11–12, 17, 18, 36, *37*, 65, 66, 83, 92, 94,
  109, *110*, 121, *122–3*, 124, 128, 151, 152, *153*, *167*, 182, *182*,
  183, 187, 247, 248, 279, 282, 283, 284, 285, 413–44,
  423, *426*, *436*, *438–9*, 455, 470, 471, 518
flint scatter 12–13, 17–18, 161, 247, 250–1, 297, 416
grinder 451, 454, 455, 463, 466, 470, 472
  'Knap of Howar' 55, 58, *58*, 137, 445, 450, 451, 454,
    456, 457, 458, *460*, 463, 464, 465, 466, 467, 468,
    469, 469, 472
grinding slab 109, 445, 450, 464, 476
grinding stone 109, 126, 445, 450, 454, 465, 470, 484
haematite 14, 173, 183, 194, 195, 248, *249*, 475–84, *476*,
  479–81, 483–4, *483*
hammerstone 53, 73, 137, *137*, 353, 417, 420, 449, *446–7*,
  450, 451, 455, 457, 463, 465, 466, *467*, 470
  necked 458, 462, 463, 465
incised slab 470, *471*, 471–2
jet 14, 283
knapping debris/waste flakes and blades 92, 109, 126, 137,
  146, 152, 416, 417, 420, 421, 424, 426–8, 430, *430*,
  433, 436, 439, 440–2, 445, 450–1, 455, 458, 462, 464,
  465, 470, 518
knapping hammer 137, *139*, 445, 451, 455, 463
knapping techniques/reduction strategies 217–21, 417,
  420, 424, 426, 427, 428, 429, 433, 442, 443, 445,
  449–50
knife 142, 146, 283, 284, 285, 413, 417, 421, 422, 424, 426,
  427, 428, 429, 430, 431, 433, 436, 438, 439, 442, 443,
  448, 450, 470
  plano-convex 424, 426, 442–3, 429
  Skaill 182, 286, 378, 445, 450, 451, 454, 455, 456, 457,
    458, 462, 464–5, 466, 468, 470, 471, 472
macehead 10, 14, 82, 83, *83*, 238, 241, *242*, 248, *249*, 281,
  283, 424
Mesolithic 18, 38, 224, 282, 297, 413, 416, 420, 421, 427,
  429, 442
miscellaneous flake tools 422, 424, 427, 428, 431, 433,
  438, 443
mortar 176, *177*, 194–5, 350, 393, 457, 458, *459*, 464,
  476, 478, 484
pebble tools 54, 109, *453*, 454, 455, *462*, 464, 468
?pestle *448*, 450
piercer/borer (inc. 'Knap of Howar' type) 393, 431, 438,
  456, 468, 469, 470, 471, 472, 476
polished camptonite object *238*
polished 'finger' stone 73, *75*, 468, *469*
polished/ground tool/fragment 238, 421, 450, 451, 455, 456,
  462, 464, 465, 466, 468–9, 470, 472
polissoir 82, 108, 468, 469, 472
pounder/grinder 451, 455, 463, 470, 472
pumice 183, 466, 470, 471, 473, *473*
quern 82, *82*, 89, 120, 121, 25, 232, 279
  saddle 89, *89*

raw materials 416–9, 421, 424, 425, 426, 429, 436, 441, 442–4, 449, 450, 455, 462, 474
reworking 417, 420, 421–2, 469
scatter 12–13, 17–18, 161, 247, 250–1, 297, 416
scraper 156, 283, 284, 413, 416, 417, 421, 422–4, 424–6, 427, 428–9, 430–3, 438–9, 443
  'Stonehall farm type' 146, 416, 420, 426, 427, 433, 436, 438, *440*, 442, 443
sculpted stone 457, 458, 464, *465*
sharpening stone 58, 265, 465, 466, *477*
smoother 109, 445, *448*, 450, 457, 458, 462, 463, 464, 465, 466, *467*, 470, 471, 472
stone, tools/objects 11, 12, 18, 36, *37*, 65, 66, 83, *110*, *122–3*, 126, 128, 151, 152, *153*, 161, *167*, 182, *182*, 187, 212, *213*, 238, 247, 248, 250, 285, 413–44, 445–84, *446–8*, *452–3*, *459–62*, *465*, 467, *469*, *471–2*, *473–4*, *476*, *479–81*, *483*
  and flint object hoard 137, 145–6, 449, 450
  unworked pebbles/cobbles 421, 424, 426, 436, 440, 443, 455
  used in butchery 451, 455, 462, 472, 486, 487
  use wear 451–2, 462, 463, 465, 466, 468, 469, 470, 471, 473

Maes Howe 60, 63, 193, 197, 209, 210, 237, 239, 241, 256, 263, 271, 273, 286–7, 293, *294*, *296*
magnetic susceptibility *102*, 106, 107, 130, 131, *132*, 139, *141*, 183–4, *183*, 187, 214–5, *217*, 330, 380–1, *382*
  on pottery 304
materiality 14, 219, 221–2
  of house/settlement 8, 13–4, 38, 39, 40, 90, 228, 229–30, 235
  of middens 151–9, 165–6, 238–9
  of passage graves 211, 212, 219, 220–2, 229, 240–1
  of stalled cairns 40, 64, 229–30
Mesolithic 4, 224, 226, 255, 297, 301
  flintwork 18, 38, 282, 297, 413, 416, 420, 421, 427, 429, 442
  Links House, Stronsay 297, *298*, 299
  Long Howe, Tankerness 297, 299
  Point of Cott, westray 282
  radiocarbon date 297
  South Ettit 224
midden 4–5, 11, 14, 17, 40, 60, 61, 143, 152, 154, 157, 161, 162, 163–4, 232, 280, 281, 287, 301, 302, 305, 465; *see also* individual sites
  and nucleation of settlement 128, 158–9, 160–1, 238–9
  as fertiliser 157
  as wall core material 16, 115, 125, 156, 157–8, 165, *179*, 190, 232, 244, 279, 354, 355, 496, 539
  materiality of 151–9, 165–6, 238–9
mortuary practices/rituals 198–223, 228, 239
  bone/body curation and circulation 198–9, 206–7, 209, 211
  cremation 41, 145, 176, 177, 202, 212, 213–4, *213*, 223, 396, 487, 489–94, 514, 517
    pyre technology and ritual 493–4, 517
  Cuween 200–2, *201*, 207–8, 209, 211

    dog skulls 200–1, 295, 296
    other animal bone 201
    radiocarbon dates 201, 202
  dismemberment 204
  exposure/excarnation, 'half-cremation' and secondary burial 198, 200, 202, 203–11
  inhumation 198, 199–202, 204, 207, 208
  deposition of body 209–10, 281
    sensory experience 210
  osteological study and interpretation 202–223, *203*, *205*, *208–9*, 285
    age range 205
    'normal' patterns of preservation and taphonomy 202–7
    quantification and skeletal element representation 202–3, *203*, 204–7, *205*, 285
  Quanterness 199–200, *200–1*, 201, 202–7, *203*, 204–7, *205*, 208, *208–9*, 209–10, 211, *212*, 285
    relationship with Crossiecrown settlement 211
  Wideford Hill 202, 208, 209, 211
    animal bone 202
  see also human bone/remains
Mousland *144*, 466, 468, 489, 493, 494
Muckquoy, Redland, Neolithic settlement 13, 14, 15, 62, 64, 128, 131, 160, 162, 195, 196, 224, 246, 247–52 *247–9*, *251–2*, 287
  burnt bone 248
  ditch/slot/palisade 14, 248–50, *251–2*
  excavation 14–15, 249
  fieldwalking 14, 247–8, 253, 475
  flint and stone tools and scatters 14, 247, 248, 250–1, 456, 465, 471–2, *472*
  geophysical survey 14, 248–50, *250*
  houses 248
  midden 14, 128, 249, 250, *251–2*
  mound 247, 248, 249, 250
  old ground surface 249
  postholes 249, 250, *251*
  pottery 14, 248, 304, 399–404, *400–1*, *404*, 407
  surface collection 14, 247–8
  walled enclosure 14
  late Neolithic
  charcoal 503, 508
  house/domestic architecture 4, 8, 14, 15 23, 126, 134–6, 143–4, 145, 148, 150, 160, 174, 193, 194, 244, 299
  lithics 416, 420, 421, 424, 426–9, 433, 436, *436*, 439, 443, 456, 45–9, 462, 464, 465, 467, 598
  midden 14, 154, 157, 158; *see also* Crossiecrown *and* Stonehall Farm
  monument 64, 194, 240–1, 302
  pottery 193, 212, 213–4, *213*, *215–6*, 217, 393, 398, 399, 404, 408
    Impressed ware 393, 421, 443
    Peterborough ware 393, 421, 443
    Grooved ware 6, 14, 138, *139*, 144, 152, 160, 161, 163, 164, 166, *167*, 168, 169, *170–1*, 182, *182*, 183, 187, 194, 195, 236, *237*, 245, 248, 254, 256, 279, 280,

pottery, Grooved ware *continued*
   281, 282, 285, 286, 301, 302, 303, 304, 305, 315–24,
      321–2, 327, 328–30, 331, 332–4, 336–47, *339–41*,
      344–6, 348, 350, 351–4, *353*, 356, 365, 377, 382,
      392, 393–4, 395, 396, 399–404, *401*, 406, 408, 409,
      410–11, 412, 443, 464, 503
   settlement/village 8, 11, 13, 16, 85, 122, 128, *129*, 143, 145,
      161, 170, 195, 238, 243, 244, 245, 248, 303, 327, 332,
      357, 372, 409, 410, 412, 413, 445, 465, 487, 498; *see
      also* Crossiecrown *and* Stonehall Farm

Ness of Brodgar 4, 10, 12, 14, 16, 85, 88, *88*, 128, 146, 161,
   172, *172*, 173, 188, 194, 225, 238, 242, *243*, 248, *249*, 250,
   255, 258, 286, 287, 291, 292, 327, 331, 332, 357, 424, 429,
   433, 439, 443
nucleation/conglomeration of settlement 127–9, *129*, 158–60,
   232–9, 244–5, 252–3

Orkney Archaeological Society 14, 247–8
orthostat
   decorated 239
   in funerary monument 61, 62
   threshold/entrance & passage 46, 48, 50, 70, 94, 100, 120,
      136, 239
   'stalled'/internal house division 4, 30, 34, 44, 46, 47, 50,
      51, 53, 54, 61, 66, 67, 69, 71, *71*, 76, 81, 82, 83, 94, 96,
      99, 100, *100*, 101–4, 105, 109, 112–8, 120, 122, 124, 126,
      135, 136, *137*, 138, 142, 149, 150, 175, 176, 178–9, 188,
      190, 193, 219, 235, *235*, 237, 256, 279, 281, 282, 284,
      286, 354–5, 428, 436, 490, 497, 539

passage grave *see* chambered cairn
peat 1, 4, 286, 532
   as fuel peat 51, 52, 53, 54, 56, 60, 330, 379, 502, 517–8, 526
   core 520–6, *520*, *523–4*
Pentland Firth 1, 5
phosphates *102*, 106–7, 118, *119*, 131, 139, 183, *183*
phytoliths 52, 530, 534, 541
Pictish 'figure-of-eight' house (House 4–5, Stonehall Knoll)
   92–6, *94–5*, *100*
Piggott, Stuart 6, 16–17, 197
pigment 12, 173, 193–4
   haematite 173, 183, 194, 195, 475, 476–84, *479*, *481*
   mortar/'paint pot' 194–5, 483
pit 34, 35, *35*, 48, *48*, 73–6, *74–6*, 77, 80, 94, *100*, 116, *117*,
   118, 138, 139, 188, 228, 276, 279, 301, 498, 510, 516
plant remains 54, 166, 278, 484, 495–526, *512*, *524*, *528*, 531,
   534, 537, 538, 539, 541
   charcoal 18, 23, 27, 30, 33, 38, 47, 48, 52, 53, 54, 56, 80,
      82, 85, 94, 116, 120, 121, 139, 140, 144, 151, 152, 166, 169,
      177, 178, 217, 232, 278, 371, 494, 495–526, *511*, 512, 524,
      524, 526, 530, 531, 532, 533, 534, 537, 538, 539, 541
   birch 23, 30, 38, 47, 48, 52, 54, 109, 140, 144, 152, 169,
      278, 495, 496, 497, 498, 503, 506, 509, 510, 511,
      513, 514, 515–7
   blackthorn type 503

cherry type 495, 503, 511, 516
grasses/sedges (rhizomes/nutlets) 498, 503, 509, 510,
   511, 514, 516, 517
hazel 23, 38, 232, 297, 495, 496, 503, 506, 509, 510,
   515, 516
heather/heather family 54, 109, 177, 495, 498, 502, 503,
   506, 509, 510, 511, 513, 514, 516–7, 518, 526
pine 38, 514
rowan 109, 502, 516
Scots pine 177, 503, 517
seaweed 109, 111, 379–81, *380*, 502
spruce/larch 503, 514, 51
willow 23, 38, 94, 109, 232, 297, 495, 496, 498, 502,
   503, 506, 509, 512, 513, 514, 515, 516
charred/carbonised
   cereals 23, 27, 30, 89, 150, 230, 232, *233*, 256, 297,
      495, 496, 497, 502, 506, 510, 514, 526
   grasses and sedges 496, 498
   hazelnut 232, 297, 512
   weed/grassland 509, 510, 512, 514, 515, 516, 517, 519
pollen 1, 517, 519, 520–6, *520*, *522–3*
   alder 525
   aquatic taxa 522, 525
   birch 523, 525
   cereal 522, 524
   fen/marshland taxa 523, 524, 525
   grassland/heathland 522, 523, 526
   ?hazel 525, 526
   heather 524
   mosses 522, 525
   oak 525
   pine 523, 525
   sedges 522, 523–4, 525
   weeds of cultivation 522, 524, 526
   woodland taxa 522–3
Pool, Sanday 16, 62, 85, 97, 98, 125, *125*, 128, 131, 151–2, 157,
   158, 160, 161, 163, 190, 194, 195, 233, 239, 245, 258, 301,
   304, 318, 330, 331, 332, 333–4, 357, 379, 398, 409, 450,
   456, 458, 462, 463, 464, 465, 472, 473, 484
posthole 18, 21, 22–3, *22*, 24–30, *24–6*, *28–9*, 38, 40, 48, 50,
   72, 73, *75*, 89, *95*, 96, 125, 228, 230, 249, *252*, 271, 281,
   289, 292, 371, 372, 375, 506, 515
pottery 17, *37*, 65, 73, 126, 151, *167*, *170–1*, 304–412, *306*, *308–
   10*, *313*, *316–8*, *320–2*, *324*, *326*, *329*, 494, 530, 531, 536
   clay sourcing and prospection 305, 326, 327–9, 350, 353,
      357, 365, 369–71, 375–8, *376*, 390, 398, 406, 407,
      409, 411
   decoration 304, 308, 311, 318–24, 327–8, 331, 333–5, 344,
      344, 347–8, 351, 352, 354, 357–8, 361, 362, 364–7,
      371–4, 375, 379, 400, 404, 409–11, 412
   deposition processes 408
   experimental work/replication 303, 328, 330, 332, 375,
      377– *378*, *380–1*
   fabrics 126, 305, 308–9, 310, *310*, 314, 325–7, *326*, 328–9,
      329, 336, 345–8, *346*, 351, 356, 357, 369 *369*, 371–2,
      378, 398, 404, 406, 407, 410

form and diagnostic features 304, 306–8, *306*, *308*, 310–18, 324–7, 333–44, *339*, 345, 347–8, 351, 352, 357–63, 365–8, 371–4, 398, 404–5, 406, 410–11

function 304, 329, 332, 346–7, 351–4, 355, 356, 406

in chambered tombs 333, 357, 358, 374

life cycle/history of pots 303, 333, 352–4, 375, 408

magnetic susceptibility 304

petrographic analysis 303, 305, 310, 314, 315, 326, 328, 349–51, 365–71, 377, 382–92, *386*, *388–9*, 397–8, 409–10

sherd size 306, *306*, 311, 327, 404, 405

'signature' (personal/group identity) 304, 329–31

techniques/manufacture 324–5, 327–31, 351–2, 356, 373, 396, 404

chaîne opèratoire 375

traditions 303, 329–32, 373–4

use wear 308, 314, 324, 336, 346, *346*, 348–9, 368, 374, 406, 411

organic/carbonized residues 304, 305, 314, 324, 331, 332, 336, 346–7, 348–9, 351, 352, 356, 368, 371, 372, 374, 393–6, *394*, 411

vessel size 308, 327, 329, 346–7, *346*, 351–2, 354, 355–7, 362–4, *364*, 369, *369*, 373, 374, 408, 409, 411, 412

see also individual sites

pottery dates and types

early Neolithic (round-based) 4, 5–6, 15, 48, 54, 55, 57–8, 92, 109, *110*, *122–3*, 127, 160, 254, 279, 281, 282, 284, 301, 302, 303, 305, 308, *309*, 311, *313*, 315, 327, 328, 329, 332, 333, 334, 382, 392, 393–4, 395, 398, *399*, 405

Carinated Bowl 300

Neutral bowl 172, 335, 357–8, 362, 364, 365, 368, 373–4, 406, 409, 410, 411

Unstan wear 4, 6, 13, 14, 16, 17, 18, 22, *23*, 44, *47*, 127, 163, 165, 248, 254, 256, 279, 283, 285, 303, 305, 327, 330, 332, 333, 334–6, *335*, 349–50, 351, 354, 357–75, *359–61*, 377, 393, 395, 404, 405, 406, 407, 408, 409, 410, 411, 439, 442, 463

late Neolithic 193, 212, 213–4, *213*, 215–6, 217, 393, 398, 399, 404, 408

Impressed ware 393, 421, 443

Peterborough ware 393, 421, 443

Grooved ware 6, 14, 138, *139*, 144, 152, 160, 161, 163, 164, 166, *167*, 168, 169, *170–1*, 182, *182*, 183, 187, 194, 195, 236, *237*, 245, 248, 254, 256, 279, 280, 281, 282, 285, 286, 301, 302, 303, 304, 305, 315–24, *321–2*, 327, 328–30, 331, 332–4, 336–47, *339–41*, *344–6*, 348, 350, 351–4, *353*, 356, 365, 377, 382, 392, 393–4, 395, 396, 399–404, *401*, 406, 408, 409, 410–11, 412, 443, 464, 503

Beaker 164, 193, 245, 281, 284, 303, 332–3, 334, 347–9, *348*, 350–1, 352, 354, 356, 364, 393, 394, 395, 396, 397, *397*, 404, 408, 409, 410, 411

Early Bronze Age 332, 393, 398

Food Vessel 284, 406

Bronze Age 248

see also individual sites

radiocarbon dates 5, 22, 23, 30, 31, 36, 38, 40, 47, 48, 52, 54, 60, 94, 105–6, 108, 116, 117, 120, 124, 125, 140, 144, 146, 150, 152, 169, 178, 181, 191–2, 195, 201, 202, 211, 213, 232, 254–302, *255*, *258*, *274–7*, *288–90*, *294–5*, *298–301*, 303, 305, 375, 409, 424, 457, 495, 497, 498, 503, 509, 510, 511, 515, 520, 521, 522 *see also* individual sites

Bayesian modelling 257–302, *258*, *274–7*, *288–90*, *294–5*, *298–301*

Irish 293–5, *300*

Mesolithic 297, *298*

Scottish 300–1

Ramberry Head barrow cemetery 212–23, *213*, 396

burnt/cremated bone 212, 213–4, *213*, 489–94

animal 214, 491

flint and stone artefacts 440–2, 470–2, *471–2*

geophysical survey 212, *213*

passage structure 215–8, *218–22*, 396, 470–1

entrance and passage 216, 218

flagstone paving 216, 217, 396

flooring (clay) 217, *220*

old land surface 216

pivot stone 217

stone arc 218, 470

threshold stone 216, 217

walling 215–6, 218

pottery 212, 213–4, *213*, 215–6, 217, 304, 396–8, *397*, 407

ring cairn 212–6, *213–8*, 219–20, *223*, 396, 470–1

basal slab 212–3, *215*, 219

beach pebble surface 214, *215*, 219

flagstone paved curb 214, *215*, 219–20, 396

foundation deposit (clay) 212, 213, 214–5, *215*

magnetic susceptibility 214–5, *217*

stone bank 215, *217–8*

stone setting 213–5

radiocarbon date 213

relationship with Crossiecrown settlement 220–2

relationship with sea 218–22, *218*, *222*

stone tools 212, 213, 215, 218, *218*

Rendall, Robert 12, 17–18, *18*, *20*, 21, 38, 161, 224, 416

Renfrew, Colin 6, 10, 12, 161, 199, 200–2, 205, 228, 254, 256, 285, 286, 409

Ring of Brodgar 194, 241–2, *242*, 286

Rinyo, Rousay 16, 62, 63, 128, 140, 160, 161, 195, 245, 248, 250, 301, 332, 334, 355, 484

Ritchie, Anna 4–5, 17, 40, 156, 228, 279

Rousay 162, 194, 198–9, 219, 390, 424

chambered cairns 194, 198–9, 207, *229*, 243, 256, 2588, 283–4, 293

Rinyo 16, 62, 63, 128, 140, 160, 161, 195, 245, 248, 250, 301, 332, 334, 355, 484

Saverock, St Ola 15, 64, 196, 225, 287,

seaweed 58, 379, 380, 473

charcoal 109, 111, 379–81, *380*, 502

as fuel 109, 111, 186, 330, 379–81, *380*, 502, 514, 515, 518

sea, importance of 218–22, *218*, *222*

sea level/sea level change 9, *11*, 62, 218, 224, 390
settlement mound 11, 14, *14*, 15, 16, 18, 40, 55, 65, 90, *90*, 92, 111, 120, 122, 128–30, *129–30*, 131, 146, 152, 157, 159, 160–2, 164, 165, 166, 168, *168*, 246–8, 249, 250, 305, 445
Shetland 1, 161, 164, 165, 193, 223, 245, 57, 282, 398, 463, 518
Skara Brae 4, 16, 34, 62, 85, 128, 143, 144, 146, 148, 150, 154, 157–8, 159, 160–1, 170, 186, 188, 193, 194–5, 209, 238, 239, 243–4, *243–4*, 245–6, *245*, 250, 254, 256, 257, 258, 287, 292, 304, 355, 372, 417, 436, 444, 456, 458, 464, 465, 472, 474, 475, 481–2, 483, 484, 517, 519, 542
Smerquoy, St Ola, *see* Brae of Smirquoy
social/group/kin identity and status 7, 38–40, 64, 124–7, 145, 157–8, 160, 173, 194–6, 197, 224–6, 228, 230, 234, 236–8, 241–3, 252–3, 331
    in pottery 304, 331, 375, 407, 411–2
social processes, strategies and practices 6, 13–14, 63–4, 91–2, 109, 111, 123–7, 195, 197–8, 226–7, 234–5, 239, 241–2, 252–3, 288, 304, 330–1, 333–51, 411, 412
social relations 7, 8, 31, 38–40, 64, 111, 124–7, 158–9, 226–7, 234–6, 241, 243–5, 352, 412
social organization and position 7–8, 109–11, 124–7, 145
sociéte à maisons (house society) 7–8, 14, 15, 31, 40, 60, 63, 64, 89, 90, 111, 124–5, 127, 145, 146, 158, 159, 160, 195, 212, 225–30, 232–4, 331
soil 157
    buried (old land surface) 4, 101, 166, 216, 231, 249, 278, 506
    burnt 60, 531, 536
    erosion/hillwash 524, 526, 530, 531, 532, 533
    micromorphology 56–7, 60, 166–7, 231–2, 406, 511, 527–42, *529*, *535*, *541*
staple isotopes 257, 395
stone (non-structural)
    and flint tools *see* lithics
    burnt 77, 85, *85*, 119, 120, 154, 231–2
    decorated *70*, 85–8, *87–8*, 339 229, 238, 239, 285, 286, 470
    sculpted 457, 458, 464, *465*
stone circle 8, 92, 226, 240, 241–2, 254, 255, 256
Stonehall Farm, Firth 10, 13, 15, 60, 62, 91, 92, *93*, 100, 109, 122–7, *123–4*, 128–59, *130*, 160, 196, 233, 238, 303, 486–7
    burnt deposits 139, 146, 498
    clay
        ball 315, *317*, 325, 328, 331
        bead 315
        prospection 10
    excavation 11, 13
    flagstone paving in Trench F 154
    flint and stone artefacts 10–11, 124, 137, 142, 145–6, 151, 152, *153*, 154, 413, 416, 421, 429–36, *434–6*, 442, 442, 464, 474, *474*
    geophysical survey 10, 11, 122, 130, *132*
    haematite 475, 482, 483
    house 30, 43
    House 1 131, 139, 146–51 *147–51*, 278, 291, 315, 327
        ?'box–bed' 150
        drainage system/hydrology 134, 146, 148, 159
        entrances 146–8, *148*, 150

        ?'dresser' 138, 143, 150, 188
        flooring and foundations (clay and flagstones) 146, *148*, 149–50, 151, *151*
        hearth 146, *148*, 150, *150–1*, 151
        internal features/division of space 146, 149–50
        paving/path 148, 154, 159
        remodelling 151
        stone box 150
        threshold stone 145, 148
        walling 148–9, 157
    House 2 122–4, *124*, 125
    midden 11, 122, 125, 128, 130, 131–6, *136*, 143, 144, 146, 151–9, *154–6*, 238, 278, 305, 315, 318, 327, 329, 331, 430, 433, 498, 528–31
    mound 11, 129–30, *130*, 131, 146, 152
    plant remains 498–501, 514, 516–7
    pottery 126, 138, *139*, 144, 151, 165, 303, 305, *306*, *309*, 314–26, *316–8*, *320–2*, 324, 326–32, *326*, 400, 404, 408
    radiocarbon dates 124, 125, 140, 144, 146, 150, 152, 272, *274*, 277–8, 305, 498
    red ash 150, 151, 154
    soil micromorphology 528–33, *529*, *535*
    Structure 1 52, 60–1, 124, 131, 133–46, *133–42*, 144, 153–7 *153–4*, 179, 256, 277–8, 305, 445, 450, 464, 474, *529*
        as a 'big house' 143–6, *144*, 238, 239
        bone 142
        clay bowl/'oven' 140, *141*, 144, 278, 498, 514, 516
        drainage system/hydrology 131–4, *134*, 135, 144, 159
        entrance 136
        evidence of burning 139
        flagstone paving 131, 133, 135, 138, 142, 143, 144, 159
        flooring and foundations (clay and flagstones) 124, 131, 134, 135, 136, 137, 138–40, 142–3, 145, 146
        hearth 60, 61, 134, 135, 138, 139–40, 143, 144–5, 474, 498
        hoards of flint and stone objects 137, 142, 145–6, 445, 449, 450, 474, *474*
        internal features/division of space 134, 135, *137–8*, 138, 141–2, 143, 176
            orthostats 124, 135, 136, *137*, 138, 142
        magnetic susceptibility 139, *141*
        phosphates 139
        pit 138, *139*
        rebuilding 140–3, 144
        stone box/cist (central) 60, 61, 134, *135*, 136–7, *137–8*, 138–9, 140, *142*, 143, 144–5, 238, 278, 498
        stone box (SW) 142, 144, 146
        walling 134, 135–6, 138, 141–2, 143, 450, 487
Stonehall Knoll 50, 91, *93*, 115, 121, 124, 125–7, 128–33, 144, 158, 230, 233–4, 256, 303, 482
    flint and stone artefacts 92, 94, 109, *110*, 417, 421, 426–7, *428*, 430, 433, 442, 445, 466
    House 2 69, 97, 98–101, 126, 405, 449
        drainage/hydrology 100
        entrance 100
        flooring and foundations (clay and flagstones) 99, 100

hearth 99, 100, *100*, 126, 514
    internal structure/division of space 99–100, *100*, 126
        orthostats 99, 100, *100*, 102, 126
House 3 45–6, 61, *100*, 101–11, *102–8*, 111, 126, 128, 230, 275, 292, 306, 405
    drainage/hydrology 105
    entrance 103, 104, *105*
    flooring and foundations (clay and flagstones) 103–4, 105, 106, 107, 108–9, 275
    hearth 103, 104, *105*, 106–7, 110–11, 518, 533–4
    internal features/division of space 104, 105, 109, 111, 126, 235
        orthostats 101, 104, 105, 109
    pathway 105
    stone box 105, *105*, 109
    stone tool 108, 109, *110*
    structural failure 60–1, 101, 103, 105, 107–8, *108*, 109, 111, 128, 230
    topographical location 102, 111, 126
    walling 103, 104, 107, *107*, 108, 126, 230
midden 92, *95*, 100–1, *101*, 102, 109–10, 305–6, 329, 405, 533
mound 92, 96, 122
paved area 96, *96*, 98, *98*, *100*, 101, 104, 109, 126
    clay spread 98–9
Pictish 'figure-of-eight' house (Houses 4–5) 92–6, *94–5*
    entrances *94*
    flooring (clay and flagstones) 94
    hearth 94
    pit 94, *100*
    walling 94–5
plant remains 498, 502–3
pottery 92, 109, *110*, 126, 303, 305–9, *306*, *308*, *309*, 315, *326*, 326–32, 358
radiocarbon dates 94, 105–6, 108, 260, *274*, 275–6, 291, 292
soil micromorphology 533–4, *535*
Structure 1 96–8, *95–7*, 111, 126, 292
    flooring and foundations (clay and flagstones) 96
    hearth 96–7, 126
    internal features 96–7
    postholes *95*, 96, 292
    threshold stone 94
    timber phase 95, 96
    topographic location 97
    walling *95*, 96
task/activity (areas) 109
Stonehall Meadow 48, 50, 66, 76, 91, 92, *93*, 100, 104, 109, 111–22, *111–22*, 124, 125–7, 127, 128–33, 144, 158, 233–4, 303, 482, 487
    flint and stone artefacts 121, *122–3*, 417, 427–9, *430*, 430, 433, 442, 443, 445, 466
    geophysical survey 111, 119, 130, *132*
    House 1 111–3, *112–3*, 116, 126, 496
    House 2 111, 113–5, *114–5*, 116, 125, 496, 498
    House 3 47, 69, 79, 80, 99, 111, *111–2*, 115–8, *114–9*, 121, 125, 229, 232, *234*, 276, 327, 445, 450, 495, 496–8

    activities 121
    'box-bed' 117, *118*
    charred cereal remains 116, *117*, 120, 125, 126
    drainage/hydrology 118
    entrance 116, 120
    flooring and foundations (clay and flagstones) 115, 116–8, 119, 120–1, 327
    hearth 117, *117*, 118, 276–7, 495, 497–8, 502, 534
    internal features/division of space 115–8, *116*, *118*, 127, 497
        orthostats 237
    paving *114*, *116*, 128
    pit 116, *117*, 118, 276, 498
    stone box 116
    threshold stone 112, 116
    walling 115–6, 120
House 4 119–20
midden 118, 119, 120–1, 128, 130, 310, 495, 496
mounds 111, 120
plant remains 495–8
pottery *122–3*, 126, 303, 305, *306*, *308*, 309–14, *310*, *313*, 315, 326–32, *326*, 358, 382–7, *386*, 390–2, 398
other features 119–21, *121*, 123
    clay surface 120–1
    hearth 120
radiocarbon dates 116, 117, 120, 261, 272, *274*, 276–7, 290–1, *298*, 495, 497
red ash 111, *117*, 118, 119, 120, 128
soil micromorphology 534, *535*
Stonehall peat core 520–6, *520*, *522–4*
    plant macrofossils and charcoal 520, 521–6, *524*
    pollen analysis 520, 221–6, *223*
    radiocarbon dates 520, 521, 522
Stonehall sites (general and comparisons) 233–4, 238, 258, 275, 527
    animal bone 485–8
    comparative analysis 125–7, 128–59
    geophysical survey 130–1, *132*
    lithic assemblages 416, 442, 445–51, *446–7*, 456, 458, 464–5, 469, 470, 472, 473, *473*
    magnetic susceptibility 131, 139, 281, *282*
    midden extent and structure 130–3, 146, 151–9, *154–6*
    phosphates 131
    plant remains 495, 514, 515, 516–7, 518
    possible pottery firing area 130
    pottery 303–32, *306*, *308–10*, *313*, *316–8*, *320–2*, *324*, *326*, *329*, 358, 375, 379, 393, *394*, 395, 407, 408–12
    settlement structure and organisation 128–3, 238, 239
Stones of Stenness 236, *337*, 241, *241*, 242, 286
stone, standing 8, 254, 286
stone, tools/objects *see* lithics
superimposition/succession of houses/settlement 25–8, 38, 129, 131, 160, 195, 228–30, 232–8, *233*, 244, 277–8, 280, 281

Tankerness House Museum, Kirkwall 10, 13, 17, 18
timber house/architecture 4, 5, 14, 15, 16, 18, 40, 64, 229, 254–5, 257, 280, 287, 301, *301*

timber house/architecture *continued*
    Brae of Smerquoy 84–5, *85*, 87, 89, 96, 103, 228, 255, 288
    Bronze Age 4, 161, 162, 193
        early (Crossiecrown) 13, 162, 163, 164, 165, 170, 190–2, *192*, 354, 457, 462, 503
    in Ireland 228
    Stonehouse Knoll 95, 96
    transformation to stone architecture 26, 38–40, 229–30, 232, 280
    Wideford Hill timber structures 18, 20–30, *21–2*, *24–6*, 27, *28–9*, 31, 35, 38–9, 40, 89, 90, 96, 125, 227–8, 229, 230, 232, 252, 255, 256, 278, 287, 288, 289, 290, *298*, *301*, 357, 369, 371–2, 408, 506, 515
Tofts Ness, Sanday 131, 157, 158, 160, 161, 194, 258, 291, 450, 456, 458, 462, 463, 464, 465, 452
topography 9–10, *10*, 13, 65, 224, 225
topographic/landscape location of settlements/buildings/monuments 13, 60, 62, 63, 65, *65*, 77, 91–2, 97, 102, 111, 125, 126, 223, 228, 235, 239, 240–1, 248, *248*
topographic survey *20*, 65, *65*, *218*, *248*
transformation 6, 7, 92, 154, 156,–7, 194, 235, 478
    from life to death 145, 196, 210, 211–2, 220–3, 228–9; *see also* mortuary practices
    from timber to stone architecture 26, 38–40, 229–30, 232, 280
    of house 60, 145, 238, 246
turf (as fuel) 52, 54, 56, 109, 121, 126, 156, 330, 496, 498, 502, 503–4, 510, 511, 514–5, 516, 517–8

Varme Dale, Evie, barrow 60, 61, 230–2, *230–1*
    baked clay layer 231
    burnt layer/deposit/stone 230, *230*, 231–2, *233*, 511–2
    plant remains 512
        charred grain deposit 230, 232, *233*, 256, 512
    radiocarbon date 232, 255, 297, 298, *298*, *301–2*
    soil micromorphology 231–2
    stone kerb 231, 232, *233*, 512

Whale ivory/bone 282, 483
Wideford Hill passage grave 161, 196, 198, 199, 201, 202, *202*, *196*, *198*, *199–201*, *202*, *202*, 207, 208–9, 211, 219, 222, 256
Wideford Hill settlement 9, 10, 12, 14, 15, 17–18, 62, 65, 77, 91, 161, 196, 224, 225, 238, 275, 287, 303, 484
    excavation 13, 18, *19*
    flint and stone
        artefacts 416, 417, 421–4, *423*, 426, 439, 443, 445, 451–6, *452–3*, 458, 464, 465, 466, 467, 468, 469, 470, 472
        scatters ('fields') 12–13, 17–18, *18*, *20*, 38, 161
        Mesolithic material 18, 22, 38, 224, 421, 442
    geophysical survey 13, 18, *19*

hearth 22, *22*, 24, 25, 26, 27, *29*, 30–1, *32–3*, 35, 40, 48, 79, 89, 278, 371, 506, 515
midden 371–2, 373, 408, 506, 515
plant remains 495, 506–9, 515, 516–7, 518–9
pottery 17–18, 22, *23*, 36, *37*, 127, 165, 303–4, 305, 307, 327, 328, 330, 332, 333, 357–74, *359–61*, *364*, *369*, 375, 393, *394*, 395, 398, 404–5, 406, 407, 408–12
radiocarbon dates 22, 27, 30, 31, 36, 40, 261, 272, 275, *274–5*, 278, 289–90, 292
rammed stone surface *35*, 36–8, *39*, 40, 372–3, 374, 405, 408, 454, 455, 466, 506
Stonehouse 1 23, 24, 25–6, 30–5, *31–6*, 38, 40, 48, 50, 80, 82, 111, 229, 278, 292, 372–3, 374, 405, 408, 455, 456, 506–9, 515
    clay bowl 33, *33*
    drainage system/hydrology 31, 34–5, *34–5*, 77, 507
    flagstones 27–9, *29*, 34, *35*, 48
    flooring and foundations (clay) 25, *25*, 30–1, 38, 40, 278, 506
    orthostats 30, 34, 126, 229
    pit/cistern 34, 35, *35*, 48
    stone box 33, *33*
    walling 35, *35*
Stone structure 2 29, 30, 35–8, *35–6*, *39*
    flagstones 35
    walling 35
timber structures 18, 20–30, *21–2*, *24–6*, *28–9*, 31, 38–9, 89, 90, 96, 227–8, 229, 232, 252, 255, 256, *298*, *301*, 357, 408, 515
    clay surfaces/floors 27, 369, 506
    postholes 18, 21, 22–3, *22*, 24–30, *24–6*, *28–9*, 38, 40, 89, 228, 230, 289, 371, 506, 515
    roofing 23
    structure 1 22–3, *21–4*, 38, 230, 278, 290, *298*, 371, 506
    structure 2 24–6, *25*, 30, 38, 40, 278, 506, 515
    structure 3 26–30, *26*, *28–9*, 35, 38, 125, 230, 278, 287, 288, 289, *298*, 371–2, 408, 506, 515
    walling 23
topographic survey *20*
willow 4, 23, 515, 516, 526
    charcoal 38, 94, 109, 232, 297, 495, 496, 498, 502, 503, 506, 509, 514, 515, 516, 526
woodland/woodland resources 1, 4, 9, 38, 90, 498, 503, 513, 514, 515, 516–7, 522, 524, 525–6
wrapping
    the cairn 219
    the dead 145, 209
    the house/'big house' 158, 193–4, 195, *215*, 219, 241, 244
    the passage grave 239, 241
    the villages 250–1, 252